**the MULTIMEDIA guide to UK UNIVERSITIES 99**

`windows cd-rom`

So many universities to choose from - so little time to visit them all... But don't fret - we have the only ticket you'll need.

Now in its fifth edition *PUSH CD* is the definitive guide to choosing a university in the UK. Packed full of information, it not only provides searchable course information, an interactive map, virtual tours of every university and the complete text of the best-selling *The PUSH Guide to Which University 99*, it also has a unique feature which allows you quite literally to design your own perfect university and find the closest match.

If a university is worth choosing, it's worth choosing properly - and all from the comfort of your own PC.

ISBN: 0 07 70944611   RRP £39.99 inc VAT

Available from McGraw-Hill and all good book and computer stores

"This is the University and Colleges Admissions Service with attitude, and students love it" *TES*

[http://www.push.co.uk]

Essential Purchase Textbooks from McGraw-Hill Publishing Company

A Division of The McGraw·Hill Companies

Economics, 5/e
David Begg, Stanley Fischer, Rudiger Dornbusch

Shaping the teaching of introductory economics for more than a decade and a half with its judicious even handed approach.

August 1997   800pp
0 07 709412 3   £21.99 PB

Principles and Practice of Marketing, 2/e
David Jobber

This exciting new edition combines comprehensive coverage of theory of marketing with a unique emphasis on its practical implementation within European business.

July 1998   860 pp
0 07 709435 2   £24.99 PB

Human Physiology, 7/e
Vander, Sherman, Luciano

This text continues its tradition of clear, up-to-date, and accurate explanations; rewarding students with a more thorough understanding of how the body works.

November 1997   768 pp
0 07 115624 0   £23.99 PB

Introduction to Thermodynamics and Heat Transfer
Yunus A. Cengel

Lavishly illustrated; this text presents key topics in thermodynamics and heat transfer in a highly accessible and student-friendly fashion.

January 1997   800 pp
0 07 114109 X   £22.99

http://www.mcgraw-hill.co.uk

the push guide to WHICH UNIVERSITY 99

Edited by: Sophie Dennis

Written by: Joe Flintham with Johnny Rich

7th Edition
Managing Editor: Johnny Rich
Executive Editor: Ben Rich
Researchers ('99 edition): Helen Adedotun, Scott Appleton, Wendy Atkins, Matthew Barker, John Barratt, Penny Brereton, Martin Burrows, Roma Cassidy, Jenny Clark, Joanna Clarke, Emma Clegg, Jon Clements, Sally Cockerton, Helen Cooper, Jane Cosher, James Diamond, Rebecca Dickinson, Amy Donnellan, Emily Fowke, Ben Gelblum, Katy Harrison, Jeanette Hurdle, Jessica Jacobs, Sudip Kar-Gupta, Julie Knox, Jennifer Lee, Sophie Lloyd, Rowena Macdonald, Paula McManus, Joanne O'Connell, Nick O'Meally, Anna Perkins, Joanna Quinn, Nikki Ratcliffe, Skeena Rathor, Arlene Russo, Elaine Sinclair, Kate Sleeman, Katheryn Smith, Ben Spriggs, James Toner, Paula Vincent, Mike Williams
Special thanks to: Liz Nuttall, Andy Robinson, Tim Footman, Lisa English
Published by: McGraw-Hill Publishing Company
Design by: David Eyres

THREE CHEERS FOR LLOYDS BANK...
To research information of the range and detail provided by **push** is a long and challenging process, which is why the publishers and editors of **push** would like to acknowledge with gratitude the generous support of Lloyds Bank who have helped **push** to help prospective students towards a better informed choice of university.
...HIP, HIP HOORAY.

McGraw-Hill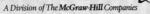

A Division of The McGraw·Hill Companies

Copyright © Johnny Rich & Ben Rich, 1992, 1993, 1994, 1995, 1996, 1997, 1998.

First published in 1992 as *PUSH 93 (The Polytechnic & University Students' Handbook)*.

2nd edition published in 1993 as *PUSH 94 (The University Students' Handbook)*.

3rd edition published in 1994 as *The PUSH Guide to Which University 95*.

4th edition published in 1995 as *The PUSH Guide to Which University 96*.

5th edition published in 1996 as *The PUSH Guide to Which University 97*.

6th edition published in 1997 as *The PUSH Guide to Which University 98*.

This edition published in 1998 as *The PUSH Guide to Which University 99*.

ISBN 00 77094638

No part of this publication may be copied or reproduced, stored in a retrieval system or transmitted in any form or by any means electronic or mechanical or by photocopying, recording or otherwise without prior permission of the copyright owners.

Flunk rates:
Source: HESA Individualised Student Record 1994/95, reference July 1995
HESA Individualised Student Record 1996/97, reference July 1997
Copyright Higher Education Statistics Agency Limited, 1995
Reproduced by permission of the Higher Education Statistics Agency Limited
HESA cannot accept responsibility for any inferences or conclusions derived from the data by third parties.

Editorial:

PUSH
McGraw-Hill Publishing Company
Shoppenhangers Road
Maidenhead
Berkshire SL6 2QL
Tel: (01628) 502970
Fax: (01628) 502971

Ordering:

Customer Services
McGraw-Hill Publishing Company
Shoppenhangers Rd
Maidenhead
Berkshire SL6 2QL
Tel: (01628) 23432
Fax: (01628) 35895

E-mail: push@mcgraw-hill.com
Web site: http://www.push.co.uk/

Contents

 ## 33-724 College profiles

p u s h power

push is an independent organisation that collects the largest ever resource of information about student life in the UK.

push distributes that information through four services:

- **The PUSH Guide to Which University** – the best-selling guidebook.
- **PUSH CD** – the ultimate multimedia guide to UK universities on CD-Rom.
- **The PUSH /Lloyds Bank Tour** – **push** experts visit sixth forms and provide specialist advice.
- **PUSH Online** – regularly up-dated information on the internet.

DID YOU KNOW?

- Over the past five years, **push** has employed more than 250 researchers, photographers and writers.
- **push** researchers visit every university in the UK every year.
- **push** research involves the universities themselves, the students' unions, Government bodies and thousands of students.
- Each year **push** generates over 10,000 pages of research.
- **push**'s entire database of information is fully updated every year.
- The information **push** distributes has been checked three times.
- **push** staff are all high-flying students and recent graduates.
- **push** is the UK's most widely used resource to student life, used by students, teachers, careers advisers, parents, universities, Government bodies, political parties, media organisations and many others.
- **push** always strives to provide the most up-to-date information in the most accessible style at an affordable cost. Everything we do is **by students for** students.

p u s h ing

Lloyds Bank

One thing you can expect to have a lot of at university is fun. Unfortunately the same can't be said of money.

In a way you can't help getting in some debt. That's why it's important that you find a bank which looks after you long term.

LONG TERM SURVIVAL FOR STUDENTS

You'll learn that at university there are many necessities to pay for, such as beer, take-aways, gigs (not to mention luxuries like books and food). And only one person to pay for them.

That's where a Lloyds Bank Student Account can help. It's been specially designed to look after your short term needs (university) as well as your long term survival (we offer a 2 year graduate package to help you when you start work).

GET SMART. GET A LLOYDS BANK STUDENT ACCOUNT

Come in and open an account before you even go to university. We can convert it to a student account later when you show us a copy of your Local Education Authority letter or other proof of your college status.

You'll have access to a network of over 9,000 cashpoints including TSB, Barclays, Bank of Scotland and Royal Bank of Scotland.

So come in and see us at your local branch. And we'll see that you survive till Finals.

push start

Foreword from the President of the National Union of Students

▶▶ Choosing the college or University that suits you best is no easy decision. That's why so many would-be students turn to **push** for advice and information. Over the years **push** has generated something of a reputation with students and the media - the offbeat statistics and irreverent information aren't the sort of thing you'd find in any other guide to universities, or in any of the university prospectuses.

But whatever your motivation remember there's a great deal more to student life than studying. **push** is packed with crucial information on courses, accommodation, entertainments, sports and welfare facilities available at hundreds of campuses.

When it comes to making your mind up try to pay a visit to the colleges you like the sound of and take time to visit the student union and talk first hand with students there for the real lowdown on student life. **push** uses information from real students but at the end of the day, the decision is all yours and from now on in, it will be your opinions that count.

Good luck and I wish you all the best for your time at college

Andrew Pakes,

NUS National President

p u s h over

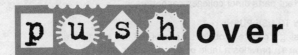

How to use PUSH

Using **push** is a pushover. A 5-year old child could understand it, but, before you rush out to find a 5-year old child, because you can't make head nor tail of it, here's the idiots' guide to **push** - also invaluable for gifted 5-year olds, vastly over-qualified academics and you...

push has been designed and devised to make it as easy to use as possible, whatever you want to do with it.

Well, maybe if you want to use it as a pet, you're probably better off with a goldfish, but as a guide to real life at the UK's universities and colleges, it's the best there is.

push isn't trying to replace the UCAS Handbook or the colleges' own prospectuses, it's just lending a hand in what is frankly the sort of decision that has most people reaching for the pin cushion. **push** provides the sort of information you really want to know in order to decide, not all that stuff about course codes and quotas which appears everywhere else.

And don't let anyone tell you your decision doesn't matter. Manchester Metropolitan, Warwick University and Christ's College, Cambridge may each do a maths course, but students are letting themselves in for more than algebra and calculus. Differentiation and integration mean something quite different when a student's chosen college becomes their home for the next few years.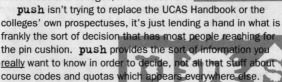

push tells you the real story and tells it straight. But there's no point just telling you that one college is the best and that everyone should go there. Everyone wants something different and every college offers something unique. What **push** does is match students with the college of their dreams... or near enough.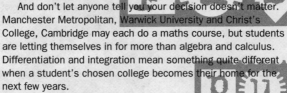

push backs up nearly everything with facts, figures and statistics and when nothing tells it better than an honest opinion, we're not ashamed to admit that it's a personal view - even if it is the best informed opinion available anywhere. In fact, we slap it in italics just so you know. Although our judgements are scrupulously researched and representative, we still advise a pretty hefty accompanying dose of salt. After all, even **push**'s opinion is still only an opinion.

With **push**, students can make comparisons and pin-point the features that they're looking for. The symbols, charts and maps give a quick and easy reference to the sort of factors that might really sway their decision, not least, courses. The profiles for each college allow comparisons and make it possible to check out whether they make the grade in the important parts other colleges cannot reach.

WHEN TO USE PUSH:

Choosing a course is obviously one of the first things to do and **push** provides a table of all courses on offer (see '**push**, of course', page 762). Since students don't want to see essentially the same course listed under 93 different names in 203 different places, **push** has standardised the names and listed them alphabetically by subject areas.

This means that students don't have to wade through pages of different institutions to find the few that offer the course they're looking for. A word of warning: the standardisation of nearly 10,000 degree courses means that some get grouped together in a way which would perhaps be objectionable to those who appreciate the finer differences between Phonic Linguistics and Linguistic Phonemics. For exact details of any course, its contents and with which other courses it may be combined, check availability with the institutions themselves, their prospectuses or the UCAS Handbook.

If the prospective student knows more or less what course they want to study and that course is not unusual - like Maths or English Literature, but not Cartesian Astrophysics with a side order of Sewage Managment - then, no problem, they can choose entirely on the strength of other factors as outlined in each college's **push** profile. However, if the course is only offered at a few colleges, students should make a shortlist from the '**push**, of course' lists (page 762) and then turn to the profiles for the clinching factors: Where is it? Is there any social life beyond a non-alcoholic cocktail bar and regular bus-spotting conventions? Is there a croquet club? Will it be possible to buy cigarettes at 3 in the morning?

Even for quite unusual courses, there are so many colleges to choose from that students should take the opportunity to get **push**y - to demand exactly what they want, or as near as damn it.

But maybe the prospective student doesn't know what course s/he wants to study, doesn't care or just hasn't exactly finalised it yet (it's still a toss up between Fine Art or Chemical Engineering for example). Well, then there are no constraints - students can choose entirely on the basis of where they'd like to study and in what environment, rather than what they'd like to study.

Either way, **push** is the best key to all the vital factors students have to put up with on a day-to-day basis. It's easy enough to chose the right course from a list of titles on a page, but to chose a place to live, to work, to rest, to play, to eat Mars bars, **push** is needed.

NAMES AND CROSS-REFERENCING:

When all the old polytechnics became universities way back at the start of the 90s, we suddenly found ourselves with lorry-loads of universities with wacky names like De Montfort University (formerly Leicester Poly) and Liverpool John Moores University (formerly Liverpool Poly) which is named after the bloke who founded the Littlewoods Pools. However, since old habits die hard, if you look up a college under the old name you will find it cross-referenced to its new name anyway. All the profiles are arranged alphabetically (ignoring the words 'University' or 'University of'), but some places like UEA (University of East Anglia) are sent as a trial of the brains behind **push**. Should it be U for 'UEA'? E for 'East'? Or A for 'Ah, we're in Norwich'? Well, if you can't beat 'em... put it under all three. However you try to look up even the most awkward of names you should find it cross-referenced.

BACKFLAP:
You can use it as a bookmark and it's also the key to the **push** symbols - handy and at hand.

GLOSSARY & ABBREVIATIONS:
It's a jargon jungle out there. Everything in higher education would be so easy to understand if the colleges didn't insist on using acrid acronyms and tedious terminology all the time. In fact, it's a plot to stop the unemployed from becoming professors, but that's another (paranoid) story. **push** unleashes the lingo in its 'Short, sharp **push**' (Abbreviations, page 799) and 'When **push** comes to shove' (Glossary, page 792).

OTHER OPTIONS:
Even though all the old polytechnics are now universities, you should still remember that higher education doesn't begin and end there. The choice for prospective students is bigger than Gazza's bar tab. We've included most of the non-university institutions which offer degree courses in a separate chapter (see page 725). There's thousands more universities abroad. And how about vocational training, rather than a degree? Free your mind and your pants will follow.

   push can't include all the options - it would be thousands of pages long, years out of date, cost the earth and be impossible to pick up, let alone read. Apart from that, we like the idea.

GETTING IN TOUCH:
We crave feedback. We love it. We would crawl naked over splintered glass to hear what you have to say about **push**. Unless, that is, you just want to slag us off or sue us for libel. Please then keep your comments to yourself. (Unfettered and pointless flattery is very welcome.) However, assuming you have some worthwhile and constructive response, not necessarily positive, please feel free to write to **push**, McGraw-Hill Companies, Shoppenhangars Road, Maidenhead, Berkshire, SL6 2QL, or e-mail us on push@mcgraw-hill.com.

   For next year's edition, we will again need researchers with an unassailable sense of duty and a streak of masochism - if you think we might not slam the door in your face whilst doubling up in fits of giggles, please drop us a line with reasons why you meet **push**'s exacting standards.

Text in italics is PUSH's point of view - take it or leave it.

Making the most of the college profiles

NAMES:
As a headline, **push** uses the name most students use or the most convenient title. So, for example, LSE is LSE, not the London School of Economics & Political Science. The college's exact name is used in the address, if you really need to know.

ADDRESSES:
For each college, **push** lists the address and telephone number of the administration and of the students' unions, as well as any fax numbers or e-mail addresses there might be. If there is more than one site, the address of the main site is given, or if there is more than one <u>main</u> site, we say, what the blinkin' flip, and give them all.

general

STATISTICS
All statistics were right up to the minute of going to press and **push** is really, really cut up if they're wrong later, but, hell, that's the way it goes. Some institutions, for various reasons, don't release certain statistics. Although we are not known for willingly taking 'No' for an answer, **push** follows the old journalistic maxim, 'If in doubt, leave it out'. We suggest readers should follow the cynics' maxim, 'What are they trying to hide?'

Founded: Many colleges have hazy histories either too deep in the clouds of time or involving too many complicated mergers and changes of name to have just one founding year. Some newer institutions, desperate to appear venerable and ivy-covered, prefer to give the founding date of an obscure technical college on the other side of town that eventually morphed into the current institution after 14 name changes and multiple mergers. **push**, however, has used the latest techniques (a step beyond the 'Eeny-Meeny-Miny-Mo Principle') to select just one year and, if further clarification is worthwhile, it's explained elsewhere in the profile.

Full-time u'grads: This includes students on sandwich courses, which are nothing to do with learning what to put between slices of bread, but courses where some time is spent not actually studying (usually on an industrial placement).

Part-time: Those on undergraduate courses only.

Postgrads: Full-time postgraduate students (who've already taken a 1st degree).

Non-degree: Often HND (Higher National Diploma) students but all sorts of vocational, access and pre-degree courses might be offered, especially at newer universities. Again, figures are for full-time students.

Ave course: Strictly speaking, for the pedantic statisticians out there, this is the modal length of courses. Or, in English, the most common course length.

Ethnic: Some institutions prefer not to ask their students to classify themselves into one racial box or another; others are

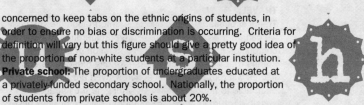

concerned to keep tabs on the ethnic origins of students, in order to ensure no bias or discrimination is occurring. Criteria for definition will vary but this figure should give a pretty good idea of the proportion of non-white students at a particular institution.

Private school: The proportion of undergraduates educated at a privately-funded secondary school. Nationally, the proportion of students from private schools is about 20%.

Flunk rate: This is the percentage of students who, for one reason or another, don't successfully complete their course by being awarded a degree. It does not include those who swap courses, but remain at the same institution. It's a good indication of how unhappy some people can get if they find themselves at the wrong college for them. Readers who use **push** properly are less likely to be adding to these statistics. Remember, science courses tend to have a higher flunk rate than others, so a higher rate in a technologically-leaning institution isn't necessarily a reason to reject it out of hand. In fact, flunk rates, just like any other single piece of information, should always be seen as only one part of the bigger picture. Figures are exclusively calculated by **push** from information supplied by HESA, the Government statistics agency. As HESA has only been around since 1994, we can only give figures for students on 3 year degree courses. Also, HESA reckon the data they collected in 1994 may not be 100% reliable. Unfortunately, it's the only data available but readers should be aware that a high flunk rate may be caused by inaccuracies in HESA's original data, rather than by lots of students flunking. Further information about how flunk rates and other statistics are calculated can be obtained from **push**.

Mature students: Those aged 21 or over at the time of starting their courses. Postgrads are not included.

Overseas students: Includes EU students from outside the UK.

Disabled students: These figures are obtained from the colleges who, if they keep records at all, often define 'disabled' differently. Some include only registered disabled students, others extend the definition to students with dyslexia, asthma or any students who, for whatever reason, choose to define themselves as disabled. **push** apologises that, for reasons of space, we haven't always used the most politically correct terms ('students with disabilities' or 'differently-abled students').

Staff/student ratios: Again, not as straightforward as it may appear. Part-time staff and students can muddy the statistical waters. But it gives you a rough idea of whether tutorials are going to be cosy little sherry sessions à deux, or rugby scrums with the tutor as the ball.

Clearing: The percentage of students who entered through the UCAS clearing system. Some institutions have (sometimes undeserved) reputations as UCAS dumping grounds. This figure should give an idea of the number of students whose presence isn't entirely by choice. Understandably, some universities are a little coy about revealing this figure.

ATMOSPHERE:
This section in the profiles, more than any other, gives the *real* feel of the place.

TRAVEL:

Trains & buses: All fares and other information are the best we can offer as we go to press - the proliferation of train companies in the wake of the privatisation of British Rail means that we can't guarantee how long these facts and figures will remain applicable. Fares given are the best we've been able to find at the time of writing, ie the cheapest possible return journey with a student railcard or apex ticket; some of these don't apply at certain times of the day and apex tickets have to be bought at least 2 weeks in advance.

Hitching: push would like to warn readers that if they don't know that hitching can be dangerous, then there is something wrong with them. push accepts no responsibility for students who have bad experiences when thumbing it, such as waiting 6 hours in the rain for a lift, being picked up by Robin Reliant-driving 'X-Files' obsessives or being made to listen to the Icelandic Eurovision entry on the car stereo.

LIBRARIES & COMPUTERS:

Unless otherwise stated, we give the total number of books in all the college libraries, not just the main library. For study places and computer workstations, we give the number available for general use and don't include places or terminals set aside exclusively for students on a particular course.

FAMOUS ALUMNI:

A bit of celebrity gossip; who went where. Just so students can boast that they're going to same college as that famous 1920s Swiss serial killer or whoever.

FURTHER INFORMATION:

Prospectuses are absolutely essential if you're seriously considering applying to an institution and invaluable for seeing what the college would like you to think of them. They are sales documents and whilst almost every word will be true, it will not be the truth, the whole truth and nothing but the truth. They are available from the address at the top of each profile.

On the other hand, some students' unions publish 'alternative' prospectuses, which present the point of view of students at the college. Also worth getting, although the views contained are almost exclusively biased and, since the writers have rarely visited a representative number of colleges, not very comparative.

We've also listed any videos, CD-ROMs, web sites or other sources of information. Some are just prospectuses dumped on the net; others are more interactive. Where possible we give you the address for the SU web site, as well as the official university one. If you've got the time and the facilities, check them out.

entertainment

Beer is:

 cheap

 average

 expensive

BEER & WINE:
Prices of beer and wine are given as the average at student bars and in towns. There are of course likely to be the usual guest ales and Mexican imports with fruit in the top which will be sold at rip-off prices.

·······social & political

The SU's activities and facilities are:

 frozen stiff

 lukewarm

 hot, hot, hot

CLUBS & SOCS:
Clubs and societies have been split into sporting and non-sporting, which isn't always easy. **push** has put them under whichever heading the college uses and you'd be well advised to check under both headings if the existence of a certain club is really important to you. Since it would get a bit repetitive otherwise, we've missed out the ones which crop up just about everywhere in the college profiles, but to be sure that the club you want is at the college you're looking at, turn to the 'clubs & societies' tables at the back (page 780). The only ones usually missed out are the course-related societies (for sucking up to tutors).

Of course, prospective students who've decided that somewhere is perfect apart from the fact that it doesn't have a 'Friends' Appreciation Society shouldn't be stopped from going there. At most colleges it's fairly easy to start a society - students only need to find between 20 and 50 others to say they want to join and the SU will often give them a packet to spend on new hairdos, a sofa and a smelly cat.

··········sports

Student sport is:

 slobbish

 average

 active and triumphant

········accommodation

The average rent is:

 cheap

 average

 expensive

RENT:
Colleges tend to transform mysteriously into conference centres the moment vacations start, which means that students living in college accommodation may well be turfed out with all their belongings to allow some pantyhose salesman to attend a corporate beerfest. **push** gives a weekly figure and, when comparing costs, it's worth considering how many weekly figures students are going to be paying. Also given are the percentages of full-time undergraduates living in catered and self-catered accommodation. Bear in mind that 'catered' can mean anything from the full-board of 3 square meals a day and a Harrods hamper for your picnics to a single 'pay-as-you-eat' canteen which you have to catch a bus to get to and serves cockroaches with the soup.

welfare

The welfare provisions is:

 poor

 passable

 pampering

FINANCIAL:
Ave debt: Debts, of course, vary from literally tens of thousands of pounds to, well, there must be some student somewhere whose bank balance isn't more vacant than Joanne Guest's grin (or wardrobe). Every year, **push** conducts the most comprehensive survey of student debt in the UK and the only one which breaks the figures down by college. We've taken a representative cross-section of students at each college and asked them how much money they owe, to banks, credit card companies, parents and friends and to the Student Loans Company. Figures show average debt accumulated per year of study, given to the nearest £50. Bear in mind that with the changes to student funding (see Hard **push**ed, page 17) debts are likely to rise dramatically.

Access funds: When student loans were introduced in 1990, the Government made some money available to colleges to help avoid the problems that were likely to arise for students who were less able to pay. The figures given are the total amount each college is currently allocated, though amounts will go up substantially in 1998/99 as maintenance grants are abolished (see Hard **push**ed, page 17). Students who want a slice of the cake should apply annually to their college, but not until they get there. Other sources of available income are listed below this figure.

Successful applications: The number of students who get a slice of the cake gives an indication of how large a slice they each got. Some colleges were only willing or able to provide figures as a percentage. Others wouldn't or couldn't give us any figures at all.

Hard pushed

Nowadays, being a student is almost the same as being in debt, but there are ways of stashing the cash and diverting the debts.

▶▶ If you're thinking about embarking on a course of study at a UK university or college, you should be thinking about debt at the same time. The two go together like... well, think of two things that go together really well and you're on the right lines. Debt has become such a fact of life for most students that some fall into a state of paralysis about the whole thing and never really deal with the problem. push can't wave a magic cliché and make debts disappear but we can come up with a few ideas to help students make the best out of a situation roughly equivalent to swimming the Atlantic with Pavarotti strapped to your knees.

At the brink of a promising career, starting with being accepted to university or college, most students don't want to think of the poverty they are going to have to put up with until they land that cushy job in merchant banking, marketing or medicine. Still less, if they are looking forward to a career where the greatest reward will be job satisfaction, such as teaching, social work or even acting.

However, there is little point starting a course you are not going to be able to afford to finish. Students have to ask themselves, 'How am I going to make ends meet?'.

If the answer is that your parents are so phenomenally wealthy and indulgent that they'll give you all the cash you need, then your problems are over. But, for those on this side of the rainbow, there are a number of alternatives to consider.

ECONOMISE

Whatever other options you take, economy is always the one that puts shoes on your feet. Decide what's important and pay for that. Then see how much money you have left and decide what else you'd like if possible. Plan expenditure – on a weekly basis if your income's tight – and stick to your plan.

Be pessimistic. Optimistic students don't check their balance when they shove their cards in the cash machine and sooner or later they get swallowed (the cards, not the students). Realists check their balance and then get out half the amount they wanted. Pessimists don't bother going to the cashpoint because they know there won't be anything there anyway. Hence they preserve enough readies to live a miserly, but not miserable existence.

As with most things, sensible moderation is the key. Students who are so desperate to economise that they never set foot in the SU bar and don't buy anything not directly related to food, shelter or academic survival may well come out the other end with a first class degree and a bank balance in the black but they might have missed out on many of the life experiences that make a degree course worthwhile. Students usually have to accept that Maserati and Armani aren't going to be on the shopping list for the next 3 or 4 years but the odd pint of beer or the next Super Furry Animals album aren't going to cast you into the fires of debt hell either.

GOVERNMENT FUNDING

Few things in life get quite so confusing as the current student funding situation. Despite the government's claims to the contrary, in March 98, 60% of sixth-formers had not even seen any of the information leaflets about the new arrangements. push, as ever, is here to help you tell the wood from the deforestation trucks and find out how you'll be affected.

First off, students have traditionally been entitled to LEA grants which come in two parts. The first part was designed to pay for tuition fees at college and the other part, the maintenance grant, was supposed to meet living costs while at university.

TUITION FEES

It will come as news only to those who have been in Timbuktu with their heads buried in an elephant's bottom, that the Government has recently decided to introduce means-testing for tuition fees. This means that a student's local LEA may no longer pay the full cost of their tuition at university.

How much lolly they have to fork out will usually depend on how much their parents earn. The DfEE estimates that if a student's parents' income exceeds about £35,000 before tax, they'll have to pay £1,000 towards their fees. If their parents' income is less than £35,000 but more than about £23,000, they'll have to pay between £45 and £1,000. If their parents' income is less than about £23,000 before tax, they won't have to pay fees at all and their LEA will carry on paying the full whack as before. This, at least, is the idea. As push went to press the NUS, the Campaign for Free Education, students all over the country and assorted rebel MPs were fighting the bill to introduce fees. Being realistic, however, push urges you to assume the worst.

There are a few exceptions to the rules outlined above:
(1) Students who started their course before 1st August 1998 will pay no fees for the duration of their course, regardless of their parents' income.
(2) Students who accepted a place on a course before 1st August 1997, but deferred their entry till 98 (aka taking a year out) won't have to pay fees for the duration of their course.
(3) Students on PGCE courses won't have to pay tuition fees.
(4) Scottish students on courses at Scottish universities and colleges which are a year longer than comparable courses in England and Wales won't pay fees for the extra year. However, students from the rest of the UK who study at Scottish institutions will have to pay fees for the whole of their course. However, even the House of Lords reckons this is crazy and it may yet be sorted out, so that all students on such courses don't have to pay fees for the extra year.
(5) Students on a sandwich course or industrial placement year will pay a reduced fee of up to £500 (again, dependent on income) for that year.

Whatever the case and whatever their parents' income, UK students should still apply to their LEA for the tuition fees part of their grant, or they could end up paying rather more than £1,000.

more
beans
when you open a student account

- £35
- Interest free (0% APR) overdraft
  – min £750
- Payment Card
- MasterCard

For more details call into
any branch of Lloyds Bank Plc.

Lloyds Bank

Lending and the issue of a Payment Card/MasterCard are subject to the Bank's assessment of your financial status and you must be 18 or over to apply. Overdraft facilities are repayable in full, on demand by the Bank. The Bank may refuse to open or continue an account, or refuse any deposit. Written quotations available on request from Lloyds Bank Plc, PO Box 112, Canons Way, Bristol BS99 7LB.

MAINTENANCE GRANTS

The maintenance grant part has always been means-tested, which means that whether you get any at all, and how much you get, depends, for most students, on how much your parents' income is. However, the 98-99 academic year is the final year that the maintenance grant will be available to new students. Since the introduction of the student loan in the early 90s, the grant has gradually been cut back while the loan has increased proportionally. This year the maintenance grant for students studying outside London and away from their parents' home is £810. Come autumn 1999, students who started their courses after 1st August 1998 won't get anything at all. Instead they'll have to find their living costs elsewhere. If they don't have a nest-egg, or their parents can't afford to pay for them, they have the option to take out a student loan. (For details see LOANS, below). So with tears in our eyes and sorrow in our hearts, **push** waves goodbye to Student Grant. Just for the record, the amounts available this time round are as follows:

For students living away from their parents, who start their course after 1st August 1998:	
in London	**£1,225**
elsewhere	**£ 810**
For students living with their parents, who start their course after 1st August 1998:	**£ 480**

As Paul Daniels would say... not a lot.

LOANS

A loan is money borrowed and don't you forget it. There are two fundamental problems with borrowing money: (i) sooner or later, whoever lent it will want it back, and (ii) they will want more than they lent in the first place. This applies whether it is borrowed from a bank, the Student Loans Company, a building society, whoever.

There are two possible exceptions. If they can afford it, students' parents often give them interest-free loans and many recognise that the likelihood of seeing it again is somewhat smaller than meeting June Whitfield at a death metal concert. On average, more than a fifth of a student's debt is to their parents. Sometimes, friends can be persuaded to lend each other a few quid to get by, but this is usually the quickest way to lose friends. Especially if they're students too, because the chances are they'll have financial problems of their own.

Student bank accounts often offer free overdraft facilities of £500 and even more. After the limit though, interest rates can be gob-stoppingly high, especially if the overdraft is unagreed. Students who intend to exceed their agreed limit, should tell the bank about it first. It's frightening as hell, but they're much nicer when they know what's going on and they send fewer rude letters and charge lower interest. They might, of course, say no, but they rarely cut students off without a penny so long as they've shown a responsible attitude.

Each year, most students can also apply for a Government-funded Student Loan from the inspiringly titled Student Loans Company. This is not, as rumour sometimes has it, interest-free. Interest is fixed at the rate of inflation; it's a cheaper loan than most, but it's not just a grant which has to be paid back.

However, just to make life that little bit more complicated, as of Autumn 1999 there will be two kinds of student loan available. Hold on to your hairdo, because here they come: the first type is for students who started their course before 1st August 1998, or who accepted a place before 1st August 1997 but chose to take a year out, and this loan is the one already in use by the Student Loans Company. The second type of loan will come into existence in the autumn of 1999 and will be available to students who started their courses after 1st August 1998. In other words, students who'll miss out on the maintenance grant from autumn 1999 will be able to get this new loan to live on while at university.

Neither loan has to be paid back until the student starts to earn money. Repayments for the first kind of loan begin when they're earning more than 85% of the average national income (currently £16,440 a year). Repayment of this loan is usually in 60 monthly installments over 5 years but can be speeded up for those who can afford it. Unfortunately, this means that the graduates' starting salary for many teachers, social workers and so on is just high enough and monthly repayments can be steep. Repayments for the new type of loan will start when a graduate is earning just £10,000 a year. However, the amount they have to pay back each month will be linked to how much they earn, rather than how much they've borrowed. This means that repayments for those on lower incomes will be smaller than at present. The downside is that it'll take them longer to pay off the loan.

Getting a Student Loan, however, is a fiendishly complicated process. Exactly how the new loans in 1999 will work is not yet set in stone, but it'll probably be similar to the current system. Students have to present their birth certificate, prove they're students where they say they are and probably do an impression of Jim Carrey dressed in a satin G-string. They're not available to postgraduates or overseas students and if in any doubt, check on your eligibility. After all this, students are currently entitled to the following amounts for each full year and for the final year (which doesn't include the summer):

	Full year	Final year
Students living away from their parents, who start their course after 1st August 1998:		
in London	£3,145	£2,565
elsewhere	£2,735	£2,265
Students living with their parents, who start their course after 1st August 1998:	£2,325	£1,970

There are other operations students can borrow from such as credit card companies and loan sharks, but if you do go down this path, check out the interest rates first and see what advance Satan will give on your soul. (It may be a better offer.)

JOBS, SPONSORSHIPS AND MORE

Earning a bob or two helps maximise income and, since working time can't be spent spending, it can even help minimise outgoings. The problem is finding a good job. For those who can find work from the employment agencies which don't have 'No Students' signs in the windows, too often it's a toss-up between valuable work experience for less than a condom machine earns in a convent, or dreadful drudgery for only reasonable readies.

There's also the problem of a job interfering with study. Students rarely find time to do more than a little bar work during term and just because some people call that five week period between terms 'the holidays', it doesn't mean they don't have dissertations, essays, field trips, projects and so on. Some unions and colleges run their own employment agencies or offer work to their own students – obviously they're much more likely to be sympathetic about the need to juggle paid work with academic commitments.

Earning extras is all very well, but except for those with a specially marketable talent (such as being bilingual, able to type at 80 wpm or having insider knowledge about the 2:30 at Chepstow), students should never rely on what they might make. Therefore, pessimism intact, it's best to leave it out of the equation when calculating budgets.

Some employers offer schemes whereby students are subsidised for the duration of their courses, usually in exchange for work during the vacation or after graduation. The armed forces and science/technology based organisations are usually the best bet for this – if you're one of those admirably and unfeasibly sussed people who mapped out what they wanted to do with their lives at the age of 12 it could be worthwhile contacting employers in your chosen field and seeing what they have to offer.

Some universities and colleges also have their own set of sponsorships and bursaries, many of which are dependent on studying a certain subject or having been born in a particular county on a Thursday when Aquarius was in the ascendant. There might not be much available but, again, it's always worth checking out the possibilities. In many cases, these schemes are being restructured to help students meet tuition fees and living costs in the wake of the new funding developments.

TOP TIPS
Finally a couple of cunning ploys to employ...
(1) Whether they need it or not, students should take up a student loan. Even for those who disagree with them from a political standpoint, the best way to abuse the system is to get one. Borrow the money and invest it elsewhere. The interest charged on a student loan at the moment is about 3.75%pa. In most building societies, it's easy enough to earn about 5% interest on investments over £500. So you're quids in, whatever.
(2) Students who can apply for state benefits, should do. Unfortunately, when student loans were introduced, students also became the only members of society not entitled to normal benefits because of their occupation. Students are not allowed to collect either unemployment benefit during their vacations if they cannot find work and are not allowed to claim housing benefit. In London, where rents are often well over £65 a week, this has proved particularly harsh. It doesn't take much maths to realise that at that level, rent alone is £3,380, leaving a princely sum of £990 for books, travel, food and so on - and that's assuming they get the full grant and loan.

(22)

However, students with disabilities or with dependents will still find they can claim some benefits.

(3) Get advice. Banks are always willing to provide a pearl or two of wisdom on budgeting and the like and students' unions have all sorts of resources to help make the most of money.

pushing
out the boat

A look at the pros and cons of taking a year out before going on to higher education.

Why do students consider taking a year off? They're only young once, so why waste time not getting on with life? Why don't they just get a degree, get a job and get an income? Why don't they choose life, choose a pension plan, choose 2.4 kids, a C&A charge account and a 34-inch telly with surround sound with a boob-job thrown in? Why don't they take the short cut and just coat themselves in compost and rot?

Why? Because it's more fun to spend a year getting up to the kind of thing they can only do when they've got the youth and the opportunity, when they haven't got kids and when slumming it round the Amazon basin doesn't leave bits of mosquito in their dentures.

But it's not all fun and opportunity-seizing, there are real practical advantages too. Far from the old view that time out is worthless bumming around, a constructive year off is now an immense asset in the competitive job market. An extended CV is better than a brown envelope stuffed with used fifties when it comes to sending out job applications. Students who've taken a year out or spent their long vacations broadening their horizons, have got more to offer to a potential employer. They stand out from the crowd at every opportunity and not just because they smell funny. It won't get them a position for which they're not qualified, but all things being equal, it helps.

With little or no real work experience, employers will have to make judgements based on qualifications and nobody's fooled for a moment into thinking that a degree in politics or an A-level in physics is relevant to a career in marketing, management or merchant banking. If they can find something to pick a student from the rest of the pack, they'll home in like wasps to alcopops. Many employers even discriminate against students who spent long summer vacations living with their parents, staying in bed and watching 'Teletubbies'.

Another reason some students take a year out is simply to work and store up their cash to see them through university. There are very few ways to avoid being in debt after graduation, but

one of them is to have cash before you start. The NUS estimate that the current average student debt on graduation is around £13,000. You might not be able to stash that sort of money away in one year before college, but you could make a dent.

But during a year out, time can be even more valuable than money. Even if money's tight, with time, students can always find a way to get away or get up to something worthwhile. Time is necessary - money isn't. Even a bout of globe-trotting doesn't have to cost the earth. It's all too easy to think cash is needed for a good time and so students sit around waiting for a job that doesn't turn up. They'd be better off using that waiting time to get out of the rut and out of the country.

Of course, some ventures do require money - for example, for a 6 month expedition across Africa several hundred quid minimum up front would be needed. But there are also ways of getting overseas for less than £100, such as crewing on a yacht to the Caribbean, being a youth leader at an American summer camp or picking fruit on a kibbutz in Israel. One thing leads to another and other opportunities open up. Travel breeds confidence, which breeds success.

If students plan to work and travel overseas, it's worth pausing to consider aims and objectives. To promote the environment? To conserve wildlife? To make some money? Or simply have a unique experience, filled with self discovery? These things are all very well, but never forget the fun factor.

Students shouldn't worry about what they think they *should* do - they should do what they really *want* to. Time out doesn't have to be politically correct - a year spent ski bumming in Switzerland is not inferior to one spent helping orphans in India or saving a rain forest in South East Asia.

Whatever they end up doing - even if they eventually decide to stay at home and get work experience (or re-sit exams) - students shouldn't expect non-stop action. They're unlikely to complete a trans-Africa expedition without getting stomach problems, very unlikely to sail across the Atlantic without getting sea sick and there's no chance of going to Australia

WORKING ADVENTURES WORLDWIDE

If you want to make the most of a 'year out' after school or a long summer vacation from university, you'll benefit from BUNAC's support and advice on work and travel overseas.

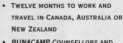

- TWELVE MONTHS TO WORK AND TRAVEL IN CANADA, AUSTRALIA OR NEW ZEALAND
- *BUNACAMP COUNSELLORS* AND *KAMP*-SUMMER JOBS IN CHILDREN'S SUMMER CAMPS IN THE USA
- SUMMER JOBS IN THE USA AND CANADA
- 3-18 MONTH INTERNSHIP WITH *OPT USA*

For full details of BUNAC's exciting work and travel programmes, send your name and address on a postcard to The Fresher's Dept. at the address below.

BUNAC • 16 BOWLING GREEN LANE • LONDON EC1R OBD
TEL: 0171. 251. 3472 EMAIL: BUNAC@EASYNET.CO.UK

without getting hungover. But new friends, knowledge, self-confidence and experience will make the sacrifices worthwhile.

When, after a year out, a student becomes a fresher, you can always tell they're not straight from school. They're the ones for whom new challenges are not quite such a fresh experience. Or maybe the insufferably arrogant ones...

ping
on a bit

A few wise words for mature students and returners to higher education.

►► First off, a mature student is not necessarily someone who wears cardigans and shakes their greying or balding head in a responsible attitude kind of way saying, 'It's not like it was in my day'. Nor necessarily are they pushing on a bit. Students can be classified as mature from as young as 21. The only generally accepted definition is that mature students are not the same age as conventional students and they are (with a few exceptions) not coming to higher education straight from school.

If you are returning to education, there are special considerations to be taken into account which vary enormously from one college to another. There's no need to accept sloppy seconds and just *make do* when it comes to higher education - there's enough choice to put your foot down and set an agenda according to your own specific needs. Most students' unions (SUs) provide some facilities for mature students such as common rooms, mature student groups and specialised welfare advice. Make a checklist of needs from housing through to entertainment which will make a difference to which college you choose. Although mature students often have roots and ties which may be an incentive to look no further than the most local college, many will find that special provisions for mature students may make a broader search worthwhile.

Some colleges provide specialised packages which are centred on people who have not just left the parental home. For example, many offer off-campus self-catering accommodation, others have specialised flats for mature students with their partner (usually only if married) and even their children, though it's rare to find places that can accommodate more than one child per couple. The college will probably also provide house hunting info for those who'd rather go it alone. The Accommodation Officer will be most handy for this - SUs' accommodation help is generally geared to conventional students.

As for social life, most entertainments centre around the

SU rather than the college. **push** gives the low-down on the goings-on, but bear in mind that bars may be full of students who, for the first time, don't have to prove their age to buy a pint and discos will be aimed at groovy young things who think that Simon & Garfunkel is a firm of solicitors. From gigs to grub, what do you want to do? And does the college you're looking at provide it?

If appropriate, check about childcare facilities as many colleges are only beginning to develop services in this area. **push** tells you whether there's a creche, but under that description can be anything from well-staffed care at subsidised cost for children from 6 months to 5 years old to some nobody who fancied a spot of babysitting, swamped by squawking brats and tipped up paint pots. In most colleges, the SU is either the main provider of childcare facilities on campus or knows best what provisions are available and will give an honest opinion of how good they are. Either get in touch in person - talk to the Welfare Officer - or ask for a copy of the SU handbook or alternative prospectus.

Although many students are aged over 21, the mainstream of facilities still caters for the 18+ age range. Mature students can feel isolated and so it's useful if there are others in the same boat and a forum for them to meet. Some SUs provide better support than others and many mature student groups organise their own functions. **push** gives the mature student percentages and, under the Welfare section, says whether there is a mature students' association.

pushing
back the
frontiers

Being disabled doesn't mean your needs cannot be met at University. Skill (the National Bureau for Students with Disabilities) points the way...

Being disabled doesn't mean going to higher education will be different for you - the other information in **push** is as relevant to you as anyone else - but if you do have a disability, medical condition or specific learning difficulty, you may have a few more things to think about before you apply.

As a disabled student you will need to know if your disability related needs can be met in colleges, but don't be tempted to make disability the only criteria you use when making choices - remember that the subject you are going to study, the social life and so on are all just as important to you as to a non-disabled student.

Skill produces a guide called 'Higher Education and Disability' which gives advice about applying and also includes profiles of some universities' facilities for disabled students. The courses database ECCTIS 2000 includes information about access and facilities for disabled students in all UK HE establishments, as well as named contacts. It's usually available in careers offices and some schools and colleges.

Don't be afraid to contact colleges before applying. If you're not sure what's available, never be afraid to ask. All colleges of Higher Education produce disability statements so if something doesn't make you feel welcome, let them know.

Sometimes it's a good idea to visit colleges before applying. 'Information visits' are a good way for you to check out the university's facilities and attitude. Consider all areas of student life - it may be just as important for you socially to get into the bar and meet other students as it is for you academically to get into the library and find books.

If you are eligible for a mandatory grant, there is a disabled students' allowance split into 3 components to help with disability related costs in studying. Skill produces a lot of information about these allowances and how to apply for them.

There's no need for you to do everything on your own. There are college advisers and union welfare officers. Some SUs have disability officers and some colleges have disabled students' groups for support and campaigning. NUS nationally has a disabled students' committee.

Skill's Information Service is available for telephone/minicom enquiries on 0171 978 9890 between 1:30pm and 4:30pm Monday to Friday, or write to: Skill, 336 Brixton Road, London, SW9 7AA. Skill also has a membership scheme and a newsletter written by and for students called 'Notes and Quotes'. So if you've any questions, meet any problems, or if you'd like to be involved in Skill's work, why not get in touch?

Women push forward

Women are entering higher education in greater numbers than ever but they still face problems...

 Women in higher education institutions often have to tackle prejudices and years of men doing things their way. It's not called the Old Boys' Network for nothing.

However, now there's a new agenda, new students, new types of student with different priorities and concerns from the traditional 18-year-old male student with no dependents on his way up the education ladder without ever having had a significant break.

Some colleges have reacted better than others to the new demands and have realised what changes they should make to policies and services. However, commitment to equal opportunities does not always live up to expectations.

In general women still have a harder time than men when it comes to personal finances and housing. For example, as women generally earn less and have different work patterns from men, the fear of student debt is greater. Or, another example, women need safe and secure, as well as affordable, housing. Too often, safety is put second to cost in seeking a place to live, especially when women students have more money worries.

On a daily basis, other problems remain sensitive issues in many colleges, such as harassment and lack of campus safety. These create genuine obstacles for many women and before applying to any, it's worth a chat to the students' union's women's officer (if it has one) to check up on a student's view of the college's attitude and past record.

Similarly, those with childcare responsibilities should check out the situation at their college well in advance of the commencement of study. At some colleges, there's a serious lack of on-site care. Often, there are no facilities at all, but even if there are, frequently they don't cater for enough children, don't take on young children, have prohibitively high costs or don't operate nurseries at suitable times of the day.

On the up-side though, nowadays, most SUs do have women's officers (increasingly, these are sabbatical positions) and there's often a women's group (not only providing support, but also offering a campaigning forum) and a safety bus, either exclusively for women students or giving them priority.

p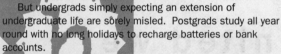grads

Some students become addicted to student life and think, what the hell, I'll do another degree. But life as a postgrad is very different from the lazy hazy daze of days as first degree students and it can be just as troubled financially. Here are some of the pitfalls for postgrads.

Whether it's because they don't think they'll get a job or not the job they want, or they want to postpone it, or being a student is just too much fun, or maybe because of a sheer commitment to their subject, more than 100,000 undergrads stay on after graduating to take postgraduate courses.

But undergrads simply expecting an extension of undergraduate life are sorely misled. Postgrads study all year round with no long holidays to recharge batteries or bank accounts.

Grants, too, are harder to come by - very few postgrads are guaranteed funding for any course (only really medics, trainee teachers and the like). This applies not only to maintenance grants (money to live on for which even first degree students are means tested), but also to tuition costs, all of which postgrads have to meet themselves, regardless of income. What grants are available are awarded on a competitive basis and so it's a good idea to have a pretty damn impressive first degree (a 2:2 is thought to be cutting it fine for most courses). It's also a good idea to be able to apply to an authority who're more generous with grants (they vary considerably).

Postgrads aren't allowed to apply for student loans, but instead there are Government-subsidised Career Development Loans, which can be large enough to help pay course fees.

At the end of the day, a postgraduate qualification may solve the financial problems it creates. Postgrads stand out from the crowd to potential employers and can expect to earn more. However, many employers prefer to train recent undergraduates and postgrads can find themselves overqualified. Many postgrads become professional academics, but the financial rewards alone are not likely to be a temptation.

Postgraduate courses split into 2 broad types - those that are taught and those that centre on research.

Students must research for 1 or 2 years to get a Masters degree or MPhil, or 3 years for a Doctorate. However, these are minimum periods - most students take a bit longer and should be prepared for a lean period writing up their work after the grant (if they have one) has stopped. Funding for research is available from Research Councils, charities or on research contracts from the institutions themselves. Commercially valuable research can often attract industrial sponsorship and delving into new types of plastic is likely to be less financially fraught than examining the philology of Philo. Although there's no teaching, postgrads' research is supervised and it's important the supervisor is appropriately clued up. Postgrads should interview whoever will be supervising them before accepting a place - it's important not only that supervisors are able to appreciate the subtleties of their postgrads' work, but also that they get on well.

As for taught courses, they are usually part of an extended career ladder or a stepping stone to a research degree. They are either for students who want to specialise in a particular field or want to convert their qualifications to a different area. Conversion courses in particular vary greatly in what they offer, so students should be sure not just that it's suitable, but also why it is. Grants for these courses are available from the same sources as for research degrees.

United we

Call them talking shops, bop shops, shopping centres or advice centres, what are students' unions? Who are they? Over to the NUS...

▶▶ Inescapable, unavoidable and absolutely essential. Within minutes of arriving at university you'll find yourself in your student union and frankly, till the day you graduate, you'll want it.

Students' unions (SUs) form the collective voice of the student body. Each student is a member of the students' union, automatically, and each student will be involved in running the union, through general meetings and electing executive officers. It costs you zero and you can't get much cheaper than that. The union represents you and your interests and whatever you want to do, you can, because you own and run your union and you can make it happen.

Students' unions work in different ways. If you want to know where to find accommodation, contraception, more money, even how to get a job, they have trained staff and student officers to help. If you want to disco till dawn, eat, drink and be merry, this is the place to be. But it's more than top bands, cheap drink, decent food and good advice. If you want to join any one of the thousands of different student sporting, social, political, cultural or special interest clubs and societies, from tiddlywinks to the lambada, then get down to the union.

And if you have a particular gripe, if there aren't enough books in the library, minibuses for the hockey teams, halls of residence or similar, then union officers will meet with the college administrators and sort it out for you. They represent your views at college meetings and make sure the student voice is heard.

Your union will also probably be a member of the National Union of Students. NUS is a confederation of unions representing over 3 million students in the UK. NUS gives you national representation, letting Parliament and the press know exactly what you think and lobbying for change. NUS also provides back-up and training for all your individual elected union officers.

p u s h ing

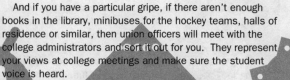

the pennies

They're a generous bunch these students. Penniless themselves they give and raise millions each year for charity. Really it's an excuse for often obscene, often illegal and always fun activity in the name of a good cause. This is how you get from charity Rags to riches...

 It's big and throbbing. Lots of people get excited about it. Much beer is drunk, many songs are sung and pots of dough are raised for charities. In fact, millions of pounds are raised every year by charity Rags across the UK.

10 years or so ago, Rags were seen as a group of students indulging in light-hearted pranks, concentrated into one week of general debauchery. Oh yes, some money was usually given to worthwhile causes as an excuse for such orgiastic goings on.

But these days, Rags are highly motivated and remarkably professional and run by students indulging in light-hearted pranks, concentrated into one week of general debauchery.

This week is known as 'Rag Week'. It's exact timing and content varies (and that even includes how many days make a week) from college to college. More often than not, there are beerfests, floats processions, collections, stunts, gungings, hit squads, parties, bands and much more. The big differences are that these days Rags focus as much on funds as fun and carry on their collection campaigns almost all year round raising ever more and more.

When students first get to college, they usually find themselves joining half a dozen societies or more. Rag is generally one of the very few that is completely free to join. At most places, students can find themselves at the heart of activities or on the organising committee early in the first term.

Rag is a most peculiar occupation. You try convincing a group of freshers that standing on a windy street corner asking Joe Public for a donation is good fun. It's not that easy, but it is a laugh. Meeting folks, chatting up the old dears, going for 'a' pint afterwards. It's all part of the job and it's addictive. Students only have to go on one 'Rag raid' (collection trip) to get caught up in it all. Before they know it, they're badgered into writing the Rag Mag (usually full of coarse humour), publicising the next big event or scrounging prizes for the raffle.

For many, Rag becomes the centre of their social life. Joining the course clubs is all well and good, but there is only so much fun that the Chemistry Society can generate and it doesn't do much to ease overloaded social consciences.

Almost every college has a Rag of some description. Of course, they're very different and **push** details them all. However, they're all guaranteed to raise a laugh, a pint glass, and not an insignificant amount of money for charity.

push

college

profiles

University of Aberdeen

University of Abertay Dundee

Aberystwyth, University of Wales

- African Studies
  see SOAS

- Anglia
  see University of East Anglia

Anglia Polytechnic University

Aston University

• •

University of Aberdeen

University of Aberdeen, Regent Walk, Aberdeen, AB24 3FX.
Tel: (01224) 272091. Fax: (01224) 272576.
E-mail: schlia@admin.abdn.ac.uk
Students' Representative Council, University of Aberdeen,
50/52 College Bounds, Aberdeen, AB2 3DS. Tel: (01224)
272965. Fax: (01224) 272977. E-mail: src@abdn.ac.uk

········**General**

The first university in the alphabet is also the most northerly,
way up there in the so-called 'Granite City'. The old stone city
(*marginally warmer than a paparazzi's welcome at the Princess
Di Appreciation Society AGM*) lies on the east coast of
Scotland, suitably placed to be the oil capital of Europe, and
spanned all round by *spectacular* castles and coastline,
beaches and lochs, the Grampians and the Cairngorms. *It's a
pretty place too*, with flowers, parks and *pleasant* architecture
in every wee nook and cranny. The University is based on 3
sites which once made up 2 separate universities. In fact,
Aberdeen had 2 universities at a time when that was the total
in the whole of England. The larger, main site is King's
College in Old Aberdeen, *a satisfying eyeful* of 15th century

**❛Text in italics is PUSH's point
of view – take it or leave it.❜**

a

buildings, modern blocks, green space and cobbled streets, ¾ mile north of the city centre where Marischal College is situated. The Medical School at Foresterhill is further inland to the west.

49% ♂♂♂♂♂♀♀♀♀♀ 51%

Sex ratio(M:F): 49%:51%	Founded: 1495
Full time u'grads: 8,351	Part time: 115
Postgrads: 1,250	Non-degree: 683
Ave course: 4yrs	Ethnic: 3%
Private/state school: n/a	Flunk rate: n/a
Mature students: 21%	Overseas students: 12%
Disabled students: 4.5%	Staff/student ratio: 1:15
Clearing: 12%	

ATMOSPHERE:
Aberdeen attracts many English, as well as Scottish students, who often find themselves further from home and more isolated than they'd anticipated. However, the University offers plenty of excitement of its own in a beautiful and relaxed environment. Students at Marischal College find that any separation from the main site is counter-balanced by being closer to the city centre, but students do complain that the only mixing they do is in the University accommodation within their own year.

THE CITY:
● Population: 201,099 ● London: 410miles
● Edinburgh: 103miles ● Dundee: 75miles
Aberdeen is busy to the point of being congested, but it's clean and is currently enjoying relative prosperity due to North Sea oil. The trade in black slippery stuff has attracted a varied cultural cocktail from all over Scotland and England, as well as industrial clusters and tankers. Consequently, the wee fishing fleet is on the wane. But Aberdeen isn't a sprawling waste, not by a long shot, and it's easy to burst out into *splendid* countryside and on to sandy beaches. Miles from anywhere, the city has more than enough shops to spend a student grant, *which takes about 34 seconds since it's not a cheap town.* It has bookshops and banks (most major branches) and several museums, including the City Art Gallery and the Maritime Museum (Aberdeen's oldest building).

TRAVEL:
Trains: Despite being so far north (the same latitude as St Petersburg), British Rail connections are quite good, but are expensive. Among many Scottish and some English towns, services are offered to London (£51.80), Glasgow (£25.95) and Dundee (£12.30).
Buses: National Express coach services to, among other places, London (£43.00), Glasgow (£11.90), Dundee (£5.90). Citylink and Stagecoach also run services.
Car: A92, A93, A94 and A96. 2 miles to the nearest junction.
Air: Aberdeen Airport offers inland flights around the UK and to some European cities.
Ferries: There's a ferry service to Lerwick in the Shetlands.
Hitching: The A92 is fairly major and once hitchers have got to

the M90, it's plain sailing. The hitches of hitching, though, are that it's a long, long road and going west inland is nigh impossible.

Local: Good bus services run anywhere in the city from 35p, useful for getting into the centre from King's.

Taxis: Useful late at night, but expensive - £4 from the station to King's, £8 from the airport.

Bicycles: Despite the heavy traffic and the cold winds, many students take to pedal power, because bikes make the ¾ mile from the halls to the campuses easy. Incidentally, bike theft is as rare as any other crime in Aberdeen which has the lowest crime rate in Britain for a city its size.

LIBRARIES & COMPUTERS:
● Books: 1,050,000 ● Study places: 1,834
● Computer workstations: 742
There are 6 libraries, including 1 at the Medical School. 24hr computer access.

CAREER PROSPECTS:
● Careers Service ● No of staff: 6full/4part
● Unemployed after 6mths (1996): 5.5%

SPECIAL FEATURES:
● Aberdeen is the only UK university offering a course in Belgian law.
● When James IV of Scotland applied to the Pope for permission to found a university in Aberdeen, he declared that the area contained 'men who are rude, ignorant of letters and almost barbarous' and that by providing higher education 'the ignorant would become informed and the rude become learned'.

FAMOUS ALUMNI:
Nicky Campbell (DJ); Iain Crichton-Smith (poet); Iain Cuthbertson (actor); Alistair Darling MP (Lab); Sandy Gall (ITV newsreader); Denys Henderson (Chair of ICI); Kenneth McKellar (singer); David McLean MP (Con); James Naughtie (BBC 'Today' presenter).

FURTHER INFO:
Prospectuses for undergrads and postgrads, a handbook for international students, a web site (http://www.abdn.ac.uk).

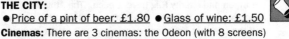

entertainment

THE CITY:
● Price of a pint of beer: £1.80 ● Glass of wine: £1.50
Cinemas: There are 3 cinemas: the Odeon (with 8 screens) and the *almost arty* Capital (1) and a new Virgin multiplex.
Theatres: His Majesty's Theatre attracts *big time* ballet and opera on tour as well as *less elite* delights like pantos. Aberdeen Arts Centre (currently under threat of closure) is smaller and hosts more fringey shows.
Pubs: A mixture of old men's pubs and pretentious glittery bars with little dance floors. **push***plugs: Bond Bar, King Street Mill, Machar Bar. Avoid Smart Alec's with its enthusiastic door staff.*
Clubs/discos: *Whilst not exactly bop city, Aberdeen has enough clubs to keep hip hips moving.* **push***plugs: Mudd*

Club at the Palace (hard rock/indie); Ministry (techno/house); L'Akimbo at Exodus (hard house); Glider at Pelican (Britpop/acid jazz); Amadeus at 'The Beach' (free buses on student nights).

Music venues: Many pubs have regular folk or rock performances, but the *top student-oriented* venues are the Music Hall, Beach Ballroom and the Lemon Tree. The Exhibition Centre pulls in *bigger* names.

Eating Out: *Eating out can be expensive compared to much of Scotland. Fish is a local speciality.* **push***plugs: Gio's, Littlejohn's, Pierre Victoire. Ashvale chippy is the best in town.*

UNIVERSITY:

● Price of a pint of beer: £1.50 ● Glass of wine: £1.30

Bars: There are 5 bars in the Union: The Dungeon (subdued lighting with messages on the wall like 'The crime is life, the sentence is death'); the Sivell's Cocktail Lounge (large, airy, domed, art deco wine bar with murals); Elf and Factory, which are mainly ents venues. Associates is a new non-smoking bar, and the New Seasons Cafe bar.

Theatres: Performers perform and actors act in the University theatre, *often to critical acclaim (and not just their mums).* Rag runs a show each year.

Cinema: 2 films a week, *nothing too esoteric.*

Music venues: The Elf (cap 473) hosts live bands, Wannadies and Death in Vegas among them recently. Folk music free in the Union on Wednesdays.

Clubs/discos: The Elf, Factory and the Dungeon share the flashing-light chores.

Cabaret: Fortnightly comedy slots at the Elf; Parrot and Alan Parker have trekked up in the past.

Food: The Central Refectory at King's offers *good value* chow 9am-6pm and the Dungeon also does snacks and lunches. The New Seasons Cafe bar does *great* grub all day.

Balls: Many departmental balls (*land economy is supposed to be the best*).

·········· social & political

STUDENTS' REPRESENTATIVE COUNCIL:
● 5 sabbaticals ● Turnout at last ballot: 15%
● NUS member

The Union's role is strictly commercial while the SRC provides representation and welfare. The SRC has 2 sabbaticals and the Union and charity Rag have 1 each. The Athletics Association has the 5th. The SRC is the body affiliated to NUS and the one that organises campaigns. *Students, though, despite being quite aware and sound, are rarely stirred into action, but when they do, ooh, when they do... It must be all the porridge. Having said that, only 150 students attended a recent demo against Tuition Fees in Edinburgh and they only went to do some shopping.*

SU FACILITIES:

The *lively* Union Building (the 2nd largest in Scotland) is in the city centre near Marischal, although it also has a mini-market at Hillhead Halls and a general shop. In the Union itself, there are 2 bars, a restaurant, 2 disco venues, a disco for hire, showers, photocopying, games room (with pool table, games machines and table football), welfare shop, large snooker hall, vending machine, cashpoint, launderette, music practice room, dark room and meeting rooms.

CLUBS (NON SPORTING):

AUSNA (Scots Nationalists); Bird; Bridge; Buddhist; Celtic; Centre Stage; Chinese Christian; CND; Creative Writing; Duke of Edinburgh; Exploration; Gilbert & Sullivan; Arabian Gulf Students; HELP (Scotland); Hong Kong Students; Jordanean; Korean; Law Mooting (legal debating); Live Music; Malaysian; Malt Whisky; Methodists; Pakistan; Parents Co-op; Red Cross; Role-playing; Re-enactment; Revelation; Ring of Fire; Scots Leid Quorum; Scroll; SNP; Sri Lankan; Street Drummers; Street Entertainers; Taiwanese; Ten Pin Bowling; Treading The Boards (musicals); Wine.

OTHER ORGANISATIONS:

Debater: Along with the Union, the SRC and the AA (Athletics Association - nothing to do with automobiles or alcoholics), students become members, automatically and for free, of a 4th organisation when they join Aberdeen University. That is Debater, one of the country's oldest mooting societies that does nothing but host discussions on topics of every hue and cry and come to conclusions (or not) about them. *It's popular fun and not as pompous as the Oxbridge debating unions.*
Others: The weekly student newspaper is 'Gaudie'. As part of the Rag, the Torcher Parade takes place each year, the largest torchlight parade in Europe. Students have 16 hours to design and make their own float and then process through the streets with folks throwing money at them. SCAG stands for Student Community Action Group and is the *energetic* local help organisation run by student volunteers.

RELIGIOUS:

● 3 chaplains (RC, CofS, Episcopal)
Within the University there are 2 chapels and a small mosque. Locally, apart from St Mary's Cathedral (Catholic), St Andrew's Cathedral (Episcopal) and St Machar's Cathedral (Presbyterian), there are local places of worship for Catholics, Anglicans, Methodists, Mormons, Christian Scientists, Quakers and, of course, members of the Church of Scotland.

PAID WORK:

Apart from the normal openings in bars, shops and restaurants, students can sometimes find work in the oil industry, particularly those whose studies are in some relevant field.

sports

● Recent successes: rowing
Sports are organised by the Athletics Association, the President of which is a sabbatical officer, *indicating the seriousness with which sport is taken. However, students are better at getting involved for a bit of a giggle than competing successfully.* There are minimal charges for facilities (eg 40p squash court hire).

SPORTS FACILITIES:

Most facilities are based on 2 sites. The Butchart Recreation Centre at King's contains a sports hall, gym, weights room, 4 squash courts and a climbing wall. Also at King's, there are a swimming pool, 2 more squash courts, playing fields and 3 all-weather tennis courts (or sometimes 1 all-weather pitch instead). However, the main sports fields are at Balgownie, 2

a

miles north, where there are more playing fields (bringing the total to just under 20 acres), a running track, golf course and dry ski slope. Elsewhere, the University has a boathouse on the River Dee, a glider at Aboyne and a mountain hut at Lochnagar.

SPORTING CLUBS:
Aikido; Boat; Boxing; Curling; Gaelic Football; Gliding; Inline Hockey; Lacrosse; Life Saving; Nordic Ski; Octopush; Potholing and Caving; Shinty; Small Arms; Trampoline; Triathlon; Weightlifting; Windsurfing.

ATTRACTIONS:
The local football team is Aberdeen FC, alias 'the Dons'.

accommodation
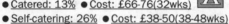

IN COLLEGE:
● Catered: 13% ● Cost: £66-76(32wks)
● Self-catering: 26% ● Cost: £38-50(38-48wks)
Availability: All first years who want it are provided with accommodation. Many 2nd years live in as well, but students are usually on their own for the last 2 years. The halls themselves, in 3 groups, are *well-equipped modern blocks set in pleasant grounds*. The Hillhead Halls are the largest set, about ¾ of a mile north of King's, a mixture of halls (with *tiny* rooms) and flats. *Hillhead is the most spirited hangout, as well as being cheaper*. Dunbar and Crombie-Johnston Halls are closer and dearer. The self-catering accommodation is split between blocks of flats, shared between 6 to 8 students, and local flats and houses either owned or leased by the University, a few of which are available for married couples.
Car parking: Parking is free with a permit and *there's enough, but only just.*

EXTERNALLY:
● Ave rent: £45
Availability: Local landlords have of late been ignoring the student trade preferring the better income from the oil industry. *There is still just about enough to go round, though, but it's expensive.* There are cheap areas like Sandilands, *but it's too rough to make it worth it*; students are better off in Ferryhill, King St, George St, Urquhart Rd and Rosemount for example.

welfare

SERVICES:
● Nursery ● Lesbian & Gay Society
● Mature SA ● Overseas SA ● Postgrad SA ● Minibus
● Women's Officer ● Self-defence classes
Apart from the 5 part-time trained staff of the University's Counselling Service, which is the universal shoulder for crying eyes to weep on, students can also get advice and support from their personal adviser, the welfare officer or the finance adviser at the SRC. For leprous outbreaks and dismembered limbs, the student health centre has 4 doctors, a dentist and a nurse.
Women: In addition to the Women's Group, there's an action group and a women's campaigning week. *Seaton Park should be avoided at night.*

Disabled: Newest halls have wheelchair access, but *the SRC is facing an uphill, cobbled, rampless struggle.* The library has a book scanner for sight-impaired students. All departments have a disabilities co-ordinator.

FINANCE:
- Ave debt per year: £1,400 • Access fund: £237,350
- Successful applications (1996): 994

There are about 150 various endowments, bursaries, external grants and trusts available for school leavers coming to Aberdeen University. *Some are very obscure*, for example, for one, applicants must be from Cabrach (a tiny village 40 miles away) and promise not to drink or smoke throughout their degree.

University of Abertay Dundee

▼
▼ • *Formerly Dundee Institute of Technology*
University of Abertay Dundee, 40 Bell Street, Dundee, DD1 1HG.   Tel: (01382) 308080. Fax: (01382) 308937. E-mail: iro@abertay-dundee.ac.uk
University of Abertay Dundee Students' Association, Bell Street, Dundee, DD1 1HG.   Tel: (01382) 227477.

General

Dundee's newest university has 3 sites, all within about 2 minutes' walk from the town centre. The large and *labyrinthine* main building is set around a grassy quad (and, *less attractively,* opposite a multi-storey car park). *It's a questionable mix of Edwardian and 70s architecture and it can be difficult to find your way around.* 500 yards away is the *nondescript* Marketgait annexe. Once upon a time it was a jute mill, then it became a bowling alley, now it houses the Students' Association and a few teaching rooms over a garage. The last building is an old house in Nichol Street which adds an extra 10 classrooms.

50% ♂♂♂♂♂♀♀♀♀♀ 50%	
Sex ratio(M:F): 50%:50%	Founded: 1994
Full time u'grads: 3,316	Part time: 349
Postgrads: 206	Non-degree: 425
Ave course: 4yrs	Ethnic: 3%
Private/state school: 3%	Flunk rate: n/a
Mature students: 31%	Overseas students: 11.3%
Disabled students: 2.6%	Staff/student ratio: 1:18
Clearing: n/a	

ATMOSPHERE:
Many students are local and most are tekkies of some description. They seem happy to be at Abertay although some

a

nurse a grudge against Dundee University. For the time being, the small numbers and cosy atmosphere mean that student/staff relations are very good.

THE CITY: see University of Dundee

TRAVEL: see University of Dundee
Dundee station is 10 minutes' walk from the University. The very comprehensive local bus service is well used by students. The bus fare from the halls to the University is 80p.

LIBRARIES & COMPUTERS:
- Books: 133,965 ● Study places: 700
- Computer workstations: 1,200

The library is also available for use by the public and Dundee University students, *who, it is sometimes complained, take all the books*. A new £8m development provides 24hr access during exams and is a *vast* improvement, but students still have to use the library at Dundee University for some books.

CAREER PROSPECTS:
- Careers Service ● No of staff: 1full/2part
- Unemployed after 6mths (1997): 6.2%

SPECIAL FEATURES:
- Among its more unusual departments, Abertay is home to the Wastewater Technology Centre (*probably what you think it is*) and the Scottish Institute for Wood Technology.

FAMOUS ALUMNI:
David Jones (invented Lemmings computer game); Maurice Malpass (Dundee Utd); Andy Nicoll, Craig Redpath, Tom Smith (Scottish rugby internationals); George Simpson (Chief Exec, GEC).

FURTHER INFO:
Prospectus, video, CD-ROM, course leaflets and web site (http://www.tay.ac.uk).

entertainment

THE CITY: see University of Dundee

UNIVERSITY:
- Price of a pint of beer: £1.40 ● Glass of wine: £1.10

Bars, clubs/discos & music venues: The bar is on the top floor of the Union and although it can hold 500 people *there are rarely that many students desperate to hang around in its pink-and-purple depths*. It does get slightly more full for the 2 discos a week, the bands (mostly locals) and the various hypnotists and self-mutilators who provide cabaret entertainment.

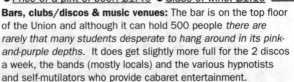

❝The Cannabis Awareness Society at UEA arranges fact-finding tours to Amsterdam, and has appeared on Radio 4 to promote the alleged benefits of the weed. ❞

Food: The University refectory, in the Kydd building, is open mornings and lunchtimes and the Union bar does lunch, dinner and snacks. *Nothing special, but does the job.*
Others: Individual departments and clubs host balls.

social & political

UNIVERSITY OF ABERTAY DUNDEE STUDENTS' ASSOCIATION:

● 2 sabbaticals ● Turnout at last ballot: 5%
● NUS member

Relations between the SA, the University administration and the student body are pretty friendly, again helped by the small size of the place, though the SA doesn't have a strong presence. This might explain why recent campaigns for a creche and against printing costs have so far been unsuccessful.

SU FACILITIES:
Gym; payphone; snooker table; games & vending machines; satellite TV; 2 meeting rooms; launderette.

CLUBS (NON SPORTING):
Dancing in Outer Space; Games Console; Goth, hippy and groovers; Jazz; Role Play; Ten-pin bowling; Vampyre.

RELIGIOUS:
● 4 local chaplains (RC, CofS, Episcopalian)
Muslim prayer sessions are offered too.

PAID WORK: see University of Dundee

sports

● Recent successes: rugby

Apart from a fitness room Abertay does not have any sporting facilities to call its own but students can purchase a £12 card which provides access to the Olympia Complex facilities for free or at reduced rates.

SPORTING CLUBS:
Hillwalking; Jiu-Jitsu; Kung Fu; Mountain Bike; Paintball; Parachute; Rowing; Tennis.

ATTRACTIONS: see University of Dundee

accommodation

IN COLLEGE:
● Self-catering: 24% ● Cost: £35-52 (36wks)

Availability: All 1st years who want to live in can do so - but this is eased by the fact that 60% of students live within a 20 mile radius, so they're usually sorted anyway. The accommodation ranges from modern purpose-built halls to converted Victorian terraces, with some halls shared with students from other colleges. The halls have single sex flats for first years only. 2-8 people share a kitchen.
Car parking: Adequate free parking near the accommodation.

EXTERNALLY: see University of Dundee
Housing help: The Student Services Unit's accommodation office exists mainly to allocate the University's own places, but also gives advice on private housing.

welfare

SERVICES:

- Lesbian & Gay Society ● Mature SA
- Overseas SA ● Postgrad SA

Health services are provided by a visiting doctor who comes to the University for an hour each morning and 3 health visitors at lunchtimes. The Student Services Unit employs 3 counsellors. Study skills workshops are a recent addition. Mature and International Students Society.

Disabled: *Disabled access is pretty poor, especially to the Union,* but all buildings have lifts and there's a dedicated counsellor. 'Phonic ears' are provided for hearing-impaired students.

FINANCE:

- Ave debt per year: £1,350 ● Access fund: £80,000
- Successful applications (1996): 626

Other sources of financial assistance (administered by the Student Services Unit) are available in the form of local trusts and legacies and there are a few bursaries for part-timers and overseas students.

●●

Aberystwyth, University of Wales

- **The College is part of _University of Wales_.**

University of Wales Aberystwyth, Old College, King Street, Aberystwyth, Ceredigion, SY23 2AX. Tel: (01970) 622021. Fax: (01970) 627410. E-mail: undergraduate-admissions@aber.ac.uk The Guild of Students, The Union, University of Wales Aberystwyth, Penglais Campus, Aberystwyth, SY23 3DX. Tel: (01970) 621700. Fax: (01970) 621701.

general

On the coast of mid-Wales is a small market town with a promenade of brightly painted houses on the sea front, a pier, the ruins of a 12th-century castle and an unspellable name. It's a *remote* place and chilly when the winter winds whistle across Cardigan Bay, but *there is a human warmth and relaxed tone about the town.* Apart from the sea front, it's not quite as quaint as it sounds, although the mountains (well, big hills) spreading inland make for an inspiring landscape. Up the side of one of these hills, less than a mile from the town centre, sits the main Penglais campus of the University. *The panoramic view is splendid:* the whole bay, the hills and the Afon Rheidol flowing through the town below. Aber, as it's known to those in the know, was one of the first of the Welsh colleges and the oldest buildings are classic Victorian stuff. Most of the College is 60s modernist architecture - ie concrete blocks, *although they're nicely spaced and you'd be surprised how interesting concrete can be with a bit of effort.* The 2nd site, a couple of miles outside town at the village of Llanbadarn, *is a pleasant scene and a secluded one, even by Aber standards.* 800 students are based there (doing Information & Library Studies and Rural Studies) and they travel frequently to the main site and the town centre.

49% ♂♂♂♂♂♀♀♀♀♀ 51%	
Sex ratio(M:F): 49%:51%	Founded: 1872
Full time u'grads: 5,335	Part time: 365
Postgrads: 859	Non-degree: 280
Ave course: 3yrs	Ethnic: 7%
Private school: n/a	Flunk rate: 9%
Mature students: 17%	Overseas students: 12%
Disabled students: 2.5%	Staff/student ratio 1:17
Clearing: 17%	

ATMOSPHERE:
Because the campus is small and there are relatively few students, it's hard to avoid bumping into friends and foes constantly, particularly when crossing the paved concourse in the middle of the campus. This is great as the students are a really friendly crowd and even though it's not the most pulsating nightspot in the Western hemisphere, the warmth of the local welcome makes up for the less hospitable weather conditions.

THE TOWN:
Aberystwyth is one of the major towns in the Welsh region of Ceredigion. *But that's a bit like saying a puddle is the largest expanse of water in the Sahara.* There are various museums, the castle ruins and public libraries with ancient Celtic records, all mixed in with the shops and banks. There are book shops (several 2nd hand), supermarkets and all the standard stores in the shopping centre. There are also a covered and a street market. Tourists often pass through, popping into the port and holiday centre and making the obligatory visit to the castle and gardens. Students make the most of the *beautiful* beaches when the sun comes out and the wind dies down. They take their books to the seashore where amazingly they seem to absorb knowledge by just lying on their backs wearing sunglasses.

TRAVEL:
Its remoteness is one of the advantages of Aber - getting away from it all to get a degree - but it's also a downer when it comes to getting to or from college.
Trains: Aberystwyth station is 1 mile from the main campus. Direct main-line connections to London (£23.10), Cardiff (£20.95) and Liverpool (£16.95).
Coaches: Traws Cambria and National Express services - London (£16.00), Liverpool (£20.00).
Car: A487 and A44 - not exactly Spaghetti Junction.
Hitching: *Without any major roads to Aber, it's mainly thumbs down although the Welsh do take pity on hitchers.*
Local: *Reliable* local buses run until 11pm. Every 20 mins, services run from the station to the main campus and to Llanbadarn. Both trips cost 60p. Britain's longest electric cliff

a

railway, which leads to a camera obscura on the headland cliff, isn't used by students on a regular basis.

Taxis: Cheaper than most places (£2.00 from the station).
Bicycles: *Students need legs like girders to pedal up the hills - worth it for those who are into physical pain.*

LIBRARIES & COMPUTERS:
● Books: 600,000 ● Study places: 1,100
● Computer workstations: 440

The Hugh Owen Library and 3 others for separate faculties. Computing facilities have 24-hr access. The National Library of Wales, a copyright library (*ie. it has a copy of every book printed in the UK*), is free to Aber students.

CAREER PROSPECTS:
● Careers Service ● No of staff: 8full/1part
● Unemployed after 6mths (1997): 5.8%

SPECIAL FEATURES:
● Students don't actually have to decide what course they're studying until they've already been doing it for a year. The course is fairly general for the 1st year, after which students choose to specialise.

FAMOUS ALUMNI:
Prince Charles (prince); Neil Hamilton (ex-Con); Dr Jeremy Leggat (Greenpeace); Simon Thorpe (editor, *Viz*); *lots of media types such as* Menna Richards (MD HTV Wales) and Huw Edwards (political correspondent, BBC); John Morris QC (Attorney General).

FURTHER INFO:
Prospectuses, video and departmental brochures all free from the admissions office. Web site (http://www.aber.ac.uk).

········· entertainment

TOWN:

● Price of a pint of beer: £1.70 ● Glass of wine: £1.40

Pubs: *Warm, cosy and somewhat pricey.* **push***plugs: Rummers, Boar's Head and, for Welsh-speakers, the Llew-Du (Welsh-speaking).*

Cinemas: 1 mainstream and 1 arthouse.

Theatres: A small theatre by the harbour hosts touring productions, everything from cabaret to Brecht, and performances by local professional groups which also appear at the University's arts centre (see below).

Clubs/discos: *Aber is not exactly at the cutting edge of entertainment. Peer Pressure, K2 and the Footie are all pretty run-of-the-mill, although the Bay has occasional indie/grunge inclinations.*

Music venues: Local bands play at a couple of the pubs and, in the true Welsh spirit, Aber has its own male voice choir.

> ❝ The rock music deploma course at Thames Valley University has a strict 'no grunge' policy. ❞

There's also an annual Jazz festival.

Eating out: Locally, there's an *excellent* variety of restaurants, especially for fresh fish. Don't expect high health after closing time - chips till 3am from the kebab van or Chinese till midnight. **push**plugs: *The Tree House, Elizabeth's (coffee house), Royal Pier Tandoori, Gannets, Spartacus.*

UNIVERSITY:

● <u>Price of a pint of beer: £1</u> ● <u>Glass of wine: £1.35</u>

Bars: The Cwrt Mawr is packed all day but there's also the Penglais Bar, aka The Joint (events 7 nights/wk) and the refurbished Outback Bar in Llanbadarn in the evenings (*more relaxed, if you can cope with karaoke, that is*).

Theatres: (2) The Arts Centre is *dead posh* and has a customised theatre, used by students and 'proper' companies. It should get a lottery funded face-lift soon. The drama students give their all in their studio theatre, including Welsh language productions.

Clubs/discos: The floors burn up 3 nights a week, everything from the Spice dance night to the monthly Funky Chicken night for rare groovers. The Wednesday night Shampoo (retro) is *pretty popular.*

Music venues: The Penglais Bar tempts tunesmiths such as My Life Story, Audioweb, Catatonia and Space.

Cabaret: *Very* occasional events, including Ben Elton and Lee Hurst.

Food: Most students who live in chow down in the dining rooms in accommodation halls (pay-as-you-eat). Munchies and Joint Food in the Union provide alternatives, as does the Refectory.

Other: Annual May Ball takes place out of town.

social 2 political
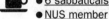

ABERYSTWYTH GUILD OF STUDENTS/ URDD Y MYFYRWYR:

● <u>6 sabbaticals</u> ● <u>Turnout at last ballot: 25%</u>
● <u>NUS member</u>

The Guild has a pretty good relationship with all the colleges' authorities. Politics comes in a fairly left-wing form, although round these parts PC means Plaid Cymru rather than Political Correctness. Only 1 in 7 students speak Welsh, which makes the strict bilingual policy a mite hard to enforce sometimes.

GUILD FACILITIES:

2 shops; a pizza bar; travel agent; bookshop; print shop; insurance; Midland Bank; car/van hire; games & vending machines; 2nd-hand bookshop once a week. There's also a building at Llanbadarn, with a bar, shop, common room and refectory.

CLUBS (NON SPORTING):

Anti-Apartheid; CND; Bell Ringers; Elizabethan Madrigal Singers; Hellenic; Kite; Methodists; Real Ale; Wargames.

OTHER ORGANISATIONS:

Aber's charity Rag is the biggest in Europe. They regularly raise 6-figure sums, but then, they do have 4 minibuses which shoot off round the country 2 or 3 times a week to hassle strangers for cash. The *excellent* Community Action group is

a

called 'Dim Prob' *which is Welsh for 'No Problem', not a reflection on the intellectual attributes of the participants.* 'The Courier' is Aber's twice termly student magazine and there's also the Welsh language 'Yr Utgorn' and the fortnightly newsletter 'Stomp'.

RELIGIOUS:

● <u>Chaplains (Christian)</u>

The town has churches for most Christian denominations and a mosque is under construction. The college has its own chapel. *The Christian Union meets outside college after it got kicked out of the Guild.*

PAID WORK:

Somewhere as small as Aberystwyth can't provide jobs for 6,000+ students, but things improve in the summer, when the tourists move in. Also a new shopping complex on the edge of town has provided opportunities for future retail operatives *(that's shelf-stackers to you and me).*

sports

● <u>Recent successes: basketball</u>

Sport is a friendly affair and half the students are members of the Athletics Union. There's a £17 charge for an AU card, which gives access to all facilities.

SPORTS FACILITIES:

Impressive: 52 acres of playing fields around the outskirts of town; 7 footy pitches, 4 rugby, 4 cricket, 3 hockey (2 grass, 1 Astroturf), 1 American football; athletics field; floodlit all-weather pitch; 2 tennis courts; 4 squash courts; 2 sports hall (with 9 badminton courts, volleyball and basketball); swimming pool; cardiovascular gym and weights room. The town doubles up on many of the University sports amenities, adding a bowling green and a golf course with which the University has a special deal. Water sports enthusiasts whet their whistles with willing both in the river (Rheidol) and the sea (Irish). These aquatic activities also provide an attraction for those who'd rather watch than do.

SPORTING CLUBS:

American Football; Ai-Kido; Caving; Clay Pigeon; Expedition; Ladies Cricket & Rugby; Lacrosse; Paintballing; Running; Sky-diving; Surfing; Tennis; Ultimate Frisbee; Water Polo; Wind-surfing.

accommodation

IN COLLEGE:

● <u>Catered: 19%</u> ● <u>Cost: £52-62(30-37wks)</u>
● <u>Self-catering: 18%</u> ● <u>Cost: £29-54(30/37wks)</u>

Availability: All 1st years can live in and 83% of finalists come back into halls, but 2nd years are usually on their own. The main sets of halls are Penbryn and Penglais. There are also 958 places in the student village at Pentre Jane Morgan. Pantycelyn Hall (260) is the Welsh hall where students speak Welsh or learn it and where a collection of Welsh treasures such as paintings and musical instruments is housed. 13% of rooms are shared, although nobody has to double up after their 1st year. *Conditions are variable and rents are increasing.*

Car parking: There's a large permit car-park on the Penglais campus (£15/yr for a permit) and *parking's not too hard around town, provided you remember your hand-brake.*

EXTERNALLY:
- Ave rent: £40

Availability: The reason the University is building more accommodation is not so that a higher percentage will be able to live in, but rather because, like many other places, the intake has expanded recently. *Aber's a bit too dinky to support all its student population and, as a result, finding places to live out isn't the easiest job in the world, but could be worse.*

Housing help: The University's residential office is lumbered with the task of helping house students. Its 4 full-time staff produce a newsletter and bulletin board.

welfare

SERVICES:
- Nursery ● Lesbian & Gay Society ● Mature SA
- Overseas SA ● Women's Officer ● Self-defence classes

In addition to the above services, there's a Welsh language group and the town provides a rape crisis line. The Guild operates a welfare department employing 2 trained counsellors and one trainee. The Medical Centre (with doctor, nurse and secretary) provides a service exclusively for students, in addition to local GPs. The Medical Officer also offers counselling.

Women: Cost-price attack alarms available.

Disabled: *Wheelchair access is problematic for geographical and historical reasons. The University has a welcoming attitude, but short of flattening the whole town, there's not much they can do*; disabled applicants are encouraged to get in touch for an individual assessment. *Facilities for sight-impaired students are good, though.*

FINANCE:
- Ave debt per year: £1,850 ● Access fund: £150,000
- Successful applications (1997): 400

Nearly 100 scholarships are available (worth up to about £3,000 apiece) by sitting Aber's own exam. Hardship Fund.

▶▶ African Studies
see SOAS

> 'Surrey Rag covered the University's geodesic dome in red sheets for Comic Relief, creating the world's largest red nose.'

●●●

▶▶ Anglia

see University of East Anglia

●●●

Anglia Polytechnic University

▼
▼ ● *Formerly Anglia Polytechnic, CCAT, Essex IHE*

(1) Anglia Polytechnic University, Chelmsford Campus, Victoria Road South, Chelmsford, Essex, CM1 1LL.
Tel: (01245) 493131. Fax: (01245) 490835.
E-mail: angliainfo@anglia.ac.uk
Anglia Students' Union, Victoria Road South, Chelmsford, Essex, CM1 1LL. Tel: (01245) 258178.
Fax: (01245) 267653.
(2) Anglia Polytechnic University, Cambridge Campus, East Road, Cambridge, CB1 1PT. Tel: (01223) 363271.
Fax: (01223) 352973.

╌╌╌╌general

Along with Ulster, De Montfort, *and* Cranfield, *this is as close as different sites get to being separate colleges.* In fact, Anglia Polytechnic University's 2 main campuses were separate colleges - Cambridge College of Art & Technology (CCAT) and the Essex Institute of Higher Education in Chelmsford - until they merged in 1989, became a poly in 1991 and a university in May 1992. All in the time it takes to get a degree. *'Merged' that is, in the loosest sense, because they're still geographically and socially quite distinct.* The courses taught at each site are different, but to confuse matters, there are smaller sites at Brentwood (soon to close), Rivermead and Danbury. It's the last institution in the UK to retain the *dreaded* 'P' word in its name although most people refer to it as Anglia or (**push**'s favourite, *because we're all big kids really*) APU. *They've recently been getting all flustered about whether to change their name to the University of Eastern England or the East England University. A nation waits with baited breath.*

40% ♂♂♂♂♂♀♀♀♀♀ 60%	
Sex ratio(M:F): 40%:60%	Founded: 1989
Full time u'grads: 7,000	Part time: 3,843
Postgrads: 330	Non-degree: n/a
Ave course: 3yrs	Ethnic: n/a
Private/state school: n/a	Flunk rate: n/a
Mature students: 48%	Overseas students: 10.8%
Disabled students: 2.8%	Staff/student ratio: 1:20
Clearing: 22%	

ATMOSPHERE & SITES:

The spirit at each site varies as much as the place names on the train tickets and there's no common overtone.

Chelmsford: (4,036 students - business; law; construction; nursing; product design; land management; IT) The administrative centre of the University is housed on this site, composed of 4 buildings (*squat, 60s, ugly, shabby and drab inside and out*) around a *token* patch of grass and *set in the main town of Essex, built with depressingly great concern for practicality. This is definitely the site for party people and sporty sorts, but not political vultures or those who mind others knowing their business. The place feels a bit like a school,* not surprising since that's what it once was. *It's planned that this site will be wound down and moved to Rivermead.*

Cambridge: (6,350 - arts; maths; music) Since Cambridge is 37 miles north-west of Chelmsford, students at the Cambridge campus have less to do with students from the other sites, socially speaking, than with those from <u>Cambridge University</u>, whose clubs they can join and whose entertainment they can attend. The campus buildings themselves are a small collection of mostly modern red brick blocks, *looking functional, smart and impressively like the home of eminent technical insight. The main problem is that there are really too many students for what's essentially a small site. It's artier, more attractive and greener than Chelmsford, but socially quieter, despite the vibrant local student population.*

Brentwood: (1,172 - education) Brentwood is 11 miles south-east in the direction of London. Courses here will be transferred to the new, green **Rivermead** site, 10 mins from the Chelmsford campus, by 1999 to the relief of many students who loathe the Brentwood site.

Danbury: (590 - part-time graduate study) 4 miles east of the Chelmsford, this is a conference centre with a few management courses added on.

CAMBRIDGE: see <u>University of Cambridge</u>

CHELMSFORD:

● <u>Population: 92,479</u> ● <u>London: 37miles</u>

Chelmsford isn't exactly Thrill City but neither is it dull beyond redemption. It's a run-of-the-mill commuter town (which of course means that London's accessible enough when things get too turgid) with an adequate selection of clubs and pubs. It isn't a student city in the sense of Cambridge and unless the students are able to integrate with the local community they might as well stay on campus for 3 years.

TRAVEL: see <u>University of Cambridge</u>

TRAVEL: CHELMSFORD:

Trains: Chelmsford Station is 2 minutes from the campus. From Chelmsford there are direct trains into London Liverpool Street (£5.00) and it is easy enough to change to services to Manchester (£30.35) and all over the country.

Coaches: Chelmsford by National Express services, which, among other places go to London (£6), Bristol (£23) and beyond.

Car: Chelmsford and Brentwood are on the A12 out of London.

a

In these towns, parking isn't a problem and many students use cars.

Air: Stansted, London's 3rd airport, is 14 miles north-west of Chelmsford and offers inland and international flights.

Hitching: *This is good hitching territory, mainly because Essex lads want to show off their turbo-powered nob substitutes.*

Local: Buses and Network SouthEast trains keep commuters commuting and shoppers shopping and are good enough for students.

Taxis: *Expensive, but you could have guessed that.*

Bicycles: *Bikes are too earthy and unnecessary in Chelmsford.*

LIBRARIES:
- Books: 296,898 ● Study places: 982
- Computer workstations: 224

Space is a problem again, but the new Rivermead campus is easing matters a little.

CAREER PROSPECTS:
- Careers Service ● No of staff: 9full/3part
- Unemployed after 6mths (1996): 5.1%

Some of the careers staff also work in the welfare department.

FAMOUS ALUMNI:
Adam Ant (80s pop icon); Fluck & Law (creators of 'Spitting Image'); Jerry Hayes MP (Con, *not gay*); Kim Howells MP (Lab); Ronald Searle (cartoonist); Tom Sharpe (writer); Mike Smith (TV presenter, Mr Sarah Greene, *bland git*).

FURTHER INFO:
Prospectuses for undergrads and postgrads, audio, Braille and enlarged versions for blind people, PC disk, web site (http://www.anglia.ac.uk). *Everything short of Morse code, really.*

entertainment

CAMBRIDGE: see University of Cambridge

CHELMSFORD:
- Price of a pint of beer: £2.00 ● Glass of wine: £1.60

Cinemas: 2 including the 8-screen Odeon, and 1 in Brentwood.

Theatres: Chelmsford has 1 mainstream theatre, the Civic, plus the Cramphorn and the Old Court for less commercial and amateur productions.

Pubs: They rely on commuters more than student trade. **push**plugs: *The Sheep; The Roundhouse; The Bayhorse; The Rat and Parrot.*

Clubs/discos: *Mostly towny.* **push**plugs: *Dukes (house); Zeus (student nights); Y Club (indie); Enigma (Gothy, runs buses to London).*

Music venues: Some pubs host live bands (especially the Army & Navy) and some of the clubs above also ditch the decks for a few minutes. Hylands Park (509 acres) has started making a pitch for the festival season, with large-scale gigs by Blur and The Prodigy in the summer of 1997; **push**plugs: *The Basement (various theme nights eg Blues).*

Eating out: *Not the most thrilling selection.* **push**plugs: *Duke Street Tandoori; Cod Father (late night chippy); Chicago's (nice but pricey); Back in Time.*

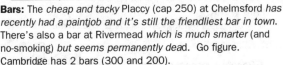

UNIVERSITY:
- Price of a pint of beer: £1.40 ● Glass of wine: £1.20

Bars: The *cheap and tacky* Placcy (cap 250) at Chelmsford *has recently had a paintjob and it's still the friendliest bar in town.* There's also a bar at Rivermead *which is much smarter* (and no-smoking) *but seems permanently dea*d. Go figure. Cambridge has 2 bars (300 and 200).

Theatres: The theatre in the Mumford Building at Cambridge *is excellent - well equipped and big for a student theatre* (the biggest in Cambridge). *Standards of am dram reflect this - and highlight the thespian dead zone that is Chelmsford.*

Clubs/discos & music venues: Chelmsford pumps up various volumes in the Placcy and the Gym (800) 3 nights a week. Cambridge's Big Bar has live music *(Judge Jules and Jools Holland, indeed)* and discos twice a week.

Food: The college refectory at Chelmsford serves a *good value* range of meals and snacks and the Placcy does more of the same. The SU runs a canteen at Cambridge.

Others: The Anglia Summer Ball, and 2 or 3 all-nighters a year at Cambridge.

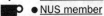

social & political

ANGLIA STUDENTS' UNION:

- 5 sabbaticals ● Turnout at last ballot: 10%
- NUS member

ASU operates on all sites and each branch is as separate from the others as the sites themselves. SU campaigning concentrates on charity fundraising and awareness of issues such as Aids, drugs etc. The SU describes itself as centre left, *whatever that means these days.* At Cambridge, students are allowed to join Cambridge University's clubs. *However the initiative is in their hands - the clubs aren't going to come looking for them. Relations between the SU and the University staff are pretty good, especially at Cambridge. 8 out of 10 students who expressed a preference said they thought the SU was OK - but many don't have a preference.*

SU FACILITIES:
Chelmsford: Bar; photocopying; minibus hire; general shop; games room; common room; vending machines.
Cambridge: Canteen; bar; catering; general shop; photocopying; minibus hire; launderette.
Brentwood: Bar; general shop; photocopying.

CLUBS (NON SPORTING):
European Cinema; Exhibition; Groove; Japanese; Law; Optics; Philosophy; St Lukes; Theatre; Writers.

OTHER ORGANISATIONS:
The SU newspaper 'Apex' is distributed on all sites with a circulation of 2,500.

> **❝Hitler planned to make Oxford the capital of the UK, with Christ Church as his palace.❞**

RELIGIOUS:
● 3 chaplains (2 CofE, 1 Catholic)

PAID WORK:
Only the usual bar work, restaurants and so on.

sports

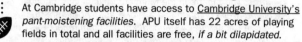

● Recent successes: fencing, hockey, rowing

At Cambridge students have access to Cambridge University's *pant-moistening facilities*. APU itself has 22 acres of playing fields in total and all facilities are free, *if a bit dilapidated*.

SPORTS FACILITIES:
Chelmsford: Gym; 2 hockey pitches; badminton and basketball courts; sports hall; playing fields.
Cambridge: 1 tennis court; playing fields; sports centre; the small multigym is being moved (*brick by brick?*) to make way for an accommodation block.
Brentwood: 2 tennis courts; gym; pool; playing fields.

SPORTING CLUBS:
Lacrosse; Mountain Bike; Rowing.

accommodation

IN COLLEGE: CAMBRIDGE:
● Self-catering: 15% ● Cost: £53-59(40wks)

The halls in Cambridge are *rather good*, but they have to be bolstered by local flats and houses, under a head tenancy arrangement and 60 places in the YMCA.

IN COLLEGE: CHELMSFORD:
● Self-catering: 15% ● Cost: £45-57(40wks)

The housing at Chelmsford is also good quality but overpriced; rooms at the *plush* new Rivermead development have been left empty because it's more cost-effective to live out. There's no University housing at Danbury and only 40 places at Brentwood.

EXTERNALLY: see University of Cambridge

EXTERNALLY: CHELMSFORD:
● Ave rent: £50

Availability: *Chelmsford is still adapting to its expanded student population, so some landlords are still a bit wary of renting to people perceived as doped-up traffic-cone shaggers. Most places are safe but the Broomfield estate is best avoided.*
Housing help: There are Accommodation Services at Chelmsford and Cambridge and a part-time office at Brentwood. They all keep registers of vacancies and post lists on bulletin boards. They also provide help and advice on contracts.

welfare

SERVICES:
● Creche ● Mature SA ● Overseas SA

● Women's Officer ● Self-defence classes

With the exception of the nurse and health clinic, ASU (which has 1 University-wide welfare adviser and 1 at each teaching site) offers the only special provision. There is no doctor at the Rivermead site. The University-run counselling unit employs 3 full-time counsellors, 5 part-timers and a registered doctor. Study skills are taught on all sites.

Disabled: Cambridge students can apply to live at St Bridget's Hall *(full care support). Access is good in Cambridge and Rivermead. Induction loops are installed in lecture theatres.*

FINANCE:
- Ave debt per year: £1,350 ● Access fund: £162,000
- Successful applications (1996): 432

Small welfare fund for short-term loans.

● ●

Aston University

▼
▼ Aston University, Aston Triangle, Birmingham, B4 7ET.
Tel: (0121) 359 3611. Fax: (0121) 333 6350.
E-mail: prospectus@aston.ac.uk
Aston Students' Guild, Aston Triangle, Gosta Green,
Birmingham, B4 7ES. Tel: (0121) 359 6531.
Fax: (0121) 333 4218. E-mail: president@aston.ac.uk

General

About a Steve Backley welly-lob (or 10 minutes' walk) from the centre of Birmingham is the Aston Triangle, which is really a parallelogram but don't tell anyone. The 'Triangle' is the modern green landscaped campus of brown brick buildings which make up Aston University. The campus's *more thoroughly modern excesses* include the *startling* red and blue glass entrance with 2 towering *Buck Rogers-style* sky lifts on the outside, and inside, the 21st century continues. *Despite being so compact, the campus has room for the Vice-Chancellor's Lake.*

52% ♂♂♂♂♂♀♀♀♀♀ 48%	
Sex ratio(M:F): 52%:48%	Founded: 1966
Full time u'grads: 4,403	Part time: 0
Postgrads: 504	Non-degree: 229
Ave course: 4yrs	Ethnic: 25%
Private/state school: n/a	Flunk rate: n/a
Mature students: 5%	Overseas students: 16%
Disabled students: 6%	Staff/student ratio: 1:18
Clearing: 8%	

ATMOSPHERE:
It's unusual to find a university that's always been a university (as opposed to a former poly) that has such a large vocational element to its courses. Most courses are linked to careers and involve a year on a work placement. *This sets the tone for the students - they have a heavy workload and are career-*

minded, refined and business-like. When students do lift their bloodshot, baggy eyes from the screen to have a spot of fun, the advantages of being in an environment this size show through - it's small enough to be cosy but large enough to let them avoid the people they can't stand.

THE CITY: see University of Birmingham

TRAVEL: see University of Birmingham
Aston's nearest station is New Street.

LIBRARIES & COMPUTERS:
- Books: 350,000 ● Study places: 600
- Computer workstations: 750

Some computer labs have 24-hour access, but the library is closed on Sundays.

CAREER PROSPECTS:
- Careers Service ● No of staff: 6full
- Unemployed after 6mths (1996): 5.3%

The vocational nature of the courses, as well as the placements system, gives Aston students a definite edge.

FAMOUS ALUMNI:
Jeff Rooker MP (Lab). Jasper Carrott has an honorary scroll.

FURTHER INFO:
Prospectuses for undergrads and postgrads. Web site (http://www.aston.ac.uk/home.html).

entertainment

THE CITY: see University of Birmingham

UNIVERSITY:
- Price of a pint of beer: £1.40 ● Glass of wine: £1.10

Bars: The drinking-holes include: Einstein's (capacity 250, *pubby and popular*); Sack of Potatoes (really is a pub); Monks (mainly for events); The Loft (balti nights on Thursdays).

Clubs/discos & music venues: The Guild Hall (940) *caters for all dancey tastes* 4 nights a week (£2-3). This includes Euphoria (house), Shine (indie), Revive (70s & 80s), Snog (easy listening) and Club Soda (anything at all). They get *big* names for the Balls (eg. Louise, Olive) but not much beyond that. There is *some* live music every Thursday, *to blast your ears while the balti blasts your buds.*

Cabaret: Stand-up twice a term *but, again, nobody you might have heard of.*

Food: Einstein's does pub grub *and the Lean Too is good for baguettes.* The new Oscar's Diner does its fast food thing and La Serre offers takeaway baguettes.

Others: Balls are held several times a year, including the Freakers' Ball (perverse), and the May Ball. There are other one-off events, such as Pyjama Hops (Rag-related bops in jim-jams) and so on. Also runs *one of the best Fresher's Weeks around.*

social & political

ASTON STUDENTS' GUILD:
- 5 sabbaticals ● Turnout at last ballot: 35%
 ● NUS member

The Guild is pretty apolitical and maintains good relations with

the students and, increasingly, the University authorities. Recent campaigns against Tuition Fees cobbled together 1,000 signatures and 200 attendees to a demo. Might not sound much, but it's better than most other places.

SU FACILITIES:
The purpose-built Guild Building contains a general shop, print shop, post office, NatWest Bank, Link and Barclays cash machines, insurance office, travel centre, hairdresser, 2nd-hand bookshop, darkroom, cafeteria, games room and launderette.

CLUBS (NON SPORTING):
Aiesec; Artificial Intelligence (drum & bass); Ballroom Dancing; Bengali; Cardsoc; Chinese; Football Supporters; Fusion; Hellenic; Hindu; India; Jazz; Juggling; Kenya; Links (First Aid); Motorsport; New Musicians; Optics; Retro; Sikh; Wargames and Roleplay; Zulu Warriors.

OTHER ORGANISATIONS:
'The Birmingham Sun' is the Guild's student newspaper, and there's a weekly info sheet, 'Wot's Up?' The student Community Action scheme is run by a new Volunteers Officer, and organises events like kid's football tournaments. RAG raised £27k in just three months last year. *Hurrah!*

RELIGIOUS:
Chaplains operate on a non-denominational basis. There is a Muslim prayer room.

PAID WORK:
The Aston Students' Guild runs a job-shop.

sports

● Recent successes: football, basketball
Sport is reasonably successful and popular but nothing out of the ordinary.

SPORTS FACILITIES:
95 acres: 2 indoor playing fields; swimming pool; 2 squash courts; sauna and solarium; 2 multigyms; snooker and table tennis tables and sports shop. Shustoke: 15 playing fields; 2 hard all-weather pitches; 3 tennis and 4 squash courts; cricket square; a large pavilion with 3 bars and social facilities.

SPORTING CLUBS:
Aikido; American Football; Caving; Handball; Ice-Skating; Jiu-Jitsu; Lacrosse; Parachuting; Rifle; Snooker; Surfing; Tennis; Tenpin Bowling; Windsurfing; Weight Training.

ATTRACTIONS: see University of Birmingham

accommodation

IN COLLEGE:
● Catered: 2% ● Cost: £41-48 (38wks)
● Self-catering: 45% ● Cost: £41-48 (38-39wks)
Availability: All 1st years and most finalists are guaranteed

❮Led Zeppelin played their first ever gig at Surrey University.❯

accommodation if they apply in time, mostly on campus in 3 20-storey towers and 4 low-rise blocks of self-catering flats and at the University Village at Handsworth Wood, 4 miles from the campus. Most 2nd years will need to find their own places - 3rd years tend to be out on placements. The Village offers the choice of catered hall places in Handsworth Hall (178 places) or 2 smaller houses, or self-catering flats (in groups of 3-12), often reserved for mature students. Handsworth Hall is being sold soon so that all college accommodation will be on campus. There is limited provision (66 places) for married couples (without children) and free parking at the Village only. Security on campus is *good*.

EXTERNALLY: see <u>University of Birmingham</u>
Housing help: The Students Advisory Centre offers standard renting contracts, help with landlords and checks out safety certificates.

welfare

SERVICES:
● <u>Creche</u> ● <u>Lesbian & Gay Society</u>
● <u>Mature SA</u> ● <u>Overseas SA</u> ● <u>Postgrad SA</u> ● <u>Minibus</u>
● <u>Women's Officer</u> ● <u>Self-defence classes</u>

The Guild's Student Advisory Centre (SAC), run by a full-time officer and student sabbatical, is *the prime source of help and advice* for students. The Health & Dental Centre on campus provides a counselling service for students employing 1 full-time and 6 part-time professional counsellors.
Women: The minibus (£1), which runs after 11pm on event evenings between the Triangle and the Handsworth student village, is open to all students but offers a priority service for women.
Disabled: *Provisions and access are better than average,* with a small number of specially adapted rooms for disabled students on the campus, and departmental provisions for sight and hearing impaired students.

FINANCE:
● <u>Ave debt per year: £1,850</u> ● <u>Access fund: £67,000</u>
● <u>Successful applications (1996): 115</u>
2 hardship funds operate, interest free loans and travel bursaries, *if you really, really need it.*

❝'It looks like bleedin' Marbella' - unidentified visitor to an HE Fair, upon seeing an aerial photo of Swansea.❞

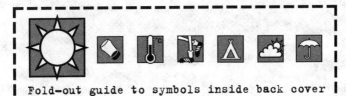

Fold-out guide to symbols inside back cover

'If you have any comments about PUSH or fancy being involved in the next edition, please write to PUSH, McGraw-Hill Publishing Company, Shoppenhangers Road, Maidenhead, Berkshire SL6 2QL.'

 'Freaked out by finance? Why not pop into your local branch of Lloyds Bank and see what they have to offer.'

Bangor, University of Wales

University of Bath

Bath Spa University College

- Bedford College
  see De Montfort University

- Bedford New College
  see Royal Holloway, London

- Belfast, Queen's University
  see The Queen's University of Belfast

Birkbeck College, London

University of Birmingham

- Birmingham Conservatoire
  see University of Central England

- Birmingham Poly
  see University of Central England

- Bishop Grosseteste College
  see Other Institutions

Bolton Institute of Higher Education

Bournemouth University

University of Bradford

- Bretton Hall
  see Other Institutions

University of Brighton

University of Bristol

- Bristol Poly
  see Bristol, University of the West of England

Bristol, University of the West of England

- Brookes University
  see Oxford Brookes University

Brunel University

Continued next page ▶▶

▶▶ *Continued from last page*

University of Buckingham

Buckinghamshire University College

● ●

Bangor, University of Wales

▼ ● **The College is part of <u>University of Wales</u>.**
▼ University of Wales Bangor, College Road, Bangor, Gwynedd,
LL57 2DG. Tel: (01248) 351151. Fax: (01248) 370451.
E-mail: admissions@bangor.ac.uk
Students' Union, University of Wales Bangor, Deiniol Road,
Bangor, Gwynedd, LL57 2TH. Tel: (01248) 353701.
Fax: (01248) 361418. E-mail: union@bangor.ac.uk

General

Squeezed between the *magnificent* mountains of the
Snowdonia National Park - an official area of outstanding
natural beauty - and the Menai Strait (the broad stretch of
water cutting off the Isle of Anglesey from mainland Wales), is
Bangor. Officially, it's a city (qualifying on the strength of its
8th century cathedral), but with a tiny population *who all seem
to know each other, it's more like a small town.* Whichever,
it's a pretty fishing port with a few shops (*although the Ivana
Trumps of this world may find it insufficient*) and - as the
estate agent said - *some delightful features*: the harbour, pier,
scenic views of Anglesey and the mountains. The main
University buildings rest on a hill in town, *resembling a grand
Victorian hotel.* The rest of the buildings (almost all within ½
mile of each other) are a mixture of more modern stone and
concrete constructions.

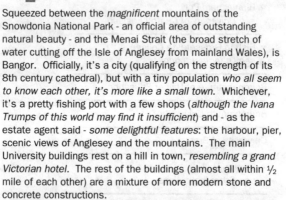

49% ♂♂♂♂♂♀♀♀♀♀ **51%**

Sex ratio(M:F): 49%:51%	Founded: 1884
Full time u'grads: 5,223	Part time: 97
Postgrads: 854	Non-degree: 475
Ave course: 3yrs	Ethnic: n/a
Private school: n/a	Flunk rate: n/a
Mature students: 20%	Overseas students: 4.7%
Disabled students: 5%	Staff/student ratio: 1:18
Clearing: 11%	

ATMOSPHERE:
*Bangor students are definitely not at the cutting edge of fashion,
but they're quite alternative nevertheless. Strong on
environmental courses and well stocked locally with the wonders*

of nature, the University attracts the outdoor type, more at home in a cagoule than a Babe Power T-shirt and, bearing in mind the rugged environment, that's only sensible. But they keep themselves fairly busy and know how to have a good time.

OTHER SITES:

Faculty of Education: (539 students) Until 1996 this was a separate teacher training college. The faculty is based on 2 sites, 1 just outside Bangor near the Menai Bridge and 1 near the centre of town.

Wrexham: (350 students) Radiography and midwifery students are taught at Wrexham Maelor Hospital, but since that's 63 miles from Bangor, *they often get left out of the social equation.*

THE TOWN:

- Population: 17,000 ● London: 236miles
- Cardiff: 180miles ● Manchester: 85miles

Bangor is a *truly sublime* rural harbour town which attracts plenty of tourists. *Such a cosy community and such beautiful scenery make it a fine place to live as well as visit, although there's a strong Welsh nationalist element. Its amenities are okay for everyday needs and apart from the usual high street shops it more or less ends there*: a museum, the recently renovated Victorian pier, supermarkets, 1st and 2nd hand book shops, a few shops open as late as midnight, banks and a street market.

TRAVEL:

Trains: Bangor station is ½ mile from the main buildings. To get almost anywhere, it's got to be via Crewe (£14.20), but without changing it's possible to go to London (£27.50).

Buses: National Express services to London (£28), Birmingham (£18) and other destinations.

Car: *Despite being a bit out on a limb, the roads to Bangor* (A5, A55 & A487) *are quite direct and very scenic.*

Hitching: *Quite easy.* The A55 to Chester and then the M56 which goes within 2 miles of the city centre.

Ferries: £6 returns to Ireland are offered from Holyhead (½hr by train).

Local: The buses are fairly regular and for a quid it's possible to get about 6 miles out of town till 11pm. They also go all over Gwynedd (the county). Trains run every hour to towns all along the coast of north Wales and there's an *incredible* journey by a single carriage steam train up Wales's highest mountain on the Snowdon Mountain Railway - *a journey to absolutely nowhere, but worth it.*

Taxis: *Bangor's small enough to make taxis a viable option for group trips or for getting home after the buses.*

Bicycles: *Bangor is hillsville, but for those with thighs with a mission, a bike is handy. There are plenty of sheds and stands and theft is a rarity.*

LIBRARIES & COMPUTERS:

- Books: 500,000 ● Study places: 900
- Computer workstations: 153

6 big faculty libraries. Having your own PC is handy.

CAREER PROSPECTS:

- Careers Service ● No of staff: 10full
- Unemployed after 6mths (1996): 7.4%

SPECIAL FEATURES:
● *Anally-retentive Beatles fans may be interested to know that* the Fabs were staying at Bangor with the Maharishi Mahesh Yogi when Brian Epstein (their manager) died.

FAMOUS ALUMNI:
Frances Barber (actress); Ann Clwyd MP (Lab); John Sessions (comedian/actor); Roger Whittaker (*cheesy* singer).

FURTHER INFO:
Prospectuses for undergrads and postgrads and videos (all bilingual) from the PR unit. The SU does an info pack. Further information on the web site
(http://www.bangor.ac.uk/home.html).

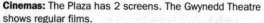 entertainment

CITY:
● Price of a pint of beer: £1.50 ● Glass of wine: £1.40
Cinemas: The Plaza has 2 screens. The Gwynedd Theatre shows regular films.
Theatres: The Gwynedd Theatre hosts touring shows from music to mime and plays in both English and Welsh.
Pubs: *The key pubs are by the quay and on the High Street, small and personable.* **push***plugs: Fat Cat (trendy); Y Glôb (Welsh); Belle Vue; Rascals; Greek Taverna.*
Clubs/discos: Most students rely on the University for club sounds and sways. The Octagon has student nights (Wednesdays) and there are occasional illegal raves in the local quarries when the weather allows.
Music venues: A few local bands play in a few local pubs, and at Powys Hall.
Eating out: *The best value is probably pub grub.* **push***plugs: Bella Pasta; Fat Cats.*

UNIVERSITY:
● Price of a pint of beer: £1.35 ● Glass of wine: £1.30
Bars: 6 bars frequented, not only by students but also, as with all the University entertainments, by locals who recognise that *the student ents are the most happening thing around.* 3 are run by the SU: the Jocks Bar (capacity 250, often packed with Trekkies and sporties watching Sky); the Main Bar (350, *uninspiring*, popular during evenings); the Curvy Lounge (*er... curved*).
Theatres: The Gwynedd Theatre (see above) is right next door. Student groups often hire it, *providing them with an excellent venue for student drama.*
Cinemas: SU film club shows *mainstream* films.
Clubs/discos/music venues: 'Time' is a new nightclub which cost £1m, hosts big dance nights *and looks like a ferry.* About 5 times a week, a club of some sort is held here or in the Main Bar. Dannii Minogue and Catatonia stopped off here recently.
Cabaret: Comedy nights got axed in favour of line-dancing

❛Text in italics is PUSH's point of view – take it or leave it.❜

which was more popular. *And nearly as funny.*

Food: Freddy's, the SU's fast food outlet, keeps the pizzas pumping out, Mrs P's is a deli and Mrs Q's does hot meals. *Cerys' Diner is also a good bet.*

social & political
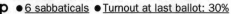

BANGOR STUDENTS' UNION/COLEG PRIFYSGOL GOGLEDD CYMRU UNDEB Y MYFYRWYR:
- 6 sabbaticals ● Turnout at last ballot: 30%
- NUS member

Party affiliations aren't bandied around but there's a general leaning to Labour and Plaid Cymru. There's a strong stance on 3rd World debt, although a boycott of Midland and Lloyd's Bank had to be lifted because no-one had any cash. The SU's most direct influence on students is through the services it provides.

SU FACILITIES:
The new SU has some *smart* facilities: 4 bars; cafeteria; snack bar & deli; restaurant; NatWest (plus cashpoint); night club; library; launderette; showers; travel agency; general shop; bookshop; print shop; photocopying; photo booth; pool & snooker tables; 6 minibuses for hire; parking; games room; creche; vending machines; juke box.

CLUBS (NON SPORTING):
Arts; Bar Staff; Big Nasty Carrot Performers; Bird; Chinese; Concert; Cymdeithas Y Cyfathrebwyr; Duke Of Edinburgh; Hellenic; Industrial; Japanese; Marine Archaeology; Malaysian; Methodist; Mountaineering; Pakistan; Rostra; Scout & Guide; Second Lanuage; Stewrads; Wargames; Yoga.

OTHER ORGANISATIONS:
Weekly free English-language magazine, 'Seren', and the fortnightly 'Y Ddraenen', in Welsh. The charity Rag was less successful than usual last year. The *highly active* student community group employs a full-time co-ordinator, has over 300 members and works on more than 40 projects.

RELIGIOUS:
- Team of chaplains

The College has an Anglican and Catholic chaplaincy. Local ministers of various denominations can be contacted in times of spiritual need. Locally, there's the Cathedral and Catholic, Methodist, Church of Wales and Baptist churches, a Quaker house and a mosque.

PAID WORK:
Apart from the usual bar work and restaurant waiting, there's the local Outdoor Pursuits Centres and other tourist trade which offers jobs to the early bird. The Student Services-run Job Mart finds part-time work.

sports

- Recent successes: hockey, canoeing

With the Menai Strait and Snowdonia, it comes as no surprise that Bangor offers exceptional opportunities for outdoor sports, particularly climbing, mountaineering, sailing, rowing and all sorts of water sports. The priority is wide involvement rather than great success. With a Union card, amenities aren't *too expensive* (60p for weights, £1 for squash). A new £800,000 sports hall provides 4 badminton courts, cardiovascular room, weights, gym and astroturf pitch.

SPORTS FACILITIES:

Bangor is very compact, nudged from every side by geographical limitations, and all the facilities are right on campus and next to the residential halls. 50 acres of playing fields (8 soccer, 4 hockey and 3 rugby pitches) and a flood-lit all-weather pitch; 2 sports halls; athletics tracks; 2 gymnasia; squash and tennis courts; archery range; multigym and, of course, the Menai Straits and the mountains. The town has a leisure centre, a swimming pool, golf course, bowling green and, about ½ an hour from the campus, the Outdoor Pursuits Centres. Also, at Llandudno, a few miles along the coast, there's a ski slope.

SPORTING CLUBS:

Caving; Gaelic Football; Gliding; Gymnastics; Jiu Jitsu; Ki-Aikido; Lacrosse; Lifeguard; Mountain Walking; Octopush; Rifle & Pistol; Rowing; Ski & Snowboarding; Surf; Tennis; Water Polo; Weights; Windsurfing.

accommodation

IN COLLEGE:

- Catered: 3% ● Cost: £56-62(30wks)
- Self-catering: 34% ● Cost: £37-46(38wks)

Availability: 76% of 1st years live in, 12% of 2nd years and finalists. There are 5 catered halls of residence or 'Neuadds' as the Welsh call them; 1 all-male hall, 1 all-female, 1 all-Welsh speakers (or those learning it) and 2 others. There are 7 self-catering buildings. *For those who want a room with a view, odds on it'll happen.* Nobody has to share.

Car parking: Permits are required, which are free but whether there are any varies from hall to hall. *Cars are only really useful in Bangor for students who find themselves living out of town.*

EXTERNALLY:

- Ave rent: £35

Availability: *Rentable accommodation in a town this small is finite and many students find themselves living further out than they would wish. Landlords tend to own more than one house, so accommodation shifts by word of mouth as much as anything. Upper Bangor is a popular area with students. The local population tends to be friendly but Maesgerchen is a bit hostile, as well as hard to say.*

Housing help: The University Accommodation Office provides a landlord and vacancy lists on the internet, seminars on safety and rights, a bulletin board and friendly staff to moan to.

welfare

SERVICES:

- Creche ● Nightline ● Lesbian Gay & Bisexual Society
- Mature SA ● Overseas SA ● Minibus ● Women's Officer
- Self-defence classes

The new Student Services unit brings together Welfare, Careers and Accommodation assistance under one roof. There are 2 full-time counsellors and a Finance Advisor.

Disabled: *Despite being quite hilly, an effort has been made*

for better access, particularly in the Arts faculty which has ramps and lifts. Some accommodation has been specially designated. *Good* facilities are also being developed for sight and hearing impaired students (loops, sign language, white lines on steps). The Dyslexia Unit is internationally renowned.

FINANCE:
- Ave debt: £3,450 ● Access fund: £152,050
- Successful applications (1997): 400

Help may be available from a small welfare budget in emergency cases.

University of Bath

University of Bath, Claverton Down, Bath, BA2 7AY.
Tel: (01225) 323019. Fax: (01225) 826366.
E-mail: admissions@bath.ac.uk
Bath University Students' Union, Claverton Down, Bath, BA2 7AY. Tel: (01225) 826612. Fax: (01225) 444061.
E-mail: union@union.bath.ac.uk

General

The Romans may have built the first settlement in Bath, but it was in Georgian times that it became the *truly beautiful* city it now is. *Radiant* golden local stone is everywhere - hardly a brick building to be seen. Now it's one of the country's top tourist resorts. They don't come just to see the Roman Baths and *pretty* city, but also the local countryside, the Mendip Hills, the Cotswolds and the Severn Estuary. *Unfortunately,* the University, being on a small 60s campus 2 miles from the city centre, *shares very little of this elegance. It's a disorienting place at first, with no immediately apparent focus or entry point. The buildings, with all the concrete charm of a suburban shopping precinct, are definitely not the University's best feature, but students soon become anaesthetised to them.* After all, there's the *pleasant* greenery of the extensive grounds and the small University lake, *compensating somewhat for the remote, windy situation.* The University offers mainly science and technology courses (often with a language element) and many include a sandwich placement in industry.

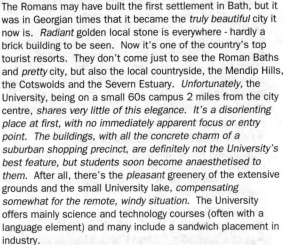

59% ♂♂♂♂♂♂♂♀♀♀♀ 41%

Sex ratio(M:F): 59%:41%	Founded: 1966
Full time u'grads: 5,108	Part time: 0
Postgrads: 1,097	Ave course: 3/4yrs
Ethnic: 13%	Private school: 21%
Flunk rate: 30%	Mature students: 10.6%
Overseas students: 14%	Disabled students: 2%
Staff/student ratio: 1:12	Clearing: 2%

ATMOSPHERE:

The campus is a bit isolated from the city (which isn't exactly Sodom and Gomorrah to start with) and the students (mainly scientists) tend to be quite serious about their studies. They know how to make use of their limited spare time, though; sport and other extra-curricular goings-on are a popular diversion.

THE TOWN:

- Population: 79,900 ● London: 100miles
- Bristol: 11miles

Tourism not only means that Bath has plenty of amenities, museums, galleries and entertainment facilities, *but also that these things cost a lot. The Roman Baths have to be visited at some time, especially if you're a bit smelly.* The Victoria Art Gallery and The Royal Photographic Centre *are also worth a look.* Bath is also the home of the fattest man in Britain, Mr Derek Snoggs.

TRAVEL:

Trains: Bath Spa station offers services to London Paddington (£17.80), Bristol (£4.80), Birmingham (£15.70) and beyond.
Buses: National Express and Badgerline services from Bath to a number of destinations including London (£13) and Bristol (£3).
Car: Bath is 9 miles off the M4 down the A46 and on the A4.
Air: Bristol Airport 18 miles away has flights inland and to main European destinations.
Hitching: Many students cadge lifts to the city centre and *the M4's good for thumbing down to London.*
Taxis: *Not cheap, but special offers for students.*
Bicycles: Bath's a humpy bumpy ride - *okay for turbo-powered limbs and it does mean it's not worth nicking bikes.*
Local: *A bus service operates between the town, Bath University and Bath Spa.* The SU has negotiated a frequent bus service between the campus and the train station (75p return).

LIBRARIES & COMPUTERS:

- Books: 275,000 ● Study places: 650
- Computer workstations: 500

Library and computer services have recently been completely revamped and expanded, with computing facilities open 24 hours in term-time.

CAREER PROSPECTS:

- Careers Service ● No of staff: 4full
- Unemployed after 6mths (1995): 11%

SPECIAL FEATURES:

- Bath operates a mixed system of terms and semesters but each system has the same Christmas and Easter breaks.

FAMOUS ALUMNI:

Neil Fox (Capital Radio DJ); Russell Senior (ex-Pulp guitarist).

FURTHER INFO:

Undergrad and postgrad prospectuses and an alternative one from the SU. Also video and a web site (http://www.bath.ac.uk).

entertainment
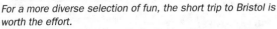

TOWN:
● <u>Price of a pint of beer: £2.00</u> ● <u>Glass of wine: £1.55</u>

For a more diverse selection of fun, the short trip to Bristol is worth the effort.

Cinemas: (3) Cannon Beau Nash, Robins Cinema and Little Theatre. Bath Film Festival is becoming more high profile.

Theatres: The elegant old Theatre Royal presents *high-brow* arts like opera, ballet and pre-West End runs, *but isn't above the occasional low-brow dross.*

Pubs: *Quaint and plentiful with many a potent pint, but expensive. Many are designed purely to part the tourist trade from their money, but most are welcoming enough.*

*push*plugs - or maybe bathplugs: *The Boater; The Huntsman; The Hobgoblin; PJ Peppers; The Hush Club has a 2am license.*

Clubs/discos: *Not a huge deal going on, but things are more lively than the staid, touristy image might suggest.*

*push*plugs: *Cheese at Moles (Tuesday irony); Po-Na-Na (cod-African decor, rare groove); Babylon.*

Music venues: *The only decent venue is Moles Club, a pretty good indie hangout.*

Eating out: *There are dozens of chintzy tea rooms aimed at tourists, but just as good for fond, visiting parents (and their wallets). Other, more student-friendly push*plugs: *Cafe Retro (lively and cheap); Cafe Piazza (on a roof); Maxsons (cosmo style).*

UNIVERSITY:
● <u>Price of a pint of beer: £1.30</u> ● <u>Glass of wine: £1.10</u>

Bars: (3) *The main bar, The Plug (cap 400), is a classic, dingy, nicotine-soaked student boozer. There's also a bar in the Venue which doesn't smell quite so bad, maybe because it's not open as often, and the Sports Bar in the Training Village.*

Theatres: Despite the fact that there are no real artists (a few linguists, though), *the students still muster a little amusement from the muses.* The Arts Barn has a fully equipped studio theatre and rehearsal space for drama, dance and music and an arts workshop. There are regular trips to the Edinburgh Fringe.

Cinemas: There's a 200-seat, stereo-equipped cinema, showing a blockbuster a week.

Clubs/discos: The Venue (800) does its bit for the disco dollies 6 times a week. Fries to Go (cheesy pop); Student DJ nights every Saturday.

Music venues: The Wannadies, My Life Story and Tony De Vit have played the Venue recently.

Food: The main University refectory is backed up by smaller departmental facilities and the SU-run Melting Pot which does *great* baguettes.

Others: Plenty of balls and occasional cabaret.

social & political
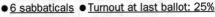

BATH UNIVERSITY STUDENTS' UNION:

● <u>6 sabbaticals</u> ● <u>Turnout at last ballot: 25%</u>
● <u>NUS member</u>

BUSU's quite carefully apolitical even though its

representative role is important and the exec is quite vocal about bringing grievances to the University's notice. A fare rise by a local bus company was warded off after protest, as was a merger with <u>Bristol, University of the West of England.</u>

SU FACILITIES:

BUSU is based in Norwood House where it offers a coffee bar, travel agency, shop, 4 minibuses for hire, printing & photocopying, photo booth, games and vending machines, TV lounge, pool tables and a juke box. All 4 major banks also have branches on campus (with cash machines).

CLUBS (NON SPORTING):

Adventure Gaming; Anglican; Arab; Astrosoc; Backstage; Bahai (religious and cultural); Baptist; Chinese; Cocktail; Clubbing; Computers; Folk Dancing; Guides & Scouts; Hellenic; Malaysian & Singapore; Methodist; Motorcycle; Musicals; Opera; Orchestral & Choral; Samba; Scandinavian; Tarts; Theatre; Visual Arts; Wine.

OTHER ORGANISATIONS:

BUSU publishes the weekly 'Sponge' and 'Spike', a free magazine. University Radio Bath, run by BUSU, is the *successful and well-equipped* student radio station. Campus Television (CTV) broadcasts on a closed circuit network, showing its own programmes and movies courtesy of satellite stations. Students take part in the Bath area charity Rag which has a sabbatical co-ordinator. They also operate their own Community Action group which runs a number of projects in the local area.

RELIGIOUS:

● <u>6 chaplains (CofE, RC, Baptist, Methodist, Quaker, Jewish)</u>
The Chaplaincy Centre in the middle of the campus is the base for all religions (but with a Christian slant). The city, with its Abbey, churches, Hindu temple and mosque, provides for other religious needs.

PAID WORK:

Tourism always provides a little seasonal work.

···· sports

● <u>Recent successes: tennis</u>

Sport takes a high priority at Bath - none of this wimpy crap about 'it's only a game'. The facilities, the expert tuition and the fact that there are no charges for any amenities are enough to make you want to run and jump and wave your athletic support in the air. There is a sports scholarship scheme where students of exceptional standards take an extra year to do their degrees which are combined with intensive training and the University is hoping to become a Regional Centre for Sporting Excellence.

SPORTS FACILITIES:

The *excellent* amenities are all on campus: sports hall; 95 acres of playing fields; 50m pool; squash court; grass ski slope; cross-country course and dressage area for horse-riding; astroturf pitches; 4 indoor tennis courts; 2 all-weather pitches; athletics field; tennis courts; climbing wall; weight room; multigym; and 30 coaches for sporting trips. Next door there's a golf course and in town further facilities like a bowling green, river and so on.

SPORTING CLUBS:
American Football; Boxing; Caving; Gliding; Gymnastics; Handball; Hot Air Balloon; Korfball; Lacrosse; Life Saving; Motor; Motorcycle; Parachuting; Rifle; Rowing; Snooker; Surfing; Tai Chi Chuan; Trampoline; Triathlon; Water Ski; Wind Surfing.

ATTRACTIONS:
Bristol Rovers, based in Bath, are the local football team (*so why aren't they... oh, never mind*), and there's also Bath Rugby Club. Bath City FC is in the Vauxhall Conference. *Lucky Vauxhall Conference.*

accommodation

IN COLLEGE:
● <u>Self-catering: 29%</u> ● <u>Cost: £41-73(39wks)</u>
Availability: All 1st years are offered a place in the University housing (a couple of concrete *beehive* tower blocks and a few smaller buildings, all on or near the campus) but expansion in student numbers could put pressure on this provision. Few other undergrads live in. Each block has its own launderette and one even has a hairdresser. Kitchens are shared between 8 and 13 students *but many can't be bothered to cook all the time* and make regular use of the 2 refectories. The top-price rooms have en suite bathrooms and phone lines.
Car parking: The parking on campus is *inadequate* and a permit is needed for which there is a charge. Clamps abound.

EXTERNALLY:
● <u>Ave rent: £48</u>
Availability: *Bath is a wealthy town and house prices reflect it but it's still possible to find the odd habitable hovel. Provided students put any thought of the gracious Georgian terraces out of their minds and concentrate on the less central areas (Twerton, Oldfield Park and Coombe Down are good bets), living out is manageable.*
Housing help: The University Accommodation Office has 8 full-time and 4 part-time staff who help with the annual home hunt, provide a landlord accreditation scheme and advise on the pitfalls of renting.

welfare

SERVICES:
● <u>Creche</u> ● <u>Nightline</u> ● <u>Lesbian & Gay Society</u>
● <u>Mature SA</u> ● <u>Overseas SA</u> ● <u>Postgrad SA</u> ● <u>Minibus</u>
● <u>Women's Officer</u> ● <u>Self-defence classes</u>
The University employs 2 counsellors, the SU 1. Every student has a personal tutor. The Medical Centre employs 3 doctors, a dentist, and a psychiatrist. There's also a money advice centre.
Disabled: *Wheelchair access on campus isn't great - the library is a nightmare to negotiate - but things are improving slowly.* Talking-book facilities exist for sight-impaired students.

FINANCE:
● <u>Ave debt: £2,400</u> ● <u>Access fund: £181,000</u>
● <u>Successful applications (1997): 359</u>
Some students who have to do vacation and field study as part of their course can apply for special awards. There's a hardship fund.

Bath Spa University College

▼ ● *Formerly Bath College of Higher Education*

▼ (1) Bath Spa University College, Newton Park, Bath, BA2 9BN.
Tel: (01225) 875875. Fax: (01225) 875444.
Bath Spa University College Students' Union, Newton Park,
Bath, BA2 9BN. Tel: (01225) 872603. Fax: (01225) 874765.
E-mail: studentsunion@bathspa.ac.uk
(2) Bath Spa University College, Sion Hill, Lansdown, Bath,
BA1 5SF. Tel: (01225) 875533. Fax: (01225) 875666.

General

Just like <u>Bath University</u>, the main site of Bath Spa isn't
actually in Bath, one of the most beautiful, unspoilt cities in
England (although, as all you tight-trouser fans will know, Jane
Austen considered it 'a monstrosity of epic proportion'). The
main site of Bath Spa isn't even in the town of Keynsham. In
fact, the centre of either Bath or Keynsham is as far as 5
miles away and the main Newton Park site is set in hilly
countryside; *more National Trust than NUS*. The buildings
themselves are, for the most part, built with the *almost golden*
Bath stone in the *classic* Georgian style. *There are a few
newer additions that don't really match* - mainly the
residences. There is an unwritten rule obeyed by all the
students that no one throws litter, *which preserves the beauty
of the place.*

550 students are based at the 2nd smaller site at Sion Hill,
5 miles away and much further into Bath in a different part of
the city. It has some residences, a library and canteen in a
converted Georgian crescent and a main 1960s building
housing the College's Art & Design subjects and a purpose-
built sculpture studio.

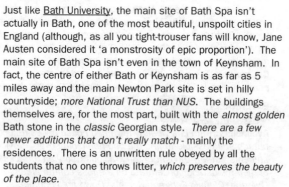

Sex ratio(M:F): 27%:73%	Founded: 1983
Full time u'grads: 2,274	Part time: 38
Postgrads: 262	Non-degree: 0
Ave course: 3yrs	Ethnic: 2%
Private/state school: 5%	Flunk rate: n/a
Mature students: 40%	Overseas students: 7%
Disabled students: 1%	Staff/student ratio: 1:20
Clearing: 2%	

ATMOSPHERE:
*The high percentages of female and mature students has
a significant effect, shifting the focus from traditional
alcoholic boisterousness towards a more quiet and friendly
little college, where everyone knows everyone else. It's
the sort of place that you wouldn't mind having in your own
backyard, if you had a backyard big enough. Although the*

Sion Hill site is, in some ways, the poor relation, many students prefer its city centre location to being out on a limb at Newton Park. In fact, most Newton Parkies who don't live in find somewhere in town, and commute. The campus dies socially at weekends, adding to the isolation of those who live there.

THE TOWN: see <u>University of Bath</u>
The Newton Park area itself is somewhere close to nowhere, *but there's the occasional pub worth visiting en route to Bath.*

TRAVEL: see <u>University of Bath</u>
Buses are the best way of getting from Newton Park into Bath. They run, *quite reliably,* every hour until midnight or later if necessary. The Orange Bus runs between town, Bath Spa and <u>Bath University</u> and does season tickets (£7.50 for 20 journeys, £145pa).

LIBRARIES & COMPUTERS:
● <u>Books: 135,000</u> ● <u>Study places: 246</u>
● <u>Computer workstations: 100</u>
There's a library at each site.

CAREER PROSPECTS:
● <u>Careers Service</u> ● <u>No of staff: 1 full/1 part</u>
● <u>Unemployed after 6mths (1996): 10%</u>

SPECIAL FEATURES:
● The Newton Park campus is built on Duchy of Cornwall land, so, although there is plenty of space, *getting planning permission for new buildings is nearly impossible.*

FAMOUS ALUMNI:
Andy Bradshaw (novelist); Howard Hodgkin (painter); Anita Roddick (Body Shop).

FURTHER INFO:
Prospectuses from the College. Web sites (http://www.bathspa.ac.uk & http://www.bathspa.ac.uk/su1.html).

entertainment

TOWN: see <u>University of Bath</u>

COLLEGE:
● <u>Price of a pint of beer: £1.35</u> ● <u>Glass of wine: £1</u>
Bars: (2) The Newton Park bar (cap 200) *is especially popular on Fridays.* Sion Hill bar is being redeveloped and will reopen in September 1998.
Theatres: (2) Newton Building and Assembly Hall both host a few student thespian efforts.
Clubs/discos: There are 1 or 2 dance nights a week in the SU at Newton Park which has a new sound system: Frisky (cheesy pop) and band/society nights.
Music venues: The Michael Tippett Centre (250) is the College's serious sound saloon, but bands also strut their stuff in the SUs at Sion Hill (150) and Newton Park. It's usually just local and tribute bands *and Shed Seven.*
Cabaret: Occasional cabaret evenings in the Newton Park SU. Charlie Cheese did the last Freshers' fortnight frippery.
Food: *Somerset Place at Sion Hill is the spot for salivating*

students. The canteen at the main site staves off starvation in an otherwise uninspiring fashion.

Others: 3 balls a year, culminating in the Summer extravaganza.

﹍﹍﹍﹍social & political

BATH SPA UNIVERSITY COLLEGE:

● 3 sabbaticals ● Turnout at last ballot: 10%
● NUS member

There are branches of the SU on both sites. *If this lot have party political leanings they enjoy them in the privacy of their own homes. They've coerced the campus shop into a longer hours trial, though. Another victory for rampant consumerism.*

SU FACILITIES:

2 bars; minibus hire; 1 shop; visiting Barclays bank; photocopiers; pool table; juke box; vending machines; satellite TV; meeting and function rooms; customised nightclub; student car parking.

CLUBS (NON SPORTING):

Follicle Awareness *(promoting the growth of facial hair)*; Human Rights; Pagan; Real Ale.

OTHER ORGANISATIONS:

The SU manages to distribute a weekly newsletter, *but that's it;* there is a Rag organised in conjunction with Bath University, which extracts several grand a year.

PAID WORK: see University of Bath

﹍﹍﹍﹍sports

● Recent successes: football
More aesthetes than athletes.

SPORTS FACILITIES:

Sports hall; tennis courts; rugby, five-a-side and all-weather pitches; gym; multi-gym.

SPORTING CLUBS:

Jiu Jitsu; Rowing.

ATTRACTIONS: see University of Bath

﹍﹍﹍﹍accommodation

IN COLLEGE:

● Self-catering: 26% ● Cost: £38-43(40wks)

Availability: The College has places in halls or shared houses for 575 students, housing all 1st years who request it and very few others. At Newton Park there are 5 60s courts of which 2 courts are single sex only and 3 more courts built just a few years ago. At Sion Hill, the *beautiful* converted Georgian Crescent provides 100 spaces. En suite and disabled accommodation being built for entry in '99.

Car parking: Free parking is available, *but not sufficient.*

> ❮ 10% of London's young homeless are graduates. ❯

EXTERNALLY: see <u>University of Bath</u>
Housing help: The College and SU Accommodation Offices employ 2 full-time staff who can help with emergency housing, blacklisted landlords and properties and *most other impediments to inhabitancy.*

 welfare

SERVICES:

- <u>Nursery</u> ● <u>Lesbian & Gay Society</u>
- <u>Mature SA</u> ● <u>Overseas SA</u> ● <u>Minibus</u> ● <u>Women's Officer</u>
- <u>Self-defence classes</u>

1 full-time counsellor employed by the College and a weekly surgery on the campus with a doctor and resident nurse.
Disabled: *The listed buildings don't help, but access is improving.* The college can arrange to pay for dyslexia assessment.

FINANCE:
- <u>Ave debt: £2,250</u> ● <u>Access fund: £60,525</u>
- <u>Successful applications (1997): 295</u>

- -

▶▶ Bedford College

see De Montfort University

- -

▶▶ Bedford New College

see Royal Holloway, London

- -

▶▶ Belfast, Queen's University

see The Queen's University of Belfast

- -

Birkbeck College, London

▼ ● *The College is part of <u>University of London</u> and students are entitled to use its facilities.*
▼ Birkbeck College, University of London, Malet Street, London, WC1E 7HX. Tel: 0845 601 0174. Fax: (0171) 631 6270.
Birkbeck College Students' Union, Malet Street, London, WC1E 7HX. Tel: (0171) 631 6335. Fax: (0171) 631 6349.
E-mail: president@bcsu.bbk.ac.uk

general

Birkbeck College, founded as the London Mechanics' Institution in 1823, is part of the complex of London University buildings in Bloomsbury, convenient for both ULU and Senate House, and just a mile from Trafalgar Square. It specialises in part-time courses for mature students with jobs or other daytime commitments. All the undergraduates are part-time and teaching takes place in twilight hours, between 6 and 9pm (3 days a week for most courses). The main building is a redbrick block, *starkly bauhausian, or, if you prefer, just stark*, but don't be put off; *courses have an excellent reputation and results are good.*

49% ♂♂♂♂♂♀♀♀♀♀ 51%

Sex ratio(M:F): 49%:51%	Founded: 1823
Full time u'grads: 0	Part time: 2,982
Postgrads: 2,373	Non-degree: 18,000
Ave course: 4yrs	Ethnic: n/a
Private school: n/a	Flunk rate: n/a
Mature students: 100%	Overseas students: 0.03%
Disabled students: 0.15%	Staff/student ratio: 1:23
Clearing: 0%	

ATMOSPHERE:
Everyone's friendly enough, but it's a long way from the standard student scenario. Since most students have pretty heavy commitments (such as jobs and families), there's not much of a community - everyone is just passing through. The work ethic is strong as most students have had to make sacrifices to study, but there is a quiet vitality which springs from such a diverse collection of individuals. Any real social buzz has to be picked up from other nearby colleges by osmosis.

THE CITY: see University of London

TRAVEL: see University of London
Trains: Nearest BR station is Euston, 750yds away.
Buses: 10, 14, 14A, 24, 29, 73 and 134. Night buses: N1, N2, N5, N9, N29, N73 and N90.
Underground: Goodge Street (Northern Line); Russell Square (Piccadilly Line).

LIBRARIES & COMPUTERS:
● Books: 250,000 ● Study places: 300
● Computer workstations: 25
2 libraries: The Main Library and the Gresse Street Library.

CAREER PROSPECTS:
● Careers Service ● No of staff: 1 part
Most students have already got jobs, although quite a few are unemployed. Often the reason they're studying is that they want to develop professionally or switch careers and a degree helps with that kind of stuff. Those who really need to can use the University of London Careers Service.

FAMOUS ALUMNI:
Elizabeth Esteve-Coll (V&A Museum Director); Helen Sharman (1st British astronaut); Frank Sidebottom (papier-maché-headed singer); Laurie Taylor (media sociologist).

FURTHER INFO:
Prospectus for undergrads and postgrads. Web site (http://www.bbk.ac.uk).

entertainment

IN LONDON: see <u>University of London</u>

COLLEGE:
● <u>Price of a pint of beer: £1.25</u> ● <u>Glass of wine: £1.10</u>
Bars: *The bar* (run by ULU, capacity 100) *is good for a swift drink before heading home, but not much more.*
Music venues/clubs/discos: The SU organises discos and/or bands in the bar (cap 100) on Fridays.
Food: The College snack bar and the dining club are the main scoff stops.
Others: There's an annual ball.

social & political

BIRKBECK COLLEGE STUDENTS' UNION:
● <u>1 sabbatical</u> ● <u>Turnout at last ballot: 20%</u>
● <u>NUS member</u>
Students have a great sense of loyalty to the College because, for many, it offers a life-changing opportunity. The staff return the compliment. Students also tend to be too busy to exert much energy in political activity or to get socially involved in the SU.

SU FACILITIES:
Bar; common room (JCR); TV room; pool table; photocopier; DTP facilities; table football; and a stationery shop.

CLUBS (NON SPORTING):
Debating; Hiking; Spanish & Latin American.

OTHER ORGANISATIONS:
The magazine is the 'Lamp & Owl'.

sports

● <u>Recent successes: football</u>
Sport is almost purely recreational and not seriously competitive, although Birkbeck has sports clubs of its own (as well as access to University facilities).

ATTRACTIONS: see <u>University of London</u>

accommodation

IN COLLEGE:
Because of its peculiar role, teaching predominantly part timers, Birkbeck has no accommodation of its own, but the University has intercollegiate housing.

EXTERNALLY: see <u>University of London</u>

welfare

SERVICES:
● <u>Creche</u> ● <u>Nightline</u>
Some services are available through ULU and the University (see <u>University of London</u>). Birkbeck's own SU operates some welfare services including 2 part-time counsellors and there's a sick room on site.
Disabled: *The College goes as far as it can in making provisions on an individual basis* and the main building has

ramps, lifts and other facilities. *Other buildings are not so hot, but no worse than usual. There are induction loops, IT equipment for the partially sighted.*

FINANCE:
Entrance fees awards scheme and a hardship fund.

● ●

University of Birmingham

▼ University of Birmingham, Edgbaston, Birmingham, B15 2TT.
Tel: (0121) 414 3344. Fax: (0121) 414 3850.
E-mail: prospectus@bham.ac.uk
Birmingham University Guild of Students, Edgbaston Park
Road, Edgbaston, Birmingham, B15 2TU. Tel: (0121) 472
1841. Fax: (0121) 471 2099. E-mail: pres@guild.bham.ac.uk

General

Birmingham, midway between Manchester and Bristol and almost as far from the coast as it's possible to be in Britain, is arguably the 2nd largest city in Britain. This depends on how you count, because, together with the surrounding towns, the Birmingham conurbation covers an expanse of land not small even by the standards of London. *Until recently, it was famous for its urban splat and sprawl; stinking factories, stagnant canals and that monument to sociopathic traffic planning, Spaghetti Junction. But now the city's moving on, moving up, developing and redeveloping and consequently, with only a little hesitation, we would actually go so far as to say it's an... an... attractive city.* The landscaped University Campus is about 2½ miles from the centre of Birmingham in Edgbaston in a little island of green trees and grassy banks, close to an abundance of shops, pubs and markets. The buildings are redbrick and red brick, although there's some more modern concrete *thrown in for bad measure.* The campus is dominated by the Old Joe clock tower, nicknamed after Joseph Chamberlain, who was a local hero turned politician.

51% ♂♂♂♂♂ ♀♀♀♀♀ 49%

Sex ratio(M:F): 51%:49%	Founded: 1900
Full time u'grads: 13,197	Part time: 529
Postgrads: 3,250	Non-degree: 483
Ave course: 3yrs	Ethnic: n/a
Private school: 25%	Flunk rate: n/a
Mature students: 14%	Overseas students: 10.6%
Disabled students: 3.3%	Staff/student ratio: 1:14
Clearing: 0%	

ATMOSPHERE:
If variety is the spice of life, Birmingham University is the vindaloo with a dollop of tabasco on the side. Although

Birmingham itself is a big place, the University is large enough to dominate its own chunk of the city, creating a touch of antipathy with one or two of the locals. Most, however, reciprocate the cheerful, chummy nature of the student body, unlikely to get worked up about much except sport.

THE CITY:
- Population: 2,200,000 ● London: 105miles
- Manchester: 75miles ● Bristol: 75miles

Birmingham is best known for being ugly and run down - the Handsworth Riots and the Birmingham Six (you can still visit the pub they didn't blow up - now called The Yard of Ale by the Odeon). Then there's the vowel-boiling accent, conjuring up images of Slade quaffing Cup-a-Soup.

But (courtesy of EC cash) Birmingham is on the up, like a phoenix rising from the fag ash of the Industrial Revolution, coughing and spluttering and spreading brand new space age wings. The canals (of which there are more in Birmingham than Venice) have been cleaned up. Grotty alleys have been cobbled or paved and pedestrianised (and often dehumanised as a result). The Broad Street area in the centre now has the new Convention Centre, one of the best venues for miles with some of the best acoustics. It has the Birmingham Rep Theatre, Ronnie Scott's Jazz Club, a new indoor arena and a modern modish piazza full of well cool cafes and chic shops. Birmingham Museum and Art Gallery has the kind of collection (particularly Pre-Raphaelites) that turns Lloyd Grossman's drawl into a drool. The Sadlers Wells Ballet has moved back to 'Brum' (as those who know it, know it) and the D'Oyly Carte Opera has joined them here. The Bull Ring shopping centre, the ugliest ever spewed onto Britain's streets, is destined for demolition and monstrosities are being replaced by swish shopping centres like the Pallisades (incorporating New Street Station), the Pavilions and City Plaza, which usually has a man playing Grand Piano at the bottom of the escalator as well as a humungous new Tower Records.

Most residential areas of the Birmingham conurbation have always tended to shelter those who can't afford to lugubriate in luxurious largesse, and now they house a friendly multi-racial, multi-cultural society and a student population of over 40,000. Brum lacks one main feature - pretension. Unlike Manchester, it's spent too long in the dumps to start preaching or teaching other cities how to be hip (but not for want of trying). If you haven't got the idea by now, the message is: forget your prejudices, Brum is buzzing bouyantly. Owroight?

TRAVEL:
Trains: *Being the belly button of Britain, Brum is brilliantly placed for rail links.* Inter City links from London (£18.50), Manchester (£10.15) and just about every city in the country come into New Street Station.
Buses: National Express services to London (£10), Manchester (£8), Edinburgh (£25) and, well, all over the shop, really. Also West Midlands Travel and London Liner.
Car: From the north-west and north Wales: M6, M54 and A41. From the south-west and south Wales: M5, A38 and A456. From London and south-east: M6 (to the M1), M40, A45. From north-east: M42 and A38.

Air: Birmingham International Airport, 9 miles from the campus to the east of the city, operates flights to the USA, Europe and Ireland as well as inland services.

Hitching: *Well located for branching out to the whole country - plenty of traffic and a motorway ring road all round the city as a launch pad.*

Local: *Bus services are very comprehensive, but all too often crowded (especially in rush hour). However, while there are plenty of services from the outskirts to the centre, it's quite difficult to skirt the edge.* They run late into the night and are quite cheap. Overground trains run around the city - *they're faster than buses, but more expensive and very unreliable. Not worth using, except by students who live in Selly Oak.*

Taxis: *The cowboy outfits are cheaper than the black cabs (minimum charge £2) but when God invented taxis, she wasn't thinking of students.*

Bicycles: *Routes are juggernaut jungles but cycle lanes are appearing.*

The Guild and the University between them run a bus service between halls and campus (40p for the round trip).

LIBRARIES & COMPUTERS:
- Books: 2,069,000 ● Study places: 1,820
- Computer workstations: 2,500

The Main Library is massive and there are various other faculty libraries, *and you need a degree just to understand the classification system. Students still complain about overcrowding, but computer provisions seem satisfactory.*

CAREER PROSPECTS:
- Careers Service ● No of staff: 19full
- Unemployed after 6mths (1996): 3.6%

FAMOUS ALUMNI:
Hilary Armstrong MP (Lab); Mark Cameron (Sean the chef in 'Emmerdale'); Tim Curry (Rocky Horror star); Philippa Forrester ('Tomorrow's World' presenter); Simon Le Bon (Duran Duran); Desmond Morris (zoologist); Chris Tarrant (TV and radio presenter); Victor Ubogu (rugby player); Ann Widdecombe MP (Con); Victoria Wood (comedian).

FURTHER INFO:
Prospectuses for undergrads and postgrads. For £1.50, an alternative prospectus is available from the Guild. Also, a Uni web site (http://www.bham.ac.uk) and a Guild site (http://www.guild.bham.ac.uk).

entertainment

CITY:

- Price of a pint of beer: £1.70 ● Glass of wine: £1.50

Cinemas: In and around the city, there are 4 multiplexes with a total of 38 screens and various smaller cinemas, including specialist Indian cinemas and the *arty-ish* Electric. *If students can't find a film they want to see, they're impossible to please.*

Theatres: The Birmingham Rep is one of the *best* rep companies in the country, but it's not the only one in Birmingham - there's also the Alexandra Theatre and the Hippodrome for ballet as well as numerous *left-field, shoestring* operations.

Pubs: *Brum pubs are plentiful, varied and vital.* push*plugs: The Farce & Firkin; The Brook (both in Selly Oak); Three Horseshoes. The Station is best avoided, as students are less than welcome.*

Clubs/discos: *A place this size is guaranteed to have umpteen foot-shifting palaces but, equally, a high proportion are liable to be naff, generic, chart-oriented dives.* push*plugs: 'Slag' at the Steering Wheel (acid jazz); The Que Club; 'Jellybaby' at Bonds; 'Republica' at Bakers (house); Snobs (indie/Britpop); Spacehopper; student nights at The Dome II and Pulse.*

Music venues: *The trouble with Brum's music scene is the lack of a decent medium-sized venue. For most decent acts the NEC and Aston Villa Leisure Centre are too big and indie venues like The Foundry, the Sanctuary and the Jug of Ale are too pokey. Nevertheless, live sounds are all around and the city has managed to spawn acts as diverse as Duran Duran, Ocean Colour Scene and, um... UB40. The Hibernian and the Irish Centre feature Irish music, Ronnie Scott's caters for jazzers, and there's a Jazz festival come the summer. The Symphony Hall is home to Simon Rattle's CBSO, but can adapt itself to less classical delights.*

Eating out: *Birmingham deserves special culinary kudos for introducing balti - a coriander-heavy style of Indian cookery, accompanied by vast, duvet-like naan breads - to the Western world. But there's more - in addition to the Hurst Street Chinese places and numerous fast food stations, many open until dawn,* push*plugs go to: Baltitastic; Magic Bean (cheap veggie); The Mud Bar (good value Italian); Selly Sausage (huge portions); Gun Barrels (Sunday lunch).*

Others: Other pastimes to pass the time include the Silver Blades Ice Rink and Merry Hill (out of town), which is one of the largest shopping centres in Europe and houses a multiplex cinema and a bowling alley. The Glee Club is a big comedy club, recently offering Jack Dee's *meretricious mirth*. And you can *always* go and see 'Gladiators' at the Indoor Arena.

UNIVERSITY:
● Price of a pint of beer: £1.50 ● Glass of wine: £1.05

Bars: There are 12 bars around the University including 1 in each hall of residence and 3 Guild bars: Old Joe's (capacity 700, *quite rowdy*); Fingal's (150, Oirish-themed); Berlin's (400, doubles as a club/venue).

Cinemas: The Black Lodge film society shows a mix of cult movies and recent releases in the Debating Hall 4 times a week.

Theatres: The University Studio Theatre is frequently used by the Guild's Theatre Group and the Drama Department. There are also 2 other theatres around the campus. Trips to Edinburgh Fringe have occurred recently.

❝Members of the Newcastle University rugby club appeared naked in Margi Clarke's Good Sex Guide.❞

Clubs/discos/music venues: There are 5 regular club nights to cater for most tastes, *popular ones* include the Club Tropicana 80s night, Martha's Yard (acid jazz), Frenzy and Club Shine (indie). There are plans to make improvements to the Debating Hall in order to lure bigger bands but nothing's happened yet.

Cabaret: The Joke Joint at Berlin's fronts a fistful of funnies, such as Junior Simpson and Will Smith.

Food: The bars produce all manner of solid fuel and there are 4 other food stops, including Dixie's donut bar. *All Guild outlets are franchised, so the quality costs.*

social & political

BIRMINGHAM UNIVERSITY GUILD OF STUDENTS (BUGS):

● 6 sabbaticals ● Turnout at last ballot: 15%
● NUS member

Most students perceive the Guild as a building where fun things happen, rather than as BUGS, a big, cheerful, all-inclusive band of diverse people out to battle for student interests. Facilities take precedence over political intrigue, although a massive campaign against the A38 relief road has so far cramped the constructors' style.

SU FACILITIES:

The Guild building provides 3 bars, cafeterias, sandwich bar, general shop, travel agency, photo shop, print shop, opticians, hairdressers, a greengrocers, IT shop, Endsleigh Insurance office, car and bus hire, meeting rooms, debating chamber, customised club venue, Midland & Co-op banks, video rental, video hire, juke box, vending and games machines.

CLUBS (NON SPORTING):

Anglicans; Arab; Astronomical; Bangladesh; Black Lodge (films); Change Ringers; Chinese Christian; Chinese; Comedy; Co-operative; Cypriot; Dead Parrot; Duke of Edinburgh; Egyptian; Freak Bros (hippy); Gothsoc; Hellenic; Hispanic; Indian; Italian; Japan; Jazz; Korean; Links; Living Marxism; Manga Anime; Methodist; Mexican; Motor; Musicians; Navigators; Newman Catholic; Nigerian; Pakistan; Pro-life; Pro-session (muso); Radio; Recycling; Scout and Guide; Sikh; Singapore; Sri Lankan; Stratford; Students with Disabilities; Taiwan; Talking Hands; Treasure Trap; Turkish; Welsh.

OTHER ORGANISATIONS:

Based at the *impressive* Media Centre, the free student magazine 'Redbrick' is *unusual and quite professional.* 'Bugs' is the Guild's info-sheet. BURN FM broadcasts for 2 months a year *to great popular acclaim* and is angling for a permanent licence; Guild TV wins awards *but is less popular with students, mainly because of limited transmission.* There's also a successful Community Action Group and an annual charity carnival. RAG raised £42,000 last year.

RELIGIOUS:

The University's St Francis Hall is a multi-denominational religious centre which the various chaplains use as a base. There's also a Muslim prayer room. Birmingham itself is a multi-cultural city and so not only has cathedrals and churches of all types, but also mosques, temples and synagogues.

PAID WORK:

The Guild's the best bet for a fuller pocket, employing over 300 students on a casual basis at any one time.

·········· sports

● Recent successes: hockey, lacrosse

Both the city and the University are full of facilities for those who like nothing better than sliding through mud, zooming round tracks and building pecs à la Peter Andre. The University's record in just about every sport is among the best in the country - they came second overall in the country in last year's BUSA competition. This emphasis on achievement is not to the detriment of the less able athletes who can and do take part on a broad level even if they don't win. Departments will even shift their timetables to allow participation in the University's Recreation Programme. As for facilities, they would ease a decathlete's soul and the ones that aren't free are cheap (eg swimming or tennis court hire 50p).

SPORTS FACILITIES:
On campus the Munrow Sports Centre has a *humungous* sports hall, martial arts dojo, squash courts, 2 gyms, dance studio, a pool, multigym and free weights and facilities for all manner of indoor sports. Near the Centre are outdoor amenities such as an all-weather athletics field, floodlit pitch, astroturf pitches, canals for canoeing and tennis courts. There are another 70 acres of fields further afield at Wast Hills, about 15 minutes from the campus by University minibuses. Out on a limb about 165 miles north, at Coniston Water in the Lake District, the University has a centre for *cable-knit sweater* sports like sailing and rock climbing. There are about a dozen scholarships for serious contenders.

SPORTING CLUBS:
American Football; Ballroom and Latin Dancing; Bridge; Clay Pigeon; Diving; Hang-Gliding; Kayak; Kite; Kung Fu; Lacrosse; Motor; Mountain Bike; Mountaineering; Ninpo Budo *(no idea either)*; Parachuting; Pool/Billiards; Rifle; Rowing; Skating; Speleological; Surf; Swimming & Water Polo; Tennis; Ten Pin Bowling; Thai Boxing; Triathlon; Wind Surfing.

ATTRACTIONS:
Footie fans will of course know all about local teams, Aston Villa and Birmingham City, and nobody can ignore the cricket at Warwickshire's main ground at Edgbaston. There's also Moseley Rugby Football Club, the Alexander Athletics Stadium, the Horse of the Year Show, figure skating at the NEC, and athletics at the Indoor Arena, when Wolf and Saracen aren't hogging it.

·········· accommodation

IN COLLEGE:

● Catered: 19% ● Cost: £66-84 (35wks)

● Self-catering: 18% ● Cost: £53 (35wks)

Availability: Most 1st years live in (and all who want to can), after which most students choose to live out. The halls themselves are based mainly on the Vale Campus about 10 minutes from the main campus. Others are spread around the south-west area of Birmingham all within 2 miles of the campus.

❝ The Sheffield Rag once tried to paint a zebra crossing on the M1. ❞

There is one, University House, the smallest, actually on the edge of the campus with some facilities for students with disabilities. Students can choose between all-male, all-female or mixed blocks. 12% of rooms are shared. There are also 6 blocks of self-catering student flats. A £15m residences development over the next 5 years *might add a room or two.*

EXTERNALLY:
- Ave rent: £33

Availability: *Accommodation is cheap and easy to find, and the quality's improving.* Selly Oak and Selly Park are the most student infested. *Moseley is also popular, but less of a ghetto. Edgbaston is Brum's poshest part, but the part of Edgbaston that's near the cricket ground is a red light district, quite run down, poor, multi-racial - being so cheap, it's ideal for students. The scuzzier parts of Balsall Heath, Northfield and North Birmingham generally are best avoided.*

welfare

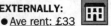

SERVICES:
- Nursery ● Nightline ● Lesbian & Gay Society
- Mature SA ● Overseas SA ● Minibus ● Women's Officer
- Self-defence classes

The ARC (advice and representation centre) offers 7 trained counsellors, the SU 3. The student health clinic provides medical support from full-time doctors and nurses.
Information room with pamphlets about the city, its services, welfare issues and finance.
Disabled: A Mobility Map is available for wheelchair users, showing the location of ramps, lifts etc. All new buildings have *good* access *but there are still no-go areas, which preclude study of some subjects completely.* Provision for sight-impaired students is good.

FINANCE:
- Ave debt per year: £1,600 ● Access fund: £250,000
- Successful applications (1997): 414

In addition to numerous scholarships and prizes there's a hardship fund administered jointly by the University and BUGS and special support to help student parents.

▶▶ Birmingham Conservatoire
see University of Central England

▶▶ Birmingham Poly
see University of Central England

▶▶ Bishop Grosseteste College
see Other Institutions

Bolton Institute of Higher Education

 Bolton Institute of Higher Education, Deane Road, Bolton,
BL3 5AB. Tel: (01204) 528851. Fax: (01204) 399074.
E-mail: enquiries@bolton.ac.uk
Bolton Institute Students' Union, Deane Road, Bolton,
BL3 5AB. Tel: (01204) 900850. Fax: (01204) 900860.

General

 *Bolton grew up amidst the urban giants of the north-west and if
it had been among less towering company, it would have
gained more credit as a sizeable civic centre on its own merits.*
Between Liverpool, Preston and Manchester (including
Salford), there are now 8 universities - one of the highest
concentrations of students in Europe. The newest is Bolton
Institute which is on course for university status and can
already award its own degrees. The Institute's main site, the
Deane Campus, is outside the town centre on 2 main roads,
consisting of a high glass tower and lower surrounding blocks
built in the late 60s. Apart from a *scruffy* stretch of grass in
front of the tower, *there isn't a lot of greenery.*

54% ♂♂♂♂♂♂♀♀♀♀ **46%**

Sex ratio(M:F): 54%:46%	**Founded: 1982**
Full time u'grads: 4,000	**Part time: 3,000**
Postgrads: 950	**Non-degree: 1,264**
Ave course: 3yrs	**Ethnic: 13%**
Private school: n/a	**Flunk rate: n/a**
Mature students: 72%	**Overseas students: n/a**
Disabled students: 6%	**Staff/student ratio: 1:14**
Clearing: 10%	

ATMOSPHERE:
*The tone is set by the massive proportion of mature students -
one of the highest in the country. Conventional student
activities and adolescent high jinks still take place, but not on
a huge scale. People are friendly but focused - they tend to
come in for their lectures and then leave fairly rapidly. If life
gets too dull, Manchester is only 10 miles away.*

THE SITES:
Deane Campus: The main campus, see above.
Chadwick Street Campus: (700 students - Humanities, Health
& Education) ½ mile from the main campus on the outskirts of
Bolton.
Eagle Mall: (700 - Textiles, IT) Just 50 yards from the main
site, the second library is also based here.
Great Moor Street Campus: (200 - Art & Design) 10 minutes'
walk from the Deane Campus is this converted Victorian red
brick school. *Moving this faculty is on the cards, but a
decision hasn't been made yet.*

TOWN:
- Population: 253,300 ● London: 182miles
- Manchester: 10miles ● Blackpool: 35miles

Bolton is blessed with lots of modern amenities including a large shopping centre with 3 arcades and branches of all the major chains. The Market Place development has given modern fronts to various old shop buildings. Relics of the cloth industry include the Tonge Moor Textile Museum. Also worth a look, the Last Drop Village, an 18th-century converted farmhouse extended to create a picturesque village with cottages, pub, restaurant, hotel, craft shops and other would-be tourist traps (if there were any tourists).

TRAVEL:
Trains: The Institute is ½ mile from Bolton mainline station with direct connections to Manchester (£1.40) every 15 minutes, Blackpool, Wigan and Blackburn. Via Manchester, the whole country can be accessed, including London (£20.45) and Birmingham (£12.60).
Coaches: National Express and Timeline Travel run services to London (£21), Birmingham (£13) and all over.
Car: The *devilish* A666, M61, M62 and A679 all serve Bolton.
Air: Manchester Airport is only a 30-minute drive or a £2.25 train journey away.
Hitching: *A good selection of main roads nearby to chose from, but students don't really try.*
Local: Students often use the buses which go from the Institute to the halls every 10 or 15 minutes until 11.30pm. A nightbus from Manchester pulls in at 1am or 2.30am on Fridays and Saturdays. There are also plans to expand Manchester's *excellent* Metro service westwards to Bolton.
Taxis: On average, taxis cost £2 from the town to the halls.
Bicycles: Not many students use bikes; *the town centre is very busy and has no cycle lanes. Nevertheless, people still seem to have enough incentive to steal bikes regularly.*

LIBRARIES & COMPUTERS:
- Books: 129,543 ● Study places: 530
- Computer workstations: 700

There are libraries at Deane Street and Eagle Mill. Computer access is 24 hours and further computers are held in individual departments.

CAREER PROSPECTS:
- Careers Service ● No of staff: 2part

The *diminutive* Careers Service is run jointly by students and the University.

FURTHER INFO:
Prospectuses for undergrads and postgrads; alternative SU prospectus; web site (http://www.bolton.ac.uk).

entertainment

TOWN:
- Price of a pint of beer: £1.60 ● Glass of wine: £1.50

When Bolton falls short, Manchester never fails to satisfy.
Pubs: *North-westerners were never ones to shirk a pint and Bolton has a goodly selection of pubs. Some town centre pubs don't welcome students (especially at weekends) but*

there are plenty that do. **push***plugs: Durty Nellie's; Cattle Market (close to halls); The Hogs; Three Crowns; Old Man & Scythe; O'Neill's.*

Theatres: The Octagon puts on a mixture of modern plays, the occasional Shakespeare and Xmas panto.

Cinemas: The only flicks is now Warner Bros which is 5 miles from campus, *leaving students cynically cinemaless.*

Clubs/discos: The Ritzy and the Crown & Cushion have student nights and Hawthorn's is an indie hangout. The Temple hosts dance nights with Kiss FM and 70s nights.

Music venues: Various venues provide anything from heavy rock to heavily classical. **push***plugs: Oscar's Café bar (jazz/blues/rock); Gypsy's Tent (alternative); Albert Hall Complex (classical/blues).*

Eating out: *Gustatory delights beyond the filet-o-fish are thin on the ground, but there are a few reasonably priced 'proper' restaurants.* **push***plugs: Tiggi's Pizzeria; Patagonia Café (chill-out zone); Taj Mahal (Indian); Cook in the Books is a venerable veggie victual vendor.*

INSTITUTE:
● <u>Price of a pint of beer: £1.30</u> ● <u>Glass of wine: £1.10</u>

Facilities are based in the new SU building at Derby Street.

Bars: (2) The South Bar is the main daytime hangout; the North Bar (*no prizes for imagination here*) is used in the evenings and when there are ents on.

Theatres & cinema: The theatre at Chadwick Street is used for student productions. 1 or 2 films shown each week.

Clubs/discos/music venues: The North Bar (cap 275) is the main venue. There are 2 club nights a week, including the *self-explanatory* Vodka Karaoke, plus occasional special events and local bands.

Food: The Institute provides *good value* refectories on 3 sites and the bars serve spuds and pizzas.

Others: Quiz nights and 2 balls a year.

········· social & political

BOLTON INSTITUTE STUDENTS' UNION:
● <u>3 sabbaticals</u> ● <u>Turnout at last ballot: 10%</u>
● <u>NUS member</u>

The students' overall perception of BISU has improved greatly since the new HQ at Derby Street was opened. Politics revolve around single issues, such as finance and the long wait for university status, rather than party affiliations.

SU FACILITIES:
Bars; cafeteria; minibus hire; travel agency; printing services; bookshop; general shop; bank (Co-op); photocopiers; library; games room; pool table; juke box; fax service; vending machines.

> ❝Lancaster University owns a peahen and two peacocks which wander around the campus.❞

CLUBS (NON SPORTING):
Live Role Play; Psychology.

OTHER ORGANISATIONS:
'Inspire' is the *optimistically titled* student mag. *Well, it has a glossy cover.* The Union is involved in Community Action Groups and Safer City projects.

RELIGIOUS:
● 1 chaplain
Local prayer palaces for Muslims, Hindus, Anglicans, Baptists, Catholics, Methodists, URC, Quakers and Scientologists. Female chaplain.

PAID WORK:
Usual bar and shop work etc, etc, etc... but not much of it. There is a jobshop run by the SU.

sports

● Recent successes: trampolining, cricket
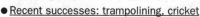
Charges for the use of facilities are minimal. It usually costs about £1.50 to join a sports club. All students are eligible for a Bolton Leisure Card.

SPORTS FACILITIES:
Sports hall; athletics field; tennis court; climbing wall and 3 acres of sports fields. Bolton adds a swimming pool complex.

SPORTING CLUBS:
Frisbee; Kung Fu; Motor Sports; Self Defence; Snow-boarding; Surf.

ATTRACTIONS:
The newly promoted Bolton Wanderers FC, in their brand new stadium, and Bolton Harriers (athletics).

accommodation

IN COLLEGE:
● Self-catering: 18% ● Cost: £41 (40wks)
Availability: Accommodation for 700 is sited on the Orlando campus, in 'The Hollins' halls on the Chadwick campus and more off campus. *Bearing in mind that most mature students look after themselves, these provisions leave only few students in the lurch.*
Car parking: Adequate free parking at the halls.

EXTERNALLY:
● Ave rent: £27
Availability: *Accommodation is reasonably easy to find, but some students have to live further out than they might have hoped. In the Great Home Quest, the first clue is to look for a shared house preferably in Chorley Old Rd, Chorley New Rd, Park Road, Deane Road or the Haulgh. Avoid the crime-ridden Mencroft Avenue area, unless you're Robocop.*

welfare

SERVICES:
● Nursery ● Lesbian & Gay Society
 ● Mature SA ● Overseas SA ● Women's Officer
There are 2 full- and 2 part-time counsellors and several other advisors.

Disabled: Facilities include a Special Needs Advisor, easily readable signs, braille on lifts, braille in Student Services, ramps for wheelchairs and alarms around the Institute. *The new SU building is particularly good.*

FINANCE:
- Ave debt: £1,700 ● Access fund: £81,274
- Successful applications (1997): 379

The access fund is concentrated on childcare support.

Bournemouth University

● *Formerly Bournemouth Polytechnic, Dorset Institute*
Bournemouth University, Fern Barrow, Poole, Dorset, BH12 5BB. Tel: (01202) 524111. Fax: (01202) 593287.
E-mail: prospectus@bournemouth.ac.uk
Students' Union at Bournemouth University, Fern Barrow, Poole, Dorset, BH12 5BB. Tel: (01202) 523755.

General

Bournemouth is the largest of 3 towns rolled into 1, with Poole to the west and Christchurch to the east and a collective population of 350,000. Following the coast east, the New Forest stretches inland. The University is technically in Poole, 2½ miles from Bournemouth town centre. It's a modern campus University, *looking like beige Lego linked by brick pathways and this is reflected in its vocational, single-mindedly career-oriented remit.*

Sex ratio(M:F): 53%:47%	**Founded: 1976**
Full time u'grads: 7,714	**Part time: 2,813**
Postgrads: 454	**Non-degree: 0**
Ave course: 4yrs	**Ethnic: 6%**
Private school: n/a	**Flunk rate: n/a**
Mature students: 25%	**Overseas students: 8%**
Disabled students: 7%	**Staff/student ratio: 1:21**
Clearing: 14%	

ATMOSPHERE:
The student body tends to be middle-class, politically apathetic, clean-cut and car-owning, the most radical style statement being the occasional surf dude look. It's a high-spec world, teeth gritted for the free market, a more economic plastic substitute for the original ivory tower. A plaque in the entrance hall declares the mission of the University is 'to become a pre-eminent vocational university, well-founded in terms of educational quality and student appeal'.

OTHER SITES:
Bournemouth House: (health and community studies, business) In the city centre, 1,800 students are based here.

Studland House: (design, engineering, computing) Also a high rise block, in the centre of town.

TOWN:
- Population: 154,400 ● London: 100miles
- Southampton: 26miles ● Bristol: 60miles

In summer, Bournemouth's *a bristling, bustling town* full of tourists, little hotels, sandy beaches, sea and ice-cream melting down your wrist. *It doesn't totally close down in winter, but there's definitely less fun to be had.* It doesn't lack space though (2,000 acres of parks in town) and has *enough shops to keep students kitted out, although for the true shopaholic, a big city trip is needed.* The urban village of Winton, ⅔ mile from the campus, has all the shops for mundane necessities.

TRAVEL:
Trains: From Bournemouth station, 2 miles from the campus, to London (£16.50), Southampton (£4.80) and all over.
Coaches: National Express services to London (£12) and more.
Car: The A38, A31 and A35 - many Bournemouth students have cars, despite parking shortages.
Air: Bournemouth airport operates flights internally and to the continent.
Ferries: Ferries go from Poole's busy port to the Channel Islands.
Hitching: The ferries attract quite a lot of long distance travel and so, from out of town or the ferry port, *chances are fair.*
Local: Buses run regularly until about 11pm. As for trains, there are frequent stops along the coast, *but few students bother.*
Taxis: Numerous firms charging £1.40 minimum fare and about £4 from the campus to the station.
Bicycles: *Even more students cycle than drive,* and there's space to park 600 bikes on campus.

LIBRARIES & COMPUTERS:
- Books: 185,000 ● Study places: 1,200
- Computer workstations: 1,000

Despite all those computers being available 24 hours a day, *shortages still occur* because students are expected to do most of their coursework on them.

CAREER PROSPECTS:
- Employment Centre ● No of staff: 6full/2part
- Unemployed after 6mths (1997): 9.8%

SPECIAL FEATURES:
- The University is the home of the National Centre for Computer Animation.
- Most courses have a language component.

FAMOUS ALUMNI:
Rick Adams (ex-'Big Breakfast' presenter); Matthew Kelly ('Stars In Their Eyes' star); Stuart Miles ('Blue Peter' presenter); Tim Vincent ('Clothes Show' presenter).

FURTHER INFO:
Prospectuses for undergrads, part-timers and postgrads. Web site (http://www.bournemouth.ac.uk).

entertainment

TOWN:

● Price of a pint of beer: £1.85 ● Glass of wine: £1.60

Cinemas: (3) 2 mainstream in Bournemouth, 1 of which is a 10-screen multiplex and 1 art-house in Poole.

Theatres: *The Pavilion and Pier Theatres are more interesting in winter because when the tourists are in town, it's just one long summer spectacular run. The Bournemouth International Centre and Poole Arts Centre offer better prospects.*

Pubs: *The local brew, Old Thumper, is a pint with punch. Places near the clubs are becoming more student oriented.* **push***plugs: Hogshead; Moon on the Square; Pumphreys (cocktail bar); Hop & Kinderlin; Bar Med; Legend (gay-friendly).*

Clubs/discos: *Don't think that Bournemouth is just blue-rinse foxtrots and the Roly Polys' summer season. There's real dancing to be done.* **push***plugs: Academy (mainstream); The Cage (studenty); Berlins (all varieties of cheese); Xtreme (hip-hop, trance, drum & bass); The Manor (out of town rave mecca); Cheekie at the Show Bar.*

Music venues: Bournemouth International Centre (BIC) is the town's biggest venue. Poole Arts Centre is a bit smaller *and more eclectic.* Some clubs also host live sounds.

Eating out: *For those at the main site, Bournemouth is a bit too far to pop out to lunch. Apart from the standard array of Indian, Chinese and fast polystyrene,* **push***plugs go to: Nouveau II Mondo (Italian); HotRocks (on the seafront); Coriander; Lorenzo's (Italian); Legends (legendary milkshakes); Giant Pizza Co. The Old Christchurch Road offers eats till at least 2am.*

Others: In summer, the tourist delights include sailboarding on the beach and seaside fairs.

UNIVERSITY:

● Price of a pint of beer: £1.30 ● Glass of wine: £1.10

Activities are centred on the SU's Fire Station (1,200) in the centre of town. It did actually used to be a fire station and has the longest brass pole in Europe.

Bars: (3) The Fire Station has the largest bar. Alternatives on campus are the Attic Bar and the *smokey but characterful* Dylan's.

Cinemas: 1 or 2 movies a week, *mainly studenty/cult fare.*

Clubs/discos: Thrice a week the Fire Station *turns into a sweaty pool of wiggling bodies.* Darren Emerson was a guest DJ recently.

Music venues: The Fire Station also provides the main gig focus, recent acts including Dust Junkies, Space and Audioweb.

Food: *The University refectory has been criticised for its cost but it's always full anyway. The campus bars offer cheaper (but still not cheap) eats.* The Fire Station does Sunday Roasts.

Balls: At least 3 balls a year.

social & political

STUDENTS' UNION AT BOURNEMOUTH UNIVERSITY (SUBU):

● 4 sabbaticals ● Turnout at last ballot: 5%

● NUS member

Bournemouth is not a hotbed of radicalism, Trotskyism or any kind of -ism. Except maybe careerism.

SU FACILITIES:
In the SU building, there is a variety of sporting facilities, a new travel agent, cafeteria, hall, bar, video games, pool tables and 4 minibuses. Elsewhere on campus, there's a Barclays Bank with cashpoint and, of course, the Fire Station in town.

CLUBS (NON SPORTING):
Arts Appreciation; Catering; Choir; Concert Band; Gig; Star Trek; Television.

OTHER ORGANISATIONS:
The SU publishes the monthtly 'Nerve' mag. Nerve FM has received a temporary licence.

RELIGIOUS:
- 2 chaplains (CofE, RC, Free Church, 2 Jewish, Muslim)

PAID WORK:
Tourism brings many vacancies for deck-chair attendants, ice-cream vendors and hotel work, but most students go home in summer. Some teach English to foreigners.

sports

- Recent successes: rugby

The most popular (semi) athletic pursuit is probably trying to recreate 'Baywatch' on Bournemouth beach but some teams put in solid performances. The University's insistence on scheduling lectures on Wednesday afternoons hampers activity. What do they think this is, an educational institution?

SPORTS FACILITIES:
Sports hall; squash courts; badminton; all-weather pitch; floodlit astroturf; climbing wall; gym; multigym. Students pay for a Sports Card (£10 for a year).

SPORTING CLUBS:
Boat; Duke of Edinburgh; Kick-boxing; Motor Sports; Mountain biking; Parachute; Shorinji Kempo; Skateboard; Surf; Windsurfing.

ATTRACTIONS:
Bournemouth FC. *Hooray.*

accommodation

IN COLLEGE:
- Self-catering: 9% ● Cost: £52-59 (34-40wks)

Availability: The student village on campus only has places for 819 1st years (40% of them) with a quarter of those sharing. The houses in the no-smoking village, *which look like the set of Brookside,* are shared between 4, 5 or 7 students. *They're not cheap, though, and a bit far from shops - a bit far from anything except the campus for that matter.*
Car parking: Adequate free permit parking.

EXTERNALLY:
- Ave rent: £43

Availability: The University helps the 1st years it can't fit in the student village to find their feet. Most are accommodated in local University-approved guest houses, hotels and B&Bs in Boscombe and Bournemouth (which can cost up to £77 all in). By the time the summer season is over, there is so much housing that landlords sometimes have to advertise for tenants. The best areas are Winton and Charminster (both near the campus) and Lansdowne (near the Fire Station).

Housing help: The SU gives advice on contracts and how best to hunt, but the main help is from the University accommodation service which has 1 full- and 2 part-time staff who run a housing accreditation scheme.

welfare

SERVICES:

● Nursery ● Nightline ● Lesbian & Gay Society
● Minibus ● Self-defence classes

All counselling has been contracted out to the local authority. The medical centre in Talbot House has a doctor and nurses and is also the site of the day nursery. No-one stood for Women's Officer last year.

Disabled: The University shows concern for students with any form of special need including epileptics, students with dyslexia, partially sighted students and so on. There is a Disability Co-ordinator, some specially adapted accommodation on campus and the facilities are currently being improved. *Access to all buildings is good.*

FINANCE:
● Ave debt: £1,950 ● Access fund: £161,270
● Successful applications (1995): 420

SUBU runs a hardship fund providing loans.

University of Bradford

University of Bradford, Richmond Road, Bradford, West Yorkshire, BD7 1DP. Tel: (01274) 233082.
Fax: (01274) 236260. E-mail: ug-admissions@bradford.ac.uk
University of Bradford Students' Union, Richmond Road, Bradford, West Yorkshire, BD7 1DP. Tel: (01274) 233300.
Fax: (01274) 235530.

general

In a gap in the Pennines, not far from the Yorkshire Dales, is a city that bloomed and boomed during the Industrial Revolution because of sheep or, more accurately, wool. The University is in the thick of it, less than a mile from the city centre and mega roundabouts which trap cars in ever repeating circles. *The campus is as compact as a Swiss Army knife although it can't get a pebble out of a horse's hoof.* Most of the modern building blocks rise into the sky leaving room to park cars in between. There's also the Management Centre at Emm Lane which consists of a former religious training college and 2 modern extensions.

54% ♂♂♂♂♂♂♀♀♀♀♀ **46%**

Sex ratio(M:F): 54%:46%	**Founded:** 1966
Full time u'grads: 6,300	**Part time:** 250
Postgrads: 1,460	**Non-degree:** 285
Ave course: 3-4yrs	**Ethnic:** n/a
Private school: n/a	**Flunk rate:** 5%
Mature students: 20%	**Overseas students:** 16%
Disabled students: 6%	**Staff/student ratio:** 1:15
Clearing: 18%	

ATMOSPHERE:

Bradford's a small, friendly and relatively quiet University - having one main self-contained campus helps keep student spirit from dissipating into the city which would otherwise swallow it with friendliness. Students at Emm Lane are less a part of the party. Most students are involved in science and technology based subjects, with 50% on sandwich courses, so there's an air of hardworking practicality - students are either working, on their way to work or maybe having a swift half while they think about what work they should do next.

THE SITES:

Emm Lane: (1,000+ students) The University Management Centre is 2 miles from the main campus, *in the posher suburbs of Bradford*. There's a refectory and accommodation for 25 students *but for most entertainments, the main site is easy enough to get to.*

THE CITY:

- Population: 449,100 ● London: 180miles
- Leeds: 9miles ● Manchester: 30miles

Bradford is one of the cheapest places to live in the whole country, but there are still many number of ways to blow what little money you have. It has all the trappings of cosmopolitan commerce and culture, with a rich and vibrant ethnic mix. The streets are criss-crosses of Victorian terraced housing, except in the city centre, a jigsaw of big civic centres and buildings from the *brilliant* National Museum of Photography to the *fantastic* Alhambra Theatre. *If it does get a bit dull, don't forget Leeds and Manchester are almost on your doorstep.*

TRAVEL:

Trains: Bradford Interchange is just ½ mile from the campus. Services to London (£32.75), Manchester (£7.20), Birmingham (£17.85) and more.

Coaches: National Express services to, among other places, London (£13.75) and Manchester (£4.50).

Car: Just a few minutes off the M62 down the M606, on the A58, A658 and A650.

Air: Leeds & Bradford Airport (6½ miles away) operates flights inland and to Europe, Ireland and, *strangely*, Canada.

Hitching: *Not too many lifts - the beginning of the M606 is the place to try though.*

Local: Regular *and cheap* bus services from the campus to the city centre, but everybody walks if it isn't raining. There are 3 stations around the city (including neighbouring Shipley) which are useful for getting to Leeds (60p). A West Yorkshire

Metrocard gives unlimited travel on trains and buses; students can get one for a *bargain* £29.70 a month.

Taxis: *Not too expensive* costing £2 from the campus to the station. Bradford is too compact to clock up a significantly larger tab for any local journey.

Bicycles: *Bradford and the campus are a bit hilly and anything but a mountain bike is about as useful as chocolate bagpipes.*

LIBRARIES & COMPUTERS:
- Books: 425,000 ● Study places: 1,400
- Computer workstations: 250

The main book repository is the J B Priestley Library and there's a smaller Management library at Emm Lane. Every room in halls has a computer socket for linking up to the University network.

CAREER PROSPECTS:
- Careers Service ● No of staff: 10full/1part
- Unemployed after 6mths (1996): 9.6%

Bradford's emphasis on vocational training means it's popular with employers, especially in the engineering and technology sectors.

SPECIAL FEATURES:
Goths still haunt the streets of Bradford in admirable numbers.

FAMOUS ALUMNI:
Roland Boyes MP; David Hinchliffe MP; Alice Mahon MP; Ann Taylor MP (all Lab); *Rt Hon Lord Viscount Sir Earl Baron etc (we can't remember which)* David Puttnam has an honorary scroll.

FURTHER INFO:
Prospectuses for undergrads, postgrads and mature students, as well as individual course booklets, CD-ROM, video, web sites (http://www.brad.ac.uk and http://www.ubu.brad.ac.uk) *and for all we know, an interactive movie starring Alicia Silverstone as the Vice-Chancellor.*

entertainment

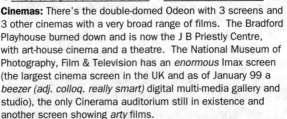

THE CITY:
- Price of a pint of beer: £1.60 ● Glass of wine: £1.50

Cinemas: There's the double-domed Odeon with 3 screens and 3 other cinemas with a very broad range of films. The Bradford Playhouse burned down and is now the J B Priestly Centre, with art-house cinema and a theatre. The National Museum of Photography, Film & Television has an *enormous* Imax screen (the largest cinema screen in the UK and as of January 99 a *beezer (adj. colloq. really smart)* digital multi-media gallery and studio), the only Cinerama auditorium still in existence and another screen showing *arty* films.

Theatres: (3) The Alhambra Theatre, with *excellent* foyer facilities, features some of the *best* productions outside the West End.

Pubs: Some of the country's *best* bitters are native to Yorkshire: Theakstons, Tetleys, Websters and Sam Smiths as well as less well-known local brews. **push**plugs: *The Shearbridge; Scruffy Murphy's; The Peel; The Blob Shop.*

Clubs/discos: *Out of Bradford's top bop houses, the* **push**plugs *go to Rio's (indie, 50p), Pickwick's (3 level club* run by former students, £1.50), Maestro's (vast).

Music venues: St George's Hall hosts a mangled mix of classical, MOR, comedy and bands.

Eating out: Locally, curry is the predominant aroma - 38 places within the campus area, to be precise, many open till 4am. But the choice is wider: there's every kind of restaurant including cheap chippies and value veggie joints. **push***plugs: Mr Papadom's (balti); Shezan (best of the Indians); Java Café (pretty cool); Angelo's Pizza; Hanser's (Asian); The Love Apple (groovy veggie).*

UNIVERSITY:
● Price of a pint of beer: £1.10 ● Glass of wine: 90p

Bars: (4) The SU bars are even cheaper than local pubs. The SU's Biko Bar is recommended by CAMRA for its range of real ales. The Mainline bar (recently refurbished *but still dingy though atmospheric*, about the only smoking venue on campus) is situated below Student Services and there's also the Escape, mainly a gig/club venue, and the Commie bar.

Cinema: Bradford Student Cinema (cap 900) shows mainstream and cultish fare 4 or 5 times a week.

Theatre: *Drama's quite a big deal, especially for a place with no drama department.* The Theatre Group runs a venue at the Edinburgh Fringe and also arranges exchanges with Eastern European groups. The Theatre In the Mill on campus hosts student and pro productions.

Clubs/discos/music venues: The Commie (formally the Communal Bar) has a capacity of 1,600, large enough to attract biggish bands; recently, Cardigans, Metalheadz and Chumbawumba. Regular clubs include the self-evident Friday Night Discos (FND) and the dancey Bliss at the Escape on Thursdays. There's also the occasional M&M disco/funk club.

Cabaret: 2 or 3 comedy gigs a term; Rhona Cameron and Sir Bernard Chumley have visited recently.

Food: The Refectory opens for lunch (11.45-1.40) *and snacks are served at the Union bars too.*

⋯⋯⋯ social & political

BRADFORD UNIVERSITY STUDENTS' UNION:
● 6 sabbaticals ● Turnout at last ballot: 19%
● NUS member

While relations with the authorities are OK, they're not afraid to get motivated if the circumstances demand. Students tend to be too wrapped up in their work to agitate, unless their

❝ Students at Lancaster claim that Alex Square on campus is named after Alex 'Hurricane' Higgins, the bad boy of snooker. Sadly, it's really named after Princess Alexandra, the University Chancellor. ❞

personal finances are under threat, and their recent rent strike proved successful. BUSU is one of the first unions to introduce on-line voting for elections.

SU FACILITIES:
Facilities are centred in the Commie, the University's social centre, where the SU has offices, 3 bars (with satellite TV), printing and photocopying, a common room, travel shop, NatWest bank (with cashpoint), photo booth, pool tables, juke boxes, vending and games machines, customised night club and meeting rooms. In the Richmond Building, the University's administrative centre, the Union still runs the Biko Bar and a shop.

CLUBS (NON SPORTING):
African; Anti-Abortion; Chinese; Gilbert & Sullivan; Greek; Hong Kong; Indian; Iranian; Kashmir; Malaysian and Singaporean; Modern Dance; Nigerian; Pakistan; Real Ale; Role Play; Spanish; Vampyre.

OTHER ORGANISATIONS:
Somebody must have been selling off a bulk load of newsprint round here. There's the *charmingly titled* union paper, 'Scrapie'; 'Ram', a daily message sheet; 'Shout', for women. There's also an independent student radio station, 'Ramair'. BUSCA, the Community Action group, provides practical help for the young, the old, the disabled and so on. The *hitherto modest* Rag is scheduled for expansion in 98-99.

RELIGIOUS:
● 3 chaplains (RC, CofE, Methodist)
The University has a quiet room, a Muslim prayer room and the city has an Anglican cathedral and other places of worship for Christians of all sorts, Jews, Muslims, Sikhs and Hindus.

PAID WORK:
Having plenty of pubs and restaurants spells opportunity.

sports

● Recent successes: netball, sailing
Bradford has a few Corinthians but most are persuaded to don trainers only on the offchance of post-match debauchery, which is perhaps why the well-supported campaign to keep Wednesdays free of lectures has not proved successful yet. There is a general charge of 65p to students for facilities.

SPORTS FACILITIES:
The campus sports centre includes badminton and squash courts; climbing wall; dance/martial arts studio; pool; gym; sauna; solarium and *seriously flash* new Nautilus suite. Just off campus, there are outdoor facilities at Laisteridge Lane: 8 tennis courts; 4 artificial turf floodlit playing fields and there are 35 acres of grass pitches 4 miles away at Woodhall. Locally and in the region, students can also enjoy the delights of a bowling green, golf course, ski slope, an ice rink and hills.

SPORTING CLUBS:
Bridge; Frisbee; Gliding; Hiking; Kobudo; Potholing; Powerlifting; Rugby League; Skydiving; Snowboarding; Trampoline.

ATTRACTIONS:
Bradford City FC is the local team and there's also Bradford

Bulls Rugby League, Bradford Dukes (speedway) and the Bradford Bulldogs (ice hockey).

accommodation

IN COLLEGE:
- Catered: 6% ● Cost: £64(30wks)
- Self-catering: 30% ● Cost: £37-53(30wks)

Availability: Almost all 1st years are guaranteed a place in halls, but few others are able to live in. Most places are in single rooms in self-catering blocks on the campus (1% have to share), although 406 are in catered halls a short walk away. 2 of the halls have blocks devoted to single-sex accommodation for both men and women and elsewhere all corridors are segregated. Kitchens are shared between as few as 7 or as many as 23. *Prices are reasonable, although the privately rented market is cheaper still.*

Car parking: *Adequate permit parking, but cars aren't needed.*

EXTERNALLY:
- Ave rent: £27

Availability: *Cheap and fairly easy to find, the popular areas being Great Horton and Laisteridge Lane which are close and Heaton which is attractive. In Buttershaw, even the muggers go in pairs.*

Housing help: The University Accommodation Office's 2 staff help and advise in the search.

welfare

SERVICES:
- Creche ● Lesbian & Gay Society ● Mature SA
- Overseas SA ● Minibus ● Women's Officer
- Self-defence classes

The University shares a service of 45 part-time voluntary counsellors with Bradford & Ilkley Community College and the Union has two advisors. There is a Health Centre with 4 doctors and several nurses.

Disabled: There's ramp access and a chair lift to the Richmond Building, extensive braille facilities and loop systems in some lecture theatres. *Not a comprehensive service and a lot of problems present themselves, but it has improved since the setting up of a Disability Office with 3 staff members, including a Disability Co-ordinator. 5p of each drink sold in the Union goes to the Disability Fund.*

FINANCE:
- Ave debt: £950 ● Access fund: £166,000
- Successful applications (1996): 564

The University operates its own hardship fund and there's a £10,000 trust fund for female students.

● ●

 Bretton Hall

see Other Institutions

● ●

University of Brighton

▼ ● *Formerly Brighton Polytechnic*

University of Brighton, Mithras House, Lewes Road, Brighton, BN2 4AT. Tel: (01273) 600900. Fax: (01273) 642825.
E-mail: admissions@brighton.ac.uk
University of Brighton Students' Union, Cockcroft Building, Lewes Road, Brighton, BN2 4GJ. Tel: (01273) 642870.
Fax: (01273) 600694.

General

Once every year a rally of vintage cars drives from central London over the South Downs to Brighton on the coast. The ones that make it have a party in one of the many hotels on the sea front, which is dashed all along with pebble beaches and marked by the Pavilion Pier. Every year, hundreds of cyclists make the same pilgrimage in aid of charity and thousands of tourists in the name of sea air *and the town's unique mix of shabby gentility and pulsating subculture.* Less joyfully, Brighton has a very large proportion of homeless. *However, the permanent residents are not all homeless, nor are they retired old fuddy duddies. There's a throbbing youth culture and a wholesome happening scene. This makes Brighton a good place for a University - it's fun and genteel, if a little shabby, and the weather's good.* However, one of the Unis is a bit outside town and the other (this one) isn't entirely in Brighton either. Okay, so 3 of the 4 sites are, but the 4th is east along the south coast in the resort of Eastbourne - Brighton's similar baby brother. *Each site is distinctly different - different characters, different building styles and different courses.* None can claim to be the main site *and it would be a bad move for students to apply without knowing where they'd be based.*

42% ♂♂♂♂♂♀♀♀♀♀ 58%

Sex ratio(M:F): 42%:58%	Founded: 1976
Full time u'grads: 7,929	Part time: 875
Postgrads: 641	Non-degree: 5,419
Ave course: 3yrs	Ethnic: 8%
Private school: n/a	Flunk rate: 39%
Mature students: 48%	Overseas students: 14%
Disabled students: 1%	Staff/student ratio: 1:17
Clearing: 20%	

ATMOSPHERE:
The social mix varies between sites but overall it's a vibrant, cosmopolitan mix, with a more creative bent than some of the other new universities. Wherever the facilities in the University fail to come up to scratch, the temptations of the town are there for the taking. The atmos is nothing like that portrayed in Lynda La Plante's dire Killer Net, which incidentally bore no

resemblance to anything in reality whatsoever, including the concept of good TV. Just by way of digression, you see.

THE SITES:

Grand Parade: (1,436 students - art, design, humanities) The only site in the centre of Brighton *and the most attractive* consists of a large 60s block with a small grassy central courtyard and a few other older buildings. *The Grand Parade site is full of arts students acting as arts students do - pseudo-radical and creative (but friendly) poseurs.*

Moulsecoomb: (5,495 students - engineering, pharmacy, computing, business studies, sciences, accountancy, maths, interior design, building, architecture) In one of Brighton's less grand suburbs, 3 miles from the town centre, the Moulsecoomb site comprises 2 small tower blocks of light brick, white concrete and glass and a converted factory. *Fairly characterless and little more than a busy work place.* Most of the overseas students are based here.

Falmer: (2,747 students - community studies, library studies, multicultural studies, languages, education) Just over the rail line from the large campus of <u>Sussex University</u> are the post-war buildings of this green field site. It's 3 miles from the city centre and *feels vaguely remote despite the easy rail connection. Even less character than Moulsecoomb.*

Eastbourne: (1,825 students - sports, PE, physiotherapy, podiatry, hotel & catering management) The Eastbourne site is itself split into several buildings spread around the town centre: a mixture of Victorian mock Tudor and newer buildings, set in some *pleasant* gardens and within a brisk walk of the seashore. *A lot of the students here are sporty and many display a little disappointment about having applied to Brighton, but ending up relatively far away, in an area cruelly, but not inaccurately, known to some as Crumblybourne; some do end up loving it, though.*

THE TOWN:
- <u>Population: 250,000</u> ● <u>London: 55miles</u>
- <u>Southampton: 56miles</u> ● <u>Eastbourne: 26miles</u>

Brighton: Sometimes called 'London by the sea', *Brighton is a truly cosmopolitan town that feels a bit like a city crushed into a village, because of the local variety and life. Homeless people beg outside swanky antique shops and leather-clad representatives of the large gay community stroll alongside well-dressed country ladies of a certain age. It's not as tacky as you might expect one of the kiss-me-quick and candy floss coastal resorts to be - it's a bit too posh for all that. Most of the touristy bits are of the quaint, craft work variety rather than the Blackpool Illuminations' bedazzling unsubtlety.* Brighton has all the daily trade and shopping stocks for most needs although there's no big shopping mall. Instead, there's North Laines (*vastly preferable*) with *terminally trendy* clothes, jewellery and antique shops, cafés and buskers. Some of the more notable features include the *excellent* selection of 2nd hand bookshops, the *bizarre* Brighton Pavilion (Indian colonial throwback) and the Palace Pier with its permanent funfair.

EASTBOURNE:
- <u>Population: 83,200</u> ● <u>London: 57miles</u>

In many ways similar to Brighton, but less so. It's smaller for

a start and, with the exception of the sea front, is *less quaint.*
It has a deserved reputation as part of the Costa Geriatrica,
but mauve rinses aren't compulsory. It has plenty of shops, an
Arndale Shopping Centre and a number of 2nd-hand spending
spots. *What nightlife there is, is student-oriented, and*
although it's not as pulsating as Brighton, it's still better than
picking out Noel Edmonds' navel-fluff with your teeth.

TRAVEL:
Trains: Connections from Brighton station to London (£8.80),
Southampton (£9.75), Manchester (£31.50) and elsewhere.
Coaches: All over the country including London (£10).
Car: The A23 connects Brighton with London. Within Brighton
beware the voucher system and zealous wardens.
Air: Gatwick, Britain's 2nd largest airport, is 23 miles north on
the A23.
Ferries: Ferries from Newhaven (8 miles east) to Dieppe.
Hitching: Students often hitch to London, although getting a
lift can be a hitch (ho, ho).
Local: The local buses are reliable but take forever. Trains
provide a comprehensive local service inland and along the
coast linking Brighton and Eastbourne.
Taxis: Not the country's cheapest.
Bicycles: *New cycle lanes have improved matters but the*
traffic's a bit mad and the hills are a bit hilly.

LIBRARIES & COMPUTERS:
● Books: 550,932 ● Study places: 1,193
● Computer workstations: 3,300
There's a major library on each site and 3 further support
libraries.

CAREER PROSPECTS:
● Careers Service ● No of staff: 9full/3part
● Unemployed after 6mths (1995): 10%

SPECIAL FEATURES:
● The University runs some very unusual courses, such as a
BA in Editorial Photography and a BSc in Podiatry (that's feet).

FAMOUS ALUMNI:
Neil Adams (judo champ); Helen Chadwick (artist); Harvey
Goldsmith (promoter); Helen Rollason (BBC sports reporter); Jo
Whiley (DJ).

FURTHER INFO:
Prospectuses for undergrads and postgrads from the Registry.
There's a video (for schools and careers offices) and the SU
has an alternative prospectus on the University's web site
(http://www.brighton.ac.uk).

entertainment

TOWN:
● Price of a pint of beer: £1.95 ● Glass of wine: £1.45
Cinemas: 3 cinemas including an MGM multiplex and the Duke
of York's cinema club.
Theatres: Theatre Royal puts on pre-West End runs, summer
spectaculars and Xmas pantos. The Gardner Arts Centre
hosts *less mainstream* productions and there are several
smaller venues as well.

Pubs: *Expensive but* **push***plugs: Hector's Horse; The Bear; Leek & Winkle; Pill & Pump; Finnegan's Wake; Zanzibar (gay).*

Clubs/discos: Some of Brighton's best clubs are nationally renowned, such as the *trendy and cavernous* Zap Club with its cabaret nights and gay nights *(£6-8 though and attracts rich, dim Sloanes).* Other clubs *rising above ankle-chained purgatory include The Escape (kitsch nights Saturday, £3-6), Jazz Place (£3) and Passion (gay, student nights Wednesdays and Thursdays).*

Music venues: *For a bit of Brighton rock, the silver sounds emanate from many a cranny and nook: The Event and the Brighton Centre are the big name venues; the Theatre Royal does classical and opera; and the Richmond pub, the Concorde and the Zap provide indie and dance stuff.*

Eating out: Brighton has a choice *as wide as Tony Blair's cheesiest grin,* including fish and chips and seafood, veggie and wholefood, pizzas and burgers, Indian, Thai, Chinese, Mongolian and of course, traditional British restaurants *to every degree of daintiness. It's almost as good and almost as expensive as London.* **push***plugs: Donatello's (student specials); Cactus Canteen (Mexicans); Food For Friends (veggie).*

Other: The Brighton Festival each May is one of the country's biggest arts and entertainment festivals - *an excellent distraction from exams.* It is accompanied by the Festival Radio station, which employs a fair few students. Also in May is the Essential Music Festival, the start of the naked mud-rolling outdoor music season.

UNIVERSITY:
● Price of a pint of beer: £1.40 ● Glass of wine: £1

Ents facilities have been somewhat hampered by the demolition of the SU's main venue, the Basement. The Komedia on the seafront has been used as a replacement, but isn't big enough for more than minor events (cap 170 bar).

Bars: There are 2 bars run by the SU at Falmer and Eastbourne and 2 smaller boozers at Moulsecoomb.

Theatres: There are 2 *enthusiastic* drama societies, and the Komedia has a *tiny* (cap 90) theatre.

Clubs/discos/music venues: The bars at Falmer and the Komedia are the only base for noisemaking these days *and it doesn't happen often. It'll take more than a big venue to compete with the ents in the city, though.*

Food: All SU bars do a *wide* range of grub, as do the *expensive* University-run refectories.

Others: Eastbourne and Brighton sites host annual balls.

⋯⋯⋯ social & political

UNIVERSITY OF BRIGHTON STUDENTS' UNION:
● 6 sabbaticals ● Turnout at last ballot: 1%

● NUS member

The University seems committed to pissing the SU off; the demolition of the Basement and recent pressure on the SU shop to stop selling cigarettes and even chewing-gum don't go down too well but students as a whole are too apathetic to organise politically. Apart from social facilities, the Basement was the SU's main moneyspinner, *so purse-strings are a wee bit tight these days.* The SU's main offices are with the University's on the Moulsecoomb site, but there are at least some facilities on each site.

SU FACILITIES:
Falmer: bar, shop, meeting room. Eastbourne: SU office, bar, satellite TV.

CLUBS (NON SPORTING):
Chinese; International; Mature.

OTHER ORGANISATIONS:
'Babble' is the monthly glossy mag.

RELIGIOUS:
● <u>2 chaplains</u>
Students can find all the world's major religions represented locally. New Muslim prayer room.

PAID WORK:
Although the jobs are no different from other towns, prospects are more hopeful, especially during the tourist season.

sports

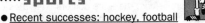

● <u>Recent successes: hockey, football</u>
Facilities at Eastbourne are good (thanks to the presence of sports studies) and they're not bad at Falmer either, but elsewhere, they're nothing to write home about. Participation is high, especially in women's sports.

SPORTS FACILITIES:
3 sports halls; playing fields; athletics track; Olympic-size swimming pool (at Eastbourne); floodlit tennis courts; floodlit 5-a-side football pitch; floodlit netball court; climbing wall; gyms; multigym; putting green; sauna; cardiovascular gym (at Moulsecoomb); Sport & Racquet club (£10 membership for students at Falmer). *As for future developments, long-term plans abound, but aren't yet a-built.*

SPORTING CLUBS:
Aikido; Gaelic Football; Sports Acrobatics; Windsurfing.

ATTRACTIONS:
Brighton & Hove Albion is the *dire* local football team and of course, there's also Sussex County cricket and Brighton races.

accommodation

IN COLLEGE:
● <u>Catered: 2%</u> ● <u>Cost: £62-70(35wks)</u>
● <u>Self-catering: 18%</u> ● <u>Cost: £42-57(35-40wks)</u>
Availability: The University accommodation is almost all snapped up by 1st years and with its other options, it can house 68% of them, with 3% sharing. The buildings range in size from the Varley Halls (capacity 495) in Brighton to the Whitworth house in Eastbourne (40). There are also 520 places in University-run head tenancy schemes.
Car parking: Free spaces *if students can find them.*

EXTERNALLY:
● <u>Ave rent: £43</u>
Availability: *It used to be hell trying to find affordable accommodation. Prices weren't much cheaper than outer*

London and were more scarce. Things have become easier (a number of agencies now deal with students) although prices are still steepish. The most hopeful spots for bedsits and shared houses are London Rd (near station and the best pubs), Lewes Rd/Elm Grove (good for Falmer), Seven Dials (near another station and the town centre) and Kemptown (just cos it's nice). Hove is a bit far and Moulsecoomb is a bit rough. Having a car doesn't help - there's nowhere to park it.

Housing help: The Student Services organisation allocates the University's spaces and lends a hand in finding places in the private market as do a number of private agencies.

welfare

SERVICES:

- Playscheme ● Nightline ● Lesbian & Gay Society
- Mature SA ● Minibus ● Women's Officer
- Self-defence classes

Student Services employs 3 full- and 2 part-time counsellors and the SU Welfare Unit does touring surgeries around the sites. For health provisions, there are doctors' surgeries and a nurse on each site. Also an Aids Awareness worker jointly funded by Sussex University. Drugs (particularly cannabis and ecstasy) are especially prevalent locally.

Disabled: Facilities are pretty feeble, especially at Falmer and Eastbourne. The University insists the situation is improving and have recently provided 6 specially designed rooms.

FINANCE:

- Ave debt: £1,700 ● Access fund: £266,087
- Successful applications (1997): 1,213

University of Bristol

University of Bristol, Senate House, Tyndall Avenue, Bristol, BS8 1TH. Tel: (0117) 928 9000. Fax: (0117) 925 1424. E-mail: admissions@bris.ac.uk
University of Bristol Union, Queens Road, Bristol, BS8 1LN. Tel: (0117) 973 5800. Fax: (0117) 946 6952. E-mail: president-ubu@bris.ac.uk

general

Just as the mouth of the Severn begins to yawn, before being swallowed by the Bristol Channel, the Avon river drops off into the south-west of England. Within a few miles it flows through the traumatically spectacular Avon Gorge at Clifton before reaching the heart of Bristol. It's an attractive stirring of old and new buildings, surrounded by green hills, which can only be described as countryside. In the middle of all this is the University Precinct and no one can forget it, what with the splendid gothic tower of the Wills Memorial Building dominating the city skyline. *Many of the other buildings are equally inspiring such as the large tea-with-crooked-pinkie* Victorian houses converted to form the arts departments and the 18th-century mansion, Royal Fort House. The Union Building, however, *lets the side down* - an *ugly*, concrete, squat, grey, *eminently demolishable* tower block.

52% ♂♂♂♂♂♀♀♀♀♀ **48%**

Sex ratio(M:F): 52%:48%   Founded: 1876
Full time u'grads: 9,112   Part time: 975
Postgrads: 3,465   Ave course: 3yrs
Private school: 38%   Flunk rate: 5%
Mature students: 11%   Overseas students: 16%
Disabled students: n/a   Staff/student ratio: 1:12
Clearing: 1%

ATMOSPHERE:
Bristol is trying to shed its image as one of the so-called green welly universities but it is nevertheless still popular with Sloanes and Oxbridge rejects (although most students would rather be here than Oxbridge any day). However, it's big enough, and the SU is buzzing enough, to blur the edges of any social stereotypes that might be encountered. The 2 great social unifiers are sport and alcohol.

THE CITY:
● Population: 370,300 ● London: 111miles
● Birmingham: 77miles ● Cardiff: 29miles
Bristol is effectively the capital of the south-west. It was, until the 19th century, as important as the big boys like London, Brum or Manchester, but the old maritime industry has gone now and the docks have been redeveloped with offices for yuppies. *Bristol's highlights include*: the Cabot Tower (which, from below, can be seen from almost anywhere, and from the top of which almost anything can be seen) and the *outrageous* Clifton Suspension Bridge, designed by Brunel. Also designed by Brunel in 1843 is the SS Great Britain, now in dry dock at the Maritime Heritage Museum. For science with fun buttons to press, try the Exploratory; for art and nature, the City Museum & Art Gallery; and for caged animals (and one of England's only hippos), Bristol Zoo. *In some ways, Bristol is the British San Francisco; beautiful, quirky, culturally thriving, slightly hippy-dippy and too many hills.*

TRAVEL:
Trains: Bristol Temple Meads station is one of the country's centres for Intercity routes with direct services all over the shop including London (£12.90), Birmingham (£13.55) and elsewhere. Bristol Parkway for Wales.
Coaches: Bristol is similarly well served by coach services, including National Express buses to, among other places, London (£7) and Manchester (£14.25). Arrow and Bakers Dolphin also offer cheap return trips to London.
Car: How do you get 2 whales in a mini? Down the M4. On the way to the Severn Bridge, the M4 also bypasses Bristol with the M32 going into the city. The M5 comes down from the Midlands, and the A38, A4 and A37 also all visit Bristol.

Air: Bristol Airport, 7 miles outside the city centre, has flights inland and to Europe.

Hitching: *The M4 and M5 are both good for long distance thumbsters.*

Local: There are several British Rail stops in and around the city and this provides a *reliable,* frequent and comprehensive service without staggering cost. Local buses fill in where trains can't go, costing £1 from Temple Meads station to the Union.

Taxis: At about £1 per mile, *useful for late night tripping.*

Bicycles: *The city's hilly nature presents a few ups and downs, but the busy roads present downright danger, although there are now an increasing number of cycle lanes. Bikes also have a tendency to cycle off on their own. Nevertheless pedalling is a popular pastime.*

LIBRARIES & COMPUTERS:

- Books: 1,200,000 ● Study places: 2,100
- Computer workstations: 1,050

The SU complains that the library's too small - plenty of students at other universities would disagree. There are network links in all residential hall rooms.

CAREER PROSPECTS:

- Careers Service ● No of staff: 13full/11part
- Unemployed after 6mths (1996): 3.7%

SPECIAL FEATURES:

- Bristol has some of the best recycling facilities and one of the highest proportions of local ex-students of any British city.

FAMOUS ALUMNI:

Paul Boateng MP (Lab); Hugh Cornwell (ex-Strangler); Alex Cox (film director); Frances Horovitz (poet); Sue Lawley (broadcaster); Matt Lucas (aka George Dawes); Alistair Stewart (newsreader); Chris Woodhead (schools inspector).

FURTHER INFO:

General prospectus from the University and alternative prospectus from UBU (£3); web site (http://www.bris.ac.uk).

entertainment

TOWN:

- Price of a pint of beer: £2.10 ● Glass of wine: £2.00

Cinemas: (12) A wide range of flicks in all kinds of picture palaces. *Some of the specially special include the Arts Centre Cinema, The Watershed and the arthouse cinema at the city's superlative dockside arts complex, the Arnolfini.*

Theatres: pushplugs: *the Old Vic (the country's oldest working theatre) which hosts high profile high brow shows, The Hippodrome (West End re-runs, pantos, occasional ballet and opera) and the Arnolfini again.* There are several fringe theatres as well.

Pubs: The local ciders and Smiles Brewery beers *are worth checking out.* pushplugs: *Berkeley (huge, cheap and close); Bohemia (Australian theme, actually); Henry J Beans.*

Clubs/discos: *Bristol used to be a dozy layby on the UK's musical autobahn but local dance acts such as Portishead, Tricky and Massive Attack have caused ripples worldwide in* recent years. It's not just trip-hop, though – **push**plugs: Lakota (hard house); Odyssey; Thekla (boogie on a boat); Bierkeller (indie and 70s); Blue Mountain (drum'n'bass); Club IQ (meat market); Lizard Lounge. 'The Strip' is a mile-long stretch on Whiteladies Road, containing 41 nightspots of varying tack levels.

Music venues: The Bierkeller, Fleece & Firkin and New Trinity all keep live sounds pumping, often of an indie persuasion. Colston Hall is more mainstream and along with St George's Hall (free at lunchtimes) is the scene for classical concerts.

Eating out: A wide range of eateries, some doling out the dogmeat till the early hours. **push**plugs: Sultans (Indian); Hullabaloo; Tequila Worm (Mexican cocktails); Planet Pizza; St Michael's Cafe (greasy spoon); York Cafe (legendary English breakfast); Boston Tea Party (bohemian).

UNIVERSITY:
● Price of a pint of beer: £1.30 ● Glass of wine: £1.00

Bars: 2 bars in the Union, namely: the Epicurean ('The Epi', cap 650) on the 3rd floor of the Union Building, which is the gravitational centre of student social life (which probably explains why so many are lying on the floor); the Mandela Bar, smaller and more intimate. The University runs a number of other bars in the halls.

Theatres: (4) Budding actors burst into full bloom at Bristol, one of the strongest universities in the country for student theatre. The Winston Theatre and the Lady Windsor Studio are both run by the Union; the drama department uses the Glynn Wickham Studio (Cantocks Close); and the Victoria Rooms (700) are used for large scale productions. Bristol usually sends something to the Edinburgh Fringe.

Cinemas: Bristol Filmhouse and the Fine Film society show anything and everything in the Union's Winston Theatre.

Clubs/discos: The Union has several rooms that can be used by ravesters on a roll. The larger Anson Room (900) and occasionally the Epi are also used. Mojo Lounge in the Mandela bar is very popular.

Music venues: The Anson Room is the largest music venue, attracting some big names, such as Roni Size, Teenage Fanclub and Super Furry Animals.

Food: Café Zuma is the focus for face-fillers, offering a vast range including its famous all-day breakfast (£2).

⋯⋯⋯ social & political

UNIVERSITY OF BRISTOL UNION (UBU):
● 6 sabbaticals ● Turnout at last ballot: 25%
● NUS member

UBU's building is one of the largest and best equipped in the country and the Union has a significant say in the University, but it still doesn't manage to attract interest from students who get most wound-up by the question of bar extensions. Incidental iniquities such as rising hall fees get their goats, though.

SU FACILITIES:
At the Union Building: 3 bars; restaurant; snack bar; vending machines; travel agent; general shop; wholefood shop; 2nd-hand bookshop; NatWest and Lloyds Bank cash machines;

video arcade; market stalls; swimming pool; 2 dark rooms; music rooms; pottery workshop; art studio; snooker, billiards and pool; 2 theatres; TV room; launderette; hairdresser and barber; music and video library; study rooms; photo booth.

CLUBS (NON SPORTING):

Art; Balloon Debates; Baptist; Bewilderebeeste (Monty Python appreciation); Bottled Beer; Buhabs (ballooning); Chinese; ChocSoc; Christian Science; Circus; CND; Dr Who; 007; Duke of Edinburgh; Erasmians; Expeditions; Falstaff; Hellenic; Hispanic; Malaysian; Marxist; Massage; Meditation; Methodist; Mr Men; Opera; Panto; Pottery; RAG Morris (*silly bells and bouncing for charity*); Red Cross; Scandinavian; Silly Walk; Speleological; Tibet; Turkish; War Games; Welsh.

OTHER ORGANISATIONS:

UBU's 2 regular (free) publications are 'Epic', the weekly newsletter, and 'Epigram', the *excellent* fortnightly newspaper. Burst FM is the student radio station. Do-gooders do good through the Bristol-wide charity Rag and the *active* SCA (Students Community Action), involved in over 20 local projects.

RELIGIOUS:

● Chaplains (most flavours)

Ecumenical University chaplaincy centre. In town, worshippers of every species can worship anywhere; from Sikh temples to the Salvation Army, from the Vedanta Movement to synagogues.

PAID WORK:

There's always begging and go-go dancing, but otherwise just the normal limited selection of bar work and restaurants.

.... sports

● Recent successes: riding, lacrosse

Pull on your boots and flex those pecs – this is one of those places where students are as likely to be carrying a tube of Deep Heat as anything dodgy. Bristol came 5th overall in last year's BUSA league and the emphasis is strongest on providing sports for the sporty, but the slobbiest couch tubers turn into Mr Motivator in this environment.

'When I started at Cambridge, I was anxious to be Prime Minister but uncertain through which political party this might best be arranged. I therefore joined the Liberals, the Labour Party and the Conservative Party as it seemed wise not to put all my eggs in one basket.'
-Matthew Parris, journalist and ex-MP.

SPORTS FACILITIES:
If a sport's worth playing, facilities are probably slotted in for it somewhere around the University. The sports centre at Woodland House by the main University buildings houses a gym and facilities for many indoor sports. The Victoria Rooms are also used for aerobics, dance and fencing. Under the Union Building is a swimming pool and further out, by the halls of residence at Stoke Bishop and at Coombe Dingle there are 38 acres of playing fields, a floodlit artificial grass pitch and 16 tennis courts. There are further sports provisions at the halls including squash and tennis courts. Sailors swing their booms down at the Baltic Wharf Marina near the city centre and rowers pull their oars at the boathouses on the Avon.

SPORTING CLUBS:
Clay Pigeon; Hang Gliding; Mountain Bike; Snow-boarding; Triathlon; Ultimate Frisbee; Waterskiing; Weight & Power-lifting; Windsurfing.

ATTRACTIONS:
In Bristol, rugby and football keep the fans flapping. There's Bristol Rugby Club, and, with round balls, Bristol Rovers and Bristol City FC. Nevil Road is the main ground for Gloucestershire County Cricket Club and other balls fly at the Redland Lawn Tennis Championship. Greyhounds race at Eastville Stadium - and look out for the Bristol Packers, the local American Football team.

accommodation

IN COLLEGE:
- Catered: 20% - Cost: £56-76(30wks)
- Self-catering: 20% - Cost: £30-64(30-38wks)

Availability: 90% of 1st years are given a place in halls (almost everyone who wants one), but after that very few live in. The choices are based in 3 areas: 6 large halls at Stoke Bishop (just under 2 miles north of the University Precinct); 3 halls near the *gorgeous* gorge in Clifton (⅔ mile west); and student houses in and around the Precinct itself, which are all self-catering *and scarce*. In all, there are 5 catered halls, 4 self-catering halls (2 of which are blocks of shared flats) and 19 houses for between 9 and 125 students. 6% of livers in have to share and some corridors in some halls and some student houses are single sex.

Car parking: The demand for spaces is kept down by requiring drivers to buy a permit, which means that *parking is adequate at most, if not all, halls for those who can afford it.*

EXTERNALLY:
- Ave rent: £45

Availability: *Finding suitable accommodation in Bristol is almost a* pushover, *although the relative affluence of students has edged the price up a bit. Although local relations are quite good, some areas of Bristol are rough 'n' tough: St Paul's has drug dealers on street corners but some students live there for the gutter cred. South Bristol is generally best baulked. Areas worth trying include Bishopston, Cotham, Clifton and Redland (where external scenes for 'The Young Ones' were shot). Wherever students lay their hat, they find it hard to park their car.*

Housing help: The University Accommodation Office's 6 staff keep a vacancies register and provide general help, a landlord blacklist and advice in home-hunting.

welfare

SERVICES:
- Creche ● Lesbian & Gay Society ● Mature SA
- Overseas SA ● Minibus ● Women's Officer
- Self-defence classes

The University employs 2 counsellors and UBU enlists the services of several part-time volunteers. The University Health Service has 5 doctors and nursing staff and the physical recreation centre keeps students fit in the first place.

Disabled: *Bristol is quite hilly, making it very difficult for students with mobility problems to get between the buildings where, ironically, access is quite good.* The University has an Access for Deaf Students Initiative and some special equipment for hearing-impaired students, induction loops and signers. There is a Disability Unit which offers support and information.

FINANCE:
- Ave debt: £1,050 ● Access fund: £352,321
- Successful applications (1997): 885

▶▶ Bristol Poly

see Bristol, University of the West of England

Bristol, University of the West of England

- ***Formerly Bristol Polytechnic***

University of the West of England, Bristol, Frenchay Campus, Coldharbour Lane, Bristol, BS16 1QY. Tel: (0117) 965 6261. Fax: (0117) 976 3804. E-mail: admiss@uwe.ac.uk
Students' Union, University of the West of England, Bristol, Frenchay Campus, Coldharbour Lane, Bristol, BS16 1QY. Tel: (0117) 965 6261. Fax: (0117) 976 3909.

general

The University has 5 sites with its main campus 5 miles north of the city centre at Frenchay. It was purpose-built in 1975 *in a style that suggests that built with a purpose means 'built with an excuse' - it doesn't do any favours for eye strain, although certain features like 'the Octagon', the HQ building of the HEFCE (the quango funding body of higher education) and the 2 accompanying 'student villages' are pleasant and even innovative. The prospectus has the buildings photographed through some bullrushes, which makes it look a touch more idyllic than reality would allow.* The other campuses, described below, are spread out around Bristol nearer the centre. They have their own courses and are roughly self-contained, although all students are allowed to use the facilities of the main site.

49% ♂♂♂♂♂♀♀♀♀♀ **51%**

Sex ratio(M:F): 49%:51%   Founded: 1969
Full time u'grads: 11,992   Part time: 1,917
Postgrads: 988   Non-degree: 6,520
Ave course: 3yrs   Ethnic: 3%
Private school: n/a   Flunk rate: n/a
Mature students: 56.5%   Overseas students: 5%
Disabled students: 3.2%   Staff/student ratio: 1:28
Clearing: n/a

ATMOSPHERE:
The University lacks a single focal point for all students at all campuses – Frenchay ends up ignoring the others a bit and the advantages of Bristol as an attractive and fun city come into play. There's a relatively high proportion of students from the private sector, especially for an ex-poly; some, aiming for social cachet, see UWE as the next best thing to Bristol University, *without the unnecessarily stringent A-level requirements.*

THE SITES:
Frenchay: (8,500 students - most courses) The main campus.
Glenside: (500 students - Health & Social Care) This is the former Avon & Gloucestershire College of Health, which before that was a psychiatric hospital. It's an imposing Victorian edifice, 1½ miles from Frenchay.
St Matthias: (1,000 students - Humanities, Health & Social Care, Psychology) 2½ miles from Frenchay with 2 halls of residence, *this is by far the best-looking site* with a gothic style listed building and a sunken lawn. *This is a tight knit community, almost a college in its own right.*
Bower Ashton: (1,200 students - Art, Media & Design) 2 miles south-west of the city centre over the Clifton Suspension Bridge and 7½ miles from Frenchay, this is an *overwhelmingly* white concrete and glass oblong, *not built to appeal to the aesthetic nature of the students based here.* It is surrounded by *pleasant* fields, though, and the students *consider themselves almost separate from the main site.*
Redland: (2,000 students) *The building does a good impersonation of Grange Hill School – fair enough, really,* since it is the base for the Faculty of Education. It is 5 miles from Frenchay near the city centre.

THE CITY: see University of Bristol

TRAVEL: see University of Bristol
Bus services link the Frenchay campus to the city centre (80p return) and run between the sites (which isn't often necessary). The most convenient station for Frenchay is Bristol Parkway.

LIBRARIES & COMPUTERS:
● Books: 500,000 ● Study places: 2,000
● Computer workstations: 1,600
There are libraries on all campuses relating to the studies

based there. The University's *extensive* computer provision is spread around the sites, open 24 hours a day, 7 days a week.

CAREER PROSPECTS:
- Careers Service ● No of staff: 5full/2part
- Unemployed after 6mths (1997): 11.4%

Amongst its other services, the careers office publishes a service on the net (http://www.uwe.ac.uk/careers/).

FAMOUS ALUMNI:
Kyran Bracken (rugby pin-up); Mark Knopfler (of Dire Straits); Nick Park (Oscar-winning animator); Dawn Primarolo MP (Lab); Jack Russell (cricketer).

FURTHER INFO:
Undergraduate prospectus. Web site (http://www.uwe.ac.uk).

entertainment

CITY: see University of Bristol

UNIVERSITY:
- Price of a pint of beer: £1.40 ● Glass of wine: £1.10

Bars: (8) There are 4 bars at Frenchay and 1 each on the other sites. The main SU-run Escape Bar is the primary social hub.
Theatre: Several performances a year at the Redland campus.
Clubs/discos/music venues: *This is not the place to hang out if you think dance music is just a lot of banging with no tunes.* 'Sin' brings on that Friday feeling at Frenchay (cap 700). 'Juicy' is a monthly dance event at The Venue bar, which also hosts live music and karaoke. China Drum, Paul Oakenfold and Alison Limerick have played here in recent months.
Food: The SU's main food stop, in the Escape Bar, is usually packed out; new nosh stops are a sandwich bar and Pizza Towers (pizza and nachos). *The University-run Refectory is cheap but the food is pretty drab. Sign of the times: 'budget meals' for hard-up students. Local eateries are fewer, further between and duller away from the city centre.*
Others: 3 balls a year.

social 2 political

UNIVERSITY OF THE WEST OF ENGLAND STUDENTS' UNION:

- 6 sabbaticals ● Turnout at last ballot: 10%
- NUS member

The SU has at least an office on each campus and usually a bar and common room as well, but the main centre is on the Frenchay campus. Relations with the university administration were pretty edgy until recently, but things are getting cosier.

SU FACILITIES:
With most facilities at Frenchay, the collected provisions of the SU include: 4 bars; minibus for hire; travel agency; post office; advice centre; 4 general shops; NatWest Bank (with cashpoint at Frenchay); Endsleigh Insurance office; photocopying; library; photo booth; games and vending machines; pool and snooker tables; juke box; jobshop; computing facilities.

CLUBS (NON SPORTING):
Buddhist; Chess; Chinese; Greek; Hempology; International; Law; Live Role Play; Malaysian; Poly Players; Spanish & Latin American; Wine.

OTHER ORGANISATIONS:
The SU publishes 'Bacus' for all students in the city. There's also a charity Rag and a Student Community Action group which involves students in local help activities.

RELIGIOUS:
The 'Octagon' houses the University's chaplaincy centre for all versions of Christianity and available for use by other faiths such as Muslims and Jews.

sports

● <u>Recent successes: squash</u>
Despite the fact that the uni has been in the shadow of its notoriously sporty neighbour for some time and facilities aren't really up to much, UWE produced four individual BUSA champions last year (judo, fencing, cycling and athletics). Team performances don't fly quite so high.

SPORTS FACILITIES:
Frenchay: 4 squash courts; fitness room; floodlit artificial pitch. Redland: small gym. St Matthias: small gym; 2 soccer pitches; cricket square. The University had the *bright* idea of turning the netball pitch into a car park. *Great PR move there, guys.*

SPORTING CLUBS:
Mountain & Hill Walking; Tennis; Ten Pin Bowling.

ATTRACTIONS: see <u>University of Bristol</u>

accommodation

IN COLLEGE:
● <u>Self-catering: 9%</u> ● <u>Cost: £36-46(40-46wks)</u>
Availability: *Although the above figures look a tad weedy*, 85% of 1st years can be accommodated, many of them under the University's head tenancy scheme (2,200 leased places). Apart from these, there's a choice: halls at Redland and St Matthias; student village at Frenchay; and some new developments in the city centre (*better for all the fun of Bristol, worse for making that 9am lecture*).
Car parking: *Extremely inadequate.* Permit required.

EXTERNALLY: see <u>University of Bristol</u>
Availability: *Accommodation works out just a bit cheaper than for those at <u>Bristol University</u>, because they can live a little further out and still be close to the campus, but otherwise details of accommodation in Bristol remain the same. A car certainly helps.*
Housing help: The 19 full-time staff of Student Accommodation Services provide aid and advice.

welfare

SERVICES:
● <u>Creche</u> ● <u>Lesbian & Gay Society</u> ● <u>Overseas SA</u>
● <u>Postgrad SA</u> ● <u>Minibus</u> ● <u>Women's Officer</u>
● <u>Self-defence classes</u>
The University's Centre for Student Affairs employs 3 full-time and 20 part-time counsellors providing help and advice to students. The SU also has its own welfare centre and staff *providing more information-based help.* The student health

service provides a nurse at the Redland campus and a visiting GP at other sites.

Disabled: *For every ramp, there seems to be an annoying hump.* The Disability Resource Centre attempts to even out the odds.

FINANCE:
- Ave debt: £2,600 • Access fund: £340,000
- Successful applications (1996): 800

●●●

▶▶ Brookes University

see Oxford Brookes University

●●●

Brunel University

▼ Brunel University, Uxbridge, Middlesex, UB8 3PH.
▼ Tel: (01895) 274000. Fax: (01895) 203096.
E-mail: courses@brunel.ac.uk
Brunel University Students' Union, Cleveland Road, Uxbridge, Middlesex, UB8 3PH. Tel: (01895) 462200.
Fax: (01895) 810477.

⸱⸱⸱⸱⸱⸱⸱⸱ General

Fettered by London's influence, Uxbridge is a *metallic* satellite town with space-age offices, a *slick, spick'n'span* shopping mall and a few *quaint, genteel* streets. A mile south of Uxbridge proper are the redbrick and grey concrete buildings of the main campus of Brunel University, *designed to be more practical than good-looking*, although grassy patches and a stream (the *optimistically* titled River Pinn) help create *a feeling of space.* It is a university that has traditionally taught sciences, social sciences and engineering, usually in the form of so-called 'thin sandwich' courses (see below), but has an increasing number of arts and humanities. There are also 3 smaller sites, none within walking distance.

57% ♂♂♂♂♂♂ ♀♀♀♀ **43%**		

Sex ratio(M:F): 57%:43%	**Founded: 1966**
Full time u'grads: 7,886	**Part time: 678**
Postgrads: 1,171	**Non-degree: 1,425**
Ave course: 3/4yrs	**Ethnic: 37%**
Private school: 10.4%	**Flunk rate: n/a**
Mature students: 36%	**Overseas students: 7.5%**
Disabled students: 4%	**Staff/student ratio: 1:17**
Clearing: 24.5%	

ATMOSPHERE:
Brunel used to be derided as the anorak capital of British studentdom, overrun with physicists in tight jeans who could

recite whole chapters of 'Lord of the Rings'. This has been tempered in recent years by the addition of humanities departments, but students still tend to be focused on careers rather than the idea of a degree course being valuable in its own right. Split sites create a slightly disorganised social set-up although most ents are based at Uxbridge.

THE SITES:
Twickenham & Osterley: (3,042 students - arts, education, health, sport, geography) The former Brunel University College (and, before that, West London Institute) is split between 2 sites in Middlesex, 13 and 11 miles from Uxbridge. Because of the different subjects, the mood is less intensely tekky and female students outnumber the blokes.

Runnymede: (450 students - design) 65 acres including *beautiful* 19th-century gardens and Victorian buildings, it's situated in Egham, 11 miles from Uxbridge.

TOWNS:
Uxbridge is a modern town with all the latest mod cons, like Tesco's, Sainsbury's, banks and so forth. The home towns on the smaller sites are pretty similar and all equally accessible to London, *which is necessary for any serious stimulation.*

THE CITY: see University of London

LOCAL TRAVEL:
Trains: West Drayton and Hayes are the BR stations nearest to the Uxbridge site (Uxbridge tube station is closer, though); both are less than 2 miles away. There are trains to Bristol, Cardiff, Slough and other cities in the south-west served by trains out of London Paddington (at least 45mins away). For other services, the quickest route is usually via London mainline stations. For trains to and from Egham, which is the nearest station to the Runnymede site, see Royal Holloway College.

Buses: National Express and London Country coach services bypass both Uxbridge and Egham. The nearest stop is Heathrow Airport (25mins by bus). Connections with London are *good enough* to make London Victoria a possibility.

Car: Both sites are on the London escape route to the west, near the M25 (2 miles), and on the M4, M40, A4, A40 and A30.

Air: Heathrow, the world's busiest airport, is 4 miles from the Uxbridge campus.

Hitching: *No shortage of main roads (although hitchers have to get on to them to start with), but drivers round here are real possession heads and pick-ups take time.*

Local: Uxbridge is still within London's local transport network, which is convenient but expensive. Numbers 207, 222, U3, U4, Express Coach 607 and Night Bus N89 (which goes right into London's West End). On the London Underground, Uxbridge station is the last stop on the Metropolitan and Piccadilly Lines and offers a *fast but expensive* service into London during the day, but is a mile from the main campus. The University runs a coach and minibus service between the sites, *which isn't quite enough.*

Taxis: Cabs charge London and Heathrow prices, but £2 from the campus to Uxbridge *is okay between a couple of people.*

Bicycles: *Bikes are useful for local trips although the busy roads make it hell for sorties into London.*

TRAVEL: see <u>University of London</u>

TRAVEL:

LIBRARIES & COMPUTERS:
- <u>Books: 400,000</u> ● <u>Study places: 1,100</u>
- <u>Computer workstations: 1,000</u>

1 library on each campus. There are plans to upgrade the libraries at Osterley and Twickenham and to expand the library at Uxbridge, *though, somewhat predictably, the SU insists that this will still not address all the access problems.*

CAREER PROSPECTS:
- <u>Careers Service</u> ● <u>No of staff: 9full/1part</u>
- <u>Unemployed after 6mths (1997): 8%</u>

Since so many students go on placements they have a highly employable mix of qualifications and experience.

SPECIAL FEATURES:
● Half of the students study 'thin sandwich' courses which are made up of a slice of industrial placement for 2 semesters out of the 6 in the first 3 years of 4-year courses, and slices of academic study for the rest of the time.

FAMOUS ALUMNI:
Jo Brand (comedian); Alan Pascoe, Kathy Smallwood (athletes).

FURTHER INFO:
Prospectuses for undergrads and postgrads, departmental brochures, web site (http://www.brunel.ac.uk).

entertainment

UXBRIDGE:

- <u>Price of a pint of beer: £2.00</u> ● <u>Glass of wine: £1.80</u>

Pubs: *Local pubs are expensive and students tend to steer clear. Scruffy Murphy's and The Old Bill are exceptions.*
Cinemas: The Odeon in Uxbridge does a 10% student discount.
Theatres: The Beck Theatre in Hayes (1½ miles away) is *outshone by London's bright lights,* but it still serves up a regular diet of musicals, plays and jazz and classical concerts.
Music venues: *Royale is a low-class pick-up joint, but does a student night on Thursdays. Students prefer to go into London to the better class pick-up joints.*
Eating out: *Pub grub is usually a good deal.* push*plugs: Grand Union (steaks); Nona Rosa (Italian).*

> ❛The University of East London forced the BBC to announce that the university in ❛EastEnders❜ is entirely fictional, and that no member of staff at UEL has ever slept with a fictional character.❜

IN LONDON: see <u>University of London</u>

UNIVERSITY:

● <u>Price of a pint of beer: £1.70</u> ● <u>Glass of wine: £1.50</u>

Bars: (8) The main Union bar (cap 400) is at Uxbridge. Runnymede has 2 newly refurbished bars.

Theatres: The addition of Performing Arts students from BUC has raised Brunel's performing profile. There are several productions in conjunction with the University arts centre.

Music venues: The Beehive (400) is the University's largest site for sounds, including, recently, Mr C.

Clubs/discos: Every Friday the SU's Now Dance extravaganza pulls potential bees into the Beehive and makes them buzz in a vaguely rhythmic manner.

Cabaret: *Brunel is a serious spot on the alt. com. circuit,* with recent mirthsters including Alan Parker and Ed Byrne.

Food: The University-run Refectory and the SU's Gallery Café provide the full meal scenario while the Pinn Inn and the sandwich bar serve snacks. SU outlets are much cheaper than the Uni's.

Other: Balls at all sites and in posh hotels, regular fireworks at Runnymede.

········· social & political

BRUNEL UNIVERSITY STUDENTS' UNION:

● <u>5 sabbaticals</u> ● <u>Turnout at last ballot: 8%</u>

 ● <u>NUS member</u>

Emphasis and energy is devoted to clubs and societies, which maintain a broad involvement in the Union's gamut of goings on and go some way to uniting the disparate sites. Politically speaking, Brunel students are notoriously apathetic, although the recent conferral of an honorary degree on Baroness Thatcher went beyond a joke for some.

SU FACILITIES:

In the Students' Union Building there are bars, catering outlets, The Academy music venue, Endsleigh Insurance office, launderette, 4 minibuses, photobooth, vending and games machines, juke box, pool tables, conference and function rooms. Also on campus, there's a travel agent, mini supermarket (open at weekends) and Midland Bank (cash machine). The SU has another little pad at the Runnymede site with a bar, barbecue, pool table, games and vending machines.

CLUBS (NON SPORTING):

Amateur Radio; Ballroom Dancing; Debating; Egyptian; Hellenic; Indian; Nutters; Oriental; Pakistani; Punjabi; Radio; Role Playing; Sikh; Sons of the Desert; Theatre Appreciation.

OTHER ORGANISATIONS:

The SU's newspaper is 'Route 66', a *slick* glossy. The B1000 radio station has some *pretty flash* equipment. The Community Action Group is funded by the SU to help the elderly and the young.

RELIGIOUS:

The University Christian chaplaincy welcomes believers of all faiths and there is a mini mosque in the SU building. There are local churches for most flavours of Christian, but for specialities like chocolate chutney and for different religions altogether, a pilgrimage to London is required.

PAID WORK:
With the placements, very few students find any necessity to earn an extra buck, *which is lucky, since the local opportunities are only slightly more common than the local amphibious giraffes.*

········ sports

● Recent successes: rugby

For a small university, Brunel has some big-time facilities and has had several successes in recent years.

SPORTS FACILITIES:
The sports centre has: a sports hall with scoreboards; a gymnasium; 7 squash courts; a *brilliant* climbing wall; solarium; multigym and free weights. Outside, there are 2 floodlit pitches (1 artificial grass), netball courts, cricket nets, 6 tennis courts, an astroturf pitch and many acres of playing fields. (Watch out for the nominal charges.) Osterley has a sports centre and a running track. Students who like their sports with liquid can either use the Queen Mother Reservoir, 7 miles from the campus (windsurfing and sailing), the boathouse on the Thames at Runnymede (rowing, canoeing) or the pavilion bar. As if that weren't enough, locally there's an ice rink, an artificial ski slope, a golf course, Thorpe Park water world and so on...

SPORTING CLUBS:
Chinese Boxing; Circuit Training; Climbing; Hang-Gliding; Ice Skating; Real Outdoor (hill-walking, orienteering, cross-country); Sub Aqua; Ten Pin Bowling; Weight Training; Windsurfing; Wrestling.

ATTRACTIONS:
The MCC's 2nd cricket ground is in Uxbridge and Queen's Park Rangers are the local football team. Twickenham is, of course, the home of English rugby. For a flutter on the nags there's nearby Kempton and Sandown.

········ accommodation

IN COLLEGE:
● Catered: 5% ● Cost: £58(35wks)

● Self-catering: 31% ● Cost: £37-56(37-40wks)
Availability: 68% of 1st years and 37% of finalists can be accommodated in halls. Catered halls are at Osterley and Twickenham and only include 5 main meals per week. *Faraday Hall at Uxbridge is the most sought after, with big en-suite rooms. A lot are left out in the cold, though -* 8% of 1st years who want to can't live in and 4% have to share.
Car parking: Plenty of free parking (permit required) *but students will insist on trying to park as close to the hall doors as possible and complain if they have to walk 10 yards.*

EXTERNALLY:
● Ave rent: £50

Availability: Many students set up camp in Hayes, within 3 miles of the campus, mostly in shared houses and flats. *There are enough vacancies for students to have some choice in the matter. Uxbridge is not enormously welcoming, but not*

as bad as Egham. Twickenham is more expensive; Hounslow may be a more realistic option for students based here.
Housing help: The University operates an Accommodation Office with full-time staff. Students get 3 names and have to go back if none of them come up trumps (*none too helpful*). The SU helps with contracts and provides a housing pack.

welfare

SERVICES:
● <u>Nightline</u> ● <u>Lesbian & Gay Society</u> ● <u>Mature SA</u>
● <u>Overseas SA</u> ● <u>Postgrad SA</u> ● <u>Minibus</u> ● <u>Women's Officer</u>
There are 11 (1 full-, 10 part-time) counsellors. The Medical Centre for students' ailments is an NHS-run practice with 3 doctors (1 female), 2 nurses, a night nurse and psychiatrist. They offer a students-only surgery for a couple of hours a day.
Disabled: *Toilets and some rooms have been adapted for wheelchair users. A few ramps have been installed. There is a Disability Officer. All this makes Brunel, well, a notch above adequate.*

FINANCE:
● <u>Ave debt: £3,050</u> ● <u>Access fund: £210,873</u>
● <u>Successful applications (1997): 790</u>
Welfare loans (up to a maximum of £150) are available from the SU. Sponsorships and placement pay ease the financial burden for many.

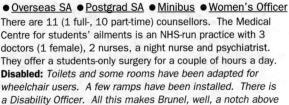

University of Buckingham

University of Buckingham, Buckingham, MK18 1EG. Tel: (01280) 814080. Fax: (01280) 822245. E-mail: admissions@buck.ac.uk
Students' Union, Tanlaw Mill, University of Buckingham, Hunter Street, Buckingham, MK18 1EG. Tel: (01280) 822522.

general

The county of Buckinghamshire, stretching from the north-west of London, contains many towns larger than Buckingham - not least, Milton Keynes (the largest) or Aylesbury (the county town). But for over 1,100 years, the county has been named after Buckingham - *Milton Keynesshire really doesn't have the same ring.* But Buckingham is *little more than a village*, a retreat for city folk. The University, based on 2 8-acre sites on the edge of town, is unique. For a start, it is Britain's only private university - that is to say, it gets no Government funding and so most students end up paying over £9,000 a year in fees (before the cost of living). Courses are only 2 years long, though, starting in January, with 4 10-week terms in each year. *This, combined with the facts that students are customers first and foremost and that UB's independent status means it requires less rigorous inspection and*

supervision from outside bodies has led to unfounded accusations that a Buckingham degree is somehow of less value than others. The Hunter Street site has the University's main facilities and some departments, such as business and humanities. Other departments are at Verney Park. The buildings are mostly modern, but *very attractive*. There's a converted mill and church, some purpose-built new blocks, with one of the sites set amidst the banks of the Ouse. Fields, trees and the old stone buildings of Buckingham surround, and *it all seems a far cry from anywhere*.

55% ♂♂♂♂♂♀♀♀♀♀ 45%	
Sex ratio(M:F): 55%:45%	Founded: 1976
Full time u'grads: 544	Part time: 41
Postgrads: 116	Non-degree: 13
Ave course: 2yrs	Ethnic: n/a
Private school: n/a	Flunk rate: n/a
Mature students: 40%	Overseas students: 70%
Disabled students: n/a	Staff/student ratio: 1:10
Clearing: 5.5%	

ATMOSPHERE:
Imagine what sort of people can afford £20,000 over 2 years, with little time to earn money in the meantime... Students fall into 3 groups - either (1) overseas students, (2) rich students or (3) a mixture of the above. There are, of course, exceptions (such as students with big bank loans), but that rather proves the rule, doesn't it? Because of the 2-year courses, it actually works out cheaper for those overseas students who'd have to pay whatever university they decided to attend. *But these courses mean the workload is heavy and, in their own words, long vacations are 'perceived as an obsolescence'. Students rise to the challenge of the burden, often because they're footing the bill. The short courses also mean there's a lot less time to get involved in non-academic stuff - fine for those who believe that getting a degree is all that being a student is about. There is, however, a variety of extra-curricular activities and, although political activism is zilch, political opinion often comes in a brighter shade of blue than at 'normal' universities. Being very small, it's easy to get to know almost all the other students and staff and having so many overseas students, makes it almost incomparably multicultural.*

TOWN:
● Population: 12,620 ● London: 50miles
● Milton Keynes: 14miles ● Oxford: 21miles
Buckingham may look pretty but it ain't up to much when it comes to fun and convenience: a Tesco's and high street shops, including Mike & Marian's open till 10pm; 1 bookshop; banks, beauticians and boutiques; and a street market. *For glizty glamour gladrags and funky threads try catching a plane to Milan. Milton Keynes (or, as it's known, 'MK'), on the other hand, is all convenience, but has the urban charm of a large eggbox. Its greatest attraction is one of the country's largest cinema multiplexes. Bicester is 11miles in the other direction, but doesn't offer much more than Buckingham except a station.*

TRAVEL:

Trains: The nearest stations are at Bicester and MK (London to MK £2.10 rtn).

Buses: Buses take 40mins to get to MK and National Express services go from there all over the country. The new X5 Stagecoach Express goes between Oxford and Cambridge, taking in Buckingham, Bedford and MK en route. Also 2 coaches a day to Northampton and Leicester, 1 a day to Nottingham.

Car: *Students who can afford UB's fees can often afford a car as well - the car-park can look like an MG rally. Parking presents few problems.* Routes often involve the M1, which bypasses MK, the A5, going straight through it, or the A43. Direct roads include A413, A421 and A422.

Air: Luton Airport, 36 miles away, is the closest international airport offering flights to most major destinations.

Hitching: *Hitching in the home counties is like trying to eat spaghetti through a straw - it's just about possible, but it takes a long time and there are easier ways.*

Local: A shuttle runs between the bus station, the campus and Tesco's.

Taxis: Several companies offer student discounts, but still, it's quite a journey to MK or anywhere else that students might want to go and distance makes the fares grow bigger.

Bicycles: *What with the quality and quantity of fresh air, the rural rarity of traffic and the ½ mile between the 2 sites, a bike is an asset to be wished for.*

LIBRARIES & COMPUTERS:
- Books: 65,000 ● Study places: 250
- Computer workstations: 42

As far as the 2 libraries go, Buckingham suffers from one of the disadvantages of small universities: they sometimes have more books per head, but it doesn't help choice. 24hr access to some computers.

CAREER PROSPECTS:
- Careers Service ● No of staff: 2full
- Unemployed after 6mths (1994): 5%

The careers service is open to the public - *for a small charge, of course, in the best free market tradition.*

SPECIAL FEATURES:
- Most courses start at the beginning of the calendar year which leaves the period from September to January before the 1st year for other activities. Many students go abroad, often on programmes in Europe arranged by the University or as far as Japan. Overseas students often arrive early for courses to improve their English.

> ‟A candidate for the Presidency of Cardiff Student's Union was forced to withdraw when it was revealed that his campaign t-shirts were sponsored by the 'Sunday Sport'.„

FURTHER INFO:
Prospectuses for undergrads and postgrads and course leaflets. Website (http://www.buckingham.ac.uk).

entertainment

TOWN:

● Price of a pint of beer: £1.60 ● Glass of wine: £1.70

For a fix of fun or culture, Buckingham is as happening as a pork chop in a synagogue. In fact, for films, students go to MK, for night clubs to Oxford (see University of Oxford) and for a treat to London (see University of London).

Theatres: *Serious-minded* local amateur dramatics and more theatres in MK.

Pubs: There are 12 pubs within walking distance of the University, *but this is rural Tory Range Rover country and so the log fires and horse brasses-type pubs are expensive and still coming to terms with a student clientele.* **push***plugs: Grand Junction; Tudor Rock; New Inn; Mitre.*

Music venues: Stowe School and the Community Centre host classical concerts and the Seven Stars in Twyford, 6 miles away, has live rock'n'roll. The pubs above have occasional bands... *occasionally.*

Eating out: *Not a great deal to tempt the discerning budget diner but 'budget' isn't always a relevant concept round here.* **push***plugs: Buckingham Tandoori (student discounts); Chen Du, Beijing (Chinese); Posties Café.*

UNIVERSITY:

● Price of a pint of beer: £1.30 ● Glass of wine: £1.75

Bars: George's Bar (cap 70) is open lunchtimes and evenings - *the academic pace is evidently too intense for all-day quaffing sessions.* There are usually *small* events on every Friday.

Theatres: Rare productions in the Radcliffe Centre (250) or the open air.

Clubs/discos: The Refectory which, *uncannily*, is used as the refectory during the day, is turned into a disco 3 times a week during term time (cap 200), often with a theme (eg vicars and tarts).

Music venues: Local and student bands appear at the Tanlaw Mill Bar. Classical concerts regularly crop up at the Radcliffe centre.

Food: The University-run Refectory provides *reasonably priced* meals till 2.30pm, with snacks in the afternoons.

Others: Karaoke, quizzes and the *posh* Graduation Ball.

social & political

UNIVERSITY OF BUCKINGHAM STUDENTS' UNION:

● Turnout at last ballot: 40%

The student body is either apolitical (the majority) or devoted to the free market ideals which underpin the University's existence - no self-respecting lefty would be seen dead here - so political agitation is a non-starter. However, the international nature of the student body has more effect on political attitudes than party labels do. Combined with the restricted amount of leisure time, there's not a lot the SU can do. Its main roles are providing services, co-ordinating clubs and running the annual Rag week and Ball, but beyond that, many students aren't particularly aware of its existence.

SU FACILITIES:
The SU is based on the Hunter St site in the converted Tanlaw Mill which also houses the refectory and some indoor sports amenities. The SU runs a travel information service, late minibuses in the exam term, weekly trips to Tesco all year round, jukebox, Sky TV, games machines, disco and pool tables.

CLUBS (NON SPORTING):
Arabic; Bahamian; Busbi; Chinese; Entertainment; Gospel Choir; Hellenic; Malaysian; Mauritian; Nigerian; Pakistani; Singapore; Sri Lankan; Tourism; Wine.

OTHER ORGANISATIONS:
The SU publishes very little and only when interested students can be bothered. The annual charity Rag week is *rather more* productive and raised £5,500 last year.

RELIGIOUS:
The Islamic Society has access to a prayer room. Mainstream Christian denominations only are catered for in Buckingham.

PAID WORK:
Nothing original here and fewer opportunities for conventional student jobs - but very few UB students need fast cash or have the time to earn it. That comes later...

sports

- Recent successes: nothing special

Courses are so intense many students don't find the time to hit the pitch/court/track. However, this means that those who play sports can do so for fun without any serious competitive urges intruding.

SPORTS FACILITIES:
In the Tanlaw Mill, there's a fitness centre (£30/year), aerobics/martial arts room and a snooker room. There are also table tennis tables, basketball, netball and tennis courts, all-weather 5-a-side pitch, a floodlit training area, and 32 acres of playing fields. Local sports centres, which provide a broader choice of provisions including a swimming pool, cost cash.

SPORTING CLUBS:
Aerobics; Bridge; Health & Fitness; Jiu Jitsu; Kick boxing; Polo; Snooker; Tennis; Windsurfing.

accommodation

IN COLLEGE:
- Self-catering: 83% ● Cost: £60(40-52wks)

Availability: All first years live in and 30% of finalists. *The rooms themselves are comfy and pleasant* and no-one has to share. *Students prefer the accommodation at the Hunter St site* because Verney Park has no bar or refectory and few other facilities. For a price, students can have phones connected in their rooms. All the accommodation is mixed and there is little provision for married couples. Students can have rooms for term-time or for the full year.
Car parking: *Adequate*, but a permit's needed.

EXTERNALLY:
● <u>Ave rent: £70</u>

Availability: Local housing is limited, which pushes prices up and the University requires that students live within 10 miles. *Since many have cars and/or cash though, the housing problems don't worry many students.* Some have the funds to buy a place.

Housing help: The Accommodation Officer forges links with local estate agents for renting.

welfare

SERVICES:
● <u>Mature SA</u> ● <u>Overseas SA</u>
● <u>Postgrad SA</u> ● <u>Minibus</u> ● <u>Women's Officer</u>

The University has a student counsellor and a Learning Support Advisor and the SU provides a few *scant* provisions for students' welfare. There is, however, a dyslexia specialist. For help with your health there are drop-in surgeries in town every Wednesday.

Disabled: *Converted buildings have very poor access. Modern buildings are just a little better.*

FINANCE:
Average debts vary beyond belief since some students owe nothing while others are in debt to the tune of their entire course costs. Being a private university, Buckingham has no Government access fund provisions. Instead, a limited hardship fund provides up to £750 to students who can present a good case.

Buckinghamshire Chilterns University College

(1) Buckinghamshire Chilterns University College, Queen Alexandra Road, High Wycombe, Bucks, HP11 2JZ.
Tel: (01494) 522141. Fax: 524392.
Buckinghamshire Chilterns University College Students' Union, Queen Alexandra Road, High Wycombe, Bucks, HP11 2JZ.
Tel: (01494) 446330. Fax: (01494) 558195.
(2) Buckinghamshire Chilterns University College, Wellesbourne Campus, Kingshill Road, High Wycombe, Bucks, HP13 5BB. Tel: (01494) 522141. Fax: (01494) 465432.
(3) Buckinghamshire Chilterns University College, Newland Park Campus, Gorelands Lane, Chalfont St Giles, Bucks, HP8 4AD. Tel: (01494) 522141. Fax: (01494) 871954.

general

Buckinghamshire College is named after the county rather than the town - that honour is reserved for University of Buckingham *which is an entirely different kettle of private fish.* This one is based in High Wycombe, a town which grew mostly out of the industrial age, though parts of it date back to the 13th-century.

It was granted the power to award its own degrees in 1996, making it one of those *anomalous beasts*, 'University Colleges'. The Chiltern part comes from the fact that those rolling hills start rolling not far away. Hence there is a lot of green belt countryside in the area, *whose charms are more manicured than rugged splendour*. There are 2 other sites: Wellesbourne campus is just outside town, while Newland Park is in Chalfont St Giles, a small village about 9 miles away. John Milton moved to Chalfont St Giles when the plague broke out in London, *and wrote Paradise Lost because there was nothing better to do there.*

50% ♂♂♂♂♂ ♀♀♀♀♀ 50%

Sex ratio(M:F): 50%:50%	Founded: 1893
Full time u'grads: 6,000	Part time: 2,000
Postgrads: 600	Non-degree: 2,000
Ave course: 3yrs	Ethnic: n/a
Private school: n/a	Flunk rate: n/a
Mature students: 20%	Overseas students: 12%
Disabled students: 2%	Staff/student ratio: n/a
Clearing: 20%	

ATMOSPHERE:
The commitment to their courses which the students evidently have doesn't stop them being chilled out: hence there isn't the rampant careerism and ambition evident at other colleges with a similarly predominantly middle-class make-up. Fun and games are concentrated heavily around the College, especially the SU, since High Wycombe doesn't offer much in the way of diversion except for a chair museum.

THE SITES:
Wellesbourne campus: (1,000 - leisure and tourism) About 2 miles away on the outskirts of town are some mainly 60s buildings which pass for Wellesbourne campus. There are buses to the main site every 10 mins (£1 rtn).
Newlands Park: (2,500 - business, health studies) Students based in this 18th-century mansion don't have to travel to High Wycombe for their course, *but might want to if they want a life outside the college, since all there is here is some woods and farmland.* Evening minibuses will get you home free if you do go to the main site where the main SU events take place.

TRAVEL:
Trains: High Wycombe station is ¼ of a mile from campus. London is 35 mins by train.
Coaches: 1 National Express service a day to London (£3.30), Birmingham (£10.25) or Heathrow (£3.30). Local buses go to Oxford, Cambridge, Reading and all over.
Car: High Wycombe is on the A40 near junction 4 of the M40, while Newlands Park is right by M25 junction 17. The M4 is also close by to the south.
Air: Heathrow is 40 miles away.
Hitching: *Hitching isn't recommended unless you want to spend the rest of your life on the roundabout at junction 4 of the M40.*
Local: Good local buses - *but, hell - where are you going to go?*

Taxis: £2 from station to campus. High Wycombe isn't a big place, so sharing makes it viable.

Bicycles: Okay around town, but the surrounding area is rather hilly. Theft isn't much of a problem.

LIBRARIES & COMPUTERS:
- Books: 150,000 ● Study places: 937
- Computer workstations: 1,760

Students seem very happy with provision - computers can be booked for ½ hour sessions.

CAREER PROSPECTS:
- Careers Service ● No of staff: 4full/1part
- Unemployed after 6mths (1996): 6.9%

FAMOUS ALUMNI:
Howard Jones (80s teen idol).

FURTHER INFO:
Undergrad, postgrad and part-time prospectuses, course leaflets, video and web site (http://www.buckscol.ac.uk).

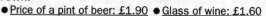

entertainment

TOWN:
- Price of a pint of beer: £1.90 ● Glass of wine: £1.60

Cinemas: There's a UCI 6-screen job in town and another at Gerard's Cross.

Theatres: As well as *low-brow* theatre the Wycombe Swan hosts comedy nights - recently, Lenny Henry, Sean Hughes and Lee Hurst.

Pubs: *High Wycombe isn't what you'd call a student town, but one or two pubs offer them bibulous benefits.* push*plugs: Antelope; Firkin; Hobgoblin. Avoid the White Horse and Saracen's Head unless you want to eat fist pie.*

Clubs/Discos: Club Eden has a student night on Mondays (dance) *but that's about it.*

Music venues: The Nag's Head hosts a bit of rock and indie - *for anything big, go to London.*

Eating out: More pragmatic than bohemian. push*plugs: Bella Pasta; Francesco's (Italian); all you can eat for a fiver from Pizza Hut is popular. The Disraeli and Wendover Arms do good pub grub.*

UNIVERSITY:
- Price of a pint of beer: £1.45 ● Glass of wine: £1

The SU makes up for the lack of entertainment in High Wycombe.

Bars: There are bars on all sites - Footprints and Junction 4 are both in The Venue at the main site. The Final Whistle at Wellesbourne *is a little more cosy and intimate.* There is an SU bar at Newlands Park.

Film: 1 film a week - *usually arty or studenty flicks.*

Music venues/clubs/discos: Junction 4 in The Venue is the nightclub: Friday night is club night, Wednesday night is run by clubs and societies, while Saturday varies between drum'n'bass and soul and swing. Byron Stingley played recently.

Cabaret: *Comedy doesn't tend to go down too well. Harry Hill lasted 90 seconds and Jo Brand courageously fought the hecklers.*

Food: The Solar Café does breakfast till 11.30 and otherwise *standard* meals (fish and chips on a Tuesday night). The Grapevine does baguettes and alternative *healthy* options. Newland Park has Megabites the burger bar and there are refectories at each site.

Other: The May Ball is the *big deal*, with Robbie Williams playing in 1998.

social & political

STUDENTS' UNION:
- 5 sabbaticals ● Turnout at last ballot: 8%
- NUS member

The SU enjoys a good relationship with the college authorities since they concentrate mainly on ents, although a successful demo against poor accommodation got them a reduction in hall fees and free food for the rest of the term. The NUS national shutdown went down well cos it got them a day off.

SU FACILITIES:
Bars; nightclub; photocopier; payphone; video games; fax; juke box; sandwich bar; late-night minibus; vending machines; photobooth; pool tables.

CLUBS (NON SPORTING):
Clubbing; DJ; Red Shed No Knickers.

OTHER ORGANISATIONS:
'Intercourse' magazine comes out every month. Rag raised £4,600 last year.

RELIGIOUS:
- 1 chaplain (CofE)

Places of worship for Christian, Muslim and Sikh persuasion.

PAID WORK:
About 45% of the students have jobs - *there are plenty in this home counties suburbia if you don't mind a bit of temp work or shelf-stacking.*

sports

- Recent successes: nothing special

Sport isn't a big thing here and participation is recreational rather than competitive.

SPORTS FACILITIES:
The £15 a year fee for a recreation card gets you access to all facilities.

❝'Always plan for practice fire alarms at 3 in the morning, as extra bodies in a hall of residence are difficult to explain.'
-Michael Fish, weatherman.❞

High Wycombe: Fitness, aerobics and weights room; gym; tennis courts; football pitches. In the local area: leisure centre; golf course; sauna and solarium; dry ski-slope.
Newlands Park: Sports hall; swimming pool; multigym; tennis courts; athletics field; all-weather pitch; gym.

SPORTING CLUBS:
Aerobics; Kick-boxing; Outdoor Pursuits; Trampolining; Water Sports.

accommodation

IN COLLEGE:
- Catered: 3% ● Cost: £65(38wks)
- Self-catering: 20% ● Cost: £51-57(38wks)

80% of first years live in (15% of those who want to can't) and 10% from each other year. Brook Street Hall and John North Hall house 500 students in High Wycombe town centre and there are 700 places at Newland Park. Self-catering kitchens are shared between 5 - 9 students.
Car-parking: *Impossible at Wycombe, but okay at Newland Park.*

EXTERNALLY:
- Ave rent: £48

Availability: It's possible to get *decent* accommodation in the area for upwards of £40. The most popular areas are Wycombe town, Desborough, Green St and Upper Street.
Housing help: The accommodation office has a team of staff who endeavour to ensure everyone's housed: noticeboard, vacancy, recommended and blacklisted landlords lists, legal help and advice, emergency housing, safety checks.

welfare

SERVICES:
- Lesbian & Gay Society ● Mature SA
- Overseas SA ● Minibus

The College's Student Advisory Service has 3 full- and 2 part-time counsellors. GP referral programme, sports and therapeutic massage service. Legal surgery every month. Support groups for women.
Disabled: *Reasonable* disabled access to most of the buildings.

FINANCE:
- Ave debt per year: £2,600 ● Access fund: £150,000
- Successful applications (1997): 650

> **The Greenwich University Rag was banned when students blocked the Dartford tunnel with the cannon from Woolwich barracks.**

❝If you have any comments about PUSH or fancy being involved in the next edition, please write to PUSH, McGraw-Hill Publishing Company, Shoppenhangers Road, Maidenhead, Berkshire SL6 2QL.❞

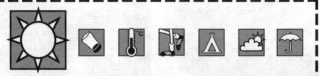

Fold-out guide to symbols inside back cover

❝Text in italics is PUSH's point of view – take it or leave it.❞

 ❝Freaked out by finance? Why not pop into your local branch of Lloyds Bank and see what they have to offer.❞

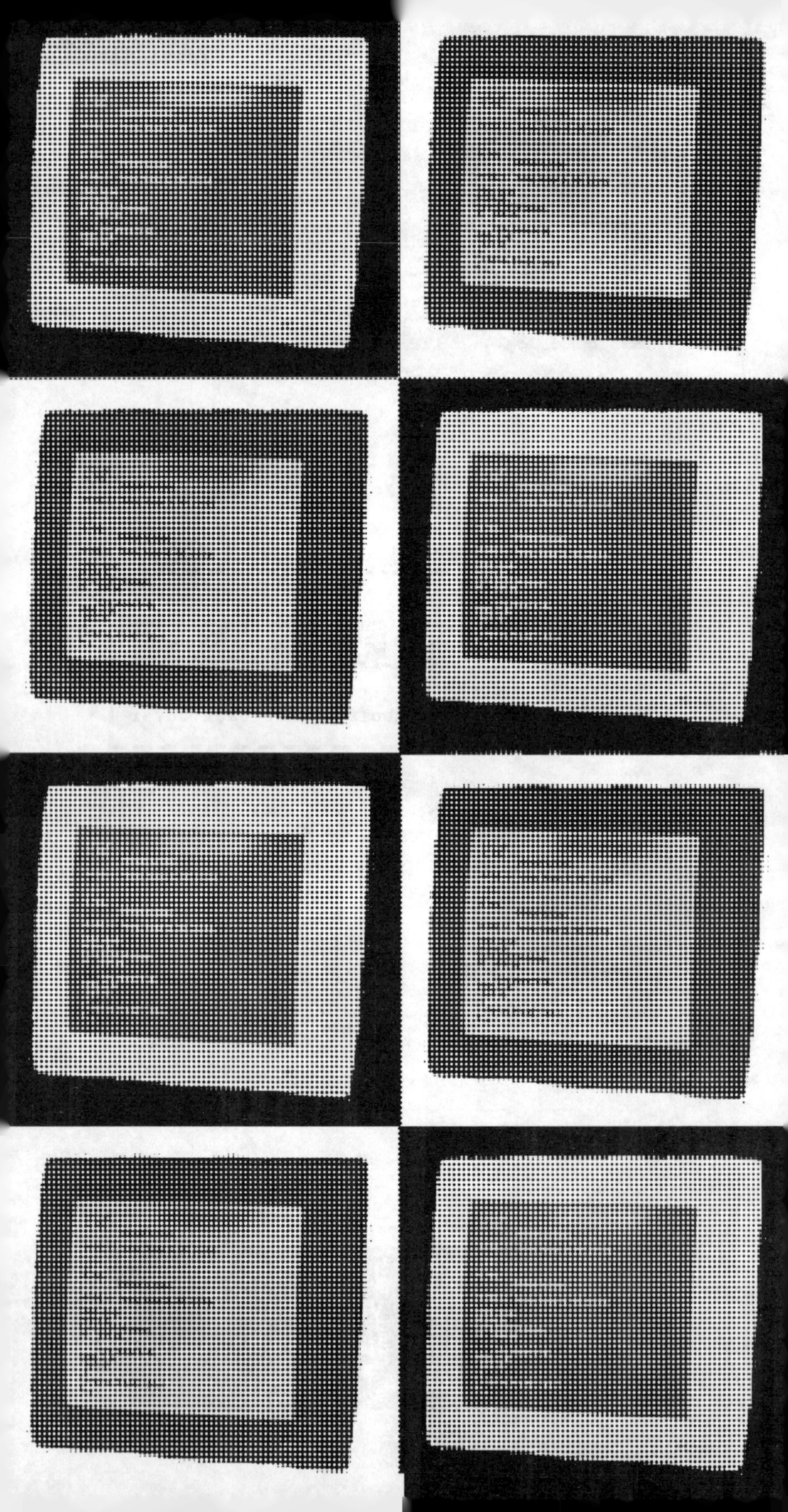

C

- Caledonian University
  see Glasgow Caledonian University

- Camberwell College of Arts
  see The London Institute

- Camborne School of Mines
  see University of Exeter

University of Cambridge
  Christ's College, Cambridge
  Churchill College, Cambridge
  Clare College, Cambridge
  Corpus Christi College, Cambridge
  Downing College, Cambridge
  Emmanuel College, Cambridge
  Fitzwilliam College, Cambridge
  Girton College, Cambridge
  Gonville & Caius College, Cambridge
  Homerton College, Cambridge
  Jesus College, Cambridge
  King's College, Cambridge
  Lucy Cavendish College, Cambridge
  Magdalene College, Cambridge
  New Hall, Cambridge
  Newnham College, Cambridge
  Pembroke College, Cambridge
  Peterhouse, Cambridge
  Queens' College, Cambridge
  Robinson College, Cambridge
  St Catharine's College, Cambridge
  St John's College, Cambridge
  Selwyn College, Cambridge
  Sidney Sussex College, Cambridge
  Trinity College, Cambridge
  Trinity Hall, Cambridge

- Canterbury
  see University of Kent at Canterbury

- Canterbury Christ Church College
  see Other Institutions

Cardiff, University of Wales

- Cardiff Institute
  see Other Institutions

- Caythorpe
  see De Montfort University

Continued next page ▶▶

Continued from last page

- CCAT
  see Anglia Polytechnic University

University of Central England

University of Central Lancashire

- Central St Martins College of Art
  see The London Institute

- Charing Cross & Westminster Hospital
  see Imperial College, London

- Charlotte Mason
  see Lancaster University

- Chelsea College of Art
  see The London Institute

Cheltenham & Gloucester College of
Higher Education

- University College, Chester
  see Other Institutions

- Chichester Institute
  see Other Institutions

- Cirencester
  see Royal Agricultural College

- City of London Poly
  see London Guildhall University

City University

- Coleraine
  see University of Ulster

Courtauld Institute of Art, London

Coventry University

Cranfield University

❝The new offices of Nottingham
Trent SU were opened in 1995 by
Torvill and Dean but the plaque
spelled their names wrong.❞

Caledonian University
see *Glasgow Caledonian University*

 Camberwell College of Arts
see *The London Institute*

 Camborne School of Mines
see *University of Exeter*

University of Cambridge

University of Cambridge, Intercollegiate Applications Office, Kellet Lodge, Tennis Court Road, Cambridge, CB1 1QJ.
Tel: (01223) 333308. Fax: (01223) 366383.
E-mail: ucam-undergraduate-admissions@lists.cam.ac.uk
Cambridge University Students' Union, 11/12 Trumpington Street, Cambridge, CB2 1QA. Tel: (01223) 356454. Fax: (01223) 323244.
E-mail: info@cusu.cam.ac.uk

 General

If it weren't for the University, Cambridge would have remained pretty much as the Romans left it: a fairly insignificant village, surrounded by flat fenlands, where East Anglia starts to bulge from the rest of England. It would just have been blown by cold winds from Siberia in winter and the river Cam would have flowed through gently, uncluttered by tourists' punts in summer. However, about a century after the trend started in Oxford, higher education sprouted in Cambridge and now, more than 700 years later, these are the most famous, most highly revered and *possibly the most extraordinary* universities in the world. The University remains (much more than at Oxford) the focal point of the city, which *is very pretty, with lots of attractive buildings* in light golden stone. The University buildings are its colleges - 31 in all (depending what you count as a college) - *and they are as attractive examples of English architecture spanning 8 centuries as are likely to be found anywhere. The area they cover is remarkably compact and has an utterly surreal feel about it, aided and abetted by the bizarre (to an outsider) language at play - backs, cuppers, bedders, bumps. These words occupy this separate world inhabited by the elite - a controversial word to which the University objects. They are elite not necessarily because of their astonishing intellect, social background and astounding talent in sport, music, drama or whatever, (although one or*

more of these may be true), but elite by the mere fact that they are students here. More or less, the centre point of Cambridge (for the purpose of distances to the colleges in push *entries, at any rate) is the breath-takingly beautiful King's Parade with a view of King's and Caius.*

56% ♂♂♂♂♂♀♀♀♀ 44%	
Sex ratio(M:F): 56%:44%	Founded: 1284
Full time u'grads: 11,223	Part time: 0
Postgrads: 4,688	Non-degree: 0
Ave course: 3yrs	Ethnic: 11%
Private school: 48%	Flunk rate: n/a
Mature students: 5.2%	Overseas students: 6.3%
Disabled students: 2%	Staff/student ratio: 1:12
Clearing: n/a	

ATMOSPHERE:

Okay, so Cambridge and Oxford are more similar than Uma Thurman and a piece of papaya. If you want someone to say they're completely different, go look in their prospectuses. push*, however, is quite happy to concede that, whilst they have their similarities, (1) it is not sufficient to dismiss them both as 'Oxbridge', (2) they are unlike each other in as many respects as they are alike, and (3) 'Hillbilly Rock, Hillbilly Roll' by the Woolpackers isn't a very good record. Like Oxford, most of the students' social concerns and the intense academic life revolve around the colleges which run themselves and arrange their own admissions. However, unlike Oxford, there are plenty of opportunities to switch courses and an even stronger sense that this is a student city.*

3 years at Cambridge is one of the most intense educational experiences you can hope to have with your clothes on. There is virtually no escape. It can be challenging, it can be claustrophobic and it can be compared to watching every episode of 'Beverly Hills 90210' end to end. The city (the beauty of which cannot be praised too much) is overwhelmed by the University. It offers little by way of diversion that is not connected somehow and it's rare for students to walk through the streets without meeting faces they know at every other step (unless of course they're sad cases with no friends, and sad cases don't read push*, do they?). Talking of friends, a recent spate of mugging and student-bashing shows that, despite the tourist-friendly image, Cambridge does have its nasty side and ambling drunkenly through town is not the carefree delight it once was, at least not on your own.*

Students have no spare time, not because they're working (although, in Cambridge, the words 'doss' and 'course' rarely go together), but because their leisure time is spent buzzing away in some hive of activity: sport; drama; journalism; music; politics; archaic drinking clubs; whatever. Cambridge students do a lot of whatever. They need to have good time management skills or learn them pretty quick.

Life in the colleges is even more cosseted, closeted and all-consuming: ranging in size from Lucy Cavendish with under 80 undergrads, to Trinity College with over 600. Most colleges have around 400 undergraduates (slightly larger than Oxford on average) and many students experience a little shock when they enter the big bad real world. The colleges themselves vary enormously and it's a foolhardy fool who uses the pinprick method of picking. Odd ceremonies and traditions persist, and it remains the case that students from atypically 'Cambridge' backgrounds (state schools, women, ethnic minorities) may take longer to adjust than others, whatever the prospectuses may say. The following push *entries expose the naked truth and the neatly garbed falsehoods about each of the undergraduate colleges.* push *doesn't cover Darwin, Hughes Hall, St Edmund's or Wolfson, which are postgrad colleges. We suggest you write to the above address or the colleges themselves if this upsets you (letters of complaint to* push *will be duly noted and used as coffee filters).*

THE CITY:
- Population: 100,000 ● London: 58miles
- Oxford: 77miles ● Norwich: 57miles

People in Cambridge seem to be either students or tourists. The permanent residents just get lost in the throng and, although there are all the basic ingredients you'd expect in a relatively prosperous city of Cambridge's size. Superficially, at least, most of the shops are trying to appeal to a passing trade: quaint shops and tea rooms, pubs with horse brasses, that sort of thing. The river Cam couldn't have been better designed if it had been put there especially for tourism. It's littered with ducks and drunken punters at almost every turn. On a more sober note, the local amenities including the Grafton Shopping Centre, big book shops (1st and 2nd hand), a street market, the Kettles Yard Art Gallery and a mass of museums: the Fitzwilliam, Zoology, and Archaeology Museums; Museum of Technology; Folk Museum and so on. There is, however, a shortage of supermarkets (1 small and busy Sainsbury's) and convenience shops in the city centre.

TRAVEL:
Trains: Cambridge Station connects to London King's Cross and Liverpool Street (£8.45), Birmingham (£30.60), Bristol (£41) and more. Incidentally, the station is some way beyond the city centre because the University authorities didn't want rough common London folk coming too close to the sensitive young undergraduates.

Coaches: Plenty of *competitive* services, for example, Greenline, Premier Travel and National Express who offer runs to London (£7.50), Bristol (£17) and elsewhere.

Car: Just a few minutes off the M11 from London. Also A45, A10 and A604.

Air: There's Cambridge Airport, but unless you own your own jet, you'd better think more in terms of Stansted, 23 miles down the M11 and on a direct train link, with domestic and European flights and flights to the Channel Islands.

Hitching: *Variable; aim towards M11 junctions, or A10/Trumpington Road for London.*

Local: The local buses, *which are regular as prunes*, go round the surrounding villages, the station and the outer colleges. Cambridge is too small to need much more.

Taxis: *They work out quite cheap (mainly because it doesn't* take too long to get anywhere). *Some colleges have free taxi arrangements at night. See separate entries.*

Bicycles: *The Cambridge student on a bike, college scarf flapping in the breeze, has been a cheesy stereotype for so long, it came as something of a shock when a bike ban was imposed in the city centre and around the Grafton. This ban is still largely ignored, though the police also take great pleasure in hauling cyclists up for having no lights.*

LIBRARIES & COMPUTERS:
- Books: 6million • Study places: 988
- Computer workstations: c2,600

The University Library is one of 5 copyright libraries in the country and as such has the right to claim a copy of every new book published in the UK. Every year, the number of new additions, if laid end to end, would extend the collection by a mile. As if that weren't enough, every college has its own library and there are more than 30 libraries devoted to individual subjects. *Quite a few books, then.* The general level of computer facilities is *good* but varies between colleges.

CAREER PROSPECTS:
- Careers Service • No of staff: 6full/2part
- Unemployed after 6mths (1995): 5%

Although (Cantab.) after your degree might not be the surefire guarantee of a top job it once was, a Cambridge education rarely does harm on a CV and, supposedly, employers find Cambridge students more down to earth than those from Oxford (who must surely then be abject space cadets). Although Cambridge was the spawning ground for most of the spies on every side of the Iron Curtain during the Cold War, vacancies for budding Bonds and Burgesses are not advertised on the careers vacancies board (though you might want to try the national press...)

SPECIAL FEATURES:
- Cambridge runs STEP (Sixth Term Examination Paper), after A-levels; see the prospectus for details, or contact STEP Office, Purbeck House, Purbeck Road, Cambridge, CB2 2PU. Tel: (01223) 411211.
- Cambridge has 8-week terms, but this doesn't mean any lazy days - exams and work pressure manage to ruin all hopes of long vacations with nothing to do.
- All undergraduate degree courses (except a BEd for education and a 4-year MEng in Engineering) lead to a BA, and, 3 years after graduation, an MA can be bought (yup, bought) without any further work.
- Undergrads have to 'keep term' which means that they may not live more than 3 miles from the city centre and they must get permission before going away during term time.
- An expansion masterplan is afoot which would site the University's science and technology departments on a campus 1½miles west of King's, potentially doubling the size of the student body.

FAMOUS ALUMNI:
See individual colleges. *Cambridge seems particularly strong on spies, Tory MPs and comedians. Draw your own conclusions.*

FURTHER INFO:
Prospectuses for undergrads and postgrads from the Cambridge Intercollegiate Applications Office (*aka CIAO... cue bad Italian joke...*) and the individual colleges as well as a web site (http://www.cam.ac.uk/index.html). CUSU also produces an alternative prospectus, costing £3.50.

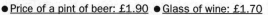
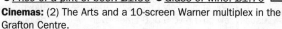

entertainment

THE CITY:
● <u>Price of a pint of beer: £1.90</u> ● <u>Glass of wine: £1.70</u>
Cinemas: (2) The Arts and a 10-screen Warner multiplex in the Grafton Centre.
Theatres: Apart from student venues, the Corn Exchange does a *wide mixture of* thespy stuff.
Pubs: *Cambridge has many good pubs, despite the fact they're pretty expensive. The pubs along the riverside are most popular among students.* push *would just like to plug the places where we've fallen over most often: The Mill; Anchor (watch fat American tourists fall off their punts); The Eagle; Town & Gown (gay-friendly); King's Run. Some town centre boozers should be treated with caution at weekends.*
Clubs/discos: *Considering a local student population of something over 20,000, Cambridge is poorly equipped in this field.* push*plugs: Big Holy Noise at Fifth Avenue (cheesy but cheery); Mad Sheep at the Q Club (indie).*
Music venues: The Junction (cap 700) is a purpose-built venue *with as much character as a goldfish, although the big (especially indie) names make it worthwhile.* The Corn Exchange has a capacity of 1,500 *and has a more mainstream roster.* The Boat Race is more geared to local bands - *Cambridge, contrary to outside appearances, has a thriving indie scene.*
Eating out: *It's customary to take one's parents, or at least their credit cards. Many cafés are just pricey tourist traps but several curry houses in Castle Hill offer sound value.* push*plugs: Varsity (Greek); India House; Henry's Café; Livingstone's.*

UNIVERSITY:
● <u>Price of a pint of beer: £1.30</u> ● <u>Glass of wine: £1.20</u>
Bars: Each college has at least 1 bar, often shamefully cheap, although some don't allow anyone but college members and their guests (*but it's never too hard to crash*). *Usually the bar is the gravitational centre of college life, which may explain the number of people lying on the floors (physics joke). Rumour has it that some of the jukeboxes still take half-crowns and play 78rpm records...*
Theatres: Drama is all over the place in Cambridge. The *pokey* ADC (cap 250) is run professionally for student productions and aims at a wider audience than simply students. It's got good facilities such as its own lights, bar, club room and workshop. At ADC, along with Fitzpatrick Hall (in Queen's College) and the Robinson Theatre, a handsome number of pretty big shows are performed each term of an extremely variable standard. There's also an enormous proliferation of other smaller venues throughout the University, including The Cambridge Playroom and about 4 others and more

experimental productions continue virtually non-stop all year.

Cinemas: Most colleges have their own film club, which usually amounts to rented videos in the JCR, although some are more professional (especially at St John's, Queens', Peterhouse and the Cambridge Union Society). Being run by students, these, of course, show just about anything students might want to see *and often just what the projectionist wants to see (The 'Ooh, let's do 'Star Wars' again' factor).*

Clubs/discos: The biggest regular club night is the weekly Big Holy Noise held at Fifth Avenue (800) run by CUSU (and often attended by Anglia Poly University students) but students can usually rely on a rave 5 or 6 times every week by doing the rounds of the college bops. push*plug bops at Queens' and Fitzwilliam.*

Cabaret: The Cambridge Footlights Revue has given birth to some of the world's best chuckle-mongers. For example, half the Monty Python Team, Peter Cook, Smith & Jones, Fry & Laurie, Clives Anderson and James, Emma Thompson, Tony Slattery and so on ad ridiculum, *although the talent scouts haven't been so ready with their cheque-books in recent years. Cambridge Comedy is unkillable, though, and the Footlights show goes on (and on, and on...).*

Music venues: The University Concert Hall (650) hosts mainly classical concerts including the University's many orchestras, choirs and chapel music groups. For more contemporary sound-waves the one to watch is Queens' Fitzpatrick Hall (again) with a capacity of 300.

Balls: *Oo-er, sounds a bit rude. Wild parties in penguin suits and ball frocks which usually end up covered in strawberries and vomit.* Most colleges have 1 (or share 1 with another college) and some are huge (such as Trinity's). *The one thing they almost all have in common is a discussion with the bank manager - a double ticket can cost in excess of £140 (plus the dry-cleaning bill - see above).* Some colleges have cheaper versions by cutting back the thrills and frills. Most students end up deciding they're only young once and only a student once and what the hell and go to at least 1 ball a year anyway. For really top names in music and cabaret, balls are the crunching ground since the organisers are often willing to splash out on chart bands. The odd thing is the balls are almost all in June and yet are called May Balls. Answers on a postcard... May Week also includes 'Suicide Sunday'; not, as some presume, anything to do with exam pressure but a day to begin alcoholic consumption at 9am and carry on until oblivion.

Others: Terribly civilised entertainments flourish, such as garden parties and cocktail parties and cheese and wine parties and possibly even S&M Tupperware parties for all we know. Students should remember to pack their cravats and Laura Ashley dresses.

Food: During the day, livers-in generally eat lunch in the college dining halls, but there are also cafeterias and sandwich bars in some of the departments and in the University Library. Evening meals are provided by the colleges - they're cheap but don't forget they're subsidised by the Kitchen Fixed Charge which all students pay at the beginning of term. So, even if you go out for the other kind of KFC, you've paid for your meal already. The big, candle-lit, roast-pig-with-fruit-rammed-up-every-orifice type of Cambridge dinner still goes on but it's not an everyday occurrence.

social & political

CAMBRIDGE UNIVERSITY STUDENTS' UNION:
● 5 sabbaticals ● Turnout at last ballot: 30%
● NUS member

The colleges' JCRs have really plugged the gap that students' unions usually fill and CUSU (which, to be fair is good at what it does) is a bit of a stranded fish. Its facilities don't reflect Cambridge's stature and, as far as most students are aware, CUSU's activities are limited to the publication of various handbooks (Societies Guide, Diary, Alternative Prospectus, termly paper, Sex Guide and Green Guide) and lashings of political hackery. However, even the politics is limited, because most students get all the (non-party) politics they need through their own JCR. On the quiet, CUSU does all sorts of valiant representation and welfare work in the University, trains and advises JCR officers and co-ordinates more societies than there are days in the academic year.

SU FACILITIES:

CUSU facilities include; cheap photocopier, shop, fax, stationery, condoms; minibus hire. Practically speaking, it aims at providing for JCRs who then provide amenities for individual students.

CLUBS (NON SPORTING):

This list doesn't include college-based societies. What do you want, the moon on a stick?

Abacus; Action Aid; Air Squadron; Anglo-Japanese; Anti-Bloodsports; Archimideans; Art; Assassin's Guild; Baby Milk Action; Backgammon; Baha'i; Ballet; Bangladesh; Birders; Black & Asian Caucus; Bone Marrow; Brass Band; Bridge (community); Buddhist; Campus Children's Holidays; Canadian; Canal; Cannabis Legalisation; Ceilidh; Chamber Choir; Chocolate; Christian Music; Christian Science; Cobblers; Cognitive Science; Comic (the paper variety not stand-up); Community Church; Computer; Contact (helping the elderly); Cuba; Cycle Safety; Dance; Detective Fiction; Diamond Way; Diplomacy (game); Disabilities; Dr Who; Duke of Edinburgh Award; Early Music; Eating Disorders; Enterprise (Star Trek); Environment Action; Esperanto; Essex; European; European Theatre Group (international touring company); Excitium; Explorers & Travellers; Field Sports; Film & TV; First Aid; Fisher Society (Catholic); Footlights; Freaky Comics; Free (libertarian); Freemasonry; French; Friends of the Earth; Gamelan (gongs); German; Go (game); Greenlink; Grimsoc (professional Northerners); Hellenic; Heraldic; Hillwalking; Hindu; Hispanic; Holistic Medicine; Hong Kong & China; Hungarian; Imfundo (South African Educational Trust); India; International; Iran; Israel; Italian; Jews & Christians; Jomborg the New (fantasy); Jugglers; Kettle's Yard (visual arts); Light Entertainment; Link Africa; Linkline; Literary; Madhouse Theatre; Mah-Jong; Malaysia & Singapore; Marlowe Dramatic; Massage; Medical Action; Methodist; Middle East; Mummers; Mystical; Officers' Training Corps; Opera; Orthodox; Overlanders (rough travel); Oxfam; Pakistan; Poetry; Pottery; Progressive Jewish; Punjabi; Quorum; Radio; Railway; Raleigh; Revolver & Pistol; Role-playing; RN; Science Fiction; Scientists for the Earth; Scottish & Irish; Scouts & Guides; Seres (Chinese magazine); Sheila & Her Dog (relapse into childhood); Slavonic & East European; Sri Lanka; Strathsprey & Reel (Scottish dancing); Student Christian Movement; Support for the Homeless; Survival (tribal rights); Third World First; Tibet Support; Tolkien; Transcendence; Troubadors; Ugandan Children; Underwater Exploration; Union Society; Union Society Boycott; United Nations; Up Shit Creek Without a Paddle (ignore exams); Visual Arts; Welsh; West End; Wine; Young Friends (Quakers).

OTHER ORGANISATIONS:

Media: The award-winning 'Varsity' is the first student newspaper to have gone into full colour and now produces an annual Year Book too. There are endless magazines which rise and die, some surviving longer than others. College magazines, which are usually no more than crude gossipy muck-rakers, 'Spark' (arts), 'Quorum' (politics), 'Sprocket' (film) and 'Corridor' (feminist) deserve a mention. Cambridge University Radio broadcasts from Churchill to a very small area although expansion is in the air waves.

Cambridge Union Society: The 2nd oldest university debating society (after Oxford) and a right-wing stronghold. With a few student facilities (bar, café, reading room, etc) *the Union can lay some claim to having scuppered CUSU. But the Union's on a rocky road itself these days, not attracting speakers of quite the same calibre any more and membership flagging (partly 'cos it costs a packet to join). The Cambridge Union Boycott Society looks on, grinning.*

Rag: Colleges compete in raising money for the University's charity Rag. With competition spurring them on, they raised a total of £90,000 last year.

Student Community Action: You'll notice from the list above that there's a number of Cambridge clubs with a conscience. Some of these and other organisations - in all about 50 - do voluntary work in all sectors of the community. *Unlike at many universities, this is not a public relations exercise to improve local feeling towards students. That relationship is already fairly good, it's a genuine and high profile attempt to do something about local problems.*

Music: Cambridge offers the perfect chance to get together and make sweet music, mostly of the classical variety with the Chamber Orchestra (CUCO), the Music Society (CUMS) or in any of the many college orchestras, choirs, etc. Contemporary musicians, ie poppers and rockers, either form bands the usual way or use the Musicians Directory to find each other. If they're any good or know the student ents officer concerned or both, student bands can reckon on a gig or 2 at college bops. Jazz is also pretty big, *but not like it was in the late fifties, daddio.* And the list goes on, opera, Gilbert & Sullivan, Christian singers, brass bands, bells, gongs, guitars, Tibetan nose flutes and so on and on and...

RELIGIOUS:

It's not enough to say Anglican Christianity is the norm (although it's true that most colleges have a CofE or inter-denominational chapel and chaplain - Corpus Christi has a mosque). Even this takes every form from incense swingers to rockin' vicars. Every denomination of Christianity is here with Catholics close behind the Anglicans in the spiritual charts and virtually no religion unrepresented (including a few religious orders started by students wanting to avoid poll tax). Try the following for some communal God squadding: The Christian Union (Anglican); the Fisher Society (Catholic); the Methodists; the Islamic Society (linked to local mosque); not 1, but 2 Jewish societies, Progressive and Orthodox (with a synagogue, rabbi and kosher restaurant of their own) and so on. There are local places of worship for Hindus, Sikhs and Buddhists.

PAID WORK:

It's actually against the University statutes (the 2,372 commandments God forgot to give to Moses) to do a job during term time and technically, students can be rusticated for it (*ooh, painful, madam*) but with the economic climate what it is, blind eyes are having to be turned all over the place. The tourist trade provides the only opening beyond the ordinary.

.... sports

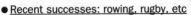
● <u>Recent successes: rowing, rugby, etc</u>

Oxford's grip on the Boat Race slipped a few years ago, a Downing alumnus captained England at cricket till just recently; face it, Cambridge breeds many more than its fair share of sports gods. Many of the rulers of rugby and the angels of athletics have come running from Cambridge's sporting fields. *But all this is for a few bionic heroes at a University-wide level. Cambridge and its colleges also encourage even the weediest wimp to exert themselves in anything from tiddlywinks to boxing, but most often, rowing.* Whatever the game, it's probably played in a college society or team and, if not there, in the University as a whole.

SPORTS FACILITIES:
Every college has its own facilities to a varying degree, so read their individual entries for details. *The University doesn't actually have all that many facilities to call its own, beyond endless playing fields. But if there's something somebody wants to do there's funding galore to redress any deficiencies. Anyone for competitive plate-spinning?*

SPORTING CLUBS:
American Football; Boxing; Caving; Clay Pigeon Shooting; Croquet; Drag Hunt; Eton Fives; Field Sports; Gymnastics; Hang Gliding; Hill Walking; Korfball; Lacrosse; Life Saving; Parachuting; Petanque; Polo; Power Lifting; Rambling; Real Tennis; Revolvers & Pistols; Rifles; Rugby League; Surf Squad; Trampoline; Ultimate Frisbee.

ATTRACTIONS:
As if the University's own sports didn't satisfy every possible desire to watch sport, there's always Cambridge United Football and Rugby Clubs. The more Sloaney set can don their toff hats and pop off to Newmarket for the races *and lose all daddy's money - hee hee.*

.... accommodation

IN COLLEGE:
● <u>Catered: 95%</u> ● <u>Cost: £35 (30-52wks)</u>

Availability: To an even greater extent than at Oxford, *one of Cambridge's best benefits is the opportunity to live in college accommodation.* All colleges offer rooms to all 1st years and finalists and 2nd years who can't be squeezed into the college itself will be offered some kind of college-owned housing nearby. *The rooms vary from palatial suites to pokey cupboards without central heating although most are fairly impressive.* Older rooms around the college courts can look spectacular from the outside, but the more modern rooms tend to offer better living conditions. It's rare to have to share a room, however, double sets (2 linked rooms) are fairly common. There is only limited availability for couples and even less for students with children. Each college makes its own arrangements - for example, Newnham, Lucy Cavendish and New Hall are for women only - but for the petty particulars, take a peek at the college entries.

Car parking: Students aren't technically allowed to bring cars to their colleges, but, in fact, some outer colleges (where parking is less impossible) don't bother too much.

EXTERNALLY:

● <u>Ave rent: £55</u>

Availability: *With so many students based in a city not purpose built for the little darlings, accommodation can be tough to source. The hand-me-down housing method has kept the severest problems at bay but students do have to keep an eye open for a few landlords who're willing to make a fast buck from a student's bad luck.* Usually, livers out share houses of between 3 and 6 people, but digs (a room in a landlord's house) are not uncommon. *Relations with the local community are generally pretty good and there are no student ghettoes, although Mill Road and Huntingdon Road are popular. The only place which students should rule out is the north of the city, because it's easy enough to find something closer.* For fast relief students can refer to the Accommodation Syndicate (18 Silver Street) for a prescription with a roof. They keep a list of suitable accommodation, often a little pricier than those on the open market but always up to scratch. *Students who choose to live out have to find somewhere within 3 miles of the city centre.*

welfare

SERVICES:
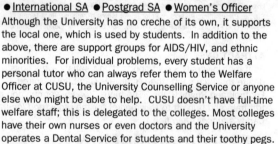
● <u>Nightline</u> ● <u>LesBiGay Society</u> ● <u>Mature SA</u>
● <u>International SA</u> ● <u>Postgrad SA</u> ● <u>Women's Officer</u>

Although the University has no creche of its own, it supports the local one, which is used by students. In addition to the above, there are support groups for AIDS/HIV, and ethnic minorities. For individual problems, every student has a personal tutor who can always refer them to the Welfare Officer at CUSU, the University Counselling Service or anyone else who might be able to help. CUSU doesn't have full-time welfare staff; this is delegated to the colleges. Most colleges have their own nurses or even doctors and the University operates a Dental Service for students and their toothy pegs.

Women: Most colleges have only started to allow women students over the last 2 decades *and some are still reeling from the shock. As female numbers grow the situation and the facilities improve, but the academic staff of many departments and colleges are still ominously all male. The prevailing chauvinism is that of a previous generation and some women end up pedalling on a lower gear just to show they can. The most blatant m-c-piggery rears its head in college bars where the tone can be frankly oppressive.* But, in the face of aggression, women have taken steps. There's a Women's Council, Women's Executive, Women's Handbook, free rape alarms and strong campaigns.

Lesbian/Gay/Bisexual: Cambridge has the largest LGB Society in the UK *and there's a long tradition of relative sexual tolerance in the University; gay icons such as EM Forster, Ian McKellen and Stephen Fry have passed through its portals.*

Disabled: Cambridge was not originally built with wheelchairs in mind, although it is blessed with a lack of hills. However, a fair amount of building has been going on over the last 20 years and there has been a genuine attempt to make these new buildings accessible at least. Bridget's hostel, on Tennis Court Road, which has special facilities for people with disabilities, offers ground floor accommodation, a care attendant and an independent life. Professor Stephen Hawking is a regular sight, in his electric chair. For sight-impaired students, large print or braille exam papers are available.

FINANCE:
● Ave debt: £800
Financial assistance usually comes from individual colleges.

Christ's College, Cambridge

▼ ● *The College is part of <u>University of Cambridge</u> and students are entitled to use its facilities.*
Christ's College, Cambridge, CB2 3BU. Tel: (01223) 334953.
Fax: (01223) 334967. E-mail: admissions@christs.cam.ac.uk
Christ's College Students' Union, Cambridge, CB2 3BU.
Tel: (01223) 334900.
Web site: http://www.christs.cam.ac.uk

Christ's is only 300 yards from King's Parade and is slap bang in the middle of the city, right by the shops and the bus station (and Burger King). It is one of the older and *most beautiful* colleges, built around 4 courts (with some parts dating back to the 15th century), except for 'the Typewriter', the 1970s accommodation block, *which has to be seen to be hated. Academic standards are very high which can cause pressure but there's a cheerful, supportive atmosphere.*

63% ♂♂♂♂♂♂♀♀♀♀ **37%**

Sex ratio(M:F): 63%:37%	**Founded: 1448**
Full time u'grads: 390	**Postgrads: 100**
Private school: 45%	**Mature students: 1%**
Overseas students: 15%	**Disabled students: n/a**

Buttery Bar (cap 100) closes early. New Late Night Bar opens 8.30-11pm or students descend on the town; theatre/venue (200); Plumb auditorium for recitals; *drama strong.* 'Christ's Pieces' for gossip and an SU newsletter; Milton Society for dining/debating. 3 libraries (120,000 books); 65 computers; *strong* Christian Union; CofE chapel. Squash courts on site, but most sports facilities 1 mile away. All live in College or in Jesus Lane hostels. Canteen and formal meals. College sick bay; nurse; late night taxi service and women's escort service; free rape alarms.

FAMOUS ALUMNI:
Charles Darwin (evolutionist); John Milton (poet); Lord Mountbatten; CP Snow (writer); Richard Whiteley (Countdown love god).

Churchill College, Cambridge

● *The College is part of <u>University of Cambridge</u> and students are entitled to use its facilities.*
Churchill College, Cambridge, CB3 0DS.
Tel: (01223) 336202. Fax: (01223) 336180.
Junior Common Room, Churchill College, Cambridge, CB3 0DS.
Tel: (01223) 465545.
Web site: http://www.chu.cam.ac.uk

Just under a mile from King's Parade, Churchill is one of Cambridge's larger, more modern and less central colleges. The buildings are stark modern blocks (but still Grade II listed), based on the old college format of courts and staircases, set in large grounds (40 acres). The modernity offers some advantages over Cambridge's more traditional colleges in terms of facilities and space. There are more scientists at Churchill than most colleges and also more state-educated students *which means poncing about like a Cambridge stereotype attracts more funny looks than admiration.* Churchill was also the first men's college to admit women.

68% ♂♂♂♂♂♂♂♂♀♀♀ **32%**

Sex ratio(M:F): 68%:32%	Founded: 1960
Full time u'grads: 420	Postgrads: 220
Private school: 20%%	Mature students: 2
Overseas students: 7%	Disabled students: 1

2 bars, bops on Thursdays; film theatre (cap 300; film soc voted best in Varsity); soundproof rooms for music practice/recitals; party room. 'Winston' mag for gossip; College Broadcasting Club. 4 libraries (45,000 books); 40 computers; free language and computing courses offered to all students; chapel; art loan scheme for student rooms. *Sport good, but better pool teams.* Everyone lives in; some smoking areas; phone and computer sockets in all rooms; pay-as-you-eat cafeteria and access to self-catering; veggie option; *kitchens unexciting but OK. Good* SU welfare; nurse; *okay* disabled access; scholarships, hardship and travel grants.

❝ 'The people who went into politics were those who couldn't get in the Footlights or were no good at journalism.'
–Peter Cook on his Cambridge contemporaries. ❞

❝ The bar at Emmanuel, Cambridge has been renamed the Parkinson/Yeo, to commemorate two of its more notoriously heterosexual alumni. ❞

• •

Clare College, Cambridge

▼ ● *The College is part of <u>University of Cambridge</u> and students are entitled to use its facilities.*
Clare College, Cambridge, CB2 1TL. Tel: (01223) 333246.
Fax: (01223) 333219.
Union of Clare Students, Junior Common Room, Clare College,
Cambridge, CB2 1TL. Tel: (01223) 333749.
Web site: http://www.clare.cam.ac.uk

About 100 yards from King's Parade, Clare is Cambridge's 2nd oldest college. Its buildings are traditional, focussed around the 17th century Old Court and spanning both sides of the river (linked by Cambridge's oldest bridge) on the Cambridge 'Backs' (the college-crusted banks of the River Cam). *The College has a reputation for insularity and a degree of poshness but it's unpretentious and there is increasing involvement with the University and especially CUSU.*

52% ♂♂♂♂♂♂♀♀♀♀♀ **48%**

Sex ratio(M:F): 52%:48%	Founded: 1326
Full time u'grads: 430	Postgrads: 175
Private school: 45%	Mature students: 0
Overseas students: 8%	Disabled students: 0

Atmospheric cellars (bar cap 200) give a university-wide ents reputation; free pool table, jukebox; weekly theme nights, DJs and jazz. 2 libraries (33,000 books); 30 computers; CofE chapel used for classical recitals; extensive gardens used for annual May Ball attended by 1,500 students (*most romantic in Cambridge*). Sports fields (4 acres) 1½ miles away; *women's football and rugby strong.* 1st to 3rd years are guaranteed rooms but 20% of 4th years live out (subsidised by College). Most students eat in the dining hall (with veggie option). Nurse; self-defence and assertiveness classes; counselling; hardship fund and travel and book grants.

FAMOUS ALUMNI:
Sir David Attenborough (TV naturalist); Chris Kelly ('Food and Drink'); Peter Lilley MP (Con); Paul Mellon (philanthropist); Matthew Parris (ex-MP, Times sketch writer); Siegfried Sassoon (poet); Cecil Sharp (folk music historian); Richard Stilgoe (entertainer/lyricist); James Watson (discovered DNA).

Corpus Christi College, Cambridge

▼▼ ● *The College is part of* <u>*University of Cambridge*</u> *and students are entitled to use its facilities.*
Corpus Christi College, Cambridge, CB2 1RH.
Tel: (01223) 338000. Fax: (01223) 338061.
Junior Common Room, Corpus Christi College, Cambridge, CB2 1RH.

Corpus Christi, founded by and for the townsfolk, is found downtown (on the King's Parade). The 'Old Court' is mid-14th century and its hardly modern equivalent 'New Court' was completed in 1827 by the designer of The National Gallery. *There's a certain insularity at play here and interaction with other colleges isn't the norm but things are improving.*

63% ♂♂♂♂♂♂♀♀♀♀ 37%	
Sex ratio(M:F): 63%:37%	Founded: 1352
Full time u'grads: 251	Postgrads: 160
Private school: 45%	Mature students: 1%
Overseas students: 10%	Disabled students: 1

Playroom theatre; student bands in bar (190); new lecture theatre/concert venue; film soc; biennial May Ball. 2 libraries (over 100,000 books including largest collection of Medieval manuscripts in UK); 15 computers; CofE chapel. Sports fields (3 acres) 10mins away; squash courts, ergo machines, outdoor swimming pool, snooker room. All students can live in; all rooms are networked, most have phone connections; cafeteria and 3 formal meals/week; veggie option. Nurse; self-defence classes; 3 rooms with wheelchair access; *sympathetic* Senior Tutor; hardship funds and scholarships.

FAMOUS ALUMNI:
Christopher Isherwood (writer); Christopher Marlowe (playwright); Lord Sieff (Marks & Spencer); EP Thompson (historian).

Downing College, Cambridge

▼▼ ● *The College is part of* <u>*University of Cambridge*</u> *and students are entitled to use its facilities.*
Downing College, Cambridge, CB2 1DQ.
Tel: (01223) 334800. Fax: (01223) 362279.
E-mail: pcm1000@cam.ac.uk
Junior Common Room, Downing College, Cambridge, CB2 1DQ.
Tel: (01223) 334825. Fax: (01223) 358674.

500 yards from King's Parade is the *elegant* Downing College, an expanse of spacious lawns and classical architecture of the

last 200 years. *It's noted for sporting achievements, but there is plenty of opportunity at a lower level if your idea of exertion is feeding the vast squirrel population. Social indulgence can take precedence over banner-waving, but Downing students are active on the University-wide hack scene as well and music is also increasingly strong.*

63% ♂♂♂♂♂♂♀♀♀♀ 37%	
Sex ratio(M:F): 63%:37%	Founded: 1800
Full time u'grads: 400	Postgrads: 150
Private school: 45%	Mature students: 1%
Overseas students: 9%	Disabled students: 2%

Large *plush* bar, longest hours in the Uni; student bands in Howard Building (theatre, cap 120) and Dining Hall (400); bops weekly in Party Room (100); music practice rooms; annual June 'event' (cap 1,200). 'Griffin' college mag bi-termly. New library (46,000 books); 12 computers; CofE chapel. Successes in rowing, football, rugby and others. Sports fields (9 acres) 1 mile away; *good* sports facilities on site. Students guaranteed rooms in the 1st year, 93% live in thereafter; College owns surrounding houses for single sex 2nd and 3rd year housing. Pay-as-you-eat dining hall (KFC £106); 3 formal meals/week; veggie option. Nurse; counselling; free taxi service for women; rape alarms; good security (CCTV); room for disabled student; hardship fund; travel grant.

FAMOUS ALUMNI:
Mike Atherton (former England cricket captain); Quentin Blake (illustrator); John Cleese (funnyman); Thandie Newton (actress); Trevor Nunn (theatre director); Michael Winner (director/restaurant critic).

• •

Emmanuel College, Cambridge

● *The College is part of* <u>University of Cambridge</u> *and students are entitled to use its facilities.*
Emmanuel College, Cambridge, CB2 3AP.
Tel: (01223) 334200. Fax: (01223) 334426.
Emmanuel College Students' Union, Junior Common Room, Cambridge, CB2 3AP. Tel: (01223) 314790.
E-mail: ecsu@emma.ac.uk.
Web site: http://www.emma.cam.ac.uk

'Emma' (as Emmanuel is affectionately known), 500 yards from King's Parade, is a collection of *dignified* buildings from the 16th century, 1960s accommodation blocks, *elegant* gardens and a duck pond (into which freshers are ritually ducked), replete with 50 resident ducks and cute but stupid ducklings every spring. *Emmanuel is perceived by other students as unpretentious and approachable and its students are well represented in University activities.*

58% ♂♂♂♂♂♂♀♀♀♀ 42%	
Sex ratio(M:F): 58%:42%	Founded: 1584
Full time u'grads: 437	Postgrads: 173
Private school: 55%	Mature students: 2%
Overseas students: 10%	Disabled students: 0

Refurbished bar (cap 200); ball/event every year; theatre in new Queen's building; films, DJ nights, quizzes, live jazz every week. 'Roar' mag. Library (50,834 books); 30 computers; CofE chapel designed by Christopher Wren. Sports fields (2½ acres) 20mins away; *reasonable* sports facilities on site, women's rowing, tennis and hockey *strong*. All undergrads live in; College owns houses nearby; internet connections in most rooms. Optional formals daily; vegetarian option. 2 part-time nurses; part-time counsellor; free condoms; bursaries and scholarships.

FAMOUS ALUMNI:
Graham Chapman (Monty Python's Brian); Michael Frayn (playwright); Eddie George (Governor, Bank of England); Griff Rhys Jones (comic); FR Leavis (lit crit); Lord Parkinson.

● ●

Fitzwilliam College, Cambridge

▼ ● *The College is part of* <u>University of Cambridge</u> *and students are entitled to use its facilities.*
Fitzwilliam College, Huntingdon Road, Cambridge, CB3 0DG. Tel: (01223) 332030. Fax: (01223) 332057.
Junior Members Association, Fitzwilliam College, Huntingdon Road, Cambridge, CB3 0DG. Tel: (01223) 353382.

Fitz isn't a typical Cambridge college. For a start, its main buildings are modern and redbrick. It admits more state school students than most - indeed, the national average in universities (*oh, well done*). *It's friendly, down to earth and not at all claustrophobic or overwhelming.* It's also set apart from the other colleges, a mile from King's Parade at the top of Cambridge's only 'hill' (shallow slope) next to New Hall in the city's businessy area.

60% ♂♂♂♂♂♂♀♀♀♀ 40%	
Sex ratio(M:F): 60%:40%	Founded: 1869
Full time u'grads: 440	Postgrads: 184
Private school: 30%	Mature students: 1%
Overseas students: 15%	Disabled students: 3%

Large *departure-loungey* bar; small theatre; bands and discos twice a term in Central Block, *very popular*; concerts in dining-hall; termly 'events' (mini-balls). 'Fitz News'; library (35,500 books); 20 computers; CofE chapel. *Good* sports fields (7 acres) ⅓ mile from College; sports facilities on site; tennis courts, multigym. All years can live in College or College-owned rooms. Most students eat in; *decent* food, veggie option. Shared nurse; free taxis and attack alarms; travel grants and hardship funds.

FAMOUS ALUMNI:
Nick Clarke (broadcaster); Phil Edmonds (cricketer); Norman Lamont (ex-Chancellor); Christopher Martin-Jenkins (cricket commentator); Derek Pringle (cricketer); Lord St John of Fawsley; Dr David Starkey (historian).

Girton College, Cambridge

● *The College is part of <u>University of Cambridge</u> and students are entitled to use its facilities.*
Girton College, Cambridge, CB3 0JG. Tel: (01223) 338999. Fax: (01223) 338896.
Junior Combination Room, Girton College, Cambridge, CB3 0JG. Tel: (01223) 338898.

Girton is 2¼ miles from King's Parade and the city centre (*a bike is pretty much compulsory*). It started life as a women-only college, before going mixed in 1977. Nowadays, *it's one of Cambridge's most liberal, relaxed and actively fun colleges*. Being out of town gives it over 50 acres of grounds with gothic redbrick buildings *and the distance means integration with the rest of the University is rare, although Girtonians seem quite proud of their distinct lifestyle.*

47% ♂♂♂♂♂♀♀♀♀♀ 53%

Sex ratio(M:F): 47%:53%	Founded: 1869
Full time u'grads: 489	Postgrads: 170
Private/state school: 39%	Mature students: 1%
Overseas students: 9%	Disabled students: 1%

2 bars; bop and/or band every week or 2; annual garden party; annual revue. JCR newsletters: termly 'Angle' and fortnightly 'Bog Sheet'; *green* JCR policies. 2 libraries (80,000 books); 20+ computers; chapel. Sports facilities on site and the bike ride into town keeps Girtonians fit (JCR lends some bikes); various sporting successes. Rooms guaranteed to all years; 2nd years and finalists live in College or in College-owned housing; cafeteria of *celebrated standard* ; *good* self-catering. 2 nurses; counsellors; self-defence classes; various financial help.

❝A rowing VIII from Magdalene College, Cambridge recently apprehended an escaped criminal during a training session.❞

FAMOUS ALUMNI:
Queen Margarethe of Denmark; Joan Robinson (economist);
Arianna Stassinopoulos (writer); Angela Tilby (writer & TV
producer); Sandi Toksvig (short comedian); Baroness Warnock
(of Warnock Committee fame).

• •

Gonville & Caius College, Cambridge

● *The College is part of <u>University of Cambridge</u> and*
students are entitled to use its facilities.
Gonville & Caius College, Cambridge, CB2 1TA.
Tel: (01223) 332447. Fax: (01223) 332456.
E-mail: admissions@cai.cam.ac.uk
JCR, Gonville & Caius College, Cambridge, CB2 1TA.
Tel: (01223) 332400.
Web site: http://www.cai.cam.uk

*The most important thing about Gonville & Caius is to
pronounce its name correctly.* Gonville's okay, *apart from
sounding like a Muppet character* and most people drop that
bit anyway, but Caius is pronounced 'keys'. Caius is based on
2 sites, 8 mins walk apart. The main building is at one end of
King's Parade and is centred on the *fine* old renaissance Caius
Court, next to Tree Court, the only college court in Cambridge
with, er, trees. *Or traius?* The other site is Harvey Court, the
1st year accommodation, designed in the 1960s in concrete
and grey brick *(and the worse for it)* and situated on the other
side of the river on the Backs (meadow banks). *The
state/private school ratio is healthier than others in
Cambridge and it's one of the friendliest colleges, although an
old-school tie reputation still adheres.*

61% ♂♂♂♂♂♂♀♀♀ 39%	
Sex ratio(M:F): 61%:39%	**Founded: 1348**
Full time u'grads: 472	**Postgrads: 250**
Private school: 45%	**Mature students: 0**
Overseas students: 9%	**Disabled students: 0.2%**

2 bars; Shreddies dance night 3-4 times a term *(used to be
called Orgasm but the council didn't like that)*; Bateman
concert room; biennial ball. Newsletter twice a term; many
drinking/dining clubs. Library (40,000 books); 40 computers;
chapel. *Good* sports facilities in College and ¼ mile away (3
acres and a bar). All 1st and 3rd years live in hall, 2nd years
in college hostels; *worst food in Cambridge.* Nurse; hardship
funds, travel, study grants.

FAMOUS ALUMNI:
Harold Abrahams (runner in 'Chariots of Fire'); Kenneth Clarke
MP (Con); Francis Crick (Nobel prize winning medic); David
Frost (broadcaster); William Harvey (who discovered circulation
of blood); Sir Nevill Mott (Nobel prize winning physicist); Dr
Venn (as in 'Venn diagram').

Homerton College, Cambridge

● *The College is part of <u>University of Cambridge</u> and students are entitled to use its facilities.*
Homerton College, Cambridge, CB2 2PH.
Tel: (01223) 507114. Fax: (01223) 507140.
E-mail: nt204@cus.cam.ac.uk
Homerton Union of Students, Homerton College, Cambridge, CB2 2PH. Tel: (01223) 507235.

Homerton is probably the least 'Cambridge-y' Cambridge college, because of its location (2 miles out of town) and its academic set-up (education and nursing students). *It's less rich than some other colleges and some feel undue emphasis has been put on the conference trade.* Students tend to socialise within the College but Homerton people have made their University-level mark in sport, journalism and more.

40% ♂♂♂♂♀♀♀♀♀ 60%	
Sex ratio(M:F): 40%:60%	**Founded: 1695**
Full time u'grads: 570	**Postgrads: 410**
Private/state school: 20%	**Mature students: 8%**
Overseas students: 2%	**Disabled students: 5%**

Bar; bops in the Union Room (100), which, with the Main Hall (500), is also used for live bands; function room (200); annual ball. 'Bed Times' College mag. Library (70,000 books); 70 computers. Sports fields (12 acres) on site; Cambridge's only College dance/drama studio; *sport for fun rather than glory*, but successful rugby and women's football. All-day buttery; dining hall; food *could be better.* Accommodation for 500 on-site. Nurse; hardship fund, bursaries and childcare fund.

FAMOUS ALUMNI:
Carly Carter (Brucey's assistant on 'Play Your Cards Right'); Julie Covington (actress/singer); Nick Hancock ('They Think It's All Over'); Cherie Lunghi (actress); Ben Oakley (British windsurfing coach).

❝'If I was called upon to mention the prettiest corner of the world, I should draw a thoughtful sigh and point the way to the Gardens of Trinity Hall.'
– Henry James.❞

Jesus College, Cambridge

● *The College is part of <u>University of Cambridge</u> and students are entitled to use its facilities.*

Jesus College, Cambridge, CB5 8BL. Tel: (01223) 357626. Fax: (01223) 339339.

Junior Common Room, Jesus College, Cambridge, CB5 8BL. Tel: (01223) 339447.

Jesus College, built around an old convent with buildings dating from the 12th century, is 5 mins walk from King's Parade and the 1140 chapel is the oldest building in Cambridge. *Jesus combines sporting enthusiasm with a liberal, if not radical, ethos and it makes a genuine effort to recruit more women and students from state schools. The bar is the College's social suction point and is usually full by nightfall.*

58% ♂♂♂♂♂♂♀♀♀ **42%**

Sex ratio(M:F): 58%:42%	Founded: 1496
Full time u'grads: 466	Postgrads: 238
Private school: 50%	Mature students: 0
Overseas students: 13%	Disabled students: 0

Bar (cap 175) - *cliquey and members only*; classical concerts in the Chapel (250); dining hall for occasional gigs (200); May Ball and lower-key 'event' on alternate years; music practice rooms. Students holding orchestral awards have high quality tuition provided; *excellent drama and music.* College mag: 'Red & Blackmail'. Library (25,000 books); 40 computers; CofE chapel. *Excellent* sports; sports fields (4 acres) and facilities on site. All 1st and 3rd years live in; 2nd years in converted houses on College perimeter; eat in dining hall. Nurse; rape alarms, self-defence courses; no disabled facilities; hardship fund and loans.

FAMOUS ALUMNI:

ST Coleridge (poet); Alistair Cooke (broadcaster); Thomas Cranmer (former Archbishop of Canterbury); Ted Dexter (cricketer); Prince Edward (showbiz impresario); Wilfred Hadfield (invented double yellow lines); Nick Hornby (writer); Richard Lacey (food safety guru); Thomas Malthus (economist).

❝The Kipper Memorial Prize For Contribution To College Atmosphere at Clare, Cambridge, has been set up to commemorate late lamented college cat.❞

❝When Magdalene College, Cambridge, admitted women, in 1988, some male members of the College wore black armbands.❞

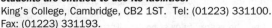

King's College, Cambridge

● *The College is part of <u>University of Cambridge</u> and students are entitled to use its facilities.*

King's College, Cambridge, CB2 1ST. Tel: (01223) 331100. Fax: (01223) 331193.

King's College Student Union, King's College, Cambridge, CB2 1ST. Tel: (01223) 332320.

Web site: http://www.kings.cam.ac.uk

King's College, on King's Parade, has many a dreaming spire and the famous King's chapel (started in 1446). *There's a good mix of all Cambridge's different types, with the same staid hierarchy*, such as a court for fellows and ducks only. *Despite this, and the awe-inspiringly ancient surroundings, King's has a somewhat leftist tradition, relaxed and down to earth* with it's relatively high proportion of state school students.

60% ♂♂♂♂♂♂♀♀♀♀ 40%	
Sex ratio(M:F): 60%:40%	**Founded: 1441**
Full time u'grads: 381	**Postgrads: 259**
Private school: 25%	**Mature students: 4%**
Overseas students: 4%	**Disabled students: 1%**

The biggest college bar in Cambridge (cap 300); Cellar Bar (150); VAC bar (*cheap cocktails, open Tues and Suns*); all bars, dining hall, chapel (250) and Keynes Hall (200) are used for bands; bops in Cellars (150) are *more hip than something very hip indeed*. Every term there is a 'Mingle' (a mini ball); 'June Event' is a deluxe 'Mingle'. Art room with resident artist. 'Red Dragon Pie' student magazine and 'King's Things' newsletter. Library (100,000 books); 20 computers; ecumenical chapel. Sports fields (6 acres) 15 mins walk; multigym; *enthusiastic but not one of the big winners*. All students can live in and eat in the dining hall; vegans can opt out of KFC; *not bad* self-catering provisions. Nurse; a few rooms for wheelchair users.

FAMOUS ALUMNI:
David Baddiel (comedian, *unlikely* pop star); Martin Bell MP (Ind); Rupert Brooke (poet); EM Forster (writer); John Maynard Keynes (economist); Michael Mates MP (Con); Salman Rushdie (writer).

Lucy Cavendish College, Cambridge

▼▼ ● *The College is part of <u>University of Cambridge</u> and students are entitled to use its facilities.*
Lucy Cavendish College, Cambridge, CB3 0BU.
Tel: (01223) 332190. Fax: (01223) 332178.
E-mail: lcc-admission@lists.cam.ac.uk
Students' Association, Lucy Cavendish College, Cambridge, CB3 0BU.

4 of the buildings of Lucy Cavendish College (½ mile from King's Parade) date from the end of the 19th century, the 5th from the years of flower power. They house a single sex college created to provide an equal opportunity for women at Cambridge. Only women students over 21 years old are admitted and the average age is 30. The site is full of trees, *tranquil and quite beautiful,* complete with a tiny Anglo-Saxon herb garden - *perfect for peaceful study. But don't think this is the academic wing of the Women's Institute; many of the students are keen to get as much as possible from their fresh start and this means a healthy dose of partying along with the intellectual exertions.*

0% ♀♀♀♀♀♀♀♀♀♀ 100

Sex ratio(M:F): 0%:100%	Founded: 1965
Full time u'grads: 76	Postgrads: 103
Private school: 40%	Mature students: 100%
Overseas students: 10%	Disabled students: 0

Bar; end-of-term parties. Music room; meditation room. Library (19,000 books); 10 computers. 'Lucy News' College mag; 24-hour gym; *solid* sporting record. 75% of students accommodated in college or town; self-catering facilities; catered means all lunches and two evening meals; weekly formal dinners; no hierarchical top table; *food and rooms are good.* Nurse; hardship fund, travel grants and scholarships; some room for disabled students. Permit car parking.

Magdalene College, Cambridge

▼▼ ● *The College is part of <u>University of Cambridge</u> and students are entitled to use its facilities.*
Magdalene College, Cambridge, CB3 0AG.
Tel: (01223) 332100.
Junior Common Room, Magdalene College, Cambridge, CB3 0A6.

If you want to cause a sudden embarrassed hush at parties say 'Maggdallin', but to flow with wit and wisdom pronounce it correctly as 'Maudlin'. The atmosphere at this college, 700 yards from King's Parade and with more river frontage than any other, is *certainly not maudlin and the social scene, which revolves around the bar, is simply spinning.* Magdalene is one of the smaller colleges *and tradition and camaraderie pervade.* The College includes *pleasant* features such as the medieval and 15th and 16th century courts and Pepys' Library, but *unfortunately, it hasn't escaped clumsy* post-war architecture for some residential blocks.

Sex ratio(M:F): 58%:42%	Founded: 1542
Full time u'grads: 311	Postgrads: 136
Private school: 56%	Mature students: 1%
Overseas students: 20%	Disabled students: 0

Bar; concerts in Benson Hall (cap 100) and student bands in Ramsay Hall (150); 3 discos a term; biennial ball (*very posh*). 'Ars Magna' College mag and 'Magd Out' newsletter. 4 libraries (25,000 books); 20 computers, *hope* to have all rooms networked by summer 98; CofE chapel. *Good* sports fields (8 acres) 500 yards shared with <u>St John's</u>; boathouse shared with <u>Queens'</u>. All students live in; *okay* self-catering facilities; most eat in the college dining halls (*mediocre food, except for formal hall - candlelit, because the hall doesn't have electricity*). Nurse; hardship funds, scholarships, travel grants and prizes; subsidised rape alarms.

FAMOUS ALUMNI:
William Cash (journalist); Bamber Gascoigne (quizmaster, writer); Gavin Hastings (Scottish rugby captain); Anthony Jay (writer, 'Yes Minister'); Charles Kingsley (author); Charles Stewart Parnell (C19th Irish nationalist); Samuel Pepys (diarist); Alan Rusbridger (editor, 'The Guardian'); John Simpson (TV reporter).

• •

New Hall, Cambridge

● *The College is part of <u>University of Cambridge</u> and students are entitled to use its facilities.*
New Hall, Huntingdon Road, Cambridge, CB3 0DF.
Tel: (01223) 762100. Fax: (01223) 352941.
New Hall Union, New Hall, Huntingdon Road, Cambridge, CB3 0DF.
Web site: http://www.newhall.cam.ac.uk

³⁄₄ mile from King's Parade, most of New Hall was built in the 60s. The white brick is turning grey and the huge dome, which dominates the centre of the College is, shall we say, *an acquired taste.* Inside it, there's a display of women's 20th century art and a large sculpture of a saucepan, called 'Skin and Blister', arrests attention in the lawn. *Apart from the freedom from history and tradition, New Hall differs from many*

other Cambridge institutions in maintaining its single-sex status. The students seem pretty happy with this but most look beyond the college walls for entertainment and socialising. Recent worst ever score on University Challenge is still a sore point so we won't mention that.

0% ⚥⚥⚥⚥⚥⚥⚥⚥⚥ 100
Sex ratio(M:F): 0%:100%   **Founded: 1954**
Full time u'grads: 343   **Postgrads: 76**
Private school: 45%   **Mature students: 0.6%**
Overseas students: 12%   **Disabled students: 0.3%**

Bar (cap 100, open 3 times a week) holds bops after formal dinners (1/wk); concerts and student bands at the Dome (cap 300), Vivien Stewart Room (60), Fellows' Drawing Room (45 and a Steinway) or the Party Room (80), which also hosts fortnightly bops. Cabaret occasionally; balls, socials, cocktail parties, ceilidhs; music room. Fortnightly JCR newsletter 'Little Juicy Bits'; 2 libraries (60,000 books); 20 computers, 24hrs; art room (largest collection of modern women's art in Europe); sewing room; dark room. *Strong* boat club; multigym. 93% of students live in and in College-run properties; 10% of rooms are shared; almost all rooms have internet and phone connections; pay-as-you-eat at canteen (*good for veggies*), formals once a week; permit parking. Nurse; various support funds *but it's not one of the richest colleges.*

FAMOUS ALUMNI:
Jocelyn Bell-Burnell (discoverer of pulsars); Frances Edmonds (writer); Joanna McGregor (pianist); Su Perkins (comedienne); Tilda Swinton (actress).

• •

Newnham College, Cambridge

● **The College is part of <u>University of Cambridge</u> and students are entitled to use its facilities.**
Newnham College, Cambridge, CB3 9DF.
Tel: (01223) 335783. Fax: (01223) 357898.
E-mail: adm@newn.cam.ac.uk.
Junior Combination Room, Newnham College, Cambridge, CB3 9DF. Tel: (01223) 335700.
Web site: http://www.newn.cam.ac.uk

Newnham is a warm brick Victorian college with distinctive white window frames set in huge gardens, ¾ mile from King's Parade near the arts faculties (*beyond most tourists' curiosity*). *Being female is the only stereotype you can apply to Newnham students and the all-female cast exudes more confidence than counterparts in mixed Colleges; they know exactly what they want, what they rilly rilly want. The College is supportive and liberal - students are thoroughly involved and successful in University-wide activities but still come 'home' to put their feet up.*

| 0% | | 100 |

Sex ratio(M:F): 0%:100%   **Founded: 1871**
Full time u'grads: 417   **Postgrads: 119**
Private school: 46%   **Mature students: 2%**
Overseas students: 10%   **Disabled students: 0**

New Boilerhouse bar; fortnightly drum'n'bass and garage, bands and classical concerts in the College Hall (cap 250); new performing arts studio; biennial ball; garden parties; plays performed in hall or garden. Observatory; artist in residence; library (85,000 books); 35 computers. Weekly JCR 'N-Files' magazine. Success at rowing and women's rugby; sports fields on site, multigym; squash courts shared with <u>Selwyn</u>. 92% of students live in; *good* self-catering facilities. Nurse; rooms for wheelchair users; grants for books, sport and travel; scholarships and hardship funds.

FAMOUS ALUMNI:
Dianne Abbot MP, Patricia Hewitt MP (Lab); Joan Bakewell (broadcaster); Eleanor Bron, Emma Thompson (actresses); AS Byatt, Margaret Drabble, Germaine Greer (writers); Baroness Mallalieu (Lab); Suzie Menkes (fashion writer); Rabbi Julia Neuberger; Sylvia Plath (poet); Baroness Seear (Lib Dem).

• •

Pembroke College, Cambridge

▼ ● *The College is part of <u>University of Cambridge</u> and students are entitled to use its facilities.*
Pembroke College, Cambridge, CB2 1RF.
Tel: (01223) 338154. Fax: (01223) 338163.
E-mail: admissions@pem.cam.ac.uk.
Junior Parlour, Pembroke College, Cambridge, CB2 1RF.
Tel: (01223) 338110.
Web site: http://www.pem.cam.ac.uk

Pembroke's buildings range from 14th century dreaming spires to 50s redbrick and more recent buildings of an *indeterminate 90s style*, just off King's Parade and surrounded by beautiful gardens. *Students are fairly well-integrated with University life. Sport, music and alcohol are the main pastimes, not necessarily in that order.*

| 60% | ♂♂♂♂♂♂♀♀♀♀ | 40% |

Sex ratio(M:F): 60%:40%   **Founded: 1347**
Full time u'grads: 386   **Postgrads: 183**
Private school: 55%   **Mature students: 1%**
Overseas students: 9%   **Disabled students: 0**

Refurbished bar (with Carlos the Basque Separatist barman); Old Reader (cap 50, theatre); concerts in Old Library (90); student bands in Junior Parlour (80) and Old Lodge Cellars

(80), used also for discos 3 times termly; annual 'ball-like event'. Library (50,000 books); 36 computers; CofE chapel; 'Pembroke Street' newsletter, 'Pem' arts; Pembroke runs a community centre in South London (where students can stay). Success in netball and rugby; sports fields (4½ acres) 1½ miles away; oldest bowling green in Europe. All students live in College or College houses; students eat in canteen ('Trough'); optional formal dinner every night; veggie option; *limited* self catering in college. Nurse; grants and scholarships; subsidised attack alarms and self-defence classes for women.

FAMOUS ALUMNI:
Tim Brooke-Taylor, Bill Oddie (Goodies); Peter Cook (late comic genius); Raymond Dolby (audio inventor); Thomas Gray, Ted Hughes, Edmund Spenser (poets); Eric Idle (Monty Python); Clive James (writer, presenter); Jonathan Lynn (writer, director); Pitt the Younger (PM); Tom Sharpe (writer); Chris Smith MP (Lab).

• •

Peterhouse, Cambridge

▼ ● *The College is part of <u>University of Cambridge</u> and students are entitled to use its facilities.*
▼ Peterhouse, Cambridge, CB2 1RD. Tel: (01223) 338223.
Fax: (01223) 337578.
Junior Common Room, Peterhouse, Cambridge, CB2 1RD.
Web site: http://www.pet.cam.ac.uk

Peterhouse, 500 yards from King's Parade, is Cambridge's smallest and oldest college, with *beautiful and well-kept gardens. The old Peterhouse image of reactionary posh kids is fading fast and there's room for everybody although teetotallers might get a bit bored. Because the college is so small, energetic movers and shakers tend to use their talents on the wider University stage.*

70% 30%

Sex ratio(M:F): 70%:30%	Founded: 1284
Full time u'grads: 252	Postgrads: 95
Private school: 50%	Mature students: 1%
Overseas students: 8%	Disabled students: 0

Bar; Music Room (cap 100) for discos and student bands *but college admin not too keen on big events*; the theatre (180) for classical concerts; annual ball; many dining and debating societies. Termly mag 'The Sex'. 2 libraries (45,000 books); 8 computers; CofE chapel. Sports facilities (8 acres shared with <u>Clare College</u>), 1 mile away. All students live in except a few 2nd years; many live in housing arranged or maintained by College not on site (including Parkside); most eat in *gorgeous* dining hall; *limited* self catering (especially at Parkside). Nurse; women's advisors; hardship fund, *generous* prizes and scholarships.

FAMOUS ALUMNI:
Charles Babbage (computing pioneer); Richard Baker
(broadcaster); Thomas Campion, Richard Crashaw (poets); Sir
Christopher Cockerell (invented the hovercraft); Colin
Greenwood (Radiohead); Michael Howard MP; James Mason
(actor); Sam Mendes (theatre director); Michael Portillo (ex-
minister); Frank Whittle (inventor of the jet engine).

● ●

Queens' College, Cambridge

● *The College is part of <u>University of Cambridge</u> and
students are entitled to use its facilities.*
Queens' College, Cambridge, CB3 9ET. Tel: (01223) 335548.
Fax: (01223) 335522. E-mail: admissions@cam.ac.uk
Junior Combination Room, Queens' College, Cambridge, CB3
9ET. Tel: (01223) 335511. E-mail: jcr_ctte@quns.cam.ac.uk
Web site: http://www.quns.ac.uk

Queens' College's medieval appearance - Elizabethan and early
17th century buildings - 200 yards from King's Parade, make it
a *good-looking and convenient* place to be, close to The Anchor
pub. *The bar is a strong magnet, aesthetically unappealing as it
may be. Students are getting more involved in the University
than they used to (especially in drama and music) but always
return to the laid-back charm of their college. Recent years have
seen a strong emphasis on applications from state schools.*

60% **40%**

Sex ratio(M:F): 60%:40%	Founded: 1448
Full time u'grads: 489	Postgrads: 281
Private school: 42%	Mature students: 0
Overseas students: 7.4%	Disabled students: 0

Bar; Fitzpatrick Hall (380, theatre) for student bands and *the
best college club nights in Cambridge* (2 per week); films;
biennial ball. 'The Drain' student mag; JCR newsletter. 2
libraries (70,000 books); 14 computers; CofE chapel. *Big*
sports fields (15 acres shared with <u>Robinson</u>) ½mile away;
very modern boathouse. All undergraduates can live in except
a few 4th years; students eat in dining hall; *very limited* self
catering. Nurse; creche; hardship fund (usually pays creche
fees); scholarships.

❝A building at New Hall, Cambridge,
was funded by businessman Yasuto
Kaetsu, who was director of the
Japanese anti-student riot police
in the 1960s.❞

FAMOUS ALUMNI:
Erasmus (Renaissance scholar); Mike Foale (1st British man in space); Stephen Fry (polymath); Michael Gibson, John Spencer (rugby players); Graham Swift, TH White (writers).

Robinson College, Cambridge

● *The College is part of <u>University of Cambridge</u> and students are entitled to use its facilities.*
Robinson College, Cambridge, CB3 9AN.
Tel: (01223) 339143. Fax: (01223) 339743.
E-mail: undergraduate-admissions@robinson.cam.ac.uk.
Robinson College Students' Association, Robinson College, Cambridge, CB3 9AN.
Web site: http://www.robinson.cam.ac.uk

The only Cambridge college (so far) to be founded by a TV salesman cum horse fancier, Robinson College is one of the youngsters and mainly redbrick. It is set in *good* gardens ½ mile from King's Parade and handy for the arts faculties, the University Library and the Real Tennis court. *Although it lacks the grand buildings of some other colleges, it also lacks their affectations and reflects the policy of admitting those who'll contribute most to College life.* The catering and the rooms are *good*, there's a large common room and an *excellent* auditorium.

58% ♂♂♂♂♂♂ ♀♀♀♀ 42%

Sex ratio(M:F): 58%:42%	Founded: 1979
Full time u'grads: 361	Postgrads: 120
Private school: 41%	Mature students: 1%
Overseas students: 11%	Disabled students: 1%

2 bars; bands, concerts and many plays in the Auditorium (cap 250); frequent club nights. Fortnightly newsletter, termly mag; 2 libraries (48,000 volumes); 15 computers; chapel with famous organ. Sports fields (15 acres shared with <u>Queens'</u>) ¾ mile; some sports on site. All students live in; *good* rooms, most en-suite with phone and internet connections, *good* self-catering. Doctor and nurse; *good* JCR welfare; free rape alarms and taxis for the stranded; financial tutor and various funds and scholarships; *excellent* disabled access.

FAMOUS ALUMNI:
Adrian Davies (Welsh rugby); Charles Hart (lyricist); Gary Sinyor (film director).

❛Newnham college, Cambridge contains the second-longest corridor in Europe.❜

❝The official name of Jesus College, Cambridge, is the College of the Blessed Virgin Mary, Saint John the Evangelist and the Glorious Virgin Saint Radegund. ❞

St Catharine's College, Cambridge

▼ ● *The College is part of <u>University of Cambridge</u> and students are entitled to use its facilities.*

St Catharine's College, Cambridge, CB2 1RL.
Tel: (01223) 338300. Fax: (01223) 338340.
Junior Common Room, St Catharine's College, Cambridge, CB2 1Rl. Tel: (01223) 338300.
Web site: http://www.caths.cam.ac.uk

Catz, as it's known, is at the beginning (or the end) of King's Parade and was founded in 1473. Its buildings bear witness to the many centuries since, including the last 50 years. *There's a strong sporting tradition, but non-jocks will not feel excluded. Political agitation is limited to campaigning for a new ironing board. Catz is conveniently close to most major facilities.*

60% ♂♂♂♂♂♂♀♀♀♀ 40%

Sex ratio(M:F): 60%:40%	Founded: 1473
Full time u'grads: 422	Postgrads: 130
Private school: 40%	Mature students: 1%
Overseas students: 8%	Disabled students: 1%

Bar (which makes c£2,000 a week - admin concerned); bops every 3 weeks; The Octagon (theatre, cap 150) and chapel (100) used for concerts; biennial ball. Fortnightly newsletter. 2 libraries (40,740 books); 20+ computers; record library; CofE chapel. Sports fields (3 acres) ¾ mile; only astroturf pitch in a Cambridge college. All students live in (all 2nd years in the octagonal St Chad's building); eat in dining halls; *self-catering very limited.* Nurse; sick bay. 5 rooms for wheelchair users; *good* access; some financial support; prizes.

FAMOUS ALUMNI:
Morwenna Banks ('Absolutely' comedian); Peter Boizot (founded Pizza Express); Howard Brenton (playwright); Kevin Greening (Radio 1 DJ); Sir Peter Hall (director); Malcolm Lowry (writer); Ian McKellen (actor); Jeremy Paxman (BBC newscaster); Steve Punt (*cat's-bum-mouthed* comedian).

> ❛The Trinity Foot Beagles at Cambridge kill hares. The Trinity Foot Bagels, however, smear each other with cream cheese.❜

•••

St John's College, Cambridge

▼▼ ● *The College is part of <u>University of Cambridge</u> and students are entitled to use its facilities.*
St John's College, Cambridge, CB2 1TP.
Tel: (01223) 338685.
Junior Combination Room, St John's College, Cambridge, CB2 1TP. Tel: (01223) 338600.
Web site: http://www.joh.cam.ac.uk

St John's College, 200 yards from King's Parade, is the home of the Bridge of Sighs, a tourist Mecca. It's one of the 'River Colleges' - old, large and set in *majestic* grounds. Its courts *harmonise tunefully (as does the famous choir), until, that is, you reach the Cripps Building, which looks as bad as it sounds. There's a posh, sporty stereotype but it's not much more representative than anywhere else. The size and wealth of the place means there's a niche for everyone and usually funds to do things but the bar still has more pulling power than Geri Spice.*

63% ♂♂♂♂♂♂♀♀♀♀ **37%**

Sex ratio(M:F): 63%:37%	**Founded: 1511**
Full time u'grads: 535	**Postgrads: 262**
Private school: 43%	**Mature students: 2%**
Overseas students: 8%	**Disabled students: 2%**

Bar; Pythagoras Building (theatre); art rooms; Palmerston Room (cap 350) for bands; Old Music Room (100) for concerts; Boiler Room (120) for fortnightly bops; annual ball. Weekly JCR newsletter and twice termly 'Cripptic' magazine; Sky TV. 2 libraries (60,000 books); 40 computers; *large cathedral-like* CofE chapel. *Large* on-site sports hall, *superb* hockey club and *extensive* sports fields 200 yards away; success in rowing. Everyone lives in or in hostels; *good* self catering. Nurse; *very good* disabled access and provisions. *Excellent* financial support, grants and scholarships (*well, they can afford it*).

FAMOUS ALUMNI:
Douglas Adams (author, 'Hitch Hiker's Guide to the Galaxy'); Rob Andrew (rugby player); Mike Brearley (cricketer); Thomas Clarkson, William Wilberforce (anti-slavery campaigners); Derek Jacobi (actor); Lord Palmerston (PM); William Wordsworth (poet).

Selwyn College, Cambridge

- **The College is part of <u>University of Cambridge</u> and students are entitled to use its facilities.**

Selwyn College, Cambridge, CB3 9DQ. Tel: (01223) 335896.
Fax: (01223) 331720. E-mail: admissions@sel.cam.ac.uk
JCR Society, Selwyn College, Cambridge, CB3 9DQ.
Tel: (01223) 335846.
Web site: http://www.sel.cam.ac.uk

Selwyn College is on the outskirts of Cambridge, 1/2 mile from King's Parade, adjacent to the University Arts lecture halls and <u>Newnham</u>. Old Court - the focal point of the College - is *an attractive* example of neo-gothic Victorian architecture. A more recent addition, the Cripps Building has won an award, *but not from* push. *Selwyn is some distance from other colleges, which doesn't always encourage involvement in University activities. However, students are easy going, and there's a fun, tolerant atmosphere.*

58% ♂♂♂♂♂♂ ♀♀♀♀ **42%**

Sex ratio(M:F): 58%:42%	Founded: 1882
Full time u'grads: 370	Postgrads: 150
Private school: 40%	Mature students: 2%
Overseas students: 5%	Disabled students: 1%

3 bars (2 for events only); theatre and 2-3 bops a term in Selwyn Diamond (cap 175), also live music and in Main Hall (200) and JCR (100); alternate May balls and Snowball at Xmas. *Excellent* college mag 'Kiwi'; library (35,000 books); 16 computers; CofE chapel. Sports facilities 1/4 mile, shared with other colleges; *netball and women's football strong.* All years live in; *very limited* self catering; 3 formals a week (non-compulsory). Nurse; sickbay; hardship fund, scholarships, prizes; free rape alarms; parenting; *some disabled facilities.*

FAMOUS ALUMNI:
Clive Anderson (TV host and lawyer); John Gummer MP (Con); Simon Hughes MP (Lib Dem); Hugh Laurie (comedy actor); Malcolm Muggeridge (journalist); Rob(ert) Newman (comedian, novelist).

> ‘Oliver Cromwell's skull is buried in the ante-chapel of Sidney Sussex, Cambridge, and when the fellows toast the Queen, they draw a curtain across his portrait.’

Sidney Sussex College, Cambridge

● *The College is part of <u>University of Cambridge</u> and students are entitled to use its facilities.*
Sidney Sussex College, Cambridge, CB2 3HU.
Tel: (01223) 338872. Fax: (01223) 338884.
Students' Union, Sidney Sussex College, CB2 3HU.
Web site: http://www.sid.cam.ac.uk

Behind the dreaming spires of Sidney Sussex's 16th century buildings there lurks red brick. The College is central (200 yards from King's Parade; its proximity to the supermarket has led to the nickname Sidney Sainsbury's), small, and *everyone's familiar. It has some of the best sports grounds in Cambridge and one of the most active JCRs with considerable say in the running of the College. Sidney students also venture forth into the University, especially for drama and Rag, and academic standards are also high.*

56% ♂♂♂♂♂♂ ♀♀♀♀ 44%	
Sex ratio(M:F): 56%:44%	**Founded: 1596**
Full time u'grads: 319	**Postgrads: 130**
Private school: 50%	**Mature students: 3%**
Overseas students: 8%	**Disabled students: 3%**

The only student-run bar in Cambridge (cap 175) is used for fortnightly bops; Knox Shaw Room (40 seated); biennial ball. College mags: 'Sid News', 'El Sid', Yearbook and their own Rag mag. Library (40,000 books); 36 computers; chapel. Sports fields (22 acres) 1½ miles; *standards OK, considering size.* Majority of students live in, with most 2nd years in College-owned housing; eat in dining hall (food *improving*, veggie option); *adequate self-catering.* Nurse; hardship fund, bursaries, book grants, prizes; 1 room for a disabled student, some lifts.

FAMOUS ALUMNI:
Asa Briggs (historian); Oliver Cromwell (Lord Protector); Lord Owen (ex SDP leader); Carol Vorderman (mathematician and sex symbol).

Trinity College, Cambridge

● *The College is part of <u>University of Cambridge</u> and students are entitled to use its facilities.*
Trinity College, Cambridge, CB2 1TQ. Tel: (01223) 338400.
Fax: (01223) 338584.
Students' Union, Trinity College, Cambridge, CB2 1TQ.
Tel: (01223) 338410.

Trinity is Cambridge's largest College, situated a hop, skip and jump from King's Parade. *It's grand and imposing,* with a *prestigious* history. *Trinity is big enough for all individuals to find somewhere to fit in but it appears to have adapted to a changing society less well than some other colleges, with state school and female representation low even by Cambridge standards. This isn't for want of trying, but it's hard to shake off a reputation. The flip side is that Trinity's so rich, less well-off students will always be assured of some level of assistance. There's a strong academic reputation, especially in sciences.*

68% ♂♂♂♂♂♂♂ ♀♀♀ 32%	
Sex ratio(M:F): 68%:32%	Founded: 1546
Full time u'grads: 650	Postgrads: 300
Private school: 55%	Mature students: 3%
Overseas students: 10%	Disabled students: 2%

Bar; Theatre (cap 150), Chapel (200) and Combination Room (100) for live music (*prestigious* choir) and sweaty fortnightly bops in Wolfson Party Room (200); biggest annual Oxbridge ball (2,000 tickets). Termly mag; SU newsletter. 2 libraries (300,000 books); 60 computers; CofE chapel; 2 chaplains; charity fund-raising. *Extensive* sports fields ½ mile from College; success in most rowing, rugby, hockey. Everyone lives in; rooms vary (attics with oak beams, grand rooms with high ceilings, modern with en suite facilities); mixed sex couples can choose to share; eat in dining hall (optional formal dinner every night) or in cheap buttery. Nurse; *generous financial support;* rooms for wheelchair access.

FAMOUS ALUMNI:
Lord Byron (*mad, bad* poet); Prince Charles; Lord Hurd (former Foreign Secretary); Lord Macaulay (historian); Vladimir Nabokov (writer); Isaac Newton (scientist); Enoch Powell (ex-MP); Bertrand Russell, Ludwig Wittgenstein (philosophers); Tennyson (less mad poet); Lord Whitelaw.

• •

Trinity Hall, Cambridge

▼ ● *The College is part of <u>University of Cambridge</u> and students are entitled to use its facilities.*
▼ Trinity Hall, University of Cambridge, Cambridge, CB2 1TJ.
Tel: (01223) 337535. Fax: (01223) 337537.
E-mail: admissions@trinhall.cam.ac.uk
Junior Common Room, Trinity Hall, Cambridge, CB2 1TJ.
Tel: (01223) 332534.
Web site: http://www.trinhall.cam.ac.uk

'Tit Hall', as Trinity Hall is widely (*but not abusively*) known, is a 'River' college, 200 yards from King's Parade in the centre of town, but away from the shops. It's the 4th smallest - *nice and intimate (ie short on privacy)* - with a Georgian courtyard and 17th century buildings and shouldn't be confused with its larger, richer neighbour, <u>Trinity College</u>. *It's a friendly place*

where tedious academic pursuits don't get in the way of drinking and messing about in boats.

Sex ratio(M:F): 50%:50%	Founded: 1350
Full time u'grads: 340	Postgrads: 150
Private school: 46%	Mature students: 2%
Overseas students: 8%	Disabled students: 1%

Bar; lecture theatre for drama and live music (cap 270); indie and dance bands and fortnightly Global nights with London DJs. 'New Moon', 'Titler' college mags, weekly newsletter; *active* Rag. 2 libraries (80,000 books); 12 computers; CofE chapel. Sports fields (3 acres) 1 mile away; *quite 'boaty' reputation*. All live in; accommodation split between college and sites on Huntingdon Road, 1 mile away. Nurse; hardship fund, book loans and scholarships.

FAMOUS ALUMNI:
Lord Howe (former Cabinet Minister); Nicholas Hytner (theatre/ film director); Donald Maclean (spy); JB Priestley (writer); Tony Slattery (*chunky* comedian); Terry Waite (former hostage).

● ●

▶▶ Canterbury

see University of Kent at Canterbury

● ●

▶▶ Canterbury Christ Church College

see Other Institutions

● ●

Cardiff, University of Wales

● The College is part of <u>University of Wales</u>.
Cardiff University, PO Box 921, Cardiff, CF1 3XQ. Tel: (01222) 874000. Prospectus requests: (01222) 874899.
Fax: (01222) 874457. E-mail: prospectus@cf.ac.uk
Cardiff University Students' Union, Park Place, Cardiff, CF1 3QN. Tel: (01222) 781400. Fax: (01222) 781435.
E-mail: studentsunion@cf.ac.uk

General

Cardiff, over the Channel from Bristol, is Wales's largest city and, since 1955, its capital. Around the northern outskirts is industry and housing, built with the riches from the coal mines. Nearer Cardiff's centre, splendid Victorian and Georgian buildings are *thoughtfully* interspersed with greenery. *Amid this elegance* - the museums and buildings of civic significance

- are the University's buildings, *very attractive* and mostly typical of the *tasteful* local white and grey stone architecture. Some are more modern, but still *very pleasant* with gardens and walkways between. Ornate gates and doorways abound, all clean and quiet despite being at the city's heart.

49% ♂♂♂♂♂♀♀♀♀♀ 51%

Sex ratio(M:F): 49%:51%	Founded: 1883
Full time u'grads: 11,468	Part time: 0
Postgrads: 2,404	Non-degree: 0
Ave course: 3yrs	Ethnic: n/a
Private school: n/a	Flunk rate: n/a
Mature students: 16%	Overseas students: 11%
Disabled students: 3%	Staff/student ratio: 1:12
Clearing: 3%	

ATMOSPHERE:
Cardiff is a vibrant, action-packed city with vibrant, action-packed students who party hard and don't care who gets caught in the headlights. There are plenty of ways of passing one's days with a wide range of facilities and activities. The Students' Union spends more time being a successful multi-million pound company than a political fighting force.

THE CITY:
- Population: 272,600 ● London: 143miles
- Bristol: 30miles ● Swansea: 40miles

The University along with the civic buildings, dominates the city centre, most of which is closed to cars. But the traffic flows through unfussed and the people leave little litter. It's just 5 miles into the South Wales countryside. As the major urban centre for the whole of Wales, Cardiff is well kitted out: shopping malls and supermarkets; banks and book shops (including 2nd hand); late-night shopping and many provisions designed for the tourists, including lots of museums, galleries (National Museum of Wales, Turner House Gallery, Welsh Industrial & Maritime Museum, etc) and the Castle ($\frac{1}{2}$ Roman, $\frac{1}{2}$ Norman, $\frac{1}{2}$ medieval, $\frac{1}{2}$ mathematical impossibility).

TRAVEL:
Trains: Direct trains from Cardiff Central: London (£22.45); Bristol (£4.35); Manchester (£24.55) and so on.
Coaches: National Express to most places: London (£16), Bristol (£5.50) and all over.
Car: Parts of the city centre are for pedestrians only. To get to Cardiff, there's the M4, A470 and A48. A car's not really necessary since the invention of feet. Nice for the countryside, though.
Air: Cardiff International Airport has flights to the Channel Islands, Ireland, and even the USA, as well as inland trips.
Hitching: The A48's a bonus - only 5 mins walk from the campus - and the Welsh are willing.
Local: Local bus services run every 20-30 mins all round town. They're reliable with an average trip costing 50p.
Taxis: Lots of firms will happily extort about £1.60 for the privilege of a ride it'd take 10 mins to walk.
Bicycles: Everything's within cycling distance and there are

sheds at all the halls. *Bikes have been known to ride off by themselves, though.*

LIBRARIES & COMPUTERS:
- Books: 1,000,000 ● Study places: 2,223
- Computer workstations: 2,500

There are 10 libraries in all but only 3 main ones: the Arts & Social Science Library, the Aberconway Library and the Science Library. Co-stars: Law and Architecture. 24hr access to some computer labs.

CAREER PROSPECTS:
- Careers Service ● No of staff: 7full
- Unemployed after 6mths (1996): 6%

SPECIAL FEATURES:
● 34% of Cardiff students are from Wales, but less than 5% are Welsh-speaking. There is provision for Welsh-speaking study, but it has to be arranged separately.

FAMOUS ALUMNI:
Richie Edwards (missing manic); Arwel Hughes (conductor); Karl Hyde, Rick Smith (Underworld); Lord Jenkins (Lib Dem); Neil and Glenys Kinnock (Europe's First Couple); Mark Lamarr (*cheeky cockney bin-man*); Sian Lloyd (weatherperson); Philip Madoc (actor); Sian Philips (actress); Denise Rubens (Booker prize winner); Tim Sebastian (BBC reporter).

FURTHER INFO:
Undergraduate prospectus, video and web sites (http://www.cf.ac.uk and http://www.cf.ac.uk/uwcc/suon).

entertainment

THE CITY:
- Price of a pint of beer: £1.80 ● Glass of wine: £1.45

Cinemas: (6) 5 mainstreamers and the Chapter Arts Centre (*showing more arty alternative flicks and selling 80 different bottled beers*).

Theatres: Cardiff has 4 theatres. There's the Chapter Arts Centre (which also has a dance studio, exhibition centres and so on). There's also the New Theatre (home of the Welsh National Opera) and the Sherman Theatre (see below). Everything available from panto to Pinter.

Pubs: *Some excellent boozers.* push*plugs: Clancey's (Irish, good fun); Rat & Carrot; The Woodville Arms (aka the Woody - very studenty); Sam's Bar; Macintosh (skittles in the summer). One or two tacky theme pubs aren't worth the effort and the docks area is best avoided by anything resembling a student.*

Clubs/discos: *There's a high proportion of naff flesh-arcades but despite this* push*plugs go to: Ibiza Foam Night at the Astoria (very popular Balearic madness); Slam at Zeus; Love Shack at the Astoria (free with NUS card); Spectrum (jazz/soul) and Rock Inferno at Club Ifor Bach. Tuesday night tends to be student night.*

Music venues: Really big bands include the International Arena on their tours (Cardiff Arms Park is currently closed) but for more down-to-earth tunes there's the Astoria, St David's Hall, FBI (jazz), Gassy Jacks (indie) and plenty more.

Eating out: *You want, you got, including the obligatory post-*

club kebab at 4am. **push**plugs: *Ethnic Deli (£10 for 5 dishes); Las Iguanas & Old Orleans (Tex-Mex); Ramon's (greasy spoon); The Pear Tree (Cathays community centre); Tarus (steakhouse).*

UNIVERSITY:
● Price of a pint of beer: £1.40 ● Glass of wine: £1.15
The Union has some of the best facilities in the country. A sackful of fun bursts every week during term time with frequent clubs and socs bashes and bops, Rag romps and occasional cabaret. The Union accounts for 1% of annual national Red Bull sales and can also afford to book just about any venue around the city.
Bars: (22) Each residential hall has its own bar and there are 6 in the Union, the most popular of which is the stained-glass enhanced, oak-beamed Tafarn.
Theatre and film: The Act One drama group puts on 4 or 5 productions annually. One, *usually culty*, film is shown per week.
Clubs/discos: There are 4 regular, *mainstream* club nights, in Terminal 396 (cap 1,600) every week. *More sophisticated party people have the occasional pleasure of* guest DJs such as Roni Size and Danny Rampling.
Music venues: The Great Hall (1,500) is the main live auditorium but the railway-themed Junction in Terminal 396 (1,600) also does its bit. *Between them they can pull in big-league acts to make most SUs go pale green*, recent examples being Beck, Placebo, Mansun, Kula Shaker, Gene, the Chemical Brothers, Ash and Catatonia. Finistere (320) puts on *lower-key* events.
Cabaret: Fortnightly cheeriness from, recently, Al Murray and the Bastard Son of Tommy Cooper.
Food: During the day the university refectories serve full meals and snacks (pay-as-you-eat) and the various snack bars in the Union *do a fine but not exactly cheap* spread of filled rolls, baked spuds and stuff.
Other: Several balls, culminating in the June Ultimate event.

social & political
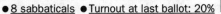

CARDIFF UNIVERSITY STUDENTS' UNION:

● 8 sabbaticals ● Turnout at last ballot: 20%
● NUS member
This Union's plat du jour is commercial rather than political but the emphasis has been shifting in recent years. The Union has a Welsh language policy and all signs and many publications are bilingual. Every year there's a Welsh Awareness Week (*maybe for people who think they're actually in Belgium*).

SU FACILITIES:
Ready, steady, go... 9 bars, 5 cafeterias and sandwich bars, minibus hire, printing service and photocopying, 2 shops (general, food, new and 2nd-hand books and stationery), Midlands & Lloyds Bank, payphones, phone messaging service, photobooth, video games and vending machines, juke box, 8 pool tables, 4 snooker tables, launderette, study rooms, tv lounges, function rooms, conference hall, customised nightclub, Endsleigh Insurance and probably a small sub-continent in the basement.

CLUBS (NON SPORTING):

Anglican; Arthurian; Bellringing; Brazilian; Canadian; Chinese; Clubbing; Debating; European; Film; French; Friends of Bosnia; Friends of Kurdistan; Handbell Ringing; Hindu; Hispanic; Iranian; Italian; Japanese; Jazz Funk; Journalism; Kenyan; Korean; Libyan; Links; Live Role Play; Liverpool Supporters; Malaysian; Meditation; Methodist; Motorcycle; North America; Pabio; Pagan; Paintball; Pakistani; Sikh & Punjabi; Sri Lankan; Tai Chi; Taiwanese; Welsh History; World Development.

OTHER ORGANISATIONS:

The Union publishes the multiple award-winning newspaper 'Gair Rhydd' which is distributed to other colleges in Cardiff and the radio station Express FM broadcasts to the SU in the afternoons. The Cardiff charity Rag (Caerdydd) raised over £20,000 last year with the aid of the usual kidnapping pranks and Student Community Action performs many a good deed locally, *helping to ease occasionally frayed town/gown relations.* It has a full-time organiser and a high level of involvement.

RELIGIOUS:

Cardiff has 2 cathedrals (Anglican and Catholic) and churches of most sorts, including Church of Scotland, Orthodox, Methodist, Quaker, United Reform. There are also places of worship for Muslims, Jews, Hindus, Sikhs and Buddhists.

PAID WORK:

Cardiff, particularly during the tourist season, has lots of opportunities for casual cash raising. Unfortunately, it also has more than lots of students going for them.

sports

● <u>Recent successes: cricket</u>

The level of involvement was high even before they got their spanking new sports hall, partly because the facilities were pretty good anyway. Student sports are run by the SU Athletic Union.

SPORTS FACILITIES:

In 4 sports centres, there are 33 acres of playing fields for all the usual field games and a small athletics track, floodlit artificial pitch, tennis and squash courts. Astroturf for 99. Refurbished indoor facilities at Talybont, one of the residential complexes (about 1½ miles from the main campus), include 2 sports halls, a fitness studio, free weights room and 5-a-side soccer pitch. The Union also has further facilities for table-tennis, squash, fencing, darts, snooker and pool. Expert advice, including fitness assessment, is usually to hand. Other facilities, such as a swimming pool, shooting range, sailing centre and boat house are hired locally by the University. The local area also adds an ice rink, ski slope, bowling green and the mountains of the surrounding countryside. For water sports, there are the River Taff, the sea (the Bristol Channel) and a lake - a fair choice. *Facilities are such that a full body work-out can be arranged for disabled students.*

SPORTING CLUBS:

Aerobics; Aikido; American Football; Caving; Hang-Gliding; Korfball; Kung Fu; Lacrosse; Mountain Bike; Rifle; Roller Skating; Snooker; Softball; Surf; Trampoline; Waterpolo; Water-Ski; Windsurfing; Yoga.

ATTRACTIONS:

There's also round ball action at Ninian Park (the National Stadium is currently being redeveloped for the Rugby World

Cup in 99), Glamorgan Cricket Club at Sophia Gardens and the Cardiff Devils ice hockey team.

accommodation

IN COLLEGE:
- Catered: 6% ● Cost: £54-62(33wks)
- Self-catering: 32% ● Cost: £39-47(39-52wks)

Availability: All 1st years are guaranteed accommodation in halls, after which only about 14% of students live in. There are 11 halls (including the all-female Aberdare) within a mile of campus and 7 more up to 2 miles away. *The standard's pretty good*, especially in the *flash* new halls with en suite facilities. £40m has been spent on accommodation in the last 6 years. Nobody needs to share, *and we should bloomin' well hope not.*
Car parking: There's limited parking and cars need permits.

EXTERNALLY:
- Ave rent: £40

Availability: *The search is most fruitful on the north side of town* (eg the Cathays student ghetto and Roath) in shared houses and flats. *Splott also looks damn good as an address.* push *recommends avoiding Grange Town and nearby Riverside.*
Housing help: The University operates an Accommodation Office with 2 full-time staff who provide vacancy and landlord lists. They also help students get legal advice.

welfare

SERVICES:
- Creche ● Lesbian & Gay Society
- Mature SA ● Overseas SA ● Postgrad SA ● Minibus
- Women's Officer ● Self-defence classes

The Dean of Students is in charge of the counselling service with 2 full- and 3 part-time staff, whom the Union supplements with its own welfare provision. The University also runs a Health Centre with 3 doctors and 3 nurses. Special provision is made for overseas students.
Disabled: *Access is pretty good all round but improvements could still be made in the SU and halls of residence.* There's also a Dyslexia Resource Centre.

FINANCE:
- Ave debt: £1,350 ● Access fund: £287,580
- Successful applications (1997): 843

The Oldfield Davies Trust can help women with health problems and there are also short-term loans and small grants, usually limited to finalists.

> ❛ The grounds of Heriot-Watt University contain a disused ticket office, all that remains of Edinburgh's proposed underground train system. ❜

▶▶ Cardiff Institute
see Other Institutions

▶▶ Caythorpe
see De Montfort University

▶▶ CCAT
see Anglia Polytechnic University

University of Central England

● *Formerly Birmingham Polytechnic*
University of Central England, Perry Barr, Birmingham, B42
2SU. Tel: (0121) 331 5000. E-mail: recruitment@uce.ac.uk
Students' Union, University of Central England, Perry Barr,
Birmingham, B42 2SU. Tel: (0121) 331 6801.
Fax: (0121) 331 6802.

General

Perry Barr is an area of Birmingham 3 miles to the north of the
centre. UCE's main site is planted here, but fewer than ½ the
students are here. There are 9 sites in all, most around the
city centre but one out on a limb at Bournville. Sites differ in
atmosphere and looks as much as the Hilton and a Happy
Eater - from the *elegant* Victorian gothic College of Art in
Margaret Street to the brown brick and dark glass slab at Perry
Barr. *Over the last few years, UCE has undergone the kind of
face-lift that would make Cher jealous.*

43% ♂♂♂♂♂♀♀♀♀♀ 57%	
Sex ratio(M:F): 43%:57%	Founded: 1971
Full time u'grads: 10,111	Part time: 9,014
Postgrads: 3,474	Non-degree: 1,284
Ave course: 3yrs	Ethnic: 23%
Private school: n/a	Flunk rate: n/a
Mature students: 61%	Overseas students: 4.7%
Disabled students: 6.4%	Staff/student ratio: 1:14
Clearing: 4.2%	

ATMOSPHERE:
*The University offers many FE courses (especially NVQs) and
free part-time courses to the unemployed, so the social mix
isn't just the usual array of undergrads. As for University
facilities, there's the Union services and... okay, so they're*

> **A group of 45 students at Leeds Metropolitan University claims to be the most unlucky Lottery syndicate ever after paying out £2,880 and winning nothing.**

limited, but that just broadens students' horizons. Doesn't it? Maybe not, but it does mean they have to get out and explore their city.

THE SITES:

Perry Barr: (3,780 students - most courses) *Despite being the main site, it isn't all that big and its students are very business-like.* Perry Barr itself is a fairly scruffy, grubby part of the city (although the campus itself is a large enough and pleasant enough island). Its best features are a good number of local shops, a greyhound stadium (opposite the campus) and a station to get you out of there.

Westbourne Rd/Edgbaston: (2,000 students - education and nursing) 6 miles from Perry Bar, *one of the main benefits of this site seems to be the crammed Crow Bar, which attracts students from all over.*

Bournville: (art & design) 4 miles from the centre, near the choccy factory, Bournville is one of 4 sites housing art & design courses, and *unsurprisingly, the students here are arty and exciting.*

Others: Gosta Green (art & design), Margaret St (art & design), the Birmingham Conservatoire (music) and the Jewellery School in the city's Jewellery Quarter *which is turning touristy.*

THE CITY: see University of Birmingham

TRAVEL: see University of Birmingham

LIBRARIES & COMPUTERS:
- Books: 300,000 ● Study places: 934
- Computer workstations: 900

The main Kenrick Library is at Perry Barr with 7 specialist libraries on other sites for the courses based there. *Students are happy with the library except when they all have to fight over the same book.* There are computer rooms at each faculty site (IBMs and Macs), all linked through 1 network.

CAREER PROSPECTS:
- Careers Service ● No of staff: 4full/2part
- Unemployed after 6mths (1996): 7.4%

FAMOUS ALUMNI:
Apache Indian (Bhangramuffin); Zoe Ball (TV & Radio new ladette); Alfred Bestall (Rupert Bear's creator); Betty Jackson (fashion designer); Larry (cartoonist); Jas Mann (Babylon Zoo); Judy Simpson (Nightshade in 'Gladiators').

FURTHER INFO:
Prospectuses for undergrads, postgrads and part timers, faculty videos and a web site (http://www.uce.ac.uk).

entertainment

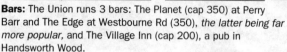

CITY: see <u>University of Birmingham</u>

UNIVERSITY:
● <u>Price of a pint of beer: £1.40</u> ● <u>Glass of wine: £1.30</u>

Bars: The Union runs 3 bars: The Planet (cap 350) at Perry Barr and The Edge at Westbourne Rd (350), *the latter being far more popular,* and The Village Inn (cap 200), a pub in Handsworth Wood.

Cinemas: The film club shows recent hits, world cinema and cult faves twice a week.

Clubs/discos/music venues: There are 2 club nights a week at Perry Barr, Toons (indie/dance) on Fridays being popular, as well as Sports Night, when everyone gathers at the Edge bar and heads to XLS nightclub in town. Only local/student live bands appear.

Cabaret: Fortnightly foppery from fools such as Martin BigPig, Brendon Burns and Adam Bloom.

Food: Scholars in the SU offers, among other *rudimentary rations,* an all-day breakfast for £1.25. There are eateries at all sites except Margaret Street

Others: 2 sports balls a year, various faculty/society events and Sunday pub quizzes.

social & political

UNIVERSITY OF CENTRAL ENGLAND STUDENTS' UNION:
● <u>9 sabbaticals</u> ● <u>Turnout at last ballot: 6.5%</u>
● <u>NUS member</u>

UCESU was the 1st student union to become a limited company, with the sabbaticals as directors. So far this has failed to impress the punters, as the voting figures indicate. Split sites, limited facilities and downright disorganisation don't help to foster a spirit of cohesion either. Racial issues do motivate a few to some kind of political awareness as does student funding.

SU FACILITIES:
The Union has facilities on 5 sites. At the Union's main centre at Perry Barr, there's a cheap bar, shop, advice centre, Endsleigh Insurance office, games machines, photobooth and photocopier. There's also a NatWest bank.

CLUBS (NON SPORTING):
Campaign For Free Education; Chinese; Live Music; Sikh.

OTHER ORGANISATIONS:
'DeUCE' is the student magazine, published by the Union. The charity Rag has come back to life, after a hiatus. The Community Action Group is involved in projects to help the homeless and *paint pictures on primary school walls.*

> ❝University of Kent Radio began as a pirate station in 1967, broadcasting through the radiators in Rutherford College.❞

RELIGIOUS:
- <u>6 chaplains</u>

4 Christian and 2 Jewish chaplains and a Muslim prayer room.

sports

- <u>Recent successes: jiu jitsu, rugby</u>

Having virtually no facilities of its own, unsurprisingly, the University isn't going to be taking on the big boys and girls and winning hands down. Unlike many universities, Wednesday afternoons aren't kept free for sporting endeavours, which gives them even less of a chance. But the Union has a student sports sabbatical, whose job it is to spend a large proportion of the Union's annual budget hiring local facilities so students can actually take part in competitions. Charges for facilities vary between 30p and £2.

SPORTING CLUBS:
Aerobics; Jiu Jitsu; Kick Boxing; Snowboarding; Surf; Tennis; Thai Boxing.

ATTRACTIONS: see <u>University of Birmingham</u>

accommodation

IN COLLEGE:
- <u>Catered: 1%</u> ● <u>Cost: £55(40wks)</u>
- <u>Self-catering: 14%</u> ● <u>Cost: £36-55(40wks)</u>

Availability: The self-catering halls are based at the Westbourne Road site and in The Coppice in Perry Barr. Overseas students get special preference at Cambrian Hall in the city centre. There's also a 'student village' with 432 study bedrooms at Perry Barr and university-leased houses and flats for 850 students.
Car parking: Easy enough, *but a car isn't really necessary.*

EXTERNALLY: see <u>University of Birmingham</u>
Housing help: The Accommodation Service runs the head tenancy scheme and there's a register of approved private housing.

welfare

SERVICES:
- <u>Nursery</u> ● <u>Lesbian & Gay Society</u>
- <u>Mature SA</u> ● <u>Overseas SA</u> ● <u>Minibus</u>

There are 2 nurseries (1 at Westbourne Road and 1 at Perry Barr) for children aged 12 months to 5 years. The University's Student Services Section provides 4 counsellors for all kinds of problems except medical ones. These are dealt with by nurses based on 3 of the sites or by the usual NHS practices.
Disabled: A Disability Sevices Advisor has made improvements to access. There's also a student services co-ordinator, for students with special needs, and library facilities for sight- and hearing-impaired students. Part-time Union executive posts are planned for 98-99 for Disability Action, International Student and Equal Opportunity Officers.

FINANCE:
- <u>Ave debt: £1,400</u> ● <u>Access fund: £203,000</u>
- <u>Successful applications (1997): 500</u>

UCE has its own non-Government Access Fund and there are Chaplaincy and Hardship Funds.

University of Central Lancashire

▼ ● *Formerly Preston Polytechnic, Lancashire Polytechnic*
University of Central Lancashire, Preston, PR1 2HE.
Tel: (01772) 892400. Fax: (01772) 892935.
E-mail: enquiries@uclan.ac.uk
University of Central Lancashire Students' Union, University of
Central Lancashire, Fylde Road, Preston, PR1 2TQ.
Tel: (01772) 513200. Fax: (01772) 908553.
E-mail: s.u.soc@uclan.ac.uk

General

Preston on the River Ribble is the 2nd largest town in
Lancashire and the county's administrative capital. It's
bigger than Lancaster, the county town, but not as big as
Blackpool, which illuminates England's north-west coast.
Preston is old (although the centre's been redeveloped)
and attractive with parks stuffed between some
interesting buildings and churches. The University is
almost in the very middle of Preston on a 38-acre campus
in 2 main blocks of buildings encompassing a variety of
modern styles (mostly red bricks, concrete and glass,
smart but about as remarkable as a balti in Birmingham)
with paved squares and a few outpost buildings. In the
midst of the campus, there are a few noteworthy features,
such as the Arts Centre - a converted church - and the SU
Building, a *stumpy* russet place with odd angles and a
light pyramid on top. There's a *strange fish tank-like*
structure *jutting out* at the front of the main building.
Maybe it's a fish tank.

43% ♂♂♂♂♀♀♀♀♀ **57%**

Sex ratio(M:F): 43%:57%	Founded: 1828
Full time u'grads: 11,581	Part time: 7,304
Postgrads: 409	Non-degree: 5,773
Ave course: 3yrs	Ethnic: 18%
Private school: n/a	Flunk rate: n/a
Mature students: 53%	Overseas students: 6%
Disabled students: 3%	Staff/student ratio: 1:18
Clearing: n/a	

ATMOSPHERE:
*The student body is a synthesis of the large number of mature
students who tend to knuckle down but not hang around and
their younger, thrusting colleagues who see everything as a
potential line on the ol' CV. Most courses include a sandwich
year, working for industry in a course-related field. A recent
survey indicated that 25% of students would not return to
Central Lancashire if they could choose again - on the other
hand, that's 75% who would.*

TOWN:
- Population: 147,109   ● London: 202miles
- Blackpool: 15miles   ● Manchester: 25miles

Granada TV awarded Preston the *staggering* accolade of being the '*best and cheapest shopping centre in Britain with a marvellous mixture of modern and old style shops and an excellent market hall*'. *And who are we to argue with the company that gave us Richard and Judy? It is true that the cost of living in Preston is low and the quality of life high.* Its long history goes further back than its boom time as a cotton town during the Industrial Revolution. It's been redeveloped in recent years, particularly the centre and the docks. Preston has 6 museums, *the least uninteresting being the exhibitions of local relevance at the Harris Museum.*

TRAVEL:
Trains: Preston Station, $\frac{1}{2}$ mile from the campus, runs direct trains to London (£28.40), Manchester (£6.55) and beyond.
Coaches: National Express services to, among other places, London (£18.50), Birmingham (£13.50).
Car: Preston is on the A6, A49, A59 and A677, and just off the M6, M55 and M61.
Hitching: *These main roads are the wheels on the hitcher's skateboard. Easy routes to London, Manchester or Glasgow.*
Local: Local buses keep to an exact fare (no change given) system. Discounted Rambler tickets (anywhere in town, £5.20/week) are available.
Taxis: *Cheap enough even for students, occasionally.*
Bicycles: *There's many a hump and bump in Preston and there's rain and poor bike parking facilities. Nevertheless, bikes are popular for getting round the campus.*

LIBRARIES & COMPUTERS:
- Books: 350,000   ● Study places: 928
- Computer workstations: 1,028

The library, centrally placed on campus, is one of the most modern buildings (built in 1979) and has, as well as books, 100,000 audio-visual items. A survey carried out by the University shows that 88% are satisfied with computer facilities, 35% with availability. *So, they're great when you can use them.*

CAREER PROSPECTS:
- Careers Service   ● No of staff: 3full/4part
- Unemployed after 6mths (1996): 15%

Another survey (*they do seem to like this survey lark, don't they?*) suggests that 80% are satisfied with the careers service.

FAMOUS ALUMNI:
Mark Beaumont (NME hack); Joe Lydon (rugby league); Phil MacIntyre (pop promoter); Tjinder Singh, Ben Ayres (Cornershop).

❝Text in italics is PUSH's point of view – take it or leave it.❞

FURTHER INFO:
Prospectuses for undergrads, part-timers and postgrads, and a web site (http://www.uclan.ac.uk).

entertainment

TOWN:
● Price of a pint of beer: £1.60 ● Glass of wine: £1.30

Pubs: *Pubs as a whole are student-friendly, or at least tolerant, especially those near the University.* pushplugs: *The Variety; The Adelphi; The Ship.*

Cinemas: (2) 17 screens between them. The UCI does a student discount.

Theatres: The Charter Theatre, within 15mins' walk of the campus, *offers a fairly straightforward bill of Shakespeare 'n' stuff.*

Clubs/discos: *Most are too tacky for words. Well, no, 'tacky' will do.* pushplugs: *The Mill (alternative, free bus service); Squires, Tokyo Jo's (student nights Monday and Wednesdays respectively).*

Music venues: *The Guild Hall hosts anything to which you might wish to tap a toe (and plenty you wouldn't). The Adelphi is the indie HQ. A new event called Prest Fest is organised between the University and various local venues.*

Eating out: *Preston's culinary scene is varied and usually very cheap and there are plenty of ethnic eateries and burger bars to satisfy those post-midnight longings.* pushplugs: *Ali's Bengal; Tiggi's Pizzeria (50% student discount); Heathcoats (perfect for parents).*

UNIVERSITY: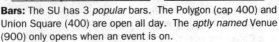
● Price of a pint of beer: £1.30 ● Glass of wine: £1.50

Bars: The SU has 3 *popular* bars. The Polygon (cap 400) and Union Square (400) are open all day. The *aptly named* Venue (900) only opens when an event is on.

Theatres: The Drama society sends a play to the Edinburgh Fringe every year.

Cinemas: 2 films a week, varying between mainstream new(*ish*) releases and theme weeks.

Clubs/discos/music venues: The Venue hosts club nights 3 or 4 times a week, the fortnightly Feel (garage/house), on Saturdays, *being the biggest thing around - in fact, 'The Observer' described it as the number one student club in the country, so don't be surprised if you see a load of journalists waving their hands in the air like they just don't have a clue.* Recent live acts include Cast, Coolio and Soul II Soul, and there's also a regular tribute band night, Timetrip.

Food: During the day students choose their chews in the University's 3 refectories, open all day, the SU's 3 eateries (Mr Nibbles for sarnies, the Polygon for pub lunch and Union Square for all-day breakfast) and local pubs.

social & political

UNIVERSITY OF CENTRAL LANCASHIRE STUDENTS' UNION:
● 5 sabbaticals ● Turnout at last ballot: 3%
● NUS member
The University's growth in numbers has rather outstripped its resources but the SU and the University are doing an OK

job, working together to deal with some of the fallout. Issues are more important than labels with environmental and racial concerns being particularly high on the agenda. Most students are more concerned with their own life-plans, though.

SU FACILITIES:
The modern SU Building has 3 bars, a cafeteria, sandwich shop, service restaurant, 4 minibuses for hire, printing service, 3 shops (selling stationery, sweets and general goods), Midland Bank and cashpoint, photocopying, photo booth, games, video and vending machines, pool tables and juke boxes and TV lounge.

CLUBS (NON SPORTING):
AISEC; Chinese; Computer; Film; Franglais; Hellenic; Juggling; Law; Rock and Thrash; Spanish; Transcendental Meditation.

OTHER ORGANISATIONS:
'Pluto' is the *better-than-average* SU tabloid (every fortnight) and other media goes on in an academic sort of way at the Journalism Department. The do-gooders of the student community group do good all over the place; priority is given to local charities.

RELIGIOUS:
● <u>1 chaplain</u>
The Multi-Faith Centre is there for all religions to do their thing. Locally, there's the Cathedral, churches and places of worship for Muslims, Hindus, Sikhs, Buddhists and Jews.

PAID WORK:
Although Preston's in the historically depressed North-West there's an abundance of pubs and restaurants hungry for part-time staff.

sports

● <u>Recent successes: golf, hockey, squash, and more</u>
The sports facilities are limited, but students make use of anything they can find locally and achieve a lot on a little, indeed the college has produced a number of BUSA champions recently.

SPORTS FACILITIES:
On campus, in the small sports centre, there's a sports hall, activities room, multigym and fitness area. £8m has been awarded from Lottery funds to develop a new complex 2 miles from campus. Preston adds goodies like tennis courts, a golf course and there's the Lake District nearby. Mobile phones are provided for dangerous sporting activities, *such as grenade-hurling and croquet.*

SPORTING CLUBS:
Aikido; Baseball; Handball; Kung Fu Hung Kuen; Rugby League; Snowboarding; Ten Pin Bowling; Windsurfing.

ATTRACTIONS:
Preston North End FC are the local soccer heroes and the town is also the home of the National Museum of Football.

accommodation

IN COLLEGE:
● <u>Self-catering: 13%</u> ● <u>Cost: £45-53(37wks)</u>
Availability: The University can house 50% of 1st years (which accounts for all who need it) but no others. The halls are on

campus, but there are also blocks of student flats 2 miles away, where 6 share a kitchen and bathroom. There are also 120 places in local houses owned by the University and rented to students, but, still, almost everything goes to 1st years. 1% of livers-in have to share.

Car parking: There is limited, permit-only parking (£36 per year).

EXTERNALLY:
- Ave rent: £35

Availability: *Preston is not pressed on too heavily to provide housing and students should find something adequate with the most moderate of hassle. Ashton and Broadgate are the most popular areas; Deepdale is the bit to avoid.*

Housing help: The University Accommodation Service has 13 full- and 1 part-time staff whose collective mission in life is to provide students with vacancy lists, bulletin boards, contract advice and rat'n'rising-damp checks of student housing.

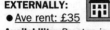

welfare

SERVICES:
- Creche ● Lesbian & Gay Society ● Mature SA
- Overseas SA ● Minibus ● Women's Officer
- Self-defence classes

Troubled students, they head for the SU Welfare Unit or the University Counselling Service's 9 counsellors (2 full- and 7 part-time). There are also 4 doctors and 2 nurses at the health service on campus.

Disabled: *Wheelchair access is no worse than most places, but facilities for hearing-impaired and, more particularly, sight-impaired students are good. The University became a member of NFAC (National Federation of Access Centres) as of 1997.*

FINANCE:
- Ave debt: £1,900 ● Access fund: £220,000
- Successful applications (1997): 630

There's also a Hardship Fund and postgraduate bursaries.

● ●

Central St Martins College of Art
see The London Institute

● ●

Charing Cross & Westminster Hospital
see Imperial College, London

● ●

Charlotte Mason
see Lancaster University

● ●

Chelsea College of Art
see The London Institute

● ●

Cheltenham & Gloucester College of Higher Education

Cheltenham & Gloucester College of Higher Education, PO Box 220, The Park, Cheltenham, Gloucestershire, GL50 2QF.
Tel: (01242) 532700. Fax: (01242) 256759.
E-mail: admissions@chelt.ac.uk
Cheltenham & Gloucester College Students' Union, PO Box 220, The Park, Cheltenham, Gloucestershire, GL50 2QF.
Tel: (01242) 532848. Fax: (01242) 261381.
E-mail: pksu@chelt.ac.uk

General

Cheltenham and Gloucester are 2 towns of similar size, of similar style (mostly elegant Regency stone, Gloucester less so) and similarly placed. They're less than 7 miles apart in the tumbling humps of Gloucestershire, the county placed beyond the end of the Bristol Channel, where it gives up being the Severn Estuary and resorts to being the not-so humble Severn River. Cheltenham and Gloucester are a college. The main site, the Park Campus, was originally a botanic and zoological garden, 1½ miles from Cheltenham town centre. On this urban island, there are *elderly* buildings, *elegant* grounds and an *extraordinary* garden. Among the tennis courts and the large pond where the ducks occasionally allow students to row, it's one of the few places in England where Wellingtonia trees can be found. They have very soft bark which can be punched or head-butted without fear of pain - *handy for students wandering home drunk.* This is 1 of 3 main sites, all of which are in Cheltenham and none are in Gloucester *which rather begs the question, why... oh never mind.*

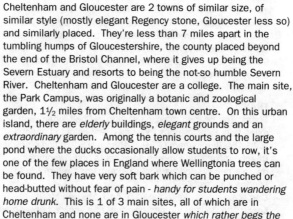

Sex ratio(M:F): 41%:59%	**Founded: 1990**
Full time u'grads: 4,413	**Part time: 702**
Postgrads: 366	**Non-degree: 1,238**
Ave course: 3/4yrs	**Ethnic: 12.4%**
Private school: n/a	**Flunk rate: 23%**
Mature students: 52%	**Overseas students: 1.7%**
Disabled students: 1.9%	**Staff/student ratio: 1:24**
Clearing: 13.5%	

ATMOSPHERE:
The separateness of the sites tends to create a slightly fragmented community, but each site is a fun place to be, full of keen, helpful and quite sporty people. Relations with the nice, Laura Ashley-clad folk of 'Chelters' are OK, because (1) the kids bring money with 'em and (2) the students know not to push it.

THE SITES:
Pittville: (art, design: 950) This *unfortunately named* site, 2.4

miles from the main Park Campus, has recently been expanded by adding a new media block (*which looks like a blue and white spaceship*) and some self-catering accommodation (274 places). *Being full of arty types*, there's a gallery and exhibition space.

Francis Close Hall/ Hardwick: (3000 – environment, sport, catering, geography, geology) 1.8 miles from Park Campus, FCH is *picturesque and classically academic-looking*. There's accommodation for 51 students and, because of the catering students, a training restaurant.

TOWN:
● Population: 107,300 ● London: 95miles
● Bristol: 40miles ● Birmingham: 43miles

Cheltenham is famous for 3 things: (1) its racecourse; (2) its spa; and, *ironically, since it's supposed to be clouded in secrecy* (3) GCHQ. The spa more than the spies were responsible for its growth in the early part of the 19th century into what is now a *very safe, Middle England* town with a *satisfactory* number of public amenities (*but certainly not a glut*). Among *the most serene* sights are the art gallery in the centre of town, the numerous parks and the Pittville Pump Rooms *where the water is brown and tastes disgusting* - although **push** is not sure whether we were drinking from the right outflow.

TRAVEL:
Trains: The nearest mainline station is Cheltenham Spa, 2 miles from Park Campus, offering direct links to London (£20.45), Birmingham (£7.90), Bristol (£5.20) and elsewhere.
Coaches: National Express, Marchants and Swanbrook operate coach services from Cheltenham; a return trip to London will cost £7.75.
Car: Main road links to the A10, A40, M5 and M40.
Local: The College runs its own free bus service between all the sites. *It's quite reliable and runs until 11.30.* Local buses take up the slack and run till midnight, but cost 40p from Park Campus to the town centre.
Bicycles: *Most students like to get the real feel of a wheel between their thighs.* The College offers a subsidy to students who want to buy bikes.

LIBRARIES & COMPUTERS:
● Books: 350,000 ● Study places: 955
● Computer workstations: 550
3 libraries - 1 at each site.

CAREER PROSPECTS:
● Careers Service ● No of staff: 1full/3part
● Unemployed after 6mths (1995): 7.9%

SPECIAL FEATURES:
● As well as pressing for full University status, the college is looking to set up a site in Gloucester *which would make the name more accurate, at least*.

FAMOUS ALUMNI:
Chris Broad (cricketer); David Bryant (bowls champion); Jonathan Callard (rugby international); Roger Lovegrove (wildlife broadcaster); PH Newby (writer); Sarah Potter (cricketer).

FURTHER INFO:
Prospectuses for undergrads and postgrads, video for schools, web site (http://www.chelt.ac.uk).

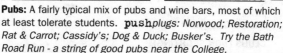

entertainment

TOWN:

● Price of a pint of beer: £1.90 ● Glass of wine: £1.80

Pubs: A fairly typical mix of pubs and wine bars, most of which at least tolerate students. **push**plugs: Norwood; Restoration; Rat & Carrot; Cassidy's; Dog & Duck; Busker's. Try the Bath Road Run - a string of good pubs near the College.

Theatres: (2) An annual 6-night production by the college is put on at the Everyman, which hosts all kinds of productions and is a bit more ambitious than the Playhouse.

Cinemas: There's a 7-screen Odeon but discerning cinéastes trek to the Guildhall in Gloucester.

Clubs/discos: Enigma and Time are chart/dance oriented; Gas is more indie. All do student nights (£1). The Axiom Arts Centre in Cheltenham does a drum'n'bass night.

Music venues: The Town Hall presents mainstream acts, while the Axiom has a more left-field programme. Cheltenham hosts three annual festivals: Jazz, Folk and Classical, if that's your thang

Eating out: There are the usual fast food chains and plenty of pubs do better than average grub. **push**plugs: Café Uno; Il Bottelino; Norwood (new student menu); Valentino's.

COLLEGE:

● Price of a pint of beer: £1.20 ● Glass of wine: £1

Bars: The Park SU Bar (capacity 840) is the centre of most activities and is usually heaving, although it closes between 2 and 5.15pm. There are also bars at FCH (180; small and cosy) and Pittville (220). A new union policy is to make all events (except balls) in the SU free entry.

Cinema: Each site has a big video screen, showing a mix of arty and mainstream fare.

Theatre: As well as the annual show in town, there is also the Sweet Charity Drama Group who make the odd trip to the Fringe.

Music venues: The Park Bar and the Refectory (500) are the main venues but the biggest names (eg D:Ream, Lightning Seeds) tend to be restricted to the Summer Ball.

Clubs: There are 4 club events a week, 2 in the Park Bar and 2 in Pittville but the SU only gets 3 late licences a year, which rather puts a dampener on things.

Food: All university outlets are contracted out to Sutcliffes, so the food is good but pricey in a service station kind of way. There is food at the bars too, plus the training restaurant at Francis Close, which is also open to the public.

Balls: The annual Freshers' Xmas and Rag Balls pack 'em in, but the Summer Ball is the biggie with a capacity of 6,000.

social & political

CHELTENHAM & GLOUCESTER COLLEGE OF HIGHER EDUCATION STUDENTS' UNION:

● 4 sabbaticals ● Turnout at last ballot: 20%
● NUS member

The bright and welcoming SU is on a mission to entertain and

politics would be a hindrance. There are facilities on all sites.
The SU headquarters is based in a *plush* new building.

SU FACILITIES:
Park Campus: Bar; 2 minibuses and 1 car for hire; shop,
photocopying; photobooth; games, video and vending machines;
pool table; juke box; launderette; computer facilities.
Pittville: Bar; photocopier; disco; juke box; vending machines;
pool table.
Francis Close Hall: Bar; shop.

CLUBS (NON SPORTING):
Archaeology; Parapsychology; Fashion.

OTHER ORGANISATIONS:
The SU publishes a *pretty good* newspaper called 'Junction'.
The Student Community Action group has a permanent staff
co-ordinator, and is involved in schemes to help deprived
children as well as a local youth club for children with learning
disabilities. Last year, the charity Rag raised £14,362.

RELIGIOUS:
The College was originally an Anglican institution and has its own
CofE chapel. *A debate is currently raging as to whether to have
multi-faith provision despite the college's heritage. My, isn't
moving with the times difficult, eh?* Most shades of Christian are
represented locally and there's a mosque in Gloucester.

PAID WORK:
The Union runs an Employment Agency. UCAS, the University
applications processing body, has its headquarters locally and
during the vacations it often takes on temporary clerical help.
The racecourse sometimes uses casual labour, *but don't put
your grant cheque on a surefire tip for the 2.30. The
employment policies of GCHQ are a different matter.*

⋯⋯⋯ sports

● Recent successes: rugby

Successes across the board. Facilities are pretty good, and
are free, *and sport is much higher on the agenda than in most
colleges of HE. The new annual Varsity rugby match against
Royal Agricultural College helps raise cash for Oxfam.*

SPORTS FACILITIES:
3 football pitches; 2 rugby pitches; 3 hockey pitches; sports
hall; swimming pool; multigym. The town provides facilities for
most other sports.

SPORTING CLUBS:
Aerobics; Gaelic Football; Gymnastics; Kendo; Kickboxing; Korfball; Kung-Fu;
Lacrosse; Rugby League; Surfing; Waterpolo; Windsurfing.

ATTRACTIONS:
Cheltenham Racecourse; Gloucester Cricket Ground;
Cheltenham Town FC.

⋯⋯⋯ accommodation

IN COLLEGE:
● Catered: 7% ● Cost: £62-75 (37-40wks)
● Self-catering: 5% ● Cost: £53-56 (40wks)
Availability: There are 720 places in head tenancy schemes.
The cost, however, is rather high, as are the tempers of the

30% of 1st years who want to live in but can't. At least nobody has to share. The 2 main accommodation blocks are on Park Campus, with more at Hardwick and and there's a new development at Pittville, *viewed by some as being excellent for its target market - the conference trade.* Also planned is a new hall with 180 places ready for 99 entry.
Car parking: There's roadside parking only, but livers-in aren't supposed to bring cars *and no one really needs them.*

EXTERNALLY:
● <u>Ave rent: £43</u>

Availability: *Housing comes on the market on a very seasonal basis, which means students need to get in there quick for the best shot, although most places tend to be of a decent standard. Leckhampton, St Paul's or Bath Road are the places to be. There are student pockets, but no ghetto.*
Housing help: The 7 full-time staff of the College Accommodation Office lend a hand with contracts and vacancy lists and they also provide a list of recommended properties (currently around 800) which have all been vetted by the college.

welfare

SERVICES:
 ● <u>Pre-school Centre</u> ● <u>Lesbian & Gay Society</u>
● <u>Mature SA</u> ● <u>Overseas SA</u> ● <u>Gender Awareness Officer</u>
The SU has a drop-in welfare and advice centre providing leaflets on useful topics, but the main welfare provisions are from Student Services where there are 3 full- and 1 part-time counsellors. There are also 3 part-time nurses and a pool of visiting doctors on site.
Disabled: 2 executive Disabled Officers. *The new SU Building has very good access, which makes up for the rest of the place.* 10% of college accommodation is specially adapted. There are induction loops.

FINANCE:
● <u>Ave debt: £1,700</u> ● <u>Access fund: £118,378</u>
● <u>Successful applications (1996): 660</u>
Student Services provides small short-term emergency loans.

▶▶ **University College, Chester**
see Other Institutions

▶▶ **Chichester Institute**
see Other Institutions

▶▶ **Cirencester**
see Royal Agricultural College

▶▶ City of London Poly

see London Guildhall University

City University

▼ City University, Northampton Square, London, EC1V 0HB.
Tel: (0171) 477 8000. Fax: (0171) 477 8560.
City University Students' Union, Northampton Square, London,
EC1V 0HB. Tel: (0171) 505 5600. Fax: (0171) 505 5601.

General

Northampton Square, 2 miles north-east of Trafalgar Square, is
just too far north of the square mile of the City of London -
Britain's financial heartland - to be part of it and is just too far
south of Islington to be part of that either. This is the site of
City University's main buildings with the rest dotted around the
area, fragmented but all within a mile of the Square, which is
the University's most attractive part. Its redbrick buildings
surround a small tree-lined grassy patch, space enough for
students to sunbathe in summer. The University's other
buildings are *less good-looking*: urban concrete. City was one
of the first universities to leap wholeheartedly into vocationally
relevant courses; *its journalism department, for example, is
world-renowned*.

50% ♂♂♂♂♂♂♀♀♀♀♀ 50%	
Sex ratio(M:F): 50%:50%	Founded: 1893
Full time u'grads: 4,465	Part time: 279
Postgrads: 1,692	Non-degree: 0
Ave course: 3/4yrs	Ethnic: n/a
Private school: n/a	Flunk rate: 28%
Mature students: 35%	Overseas students: 15%
Disabled students: n/a	Staff/student ratio: 1:18
Clearing: 12%	

ATMOSPHERE:
*The work ethic is strong at City. Number 1 priority is to get a
degree (preferably a good one) and the schedule doesn't allow
for much free time. Extra-curricular activities take second
place and political posturing comes last and definitely least.
With the University physically fragmented, a high proportion of*

❝Saggy old cloth cat Bagpuss has
an honorary degree from the
University of Kent.❞

postgrads and competition from the strong draw of London's own entertainments, the social profile is poor. But the common cause does create a certain sympathy and a lot of friendliness around the halls of residence.

THE CITY: see University of London

LOCAL AREA:
The City is full of big business and big buildings, Britain's closest competitors to Manhattan's skyscrapers. *This is the stamping ground of the sad git who hands back the keys to the Audi and says it's 'not my style'. There's a plethora of extremely expensive wine bars and chintzy sandwich bars but little else; thankfully,* the West End is just a bus ride or brisk walk away. Nearby Islington, on the other hand, *is a different kettle of fishsticks.* It is one of the *trendier* bits of north London: wholemeal cafés; antique shops; the Chapel Market; *groovy* pubs. It is largely residential and, *if you keep your ambitions on a leash, even affordable.*

TRAVEL: see University of London
Trains: Liverpool Street and King's Cross mainline stations are both within 20 minutes' walk of the University.
Buses: 4; 19; 30; 38; 43; 55; 56; 73; 171; 171A; 196; 214; 243; 279; and 505. Night buses: N19; N21; N73; N92; and N96.
Car: *Parkers beware: clamps and tickets.*
Underground: Angel (Northern Line), Farringdon or Barbican (both on the same lines: Hammersmith & City; Circle; Metropolitan; and Thameslink).

LIBRARIES & COMPUTERS:
● Books: 332,000 ● Study places: 905
● Computer workstations: 2,000+
2 main libraries - the Skinners Library and the Frobisher Crescent Branch Library - as well as various departmental libraries. Facilities are very good after the recent expansion of the library.

CAREER PROSPECTS:
● Careers Service ● No of staff: 4full/2part
● Unemployed after 6mths (1996): 6.5%
The University's vocational emphasis is rewarded by a *good* graduate employment rate.

SPECIAL FEATURES:
● City's motto is 'To Serve Mankind' - **push** *wonders how the women students feel about that.*
● The University validates degrees at colleges as diverse as the Guildhall School of Music and Drama, Laban Centre for Movement and Dance and Cordwainers College (that's cobblers to you).

FAMOUS ALUMNI:
Michael Fish (weatherman); Dermot Murnaghan (newsreader); Jack Warner (Dixon of Dock Green - *ask your gran*); Kate Adie (reporter) has an honorary degree.

FURTHER INFO:
Prospectuses, SU prospectus and web site (http://www.city.ac.uk) and a guide to courses (http://www.city.ac.uk/city/ugcourse).

entertainment

IN LONDON: see <u>University of London</u>

THE CITY AND ISLINGTON:

The Barbican contains theatres, cinemas, restaurants, bars, *and not enough loos*, all under one roof, *more than making up for the dearth of affordable ents in this neck of the woods*. In Islington, The Walkabout, the Leopard and the King's Head are all good for a pint or 5; the Hope & Anchor has indie bands while the Bull & Gate has dance nights; the Complex is a banging club in Angel and the Rhythmic is a popular new jazz/blues club.

UNIVERSITY:

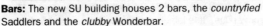

- <u>Price of a pint of beer: £1.50</u> ● <u>Glass of wine: £1.10</u>

Bars: The new SU building houses 2 bars, the *countryfied* Saddlers and the *clubby* Wonderbar.

Theatre & film: One major production a year plus a trip to the Fringe. 1 culty or mainstream film a week.

Music venues/clubs/discos: The Wonderbar (cap 550) has been revamped and hosts live gigs (mainly tribute bands) and doubles as a dance venue, with a weekly dose of swing, hip-hop and more chart-oriented noise. Roni Size, Daft Punk and Jamiroquai have all ventured here recently.

Comedy: *The slapstick scene has improved recently with shows every fortnight courtesy of the Newcastle Brown Comedy Network.*

Food: The University runs 2 refectories (*which have a good vegetarian range*) throughout the day. Ponchos in the Wonderbar serves Mexican food, while the Saddlers Bar serves snacks and sandwiches - *try saying that after 7 pints and a tuna bap.*

Others: The Union tries to keep up a programme of at least 3 events per week and generally churns out some *worthwhile* budget fun, the biggest source of merriment being the President's Ball.

social & political

CITY UNIVERSITY STUDENTS' UNION (CUSU):

- <u>4 sabbaticals</u> ● <u>Turnout at last ballot: 10%</u>

- <u>NUS member</u>

The new SU building has done a lot to put entertainments and socialising centre stage and the Union's extra efforts to liven up the party have been fairly successful (not hard, since it had been as fevered as a fossilised flatworm in the past). A new ents manager has remedied the situation, although the facilities suffer by comparison with ULU, which City students aren't entitled to use (but many do).

SU FACILITIES:

2 bars; general shop; computer shop; games area; dark room; minibus hire; committee room; snooker and pool tables; vending machines and video games; travel and insurance shops; 2nd-hand book stall.

CLUBS (NON SPORTING):

Aerospace; Business; Chess; Economic; First Aid; Hellenic; Hindu; Iranian; Malaysian; Punjabi; Role Play; Tamil; Vedic.

OTHER ORGANISATIONS:
The glossy student mag, 'Massive', is also available on the net. There isn't a main Rag event, but various charity events coincide with awareness campaigns.

RELIGIOUS:
● Chaplain
The University has some *active* religious clubs, but otherwise, students rely on London's religious amenity overload. The University provides a 'mosque facility'.

PAID WORK: see University of London

sports

● Recent successes: fencing, hockey, netball
For a small inner-city university, City has access to some fairly good facilities and the overall level of interest is high.

SPORTS FACILITIES:
A sports ground in south London is shared with King's College London and includes 26 acres of playing fields. Close to Northampton Square, the University owns the Saddler's Sports Centre where there are facilities for a variety of indoor sports including a swimming pool, 2 squash courts, gym, sports hall, martial arts room, multigym, sauna and solarium. There's a boathouse for the rowing club on the Thames at Chiswick and sailors and surfers can use facilities at the Queen Mary Sailing Club.

SPORTING CLUBS:
Extreme Sports (bungi, parachuting, stock car); Sailing; Shorinji Kempo; Tennis; Women's Football; Wrestling.

ATTRACTIONS: see University of London

accommodation

IN COLLEGE:
● Catered: 7% ● Cost: £81(31wks)
● Self-catering: 13% ● Cost: £69-71(39-48wks)
Availability: The University guarantees accommodation to 1st years subject to some *fairly strict* conditions (early application, non-Londoners only). In practice, about 80% live in. That leaves few places for 2nd years, finalists and postgrads. There are 2 catered halls and 3 blocks of self-catering flats (mainly for postgrads and not available for 1st years). *The centres of sociability and spirit in the University revolve around the halls, or, more precisely, around the halls' bars. Accommodation is very expensive but this reflects property costs locally.*

> ❝One idea for a name for Newcastle's second university was the City University of Newcastle-upon-Tyne, until somebody decided the acronym wouldn't look good on letterheads.❞

EXTERNALLY: see <u>University of London</u>
● <u>Ave rent: £80</u>
Housing help: The University Accommodation Office helps students find housing in London. Camden, Finsbury Park and Manor House are popular areas and cheaper than the immediate locality.

welfare

SERVICES:
● <u>Lesbian & Gay Society</u> ● <u>Mature SA</u> ● <u>Overseas SA</u>
● <u>Postgrad SA</u> ● <u>Minibus</u> ● <u>Women's Officer</u>
● <u>Self-defence classes</u>

The University runs a student counselling service which is the principle problem post for students, employing 1 part-time and 3 full-time counsellors. CUSU also has a welfare advisor. The health service has a doctor, dentist and sister.
Disabled: *All new buildings are wheelchair accessible and things are improving in the older ones. Some accommodation has been adapted. There is a Disability Officer.*

FINANCE:
● <u>Ave debt: £1,600</u> ● <u>Access fund: £172,000</u>
There is a hardship fund and the SU can make short-term loans of £50.

● ●

▶▶ Coleraine

see University of Ulster

● ●

Courtauld Institute of Art, London

● *The Institute is part of <u>University of London</u> and students are entitled to use its facilities.*
The Courtauld Institute of Art, Somerset House, Strand, London, WC2R 0RN. Tel: (0171) 873 2645.
Fax: (0171) 873 2410.
Courtauld Students' Union, Somerset House, Strand, London, WC2R 0RN. Tel: (0171) 873 2717.

general

Right by Waterloo Bridge, in the elegant 18th century Somerset House, are the main offices of the Inland Revenue. Totally unconnected, but sharing the same building (round the corner, facing onto the Strand), is the Courtauld Institute of Art. To the east is Fleet Street and the City (London's financial centre), to the west, the West End and (at the other end of The Strand, about 500yds) is Trafalgar Square and the National Gallery. Also in Somerset House, which is strewn with *splendid* sculptures and architectural features, is the Institute's remarkable collection of art, books and manuscripts which is open to the public. It is hardly surprising then to know that the Institute is the UK's only college specialising solely in the teaching of the history of art. It's only a bus ride/tube trip/energetic walk to ULU, whose facilities Courtauld students are entitled to use. King's College, London is next door and LSE just round the corner.

25% ♂♂♀♀♀♀♀♀♀♀ 75%

Sex ratio(M:F): 25%:75%	Founded: 1932
Full time u'grads: 115	Part time: 0
Postgrads: 125	Non-degree: 0
Ave course: 3yrs	Ethnic: n/a
Private school: 37%	Flunk rate: n/a
Mature students: 16%	Overseas students: 2%
Disabled students: 1%	Staff/student ratio: 1:8
Clearing: 0%	

ATMOSPHERE:
Women outnumber men 3:1 and the intake from the private education sector is high which leaves a subtle hint of Swiss finishing schools. The main influences on the atmosphere, however, are its size and intimacy, its proximity to King's (which makes up for the Institute's lack of facilities) and the shared interests of the students. The atmosphere is detached from the rest of the University and cliques can form but the students present a unified bastion of cheerfulness against the sour-faced minions of the Inland Revenue.

THE CITY: see University of London

ALDWYCH:
Aldwych and The Strand are close to Covent Garden, the West End and, over the Thames, the South Bank Complex (National Theatre, Hayward Gallery, National Film Theatre, Royal Festival Hall, etc). This is not a residential area and *it's an expensive place to buy a canned drink, let alone bread and cheese. It's extremely well served for entertainments and culture though.*

TRAVEL: see University of London
Local Trains: The nearest mainline BR stations are Waterloo, Charing Cross and Blackfriars.
Buses: 1; 4; 6; 9; 11; 13; 15; 15B; X15; 68; X68; 77A; 168; 171; 171A; 176; 177Ex; 188; 196; 501; 502; 505 and 513 and endless night buses.
Car: Very limited parking. Forget the car.
Underground: Covent Garden (Piccadilly Line); Temple (Circle and District Lines).

LIBRARIES & COMPUTERS:
● Books: 215,000 ● Study places: 139
● Computer workstations: 10
The Institute's libraries are among the country's major sources for art history. The Witt, Conway and Slide Libraries have over 1.6 million reproductions and 800,000 photographs.
However, specific undergraduate course books are in short supply. Computer facilities are also limited, but students have access to those at King's College, London.

FAMOUS ALUMNI:
Anita Brookner (writer); Andrew Graham-Dixon (art historian); Neil MacGregor (National Gallery); Vincent Price (actor); Nicholas Serota (Tate Gallery); Brian Sewell (art critic). Anthony Blunt (spy) was the Director here for several years, before he was fingered.

FURTHER INFO:
Prospectuses for undergrads and postgrads and a web site (http://www.courtauld.ac.uk).

entertainment

IN LONDON: see University of London

INSTITUTE:
There's no bar, so Courtauld students pop into the King's College bar next door. About once every 3 weeks there'll be a disco, party or, more likely, a *sedate* wine evening in the refectory, often with a jazz band or a string quartet - something like that anyway. Ball every summer.
Food: There's a glass-roofed refectory (cap 100) with contract caterers and there's always King's.

social & political

COURTAULD STUDENTS' UNION:
● No sabbaticals ● NUS member

The SU is an entertainment-based organisation, but its representatives do attend staff meetings and act as a conduit for academic complaints. **Also ULU:** see University of London.

SU FACILITIES:
Lounge; *very popular* pool table.

CLUBS (NON SPORTING):
Life Drawing.

OTHER ORGANISATIONS:
'Dr No' magazine once a year. No Rag, but the official Institute charity is Centrepoint, which helps the homeless.

sports

The Courtauld Institute has no sports facilities of its own. Students are eligible to use ULU and London University facilities, *but don't*. Sporadic attempts at mixed-sex football crop up, and someone played hockey for the University. *Once. They think.* **Sports in London:** see University of London.

accommodation

EXTERNALLY: see University of London
No accommodation of its own. 56% of 1st years and 10% of finalists live in the University's intercollegiate housing and nearly 10% have their own flats.

welfare

SERVICES:
There's a student welfare officer, and students can also turn to the University of London Central Health Service.
Disabled: Although the Courtauld currently has no disabled students, it does have lifts and wheelchair access *is good.*

Lesbian, gay & bisexual: *The Institute used to have a bit of a reputation for accommodating a loud gay clique, but things are quieter of late. There's no Gay Society, but the atmosphere is probably more tolerant than many.*

FINANCE:
- Access fund: £13,000

Travel grants and course trips are subsidised.

Coventry University

- *Formerly Coventry Polytechnic*

Coventry University, Priory Street, Coventry, CV1 5FB.
Tel: (01203) 631313. Fax: (01203) 838638.
E-mail: cor003@coventry.ac.uk
Coventry University Students' Union, Block E, Priory Street, Coventry, CV1 5FT. Tel: (01203) 221167.
Fax: (01203) 559146. E-mail: suexec@coventry.ac.uk

General

Coventry has a much longer history than most cities in the Midlands and, what with good connections all over the country, being sent to Coventry is far from the isolation it's supposed to be. This is where Lady Godiva did her famous bareback horse ride, but trotting naked through the streets has fallen off somewhat as a local sport since the city was almost completely destroyed in a single night's bombing during the 2nd World War. Despite the speed with which it was resurrected, there was some thought involved and *it's interesting to look at if not exactly attractive - a huge futuristic machine with giant chimneys and intestinal roads woven among the buildings. The city's heart is a shopping centre maze although wheelchair access is among the best in the country.* This is where the University campus is spread, across 25 acres (only about 10mins' walk), near other civic buildings like the sports centre, the Art Gallery & Museum and the very impressive Cathedral opposite the SU Building. The University buildings are made of red bricks and look modern, *but are not brash or brutal. An effort has been made to make them blend.* There are lots of sculptures, flower beds, paved squares and, bizarrely, gravestones.

55% ♂♂♂♂♂♂♀♀♀♀ **45%**

Sex ratio(M:F): 55%:45%	**Founded: 1970**	
Full time u'grads: 9,785	**Part time: 3,694**	
Postgrads: 1,576	**Non-degree: 1,000**	
Ave course: 3/4yrs	**Ethnic: 20%**	
Private school: n/a	**Flunk rate: 24%**	
Mature students: 47%	**Overseas students: 16%**	
Disabled students: 1.5%	**Staff/student ratio: 1:21**	
Clearing: n/a		

ATMOSPHERE:
The silly but fun, first-freedom-from-home attitude is less common than just getting on with the task in hand - students are here to get a qualification, preferably job-related.
Relations with the locals are reserved but not as nasty as they once were.

COVENTRY:
- Population: 322,573 ● London: 88miles
- Birmingham: 16miles

Rebuilt, Coventry's a new city with an old spirit which doesn't let the modern design interfere with the ancient heritage.
There are archaeological digs on view close to the campus and in the city centre. There's a mile-long pedestrianised shopping centre, big enough to provide more shops than a student grant can withstand (including several bookshops and a number of stores open after 10pm). The local heritage can be viewed in the city's museum and tourist attractions (*although Coventry is hardly what you might call 'a holiday resort'*), notably the Herbert Art Gallery, the Toy Museum, the Museum of British Road Transport, the Cathedral (restored and built anew by Basil Spence), the olde world shops, Lunt Roman Fort and statue of Lady Godiva. *It's hoped that a millennium project currently underway will transform Coventry into a truly cosmopolitan 24 hour city, which, if successful, will be an astounding feat of triumph over adversity.*

TRAVEL:
Trains: The Grade II-listed Coventry Station is about 1 mile from the Coventry University campus and on the main London (£11.60) to Birmingham (£2.20) line.
Coaches: National Express, Bharat and Harry Shaw services all over the place, including London (£12) and more.
Car: The usual Midlands ease of accessibility, via the M6, M69 and M45/A45, and just a few miles from the M1, M40 and A5. The one-way systems aren't good for the blood pressure.
Air: Coventry Airport isn't terribly helpful, but Birmingham International is a big one, 9½ miles away.
Local: There are 3 BR train stops within the confines of Coventry, but the *reliable* local bus services are more useful for getting to places students haven't got the welly to walk to.
Taxis: Coventry's small enough to mean £2 will get students *a worthwhile whack* across town by taxi.
Bicycles: The roads are busy, the thefts frequent. But it's flat.
Others: Summer brings 'Lady Godiva Topless Tours'; for £3.50, visitors can tour Coventry in an open-topped bus *(but they're allowed to keep their vests on).*

LIBRARIES & COMPUTERS:
- Books: 300,000 ● Study places: 1,200
- Computer workstations: 1,564

Apart from the main Lanchester Library, which also includes a specialist collection, there's the Art & Design Library.
Facilities have increased in recent years but they're still under-resourced as far as books and computers go. A new Learning Resource Centre due to open in 1999 should address this *provided it opens on time.*

CAREER PROSPECTS:
● <u>Careers Service</u> ● <u>No of staff: 6full/2part</u>
● <u>Unemployed after 6mths (1995): 8%</u>
The Careers Office is some distance off campus *and many students seem unaware of its existence.*

FAMOUS ALUMNI:
Mark Chase (TV presenter); Jerry Dammers (ex-Specials); John Kettley (*is a weatherman, a weatherman, a weatherman and so is Michael Fish*); Steve Ogrizovic, Alan Smith (footballers); Michael Rodber (designed the *distinctly unprofitable* Eurostar); Alison Snowden (Oscar-winning animator).

FURTHER INFO:
Prospectuses, accommodation video (£6), alternative prospectus and a web site (http//www.coventry.ac.uk and http://www.coventry.ac.uk/sandf/s_union/coventry.htm).

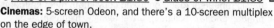

entertainment

COVENTRY:
● <u>Price of a pint of beer: £1.80</u> ● <u>Glass of wine: £1.85</u>

Cinemas: 5-screen Odeon, and there's a 10-screen multiplex on the edge of town.

Theatres: The Belgrade Theatre offers *competent* dramatic fare.

Pubs: *Some pubs are no-go areas; the local name for them is 'playschool pubs', because you have to guess which window you're going to be chucked through. Wise students have their own supping sanctuaries.* **push**plugs: *Oak Inn; The Campbell; Bar Coast.*

Clubs/discos: *Mainly a refuge for stiletto fetishists.* **push**plugs: *Browns (good soul night Thursdays); Foundry (techno, drum'n'bass); Coliseum (mainstream).*

Music venues: *Not exactly throbbing.* **push***plugs: Browns (jazz, soul); West Indian Centre (world music); Dog & Trumpet.*

Eating out: *Cheap and cheerful or more money than Rennies, Coventry has something to offer any gourmet.* **push***plugs: Oysters (veggie); Brown's (parent-friendly); Corks Wine Bar; Hope & Anchor (good grub, cheap Sunday roast); Gringo's (cheap pizza).*

UNIVERSITY:
● <u>Price of a pint of beer: £1.55</u> ● <u>Glass of wine: £1.60</u>

Ents are dominated by the spanking new 4-storey Planet venue, with a total capacity of 1,700.

Bars: There are 5 bars in the Planet and the Oasis (cap 350) in the old Union building.

Theatre: The Performing Arts school puts on lots of productions *but extra-curricular drama is pretty well non-existent.*

Music venue: Planet has raised the stakes for live ents in the last few months, with acts such as Dannii Minogue and Supersonics luring the punters.

Clubs/discos: 4 regular club nights a week, 2 mainstream and 1 each for dance and indie sounds. Recent visiting DJs/clubs have included Pete Tong, Sasha and Boy George.

Cabaret: Coventry is a stop-off for the National Comedy Network and Craig Charles, Rory McGrath and Hugh Lennon have all tickled tums recently.

Food: *Oasis has a good value selection of standard pub/fast food; the platter at Planet's bistro bar is more comprehensive and cosmopolitan (and also more costly).* Also around college are the Best Cellar, Fads and the most recent addition, the William Morris Bistro, *named with an alarming absence of irony.*

Others: 2 balls a year.

social & political

COVENTRY UNIVERSITY STUDENTS' UNION:
- 5 sabbaticals ● Turnout at last ballot: 10%
- NUS member

CUSU has been making a real effort to stir the student body from its cryogenically-frozen attitude to politics. Now they're just apathetic and uninformed, which is a vast improvement.

SU FACILITIES:
The SU Building provides a general shop, bars, activities and development centre (nicknamed 'the Junction' and providing a music rehearsal room, print and copy shop, meeting rooms, IT, printing and fax facilities), travel agency, nightclub, 4 minibuses for hire, photo booth, video games, vending machines, pool tables, juke boxes and 2 meeting rooms and the new Planet venue.

CLUBS (NON SPORTING):
Afrique; Choir; Circus Skills; Debating; Hellenic; Norwegian; Roleplay; Scout & Guide; Soul; Star Trek.

OTHER ORGANISATIONS:
The student magazine is called 'Elephant & Castle' and pops off the presses every month. The Community Action group does *much-needed good for students' local image* by raising funds and helping volunteer projects.

RELIGIOUS:
- 3 chaplains (CofE, RC, Free Church)

There's a non-denominational prayer room. Locally, Coventry has many a prayer palace and creed cabin for god-squadders of every hue, most notably, the Anglican Cathedral.

PAID WORK:
CUBE (Coventry University Bureau of Employment) is run by students to help them find part-time and vacation work, from bar work to market research.

sports

- Recent successes: badminton

Coventry students get marginally more interested in sport than about politics, which isn't saying much. That said, facilities are OK and there are usually enough people to make up a team.

SPORTS FACILITIES:
The University has facilities at Westwood Heath and at a new building in Raglan St. Westwood Heath: 37 acres of playing fields (3 football pitches, 3 rugby pitches, cricket pitch, etc); floodlit hockey pitch; cricket nets; 9-hole golf course; 4 tennis courts. Raglan St: gym; weights; martial arts dojo; table

tennis; sunbed. Coventry makes up for any shortfalls by providing student discount rates for use of the local sports centre including the Olympic standard swimming pool and squash courts. There are now sports bursaries worth £4,000.

SPORTING CLUBS:
Aikido; Caving; Jiu Jitsu; Kung Fu; Leisure Pursuits; Parachute; Rowing; Ten Pin Bowling; Thai Boxing; Windsurfing.

ATTRACTIONS:
Coventry City FC are the local footie boys. There's also horse-racing at Warwick and 2 council-owned golf courses.

accommodation

IN COLLEGE:
- Catered: 6% ● Cost: £66(40wks)
- Self-catering: 12% ● Cost: £49-53(40wks)

Availability: 4 halls of residence and 1,100 places in head tenancy schemes. Priority is given to 1st years but 10% are unlucky; lots of local and mature students are already sorted. 2% have to share. Most hall places are in Priory Hall on campus, although Caradoc Hall (64 single bedsits and 62 twin flats) is 3 miles away and there are 350 places in University-owned houses in town.

Car parking: Like Monopoly - occasional free parking.

EXTERNALLY:
- Ave rent: £32

Availability: *With a bit of work, students can find somewhere suitable and when they do, the cost is sweet, grant-wise. The best areas are Earlsdon, Poleshill and Whitton Ash. Hillfields is Coventry's Bronx. The cost and availability of parking spaces renders cars pointless.*

Housing help: The Accommodation Office checks out every place it recommends on its list of houses and also offers a handbook, bulletin board, full-time staff and contract advice.

welfare

SERVICES:
- Creche ● Nightline ● Lesbian & Gay Society
- Mature SA ● Overseas SA ● Minibus ● Women's Officer
- Self-defence classes

The SU runs an *excellent* Advice Centre which offers to help students with anything. The University also employs 8 counsellors. The Medical Centre on the campus has 6 doctors and 1 nurse.

Women: The SU produces a women's rights booklet. Women have priority on the minibus, although men are allowed to use it too. It's free, *but can be irregular and could run later sometimes.*

Disabled: There is a Disabled Students' Forum, a Disability Unit with 4 staff and facilities for students with various forms of disability: orthopaedic chairs; print enlargers; computer braillers; software for the sight impaired; a wheelchair-only computer terminal; student officer. *Wheelchair access has improved considerably over the last few years.*

Drugs: *The city is getting a bit of a reputation for drug gangs and associated nastiness and if you're not used to the* *prevalence of dodgy substances, you might experience something of a culture shock. The University remains relatively untouched.*

FINANCE:
- Ave debt: £1,200 ● Access fund: £193,681
- Successful applications (1997): 178

As well as the access fund there's a small welfare fund for the desperate, short term loans of up to £50 and there are arts and sports bursaries worth £500 each.

●●

Cranfield University

(1) Royal Military College of Science, Shrivenham, Swindon, Wiltshire, SN6 8LA. Tel: (01793) 785400.
Fax: (01793) 783966.
Association of Students, Royal Military College of Science, Shrivenham, Swindon, Wiltshire, SN6 8LA.
Tel: (01793) 785702. Fax: (01793) 783966.
(2) Silsoe College, Silsoe, Bedfordshire, MK45 4DT.
Tel: (01525) 863318. Fax: (01525) 863316.
Student Union Society, Silsoe College, Silsoe, Bedfordshire, MK45 4DT. Tel: (01525) 863075. Fax: (01525) 863001.
E-mail for both sites: recruitment@cranfield.ac.uk

·······§eneral

There are several multi-site universities in **push** but few as odd as Cranfield. Not only are the 2 sites separated by more than 100 miles, *but they're as unalike as 2 peas in a pod aren't.* They have their own social peculiarities which may put some potential applicants off but the academic and vocational reputation compensates for many. Silsoe is the gentle, Yin bit, sometimes known as School of Agriculture, Food and the Environment (SAFE). It's a rural backwater between Luton and Bedford, *without much in the way of high-calibre entertainments.* The Yang side, RMCS, as the name suggests, revolves around the scientific requirements of the armed forces *and is more akin to a military establishment than a university* (although civilians are admitted). It's about 8 miles from Swindon, *again not exactly at the social heart of things.*

75% ♂♂♂♂♂♂♂♀♀♀ **25%**

Sex ratio(M:F): 75%:25%	Founded: 1975
Full time u'grads: 613	Part time: 0
Postgrads: 642	Non-degree: 114
Ave course: 3/4yrs	Ethnic: 1%
Private school: 20%	Flunk rate: n/a
Mature students: 32%	Overseas students: 13%
Disabled students: 6%	Staff/student ratio: 1:8
Clearing: 3%	

ATMOSPHERE:

Silsoe is a quiet, contemplative place, where students tend to be very committed to their courses; social activity rarely extends beyond a few pints on a Saturday night. It's a tight-knit, supportive atmosphere and if things start to get claustrophobic, a car is indispensable. Shrivenham is equally remote and tight-knit, but considerably less quiet. Although not all the students have specifically military connections, the dominant ethos is that of the forces personnel and potential students who aren't into rules, regulations and dress codes should think long and hard before applying. Students at each site appear to go about their business in blissful ignorance of their nominal colleagues and they probably wouldn't have that much in common if they did meet up.

TOWNS:

Silsoe Village itself has little going beyond a couple of pubs. For the nearest thing to fun see <u>Luton University</u> and, for Bedford, <u>De Montfort University</u>. Swindon, the nearest centre of population to Shrivenham, is another commuter commune for London and the historical home of the Great Western railway. It has all the usual accoutrements - pubs, clubs, supermarkets and so on - *but it's not a 'student town' in the conventional sense. Not that RMCS people are conventional students...*

TRAVEL:

At both sites non-drivers are at a distinct disadvantage. Silsoe's nearest train station is Flitwick, 3 miles away, *but it's way off the beaten track*, so <u>Luton's</u> the best bet; a day return by bus costs £2.70. The A6 passes through the village. Local buses *supposedly* run every hour or so, *but don't count on it.* Shrivenham is even more remote, but at least Swindon has rail and coach connections to most major cities. Train from Shrivenham to London (£15.50), coach (£12.50). The A420 runs near the college and local buses go from the main gate every hour.

LIBRARIES & COMPUTERS (SILSOE):
- <u>Books: 65,000</u> ● <u>Study places: 79</u>
- <u>Computer workstations: 81</u>

LIBRARIES & COMPUTERS (RMCS):
- <u>Books: 100,000</u> ● <u>Study places: 75</u>
- <u>Computer workstations: 200</u>

The Ministry of Defence provides free stationery and books for students at Shrivenham.

CAREER PROSPECTS (SILSOE):
- <u>Careers Service</u> ● <u>No of staff: 1full/2part</u>
- <u>Unemployed after 6mths (1996): 6%</u>

CAREER PROSPECTS (RMCS):
- <u>Careers Service</u> ● <u>No of staff: 1part</u>
- <u>Unemployed after 6mths (1996): 0%</u>

Although the armed forces have been cutting back in recent years, Shrivenham graduates don't appear to have been touched.

FAMOUS ALUMNI:
Prince Andrew.

FURTHER INFO:
Prospectuses from both sites. Silsoe has an Alternative Prospectus. The web sites (http://www.silsoe.cranfield.ac.uk and http://www.rcms.cranfield.ac.uk).

entertainment

SILSOE VILLAGE:

● Price of a pint of beer: £2.00 ● Glass of wine: £1.80
Silsoe is not the sort of place that attracts coachloads of up-for-it clubbers. There are 3 good pubs. That's it - try Luton or Bedford for burning off excess energy.

SHRIVENHAM VILLAGE:
● Price of a pint of beer: £1.80 ● Glass of wine: £1.20
...and Shrivenham's much the same, if a bit bigger. The Royal Oak and the Eagle sometimes host live music. The Indian Brasserie is expensive but worth a splurge once in a while.

COLLEGE: SILSOE:
● Price of a pint of beer: £1.30 ● Glass of wine: £1.35
Bar: (cap 350). Open lunchtimes and evenings only.
Cinema: 1 or 2 films a week.
Clubs/discos/music venues: The common room and bar are turned over to dance antics on Fridays and local bands are occasional visitors.
Food: A food card (£200/term) entitles students to eat in the one cafeteria. *It's OK but limited, especially for vegetarians, and there isn't much alternative.*
Others: 4 balls a year, plus International Week.

COLLEGE: RMCS:
● Price of a pint of beer: £1.40 ● Glass of wine: 60p
Bars: (3) *The main social magnet for the student body, especially the army types.*
Theatre: 4 productions a year, plus a panto and 2 or 3 shows from the choral society.
Clubs/discos/music venues: 1 foot-moving fiesta a week, plus some *obscure* bands once a month.
Food: The Mess (note military terminology) comes up with four 5-course meals a day. Dress codes are enforced at all times, even for non-military students. There is also a cafe.
Others: 3 balls a year.

social & political

STUDENTS' UNION:
● Turnout at last ballot: 47% ● NUS member
Politics is an irrelevance at both sites, although the private opinions of RMCS students, unsurprisingly, tend rightwards. The Union's officers are non-sabbatical, so they're juggling the intensive work-load too.

SU FACILITIES:
Silsoe: Bar; cafeteria; shops; TV lounge; function room; snooker & pool tables; launderette; minibus hire.
RMCS: Bars; TV lounge; photocopier; launderette; function rooms.

CLUBS (NON SPORTING):
Silsoe: Brewing; Film; Greek; International; Motor; Music.

RMCS: Arts; Bridge; Choral; Flower; Good Neighbours; Military; Painting; Re-enactment; Record Collectors; Saddle; Scottish Country Dancing; Scouts; Shrivenham.

OTHER ORGANISATIONS:
Silsoe has the 'Nameless Newsletter' and runs a charity called SAFAD (Student Aid For Appropriate Development) which raises funds for projects abroad. RMCS has a Rag and a number of periodicals, including 'Student Matters'. *Neither site has picked up any Imaginative Name awards recently.*

sports

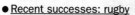
- Recent successes: rugby

Students pay £1/month towards the sports fund. Sporting success is hampered by low numbers, but facilities and attitude are good, especially at RMCS. The fact that there's not much else to do may help...

SPORTS FACILITIES:
Silsoe: Sports Hall with climbing wall; running machine; Courts for squash, badminton, tennis (4); rugby, football and hockey pitches; gym.
RCMS: Astroturf pitch; gym with jogging, rowing and step machines.

SPORTING CLUBS:
Aerobics; Beagles; Boat; Boxing; Caving; Fishing; Gliding; Gun; Hang Gliding; Karting; Lawn Tennis; Motor; Mountaineering; Outdoor Activities; Parachute; Powered Flying; Rifle & Pistol; Shooting; Soak (Silsoe Outdoor Activity Klub); Triathlon; Weights; Women's rugby & football.

accommodation

IN COLLEGE (SILSOE):
- Catered: 88% ● Cost: £58(30 wks)
- Self-catering: 12% ● Cost: £45-65(40-50 wks)

All undergrads can be housed, except for those on work placements. 200 self-catering places are available in a purpose-built student village.

IN COLLEGE (RMCS):
- Catered: 49% ● Cost: £79(32wks)
- Self-catering: 31% ● Cost: £45-50(32wks)

Again, all who want to live in can do so, mostly in the Mess or its Annexe.

EXTERNALLY:
- Ave rent: £45

Silsoe & RCMS: *There's plenty of attractive housing for those who choose to strike out on their own, although at this point the status of a car moves from handy to indispensible.*

welfare

SERVICES:
- Nightline ● Overseas SA ● Women's Officer

FINANCE:
Many RMCS students are sponsored by the forces.

- Dartington College of Arts
  see Other Institutions

De Montfort University

University of Derby

- Distributive Trades
  see The London Institute

- DIT
  see University of Abertay Dundee

- Dorset Institute
  see Bournemouth University

University of Dundee

- Dundee Institute of Technology
  see University of Abertay Dundee

University of Durham

▶▶ Dartington College of Arts

see Other Institutions

De Montfort University

- **Formerly Leicester Polytechnic**

Telephone hotline to all campuses: (0645) 454647.
E-mail: mardiv@dmu.ac.uk
(1) De Montfort University Leicester, The Gateway, Leicester, LE1 9BH. Tel: (0116) 255 1551. Fax: (0116) 255 0307.
(2) De Montfort University Bedford, 37 Landsdowne Road, Bedford, MK40 2BZ. Tel: (01234) 351966.
Fax: (01234) 350833.
(3) De Montfort University Milton Keynes, Hammerwood Gate, Kent's Hill, Milton Keynes, MK7 6HP. Tel: (01908) 695511.
Fax: (01908) 695581.
(4) De Montfort University Lincoln, School of Agriculture and Horticulture, Caythorpe Court, Caythorpe, Grantham, Lincolnshire, NG32 3EP. Tel: (01400) 272521.
Fax: (01400 272722).
(5) De Montfort University Lincoln, School of Applied Art and

Design, Lindum Road, Lincoln, LN2 1NP.
Tel: (01522) 512912. Fax: (01522) 895147.
De Montfort University Students' Union, 4 Newarke Close,
Leicester, LE1 9BH. Tel: (0116) 255 5576.
Fax: (0116) 257 6309.

general

*When Leicester Polytechnic stopped being Leicester
Polytechnic in the early 90s, the powers that be obviously had
bigger and better ideas than their colleagues at the other 'new
universities' and started putting feelers out way beyond to*
Bedford, Lincoln and Milton Keynes. So DMU currently has 4
centres in all, 3 of which in turn have more than one site.
Students don't need to travel between the various towns for
their courses. *The advantage to DMU's 'distributed' status is
that it can offer one of the widest ranges of courses in the UK.
The drawback is that there's very little sense of a central
university identity; students are loyal to their centres rather
than to DMU.*

49% ♂♂♂♂♂♀♀♀♀♀ 51%	
Sex ratio(M:F): 49%:51%	Founded: 1969
Full time u'grads: 15,650	Part time: 3,100
Postgrads: 1,500	Non-degree: 1,825
Ave course: 3yrs	Ethnic: 28%
Private school: n/a	Flunk rate: n/a
Mature students: 25%	Overseas students: 9%
Disabled students: 2.5%	Staff/student ratio: 1:17
Clearing: 19.5%	

ATMOSPHERE:
*Students tend to be committed to having a good time, getting
a good degree then going on to a good job. The University is
just too spread out to make generalisations, however.*

THE SITES:
Leicester: (16,209 students - most courses) The large City
Campus, in the *groovy* bit of town, is *pretty ugly in a 60s
brutalist style*, although it does include the medieval Trinity
building. There are also sites at: Scraptoft, 6 miles away, in a
rather nice wooded setting *but with fairly basic facilities*; and
the Charles Frears Campus (for nursing) a *brisk* walk away.
There are regular bus services between the Leicester sites.
Bedford: (3,115 - humanities, education, sports, leisure,
performing arts) 65 miles from Leicester there are 2 campuses,
2 miles apart: Lansdowne (*sporty*); and Polhill (*less so*).
Milton Keynes (MK): (1,268 - business, computing, social
science, engineering). The smallest centre, about 60 miles
from Leicester. MK itself, *the new town to end them all, is an
acquired taste, with pretty good leisure facilities but little
acknowledgement of a student market.*
Lincoln: (2,285 - agriculture, horticulture, art and design, FE
courses). Approximately 60 miles from Leicester. The artists
are based in the city of Lincoln itself, with the various diggers
and planters in Caythorpe, Riseholme and Holbeach in the
Lincolnshire countryside.

THE CITY: see <u>University of Leicester</u>

TRAVEL: see <u>University of Leicester</u>

LIBRARIES & COMPUTERS:
● <u>Books: 440,000</u> ● <u>Study places: 1000</u>
● <u>Computer workstations: 400</u>

There's 1 library on each site. MK has only 23,000 books, but the library is set up so that students at any site can order a book from another site if necessary. *And if they can be bothered.* Students in MK can also use the library at the headquarters of the <u>Open University</u>. *An extension to the Kimberlin library has improved facilities somewhat, but talk of a new Digital Library remains very much in terms of 'could', 'might' and 'should'.*

CAREER PROSPECTS:
● <u>Careers Service</u> ● <u>No of staff: 11full/3part</u>
● <u>Unemployed after 6mths (1996): 7.5%</u>

The Careers Service publishes the fortnightly 'Grapevine', listing job opportunities, which is distributed to all sites. They also arrange workshops and talks from employers.

SPECIAL FEATURES:
● *De Montfort takes its name from Simon De Montfort, the 13th-century Earl of Leicester. The Earl was anti-semitic and banned Jews from Leicester. He also wanted to overthrow the King and led the baronial revolt, kidnapping Henry III and his son, before he finally got his head chopped off and put on a spike. His father, also called Simon, fought in the 4th crusade slashing his way through Jews and Muslims. His son, also called Simon, may or may not have fornicated his way through Kent. None of them, however, had any firm policies on lifelong education, the rights of all to get academic and professional qualifications, or indeed the merits of charity shop clothing.*

FAMOUS ALUMNI:
Charles Dance (actor); Engelbert Humperdinck (*cheesy* 60s singer); Prolapse (indie band); Janet Reger (*nice knicks*); Kendra Slawinski (netball player); Liz Tilberis (Editor, 'Vogue').

FURTHER INFO:
Prospectuses for undergrads, postgrads and part-timers. Web site including interactive prospectus (http://www.dmu.ac.uk).

⠄⠄⠄⠄⠄⠄⠄ entertainment

THE CITY: see <u>University of Leicester</u>
De Montfort's smaller outposts tend to be based in towns less cosmopolitan and student-oriented than Leicester.
Bedford: *Local student faves include the Barley Mow gay-friendly pub, Esquires club (garage and acid jazz nights) and Gulshan's Tandoori. There's also an annual regatta and a notorious beer festival. The Aspects Complex near Polhill includes a 6-screen cinema and ten-pin bowling.*
Milton Keynes: MK has an *excellent* multiplex cinema *but the pubs and clubs tend to be a bit cleancut.* The National Bowl is a *good* music venue *for those who like to wave their lighters in the air.*

Lincoln: *Lincoln is never going to challenge Leeds or Manchester as a student Mecca but the new* <u>University of Humberside</u> *site has increased the number of funseekers, so the level of entertainment should progress in coming years beyond the current pub culture. Those based at the rural outposts have to hike in to the city or make do with maypole dancing and satanic worship.*

UNIVERSITY:

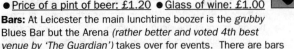

● <u>Price of a pint of beer: £1.20</u> ● <u>Glass of wine: £1.00</u>

Bars: At Leicester the main lunchtime boozer is the *grubby* Blues Bar but the Arena *(rather better and voted 4th best venue by 'The Guardian')* takes over for events. There are bars at the other main centres.

Theatres: The DM Players put on performances in the Y Theatre and often take shows to Edinburgh. At Bedford the Bowen West Centre on the Lansdowne site is run by DMU. The University drama course is based at Scraptoft.

Clubs/discos: The Arena has recently been expanded to a capacity of 1,200 with an *ear-scraping* sound system. Regular nights range from the fortnightly Pandora's Box mishmash of techno and triphop to the Big Cheese, *(Saturdays, 70s cheese)*. There are 2 club nights a week at Polhill (Bedford) and weekly discos at other sites.

Music venues: The Arena can pull in *big names* of the calibre of Dodgy, Chemical Brothers, Boo Radleys, Gene, Audioweb and Black Grape. John Peel has called it the best student venue for live bands in the country *and we wouldn't want to run the risk of offending his many devout followers.* Lower-profile gigs at the other sites, such as Supercool, a jazz night on Sundays at Bedford.

Food: At Leicester the Blues Bar and the Servery fulfil most hot and cold requirements but there are also facilities in the Arena. MK has a *pretty expensive* refectory, run by outside caterers. Bedford has a canteen on each site - *the Polhill bacon rolls come recommended.* The Caythorpe and Lincoln sites have a *well-stocked* refectory and a smaller canteen respectively.

Other: 2 balls a year.

·········· social & political

DE MONTFORT UNIVERSITY STUDENTS' UNION:

● <u>13 sabbaticals</u> ● <u>Turnout at last ballot: 10%</u>

● <u>NUS member</u>

DSU has a 2-tier system to cope with the fragmented nature of its student body. The Global Union (which sounds like something created to fight the Darkside) acts as a representative body for all students but there are individual unions at all sites, which are encouraged to maintain a level of autonomy. This sounds great on paper, but in reality the whole shebang has been in disarray, with students on the smaller sites feeling cut off from the Global Union in favour of the Leicester site. Recent resignations and intra-political turmoils have left precious little time for addressing any issues of real concern. On the up side, these problems are being tackled and the GU is being restructured to better reflect the disparate sites. Only time will tell how successful this will be.

SU FACILITIES:
City Centre Union Building: 2 bars; 1 café; coffee bar; restaurant; 2 minibuses; travel agent; printing services and photocopier; general shop (including newsagent); games, vending and video machines; photobooth; pool tables; juke box; meeting room.
Scraptoft: 2 bars; 1 coffee bar; photocopying; games machines; pool table; juke box; TV lounge; launderette; parking.
Bedford: Bar, 2 shops, 2 games rooms, video machines, pool table, juke box, 2 minibuses.
Milton Keynes: Bar, shop, ents facilities, minibus, cashpoint.
Lincoln: 3 bars.

CLUBS (NON SPORTING):
Alcohol Appreciation; Amateur Radio; Art Appreciation; Chinese; Hellenic; Hindu; Melting Pot; Pagan; Sikh.

OTHER ORGANISATIONS:
'The Voice' newspaper is distributed every 2 weeks to all sites. Radio Demon broadcasts on FM 1 month a year. No Rag at the moment due to the *embarrassingly* poor sums raised in the past, but may be resurrected next year by a new committee.

RELIGIOUS:
● 5 chaplains (2 CofE, RC, Jewish, Methodist)
There's a Centre for Religion by the Union for Catholics, Anglicans and Muslims. **Religion in Leicester:** see Leicester University.

PAID WORK: see University of Leicester

sports

● Recent successes: hockey, volleyball, ladies' rugby.
Again, distance precludes University-wide enthusiasm; sport is popular at Leicester, but Bedford is the prime pillar of sporting success (women's teams are particularly strong) along with Caythorpe (for posh country pursuits, especially).

SPORTS FACILITIES:
Leicester: There are sports facilities at both Leicester sites, but at Scraptoft, it only amounts to 7 acres of playing fields and a gym. At the John Sandford Sports Centre, a few minutes walk from the City site, there are squash and badminton courts, a sports hall, a multigym and sauna. The River Soar which runs by the campus is also useful for watersports.
Bedford: *Huge* sports hall, swimming pool, 3 gyms, fitness suite, dance studio, astroturf pitch, football & rugby pitches, cricket field.
MK: Access to local sports centre and Open University facilities. A new watersports centre is co-managed by DMU.
Lincoln: Riseholme has a weights room, swimming pool, sports hall, pitches and a golf course, *handy for those doing the course in Golf Studies*. Caythorpe has a pool. Students also have access to pitches and sports halls in the locality.

SPORTING CLUBS:
Leicester: Aikido; American Football; Caving; Juggling; Motor Biking; Mugendo; Parachuting; Rowing; Rugby League; Snowboarding; Windsurfing.
MK: Surfing; Windsurfing.

Bedford: Boxing; Korfball; Lacrosse; Martial Arts; Rowing; Rugby League.
Lincoln: Polo (at Caythorpe).

ATTRACTIONS: see University of Leicester

accommodation

LEICESTER:

● Catered: 7% ● Cost: £55(37wks)
● Self-catering: 8% ● Cost: £41(37wks)

Only about ³/₄ of first years are given accommodation in halls of residence at the moment, and 3% have to share, but this should improve when Bede Hall (240 places) is opened for the 98-99 session. *Catered halls only actually cater on weekdays.*

MK:
● Self-catering: 25% ● Cost: £47(37wks)

There is 1 hall of residence at Milton Keynes which only offers 180 self-catering places.

BEDFORD:
● Catered: 16% ● Cost: £48(37wks)
● Self-catering: 1% ● Cost: £40(37wks)

Most places at Bedford are catered and usually only people with special dietary requirements will get into a self-catered hall. *An allergy to canteen food probably doesn't qualify.* There are also limited head tenancy schemes. 370 are accommodated in total.

LINCOLN:
● Catered: 73% ● Cost: £74(31wks)
● Self-catering: 9% ● Cost £41(31wks)

Halls are at Riseholme and Caythorpe and there are a number of head tenancy schemes. *Caythorpe also houses under-18s so you'd better set a good example.*

The figures above show the percentages of full-time undergraduates at each site who are in college accommodation. Overall, 19% of De Montfort full-time undergraduates are housed. Many students are local anyway, especially in Leicester, and so are alright for digs.

EXTERNALLY: see University of Leicester
Housing help: The University Accommodation Office at all sites has a bulletin board and newsletter. The Union provides help and advice.

welfare

SERVICES:

● Creche ● Nightline ● Lesbian & Gay Society
● Mature SA ● Overseas SA ● Minibus ● Women's Officer
● Self-defence classes

The Union and University provide welfare services on all sites. They are organised by the Union's Student Support Unit and Welfare Officer and the University's Counselling & Welfare Service (with 4 counsellors), Law Clinic, Student Health Centre (with 2 doctors and nurses) and the sick bay run in conjunction with Leicester University (costing students £7 a year). The creche is at Bedford only.
Disabled: *Poor access at Leicester* - there are chair lifts and

ramps, but the ramps are designed for goods rather than people. It does have a 'Disability Statement', however, and a new Disabled Committee. *Which is nice. MK, by contrast, is excellent. Bedford, OK.*

FINANCE:
- Ave debt per year: £2,150 ● Access fund: £375,000
- Successful applications (1997): 500

Bursaries are available in science and engineering subjects. Debts are higher overall at Leicester, *maybe because there are more spending temptations in town.*

University of Derby

● *Formerly Derbyshire College of Higher Education*
University of Derby, Kedleston Road, Derby, DE22 1GB.
Tel: (01332) 622222. Fax: (01332) 294861.
University of Derby Students' Union, University of Derby, Kedleston Road, Derby, DE22 1GB. Tel: (01332) 622238.
Fax: (01332) 348846. E-mail: s.union@derby.ac.uk

General

At the southern tip of the beautiful Derbyshire Peak District is the *eminently less beautiful* city of Derby. For those for whom the exact position of the Peak District has always remained a mystery, this places Derby in the north of the Midlands. The university is based at 5 sites around this city, the main one being the Kedleston Road campus just outside town to the north-west amidst *rather pleasant* open countryside. But descriptions of the University are somewhat difficult right now, since, having taken the step from a College of Higher Education to University in 1992, it is still undergoing tremendous changes. By the turn of the century, if work goes to plan, a complete face-changing building programme will have been finished.

45% ♂♂♂♂♂ ♀♀♀♀♀ 55%	
Sex ratio(M:F): 45%:55%	Founded: 1851
Full time u'grads: 9,300	Part time: 3,500
Postgrads: 1,000	Non-degree: 500
Ave course: 3yrs	Ethnic: n/a
Private school: n/a	Flunk rate: 30%
Mature students: 52%	Overseas students: 5%
Disabled students: n/a	Staff/student ratio: 1:16
Clearing: 30%	

ATMOSPHERE:
The Kedleston campus is a friendly, buzzing environment. The large fashion department polarises students into those who look cool and those who wear anoraks, but even among those

who still think terylene is trendy, there's a generally good buzz. Derby has tackled the transformation into a university very well since '92 and is facing the millennium with a wicked grin on its face.

OTHER SITES:
The much-improved bus service has made inter-site travel much easier.

Mickleover: (1,000 students - health & community studies, education, social science) This mainly concrete site, 2 miles to the west of the city centre, has some halls of residence as well as departments. It used to be the Bishop Lonsdale College for Teacher Training.

Green Lane: (300 students - film & TV) Right in the city centre, 3 miles from Kedleston, is this listed Victorian building - a purpose-built art college.

Britannia Mill: (500 students - art & design) *Arty atmosphere* in a converted mill, also in the city centre. There are rumours of a new base for art students, but nothing tangible yet.

Cedars: (200 students - occupational therapy) An Edwardian building and a modernist chunk side by side, also 3 miles from the main site.

THE CITY:
- Population: 220,681 ● London: 120miles
- Birmingham: 37miles ● Nottingham: 14miles

Those who dismiss Derby as being as ugly as a warthog with acne are missing the historical significance of the place. After all, Derby played an important role in the Jacobite Rebellion and a crucial part in the Industrial Revolution. It has got 600 listed buildings, a good number of parks and lots of useful shops and amenities, including a number of bookshops (not least a Dillons at the Kedleston campus). Derby also has 3 museums - the Derby Museum, Industrial Museum and Pickford House - and other attractions like the Arboretum Park and, outside town, Elvaston Castle and Chatsworth House. Note for American readers: it's pronounced 'D*arr*by', not 'D*err*by'.

TRAVEL:
Trains: Derby BR station is 2½ miles from Kedleston Road. Services to London (£22.40), Sheffield (£5.95), Bristol, Edinburgh and beyond.

Coaches: National Express and other services operate to London (£14.25), Sheffield (£4.35), among other places.

Car: Derby is 8 miles from the M1, and also on the A6, A38, A50 and A52.

Air: East Midlands is the closest airport, 8 miles south east of town, with flights inland and to Europe.

Hitching: *Kindly motorists on long hauls on the main roads.*

Local: Reliable buses run every 15 minutes to the town centre from the main campus. Weekly passes are available.

> **❛Mick Jagger, who dropped out of the LSE, is now honorary President of the SU.❜**

Taxis: *£2-3 between sites and city centre; several companies offer 10% student discounts.*
Bicycles: *There are plans for a bike link between city and sites but at the moment roads are too busy for all but the most bloody-minded cyclist.*

LIBRARIES & COMPUTERS:
● Books: 250,000 ● Study places: 1,200
● Computer workstations: 250

There are 5 libraries, 1 at each site. *Study space is pretty cramped* but the new Learning Centre at Kedleston has added more space. Green Lane and Cedars Libraries are closed at weekends. Computer access is 24-hour.

CAREER PROSPECTS:
● Careers Service ● No of staff: 6full/3part
● Unemployed after 6mths (1995): 24%

There's a Student Employment Service to assist in the search for part-time work.

SPECIAL FEATURES:
● 55% of Derby students are local to the area.

FAMOUS ALUMNI:
Cedric Brown (former British Gas fatcat); Jyoti Mishra (White Town).

FURTHER INFO:
Prospectuses for undergrads and part timers. Also course leaflets for some departments. Web site (http://www.derby.ac.uk).

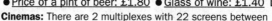

entertainment

THE CITY:
● Price of a pint of beer: £1.80 ● Glass of wine: £1.40
Cinemas: There are 2 multiplexes with 22 screens between them, as well as the *artier* Metro.
Theatres: The Derby Playhouse hosts all sorts and has its own repertory company.
Pubs: *Nearby Burton is the brewing capital of England.*
push*plugs: Ryan's; O'Neil's; The Flamingo & Firkin. The Ashbourne mile is a renowned bar crawl.*
Clubs/discos: Derby is picking up speed on the club front. The SU runs Bonk at the Pink Coconut (happy house/indie) and Disco 2000 at the Eclipse (handbag/chart). *Other*
push*plugs: Bluenote (indie); Progress (techno); Swamp Club (cajun).*
Music venues: No massive venues, but several large enough to attract more than local strummers and drummers. The Assembly Rooms has major bands *but they charge the earth. The Wherehouse is a popular indie venue.*
Eating out: The pizza chains do student discounts and Curzon Street and Normanton Road provide the curry nexus.
push*plugs: Friargate (Cantonese); Excelsior (Chinese); Moghul (Indian).*

UNIVERSITY:
● Price of a pint of beer: £1.30 ● Glass of wine: £1.20
Bars: (6) The Riverside (capacity 700) next to Britannia Mill is the social focus for the student body and there's the Union

Arms at Kedleston Road. Smaller outlets at Mickleover and in halls of residence.

Theatres: (1) *The Musical Productions Society is particularly strong, and Mickleover Student Theatre put on around 5 productions a year.*

Cinema: Derby's Metro cinema is on the Green Lane site.

Clubs/discos/music venues: Union 1 and... *wait for it...* Union 2 are the top venues, luring the likes of Sneaker Pimps, My Life Story and Shed Seven recently. In addition there's some sort of dance event every night.

Food: The Atrium does *inexpensive* snacks and meals.

Others: 3 balls a year, plus various club and society dos and an annual beer festival. 'Week in the Sun' *is a theme week in the summer.*

social & political

UNIVERSITY OF DERBY STUDENTS' UNION:

- 5 sabbaticals ● Turnout at last ballot: 16%
- NUS member

Relations with the university administration have been very cosy indeed, although the Vice-Chancellor's support for top-up fees caused annoyance, as well as the decision to charge the SU rent on two of its bars, now that it's become so successful. Oh, the price of success....

SU FACILITIES:

At Kedleston and in the Mickleover Students' Union Block, the Union provides: bars; minibuses; general and stationery shops; advice centre; fax service; payphone; photocopier; games and vending machines; pool tables; juke box; TV lounge; conference hall; parking.

CLUBS (NON SPORTING):

Grape & Grain; Hellenic; Heritage Conservation; Masters; Mind Games; Pagan; Sikh; Student Chamber of Commerce; Writing.

OTHER ORGANISATIONS:

There's 'Eclipse' magazine (*which is pretty good*) and a charity Rag which raised £10,000 in 1997. There is now a permanent member of staff in charge of the charity Rag, so the figures are set to grow.

RELIGIOUS:

- 1 chaplain (CofE)

The Religious Resource & Research Centre has prayer facilities at both Kedleston and Mickleover and there's a Muslim prayer room at Kedleston. In Derby, there's an Anglican cathedral and provisions for Christians of every hue and Hindus, Muslims, Sikhs and Jews.

sports

- Recent successes: rugby

Facilities are cramped but a new 21-acre site has been acquired. Things were set to perk up, but the SU is currently upset about the lack of facilities.

SPORTS FACILITIES:

Facilities are based at Mickleover. 6 football pitches; athletics field; swimming pool; all-weather pitch; climbing wall;

multigym; running track; badminton court; American football pitch; hockey pitch. Derbyshire adds various other goodies like golf courses, cricket facilities, the river and, of course, the Peak District.

SPORTING CLUBS:
American Football; Dance; Jiu Jitsu; Mountainbiking; Mountaineering; Muay Thai; Parachuting; Snowboarding; Surf; Tennis; Yoga.

ATTRACTIONS:
Derby County FC, and Derbyshire Cricket Club as well.

accommodation

IN COLLEGE:
● Self-catering: 28% ● Cost: £38-£56(35wks)
Availability: 85% of 1st years can be accommodated and 8% of students have to share. The residences are purpose-built in the last few years, all a healthy walk away from the main campuses. *St Christopher's Court is a groovy cosmopolitan place to live. Students should beware late-payment fines, which are rather strictly observed.*
Car parking: *Space for parking is at a premium and not available to most students.*

EXTERNALLY:
● Ave rent: £35
Availability: *The rental market has settled down after the explosion of student numbers encouraged some pretty sub-standard flats onto the scene. The West End, Duffield Road and Kedleston Road are the main pockets of student habitation. Normanton and Peartree are the red-light districts - if that's of any interest.*
Housing help: The 6 staff in the Residential Services Department can offer advice and assistance, as can the SU.

welfare

SERVICES:
● Nursery ● Nightline ● Lesbian & Gay Society
● Mature SA ● Minibus ● Women's Officer
● Self-defence classes
The college provides 10 counsellors in a new advice centre. There's a 40-place nursery at Mickleover, *with a long waiting list.* Drop-in surgeries are held by a nurse.
Disabled: *Wheelchair access is variable according to the site; all new developments are excellent. The University is rightly proud of its Deafness Studies Unit and there's help available for students with dyslexia.*

FINANCE:
● Ave debt per year: £2,250 ● Access fund: £134,000
● Successful applications (1996): 460

▶▶ **Distributive Trades**
see The London Institute

● ●

▶▶ DIT

see University of Abertay Dundee

● ●

▶▶ Dorset Institute

see Bournemouth University

● ●

University of Dundee

▼
▼ University of Dundee, Dundee, DD1 4HN. Tel: (01382) 344160. Fax: (01382) 221554. E-mail: srs@dundee.ac.uk Dundee University Students' Association, Airlie Place, Dundee, DD1 4HP. Tel: (01382) 221841. Fax: (01382) 227124.

General

On the northern side of the Firth of Tay, down the eastern coast of Scotland from Aberdeen, is Dundee. The Tay estuary, the surrounding miles of beaches and highlands rising inland *are very picturesque. Unfortunately, the same cannot be said for Dundee. It's a fairly dour city, a hotch-potch of architecture.* In an area of town with some *lovely* views over the Tay, 1 mile west of the city centre, is the self-contained campus of Dundee University. Its buildings have sprouted over the last 100 years or so and provide examples of most styles over that period - *some of the best and worst excesses. The Union Building, for example, is a modernist glass-fronted thingy.* Despite a sense of space, there are few green areas, but the parks of Riverside are only ¼ mile away.

43% ♂♂♂♂♂♀♀♀♀♀♀ 57%	
Sex ratio(M:F): 43%:57%	Founded: 1967
Full time u'grads: 7,524	Part time: 424
Postgrads: 749	Non-degree: 1,524
Ave course: 4yrs	Ethnic: 6%
Private school: 10%	Flunk rate: n/a
Mature students: 32%	Overseas students: 9%
Disabled students: 3%	Staff/student ratio: 1:10
Clearing: 10%	

ATMOSPHERE:
The campus is compact and the University untraditional. The mix of students on campus is broad - full of normal, unpretentious people and there is fun to be had, but the atmosphere isn't exactly rocking. By all rights, the main centre of activity should be the Union, but it feels a bit flat and characterless. So students find their own entertainment, forming clubs and losing themselves in their work.

THE CITY:
- Population: 165,548 ● London: 384miles
- Edinburgh: 50miles ● Aberdeen: 60miles

The city has recently had a *long overdue* facelift. The Tay itself, Riverside and the port area have certain attractions and there are 1,300 acres of parkland including golf courses, a zoo and a nature trail. There are 2 bridges over the Tay - a railway and a road bridge, both of which are more successful than the first bridge which collapsed in 1879 shortly after it was built, killing 75 people *(as described in the profoundly moving poem by McGonagall). The people are friendly enough too.* The city has several museums, galleries and historic buildings including Bonar Hall (a University-owned exhibition centre). *Worth a mention* are the Observatory on Balgay Hill and Captain Scott's ship 'Discovery'.

TRAVEL:
Trains: Dundee BR Station has services to London (£42.90), Glasgow (£15) and routes to most parts of Scotland and England.

Coaches: National Express, Stagecoach and Citylink services to many destinations including London (£27), Glasgow (£6.50) and Edinburgh (£6).

Car: From the south, the M90 goes up to Perth (19 miles west) from where there's the A90, or the A914 which crosses the Tay. From the north, there's the A92, A929 and A923.

Air: Dundee (Riverside Park) Airport.

Hitching: *Not easy. Around Dundee there are too many roundabouts where hitchers can get stuck all day. The best bet is to get a lift on the A92 along the coast and, if heading south, to try to pass close by Edinburgh.*

Local: There's a *good* bus service and it's *fairly cheap* (80p across town), but the last is at around 11.15pm. There's only 1 train stop in Dundee; 1 line comes along the Tay from Perth and the other crosses the Tay heading south.

Taxis: Cheapest in Scotland.

Bicycles: *Not too hilly and theft isn't a major problem, but bikes aren't really that necessary.*

LIBRARIES & COMPUTERS:
- Books: 700,000 ● Study places: 1,350
- Computer workstations: 875

More than ½ of the books are in the Main Library, but there are 3 others specialising in Medicine, Art and Law, as well as departmental libraries. There's also a computer suite, with *limited* 24hr access.

CAREER PROSPECTS:
- Careers Service ● No of staff: 7full
- Unemployed after 6mths (1996): 4.8%

There are lots of resources available and the Careers Office is open during the vacations but personal help is perceived to be in short supply.

SPECIAL FEATURES:
● Tony Slattery is the new Rector of the University, *which is a shame because his predecessor, Stephen Fry was much funnier.* 'I have an assessor, there is a Students' Association, there is a chaplain, there are tutors. All these fine men and

women may be able to do things for you. I am, to some
extent, the almonds lying atop the Dundee cake, not the rich
body of the cake itself.'
● Comedian Jerry Sadowitz describes the residents of
Dundee: 'They're so thick, if you pour hot water on their heads,
you get Pot Noodle.'
● The University has taken over the School of Nursing and
Midwifery in Kirkcaldy, Fife, about 30 miles away.

FAMOUS ALUMNI:
Sir James Black (Nobel laureate, medicine; current
Chancellor); Brian Cox (actor); David Leslie (rugby); George
Robertson MP (Lab).

FURTHER INFO:
Prospectuses for undergrads and postgrads. SA Handbook.
There are also web sites for the University
(http://www.dundee.ac.uk) and DUS
(http://www.dundee.ac.uk/dusa).

entertainment

THE CITY:
●Price of a pint of beer: £1.80 ●Glass of wine: £1.45
Cinemas: 10-screen Odeon, 2-screen independent and a small
art-house cinema.
Theatres: The Dundee Rep hosts transfers from the West End,
Scottish plays, Xmas pantos and so on, often starring
household names. On Sundays, it has comedy nights.
Pubs: *Many of the city's best pubs are quite student-friendly.
Of course, being Scotland, they're open virtually all the time.*
push*plugs: The Globe (friendly, good food); Tally-Ho (beer
yard out back); Lucifer's Mill (cheap cocktails, live music);
Freelance & Firkin; Balgay (cheap). Avoid the Speedwell and
the Taybridge - old men alert.*
Clubs/discos: *Dundee's clubs may not be world-renowned, nor
indeed cheap, but that doesn't stop students having a good
time.* **push***plugs: Fat Sam's; Mardi Gras; Cooler (new funk
club opened at Lucifer's Mill).*
Music venues: *Lucifer's Mill is the indie stronghold, while Fat
Sam's is more rock'n'roll. Recent acts to do it in Dundee
include Cast, the Charlatans and Radiohead. Caird Hall has
classical and pop on a regular basis. The West Port pub
swings to cajun and Mexican sounds.*
Eating out: *Pubs are usually a good starting-point - most of the
student favourites do food beyond the pork scratching stage.
Other* **push***plugs: DD1's (good value); Raffles; Rat & Parrot.*

❛One of the entrances to
Loughborough University is
nicknamed 'The Bastard Gates'
because they were presented by Sir
William Bastard, a former chairman
of the University governors.❜

Others: For fun before nightfall, there are the zoo and wildlife sanctuary and the beaches.

UNIVERSITY:

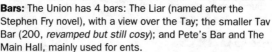

● Price of a pint of beer: £1.20 ● Glass of wine: £1.00

Bars: The Union has 4 bars: The Liar (named after the Stephen Fry novel), with a view over the Tay; the smaller Tav Bar (200, *revamped but still cosy*); and Pete's Bar and The Main Hall, mainly used for ents.

Theatres: (2) There are theatres in the Union and the Bonar Hall (500), which is run as a commercial venture by the University. There are *active* student drama and opera companies.

Cinema: 1 film a week, *usually arty, culty, fringey or world-cinema-y.*

Music venues: The Main Hall and Pete's Bar both pull in *OK* live acts; recently, Death in Vegas, Space.

Clubs/discos: The main club nights (£3) are Lollipop (Britpop/60s), Nightfever (70s) and Dallas (cheese central).

Cabaret: Occasional comic turns (eg Graham Norton, Rhona Cameron)

Food: The Filling Station is open for breakfast and lunches. There's also a Pizza/Snack bar, and the Liar and the Tav do *good value* meals.

Others: Annual 12-hour Graduation Ball, faculty balls and termly, *less dressy* affairs.

⸳⸳⸳⸳⸳⸳⸳⸳ social & political

DUNDEE UNIVERSITY STUDENTS' ASSOCIATION:

● 3 sabbaticals

The Union is the name of the *horribly mirrored* building where DUSA, the representative and organisational body is based. The students can be a bit complacent about the services they get out of the SA. *Politically, most students don't care if they're right, left or hanging from the ceiling by their ankles, so long as the beer doesn't run out.*

SU FACILITIES:

In the Union: 4 bars; coffee lounge; advice centre; meeting room; minibuses; travel agency; photocopying and printing service; banks & cashpoints (Clydesdale & Royal Bank of Scotland); pool tables; swimming pool; bookshop; launderette; hairdressers; photo booth; vending machine; large games room; juke-box. Outside the Union, but also on campus, there's a general shop.

CLUBS (NON SPORTING):

Buddhist; Chinese; Cumbrian Roads; European; Hellenic; Juggling; Malaysian; Operatic; Role Playing.

OTHER ORGANISATIONS:

The official, DUSA-sponsored paper is the three-weekly 'Student Times' - there's also 'McDougall', an independent mag, and 'Blunt Instrument', an ents publication.

RELIGIOUS:

● 8 chaplains (CofE, RC, Baptist, Methodist, CofS)

In the University, there are a large chaplaincy *(which also hosts things like line-dancing events)*, inter-denominational chapel and Muslim prayer room. In town, there are other churches and places of worship, catering for most types of Christian, as well as Muslims, Jews, Sikhs and Hindus.

PAID WORK:

Some seasonal work at the local Outdoor Pursuits Centre and tourist spots across the Tay in Fife. *Local part-time work is as hard to find as a good heart.*

sports

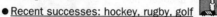

- <u>Recent successes: hockey, rugby, golf</u>

Sport is a major topic of conversation; even those not keen to get their knees dirty are quite happy to swing a club or two (that's golf, not armed combat).

SPORTS FACILITIES:

The Riverside sports facilities include 33 acres of playing fields and an all-weather pitch. On campus, there are 2 refurbished sports halls, 4 squash and tennis courts, a gym, a swimming pool and a sauna. Overall Dundee has the most extensive indoor facilities of any Scottish university. At Newport, there is a watersports centre. There's a set of bursaries from the St Andrews Royal & Ancient Golf Club worth £1,500 each to 8 students hot with a 3 iron.

SPORTING CLUBS:

Gaelic Football; Jiu Jitsu; Kickboxing; Tennis; Ultimate Frisbee.

ATTRACTIONS:

Dundee United and Dundee FC are the local soccer heroes. There are also 3 local sports centres.

accommodation

IN COLLEGE:

- <u>Catered: 7%</u> ● <u>Cost: £64(31wks)</u>
- <u>Self-catering: 14%</u> ● <u>Cost: £35-52(38wks)</u>

Availability: All 1st years who live outside Dundee are guaranteed accommodation but it gets a bit tougher after that, and only 64% of 1st years live in. Halls tend to be for freshers only *and the catered food is dire*; then there's self-catering accommodation, *some of it very new and flash, with en suite, good security and everything;* and there are also a number of leased houses around the city, that the University administers. 4% have to share, most of them in halls.

Car parking: *There's a desperate shortage of parking on and around the campus.* Permits, at £5 a year, are needed.

EXTERNALLY:

- <u>Ave rent: £37</u>

Availability: Many students who live out live in their parents' or their own home and so they are alright, Jack (or Jackie). *There's enough choice around for students to be able to pick somewhere near where they have to study. Good places include Perth Road, but even this is getting to be quite expensive, and students are moving further and further out. The east side and city centre are a bit too rough for more sensitive souls. Certainly, it's better to be safe than sorry.*

Housing help: The University Residences Office, apart from allocating University places, offers bulletin boards, advice and booklets, provided by 8 staff.

welfare

SERVICES:

● Nursery ● Lesbian & Gay Society ● Mature SA
● Minibus ● Women's Officer ● Self-defence classes

The 1 part- and 2 full-time professional counsellors at the University Counselling Service deal with all manner of troubles, while the new Student Advisory Service concentrates on financial matters. There are lunchtime drop-in sessions and police and solicitor's clinics. The Student Health Service has visiting doctors and a nursing officer.

Women: Personal safety alarms are subsidised and there are security patrols.

Disabled: *The University has a good record for making provision for sight-impaired students, but wheelchair access isn't so great.* One hall has some specialised rooms. There is also a Disabled Support Unit, a Special Needs Advisor and 'Dudes' Support Group.

FINANCE:
● Ave debt per year: £1,400 ● Access fund: £167,000
● Successful applications (1997): 514

The University doles out various bursaries and DUSA has its own hardship fund (£13,000).

▶▶ **Dundee Institute of Technology**
see University of Abertay Dundee

University of Durham

(1) The University of Durham, Old Shire Hall, Old Elvet, Durham, DH1 3HP. Tel: (0191) 374 2000.
Fax: (0191) 374 7250.
Durham Students' Union, Dunelm House, New Elvet, Durham, DH1 3AN. Tel: (0191) 374 3310. Fax: (0191) 374 3328.
E-mail: student.union@durham.ac.uk
(2) University College Stockton, University Boulevard, Thornaby, Stockton-on-Tees, Cleveland, TS17 6BH.
Tel: (01642) 335300. Fax: (01642) 618345.
University College Stockton Students' Union, University Boulevard, Thornaby, Stockton-on-Tees, Cleveland, TS17 6BH.
Tel: (01642) 335344.

general

Durham City, laced by the River Wear, lies in the heart of the Geordie-speaking North East, near the Northumbrian moors, 10 miles from the North Sea and 52 south of the Scottish border. The University is planted in the middle of the ancient, small city, and *on weekdays during term time, students*

dominate it socially as much as the cathedral and castle do physically. The Castle is one of the University's colleges, which are spread out in 3 main groups *giving the advantages of a collegiate, a civic and a campus university.*

50% ♂♂♂♂♂♀♀♀♀♀ **50%**

Sex ratio(M:F): 50%:50%	Founded: 1832
Full time u'grads: 7,843	Part time: 553
Postgrads: 1,214	Non-degree: 572
Ave course: 3yrs	Ethnic: 4%
Private school: 33%	Flunk rate: n/a
Mature students: 13%	Overseas students: 4%
Disabled students: 5%	Staff/student ratio: 1:13
Clearing: 2%	

ATMOSPHERE:
As England's 3rd oldest university, there's something of the Oxbridge about Durham, with its traditions, its formal dinners and balls (the black-tie variety). One major difference though is the strength of its central SU. Although the weather's chilly, the hearts are warm. The college system and the size of the city certainly create a communal atmosphere that some find claustrophobic, but the city's becoming more student-friendly so there's more chance to escape.

THE COLLEGES:
Much of a student's social life is centred around the college where they eat, sleep and drink. However, unlike Oxbridge, teaching is not college-based. The colleges are grouped into 3 areas *and each group has a flavour of its own. It is important to pick the right college - they do vary.*
The oldest colleges are on 'the Peninsula' and *they appeal particularly to those who admire their architecture and tradition, if not their facilities:*
University College or 'Castle' (523 students): *predominantly public school students sacrifice a few creature comforts to live in a castle in their 3rd year.* The Castle (founded in 1072) is the oldest building used for student accommodation in the country *and can get a bit sloany.*
Hatfield (617): *rugby and beer.*
St Chad's (279): *croquet and Pimms.*
St John's (364): *church links, largely Christian.*
St Cuthbert's Society (906): 80% live out of college, many mature students but this is balancing out.
'The Hill Colleges', near the science departments, were mostly built in the 60s *and tend to be more progressive:*
St Aidan's (704): *motivated and progressive students; they have to be to climb that hill.*
Van Mildert (645): *like Aidan's, but perhaps less motivated and not on a hill.*
Trevelyan (499): *honeycomb maze architecture.*
St Mary's (522): all female, *sporty party monsters.*
Grey (707): *slightly more character than its name suggests.*
Collingwood (944): *media hacksville.*
The 3rd area is the hilly north bank of the Wear where
Hild/Bede (858) stands alone, *a mixture of all sorts, accused*

variously of being too insular or too dominant.

There are also **The Graduate Society** (811) for postgrads and **Ushaw College** (4), a Catholic seminary 4 miles outside the city.

The 15th college, **University College, Stockton** (905), *is completely unlike the main site, in terms of atmosphere, history and geography.* It only accepted its first intake in 1992. It has 700 undergraduates, many from the local area, and about 40% mature. Stockton is about 21 miles south of Durham, and 3 miles from Middlesbrough. It's expanding at a rate of knots and should have 1,750 students by 1999. There's self-catering accommodation with 240 places.

THE CITY:
- Population: 85,000 ● London: 240miles
- Newcastle: 15miles

Durham used to be the epicentre of the north-east's mining tradition. There was a time when the annual Durham Miners' Gala (pronounced GAY-ler) was the country's largest Labour meeting - recently though, it has only attracted 5,000 people and no Labour leaders. *Nowadays (as far as it seems to students at any rate), there's not much in Durham that isn't connected to the University or the Cathedral:* a shopping mall, lots of quaint shoppes, DLI arts museum, open air and covered markets, but no shopping after 5.30pm. *Things are picking up a bit but the fun-seekers and money-spenders take themselves to Newcastle.*

Stockton: Stockton is part of the Teesside conurbation, and was the birthplace of commercial passenger railways in 1825. It's now an area of bigtime urban renewal, with a couple of shopping malls, and easy access to Middlesbrough (see University of Teesside).

TRAVEL:

Trains: Main-line connections to London King's X (£41.60), Newcastle (£2.60) and more.

Coaches: National Express and Blue Line services to many destinations: London (£20), Newcastle (£1.50) and so on.

Car: 5 mins off the A1.

Air: Newcastle Airport on the A691 - flights to London, Northern Ireland and Europe.

Hitching: *Good grooving from the A1.*

Local: *Good* buses around town and surrounds which lazy students use to get to the hill colleges (most walk). Fares from 32p. No trains around the city but a *useful* service into Newcastle.

Taxis: Some of Britain's cheapest taxis (minimum fare £1; only £15 to Newcastle, making it a worthwhile share).

Bicycles: *A bit hilly for bikes.*

LIBRARIES & COMPUTERS:
- Books: 1,140,000 ● Study places: 1,200
- Computer workstations: 620

In addition to the University's recently extended main library with 540,000 books, there are 3 other libraries (education, ecclesiastical texts and special collections). Each college has its own library as do many departments. There are 6 classrooms of computers around the University and computer rooms in most colleges as well as a computer centre. *Even so, access to computers can get difficult at peak times.* All students can do an optional computer literacy course.

CAREER PROSPECTS:
- <u>Careers Service</u> ● <u>No of staff: 8full/3part</u>
- <u>Unemployed after 6mths (1996): 6%</u>

SPECIAL FEATURES:
- Durham has one 9-week and two 10-week terms.
- A new £30 million, 17-acre science park is on the cards, as is a new college, at Howlands Farm.
- A Japanese university has a campus in Durham for the purpose of forging cultural links with British students.
- 1994 saw the launch of the UK's first degree course in classical ballet, in conjunction with the Royal Academy of Dancing.

FAMOUS ALUMNI:
George Alagiah, Jeremy Vine (BBC reporters); Nasser Hussein (cricketer); Biddy Baxter (ex-producer of 'Blue Peter'); Will Carling, Phil de Glanville (England rugby captains); Jack Cunningham MP, Mo Mowlem MP (Lab); Hunter Davies (journalist); Jonathan Edwards (triple jumper); Harold Evans (ex-Sunday Times editor); Cmdr Tim Lawrence (Princess Anne's hubby); Edward Leigh MP (Con); James Wilby (actor); Glenda Jackson (actress and MP); Johnny X (Kenickie); Steve Redgrave (4 times Olympic hero) has an honorary scroll.

FURTHER INFO:
Prospectuses for undergrads, postgrads and adult students. SU Handbook. Alternative Prospectus from SU (£3.50). Web site (http://www.dur.ac.uk and http://www.dur.ac.uk/DSU).

entertainment

THE CITY:

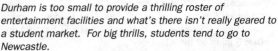

- <u>Price of a pint of beer: £1.70</u> ● <u>Glass of wine: £1.40</u>

Durham is too small to provide a thrilling roster of entertainment facilities and what's there isn't really geared to a student market. For big thrills, students tend to go to Newcastle.

Pubs: *Although students aren't welcomed everywhere, there are still plenty of traditional northern pubs serving bitters with bite like the ubiquitous 'dog' (Newcastle Brown).* **push***plugs: The Court Inn (good grub); Colpitts; The Shakespeare; Dun Cow (real ale); Market Tavern; New Inn; Saints (Internet café); Scruffy Murphy's. The aptly-named Fighting Cocks is best avoided.*

Cinemas: *1 independent with 4 screens. Robin's Cinema on North Street has a student night on Thursdays and shows arty stuff.*

Clubs/discos: *Café Rock is the mainstream chartbound venue.* **push***plugs: Funky Slug (indie); Klute (70s/80s nights, Drum & Bass); Club Elysium.*

Music venues: *No big venues, but local bands play at the Working Men's Club and local pubs (plenty of folk and R&B).*

Eating out: *Not a great deal of choice but one or two places to take your mind off college food for a few hours.* **push***plugs: La Spaghetatta (Italian); Pierre Victoire; Market Tavern (great pies).*

UNIVERSITY:

● <u>Price of a pint of beer: £1.15</u> ● <u>Glass of wine: 90p</u>

Bars: (16) Each college has its own bar, *where college spirit comes in doubles*, and the Kingsgate Bar in Dunelm House (the SU) is open on a regular basis, *though it has been said that the seating is bad, music too loud and the staff rubbish.* There's a club bar - ie a small one - at DUS (which isn't the same as DSU, see below).

Theatre: *Durham Student Theatre is very active, putting on big, expensive productions in the University theatre and at the Edinburgh Fringe.* The Castle Shakespeare Theatre Company and Fountains Theatre Company based at Grey College are developing quite a reputation.

Cinemas: Hild/Bede and the SU each show recent films.

Clubs/discos/music venues: Dunelm House has 3 halls to use as club and live music venues (caps 750, 250, 100) and colleges have smaller facilities *but round these parts 'bangin' choons' means hitting menthol sweets, though St Aidan's puts on a good dance night. Visiting bands are conspicuous by their absence - according to an ents officer 'apathetic students would rather get trolleyed for a tenner'.*

Food: *The Riverside Cafe is a bit shabby and institutional, and Kingsgate does pretty standard stuff.*

Balls: Each college has at least 1 ball a year, costing from a few quid to £130 for a double ticket at Castle's *elitist* June bash. The SU also holds a Freshers' Ball. *Durham's raucous 'Rah' contingent (chinless posh kids) use these as an excellent opportunity to behave badly in expensive frocks. As if they need an excuse.*

Comedy: Comedy club every Thursday - recent giggle-givers include Jenny Eclair as well as the Union's own Durham Review.

Others: Musicon organises regular classical and more populist concerts (but not pop) in the Cathedral and around the University.

social & political

DURHAM STUDENTS' UNION:

● <u>3 sabbaticals</u> ● <u>Turnout at last ballot: 25%</u>
● <u>NUS member</u>

Although DSU is a politically shrewd union with a representative voice in the University, active members don't often have party affiliations (at least not on their sleeves, although many students feel the sabbatical posts are just stepping stones for political careers). On the other hand, the executive feel the students sometimes forget who provides the many SU services. There are 7 JCR Chair sabs as well as the 3 in the executive. 25% of the student body voted in a referendum against Tuition Fees. Stockton has its own Union.

SU FACILITIES:

The large union building, Dunelm House, is placed right in the middle of the city where it offers 3 bars, a ballroom, Riverside Room cafeteria, small hall, shop, travel agent, launderette, stationery shop, 2nd-hand bookshop, advice centre, ticket agency, pool tables, minibuses, car & van hire, fax, print and photocopier service, meeting rooms, games and vending machines, juke box, public phones, photo booth.

CLUBS (NON SPORTING):

Anglo-Japanese; Archaeology; Assassins; Beatles; Belly-dancing; Blondes; Buddhist Meditation; Change Ringers; Choral; Circus; Club Scene; Football Supporters; Free Tibet; Hellenic; Hot Curry; Indie; Industrial; Line Dancing; Mah Jong; Merhaba; Methodist; Motor Sports; Oriental; Real Ale; Rock; Russian; Ruth First; Scouts & Guides; Tibet; Treasure Trap; Walking; Wine; Wodehouse *(as in PG)*.
Each college also has its own set of societies.

OTHER ORGANISATIONS:

DSU publishes the *excellent* independent student newspaper 'Palatinate' and there's also 'ON', the *similarly impressive* student arts magazine. There's also Purple FM radio. The charity Rag was banned in 1976 for breaking <u>into</u> Durham's top security prison and so students just changed the name to 'DUCK' (Durham University Charity weeK). Student Community Action acts as an umbrella group for many town-gown projects including SPARK which promotes work with local youngsters. The Durham Union Society (DUS) is the long-standing debating society which offers more than just debating. It also runs a bar, TV room, café and a range of events. *It's often seen as a right-wing alternative to DSU or a refuge for the sophisticated Sloane -* either way it costs £35 to get in.

RELIGIOUS:

There is a 1,500 year-old Christian heritage, so finding a church is easy: as well as the Cathedral there are Anglican, Catholic, Methodist, Quaker and United Reformed churches. Most colleges have their own chapel. For Muslims, a prayer room is provided, but the nearest mosque is in Sunderland. Anyone else has to venture to Newcastle for places to worship.

PAID WORK:

Very few openings, although the SU runs a job-shop. Last year only 383 students sought work through the job-shop, and 192 of them found it.

sports

● <u>Recent successes: cricket, rowing</u>

Durham has an excellent sporting record as a glance at the alumni list will testify. The large amount of money spent on sports by the University may have something to do with this. There's a sabbatical student sports president.

SPORTS FACILITIES:

Sports hall; 60 acres of playing fields; all-weather pitch; multigym; athletics and running track; gym; croquet lawn and bowling green, tennis and squash courts and the River Wear. Outdoor pitches are floodlit. Durham City also has a public baths and an ice rink. Stockton, by contrast, has no facilities.

> ❛Leeds University contains the longest corridor in Europe and scenes from 'Blake's 7' were filmed there.❜

SPORTING CLUBS:

Bridge; Chess; Croquet; Fives; Free Fall; Gliding; Golf; Guns; Hang Gliding; Ice Hockey; Ice Skating; Kendo; Lacrosse; Mountaineering; Real Tennis; Rowing; Rifles; Speleological (Pot-Holing); Tang Soo Do; Ten-pin Bowling; Water Polo; Windsurfing. Each college also has its own sporting clubs, including a boat club each.

ATTRACTIONS:

The Durham Regatta is *one of the top annual university rowing events (Henley and the Varsity Boat Race are more top).* The ice rink is the home of the Durham Wasps ice-hockey team and Durham is now a 1st class cricketing county *(but not a very good one).* Some of Durham's Sloanes like to flutter daddy's money on the geegees at Thirsk. *As with most things, Newcastle offers more.*

accommodation

IN COLLEGE:

- <u>Catered: 53%</u> ● <u>Cost: £74(28wks)</u>
- <u>Self-catering: 5%</u> ● <u>Cost: £43(28wks)</u>

Availability: Almost all 1st years live in and colleges can usually provide accommodation for at least 1 further year. Overall, 17% have to share. Except in St Mary's, all accommodation is mixed. 41% of postgrads are already housed, and another hall is being planned for them.

Catering: Living in means having to suffer or enjoy the variable standards of mass-catering *(University College is the worst, Collingwood the best - bring your vitamin supplements, either way).* Except for the self-catering places (post-grads and Stockton only), the shared kitchens are only adequate for tea and toast.

Amenities: Launderettes; bars; libraries; chapels; common rooms; TV and games rooms; music rooms; some colleges also have halls and large theatre-style venues.

Car parking: Permit required for the limited spaces at some colleges.

EXTERNALLY:

- <u>Ave rent: £45</u>

Availability: *It's difficult but feasible to find private housing for rent.* Some choose to resort to the surrounding villages where rents are lower and places are more available. What there is is in Victorian houses shared between about 3 and 5, *the Viaduct being a sought-after spot, closely followed by Bowburn and Langley Moor. The surrounding pit villages should be avoided.* Cars are unnecessary and are the cause of much local tension, but many still bring them.

Housing help: DSU employs 1 part-time accommodation officer who runs an office with vacancy lists, standard contracts, legal help and postgrad house-hunting days. St Cuthbert's Society gives a bit of a boost to its own students.

welfare

SERVICES:

- <u>Creche</u> ● <u>Lesbian & Gay Society</u>
- <u>Mature SA</u> ● <u>Overseas SA</u> ● <u>Postgrad SA</u> ● <u>Minibus</u>
- <u>Women's Officer</u> ● <u>Self-defence classes</u>

There is a student health centre run by the University with 1 doctor, a psychotherapist and nurses. Students are also allocated to local NHS practices by their colleges. There's an *excellent* welfare service employing 6 full-time counsellors. Each student is also assigned a moral tutor by their college and there's even a legal advice surgery, run by a local solicitor. Race Awareness Officers are a recent introduction.

Disabled: Special provisions have been made for hearing impaired students and, with a few partially sighted students, these make up most of the University's disabled population. *However, the city's topsy topography makes it a toughie for students with mobility difficulties.* Students with disabilities are allowed to use the women's minibus.

FINANCE:
- Ave debt per year: £1,650 - Access fund: £200,000
- Successful applications (1997): 350

There's a hardship fund of £30,000 *but a student has to be in seriously deep poo to benefit from it.* There are also scholarships, bursaries and prizes galore.

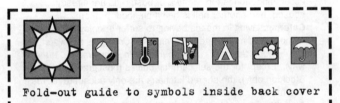

Fold-out guide to symbols inside back cover

> ❝'I bleed for these students' unions that have been hijacked by a bunch of lefties. We're sick of them wasting our money on their pathetic marches, demos and women's things. We should tell students' union leaders to go stuff themselves.'
> -Brian Hitchens, editor of the 'Daily Express' and profound educational philosopher.❞

❝Huddersfield University is building a teaching and accommodation block on the site of the largest psychiatric hospital in Europe.❞

❝Get your money's worth... read 'PUSHover: how to use PUSH' at the front of the book.❞

❝Freaked out by finance? Why not pop into your local branch of Lloyds Bank and see what they have to offer.❞

e

Ealing College
see Thames Valley University

East Anglia
see University of East Anglia

East European Studies
see SSEES

❛The Rector of Glasgow University, elected by the students, is Richard ʼVictor Meldrewʼ Wilson.❜

229

University of East London

● *Formerly Polytechnic of East London, North East London Polytechnic*

(1) University of East London, Barking Campus, Longbridge Road, Dagenham, Essex, RM8 2AS. Tel: (0181) 590 7700. Fax: (0181) 590 7799.

University of East London Students' Union, Longbridge Road, Dagenham, Essex, RM8 2AS. Tel: (0181) 590 6017.

(2) University of East London, Stratford Campus, Romford Road, London, E15 4LZ.

General

For general information about London: see <u>University of London</u>. The University of East London (UEL) isn't just in east London. In fact, it's in 6 places, grouped into UEL's 2 main sites, 4 miles from each other: the Stratford Campus (nothing to do with Avon or Shakespeare) and the Barking Campus *(nothing to do with dogs - oh dear, sorry)* in the huge area of *sprawling suburbia,* east of London that is Ilford and Barking. 5½ miles north-east of Trafalgar Square at Stratford, the Main Building is *a fine example* of Victorian municipal architecture (a listed building), surrounded by London's East End, which, *with toned down stereotypes, is pretty well represented by a certain well-known soap.* The Barking site is bigger and *more attractive, despite the surrounding area. This is partly because* it is set in Goodmayes Park, *an oasis in the suburban desert of Essex.*

50% ♂♂♂♂♂♀♀♀♀♀ 50%	
Sex ratio(M:F): 50%:50%	**Founded: 1970**
Full time u'grads: 8,400	**Part time: 2,900**
Postgrads: 1,820	**Non-degree: 850**
Ave course: 3yrs	**Ethnic: 49%**
Private school: n/a	**Flunk rate: n/a**
Mature students: 80%	**Overseas students: 16%**
Disabled students: 2%	**Staff/student ratio: 1:19**
Clearing: n/a	

ATMOSPHERE:
Probably the best part of UEL is that students can get on with their own lives without being bothered with the delights and distractions of student culture. A real disappointment for those in quest of the cliché lifestyle of baked beans, bars and books, but a definite bonus for some, particularly the huge proportion of students who qualify as mature, which means they're returners to education, not that they smell of cheese. In fact, although facilities may be wanting, the social mix is an interesting cocktail - half the students come from ethnic minority backgrounds and many come from the local area.

There's a positive atmosphere of vibrant tolerance, but most people see this as a friendly environment in which to study, rather than as a political statement.

BEING A STUDENT IN LONDON: see <u>University of London</u>

THE SITES:
There's a fair amount of travelling between sites (by London's public transport, see below). It is, however, important for students to check out which site their courses are based at and what's there: Barking (engineering, business, social sciences and design); Maryland (new technology); Duncan House (management); Holbrook and Greengate (art and architecture). *As sites go, the Stratford campus is a bit incohesive, while Barking is much more bustley.* A new site is planned to open in Docklands in September 99.

THE CITY: see <u>University of London</u>

THE EAST END AND DAGENHAM:
Stratford and the surrounding areas of London's East End are, traditionally, the home of London's dispossessed: first, Jews; nowadays, Asians and yuppies. *They have a lively community atmosphere which is hard to find elsewhere in inner city London.* The market in Petticoat Lane *may be a bit more gimmicky than once upon a time,* but Brick Lane is a *massive overdose for the shopaholic,* even late into the night. Local attractions *worth noting* include the labyrinthine Barbican Centre, one of the country's largest arts centres.

Barking and Ilford are the stomping grounds of the Essex Girl and where Essex Man parks his Capri. There are the bare necessities of shops and pubs but for history and broadened horizons they pale beside Stratford.

TRAVEL: see <u>University of London</u>
Local travel: *One thing that would really make UEL seem like a real University would be a decent bus service between sites and this may happen at some stage. Until then students often bring cars, the parking implications of which cause friction with the locals.*
Trains: For Stratford the nearest rail station is Maryland (10mins from London Liverpool St). Barking Station is 13 minutes from London Fenchurch St Station.
Buses: The only buses that run between the 2 sites are the 238 and the 25 (more or less), which run from the Aldwych (in the West End), past the Stratford site's Main Building to Ilford. Other buses for Stratford include 69, 173, 241, 262 and a number of Night Buses. And for Barking: 5, 87, 162, 287 and N95.
Docklands Light Railway: *The somewhat unreliable DLR runs services into the City and Docklands, when it runs.*
Underground: Stratford is on the Central Line. Barking on the District Line (and, at peak hours, the Hammersmith & City) and Plaistow (on the same lines) are useful for some of the other buildings.
Hiking: *Impossible from inside London - hitchers have to get to the outskirts, but Essex is a no go area for the thumb traveller, even the freight terminal near the University.*
Bicycles: *For those students who can stand the filth and traffic, biking it is a great deal cheaper than public transport, until they have to replace their stolen bike.*

LIBRARIES & COMPUTERS:
- Books: 252,000 ● Periodicals: 1,660
- Study places: 861 ● Computer workstations: 684

Students are remarkably understanding about the limited resources.

CAREER PROSPECTS:
- Careers Service ● No of staff: 3full/4part
- Unemployed after 6mths (1996): 15%

Many of the courses are vocationally based which doesn't necessarily mean students get jobs, but does increase their chances of going into certain areas.

FAMOUS ALUMNI:
Hilary Armstrong MP (Lab); Garry Bushell ('Sun' TV 'critic'); Ken Russell (film director); Christopher Wenner (ex-'Blue Peter' presenter).

FURTHER INFO:
Prospectuses for undergrads and postgrads.

entertainment

CITY: see University of London

EAST LONDON:
- Price of a pint of beer: £1.80 ● Glass of wine: £2.20

Cinemas: Multiplexes at Barking and Gant's Hill, Ilford (10 screens in all). Barking's pic house has student discounts and there is a new 4-screen cinema at Stratford.

Theatres: The Theatre Royal Stratford East has many productions which transfer to the West End - those who have the foresight to see them here first, see them cheaper.

Pubs: *In the East End, there are plenty of pubs passing cheerfully for the stereotypical (and fictional) Queen Vic; Viz's Cockney Wankah would be comfy in many. In Barking every pub's a pitiful pulling joint for Essex Men and Girls. These are outrageously unfair generalisations and at least they're cheaper than most London pubs.* **push***plugs: the King Edward, Princess Alice and The Pigeons are all earmarked as student pubs.*

Eating out: *The best local cuisine comes from the Indian, Chinese and other ethnic restaurants in the East End. Other* **push***plugs: Sombrero Steak House (Ilford); Raj (Barking).*

Clubs/discos: *There are endless nightclubs in east London that score high on the snog, vomit and fight factor. Most students avoid them like a sewage dump in summer. They flock instead to Benjy's on the Mile End Road, the Princess Alice (indie nights) or The Pigeons pub, which tends to deliberately complement SU events and has indie, gay & lesbian and student nights.*

UNIVERSITY:
- Price of a pint of beer: £1.40 ● Glass of wine: £1

Bars: (3) 2 in Barking, 1 in Stratford. Maryland House (800) *is a popular drinking den but the Barking Bar (600) is more ents-related. The bars provide something of a refuge where local pubs aren't entirely student-friendly.*

Cinema: 1 film is shown every week (*not the same one*) by the student film society 'Reels'.

Clubs/discos/music venues: Weekly Sabotage night (techno/house) in the Barking Bar. Bands aren't so common.
Cabaret: Regular acts in Maryland House and the Barking SU bar.
Food: There are refectories and snack bars at several sites, namely the A Block at Barking, one half of the SU bar in C Block, the top floor at the Stratford Main Building (*where the mural is more memorable than the food*), *the friendly coffee bar* at Greengate House, Holbrook House, the Green and *the best one at the swish* management course centre at Duncan House.
Others: Quiz nights, Freshers and May Ball, cultural nights.

e

social & political

UNIVERSITY OF EAST LONDON STUDENTS' UNION:
● 6 sabbaticals ● Turnout at last ballot: 10%
● NUS member

The *dingy,* graffitied C Block is the SU's administrative, welfare and finance centre. Ents, communications and more welfare are based on the ground floor at Maryland House. It also has offices on most other sites. *The Union is particularly strong on welfare, and specific issues such as racism and the 'no means no' campaign, but there is some mistrust on the part of the student body.*

SU FACILITIES:
Collectively, the various sites of the SU offer 2 bars, 2 cafeterias, bookshops at both sites, minibus hire, general shop, Barclays bank, Endsleigh Insurance office, photocopying, phones, photo booth, pool table, vending machines and juke box.

CLUBS (NON SPORTING):
Barking Union Student Staff; Bengali; Chinese Oriental Cookery; Cultural Awareness; European students; Fashion; Finnish; Kegites; Law; Live Music; Malaysian; Meditation; Nursery; Punjabi; Reels (film); Rock Musicians; Samba; Sikh; Social Equality.

OTHER ORGANISATIONS:
The SU's 'FUEL' magazine is good-looking, if sloppily written. The hitherto dormant Rag is set to spring into action this year.

RELIGIOUS:
● 1 chaplain (CofE)
The Christian Union is large and active, but apart from the Muslim prayer room in Barking's T Block, students rely on East London's *plentiful* religious facilities. There's a particularly strong Asian community and corresponding religions.

PAID WORK: see University of London

sports

● Recent successes: nothing special
The sporting record is okay, but Norris McWhirter isn't about to show an interest. Charges for facilities are about £1 per session.

SPORTS FACILITIES:
Most sports facilities are around Goodmayes Park at the Barking site, where there's a sports centre, swimming pool, 2 gyms, 1

squash court, multigym, weights, minibus, sauna and solarium, and 1 playing field. A further 4 playing fields are at Little Heath, 3 miles away. *Optimistically*, there's an Injuries Clinic with built-in physio. For other sports, London is the answer and Newham Sports Centre is nearby. Near both sites there's a dry ski slope, athletics track and amenities for most sports.

SPORTING CLUBS:
Jiu Jitsu; Tennis.

ATTRACTIONS:
West Ham is, of course, the local football team, but there's also Leyton Orient. Sports fans can fan their fanaticism all over London, see <u>University of London</u> for details.

accommodation

IN COLLEGE:
● <u>Self-catering: 10%</u> ● <u>Cost: £36-51(52wks)</u>
Availability: Pressure is eased by the fact that the majority of students live locally anyway. There are 3 developments, with a total of 1,062 places. Students are accommodated at Park Village (next to an international freight terminal) about 20mins walk from the Stratford site. There are 508 places on the Barking site, which includes some purpose-built rooms for disabled students. Kitchens are shared between 6 people.
Car parking: *It's far enough from central London to be free and adequate*, although a permit is needed.

EXTERNALLY: see <u>University of London</u>
Local Availability: Most students are mature and have their own homes already sorted. East London is cheaper than many other parts of the capital and at UEL, it's possible to live quite far out (and so more cheaply) and still be right on the doorstep. *Stratford itself is a likely locale, as are Leyton, Forest Gate and East Ham. Also Leytonstone and Walthamstow, but they're quite a trek.*
Housing help: There are 3 accommodation offices, which between them employ 6 full- and 3 part-time staff. They provide vacancies boards and newsletters.

welfare

SERVICES:
● <u>Nursery</u> ● <u>Lesbian & Gay Society</u> ● <u>Mature SA</u>
● <u>Overseas SA</u> ● <u>Postgrad SA</u> ● <u>Women's minibus</u>
● <u>Women's Officer</u> ● <u>Self-defence classes</u>
The Student Services Department provides advice and counselling for students with all sorts of problems, employing 6 counsellors. The SU is *very eager* to help with a range of issues, although it has no professional counsellors so concentrates on financial, legal and academic advice and representation. There are medical centres at both campuses, staffed by nurses, offering GPs and family planning.
Women & ethnic minorities: UEL has a crusading equal opportunities policy, reflected in the high proportion of students from ethnic minorities and the equal gender balance. *This is particularly important as the local area is seething with racial and social tensions.* There is a **strong** Women's Unit run by the SU and the student Women's Officer is a sabbatical

position. There's also a Black Mentor scheme to pair up black students with successful black people in their chosen career.
Disabled: The University employs a disability advisor and provides *fairly good access.* New accommodation takes students' disabilities into account. In the largest library there are 2 Arkenstone readers for the sight-impaired and Minicom equipment for the hearing-impaired. There's also a workshop for dyslexic students.

FINANCE:
- Ave debt: £1,950 ● Access fund: £303,000
- Successful applications (1995): 1,324

There are 7 scholarships for part-time unwaged students, as well as partial fee remission schemes.

••

▶▶ Economics
see LSE

••

▶▶ Edge Hill
see Other Institutions

••

University of Edinburgh

 The University of Edinburgh, Old College, South Bridge, Edinburgh, EH8 9YL. Tel: (0131) 650 4360.
Fax: (0131) 668 4565.
Edinburgh University Students' Association (EUSA), 5/2 Bristo Square, Edinburgh, EH8 9AL. Tel: (0131) 650 2656.
Fax: (0131) 668 4177. E-mail: eusa.enquiry@ed.ac.uk

General

It's on the east coast of Scotland. It is the country's capital. *It is one of the most cultural, beautiful and vibrant cities in the world.* It has been called 'the most ideal city to live in'. It is Edinburgh. Enough from the Edinburgh Tourist Office, see below for a fuller advert... There are 4 universities in Edinburgh: Napier, Heriot-Watt, Queen Margaret College, and, of course, Edinburgh University, itself - the 6th oldest in Britain, situated in buildings throughout the city. There are 3 main areas, but departments and halls are dotted all over the place. The largest concentration of departments is in the George Square/Old College area in the city centre and there are almost as many at King's Buildings - the science campus - 2 miles south. The largest group of residences, the Pollock Halls, are east of the centre near Holyrood Park. The University buildings have steadily developed over the last 2 centuries, many appearing in the last 40 years, *but almost all have been built with a love for the city's beauty and in local stone.*

53% ♂♂♂♂♂♀♀♀♀ 47%	
Sex ratio(M:F): 53%:47%	Founded: 1583
Full time u'grads: 13,228	Part time: 379
Postgrads: 3,560	Non-degree: 0
Ave course: 4yrs	Ethnic: n/a
Private school: n/a	Flunk rate: n/a
Mature students: 13%	Overseas students: 10%
Disabled students: 5%	Staff/student ratio: 1:5
Clearing: 0	

ATMOSPHERE:

There are over 50,000 students from various colleges in Edinburgh and just as the University buildings are spread throughout the city and reflect its beauty, so the students live as a part of the city - rather than simply in it - and they reflect and merge with its lively culture, combining study and fun as if there aren't enough hours in the day. Students are often from the south (40% are English) but get on with the locals nevertheless.

THE CITY:

- Population: 421,213 ● London: 391miles
- Glasgow: 44miles ● Newcastle: 93miles

Edinburgh is a stunning city with a tremendous heritage. *Like all the best cities,* it is built on 7 hills, overlooked by Arthur's Seat, a mini-mountain. The centre hill is peaked by the castle and old city walls. There are over 16,000 listed buildings, mostly built of the local stone *that picks up something ethereal in the quality of the light.* These buildings date mainly from 2 periods of expansion: the formation of the centre from the 11th century onwards; and later, the New Town, mainly to the north. The broad streets, garden squares, cobbled alleys, parks and *gasping* views are *well planned* (all by one guy, George Drummond) with 3 main roads running parallel (Queen Street, George Street and Princes Street). The Royal Mile, a straight stretch of linked roads, runs through the city's heart. 4-storey tenements line the Royal Mile. *The Old Town is unique in its ability to look as though Nature intended it to be there, and the names evoke the charm:* Grassmarket; Lawnmarket; The Pleasance; Cowgate; The Mound. Among the sites that should be first on any tour of the city are the Holyrood Palace, the Royal Museum of Scotland, the National Gallery, the Castle and more. *Despite the history all around, it's a living, breathing 24-hour city with a pumping nightlife and there's always somewhere to be seen at any time of day or night. It's not just a tourist trap of course; there are some rough areas that don't turn up on the lids of shortbread gift boxes. But stay safe and it's one hell of a place to be a student.*

TRAVEL:

Trains: Edinburgh Waverley Station is the most central in Edinburgh. There is a direct line to Glasgow (£6.50), another to the north and another to the south through Newcastle and York to London (£40.25). Regular connections also to Birmingham and Bristol.

Coaches: National Express, Stagecoach and Citylink services to London (£23.50), Glasgow (£6.50) and so on.

Car: The M8 and M9 connect with the A8 on the west of Edinburgh. It is also served by the A1, A7, A68, A70, A71, A702, A703 and A90.

Air: Edinburgh (Turnhouse) Airport, 5½ miles west of the city centre, has a range of international and internal flights (from £69rtn to London).

Hitching: *The A1 is a popular road for hitchers. Unfortunately, this part of the A1 isn't so popular with the sort of driver who gives lifts. But the lifts are there - eventually. It's easier to get into Edinburgh than out of it. The M8 and M9 are good for routes to Glasgow and Perth.*

Local: *Bus services are good all round the city and quite cheap* (from 40p). *They run less frequently after 7pm until midnight.*

Taxis: *Useful for late night trips, otherwise they're a bit extravagant* (£3 across town).

Bicycles: *Very useful, but remember Edinburgh is built on 7 hills. Bicycles also have a severe tendency to wheel themselves away.*

LIBRARIES & COMPUTERS:
- Books: 2,286,000 ● Study places: 3,500
- Computer workstations: 1,500

There's an *enormous* Main Library and 6 other more specialised ones (Divinity; Law; the Europa Institute; Medicine; Music; Science & Veterinary Medicine).

CAREER PROSPECTS:
- Careers Service ● No of staff: 15full/11part
- Unemployed after 6mths (1995): 8%

SPECIAL FEATURES:
- Past Rectors (elected every 3 years by the students) have included Magnus Magnusson, Winston Churchill, Muriel Gray, Donnie Munro (of Runrig), Sir David Steel and James Robertson Justice (the fat bearded one who bullied Dirk Bogarde in 'Doctor' movies).
- The Moray House Institute of Education (education and 'people-centred profession' courses) will merge with Edinburgh University as of August 98. 2,000 students are based at Moray House's 2 campuses, one at the end of The Royal Mile near Edinburgh's city centre, the other on the seashore. Accommodation for 300 students is about 2 miles away.

FAMOUS ALUMNI:
James Barrie, Arthur Conan Doyle, Walter Scott, Robert Louis Stevenson (writers); Dr Barry (world's first qualified woman doctor who impersonated a man in order to study and practice); David Brewster (who invented the kaleidoscope); Gordon Brown, Robin Cook, Malcolm Rifkind (MPs); Thomas

❝The first person to be caught for speeding in a Sinclair C5 was a student at the University of Kent.❞

e

Carlyle (historian/philosopher); Charles Darwin (revolutionary evolutionary); David Hume (philosopher, who had a nervous breakdown shortly after graduating); Eric Liddel ('Chariots of Fire' runner) and Ian Charleson, who played him; Lord Mackay of Clashfern; Julius Nyerere (ex-President, Tanzania); Peter Roget (of Thesaurus fame); Kirsty Wark (TV presenter); James Watt (engineer/inventor); and so on.

FURTHER INFO:
Prospectuses for undergrads, postgrads, mature students and those from overseas. Web site (http://www.ed.ac.uk and http://www.ed.ac.uk/~eusaweb/).

entertainment

CITY:

● Price of a pint of beer: £2.20 ● Glass of wine: £1.60

Festivals: *Edinburgh is never short of entertainments*, but there is *a positive festglut* during August, not just the main Edinburgh Festival (in itself the largest arts event in the world), but at the same time the Fringe (which includes hundreds of student productions), Film, Dance, Jazz and Book Festivals (and probably many others; the whole thing has been described by Robert Llewellyn (aka Kryten from 'Red Dwarf') as the 'Festival of theatre, music, dance, poetry, opera, jazz, film, television and shagging'). *The city springs into life with buskers and performers and it's impossible to enjoy it, even if all you do is walk (slowly) around the streets.* Of course, this is outside term time, but students should take advantage of their situation at least 1 year out of their 4-year stay. (See 'Accommodation' below for a money-making idea for students who don't stick around for the Festivals.)

Cinemas: There are 7 cinemas around town with a total of 40 screens. The Filmhouse and the Cameo are both fairly arty and host the Edinburgh Film Festival.

Theatres: Strictly speaking there are 13 theatres, but each year the Festivals find literally hundreds of performance venues. The Festivals have a knock-on effect for the rest of the year and Edinburgh brims with exciting and experimental theatre and dance, as well as mainstream arts, throughout the year. The Royal Lyceum, King's Theatre and the relocated Traverse are among the hardy perennials and now there's the magnificent new Festival Theatre which does everything from Rocky Horror to Harry Secombe.

Pubs: *Quite apart from being as popular as Pammy Anderson's silicon bits*, most pubs are open till 1am. *Students who want to make the most of an Edinburgh education will develop a taste for whisky. The best places to do it are most pubs in the Grassmarket area; Maggie Dicksons (good grub); Sneaky Pete's and Whistlebinkies (for the serious quaffer); Iguana, Bar Kohl (studenty); Black Bo's (cheap); The Kitchen (funky music); Jekyll & Hyde (in the New Town).*

Clubs/discos: *Just because there's so much fun to be had watching and listening, Edinburgh doesn't slack on more active entertainment.* **push**plugs: *Pure (legendary hardcore at The Venue, £3-£5); Mercado (dance of all sorts); Shaft and FBI at Moray House (alternating retro and indie at a fun student venue, £2.50); Joy (gay/Hi-NRG) and Bound To Please (house) at the New Calton Studios; Café Graffiti; JP's.*

Music venues: *The remarkable thing about the number of live music venues is how they can all continue to make a profit. Maybe they don't. Maybe they do it for fun.* Apart from the following, live music spills out from many a pub, club and meeting place. **push***plugs: Usher Hall (classical, including the Scottish National Opera); Queen's Hall (indie and more); Playhouse (AOR); The Venue (indie); Rocking Horse (metal mayhem).*

Eating out: *Some of Scotland's best restaurants are in Edinburgh,* serving everything from cordon bleu cuisine to brown sauce cookery. *The only drawback is that eating out in Edinburgh will unfill students' pockets faster than it fills their stomachs.* **push***plugs (among many others): Henderson's (veggie hangout); Pierre Victoire and Chez Jules (bistro); Mamma's (value Italian); Kalpna (gorgeous Indian veggie).*

Others: Among the many other *endless* entertainments, it's worth mentioning the *phenomenal* amount of cabaret and the Tattoo, a military parade at the castle. *Americans and old people seem to like it.*

UNIVERSITY:
● Price of a pint of beer: £1.35 ● Glass of wine: £1.25
Union facilities at Potterow are being updated, which should create a 900-capacity music venue.

Bars: There are 11 bars in the various sites of EUSA (see below) and at the King's Buildings Union. The major ones are the Teviot main bar and the *pubby* Pleasance Bar.

Theatres: There are 3 theatres around the University and its students staged more shows at last year's Edinburgh Fringe Festival than any other university, *but then, it does have a slight geographical advantage.* The Bedlam Theatre Company runs its own theatre.

Cinemas: The University film club - the largest in the country with more than 2,500 members - shows about 6 films a week, a *broad range beyond the usual pap.* Annual membership also gets you cheap tickets to the Cameo *arty* cinema.

Clubs/discos: There are dance venues all over the place in EUSA's various centres, the biggest being 'Juice' at Teviot Row (capacity 1,800).

Music venues: The Teviot Debating Hall features regular live bands including recently Space, Urusei Yatsura and the Supernaturals, as well as local wannabes.

Cabaret: At the Pleasance, weekly cabaret nights keep those tums vibrating with chuckles, featuring recently Boothby Graffoe.

Food: The University itself doesn't actually provide any eateries, but there are cafeterias in all EUSA's main sites open from 8.30am till late at night. In total, there are 13 EUSA food outlets.

Others: Regular quiz nights and several balls a year, the highspot being the President's Ball in November.

········ social & political

EDINBURGH UNIVERSITY STUDENTS' ASSOCIATION:
● 5 sabbaticals ● Turnout at last ballot: 20%
Forget any other structures of student representation and services, Edinburgh is different. EUSA is an umbrella organisation formed from the merger of the SRC (Student

Representative Council) which does political and representative work, with the Union which provides student services. *To make matters more complicated* there's also the Sports Union which is separate, although membership is simultaneous with automatic free membership of EUSA. This entitles students to use the Union centres (see below). There's also 'The Advice Place' (see Welfare below), *which is particularly important as EUSA is not affiliated to NUS, and doesn't have its services as a back up. Enthusiasm pervades the Unions (as with everything else) and students appreciate the choice of service centres.* When Moray House Institute of Education merges with Edinburgh in the autumn, there will be a referendum on NUS affiliation: EUSA, currently disaffiliated, will subsume MHSU, who are affiliated, *which will confuse everybody even more.*

SU FACILITIES:

Teviot Row: 4 bars; juke boxes; snack bar; 2 cafeterias; restaurant; showers; games room; music room; satellite TV; largest lighting rig in Scotland; shop; launderette; free showers.

King's Buildings House: Currently closed for redevelopment but will re-open late 1999.

Potterrow: Due to re-open in October 1998 and offer a new nightclub and music venue, games room and catering outlets.

PAM's House: Geared to postgrads and mature students - 1 bar; sound system; TV; newspapers; kitchen and catering.

The Pleasance: bar; The Societies Centre; catering; technical equipment hire; theatre (cap 270); meeting rooms; function room.

Also: travel agencies; print service; 4 shops; NatWest and Bank of Scotland cashpoints; Endsleigh Insurance office; photocopying; library; employment services; photo booths; pool tables; games and vending machines; TV lounges; meeting rooms; launderettes.

CLUBS (NON SPORTING):

A-Ha Revival; Asylum & Immigration Bill; Celtic Supporters; Chess; Children's Holiday Venture; Chinese Cultural; Cyborg; Duke of Edinburgh Award; European; Fabian; Folk Song; Football Supporters; Footlights (revue); Friends of Edinburgh Direct Aid; Games & Recreational; GEAS (role-playing); Goth & Rock; Hearts Supporters; Hellenic; Help (Scotland); Highland; Hispanic; Huggabugga Jaffa Cake Appreciation; Hungarian; Indonesian; Japanese; Jazz Orchestra; Juggling; Korean; Malaysian Students; Methodist; Mooting; Motorcycle; New Philosophy; New Scotland Country Dance; Norwegian Students; Opera; Perfidious Albion; Pie-Eaters; Piping; Poetry; Politics; Rajayoga Meditation; Red Cross; Reel; Renaissance Singers; Revelation; Savoy Opera; Scottish Militant; Sign Language; Singaporean; SNP; Sri Chimnoy; Student Action for Refugees; Student Christian Movement; Suave; Tibet Support; Turf; UNICEF; Untapped Talent; Up the Kilt Productions; Virtual Trading & Investment; Wargames; Water of Life (whisky appreciation); Wind Ensemble; Wind (kite-flying); Wine; Yoga.

OTHER ORGANISATIONS:

EUSA produces a number of *excellent* publications including the weekly 'Members Only' and many student society magazines. Among Edinburgh's other award-winning media are 'Student' (independent newspaper) and Fresh Air FM (24hrs). Another couple of acronyms to learn: ESCA, the charities appeal *which, despite the more reserved name, is wackier than many of the wildest rags* and raised £75,000 last year; and SCAG (the Student Community Action Group), the high-profile local help organisation. Other groups include

'Settlement', a help group that, together with members of the community, provides for the deprived and disadvantaged in the local area. The Debates Committee is a *popular* talk shop and *much more than just another club.*

RELIGIOUS:
There is a chaplaincy centre staffed by Anglican, Church of Scotland, Methodist and Catholic chaplains. Local worship shops include all manner of churches as well as facilities for Sikhs and Jews.

PAID WORK:
Apart from the usual bar and restaurant work, during the summer, there's plenty of work revolving around the Festivals trade for those who get in early enough.

sports

● Recent successes: badminton, football, rugby

Edinburgh students are stronger at cultural pursuits than sporting ones, but that isn't to say they don't have the facilities or the successes. It's just that with all the other distractions, sport isn't quite the collective obsession to be found in some other universities.

SPORTS FACILITIES:
The University has outdoor facilities at Peffermill Sports Ground (including 24 acres of playing fields and 3 new clay tennis courts) and at the Pollock Sports Centre (10mins from Pollock Halls), where there is a sports hall, a small hall, fitness room, 10 squash courts, table tennis studios, a combat salle, a rifle and archery range. The 25-acre playing fields at Peffermill include a floodlit synthetic grass pitch, tennis courts and golfing facilities. There are further outdoor amenities at the Firbush Point Field Centre, 80 miles from Edinburgh, including sailing, canoeing, skiing and hills to walk. The city has many golf courses, a large swimming pool, ice rink and the Meadowbank Stadium. 50% of the city is made up of parks and open spaces (including Queen's Park and Arthur's Seat).

SPORTING CLUBS:
Aikido; Jiu Jitsu; Tai Chi; Yoga.

ATTRACTIONS:
Hearts and Hibs FCs each have a home turf in Edinburgh and there're also Murrayfield rugby, athletics at Meadowbank and speedway.

accommodation

IN COLLEGE:
● Catered: 15% ● Cost: £81-91(30wks)
● Self-catering: 28% ● Cost: £52-66(30-50wks)

Availability: It's almost exclusively 1st years who live in the modern catered *rabbit-hutch-like* Pollock Halls of Residence which house 1,794 students in 10 halls, ½ mile from the city centre. The ½ of 1st years who can't get into Pollock are spread between student houses, which accommodate 9 to 77 students each, and the University-owned flats. Only 1% have to share. There is room for about 20% of students from other years, particularly in the flats, but also in Mylne's Court, a *beautiful* old building on Princes Street housing 230 students, mainly postgrads and 2nd years.

Car parking: *Because so much of Edinburgh's residential housing is in tenements, there is a tremendous parking problem all round the city.* For those who really think it necessary, limited permits are available, costing £39 a year at Pollock Halls and £15 at the King's Buidings.

EXTERNALLY:
● Ave rent: £45

Availability: Living out presents as many options as living in. Most students opt to live in privately rented flats, some of which are *very good value*, but some end up (for at least part of a year) in lodgings with a live-in landlord/lady who cooks and cleans. *Often this is like a home from home, but students complain that rather than making them homesick, this arrangement more frequently makes them sick of home.* Talking of home, many students are local and live with their parents and/or families. *With all these options, most of the year it's not too difficult to find somewhere, until it comes to September when everybody else is looking, or August when landlords with any sense don't want to know because all their properties are on profitable short-term rents to Festival-goers. Students with nous can get a piece of this action themselves. The trick is to avoid the crush and start a rental period at the beginning of the summer and to ensure subletting's allowed. Then get some am dram group doing a Fringe show to pay £50 per person per week, cramming in a cast of 20, during the Festival and suddenly student debt is a thing of the past. The best places to be are Marchmont, Bruntsfield and Newington, particularly studenty areas, close to the centre with high quality housing. Niddrie, Pilton and Wester Halls are a bit rough.*

Housing help: The 4 full-time staff of the Allocations Office of the Accommodation Service, apart from allocating and managing University-run properties, keep a register of approved flats and lodgings, help negotiate contracts and provide general advice.

·········· welfare

SERVICES:
● Creche ● Nightline ● Postgrad Union
● Equal Opportunities Officer ● Self-defence classes

EUSA's Advice Place operates as a drop in centre providing help *of a high standard.* The University, however, does have some services of its own, including the Legal Dispensary, the Student Counselling Service, which employs 2 full- and 6 part-time counsellors, and the Student Health Centre, which has 6 doctors, as well as nurses, a psychologist, physiotherapist, pharmacist and a family planning unit. Edinburgh itself has a large gay and lesbian community, *which, although it doesn't necessarily make coming out any easier, means there's more fun to be had for those who have done.*

Disabled: *The access is inherently restricted by the nature of the many old buildings,* but the University has an advisor and a Special Needs committee who, if informed early enough, will do everything in their power to meet the needs of individuals, even to the point of making some structural changes to buildings. Many lecture theatres do have audio loops. There is a Dyslexia Study Adviser.

FINANCE:
- Access fund: £414,966
- Successful applications (1996): 886

EUSA can offer a small crisis loan (up to £100) on a 6-month repayment scheme and limited grants are available from the University Common Bursaries Fund.

▶▶ Edinburgh College of Art
see Heriot-Watt University

University of Essex

University of Essex, Wivenhoe Park, Colchester, CO4 3SQ.
Tel: (01206) 873666. Fax: (01206) 873423.
E-mail: admit@essex.ac.uk
Essex University Student Union, Wivenhoe Park, Colchester,
CO4 3SQ. Tel: (01206) 863211. Fax: (01206) 870915.
E-mail: su@essex.ac.uk

general

Forget the Essex girl jokes – the University isn't in the famously maligned part of Essex, *full of parked Ford Capris and peroxide blondes*. It's 2½ miles from Colchester, a thoroughly modern Roman town, a bit further from London. It's the smallest fully fledged university in England and Wales, set amidst 3 large lakes in 200 acres of *scenic* parkland designed to hold a much larger institution - the University slowed its ambitious expansion a few years after it was founded. It has remnants of the big plans, though: the campus contains shops, eating places and facilities *which betray the grander designs for the place.* They're all set in a *confusing* series of interlinked courtyards and modern concrete buildings, flanked by towering multi-storey residential blocks.

53% ♂♂♂♂♂♂♀♀♀♀ **47%**

Sex ratio(M:F): 53%:47%	Founded: 1964
Full time u'grads: 4,175	Part time: 35
Postgrads: 1,535	Non-degree: 373
Ave course: 3yrs	Ethnic: n/a
Private school: n/a	Flunk rate: 16%
Mature students: 28%	Overseas students: 37%
Disabled students: 1%	Staff/student ratio: 1:15
Clearing: n/a	

ATMOSPHERE:

Being such a small university, based in a big campus (if you include the parkland), there's quite a sense of community. This can either be seen as friendly solidarity or as busy-body nosiness, close knit groups or cliques. Whichever, most of it is tightly focused on the bars. Less gregarious students can have a hard time and relations with the locals aren't particularly warm, particularly the large contingent from the nearby barracks.

COLCHESTER:
- Population: 88,847 ● London: 40miles
- Ipswich: 16miles

Like we said, Colchester is a thoroughly modern Roman town - that is to say, the Romans started the place, although they went home some time ago. It's the oldest recorded town in the country - *and the town plan hasn't been greatly changed since.* But, as when all the bits of a car have been replaced so many times that you have a new car, Colchester has established many modern pockets: shopping centres and light industry, busy roads and modern architecture and now a new leisure centre. There are still many *pretty* parts, old houses and ancient buildings, not least the original Roman Wall and the castle (built by William the Conquerer) which houses the town Library and Museum. The area's most recent claims to fame, *ex-Mods/reborn slackers* Blur, have left less of an impression on the town.

TRAVEL:
Trains: The nearest mainline station to the campus is Colchester North, 3 miles away (there are 2 other stations in town). Direct services run into London Liverpool Street (£8.70). Connections via London are possible all over the country including Birmingham, Bristol and Edinburgh.
Coaches: National Express services to London (£6.75), Birmingham (£16.75) and more.
Car: Colchester is visited by the A120, A12, A133, and A604.
Air: Stansted International is 32 miles west on the A120.
Ferries: To the continent from Harwich and Felixstowe, 16 miles away.
Hitching: *The slip roads of the A12 are the best bet, but trying to get a lift in Essex is like sucking an iron bar.*
Local: Buses are *expensive* (£1 return to the town centre), *but*

❝Newcastle SU produced a caricature of Liz Hurley saying 'Don't Suck My Grant' for their anti-poverty campaign. The actress asked for it to be withdrawn but she was so nice about it that the Union is pushing for her to be awarded an honorary degree. ❞

they are reliable and they tour the local villages *which can be useful for those living there.*

Taxis: Some firms are less expensive than others, *but we wouldn't use the word 'cheap' for any of them.* From £2.50 from the station to the campus.

Bicycles: There's a cycle network around Colchester, Essex is quite flat *and distances are cycle-able.*

LIBRARIES & COMPUTERS:
- Books: 705,000 ● Study places: 950
- Computer workstations: 395

The Albert Sloman Library has a Paternosta lift - just step on and step off while the open lift keeps moving. *If you ever get bored of that,* there are computer terminals in the library and in 9 departmental libraries - *however, access is not always easy.*

CAREER PROSPECTS:
- Careers Service ● No of staff: 4full/4part
- Unemployed after 6mths (1996): 8.8%

SPECIAL FEATURES:
- There are a lot of ducks on the 3 lakes and around the campus there are more rabbits than students. Each year, much to the distress of the students, the University carries out a bunny cull.

FAMOUS ALUMNI:
Oscar Arias (former President of Costa Rica & Nobel prize winner); Tony Banks (Genesis); John Bercow MP, Virginia Bottomley MP (Con); Ivor Dembina (comedian); Brian Hanrahan (BBC reporter); Jane Heptonstall (actress); Ben Okri (writer, Booker Prize winner).

FURTHER INFO:
Prospectuses for undergrads and postgrads; video and web site (http://www.essex.ac.uk).

entertainment

THE TOWN:
- Price of a pint of beer: £1.90 ● Glass of wine: £1.80

Cinemas: The Odeon shows mainstream films and St Mary's Arts Centre sometimes features more arty flicks.

Theatres: The Mercury Theatre hosts a rep company.

Pubs: *Students more usually stick to their own bars or the pubs close by, since the local pubs are full of soldiers. A few* **push***plugs: The Lamb (noisy); The Flag; Hole in the Wall; Wig & Pen; Horse & Groom (aka the Doom & Gloom).*

Clubs/discos: *The real stiletto-heeled, mini-skirted cattle markets are in Southend (28 miles away) and Chelmsford (24 miles). Colchester's clubs are slower lane, more down-to-earth, but still tacky. Students often don't bother. Terrace (student DJs but no student groovers, sadly); Hippodrome (large, crowded, £5); Club Valentino's (small, a bit Costa Del Sol, £2); L'Aristo's (expensive) are all Sharon Central. The housier King's Club earns a* **push***plug out of desperation.*

Music venues: The Hippodrome has naff PAs. Better stick to Oliver Twist (blues and rock), Arts Centre (indie, reggae), Charterhall (various). *Better still, stick to London.*

Eating out: Colchester has restaurants of every description - *worth checking out those with student discounts* - and junk yards of fast food. **push***plugs: Jade Garden (cheap Chinese); Chicago's; Rose & Crown for parental purchasing; Playhouse, Wig & Pen (cheap pub grub); Sloppy Joe's (Tex-Mex).* Some kebab shops and the like are open till 4am.

UNIVERSITY:

●<u>Price of a pint of beer: £1.20</u> ●<u>Glass of wine: £1.00</u>

Bars: (5) The SU's Main Bar is, unsurprisingly, the chief quaffing spot, holding 1,000 thirsty people when it's chocka. *The Level 2 bar is a bit posh and cocktaily for an SU boozer* and the Dance Hall Bar is only open during events.

Theatres: The University is *well-equipped* and the Lakeside Theatre has many visits from national companies. Student shows are also *enthusiastically* produced.

Cinemas: 2 mainstream films a week.

Clubs/discos: The main, charty club night is the Jump Club on Fridays (£3) and there are other, less regular dance events, including recent visits from the likes of Digweed and Rampling.

Music venues: Underground (850) is the main live venue but there are also frequent band nights in the bar and the Party Room. Recent giggers include Mansun and Embrace. The various student music societies put on concerts and there are professional classical concerts.

Food: *The meals in the Hexagon restaurant and the snacks in the Blue's Cafe are beyond the pockets of many students, who tend to stock up on eats in the Main Bar.*

Others: The University has a purpose-built exhibition gallery. Loads of balls organised by societies, with a main one in the summer.

......**sociaL 2 poLiticaL**

UNIVERSITY OF ESSEX STUDENTS' UNION:
●<u>5 sabbaticals</u> ●<u>Turnout at last ballot: 25%</u>
●<u>NUS member</u>

Essex had a radical reputation as a red-hot hot-bed, then became known for a few blue-eyed Thatcherites, but the students are somewhat more apathetic nowadays, although UESU is a major player in the campaign against tuition fees.

SU FACILITIES:
In SU Building: 2 bars; 5 minibuses for hire; printing services; general shop; Lloyds/NatWest cashpoint; Endsleigh Insurance office; function room (cap 100); TV room; 3 meeting rooms; *and a bloody Lottery terminal.* On campus, there is another general shop, jointly run with the University to challenge the *huge* Tesco's at the bottom of the hill.

CLUBS (NON SPORTING):
1960s; Ballroom Dancing; Buddhist; Comedy Workshop; Choir; Chinese Christian; Classical; Cocktail; Cypriot; DiscWorld Companions; DJ; Fifth Monarchists; Gigsoc; Goth; Gregsoc; Hellenic; Human Rights; Italian; Japan; Jungle; Latin American; Magic Gathering; Malaysian; Mexican; Musoc; Nigerian; Poetry; Silly; Soul; Star Trek; Stop the Fees; Turkish; Wine & Beer.

OTHER ORGANISATIONS:
The student media include the SU's newspaper 'Parklife' and URE (University Radio Essex), which broadcasts 24 hours a day. ESCA, the Community Action group, started up last year.

RELIGIOUS:
- 2 chaplains (RC, CofE)

There is a worship area in the University chaplaincy centre for use by all religions. During term, there are Anglican services each Sunday and Mass 3 times a week. The Islamic Society organises a prayer schedule and has a deep freeze with Halal meat. A kosher kitchen supplies the general shop.

PAID WORK:
The SU has a policy of giving students paid work in shops, bars and the Dance Hall.

sports

- Recent successes: rugby, judo

As with many other things, the University has sports facilities that were intended for somewhere much larger. But who's complaining? The number of students means that the University is less likely to boast as many bionic men and women as larger colleges, but it still holds its own (and sometimes other people's) in competitions, while maintaining a good overall level of participation.

SPORTS FACILITIES:
40 acres of the parkland are used for sports fields including playing fields, a grass athletics track, a floodlit synthetic sports pitch; 3 all-weather tennis courts; 4 new squash courts; new fitness room; archery range; an exercise circuit ('the Squirrel Run'), the only 18-hole frisbee golf course in the country and, of course, the 3 lakes. Also a gym and sports hall including 6 badminton courts, another tennis court, a climbing wall (largest in the south-east), 6 squash courts (4 elsewhere on campus), weights and other indoor sports facilities. Colchester also provides swimming pools and a roller rink.

SPORTING CLUBS:
Canoeing; Jazz Dance; Kickboxing; Korfball; Ten-Pin Bowling; Trampolining; Yoga.

ATTRACTIONS:
Colchester United are the local football team, and need we mention Essex County Cricket Club? We did anyway.

accommodation

IN COLLEGE:
- Self-catering: 65% ● Cost: £39-55(39wks)

Availability: There are 6 tower blocks on campus which are the highest brick buildings in the whole of Essex. Evidently, the architect was a bit eccentric and based the campus design on an Italian hill town. Also, a low-level court, 276 rooms in houses, 360 places in off-campus halls and flats, and 3 houses off-campus for overseas postgrads. *Not a bad selection,* meaning that the University is able to guarantee accommodation (usually on the campus) to all 1st years who apply in time and 60% of all other students too. All rooms are single, mostly in shared flats for between 4 and 6 students. *Many are quite spacious and well-equipped, but the room numbering system is quite incomprehensible.* Most flats are mixed, although some single-sex flats are available. No loud music is allowed after midnight. The 39-week rentals have the advantage that students aren't required to move their lives out of their rooms at the end of every term, but on the down side, it stretches the cost through the 2 short vacations.

Car parking: Automotive students living on or near campus have to pay and display.

EXTERNALLY:
- Ave rent: £40

Availability: The University runs a contract housing scheme where it rents from private landlords and then sublets to students on *favourable* terms. In this way it currently provides space for 444 students. *But anyway, finding suitable accommodation in Colchester, Wivenhoe or other surrounding villages presents few problems. Students should avoid Lexden (too close to the barracks) and Tollgate is just too far. If living out, a car is handy, but the cost of parking should be brought into the reckoning.*

Housing help: The University Accommodation Office, apart from running its own contract housing scheme and providing general help, approves some houses and flats and can fix students up in lodgings (with live-in landlord/lady).

welfare

SERVICES:
- Day nursery ● Nightline ● Mature SA
- Lesbian, Gay & Bisexual Society ● Overseas SA
- Postgrad SA ● Minibus ● Women's Officer

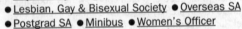

The SU Advice Centre provides help and referral for students with all manner of difficulties. It is staffed by student volunteers, trained and supported by professional staff. The University has a welfare advisor in the Student Support Office and the Health Centre provides 1 full- and 2 part-time counsellors, 3 nurses, 5 doctors, 2 physiotherapists and 1 administrator. *In general, the welfare provision is extensive and well-structured at every level.* There is both a University-run nursery and a Union-run creche *(a nursery is for toddlers and a creche is for babies. Both can get very smelly).*

Disabled: There are special provisions and representative channels for students with all forms of special needs, including induction loops in lecture theatres and adapted housing for wheelchair users in the houses on campus. *Accessibility and provisions are generally among the best in the country.* Colchester Council recently gave the University an award by way of recognition.

FINANCE:
- Ave debt per year: £1,600 ● Access fund: £100,000
- Successful applications (1997): 165

Hardship funds are available from the Student Support Office and the SU provides loans.

 Essex IHE

see Anglia Polytechnic University

University of Exeter

(1) University of Exeter, Northcote House, The Queen's Drive, Exeter, EX4 4QJ. Tel: (01392) 263263.
Fax: (01392) 263108.
Guild of Students, Exeter University, Devonshire House, Stocker Road, Exeter, EX4 4PZ. Tel: (01392) 263536.
Fax: (01392) 263531.
(2) Camborne School of Mines, Pool, Redruth, Cornwall, TR15 3SE. Tel: (01209) 714866. Fax: (01209) 716977.

General

The River Exe flows out into the English Channel in a wide estuary with the golden, sandy beaches of south Devon all round. The river springs inland amidst the windy wilds of Exmoor, in the heart of the West Country. 9 miles from the coast, where the river starts to widen, is Exeter, not a big city, *but a pretty one.* Although the city was almost wiped out by a single night's bombing in World War II, the Luftwaffe didn't manage to destroy any major landmarks, such as the ancient cathedral (built in 1050), the city walls (built by the Romans) or the Guild Hall. Among the other things not destroyed by bombing was the University - mainly because it wasn't built until 1955. Some of the University's buildings date from the last century though, but most were built in the 50s and 60s and are low-rise blocks in light stone. The University is about a mile from the city centre in a particularly hilly and green area. *The setting is stunning, perfect for both town and country,* with 2 streams and ponds dotted about the campus. There are 2 other sites: St Luke's, 1½ mile away, is the School of Education; and the Camborne School of Mines in Redruth, Cornwall is now part of the University.

46% ♂♂♂♂♂♀♀♀♀♀ 54%

Sex ratio(M:F): 46%:54%	Founded: 1955
Full time u'grads: 6,943	Part time: 35
Postgrads: 1,462	Non-degree: 1,010
Ave course: 3yrs	Ethnic: 4%
Private school: 29%	Flunk rate: 17%
Mature students: 11.8%	Overseas students: 7%
Disabled students: 5%	Staff/student ratio: 1:16
Clearing: 6%	

ATMOSPHERE:
Exeter has a reputation for attracting rich kids who couldn't make it to Oxbridge. As with most reputations this is probably overstating things but there is a higher-than-average concentration of GTis, double-barrelled names and braying laughter. There are plenty of real people as well, though, and the gorgeous setting is more than enough compensation for

the odd bit of social friction. Students are tolerated by the local populace (maybe because they spend so much) rather than welcomed with open arms - the local endearment 'm'lover' isn't as amatory as it sounds.

THE SITES:

St Luke's: (1,800 students - education) Although it's only 1½ miles from the main campus, opposite the police station, *the Education site feels a bit like a separate institution and there's a constant battle to include the 'Lukies' in Guild activities, though it does have a community spirit all of its own.* St Luke's Hall can house 209 students.

Camborne School of Mines: (350 students) Camborne covers courses like geology, engineering and so on. It's 100 miles from Exeter in the *pretty* countryside near Camborne and Redruth and teaches 350 students in purpose-built blocks thrown up in the mid 70s. The students have no practical connection with Exeter or the University's main site. They have their own Student Club with a bar and *limited* social and sporting facilities, although the Guild provides welfare and counselling services. There is accommodation for 52 students and plenty of rented places nearby.

EXETER:

- Population: 101,100 ● London: 170miles
- Bristol: 69miles ● Plymouth: 46miles

Exeter is quaint and quiet and, according to the EC, has the highest quality of life of any English city. In part, this must be due to the ample selection of high street shops, supermarkets and banks, and to the numerous wholesome cafes and *cute little hippy-dippy shops run by people who came to Glastonbury 25 years ago and haven't moved far away.* Tourist attractions include the ancient cathedral, the historic Guild Hall, and various museums, including the Maritime Museum and the Royal Albert Museum and Art Gallery, with its *amusing* giraffe.

TRAVEL:

Trains: Exeter St Davids Station is ½ mile from the University. There are direct lines to London (£32.80), Bristol (£13.60), Manchester (£51.50) and connections all over.

Buses: National Express services all over the country, include London (£18.50), Manchester (£26) and more.

Car: Exeter is at the southern end of the M5, or there's the A30, A377 and A38.

Air: Exeter Airport (6 miles) offers inland and European flights.

Hitching: *The M5 is good for heading north.*

Local: *Local buses are reliable and quite comprehensive, but not cheap. The same can be said of local trains -* there are 4 stations around the city, *but they're not very usefully placed.*

Taxis: *Numerous, reliable and relatively cheap.*

Bicycles: *The city's not the flattest around and the University's in the hilly part, but students with legs like steam pistons find bikes useful.*

LIBRARIES & COMPUTERS:

- Books: 1,020,000 ● Study places: 1,733
- Computer workstations: 650

The main library (9am-10pm) has 690 places and the rest are in the departmental libraries. 5 computer rooms have 24-hour access, with a special emphasis on computers in Arts departments (aka Project Pallas).

CAREER PROSPECTS:
- Careers Service ● No of staff: 4full/5part
- Unemployed after 6mths (1996): 6.3%

FAMOUS ALUMNI:
Toby Amies (MTV VJ); Anastasia Cooke, Juliet Morris (TV presenters); Paul Jackson (TV producer/bigshot); Stewart Purvis (ITN chief exec); Sam Smith (tennis player); Thom Yorke (head Radiohead).

FURTHER INFO:
Prospectuses for undergrads, postgrads; web sites (http://www.exeter.ac.uk and http://gosh.ex.ac.uk); video and alternative prospectus from the Guild (£1.50).

entertainment

THE CITY:
- Price of a pint of beer: £1.60 ● Glass of wine: £1.50

Cinemas: There's a 3-screen Odeon and the *arty* Picture House.
Theatres: The Northcott on campus is the main regional theatre, but the Barnfield and the Arts Centre encourage less commercial fare.
Pubs: push*plugs: Victoria Inn; Jolly Porter; Mount Radford (for Lukies); Double Locks (a bit far, but worth it in summer); Black Horse (sportsnights); Bowling Green (live music); Walkabout Inn (Aussie theme pub). Avoid the Turk's Head (it's a Royal Marines pub).*
Clubs/discos: *Most clubs, such as Warehouse, Volts and Humphrey Bees are quite mainstream;* push*plugs: Rococco's; The Cavern and Timepiece (eclectic indie); Empire (dance).*
Music venues: West Point is a *big* venue and the University is also a main venue for the town, *but again The Cavern provides a more intimate, less mainstream alternative.*
Food: *Not a huge selection of cheap eats but you won't starve either. Late night food can be hard to come by unless you're near a 24-hour garage.* push*plugs: Waterfront (vast, good value pizzas); Mad Meg's (supposedly haunted by a medieval cook); Herbies (veggie); House of Wong; Double Locks (pub lunches by the river).*
Others: Bowling alley. *Exeter pretty much shuts down when pubs close.*

UNIVERSITY:
- Price of a pint of beer: £1.20 ● Glass of wine: £1.15

Bars: *The Ram is hugely popular throughout the day; its sister bar, the Ewe, is OK for more reflective supping.* There are smaller bars in 4 of the halls.
Theatres: Northcott Theatre (cap 433) is based on campus and student companies put on occasional productions there, as well as jaunts to Edinburgh.
Cinema: CinSoc shows 3 films a week, mostly mainstream.
Clubs/discos/music venues: The Lemon Grove (cap 700) hosts varied club nights twice a week. Live sounds pound there and in the Great Hall (cap 1,800), which doesn't actually belong to the Guild, but is regularly borrowed from the

University and is one of the biggest venues in the South West.

Recent bands: Prodigy, Manics, Ocean Colour Scene, Charlatans, Space, Divine Comedy, Mansun, Jamiroquai, Dodgy, Chemical Brothers.

Cabaret: Occasional comic stops, recent offenders being Harry Hill and Lee Hurst.

Food: The Refectory is open for lunch and dinner and the *grim but good-value* Coffee Bar is popular for elevenses. The bars do a *good* selection of snacks and hot meals and there's even an on-campus pizza delivery service.

Others: *According to the SU 'we're big on balls', the high spot being the Summer do.*

social & political

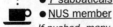

UNIVERSITY OF EXETER GUILD OF STUDENTS:

● 7 sabbaticals ● Turnout at last ballot: 20%
● NUS member

If pushed, many students would describe themselves as more right-wing than their contemporaries elsewhere but nobody can be bothered to push them, so let's put that one down as 'don't know', shall we? They've recently taken a stalwart stand against tuition fees, though, which may have caused the machine that goes 'ping' to go 'ping'. The Guild's facilities are based in Devonshire House, shared with various University activities.

SU FACILITIES:

2 bars; a shop; travel agency; coffee shop; launderette; 2nd-hand bookshop.

CLUBS (NON SPORTING):

Arts & Crafts; Ballroom Dancing; Change Ringing; Circus Skills; Cocktail; Debates; Folk Dance; Gilbert & Sullivan; Malaysian; Out of Doors; Pro-Life; Turkish; Welsh; Wine; XTV; Yoga.

OTHER ORGANISATIONS:

There's a newspaper, 'Exeposé', the XTV station broadcasting to the bars and an *excellent* award-winning radio station. There are also a charity Rag (which raised £40,000 last year) and a *major league* Community Action organisation, which manages 36,000 hours of voluntary work a year, including work with kids' camps.

RELIGIOUS:

Anglicans and Catholics don't have to leave the campus to find a place to bow their heads and there are numerous chaplains too, for most Christian denominations, and a Muslim prayer room. The town also keeps them prayerful and there's an Anglican Cathedral.

PAID WORK:

A few local jobs for students in the tourist trade and some bar and clerical work in the Guild.

> **Central St Martin's (London Institute) is mentioned in Pulp's 'Common People'.**

sports

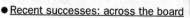

- <u>Recent successes: across the board</u>

Exeter has an excellent sporting reputation and facilities; women's sports in particular have enjoyed great success in recent years.

SPORTS FACILITIES:

64 acres of playing fields; 29 tennis courts; big sports hall; 2 all-weather pitches; 2 gyms (at St Luke's); climbing wall; indoor cricket nets; 8 squash courts; 2 fives courts; a multigym; indoor swimming pool (at St Luke's); a *beezer* outdoor swimming pool at the main site. The sea and moors are also assets. Exeter has sports bursaries for the gamesome gifted.

SPORTING CLUBS:

Aikido; American Football; Boardsailing; Boat (rowing); Fives; Gliding; Kendo; Kuk Soo Woon; Lacrosse; Nin Jitsu; Rifle; Snooker; Speleology (caving); Snooker; Sport Parachute; Street Hockey; Surf; Ultimate Frisbee.

ATTRACTIONS:

Exeter FC is the local footy team and there are rugby and hockey outfits as well. The races are also popular round here - horses at Newton Abbott, speedway, dogs and people in town.

accommodation

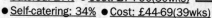

IN COLLEGE:

- <u>Catered: 27%</u> • <u>Cost: £74-90(30wks)</u>
- <u>Self-catering: 34%</u> • <u>Cost: £44-69(39wks)</u>

Availability: All 1st years are guaranteed a place in University accommodation if they want it and there's still space for over ½ the students from other years. The 1st years live in the catered halls, which, with the exception of St Luke's Hall, are right next to the campus and vary in style from 19th-century buildings to new halls. 10% of 1st years have to share. Most students who live in after their 1st year are housed in the self-catering flats, including a new development near St David's Station. *Prices are steep but standards, especially in the newer accommodation, are very high.* There are also 201 places in a head tenancy system.

Car parking: Free permit parking is only available for students living more than 1½ miles from campus, or those with a medical excuse.

EXTERNALLY:

- <u>Ave rent: £47</u>

Availability: *Finding private accommodation in Exeter doesn't present a major problem. Some car-owners travel quite a way into the countryside (but find beautiful country homes there). The best places are St James and Pennsylvania near the campus and Newtown nearer the School of Education.*

Housing help: The Accommodation Office keeps a list of lodgings.

welfare

SERVICES:

- <u>Creche</u> • <u>Nightline</u> • <u>Lesbian & Gay Society</u>
- <u>Mature SA</u> • <u>Overseas SA</u> • <u>Minibus</u> • <u>Women's Officer</u>

The Guild has a Student Advice Centre with a Welfare Officer who helps with all sorts of upsets and an Academic Affairs Officer *(whose job probably isn't to tell you which lecturers are having hanky-panky).* Personal tutors are assigned to each student, and there are 2 full- and 5 part-time counsellors. For a game of doctors and nurses, join the staff of the health centre.

Disabled: *Wheelchair access is not good - the hilly campus doesn't help.* Bearing that in mind, some halls and houses have adapted facilities *and provisions are pretty good for students with sight or hearing problems.*

FINANCE:
- Ave debt: £1,750 ● Access fund: £257,105
- Successful applications (1997): 840

There are bursaries of £1,000 for some education courses.

‘ Freaked out by finance? Why not pop into your local branch of Lloyds Bank and see what they have to offer. **’**

‘ Cilla Black declined an honorary fellowship of Liverpool John Moores University, after students objected. **’**

'There's more to student life
than poverty and fun... see the
courses tables at the back of
the book.'

e

Fold-out guide to symbols inside back cover

'If you have any comments about
PUSH or fancy being involved in
the next edition, please write to
PUSH, McGraw-Hill Publishing
Company, Shoppenhangers Road,
Maidenhead, Berkshire SL6 2QL.'

- George's Hospital
  see St George's Hospital Medical School, London

University of Glamorgan

Glasgow University

Glasgow Caledonian University

- Glasgow Poly
  see Glasgow Caledonian University

- Gloucester
  see Cheltenham & Gloucester College of Higher Education

Goldsmiths College, London

- Gordon University
  see Robert Gordon University

University of Greenwich

- Guildhall
  see London Guildhall University

- Guy's Hospital
  see King's College, London

●●●

▶▶ **George's Hospital**
see St George's Hospital Medical School, London

●●●

 'If you want a sound education in Britain, the safest way is to buy it. That's no way to run a country at the end of the 20th century.'
- George Walden MP. "

University of Glamorgan

● *Formerly Polytechnic of Wales*

University of Glamorgan, Treforest, Pontypridd, Mid Glamorgan, CF37 1DL. Tel: (01443) 480480. Fax: (01443) 480558. University of Glamorgan Union, Forest Grove, Treforest, Pontypridd, Mid Glamorgan CF37 1UF. Tel: (01443) 408227. Fax: (01443) 491589.

General

In south Wales, up the Taff Valley from Cardiff, is the market town of Pontypridd. A mile away is the slate and stone village of Treforest and overlooking it on a steep hillside are the 70 acres of the University of Glamorgan campus. It's a mixture of building styles with a few attempts to prettify the place, such as piazza steps and seating areas. *The main attraction isn't the University itself, but the extraordinary views it affords over the valley, especially when it's not raining. Those who are struck with a desire to listen to Tom Jones singing 'Green Green Grass of Home' will be forgiven.*

60% ♂♂♂♂♂♂♀♀♀♀ 40%

Sex ratio(M:F): 60%:40%	Founded: 1913
Full time u'grads: 10,879	Part time: 6,269
Postgrads: 1,607	Non-degree: 3,520
Ave course: 3yrs	Ethnic: n/a
Private school: n/a	Flunk rate: 17%
Mature students: n/a	Overseas students: 9.1%
Disabled students: 3.5%	Staff/student ratio: 1:16
Clearing: n/a	

ATMOSPHERE:

It's a fairly self-contained place and the high proportion of business and technology students makes for a pretty down-to-earth environment. The only real social outlet is sport. There's a friendly, almost family atmosphere, especially because relations with the locals aren't too wonderful. This can be reassuring to nervous newcomers but it does mean everybody knows who you copped off with last night.

PONTYPRIDD:

●Population: 35,000 ● London: 145miles
● Cardiff: 15miles ● Birmingham: 90miles

There are 3 towns to consider: (1) Treforest. Corner shop, post office, train station. Consider it considered. (2) Pontypridd, which is, of course, Welsh for 'the bridge near the earthen cottage', and is familiarly known as 'Ponty'. It's an old town, built mainly on the money of local coal mining in the last century which has now been spent, leaving a depressed, working class community. Although it's still small, Ponty's got enough amenities for daily needs: shops, supermarket, book shops, banks, market and a local history museum for the sizeable tourist trade. And (3) Cardiff. Only 20 minutes away by train. See <u>Cardiff, University of Wales</u>.

TRAVEL:
Trains: From Treforest station, only 400 yards from the campus, trains go every 20 mins to Cardiff (£1.55). Unfortunately the last return train is just after 10pm. From Cardiff, it's possible to get trains all over the country (see <u>Cardiff, University of Wales</u>).
Coaches: National Express to London (£18.50) and Cardiff (£1.30), which is a better bet for getting elsewhere.
Car: Treforest is on the A470 and about 8 miles off the M4.
Hitching: The Welsh take pity on hitchers and once on the M4 *prospects are good (except if dropped in the home counties).*
Local: There are local bus services going every 20 mins to Ponty and every 25 mins to Cardiff - last bus from Cardiff is at 11.30pm. A free shuttle bus within a 10-mile radius of the campus is run for students after 10.30pm.
Taxis: Cabs to Ponty work out at about £1.50.
Bicycles: The roads have hills and holes and bike theft is a bit of a problem.

LIBRARIES & COMPUTERS:
● <u>Books: 223,340</u> ● <u>Study places: 850</u>
● <u>Computer workstations: 1,000</u>
The Learning Resources Centre contains the main library (open until 11.45pm), a book shop, TV and sound studios and photographic darkroom. *Could do with some more books, too.*

CAREER PROSPECTS:
● <u>Careers Service</u> ● <u>No of staff: 5full/2part</u>
● <u>Unemployed after 6mths (1996): 7.2%</u>

FAMOUS ALUMNI:
Max Boyce (comedian); Ian Hamer (Olympic athlete); Nigel Davies, Jonathan Humphreys, Rupert Moon (Welsh rugby union caps).

FURTHER INFO:
There are prospectuses for undergrads and part-timers, a video and a web site (www.glam.ac.uk/home.html).

entertainment

TOWN (PONTYPRIDD):

● <u>Price of a pint of beer: £1.65</u> ● <u>Glass of wine: £1.20</u>
Entertainment in Ponty goes about as far as a drink in one of the pubs, a little music or a stroll through the very pleasant park or maybe a ramble in the hills. These limitations and the somewhat cold local shoulder mean that most students resort to the resort of Cardiff (see <u>Cardiff, University of Wales</u>).
Cinema: (1) *Pretty mainstream.*
Theatre: The Muni Arts Centre puts on community-based shows.
Pubs: *With a few exceptions, students tend to stick to the SU.* **push***plugs: The Otley (full of photos of local boyo Tom Jones), Pick & Shovel, The Forest. Just don't act like Student Grant.*
Clubs/discos/music venues: *For more than Welsh choirs, go to Cardiff.*

Eating out: *Beyond the usual variants on unidentifiable meat, grease and chips, not a lot of variety, especially for veggies and health-food freaks.* **push**plugs: *John & Maria's (Italian); Prince's Café; Pick & Shovel.*

UNIVERSITY:

● Price of a pint of beer: £1.30 ● Glass of wine: £1.10
Even though it's none too big, the SU building is a well-equipped, modern, yet atmospheric venue for a variety of ents, but that's about as far as the entertainment on campus goes.
Bars: (3) *The SU bars provide a cosy refuge from the sort of reception students might face in Ponty pubs.* They are the George Knox Tavern (cap 200, *Irish-esque*, named after the first principal, who happened to be teetotal), Smith's Café Bar (500, named after the late John Smith MP) and Shafts Disco Bar (500, *very purple*).
Theatres: 1 studio theatre. Shows often go to the Edinburgh Fringe and the National Student Drama Festival.
Cinemas: Movies every month in Shafts.
Clubs/discos: Every night is dance night in Shafts, including chart and easy-listening nights.
Music venues: Shafts is also the main site for live gigs, Space, Dodgy and the Sneaker Pimps being recent visitors. Jazz nights once a month in Smith's.
Cabaret: Once a month featuring circuit comedians such as JoJo Smith.
Food: The refectory does a range of main meals and salady things; the SU responds with a sandwich bar plus a veggie range in Smith's.
Others: Quizzes, karaokes and 4 annual balls.

......·social & political

UNIVERSITY OF GLAMORGAN UNION/
UNDEB PRIFYSGOL MORGANNWG:
● 6 sabbaticals ● Turnout at last ballot: 8%
● NUS member
The SU focuses most of its energies on its campaigning, especially on issues close to home, such as the University's facilities. Even this goes over the heads of most of the students, although 80% stuck to a lecture boycott to protest against tuition fees, which was only slightly predictable regardless of their real views.

SU FACILITIES:
The facilities don't need much management because they're generally pretty successful and limited by the size of the SU building (although expansion is on the agenda). *Plenty of goodies*: 3 bars; cafeteria; restaurant; customised night club/theatre; 4 minibuses for hire; travel agency; general shop (also sells new books); cashpoints; minibus; Endsleigh Insurance office; photocopier; photo and phone booths; video and vending machines; pool tables; juke box and launderette.

CLUBS (NON SPORTING):
Arthurian; Chinese; Chiropractic; Cum Cym (Welsh); Dance; Darts; FROGS (Foreign Residents of Glamorgan Students); Gaming & Telefantasy; Ghost & Paranormal; Greenpeace; Hellenic; Hot Lips; Links; Malaysian; Pool; Regia Anglorum (war re-enactment); Taff Conservation; Taskforce (paintballing); Trespass (multi-cultural); Voice.

OTHER ORGANISATIONS:

'Leek', the monthly independent student tabloid, *is good for a free publication.* Involvement in Rag is good, and a Community Action group is being set up to redeem the University's image in the locality.

RELIGIOUS:

● <u>2 chaplains (Christian, Jewish)</u>

In college, there's an Anglican and a Catholic Chapel and a Mosque. Locally, there are churches for all flavours of Christian endeavour from Methodist to Ben and Jerry's Rainforest Crunch. For other godly grace, a trip to Cardiff is called for.

PAID WORK:

A Union-run employment service finds students jobs at open days and in college bars, but that's about your lot.

sports

● <u>Recent successes: football, rugby</u>

Everyone is very proud of the sports facilities and not without reason. The 3-storey Recreation Centre makes muscles bulge in the strangest places just looking at it. A new sports science course can only add to the influx of pec-flexers.

SPORTS FACILITIES:

30 acres of playing fields (some floodlit); all-weather pitch; floodlit trim trail; sports hall; 4 squash courts; climbing wall; fitness room with multigym; sauna/solarium/steam suite; 2 gyms; golf practice area; archery range; boules, bowls and croquet lawns; floodlit tennis court; new astroturf pitch for '98 entry. All for a £10 membership fee. And locally: mountains; caves; lakes; the River Taff among others; golf course; and in Ponty, a swimming pool.

SPORTING CLUBS:

Aikido; Gaelic football; Jiu Jitsu; Rugby League; Surf; Tennis; Triathlon; Windsurfing; Women's football & rugby.

ATTRACTIONS:

Rugby union in Pontypridd.

accommodation

IN COLLEGE:

● <u>Catered: 1%</u> ● <u>Cost: £67(37wks)</u>
● <u>Self-catering: 8%</u> ● <u>Cost: £36-48(37wks)</u>

Availability: *The new Glamorgan Court development has eased things a little but it's still not enough.* There are other developments on campus and 2 halls 3 miles away.

Car parking: Permits are needed although there's a lack of space around the halls. There's a car park just down the hill, which means that parking on campus doesn't present dilemmas of any epic proportion.

EXTERNALLY:

● <u>Ave rent: £35</u>

Availability: Most students try to get a place in Treforest, it being nearest the campus (*Queen St is the golden prize*), but inevitably many end up in Ponty which is not only further, *but also not that welcoming and the houses themselves can be a* *bit crappy. Merthyr is worse. With a car, the surrounding villages become an alternative and it's quite useful for jaunts to Cardiff, Ponty or the surrounding hills. Parking isn't too easy in Treforest.*

Housing help: The University Accommodation Office has 1 full-timer who offers a very friendly service, trying to set students up with approved landlords and negotiated contracts, in conjunction with an outside consultancy.

welfare

SERVICES:
● Creche ● Lesbian & Gay Society
● Mature SA ● Overseas SA ● Postgrad SA ● Minibus
● Women's Officer ● Self-defence classes

Both the University and the SU offer welfare provisions. In the SU, there's the Welfare sabbatical and the University employs 2 counsellors and a number of nurses to staff the campus sick bay.

Disabled: There is a desire to do better which has meant that the newest buildings (for example, the Union Building and Recreation Centre) have improved access. *Unfortunately, there's still been a lack of funds to do anything about the older buildings.* A special effort has been made for sight-impaired students who should find the facilities *pretty good.*

FINANCE:
● Ave debt per year: £2,100 ● Access fund: £161,000
● Successful applications (1995): 234

There's a specialist finance advisor in the Department of Student Services.

Glasgow University

University of Glasgow, Glasgow, G12 8QQ.
Tel: (0141) 339 8855. Fax: (0141) 330 4808.
Student Representative Council, University of Glasgow, 32 University Avenue, Glasgow, G12 8QQ. Tel: (0141) 339 8697. Fax: (0141) 334 2216.

general

We'll get in trouble with the Glaswegians if we describe their city as Scotland's 2nd, so we'll just say it's the largest and the unofficial capital of the west of Scotland. It's an industrial city with a ring of tower blocks and factories around the outside, but more up market in the city centre with a spattering of large busy parks. To the north of just such a park, 2 miles west of the city centre on Gilmorehill, is the campus of Glasgow's oldest and the UK's 4th oldest university. (There's also Strathclyde University, Glasgow Caledonian University and, a few miles out of town, Paisley University). Some campus buildings were erected in the 50s and 60s, but many date back to when the University relocated to its present site in 1870. The older buildings *of particular note* include the *splendid* chapel (built in 1921), set by *secluded* quadrangles. It is next to the administrative centre, which also houses the Hunterian Museum.

Sex ratio(M:F): 45%:55%	Founded: 1451
Full time u'grads: 15,721	Part time: 2,932
Postgrads: 1,948	Non-degree: 4,055
Ave course: 4yrs	Ethnic: n/a
Private school: n/a	Flunk rate: n/a
Mature students: 18%	Overseas students: 7%
Disabled students: 4%	Staff/student ratio: 1:14
Clearing: 2%	

ATMOSPHERE:
Glasgow students are almost as much people of this city as the Glaswegians. Both groups get on famously, partly because 40% of the students live at home and partly because the University happens to be in a formerly middle-class (now fairly déclassé) area - it'd be interesting to see how students coped in the city's rougher areas. However, we don't want to give the impression there is any pretentiousness about the students - there isn't. The University has the odd advantage of being very near the city centre while at the same time being an exclusive haven, which makes for a friendly campus community - students make less use of the city than those at the other universities nearby. There's also the Garscube site, at Bearsden, about 4 miles away, which houses the Faculty of Veterinary Medicine.

THE CITY:
- Population: 654,542 ● London: 367miles
- Edinburgh: 52miles

The Clyde flows out to sea from Glasgow to its Firth and towards the Isle of Arran. Inland, the city is surrounded by the rolling hills of Strathclyde. It used to be a centre for shipping and steel, before the city dropped into a recession as deep as a saying by Confucius. *With enormous effort in recent years, Glasgow has been dragging itself up from the gutter, and has shown itself to be a thoroughly cultural, modern European city.* In fact, in 1990, it was declared Cultural Capital of Europe and in 1999 will be the City of Architecture and Design. In the city centre, there is some *magnificent* architecture (with many buildings designed by home-grown Charles Rennie Mackintosh) and there are 35 museums and art galleries, including *notably*

❝The catering staff and Chemistry Department at Sheffield University have appeared on a TV soap powder advert with Carol Vorderman❞

the Art Gallery & Museum in Kelvingrove Park, the Burrell
Collection, the McLellan Galleries, the Tobacco Lords House
and many National Trust properties. You might expect a city of
this size to have loads of shops, public amenities and stuff
like that - you wouldn't be wrong. *In the under-belly of Glasgow
life, especially around the East End, there is a considerable
amount of drug abuse with both hard and soft drugs easily
available. There is a considerable problem with related crime.*

TRAVEL:

Trains: Queen's Street and Central Stations are the mainline
stops and run regular services to London (£35), Edinburgh
(£5.50), Birmingham (£30.50) and most other major stops.

Coaches: Services to London (£23.50), Birmingham (£25) and
all over Scotland and beyond.

Car: Good connections all over the country by road, including
the M74, A8/M8, A80/M80, A82, A77,and A736.

Air: Direct flights to Europe and the US, as well as shuttle
links to Heathrow and Gatwick (London £69), from Glasgow
Abbotsinch Airport, 8 miles from the city centre.

Hitching: *If you bus it out to the main roads, you may be OK,
but it's not a thumber's paradise.*

Local: Buses are frequent, cheap and comprehensive - fares
from 45p. The local trains are fast and efficient, with several
stops around the city. A 10-week Zonecard covering all travel
in the city costs £316.

Underground: There's an *efficient* underground system costing
60p a trip.

Taxis: *Only worth it late at night.*

Bicycles: Glasgow is hilly and traffic is heavy. *Bikes are useful,
but not essential.*

LIBRARIES & COMPUTERS:
- Books: 1,500,000 ● Study places: 2,700
- Computer workstations: 2,000

There are something over 50 libraries in departments around
the University (notably the Modern Languages, the Adam Smith
Social Science, Chemistry, Dental & Veterinary Libraries) as well
as a main library. *Computer facilities are excellent; the only
problem seems to be that students aren't informed about them.*

CAREER PROSPECTS:
- Careers Service ● No of staff: 10full
- Unemployed after 6mths (1996): 6.8%

The Careers Service holds information about part-time work as
well as opportunities after graduation.

SPECIAL FEATURES:
- The teaching week runs from Monday to Saturday.
- The Rector (the senior student representative) is Richard
'Victor Meldrew' Wilson.

FAMOUS ALUMNI:
William Boyd, AJ Cronin (writers); Menzies Campbell, Charles
Kennedy, Teddy Taylor (all MPs and ex-Presidents of the Union);
the Delgados; Donald Dewar MP (Lab); James Herriot (vet); Pat
Kane (Hue & Cry); Joseph Lister (pioneer of antiseptics); John
Logie Baird (invented TV); Anne Louise McIlroy (pioneer of
women in medicine); Adam Smith (economist); John Smith (late
Labour leader); James Watt (inventor).

FURTHER INFO:
Undergraduate prospectus and various handbooks from the various unions. Web site (http://www.gla.ac.uk).

entertainment

THE CITY:

● Price of a pint of beer: £1.80 ● Glass of wine: £1.40

Cinemas: (8) *Enough cinemas to keep eyes squared for ages,* including everything from 21st century multiplexes to old-fashioned flea pits. There are a few which specialise in arty flicks, including the Glasgow Film Theatre.

Theatres: Take your pick from the Theatre Royal (classical repertoire, Scottish Opera), King's (mainstream and musicals), Citizens' (special offers for students), Tramway (avant-garde), Tron (studio) and any number of fringe and amateur set-ups. Every May, there's the Mayfest, which, although a lot smaller (*and more radical*) than the Edinburgh Festival, has the advantage of being during term.

Pubs: *Some of the city's best beer bars are more fun than a jelly-fight on a bouncy castle.* **push***plugs (among many others): Maxaluna (trendy, arty); Bon Accord (real ales); O'Neill's (Irish); Chimichanga's (Tex-Mex décor). Ashton Lane for Cul De Sac, Curler's and Jinty McGuinty's. Don't try your luck in the East End if you're English.*

Clubs/discos: *Glasgow's clubs may not be cheap but they're varied.* Many have student nights. **push***plugs: The Velvet Rooms (house/Britpop); The Garage; Trash; Ark at the Tunnel (hard house); Ice at Archaos (garage/techno).*

Music venues: Many local bands have made it big, often starting out at some of the *vibe-ridden* venues. **push***plugs: Barrowlands, King Tut's Wah Wah Hut, The Garage (all indie hangouts) and the vast SECC.*

Eating out: *Glasgow has plenty of restaurants but Ainsley Harriott wouldn't get hyperactive over the ones that students can afford.* Pub lunches offer the best value. **push***plugs: Change at Jamaica (all-night caff); Maw Broom's (traditional Scottish); Java Internet Café; Fire Station (student discounts); California Gourmet (eat standing up).*

UNIVERSITY:

● Price of a pint of beer: £1.35 ● Glass of wine: £1.10

Bars: (7) There are bars at both of the university's 2 unions (see 'Social & Political' for an explanation). The most popular are Deep Six (recently refurbished) and the Beer Bar (*sporty*), at GUU, and Jim's Bar (*trendy*, hosts bands), at QM.

Theatres & cinema: The University's theatre hosts regular productions. Last year, students took 3 shows to the Edinburgh Fringe (*but it's not such an effort for them is it?*). The University drama course is *highly regarded* and over-subscribed. The *brand new* Gilmorehill Centre has facilities for theatre, TV and film studios as well as public performances.

Clubs/discos: Qudos (capacity 1,100) at QM and The Hive (800) at GUU each host 3 club nights a week, with cheese, indie and dance themes. *Cheeze at The Hive creates the most pungent perspiration.*

Music venues: *QM has a definite edge on the live action front.* The Supernaturals and Supergrass have both played recently.

Food: The Hub is the SRC outlet, offering *slightly pricey* snacks and full meals from 9 to 5.

Others: The highlight of the entertainments year is 'Daft Friday', the last day of the 1st term, when GUU holds a *posh* ball for its members only. In retaliation, QM started the 'Dafter Friday Ball' which is *much less formal* and geared around bands and discos. Both unions have other occasional events like the unavoidable karaoke and so on. Friday night is Newky Brown comedy night at QM.

social & political

STUDENT REPRESENTATIVE COUNCIL/GLASGOW UNIVERSITY UNION/QUEEN MARGARET UNION:

● <u>4 sabbaticals</u> ● <u>Turnout at last ballot: 10%</u>

Glasgow has the most confusing set of student organisations in the country, but you can always rely on push *to unmuddy.* In Glasgow, there are 5 student unions, with 2 in competition. First, there's the SRC (all students are automatically members when they first come to Glasgow, so there) which organises student representation, welfare and the student clubs and societies. *It's gently left-wing and not very high profile.* Next come the 2 services unions. A student can be a member of only 1 of these and they must choose in their first few days. Very few opt out altogether. *The rivalries are not too distinct* and students can use the facilities at both most of the time, but can vote in their own union. GUU, originally a men-only affair, is bigger (66% of students) with a large centre in a listed building near the centre of the campus. It organises debates as well as services *and rates with the Oxbridge Unions for the speakers it attracts. Fans of QM* (formerly the women's union) *would argue that, despite its size, it's where the cool people who don't like rugby hang out and ents are given priority over laddish drinking games.* The 4th union is the Athletics Union (see Sports below). Finally, there is the Postgraduate Research Club. None of the unions is a member of NUS.

SU FACILITIES:

GUU: 5 bars; cafeteria; restaurant; minibus; travel agency; print shop; photocopying; games machines; pool; juke box; vending machines; 2 libraries; meeting and conference rooms; launderette; Bank of Scotland and Royal Bank of Scotland cashpoint.

QM: 2 bars; cafeteria; restaurant; sandwich bar; print shop; photocopying; shop; games and vending machines; pool table; juke box; TV lounge; meeting rooms; customised nightclub; launderette; Bank of Scotland cash machine.

CLUBS (NON SPORTING):

Alchemists; Alexandrian; Debating; Dialectic; East Timor & Indonesia; Gaming; Humanist; Monty Python; Pakistani; SNP.

OTHER ORGANISATIONS:

The SRC publishes 'The Guardian' newspaper - no not that one - and there's also the independent GUM and Niche. The student TV station, GUST, and Sub City radio (with an FM licence 2 months a year and official radio station of the 'T in the Park' festival) have both won national awards recently.

RELIGIOUS:
● Team of chaplains
There are Anglican, Methodist, Free Church, Baptist, Jewish, Catholic and Church of Scotland chaplaincies. *In town there are enough churches of different denominations to wear out the knees of any good pair of jeans*, including, notably, Glasgow Cathedral (Church of Scotland) and St Andrew's Cathedral (Catholic). There are other places of worship locally for Muslims, Jews, Buddhists, Hindus and Sikhs.

PAID WORK:
Glasgow has been heaving itself out of the doldrums for more than a decade now and is still heaving. There is work around in bars and so on but there's others than students looking for it.

sports

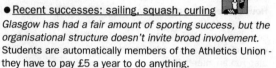

● Recent successes: sailing, squash, curling
Glasgow has had a fair amount of sporting success, but the organisational structure doesn't invite broad involvement. Students are automatically members of the Athletics Union - they have to pay £5 a year to do anything.

SPORTS FACILITIES:
Indoor facilities are available on campus in the Stevenson Building where there are squash courts, a swimming pool, saunas, multigym and a sports hall. Just a short way off is the Kelvin Hall sports centre with an indoor running track, fitness rooms, climbing wall and multigym. At the Garscube site: 3 artificial tennis courts, synthetic pitch and cricket wicket. A new sports hall is being developed and will open in 2 years.

SPORTING CLUBS:
Aikido; Curling; Shinty; Trampolining.

ATTRACTIONS:
Glasgow is one of the world's great football battlefields housing both Rangers and Celtic FCs *and Glaswegians won't understand it if soft southern students can't say which team they support.* There are 8 *lovely* golf courses around town feeding the Scottish habit and a dry ski slope locally.

accommodation

IN COLLEGE:
● Catered: 6% ● Cost: £54-62(31wks)
● Self-catering: 13% ● Cost: £34-42(38-52wk)
Availability: 33% of 1st years are housed in the University accommodation. The rest are mostly 'home students', ie they live either with their parents or in their own homes. 15% have to share. The halls of residence are all within 20 minutes' walking distance of the campus, with the exception of Wolfson Hall, 3 miles away, which has a University-run shuttle bus. There are 11 Student Houses, housing between 8 and 28 students in self-catering places. There are 1,875 places in flats which the University rents to students on a private basis but on favourable terms (housing 1st years and about 14% of the 2nd, 3rd and 4th years). There are also 70 flats for couples (140 places) and the Murano Street student village (1,100 places) with a shop 15 minutes' walk from the campus

(downhill) and 25 minutes back (uphill).

Car parking: *Parking for residents only is limited but adequate.* A £15 permit is needed for the Hillhead area.

EXTERNALLY:
● Ave rent: £50

Availability: For those students not living at home or in University accommodation, *it's best to look as early as possible. Around September, all the students who don't heed our wise advice will be looking just when it's getting toughest. Despite it's rundown image, housing in Glasgow is far from cheap, although it's possible to get good value in suburban tenement flats. Glasgow has its rough areas, but gentrification is cleaning up some of the former slum areas and students can live happily, although there are still some no-go areas. Parking is not easy and having a car is more hassle than help.*

Housing help: The *massive* Accommodation Office has weekly vacancy lists (daily in the peak period), bulletin boards, selective advertising on landlords' behalf, standard renting contracts and various other pearls of advice and help. They also run an inter-halls bus.

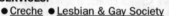

welfare

SERVICES:
● Creche ● Lesbian & Gay Society
● Mature SA ● Minibus ● Women's Officer

The SRC runs a welfare service, *but it suffers from the division of resources across the unions. That said, it is helpful on all sorts of problems, and runs the LGB Pride week.* The Accommodation Office also offers debt counselling and the University has a Counselling Service with 1 part- and 2 full-time counsellors. The Student Health Service employs a doctor, a psychiatric counsellor, a nursing sister and a visiting psychiatrist and the new student village has its own health centre.

Disabled: *The University is spending £50,000 a year on making buildings more accessible, but some, like the library, are still a joke (and not a very funny one at that).* There's a Special Needs Adviser *to make things a little less farcical.*

FINANCE:
● Ave debt: £900 ● Access fund: £894,508
● Successful applications (1997): 1,584

Student Hardship Fund as well as the access fund. Also, plenty of little grants and bequests.

> ❝ 'The Constitution of the NUS is meant to be the bible of the Union but I've never got past the front page.
> – Jim Murphy, former NUS President. ❞

Glasgow Caledonian University

● *Formerly Glasgow Polytechnic*

Glasgow Caledonian University, City Campus, Cowcaddens Road, Glasgow, G4 0BA. Tel: (0141) 331 3000. Fax: (0141) 331 3005.
Glasgow Caledonian University Students' Association, Cowcaddens Road, Glasgow, G4 0BA. Tel: (0141) 331 3886.
president@sa.gcal.ac.uk

general

For general information about Glasgow: see University of Glasgow. The University is split into 2 sites. Slap bang in the heart of Glasgow near the main shops and various housing estates, is the main site, the City Campus, made up of 4 1960s' concrete and glass towers and a newly-built library. The Park Campus is two miles away, used to be The Queen's College and overlooks Kelvingrove Park. It's made up of a *happy* mixture of Victorian and sandstone buildings with modern extensions.

41% ♂♂♂♂♂♀♀♀♀♀ **59%**

Sex ratio(M:F): 41%:59%	Founded: 1971
Full time u'grads: 9,564	Part time: 1,960
Postgrads: 883	Non-degree: 518
Ave course: 4yrs	Ethnic: 3%
Private school: n/a	Flunk rate: n/a
Mature students: 24%	Overseas students: 5.2%
Disabled students: 1.4%	Staff/student ratio: 1:18
Clearing: 16%	

ATMOSPHERE:
Many of the students are locals and/or mature students, which tends to make the place feel like a means to an end rather than a cohesive, self-contained environment - students are here to get a course and everything else is secondary. Interaction between the sites is limited, with students at Park Campus feeling socially hard done by.

THE SITES:
City Campus: The main site.
Park Campus: (1,345 students - hospitality & tourism, consumer management). *Students here tend to be career motivated and flash cars are much in evidence.*

THE CITY: see University of Glasgow

TRAVEL: see University of Glasgow
Queen Street station is 10 minutes' walk from the City Campus.

LIBRARIES & COMPUTERS:
- Books: 300,000 ● Study places: 1,500
- Computer workstations: 1,500

There's a library on each site. *The main library seems to double as a social venue, so a studious atmosphere is hard to maintain. Pressure on computer facilities can be a tad intense, but the opening of the new Caledonian Library & Information Centre should ease the strain.*

CAREER PROSPECTS:
- Careers Service ● No of staff: 6full/3part
- Unemployed after 6mths (1996): 8.6%

FAMOUS ALUMNI:
Jim Delahunt, Louise White (Scottish TV); Pat Nevin (footballer).

FURTHER INFO:
Prospectuses for undergrads, part-timers and a handbook for mature students. Web Site (http://www.gcal.ac.uk and http://www.sa.gcal.ac.uk).

entertainment

THE CITY: see University of Glasgow

UNIVERSITY:

- Price of a pint of beer: £1.40 ● Glass of wine: £1.10

Bars: (4) There are 3 bars on the City Campus. Park Campus has the Bedsit bar *which is also used by the canny locals.*
Cinema: Big video screens at City and Park campuses but these are used as much for sporting events as for movies.
Clubs/discos/music venues: *Clubbing seems to be the only form of social activity that can keep students on campus beyond nightfall* and to that end there are various club nights in the Asylum (650, adm free-£3), with regular events including X-rated and Stereo plus live student and 70s cover bands every month. At the Bedsit, boogies include Uptight (northern soul) and Club Cubana (Latin American) every fortnight; monthly musical ministration at Bongo Fury (funk), Under the Influence (techno) and Crucial Vibes (reggae). Space played the last Freshers' Ball.
Food: *The City Campus Refectory is pretty expensive but the Park Café is more realistic. The training restaurant at Park Campus is worth a try.*
Others: At least 3 balls a year and the Final Fling - another all-nighter. Also quiz nights, karaoke and occasional cabaret.

social & political

GLASGOW CALEDONIAN UNIVERSITY STUDENTS' ASSOCIATION:
- 5 sabbaticals ● Turnout at last ballot: 13%
- NUS member

The addition of 2 new sabbatical posts and a slightly more radical, left-wing tone to the SA's campaigning has woken up a

> ❛Pembroke College, Cambridge has the oldest bowling green in Europe.❜

generally politics-free student body to the extent that they're peeping drowsily over their duvets and looking curiously at the fried breakfast of agitation.

SU FACILITIES:
The Association is housed in the Union at the City Campus, with a few further facilities at Park Campus.
City Campus: 3 bars; cafeteria; pizza cafe; 2 shops (general and stationery); games, video and vending machines; pool table; TV; conference hall; customised nightclub; welfare centre.
Park Campus: Shop; bar; vending and video machines; pool tables.

CLUBS (NON SPORTING):
Campus TV; ENEMA (Entertaining Nurses and Entertaining Midwives Association); Radio; Scottish Socialist Alliance; Stop the Fees.

OTHER ORGANISATIONS:
The SA publishes 'UNI' the monthly student newspaper.

PAID WORK: see University of Glasgow

sports

● Recent successes: nothing special

Apart from a committed hardcore, sport isn't an abiding passion. Limited facilities don't help but a new £4m sports centre is due to open in 1999 (a year late already).

SPORTS FACILITIES:
City: A sports hall with multigym.
Park: Multigym.

ATTRACTIONS: see University of Glasgow

accommodation

IN COLLEGE:
● Catered: 1.5% ● Cost: £57(37wks)
● Self-catering: 3.3% ● Cost: £34-52(37wks)
Availability: 1st years get priority in the University's *haphazard* mix of accommodation, which ranges from the study bedrooms at Gibson Hall to 320 self-catering flats just off City Campus in Caledonian Court. There are also 340 spaces in a head tenancy scheme *but in all, provisions aren't great.*
Car parking: Staff and disabled students only.

EXTERNALLY: see University of Glasgow
Housing help: Student Services provide an accommodation service, with 1 full- and 1 part-time member of staff who allocate the University-managed rooms and can help with rent difficulties. *Compared to services at other universities, this is more of an internal than an external accommodation service, although some work is done housing students in the private sector.*

welfare

SERVICES:
● Creche ● Nightline ● Mature SA
● Overseas SA ● Postgrad SA
The Counselling Service has 2 full- and 3 part-time employees, while the SA has 1 advisor. The University Health Service

provides a nurse and visiting doctor. Tutors are also a good
source for help.

Disabled: *Access is improving.* There are induction loops in
the largest lecture theatres and the University, together with
the Royal National Institute for the Blind, has established a
resource centre for sight-impaired students and help is
available for those with dyslexia.

FINANCE:
- Ave debt per year: £1,350 ● Access fund: £240,000
- Successful applications (1995): 1,319

University Hardship Fund and Childcare Fund.

••

 ▶▶ **Glasgow Poly**

see Glasgow Caledonian University

••

▶▶ **Gloucester**

see Cheltenham & Gloucester College of Higher Education

••

Goldsmiths College, London

▼ ● *The College is part of <u>University of London</u> and students
are entitled to use its facilities.*

Goldsmiths College, New Cross, London, SE14 6NW.
Tel: (0171) 919 7282. Fax: (0171) 919 7509.
E-mail: admissions@gold.ac.uk
Goldsmiths College Students' Union, New Cross,
London, SE14 6NW. Tel: (0181) 692 1406.
Fax: (0181) 694 9789.

General

New Cross, 5 miles south east of Trafalgar Square, is a
shabby part of London, with traffic trundling through
interminably. *It's a bit like a tattered teddy bear, torn at the
seams, but still with character. Some nearby areas, such
as Greenwich, are lively cultural toy boxes, but most are
busted Airfix models and broken Tonka toys, such as
Lewisham, Catford, Deptford and New Cross itself.*
Goldsmiths College, in the midst of all this, is *a walking,
talking doll.* The main building is *clean (considering its
location), attractive,* 3 storeys and redbrick with a big, busy,
white pillared, entrance at the front and creeper covered
walls and a flat lawn to the rear. The rest of the College's
buildings are more modern and in keeping with the
surrounding urban sprawl, *but unassuming enough to be
ignored.* Most of the students are arty types from a collage
of different backgrounds.

34% ♂♂♂♀♀♀♀♀♀♀ **66%**

Sex ratio(M:F): 34%:66%	Founded: 1891
Full time u'grads: 3,797	Part time: 1,141
Postgrads: 992	Non-degree: 1,842
Ave course: 3yrs	Ethnic: 19%
Private school: n/a	Flunk rate: 27%
Mature students: 40%	Overseas students: 17.5%
Disabled students: 4.3%	Staff/student ratio: 1:16
Clearing: 17%	

ATMOSPHERE:

Goldsmiths is unique in London. It combines a buzzing and vividly vibrant student culture with local community links. The College is friendly, open and bristling with fun, a self-contained oasis of expressive, creative people and most are doing courses because they're interested rather than as a means to an end. Earnest careerists in suits are noticeably absent. The College's academic standard, shaky in recent years, has now taken a substantial turn for the better.

THE CITY: see <u>University of London</u>

NEW CROSS, LEWISHAM, GREENWICH:

New Cross, Lewisham and most of the surrounding areas are *dingily* residential, with shops on every corner and paving stones cracked and littered. *They're not inner-city hellholes, though, and what they lack in tourist appeal they make up for with a friendly, vibrant local community and a relatively low cost of living.* Greenwich provides culture: the famous park with the Observatory and Planetarium; the Maritime Museum; the Cutty Sark; a *fun* Sunday market; and *one of London's best theatres outside the West End.*

TRAVEL: see <u>University of London</u>

Local Trains: Trains from New Cross and New Cross Gate go straight into London Bridge, Waterloo and Charing Cross in less than 1/4 hour.

Buses: 21, 36, 36B, 142, 171 (to the West End), 225 and Night Buses N53, N62, N72, N82, N85 and N86. Bingo!

Car: Close to the South Circular (the bottom bit of London's inner ring road), which helps, and *parking is easier than in some parts of London, but a lot harder than brie in sunshine.*

Underground: *Oddly ill-served* by the tube; the East London Line ends with stations at New Cross and New Cross Gate, but it's not a very direct route into London.

Bicycles: *A lot of theft and pollution, but many students use bikes because they're more sound (and cheaper) than cars.*

> ❝In 1969 the SOAS Union disaffiliated from NUS (because it was too reactionary) and allied itself to the Black Panthers.❞

LIBRARIES & COMPUTERS:
- Books: 230,000 ● Study places: 430
- Computer workstations: 250

CAREER PROSPECTS:
- Careers Service ● No of staff: 3full
- Unemployed after 6mths (1996): 9%

Despite its arts bias, Goldsmiths' employment record is better than many 'vocational' universities. Students also have access to the University's careers service.

FAMOUS ALUMNI:
Most of Blur; John Cale (Velvet Underground); Julia Carling (TV presenter); Vic Charles (karate champ); Julian Clary (comedian); Wendy Cope (poet); Lucien Freud, Damien Hirst, Tom Keating, Bridget Riley (artists); Tessa Jowell MP (Lab); Linton Kwesi Johnson (dub poet); Malcolm McLaren (Sex Pistols manager, manipulator); Brian Molko (Placebo); Mary Quant (designer); Lord Merlyn-Rees (former Home Secretary); Gillian Wearing (Turner prize-winner 1997); Colin Welland (playwright/actor).

FURTHER INFO:
Prospectuses for undergrads and postgrads, a video and a web site (http://www.gold.ac.uk).

entertainment

IN LONDON: see University of London

NEW CROSS:
- Price of a pint of beer: £1.90 ● Glass of wine: £1.60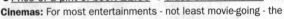

Cinemas: For most entertainments - not least movie-going - the West End has more to offer than the locality.

Theatres: Again the West End, although Greenwich Theatre has, in the past, fed the West End with some of its *most moist morsels.*

Pubs: *A few are worthwhile.* **push***plugs: New Cross Inn, Marquis of Granby, Rosemary Branch, Paradise Bar, Goldsmiths Tavern.*

Clubs/discos/music venues: *Live music and spinning sounds are soundest in some of the less unwholesome local pubs and clubs. Recommended: The Venue; Amersham Arms; Up the Creek (regular comedy slot).*

Eating out: *Not the hautest of cuisines but most tuck shops are cheap and there's a good range of ethnic and cultural taste experiences to be had.* **push***plugs: Marie's Café, Gem's (greasy spoons), Mr Cheung, Raj Bhujan.*

COLLEGE:
- Price of a pint of beer: £1.65 ● Glass of wine: £1.20

Bars: *The main SU bar is usually packed but everything closes down at weekends.*

Theatres: With lots of drama and arts students, it's not surprising that Goldsmiths is well-equipped: a proscenium stage in the George Wood Theatre and 3 studios used for thespian pursuits by the Players, and Stage & Musical Societies, *dished up with buttock-toughening regularity.*

Cinema: 2 blockbusters shown every week.

Clubs/discos/music venues: 2 club nights a week, including the housey 'Jetset', plus latin and funky stuff. Live acts do their stuff at the top of the SU building.

Food: *Loafer's Corner and Sutcliffe's are surprisingly health-oriented, but pricey. The more junk-laden Panhandle, run by the SU, is cheaper. Take your pick: overdraft or arteries?*

Others: At least 4 balls a year, plus hall and society events.

social & political

GOLDSMITHS COLLEGE STUDENTS' UNION:

- <u>4 sabbaticals</u> ● <u>Turnout at last ballot: 15%</u>
- <u>NUS member</u>

Goldsmiths' SU is one of the most politically vocal in London but the broad left consensus within the ranks of the hacks doesn't necessarily translate to the student body in general – they're more likely to be getting down to studying and partying. Campaigns to keep beer cheap and keep the earth clean (more long-term wishful thinking than the former motion) have met with success.

SU FACILITIES:

It's quite a trek to Bloomsbury from New Cross so Goldsmiths students rarely use the University and ULU facilities, but, in its own Tiananmen Building, GCSU provides The Panhandle snack bar and coffee shop, 3 bars, a general shop, photocopier, launderette, 4 pool tables, games machines; CD juke box and 2 minibuses. On campus there's a Waterstones bookshop and a NatWest Bank.

CLUBS (NON SPORTING):

Band; DJ; Free Speech; Japan International; Kickin' Party; Korean; Mature Students; Meditation; M.F. Club; Muslim Women; Radio; Rebel Music; Roleplaying; Singaporean; Stage Musical; Stop the Fees; Student Assembly Against Fascism; Young Socialists.

OTHER ORGANISATIONS:

The monthly 'Smiths' magazine *is an excellent example of what can be achieved without gloss and gimmick.* Radio station 'Wired!' is being set up *even as we speak.*

RELIGIOUS:

Catholic and Anglican chaplaincies and a rabbi.

PAID WORK: see <u>University of London</u>

sports

- <u>Recent successes: football, karate</u>

Sporting enthusiasm at Goldsmiths has taken an upturn lately although the facilities leave something to be desired. Fortunately, students are entitled to use <u>University of London</u> amenities.

SPORTS FACILITIES:

Facilities on site include 2 small gyms, tennis courts, cricket nets and a rugby scrum machine (*whacking fun*). Wavelengths Baths in Deptford are just down the road. There are 21 acres of playing fields at the Loring Sports ground in Sidcup, Kent (8 miles away).

SPORTING CLUBS:

Aikido; Male, female and mixed Basketball; Kick-boxing; Self-Defence; Ski/Snowboard; Women's Football & Hockey.

‹Vimto was invented at UMIST.›

ATTRACTIONS:
The local football team is Millwall. Also nearby are Crystal Palace and Charlton Athletic.

accommodation

IN COLLEGE:
- Catered: 5% ● Cost: £62(31wks)
- Self-catering: 27% ● Cost: £45-57(39-52wks)

Availability: All 1st years who want it are accommodated in halls close to campus. Chances for other years are less good, but 28% of 2nd years and 16% of finalists were lucky last year. Nobody needs to share. New halls are being developed to improve provisions.

Car parking: Free parking is available at halls but there's not much space to go round.

EXTERNALLY: see University of London
Availability: South London usually works out cheaper than north because of the capital's own topsy-turvy north/south divide. Brockley, Lewisham and Brixton are all quite popular.
Housing help: The College runs an accommodation office in addition to the University's.

welfare

SERVICES:
- Creche ● Lesbian & Gay Society
- Mature SA ● Overseas SA ● Minibus ● Women's Officer
- Self-defence classes

The University provides some services but so does Goldsmiths itself and the SU. Health services (from doctors and nurses) are based at the College's Medical Centre just round the corner and there are 2 counsellors available. There is also a tutor support system. The International Office takes particular care of overseas students.

Women: For once, men are in the minority and *the provisions for women are excellent.* The SU subsidises personal attack alarms and provides women's safe transport after events.

Disabled: *Wheelchair access is good in the learning centre and the SU, but elsewhere you have to cope with stairs and old Victorian houses.* Braille signs have been fitted recently and there are induction loops in College. 1 bar has been specially adapted. A Dyslexia Support Group is in place.

FINANCE:
- Ave debt: £3,950 ● Access fund: £135,750
- Successful applications (1997): 1000+

▶▶ **Gordon University**
see Robert Gordon University

University of Greenwich

● *Formerly Thames Polytechnic*
University of Greenwich, Bexley Road, Eltham, London SE9
2PQ. Tel: 0800 005006. Fax: (0181) 331 8145.
E-mail: courseinfo@greenwich.ac.uk
Greenwich University Students' Union, Bathway, Woolwich,
London, SE18 6QX. Tel: (0181) 855 8268.
Fax: (0181) 331 8591.

General

Don't be fooled by the name 'Greenwich'. Only Americans
pronounce it 'green-witch'. *It's 'grennidge' - get it right. Also,
forget any images of the Cutty Sark, Maritime Museum and
Sunday markets - you won't find the University there.* The largest
site is in *un-touristy* Woolwich, 8½ miles east of Trafalgar
Square, and some sites aren't even in the Borough of
Greenwich, including Dartford (in Kent). In all, the sites are
spread over 23 miles, never far from the river, *which seems to
suggest that the old name (Thames Poly) was closer to the
mark.* However, the University is intending to acquire the Royal
Naval College, which really is in Greenwich, *so at last the name
might be appropriate.* The different sites offer different courses
and students considering applying to the University should
check which one they'd be based at, since *they are largely self-
contained and as different as chalk and chutney.*

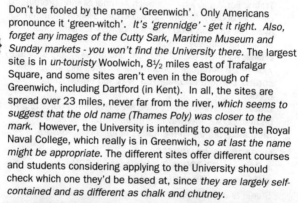

50% ♂♂♂♂♂♀♀♀♀♀ 50%	
Sex ratio(M:F): 50%:50%	Founded: 1890
Undergrads: 8,577	Part time: 3,067
Postgrads: 1,244	Non-degree: 2,637
Ave course: 3yrs	Ethnic: 26%
Private school: n/a	Flunk rate: n/a
Mature students: 58%	Overseas students: n/a
Disabled students: 1.2%	Staff/student ratio: 1:19
Clearing: n/a	

ATMOSPHERE:
*The 2 major SU venues provide a social focus which otherwise
fall prey to the distances between sites. This helps
to provide a sense of fun and an extra-curricular buzz that's
missing at some of the other 'new' universities.*

THE SITES:
Woolwich: (6,000 students - humanities, business, technology
and sciences) Almost ½ the students are based at the
Woolwich campus. Local attractions include the Thames
Barrier (the world's largest flood gate), the Woolwich Ferry
across the Thames and the Woolwich Arsenal.
Avery Hill: (6,000 - law, health, teacher training, social
sciences) *The most attractive site,* 3 miles south of Woolwich,

set in an 86-acre park with a listed mansion as the main building. The nearest major shopping area is Eltham, a mile away.

Dartford: (2,000 - architecture, surveying, civil engineering) In Kent, 13 miles from Woolwich (40mins by train from Charing Cross), it's a collection of modern rectangles with 5 halls of residence and some amenities including *good* sports facilities. It's actually about a mile from Dartford. Dartford is a fast expanding industrial town with a few shops and a direct escape route by train into London.

Medway: (1,200 - earth sciences, engineering) A relatively new development in association with the Natural Resources Institute.

THE CITY: see University of London

TRAVEL: see University of London

Trains: For Woolwich - Woolwich Arsenal Station (25mins to central London); for Dartford - Dartford Station (40mins); for Avery Hill - Falconwood (30mins) or New Eltham. Chatham station for Medway.

Buses: All sites, except Dartford and Medway, are served by a wide range of regular London bus services including night buses. Dartford is connected by Green buses with central London.

Car: Dartford is just within the M25 (London's outer ring road) on the M2/A2. Medway is 3 miles from the M2.

Bicycles: *Your life in the hands of juggernaut drivers.*

LIBRARIES & COMPUTERS:
- Books: 600,000 ● Study places: 1,600
- Computer workstations: 1,000

Students aren't exactly jumping over moon about library facilities, given the scrums over primary texts and the fact that they're closed on Sundays.

CAREER PROSPECTS:
- Careers Service ● No of staff: 3full
- Unemployed after 6mths (1995): 14%

Careers services at each site.

FAMOUS ALUMNI:
Hale & Pace (*unamusing* double act); Rachel Heyhoe Flint (cricketer); Prof Charles Kao (inventor of fibre optics); Graham Ingham (BBC TV reporter); Brian Jacks (former judo champ); Matt James (Gene drummer).

FURTHER INFO:
Prospectuses for undergrads and postgrads, guide for mature students, video and web site (http://www.greenwich.ac.uk).

entertainment

IN LONDON: see University of London

LOCAL AREAS:
There is nothing to do outside college as the sites are not in London's most jumping joints. There's more or less the level of entertainment facilities you might reckon to find in London's inner cities and outmost commuter reaches. Many students avoid the local pubs, especially those popular with local

squaddies. Solitary **push***plug: Earl of Chatham in Woolwich. For other ents, the SU and the West End provide more than enough compensation.*

UNIVERSITY:
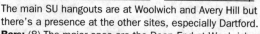
● Price of a pint of beer: £1.55 ● Glass of wine: 85p

The main SU hangouts are at Woolwich and Avery Hill but there's a presence at the other sites, especially Dartford.

Bars: (8) The major ones are the Deep End at Woolwich and the Jesters bar in the Dome at Avery Hill.

Cinema: 1 blockbuster a week.

Clubs/discos: There are 3 or 4 club nights a week, including Millennium, which has featured Danny Rampling and Graham Gold in the past, and Warp at the Deep End (jungle).

Music venues: The Deep End at Woolwich and the Dome at Avery Hill can hold 1,000 punters each and the Zone at Dartford can take 300. Recent acts have included Gina G, Jools Holland and Dannii Minogue.

Cabaret: Fortnightly stop offs at the Dome from London circuit regulars such as Rob Newman and Charlie Chuck.

Food: A range of eateries across the expanse, *the best being Woolwich's Snorkels Cafe.*

Others: 2 main balls (Christmas and May) and the more outlying sites do their own spherical things.

social & political

UNIVERSITY OF GREENWICH STUDENTS' UNION:
● 5 sabbaticals ● Turnout at last ballot: 8%
● NUS member

The concentration of SU facilities at Woolwich and Avery Hill tends to leave the further-flung members somewhat out of the equation. The entertainment facilities are well used, maybe because there's not much competition in the local area, but politics isn't really on the agenda.

SU FACILITIES:
8 bars (on 5 sites); 4 minibuses; 3 shops; vending and games machines; pool tables; juke box; library; photocopying; hairdressers; 3 meeting rooms; customised disco venue.

CLUBS (NON SPORTING):
Chinese; DJ; Malaysian.

OTHER ORGANISATIONS:
There's a monthly student magazine, the 'Sarky Cutt'. The fortnightly ents sheet is called 'Get Out'.

RELIGIOUS:
● 2 chaplains (CofE, RC)
Meeting rooms available for students of any denomination. Muslim prayer room at Woolwich.

PAID WORK: see University of London

sports

● Recent successes: nothing special

For a university inside the M25, Greenwich has some pretty good sports facilities, but only a certain proportion of the students get into the spirit. Most sites have something to offer.

❝ One of the modern sculptures at Southampton University was designed to moan in the wind but it disturbed the law department, so the holes were blocked up. **❞**

SPORTS FACILITIES:
Avery Hill: sports centre with multigym, squash courts, snooker tables; 2 gyms; cricket, football, rugby, hockey pitches; tennis courts; running track; swimming pool.
Woolwich: sports hall; fitness room; 2 squash courts.
Dartford: swimming pool; sports hall; netball and tennis courts; playing fields; cricket nets.
Medway: sports hall.

SPORTING CLUBS:
Horse-riding.

ATTRACTIONS:
Charlton Athletic, Millwall and Gillingham are the local football teams.

accommodation

IN COLLEGE:
● Catered: 3% ● Cost: £69(33wks)
● Self-catering: 25% ● Cost: £42-67(40wks)
Availability: The University guarantees to house all 1st years who request it, although this might mean private accommodation (head tenancy or housing association schemes). The majority of Uni-owned housing is at Avery Hill but there's something at each site, and all sites have disabled facilities.

EXTERNALLY: see University of London
● Ave rent: £50
Availability: *East and south-east London, especially Woolwich and Plumstead, are cheaper than north of the river, but you get what you pay for. Some parts, such as Thamesmead, are a bit deficient on the safety front.*
Housing help: The University runs an accommodation service with a vacancies board and an approval scheme.

welfare

SERVICES:
● Creche ● Lesbian & Gay Society
● Overseas SA ● Women's Officer
The SU runs a Welfare and Advice Department with 2 advisors, and the University runs a Counselling Service employing 3 full- and 4 part-time staff, *easily accessible on the larger sites only.* They organise workshops for coping with stress, anxiety and so on. The Medical Service operates at Woolwich, Dartford and Avery Hill offering a nurse and medical officer.
Disabled: *There are a few ramps, designated parking spaces and faulty lifts, but generally the facilities have discouraged*

disabled students. A new disability advisor is working to
reverse this.

FINANCE:
- Ave debt: £2,800 ● Access fund: £350,000
- Successful applications (1996): 1,500

●●●●●●●●●●●●●●●●●●●●●●●●●●●●●●●●●●●●●●●

 **Guildhall**
see London Guildhall University

●●●●●●●●●●●●●●●●●●●●●●●●●●●●●●●●●●●●●●●

 **Guy's Hospital**
see King's College, London

❝Freaked out by finance? Why
not pop into your local branch of
Lloyds Bank and see what they
have to offer.❞

❝If you have any comments about
PUSH or fancy being involved in
the next edition, please write to
PUSH, McGraw-Hill Publishing
Company, Shoppenhangers Road,
Maidenhead, Berkshire SL6 2QL.❞

i teach you the superman

man is something that

should be overcome

thus spake zarathustra

Hallam
see Sheffield Hallam University

Harper Adams
see Other Institutions

Hatfield
see University of Hertfordshire

'Text in italics is PUSH's point of view – take it or leave it.'

Heriot-Watt University

Heriot-Watt University, Riccarton, Edinburgh, EH14 4AS.
Tel: (0131) 451 3450/1. Fax: (0131) 451 5153.
E-mail: e.lister@hw.ac.uk
Heriot-Watt University Students' Association, The Union,
Riccarton, Edinburgh, EH14 4AS. Tel: (0131) 451 5333.
Fax: (0131) 451 5344.

General

For general information about Edinburgh: see <u>Edinburgh University</u>. Heriot-Watt is based on a *beautiful* 380-acre parkland site 6½ miles outside Edinburgh at Riccarton. This green and wooded campus, which was only completed in 1992, is on the site of an old mansion. The gardens of the mansion remain, surrounding the library which now stands where the house once did. The University buildings, built mostly from *smart* light brick in the 70s and 80s, lie among the old trees and around an artificial lake or, since this is Scotland, artificial loch, with bad-tempered swans. The campus is still growing and now includes a research park and the Edinburgh Conference Centre. *The countryside around the campus is not exactly the purple flower of Scotland's thistle. It's fairly uninteresting.* There is also an associated college of the University based in Edinburgh centre and another site in Galashiels, 26 miles away.

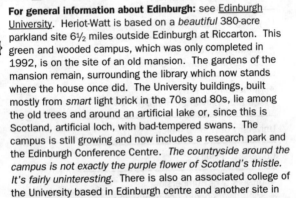

71% ♂♂♂♂♂♂♂♀♀♀ 29%	
Sex ratio(M:F): 71%:29%	Founded: 1966
Full time u'grads: 4,750	Part time: 465
Postgrads: 900	Non-degree: 0
Ave course: 4yrs	Ethnic: 7%
Private school: n/a	Flunk rate: n/a
Mature students: 18%	Overseas students: 15%
Disabled students: 4%	Staff/student ratio: 1:13
Clearing: 10%	

ATMOSPHERE:
It's a science-based, 9-5 type place and most students who live off campus don't hang around come tea-time, leaving the place a bit bleak except for the lesser-spotted fresher who can be spotted, flitting nervously through his (and it's mainly blokes) concrete-block habitat. By Scottish university standards, Heriot-Watt is very cosmopolitan: only 59% of students are native Scots and there is a large number of overseas students who take an active role in student life.

THE SITES:
Although the associated colleges are technically part of Heriot-Watt, *students often try to disown their 'big brother' institution, regarding it as a bit nerdy and unhip.* Students are

entitled to use HW facilities for sports and other pursuits but few do.

Moray House was an associated college but is now part of the University of Edinburgh.

Edinburgh College of Art: (architecture, landscape, planning & housing, art & design) Situated in Edinburgh's centre, the 1,500 students here are *very arty*. Funny, that...

The Scottish College of Textiles: (textile design, management & technology) SCOT (as it's abbreviated) is merging with Heriot-Watt this year. There are 750 students based here, some of whom study for part of their courses at Riccarton. SCOT is in Galashiels, a *small but attractive* town, 29 miles from Riccarton, *somewhat limited in facilities*.

THE CITY: see University of Edinburgh

TRAVEL: see University of Edinburgh
Local buses: Buses to the city centre cost 80p and take 30 minutes. There is a night service until 4.30am.
Car: The Riccarton campus is about 1 mile outside the A720 Edinburgh ring road, just off the A71 on its way out of the city. There are parking spaces on the campus, but very few in the city centre.
Taxis: By taxi to Waverley Station in the city centre only takes about 15 minutes but costs around £7.
Hitching: *Not a safe way of getting into town and so most students take the bus.*
Bicycles: *A bit far to the city centre and Edinburgh is generally too hilly and too windy. Theft is also a problem.*

LIBRARIES & COMPUTERS:
- Books: 111,000 ● Periodicals: 1,500
- Study places: 650 ● Computer workstations: 1,070
There's a main library at the Riccarton campus as well as further collections in some departments and at least 1 library at each of the other colleges.

CAREER PROSPECTS:
- Careers Service ● No of staff: 7full/1part
- Unemployed after 6mths (1995): 7.8%

SPECIAL FEATURES:
- The name Heriot-Watt has nothing to do with TV vet James Herriot. James Watt (1736-1819) was one of the innovators of the Industrial Revolution with his work on steam engines. George Heriot (1563-1623), known as 'Jinglin' Geordie', was a jeweller and financier to James VI of Scotland (James I of England).

❝In 1953, just before the Coronation, students from Glasgow University pinched the Stone of Scone from Westminster Abbey, and took it back to Scotland. Sure beats traffic cones.❞

● The country's only degree course in Brewing & Distilling. Cheers.

FAMOUS ALUMNI:
Ronnie Corbett (diminutive comedian); Bernie Grant MP, Martin O'Neill MP (Lab); Craig Joiner (rugby player); Archy Kirkwood MP (Lib Dem); Irvine Welsh ('Trainspotting' author).

FURTHER INFO:
Prospectuses for undergrads and postgrads and web sites (http://www.hw.ac.uk and http://www.hw.ac.uk/exuwww/).

entertainment

TOWN: see University of Edinburgh

UNIVERSITY:
● Price of a pint of beer: £1.35 ● Glass of wine: £1.15
Bars: (7) There are 3 bars in the University, 1 in the Conference Centre and 3 in the Union, which are the *popular* Jinglin' Geordies (cap 250), Liberty's (170, *recently refurbished*) and Dr Connery's (450), named after the recipient of an honorary doctorate. *Clue: it wasn't Pearce Brosnan.* All the associate colleges also have their own bar arrangements.
Clubs/discos: Dr Connery's is the dance dive 2 or 3 times a week, running themed nights from acid jazz to mainstream chart fodder (free-£3).
Music venues: The Conference Centre (452) hosts occasional gigs, including, recently, Shiner, Arkana and the Dharmas.
Food: The University refectory does 3 meals a day at *reasonable* prices and the SA bars also serve hot and cold food.
Others: There are weekly pub quizzes, occasional balls, and the usual posse of hypnotists.

social & political

HERIOT-WATT UNIVERSITY STUDENTS' ASSOCIATION:
● 3 sabbaticals ● Turnout at last ballot: 15%
● NUS member
Politics is generally a bigger turn off for Heriot-Watt students than a tongue sandwich from John Prescott, although environmental issues can sometimes create rustles in the activist undergrowth. Students regard their Student Association first and foremost as a services organisation.

SU FACILITIES:
The Student Association's building is called the Student Union (so that's 'the Association' that's the organisation and 'the Union' that's the building, got that? Right.): 3 bars; disco; cafeteria; shop; travel agency; PA hire; welfare library; meeting rooms.

CLUBS (NON SPORTING):
Bands & Recording; Brewing (biggest beer fest in Scotland); Bookworm; Celtic Supporters; Collectable Card Players; Duke of Edinburgh; Ents Volunteers; French Students; German Theatre; Gaming; Hong Kong Students; Malaysian/Singaporean; Norwegian; Offshore; Orkney; Parthenon Hellenic; Red Cross; Venture Scouts; Watt Gamers; Watt No Batteries; Watt Wheelers; University Pipe & Dance.

OTHER ORGANISATIONS:
The free student newspaper is called 'Watt's On' and comes out 3 times a term.

RELIGIOUS:
- **6 chaplains**

Multi-faith chaplaincy centre (with 6 honorary chaplains of various denominations) and a Muslim prayer room.

PAID WORK: see University of Edinburgh

sports

- **Recent successes: badminton, football, hockey, volleyball**

With such large grounds, the University has provided some excellent sporting facilities which have attracted a fair number of muscle-bound Olympians. Student sports are co-ordinated by the Sports Union (independent of the SA). Sports scholarships are available for badminton, golf and squash.

SPORTS FACILITIES:
The Riccarton campus boasts the impressive National Squash Centre, but also has a number of large playing fields (6 football, 2 rugby, 1 cricket), a floodlit training area, jogging track, 3 tennis courts and a sports hall, climbing wall, 2 multigyms, golf driving nets, croquet pitch, weights and fitness rooms and indoor sports courts.

SPORTING CLUBS:
Nin Jutsu; Sea Anglers; Sui Bukan Karate.

ATTRACTIONS: see University of Edinburgh

accommodation

IN COLLEGE:
- **Catered: 7%** • **Cost: £63-72(32wks)**

- **Self-catering: 16%** • **Cost: £31-48(34/38wks)**

Availability: All 1st years from outside the region can be accommodated and most of those who want it from other years (although this only comes to about 20%). The accommodation is divided into 4 'phases', I to IV, which differ according to cost *and levels of concrete ghastliness.* There's also a head tenancy scheme, whereby the University rents out 100 flats in town.

Car parking: Car ownership is increasing, and *the situation sometimes approaches a shoehorn/vaseline scenario.*

EXTERNALLY: see University of Edinburgh
Housing help: The *excellent* Accommodation Office has 5 staff providing a bulletin board, approval scheme and advice.

welfare

SERVICES:
- **Nursery** • **Lesbian & Gay Society**

- **Overseas SA** • **Women's Officer** • **Self-defence classes**

The Student Association has a drop-in advice centre. The University provides 'mentors', tutors or members of staff with some welfare training, as well as a counsellor. The Health Service at Riccarton has doctors, nurses and a dentist, plus a sports doctor and physiotherapist on site.

Disabled: *Access to some departments and buildings is very good and there is a good degree of awareness, but considering how modern a campus this is, there have been*

some serious design errors, such as limited access to the
Union. Some specially adapted accommodation and there's a
Special Needs Adviser.

FINANCE:
- Access fund: £116,500
- Successful applications (1996): 500

The Student Association runs a crisis fund. There are sports
bursaries worth between £500 and £1,500.

University of Hertfordshire

● *Formerly Hatfield Polytechnic*
University of Hertfordshire, College Lane, Hatfield,
Hertfordshire, AL10 9AB. Tel: (01707) 284000.
Fax: (01707) 284870.
Hertfordshire University Students' Union, Hatfield Campus,
College Lane, Hatfield, AL10 9AB. Tel: (01707) 285000.
Fax: (01707) 251118.

General

Hatfield is hardly outside London, less than 8 miles from the
outskirts. It's an *uninteresting* satellite, but Hertfordshire i*s
one of the less trite Home Counties with many pretty rural
villages* and the *attractive* town of St Albans. The University's
main campus *seems divorced from everything but the A1*,
which runs right along one edge. It's a couple of miles away
from the train station in Hatfield - *and in Hatfield, the station is
all you'll want.* The campus buildings are *uninspiring* blocks
from the last 30 years, dotted *spaciously* around the green
and wooded site. Fortunately, this is just the main campus
out of 4, not including the Bayfordbury site where a field centre
is based.

50% ♂♂♂♂♂♀♀♀♀♀ **50%**

Sex ratio(M:F): 50%:50%	Founded: 1952
Full time u'grads: 10,655	Part time: 4,342
Postgrads: 2,269	Non-degree: 2,866
Ave course: 3/4yrs	Ethnic: 20%
Private school: 10%	Flunk rate: n/a
Mature students: 39%	Overseas students: 6%
Disabled students: 6%	Staff/student ratio: 1:18
Clearing: 12%	

ATMOSPHERE:
*The fact that the immediate vicinity isn't the most socially
happening slab of commuterland hasn't dampened students'
spirits; in fact, it galvanises them to build fun factories of their
own. This doesn't, however, distract from the main purpose of
coming to Herts which is the old 'Choose University. Choose*

Degree. Choose Career.' progression. Not the most spiritually fulfilling prescription for life but this lot seem to be doing all right.

THE SITES:

Hatfield: (all courses not based at other sites) This 93-acre site is the main campus, *but the least attractive. It's the sort of place that will probably never look as though the building has been completed.* Among the more recent additions are some modern brick student houses on the edge of the campus, brightly adorned with colourful drainpipes.

Hertford Campus: (Business School) About 1,500 students are based at this *stunningly beautiful and seemingly remote* site, ½ mile from Hertford and 11 miles from the Hatfield campus. Its main building is a mansion dating from 1640, edged by some *inconspicuous* more modern buildings and 100 acres of parkland, ponds, topiaried hedges and so on, known as balls park (*and yes, thanks, they've heard all the jokes*).

Watford: (Education, Humanities) 1,900 students are based in this rural site at the village of Aldenham near the little town of Radlett, about 2 miles from Watford (the most north-westerly reach of London). It's 12 miles from the Hatfield campus and, like Hertford, also has a mansion as its main building. This one looks like a castle and, having been built in 1799, is modern by comparison. *The grounds are pleasant and the contemporary additions are imposing.*

St Albans: About a mile from Hatfield is the *pretty* Roman town of St Albans, which houses the Law department. *Leisure facilities on site aren't that great, but it's so close to the main campus this rarely matters.*

Bayfordbury: 5 miles east of the Hatfield campus, in the grounds of yet another mansion (Bayfordbury House). This time only *a mildly splendid* white affair, host to the University's observatory and biology field station.

THE TOWNS:

None of the nearby towns is totally devoid of attractions; conversely, none is so well-provided that London's proximity isn't a bonus. The only part of Hatfield that has any real character is Old Hatfield with some village charm and an almost separate identity. Hatfield House is here, a *handsome* Elizabethan palace. The new town is larger, *but pretty nondescript, except that (or, perhaps, because) it is at the centre of the UK pharmaceutical and computing industries, which is useful for the many students on sandwich placements.* Lots of grass verges are *a nice idea,* but they play havoc with residential parking. The massive Galleria shopping mall on a bridge above the A1 on the outskirts of town has distracted shoppers.

7 miles away, Hertford is a *pleasant, sleepy, middle-class* market town, which despite a long history, *hasn't got much of*

> **The mascot of City University Rag is a lifesize carrot which went to the Lord Mayor's Ball and met Mr Blobby.**

a story to tell. It's not the largest, nor the most important, *nor the most exciting* town in Hertfordshire, despite providing it with its name. However, it has *a surprisingly good number* of shops, is *one of the prettiest towns and is surrounded by lovely countryside. St Albans is prettier still. Watford may have its architectural fans but* push *isn't one of them.*

TRAVEL:
Trains: Hatfield station is 1½ miles from the main campus - *useful* for the direct service to London King's Cross to the south and Stevenage to the north. From these stations, there are also direct services all the way to York, Newcastle and Edinburgh and connections to the rest of the country. Hertford station is about ½ hour from London.

Coaches: No National Express service to Hatfield or Hertford - the nearest stops are London's Victoria Coach Station and Luton (12 miles away). London Country and Greenline buses run services to and from London.

Car: The A1(M) runs right by the campus (but through a cutting, *so the noise and fumes pollution aren't too bad*). The A1000 passes through Hatfield, as does the A414 which also goes to Hertford. All sites are within 5 miles of the M25.

Air: Luton Airport, offering international and inland flights, is 11 miles north-east.

Hitching: *The Home Counties as a rule are not good for picking up lifts, but if that's where you've gotta hitch from, the A1 is just about the best road to be on. Try the junction with the M25, 6 miles down the road.*

Local: Buses aren't the cheapest in the country, *but are useful for quick trips into Hatfield.* The University also provides a bus service between sites, free to students.

Taxis: Numerous firms, *but they can work out expensive beyond any of the town boundaries.*

Bicycles: *Provided you've got a hefty padlock, a bike's a useful way of rolling around the campuses.*

LIBRARIES & COMPUTERS:
- Books: 260,000 ● Study places: 450
- Computer workstations: 278

The Learning Resources Centre at Hatfield, in the Todd Building, is one of the main features of the campus. Other libraries relate to the subjects taught at each site.

CAREER PROSPECTS:
- Careers Service ● No of staff: 4full/5part
- Unemployed after 6mths (1994): 9.1%

SPECIAL FEATURES:
- Students who can claim a loan, can claim a bigger one at the Watford campus because it is 2 miles within the M25 ring road and qualifies as London (*despite the fact that Hertford's more expensive*).

FAMOUS ALUMNI:
Ian Dowie (footballer); Helen Lederer (comedian); Lady Parkinson (wife of Cecil); Jayne Zito (mental health campaigner).

FURTHER INFO:
Prospectuses for full- and part-time undergrads and postgrads, faculty booklets, video, web sites (http://www.herts.ac.uk and

http://uhsy.herts.ac.uk). The undergrad prospectus is also available in enlarged print, braille and on tape and disk.

entertainment

TOWN:

- Price of a pint of beer: £1.80 ● Glass of wine: £1.60

Hatfield and Hertford are pretty minimally equipped for entertainments. Welwyn Garden City (3 miles up the A1 and easily accessible by train) offers more by way of a good time and there's also the garish Stevenage Leisure Park and (sorry about this) London.

Cinemas: At the Galleria, there's a 9-screen multiplex offering student discounts during the week.

Theatres: The Forum Theatre shows anything that comes its way from panto to Pinter.

Pubs: *The Eight Bells in Hatfield, The Philanthropist & Firkin in St Albans, and The Duncan in Hertford are worth a wet whistle stop. Some other places are less than welcoming to the student population.*

Clubs/discos: *Kudos in Watford is the nearest club with any merit – a bus runs from the University but not back, oddly enough. Zero's (house/garage) is the closest thing to a non-mainstream dance venue round here, so most serious party animals seek their kicks in London.*

Music venues: Very occasional live music at The Forum. Wembley and Knebworth are both within $\frac{1}{2}$ an hour's drive.

Eating out: Students chase a chomp at the Galleria's many eateries (including MacDonald's and other plastic food in plastic packs). Hatfield has a few restaurants (Indian, Italian, Greek and Chinese) and snack shops, such as burger bars, chippies and spud places *but there's nothing to make a seasoned gourmet drop her fois gras butty.*

UNIVERSITY:

- Price of a pint of beer: £1.30 ● Glass of wine: £1.00

Bars: There are 5 SU bars - 3 at Hatfield and 1 each at Hertford and Watford. The Font Bar (cap 900) at the main site is the most popular.

Theatres: *Pretty strong dramatic activity* and a theatre.

Cinemas: New releases on different days across the sites.

Clubs/discos/music venues: At Hatfield, Hutton Hall and the Font Bar combine to create a capacity of 1,200 for twice-weekly club action and occasional gigs. *The latest fad is 70s and 80s cheese.*

Cabaret: Occasional comedy at the Elephant House in Hatfield.

Food: The Font Bar and the Elephant House do all manner of speedy snacks *which usually work out cheaper than the Uni Refectory.* The Hertford bar serves snacks.

Others: 3 balls a year at each campus (except St Albans).

social & political

HERTFORDSHIRE UNIVERSITY STUDENTS' UNION:

- 5 sabbaticals ● Turnout at last ballot: 13%

 ● NUS member

The Elephant House is the SU's own building, but it also has offices in the University's Hutton Block. *This is the low*

ceiling-ed venue for some of the University's most lively moments but if the students were any more middle of the road they'd be white lines. The SU magazine devotes more space to the Spice Girls than to politics and potential hacks stand for SU posts on a platform of introducing telephone ticket booking. There are facilities on all the teaching sites.

SU FACILITIES:
Bars, snack bar, general shop, stationery shop, Endsleigh Insurance office, travel office, games and vending machines, satellite TV, juke boxes, photo booth, photocopier, NatWest Bank, 2 meeting rooms, 2 conference halls. All SU facilities are due for new developments in the near future.

CLUBS (NON SPORTING):
Amateur Radio; Arts & Theatre; Hellenic Cypriot; Irish; Kyshatiya Dharma; Myth & Magic; Paintball; Turkish.

OTHER ORGANISATIONS:
'Uni Verse' is the SU-published newspaper, out every 3 weeks. CRUSH AM broadcasts each morning to all the halls and houses on the main site and has regular slots in the Union bars. It's been running for 20 years. There's also a charity Rag.

RELIGIOUS:
On campus there are facilities for Muslim and Christian worship, including an ecumenical chaplaincy and a full-time chaplain at Hatfield and part time at the other sites. In Hatfield, there are Anglican, Catholic and Evangelical churches.

PAID WORK:
There are many local temping agencies and the Galleria offers some hope, *but luck still plays a large part. The SU temp agency tries to make you lucky.*

········ sports

● <u>Recent successes: judo, basketball</u>
Quite good facilities + overall level of keenness = some not bad results.

SPORTS FACILITIES:
Hatfield: There's a large sports hall with facilities for all manner of indoor sports and a viewing balcony, which can be curtained off for other sports such as aerobics. There's also a climbing wall, 2 squash courts, minigym, trim trail, 2 floodlit tennis/netball courts and playing fields. Further playing fields are 15 minutes walk away at Angerland Common. Hatfield has a leisure centre 10 minutes walk from the campus.
Hertford: Swimming pool; gym; tennis and netball courts; cricket pitch; trim trail; golf practice area.

> ❝'I just didn't have anything in common with students. I thought that the people I knew in my home town were brighter.'
> –Rob Newman.❞

SPORTING CLUBS:
Aerobics; Aikido Yoshinkan; American Football; Climbing & Walking; Kung Fu; Lacrosse; Water Polo; Weight Lifting.

ATTRACTIONS:
Wembley Stadium is just 20 minutes drive away. Choose between Barnet, Luton and Watford for the local footie team.

accommodation

IN COLLEGE:
● Self-catering: 33% ● Cost: £38-52(40wks)

Availability: There is accommodation on 3 sites. On the Hatfield campus, the choice includes single rooms in halls, flats with 2-6 places or shared houses for 6 in the new student village. All 1st years are accommodated, but few others. *The houses and flats are quite plush, but many of the hall rooms are quite small.* The flats (in Chantry Court) are let to couples and other areas are all mixed sex.

Car parking: There is inadequate free parking - a permit is needed. *Cars are useful, but parking all round town is a problem.*

EXTERNALLY:
● Ave rent: £45

Availability: *Finding places in September, when most people look, can be difficult and students may well not start the academic year in the same place that they finish it. By November, it gets a bit easier.* The University comes to the rescue of a large proportion of students with its head tenancy scheme, whereby it rents local accommodation for 1,000 students. The University also has arrangements with landlords/ladies placing 300 students in digs, living with their host. *South Hatfield and St Albans are the best places to look.*

Housing help: The Accommodation Office has 5 full-time staff, which apart from the head tenancy scheme, provides advice, and help in the house hunt.

welfare

SERVICES:
● Creche ● Nightline ● Lesbian & Gay Society
● Mature SA ● Overseas SA ● Postgrad SA ● Minibus
● Women's Officer ● Self-defence classes

A full-time welfare adviser at the SU provides help (usually for cases where the University's help might be inappropriate, such as appeals) and the University runs the *excellent* Student Services Unit, which employs 10 staff including a legal adviser and 3 part-time and 2 sessional counsellors. On each site there is a Medical Centre, staffed by nurses and doctors who hold surgeries 2 or 3 times a week, as well as facilities such as Alexander technique, aromatherapy, and First Aid training.

Disabled: The Hatfield campus has *comparatively excellent access* and special accommodation provisions. *Other sites aren't too bad either.* What's more, there are various amenities for hearing- and sight-impaired students.

FINANCE:
● Ave debt: £3,500 ● Access fund: £250,000
● Successful applications (1997): 275

Heythrop College, London

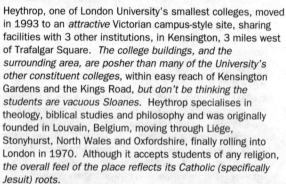

▼ ● **The College is part of <u>University of London</u> and students are entitled to use its facilities.**
Heythrop College, Kensington Square, London, W8 5HQ.
Tel: (0171) 795 6600. Fax: (0171) 795 4200.
E-mail: a.clarkson@ic.ac.uk
Heythrop Students' Union, Kensington Square, London,
W8 5HQ. Tel: (0171) 795 6600. Fax: (0171) 795 4200.

General

Heythrop, one of London University's smallest colleges, moved in 1993 to an *attractive* Victorian campus-style site, sharing facilities with 3 other institutions, in Kensington, 3 miles west of Trafalgar Square. *The college buildings, and the surrounding area, are posher than many of the University's other constituent colleges,* within easy reach of Kensington Gardens and the Kings Road, *but don't be thinking the students are vacuous Sloanes.* Heythrop specialises in theology, biblical studies and philosophy and was originally founded in Louvain, Belgium, moving through Liége, Stonyhurst, North Wales and Oxfordshire, finally rolling into London in 1970. Although it accepts students of any religion, *the overall feel of the place reflects its Catholic (specifically Jesuit) roots.*

60% ♂♂♂♂♂♂♀♀♀ **40%**

Sex ratio(M:F): 60%:40%	Founded: 1614
Full time u'grads: 140	Part time: 0
Postgrads: 345	Non-degree: 25
Ave course: 3yrs	Ethnic: 10%
Private school: 20%	Flunk rate: n/a
Mature students: 75%	Overseas students: 4%
Disabled students: 2%	Staff/student ratio: 1:12
Clearing: 20%	

ATMOSPHERE:
Heythrop is not the first place to start looking for Shi'ite Muslim fundamentalists, devil worshippers or Ian Paisley. It's a very cosy, informal, largely Catholic community, with a significant number of mature students and postgrads, which means the distinction between staff and students is less important. The building is shared with an American college and LAMDA which adds to the social pot-pourri. Many of the students and staff are members of religious orders or hoping to join one. *Being so few in number and having so much in common means everyone is very friendly, familiar and homely. The flipside, of course, is that claustrophobia can set in.*

CITY: see <u>University of London</u>

KENSINGTON:

Kensington is very posh and very expensive. Georgian squares, parking meters everywhere and homeless people moved on by the police. Applicants should not expect to live round the corner from the College. Earl's Court (*Australians*), Notting Hill (*rastas and rich kids slumming it*) and Battersea (*yuppies, dogs*), are nearby and considerably cheaper. The University buildings in Bloomsbury are about 20 minutes by tube (nearly 4 miles) or not much slower by bus.

TRAVEL: see University of London
Trains: Nearest mainline BR stations are Victoria and Paddington.
Buses: To Kensington: 9; 10; 27; 31; 49; C1; etc...
Car: Getting a clamp every day works out about £100 a time and *in Central London clamps prowl the streets like pigeons.*
Underground: High Street Kensington (District & Circle Lines) and Gloucester Rd (District, Circle & Piccadilly).
Bicycles: There's a cycle rack at Kensington.

LIBRARIES & COMPUTERS:
● Books: 250,000 ● Study places: 150
● Computer workstations: 10
Heythrop has the largest theological library in the country. In addition to the computer provisions above, students can use the *far more impressive* facilities at Imperial College (including internet access).

CAREER PROSPECTS:
For a life in the clergy or teaching religion, a Heythrop degree goes a long way. The College uses the University's careers service. See University of London.

SPECIAL FEATURES:
● Heythrop will not be charging the £1,000 tuition fee to students for the 98-99 academic year.
● There are 2 12-week terms and 1 of 6 weeks.
● Tutorials are almost always on a 1 to 1 basis.

FAMOUS ALUMNI:
Frederick Copleston (philosopher); Gerard Manley Hopkins (poet); Nick Stuart (TV presenter).

FURTHER INFO:
Prospectus, web site (http://www.heythrop.ac.uk).

entertainment

LONDON: see University of London

KENSINGTON:
Kensington is only 15 minutes by bus or tube from the West End and even has some of its own entertainments, *mainly aimed at the filthy rich. Earl's Court is more down to earth, as is Victoria.* The Lyric Theatre, Hammersmith *is worth a look-in and for those who don't cringe at the sound of Sloane Rangers in full flow, their stomping ground actually has some pretty happening nooks, although it is expensive, even by London standards. For drama-lovers the Royal Court Theatre (Sloane Square) is particularly useful.* Kensington has plenty of *extravagant* wine bars and delicatessens, as well as Garfunkels and numerous pizza places. The Next café is *good*

(*and cheap by local standards*) for coffee and squidgy cakes.
Pub **push***plugs: Greyhound (theologians); Builders' Arms
(philosophers).*

COLLEGE:
Heythrop has no licensed bar of its own, but students do make
use of <u>Imperial College</u> and ULU, and the Union has recently
started hiring a club in Kensington Square. The Maria
Assumpta Centre provides *good-value* meals during the day.
The Summer Ball is held at the Kensington Park Hotel, and
they have a jazz band in at Christmas.

social & political

HEYTHROP STUDENTS' UNION:

● <u>Turnout at last ballot: 7%</u> ● <u>NUS member</u>
*The SU organises social events, especially at the beginning
and end of term, but has little political role. They're trying to
negotiate for a full-time sabbatical officer.*

SU FACILITIES:
Smoking and non-smoking common rooms; TV; pool tables;
drinks machines.

CLUBS (NON SPORTING):
Justice & Peace.

RELIGIOUS:
*It ought to be pointed out that not everyone is Catholic, nor
indeed, Christian, and there's room for diversity and
considerable tolerance among religious groups and beliefs.*
Unsurprisingly, religious facilities, particularly Catholic, are very
high profile. A Catholic/Ecumenical chapel is in the College.
Optional weekly Mass for students and staff. See also
<u>University of London</u>.

sports

● <u>Recent successes: not much</u>
*The Heythrop football team knocks around the London
intercollegiate league but students' minds are generally on
higher things than high jumps.* There are pool and ping-pong
tables, tennis courts and *a bit of a one-sided* agreement with
<u>Imperial College, London</u>.

accommodation

IN COLLEGE:
Only about 15% of students request college accommodation,
which is handy because Heythrop has none of its own.
Students are, however, able to use the <u>University of London</u>
intercollegiate halls and there are some places in the
chaplaincy and the Maria Assumpta Convent Hostel on site.

❝'Advice for PUSH: Never mix
grain and grape and never eat
newspaper.'
-Stephen Fry.❞

EXTERNALLY: see <u>University of London</u>
Accommodation in Kensington is exorbitant, unless you have access to the Vatican bank. Students living out are better off in Earls Court, Notting Hill or Hammersmith.

welfare

SERVICES:
● <u>Creche</u> ● <u>Nightline</u> ● <u>Mature SA</u> ● <u>Overseas SA</u> ● <u>Postgrad SA</u> ● <u>Minibus</u> ● <u>Self-defence classes</u>

Heythrop has its own Welfare Officer and chaplain who provide help and advice to students or refer them to the services provided by ULU and the University.

Women: There's a new and increasingly active women's group, raising awareness of issues such as sexual harassment.

Disabled: Signing is occasionally used during lectures and meetings and other facilities are available for hearing impaired students. There is also a Dyslexia Teaching Centre. *Access is a bit of a problem in the stair-crazy college buildings.*

FINANCE:
● <u>Access fund: £3,620</u> ● <u>Successful applications (1996): 16</u>
A small bursary fund is available for fee-paying students.

▶▶ **Holloway College**
see Royal Holloway, London

▶▶ **Homerton College**
see University of Cambridge

University of Huddersfield

● *Formerly Huddersfield Polytechnic*
University of Huddersfield, Queensgate, Huddersfield, HD1 3DH. Tel: (01484) 422288. Fax: (01484) 516151.
E-mail: prospectus@hud.ac.uk
Huddersfield University Union, University of Huddersfield, Queensgate, Huddersfield, HD1 3DH. Tel: (01484) 538156. Fax: (01484) 432333.

general

Huddersfield is on the eastern side of the Pennines in the middle of northern England. And in the centre of town is 1 of the 2 main sites of Huddersfield University. The other, Holly Bank, is 2 miles away but as far as most undergrads are concerned, the city centre site's the important one. The main building is an *overbearing* network of brown concrete boxes joined together by steps and walkways and a bridge arching over a part of a canal. There's another building a short walk from the central campus at Larchfield Mills, with light brick and glass 70s architecture, *but not too bad. It looks better at night when you can't see the buildings too well and the lights from thousands of tiny department windows make the place look like Gotham City.*

50% ♂♂♂♂♂♀♀♀♀♀ 50%	
Sex ratio(M:F): 50%:50%	**Founded: 1841**
Full time u'grads: 10,012	**Part time: 5,339**
Postgrads: 2,142	**Non-degree: 4,931**
Ave course: 3/4yrs	**Ethnic: 11%**
Private school: n/a	**Flunk rate: n/a**
Mature students: 29%	**Overseas students: 3.3%**
Disabled students: 0.5%	**Staff/student ratio: 1:18**
Clearing: 19%	

ATMOSPHERE:
If it's possible to be laid-back with attitude that's what Huddersfield students are; they want to get on with their courses and wash them down with several pints. As long as nobody gets in the way they're a happy, hospitable, cosmopolitan bunch.

THE TOWN:
- Population: 148,544 ● London: 174miles
- Leeds: 14miles ● Manchester: 23miles

Huddersfield first found its feet as an industrial town peddling textiles. It still is industrial, although cloth has turned to economic sloth and various recessions over the last 80 years have left the town in considerable recess. *There's now a slow and aged pace about the place, some might even say boring, definitely not a bright-lights-big-city - although Leeds is close enough for those who need some serious club action. The architecture reflects the tone - rather grand, though sooty, Georgian buildings, coexisting with the more modern features of the shopping centre. When God created Huddersfield, she was going through a hilly phase – breathing apparatus would be handy for some of them.*

TRAVEL:
Trains: The main site is 10 minutes walk from Huddersfield BR station which has direct lines to Leeds (£1.70) and Sheffield (£2.60) every 30mins. Intercity service to London (£33.45) via Wakefield.

Coaches: National Express services to London (£13.75), Birmingham (£11.50) and elsewhere.

Car: A few minutes off the M62, on the A62, A642, A629 and A616.

Air: Manchester Airport (International), 30 miles away.

Hitching: *Locals will pick up hitchers even if they're pretty smeggy. The A62 is probably the best pick-up point or take a bus to Junction 24 of the M62.*

Local: Buses are comprehensive charging between 35p and 80p. A Metrocard is a worthwhile investment.

Taxis: £3 to get most of the way across town.

Bicycles: *Heavy traffic, hellish hills and plenty of rain, so much* *stamina is required even going downhill. And then there's the usual problems with theft.*

LIBRARIES & COMPUTERS:
- Books: 400,000 ● Study places: 800
- Computer workstations: 1,500

The Central Library includes a new Media Centre, with *dead good* audio-visual resources and DTP facilities. There are 3 smaller libraries: Holly Bank; a music library; and a chemistry periodicals library.

CAREER PROSPECTS:
- Careers Service ● No of staff: 9full/2part
- Unemployed after 6mths (1997): 6%

FAMOUS ALUMNI:
Gorden Kaye (René in 'Allo, Allo'); Wilf Lunn (eccentric inventor); Patrick Stewart (Capt Piccard in 'Star Trek TNG').

FURTHER INFO:
Prospectuses for undergrads, part timers and postgrads, plus a video. Netties can find out more at http://www.hud.ac.uk.

entertainment

TOWN:
- Price of a pint of beer: £1.80 ● Glass of wine: £1.70

Pubs: *Some good real ale pubs - this is Yorkshire after all - and generally welcome to student custom.* pushplugs: *College Arms, O'Neill's, Thirsty Scholar (all near the University).*

Cinemas: There's a new UCI multiplex 10 mins' bus-ride from the Uni.

Theatres: The Lawrence Batley Theatre is mainstream, while the Cellar does more offbeat stuff, including comedy nights.

Clubs/discos: *Many local clubs are truly naff and the many students who frequent them do so with their tongues firmly planted in their cheeks.* pushplugs: *Visage; retro nights at Hotshots; Feel Da Funk (70s) at the Ship.*

Music venues: The Alfred McAlpine Stadium hosts occasional mega-gigs (eg REM) but for a wider choice Leeds, Manchester and Bradford are an easy trip. Classical music fans are better catered for at the Huddersfield and St Paul's Concert Halls.

Eating out: *Local eateries are not plentiful and offer more by way of value than quality. Some are worth* pushplugging *anyway: Mensahib (cheap studenty Indian); Shamus O'Donnell's (best of a good pub grub selection); Caspian takeaway; Blue Rooms (veggie).*

UNIVERSITY:
- Price of a pint of beer: £1.40 ● Glass of wine: £1.20

Bars: The SU runs 7 in all, *the most popular being the Roland and Cellar Bars, aka the Milton Hall bars.* There are 5 in the SU's own Eden nightclub, called Adams (which turns into a *cool* chill-out zone from 10pm to 2am), Eves, Orchard, Serpentine's and, um, Vodka. There are also University-run dens of iniquity at Holly Bank and Storthes Hall.

Films: The film club shows 1 or 2 'classic, cult and controversial' films a week at the Tudor Cinema.

Clubs/discos/music venues: Butt-shaking 4 nights a week at

Eden, *highspots* being Friday's 'Decade' (indie) and Saturday's 'Blaspheme' (dance). Big names on the club circuit, including Sasha, Digweed, Ministry of Sound and Byron Stingly have all stopped off here recently.

Comedy: Fortnightly giggles in Storthes Hall.

Food: The Milton Hall coffee bar is cheap and cheerful and the Refectory serves *school dinner style* permutations of pies, chips and beans all day.

Other: Various balls and dinners, providing a good range, all revolving around alcohol and usually with drinks promotions.

social ₴ political

UNIVERSITY OF HUDDERSFIELD STUDENTS UNION:
● 5 sabbaticals ● Turnout at last ballot: 12.5%

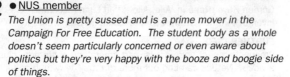

● NUS member

The Union is pretty sussed and is a prime mover in the Campaign For Free Education. The student body as a whole doesn't seem particularly concerned or even aware about politics but they're very happy with the booze and boogie side of things.

SU FACILITIES:
The Union has facilities on both sites. Its collective facilities include: the Eden nightclub; bars and coffee bars; cafeteria; travel agency; printing service; general shop; photocopying; games and vending machines; juke box; function rooms.

CLUBS (NON SPORTING):
Campaign for Free Education; Film; Juggling; Malaysian; Motor; Silver Star Cheerleaders.

OTHER ORGANISATIONS:
Milk the student newspaper, 'Udders', for all the info you can. UNITY is a campaigning organisation which holds an annual festival for Community Action and does good stuff with local residents (OAP visits, cleaning up the canal, etc), plus a *busy* Rag week and ball.

RELIGIOUS:
● 3 chaplains (RC, CofE, Free Church)

There is an interdenominational chaplaincy centre and a Muslim prayer room. The town caters for Christians of 6 different flavours as well as Muslim, Hindu, Sikh, Buddhist and Jewish religious ravers.

PAID WORK:
Local unemployment keeps opportunities limited, but the SU employs over 500 students and runs a jobshop to help the rest get some readies.

sports

● Recent successes: basketball

The University has little to offer by way of its own sports arrangements, but this is somewhat compensated for by the town's very good facilities which the students use frequently. To get in the pink, a Kirklees Passport (£6/yr) is recommended, giving discounted access to local facilities.

SPORTS FACILITIES:
There are 15 acres of playing fields, 2 miles from the campus,

a sports hall, athletics field, astroturf pitch, squash courts and multigym. The town doubles up on all of these and also has a croquet lawn, bowling green, running track, swimming pool, golf courses, tennis courts, saunas and an all-weather pitch. Close by there are also a lake, river and hills.

SPORTING CLUBS:
Caving; Jiu Jitsu; Kung Fu; Mountain Bike; Outdoor Pursuits; Surf.

ATTRACTIONS:
Huddersfield Town FC and Huddersfield Rugby League both play at the spanking new Alfred McAlpine stadium. National ballooning festivals use Storthes Hall's 100 acre back garden.

·········· accommodation

IN COLLEGE:
● Catered: 2% ● Cost: £65 (41wks)
● Self-catering: 20% ● Cost: £36-53(42wks)
Availability: There are 6 halls in all, most within gobbing distance of the main campus, although the new Storthes Hall development is 4 miles away (but free transport is laid on) - Storthes is popular because of its student village feel. 5.5% have to share (no mixed quarters), but all 1st years are guaranteed a place if they ask for it in time.

EXTERNALLY:
● Ave rent: £35
Availability: As the accommodation office points out, the further away students are prepared to look, the better value they will find. *The best student nests are Bradford Road, Springrove, Newsome, Birkby and Lockwood. Sheepridge, Deighton and Fartown are a bit rough, though, and worth avoiding.*
Housing help: The Accommodation Office allocates places in halls and, for those living out, can offer legal advice, vacancy lists, recommended landlords and safety checks.

·········· welfare

SERVICES:
● Nursery ● Nightline ● Lesbian & Gay Society
● Overseas SA ● Minibus ● Women's Officer
● Self-defence classes
The University offers 6 full- and 1 part-time counsellors, the Union 2 and 1. The University Health Centre has 3 visiting local GPs and 3 nurses.
Disabled: *What with the hills wheelchair-users don't have it easy to start with. New buildings are well thought out but the Union is a Grade II listed building which makes access difficult.* Textphone facilities are available for hearing-impaired students.

FINANCE:
● Ave debt: £950 ● Access fund: £125,000
● Successful applications (1997): 730
The Union offers emergency welfare loans of about £15/week, and there's money available for disabled and overseas students.

University of Hull

University of Hull, Hull, HU6 7RX.
Tel: (01482) 34631¼44488. Fax: (01482) 465936.
Hull University Union, University House, Cottingham Road, Hull,
HU6 7RX. Tel: (01482) 445361. Fax: (01482) 466280.
E-mail: u.president@union.hull.ac.uk

General

Hull's full name is Kingston-Upon-Hull and it's Britain's 3rd
largest port, a *sprawling* city (but not sprawling very far) on
England's north-east coast, surrounded by miles of flat, flat
land. The River Hull flows down from the north to join the huge
estuary of the Humber. *The surrounding coastline is stunning*
and the Victorian city centre is also *quite attractive*, even if the
outskirts and harbours are heavily industrialised. The
University is 2 miles from the centre in a *pleasantly leafy*
Victorian/Edwardian residential area. The large campus (94
acres) is a collection of municipal architecture from the last
100 years, but principally from the 30s and 60s. Those 60s
bits in *dull* brick *damage* the overall picture, which would
otherwise be a *good-looking,* low-lying campus with broad
spreads of paths, paving and even grass and trees.

45% ♂♂♂♂♂♀♀♀♀♀ 55%	
Sex ratio(M:F): 45%:55%	Founded: 1927
Full time u'grads: 6,466	Part time: 868
Postgrads: 1,080	Non-degree: 2,080
Ave course: 3yrs	Ethnic: 3%
Private school: 10%	Flunk rate: n/a
Mature students: 17%	Overseas students: 12%
Disabled students: 4%	Staff/student ratio: 1:16
Clearing: 5%	

ATMOSPHERE:
*Hull University is the most typical example of a civic campus
university. It has the friendly camaraderie of a self-contained
campus, but, being in a city, isn't stifling, because there's
escape into the welcoming anonymity of the centre (most
students don't bother escaping). Fun facilities are better than
average; any more and the students would be approaching
meltdown.*

TOWN:
● Population: 242,000 ● London: 165miles
● York: 34miles ● Leeds: 50miles
Back in the 19th century, fish were responsible for the
growth of Hull - the fishing industry rather than a school of
particularly adept mackerel. This century, trade has shifted
to industries, particularly chemical ones. *In a weird twist of
the old adage, Hull is an okay place to live, but you wouldn't*

want to visit there. It hasn't got much to attract tourists, but has all the paraphernalia that attend daily existence: shops, banks, VD clinics and so on (including a Waterstones bookshop). The most amazing local sights include the docks and marina, the Hull Fair, several art galleries and the Humber Suspension Bridge (the largest central span in the world). Hull is also the only town in Britain to have its own telephone system.

TRAVEL:

Trains: Hull Paragon rail station runs services to London via Doncaster or York (£29.35) and other connections to Newcastle (£20.45) and Birmingham (£20.65).

Coaches: Clipper and National Express services all over the country including London (£18), Birmingham (£15), and Newcastle (£14.25).

Car: From the south the M18 connects the M1 with the local Hull motorway, the M62. From the north, the M1 then M62 which leads into the A63 - then look out for the A1079.

Air: Humberside Airport, 12 miles south across the Humber is mainly for inland flights, although has some to Europe.

Ferries: To Holland and Scandinavia.

Hitching: There's a semi-official hitch pitch on the A63 that all traffic has to pass.

Local: There's a *fiercely competitive* number of bus companies running until midnight-ish. There are 3 train stops in Hull, 2 of which are useful for students, since 1 is in the city centre and the other is in Cottingham.

Taxis: *Sharing taxis is often cheaper than catching a bus or train.*

Bicycles: *Hull is very flat with straight wide roads between the residential and functional parts of the University. However, theft is rife.*

LIBRARIES & COMPUTERS:
● Books: 934,593 ● Study places: 1,347
● Computer workstations: 1,000

Given that most students anywhere spend their library time staring out of the window, Hull's main library is a good one – the top floor gives spectacular views over the Humber Estuary. There are 3 subsidiary libraries as well.

CAREER PROSPECTS:
● Careers Service ● No of staff: 7full/5part
● Unemployed after 6mths (1996): 3.8%

FAMOUS ALUMNI:
Sir Ron Dearing (of Dearing Report fame); Sarah Greene (TV sex goddess and Mrs Mike Smith); Jonathan Harvey (playwright); Lord Hattersley; John McCarthy (former hostage) & Jill Morrell (his campaigning ex-partner); Roger McGough (poet); Anthony Minghella ('English Patient' director); Juliet Morris, Jenni Murray (broadcasters); John Prescott MP (Lab); Ben Watt & Tracey Thorn (Everything But The Girl).

FURTHER INFO:
Prospectuses for undergrads and postgrads. Not to mention departmental pamphlets, video, CD-ROM and web site (http://www.hull.ac.uk).

entertainment

TOWN:

● Price of a pint of beer: £1.75 ● Glass of wine: £1.60

Cinemas: (4) 2 multiplexes with 8 screens each, one of which is in St Andrew's Quay; 1 with 4 screens. Also, the Film Theatre, next to the City Library, for arty flicks.

Theatres: (2) The more *highbrow* is the New Theatre for posh plays, opera and ballet. Spring Street Theatre is a rep base, the home of the *excellent* Hull Truck Theatre company and also hosts cabaret nights.

Pubs: Being a port, Hull has no shortage of pubs, some of which have stuffed fish on the walls and glass balls in nets, but *most are less naff.* **push**plugs: *Gardner's Arms (packed with students); Haworth Arms; Foxhill & Firkin; Scruffy Murphy's. The Bev Road Run, a 12-pub crawl, is a good bet for the hollow-legged.*

Clubs/discos: *Hull's selection of dance palaces leaves much to be desired. Student nights offer the best value.* **push**plugs: *Spiders (Goth/trash); Silhouette (theme nights, gay-friendly, £2); Eclipse (cheesy house).*

Music venues: *Things are better on the live front, especially for indie fans.* **push**plugs: *The Room, The Adelphi (small-scale gigs); City Hall, Tower Ballroom (bigger draws).*

Eating out: *A good range, if a little lacking on the late night snacking front.* **push**plugs: *Hitchcock (veggie); Zoo Café (hippy); Chaplin's (Tex-Mex, all-you-can-eat buffet £4); Old Grey Mare (good value pub grub).*

UNIVERSITY:

● Price of a pint of beer: £1.20 ● Glass of wine: 75p

Bars: (5) The Resnikov Bar is the main one, *especially popular at lunchtime and weekends*; the John McCarthy is the main venue boozer in the evenings; the Chico Mendes (named after a Brazilian environmental campaigner and, *ironically*, decorated with hardwood) is mainly used for society functions.

Theatres: Drama students put on 10 major shows a year in the *flash* Gulbenkian Theatre and the Z Theatre Company takes regular productions to Edinburgh.

Cinemas: 1 cult film a week.

Clubs/discos: 2 main club nights a week in the Union Main Hall (cap 1,100); the indie of Big Bang and the 2-room dance/nostalgia mix that is Twisted, costing £1.50 each. The monthly drum'n'bass do New Horizons is also popular. *Things get a bit more exciting* when the occasional Industry night attracts *big name* clubs (eg Cream).

Music venues: The Union Main Hall is the main live music venue, luring the likes of Echobelly, My Life Story and Wannadies in recent months. The John McCarthy also hosts jazz nights fortnightly.

Food: The Main Hall has yet another guise; it's a Refectory during the day, doling out *reasonably priced* chips 'n' pizza-type stuff *to willing gannets*. There's also a new continental style bar serving above-average student snap. The Resnikov has a *less enthralling* menu of fry-ups and sarnies.

Others: Numerous termly balls, fortnightly cabaret, annual Athletic and St Patrick's Day Events, etc.

········· social & political

HULL UNIVERSITY UNION:

- 7 sabbaticals ● Turnout at last ballot: 20%
- NUS member

The Union's main roles are welfare provision and commercial acumen - the building is big and the facilities are impressive - but politics of the soapbox variety seldom intrudes although green concerns such as Pepsi in Burma are high on the agenda. Last year's anti-fees campaigns were well supported.

SU FACILITIES:

Union facilities are based in University House: 3 bars; mini-mart shop (and mini-mart with limited opening hours at the Lawns Centre - see below); gift shop; travel agency; dark room; launderette; photocopying; DTP unit; Lloyds cashpoint; games machines room; vending machines; pool tables; function rooms (including 4 large halls); minibus hire. The sports centre is 1 of only 2 Union-run centres in the country.

CLUBS (NON SPORTING):

Beatles; Buddhist; Cercle Francais; Chinese; Comedy; Commonwealth; European football supporters; Eurosceptics; Evangelical; Gilbert & Sullivan; Hellenic; Hunt Sabs; Links First Aid; Malaysian; Mediterranean; Methodist; Motorcycle; Oxfam; Peace; Prince's Trust; Saudi; Singapore.

OTHER ORGANISATIONS:

The Union-financed, but editorially independent 'Hullfire' is the main student newspaper and has notched up more than its share of national awards. The student radio station JAM999 broadcasts on AM and has a 24hr license. HUSSO, the country's largest student community group, runs *some extremely active and worthwhile* projects. It employs a sabbatical co-ordinator, a full-time secretary and involves over 1,000 students.

RELIGIOUS:

- 10 chaplains (CofE, RC, Orthodox, Methodist, Baptist, URC, Friends, Jewish)

There's a chapel sort of thing under the Arts building. In Hull, most versions of Christianity are represented and there is a small Jewish community, but the city is far from multi-cultural and other religions don't get much of a look-in.

PAID WORK:

Hull has got a pretty bad unemployment problem, and students aren't first in the queue, facing resentment if they try to push in, but the Union-run jobshop helps to smuggle them in through the back door.

❛One of the proposed name-changes for the old Polytechnic South-West was the New University of Devon Institute of Science and Technology (NUDIST).❜

> **Edwina Currie is an honorary member of Liverpool Guild of Students.**

sports

● <u>Recent successes: hockey, rugby</u>

In the past, Hull didn't have the facilities to attract anybody who took sport too seriously. Now that the new Health & Fitness Centre is complete, things are improving, although it's still not one of those places where a BUSA win is of momentous importance. There is a good level of participation, though.

SPORTS FACILITIES:

At the Sports & Fitness Centre: indoor sports; fitness and weight training; 2 multigyms; sauna and solarium; jacuzzi. At the Sports Centre (5 minutes walk from the Union): gym; 2 sports halls; badminton and 7 squash courts; all-weather pitch; climbing wall. 11 playing fields on the campus and near the Lawns halls, an athletics and running track, 11 tennis courts and a boat house at Beresford Avenue. The city also provides a swimming pool nearby and an ice rink; recreation passes (£4.50) allow students to use many facilities for free during the day. There is a new sports bursary scheme.

SPORTING CLUBS:

Aikido; American Football; Boats; Clay Pigeon; Gaelic Football; Jiu Jitsu; Lacrosse; Latin and Ballroom Dancing; Parachute; Snooker; Speleological; Tennis; Ten Pin Bowling; Ultimate Frisbee; Yoga.

ATTRACTIONS:

Hull has 2 major rugby league clubs plus soccer and ice hockey teams. There is also a race track in Beverley.

accommodation

IN COLLEGE:
● <u>Catered: 12%</u> ● <u>Cost: £57-72(31wks)</u>
● <u>Self-catering: 18%</u> ● <u>Cost: £30-52(31-50wks)</u>

Availability: There are 3 types of University accommodation: the 6 Lawns halls, on a baby campus 3 miles from the University itself; the 4 traditional halls (behind the Botanical Gardens, halfway between the campus and the Lawns); but the largest number of places are in shared houses, most of which are close to the campus. All 1st years can be accommodated. 24% have to share, but some of those are *judiciously partnered* in student houses. The Lawns Halls (1 is self-catering) are accompanied by the Lawns Centre featuring all sorts of facilities. There are also 720 places in a head leasing scheme and 44 in a Housing Association scheme.
Car parking: Permit parking only - get on your bike.

EXTERNALLY:
● <u>Ave rent: £35</u>

Availability: *Finding housing is easy enough but it's advisable to start looking early. Students could do worse than Beverley Rd, Cottingham Rd, Newland Avenue and Princess Avenue.*

Among the places where they could do better are Bransholme and Orchard Park (both unwelcoming).
Housing help: Information on private housing is available from the Advice Centre of the SU.

 welfare

SERVICES:

- Creche ● Lesbian & Gay Society

- Mature SA ● Overseas SA ● Postgrad SA ● Minibus
- Women's Officer ● Self-defence classes

The Union and University give troubled and miserable students the metaphorical spoonful of sugar at the Welfare and Counselling Service, which employs 1 full- and 4 part-time counsellors and 1 student sabbatical adviser.
Disabled: *Only the major buildings are adapted with wheelchair access in mind. Learning disabilities, such as dyslexia, however, are well covered.*

FINANCE:
- Access fund: £147,550
- Successful applications (1996): 1,123

The Vice Chancellor's Hardship Fund dishes out loans as does the SU in emergencies.

●●●

▶▶ University of Humberside
see University of Lincolnshire and Humberside

> **'There's more to student life than poverty and fun... see the courses tables at the back of the book.'**

Fold-out guide to symbols inside back cover

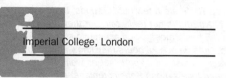

Imperial College, London

Imperial College, London

▼▼ ● **The College is part of <u>University of London</u> and students are entitled to use its facilities.**
Imperial College of Science, Technology & Medicine (University of London), London, SW7 2AZ. Tel: (0171) 594 8014. Fax: (0171) 594 8004. E-mail: admissions@ic.ac.uk
Imperial College Union, Prince Consort Road, London, SW7 2BB. Tel: (0171) 594 8060. Fax: (0171) 594 8065.

General

Jam sandwiched between The Natural History Museum and The Royal Albert Hall in South Kensington, just 1½ miles from Trafalgar Square, is Imperial College. Imperial was formed when in 1907 The Royal School of Mines, City & Guilds College and The Royal College of Science merged with the Medical School coming along in the early 90s. *The main building is what Prince Chas would call a 'carbuncle' - a towering, oversized portakabin of aluminium, smoked glass and concrete.* Inside it's well ordered - echoing walkways with glass displays and cabinets full of scientific paraphernalia which all adds to *the sense of awesome scientific knowledge.* Overshadowing all this is the Queen's Tower, which has now been locked off. *Allegedly, too many frustrated finalists were flinging themselves from the parapet, knowing at least enough physics to realise it was a sure fire way of getting out of exams.* Apart from the buildings at South Kensington and the various hospital sites, Imperial has a mine at Truro in Cornwall and a 260-acre site at Silwood Park, near Ascot, mainly for scientific field work.

69% ♂♂♂♂♂♂♂♀♀♀ 31%

Sex ratio(M:F): 69%:31%	Founded: 1907
Full time u'grads: 6,240	Part time: 0
Postgrads: 2,532	Non-degree: 0
Ave course: 3/4yrs	Ethnic: n/a
Private school: n/a	Flunk rate: 23%
Mature students: 44%	Overseas students: 27.6%
Disabled students: 1.5%	Staff/student ratio: 1:10
Clearing: 3.4%	

ATMOSPHERE:
Just because Imperial's students are overwhelmingly male and all studying science, technology or medicine, doesn't mean

they're all geeks. There are a few nerds, spods, boffins and dweebs as well. No, that's not really fair, but they do work very hard, on a 9-5 basis mostly, and academic standards are world-renowned. Outside school hours they know how to chug a pint and there's a substantial sporty set as well. Relations with the immediate locals (posh Kensingtonians) are next to non-existent.

THE SITES:

The Imperial College School of Medicine is based across 4 sites in West London:

St Mary's: (700 students) 2 miles from Imperial, in Paddington, is this medical school *and if you thought the scientists worked hard, the doctors-to-be put in even more.* Despite this, they have time to use the recreation centre on site, as well as the swimming pool and bar.

Royal Brompton: (140 students) What used to be known as the National Heart and Lung Institute is now the Royal Brompton site in Chelsea, a mile from the main site. Apart from academic facilities, *funtime is restricted to a sarnie shop.*

Charing Cross: (300 students) Not, despite its name, anywhere near Charing Cross, the newest addition to the Imperial family is 3 miles from the main site, in Hammersmith. There's a bar and a café.

Hammersmith: (300+ students) Formerly the Royal Postgraduate Medical School, this site is mostly for postgraduates.

THE CITY: see <u>University of London</u>

SOUTH KENSINGTON:

The area immediately surrounding the College is a *prim quad* with privet hedges in the relative peace of South Kensington. Kensington itself, is a *well to do area* with Harrods just round the corner in Knightsbridge *(although we don't recommend students use it for their weekly shop). It's full of expensive boutiques and delicatessens. Even the kebab joints have French names round here. It's also an erudite part of London,* brimming with museums and libraries and obscure educational institutions. *It's pricey to live in South Kensington itself; Notting Hill or Earl's Court are a likelier bet. However, it's well connected for the West End* and ULU only takes 20mins by tube or slightly longer by bus.

TRAVEL: see <u>University of London</u>

Trains: The nearest mainline BR stations are Paddington and Victoria, each about 1½ miles away.

Buses: 9; 10; 14; 51; 74; and C1. Night buses: N14 and N97.

Car: Parking at the college is limited to those with disabilities.

Underground: Gloucester Road and South Kensington (both on the District, Circle and Piccadilly Lines).

LIBRARIES & COMPUTERS:

- <u>Books: 775,000</u> ● <u>Study places: 2,000</u>
- <u>Computer workstations: 1,400</u>

There are 19 libraries in all, including the Medical School and departmental libraries. *Unsurprisingly, computer provision is better than average but the facilities still can't keep up with the eager little mouse-wielders.*

CAREER PROSPECTS:
- Careers Service ● No of staff: 6full/1part
- Unemployed after 6mths (1997): 4.6%

Potential employers, particularly in scientific and technical areas, regard Imperial as a goldmine of bright bods.

SPECIAL FEATURES:
- Imperial's mascot is a 185lb micrometer, which deters the trend among London colleges of stealing each other's mascots.
- 99% of Imperial's staff have PhDs and 20% of students get 1st class degrees.

FAMOUS ALUMNI:
Mary Archer (Lord Jeff's wife); Sir Roger Bannister (4-minute miler); Alexander Fleming (discovered penicillin); Rajiv Gandhi (former Indian Prime Minister); WG Grace (cricketer); David Irving (revisionist 'historian'); David Livingstone (explorer); Brian May (large-haired Queen guitar hero); Trevor Phillips (TV presenter); Joan Ruddock MP (Lab); Simon Singh ('Fermat's Last Theorem'); HG Wells (writer); JPR Williams (rugby player); Francis Wilson (weatherman).

FURTHER INFO:
Prospectuses for undergrads and postgrads, web site (http://www.ic.ac.uk) and handbook from SU.

entertainment

IN LONDON: see University of London

SOUTH KENSINGTON:
South Kensington has a fair level of entertainments of its own, but it's mainly wine bars and posh clubs, although the Queen's Arms is popular. The West End is within a strident stroll's distance and many of the areas around Kensington offer some thrills and spills (Notting Hill, Earl's Court, Hammersmith, Chelsea, Fulham, Putney). Local pubs with a **push**plug *include: The Queen's Arms; Rat & Parrot; Finnegan's Wake.*

COLLEGE:

- Price of a pint of beer: £1.40 ● Glass of wine: £1.10

Bars: There are 5 bars at the main site, including Da Vinci's (*looks like a Butlin's leisure lounge*); Southside (*pipe 'n' slippers pub*); Union Bar (*also pubby, popular with rugby gorillas*); and dBs (*venue bar, womb-like*). Facilities for getting incoherent and falling over are also available at St Mary's and Charing Cross.

Theatres: Imperial has 2 halls which are both *eminently suitable* as theatres for its *strangely strong* dramatic contingent. Not only do they take shows to the Edinburgh Fringe, they rent a theatre and sub-let it to other groups. There's also an opera society.

Cinemas: Imperial has the largest student cinema screen in the country, *but still only shows 1 arty or mainstream film a week.*

Clubs/discos: Several clubs every week: the mainstream Pop Tarts; Common People (indie); Hedonizm (dub); Shaft (70s) and more.

Music venues: The Great Hall has a capacity of 600 and there's also the Concert Hall (450) and dBs (250). My Life Story played recently.

Cabaret: Once a fortnight, in the Union building, there's a comic on the bill, Lee Mack and Sean Locke being recent examples.

Food: *Basics Restaurant at Southside is pretty accurately named but Da Vinci's Cafe Bar offers a wider-ranging, more edible spread.* QT in the Sherfield building sells snacks in the daytime as well as the Main Hall which serves *slightly more* substantial scoff.

Others: 2 big balls a year, occasionally in posh London hotels. Also Christmas and departmental binges.

social & political

IMPERIAL COLLEGE STUDENTS' UNION:

● <u>5 sabbaticals</u> ● <u>Turnout at last ballot: 17%</u>

The Union is politically independent, even of the NUS. It exists to provide services to its members, who lap them up when they can tear themselves away from work. Urging the students into any political activity is harder than learning Gujurati from a Martian. 30 of them attended a recent fees rally. **Also ULU:** see <u>University of London</u>.

SU FACILITIES:

The Union has facilities at the main site, St Mary's and Charing Cross. At South Kensington, the Union building, called Beit Quad, is on the other side of the road. In all, the Union offers bars, a cafeteria, sandwich bar, travel agency, resources centre, 2 shops, printing service, NatWest bank, minibus hire, photo booth, video and games machines, juke boxes, cinema and fax service.

CLUBS (NON SPORTING):

Abacus; Amateur Radio; Arabic; Arts Appreciation; Audio; Bag; Bangladeshi; Benelux; Book; Chinese; Choir; Circus Skills; Cypriot; Friends of Palestine; Hellenic; Indian; Iranian; Irish; Italian; Japanese; Jazz Big Band; Lebanese; Leonardo; Malaysian; Mauritian; Methodist; Operatic; Pakistan; Persian Gulf; Pimlico; PoetIC; Radio Modellers; Real Ale; Scandinavian; Scout & Guide; Spiritual Arts; St John's Ambulance; Sikh; Singapore; Spanish; Sri Lankan; Taiwan; Tamil; Thai; Theatre West End; Transcendental Meditation; Turkish; University Challenge; Wargames; Welsh; Wine Tasting; YHA.

OTHER ORGANISATIONS:

'Felix' is the Union's weekly newspaper and there's also a radio station (Imperial College Radio) and a TV station (STOIC - Student Television of Imperial College). *Imperial College's Rag is very energetic, although as much energy goes into oh-so-wacky stunts as into actual fund raising. There's the annual tiddlywink race down Oxford Street and legends abound of the naked parachute leap which ended in nude students being bundled out of a van at Harrods.* 'Felix' claims to have photos.

RELIGIOUS:

The West London Chaplaincy handles all Christians, whatever the denomination. Daily prayer meetings are held in the Islamic Society prayer room and Regent's Park Mosque (1 of the country's largest) is just round the corner. **Religion in London:** see <u>University of London</u>.

PAID WORK:

Imperial students can appeal to the firms constantly vying for their talents for vacation work or there's Imperial's UROP scheme where they help lecturers with their research work and can expect to earn anything up to £120 a week and many brownie points.

sports

● Recent successes: across the board

Bearing in mind that Imperial students are entitled to use ULU and the University's facilities as well as their own excellent amenities, they've got the world at their feet like a football. Imperial is top of the London colleges in BUSA.

SPORTS FACILITIES:

Imperial has 60 acres of playing fields at Harlington (15 miles from Kensington) which are also used for practice by Chelsea Football Club. The College lays on buses 2 days a week to get there where students can use the pitches, including an all-weather pitch, and the pavilion. Meanwhile, over the road from the South Kensington ranch, Imperial has a sports centre which is *a fabulous feat of architecture*. It is built underground to save space with only a transparent tardis visible on the surface. *The cavern down below looks like something from The Man from U.N.C.L.E.* and includes a 25m pool, 4 squash courts, weights room and multigym, jacuzzi, projectile hall, health suite and studio. It's hired out to the public to subsidise student use. Back above ground, Imperial has 2 tennis courts, a shooting range, martial arts centre and a boat house at Putney. What's more, the SU provides 3 training halls, 2 tennis courts and a free weights room. Charges for other facilities are minimal (40-50p). A new boat-house and sports centre are to come.

SPORTING CLUBS:

Boardsailing; Boat; Bridge; Caving; Gliding; Hang Gliding; Jiu Jitsu; Keep Fit; Kung Fu; Lawn Tennis; Motorcycle; Nippon Kempo; Parachuting; Rifle & Pistol; Roller blading; Ten Pin Bowling; Weights; Wing Chun; Wrestling; Yachting; Yoga.

ATTRACTIONS: see University of London

accommodation

IN COLLEGE:

● Catered: 3% ● Cost: £62-80 (34wks)
● Self-catering: 24% ● Cost: £33-67(34-38wks)

Availability: Imperial can accommodate all of its 1st years either in their own halls or intercollegiate halls, but college housing is limited for other students. There are 9 halls in all and 4 so-called student houses, the largest of which, Bernard Sunley House, has 98 places for men only and which we'd call large enough to be a hall. There's another all-male hall, but

> ❝Wye College is home to the Druids, a secretive drinking society of practical jokers who leave sheep in odd places.❞

women have to apply to the University for intercollegiate all-female housing. *A wopping* 26.5% of students in college accommodation have to share rooms, sometimes even in triple rooms, but they are charged less. The halls are mostly around South Kensington, but also spread throughout west London. Some self-catered places are in flats in south Ealing.

Catering: The kitchens shared by 8 students on average are usually *pretty well equipped* and cleaned every day. Catered places offer a meal a day, *ranging from bad to edible.*

Parking: *Only if you have a disability, a considerable disposable income or a magic laser-rifle that dissolves traffic wardens and clamps.*

EXTERNALLY: see University of London
Hammersmith is the closest location for those who haven't struck lucky on the scratch cards. The Union has a Housing Advice scheme and the Student Accommodation Office provides housing lists.

·········welfare

SERVICES:

● Nursery ● Nightline ● Mature SA ● Overseas SA
● Lesbian & Gay Society (aka Imperial Queers) ● Minibus
● Women's Officer ● Self-defence classes

The Health Centre is home to 6 doctors, 4 nurses, a dentist and 1 full-time and 4 part-time counsellors.

Women: *With less than 1 woman to every 2 men, the most severe problem is solitude, although the increasing number of medical students is levelling the figures out. The College is trying to encourage female applicants. Attack alarms are available, and there's a minibus. The main problem for (straight) males, of course, is intense sexual frustration.*

Disabled: Provisions have tended to be on an ad hoc basis, although buildings have been made accessible where possible and the College now employs a Disabilities Officer. There are lifts around the main building and special accommodation has been set aside for students with wheelchairs. *However, the restrictions of Imperial's location are definitely a disincentive.*

FINANCE:
● Ave debt per year: £2,150 ● Access fund: £367,712
● Successful applications (1997): 685

Many scholarships and sponsorships are available.

❛There's more to student life than poverty and fun... see the courses tables at the back of the book.❜

‘Text in italics is PUSH's point of view — take it or leave it.’

‘Freaked out by finance? Why not pop into your local branch of Lloyds Bank and see what they have to offer.’

‘If you have any comments about PUSH or fancy being involved in the next edition, please write to PUSH, McGraw-Hill Publishing Company, Shoppenhangers Road, Maidenhead, Berkshire SL6 2QL.’

Jews' College, London

- John Moores University
  see Liverpool John Moores University

- Jordanstown
  see University of Ulster

Jews' College, London

- **The College is part of <u>University of London</u> and students are entitled to use its facilities.**
Jews' College, Albert Road, Hendon, London, NW4 2SJ.
Tel: (0181) 203 6427. Fax: (0181) 203 6420.
Jews' College Students' Union, Albert Road, Hendon, London, NW4 2SJ. Tel: (0181) 203 5989.

You could pass Jews' College without realising it's there, because it's small, modern, low and purpose built, on a residential street in Hendon, *quite a quiet and pleasant* commuter suburb of north west London (6¼ miles from Trafalgar Square). Hendon has a large Jewish community with plenty of local kosher butchers and bagel bars, and even a Jewish pub (The Load of Hay) so it's *an appropriate setting* for this college which teaches Jewish Studies only, although students of any religious background will be considered, provided they read Hebrew. Over the years, most of Britain's orthodox rabbis have studied here. *Its tiny size makes it one of London's friendliest and most intense college communities. Everybody knows everybody and staff and students integrate thoroughly creating a studious air, suffused with religion and history.*

50% ♂♂♂♂♂♀♀♀♀♀ **50%**

Sex ratio(M:F): 50%:50%	Founded: 1855
Full time u'grads: 24	Part time: 3
Postgrads: 10	Non-degree: 17
Ave course: 3yrs	Ethnic: n/a
Private school: n/a	Flunk rate: n/a
Mature students: 4%	Overseas students: 8%
Disabled students: n/a	Staff/student ratio: 1:6
Clearing: 10%	

The College has no entertainment facilities of its own *although the students use any excuse for a party*. The Union of Jewish Students and local Jewish youth groups occasionally use it as a base for activities. The College provides free breakfast for everyone who attends morning prayers and serves sandwiches. There's more than a minyan of local kosher restaurants, delis and bagel bars (some of which stay open late). The SU is a member of NUS, *but completely apolitical and only really exists to represent students on College committees and that relationship's fairly informal anyway.* Apart from the facilities of ULU and <u>London University</u>, which students are entitled to use (*but generally don't*), there is a games room in the College and a synagogue (beit hamidrash), which doubles as an informal function room. Many of the students are local and others rent flats or houses within walking distance (Golders Green and Hendon). There are many rabbis among the staff to help you through trials and tribulations.

FAMOUS ALUMNI:
Lord Jakobovits (former Chief Rabbi); Jonathan Sacks (current Chief Rabbi).

FURTHER INFO:
General prospectus.

John Moores University
see Liverpool John Moores University

Jordanstown
see University of Ulster

‘Hamlet is a completely sad man: he's Danish and he's a perpetual student.’
- Arthur Smith.

'The JCR of Balliol College, Oxford once sent Prince Charles a letter applauding him over his environmental stance but then sent him another one taking it all back because they'd forgotten their standing policy against the monarchy.'

Fold-out guide to symbols inside back cover

KCL
see King's College, London

Keele University

University of Kent at Canterbury

- Kent Institute
  see Other Institutions

- King Alfred's
  see Other Institutions

King's College, London

- King's Hospital
  see King's College, London

Kingston University

▶▶ KCL

see King's College, London

Keele University

▼▼ Keele University, Keele, Staffordshire, ST5 5BG.
Tel: (01782) 584003. Fax: (01782) 632343.
E-mail: aaa20@admin.keele.ac.uk
Keele University Students' Union, Keele, Staffordshire,
ST5 5BG. Tel: (01782) 711411. Fax: (01782) 712671.

·······ｇｅｎｅｒａｌ

Keele University is situated between the North Midland towns of Stoke and Newcastle-under-Lyme *and at the same time feels like a million miles from anywhere.* It's a set of geometric blocks in a square mile of parkland, mostly modern but including the *beautiful* Keele Hall, the oldest building (19th century) on the estate. *It gained a reputation in the post-war expansion of higher education for its (at the time) unique flexibility of study, which many institutions have since copied, and its communal atmosphere. These are still true to an extent but the isolation is as important.*

48% ♂♂♂♂♂ ♀♀♀♀♀ 52%

Sex ratio(M:F): 48%:52%	Founded: 1949
Full time u'grads: 4,164	Part time: 36
Postgrads: 877	Non-degree: 3,465
Ave course: 3/4yrs	Ethnic: n/a
Private school: n/a	Flunk rate: 10%
Mature students: 18%	Overseas students: 9%
Disabled students: 1%	Staff/student ratio: 1:15
Clearing: 10%	

ATMOSPHERE:

Keele is a small, friendly and busy University, with 70% of students and many of the staff and their families living on campus. It's important that it should be friendly because escape to Newcastle-under-Lyme or even Stoke is hardly freedom, although from time to time, most students just have to get away. Social life usually takes precedence over all else. Whatever you do, you can never forget you're a student; the place can feel like a 600-acre ivory tower, made by IKEA.

LOCAL AREA:

● London: 147miles ● Manchester: 34miles
● Birmingham: 43miles

Keele is hardly a village, let alone a town. The area around Keele was built on the 19th-century pottery industry, hence the cunning name, The Potteries. Wedgewood, Spode and Royal Doulton pottery all came from round here (Habitat and Tupperware didn't). *Local facilities in the old market town of Newcastle are a little limited. However, there's more than enough to get by* - all the major banks and a fair few shops (not after 10pm, though). For more of the trappings of commercialism, Hanley in Stoke is better equipped. The Potteries Shopping Centre is full of all the national traders. Local attractions include all the various Pottery Museums, the once industrial, but now leisure canals, the Stoke City Museum & Art Gallery and Alton Towers, the *mega* theme park, $\frac{1}{2}$ an hour down the road.

TRAVEL:

Trains: There's no station at Keele, or at Newcastle *(that's the little one nearby)*. Trains from Stoke-on-Trent go to London (£18.50), Manchester (£4.55), Newcastle *(that's the big one up North* - £31.30) and all over.

Coaches: National Express doesn't go to Keele either, the nearest service being Stoke, from which there are services to London (£12) and Manchester (£3.80).

Car: The M6 is within smelling distance of the campus; in fact it runs along the southern edge of the park. The A525 runs right past the campus and the A34, A50, A52, A53 and A531 are all nearby.

Hitching: *Hitchers need to get to the M6 junctions (by bus) which is quite hopeful, if replete with drunk drivers and psychotics.*

Local: Buses run between the campus and the surrounding towns every 15mins.

Taxis: Plenty of taxis which charge between £1.50 and £3 to Newcastle.

Bicycles: *Bikes are a useful way of getting around the campus although the landscaped hills are bumptious bumps. Off-campus, there are hazardous roundabouts.*

LIBRARIES & COMPUTERS:
- Books: 502,000 ● Study places: 792
- Computer workstations: 250

All students should leave knowing how to use some kind of keyboard, since all final-year coursework has to be typed (and the University charges for printer paper), *despite there being a shortage of computers. A cybercafe might be opening soon, but it won't be free.*

CAREER PROSPECTS:
- Careers Service ● No of staff: 6full/1part
- Unemployed after 6mths (1996): 8.4%

SPECIAL FEATURES:
- Almost everybody does joint honours courses (ie more than one main subject). It is compulsory to take a cross-faculty subsidiary course in the first year - for example, if you study an arts subject, you'll have to do a science subsidiary. *The result is that students get an insight into matters they might have otherwise completely ignored.*

FAMOUS ALUMNI:
Don Foster MP (Lib Dem); Nick Partridge (AIDS campaigner); Jack Straw MP (Lab); Adelaide Tambo (ANC official).

FURTHER INFO:
Prospectuses for undergrads and postgrads, departmental leaflets and a video. An Alternative Prospectus is available from the SU (£1) and check out the web site (http://www.keele.ac.uk).

entertainment

TOWN:
- Price of a pint of beer: £1.90 ● Glass of wine: £1.40

Since students usually have to venture beyond Keele itself if they want off-campus adventure, some go the whole hog and stray as far as Birmingham and Manchester.

Pubs: There are 2 pubs within stumbling distance of the campus: the Golfer's Arms (*owned by the SU*) and the Sneyd Arms. *Other* **push**plugs: O'Neill's; Scruffy Murphy's; Firkin.

Cinemas: In Stoke, there are 2 cinemas (one with 8 screens,

> ❛'He'd got into Aberdeen University, and found the course easy, but was forced to leave mid-way through the first year after blowing his grant money on drugs and prostitutes.'
> -Irvine Welsh, Trainspotting❜

the other with 3). The odd arty pic reaches the local flicks.
Theatres: There are 5 theatres locally, in particular, the
Theatre Royal in Hanley and the New Vic Rep in Newcastle
offer a wide ranging selection.
Clubs/discos: There are numerous clubs around the towns.
Monday tends to be student night. **push***plugs: The Place
(cheesy pop); Valentino's (Bonk, free bus from SU); Void (Hanley).*
Music venues: *Stoke is the epicentre of live sounds,
especially guitar-based - recently, Sleeper, Paul Weller,
Radiohead.* **push***plugs: The Stage; Trentham Gardens.*
Eating out: *A better selection than might be expected.*
push*plugs: Dillons (veggie) in Hanley; Ossies (curry); Peaches
(Chinese); Hungry Horse and Golfer's Arms (pub grub);
Shalimar's (Indian).*

UNIVERSITY:
● <u>Price of a pint of beer: £1.40</u> ● <u>Glass of wine: £1.00</u>
Bars: (7) The main SU-run bars are the Gallery, BJs (non-
smoking) and Baldwin's (sporty and non-smoking in the
evenings).
Theatres: The University gives financial support to the *strong*
drama society which puts on about 5 major productions a year.
Cinema: 2 films a week, mainstream and world cinema.
Clubs/discos: 3 club nights a week in the Ballroom (capacity
1,000) and the Club (1,500), events with names like Luvshack
(70s & 80s), Underground (indie), Cheeky Half (cheese) and
Shag (*80s retro, does exactly what it says on the can*). Top
DJs have been lured, including LTJ Bukem and Judge Jules.
Music venues: The Ballroom plays host to various bands such
as, recently, Wannadies and Faithless.
Cabaret: Fortnightly cabaret turns in the Nightclub have
recently attracted Boothby Graffoe and Jeff Green.
Food: Multiple munch outlets across campus, the Diner (meat &
2 veg) being run by the SU and others by the University. *All offer
sound value for money. Harvey's is a continental style veggie cafe,
and Keele Hall restaurant does Binge till you Burst for a fiver.*
Others: Termly (at least) balls and various theme nights.

·········· social & political

KEELE UNIVERSITY STUDENTS' UNION:

● <u>4 sabbaticals</u> ● <u>Turnout at last ballot: 64%</u>
● <u>NUS member</u>
*Politically, the Union is full of wide-eyed interest, but very few
party affiliations. It was recently in financial difficulties but is
now starting to thrive and is a source of pride to students,
being unafraid to stand up to the University on welfare and
other issues. Recently a rent rise was fought off and they got
TV coverage of their gas safety campaign. The SU places a lot
of emphasis on its welfare role and is currently at odds with
Hospitality who take care of the conferences and are felt to
neglect student needs as soon as the academic term is over
and those fat corporate money-bags move in.*

SU FACILITIES:
The Union Building in the middle of the campus has bars, a
cafeteria and restaurant, travel agency, 2 banks and 3 cash
machines (Lloyds, NatWest, Halifax), general shop, Endsleigh
Insurance office, disco, print service and photocopying, 3

minibuses, arts and pottery studio, vending machines and video games, photo booth, pool tables, bookshop, video rental, Thursday market, juke box and function rooms.

CLUBS (NON SPORTING):
Arcana; Chapel Choir; Concert Band; Duke of Edinburgh; Film; Folk; Hellenic; Klas (role-playing); Fantasy Football; Writers; Wargames.

OTHER ORGANISATIONS:
There's a weekly student newspaper, 'Grapevine', a monthly mag called 'Green Monster' and the termly 'Concourse'. The charity Rag raises *pretty big bucks, considering the location*. Keele's radio station KUBE has been re-formed and broadcasts daily 7.30am-midnight.

RELIGIOUS:
● <u>4 chaplains (CofE, RC, Free Church, flying rabbi - what a lovely image)</u>

The big inter-denominational Christian chapel is a *bizarre* grey brick structure, rectangular with 2 cylindrical turrets at one end. Muslim prayer room provided on campus. In Newcastle and Stoke, apart from various churches, there are places of worship for Muslims, Sikhs and Buddhists.

PAID WORK:
Few opportunities in the local towns, *and even fewer in College, now that Hospitality has cut back on the number of students it employs.*

sports

● <u>Recent successes: kick-boxing, running</u>

A fairly good level of facilities and involvement. There is a small charge for some facilities if not organised through the sporting clubs.

SPORTS FACILITIES:
Close to the principle parts of the University (the halls of residence, the Union and the main teaching areas) are the sports facilities spread over 46 acres including playing fields, cricket squares, an all-weather floodlit pitch and netball and tennis courts. In the adjacent sports centre are a recently upgraded gym, sports hall, multigym, fitness centre, 7 squash courts and a climbing wall. Also, based in the sports centre, there's a sports shop and *strangely*, pizza take-away and hairdresser. The towns add extra amenities such as a golf course, ski slope, a swimming pool, lake and bowling green.

SPORTING CLUBS:
Aeroball; Caving; Frisbee; Kung Fu; Rock Climbing; Water-skiing.

ATTRACTIONS:
Locally, there's Stoke City and Port Vale Football Clubs, Uttoxeter Race Course, the Potteries marathon and, most years, the Lombard rally. Keele is also host to the National Karate Championships.

accommodation

IN COLLEGE:
● <u>Self-catering: 77%</u> ● <u>Cost: £30-51(33-42wks)</u>

Availability: Living in is the norm. *It's one of the big things about Keele as far as Keele is concerned.* 1st years actually have to apply to live out rather than to live in. As a consequence, they are almost all housed in the University's 4 halls on campus. They are all self-catering (some have pay-as-you-eat refectories and snack bars, though). They vary in size from 400 to 800 places and have single and mixed sex blocks. 2 halls are blocks of flats for 4 students each, sharing a kitchen and bathroom, although these are mainly for 2nd and 3rd years and finalists 95% of whom live in. 25% live out for their 2nd year. Some space is available on campus specially for mature students and a few single parents. Off campus, the University owns houses which can accommodate up to 99 students in groups of 4 to 6.

Car parking: *Limited* permit parking (£10) on campus with clamps.

EXTERNALLY:
● <u>Ave rent: £35</u>

Availability: *The University is expanding and may have to reduce its proportion of students living in which may well create problems in the local housing market. At the moment Newcastle is the preferred option, being on a handy bus-route, although Hanley and parts of Stoke are also options. Knutton and Cobridge are a bit rough and Parkside is getting worse. When living out a car wouldn't go unused, unless students are on the main bus routes.*

Housing help: The University's Accommodation Office has 3 full-time officers, a vacancies newsletter and a housing approval scheme.

·········· welfare

SERVICES:
● <u>Creche</u> ● <u>Nightline</u> ● <u>Lesbian & Gay Society</u>
● <u>Mature SA</u> ● <u>Overseas SA</u> ● <u>Minibus</u> ● <u>Women's Officer</u>
● <u>Self-defence classes</u>

The Keele General Practice is based on campus and employs a male and a female doctor and two nurses. As well as normal health care, it offers a psychiatry clinic. The mental even keel of Keele is also maintained by the 3 part- and 1 full-time counsellors of the University's Counselling Service (the chaplains also help out). The Union runs an independent Advice Unit with 3 counsellors who can offer a free and confidential listening service, financial and legal advice, help for overseas students, drugs information, jobshop with local vacancies, and support for lesbian and gay students.

Women: The health centre has a well woman clinic and the Union has a women's resources centre.

Disabled: *Facilities for hearing and sight-impaired students and for those with dyslexia look good but there have been complaints that they're just left to get on with it themselves. Things are hard for wheelchair users, but there is at least a Disability Officer.*

FINANCE:
● <u>Ave debt: £1,500</u> ● <u>Access fund: £75,272</u>
● <u>Successful applications (1997): 332</u>

The University loans money from the Emergency Hardship Fund and the SU and chaplains have similar arrangements.

University of Kent at Canterbury

The University of Kent at Canterbury, The Registry, Canterbury, Kent, CT2 7NZ. Tel: (01227) 764000. Fax: (01227) 452196.
E-mail: admissions@ukc.ac.uk
Students' Union, University of Kent, Canterbury, Kent, CT2 7NZ. Tel: (01227) 765224. Fax: (01227) 464625.
E-mail: union@ukc.ac.uk

General

This is the so-called Garden of England, full of hop fields, oast-houses and ruminating cows. Well actually, Canterbury, an ancient city and the seat of the Church of England, is more than a quaint slice of ye olde heritage industrie. It's still surrounded by rolling Kent countryside and little villages of pretty ivy-covered cottages but nowadays, trendy cafés and an increasing number of big chain stores have joined the long stretches of 13th and 14th century city walls to the south and east of the city. The University is 1½ miles from the city, based on a very large campus (300 acres) with 4 University colleges. For those who like ornate architecture the University doesn't offer much. The buildings are a plain collection of redbrick, with more than enough concrete, set amidst a green and pleasantly landscaped campus which has the bizarre effect of magnifying weather conditions; when the sun comes out it's baking and as soon as it goes away you might as well be in Siberia.

43% ♂♂♂♂♂♀♀♀♀♀ 57%

Sex ratio(M:F): 43%:57%	Founded: 1965
Full time u'grads: 5,898	Part time: 111
Postgrads: 1,103	Non-degree: 2,150
Ave course: 3yrs	Ethnic: n/a
Private school: 50%	Flunk rate: 8%
Mature students: 25%	Overseas students: 23%
Disabled students: 6%	Staff/student ratio: 1:10
Clearing: n/a	

ATMOSPHERE:
The collegiate system at Kent tends to encourage cliques and students remain faithful to their particular college throughout their University careers. However, the 4 colleges (each about 1,250 undergrads) aren't that different from one another and students don't normally express a preference in their application (nor is it a particularly good idea). Like most collegiate universities, the strength of the colleges and the Junior College Committees (JCCs - mini SUs) detracts from the University-wide Students' Union. Students seeking a full social life need to look for it. Since many of the students come from the Home Counties many go home at the weekends, but those who stay behind have lots of fun behind the others' backs.

❝Heinz Wolff, the professor of bio-engineering at Brunel University, has posed with glamour model Joanne Guest in the pages of 'Loaded' magazine.❞

THE CITY:
- Population: 54,500 ● London: 56miles
- Dover: 16miles ● Maidstone: 26miles

Canterbury has all the local amenities of a city with *the advantage of still being a small place amidst beautiful surroundings*. Not least of these are the many historical buildings, the medieval city walls and the *overbearing, but impressive*, ancient Cathedral. There has been a cathedral here (not the same one) since the end of the 6th century, staking an early claim to become the centre of the Anglican Church. Urban decay can be spotted on the way out of the city, although there's also a good deal of modern development and big chain stores based on the outskirts. Students (including those from various other colleges) make up more than 25% of the population.

TRAVEL:
Trains: Although Canterbury West is closer, Canterbury East is the most convenient station, with mainline connections to London (£16.10) and Dover and connections to Edinburgh, Birmingham and Bristol.
Coaches: National Express services all over the country.
Car: The A2 and, some way up the road, the M2 connects London with Canterbury while the A28 runs to the south coast.
Ferries: From Dover and Folkstone to France and Belgium.
Hitching: *The A2 and A28 should be good bets, but drivers are pretty possessive about their upholstery in Kent.*
Local: Buses from town to campus every 15 minutes and student bus cards are available.
Taxis: £2 for the mile from the campus to Canterbury.
Bicycles: *Many bikes despite the fact the campus is on a hill.*

LIBRARIES & COMPUTERS:
- Books: 830,000 ● Study places: 1,300
- Computer workstations: 450

In addition to the Templeman Library, the colleges have their own small collections and the University looks after the running of the Cathedral Library, which isn't available for general academic purposes. The campus computer network is available 24 hours a day, 7 days a week.

CAREER PROSPECTS:
- Careers Service ● No of staff: 6full/2part
- Unemployed after 6mths (1996): 4.3%

FAMOUS ALUMNI:
Alan Davies (comedian); Gavin Esler (journalist); Kazuo Ishiguro (writer); Wayne Otto (karate champ); Paul Ross (TV

presenter); David Walsh (historian); Charles Wigoder (mobile phone entrepreneur); Sir Robert May (Chief Scientific Advisor to Government and Head of Office of Science and Technology) was awarded an honorary doctorate in '97 *in an act of unexpurgated sycophancy.*

FURTHER INFO:
Prospectuses for undergrads and postgrads. Web site (http://www.ukc.ac.uk).

entertainment

THE CITY:

● <u>Price of a pint of beer: £1.90</u> ● <u>Glass of wine: £1.80</u>

Cinemas: (1) The Cannon has 2 screens, *but the flicks in Whitstable is nicer.*

Theatres: (1) The Marlowe Theatre is the city's only permanent theatre although T S Eliot's verse play 'Murder in the Cathedral' was written for and first performed in Canterbury Cathedral.

Pubs: In some parts of Kent the air is thick with the *cornflakey* stench of hops and brewing. Not all this local brew gets transported out of the county and Canterbury is full of pubs that serve a *mean* brew or two. *Testing the local tastes is a major student pastime.* **push***plugs: Simple Simons (14th century); Three Compasses (packed, wild and brash); Black Griffin; Falstaff & Tap; Franklin & Firkin; Black Griffin.*

Clubs/discos: (2) *Canterbury is not club city but Churchill's and Alberry's are worth a try.*

Music venues: Classical concerts are held in the Cathedral and the Marlowe Theatre, which also has folk music. Cuba specialises in jazz and Latin. For local bands and indie, there's the Penny Theatre and Cardinal's Cap. *Otherwise, a trip to Metronome or Leas Cliff Hall in Folkestone (over 14 miles) or Whitstable Labour Club (6 miles) is in order, but it's still mainly local bands.*

Food: Local scoff shops are geared to the student and tourist trade and there are plentiful Indian, Italian, pizza, Chinese, French and vegetarian restaurants, as well as various fish'n'chip shops and other takeaways. **push***plugs: Pinnochio's (Italian); Café des Amis, which, is, of course, Mexican; Ask (gorgeous pizzas); Caesar's (big portions).* Students who need to stuff something down their throats late at night can resort to curries and kebabs until about 1am.

UNIVERSITY:

● <u>Price of a pint of beer: £1.30</u> ● <u>Glass of wine: 90p</u>

Kent's ents provisions have been a trifle lame recently but this should change now they've got a new SU building complete with a full-time ents manager.

Bars: Woody's (a converted scout hut) was the *popular* old SU bar but the new SU (cap 1200) has 3 bars, 1 of which is part of the new nightclub 'The Venue'. *The Theatre bar is trendy.* The colleges also run their own bars.

Theatres: The Gulbenkian Theatre on campus (cap 342) *is very well equipped, but there's a price to be paid for that - it's not for the exclusive use of students.* It plays host to many touring productions, the annual Canterbury Festival and concerts of all sorts. The University does, however, have the largest drama department in the country and a new drama building. Students put on productions in makeshift theatres in the colleges when the Gulbenkian's booked.

Cinemas: Cinema 3 shows commercial and occasional arty stuff, and the cinema club shows three films a week.

Clubs/discos & music venues: Gigs and club nights have been based in JCRs and dining halls across the 4 colleges. *Now that 'The Venue' has opened, the club and live music scene should pick up* - the plan is to get big name DJs in weekly and live music every fortnight. There's some kind of event on most nights.

Food: Catering is based in individual colleges.

Cabaret: 2 or 3 funsters per term; recently, Phil Jupitus and Jeremy Hardy.

Others: Apart from college and society dos, there's at least 1 major event a term, culminating in the Grand Summer Ball. An ents card (£25) gives discounts on all SU events.

social & political

UNIVERSITY OF KENT AT
CANTERBURY STUDENTS' UNION:

● <u>5 sabbaticals</u> ● <u>Turnout at last ballot: 10%</u>
● <u>NUS member</u>

The Union is based in the small Mandela Building, and things tend to have a collegiate, rather than University feel. Students seem to be largely unaware of the SU, and social life centres around societies. The new SU building should address this though.

SU FACILITIES:

Minibus; travel agency; printing; Endsleigh Insurance office; general shop; 2nd-hand bookshop; pool table; juke box; vending machines; TV lounge; meeting room; launderette; stationery shop; photocopier; photobooth; van hire. Also banks with cashpoints on campus. One of the 2 new buildings will provide a nightclub and 3 bars with a late license, the other a larger shop and office space.

CLUBS (NON SPORTING):

Adventure Gaming; Amateur Radio; Anglican; Ballroom Dancing; Belly Dancing; Buddhist Meditation; Chess; Chinese; Comic; Creative Expression; Critical Lawyers; Film-Making; Scandinavian; Sci-Fi; Shiatsu; Singapore; Space; Spanish; Sri Lanka; Star Trek; Wine.

OTHER ORGANISATIONS:

'Kred' is the student newspaper, produced by the Union. 'Propaganda' is a handy ents listing sheet, out every fortnight. UKC Radio will soon broadcast across campus on FM. There is a charity Rag and the student community organisation works with local help projects.

RELIGIOUS:

● <u>7 chaplains (CofE, RC, Baptist, Methodist, Quaker, Orthodox, Jewish)</u>

The Eliot Chapel is the campus prayer place although there are various makeshift worship shops in the colleges as well as a Muslim prayer room. In town, there's the Cathedral, of course, *but Christians who fancy something a little less lofty don't have to worry about any kind of theological drought. Non-Christians may get a bit more spiritually thirsty.*

PAID WORK:
During the summer, the Garden of England offers a monumental set of gardening tasks such as hop and fruit picking. A new jobshop is being set up on campus, *but even so there isn't a lot going*. A foreign language is handy for *touristy* Canterbury, and it's also possible to find jobs teaching English as a foreign language.

sports

● 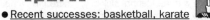Recent successes: basketball, karate

Intercollegiate rivalries come into the open when sportsmen and women get into gear but Kent's reputation in national competitions is on the up as well. The facilities are all on campus and shared between colleges. Sports bursaries worth £500 are available.

SPORTS FACILITIES:
Playing fields; sports centre including sports hall; archery range; cricket nets; gym; 2 multigyms; weights; boxing ring; sauna and solarium; 6 squash courts; athletics field; tennis courts; flood-lit all-weather pitch; climbing wall; running track. The city adds a croquet lawn swimming pool and golf course *and the coast isn't too far away.*

SPORTING CLUBS:
American Football; Boxing; Caving; Handball; Kendo; Lacrosse; Motorcycling; Mountaineering; Paintball; Street Hockey; Tennis; Ten Pin Bowling; Ultimate Frisbee.

ATTRACTIONS:
Dog racing track; windsurfing at Whitstable.

accommodation

IN COLLEGE:
● Catered: 26% ● Cost: £54-83 (30wks)
● Self-catering: 28% ● Cost: £42-47 (39wks)

Availability: Whether or not students live in, they remain members of their colleges throughout their university careers. 1st years are guaranteed accommodation if they want it. 5% share. In general, the self-catering accommodation in University Houses and Park Wood Courts - a small village of terraced purpose-built student houses on campus - is used by students beyond their 1st year. *Beckett Court is 5 star, spacious accommodation, Eliot and Keynes are popular, but other housing is a bit run down. Catered here means B+B.*

Car parking: Free, provided you live off campus.

EXTERNALLY:
● Ave rent: £46

Availability: *Students have to keep their eyes, ears and cheque books open if they're going to find anywhere to live in Canterbury.* An increasing number are moving out to Herne Bay and Whitstable (5 to 7 miles north), *where rents are cheaper, places are more plentiful and life more dull.* For those who rillyrilly want something closer to the action, Winchaep and Sturry Road are the places to aim for.

Housing help: The University Accommodation Office employs 4 staff who try to place students, especially 1st years, but its main concern is allocating places on campus.

welfare

SERVICES:
- ● Creche ● Nightline ● Lesbian & Gay Society
- ● Mature SA ● Overseas SA ● Postgrad SA ● Minibus
- ● Women's Officer ● Self-defence classes

There is a 24-hour counselling service based in Darwin which employs 2 full- and 3 part-time members of staff and a medical centre complete with residential sick-bay. There are campus escorts and new lamps are being installed all over. An Overseas Group and newsletter also operates.

Disabled: *Pretty much par for the course, but there has been an effort to improve many of the buildings.* A committee does a lot of talking. Individual advice can be sought from a special advisor.

FINANCE:
- ● Ave debt: £1,000 ● Access fund: £145,000
- ● Successful applications (1996): 1,200

Sports and music bursaries are available.

• •

▶▶ **Kent Institute**

see Other Institutions

• •

▶▶ **King Alfred's**

see Other Institutions

• •

King's College, London

▼ ● *The College is part of <u>University of London</u> and students are entitled to use its facilities.*
(1) King's College London including Guy's, King's College & St Thomas' Hospitals Medical and Dental School, University of London, The Strand, London, WC2R 2LS.
Tel: (0171) 836 5454. Fax: (0171) 836 1799.
King's College London Students' Union, Macadam Building, Surrey Street, London, WC2 2LS. Tel: (0171) 836 7132. Fax: (0171) 379 9833.

general

At one end of The Strand is Trafalgar Square and at the other is King's College, among other things. Those other things include the beginning of Fleet Street, Somerset House (the home of the Inland Revenue and the <u>Courtauld Institute</u>), Aldwych (a 5-lane crescent curving round Bush House, the HQ of the BBC World Service), the <u>LSE</u> and the handsome Wren church St Mary's-in-the-Strand. *The 70s front of the King's*

College main building is a bit of a disappointment among the splendid surrounds. It's concrete, glass and grey, *but bland enough to blend.* Hidden away at the back of the building, overlooking the Thames is much finer Georgian architecture, *but once that far into the building it's hard to find your way out again.* In addition to the Strand site there are further sites across the river from the Strand including the Waterloo and Guy's sites to the south of the river at London Bridge. These recent developments, brought about by a merger with UMDS have made it the largest life/science department in Europe. King's also has halls of residence all over central London (both north and south) *in some of the capital's most exciting, not to say valuable, locations.*

41% ♂♂♂♂♂ ♀♀♀♀♀ 59%

Sex ratio(M:F): 41%:59%   Founded: 1829
Full time u'grads: 11,500   Part time: 190
Postgrads: 4,500   Non-degree: 3,077
Ave course: 3yrs   Ethnic: 34%
Private school: n/a   Flunk rate: n/a
Mature students: 33.7%   Overseas students: 18%
Disabled students: 4%   Staff/student ratio: 1:13
Clearing: n/a

ATMOSPHERE:
It's a pulsating, multicultural social mix but the student body is too diverse, and increasingly dispersed across the capital, to create a particularly tight community atmosphere. There is, however, a strong sense of pride in the college, usually expressed in rivalry with University College, London. *The Strand site is ideally placed for enjoyment of all that London cares to offer (and attendant costs) but those based at some of the outlying sites tend to experience less of the action.*

THE SITES:
The Strand: This is the eastern end of the West End. *There's a million ways to spend money but not, however, any places to live, or anywhere to do the weekly shopping without your daily bread costing more than your dough.* The SU is based at this site and the nearest college halls are ½ mile away.
Waterloo: (1,160 students - management, health and life studies) ½ a mile from the Strand site on the other side of Waterloo Bridge on the Thames' South Bank. Café bar, common room, K4 Fitness centre.
Guy's: (biomedical sciences, preclinical medicine and dentistry) 2 miles from the Strand site on the Thames' South Bank. This will be a brand new complex at Guy's Hospital offering accommodation, a new Student Union building and welfare centre. When it is ready in 1999, over 3,000 students will be based here.
Drury Lane: (100 students - biomolecular science) ¼ mile from the main site, with only a small canteen.
Medical Schools: (1,567 students - dentistry and medicine) There are 3 hospitals at which teaching takes place: **Guy's:** A Georgian style collection of buildings close to London Bridge.

From the top of the very tall Guy's Tower there is an incredible view across the city; **St Thomas':** (aka Tommy's) ¾ mile from Trafalgar square, opposite the Houses of Parliament on the south side of the Thames is Tommy's modern 70s development with open plan, bright and clean inter-connected buildings; **Denmark Hill:** King's College Hospital in Camberwell. *A different kettle of cod altogether*, Camberwell is south of the river and, almost necessarily, shabbier as a result. *It's not London's safest area (or its worst - London gets much worse)*, but it's cheap, residential and *good* for shopping. Camberwell may not have a great deal by way of entertainment itself, but is very well connected for the West End. The hospital has its own social life, anyway.

THE CITY: see <u>University of London</u>

TRAVEL: see <u>University of London</u>
Trains: Charing Cross is the nearest mainline station for the Strand site. Denmark Hill station is the best way of getting to the St Thomas' Hospital, while Guy's is closest to London Bridge.
Buses: Denmark Hill: 12, 35, 40, 45, 68, 171, 176, 184; Night Buses N12, N62, N72, N82 & N86. 21, 35, 40 and 133 go near Guy's and 77 and 507 go to Tommy's.
Underground: Temple (District & Circle Lines) or Holborn (Piccadilly and Central) for the main site. Northern and Bakerloo lines for Waterloo; London Bridge (Northern line) for Guy's; Lambeth North (Bakerloo line) for Tommy's. The Jubilee line will serve both Guy's and Waterloo based students when it opens...
Bicycles: *Quite a popular form of transport although pollution and fatal injury aren't big selling points.*

LIBRARIES & COMPUTERS:
- <u>Books: 850,000</u> ● <u>Study places: 1,683</u>
- <u>Computer workstations: 1000</u>

There are 12 libraries in all. There are student places on the library committees and they have pressed successfully for extended opening hours and other improvements. *A new library planned at the Waterloo site should address current problems with book shortages.*

CAREER PROSPECTS:
- <u>Careers Service</u> ● <u>No of staff: 6full/1part</u>
- <u>Unemployed after 6mths (1996): 6.4%</u>

SPECIAL FEATURES:
- KCL runs a popular optional Theology course for all students. This is a relic of the College's religious foundations and there is a certificate - the AKC (Associate of King's College).

FAMOUS ALUMNI:
Rory Bremner (impressionist); George Carey (Archbishop of Canterbury); Arthur C Clarke (sci-fi writer); John Eliot Gardner (composer/conductor); Susan Hill (novelist); Hanif Kureishi (writer); Chapman Pincher (writer/journalist); Dame Angela Rumbold MP (Con); Ian Shaw (jazz singer); Desmond Tutu, Njongonkulu Winston Ndungane (past and present Archbishops of Cape Town); Maurice Wilkins (Nobel Laureate DNA Scientist).

FURTHER INFO:
Prospectuses for undergrads and postgrads, video and web site (http://www.kcl.ac.uk).

entertainment

IN LONDON: see University of London

COLLEGE:
● Price of a pint of beer: £1.60 ● Glass of wine: £1.20

Bars: The Strand site has 3 bars, the Waterfront (capacity 350, *hip & happening*), Tutu's (620) which concentrates on events and the Reach Bar, at the top of Tutu's. There's also the Penthouse at Denmark Hill and bars at Guy's and Thomas'.

Theatres: There are strong drama societies who put on shows in the theatre at the Strand site and go to the Edinburgh Fringe.

Clubs/discos: There are 2 club nights a week at the Strand, including Collide-a-Scope, *one of the best indie nights in the capital.* The Penthouse bar at Denmark Hill expands into the next room (cap 300) and makes *a hot spot to trot.* Regular club nights in Guy's bar (cap 400).

Music venues: Tutu's is used for band nights *attracting bigger names than most London colleges manage*; for example, Dust Junkies, Curve and Girls vs Boys. Reggie's at Kensington hosts smaller bands.

Food: The College-run cafeterias at the Strand have *inspiring* names like GO1 (*cliquey* snack bar), B1 (refectory) and B2 (waitress restaurant). King's Hospital at Denmark Hill has the *even less enthralling* monicker 'hospital canteen'. Still it's the food you eat, not the names. The SU runs a deli at the Strand in the Waterfront Bar and Tutu's sells cheap pizzas, baked spuds and breakfast. The Rooftop Cafe *has excellent views and only slightly less excellent food.*

Others: The SU keep trotting out a host of hoots *well-attended* by students on each site: weekly bar quizzes, karaoke. Each year there's a thoroughly formal Summer Ball at a posh hotel.

social & political

KING'S COLLEGE LONDON STUDENTS' UNION (KCLSU):
● 4 sabbaticals ● Turnout at last ballot: 10%

● NUS member

KCLSU has a tiny political core and does its little bit for student representation, but is essentially a slick organiser of student ents, bars and clubs. It remains to be seen how well the SU amalgamates over the different sites.

SU FACILITIES:
Strand: The Macadam Building (named after NUS's first president) houses bars, cafes, nightclub, shop, travel agency, Dillons, cashpoint (Barclays).

> **Researchers at De Montfort University have perfected a technique for turning pig manure into energy.**

Guy's Hospital: bar, MacDonalds, ballroom, bookshop. The new complex will have an SU building.
Denmark Hill: bar, meeting room, TV and games room, Union offices, stationery shop, medical shop.

CLUBS (NON SPORTING):

Arab Youth; Ballroom Dancing; Chinese; Debating; Film; Hellenic; Hindu; Japanese; Jazz; Liberation; Malaysian & Singapore; Mauritian; Mediterranean; Opera; Oxfam; Public Awareness; Salsa; Sikh; Sri Lankan; Taiwan; Tamil; Vegetarian.

OTHER ORGANISATIONS:

There's 'Roar', an SU mag which includes listings. King's charity Rag does all the normal *stupid* and occasionally illegal things that students get up to in the name of charity. Beer races with UCL go down well and London colleges have a penchant for pinching each other's mascots. King's mascot was Reggie, a $\frac{1}{4}$-ton red copper lion, until he was stolen by City & Guilds who castrated him. The mascot was then filled with concrete, making it such a challenge that it was quickly stolen with the aid of trucks and winches. Now they've got a copper lion again, *which is just asking for it.*

RELIGIOUS:

● 4 chaplains (CofE, Orthodox, RC, Free Church)
A chapel at the Strand and Muslim prayer rooms at both Kensington and Chelsea.

PAID WORK: see University of London

·········sports

● Recent successes: jiu jitsu, athletics
They're a sporty sort at King's, surprisingly so considering the outdoor facilities are at Berrylands in Mitcham, about 9 miles south of the Strand. 40% of University of London team members are King's students.

SPORTS FACILITIES:

Some indoor facilities are on site, including a shooting range at the Strand. The new K4 fitness centre at Stamford St has qualified trainers. There is a 6-acre ground in Dulwich, 2 miles from the St Thomas' Hospital and a sports ground at New Malden. Guy's has a swimming pool.

SPORTING CLUBS:

Aerobics; Aerosports; Boat; Boxing; Bujinkan; Capoira; Lacrosse; Polo; Rifle & Pistol; Shaolin Kung Fu; Thai Boxing; Water Polo; Yoga.

ATTRACTIONS: see University of London

·········accommodation

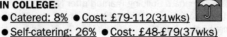

IN COLLEGE:
● Catered: 8% ● Cost: £79-112(31wks)
● Self-catering: 26% ● Cost: £48-£79(37wks)
Availability: King's has 8 halls dotted around London, all within a 4-mile radius of the Strand, with halls attached to each of the other sites. *Some are very expensive, but are correspondingly lavish.* About 13% of students share. The provision is sufficient to offer places to most 1st years who request them but 25% live out. *Hampstead Hall is the most spirited but pricey hall, King's College Halls are a little less desirable.*

Car parking: *Almost impossible at almost all the halls.*

EXTERNALLY: see University of London

Housing help: The College has its own Accommodation Office as well as the University's *excellent* service.

welfare

SERVICES:

● Nursery ● Lesbian & Gay Society

● Overseas SA ● Minibus ● Self-defence classes

For most services, the University's provisions are more extensive than those available in the College. However, KCLSU offers a Welfare Department and the College runs a Counselling and Medical Centre, employing 12 full-time staff, including trained counsellors, 2 doctors, 3 nurses and a psychotherapist. The personal tutor system also operates in a caring kind of way.

Disabled: *Hit and miss wheelchair access.*

FINANCE:

● Ave debt: £1,500 ● Access fund: £317,000

● Successful applications (1997): 650

Also Principal's and Overseas Students' Hardship Funds.

▶▶ King's Hospital

see King's College, London

Kingston University

● *Formerly Kingston Polytechnic*

Kingston University, 53-57 High Street, Kingston upon Thames, Surrey, KT1 1LQ. Tel: (0181) 547 2000.
Fax: (0181) 547 7093.
Kingston University Guild of Students, Penrhyn Road, Kingston upon Thames, Surrey, KT1 2EE. Tel: (0181) 255 2222.

general

The address may say Surrey, but don't be fooled - London doesn't stop between the suburban *petty prettiness* of Kingston and Trafalgar Square, 10 miles to the north east. But Kingston is one of London's *pleasantest* parts with 2 large parks breaking the alternating streets of homes and shops. Local highlights include the famous Hampton Court, one-time home of Henry VIII, and its deer-infested park. But to get to such delights from Kingston University, a trip across Kingston's *handsome* Bridge is required. The University is based on 4 main sites all within 3 miles of each other, 2 of which are in Kingston town centre. They are composed of a mangled mix of different buildings, from the new Roehampton Vale site to the *white washed charm* of the Kingston Hill site (the slightly separate one) set in 50 acres of *delightful* parkland. There's old, there's new, there's *ugly* blocks and *attractive* towers.

49% ♂♂♂♂♂♀♀♀♀♀ 51%	
Sex ratio(M:F): 49%:51%	Founded: 1971
Full time u'grads: 10,743	Part time: 1,470
Postgrads: 833	Non-degree: 947
Ave course: 3yrs	Ethnic: 26%
Private school: 9.2%	Flunk rate: n/a
Mature students: 22%	Overseas students: 9.8%
Disabled students: 3.1%	Staff/student ratio: 1:14
Clearing: 15%	

ATMOSPHERE & SITES:
Each site is very individual (different faculties are based at each one). Although there is a stronger identity than most split site colleges, it's not easy to pin it down: well-to-do and largely from the South would be a bit too harsh. Penrhyn, the largest site with 6,000 students, for example, is lively and noisy - lots of drinking and prankish japes, finding any excuse to dress up and get wasted. Knight's Park (1,000 students), though, is much more sober and sombre, full of trendy arty types in the throes of creativity. Roehampton Vale (1,000 students) has the engineers who work hard and when they're not working hard, they're sitting around just chatting. Kingston Hill (3,000 students) is the only one with halls of residence on site and so has a much stronger community unity - Sloanier too.

THE CITY: see University of London

KINGSTON:
Kingston upon Thames is about as historic as places get in this country (if it were any older, it'd have to be nearer Rome). *Its village-like character is alive and well and living* in the centre of the town where there's an old daily market. *But time has left its ticks and tocks on Kingston* and recently it has been swamped by new developments: a huge shopping centre; a great many car parks and even more cars. In retaliation, many of its streets have been pedestrianised and now it has a monster one-way system *(one way in - no way out)*. Still, it does offer a trolleyful of shops (including a bookshop in Brook Street) and a wacky sculpture consisting of old red telephone boxes toppling each other like dominoes.

TRAVEL: see University of London

LIBRARIES & COMPUTERS:
● Books: 350,000 ● Study places: 930
● Computer workstations: 1,000
There are 4 libraries, 1 on each site, devoted to the faculties based there. *There are complaints that they're disorganised and lacking in specialist tomes.*

CAREER PROSPECTS:
● Careers Service ● No of staff: 5full/3part
● Unemployed after 6mths (1997): 5%

FAMOUS ALUMNI:

Glenda Bailey (editor, 'Marie Claire'); Angie Bowie (Dave's 1st wife); Lawrence Dallaglio (rugby player); Trevor Eve (actor); Patrick Forge (DJ); Nick Hornby (novelist, 'Fever Pitch'); Richard James (the Aphex Twin); Graeme Le Saux (footballer); Steve Mason (Gene guitarist); John Richmond, Helen Storey (fashion designers); Stella Tennant (posh model).

FURTHER INFO:

Prospectus and web site (http://www.kingston.ac.uk).

entertainment

TOWN:

● Price of a pint of beer: £2.10 ● Glass of wine: £1.90

Cinemas: In Kingston, there's a large Odeon, *but for movies, as for all entertainments, it's easier to take a trip into the West End.*

Theatres: None to speak of in Kingston; *arty* productions at the Orange Tree in neighbouring Richmond.

Pubs: Many of the local pubs, *which have much more local charm than most in London,* host live music. **push***plugs: Financier & Firkin; Spring Grove, O'Neill's, Gazebo.*

Clubs/discos: Volts is the student-friendly club, along with Backers *(indie/dance in a dingy cellar - better than it sounds).*

Eating out: **push***plugs: Kelly Arms (great fry-ups); Mantana (Thai); Yellow Heaven Soup Kitchen (10% NUS discount).*

Others: Kingston offers many pastoral pastimes such as boat trips on the Thames, which can be booked for evening parties.

UNIVERSITY:

● Price of a pint of beer: £1.50 ● Glass of wine: £1.10

Bars: 4 bars, *Penrhyn Road being the liveliest.*

Comedy: *Every other Tuesday comics struggle to get a drunken audience's attention.*

Cinema: The Film and Cult TV Society put on a couple of mainstream and cult films in a lecture theatre every week.

Clubs/discos: Volts (capacity 2,000) in town hosts the weekly student stomp.

Music venues: Live music lives on in the bar at Penrhyn Rd (600); Pop Tarts and Lovetrain have played there recently.

Food: All sites have canteens and sandwich bars.

Balls: Several balls every term run by clubs and the Guild.

social & political

KINGSTON UNIVERSITY GUILD OF STUDENTS (KUGOS):

● 4 sabbaticals ● NUS member

KUGOS is a lot more active than it is radical, more into clubs than clubbing policemen, more into bars than barricades. Must be the only union to be criticised for apathy by its parent University. Definitely not to be confused with kudos.

SU FACILITIES:

The portacabinesque Guild Building is based at Penrhyn Road and offers bars with TVs, pool tables and games machines, a travel office, photocopying and printing.

CLUBS (NON SPORTING):

Bongo; Chinese & Far Eastern; Film & Cult TV; Hellenic; Kingston Kidney Choir; Literary; Meditation; Political; Punjabi; Sikh; Vedic.

OTHER ORGANISATIONS:
The weekly Guild broadsheet 'Rumours' is filled with student contributions. There's also an ents mag, 'Reverb'. Students and staff do a fair deal of community work arranging, among other things, an Xmas dinner for OAPs and an appeal for Romanian Orphans. Rag raised £2,000 last year.

RELIGIOUS:
- 3 chaplains

PAID WORK:
The many local fast food joints always need new blood as does the Guild. There might, for example, be a job in the cloakroom.

sports

- Recent successes: swimming

Sport doesn't tend to get pulses racing in more than a small minority, who are mostly on the Penrhyn site.

SPORTS FACILITIES:
The playing fields are a couple of miles away at Tolworth in Surbiton where there are also tennis courts. Other facilities are spread around the sites: a gym at Kingston Hill; and a fitness centre and aerobics studio at Penrhyn Road. There's also a local public leisure centre and swimming pool.

SPORTING CLUBS:
Caving; Croquet; Gaelic Football; Kung Fu; Mountain Bike; Mountaineering; Parachute; Rowing; Tae Kwon Do; Tennis; Ten Pin Bowling.

ATTRACTIONS:
Rugby at Twickenham is close and there's racing at Sandown Park. Wimbledon for the tennis after summer exams and, of course, all of London's sports ports.

accommodation

IN COLLEGE:
- Self-catering: 21% ● Cost: £49-57(42wks)

Availability: The University can house all 1st years who apply in time. There are 2,261 places in 5 purpose-built halls and 650 places run under a head tenancy scheme. Nobody needs to share.

Car parking: Permit parking *and not nearly enough.*

EXTERNALLY:
- Ave rent: £70

Availability: It's quite difficult to find local accommodation at an affordable price. *Surbiton and Berrylands are popular areas, but in Kingston, landlords are reluctant to rent to rowdy students.*

Housing help: The University and Guild offer a joint Accommodation Service with vacancy boards.

welfare

SERVICES:
- Creche ● Lesbian & Gay Society ● Mature SA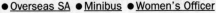
- Overseas SA ● Minibus ● Women's Officer

The Guild runs an *impressive* welfare service and employs a full-time welfare caseworker. The University employs 7 counsellors and has a medical centre at Penrhyn Rd with a visiting doctor and a nurse. There are lots of *rather nice* services including acupuncture, aromatherapy, relaxation sessions, sexual health clinic, reflexology, food and feeling group, stress clinic, hypnotherapy, sport therapy, osteopathy and chiropody clinics and free dental health checks.

Disabled: *Access and facilities are OK-ish; students with dyslexia are particularly well-served.*

FINANCE:
- Ave debt: £2,250 ● Access fund: £333,462
- Successful applications (1996): 808

 ❝ Freaked out by finance? Why not pop into your local branch of Lloyds Bank and see what they have to offer. ❞

❝ If you have any comments about PUSH or fancy being involved in the next edition, please write to PUSH, McGraw-Hill Publishing Company, Shoppenhangers Road, Maidenhead, Berkshire SL6 2QL. ❞

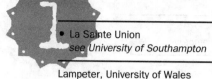

- La Sainte Union
  see University of Southampton

Lampeter, University of Wales

- Lancashire
  see University of Central Lancashire

Lancaster University

University of Leeds

Leeds Metropolitan University

University of Leicester

- Leicester Poly
  see De Montfort University

University of Lincolnshire and Humberside

University of Liverpool

- Liverpool Hope University College
  see Other Institutions

Liverpool John Moores University

- Liverpool Poly
  see Liverpool John Moores University

University of London

- London College of Fashion
  see The London Institute

- London College of Printing
  see The London Institute

London Guildhall University

The London Institute

- London School of Economics
  see LSE

Loughborough University

LSE

Continued next page

Continued from last page

● LSU
see University of Southampton

University of Luton

La Sainte Union

see University of Southampton

Lampeter, University of Wales

▼ ● **Formerly St David's College**
● **The College is part of <u>University of Wales</u>.**
University of Wales, Lampeter, Ceredigion, SA48 7ED.
Tel: (01570) 422351. Fax: (01570) 423423.
Ty Ceredig, University of Wales Lampeter, Lampeter,
Ceredigion, Wales, SA48 7ED. Tel: (01570) 422619.
Fax: (01570) 422480. E-mail: union@vax.acs.lampeter.ac.uk

general

Deep in south-west Wales, where valleys meet, is a little
market town called Lampeter, so remote it doesn't even have
a train station and quite a way from Carmarthen, *the nearest
town with anything approaching excitement.* In this virtual
village just round the corner from nowhere, is the appropriately
small college. Set in its own grounds, the *elegant* stone
buildings of Wales's oldest university college almost engulf the
town. Beyond the town's borders, you're immediately plunged
into the beautifully rugged hills from which the stones of
Stonehenge were cut and 13 miles away, the town of
Aberaeron on Wales's west coast.

Sex ratio(M:F): 50%:50%	Founded: 1822
Full time u'grads: 1,542	Part time: 182
Postgrads: 252	Non-degree: 0
Ave course: 3yrs	Ethnic: 30%
Private school: n/a	Flunk rate: n/a
Mature students: 42%	Overseas students: 7.3%
Disabled students: 5%	Staff/student ratio: 1:20
Clearing: 35%	

ATMOSPHERE:
Students (a strange mixture of sensible country folk and

zonked-out Swampy lookalikes) are happy enough to make their own entertainment, since there's little alternative. Everyone knows each other and the local community came to terms with the College about a century ago. Students who find themselves here by accident, through UCAS clearing or whatever, can have a problem adjusting but most find this extended chill-out zone a great way to spend 3 years.

THE TOWN:
- Population: 2,000 ● London: 180miles
- Aberystwyth: 30miles ● Swansea: 45miles

It depends what you consider to be the local town. Lampeter has about 20 shops *and there the excitement ends (outside the SU, of course)*, so most students look on Aberystwyth as the local big-time *even though that's pretty titchy as well;* see Aberystwyth, University of Wales. Carmarthen is 22 miles away and smaller (pop 8,500); it's a *good* shopping town serving quite a large catchment area where there are more sheep than people. The surrounding area is rich in tourist attractions: Roman gold mines; castles; Talley Abbey; Pembrokeshire National Park and the famous Devil's Bridge.

TRAVEL:
Trains: From Carmarthen you can get mainline trains to London (£25.75), Cardiff (£9.50) and Birmingham (£23.30). Aberystwyth station is better for northbound journeys.
Coaches: Aberystwyth and Carmarthen are both National Express drop-offs, with routes to London (£27), Cardiff (£7.75) and beyond.
Car: *Now there's a good idea. If you can afford it, get a car, or, failing that, a turbo-powered lawn mower. In Lampeter, it makes a big difference to the quality of life; day trips and shopping become feasible.* 18 miles (½hr) off the A40.
Hitching: *Without any major roads, it ain't easy. Allow a day to get anywhere and take a sleeping bag just in case, because it's not worth thinking, 'I can always catch a bus', because you can't because there probably won't be one.*
Local: The buses stick to the timetables, 1 every hour till about 5.30pm. It's £3.50 return to Carmarthen and a similar service to Aberystwyth.
Taxis: Sure, there are taxis, but frankly, students can't afford the cost anywhere - it's about £20 to Carmarthen. Maybe worth it to have a night out in town if 4 share the ride back.
Bicycles: There are sheds, not too many hills and virtually no theft, *but without motorised legs, most places are out of cycle reach.*

LIBRARIES & COMPUTERS:
- Books: 170,000 ● Study places: 266
- Computer workstations: 80

There are 2 libraries: the Founder's Library (with 20,000 historical books, documents and manuscripts) and the Main Library.

CAREER PROSPECTS:
- Careers Service ● No of staff: 3full
- Unemployed after 6mths (1994): 9.6%

Although there aren't many big employers on the doorstep the careers service arranges trips to Cardiff for the milk round.

FAMOUS ALUMNI:
Jack Higgins (thriller writer); Anthony Hopkins (*colossally great actor*); TE Lawrence (of Arabia).

FURTHER INFO:
Prospectus for undergrads; alternative prospectus from SU. Also, a web site (http://www.lamp.ac.uk) and a video loan service.

entertainment

TOWN:
● Price of a pint of beer: £1.60 ● Glass of wine: £1.30
Pubs/clubs/music/theatre: There are 14 pubs within a 1½ mile radius, *the Quarry being the most popular with students for its disco; Cumann Tavern for live music.* Felinfach Theatre is about 15mins away by car and puts on mostly Welsh language productions. Occasional music in the pubs but for anything else you need to get out of town.
Food: *Not a great deal.* *push*plugs: *Lloyds (fish & chips); Shapla (Indian).*

UNIVERSITY:
● Price of a pint of beer: £1.30 ● Glass of wine: £1.85
Bars: (2) Students and staff mix socially and sociably in the Main SU Bar (cap 365) and the Extension Bar (350).
Theatres: The Arts Hall (450) is used for events of all sorts, including student theatre productions.
Cinemas: The film club shows major films and cult pics.
Clubs/discos/music venues: Popular bops 3 nights a week in the Union Extension (so-called because it's been recently extended). Local bands play here on Tuesdays. NoWaySis and Dust Junkies have played here recently, *but no one knows why.*
Food: *The Refectory offers basic school dinnery stuff, but the portions are generous. Pooh's Corner and the Pizza Bar in the SU are more likely to tempt jaded palates.*
Other: 3 balls a year.

social & political

LAMPETER STUDENTS' UNION/TY CEREDIG: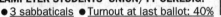
● 3 sabbaticals ● Turnout at last ballot: 40%
● NUS member
Being such a small institution, it's not hard to maintain a high level of involvement in the SU and (almost) unanimous consent. This is because no-one gets too party political at Lampeter. It's all pretty liberal and tolerant. The SU sees itself as a services and welfare organisation, although some environmental issues have provoked some political piquancy.

SU FACILITIES:
The SU building, Ty Ceredig, has a bar, cafeteria, restaurant, printing and photocopying, general shop, travel service, TV room, function room, customised night club (Union Extension), pool table, juke box and vending machines and minibus hire. The new extension provides a dancefloor, bar, nightclub facilities and conference suite.

CLUBS (NON SPORTING):
Battle Re-enactment; Cymdeithas Cymreig (Welsh); Dyslexia; Fluffy; Hellenic; Hunt Sabs; ICT; Inter-Faith Dialogue; Masquerade; Media; Meditation; Methodist; Music; Pagan; Rave; Swedish; Toc-H; Warpsoc.

OTHER ORGANISATIONS:
3 times a term the SU publishes 'Union News'. '1822' is the College's satirical magazine 4 times a term and there's a gay publication, 'Absolutely Campus'. There is no student community group; good relations make it unnecessary but there are clubs which do voluntary work.

RELIGIOUS:
● Chaplains (Christian)
The College has a chapel and Muslim prayer room and there are local churches. *Other religions will find it a bit tougher but most obligations can be fulfilled in Lampeter or nearby.*

PAID WORK:
The SU employs some student staff and there's a local organic farm, *but we're not talking major opportunities here.*

sports

● Recent successes: tae kwan do, riding
There's a high level of participation, but the emphasis is on fun, not competitiveness.

SPORTS FACILITIES:
There is a *stark* modern sports hall, 5 acres of playing fields, squash and tennis courts, an all-weather pitch, swimming pool, multigym and croquet lawn. The river (Afon Teifi) is useful for some sports but isn't large enough for any aquatic Olympics. Around town, there's a golf course and pony trekking and the mountains are excellent for rambling and hill walking, climbing and mountaineering, hang-gliding and getting cold.

SPORTING CLUBS:
Darts; Keep-Fit; Pool.

accommodation

IN COLLEGE:
● Catered: 9% ● Cost: £67(30wks)
● Self-catering: 29% ● Cost: £39-46(30-36wks)
Availability: All 1st years who want to live in can do, along with 37% of the finalists. There's a mix of catered and self-catering halls on campus and there's also a complex of ex-holiday bungalows which works out cheaper but residents need a car to make it worthwhile. A few people have to share briefly at the start of the academic year while the college finds them somewhere else to stay.
Car parking: Parking is free with a permit *and there's enough for the moment, although the situation is likely to deteriorate as numbers expand.*

EXTERNALLY:
● Ave rent: £38
Availability: Lampeter offers a mix of shared rented houses, bedsits and digs (with a live-in landlord/lady), *mostly of an OK standard. If you've got wheels of course, out in the country there are dinky little cottages aplenty, although some hippies have been known to disappear completely.*
Housing help: Help is at hand from the College's Accommodation Office which has 2 full-time staff offering standard contracts, advice and a vacancies board.

welfare

SERVICES:

- Creche ● Nightline ● Lesbian & Gay Society
- Mature SA ● Overseas SA ● Postgrad SA ● Women's Officer
- Self-defence classes

Most welfare provision is handled by the SU, with no professional support. The University has 2 part-time counsellors.

Disabled: There are a few special rooms for wheelchair users but they can't get into most departments. Similarly, although there's a wheelchair lift in the library, the aisles between books are too narrow. Structural changes are taking place *slowly; to be fair, facilities for hearing-impaired students are good.*

FINANCE:
- Average debt: £3,050 ● Access fund: £28,323
- Successful applications (1996): 45

▶▶ Lancashire

see University of Central Lancashire

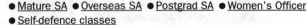

Lancaster University

Lancaster University, University House, Lancaster, LA1 4YW.
Tel: (01524) 65201. Fax: (01524) 846243.
E-mail: ugadmissions@lancaster.ac.uk
Lancaster University Students' Union, Bailrigg, Lancaster,
LA1 4YT. Tel: (01524) 593765. Fax: (01524) 846732.

general

Lancashire is typified by the industrialised urban landscape of the south of the county, but the county town, Lancaster, to the north, is quite a different proposition and only a few miles south of the *luscious* Lake District beyond. Lancaster is hemmed by countryside on most sides and reaches out to Morecambe and Heysham on the north-west coast, 4 miles away. The University is 3 miles from Lancaster and is situated on a large greenfield campus on a hill in the middle of *stunning* countryside. Despite the surroundings, however, many of the buildings were put up during the 60s *and are now looking decidedly naff.* At the centre of the campus is Alexandra Square, a large paved area with a few trees and surrounded by light-coloured brick buildings. Around this square, there are 250 acres of spacious landscaped woods, fields and geometric buildings, including the University's 9 colleges, most of which are undergoing a £26m rebuilding programme.

49% ♂♂♂♂♂♀♀♀♀♀ 51%

Sex ratio(M:F): 49%:51%	Founded: 1964
Full time u'grads: 6,981	Part time: 121
Postgrads: 2,103	Non-degree: 0
Ave course: 3yrs	Ethnic: 3.5%
Private school: 35%	Flunk rate: 19%
Mature students: 18%	Overseas students: 14%
Disabled students: 1.8%	Staff/student ratio: 1:14
Clearing: 12%	

ATMOSPHERE:

The most important factor is the small 'communities within a community' in which most students live: the colleges. The colleges don't conduct admissions (although students can voice a preference), *which means that, in atmosphere, they don't differ enormously. The main difference between them is size,* varying from 450 to 800 undergrads. *The college system is not as strong as, say, Oxbridge; they're not that much more than glorified halls of residence, although most teaching is based in them. The system, combined with the high proportion of privately-educated students who come here to avoid inner-city life, means that Lancaster sometimes feels more like a boarding school than a 90s university. The lack of an on-campus ents facility doesn't help but most students think the hike into town is worth it.*

THE CITY:

- Population: 125,600 ● London: 223miles
- Manchester: 48miles ● Blackpool: 20miles

Lancaster is an *almost quaint* tourist centre dominated by the Ashton Memorial on one hill and the castle on another. At the moment, parts of the castle are used as a prison. Some parts of it are open to the public, including the dungeons, but not the prison cells, *naturally.* The rest of the city goes up and down all over the place and is battered by wind and rain, *but is lovely when the sun dares to shine.* It has the usual facilities like a public library, supermarkets, late night shops, bookshops and the Maritime Museum. Marketgate and the St Nicholas Arcade are the favoured shopping haunts.

TRAVEL:

Trains: Lancaster station, 3 miles from the campus, has direct connections to London (£19), Manchester (£7.50), Birmingham (£18.55) and further afield.
Coaches: National Express services from the campus all over the country including London (£18.50) and Manchester (£4.50).
Car: The M6 bypasses Lancaster from north to south slicing past the edge of the campus. The A6 and A683 go right into the centre. *A car is useful around town, especially for students who live out.*
Ferries: Service from Heysham to Douglas on the Isle of Man.
Hitching: Students have set up a *great* hitching system. There is a special shelter on the campus and an established point in town for pick ups, but these are for trips to and from the University. *For longer journeys the M6 is a good bet.*
Local: There is a *reliable* minibus shuttle service to campus

every 10 minutes (£1 return) and a double decker that runs via the local estates. Bus passes covering the Lancaster area cost £120 for a year.

Taxis: There are ranks at the rail and bus stations, *but they work out expensive.*

Bicycles: *A bike is even better than a car (the fuel is free) although the squash factor from traffic is high.* There are a number of cycle paths.

LIBRARIES & COMPUTERS:
● Books: 1,000,000 ● Study places: 900
● Computer workstations: 1,500

The Library has recently been extended *but students might have preferred the money to be spent on books rather than bricks. Computer provision gets a thumbs-up.*

CAREER PROSPECTS:
● Careers Service ● No of staff: 12full/3part
● Unemployed after 6mths (1995): 6.1%

SPECIAL FEATURES:
● The 1st year of study is very flexible; students study 3 subjects. By the 2nd year, many do a course other than the one for which they originally applied.

FAMOUS ALUMNI:
Richard Allinson (DJ); Simon Smith (rugby player); Gary Waller MP (Con); Peter Whalley and Marvin Close (Coronation Street writers).

FURTHER INFO:
Prospectuses for undergrads, postgrads and mature students (all also available on audio tape), as well as a video. Alternative Prospectus available from SU Welfare Department. Web site (http://www.lancs.ac.uk and http://www.lancs.ac.uk/lusu).

entertainment

THE CITY:
● Price of a pint of beer: £1.60 ● Glass of wine: £1.50

Lancaster has a high proportion of elderly people; the liveliest entertainment is student-centred.

Cinemas: There are 2 cinemas including arty movies at The Dukes Theatre Arts Centre. New 4-screen Apollo at Morecambe.

Theatres: (2) The Dukes Theatre also hosts touring companies; the Grand Theatre is mainly amateur and shows also go on at the Gregson Centre.

Pubs: *Plenty of real ale and friendly olde worlde pubs.* **push***plugs: Water Witch (on the canal, best in summer); Blob Shop; The Priory; Friary & Firkin; Penny Bank; Gallon Drunk Club; Paddy Mulligan's. Avoid Lanky's where there's hostility to studility.*

Clubs/discos/music venues: The Sugarhouse (see below) is the main venue in town. Otherwise, there's Brookes and the Warehouse (mainstream), the Carleton (indie/dance), Springs and the Alex (rock).

Eating out: *Not a vast selection, but all bar the pickiest palates will be satisfied.* **push***plugs: Nawaab Tandoori (excellent value balti); Sultan's (Indian, in a converted church);*

Paulo Gianni's (Italian, student discounts); Whaletale Café (veggie); Marco's; Icky's; Bodrums.

UNIVERSITY:
- <u>Price of a pint of beer: £1.30</u> ● <u>Glass of wine: £1.30</u>

Bars: Each college has a bar, popular with its own students. Cross-fertilisation only usually happens when there's an event on somewhere or students do 'The 9 Hole Golf Course' (a pint in each, ending at their own).

Theatre: The Nuffield Studio is a flexible theatre space for *strong* student productions and visiting companies.

Cinemas: Blockbusters and more are shown 4 times a week by *one of the best equipped* student film clubs in the country.

Clubs/disco: The centre of all action is the Sugarhouse (cap 1,200), owned and run by the Union but situated in town. *3 nights a week the place quakes to some sound sounds*, from the indie of Star to the hard house of Lust which has attracted *serious* guest DJs such as Carl Cox. Time Tunnel is a retro night every other Friday.

Music venues: Again, the Sugarhouse stands out against the culturally bleak landscape, managing to lure names such as Shed Seven, Mansun and the Charlatans.

Food: *Students are spoiled for choice*: there's the Wibbly Wobbly Burger Bar (*we kid you not*) open till midnight, plus Pizetta Republica, Moonlight's Kebabs, Diggles sandwiches, curries, chips and even real food on the go all day.

Others: Most weeks, there's something in at least 1 of the college bars (competitions, theme parties, etc) and each year, the SU puts on a Graduation Ball. The last week of the summer term is 'Extrav Week' - *major party time*, culminating in a 'Summer Extrav' at each college (6pm-6am, drink, bands, DJs, drink, karaoke, food and drink).

social & political

LANCASTER UNIVERSITY STUDENTS' UNION (LUSU):
- <u>6 sabbaticals</u> ● <u>Turnout at last ballot: 31%</u>
- <u>NUS member</u>

LUSU has the ground floor of the plush, new Slaidburn House to administer its little empire. Representation, entertainments and services are also provided on a college level through Junior Common Rooms (JCRs). *Students here are more politically aware than some we could mention, and the SU rouses rabbles on their behalf.*

SU FACILITIES:
LUSU provides 2 general shops, a 2nd-hand bookshop, drugstore and, of course, the Sugarhouse. Also around the campus there are banks, a post office, petrol station, bookshops (1st and 2nd hand), hairdresser, chemist, newsagent, supermarket, bakery, travel agency and a few smaller shops. Each college also has a JCR.

CLUBS (NON SPORTING):
Alternative Music; Backpacker; Ballroom Dancing; Buddhist; Hellenic; Green Action; Jugglers; Motoring; Roleplay.

OTHER ORGANISATIONS:
'SCAN' (Student Comment And News) is the union-published student newspaper, with a sabbatical editor, and Bailrigg FM

broadcasts around campus. There's a full-time Rag coordinator and last year over £10,000 was raised.

RELIGIOUS:
● <u>Chaplains</u>
There is a non-denominational Chaplaincy Centre on campus which hosts visits from ministers of most religions, as well as a new Muslim prayer room. There are various places of worship in town including a number of different churches and a mosque.

PAID WORK:
Nothing unusual except some tourist jobs in summer; the SU jobshop has a minimum wage policy.

sports

● <u>Recent successes: football</u>
One of the clearest expressions of college differences is through the intercollegiate sporting competitions for the Carter Shield; when they gang up and take on other universities the story is less impressive, but not disastrous. Every year the University fights for the Roses Cup with <u>York University</u>.

SPORTS FACILITIES:
18.2 acres of playing fields (*which allegedly provide a fine harvest of magic mushrooms in season*); all-weather pitches; sports hall; 8 each of tennis and squash courts; croquet lawn; bowling green; 25m swimming pool; climbing wall; gymnasium; multigym; sauna & solarium; gym; weights rooms (male and female); dance studio; athletics area; golf practice area; archery range; floodlit hard playing area; and the University's Lake Carter. Locally, a golf course and the River Lune (where the University has a boat house). The Sailing Club uses the Glasson Dock marina.

SPORTING CLUBS:
American Football; Freefall; Frisbee; Kick Boxing; Korfball; Lacrosse; Martial Arts; Rowing; Windsurfing.

accommodation

IN COLLEGE:
● <u>Self-catering: 52%</u> ● <u>Cost: £33-55(31-38wks)</u>
Availability: All 1st years live in their colleges as do nearly half of finalists. 2nd years are almost entirely on their own, although there are no guarantees for students coming through clearing. Only about 2% share and this includes family groups. Corridors in the colleges are split into single sex areas. There are 40 rooms with en suite bathrooms at Cartmel College (costing £47 a week) - most are taken by overseas students. Alexandra Hall in town is used by postgrads. A head tenancy scheme provides 600 places, too.
Car parking: Limited free parking 5 to 10 minutes from the colleges. Even more limited permit parking nearer, but 1st years are not allowed to bring cars.

EXTERNALLY:
● <u>Ave rent: £38</u>
Availability: *The best places are Bowerham (convenient), Galgate (10mins walk) and around Blade and Dale Streets (students-ville), but the Marsh Estate and Rylands should be*

avoided. Appropriate accommodation in Lancaster is getting easier to find but a few students still find themselves in Morecambe, 4 miles away. In this instance a car comes in handy.

Housing help: The Accommodation Office is run jointly by the University and LUSU and provides a vacancy board, a list of recommended landlords, newsletter, approval scheme and standard contracts.

welfare

SERVICES:

● Creche ● Nightline ● Lesbian & Gay Society
● Mature SA ● Overseas SA ● Minibus ● Women's Officer

LUSU's Welfare Officer works in conjunction with University staff to provide help and advice with all manner of tear-jerkers. The University provides a counselling service with 7 full-time staff and a campus clinic with a medic; the Union has 4 counsellors. There's also a student parents group.

Disabled: *The University has worked wonders in improving access on campus,* earning itself a Queen's Anniversary Award for special needs provisons. There are ramps all over the place, taped information available for sight-impaired students and a loop system in lecture halls for the hearing impaired.

FINANCE:

● Ave debt: £950 ● Access fund: £181,759
● Successful applications (1997): 499

Each college administers its own hardship fund for loans and gifts. There's also a *good* selection of scholarships and bursaries for academic merit.

University of Leeds

The University of Leeds, Leeds, LS2 9JT.
Tel: (0113) 233 2332. Fax: (0113) 233 3991.
E-mail: prospectus@leeds.ac.uk
Leeds University Union, PO Box 157, Leeds, LS1 1UH.
Tel: (0113) 243 9071. Fax: (0113) 244 8786. E-mail: comms@union.leeds.ac.uk

general

From the top of the virginally white Parkinson Building clock tower, which is the University's landmark, it's possible to see Leeds City Centre, the *tidy* terraces of the inner city, the *sprawling, crawling* suburbs and the tangled spaghetti of by-passes, ring roads and the M1. Casting eyes beyond the city boundaries, the southern edge of the Yorkshire moors loom to the north. To the south and west, there are few green spaces separating Leeds from Bradford, Wakefield and Sheffield. Although founded in the late 19th century, the University has undergone spasmodic periods of growth, mainly in the 30s and

60s, which has created a campus which is *the architectural equivalent of Bombay Mix.* Together with <u>Leeds Metropolitan University</u>, the University forms a massive 'student land' conurbation of homes, halls and other academic buildings.

48% ♂♂♂♂♂ ♀♀♀♀♀ 52%	
Sex ratio(M:F): 48%:52%	Founded: 1887
Full time u'grads: 16,981	Part time: 943
Postgrads: 5,193	Non-degree: 0
Ave course: 3yrs	Ethnic: 7.8%
Private school: 23.6%	Flunk rate: 15%
Mature students: 16.2%	Overseas students: 10.1%
Disabled students: 8.7%	Staff/student ratio: 1:8
Clearing: 4%	

ATMOSPHERE:

With so many examples, it's difficult to draw a very exact picture of the Leeds University student. In such a vibrant, frantic city (Leeds' serious social scene has usurped Manchester's) the prevailing relaxed attitude is odd. A healthy scepticism, bordering on apathy, abounds in virtually epidemic proportions and an observer more cruel than push *might suggest that few students consider anything deeper than the bottom of their glass. But appearances can be deceptive and the large Union Building is always busy.*

THE CITY:

● <u>Population: 674,400</u> ● <u>Manchester: 40miles</u>
● <u>London : 189miles</u>

Although the bombs of 2 world wars missed the city, the 60s developers and town planners didn't and Leeds' one-way system provides endless entertainment. On tour, the frustrated driver will trundle round in circles, passing *glorious* Victorian civic buildings - the Town Hall, City Museum, Henry Moore Gallery and The Grand Theatre (home to Opera North). The driver, however, will miss the semi-pedestrianised, bustling main street, known as the Headrow, *the site of every local amenity a student could ever want and many they wouldn't. Soft Southerners shouldn't write Leeds off as a home to coal-munching whippet-breeders; it's a vibrant, youthful city, with some of the best clubs and venues in the country and even its own branch of Harvey Nick's. Fabulous, dahling...*

TRAVEL:

Trains: Leeds rail station is the centre of the West Yorkshire metro train network which serves all the local Yorkshire towns (Bradford, Wakefield, Sheffield and York). Many direct services operate further afield to, for example, London (£32.35), Manchester (£8.60) and more.
Coaches: National Express to London (£13.75), Edinburgh (£22) and other destinations. Also served by Blueline.
Car: 10mins off the M1 and on the M62 to Manchester. The A64 runs to the nearby A1, *but a car is unnecessary for local travel, due to the good public transport, and may get confusing with the introduction of the new 'high occupancy vehicle lane' system.*

Air: Leeds/Bradford Airport for inland and European flights.
Hitching: *Excellent prospects for long distance on the A1, M1 and M62, but as ever, there are safer ways of getting around.*
Local: *Very reliable, frequent trains and buses.* The maximum off-peak fare is 64p and a monthly student Metrocard (bus and train) is £31.30.
Taxis: *Quick and efficient.*
Bicycles: *There are cycle paths in many areas, but the place is too hilly and fume-filled and has too many light-fingered locals to make cycling a pleasurable experience.*

LIBRARIES & COMPUTERS:
- Books: 2,500,000 ● Study places: 3,500
- Computer workstations: 1,462

There are 3 main libraries and 7 departmental ones. The Brotherton library is closed on Sundays. 24hr access to computers for postgrads only.

CAREER PROSPECTS:
- Careers Service ● No of staff: 17full/6part
- Unemployed after 6mths (1996): 10.5%

Apart from the *highly efficient* Careers Service, there's also SLUGS, the Society for Leeds Under-Employed Graduates, an independent support group.

FAMOUS ALUMNI:
Steve Bell (cartoonist); Barry Cryer (writer/comedian); Andrew Eldritch (Sisters of Mercy); Gavin Esler (BBC journalist); David Gedge (Wedding Present); Andy Kershaw (DJ); Mystic Meg (who only got a 2(ii), so she obviously couldn't forecast her exam questions); Nick Owen ('Anne and...'); Gerald Ratner (former crap jeweller); Clare Short MP (Lab); Jack Straw MP (Lab, ex-SU president); Nicholas Witchell (BBC newscaster, once editor of 'Leeds Student').

FURTHER INFO:
Prospectuses for undergrads and postgrads, a guide for mature students and a web site (http://www.admin.leeds.ac.uk). The SU produces a free alternative prospectus.

entertainment

CITY:
- Price of a pint of beer: £2.05

Check out the 'Planet Leeds' freesheet for listings.
Cinemas: (5) 2 independent single-screen flea pits, 1 multiplex, 1 Odeon, 1 MGM. A new Warner Brothers complex is also being built.
Theatres: (4) Everything from grand opera at the Grand to Alan Ayckbourn and amateur dramatics. The West Yorkshire Playhouse is an *excellent* modern repertory theatre complex.
Pubs: This is the home of Yorkshire bitter *and there are few local pubs that don't serve a decent pint. Serious imbibers should contemplate the Otley Run, a 14-pub crawl of mythical proportions, including The Faversham (aka 'The Fav'), The Eldon, The Skyrack, The Original Oak and The Dry Dock (on a boat); or try the Royal Park; Hyde Park; Headingly Taps.*
Clubs/discos: *Leeds is an all-night city thanks to a tolerant council licensing policy; it's also home to some of the*

trendiest house flavours of the moment, if you can squeeze past the queues. The **push** posse is on the guestlist for: Fruit Cupboard; Majestyk; It's Obvious at the Warehouse; Up Yer Ronson at Europa; Back To Basics at the Pleasure Rooms.

Music venues: Leeds is a compulsory stop shop for touring bands from big names to the biggest and there's a thriving live scene. **push**plugs: T&C; Duchess of York; Irish Centre (indie).

Eating out: Somewhere as large and cosmopolitan as Leeds is guaranteed to have grub-stops to satisfy all palates and pockets. **push**plugs: Theo's (kebabs and the best lentilburgers in the world); Zacks (pizza/pasta buffet £4); Sala (good value Thai); Original Oak (pub lunches); Clock Café; Grove Café; Manuela's; Dino's.

UNIVERSITY:

- <u>Glass of wine: £1.50</u> ● <u>Price of a pint of beer: £1.15</u>

Bars: With 3 bars in the Union and at least 1 in most of the halls, students are in little danger of dying of sobriety. All are popular, especially the vast, sweaty Old Bar (cap 1,000). The Harvey Milk Bar doubles as the main club venue.

Cinemas: 2 mainstream movies a week.

Theatres: (3) Leeds holds its own among thespians with a workshop theatre and a selection of other potential venues. Edinburgh is a regular summer jaunt for the luvvies.

Clubs/discos/music venues: The Harvey Milk Bar (cap 450, £2) hosts club nights 3 nights a week, from indie to Irish. The live band scene isn't quite as pumping as the one at their upstart neighbours (<u>Leeds Metropolitan University</u>), probably because they can't sell beer in the gig venue and hence the concentration on clubs, but the Wannadies, Eat Static and the Chemical Brothers played in recent months.

Food: The Refectory's the best bet for full and filling meals, while the Mouat Jones coffee bar deals with all snack requirements. The bars also serve up a good range of eats.

Cabaret: Comedy every fortnight in Harvey's Milk Bar from the likes of Mark Lamarr, Hugh Lennon and Rolf 'can you tell what it is yet' Harris.

Others: Balls bounce all over the place, the biggest being the Freshers' do at the T&C and the graduation shindig (over 4,000 people).

.... social 2 political

LEEDS UNIVERSITY UNION:

- <u>13 sabbaticals</u> ● <u>Turnout at last ballot: 5%</u>
- <u>NUS member</u>

Many other students would be delighted to have an operation on the scale of LUU to represent them but size brings its own problems, not least a slight sense of remoteness from the experience of the average non-hack. Still, as long as the beer's cheap and the ents are entertaining most are happy with the set-up. Political activity is on the up, with a recent occupation of the Grants Office by fee protesters causing various shades of havoc on the Leeds streets.

SU FACILITIES:

Every facility but the kitchen sink - oh, no, we take that back, there's one of those too: bars; 6 cafeterias; a coffee bar;

> **❝The central computer system of the University of Wales crashed recently, when a student downloaded too much hardcore pornography.❞**

darkroom; opticians; minibus & car hire; ABTA travel agency; book/stationery shops; Lloyds Bank with cashpoint; hair salon; photocopying; photo booth; games and video machines; TV lounges; meeting rooms; launderette and dry-cleaning. A planned extension to the Union building will provide another venue for 1999-2000.

CLUBS (NON SPORTING):

AEGEE; Agroculture; AIESEC; Africa Direct; Alternative Cycling; Artificial Life; Arts; Backstage; Ballet; Ballroom Dancing; Boardgames and Wargames; Buddhist Meditation; Caballe and Meditation; Chao Thai; Chinese; Egyptian; Emmanuel; Euphonic; Hellenic; Hiking; Himalayas; Hindu; Iranian; Juggling; Kabal; Lemsip (satirical publication); Live Role Playing; LSR (student radio); LUST (theological, funnily enough); Malaysian; Massoc; Model UN; Motorcycle; Monkeyhouse; Music Theatre; Navigators; Norseman; Pakistani; Pelicans (creative writing); Psychedelic & Trash; RCP; Scottish Dance; Scout & Guide; Sign Language; Singaporean; SIS; Soka Gokai Buddhist; Spanish, Portuguese & Latin American; Speleological; Spurs Supporters; Stage Musical; Student Workers Aid for Bosnia; St Johns Ambulance; Taoist Arts; Theatre Group & Performing; Tibet Support; Use Your Head; Wolves Supporters.

OTHER ORGANISATIONS:

'Leeds Student' is the award-winning University and <u>Leeds Metropolitan University</u> joint weekly newspaper, with a sabbatical editor and 30,000 readers. The Union publishes a newsletter ('Action'). The Network Society runs radio and TV stations and LSR (radio) is forming a new sabbatical post. The charity Rag is also a co-production with Leeds Met. Leeds Student Community Action has a sabbatical co-ordinator and runs 30 *effective* local help projects.

RELIGIOUS:

There are *excellent* facilities for 99 different denominations and religions and the largest Jewish student community outside Manchester.

PAID WORK:

There's the usual bar work and bouncing at Union ents and a joblink scheme run by the SU.

 ## sports

● <u>Recent successes: American football, women's hockey</u>

The facilities are there for sporting success and there are more than enough healthy hopefuls with lycra bottoms and participation is fairly high.

SPORTS FACILITIES:

The Leeds Sports Centre provides facilities for everything from weight training to ballet and from table tennis to martial arts, all in a large sports centre. The Weetwood playing ground, 4 miles away, has 14 soccer, 7 hockey, 6 rugby and 5 cricket pitches. There's also an astroturf football pitch, 6 tennis courts and the Lawnswood playing fields. The Sports Centre has a climbing wall, but the Yorkshire Dales offer the real thing. *The solarium, however, is the most reliable sunshine source round here.*

SPORTING CLUBS:

Aikido; American Football; Boat; Bridge; Gymnastics and Trampoline; Hang Gliding; Lacrosse; Paragliding; Samurai Jiu Jitsu; Snooker; Sport Parachute; Surfing; Tennis; Ten Pin Bowling; Triathlon; Ultimate Frisbee; Windsurfing.

ATTRACTIONS:

In the heartland of rugby league, with Leeds United at Elland Road, international cricket at Headingley and swimming facilities only a paddle away, Leeds is fully equipped with all the mod cons.

accommodation

IN COLLEGE:

- Catered: 11% ● Cost: £63-85(31wks)
- Self-catering: 30% ● Cost: £33-48(40wks)

Availability: All 1st years who want to can live in a variety of *highly satisfactory* halls. The older halls, such as Bodington and Devonshire (both catered), require about 10% of their students to share (for whom rents are lower). The self-catering flats hold between 4 and 14 students. Students do complain about odd restrictions (against posters, in some cases) and cleaners who arrive at inopportune moments.

Car parking: *Expensive, unnecessary and in short supply.*

EXTERNALLY:

- Ave rent: £38

Most students stick to the large quantities of late 19th century back-to-back terraced housing in variable condition. The Unipol code of practice has sorted out a few problems with unscrupulous landlords. *Students who want to stay in one piece are advised to try Headingley and Hyde Park and avoid Chapeltown.*

Housing help: UniPol (*which should change its name to UniUni*) - the joint University and Leeds Metropolitan University SUs' housing service - provides some help and advice by keeping tabs on the worst landlords. With 10 full- and 4 part-time staff, *it's a dream scheme.*

welfare
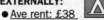

SERVICES:

- Creche ● Lesbian & Gay Society
- Overseas SA ● Women's Minibus ● Women's Officers
- Self-defence classes

With a student health service (6 full-time medics, nurses and a psychiatrist), as well as 4 full-time and 5 part-time counsellors, the University is *well-equipped* but somewhere this size needs to be.

Disabled: *The University and Union are making efforts to improve access and have shown a willingness to adapt rooms, provide equipment and so on, as necessary. However, despite all these efforts, the campus does not lend itself to easy access being on a hill with many steps and level changes.*

FINANCE:
● Ave debt: £1,850 ● Access fund: £344,961
● Successful applications (1997): 572
The Union offers emergency loans of up to £100 and there's a
range of budgeting advice, debt counselling and even help with
bankruptcy.

Leeds Metropolitan University

● *Formerly Leeds Polytechnic*
Leeds Metropolitan University, Calverley Street, Leeds,
LS1 3HE. Tel: (0113) 283 3113. Fax: (0113) 283 3114.
E-mail: course-enquiries@lmu.ac.uk
Leeds Metropolitan University Students' Union, Calverley
Street, Leeds, LS1 3HE. Tel: (0113) 243 0171.
Fax: (0113) 275 2973.

General

Right in the middle of Leeds, there is a university. Right next
door is another one. Somewhere one ends and the next
begins, *but it's not easy to tell where.* Like its older sibling,
the Met's buildings are a *jumble* of old and new, but it centres
on 7 concrete tower blocks. The central building is a 60s
block *with all the beauty of a bulldog licking a thistle and the
colour and character of John Major's pants.* Escape comes at
the Beckett Park Campus, 3 miles out in a *picturesque*
wooded site arranged *tastefully* around a cricket square.

50% ♂♂♂♂♂♂♀♀♀♀♀ 50%	
Sex ratio(M:F): 50%:50%	Founded: 1970
Full time u'grads: 11,000	Part time: 12,000
Postgrads: 690	Non-degree: 3,016
Ave course: 3yrs	Ethnic: 9%
Private school: n/a	Flunk rate: n/a
Mature students: 54%	Overseas students: 2%
Disabled students: 1.1%	Staff/student ratio: 1:17
Clearing: 20%	

ATMOSPHERE:
*Not a place to take itself too seriously, Leeds Met students
know the meaning of fun (**n.** a source of enjoyment,
amusement, diversion, etc - Collins Dictionary) and there's a
hectic party atmosphere often lacking in institutions with such
a high proportion of mature students.*

THE SITES:
City Centre: Brunswick and Calverley sites. 300 yards from
the civic centre and 200 yards from *the most unattractive
supermarket outside Moscow.*
Beckett Park Campus: 3 miles from the main site, Beckett

Park is in 100 acres of woodland and parkland, affording panoramic views across Leeds. The main building dates back to 1913. Beckett Park includes various departments (including education, IT, law, sports sciences and languages), accommodation for staff and students and the University's main sports facilities. There's a bus service between here and the main site every 6-10 minutes.

THE CITY: see <u>University of Leeds</u>

TRAVEL: see <u>University of Leeds</u>

LIBRARIES & COMPUTERS:
- <u>Books: 500,000</u> ● <u>Study places: 2,300</u>
- <u>Computer workstations: 500</u>

There are 3 main libraries. The Learning Centre at Beckett Park has a selection of sports and leisure volumes, as well as the more academic stuff. *Computer facilities okay but students still complain of difficulties getting access to books.*

CAREER PROSPECTS:
- <u>Careers Service</u> ● <u>No of staff: 4full/4part</u>
- <u>Unemployed after 6mths (1996): 9.8%</u>

The Careers Service runs development workshops, offering help with work experience and job applications, and there's also a jobshop aimed at finding temporary work during term-time.

SPECIAL FEATURES:
- 13-week autumn and spring terms allow students to get away with a 3rd term of just 8 weeks hard labour in the summer.

FAMOUS ALUMNI:
Marc Almond (singer); Glen Baxter (cartoonist); Betty Boothroyd MP (Speaker); Peter Cattaneo (film director); Ron Pickering (late sports commentator); Eric Pickles MP (Con).

FURTHER INFO:
Prospectus for undergraduates and postgrads, video and a web site (http://www.lmu.ac.uk).

entertainment

THE CITY: see <u>University of Leeds</u>

UNIVERSITY:
- <u>Price of a pint of beer: £1.68</u> ● <u>Glass of wine: £1</u>

Bars: (4) The Kirkstall Brewery (capacity 1,000) spreads over 2 floors and there's also the Beckett Park Bar (450, *popular for post-match celebrations/sorrow-drowning*), the City Bar (1,400) which has a late licence 3 nights a week and the SU bar *which looks like a gents.*

Theatre: There's a University-run studio theatre.

Clubs/discos: 3 club nights a week, *from the indie mayhem of OTT to the dance/pull-fest that is the imaginatively titled Saturday Night.*

Music venues: Recently in the Ents Hall: Kula Shaker, Divine Comedy, Roni Size, Shirehorses, Spiritualised, Stereolab, Fun Lovin' Criminals. *Leeds Met has a deserved reputation as a major indie tour date, overshadowing its more staid neighbour.* Local bands play free gigs at Beckett Park.

Cabaret: The SU occasionally attracts some *top notch* giggle jugglers: Craig Charles and Rob Newman recently packed the Ents Hall.

Food: *The main refectory 'The Depot' offers good value for limited dosh and the SU coffee bar deals with the munchies. The Grapevine is a posher affair where the lecturers hang out.* There's also a refectory at Beckett Park, also confusingly called 'The Depot'.

.... social & political

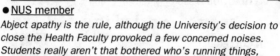

LEEDS METROPOLITAN UNIVERSITY STUDENTS' UNION:
● 6 sabbaticals ● Turnout at last ballot: 5%
● NUS member

Abject apathy is the rule, although the University's decision to close the Health Faculty provoked a few concerned noises. Students really aren't that bothered who's running things, though; they're more concerned with who scored the winning try and whose round it is.

SU FACILITIES:
The main facilities are at the City campus where there are 2 bars, 5 coffee bars, 2 print rooms and 2 shops. At Beckett Park, there's not just another bar, but also a cafe, bank, photo booth, games and video machines, pool tables, TV lounge and disco and a juke box.

CLUBS (NON SPORTING):
Bellringing; Games; Hellenic; Juggling; Malaysian; Sikh; Travel.

OTHER ORGANISATIONS:
The SU produces a fortnightly newsletter, 'Headliner'. The award-winning and widely read 'Leeds Student' newspaper, run jointly with University of Leeds Union along with the radio station, *deserves both to win awards and to be widely read.* The Rag is also a joint effort and the Action group, headed by a sabbatical officer, does all manner of good stuff in the local community.

RELIGIOUS:
● 2 chaplains (Christian)
Students can also share 6 other chaplains with University of Leeds. There is a Muslim prayer room.

PAID WORK:
Try robbing a bank or the SU for bar work and/or bouncing.

.... sports

● Recent successes: acrobatics
This lot plays to win. To use facilities there's a single charge of £15 per year.

SPORTS FACILITIES:
The *excellent* facilities (all at Beckett Park) include the

❛The Warwick University sports teams' anthem is called 'Warwick Wanking Men Are We'.❜

Carnegie Regional Gymnastics Centre, a swimming pool, squash courts, athletics and playing fields including 12 football pitches, 4 rugby, 1 lacrosse, 2 synthetic floodlit and 1 5-a-side pitch, a multigym, weights room, running track, tennis courts, and regular aerobics classes. These facilities were acquired through lottery funding which means that they are also open to the public. The city has its own leisure centre, pool, sauna, ski slope, a lake and river, a bowling green and golf course.

SPORTING CLUBS:
Acrobatics; Snowboarding.

ATTRACTIONS: see <u>University of Leeds</u>

accommodation

IN COLLEGE:
● <u>Self-catering: 20%</u> ● <u>Cost: £38-59(41wks)</u>
Availability: With the addition of the Kirkstall Brewery complex most 1st years can be accommodated; the rest are handled by Unipol, not an international crime-fighting agency, but the Leeds universities' *first-rate* joint student property management scheme.
Car parking: Plenty of parking at Beckett Park, but almost none at the city campus.

EXTERNALLY: see <u>University of Leeds</u>
Housing help: See <u>University of Leeds</u> for more details of Unipol. Leeds Met also has its own Accommodation Office which has in the past successfully avoided any students-on-gym-floors scenarios.

welfare

SERVICES:
● <u>Lesbian & Gay Society</u> ● <u>Overseas SA</u>
● <u>Minibus</u> ● <u>Women's Officer</u> ● <u>Self-defence classes</u>
The University's 2 student health centres (1 at each campus) are staffed by nurses. There are also 2 full- and 2 part-time counsellors, with additional specialists for disability, finance and other issues.
Disabled: *Despite a fine array of Equal Opportunity policies and a Disability Support service, access is poor.* Unipol (see above) makes an extra effort to accommodate students with disabilities. There are induction loops at Beckett Park.

FINANCE:
● <u>Ave debt: £2,400</u> ● <u>Access fund: £225,000</u>
● <u>Successful applications (1997): 900</u>
Debt counselling is available from the Budget Advisor and 2 part-timers.

❝According to York University regulations students can be chucked out if they eat the ducks that live on the campus lake.❞

University of Leicester

University of Leicester, University Road, Leicester, LE1 7RH.
Tel: (0116) 252 5281. Fax: (0116) 252 2447.
E-mail: admissions@le.ac.uk
Leicester University Students' Union, Percy Gee Building,
University Road, Leicester, LE1 7RH. Tel: (0116) 223 1111.

General

Leicester (along with Nottingham to the north, and Northampton to the south) is one of the principal cities of the East Midlands. *But it doesn't really feel all that big. It's something about the attitude of the people, which is generally full of small-town small-talk friendliness. The suburbs are attractive,* but the centre, steeped in history, has a few less salubrious quarters. Parts have been pedestrianised, mainly the shopping areas. 1 mile from the centre, flanked by a large cemetery and the *rather pretty* Victoria Park, is the city's older University. It's a mixture of *pleasant* old architecture, such as the original Georgian building, and new-fangled post-war *horrors.* 3 of these are particularly prominent on the skyline: the Attenborough Building, 18 storeys high, which won a design award *(but then, Germany won Euro 96);* the 10-storey Charles Wilson Building; and the Engineering block, *which looks like it's got a crane sticking out of the top* and which is Grade II listed (having won an award in the 1960s for its use of aluminium).

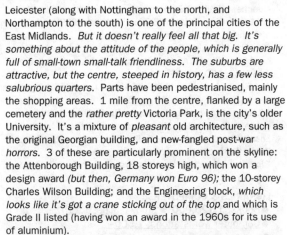

48% ♂♂♂♂♂ ♀♀♀♀♀ **52%**

Sex ratio(M:F): 48%:52%	Founded: 1921
Full time u'grads: 7,164	Part time: 64
Postgrads: 1,493	Non-degree: 0
Ave course: 3yrs	Ethnic: n/a
Private school: n/a	Flunk rate: n/a
Mature students: 14%	Overseas students: 10%
Disabled students: 3.4%	Staff/student ratio: 1:12
Clearing: 9.7%	

ATMOSPHERE:
Students are into having a good time, whether on the playing fields or in the bars. The campus is surrounded by much greenery, heightening the impression that students are slightly divorced from the rest of town, physically as well as socially.

THE CITY:
● Population: 270,600 ● London: 98miles
● Birmingham: 33miles ● Nottingham: 21miles

Leicester is large enough to have all the local amenities that a student grant can bear, yet small enough to have some kind of homeliness. Apart from the 700-year old market place, local highlights include a bookshop on Market St, the largest open-air market in Europe (for clothes, fruit and veg, fish and so on), the 2nd hand clothes stalls in Silver Arcade, Malcolm Arcade and Silver St, and Gary Lineker's dad's fruit stall. A more *touristy* tour takes in the Newarke House Museum, the City Museum & Art Gallery, Snibston Discovery Park and Rutland Water (very popular with students in summer). There's a large Asian population, adding further variety to the culinary and sartorial availables. *Leicester may not be the hottest nightspot in the land,* but Birmingham and London are close enough for day trips.

TRAVEL:

Trains: Leicester Station operates many services direct all over the Midlands and the rest of the country, including London (£21.45), Birmingham (£6.65), Edinburgh (£37.80), Bristol, Leeds and beyond.

Coaches: National Express and other services to London (£11.75), Birmingham (£3.70), Edinburgh (£29) and elsewhere.

Car: The M1 skirts the edge of Leicester and the M69 connects with the A5 from the city's outskirts. Also, the A6, A46, A47, A50 and A607.

Air: Flights from East Midlands Airport (16 miles away) inland and to Europe.

Hitching: *Excellent* for London or Birmingham. Catch a bus out to near the M1 or M69 motorway junctions.

Local: Buses are reliable, well used and run until 11pm.

Taxis: *Fairly cheap and handy after pub-shut.*

Bicycles: Leicester, 'Britain's First Environmental City', is steadily introducing cycle ways and there are racks on campus.

LIBRARIES & COMPUTERS:

● Books: 1,125,000 ● Study places: 1,115
● Computer workstations: 1,500+

The University has 3 libraries: the Main Library; Clinical Science; and School of Education.

CAREER PROSPECTS:

● Careers Service ● No of staff: 5full/1part
● Unemployed after 6mths (1996): 4.6%

The Student Employment Centre operates a jobshop.

FAMOUS ALUMNI:

Malcolm Bradbury (writer); Sue Cook (TV presenter); Heather Couper (TV astronomer); Michael Jack MP (Con); Bob Mortimer (comedian); Pete McCarthy (comedian, TV presenter); Michael Nicholson (ITN newscaster); Tony Underwood (rugby player); Sir Alan Walters (economist).

FURTHER INFO:

Prospectuses for undergrads and postgrads. Alternative prospectus from the SU. CD-ROM and web site (http://www.le.ac.uk).

entertainment

TOWN:

● Price of a pint of beer: £1.70 ● Glass of wine: £1.70

Cinemas: The 8-screen Odeon and the Cannon for mainstream movies, a Warner multiplex, the Phoenix Arts centre for arthouse flicks and Bollywood for Asian epics.

Theatres: (2) The Haymarket hosts populist productions and touring companies and, again, the Phoenix for fringe and cult productions.

Pubs: push*plugs: Fullback & Firkin; O'Neill's; Bar Gaudi (cocktails); Swan & Rushes; Loded Dog. Don't bother with the Braunstone (anti-student) or the Angel (unless you support Leicester City FC).*

Clubs/discos: *Leicester has enough clubs to suit all but the most ardent tail feather shaker although some aren't up to much.* push*plugs: Planet (trance/acid, big queues); le Palais de Danse (charty, hired by SU for Rush night); Attik (ambient/drum & bass); The Fan Club and Alcatraz (indie); Streetlife (gay); Junction 21 (hip-hop, dub); Flaming Colossas (big name DJs); Mosquito Coast (NUS night indie/retro).*

Music venues: De Montfort Hall, an *important* indie venue, shouldn't be confused with De Montfort University, which is also a *good* sound spot, as is Granby Halls. The Charlotte and the Shed have smaller indie bands.

Eating out: *Leicester's a hot favourite for curry fiends - among the dozens of cumin attractions Akash, Shireen and Manzel's stand out but there are plenty more. Other* push*plugs: Que Pasa (Mexican); Lynn's Café (greasy spoon); Café Brussels; Bread & Roses (veggie); Dino's (Italian); Fat Cat Café.*

Other: Leicester's numerous ethnic communities add to the fun with annual Caribbean and Mela (Asian) carnivals and Diwali (Hindu) celebrations. There's also a popular and successful comedy festival.

UNIVERSITY:
● <u>Price of a pint of beer: £1.00</u> ● <u>Glass of wine: £1.50</u>

Bars: There are 3 bars: the Venue; Redfearn Bar (cap 500, *popular at lunchtimes*); the Asylum (cap 300, *incredible achievement of seeming both gothy and futuristic at the same time*); and the Oasis Bar in the Venue.

Theatres: *Student drama is very strong*, with 3 productions a year, including regular Edinburgh Fringe shows.

Cinemas: The Film Society flashes mainstream flicks every Monday in Queen's Hall.

Clubs/discos: The Venue (1,600) is the *jumpingest* joint 4 nights a week, mostly chart/dance except for Thursday's 80s night. Guest DJs have included Danny Rampling and Jeremy Healy in recent months.

Music venues: The Venue can boast a *healthy* visitors' list, including Space, Sleeper, Catatonia and Kula Shaker.

Food: There are a number of food outlets including Snappers Diner, overlooking Victoria Park; Loafer's does fast food at lunchtimes; the Venue Food Court does cheap and cheerful stuff while the Café Piazza has a *pricey* continental style.

❝The Fine Art Building at Staffordshire University was painted bright pink and covered with song lyrics as a final year project.❞

Others: Regular balls throughout the year, culminating in the Graduation do.

social & political

LEICESTER UNIVERSITY STUDENTS' UNION:

● 5 sabbaticals ● Turnout at last ballot: 10%
● NUS member

The SU is pretty down-to-earth and concentrates on organising some successful services - issues revolve around awareness and information rather than all that boring politics stuff.

SU FACILITIES:
The Percy Gee Building contains a general shop, 2 bars, travel agency, Queen's Hall (cap 800), TV rooms (including satellite), launderette, snooker room, 2 banks with cashpoints, print shop, Asylum nightclub, weekly market stalls, video machines, squash court, mature and overseas students' rooms.

CLUBS (NON SPORTING):
Anglican; Ballroom Dancing; Cheezy Funk; Choral; Clubbing; Contact; Cyprus Society; Cyprus Turkish; Debating; Games; Hellenic; Indie; Juggling; Knighton Morris; Lawyers Christian; LEAF; League Against Cruel Sports; Literary; Live Role Playing; Malaysian; Murth; Navigators; Off The Page; Old Coffee Bar (student bands); Role Play; Scouts & Guides; Turkish; Wind Band.

OTHER ORGANISATIONS:
Apart from 'Ripple', the independent student newspaper (fortnightly), there's also Leicester University Student Television or LUST for short and LUSH FM. The charity Rag has a sabbatical organiser which explains the £35,000 raised last year. 'Contact' is the student community group which runs about 10 local help projects with up to 400 student volunteers.

RELIGIOUS:
● 8 chaplains
The Gatehouse Chaplaincy Centre welcomes students of all denominations. Locally, there are churches and places of worship for every brand of god-fearer including a Jain Centre, unique outside the Indian sub-continent.

PAID WORK:
Apart from bar work, etc, there's the Walkers Crisps factory.

sports

● Recent successes: riding, badminton, karate

The sports facilities are worth checking out. To do so, students have got to get a Sports Card (£25). Loughborough University, 10 miles up the A6, takes most of the honours round here, but this lot can pull a few rabbits out of the hat when required. Didn't realise that was a competitive sport but never mind...

SPORTS FACILITIES:
The main sports ground is at the Oadby halls of residence, where there is also a sports hall. In addition, there is a sports hall and fitness club on the main campus. Between them, they provide 25 acres of playing fields, *one of the best* athletics tracks in the Midlands, 2 sports halls, an all-weather pitch, 14 tennis courts and a health and fitness club. Leicester adds a croquet lawn/bowling green, 7 swimming

pools, golf course, ski slope, skating rink, basketball centre, sauna and solarium, and the River Soar.

SPORTING CLUBS:

Caving; Fell-walking; Jiu Jitsu; Lacrosse; Mountaineering; Rowing; Smallbore Rifle; Ultimate Frisbee.

ATTRACTIONS:

Apart from last year's *unlikely* Coca-Cola Cup-holders Leicester City FC, there are the Tigers (rugby), the Riders (basketball), the Panthers (American Football), Leicestershire Cricket Club, a Cycling Stadium and the racecourse (horses).

accommodation

IN COLLEGE:

- Catered: 26% ● Cost: £58-77(30wks)
- Self-catering: 29% ● Cost: £37(39wks)

Availability: 1st years are guaranteed a place in University accommodation if they want it. About 25% stay in for their 2nd year and a few finalists. The choice is between the 5 catered halls at Oadby, 2½ miles from the campus (60s blocks and Edwardian houses), the hall at Knighton (halfway to Oadby) or the self-catering student houses, mainly at Knighton, but some nearer the campus. 10% of students in halls have to share rooms and all halls are mixed, although sexes are split into corridors. The rooms themselves are a *decent* size - some are very new and have en suite facilities - and the halls are *well equipped* with bars and so on. At Oadby, they are *beautifully* set in the University's Botanical Gardens. Beaumont and Villiers have computer rooms. The houses have single rooms and each house is single sex but groups of houses are mixed.
Car parking: Limited free parking at all halls.

EXTERNALLY:
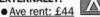
- Ave rent: £44

Availability: *A decent standard at an OK price, if you look around. The best places to look are the Tudor Road and Narborough Rd area, Clarendon and Knighton. The City Centre is also good. Highfields is the red light district with drug dealers on street corners, so only try for here if you want the seedy ambience. Parking is about as difficult as getting a needle through the eye of a camel with the RSPCA complaining.*
Housing help: The Union-run Accommodation Office provides a vacancy board and help and advice in the great home hunt.

welfare

SERVICES:

- Nightline ● Gay and Bisexual Society
- Mature SA ● International SA ● Postgrad SA ● Minibus
- Women's Officer ● Self-defence classes
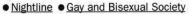

Both the Union and University provide welfare help and advice. The University employs 4 counsellors and the Union has a Legal Advice Centre. The Student Health Centre has 7 doctors, 3 sisters and a nurse and, what's more, there's 24-hour care at the Hugh Binnie sick bay.

Women: There's a Women's Committee with reps from the halls and the city and a safety minibus.

Disabled: *Access is fairly poor but it's improving.* The Percy Gee Union Building has installed a lift, *which should make things easier.* There's a disability co-ordinator and an Open Access Study Support Centre for students with learning difficulties.

FINANCE:
- Ave debt: £2,200 ● Access fund: £213,000
- Successful applications (1997): 630

Numerous hardship funds exist, some for specific groups (mature students, overseas students, etc). The SU gives hardship loans up to £100.

• •

 ## Leicester Poly
see De Montfort University

• •

University of Lincolnshire and Humberside

 ● *Formerly Humberside Polytechnic, University of Humberside*

(1) Humberside University Campus, Cottingham Road, Kingston-upon-Hull, HU6 7RT. Tel: (01482) 440550. Fax: (01482) 463310. E-mail: marketing@humber.ac.uk
University of Lincolnshire and Humberside Students' Union, The Strand, Strand Close, Hull, HU2 9BT Tel: (01482) 444584. Fax: (01482) 491911. E-mail: union@humber.ac.uk
(2) Lincoln University Campus, Brayford Pool, Lincoln, LN6 7TS. Tel: (01522) 882000. Fax: (01522) 882088. E-mail; marketing@lincoln.ac.uk
Students' Union, Lincoln University Campus, PO Box 182, Lincoln LN2 4YF. Tel: (01522) 882000. Fax: (01522) 886142. E-mail: union@lincoln.ac.uk
(3) School of Applied Science & Technology, University of Lincolnshire and Humberside, Bargate, Grimsby. Tel: (01472) 874140. Fax: (01472) 315099.

 ## General

 Now concentrate, because this bit could get confusing. In 1983, the HE colleges in Hull and Grimsby combined to create Humberside Poly. 9 years later it turned into the University of Humberside. Then Nottingham Trent University (which used to be Trent Poly - *still with us?*) dropped out of a deal to set up a new campus 44 miles from Hull, in Lincoln (see De Montfort University - which used to be Leicester Poly - *do try to keep up*). So the University of Humberside stepped in and changed its name to the University of Lincolnshire and Humberside, now based in 3 towns (although the Grimsby one isn't much longer for this world). *There, simple, isn't it? Who threw that?* The Hull site is by far the biggest *although Lincoln is flexing its muscles and trying to prove it can stand on its own two feet.*

All marketing material for the Lincoln bit refers to the 'Lincoln University campus' with the last word in a smaller, fainter typeface and the separate prospectus doesn't mention the Hull site at all.

50% ♂♂♂♂♂♀♀♀♀♀ 50%

Sex ratio(M:F): 50%:50%	Founded: 1983
Full time u'grads: 9,727	Part time: 2,474
Postgrads: 1,421	Non-degree: 1,272
Ave course: 3yrs	Ethnic: 6.5%
Private school: n/a	Flunk rate: n/a
Mature students: 57%	Overseas students: 11%
Disabled students: 4%	Staff/student ratio: 1:22
Clearing: 18%	

ATMOSPHERE:

The number of sites without cast iron links and the proportion of mature students conspire to slow down any party potential. Some students (particularly at the Cottingham and Inglemire Avenue sites) pop round the corner to <u>Hull University</u> for a social life. The Grimsby site, which is due to close in 1999 (all courses will transfer to Lincoln), has an appropriately funereal feel. It's a bit early to make judgements about Lincoln - lots of eager types keen to better themselves in a development that looks more like a conference centre than an academic facility. Oops, there goes a judgement. The University, accused by its SU of being money-oriented, may be closing down the Hull sites altogether and moving everything to Lincoln. Hope you're keeping up with all this.

THE SITES:

Cottingham Road: (business, engineering, infotech) The University's largest and *most elegant* site, next door to <u>Hull University</u>, it is constructed of brick with grass quads in front. A few *flash* additions like the modern Polygon building and the Language Centre. Many of the University's overseas students are based on this site.

Inglemire Avenue: (social & professional studies) A couple of hundred yards round the corner from Cottingham Road and surrounded by playing fields and a convent, this is a set of 4 buildings (2 dating from the 1920s) with a *bland* block of concrete and glass to the front This site is being wound down and its courses split between Cottingham Road and Queen's Gardens. *Some students who had already paid deposits on houses nearby before they were told are suitably furious.*

Queen's Gardens: (art & design, architecture) City centre site, about 2 miles from Cottingham Rd.

Lincoln: This modern *but not ghastly*, £32million development on the edge of an ancient harbour in the historic city of Lincoln is primed for expansion over the next few years - a new Learning Resource Centre will open here for entry in 98; the students there (2,300 in all at the moment) *tend to rattle around a bit in the big, airy development.*

Nun's Corner (Grimsby): (applied science, food & fisheries) All courses will transfer to Lincoln by 1999.

LINCOLN:
● <u>London: 132miles</u> ● <u>Hull: 44miles</u>

Lincoln's a beautiful cathedral city surrounded by flat, peaceful countryside but despite the presence of 2 universities in its midst (see <u>De Montfort University</u>) *local amenity providers are only just waking up to the (allegedly lucrative) student market.*

GRIMSBY:
Grimsby has a strong history and heritage as one of England's most important seaports. It's smaller than Hull and apart from supermarkets, is somewhat short on amenities or fun.

HULL TRAVEL: see <u>University of Hull</u>

LINCOLN TRAVEL:
Trains: The station, a few minutes walk from the campus, has services to London (£24.55), Birmingham (£11.20), Edinburgh (£35.95) and more.
Car: The A1 runs nearby, intersecting with the A46 at Newark and the A57 near Retford. Lincolnshire has no motorways.
Bicycles: *Flat beyond your dreams. Get pedalling.*

LIBRARIES & COMPUTERS:
● <u>Books: 210,000</u> ● <u>Study places: 1,541</u>
● <u>Computer workstations: 1,510</u>

The libraries in Hull are inadequate for the numbers of students, though provision is much better in Lincoln. Similarly, the computers are a bit dated and there's no 24hr access. The provision at the Inglemire site is better - but that's being closed down, unfortunately.

CAREER PROSPECTS:
● <u>Careers Service</u> ● <u>No of staff: 5full</u>
● <u>Unemployed after 6mths (1996): 14%</u>

SPECIAL FEATURES:
● Many courses include a sandwich year working in industry.
● It runs one of the largest and most *successful* international exchange schemes in the country with connections with 64 institutions.

FAMOUS ALUMNI:
Elliott Morley MP (Lab); Mary Parkinson (TV presenter).

FURTHER INFO:
Prospectuses for full- and part-time and overseas students, plus a separate publication for the Lincoln campus. CD-ROM and web sites (http://www.humber.ac.uk and http://www.lincoln.ac.uk).

·········· entertainment

HULL: see <u>University of Hull</u>

LINCOLN:

● <u>Price of a pint of beer: £1.85</u> ● <u>Glass of wine: £1.70</u>

Lincoln is slowly getting used to these strange student creatures and new ways to spend your money are popping up all the time.
Cinemas: (2) Both mainstream.
Pubs: *The Jolly Brewer is the only one that could reasonably be labelled a student haunt. Other* **push***plugs: Green Dragon;*

Cheltenham Arms; Cornhill Vaults (alternative); Barge; Edward's; Yate's; Martha's; the Falcon.

Music venues: Grafton House and O'Rourke's host local indie wannabes and Stadz Café has jazz nights.

Clubs/discos: There's been a recent spate of club closures *in an area that was hardly brimming with facilities in the first place.* **push**plugs: Klubhopping at Ritzy (chart dance); Milligan's (house/techno); Baracudas; the Sugar Club.

Eating out: A decent range of eateries, *although not all of them are student-oriented (or priced).* **push**plugs: Restaurant Italia; The Mint; Spinning Wheel, Wig & Mitre (for rich parents); Raj Duth (very good Indian, free if you can prove it's your birthday); Damon's Motel; the Barge does decent pub grub.

UNIVERSITY:

● Price of a pint of beer: £1.40 ● Glass of wine: £1

Bars: (3) *The Cottingham Road Flyer's Bar is the most lively and doubles as an ents venue (500). The Strand, also in Hull but soon to close, is less energetic, as is the new bar at Lincoln.*

Cinema: A weekly double-bill, *usually mainstream but not schlocky,* at Cottingham Road.

Clubs/discos/music venues: Cottingham Road resounds to the sounds 4 nights a week, ranging from 70s retro to local name DJs. *Live music (apart from local bands) is rare – stagediving enthusiasts make the journey to Hull University.* There's no venue as yet at Lincoln.

Food: The SU Café at Cottingham Road serves up *cheap 'n' cheerful* greasy spoon stuff most of the day. *The main Refectory is usually packed for some reason - can't be the food. Edibility ratings are better at Lincoln.*

Others: Occasional balls, often of a sporty nature.

social & political

UNIVERSITY OF LINCOLNSHIRE AND HUMBERSIDE STUDENTS' UNION:

● 5 sabbaticals ● Turnout at last ballot: 7%
● NUS member

Think apathy doesn't matter? This is where it leads. 4 of the 5 sabbaticals are based at Hull; while they struggle to unify the masses, with so little community atmosphere it's hard to steel students for a bout of banner brandishing. The 75-odd Lincoln-based students who turned up in their buses to the AGM in Hull accounted for 75% of the turnout. This state of affairs is driving the SU exec wild, especially since the University is pruning the Union's wings - giving them less money and closing the Strand SU building - and as long as the body as a whole remains apathetic, there's nothing they can do.

❝One of the sites of Oxford Brookes University used to be owned by Robert Maxwell.❞

SU FACILITIES:
The Union building, the Strand, *is something of a shell*; all the available funds have been sucked up by the building itself, *leaving a skeleton staff and few facilities*. There are offices, 2 bars (1 at Cottingham Road), a Health & Fitness Centre (at Inglemire) and not much else - *but this is positively sumptuous when compared with Lincoln. Still, it's early days yet.*

CLUBS (NON SPORTING):
Criminology; Dance and Club Culture; Film; Malaysian.

OTHER ORGANISATIONS:
There's a student magazine, 'Yum' (*improving on its former not-much-copness*).

RELIGIOUS:
Full-time ecumenical chaplains at each site.

PAID WORK: see University of Hull

sports

● Recent successes: nothing special

The sports facilities are still too feeble to propel Humberside into the big time, or even among the also-rans, but they've improved in recent years. Where there are shortfalls, students make use of University of Hull.

SPORTS FACILITIES:
Sports hall; gym; all-weather pitch; gravel hockey pitch; 3 football pitches; multigym; solarium; health & fitness club. Students at Lincoln don't have facilities of their own but a discount scheme has been arranged at a local sports centre. *Typically,* the new gym being built on campus next to the Learning Resource Centre will be private and cost around £200 to join. When the Inglemire site closes, so will the solarium, multigym and health club, with as yet no plans for relocation.

SPORTING CLUBS:
Dangerous Sports; Jiu Jitsu.

ATTRACTIONS: see University of Hull

accommodation

IN COLLEGE:
● Catered: 12% ● Cost: £53-57(33-38wks)
● Self-catering: 23% ● Cost: £42-53(38wks)
Availability: 85% of first years are accommodated in halls, 5% who want to be, can't. The spaces in Hull are mostly based at Cottingham Rd (including the all-female Johnson Hall) and the new Pacific Court development, near Queen's Gardens. There are also 1,000 places in a Direct Lettings scheme, where accommodation is allocated by the accommodation service. Lincoln has 310 self-catering places, adequate for the current number of undergrads but liable to be outstripped if things progress as quickly as they'd hope.
Car parking: Free permit parking, but *insufficient*.

EXTERNALLY: see University of Hull

LINCOLN:
● Ave rent: £40
Because Lincoln isn't yet swamped with house-hungry

students there's enough private accommodation going, especially the *relatively cheap* Victorian houses around Monks Road and West Parade. *The areas near the football ground are somewhat grimmer.*

········welfare

SERVICES:
- Nightline ● Lesbian & Gay Society
- Overseas SA ● Women's Officer ● Self-defence classes

The University Advice Office, with 2 full-time counselling staff (1 at Lincoln) deals with most problems that life can throw up. The Student Health Service is staffed by 3 nurses.

Disabled: *Poor wheelchair access, but some loops, braille printers etc for hearing- and sight-impaired students. The Division of Assistive Resources and Technology supports students with special needs.*

Women: Women outnumber men 2:1 at Lincoln.

FINANCE:
- Ave debt: £2,200 ● Access fund: £153,712
- Successful applications (1997): 1,500

The University waives fees for part-time undergraduates on income support. The cost of living is low in Hull.

University of Liverpool

The University of Liverpool, PO Box 147, Liverpool, L69 3BX.
Tel: (0151) 794 7000. Fax: (0151) 794 6502.
E-mail: scilas@liv.ac.uk
The Guild, The University of Liverpool, PO Box 187, 160 Mount Pleasant, Liverpool, L69 7BR. Tel: (0151) 794 6868.
Fax: (0151) 794 4174.

········general

If, when you think of Liverpool, you think of The Beatles, Bill Shankly and Brookside, you're not far wrong. Of course, the Beatles and Bill are no more and Brookie's gone a bit ridiculous of late but Liverpool lives on as one of Britain's youth culture capitals. It's always taken an independent stand politically, and it's rich with culture and art, but it's more exciting just strolling the streets. The Mersey cuts through the city, dividing it from the Wirral and skirting the jumble of streets, full of art-deco and post-industrialist architecture. Liverpool is unique, the seaway for the North West. Considering how big it is, *it seems odd that it's so close to Manchester* (28 miles) - but with 2 *great* cities for the price of 1, who's complaining?

Liverpool's 1st university (joined in 1992 by Liverpool John Moores University) is the original 'redbrick' university. The word was coined to describe the University's Victoria Building on Brownlow Hill. Many of the other buildings are redbrick too but others are more modern (60s and 70s), based on a 100-acre site (big for an inner city campus) in the Mount Pleasant area of town, on top of a hill.

51% ♂♂♂♂♂♀♀♀♀♀ **49%**

Sex ratio(M:F): 51%:49%	**Founded: 1881**
Full time u'grads: 10,200	**Part time: 250**
Postgrads: 1,650	**Non-degree: 0**
Ave course: 3/4yrs	**Ethnic: 7%**
Private school: 7.1%	**Flunk rate: 10%**
Mature students: 19%	**Overseas students: 10%**
Disabled students: 7.3%	**Staff/student ratio: 1:13**
Clearing: 4%	

ATMOSPHERE:
Liverpool University is down to earth, unpretentious and the students enjoy good relations with the local community. Not bad for starters from a town few respect for anything but its music and football. Scousers and the University students defend their city to the hilt and it's hard not to have a good time in Liverpool so, in your best Harry Enfield voice, 'Caaalm down'.

THE CITY:
- Population: 448,300 ● London: 189miles
- Manchester: 28miles ● Glasgow: 213miles

Liverpool was once a prosperous merchant town, doing deals on the docks, touting for trade inland. It still bears the legacy of former times with grand Victorian houses and old streets built for carriages, such as Princes Road lined with tall houses, but it's seen some rough times, *and some areas, such as Toxteth, have developed a reputation for being notoriously run-down and violent.* But it's far from all gloom and doom: the Albert Dock development is just one part of a face-lift programme *that makes Michael Jackson's nasal amendment look subtle by comparison. The richness and contrast of architectural styles is being revitalised and is beginning to reflect the spirit of the people, a spirit that never dwindled.* There are nightclubs everywhere *and bohemian bustle is bubbling away.* Supermarkets, shops and markets abound and there's more for tourists to do than visit Penny Lane and Strawberry Fields. There's the Liverpool Museum, the Museum of Labour History, the Walker Art Gallery (the largest art collection in the UK outside London), the Tate Gallery in Albert Dock and Liverpool University's own art gallery on campus.

TRAVEL:
Trains: Mainline links with many destinations including London Euston (£26.05), Manchester (£4.15) and Birmingham (£9.75).
Coaches: National Express to most destinations including London (£15.75) and Manchester (£4.50).
Car: M53, M56, M57, M58 and M62 (good for North West and Wales).
Air: Flights inland and to Belfast and Dublin from Liverpool Airport, 7 miles from the city centre.

Ferries: This is the main port for Belfast and there are other regular ferries to Ireland. *And, of course, there's the ferry 'cross the Mersey.*

Hitching: *Good connections and many long-haul drivers who sympathise, especially round the M62.*

Local: *Efficient bus services. Student fares, 50p.*

Underground: *The Metro is the best way of getting around town although delays can be common.*

Taxis: *Many black cabs and other dodgy merchants - a bit of a taxi city but not cheap.*

Bicycles: *Cycles lanes are being developed, but it's generally too smoggy and large and chances are the bike'll get nicked. The city came last in a recent 'New Cyclist' magazine survey.* There's a University bus service running between halls all day (50p).

LIBRARIES & COMPUTERS:
- <u>Books: 1,311,000</u> ● <u>Study places: 1,527</u>
- <u>Computer workstations: 1,500</u>

The Sydney Jones Library is the largest, but the Harold Cohen Library would be big enough for most universities. There are also 13 smaller libraries. *Facilities are excellent.*

CAREER PROSPECTS:
- <u>Careers Service</u> ● <u>No of staff: 16full/2part</u>
- <u>Unemployed after 6mths (1996): 7%</u>

SPECIAL FEATURES:
- The English Department runs a science fiction course.

FAMOUS ALUMNI:
Steve Coppell (footballer/manager); Hugh Jones (marathon runner); Chris Lowe (Pet Shop Boy); Phil Redmond (TV mogul, writer and inventor of 'Brookside' and 'Grange Hill'); Patricia Routledge (actress); Jon Snow (ITN reporter).

FURTHER INFO:
Prospectuses for undergrads and postgrads and an alternative prospectus available from the SU (£2.00). Web site (http://www.liv.ac.uk).

entertainment

CITY:

- <u>Price of a pint of beer: £1.50</u> ● <u>Glass of wine: £1.75</u>

Cinemas: (3) including the Odeon and a 14-screen multiplex out of town on the M57.

Theatres: (4) The Empire is a national touring venue for subsidised companies where you can see shows before they transfer to London's West End. Also, there are the *often controversial and innovative,* but financially threatened Everyman Theatre, the Neptune and the *small, but beautiful* Unity Theatre which hosts an *unconventional* array of drama, dance and comedy.

Pubs: *Liverpool's pubs can vary from Berni Inn style drop outs to shrines like Ye Cracke (Lennon and crew drank here). Smithdown Road is the prime student crawl route.*

push.plugs: *Finch & Firkin (vast); Baa Bar (trendy); The Philharmonic (Grade II listed loos); The Rose; Eurobar (by <u>Liverpool John Moores University</u>).*

Clubs/discos: *Cream at The Nation attracts trendhoppers from across the UK and beyond. Other* **push***plugs: Mardi Gras; Eden; Voodoo (techno) at Clear; student nights at the Cavern (next door to where the original was); L2; No Fakin' at Zanzibar; indie at Krazy House and the Razz.*

Music venues: The *premiere* venues are: the Empire (mainstream and classical); The Royal Court for top bands; Jaks for funk and soul; the Lomax (*indie bliss*).

Eating out: *Café Tabac and the Baa Bar are terminally hip but not overpriced.* **push***plugs: El Macho (Mexican); Kelly's (cheap and bohemian); Uncle Sam's (fat portions without a fat bill); Caesar's Palace; Royal Tandoori.* Chinatown keeps sizzling until 4am.

Other: *If none of the above appeal and you've checked that you still have a pulse, why not try the bowling alley or live poetry at the Largo or one of the many cabaret venues (especially the Neptune) where the legendary Scouse wit lives on.*

UNIVERSITY:

● <u>Price of a pint of beer: £1.50</u> ● <u>Glass of wine: £1.25</u>

Bars: There are 8 bars around the Guild and the University. The most notable are: the Liver Bar (pink and purpleness) and the Ken Saro Wiwa (aka the Blue bar) and the 3 lounge bars, all named after political prisoners and open during clubs and events.

Theatres: There are 2 theatres in the University: the Stanley Theatre in the Guild and the University Theatre. Most years they manage to muster a production for the Edinburgh Fringe.

Cinemas: The Guild has a large screen in the Stanley Theatre and shows a film every week.

Clubs/discos: The Time Tunnel is the Saturday night retro fest now in its 7th year *for students who think they're George Michael when they're pissed;* Religion every Friday and Double Vision on Mondays. Guest DJs have included Paul Oakenfold.

Music venues: Mountford Hall (1,530) is the main venue but the Courtyard and some of the bars are equipped for live gigs too. Recent appearances include Orbital and Republica.

Cabaret: The Guild organises the fortnightly Uncle Piehead's Comedy Parlour, usually featuring top japesters such as, recently, Harry Hill, Martin BigPig and Craig Charles.

Food: The bars all serve food of some description; the Lounge Food Court in the Ken Saro Wiwa bar rustles up a *respectable range at a reasonable rate* and this is bolstered by various fast food outlets and the Courtyard Café.

Others: All the major academic departments and halls arrange balls at least once a year (adm £8-25).

·········· social & political

THE UNIVERSITY OF LIVERPOOL GUILD OF STUDENTS:

● <u>4 sabbaticals</u> ● <u>Turnout at last ballot: 11%</u>

● <u>NUS member</u>

The Guild is the 2nd largest students' union building in Europe (the biggest is in Paris) and so it's not surprising that it offers some pretty good facilities, but also being so big, it's often difficult to fill it. Still, it's a bit rich to start complaining that the Guild's facilities are too big while too many students'

> **❝The Athletics Union at York University is sponsored by Vaseline.❞**

unions have to go without. In terms of political activity, lots goes on in the students' paper, but little seeps out into the students' body.

SU FACILITIES:
Bars; cafeterias; print shop; general shop; photographers; optician; 'Little Cohen' Library with study area; travel agency; prayer room; international lounge; launderette; hair-dresser; table tennis; snooker; Mountford Hall; Monday market (clothes, CDs, plants, etc); theatre; dark room; band practice room; function rooms; photo booth; games and vending machines; film-making facilities; photocopying.

CLUBS (NON SPORTING):
Amateur DJs; Band; Change Ringers; Cocktails; Esperanto; Hellenic; Hindu; Juggling; Life; Links; Liverpool University Show Troupe; Mountaineering; Music; The Off the Fence Fund; Welsh; Wine.

OTHER ORGANISATIONS:
There's a student newspaper 'Gazette' and an arts magazine 'Sphinx', the oldest student mag in the country. The Guild executive produce a newsletter ('Blurb') and plans are being made for a radio station. The Community Action group has a full-time paid worker who co-ordinates many local help projects including play schemes and soup runs.

RELIGIOUS:
● 2 chaplains (CofE, RC)
There's the Muslim prayer room in the Union and an Anglican chaplaincy on campus. There are 2 cathedrals in town, Catholic and Anglican, in strongly contrasting architectural styles, and both within praying distance of the Union. There are plenty of churches, more synagogues than in any other English town this size and a few mosques, as well as temples for Hindus, Buddhists and Hare Krishnas.

PAID WORK:
There is high unemployment in Liverpool, so there's lots of competition for the few places in bakeries, shops and bars. The Business Bridge scheme helps students find local placements.

sports

● Recent successes: karate, netball
Membership of the Athletics Union costs £20 for 3 years, about 1 in 3 students cough up and there are minimal charges for facilities. *The facilities are excellent, including one of the best pools in any UK university - in fact, with an infrastructure like this, it's surprising sport isn't more important to the students.*

SPORTS FACILITIES:
There are 2 main sports centres on the campus, including 1 with a pool, sports hall, 4 squash courts, a climbing wall,

dance studio, multigym and solarium. There are 3 more sports grounds near the halls, the main 1 with floodlit artificial pitches, tennis courts, lacrosse pitch and cricket squares; and naturally, a bar and café. The sports fields at Wyncote Allerton are 4 miles from the campus but not too far from the halls. Further away, there are more grounds at Maryton Grange and Widnes served by University minibuses. Added extras include the boat house at Knowsley Park and the outdoor activity centre in Snowdonia in North Wales. The town and area make up for *the few shortcomings in the University provisions.* Apart from the Mersey for water sports, there are a number of sports and leisure centres, *some of which are excellent* (Toxteth, Everton, Kirkby, among others).

SPORTING CLUBS:
Ballroom Dancing; Diving; Jiu Jitsu; Kung Fu; Lacrosse; Rifle; Ski and Snowboarding; Surf; Ten Pin Bowling; Water Polo; Windsurfing.

ATTRACTIONS:
Liverpool FC is still one of the legendary teams of world footie but don't forget Everton, or, indeed, the *feisty* Tranmere Rovers. There's Aintree Race Course and many other sporting sights.

accommodation

IN COLLEGE:
- Catered: 20% ● Cost: £67(32wks)
- Self-catering: 13% ● Cost: £42-51(40-52wks)

Availability: Students who accept an offer by May, and apply for accommodation before September are sorted for their 1st year - about 8% can't live in for one reason or another. The halls, *which are of a high standard with good amenities and truly edible food*, are on 2 *pleasant* green sites, both about 3 miles from campus. The larger, *with a strong community atmosphere*, is Carnatic, with 6 halls of about 250 spaces each. The other is Greenbank *with a social life all of its own* and 2 halls of about 500 each. Buses go to and from the halls in the mornings and evenings. 1 hall is all-female, but otherwise they're mixed.

Car parking: Limited permit parking on campus.

EXTERNALLY:
- Ave rent: £36

Availability: *There's enough housing to make it possible to get something considerably cheaper than £36, if students are prepared to take what's going. The only real competition is to find somewhere close to your place of study but even then nobody's left miles away. Some areas have developed as decidedly studenty, such as Wavertree (a veritable student ghetto), Sefton Park (more expensive, but arty, converted flats), Allerton, Mossley Hill, Aigburth, Old Swan and the famous Penny Lane. Some areas are less salubrious, such as Toxteth and Walton, but students do live there quite happily. Car parking depends very much on the area: further out of the city, it becomes easier, but public transport is fine.*

Housing help: The Accommodation Office keeps a vacancy list and provides advice. The 2 universities are running a scheme called 'Liverpool Student Homes' helping students find housing and providing grants for modernisation and building.

welfare

SERVICES:

- Creche ● Lesbian & Gay Society
- Mature SA ● Overseas SA ● Minibus ● Women's Officer
- Self-defence classes

The Guild operates a *good* Welfare Advice Centre where students can drop in and consult advisers, including 15 part-time counsellors. The University provides a further 2 full- and 3 part-time advisers. For bruised knees and severed limbs, the doctors, sister and nurses at the Health Centre can help.

Women: There are women-only swimming lessons at the pool and priority on the minibus.

Drugs: *The trade in Liverpool isn't as nasty as it was. The student body is no more or less prone to drug use than any other, anyhow.*

Disabled: *Access isn't so good,* but there's been serious investment towards ramps and lifts in some campus buildings. There is a Disabled Students' Working Party as well as particular provisions for hearing-impaired and dyslexic students.

FINANCE:
- Ave debt: £1,100 ● Access fund: £270,000
- Successful applications (1997): 572

Also Vice Chancellor's Hardship Fund (mainly for overseas students); Hillsborough Trust Memorial Bursaries (£500; must come from Merseyside); John Lennon Fund (£1,000, for environmental interests).

▶▶ **Liverpool Hope University College**
see Other Institutions

Liverpool John
Moores University

● *Formerly Liverpool Polytechnic*

Liverpool John Moores University, Rodney House, 4, Rodney Street, Liverpool, L1 2TZ. Tel: (0151) 231 5090/1. Fax: (0151) 231 3194. E-mail: recruitment@livjm.ac.uk
Liverpool John Moores Students' Union, The Haigh Building, Maryland Street, Liverpool, L1 9DE. Tel: (0151) 794 1900. Fax: (0151) 708 5334.

general

Liverpool John Moores University is built on 17 sites. Or 4. Or maybe only 3. Or possibly over 20. In fact, it's so spread out that it's hard to say exactly how many sites there are and none of them can be said to be the main one. The University definitely used to be 4 separate colleges and you can still detect the cracks where the merger took place back in the 60s. As a result, some of the University buildings are modern purpose-built constructions like the Trueman Building, while others, such as the Fine Art Department are *fine* examples of Georgian and Victorian architecture. The sites are clustered in the city centre, near <u>Liverpool University</u>, and further out in some of the *less kempt* areas of Liverpool's urban edges.

48% ♂♂♂♂♂ ♀♀♀♀♀ 52%

Sex ratio(M:F): 48%:52%	Founded: 1970
Full time u'grads: 13,652	Part time: 6,748
Postgrads: 680	Non-degree: 3,916
Ave course: 3/4yrs	Ethnic: 7.9%
Private school: 11%	Flunk rate: 26%
Mature students: 39%	Overseas students: 8%
Disabled students: 5.1%	Staff/student ratio: 1:7
Clearing: 15.4%	

ATMOSPHERE:
Students at Liverpool's newer university are very attached to their city, many being locals anyway. They're also proud of their university (if not its name) and despite the separate sites the students are united by their SU and its building, the Haigh, which is the nub of an electric social life.

THE SITES:
Although JMU can be divided into 4 main chunks, Mount Pleasant and Byrom Street each have numerous smaller annexes. There are also associated institutions throughout Merseyside and Cheshire and even as far afield as Dublin.

Mount Pleasant: (4,000 - business, design, law, modern languages, social work, architecture, media) An old building with lots of gargoyle type things, next door to the Haigh. There's a big new Learning Resources Centre here.

Byrom Street: (8,000 - bioscience, computing, engineering, maths, pharmacy, health, social and human sciences) A 60s *carbuncle* and the more attractive Georgian Mountford Building in the city's shopping district, 2 mins from the centre.

IM Marsh: (1,000 - education, sports, dance) 3 miles from the city centre, on the ruralish outskirts of Aigburth. *Usually swarming with sporty types.*

Liverpool Institute of Performing Arts: *Launched in January 1996 by Paul 'Fab Macca Thumbs Aloft' McCartney, LIPA is affiliated to JMU but the building is closed to non-LIPA students and the budding Kids from 'Fame' here tend to keep to their own patch, mulling over the subtext of 'The Frog Chorus'.*

THE CITY: see <u>University of Liverpool</u>

TRAVEL: see <u>University of Liverpool</u>

LIBRARIES & COMPUTERS:
● <u>Books: 609,308</u> ● <u>Study places: 1,619</u>
● <u>Computer workstations: 1,200</u>

Students are pretty satisfied with the facilities at the 3 libraries, also known as Learning Resource Centres or, *for all we know, Information in Tiny Silicon Objects and Bound Papery Things General Containment Facilitation. What was wrong with 'library'?*

CAREER PROSPECTS:
- Careers Service • No of staff: 11full/1part
- Unemployed after 6mths (1996): 8.1%

SPECIAL FEATURES:
- Phil Redmond - TV mogul and deviser of such series as 'Grange Hill', 'Brookside' and, um, 'Hollyoaks' - is an Honorary Professor of the University.
- In a ballot of students when it was still Liverpool Poly, 60% opposed 'Liverpool John Moores University' as the new name.

FAMOUS ALUMNI:
Caroline Aherne (Mrs Merton); Julian Cope (musician); Bill Drummond (KLF); Debbie Greenwood (ex-Miss England & TV presenter); Jim King (Cream club runner); John Lennon, Stu Sutcliffe (dead Beatles); Martin 'Chariots' Offiah (Rugby League). Liverpool and Everton FCs have honorary degrees.

FURTHER INFO:
Prospectuses for undergrads, postgrads, part-time and overseas students. Also videos and a web site (http://www.livjm.ac.uk).

entertainment

CITY: see University of Liverpool

UNIVERSITY:
- Price of a pint of beer: £1.30 • Glass of wine: £1.02

Bars: There are 2 bars in the Haigh (the SU building), including a wine bar and The Cooler - both very popular. IM Marsh and Byrom Street each has a boozer.

Theatres: 2 theatre venues around the University, plus the facilities at LIPA.

Cinemas: In the Haigh the SU shows weekly films, mostly recent mainstream releases and *surefire student hits (ones where the director's first name begins with 'Q').*

Clubs/discos/music venues: The Cooler (300) is the *prime* dance site most nights of the week, including the *Loveshack (60s, 70s, 80s and er, 90s - well yeah, the lot),* Barbarella *(charty)* and is also the venue for mainly local bands.

Cabaret: *Regular riotous assembly* in the company of, recently, Sean Locke and Lee Mack.

Food: All the bars double as food stops, *with the Cooler getting top marks for value.*

Others: *Apart from regular high-jinks in the bars and club/society parties there's a major-league Graduation Ball.*

social & political

LIVERPOOL STUDENTS' UNION:
- 6 sabbaticals • Turnout at last ballot: 25%
- NUS member

The SU manages to pull off the tricky balancing act of getting on OK with the University authorities and maintaining a level of political radicalism, most of which passes the students by completely. A small minority were up for a bit of agitation on the fees front recently.

SU FACILITIES:
In The Haigh: wine bar; Pizza Hatch; The Cooler; Café Bar; travel agency; shop; solarium; print shop; minibus hire;

meeting rooms; Barclays Bank cash dispenser; fitness centre; job shop; games room and vending machines; juke box; photo booth; photocopying. There are bars and smaller shops (including an art shop) at the other sites.

CLUBS (NON SPORTING):
Circus; Debating; Real Ale; Role Play; Wine Tasting.

OTHER ORGANISATIONS:
'Shout' is a *high quality* independent magazine published every 3 weeks. 'Scream' is a weekly newsletter. Shout FM Radio broadcasts intermittently. Community Action Now (CAN) undertakes local community projects and charity fundraising in the absence of a Rag.

sports

● <u>Recent successes: hockey, tennis</u>

Lycra and studs are donned more for pleasure than for glory but a respectable pile of silverware is being amassed. Students at IM Marsh take it all more seriously than those at other sites.

SPORTS FACILITIES:
At the IM Marsh site there are 2 gyms, 2 dance studios, a renovated sports hall, indoor swimming pool, 5 playing fields and an all-weather athletics track. Students at the other sites can choose to make the trek to IM Marsh or use The Base at the Haigh buiding which has various fitness programmes and classes, a solarium, sauna and massage facilities. Or they can try public (for which they can get a £15 discount pass) or <u>Liverpool University</u> facilities.

SPORTING CLUBS:
Gaelic Football; Hang Gliding; Kick-boxing; Mountainbiking; Parachuting; Waterpolo.

ATTRACTIONS: see <u>University of Liverpool</u>

accommodation

IN COLLEGE:
● <u>Self-catering: 13%</u> ● <u>Cost: £40-52(39wks)</u>

Availability: Students only stand any chance of living in during their 1st year and, even then, only 36% get places. The choice is between Cathedral Campus, self-catering flats for 3 people, or houses for 5 at Parkside Hall in Aigburth. The houses *are pleasant and very well situated* in the centre near the Anglican Cathedral. *The flats in Lime Street are also good.*
Car parking: *Easy enough at the houses, harder at the halls, very hard at the flats.*

EXTERNALLY: see <u>University of Liverpool</u>
Housing help: Liverpool Student Homes is run jointly by JMU and the <u>University of Liverpool</u> and offers legal help and advice, lists of recommended landlords and safety checks.

welfare

SERVICES:
● <u>Nursery</u> ● <u>Nightline</u> ● <u>Lesbian & Gay Society</u>
● <u>Mature SA</u> ● <u>Overseas SA</u> ● <u>Minibus</u> ● <u>Women's Officer</u>
● <u>Self-defence classes</u>
The University provides 3 medical centres and 4 counsellors. Each student has an academic tutor called a 'counsellor' and

the SU Welfare Unit's 3 advisers are equipped to provide counselling, legal and financial advice.

Disabled: Some buildings have been adapted for improved access and, *while there are still some major problems, the University's record is better than most. Some older parts such as Hahnamann Building have no access at all, whereas others (eg Josephine Butler House) are excellent.* There are Braille notices on all doors and loop systems in some lecture halls. There is a part-time Disabilities Welfare Advisor. The receptionist can do sign language.

FINANCE:
- Ave debt: £1,550 ● Access fund: £276,640
- Successful applications (1997): 1,110

There's also a hardship fund and emergency loans.

• •

 Liverpool Poly

see Liverpool John Moores University

• •

University of London

 • **The information which follows refers to the University of London as an amorphous blob. The services described are those provided centrally by the University and by ULU, the Union. The colleges and individual unions of the University provide services themselves, and push covers these in individual entries. Similarly, the general comments about London apply on the whole to the central area, close to ULU itself, and these are of equal relevance to the many institutions which are in the city but not part of London University itself. For more specific discussion of the differences between Norf 'n' Sarf, Hackney 'n' Hampstead, individual entries go some way to explaining the inexplicable.**
The University of London, Senate House, Malet Street, London, WC1E 7HU. Tel: (0171) 636 8000.
Fax: (0171) 636 5841.
University of London Union, ULU Building, Malet Street, London, WC1E 7HY. Tel: (0171) 664 2000.
Fax: (0171) 436 4604.

General

 The capital is a big place. A very big place. Just under 10 million people live within the boundary of the M25 (150 miles of 8-lane car park). If you've got the idea that London is basically Big Ben, Buckingham Palace and a few big shops, go back to square one. It is mile after mile of urban flood *and there is so much diversity, it is pointless to even attempt to describe the place briefly.* push *may be good value for money, but there are limits. Students who don't know London, but are serious about wanting to study there should get hold of*

one of the less touristy guides. Every year, 'Time Out' - the *essential* magazine to what's on in the capital (and they haven't paid us to say that) - produces a London Students' Guide (priced about £2.20).

Suffice it to say, that since the days of the little Roman village of Londinium on the banks of the Thames, London has come a long way, becoming the country's centre of politics, finance, arts, heritage, tourism, media, pornography, crime, bagel production and so on...

Appropriately, London University is also big. One in 10 of the country's entire higher education population is at 1 of London University's 42 colleges and associated institutions. *However, students rarely get a sense of the University as a whole especially since some of the larger constituent colleges, such as King's, Imperial and UCL, are big enough to be fairly sizeable universities on their own.*

The University's headquarters are in the *magnificent* art deco Senate House in Bloomsbury about 1 mile from Trafalgar Square. push features entries for most of the undergraduate colleges, so read this and read the separate colleges' entries too because *they vary as much as if they were different universities.* We don't cover postgraduate institutions and a medical school or other institution which is part of an individual college (eg King's College Hospital) will be mentioned under the college heading. For the record, here are those London colleges in full:

Featured in PUSH:

Birkbeck College	Royal Holloway
Courtauld Institute of Art	Royal Veterinary College
Goldsmiths College	St George's Hospital Medical
Heythrop College	School
Imperial College	SOAS (School of Oriental &
Jews' College	African Studies)
King's College London	School of Pharmacy
LSE	SSEES (School of Slavonic &
Queen Mary & Westfield College	East European Studies)
Royal Academy of Music	Trinity College of Music
Royal College of Music	(in 'Other Institutions')
Royal Free Hospital School	University College London
of Medicine	Wye College

50% ♂♂♂♂♂ ♀♀♀♀ 50%

Sex ratio(M:F): 50%:50%	Founded: 1836
Full time u'grads: 47,834	Part time: 5,114
Postgrads: 29,314	Ave course: 3yrs
Mature students: 20%	Overseas students: 11%

THE CITY:
- Population: 6,377,900
- Birmingham: 106miles
- Manchester: 172miles
- Edinburgh: 423miles

Samuel Johnson wrote 'When a man is tired of London, he is tired of life; for there is in London all that life can afford.' More recently it's been dubbed 'the coolest city on the planet' and there's a prevalent hype which says that the city's returning to its 60s 'swinging' heyday; relaxation of licensing laws, the resurgence of the UK fashion and film industries and the Britpop phenomenon have combined to create a city that's buzzing like a wasp on Hooch. It's easy to feel that you're not making the most of London if you're not spending every waking minute at the theatre, ballet, opera or cinema, in clubs or fashionable markets, and in museums and galleries, sports grounds and parks. It's a bit like the salad counter in Pizza Hut; it's up to you to make a selection from the vast selection of goodies and pile them on your plate however you like but you might end up face-down in a puddle of sweetcorn and thousand island dressing, while the waiters have a good laugh. Not everyone likes the pace or the impersonal atmosphere that many find in London. London can be oppressive and if you're not streetwise, or at least street sensible, it can be a dangerous place. While bomb scares should now be a thing of the past, violent crime is still on the up. The traffic can be manic as well and, as Morrissey pointed out, 'smoke lingers round your fingers'; it's sometimes hard to discern the capital's charms beneath the grime.

And it costs, if not the earth, then a sizeable pile of mud. There are a number of responses to the high cost of living in London: (1) burst into tears; (2) mug someone; (3) live on credit; (4) ask daddy for lashings of cash. Alternatively, if these don't appeal, you can always use the following methods: (1) Limit your spending by only going out when and where you can afford it (ULU fits the bill, offering cheap events for students). (2) Buy second hand - for books, there's ULU, Charing Cross Road and Waterloo and, for clothes, try Camden Market, Greenwich, Brick Lane and Portobello Road. (3) Get a job - more London students have part-time jobs than anywhere else. If you find yourself in London in your teens or twenties, you'd be a fool not to take advantage of the situation - but don't use this as an excuse to go on a spree. You can live within a budget but it's bloody tempting to forget this when the view from your college bar looks like the latest edition of 'The Face' and people from New York, Paris and Tokyo are telling you how lucky you are to be living at the centre of the universe.

TRAVEL:

Trains: London is the centre of the network: Birmingham (£13.55); Manchester (£26.05); Leeds (£32.35); Bristol (£18.50); Glasgow (£35) - anywhere you like, *provided the whole system hasn't completely disappeared up its own shunting yard by the time you read this.*

Coaches: London is also the centre of the National Express system and a whole variety of other national bus services (Green Line, Blue Line and so on) letting you ride to Birmingham (£13); Manchester (£21) and so on.

Local Trains: Local overground trains are a *speedy and sometimes pleasant* way to travel *and are moderately efficient. The main problems are the ease of use (a fair level of understanding is necessary), the high fares (although Travelcards are valid) and the early closing (last trains between 11pm and 1am). Trains are often the best bet south of the river.*

Underground: The 'tube' is the largest underground train system in the world and generally, *it is fast, easy to use, efficient and takes you just about anywhere you want to go,* although South-East London is a bit hard done by. However, it is often crowded, shuts down at midnight, it's often disrupted by strikes and breakdowns, though bomb scares are less common these days, and it's expensive. Talking to other tube passengers is tantamount to threatening their mother - the only people who do it are tourists and people who want to talk to you about Jesus. Also, London Underground is in the midst of a massive rebuilding phase which will put whole stretches of track into mothballs for months on end, not to mention a funding crisis which seems to have gone on longer than the escalator at Tottenham Court Road. Nearest tube to Senate House/ULU Building: Goodge St (Northern Line).

Local Buses: In the tube you can't see the real sights, so why not take the buses which are just as efficient, offer even more destinations and are slightly cheaper (50p minimum). But buses are slow and, until you know your way around, it's difficult to know which ones take you where. After midnight, buses come into their own - Night Buses are London's only form of all-night public transport and if you don't mind how long it takes, you can go almost anywhere within 10 miles of the centre.

Travelcards: For a legal way of dodging the expense of tubes, buses and trains, Travelcards are available at £3.60 for a daily pass for zones 1 to 4 of the network or, much more cost-effective, £15.70 for a weekly, £60.30 for a monthly.

Taxis: There are 2 types: the classic black cabs which are well regulated and enormously expensive, and dodgy merchants in Ford Escorts which are almost as expensive. There are now also some run by and for women. Basically though, forget all taxis, except late at night when all else fails and/or you're in a party of 4 or more.

Car: Parking in Central London is impossible, and, although there is only 1 rush hour every day it lasts from 6 in the morning until midnight. Nutters only need apply (and do).

Air: Served by 4 airports, including Heathrow, the world's busiest. Regular flights to Paris (£72), Belfast (£79), Prague (£129), New York, Timbuktu, anywhere else you care to pluck out of your WH Smith School Atlas, and back.

Hitching: Not possible from Central London, but get out a little way on to the city's escape routes or beyond the M25 and a thumb's a first class ticket.

‹Students at Wye College are convinced that the H & G blocks in the College's accommodation are haunted, due to the odd tapping sounds which rattle through the pipes. Allegations that these sounds are created by drunken jokers in the Druids club are fiercely denied.›

Bicycles: *A popular form of student travel given the pros: it's cheap and you can get through traffic. But there are the cons: London is big, full of exhaust fumes, lacking in cycle lanes and a Houdini-proof lock is advisable. It's also an easy way to die.*

LIBRARIES & COMPUTERS:
● Books: 2,000,000 ● Study places: 650

There is a vast central library at Senate House but computer provision is covered by the individual colleges, which also have their own library facilities. Check out http://www.ull.ac.uk/ull for up-to-date details.

CAREER PROSPECTS:
● Careers Service ● No of staff: 25full

The University careers service is well used and even offers job lists, careers fairs etc to non-London students for a small fee.

FURTHER INFO:
The University produces the glossy 'Guide to the University of London' which covers all the colleges. There's also an accommodation pamphlet and a Student Guide from ULU. For further details see the web sites (http://www.lon.ac.uk and http://www.ulu.ucl.ac.uk).

·········· entertainment

IN LONDON:

● Price of a pint of beer: £2 ● Glass of wine: £2.20

For a weekly guide to the Capital's entertainments, 'Time Out' magazine (£1.70) is a must.

Pubs: *Some London pubs water down their ridiculously expensive beer, but you can often find a decent pint of Young's or Fuller's, or a good selection of guest ales (the Weatherspoon chain is a reliable starting point). Beyond that, every variety of drinking den, from Irish to Jamaican, from sports bars to wine bars, from plush chrome extravaganzas serving Belgian banana beer with a free half-hour on the 'net to rough dives that serve phlegmy Carlsberg and a filthy look to any outsiders, you've got the lot.* **push** *plugs in Bloomsbury area: Jeremy Bentham; Rising Sun.*

Cinemas: *Many repertory cinemas offer student discounts and The Prince Charles Cinema just off Leicester Square shows films from £1.99.* **push** *plugs; Ritzy (Brixton); Everyman (Hampstead); Riverside (Hammersmith); NFT (South Bank); the Odeon in Leicester square is reopening and will have students discounts for some screenings.*

Theatres: Student standby tickets are sometimes available for West End shows, but they're still around £8. The National Theatre on the South Bank and the RSC at the Barbican are cheaper and feature some of the country's top talent. Also, don't forget the Fringe (the collective title for all the smaller theatres around town, ranging from back rooms at pubs to full size auditoria) *where you can often see high quality at low cost.*

Clubs/discos: Although London clubs are always at the very nub of any fashion scene, you pay for the privilege. At top nightspots, admission starts at around £6 and drinks can be anything up to 5 times pub prices. There is, however, an ever-changing set of cheaper hang-outs where the latest sounds are available without the latest prices. **push***plugs: Heaven (gay); Ministry of Sound (huge but still cool-ish); Subterania; Fridge; Los Locos (Latin); Camden Palace; Equinox (tacky beyond belief but relatively student-friendly). These are the venues; individual events move between clubs and disappear like clichés in the night, so we won't recommend any beyond saying there's anything from jungle to swingbeat, gabba to goth, to places where you can chill out and play Connect 4 while listening to Shirley Bassey, so if you can't find something to move to, you might ask yourself whether you've left your legs on the bus.*

Music venues: Many of the country's biggest *and most famous*, including Wembley Stadium and Arena, Labatt's Apollo, The Forum, The Astoria, Shepherds Bush Empire, Brixton Academy, 2 major opera houses and dozens of classical music venues. *As ever, though, it's the smaller, less publicised venues that provide for the real connoisseur*, whether it's the latest lo-fi sensation in the back room of the Camden Falcon or an uplifting cello recital in a church hall in Kensington. *If it makes a noise, you can go and hear it, sometimes for very little.*

Cabaret: *London is a hot-bed of alternative laugh-mongers.* **push***plugs: There's the Comedy Store near Piccadilly Circus or, more cheaply, Jongleurs (Camden, Battersea, Shepherds Bush), Acton Banana, Hackney Empire and many, many more. Also, keep a look out for free tickets to TV and radio show recordings.*

Eating out: Nowhere in the country has a broader choice of eateries. There is every kind of café, restaurant and fast food and then some. *Not everywhere is bank-busting either. Head for Soho and Chinatown for affordable food and late night nibbles. For budget fare in the West End, our* **push***plugs: Pollo's (madhouse Italian); Stockpot (school dinners, but superb value); Gaby's (friendly deli); Poon's (Chinese); Wagamama (Japanese noodles); Pret à Manger (imaginative sarnie chain); Cranks and Food for Thought (veggie without stodge); Bar Italia (Frith St, open till 7am); etc, etc, etc. These are ours, go find your own – and if you run out of places to eat, why not go on a diet?*

ULU:

- Price of a pint of beer: £1.20 ● Glass of wine: £1.40

Bars: (4) Gallery Bar/Diner (*very popular all day*); Duck & Dive (*more pubby*); Bar 101 (chrome design, for gigs, clubs etc); Palms (events only).

Clubs/discos: At least 2 club nights a week in Room 101, 'Lost in Music' on Fridays - *a dress-up-in-your-chintzy-curtains-and-slap-on-some-fake-sideburns kind of 70s and 80s thing -* and the chartier 'Beano' on Saturdays.

Music venues: The newly refurbished Room 101 (cap 700) *is probably the best college venue in London* and attracts some *pretty big* names, mostly of an indie persuasion; recently, Space, Super Furry Animals, Cornershop, the Longpigs and Kenickie, for example.

Food: *The Gallery Diner provides all a hungry student could desire, from spuds to fry-ups to, well, spuds, really.* Macmillans at Senate House (the University HQ) offers *decent value* meat 'n' 2 veg in a *gorgeous* art deco setting. New sandwich shop, 'Lunchbox'.

❬The head of the law course at Thames Valley University also teaches kite flying.❭

Others: Quite apart from the individual colleges' events there are annual balls (the Freshers Ball lasts all night), regular quiz nights, casinos and cultural and international social nights.

social & political

UNIVERSITY OF LONDON UNION:
● 5 sabbaticals ● NUS member

The individual colleges' SUs affiliate separately to NUS and are automatically part of ULU which offers the most extraordinary level of facilities at the building in Bloomsbury, open to 11pm or later when hosting an event. ULU is also the students' central representative body and has effective officers on most of the University's important committees. It is a politically balanced union with activists from most parties. Since the student body which ULU represents is so large and so disparate, it never operates through ballots of all members, but rather through an electoral college of representatives from the member SUs. As an inevitable result, the standard Joe or Joanne London student often isn't even aware of ULU's representative role and, relatively speaking, is not that bothered by it. This is, of course, an extremely unfair generalisation and if there's one thing that can be said about London students, it's that they're a very varied bunch. They're also a very cosmopolitan crowd with a large percentage of mature and part-time students. ULU often focuses its efforts on providing support for these groups, including running international events and campaigns.

SU FACILITIES:
The Union building (ULU Building) contains: 4 bars; cafeteria; general shop; sports shop; print shop and photocopying; coach, rail and gig tickets shop; travel agent; bank (Barclays) with cashpoint; Endsleigh Insurance office; opticians; vending machines; games and gambling machines; fax service; creche; snack-bar; sandwich shop; full-size swimming pool (favoured dip location for the Mitchell Brothers out of 'Eastenders', apparently); fitness centre; gymnasium; squash and badminton courts; launderette; theatre hall; offices and meeting rooms; *and a partridge in a pear tree.* ULU also provides training for staff and student officers of all the member colleges' SUs, and handbooks and publications for all aspects of London student life.

CLUBS (NON SPORTING):
Albanian; Arts; Baha'i; Ballroom Dancing; Bridge; Caving; Choir; Chinese; Consciousness; Debating; European; Games; Indian Dance; Lifesaving; Malaysian; Marxist; Medicus Leo; Meditation; Methodist; Muslim Women; Opera; Palestine; Refugees; St John Ambulance; Starfleet; Tai Chi; Writers. Colleges of the University also have their own clubs.

OTHER ORGANISATIONS:
The award-winning student newspaper, 'London Student', is published by ULU but is editorially independent. It has a

sabbatical editor and is aimed at all London students both in and outside the University. *There's also TFI London which is more of a listings mag and is arse.*

RELIGIOUS:
London has religious groups for every denomination from Muslims to Moonies, Jews to Jains. *If you can't find spiritual solace here, please direct your complaint upwards.*

PAID WORK:
There are more opportunities in London for part-time work than anywhere else, but there are also more people trying to get those jobs. Students find work in all the usual places like bars and restaurants and also in theatres, offices and shops.

sports

● <u>Recent successes: karate, rowing, volleyball</u>

There being so many students in London, certain features are inevitable; there are some very high sporting standards and some peerless facilities. The high standard doesn't put off beginners though, and the facilities mean that sport is an important social focus for students of all abilities. There are certain areas where London has been particularly successful, notably rowing (they've beaten both Oxford and Cambridge repeatedly over the last 10 years). Many competitions are run between the University's colleges.

SPORTS FACILITIES:
At the ULU Building, there are all the amenities mentioned above (the swimming pool, gym, fitness centre, squash court and so on). 31 acres of playing fields, a floodlit artificial pitch, 6 grass tennis courts and 1 hard court can be found at Motspur Park, ULU's sports ground in New Malden just outside London; ULU has sailing facilities at the Welsh Harp reservoir in North London and a boathouse at Chiswick-on-the-Thames.

SPORTING CLUBS:
Boat; Canoe Polo; Gymnastics; Korfball; Kung Fu; Lacrosse; Polo; Rifle; Ten Pin Bowling; Water Polo; Windsurfing.

ATTRACTIONS:
There is no end to London's sporting attractions: from tennis and strawberries at Wimbledon to football and fighting at Millwall; from cricket at Lords to croquet at Hurlingham; from athletics at Crystal Palace to rugby at Twickers; from... well, as we said, there's no end.

accommodation

IN UNIVERSITY:
● <u>Catered: 3%</u> ● <u>Cost: £84-86(30wks)</u>
Availability: The percentage of London students living in college accommodation varies enormously from college to college, but for those that the colleges don't accommodate, there's a limited number of catered places in the University's 8 intercollegiate halls and 600 places provided through a head tenancy scheme. The figures above apply to these halls only; including college halls, 28% of students at the University are accommodated and costs are usually somewhat lower. *The halls are mainly mixed but there are two (Canterbury and College) for women only, one (Connaught) for men and one*

(International) mainly for overseas students.

Amenities: Conditions in each hall are different but, mostly, it's single rooms with shared bathrooms and *minimal* cooking facilities. There is also a selection of other amenities including bars, TV rooms, function, meeting and study rooms, libraries, launderettes, payphones and so on. Depending on the hall, you may be able to enjoy the delights of a squash court, dark-room, music room, bike sheds, gardens, videos and in College Hall there is a hairdressing salon. In some halls, there is the chance to share rooms, sometimes even for mixed couples.

Car parking: *Not recommended; spaces are limited.*

EXTERNALLY:
● Ave rent: £60

London Transport (buses, tube and trains) splits the city into several 'zones' which are concentric circles from the centre. Zone 1, for example, is the area within a radius of about $2\frac{1}{2}$ miles of Trafalgar Square. Zone 2 is the next 3 miles and so on. Obviously, rents get cheaper in the outer zones, but then travel costs to the centre go up accordingly.

Availability: *Contrary to popular belief, it's really not that difficult to find accommodation in London, just buy a copy of the Evening Standard or Loot and there are hundreds of places. It is, however, a challenge of epic proportions to find anywhere that is both affordable and inhabitable. There's very little housing in Zone 1 even for yuppies, and students come a lot lower in the pecking order. Zone 2 is a bit better, particularly for single rooms in shared flats or houses in places like Wandsworth, Putney and Fulham and wherever the tube system is lacking. Zone 3 is relatively promising, but the catch is that it can take an hour to get to the centre. Zone 4 and beyond are not popular for the same reason, but, as they say, homeless students can't be choosers. Although there are many thousands of people living in cardboard boxes on London's streets, they aren't students. In fact, many students manage to find very comfortable flats for almost reasonable rents. There is also a growing number living in squats. To be safe, students coming to London should work out where they're going to stay first. Hammersmith, Camberwell and Finsbury Park all have student ghettos but it obviously depends where in the city they need to get to every day.*

Housing help: The University Accommodation Office with 8 full-time staff is *a formidable service with the formidable task of handling the external housing requirements of the University's students.* It offers a bulletin board, vacancies list and accommodation counselling. Larger colleges also have their own services.

welfare

SERVICES:
● Creche ● Lesbian & Gay Society
● Mature SA ● Overseas SA ● Postgrad SA ● Minibus
● Women's Officer ● Self-defence classes

ULU runs the above services as well as playing host to an opticians in the ULU Building and producing an *excellent* annual Welfare Handbook. Students usually go to the

University's Central Health Centre in Gower Street (Bloomsbury again), where counselling and health and dental treatment are on offer. *Generally, London students tend to use their own colleges' provisions, the local public health services, the Citizens Advice Bureau or else, suffer in silence.*

Drugs: *Many Londoners live for years in the capital without ever encountering them. Others, however, walk around with their eyes open. Every drug you've heard of and a great many beside are readily available on the streets and in the pubs and clubs of London. Cannabis is perpetually prevalent and ecstasy currently has a high profile. Heroin is more common than in most cities and the abuse/use of crack is spreading, especially in the South. They're often more expensive than elsewhere, but that shouldn't be regarded as any guarantee of quality - dangerous mixtures are common and the risks are your own.* There are a number of help centres (including Narcotics Anonymous 0171-351 6066) *and the authorities usually take a progressive but firm attitude.*

Women: *Anyone who isn't familiar with London, but particularly women, should remember that the diversity of the capital has a nasty slant - it's easy to turn a corner from a delightful residential area and suddenly find yourself in considerably less attractive surroundings. ULU's self-defence classes are not laid on as anybody's idea of a good joke. Without being sensational, in London there are risks it's best to avoid.*

Lesbian, gay & bisexual: *Far more than most places, it's possible to be out in London without experiencing constant prejudice (although that still doesn't make coming out easy, and there are plenty of sad bigots around as well). The gay community in London is sizeable and proud, and has marked out a large chunk of Soho as pretty much its own. As a result, there are plenty of entertainments which don't conform to heterosexist stereotypes and a few London boroughs make special housing provisions. Many of the best clubs have gay nights or even, for a change, straight nights. And don't forget the Pride March and Festival, every summer.*

Disabled: College facilities vary. The ULU building has a front ramp and lifts to all floors. *Getting around London can be hellish even for those who are fully mobile, but plenty have learned to cope.*

FINANCE:

College arrangements vary but if all else fails, there's the Vice-Chancellor's Hardship Fund or the ULU fund, sponsored by Dillon's bookshop.

▶▶ London College of Fashion
see The London Institute

▶▶ London College of Printing
see The London Institute

London Guildhall University

- **Formerly City of London Polytechnic**

London Guildhall University, 31 Jewry Street, London, EC3N 2EY. Tel: (0171) 320 1616. Fax: (0171) 320 1163. E-mail: enqs@lgu.ac.uk
London Guildhall University Students' Union, 2 Goulston Street, London, E1 7TP. Tel: (0171) 247 1441. Fax: (0171) 247 0618.

General

London Guildhall University is based at... um, well... 7 places, really. And they're all in the City - the financial and corporate centre of London and the UK (with the 'EC' postcodes). Except for the sites in the East End (with just 'E' postcodes). Anyway, they're all around there and they're all *fairly drab* concrete constructions. Except for some of them, like the building at Moorgate which is built in *elegant* grey stone, or the Jewry Street building. The City, the famous square mile from about ¾ to 2 miles east of Trafalgar Square, is not one of London's shopping areas, nor is it residential - we're talking big business and big buildings, the nearest Britain offers to compete with Manhattan's skyscrapers. The East End is well-known enough because of a certain TV soap. *Ironically for an institution so intimately situated in the heart of financial derring-do, London Guildhall was suffering the odd financial setback until cutbacks were made in staffing levels. Since then, they've been turning over a tidy profit, thank you very much.*

Sex ratio(M:F): 50%:50%	Founded: 1970
Full time u'grads: 7,541	Part time: 1,145
Postgrads: 400	Non-degree: 5,600
Ave course: 3yrs	Ethnic: 38%
Private school: n/a	Flunk rate: n/a
Mature students: 49%	Overseas students: 12%
Disabled students: 6.9%	Staff/student ratio: 1:24
Clearing: 20%	

ATMOSPHERE:
For such a dispersed college in the centre of London, the University has a surprisingly united identity as an open, unpretentious place, possibly because so many of the students are locals. They manage to achieve some semblance of solidarity by quite a hefty emphasis on ents, which, compared to London's bright lights, are something of a sputtering candle. Many of the courses have vocational links, some taking advantage of local money meddling, but there are also plenty with a more arts-'n'-crafts leaning.

❝When 'Mastermind' was filmed at Ulster University, students kidnapped the Black Chair. When the BBC refused to pay a ransom, the chair was pushed into the River Bann.❞

THE SITES:
Not all the sites, *but 5 of the most prominent* (some students are based at more than 1 site):
Central House: (1,513 students - art, design, jewellery) A grey 60s block *with a laid back atmosphere*, about 2 minutes walk from Calcutta House, one of the University's most essential student ports of call.
Moorgate: (2,744 - law, economics, accountancy, business studies, financial services) An 19th century building, *looking vaguely important, but very easy going.* 15 minutes walk from Calcutta House.
Tower Hill: (921 - computing, civil aviation) Opposite the Tower of London, but being 60s concrete, *hardly a reflection of its glory. Quiet with a serious work ethic.* 3 minutes from Calcutta House.
Commercial Rd: (1,500 - art, design, manufacture) Another 60s building, 8 minutes from Calcutta House.
Calcutta House: (2,174 - humanities) Once an old tea warehouse.

THE CITY: see <u>University of London</u>

THE CITY & EAST END:
The City of London is so busy making money in phallic towers, that property prices are too sky-scraping high for anything else to get a look in. There is the barest minimum of extremely expensive wine bars, theme pubs and sandwich bars which provide so much packaging you never know whether it may be part of the sandwich. *Far be it from* push, *however, to suggest it's a cultural wasteland...*
    The East End is closer to reality. Traditionally, it is the home of London's dispossessed: first, Jews; nowadays, Asians and yuppies. *It has a lively community atmosphere which is hard to find elsewhere in inner city London.* The market in Petticoat Lane may be a bit more *gimmicky* than once upon a time, but Brick Lane is a *massive overdose for the shopaholic,* even late into the night. *The University's protestations that they're not near the East End are belied by the jellied eel vendor making a killing outside the Union building.*

TRAVEL: see <u>University of London</u>
Local Trains: Liverpool St and Fenchurch St mainline stations are both within 10 minutes walk of almost all the University's sites.
Buses: The City and East End are well served by an enormous

number of buses and you must be kidding if you think we're going to list them all, but here are the ones to catch to the SU building: 8; 15; 15B; 25; 40; 67; and 253. Night buses: N6; N8; N16; N76; N95; N97; and N98.

Car: *Parking? Yeah, right...*

Underground: Moorgate (Northern, Metropolitan, Circle and Hammersmith & City Lines), Aldgate (Metropolitan and Circle), Aldgate East (Hammersmith & City and District), Tower Hill (District and Circle) and Tower Gateway (on the Docklands Light Railway) are all local. No 2 sites are further than 1½ miles apart so any of these stations will do for most sites.

LIBRARIES & COMPUTERS:
● Books: 291,640 ● Computer workstations: 800

In addition to the above figures there are 3,000 videos and 80,000 slides across 3 libraries. There are also more computers in various departments, but no study places in the libraries.

CAREER PROSPECTS:
● Careers Service ● No of staff: 6full
● Unemployed after 6mths (1996): 9%

SPECIAL FEATURES:
● *The staff who were made redundant during LGU's prior financial strife will be comforted to know that around £15,000 of last year's £3.3m surplus was spent on an ornamental mace for use in graduation ceremonies.*

FAMOUS ALUMNI:
Sonya Aurora Madan (Echobelly); Joy Gardner (victim of *over-zealous* extradition procedures); Kate Hoey MP (Lab, ex-Spurs physio); Jools Holland; Michael Jackson (of TV executive, rather than King of Pop fame); Nick Leeson (disgraced bank bloke); Terry Marsh (former boxing champ); Alison Moyet (chanteuse); Vic Reeves (comedian); Mark Thatcher (*Maggie's pride and joy*).

FURTHER INFO:
Prospectus and individual course leaflets, and a mature students' guide. Web site (http://www.lgu.ac.uk).

entertainment

IN LONDON: see University of London

UNIVERSITY:
● Price of a pint of beer: £1.50 ● Glass of wine: £1.15

Students tend to stick with the SU for fun, if only because the immediate vicinity is so expensive (although Brick Lane is very close).

Bars: (3) The main supping spot is on the 1st floor of the SU building, in *relaxing* shades of candy blue and banana. There's also the *dingy* Sub Bar (cap 450), mainly used for ents *(dead when it's not)* and there's a *more relaxed* place at Commercial Road.

Music venues/clubs/discos: The Sub Bar hosts 3 club nights a week with open DJ spots and jam sessions and *occasional* bands *(but nobody to get too ecstatic about).*

Cabaret: *Occasional selection of comics,* recent catches including Jenny Eclair and Charlie Chuck.

Food: The SU Diner doles out hot and cold food from 12 to 8, *leaving a much saner bill than you'd get at any nearby café.* The SU Bars do pizzas.

Others: At least 3 balls a year.

social & political

LONDON GUILDHALL UNIVERSITY STUDENTS' UNION:
● 5 sabbaticals ● Turnout at last ballot: 22%

● NUS member

The SU has facilities at 4 sites, but its main centre is the freshly renovated Joy Gardner House in Goulston Street. *Getting this lot interested in politics would be harder than a concrete ox.*

SU FACILITIES:

In the SU Building there are 2 bars, a diner, print shop and satellite TV. Elsewhere the SU runs 1 bar at Calcutta House, a snack bar and 3 stationery shops.

CLUBS (NON SPORTING):

Bangladeshi; Fine Arts; Hunt Sabs; Peer Support.

OTHER ORGANISATIONS:

There's a mag, 'G:Echo', which comes out every 6 weeks. *The slightly disappointing Rag raised £150 last year.*

RELIGIOUS:

● 2 chaplains (RC, CofE)

There's an ecumenical chaplaincy and a *small* multi-faith 'quiet area', mainly used by Islamic students as a prayer room. The East End is a multi-ethnic area with Judaism and most Asian religions well represented.

PAID WORK: see University of London

sports

● Recent successes: nothing special

Split sites mean that it's hard to maintain an overall level of athletic bravado. There's a new fitness centre, but the outdoor facilities are quite a trek by train or tube. By the time students get there, they're often too knackered to play.

SPORTS FACILITIES:

The fitness centre has a gym and activities rooms, for exercise classes such as yoga and funky step (*we didn't like to ask*). There's a gym on the top floor at Tower Hill. The University also has a sports ground at Grove Park (20 acres of playing fields and tennis courts), 7 miles away.

SPORTING CLUBS:

Boxing.

ATTRACTIONS: see University of London

accommodation

IN COLLEGE:
● Catered: 1% ● Cost: £70(40wks)
● Self-catering: 5% ● Cost: £48-63(40wks)

Availability: There are only 461 places in the University's accommodation, procured through an arrangement with an independent housing association, in Sir John Cass Hall, a

catered 2-storey house in Hackney (4 miles from the City), and 2 blocks of self-catering flats. No-one is guaranteed a place and about 50% of first years who want to can't get a place. *The students who are lucky enough to get such accommodation*, get single rooms in the mixed blocks. Flats are single sex. Between 3 and 5 students share cooking and cleaning facilities.
Car parking: *Limited permit parking space at the flats, but students can forget any thoughts of driving to the University.*

EXTERNALLY: see University of London
Housing help: Students appeal to the Accommodation Service and private letting firms for help in finding housing. *Leyton and Hackney are recommended areas for budget and proximity. The Isle of Dogs is pretty rough, with notorious racial and social tensions.*

welfare

SERVICES:
● Creche ● Lesbian & Gay Society
● Mature SA ● Overseas SA ● Women's Officer
The Student Advice Centre has 4 counsellors at Calcutta House. A nurse is employed to provide medical cover at Calcutta House and a doctor drops in for 3 sessions a week. The University runs a dyslexia support group and health-related workshops, including stress management and controlling eating disorders.

Women: The Fawcett Library houses The National Library for Women (including banners and unique archive material). The University also has a number of links with other organisations promoting women's educational opportunities.

Disabled: The University encourages advance visits for applicants with disabilities and has its own Equal Opportunities Adviser. *Most buildings will have reasonably good access and the University goes a fair distance to make its education open to all.* There are supplementary workshops and a Special Needs Co-ordinator based at Commercial Rd.

FINANCE:
● Ave debt: £1,850 ● Access fund: £217,000
The University targets the access fund at students with special needs (ie self-funding students and those with children or disabilities). Other bursaries and scholarships may be available.

> ❝'Go to St Andrew's for the golf, if nothing else. It is one of the town's best, and, of course, most famous attractions. Perhaps, however, I spent a little too much time playing golf, especially late at night.'
> —Alex Salmond MP, leader SNP❞

The London Institute

(1) The London Institute, 65 Davies Street, London, W1Y 2DA.
Tel: (0171) 514 6129. Fax: (0171) 514 6131.
E-mail: marcom@linst.ac.uk
London Institute Students' Union, 388-396 Oxford Street,
London, W1R 1FE. Tel: (0171) 514 6000 ext 6270.
Fax: (0171) 514 6284.
(2) Camberwell College of Arts, Peckham Road, London,
SE5 8UF.
(3) Central Saint Martin's College of Art and Design,
Southampton Row, London, WC1B 4AP.
(4) Chelsea College of Art and Design, Manresa Road, London,
SW3 6LS.
(5) London College of Fashion, 20 John Princes Street,
London, W1M 0BJ.
(6) London College of Printing & Distributive Trades, Elephant
& Castle, London, SE1 6SB.

General

Despite its *somewhat clinical* name, the London Institute is
the largest art school in Europe, comprising five separate
institutions, all of which have excellent reputations in their own
rights and attract students the world over. Although the
Institute awards its own degrees, students apply to the
individual colleges.

37% ♂♂♂♂ ♀♀♀♀♀ 63%

Sex ratio(M:F): 37%:63%	Founded: 1986
Full time u'grads: 5,942	Part time: 575
Postgrads: 555	Non-degree: 1,673
Ave course: 3yrs	Ethnic: 11%
Private school: 4%	Flunk rate: n/a
Mature students: 35%	Overseas students: 26%
Disabled students: 5%	Staff/student ratio: 1:21
Clearing: 5%	

ATMOSPHERE:
*Not only is the Institute the sum of 5 separate colleges, but
these are in turn fragmented between 18 different sites across
central and south London, which means the chance of overall
social cohesion is pretty much stifled at birth. The only
generalisations possible are the students' tendency to
trendiness and a strong level of commitment to their courses.
The days of self-conscious artists wallowing in an existential
mire of absinthe and syphilis may have passed, but many want
to keep the image going (if not the reality).*

THE SITES:
Camberwell: A large mixed modern/Victorian building, next to
the South London Art Gallery, with 2 annexes up to 15mins

walk away. Camberwell specialises in graphics. South London; *shabby, but friendly enough and relatively cheap.*

Central Saint Martin's: (2,579 students) HQ in Holborn, near Bloomsbury; further sites at Clerkenwell (shared with LCP), nearer the City; in Covent Garden; and on the Charing Cross Road. CSM has a big reputation in fine art and also runs graphic design and fashion courses.

Chelsea: (880 students) 3 sites *in and around Sloane country,* with a fourth further west, at Lime Grove.

London College of Fashion: (1,365 students) 3 sites around the western, *posher* stretch of Oxford Street. 2 more in the City, *among the financial whizzkids.*

London College of Printing: (3,405 students) The most dispersed college, LCP is based at the Elephant & Castle (see South Bank University) with other bits at Clerkenwell and Davies Street. Media, graphic design, business, retail and printing courses are taught here.

THE CITY: see University of London

TRAVEL: see University of London
Nearest Underground/rail links:
Camberwell: Peckham Rye and Denmark Hill overground stations; Oval (Northern Line) on the tube.
C St Martin's: Holborn (Central and Piccadilly) for Southampton Row. Farringdon (Circle, Hammersmith & City) for Clerkenwell. Covent Garden (Piccadilly) for Long Acre. Tottenham Court Road (Central and Northern) for Charing Cross Rd.
Chelsea: Manresa Rd: South Kensington (Circle, District, Piccadilly Lines). Bagley's Lane and Hugon Rd: Putney Bridge (District). Lime Grove: Shepherd's Bush (Central).
LCF: Oxford Circus (Central, Bakerloo and Northern) or Bond Street (Central and Jubilee) for Oxford Street sites. Barbican (Circle and Hammersmith & City) or Old Street (Northern) for City sites.
LCP: Elephant: Elephant & Castle (Bakerloo and Northern). Davies Street: Bond Street (Central and Jubilee). Clerkenwell: Farringdon (Circle, Hammersmith & City).
Yes, there are buses, and no, we're not going to list all of them.

LIBRARIES:
● Books: 274,815 ● Study places: 673
● Computer workstations: 930
There are 10 libraries in all, dotted between the various sites.

CAREER PROSPECTS:
● Careers Service ● No of staff: 7full/6part
● Unemployed after 6mths (1996): 17%
The Careers Service publishes a monthly job list.

FAMOUS ALUMNI:
Lionel Bart (composer); Dirk Bogarde (actor, writer); Neville Brody (graphic designer); Jarvis Cocker (Pulp); Terence Conran (entrepreneur); Nicole Farhi, John Galliano, Katherine Hamnett, Stella McCartney, Alexander McQueen, Bruce Oldfield, Rifat Ozbek, Zandra Rhodes, Vivienne Westwood (fashion designers); Mike Flowers (of Pops fame); Gilbert & George (artists); Mike Leigh (film director); Henry Moore (sculptor); Alexei Sayle (comedian); Vivian Stanshall (eccentric musician).

> ❝The original site of Reading
> University was the back yard of
> the Huntley and Palmer biscuit
> factory.❞

FURTHER INFO:
Prospectuses, videos, leaflets from the central
Communications and Marketing Office. Web site
(http://www.linst.ac.uk).

entertainment

IN LONDON: see <u>University of London</u>

COLLEGES:

● <u>Price of a pint of beer: £1.30</u> ● <u>Glass of wine: £1</u>
Social facilities vary between the sites. When students get a
serious urge to party as a collective mass, they take over
Heaven and the Ministry of Sound (see <u>University of London</u>).
Bars: (5) The Boiler Room at LCP; The Ophelia Suite at LCF;
99 Screwz at Camberwell; a bar above the Cochrane Theatre
for CSM bevvying; and one at the Furzedown halls of residence
in Tooting. Chelsea students have to improvise.
Cinema: There's a Videodrome at the College of Printing.
Food: Catering on all sites is handled by an outside contractor,
to less than universal approval.

social & political

LONDON INSTITUTE STUDENTS' UNION (LISU):

● <u>6 sabbaticals</u> ● <u>Turnout at last ballot: 6%</u>
● <u>NUS member</u>
Each college has its own SU, under the umbrella of LISU.
*Because of the fragmented nature of the Institute (and even of
some of the component bodies) students often become aware
of their Union only when something goes wrong.*

SU FACILITIES:
At LISU; bar; photocopier; payphones; games machines;
jukeboxes.

OTHER ORGANISATIONS:
The LISU newsletter, 'Blue', comes out monthly, *a wonderful
example of the triumph of style over content. But then they're
into style, aren't they?*

RELIGIOUS: see <u>University of London</u>

PAID WORK: see <u>University of London</u>

sports

● <u>Recent successes: not a lot</u>
*Those students who channel their creative urges into exertion
tend to steer clear of competitive team stuff.*

SPORTING CLUBS:
Pool.

ATTRACTIONS: see <u>University of London</u>

accommodation

IN COLLEGE:
- <u>Catered: 3%</u> ● <u>Cost: £75(33-39wks)</u>
- <u>Self-catering: 6%</u> ● <u>Cost: £51-60(33-40wks)</u>

5 blocks of mostly 60s design, split between Battersea (200 catered places, *bearable*) or Tooting (380 self-catering), with preference given to 1st years from outside SE England. 16% of first years are unlucky and don't get the place they're after. Students can book accommodation over the summer if they need to look for rented places.

EXTERNALLY: see <u>University of London</u>
The College Accommodation Service offers housing lists and a Find-a-Flatmate service.

welfare

SERVICES:
- <u>Creche</u> ● <u>Lesbian & Gay Society</u>

1 full- and 3 part-time counsellors are employed by Student Services; the union has 9 full- and 4 part-time advisers.
Disabled: *The Institute's facilities are pretty good overall. Support for dyslexics.*

FINANCE:
- <u>Ave debt: £1,800</u> ● <u>Access fund: £324,004</u>
- <u>Successful applications (1997): 1,163</u>

• •

▶▶ London School of Economics
see LSE

• •

Loughborough University

Loughborough University, Loughborough, Leicestershire, LE11 3TU. Tel: (01509) 222498/9. Fax: (01509) 223905. E-mail: prospectus-enquiries@lboro.ac.uk
Loughborough Students' Union, Ashby Road, Loughborough, Leicestershire, LE11 3TT. Tel: (01509) 217766.

general

Loughborough, *pronounced 'Lufbra' by the locals and 'Loogabarooga' by the self-consciously wacky and/or drunk,* is a small, industrial market town, set among wandering countryside and small suburban villages of the East Midlands. The University is set about a mile west of the town centre in green and *pleasant* parkland. It became a university in 1966, but has its origins in a technical college dating back to 1909 and continues to evolve - it merges with Loughborough College of Art & Design in August 1998. The campus buildings are mainly *inoffensive*, low-rise blocks on a landscaped, 223-acre site. *It's perfect for* the various playing fields and sporting facilities, *the University's chief extra-curricular preoccupation.*

64% ♂♂♂♂♂♂♀♀♀ 36%	
Sex ratio(M:F): 64%:36%	Founded: 1966
Full time u'grads: 8,657	Part time: 84
Postgrads: 1,047	Non-degree: 242
Ave course: 3/4yrs	Ethnic: 6.8%
Private school: n/a	Flunk rate: 5%
Mature students: 12.5%	Overseas students: 10%
Disabled students: 4.2%	Staff/student ratio: 1:12
Clearing: 5.8%	

ATMOSPHERE:
Don't believe what they say about 'it's not the winning but the taking part'. At Loughborough University, it's the winning that matters, and the training beforehand and the celebration, analysis, recriminations and loud drinking games afterwards. If you're not particularly interested in sport one way or another, don't be dismayed - there's plenty else to do, plus the influx of new arty types in the wake of the merger. However, for those who are allergic to track suits and become apoplexic at the hint of exertion, applying here could be construed as a little perverse, to say the least.

THE TOWN:
- Population: 51,000 ● London: 100miles
- Leicester: 13miles ● Nottingham: 17miles

Loughborough is not big enough to fit in more than a few sites of historic interest, but it gives its money's worth, including a few old churches and museums (eg the Bell Foundry Museum - which makes bells - the Military Museum and the Ancient Monuments Museum). Apart from all the usual shops and public amenities, there is a twice-weekly street market, some *good* independent record stores and some ethnic jewellery shops. The town is surrounded by the ancient Charnwood Forest - so ancient that there's not much forest left - and various waterways flow through the area. Of local note is the Great Central Railway, still steaming its way cross-country and there's the Quorn Hunt *who look silly and fall off horses.* Ladybird Books also have their HQ here, *which should give a warm feeling to anyone brought up on 'Peter and Jane', although it's not much help if you've got an essay crisis.*

TRAVEL:
Trains: Loughborough station, on the main InterCity line north from London St Pancras (£19.50) to Edinburgh, is 2 miles from the campus.
Coaches: Served by local coach company Paul Winson and National Express - London (£12).
Car: The A6 goes straight through Loughborough and the M1 is less than 2 miles west of the campus.
Air: East Midlands Airport (inland and European flights) is 5½ miles from the campus.
Hitching: *The M1 is good, but it's a bus ride to the junction.*
Local: Local buses run between campus and town. For 65p students can get across town to the station, or for a bit more

they can catch a ride into Leicester or Nottingham.
Taxis: £3 from the campus to the station (2 miles).
Bicycles: *Useful for getting into town (and the campus and its sports fields). The theft situation is improving, but don't bring an expensive mountain bike; you won't take it back.*

LIBRARIES & COMPUTERS:
- Books: 600,000 ● Study places: 420
- Computer workstations: 1,500

The large white library is in the centre of the campus. Some 24hr access to computers.

CAREER PROSPECTS:
- Careers Service ● No of staff: 8full/4part
- Unemployed after 6mths (1996): 3.6%

FAMOUS ALUMNI:
Steve Backley (javelin chucker); Sebastian Coe (runner); Michael Fabricant MP (Con); Lorna Fitzsimons MP (Lab, former NUS president); David Moorcroft (athlete); Carole Tongue MEP (Lab); Bob Wilson (commentator, ex-Arsenal goalie).

FURTHER INFO:
Prospectuses for undergrads, postgrads and individual departments. Web site (http://www.lboro.ac.uk/).

entertainment

TOWN:

- Price of a pint of beer: £1.50 ● Glass of wine: £1.30

Cinemas: (1) The 6-screen Curzon.
Theatres: Amateur and touring shows in the Town Hall.
Pubs: *Local pubs are popular with students who live out or want to get off campus, but Loughborough generally suffers from an embarrassing lack of swinging student spots.*
push*plugs: The Griffin and The Paget (as studenty as any round here); The Swan (live bands and real ale); Barleymow; Phantom & Firkin; Tap & Spile; Blacksmith's Arms.*
Clubs/discos/music venues: The town's mainstream clubs, TJs, Echoes and, above all, Pulse, which everyone still knows by its former name 'Crystals', all compete for student trade. Although the Town Hall has occasional bands, *Leicester and Nottingham are better bets for any form of entertainment.*
Eating out: *Again, it's necessary to go out of town for serious tastebud tingles but a few establishments are worth a look.*
push*plugs: Bar Europa (good, cheap pizza); Cactus Café (Mexican).* There are numerous Indian, Chinese and takeaway places, some open till at least 2am.

UNIVERSITY:

- Price of a pint of beer: £1.20 ● Glass of wine: £1.40

Bars: There are 9 bars around campus, 3 in residential halls and 6 in the Union Building, *which are always lively, especially on event nights and when there's something sporty to celebrate.*
Theatres: Regular presentations in the Arts Centre and a Union-funded troupe.
Cinemas: The film society shows pics and flicks thrice a week.
Clubs/discos: 2 club nights a week in Rattlers *but students tend to shake their butts on the fields more than on the dance*

floor. For those who need some ents-style excerise, the Saturday Selection rotates 70s, 80s, charty and club nights.

Music venues: The Main Auditorium tempts some *not bad* modern minstrels, recent examples being Progress Club Tour, Catatonia and the Dust Junkies. There's also live jazz at the Bocca bar on Sunday evenings.

Cabaret: Weekly cabaret in the Union Building with *top* rib-ticklers, such as, lately, Ed Byrne and Donna McPhail.

Food: In the Union and the Student Village students can find something edible (and legal) to put in their mouths from 10am to 3am. *There's an imaginative selection, from the Purple Onion pizza/burger delivery service to Greasy Joe's breakfast outlet.*

Other: *Freshers' week is a blur of entertainments from surf simulators to bucking broncos and at the other end of a student's stint is the Graduation ball (dodgems, casino and that bloody bronco again).* Occasional bingo.

⸱⸱⸱⸱⸱⸱⸱⸱social & political

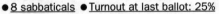
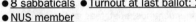
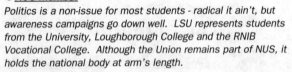

LOUGHBOROUGH STUDENTS' UNION:
● <u>8 sabbaticals</u> ● <u>Turnout at last ballot: 25%</u>
● <u>NUS member</u>

Politics is a non-issue for most students - radical it ain't, but awareness campaigns go down well. LSU represents students from the University, Loughborough College and the RNIB Vocational College. Although the Union remains part of NUS, it holds the national body at arm's length.

SU FACILITIES:
A general shop (complete, of course, with sports gear section); 6 bars; 5 catering outlets; travel agency; printing facilities; bookshop (Blackwells); market stalls; 3 banks; an insurance office; photocopier; photo booth; games and vending machines; pool tables; juke box; meeting rooms; auditorium; optician; dentist; hairdresser; taxi hire; suit hire.

CLUBS (NON SPORTING):
Aerospace; CD Library; Cocktail; Hellenic; Hiking and Hostelling; Indian; Malaysian; Real Ale; Wargames.

OTHER ORGANISATIONS:
The Rag is about the only thing that distracts anyone from sporting pursuits. There's also a Student Community Action group. Student media includes 'The Label', a weekly newspaper financed by the Union, but run independently, and a radio station, 25 years old this year. *The rather remarkable* Rag raised over £227,000 last year.

RELIGIOUS:
There's an ecumenical Christian chaplaincy and a Muslim prayer room.

❝There's more to student life than poverty and fun... see the courses tables at the back of the book.❞

PAID WORK:
There's an employment agency with a job database for students.

sports

● <u>Recent successes: it'd be quicker to list the ones they didn't win...</u>

Did we mention that Loughborough University is big on sport? Applicants who think that running around a field in shorts, chasing/catching/kicking/throwing a ball, is stupid should keep quite quiet about it if they go to Loughborough, unless they want to see grown men and women cry. The University enjoys a vast range of sporting facilities, virtually unmatched by any other, let alone by a university this size. Success in most sports has been phenomenal; they've won the British Universities Sports Association women's championship for the last 19 consecutive years and the men's version for the last 18.

SPORTS FACILITIES:
All sports clubs are fully insured against accidents, *which makes them relatively pricey to join* - even table tennis costs £8. *But many would argue that the facilities are worth it.* 4 sports centres geared up for all manner of indoor exertion; 2 gymnasia; dance studio; 2 swimming pools; 7 squash courts; 2 flood-lit all-weather areas; an all-weather athletics stadium (run jointly with the town); many acres of playing fields; the Dan Maskell tennis centre; and equipment for indoor sports of all sorts such as a multigym, martial arts dojo, badminton courts and so on and so on...

The town doesn't really need to add anything, but the surrounding area does make outdoor sports, such as fell-walking and watersports, possible.

SPORTING CLUBS:
Aerobics; American Football; Gliding; Hot Air Balloon; Karting; Kickboxing; Lacrosse; Paragliding; Rifle; Rowing; Rugby League; Speleological (caving); Sport Parachuting; Surf; Ten Pin Bowling; Tetsudo; Thai Boxing; Triathlon; Ultimate Frisbee; Water Skiing; Windsurfing.

ATTRACTIONS:
Formula 3 motor racing, motor cycle racing and the Grand Prix at Castle Donington.

accommodation

IN COLLEGE:
● <u>Catered: 42%</u> ● <u>Cost: £55-79(30-37wks)</u>

● <u>Self-catering: 22%</u> ● <u>Cost: £32-46(30-50wks)</u>

Availability: There are 10 catered and 6 self-catering halls. They are all mixed (although some blocks or corridors are single sex) and accommodate between 150 and 650 students. They are all on or adjacent to campus except 1 en route to town nearly 1km away. There are also self-catering flats arranged in courts or in the student village. Between 6 and 8 students share each kitchen. This is enough to house all 1st years who request and a good number of finalists. 9% of rooms are shared.

Car parking: Limited spaces for which a permit is needed; 2nd and 3rd years only.

EXTERNALLY:
● Ave rent: £37

Availability: *It's a renter's market and you're unlikely to be left on the pavement. The best places, plucked by the early birds, are around Ashby Road and Storer Road, between the campus and Sainsbury's.*

Housing help: The Union runs an advice service and the University's Student Accommodation Service holds an accommodation list and offers handy suggestions to new and bemused students.

welfare

SERVICES:
● Nursery ● Lesbian & Gay Society ● Mature SA
● Overseas SA ● Postgrad SA ● Nightbus ● Women's Officer

The University Counselling Service has 2 full- and 3 part-time counsellors, and there's a medical centre on campus, providing a sick bay, a doctor on call 24 hours a day and a physiotherapy clinic for sportspersons who let their exertions get the better of them. The SU also runs a student advice centre with 5 advisers.

Disabled: *Access is reasonably good to most buildings, even though the campus isn't entirely flat.* Support is also available for students with sight and hearing difficulties and there's a tutor for students with special needs.

FINANCE:
● Ave debt per year: £1,500 ● Access fund: £156,000
● Successful applications (1997): 321

There is a hardship fund and over 200 scholarships and bursaries, 70 of which are sports-related. *Quite remarkable.*

LSE

● *The School is part of University of London and students are entitled to use its facilities.*

The London School of Economics & Political Science, Houghton Street, London, WC2A 2AE. Tel: (0171) 405 7686. Fax: (0171) 831 1684.
LSE Students' Union, East Building, LSE, Houghton Street, London, WC2A 2AE. Tel: (0171) 955 7158.
Fax: (0171) 955 6789. E-mail: su-gen-sec@lse.ac.uk

general

Hot in the heartland of London's throbbing core, between the end of the Strand and the beginning of Fleet Street, is one of the bull's eyes in the world's economic and political darts board. LSE may have an international reputation for the E part of its name, but studies extend to social sciences of all sorts. *The buildings themselves don't live up to expectations, being a cross between the old and austere and your modern cake-tin type blocks.* The buildings are clustered - *well, squashed actually* - onto the pavement just opposite the BBC's Bush House, less than a mile down the road from Trafalgar Square, and just round the corner from <u>King's College London</u> and the <u>Courtauld Institute</u>. *The place is cramped and busy - not a good place to start swinging cats because you'll either (a) hit a wall, (b) hit a person, or (c) get caught by the RSPCA.*

55% ♂♂♂♂♂♂♀♀♀♀♀ 45%

Sex ratio(M:F): 55%:45%	Founded: 1895
Full time u'grads: 2,698	Part time: 56
Postgrads: 2,537	Non-degree: 0
Ave course: 3yrs	Ethnic: n/a
Private school: 37%	Flunk rate: 3%
Mature students: n/a	Overseas students: 51.7%
Disabled students: n/a	Staff/student ratio: 1:18
Clearing: n/a	

ATMOSPHERE:
It's a hectic hive of intellectual pressure, attracting the brightest social scientists from around the world. A combination of the high proportion of overseas and postgrad students and the fact that they can get very ambitious, career-minded and academically competitive tempers the potential for youthful exuberance but there are still enough traces of the radicalism for which the School was renowned in the 1960s to keep things electric. If you want to chill for 3 years, don't come to the LSE.

THE CITY: see <u>University of London</u>

ALDWYCH:
Spit east and it'll land in the eye of a businessman in the City. Spit west and you'll hit either a theatre, a restaurant, a café or a cinema in the West End. Spit north and you'll have dampened the cardboard home of one of the many homeless who live on the streets around Lincoln's Inn Fields (a small area of grass, which, until the homeless were evicted, was itself a makeshift shanty). Spit south and it'll go deservedly straight back in your face because the Thames is about 100 yards in that direction and the wind will probably be blowing from there. For more details where to spit, look up either the <u>Courtauld Institute</u>, <u>King's College London</u> or <u>University of London</u>.

TRAVEL: see <u>University of London</u>

LIBRARIES & COMPUTERS:
● <u>Books: 930,000</u> ● <u>Study places: 1,340</u>
● <u>Computer workstations: 500</u>
LSE's main library goes under the appropriately grand title of the British Library of Political Science & Economic Science. There are also several small departmental libraries. Some 24hr access to computers.

CAREER PROSPECTS:
● <u>Careers Service</u> ● <u>No of staff: 3full/2part</u>
● <u>Unemployed after 6mths (1996): 6.8%</u>
A high proportion of students go on to further training or higher degrees.

SPECIAL FEATURES:
- LSE has students from 119 countries; that's more than the World Bank and almost as many as the UN.

FAMOUS ALUMNI:
Sir David Attenborough (biologist and broadcaster); Cherie Booth QC; Carlos the Jackal (terrorist); Ekow Eshun (editor, 'Arena' magazine); Clare Francis (yachtswoman, author); Loyd Grossman (foodie TV presenter); Mick Jagger (Stone); John F Kennedy; Robert Kilroy-Silk (chat-show host); Bernard Levin (journalist); Mat Osman (Suede); Maurice Saatchi (advertising guru); George Soros (financier).

FURTHER INFO:
Prospectuses for undergrads and postgrads, alternative prospectus from the SU, video (£6) plus a web site (http://www.lse.ac.uk).

entertainment

IN LONDON: see <u>University of London</u>

COLLEGE:
- <u>Price of a pint of beer: £1.60</u> ● <u>Glass of wine: 80p</u>

Bars: (3) The Three Tuns Bar (cap 700) is *pretty popular*. The Underground (120) is primarily an events venue and the Beavers Retreat, *which looks as if it's been furnished courtesy of MFI, is expensive and only really popular with the academics.*

Cinemas: The film club shows an arthouse or cult movie every week.

Theatres: *Brimming with luvvies, LSE may not be,* but it does have a theatre which hosts 3 productions a year. Last year they took 2 shows to the Fringe in Edinburgh.

Clubs/discos/music venues: The Underground goes overboard for its Friday night disco 'Crush' and the Quad is used for bands.

Cabaret: Every Saturday the Chuckle Club chucks up comics, Mark Lamarr and Phil Jupitus being recent examples.

Food: The Union runs a café *which is unusually good for vegetarian and vegan grub,* with furniture from the next century and trendy murals. It also runs a pizzeria and restaurant. The Veggie Café is exactly that.

Others: Student society events (eg tequila and dance nights) and multi-cultural goings-on. Annual Rag and Graduation Balls (last year's Grad Ball was at the Savoy).

social & political

LSE STUDENTS' UNION:
- <u>4 sabbaticals</u> ● <u>Turnout at last ballot: 20%</u>
- <u>NUS member</u>

The SU still veers leftwards, but not at the break-neck angle it once did. It has weekly general meetings and occasionally threatens to disaffiliate from the NUS, but the fact that it attracts major political speakers from the UK and abroad is of more interest to the political junkies who infest the place. Recent campaigns against tuition fees were well supported.
Also ULU: see <u>University of London</u>

SU FACILITIES:
The SU has 3 floors and the basement in the *cramped and*

slightly claustrophobic East Building where The Three Tuns bar is based as well as the café, travel agent, general shop, printing and photocopying service. The School also has a bookshop on its grounds.

CLUBS (NON SPORTING):
Animal Aid; Arabic; Bridge; Central & Eastern European Development; Chinese; Cypriot; Dr Bike (bicycle maintenance); European; Green; Grimshaw; Hayek; Hellenic; Human Rights of Women; Indian; Italian; Jelly Baby Party (club trips); Latin American; Law; Mauritian; Mexican; Modern Dance; Pakistan; Peace; Scandinavian; Stop the Fees; Student Aid for Bosnia; Theatre Appreciation; Vedic.

OTHER ORGANISATIONS:
The weekly student newspaper 'The Beaver', is published by the SU. Ambitions to broadcast on the radio waves.

RELIGIOUS:
● 4 chaplains (RC, CofE, Free Church, Jewish)
Also Buddhist and Muslim facilities.

PAID WORK: see University of London

sports

● Recent successes: football

Most of LSE's greatest sporting moments are reserved for the Rugby Club Ball. The Aldwych is obviously not the place for vast playing fields but a *hardy* few make the 40-minute train journey to the School's 25 acres of playing fields at Berrylands near New Malden. Students can, of course, use ULU's facilities.

SPORTS FACILITIES:
On site, LSE offers 3 squash courts, a badminton court, multigym, snooker table and a circuit room. At Berrylands, 10 miles away, there are playing fields, tennis courts, a croquet lawn, pavilion, bar and restaurant.

SPORTING CLUBS:
Aerobics; Boxing; Hapkido; Kung-Fu; Muay Thai Boxing; Rock Climbing; Rowing; Tennis.

ATTRACTIONS: see University of London

accommodation

IN COLLEGE:

● Catered: 25% ● Cost: £66-85(30wks)
● Self-catering: 14% ● Cost: £63-87(39wks)
Availability: Students can use the University's intercollegiate housing (see University of London) so all 1st years from ouside Greater London can be housed where necessary. The accommodation itself is in 2 sets of self-catering flats and 4 catered (pay-as-you-eat) halls spread out between 1 and 4 miles from the School, from Holborn to Docklands. 10% of places are shared, some even in triple rooms and some flats are available for single parents or married couples. None of the School's own housing is single sex although the University offers some. In some rooms heating and/or lighting is not included.
Catering: As well as kitchens shared between 6 students, there are refectories operating a pay-as-you-eat scheme in some self-catering halls and, in catered housing, dining halls.

EXTERNALLY: see University of London
Housing help: The SU runs the student advice centre where they can help with housing problems.

welfare

SERVICES:
- Creche ● Lesbian & Gay Society ● Mature SA
- Overseas SA ● Minibus ● Women's Officer
- Self-defence classes

The School has 1 full- and 2 part-time counsellors, the Union 3 part-time advisers, who provide assistance to students in need and the Health Service provides medical support. There is a student Parents' Society. Other services are available through the Union and London University.

Disabled: *There are lifts aplenty, but often you have to climb stairs to get to them. There's also a Society for the Enlightenment of Able-Bodied Students, as well as Braille and recording facilities, and plans for voice synthesisers on library PCs.*

FINANCE:
- Access fund: £157,500

Generous hardship funds and scholarships ease the way more than a little; *maybe the economists help everyone to budget more successfully than at other colleges.*

▶▶ LSU

see University of Southampton

University of Luton

- ***Formerly Luton College of Higher Education***

University of Luton, Park Square, Luton, Bedfordshire, LU1 3JU. Tel: (01582) 489015. Fax: (01582) 486260. Luton University Students' Union, Europa House, Vicarage Street, Luton, Bedfordshire, LU1 3HZ. Tel: (01582) 489366. Fax: (01582) 457187.

general

For years, Luton has had a hard time living down the image of dropped aitches and having a local Vauxhall Cavalier car factory *as its most interesting feature.* This perception is becoming increasingly outdated, however, and Luton is metamorphosing into a *lively,* growing place with 150 acres of pleasant greenery, (winner of Britain in Bloom '97, *the highest accolade in the world, ever*), not far from the Chiltern hills and London ($\frac{1}{2}$ an hour by train). The University of Luton is now one of the most *exciting* features and is sure is going some on the expansion front, having only gained university status in 1993 and having grown unrecognisably since 1976, when it became a college of HE rather than a technical college. The last few years have seen a huge increase in degree students and expenditure of over £40 million on buildings, and the university is rated in the top 10 of the new universities for academic standards.

46% ♂♂♂♂♂♀♀♀♀♀ **54%**

Sex ratio(M:F): 46%:54%	Founded: 1957
Full time u'grads: 8,200	Part time: 1,800
Postgrads: 860	Non-degree: 800
Ave course: 3yrs	Ethnic: 21.5%
Private school: n/a	Flunk rate: n/a
Mature students: 14%	Overseas students: 14%
Disabled students: 5.5%	Staff/student ratio: 1:12
Clearing: 30%	

ATMOSPHERE:
A high proportion of students are here simply because it's their local university and a good chunk had little choice in the matter, being sucked in through clearing. That said, once they find their feet, most seem quite happy with their lot, provided they see a degree course primarily as a means to a job. Everything else, especially politics, can disappear down the cracks in the concrete.

THE SITES:
Park Square: (main site) *The brutalist architecture of the Park Square site is rather appropriate to the utilitarian philosophy of the courses taught here.*
Castle Street: (humanities) 5 minutes walk from the main site, *this is another not-terribly attractive example of 60s office block architecture,* although it does house some *nifty* multimedia equipment.
Putteridge Bury: (management) 3 miles away, *this is a much more aesthetically pleasing site,* although much of it is devoted to conferences and research, so few undergraduates get to benefit.

THE TOWN:
● Population: 167,300 ● London: 28miles
● Bedford: 25miles ● Birmingham: 80miles

Luton, which started as the centre of the hat and lace industry - *don't knock it* - is now a busy business town, not suffering the high unemployment that some are. It's the largest town in Bedfordshire, which doesn't say much since Bedford is just about the only competition. Nevertheless, it has all the cosmopolitan paraphernalia like shops, libraries, banks, markets and the rest in plentiful supply. *Worth a particular mention* are the massive modern Arndale Shopping Centre, right by the University and the development of the Artezium, a *spanking* new arts centre, which when completed in October 98 will feature music, TV and multimedia facilities, cinema, art gallery, restaurant and café.

TRAVEL:
Trains: Luton is the nearest station, 5 minutes walk from the University with trains to, among other places, London King's Cross (£8.60), Birmingham, Edinburgh, Bristol, Bedford and Milton Keynes.

Coaches: Green Line and National Express services.

Car: Luton is on the edge of the M1 at the junction where it splits with the A6 which goes straight through the town. The A1 is only 5 miles east and the end of the A5 is 2 miles south.

Air: Luton Airport operates inland and international services to Europe, Ireland and the USA.

Hitching: *Despite the good connections, it's easier to pick up the white lines on the road than pick up a lift in the Home Counties. It's none too safe either, but a few students try anyway.*

Local: Little 'hopper' buses scuttle round the town *reliably although not particularly cheaply and not late.* No local trains around the town, but an *excellent* link into London which students often use for a day trip, *however, the last train's all too early and easy to miss.*

Taxis: *Not cheap, but worth using at night because Luton's not too big or congested.*

Bicycles: *Although Luton is flat, not many students bike it. Maybe because about 3 heavy padlocks are needed to hang on to a bike for more than a week, but there's no denying it would be useful for the many students who don't live on site.*

LIBRARIES & COMPUTERS:
- Books: 200,000 ● Study places: 1,050
- Computer workstations: 700

The main library is in the Learning Resources Centre at Park Square which also houses many of the computers *and is listed by the Borough Council as a stop on the sight-seeing tour of Luton.* There's also a smaller library at Putteridge Bury.

CAREER PROSPECTS:
- Careers Service ● No of staff: 7full/1part
- Unemployed after 6mths (1996): 9%

FAMOUS ALUMNI:
Ian Dury, Paul Young (singers).

FURTHER INFO:
Prospectuses for undergrads, postgrads and part-time students, video and web site (http://www.luton.ac.uk).

entertainment

TOWN:
- Price of a pint of beer: £2.20 ● Glass of wine: £2.00

Cinemas: The Cannon has 3 screens and the country's largest multiplex is at Milton Keynes (18 miles away).

Theatres: St George's Theatre (cap 256) plays host to local professional and amateur productions, occasional music and even the RSC when on tour. The Arts Centre has a small theatre studio, *a good events programme and a congenial atmosphere.*

Pubs: *Pubs have started waking up to the student trade.* pushplugs: Dog & Donut; the Cock; Newt & Cucumber; Brewery Tap. Avoid Mr Bumbles.

Clubs/discos: *Legends is popular, but the bouncers aren't. The Zone is a better bet.*

Cabaret: Cabaret venue in Guildford Street.

Music venues: The Arts Centre has a bit of everything, especially jazz and minor league indie. The Colliseum and

Legends have regular live bands and DJing. O'Shea's has live Irish bands free 6 nights a week.

Eating out: *The Arndale Centre has a wide variety of scoff stops and Leagrave Road has the best Indian restaurants in town. Arab and Caribbean cuisine are also popular.*

pushplugs: *Cork & Bull for good pub fayre; Brooks Café Bar.*

Others: There's a Fair at Wardown Park, an annual Beer Festival in High Town (a studenty area).

UNIVERSITY:

●Price of a pint of beer: £1.30 ● Glass of wine: £1.10

Bars: (4) 3 *smallish, hot, loud and busy* bars, including the Subclub venue, *and a quieter one.*

Cinema: Weekly showings *veering between cult and mainstream.*

Clubs/discos/music venues: Swaying to sounds and moving to music 3 or 4 nights a week in the Subclub (cap 360): Fridays *cheese* and Saturdays rotate between indie, dance and soul and swing. Recent live acts include Morcheeba and Dodgy.

Food: The University has 2 refectories on Church St and Vicarage St and a restaurant. Norma Jean's Coffee Bar is *popular for its value for money.* In the halls, for the few livers in, there are canteens dishing up grub and the Union provides snack machines and titbits from behind the bar.

Others: The enormous May Ball claims to be the biggest in the country. 1997's effort lured 6,000 punters to the Luton Hoo stately home with acts such as Dodgy and Tim Westwood. Cabaret from the likes of Alan Parker once a month.

social & political

UNIVERSITY OF LUTON STUDENTS' UNION:

●4 sabbaticals ●Turnout at last ballot: 40%
●NUS member

There are no political parties (by choice, not by policy), and specifically student issues such as LRC opening times take centre stage, with fees fandangos following far behind. The Union does an OK job with limited resources, especially on the ents front.

SU FACILITIES:

The Union has its own building, Europa House, right next to the Park Square building, containing bars, nightclub, photocopier, juke boxes, video games, pool tables, vending machines, function rooms, minibus hire.

> 'When I was a student I couldn't wait to be a proper grown-up. A few years after graduating, I couldn't wait to be a student again.'
> −Zeinab Badawi, newsreader.

CLUBS (NON SPORTING):
Asian; Baha'i; Club Rev (dance); Hellenic; Hindu; Moving Image; Sikh; Student Action.

OTHER ORGANISATIONS:
The SU magazine, 'L'Uni', comes out monthly. The Rag raised over £2,000 last year.

RELIGIOUS:
Ecumenical chaplaincy. Luton is abundantly furnished with places of worship including churches, a synagogue, 2 mosques, several Sikh and Buddhist temples.

PAID WORK:
The airport sometimes needs part-time staff. The Brook Street employment agency is on campus.

sports

● <u>Recent successes: football, trampolining, volleyball</u>
The emphasis is on taking part and pecs are flexed by a good few. The University's own facilities are virtually negligible, but Vauxhall and Lucozade have recently laid on the use of recreational facilities for students and the public which has improved opportunity no end, and Luton is now climbing the BUSA ranks.

SPORTS FACILITIES:
At Park Square: fitness suite; gym; multigym; sauna and sunbed. There are 4 sports centres in Luton, 6 swimming pools, a running track, 2 golf courses and a boating lake. At Luton Regional Sports Centre (a public leisure centre 15 minutes away by bus) the University has a club room and squash club and has arranged a scheme for using other facilities.

SPORTING CLUBS:
Aerobics; Boxing; Terra Firma (Parachuting); Weight Training; Windsurfing.

ATTRACTIONS:
Luton's biggest sporting *non-attraction* are 'the Hatters' (Luton FC) who for years *cheated* with their plastic *so-called* 'pitch', until they were finally made to get rid of it and then started to slide down one division per season.

accommodation

IN COLLEGE:
● <u>Self-catering: 13%</u> ● <u>Cost: £40-52(40wks)</u>
Availability: There are 20 halls in all, ranging from terraced houses to tower blocks. Most 1st years who want University accommodation can get it, provided they apply in time. The University also has a head tenancy scheme whereby it rents houses from landlords and lets them on to students, currently providing 391 places on better terms than on the open market. Security in halls is being improved with CCTV *and all that kind of invasion of privacy stuff.*
Car parking: Permits available from the local Council.

EXTERNALLY:
● <u>Ave rent: £39</u>
Availability: *For the moment, there's no shortage of appropriate housing around Luton, although the beginning of*

the year panics are becoming a regular occurrence. The best areas are High Town, Park Town, New Town and the Town Centre which are all within walking distance of the University. Bury Park (especially Crawley Rd) is not terribly safe.

Housing help: The University Accommodation Office allocate the places in college and in the head tenancy scheme (see above) as well as providing vacancy lists and advice.

welfare

SERVICES:

- ● Nursery ● Lesbian & Gay Society
- ● Mature SA ● Overseas SA ● Minibus ● Women's Officer

The University places considerable emphasis on its student support. Counselling and advice are available from the 12 full- and 2 part-time counsellors at the Student Advisory Service. The University has an on-site nurse from the NHS Health Centre 200 yards from Park Square. The Union also offers a *busy* advice service with 3 advisers.

Disabled: *The various new buildings take disabled students' needs into consideration which is more than can be said for the older ones, although they are being adapted slowly.*

FINANCE:
- ● Ave debt: £1,550 ● Access fund: £171,000
- ● Successful applications (1997): 635

There are several bursaries, scholarships and trust funds. Funds are also available for members of specific groups, eg ethnic minorities, mature students, local students.

> **❛On one day a year all students at New College, Oxford are entitled to unlimited free mint julep.❜**

Fold-out guide to symbols inside back cover

Photos
NUS
Students Union
Vauxhall College

m

● ●

▶▶ Magee

see University of Ulster

● ●

University of Manchester

University of Manchester, Oxford Road, Manchester, M13 9PL.
Tel: (0161) 275 2000.
Manchester University Students' Union, Oxford Road,
Manchester, M13 9PR. Tel: (0161) 275 2930.
Fax: (0161) 275 2936.

General

Welcome to the 25-hour party town, the battered but on-for-it
sprawl of Britain's second largest city and the capital of the
north-west. It's a big place with a big student population.
Including the surrounding towns of the conurbation, such as
Salford, there are well over 50,000 higher education students

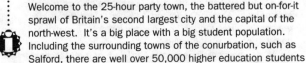

living in Manchester and the University accounts for the lion's share. It's one of the biggest universities in the country with buildings spread around a campus about a mile from the city centre. The campus is surrounded by other colleges - <u>UMIST</u>, <u>Manchester Metropolitan University</u>, teaching hospitals and so on - which together form the largest educational complex in western Europe. The buildings themselves range from the gruff and grand Victorian main building to drab blocks from the 60s and 70s and then to the stark towers of Thatcherite architecture.

50% ♂♂♂♂♂♀♀♀♀♀ 50%	
Sex ratio(M:F): 50%:50%	Founded: 1851
Full time u'grads: 15,557	Part time: 669
Postgrads: 3,072	Non-degree: 0
Ave course: 3yrs	Ethnic: n/a
Private school: n/a	Flunk rate: 14%
Mature students: 11.5%	Overseas students: 12%
Disabled students: n/a	Staff/student ratio: 1:14
Clearing: n/a	

ATMOSPHERE:
The University is big enough and compact enough to give its students the best of both worlds: city life and a campus community. They're a vibrant and diverse bunch, who often seem to think of themselves as the archetypal student. Although facilities are top-rate, the sheer size and bustle of the place can put all but the most self-assured individuals in the shade. Relations with the locals are variable but there is safety in numbers if things get unpleasant.

BEING A STUDENT IN MANCHESTER:
Manchester's late 80s heyday as youth capital of the Universe and beyond is nowt but a dim, baggy-topped memory these days but the city is still buzzing like very few others and as the Gallaghers have proved, it can still churn out music-makers and style-setters to trample over everyone else.

A job's pretty handy (there are a few about but many hunters) because life ain't cheap here. Although not on a London scale of urban extortion, there are too many temptations to look after the pennies and the pounds end up playing follow the leader. However, Manchester has very little of the crowded loneliness of London or its impersonality. The people are friendly (Paul Calf isn't representative of all locals) and, among students, local pride is a virus. At the end of term, students from the south frequently return (to their mothers' horror) sporting 'Born in the North - Die in the North' t-shirts.

While the city sprawls for about 10 miles in all directions, its centre is relatively small which makes getting out and about a cruise. With so much to do around town, there's no excuse for a Saturday night on the sofa. A bar or a club on the other side of town is only 20 minutes walk and, since the student residential areas tend to be inner-city districts, a minicab home won't be grant-busting.

At the very core, indeed, the hard core of the Manchester

Scene is ecstasy. This and other, nastier, drugs are readily available in the clubs, pubs and on the streets of Manchester. Manchester students' attitudes to drugs obviously vary enormously between individuals and although use of E, acid (LSD), cocaine and dope (cannabis) is perhaps more widespread than the norm, the pressure to partake is small and those old standbys of Cigarettes and Alcohol are still far more common.

THE CITY:
- Population: 2,454,800 ● London: 167miles
- Liverpool: 28miles ● Birmingham: 72miles

Manchester, although it's been around since the days when Caesar took his stroll in the forum, was really built out of cotton during the Industrial Revolution. Out of the money from cotton, that is. Industry flooded Manchester and the canals drained it, making the city one of the all-time boom towns. *But it didn't last, and Manchester found depression pretty depressing, scarring the city with slums. Some of these, such as Moss Side and Burnage, remain pretty bleak and the IRA bomb in 1996 rather kicked the city centre in the metaphorical goolies but many areas have been redeveloped and its chequered history has left Manchester rich in culture. Being a student here is to be rocking in the free world with every facility under the sun, from theatres to Afflecks, from museums to Old Trafford.*

TRAVEL:
Trains: Not 1 but 2 mainline stations, Manchester Piccadilly for London and the South, and Manchester Victoria for just about everywhere else. Routes go all over, including London (£26.05), Birmingham (£11.15), Edinburgh (£23.35) and more.

Coaches: All sorts of coach services to, among most other places, London (£15.75), Birmingham (£8), Edinburgh (£15) and beyond.

Car: From the North, M6 (then M61 or M62), A6 or M66; from the east, M62, A58, A62; from the South, M6, A6, A523, A34; and from Wales, the M56. Parking may well be a problem in central Manchester, *but, for the lazy or environmentally carefree, a car doesn't go amiss.*

Air: Manchester Airport is one of the UK's big ones - flights all over the world as well as inland.

Hitching: *Not possible from central Manchester, but quite good on arterial routes out of the city.*

Local: Manchester has a major bus network, running all over town, especially up and down Oxford Road. Trains are a *quicker* alternative, especially for the outskirts. The Metro Link

m

❛The architect who designed the Rutherford accommodation building at the University of Kent was also responsible for the H-block prisons in Northern Ireland.❜

tram service is now up and trundling.

Taxis: *Manchester's centre, being relatively small, means taxi trips are a viable resort. The black cabs which screech to a halt as you hail them are a lot more expensive than the private traders who are only supposed to pick up phone callers and drop ins.*

Bicycles: *Manchester's quite bike-friendly (flat with a fair few bicycle lanes), but theft is rife. A mountain bike will identify you as a drug pusher, especially if you're about 12.*

LIBRARIES & COMPUTERS:
- Books: 3,600,000 ● Study places: 2,500
- Computer workstations: 800

Despite the vast acreage of reading material, there's still a panic run on valuable books around exam time. Computer provision is more than adequate, however.

CAREER PROSPECTS:
- Careers Service ● No of staff: 9 full
- Unemployed after 6mths (1996): 6.8%

The careers service operates jointly with UMIST and is open office hours all year round.

SPECIAL FEATURES:
- Being so close, Manchester University has strong ties, both official and unofficial, with other local colleges, particularly Manchester Metropolitan University and UMIST. Students join each others' clubs and societies, use each others' facilities and go to each others' ents, *toilets, beds and therapy sessions.*
- Manchester degrees are also awarded at the Institute of Advanced Nursing Education in London, Stockport College of Further & Higher Education and University College, Warrington.

FAMOUS ALUMNI:
Robert Bolt (playwright); Sir Rhodes Boyson MP (Con); Anthony Burgess (writer); Adrian Edmonson, Ben Elton, Rik Mayall (comedians); Anna Ford (broadcaster); Peter Maxwell Davies (composer); Austin Mitchell MP (Lab); Sir Maurice Oldfield (MI6); Christabel Pankhurst (suffragette); Justin Robertson (DJ); Trevor and Simon ('Live and Kicking' anarchists); Louise Wener (Sleeper).

FURTHER INFO:
Prospectuses for undergrads and postgrads. Alternative prospectus from the SU (£3.20). Web site: (http://www.man.ac.uk).

entertainment

CITY:
- Price of a pint of beer: £1.60 ● Glass of wine: £1.35

Manchester is a cultural jamboree, bringing together the brightest and the best in theatre, food, nightlife and, most recently, music to this corner of the country. In fact, you could say the city's a bit of an Oasis.

Cinemas: A multiplicity of multiplexes and sundry cinemas, everything from the 8-screen Salford Quays multiplex and the *cool and trendy* Cornerhouse (3 screens) which shows many an *arty* flick. With a gallery and cafe thrown in, *it's a poser's paradise.*

Theatres: The old Cotton Exchange is now the *nationally renowned* Royal Exchange Theatre - some of the country's *best* shows for under a fiver on student standbys. The Palace and Opera House do good pantos while the Green Room is more experimental.

Pubs: *Manchester has historic pubs in the truest tradition of the working men's dive but there's everything from real ales to obscure liqueurs to weak lemon drinks. If you must be a poseur, pose in Manto and Dry 201 but, for those living somewhere in reality,* push*plugs go to the central Rocket Bar, Jabes Clegg, the Queen Of Hearts (Fallowfield), Retro Bar and Joshua Brooks (both near <u>UMIST</u>).*

Clubs/discos: *When God created Manchester, she created clubbing. A student night out is often a euphemism for dancing and a curry and the only problem is listing the best bop spots. The music is alive and the clubs come and go - The Hacienda, alas, continues only in spirit. Read 'City Life' for the latest.* push*plugs: Temptation at Home (Weds); the Rock 'n' Roll Bar (indie); Hallelujah at the Paradise Factory; and Thursday night is student night at the hysterically tacky Royale. Check for these cheaper NUS-only nights and watch also the flyers for the alighting points of fly-by-night clubs.*

Music venues: The Nynex Arena lures the hugest names, *if binocular-rock's your game. The Apollo, by most towns' standards, would be a best bet,* however, all over town there are live venues of every size. *Among the many others: The Academy* (run by <u>Manchester University</u> SU*); Boardwalk (indie); Jilly's (rock); Band on the Wall (rootsy); Chorlton Irish Club (folk); P J Bells (jazz); The Bridgewater Hall and the Royal Northern College of Music (classical).* Many of these clubs also stage live bands.

Cabaret: *Manchester is a breeding ground for stand-up talent. Live comedy lives and is usually high octane fun. Bernard Manning is a local boy. Well, the exception that proves rule, eh?*

Eating out: *OK, there may not be many places in the running for the Michelin Guide but if you want it good, quick, tasty and cheap, you've come to the right place. Chinatown (the oldest in Europe) is stacked with noodleries and Rusholme has half a mile of end-to-end Indian restaurants. There's the usual artery-full of kebab and burger dens but the* push*plugs go to: Generation X; Amigo's (Oxford Road, Mexican); Barca (tapas); Sangam, Shezan (Indian); Green Room (hip veggie with slack service); Dalton Cafe (greasy spoon and then some).*

Others: Millionaire students, or at least lucky or stupid ones, will, no doubt, not want to miss Manchester's many casinos. The more cultured will find many a fond hour to spend in some of the city's splendid galleries (The City Gallery, The Cornerhouse and The Whitworth, which has many of LS Lowry's best paintings, particularly of Manchester, his home turf).

UNIVERSITY:
● <u>Price of a pint of beer: £1.25</u> ● <u>Glass of wine: £1.05</u>
The Union itself is one of Manchester's main entertainment venues - no mean feat round here.
Bars: (4) The Hop & Grape pub (capacity 300) at the top of the SU building is also a music venue; The Serpent (400) comes

into its own at lunchtimes; The Cellar (600), *bizarrely enough,* is in the basement. *And of course, the Academy has a bar too.*

Theatres: (2) The University's Contact Theatre has its own resident professional company, but also provides an *impressive and versatile* venue for regular student productions and recent trips to the Edinburgh Fringe *have been very successful.* The Drama Department has its own studio theatre (Stephen Jones Studio) as well.

Cinemas: The University has its own *excellent* film club for blockbusters and cult/foreign faves, 4 times a week. Danny Boyle (*Trainspotting? Never heard of it*) is the film society president for this session.

Clubs/discos: There are 2 or 3 nights a week, mostly chart and nostalgia efforts, with occasional guest nights (eg Megadog, Paul Oakenfold) for *more serious* clubbers.

Music venues: In addition to The Academy, *one of the top live venues in the North West,* live bands also feature at the Union's Hop & Grape pub (300), the Burlington Rooms (150) and the MDH (the Union's main hall, 450).

Recent band appearances: David Bowie, Robbie Williams, Kula Shaker, Beck, Mansun, Geneva, Reef, Jamiroquai, Kenickie, Divine Comedy, Pavement, Cardigans, Space, Chemical Brothers, Bis, Bush, Lemonheads, The Orb, Placebo, Boo Radleys, CJ Bolland, Super Furry Animals... and that's just a small selection.

Cabaret: Occasional stand-up, Lee and Herring and Donna McPhail being recent attractions.

Food: The University Food Court and the SU coffee bar provide an *unimaginative* selection of burgers, sandwiches and chips *but portions are substantial and nobody's complained about the value for money.* The new Cafe Express in the Union does light lunches. The bars also do grub.

Others: Among the other *delights* are quizzes, multi-cultural events and all-night balls.

social & political

MANCHESTER UNIVERSITY STUDENTS' UNION:

● 6 sabbaticals ● Turnout at last ballot: 10%
● NUS member

The Union is well-organised and has left-wing tendencies which probably don't reflect the overall viewpoint of the student body. The punters, however, are happy enough with the Union as it is, so long as it keeps on offering the bevy of brilliant facilities in the Steve Biko Building as the Union Building is officially called - well, it's more original than Nelson Mandela. The recent Fees demo was the biggest in the country.

SU FACILITIES:

In the *impressively* big art deco Union Building there are: a general shop; a bookshop (2nd hand); an opticians; travel agency; hairdresser; customised night clubs and discos; photocopiers; coffee and snack bar; 2 burger bars; 2 bars and a pub (with satellite TV); Barclays and Halifax cashpoints; taxi freephone; video, vending and games machines; TV room; meeting and function rooms; societies resource centre; showers; sauna and solarium; and photo booth.

❝The Guild Buildings at Liverpool University house Europe's largest toilet complex.❞

CLUBS (NON SPORTING):

How long have you got? Students are also entitled to join UMIST clubs and societies and vice versa.

Arab; Backgammon; Buddhist; Campaign for Free Education; Ceilidh; Chamber Music; Chinese; Circus; Cocktail; Cuba; Cyprus; Debating; Dechen Buddhist; Egyptian; Expedition; Film; Free Tibet; Fruit; Gilbert & Sullivan; Harm; Hong Kong; Japanese; Jazz; Kurdish; Links; Living Marxism; Malaysian; Old School Theatre; Pakistan; Reach Out; Real Ale; Scout & Guide; Singapore; Spanish; Talmud; Techno; Turkish; Warped. *If your own particular interest isn't covered there's probably enough people around to find a few fellow-saddoes to set something up.*

OTHER ORGANISATIONS:

'Mancunion' is the Union's award-winning, free, weekly student newspaper, a new paper 'Student Direct' is up and running and if that's not enough for the student journo there are plenty of other opportunities including a planned city-wide radio station from 1998. The Manchester Universities Charities Association employs a full-time co-ordinator. Rag pulls in a 6-figure sum most years.

RELIGIOUS:

● 3 chaplains (CofE, RC, Jewish)

The University has both Anglican and Catholic chapels and a Muslim prayer room. *The Jewish Society is social as much as religious and is a strong political force.* The city caters for most creeds' needs: local cathedrals, churches, temples, mosques, synagogues and almost all the usual places of worship.

PAID WORK:

Because Manchester's such a big centre for entertainment there are lots of part-time jobs in bars, clubs and restaurants - but, of course, there are lots of people chasing them. Still, the situation's better than in some other parts of the North-West.

sports

● Recent successes: basketball, cycling, rowing, water polo

Quite apart from excellent facilities (not 1, but 2 sports centres), the University's size means more than a fair share of sporting stars. But choice abounds giving even the hardiest couch potato the chance to uproot and branch out into a sprouting of sports. There is a charge of just 30p for the sports centres.

SPORTS FACILITIES:

On campus there's the McDougall Centre offering a swimming pool, a sports hall, a small gym, multigym, 4 squash courts, 2 fives courts, rifle range, climbing wall, sauna, solarium and outside basketball/netball court. A small admission fee is charged. There are also facilities at a variety of other centres. The Wythenshawe Ground is the largest: 60 acres of playing fields (10 acres more, shared with UMIST, are within 4 miles of the campus), 6 tennis courts and a pavilion. Firs Athletic

Ground at Fallowfield in South Manchester has 31 acres of playing fields, 8 tennis courts, an all-weather pitch and a large pavilion, all near the main student halls of residence. Nearby, the Fallowfield Stadium has amenities for track and field events and a soccer pitch. The Armitage Centre provides a sports hall, a climbing room, sauna and solarium, 2 martial arts dojos, table tennis and a fitness room, all for a small charge. The University will host judo, squash and wrestling events for the 2002 Commonwealth Games.

SPORTING CLUBS:
Fives; Hang Gliding; Korfball; Lacrosse; Pistol; Rifle; Rowing; Speleology (caving); Ten Pin Bowling; Trampoline; Water-Polo; Yachting.

ATTRACTIONS:
Can you identify 3 football teams with swear-words in their names? Answer: Arsenal, Scunthorpe and F***in' Manchester United. *Real Mancs (like Oasis) tend to support the less successful, but less-despised Man City.* For test and county cricket, there's Old Trafford and golf at the Golf Club. Basketball (The Giants) and ice hockey (The Storm) at Nynex; speedway at Broadhurst Park, rugby at Swinton, Salford and Trafford Borough, volleyball at Sale. Manchester will be hosting the Commonwealth Games in 2002 *and the resulting facilities should be something pretty special.*

accommodation
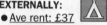

IN COLLEGE:
- Catered: 17% ● Cost: £67-84(31-38wks)
- Self-catering: 39% ● Cost: £37-54(38wks)

Availability: The University and UMIST bundle all their accommodation in one hat and pull it out together. As a result, the options vary from small houses owned by the University and shared by as few as 8 students to massive complexes of flats and rooms, providing over 1,000 places in the case of Owens Park. All 1st years who want to live in halls (with 2% sharing) and there's space for plenty of other years as well. *The demand exceeds the supply, but the opportunities are better than most places.* Out of 14 halls - all within 2½ miles of the campus - 4 are all male, 3 are for women only and in all, only about 150 1st years have to share a room. *Apart from this, just about everything depends on the individual hall and the variety is broad: fabulous facilities to bare necessities (usually good, though); no parking all the way to adequate; and so on.* Most accommodation is very central and within easy walking distance of the campus.

EXTERNALLY:
- Ave rent: £37

Availability: *At the moment, it's not too difficult to find housing without resorting to damp-ridden dives and rents are rarely extortionate. Fallowfield, Victoria Park and Withington are the studey ghettos; Didsbury is a bit more suburban but quite accessible; Rusholme can be quite rough but is improving; Hulme and Moss Side should be treated with caution, although some hardy souls do settle there.*
Housing help: The University Accommodation Office offers vacancy lists, emergency housing and help with landlord problems.

welfare

SERVICES:
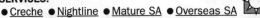
- Creche ● Nightline ● Mature SA ● Overseas SA
- Lesbian Gay & Bisexual Society ● Postgrad SA ● Minibus
- Women's Officer ● Self-defence classes

The Union's Advice Centre is *extremely effective and is one of the students' main sources of welfare support.* Its Welfare sabbatical, 2 professional advisers and weekly legal sessions will this year see over 10,000 students. The University also runs a counselling service employing trained counsellors and a health centre for students. *The Union has a particularly positive attitude to gays, lesbians and bisexuals, who are a powerfully vocal force amongst the students (Manchester as a whole is a bit of a gay mecca).*

Women: *The Union has a strong policy (often promoting positive discrimination) on women's issues and representation. Attack alarms are subsidised.*

Disabled: Some ramps around campus and lifts in many buildings (including the Union), but, generally, *access really isn't up to scratch, especially considering how good other facilities are.*

FINANCE:
- Ave debt per year: £1,900 ● Access fund: £420,000
- Successful applications (1997): 600

In future the University will distribute the access fund by giving smaller amounts to a larger number of applicants. The Union lends up to £75 (interest-free) in emergency cases, but a fellow student has to guarantee the loan.

● ●

▶▶ **Manchester Institute of Science**

see UMIST

● ●

Manchester Metropolitan University

● **Formerly Manchester Polytechnic**

Manchester Metropolitan University, All Saints, Oxford Road, Manchester, M15 6BH. Tel: (0161) 247 2000.
Fax: (0161) 247 6350. E-mail: prospectus@mmu.ac.uk
MMU Students' Union, 99 Oxford Road, Manchester, M1 7EL.
Tel: (0161) 273 1162. Fax: (0161) 273 7237.

general

The main cluster of Manchester Metropolitan University at the All Saints sites is centred on the biggest educational complex in western Europe, which also includes the HQs of Manchester University and UMIST. There are, however, further sites along the A34, in the Didsbury area and, some distance out of the city, in Crewe. The University was originally Manchester Poly, which was in turn set up in 1970 from a number of smaller colleges.

44% ♂♂♂♂♂♀♀♀♀♀♀ **56%**

Sex ratio(M:F): 44%:56%	Founded: 1970
Full time u'grads: 18,513	Part time: 6,186
Postgrads: 1,640	Non-degree: 7,537
Ave course: 3yrs	Ethnic: 13%
Private/state school: n/a	Flunk rate: n/a
Mature students: 53%	Overseas students: 6%
Disabled students: 1.4%	Staff/student ratio: 1:18
Clearing: 20%	

ATMOSPHERE:
MMU is a pretty vibrant environment, considering it's so spread out, and many students admit to picking the place for the city's party-till-you-puke atmosphere. Nearly half the students are returners to education and some feel that entertainment provision is aimed too specifically at the young, groovy and beautiful element.

THE SITES:
John Dalton: Based in Chester Street, $\frac{1}{4}$ mile from the All Saints sites, 5,500 students in the Science and Technology departments do cool stuff with Petri dishes and capacitors and all that gubbins.

Rosamond Street: (3,500 students) $\frac{1}{2}$ a mile from All Saints, various Humanities departments are sited here and there are 422 accommodation places as well.

Hollings: (1,700 students) The Clothing, Food and Hotel Management courses are based here in Fallowfield, a 3-mile bus ride from All Saints.

Didsbury: Nearly 4,000 students in the Community Studies, Law and Education faculty are based here, about 5 miles from the city centre.

Crewe: (3,300 students) 28 miles south-west of Manchester, we find Business Studies and trainee teachers.

Alsager: This site is about 34 miles from Manchester, near Stoke-on-Trent, with 1,592 students on a variety of Arts, Humanities and Sports Science courses. *Despite coach trips to Manchester, students at these last two sites don't really feel like part of the MMU experience and those applying to the University for the bright lights should check where they're going to be based; Crewe and Alsager are less than dazzling in the fun stakes.*

TOWN: see <u>University of Manchester</u>

TRAVEL: see <u>University of Manchester</u>

LIBRARIES & COMPUTERS:
● <u>Books: 1,000,000</u> ● <u>Study places: 3,245</u>
● <u>Computer workstations: 3,500</u>

There are 8 libraries in all, including those at Crewe and Alsager. *Students find library and computer facilities OK*, but occasional runs on popular titles mean students make use of <u>Manchester University</u>'s even more generous provision.

CAREER PROSPECTS:
- Careers Service ● No of staff: 9full/2part
- Unemployed after 6mths (1996): 9.4%

FAMOUS ALUMNI:
Terry Christian (ex-'Word' presenter and Oasis biographer); Bernhard Hill, David Threfall, Julie Walters (actors); Steve Coogan, John Thompson (comedians); Mick Hucknall (Simply Red soul dwarf); LS Lowry (painter); Min Patel (cricketer); Bryan Robson (footballer).

FURTHER INFO:
Prospectuses covering undergrad, postgrad and part-time courses; also a web site (http://www.mmu.ac.uk).

entertainment

CITY: see University of Manchester

UNIVERSITY:

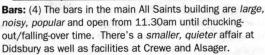

- Price of a pint of beer: £1.20 ● Glass of wine: £1.30

Bars: (4) The bars in the main All Saints building are *large, noisy, popular* and open from 11.30am until chucking-out/falling-over time. There's a *smaller, quieter* affair at Didsbury as well as facilities at Crewe and Alsager.

Theatres: (1) The Horniman Theatre is based at Didsbury. Performance students at Crewe have their own studio.

Clubs/discos: 3 or 4 times a week it's club night in Kelly's Bar (cap 900, adm £2-£3, mainly indie, chart and retro) in the Union's main building.

Music venues: Kelly's Bar is also the site of *very occasional gigs but it's mostly unknowns who play there and MMU students tend to slope off to* Manchester University *for their live kicks.*

Food: The University Refectory is open 11am-3pm *but the SU coffee bar has a more interesting selection and more sensible opening hours.*

Other: Academic departments have their own balls and the annual Athletic Union bash is always well attended.

social & political

MMU STUDENTS' UNION:

- 6 sabbaticals ● Turnout at last ballot: 7%
- NUS member

The Union's main building on Oxford Road has variously been named after Nelson Mandela, Martin Luther King and Bruce Forsyth, *which gives some idea of the level of political commitment round these parts. Party political allegiances aren't that strong and the only thing that gets the students really worked up is money (or lack of).*

> ❛A lecturer at Newcastle brought the whole admissions procedure to a standstill with his Newcastle United Supporters' Web Site.❜

SU FACILITIES:
The Union has facilities on 5 sites. In the main building there are 2 bars, 2 cafes, travel agency, shop, Barclays and Link cash machines, a bakery, vending and games machines, pool tables, photo booth, launderette, TV lounge, 2 minibuses, function rooms and recycling facilities.

CLUBS (NON SPORTING):
Anti Blood Sports; Bisexual Caucus; Campaign For Free Education; Chinese; Cuba Solidarity; Dance; Hindu; Hong Kong; Kagyu; Marxist; Radio; Role Playing; Rolf Harris; Sikh; Spiritualist; Urban Green Action.

OTHER ORGANISATIONS:
'Pulp' (no, not them) is the award-winning student mag (with a sabbatical editor) and the Athletics Union has its own weekly bulletin. 'Student Direct' is a new publication covering the whole of Manchester (*not literally, of course*).

PAID WORK: see University of Manchester

sports

● Recent successes: tennis, badminton
As with most things at MMU, keeping up with course work and having a quick half in the bar tends to take precedent over busting a gut on the track, court or pitch but there are a few brave souls prepared to strain the odd ligament in pursuit of laurels.

SPORTS FACILITIES:
There are sports halls at All Saints and Didsbury and the new Sugden sports centre is a joint venture with UMIST. The best outdoor facilities, however, are at the Crewe & Alsager sites, where there are 32 acres of playing fields and an outdoor swimming pool.

SPORTING CLUBS:
Aikido; Hang Gliding; Hung Kuen; Lacrosse; Links; Rambling; Rowing; Rugby League; Shokotan Karate; Surf; Tai Chi; Ultimate Frisbee; Volleyball; Water Polo; Weights.

ATTRACTIONS: see University of Manchester

accommodation

IN COLLEGE:
● Catered: 10% ● Cost: £64(34wks)
● Self-catering: 2% ● Cost: £42(34wks)
Bearing in mind the proportion of locals who are presumably set up elsewhere things aren't as bad as the stats might appear. However, half the first years that do want to live in have to brave the private sector from the off. Of those that get a coveted place, less than 2% have to share. A new hall with 770 self-catering places will open in September 1998. Provision at Crewe and Alsager is more generous; two-thirds of freshers can be housed.

EXTERNALLY: see University of Manchester
Housing help: The Accomodation & Welfare Office keeps vacancy lists, checks properties and contracts and attempts to resolve disputes. There is a new joint housing service between Manchester Metropolitan and the University of Manchester.

welfare

SERVICES:

- Creche ● Nightline ● Lesbian & Gay Society
- Mature SA ● Minibus ● Women's Officer
- Self-defence classes

In the case of medical emergencies or more moderate malaise, students can rush to the University's Health Centre at All Saints or the daily clinics at Broomhurst Hall, Didsbury and Loxford Hall. There are 3 full-time counsellors and 2 at Crewe and Alsager, which also have their own medical facilities. The University also employs a Learning Skills Co-ordinator.

Women: The Women's Officer is a sabbatical post and there are regular *activity-packed* Women's Weeks.

Disabled: Not only are there ramps and lifts in most places, but there are policies for disabled access *which have been a genuine help*. A guideline publication is produced specially for students and applicants with disabilities and the SU has a specialist officer. *Other places take note.*

FINANCE:

- Ave debt per year: £2,050 ● Access fund: £501,092
- Successful applications (1997): 1,444

The SU can give loans of up to £50 (or higher in exceptional circumstances), but they want the money back by the end of the year, thank you.

● ●

▶▶ **Metropolitan University**

see Manchester Metropolitan University

● ●

Middlesex University

▼
● *Formerly Middlesex Polytechnic*
▼

Middlesex University, White Hart Lane, London, N17 8HR.
Tel: (0181) 362 5000. Fax: (0181) 362 5649.
E-mail: admissions@mdx.ac.uk
Middlesex University Students' Union, Trent Park, Bramley Road, London, N14 4YZ. Tel: (0181) 362 6450.
Fax: (0181) 440 5944.

general

Middlesex used to be a county, now it only really exists as a postal district, a cricket team and an abstract band down the western side of London, which roly-poly TV starman Russell Grant is campaigning to return to county status. *The location of Middlesex University is equally non-specific.* It's based on 6 major and 2 minor teaching 'campuses' and several one-off buildings throughout London; there's also the Bedford campus which used to be *misleading* known as the London College of Dance. The London sites range from White Hart Lane campus - an urban, industrial area - to Trent Park - set in the suburbs 15 miles from Central London, a series of blocks on a campus in country grounds around an old manor house. Maintaining the dance motif, one minor site is in an old house in Golder's Green that belonged to Anna Pavlova, the famous ballerina and pudding.

44% ♂♂♂♂♂♀♀♀♀♀ **56%**

Sex ratio(M:F): 44%:56%	Founded: 1973
Full time u'grads: 16,657	Part time: 698
Postgrads: 1,027	Non-degree: 3,973
Ave course: 3yrs	Ethnic: 41%
Private school: n/a	Flunk rate: 22%
Mature students: 70%	Overseas students: 20%
Disabled students: 2.5%	Staff/student ratio: 1:24
Clearing: n/a	

ATMOSPHERE:
Having lots of mature students puts a different emphasis on things and being so spread out leads to a lack of cohesion between sites, with students, especially from Bound's Green and Hendon, having a loyalty to their own campus rather than to the University as a whole. With facilities all over the place, it's hard to know what's available and, once discovered, it can be a hassle getting to it. But many still make the effort.

THE SITES:
Bedford: (76 students - dance) 53 miles from Trent Park, *unsurprisingly, there's little social contact with the University as a whole.*
Bounds Green: (2,225 - computing, engineering) It's 80% male engineers *and feels like a degree factory.*
Cat Hill (1,349 - textiles, product design, electronic arts) In Barnet, facilities include a bar and a multigym.
Enfield: (3,975 - social science, health studies) includes ents venue the Forum.
Health 'Campus': (1,887 full-time equivalent - nursing) Teaching facilities spread across 4 North London hospitals (*so it can hardly be called a campus*).
Hendon: (4,728 - business school) the largest site in terms of numbers, 13 miles from Tottenham.
Ivy House: (163 - drama)
Quicksilver Place: (277 - fine art)
Tottenham: (2,622 - humanities, business, law) The main admin site (if there is such a thing).
Trent Park: (3,145 - arts, education, humanities) The main SU site.

THE CITY: see University of London

TRAVEL: see University of London
Car: *Parking is slightly easier than in the institutions closer to the centre of London, but it's still not really necessary.*

LIBRARIES:
- Books: 600,000 ● Study places: 1,594
- Computer workstations: 1,800

Libraries and computer facilities have *pretty restricted* opening times, for security reasons. The SU is pressuring for improved access.

CAREER PROSPECTS:
- Careers Service ● No of staff: 8full/2part

Careers advisors travel between sites.

SPECIAL FEATURES:
- Middlesex was the first university to offer a degree course in herbal medicine.

FAMOUS ALUMNI:
Adam Ant (singer); Ray Davies (Kinks mainman); Nick Harvey MP (LibDem); James Herbert (novelist); Alison Lloyd and Jomo Platt (Ally Capellino fashion house); Anish Kapoor (artist); Matthew Marsden (*Corrie*); Omar (singer); Rianna Scipio (tv presenter); Vivienne Westwood.

FURTHER INFO:
Prospectuses for undergrads and postgrads. Rough Guide for Students. Video. There's also a web site (http://www.mdx.ac.uk).

entertainment

IN LONDON: see University of London

UNIVERSITY:
- Price of a pint of beer: £1.60 ● Glass of wine: £1.25

Bars: (7) 5 are run by the SU on separate campuses, the rest by the University. The Enfield set-up is the biggest, with a combined capacity of 800 across 2 bars. There are others at Trent Park, Tottenham and Bounds Green.

Theatres: The Simmonds Theatre (cap 400) is the larger of 2. Middlesex has one of the largest drama departments in Europe but it's currently suffering serious cutbacks.

Clubs/discos/music venues: Every night there's some kind of dance or indie event occurring, either at Enfield, Tottenham or Trent Park such as Kushti (Cat Hill), Jazz night (Trent park) and occasional Salsa nights. Disco Inferno and Dom 1 get the kids kicking.

Food: All catering outlets are now operated by Sutcliffe's, a subsidiary of the Granada Group, *which is great if you like service stations. The canteen at Tottenham leaves a lot to be desired. Including edibility.*

Others: *Middlesex is big on balls.* The Summer extravaganza usually lasts 36 hours and last year's Freshers' do took place in The Forum at Enfield with appearances by the likes of Dannii Minogue and The Rocky Horror Show Band.

social & political

MIDDLESEX UNIVERSITY STUDENTS' UNION:
- 6 sabbaticals ● Turnout at last ballot: 2%

 ● NUS member

The SU is about services and ents, rather than tearing down the barricades and guillotining the University administration. They're starting to suffer for this though: the inter-site bus

service was stopped last year and the students are a little annoyed about this, especially as the chance they had to prevent it through the Union was squandered through non-attendance. Sillybillies.

SU FACILITIES:

The SU has facilities on all campuses. There are 5 bars, 3 snack bars, 6 shops, a printing service, games machines, photo booths, function rooms, prayer room, art shop, DJ equipment, TV lounges and a minibus for hire. And a sculpture of Posh Spice, made of Dairylea triangles. Also all ents are SU run, *prolific and very good*. By the way, we lied about the sculpture.

CLUBS (NON SPORTING):

Abacus; American; Bagpuss; Criminology; Exhibifionist; Greek Cypriot; Hellenic; Herb; Iranian; Journey 2000; Law; Malaysian; Meditation; Poetry; Soul; Traditional Chinese Medicine.

OTHER ORGANISATIONS:

The SU magazine is called 'Planet' *and it's still little better than crap.*

RELIGIOUS:

There is an ecumenical chaplaincy based at the Tottenham campus. At Bound's Green and Hendon (the heart of Jewish London), there is a Muslim prayer room in college, an Islamic society, a Jewish society. **Religion in London:** see <u>University of London</u>.

PAID WORK:

Apart from bar work, the SU has work for about 100 students, including decorating and so on during the holidays. The national headquarters of the Small Press Association are at the Tottenham campus. There are about 5,000 members and work placements often come up for students. **Paid Work in London:** see <u>University of London</u>.

sports

- <u>Recent successes: table tennis.</u>

The same old problems of divergent sites and students with other things on their minds means that Middlesex is never going to be kicking serious BUSA butt, although they're not sofa spuds either. Winners of British Universities Table Tennis Championships for three consecutive years...

SPORTS FACILITIES:

The University has 5 sports halls and 3 playing fields. There are indoor and outdoor tennis courts, a sauna, 6 multigyms, swimming pools, a hockey and an all-weather pitch. Recent expansion has been helped by Lottery funding.

SPORTING CLUBS:

Climbing; Wu Shu Kwan.

ATTRACTIONS:

Spurs at White Hart Lane and various sports, including ice skating at Alexandra Palace.

accommodation

IN COLLEGE:

- <u>Self-catering: 14%</u> ● <u>Cost: £49-57(41wks)</u>

Availability: There's accommodation for 65% of 1st years, a level which usually copes with the demand. There are 7 halls on separate campuses not far from most of the teaching sites. Kitchens are shared between up to 14 students. *There have been one or two cases where students have had to live at one site when their course is taught at another. Doh.*

Car parking: Parking is free with a permit, *although there's not enough.*

EXTERNALLY: see University of London
● Ave rent: £52

Availability: *Most students must find their own housing and a lot live at home. It's not difficult to find somewhere decent since the sites are far enough from the city centre. Palmers Green is a very popular and convenient area, Wood Green and Turnpike Lane are also handy.*

Housing help: The University runs an accommodation service which produces a vacancies sheet, housing database, lists of recommended landlords and they can give legal help and advice.

 ## welfare

SERVICES:
● Creche ● Lesbian & Gay Society
● Overseas SA ● Postgrad SA ● Minibus

Services include various counselling groups with 8 counsellors. There is a parents' group, an HIV/AIDS health worker and nurses on each main campus. The creche, which caters for litl'uns 6mth to 8yr-olds may get privatised. *Poor provision for bewildered overseas students has left some feeling a bit lost.*

Women: There is a women's room and a women-only disco.

Disabled: *Major improvements in access over the last 4 years, mainly facilitated by the very impressive Able Centre. Induction loops installed.*

FINANCE:
● Ave debt per year: £2,650 ● Access fund: £484,550
● Successful applications (1997): 708

▶▶ Milton Keynes

see De Montfort University

▶▶ Moores University

see Liverpool John Moores University

▶▶ Moray House

see University of Edinburgh

'Text in italics is PUSH's point of view – take it or leave it.'

n

Napier University

Nene – University College Northampton

- NESCOT
  see Other Institutions

University of Newcastle

- Newcastle Poly
  see University of Northumbria at Newcastle

- UWC Newport
  see Other Institutions

- North East London Poly
  see University of East London

- North East Wales Institute
  see Other Institutions

University of North London

- North Wales
  see Bangor, University of Wales

- Northampton
  see Nene – University College Northampton

- Northern College
  see Other Institutions

University of Northumbria at Newcastle

- Norwich
  see University of East Anglia

University of Nottingham

Nottingham Trent University

❝Chuck Berry's 1972 hit 'My Ding-a-Ling' was recorded at Lanchester College, now part of Coventry University.❞

Napier University

- **Formerly Napier Polytechnic**

Napier University, Craiglockhart Campus, 219 Colinton Road, Edinburgh, EH14 1DJ. Tel: (0131) 455 4330.
Fax: (0131) 455 4666. E-mail: info@napier.ac.uk
Napier Student Association, 12 Merchiston Place, Edinburgh, EH10 4NR. Tel: (0131) 229 8791. Fax: (0131) 228 3462.

General

For general information about Edinburgh: see <u>Edinburgh University</u>. Napier is one of the new universities, and like many others, it is growing at a rip-roaring pace and based on a number of sites. 7 sites in fact and with the exception of Sighthill Court, they're all spread around a *pleasant, predominantly middle-class area* a couple of miles to the west of Edinburgh city centre.

51% ♂♂♂♂♂ ♀♀♀♀♀ 49%	
Sex ratio(M:F): 51%:49%	Founded: 1964
Full time u'grads: 7,966	Part time: 1,965
Postgrads: 684	Non-degree: 5,189
Ave course: 4yrs	Ethnic: n/a
Private school: n/a	Flunk rate: n/a
Mature students: 30%	Overseas students: 9%
Disabled students: n/a	Staff/student ratio: 1:18
Clearing: n/a	

ATMOSPHERE:
Most students come from the local area and pride themselves on not having the self-consciously 'studenty' attitudes that sometimes bedevil older institutions. However, the seriously over-stretched facilities mean there's not much scope for such behaviour anyway; it's a pretty functional place with a distinct lack of social cohesion and, as a former SA President has said, 'People tend to come to get a job, not to hobnob with Henriettas and other Hoorays.'

THE SITES:
The problem with overcrowding has been made worse by the fact that students have to be shunted from site to site for many classes and lectures, often not knowing where they're supposed to be. Poor intersite transport doesn't help.
Merchiston: (3,700 students - science, engineering) Although most of the main campus consists of a large modern block, a paved square and a converted house for NSA, the focus is the ancient Tower of Merchiston in the centre. This is the place where John Napier - the mathematician and inventor of logarithms, after whom the University was named - was born in 1550.
Craiglockhart: (1,300 - central services, electrical engineering, maths, computing) The buildings here include the *ornate* 19th

century administrative building, an accommodation block, swimming pool and a few other sports facilities both set in *pleasant* terraced grounds 1½ miles from Merchiston. From here it's possible to see the Forth Bridge.

Sighthill: (2,000 - business) This is an *ugly great* 6-storey tower block with an even more modern extension, a sports dome and another NSA centre, all on the edge of the city near a *dodgy* housing estate, 3 miles east of Merchiston. *It's not so bad on the inside.*

Marchmont/Coates Place: (photography, film & TV) Both these sites are very small, quite close to Merchiston. A lot of students (from all 3 Edinburgh universities) live in the Marchmont area.

Craighouse: (1,000 - music, hotel management) This is a new site, 2 miles from Merchiston. It's on a hill, *with some of the best views in town.* It also used to be a lunatic asylum.

Canaan Lane: (nursing/midwifery) The former Lothian College of Health Studies, about 1½ miles from Merchiston.

THE CITY: see <u>University of Edinburgh</u>

TRAVEL: see <u>University of Edinburgh</u>

Local Trains: The closest stations are as follows: Haymarket for Merchiston, North Merchiston & Redwood House; Waverley for Marchmont; Slateford for Craiglockhart; and Wester Hailes or South Gyles for Sighthill.

Buses: Public buses offer *good* services between the sites and into the city centre from 50p upwards. *The intersite buses are too small, too infrequent and their drivers best described as 'relaxed'.*

Bicycles: There's a *big* bike rack at Merchiston.

LIBRARIES & COMPUTERS:
● <u>Books: 250,000</u> ● <u>Study places: 1,268</u>
● <u>Computer workstations: 1,400</u>

There are 8 libraries, the largest being at Merchiston (housing the Edward Clark Collection, tracing the history of printing since the 15th century), Sighthill and Craiglockhart. *Access to books and computers is fine, except at peak times when it's a mare.*

CAREER PROSPECTS:
● <u>Careers Service</u> ● <u>No of staff: 7full/2part</u>
● <u>Unemployed after 6mths (1996): 7.4%</u>

FAMOUS ALUMNI:
Mark Goodier (Radio 1 DJ); Greg Kane (of Hue & Cry); Derrick Lee (Scottish rugby player); Alison Paton (Siren the Gladiator); Jane Franchi, Bill McFarlan, Malcolm Wilson, Cathy McDonald and Jim White (all Scottish TV presenters).

FURTHER INFO:
Prospectuses for undergrads, postgrads and part-timers and a web site (http://www.napier.ac.uk).

entertainment

THE CITY: see <u>University of Edinburgh</u>

UNIVERSITY:
● <u>Price of a pint of beer: £1.45</u>

Bars: (3). The most popular drinking den is at Merchiston (cap

200), known as 'the Merky' or 'Bertie's Bar', because it's run by the *ebullient* Bert. There are also bars at Sighthill (500) and Craiglockhart (125) *but the new, smoke-free Craighouse Bar, run by the University, doesn't seem too popular.* All the bars are closed at weekends.

Theatres: *The thespian thortees have improved - 2 productionth are thtaged every year, and they finally made it to the Fringe in ninety-theven.*

Clubs/discos/music venues: *NSA club/music venue was closed in 1996 after trouble with local drug dealers, leaving a huge venue-shaped problem. Sighthill is big enough, but it's miles out of the way.* However, 'Dodgy' is a fortnightly bop at Craiglockhart and there's also an monthly meander to a club in the city - *but that's about it.*

Food: There are SA eats facilities across 4 sites; *Craiglockhart is the best and Sighthill is improving.*

Others: There are several balls a year *but they've suffered from a low turnout recently.*

social 2 political

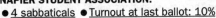

NAPIER STUDENT ASSOCIATION:

● <u>4 sabbaticals</u> ● <u>Turnout at last ballot: 10%</u>
● <u>NUS member</u>

To encourage democratic participation, NSA has resorted to a beer raffle to entice voters. *To quote another SA president, the students 'canne be bloody bothered wi' politicians'. NSA concentrates on doing the best it can to provide services, given its limited facilities.*

SU FACILITIES:
Merchiston Avenue is NSA's converted house and corporate headquarters housing 1 bar/snack bar, common room, print shop, job shop, general shop, photocopier, DTP facilities, games rooms, pool table, juke box, games machines, vending machine, function room and car park. NSA has shops, pool tables and bars at Sighthill and Craiglockhart.

CLUBS (NON SPORTING):
Debating; Men's Club; Real Ale; Role Play.

OTHER ORGANISATIONS:
The mag, *pretentiously* called 'Veritas', *is floundering in an act of pretentious justice. The president strives to keep everyone informed with a fortnightly newsletter.*

RELIGIOUS:
There is a large inter-denominational chapel and chaplaincy centre at Craiglockhart, which used to be a Catholic teaching college. Also chaplains representing the major Christian faiths. **Religion in Edinburgh:** see <u>Edinburgh University</u>.

> ❮A former head of Glamorgan University Rag holds the world record for standing in a bucket of maggots.❯

PAID WORK :
The SA runs a jobshop which has policies of minimum wages
(£3/hr) and maximum hours (18/wk). See <u>University of Edinburgh</u>

sports

● <u>Recent successes: football, fencing</u>
*Sport facilities aren't up to much and there isn't the thigh-
slapping, cold-showering enthusiasm for active activities that
is often found elsewhere. However, balls are kicked and
hamstrings are... whatever it is that happens to hamstrings.*

SPORTS FACILITIES:
The dome at Sighthill includes a sports hall, multigym,
climbing wall and tennis courts. At Craiglockhart, there's the
swimming pool *(which could better be descibed as a large
bath)* and a putting green. Other facilities must be hired.

ATTRACTIONS: see <u>University of Edinburgh</u>

accommodation

IN COLLEGE:
● <u>Self-catering: 13%</u> ● <u>Cost: £33-51(33-39wks)</u>
Availability: There are 714 places in a hall at Craiglockhart,
West Bryson Road and Morrison Circus, enough for most non-
local freshers to be housed if they want - *but 15% who want,
can't.* If they do get a place, there's an 10% chance it'll be
shared. Halls are split into single sex corridors with kitchens
for every 5 or 6 students.

EXTERNALLY: see <u>University of Edinburgh</u>
Housing help: NSA's Student Services employ a full-time
accommodation officer who keeps a list of vacancies, who
helps match students and landlords and who advises generally
on housing and contracts. *Private agencies are also worth
contacting.*

welfare

SERVICES:
● <u>Lesbian & Gay Society</u> ● <u>Mature SA</u>
● <u>Equal Opportunities Officer</u> ● <u>Self-defence classes</u>
The University employs 1 full- and 3 part-time counsellors to
help students with problems more serious than an overdue
essay. Each site has a welfare room. The Health Centre at
Craiglockart has a nurse and an occupational therapy service
is available.
Women: The Women's Group deals with family planning, rape
counselling and invites speakers. There's a Men's Group, but
they discuss men's attitudes to feminism more than beer and
football.
Disabled: *The negligible number of disabled students at Napier
is unlikely to increase until there are more facilities, which are
currently arranged on an individual basis.*

FINANCE:
● <u>Ave debt per year: £1,700</u> ● <u>Access fund: £157,905</u>
● <u>Successful applications (1997): 1,061</u>
NSA has a hardship fund of £3,000 (or 50p per undergrad)
which it dishes out as £30 loans to the desperate.

Nene

Nene - University College Northampton

● *Formerly Nene College*

(1) Nene - University College Northampton, Park Campus, Boughton Green Road, Northampton, NN2 7AL.
Tel: (01604) 735500. Fax: (01604) 720636.
E-mail: admissions@nene.ac.uk
Nene University College Northampton Students' Union, Boughton Green Road, Northampton, NN2 7AL.
Tel: (01604) 712071. Fax: (01604) 713732.
(2) Nene - University College Northampton, Avenue Campus, St George's Avenue, Northampton NN2 6JD.
Tel: (01604) 735500.

General

Northampton's a *pleasant* market town, slap bang between Brum and London, a bit too far east to be properly in the Midlands, and too far north to be in the Home Counties. Its nearest neighbour is the *dreaded* Milton Keynes, but there's some *lovely* countryside nearby to get lost in. Historically, it's the centre of the British shoe industry (this is where your DMs came from) and, more recently, Carlsberg UK has set up shop here. *Northampton; probably the most Northampton-ish town in the world.* Now we've got the town placed, Nene College is about 2½ miles away, on two landscaped campuses, with modern building developments, *tastefully arranged.* It's allowed to award its own degrees, has applied for 'University College' status (*neither a university, nor a college, but something in between, as Paddy Ashdown would say*) and is using the name anyway. Talking of names; it's pronounced 'Nenn', not 'Neen', or 'Ne-Ne', which is a Hawaiian goose, or 'Nena', who had a hit with '99 Red Balloons' in 1983, and didn't shave her armpits.

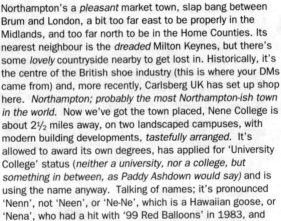

Sex ratio(M:F): 44%:56%	Founded: 1975
Full time u'grads: 7,365	Part time: 520
Postgrads: 690	Non-degree: 2,475
Ave course: 3yrs	Ethnic: 18%
Private school: 3.2%	Flunk rate: 34%
Mature students: 32%	Overseas students: 1.5%
Disabled students: 5.4%	Staff/student ratio: 1:16
Clearing: 25%	

ATMOSPHERE:
The main campus is a blend of high-tech architecture and rolling greenery and the student body is similarly disparate, a broad mix of all accents and ages. They're a friendly lot, too, though relations with the locals are as chummy as you could wish for from people who avoid each other religiously.

78910

AVENUE CAMPUS:

Arts and technology departments co-exist on this recently refurbished site, 2.4 miles from the main campus. There's a sports hall, SU bar and this is the site of regular club nights and arts events.

NORTHAMPTON:

- Population: 200,000 ● London: 63miles
- Birmingham: 52miles ● Manchester: 137miles

Northampton has managed to maintain its ancient market square (the largest in Britain) in *something approaching good nick*, and there are some *lovely* examples of Victorian and Georgian architecture around the city centre. *Some of the outer reaches are closer to prefab hell, however.* In amongst the urban planning practical, you can find the usual array of banks, malls, supermarkets, book shops (new and 2nd hand), art galleries and museums, *although the leather museum isn't as much fun as it potentially could be.* Other attractions include regular hot-air balloon festivals (*why don't they get together with the museum people and make a leather balloon?*) and one of the best-preserved Norman round churches in the country.

TRAVEL:

Trains: Northampton station is about 4 miles from the main campus, offering mainline services to London (£14.90), Birmingham (£7.60), Manchester (£35) and beyond.

Coaches: Midland Fox and National Express services to, among others, London (£9.75) and Birmingham (£4.80).

Car: The M1 goes right past Northampton, although there's about 3 miles of wiggling before you get to Nene. There's also the A45, A50, and A43.

Hitching: *Hitching is reasonably easy near the M1 junctions.*

Local: *Buses are reliable,* running every 15mins between the Park campus and the town (45p one way). There's also a free bus between the 2 Nene campuses.

Taxis: Westbridge and Favell companies offer student discounts.

Bicycles: *There are some bike lanes, but not throughout town, and the roads are pretty busy. Park campus has locked sheds (so how do you get your bike in? Ha-ha-ha).*

LIBRARIES & COMPUTERS:

- Books: 200,000 ● Study places: 1,000
- Computer workstations: 2,000

Libraries on each campus, and 24hr access to computer facilities.

CAREER PROSPECTS:

- Careers Service ● No of staff: 2full/2part
- Unemployed after 6mths (1996): 7.5%

SPECIAL FEATURES:

- There was a University in Northampton in 1261 but it only lasted 3 years.

FAMOUS ALUMNI:

Daniel Ash, David J (Bauhaus/Love & Rockets); Lord Hesketh (Formula 1 team manager); Jonn (Ned's Atomic Dustbin); Derek Redmond (athlete).

FURTHER INFO:
Prospectuses for undergrads and part-timers and a video.
More info on the web site (http://www.northampton.ac.uk).

entertainment

TOWN:

● Price of a pint of beer: £2.20 ● Glass of wine: £2

Northampton has had a bit of a renaissance recently and there are actually things to do now.

Cinemas: There's a Virgin multi just outside town; the 10-screener at Milton Keynes is popular as well.

Theatres: (3) The Royal puts on *traditional stuff, mainly rep*; the Derngate is a flexible, multi-purpose venue and the Roadmender puts on experimental stuff.

Pubs: *A sudden surge of studenty swig-spots.* pushplugs: *Chicago Rock; Smithy's Palace; Sunnyside; Frog & Fiddler; Rat & Parrot. Stay away from the Keep.*

Clubs/discos: *The revelry revival has yet to colonise the club scene.* pushplugs: *Shine at Visage (student night on Monday); Lounge (student night on Thursday); house and indie nights at the Roadmender (the only student-friendly place at weekends).*

Music venues: The Roadmender is a *fair-to-middling* indie stop-off and the Racehorse pub offers *lesser lights.*

Eating out: Northampton has the usual range of eateries, including burgers and pizzas till 4am; Wellingborough Road is the best bet, for value and variety. pushplugs: *Papa Luigi; Giggling Sausage; Frog & Fiddler (£4 Sunday lunch); Rat & Parrot; Imran's Balti (3 courses for a fiver).*

COLLEGE:

● Price of a pint of beer: £1.40 ● Glass of wine: £1.00

Bars: (4) The Venue (capacity 600) is open late on Thursdays and Saturdays; the Pavillion Bar is a non-smoking area; George's (300) is the Avenue Campus boozer.

Theatres: The Black Box theatre hosts shows by the *strong luvvy contingent.*

Clubs/discos: The Vibe hits the floor every week at George's and various other club nights get the hips gyrating (£2 till 2am) and Wednesday is sports night (*enabling rugby players to remove each others' trousers in a mutually supportive environment*). The Mixmag tour stopped off here last year.

Music venues: The Venue and George's are used *for local bands.*

❝ The new Chancellor of the University of East London is Lord (Brian) Rix, famous for a) his charity work on behalf of people with learning disabilities and b) innumerable apperances on stage and screen without his trousers. ❞

Food: *The bars are the main food stops and the value's OK.*
Others: 3 balls a year, plus the Pavilion 2-night festival.

social & political

NENE COLLEGE STUDENTS' UNION:

- 3 sabbaticals ● Turnout at last ballot: 16%
- NUS member

The SU actually managed to fill the sabbatical posts this year, which is something of a triumph, as was the campaign to get outside sponsorship for sports kits and equipment. A stunning improvement on their previous pallid performance.

SU FACILITIES:
Bars, cafeterias, minibus hire, NatWest bank, payphones, photo machine, video machine, pool table, juke box, TV lounge and a MicroChips vending machine.

CLUBS (NON SPORTING):
Law; Psychology Games.

OTHER ORGANISATIONS:
The SU newspaper is the *all-new (and somewhat optimistically titled)* 'Phenomenene' *(geddit? Yeah, you do! Nene, see, Phen-oh what the hell).* Rag raised £3,000 last year.

RELIGIOUS:
There's an interdenominational chaplaincy centre.
Northampton is big enough to support all but the most esoteric spiritual requirements.

sports

- Recent successes: rugby, hockey

Enthusiasm outstrips the facilities and trophy collection. Outside sponsorship has perked things up, though, and the rugger is going strong.

SPORTS FACILITIES:
The Park Campus has: sports hall; multigym; sauna; 25 acres of fields; pavilion. Nothing at Avenue. Access to the swimming pool in the school next door and to the River Nene.

SPORTING CLUBS:
Lacrosse; Parachute; Various Martial Arts.

ATTRACTIONS:
Northampton Rugby Club *are local heroes.* Northampton FC *(known, not entirely inaccurately, as 'The Cobblers').*

accommodation

IN COLLEGE:

- Self-catering: 20% ● Cost: £28-52(40wks)

There are around 1,600 places in purpose-built halls and blocks on campus. Most 1st years can be accommodated, but 20% are unlucky. Only about 7% of other years live in, *so don't count on it.* 3% overall have to share. It's mostly mixed-sex but there's one all-female hall with 90 spaces. A new 230-place hall is being built for 98 entry.

EXTERNALLY:

- Ave rent: £40

Student Services offer a placement service; there's an aim of each 1st year having an address at the beginning of the year. *Local housing is pretty good and reasonable, although the hike between town and campus can get a little wearisome. Kingsthorpe and Abbington are your best bet; Semilong is the red-light district but whether that's a bad thing is down to your personal predilections.*

welfare

SERVICES:

- Creche ● Lesbian & Gay Society ● Mature SA

Student Services employs 2 counsellors and there are 2 nurses and a visiting GP in the health service.
Disabled: All SU buildings are wheelchair-accessible, *and access as a whole is pretty good.*

FINANCE:

- Ave debt per year: £2,050 ● Access fund: £127,298
- Successful applications (1996): 292
Short-term loans of up to £100 are available from the Extreme Hardship Fund.

● ●

▶▶ NESCOT

see Other Institutions

● ●

University of Newcastle

▼ University of Newcastle, 6 Kensington Terrace, Newcastle upon Tyne, NE1 7RU. Tel: (0191) 222 6000. Fax: (0191) 222 6139. E-mail: admissions-enquiries@ncl.ac.uk
Newcastle University Union Society, King's Walk, Newcastle upon Tyne, NE1 8QB. Tel: (0191) 232 8402.
Fax: (0191) 222 1876. E-mail: union.society@ncl.ac.uk

general

Set in the *stunning* Northumbrian countryside and at the heart of England's Geordie country, is Newcastle upon Tyne, *the unofficial capital of the North East and, as far as the Geordies are concerned, the world.* It is most of the way up the A1, the largest town north of Leeds and south of Edinburgh. As you might expect from a city that can boast the likes of the *splendid* Alan Shearer and Viz Comic, as well as the *tiresome* Sting and Ant & Dec, Newcastle has two sides: *on the one hand it is a buzzing cosmopolitan city, with more shops, pubs and clubs than you can shake a bus-load of Texans at and, on the other, it is in parts riven by crime and unemployment. It has been a victim of economic strife, but never lost its vitality, style, spirit or pride.* Its outer areas are arranged in eras - *some quite run down,* such as Byker (of 'Byker Grove' fame), *some still remaining quite posh,* such as Jesmond (*'Jesmond*

Grove' just didn't cut it). The heart of the city is laced with *gorgeous* Georgian and Victorian architecture, alongside *uninspiring* 60s shopping centres. There are 2 universities in town: <u>Northumbria University</u> and Newcastle University, a classic redbrick campus on a 45-acre site in the city centre. The buildings are mainly 19th-century constructions formed into *attractive* blocks arranged around paved squares, but there are also some 60s concrete additions *with little to offer the aesthete.*

53% ♂♂♂♂♂♂♀♀♀♀♀ 47%	
Sex ratio(M:F): 53%:47%	**Founded: 1834**
Full time u'grads: 10,063	**Part time: 45**
Postgrads: 1,859	**Non-degree: 0**
Ave course: 3yrs	**Ethnic: 3.5%**
Private school: 30%	**Flunk rate: 31%**
Mature students: 13%	**Overseas students: 8%**
Disabled students: 3%	**Staff/student ratio: 1:14**
Clearing: 4.6%	

ATMOSPHERE:
The atmosphere is buzzing and friendly but cliquey. Despite the city's rough diamond image, the tone of the student body is predominantly middle class and relations with the locals are reserved, unlike those with nearby Durham, with whom there is an intense rivalry. The cost of living round here is quite low and so students can almost afford to enjoy Newcastle's bright lights. Haweey the ladz!

THE CITY:
- <u>Population: 263,000</u> ● <u>London: 255miles</u>
- <u>Edinburgh: 94miles</u> ● <u>Manchester: 112miles</u>

The River Tyne runs through Newcastle towards the North Sea, just 8 miles away. The city itself is the fun hub of the Tyne & Wear area and the shopping centre too. Among the modern additions to the city centre are the Haymarket Metro Station and the Eldon Square Centre, a huge shopping mall. The *trendiest* areas for shops are High Bridge Street and Old Eldon Square. There are endless banks, late-night shops and bookshops. Among the many museums and galleries, there's the Laing Art Gallery and the Zone Gallery, where students can pick up arty posters a bit different from Slapper Spice or men cuddling babies. A little bit south is the town of Gateshead, where the vast Metro Centre is based. It's more of a shopping town than a centre (the largest in Europe) with expanses of shops, a 10-screen cinema, a bowling alley, funfair, and 10 car parks, so enormous that the Centre employs someone to help confused shoppers find their cars.

TRAVEL:
Trains: The station's about 20mins walk from the city centre, or 2 by Metro. Direct lines to London (£41.60), Sheffield (£20.45), Edinburgh (£17.75) and all over the country.
Coaches: Several coach companies, including Clipper, Blue Line and National Express offer services to many other destinations, for example London (£20), Sheffield (£15), Edinburgh (£13) and so on.

Car: The A1 proper hooks round the edge of the city. The A69, A692, A696, A189 and A19 are all useful.

Air: Newcastle Airport, 6 miles from the centre, has many inland and European flights.

Hitching: Good prospects from the routes out of the city, especially on the A1.

Local: Bus routes through the city are regular, reliable and cheap.

Underground: The best underground system in the world is Moscow's, but Newcastle's Metro comes a close second - clean, cheap, reliable, and easy to use. It's noisy and not as extensive as it could be, but it serves all the essential areas for students.

Taxis: Cheaper than in most towns.

Bicycles: The city's hilly and full of traffic. There's nowhere to leave bikes off-campus, and with the high theft rate, you need somewhere.

LIBRARIES & COMPUTERS:
● <u>Books: 1,000,000</u> ● <u>Study places: 2,050+</u>
● <u>Computer workstations: 1,182</u>

The *comfy, well-stocked* Robinson Library, *interestingly,* has a Relative Humidity of 50%±10%, *just in case you were wondering*.

CAREER PROSPECTS:
● <u>Careers Service</u> ● <u>No of staff: 21full/1part</u>
● <u>Unemployed after 6mths (1996): 7.8%</u>

FAMOUS ALUMNI:
Kate Adie (BBC flak-jacketed überbabe); Rowan Atkinson (comedian, who reportedly spent 3 years in his room); Bryan Ferry (Roxy Music); Richard Hamilton (artist); Debbie Horsfield (TV writer); Miriam Stoppard (TV doctor).

FURTHER INFO:
Extensive prospectuses for undergrads and postgrads and an alternative prospectus from the SU. Video available to schools and careers libraries. Web site (http://www.ncl.ac.uk).

entertainment

TOWN:

● <u>Price of a pint of beer: £1.85</u> ● <u>Glass of wine: £1.60</u>

Newcastle is as happening a city as any, running a close race with the likes of Manchester, Leeds and London. The club and music scene is massive, both mainstream and underground. To keep a check on what's on, pick up a free copy of 'Crack' or 'Paint it Red'.

Cinemas: There's a 10-screen Warner cinema, a 4-screen Odeon and the *excellent* Tyneside Arts Cinema (2 screens), all within walking distance of the uni. There's also a multiplex at the Metro Centre, *though this isn't used much by students since it's further out.*

Theatres: Among other theatres, there's the Theatre Royal (a regular venue for the Royal Shakespeare Company) the Tyne Theatre & Opera House, the Newcastle Playhouse and the Gulbenkian.

Pubs: Newcastle has many, many pubs, some rougher than students might like, but plenty serve a welcome brew, not least a pint of the ubiquitous 'dog' - Newcastle Brown. *The Bigg Market in the city centre is popular, but this is town territory at weekends* and a bit more down-market than the Quayside, which has been redeveloped over the last few years and is now a vibrant place to hang out. **push**plugs: Beehive; Offshore; Bacchus; The Trent House; Bierrex; The Telegraph; Scruffy Murphy's.

Clubs/discos: Club life is part of the Geordie way of being. **push**plugs (among others): Shindig at the Riverside (garage); Brithop at Ikon; Carwash at Planet Earth; Tuxedo Royale (revolving dance floor on a boat, student night Mondays).

Music venues: The new Arena houses the biggest bands but there's also the Riverside (indie), City Hall (classical and pop), the Jazz Café near the station (music and cheap food) and Mayfair (mainstream/indie). Whitley Bay Ice Rink and Gateshead are easily reachable on the Metro.

Cabaret: Newcastle nurtures many a comic talent in pubs and clubs. **push**plug: Hyena Cafe.

Eating out: Newcastle's got the lot, from posh restaurants to impress your lust objects, through to bacterium bhuna in a bun. Somewhere between these extremes, **push**plugs go to: Breadcrumbs (fry-ups to die for, of heart disease if necessary); Komal Tandoori; Café Paradiso & Marco Polo's (Italian); Cradlewell (all-day breakfasts). The Playhouse and the Tyneside Coffee Rooms are the places to pose and Stowell Street is good for Chinese food.

UNIVERSITY:

●Price of a pint of beer: £1.25 ●Glass of wine: 95p

Bars: The vast Union building has 7 excellent and popular bars. The Mens Bar is not for men only, but named after the Uni motto, 'Mens agitat molem' (subterranean rodent creating havoc in the gents' or something). However, it does retain a pretty laddish, sporty atmosphere. The Cochrane Lounge is comfy and smoke-free; Twisters is the games bar; the Global has a continental cafe style; the Irish Bar is singularly un-Irish. The vast Bassment is mainly for gigs but it's also open at lunchtime.

Theatres: There are regular jaunts to Edinburgh.

Clubs/discos: The Bassment Club in the Union Building (cap 1,850, adm £1) is the dance venue to end them all. The Arcane techno/ambient night takes over the entire building once a term. Recent guests have included TWA and Metalheadz.

Music venues: The Bassment is big enough to attract some pretty impressive names, such as, recently, Cornershop, the Chemical Brothers and the Fun Lovin' Criminals. There are plans for a smaller venue at the top of the Union building.

Cabaret: Fortnightly laughalongs, Phil Kaye being a recent visitor.

Food: The Bassment eating area looks like a school dining hall but the food provokes no complaints. The bars also come up with the goods, gulletwise.

Others: At least 4 balls a year plus a 5-day freshers' binge.

·········social 2 political

NEWCASTLE UNIVERSITY UNION SOCIETY:

●6 sabbaticals ●Turnout at last ballot: 8%

●NUS member

The Union is not only as frantic as Chris Evans on Pro-Plus, but also owns its own building and so is free to do what it blimmin' *well likes with it. As of 98-99, the executive is being restructured, but the apathy of the majority of students remains unreconstructed.*

SU FACILITIES:
There's a whole floor of franchise outlets, currently hosting a travel shop and others. There's also the union shop (including a post office), advice centre, print shop, 2nd-hand bookshop, music rooms, bars, restaurant, hot food counter, salad bar, TV lounge, games, photo booth and function rooms.

CLUBS (NON SPORTING):
Baha'i; Ballroom; Bridge; Buddhist; Campaign for Free Education; Clubbing; Country Sports; Fine Art; Fringe Benefits; Gilbert & Sullivan; Irish Dance; Jazz; Juggling; Malaysian; Music; Norwegian; NOMAD (travel writing); Pakistan; Pottery; Radio; Scottish Dancers; Singapore; Spanish; UNICEF.

OTHER ORGANISATIONS:
The award-winning student newspaper 'Courier' is published by the Union and there's also an Ents guide. The charity Rag raised £18,000 last time they counted and SCAN (Student Community Action Newcastle) has a very high profile with local help projects, a full-time staff member and its own fund-raising shop and minibuses.

RELIGIOUS:
● 3 chaplains (CofE, RC, Methodist)
There is a mosque on campus. If not in Newcastle itself, most denominations are represented on the Tyne & Wear conurbation.

PAID WORK:
The Union runs a job-shop, which might be better described as a job-noticeboard. There are opportunities to augment coffers in bars, the theatres and *tedious* work at the Metro Centre.

·········· sports

● Recent successes: rugby, tennis judo
There are reasonable sporting facilities both on and off campus and some impressive achievements. However, participation is not as broad as it could be (not for lack of opportunity).

SPORTS FACILITIES:
On campus, there are facilities in the Claremont Sports Hall (sports hall, squash courts) on the edge and in the Centre for PE & Sport at the newly-refurbished Kings Walk Sports Centre with 2 gyms, weights room and 2 squash courts. There are outdoor amenities on 5 sites: Heaton (medic's playing fields); Close House (10 miles out - 18-hole golf course; hockey pitches); Cochrane Park (playing fields); Longbenton (more playing fields); and Newburn Boat House on the Tyne for rowers. Just 6 acres of playing fields in all, though.

SPORTING CLUBS:
American Football; Angling; Boat; Canoe Polo; Caving; Chinese Martial Arts; Clay Pigeon Shooting; Hang Gliding; Ice Hockey; Jiu Jitsu; Lacrosse; Mountaineering; Mountain Bike; Parachute; Real Tennis; Rifle; Surfing; Thai Boxing; Triathlon; Windsurfing.

ATTRACTIONS:
You may have heard of Newcastle United FC and their not unenthusiastic fans, the Toon Army - if not, bone up before you

get here. 'Alan who?' will not be tolerated. There's also the rugby union club and Gateshead International Stadium, Whitley Bay Ice Rink and Blaydon Races are close as well.

accommodation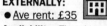

IN COLLEGE:
- Catered: 18% ● Cost: £57-64(38.5wks)
- Self-catering: 20% ● Cost: £38-56(up to 52wks)

Availability: All those who return accommodation forms in time will be housed and even students who get in at the last minute, via clearing, will usually do OK for their 1st year. There is also space for about 20% of other students. The 3 Castle Leazes halls (60s Swedish prison design) and Windsor Terrace (converted Georgian) are 5 minutes' walk from the campus, the others are 2 and 3 miles away. Castle Leazes and Henderson Hall are catered, offering 2 meals a day. There are self-catering flats in 4 main blocks in shared sets for up to 6 to a flat. Finally, there are 300 student houses at Leazes Terrace, converted Georgian houses, a 1/4 mile from the campus. *Flats seem to be preferable to halls, mainly because the food in catered accommodation is pretty dire.* Only about 2% need to share. The University also operates a head tenancy scheme housing 292 students in local private accommodation.

Car parking: Free.

EXTERNALLY:
- Ave rent: £35

Availability: *There's not much problem about finding housing in Newcastle and students can afford to be choosy. The best places to look are in Fenham (good for parties, bad for burglary), Jesmond (safe & leafy) and Heaton. Avoid Benwell and Scotswood (burnt out cars). The West End has a high crime rate and lots of drug taking. In fact, some students would be surprised if they didn't get offered something, but with cheap accommodation elsewhere, students can afford not to bother with such areas. Car parking is restricted around the city centre and it's not really worth having a car.*

Housing help: The University Accommodation Service approves houses and flats on its lists and provides help, advice and standard contracts.

welfare

SERVICES:
- Nightline ● Lesbian & Gay Society ● Mature SA
- Overseas SA ● Minibus ● Women's Officer

Both the Union and University have welfare departments. There are 2 full- and 3 part-time counsellors.

Women: There's a clause in the Union's constitution to

‘Because of an architect's error, the Psychology building at Exeter University was built back-to-front.’

provide women-only space and there's also an escort system.
Disabled: *With many 19th-century buildings access is bound to
be limited, but the Union is a good example of an old building
adapted to provide access to every level. The library's pretty
good as well.*

FINANCE:
- Ave debt per year: £1,750 ● Access fund: £192,000
- Successful applications (1997): 586

*Debt is still a problem but the relatively low cost of living takes
a few ounces of pressure off.*

▶▶ **Newcastle Poly**

see University of Northumbria at Newcastle

▶▶ **UWC Newport**

see Other Institutions

▶▶ **North East London Poly**

see University of East London

▶▶ **North East Wales Institute**

see Other Institutions

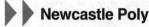

University of North London

▼ ● *Formerly Polytechnic of North London*
University of North London, 166-220 Holloway Road, London
N7 8DB. Tel: (0171) 753 3355. Fax: (0171) 753 3272.
E-mail: admissions@unl.ac.uk
University of North London Students' Union, 166-220 Holloway
Road, London, N7 8DB. Tel: (0171) 753 3200.
Fax: (0171) 753 3201.

general

Most of the University of North London is concentrated on a
cluster of buildings on the Holloway Road, dominated by the
mirror-glass Learning Centre containing the main computing
and library facilities. The University has a policy to double as a
community resource as well as an educational institution. As
a result, over 70% of students are real live Londoners, with a
very high proportion of mature students, many on part-time
courses.

44% ♂♂♂♂♂♀♀♀♀♀ **56%**

Sex ratio(M:F): 44%:56%	**Founded: 1896**
Full time u'grads: 8,232	**Part time: 2,465**
Postgrads: 724	**Non-degree: 2,957**
Ave course: 3/4yrs	**Ethnic: 38%**
Private school: n/a	**Flunk rate: n/a**
Mature students: 73%	**Overseas students: 28%**
Disabled students: 3%	**Staff/student ratio: 1:30**
Clearing: 29%	

ATMOSPHERE:

UNL has got over the initial problems of split sites and limited resources and has managed to develop an overall sense of unity. However, the high proportion of locals and mature students means that there are many people for whom 'student life' isn't the be-all and end-all and wacky student hi-jinks don't figure much.

THE CITY: see <u>University of London</u>

TRAVEL: see <u>University of London</u>
Trains: The nearest mainline station is King's Cross. Local stations near the sites include Highbury & Islington and Drayton Park.
Buses: Many bus routes to all sites and between them.
Car: *Cars are unparkable and really not necessary - clamps will work out just as expensive as London public transport.*
Underground: Nearest stations - Holloway Road and Caledonian Road (both on the Piccadilly Line) and Highbury & Islington (Victoria).

LIBRARIES & COMPUTERS:
- <u>Books: 359,000</u> ● <u>Study places: 1,400</u>
- <u>Computer workstations: 1,000</u>

There are libraries on 2 sites.

CAREER PROSPECTS:
- <u>Careers Service</u> ● <u>No of staff: 5full/5part</u>
- <u>Unemployed after 6mths (1996): 12.5%</u>

FAMOUS ALUMNI:
Miki Berenyi (Lush); Garth Crooks (journalist, ex-Spurs star); Martyn Lewis (newsreader); Sinead O'Connor (singer); Peter Tatchell (gay activist); Neil Tennant (Pet Shop Boy); Jamie Theakston ('Live & Kicking' presenter).

FURTHER INFO:
Prospectuses for undergrads and postgrads, 'Informed Choice' brochure and a web site (http://www.unl.ac.uk).

entertainment

IN LONDON: see <u>University of London</u>

CAMDEN & ISLINGTON :
Pubs: Lots of Irish pubs, *which means 3 things: they know how to run a good pub, serve a good pint and play good music.* pushplugs: The Tappit Hen (close with good grub); The Vic (Irish); Clancey's; Bartizan; Hobgoblin; Coronet. *Avoid the Highbury Barn near Ladbroke Hall.*

Clubs/discos/music venues: Many bands in local pubs and on the streets. The Electric Ballroom, the Garage and the Forum are all nearby.
Eating out: *A wide range, especially of ethnic specialities.* push*plugs: Delhi Diner; Steve's Nest (Greek).*

UNIVERSITY:

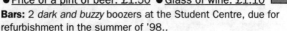

● Price of a pint of beer: £1.50 ● Glass of wine: £1.10
Bars: 2 *dark and buzzy* boozers at the Student Centre, due for refurbishment in the summer of '98..
Clubs/discos/music venues: There are events most evenings at the Rocket (capacity 1,000) in the Student Centre, the main venue for visits from *noteworthy* DJs and acts like Wu Tang Clan and the Megadog tour. Heaven on Earth is a regular 10pm-6am event. *Club culture overall is better represented than spotty boys with guitars.*
Food: There are 6 refectories and 2 restaurants (1 training) *all at what would be sensible prices if the food was any good.*
Other: Regular May Ball.

⸬⸬⸬ social & political

UNIVERSITY OF NORTH LONDON STUDENTS' UNION:

● 3 sabbaticals ● Turnout at last ballot: 12%
● NUS member
The SUs been going through a bit of an upheaval lately, ditching 4 sabbatical posts and a lot of hard left ideology with them. Most students haven't noticed.

SU FACILITIES:
Shop; 2 bars; Rocket venue; vending machines; pool tables; common rooms.

CLUBS (NON SPORTING):
Cuban Dance; Hindu; Malaysian; Scandinavian; Sikh; Spanish/Latin American; Sri Lankan.

OTHER ORGANISATIONS:
The new student magazine, 'Big Fish', is published by the SU - *currently termly but should go monthly. It's also online -* (for a taster try http://www.unl.ac.uk/su).

RELIGIOUS:
There are prayer rooms for student use for any religion.
Religion in London: see University of London.

PAID WORK: see University of London

⸬⸬⸬ sports

● Recent successes: hockey
The sporting record and facilities can be described as adequate.

SPORTS FACILITIES:
2 gyms; fitness room; sports hall; dance studio; weights room.

SPORTING CLUBS:
Aerobics; Bowls; Canoeing; Gatka; Mountaineering; Parachuting; Sub-Aqua; Tennis; Yoga.

ATTRACTIONS:
Arsenal & Tottenham are the local teams, *but it is not considered good manners to support them both.*

accommodation

IN COLLEGE:

- Catered: 3% ● Cost: £68(39wks)
- Self-catering: 8% ● Cost: £50-58(39wks)

Availability: Most 1st years who want accommodation can be housed but most are already sorted. They live in the purpose-built blocks and Victorian houses around Tufnell Park, the Caledonian Road and Holloway Road.

Car parking: No parking at Holloway Road, *otherwise unusually easy.*

EXTERNALLY: see University of London

Availability: *Islington, Wood Green, Camden and Kentish Town especially are the best areas to look,* but the majority of students are locals anyway.

Housing help: UNL provides newsletters, vacancy lists and landlord blacklists, emergency housing and general advice.

welfare

SERVICES:

- Nursery ● Lesbian & Gay Society
- Mature SA ● Overseas SA ● Minibus ● Women's Officer

The University runs a Counselling & Advisory Service employing 2 full- and 3 part-time counsellors, publishing an annual welfare help book. There are advisors to cover the whole spectrum of personal and academic problems.

Disabled: *Access is average, but no better.* Special arrangements include adjustable timetables, dyslexia support unit and a special needs co-ordinator.

FINANCE:
- Ave debt per year: £4,125 ● Access fund: £293,300
- Successful applications (1997): 776

The Student Hardship Fund provides small emergency loans. There are limited amounts for postgrads and mature students and a bursary fund is being set up.

▶▶ North Wales

see Bangor, University of Wales

▶▶ Northampton

see Nene – University College Northampton

> ❝Gourmet students at St Andrew's can join the Friends of Fondue and the Tunnocks Caramel Wafer Appreciation Society.❞

▶▶ Northern College

see Other Institutions

University of Northumbria at Newcastle

▼ ● *Formerly Newcastle Polytechnic*

(1) University of Northumbria at Newcastle, Ellison Place, Newcastle Upon Tyne, NE1 8ST. Tel: (0191) 232 6002. Fax: (0191) 227 4017.

University of Northumbria Students' Union, Sandyford Lane, Newcastle Upon Tyne, NE1 8SB. Tel: (0191) 227 4757. Fax: (0191) 227 3760. E-mail: studentsunion@unn.ac.uk

(2) University of Northumbria, Longhirst Campus, Longhirst Hall, Longhirst, Morpeth, Northumberland, NE61 3LL. Tel: (01670) 795000. Fax: (01670) 795021.

(3) University of Northumbria, Carlisle Campus, 4-5 Paternoster Row, Carlisle, Cumbria, CA3 8TB. Tel: (0191) 227 4550. Fax: (0191) 227 4820. E-mail: carlisle.admin@unn.ac.uk

General

The name of Newcastle's newer university draws attention to its intentions to expand beyond its birthplace. The main site and 1 other are in Newcastle and there are 2 other campuses, 15 and 87 miles away.

47% ♂♂♂♂♂♀♀♀♀♀ 53%

Sex ratio(M:F): 47%:53%	Founded: 1969
Full time u'grads: 11,237	Part time: 1,850
Postgrads: 832	Non-degree: 7,344
Ave course: 3/4yrs	Ethnic: 4%
Private school: n/a	Flunk rate: 14%
Mature students: 32%	Overseas students: 14%
Disabled students: 2%	Staff/student ratio: 1:22
Clearing: 33%	

ATMOSPHERE:
The architecturally oppressive environment doesn't dampen the enthusiasm of the students, even though many are mature, often with outside commitments. Any shortcomings in the Uni are more than offset by the city's ultra-bright lights. Local relations are good, unsurprisingly as many students are local, although things can get a bit hairy on a Friday or Saturday night.

THE SITES:
City Campus: (1,200) The main site is a mixture of 1880s municipal buildings, such as the original redbrick Sutherland Building, and 60s concrete architecture. Being just a

continuation of buildings and no greenery, it's fairly difficult to tell exactly where the town stops and the campus starts. In Ellison Place, the University has many *attractive* examples of early 19th century buildings.

Coach Lane: (7,355, Educational Studies, Health, Behavioural Science) 3 miles from the main site in Benton (*quite a rough suburb*), is the Coach Lane site, a modern campus, *clean and green.*

Longhirst Hall: (773, Business School) Stately home 15 miles north of Newcastle, in Morpeth, *but not made of plasticene, and not known to say 'obodoey' to Tony Hart. Newcastle students regard it as a bit like being sent to Siberia, so God knows what they make of...*

Carlisle: (564, Business Studies) Opened in October 1992, this is a set of converted buildings many of which are listed, in the town centre. For example, the library building used to be a tea warehouse. *Carlisle itself is an attractive city with a long heritage,* not far from the Lake District, Eden Valley, the west side of the North Pennines and the Solway Firth. In theory, it provides business training opportunities for the people of Cumbria, but business students from all over are able to opt to study here rather than in Newcastle, *although nobody's worried about being crushed in the rush.*

THE CITY: see <u>University of Newcastle</u>

TRAVEL: see <u>University of Newcastle</u>
Carlisle: Served by National Express coach services and by many trains on the mainline from Glasgow to London King's Cross.

LIBRARIES & COMPUTERS:
● <u>Books: 500,000</u> ● <u>Study places: 1,200</u>
● <u>Computer workstations: 2,500</u>

The main library is a brick and concrete structure with small arrow-slit windows on the edge of a quadrangle in the City Campus. *As student numbers have rocketed, book provision hasn't kept up.*

CAREER PROSPECTS:
● <u>Careers Service</u> ● <u>No of staff: 7full</u>
● <u>Unemployed after 6mths (1996): 8.7%</u>

FAMOUS ALUMNI:
Emmanuel Bajyewv (Lighthouse Family); Jeff Banks (fashion designer/former Clothes Show presenter); Steve Bell (cartoonist); Sarah Blackwood (Dubstar); Steve Cram (athlete); Vaughan Oliver (artist/designer); Sting (*pompous* pop star); Kevin Whateley (actor).

FURTHER INFO:
Prospectuses for undergrads, postgrads and part-timers, Guide for overseas students, CD-ROM and a web site (http://www.unn.ac.uk).

entertainment

CITY: see <u>University of Newcastle</u>

UNIVERSITY:
● <u>Price of a pint of beer: £1.30</u> ● <u>Glass of wine: £1.70</u>
Bars: There are 3 bars at the main centre: Reds (cap 500)

which is actually a *scary* shade of blue; Northumbria Lounge (150, *mainly mature students*); Ballroom (1,200, events only). Carlisle and Coach Lane both have 1 drinking den each.

Theatre & film: Periodic performances at the Stage 2 theatre in the Union. 1 film every week.

Clubs/discos: 4 dance nights a week at Reds, from the deep house of Electric Lounge to the charty sounds of Wiggle Wiggle.

Music venues: *Trouble attracting anything more than tribute bands recently.*

Food: The Union runs 4 eateries, offering *a wide range* from filled stotties (baps) to full breakfasts. The University has a refectory *doling out the usual greasy spoon fare*.

Others: An *impressive* art gallery in the library building, and occasional balls.

·········· social & political

UNIVERSITY OF NORTHUMBRIA STUDENTS' UNION:

- 5 sabbaticals   • Turnout at last ballot: 10%
- NUS member

The Union building, situated on the main campus's central quadrangle opposite the library, is very big with OK facilities. The students aren't the most politically committed, to put it mildly. Recent anti-racism campaigns have attracted more interest from outside organisations than from the students.

SU FACILITIES:
Ballroom; theatre; function rooms; bars; small stationery/general shop; bookshop; travel agent; employment office; launderette; photocopying; cafeteria. A new SU building with 2 bars has just opened at Carlisle.

CLUBS (NON SPORTING):
Youth Against Racism in Europe.

OTHER ORGANISATIONS:
The fortnightly 'Newcastle Student' (*how long did it take them to think that one up?*) is supplemented by some unofficial publications at the satellite sites, and there may be a radio station soon. The Community Liaison Team does noble things in the wider world.

PAID WORK: see University of Newcastle

·········· sports

- Recent successes: nothing special

As a poly, it had better facilities than most, but as a university, it doesn't rank with the seriously big boys, just the slightly chunky ones. Membership of the Sports Centre costs £7.50 a month. Recent sporting success in squash, rugby, and swimming has been on an individual rather than team level.

SPORTS FACILITIES:
There are 5 main sports sites: at the City Campus, there's the Lipman Sports Centre, the Wynne Jones Hall and a sports centre; there are further provisions at Coach Lane; and there's the 42-acre Bullockstead sports ground, 5 miles from the City Campus. They offer facilities for most sports including squash and tennis courts, sports halls, climbing wall, weights room, gym, multigym and 47 acres of playing fields. Of course, for

Carlisle students the lakes offer real watery pursuits and mountains. Bursaries for the elite.

SPORTING CLUBS:
Aikido; American Football; Gaelic Football; Ice Hockey; Jiu Jitsu; Kung Fu; Lacrosse; Mountain-Biking; Roller Hockey; Rowing; Surfing; Thai Boxing.

ATTRACTIONS: see University of Newcastle

accommodation

IN COLLEGE:
● Catered: 5% ● Cost: £54-68(33-35wks)
● Self-catering: 13% ● Cost: £32-45(43wks)
Availability: The University halls are based on the main campus, at Coach Lane, in Jesmond and Gosforth (a few miles from the city centre). Of the 1st years who request accommodation, 10% can't get it. A few rooms (4%) are shared. Jesmond Hall is an all-male hall and the Lovaine Flats have single-sex corridors. The halls are 60s high-rise blocks in an *unattractive* blend of grey concrete and grey concrete. *Students complain that they are poorly maintained and that showers never work.* The University also acts as a *benevolent* landlord, running a head tenancy scheme and allocating 387 places in houses and flats, none too far from the city centre.
Car parking: Free permit parking.

EXTERNALLY: see University of Newcastle
Housing help: The University Accommodation Office has 6 staff who operate an extensive advertising service including newsletters and providing help, information and advice.

welfare

SERVICES:
● Nursery ● Nightline ● Lesbian & Gay Society
● Mature SA ● Overseas SA ● Postgrad SA ● Minibus
● Women's Officer ● Self-defence classes
Both the Union and the University have welfare services which work together. The Union has a welfare officer and the University employs 4 full-time counsellors. There are 3 nurses at the Health Centre. The Walksafe scheme provides escorts across campus at night.
Disabled: *Wheelchair access is a mixed bag; some courses aren't suitable for wheelchair-users because the relevant buildings aren't.* Facilities for sight- and hearing-impaired students and a Dyslexic Support Group.

FINANCE:
● Ave debt: £1,450 ● Access fund: £220,000
● Successful applications (1996): 709
Assistance is available with part-time fees and there are also specialist bursaries.

▶▶ Norwich

see University of East Anglia

University of Nottingham

(1) University of Nottingham, University Park, Nottingham, NG7 2RD. Tel: (0115) 951 5151. Fax: (0115) 951 5759. E-mail: undergraduate-enquiries@nottingham.ac.uk University of Nottingham Union, Portland Building, University Park, Nottingham, NG7 2RD. Tel: (0115) 935 1100. Fax: (0115) 935 1101.
(2) University of Nottingham, School of Biological Science, Sutton Bonington, Nr Loughborough, Leicestershire, LE12 5RD. Tel: (0115) 951 5151.

General

'Robin Hood - Prince of Thieves' would have you believe that Nottingham is about ½ an hour by horse from Kent, but it is, actually, in the East Midlands. In fact, the East Midlands' largest city. As with most cities in the Midlands, it's come a long way since the days of the evil Sheriff (*and Michael Praed was better than Kev Costner any day*). It grew rich during the Industrial Revolution then got poorer again when that finished. But Nottingham didn't let a slight change of fortune get it down, not in the same way that, for instance, Birmingham did. It remained and remains a busy, cultural, *beautiful* city, about ½ an hour by horse from the Peak District. About 3 miles from the city centre, is the University Park Campus, 330 spacious acres of *charming* views, parkland, lake and a mixture of *majestic* old buildings (such as the main administrative centre and the Union) and newer blocks (such as the white concrete *flying saucer* which disguises itself as the Hallward Library). 10 miles south, at Sutton Bonington near Loughborough (see Loughborough University for general details), the University has another self-contained campus, 400 acres, devoted to the School of Biological Science.

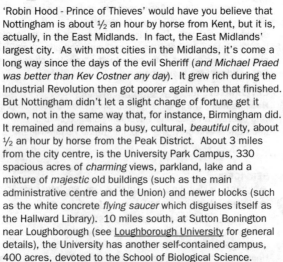

48% ♂♂♂♂♂ ♀♀♀♀♀ 52%	
Sex ratio(M:F): 48%:52%	Founded: 1881
Full time u'grads: 11,990	Part time: 6,430
Postgrads: 4,530	Non-degree: 6,200
Ave course: 3yrs	Ethnic: 6.9%
Private school: 27%	Flunk rate: 17%
Mature students: 9.1%	Overseas students: 11%
Disabled students: 6.3%	Staff/student ratio: 1:12
Clearing: 3%	

ATMOSPHERE:
The buzz and hum on the campus is like a hive of bees on speed. The social life flows with honey and the clubs milk the efforts of almost all students. Yet, a staggering proportion of students still get involved in the successful Rag and Community Action group. Undiluted essence of life is bottled

*and served in large quantities at centres around the campus
and it would take considerable effort to be bored.*

SUTTON BONINGTON CAMPUS:

(600 students) This site has its own Student Guild (funded by
the Union) which runs a shop and some social events. *The
site is self-contained and has all the basic necessities for life,
but escape into Loughborough or Nottingham is easy if it all
gets too claustrophobic.*

THE CITY:

● Population: 261,500   ● London: 117miles
● Birmingham: 47miles   ● Loughborough: 13miles

*Nottingham is big enough to have all the amenities a social
animal could desire but small and cosy enough to avoid urban
angst. It has its dank and squalid corners,* but the main areas
with shops galore and developments like the Victoria Centre
are clean, spacious and filled with *beautiful* Victorian buildings.
Areas such as Hockley, among others, offer trendy little bars,
trendy little designer shops and trendy big 2nd hand markets.
Some of the *daintiest* features include the Goose Fair every
October (the largest temporary fun fair in Europe), the famous
old lace market (an old quarter of the city where lace is still
sold wholesale), Nottingham Castle (more of a mansion really),
Slab Square for sitting amidst pigeons, and 'Ye Olde Trip to
Jerusalem' and 'Salutation Inn', 2 of the country's oldest
pubs. Students particularly enjoy 'The Tales of Robin Hood', a
heritage centre aimed at kids of all ages.

TRAVEL:

Trains: Nottingham Station offers services all round the country
(north and south is simpler than east and west), including
London (£18.50), Birmingham (£6.95) and Glasgow (£31.80).
Coaches: National Express services to, among other places,
London (£14.50), Birmingham (£4.90) and Glasgow (£27).
Car: Nottingham is 5 minutes off the M1 and is also easily
reached by the A6, A47, A52 and the A1 (20 miles away).
Air: East Midlands Airport, 12 miles outside town, has flights
inland and to Europe.
Hitching: *The M1 is a goody for wild rovers.*
Local: Buses run every 15 minutes from the campus into the
city centre until 9pm and cost between 60p and 70p.
Taxis: Pretty reasonable rates in the city centre.
Bicycles: *Flat with cycle lanes, but laxity with locks can leave
legs with little to lever.*

LIBRARIES & COMPUTERS:

● Books: 1,000,000   ● Study places: 2,047
● Computer workstations: 770

There are 7 libraries (2 of which are specialist interest
collections) including the Hallward Library (arts, social science
& education), the Science Library, Greenfield Medical Library,
Law Library and a library on the Sutton Bonington site. The
Cripps Computing Centre is the base of the University network.
24hr access to computers is *complicated.*

CAREER PROSPECTS:

● Careers Service   ● No of staff: 5full/6part
● Unemployed after 6mths (1997): 1.9%

SPECIAL FEATURES:
● The University makes a big deal out of the fact that DH Lawrence was a student here and is the foremost centre for research into his works, *although Lawrence's attitude to the University was, to say the least, ambivalent.*
● The University claims to have more applications per place than any other UK university (but others make the same claim).

FAMOUS ALUMNI:
Matthew Bannister (controller, Radio 1FM); DH Lawrence (writer); Brian Moore (former England rugby player); Tim Robinson (cricketer); Sultan Raja Azlan Shah (King of Malaysia).

FURTHER INFO:
Prospectuses for undergrads and postgrads, video for schools loan and a web site (http://www.nottingham.ac.uk).

entertainment

THE CITY:
● <u>Price of a pint of beer: £1.70</u> ● <u>Glass of wine: £1.70</u>
Cinemas: Nottingham has a 16-screen multiplex as well as 3 4-screen cinemas. The Nottingham Film Theatre shows more arty pics and the Broadway offers student discounts.
Theatres: The Royal Theatre is Nottingham's largest theatre and shows mainstream stuff, as well as opera and ballet. The Playhouse offers top rep and the Lace Market and Co-op Theatres host amateur local dramatics and fringe shows.
Pubs: The local brew is Shipstones. **push***plugs: Happy Return; Grove; Rose & Crown; White Hart; Kukamaras (for the young and the beautiful); Ye Old Trip to Jerusalem (the country's oldest pub). Some boozers in Beeston aren't that student friendly.*
Clubs/discos: *For the discerning clubber, Nottingham has many sweaty cattle markets where students can bop their socks off.* **push** *recommends, for the more discerning, student nights at the Isis; Essance (sic) at Options (house); Cookie Club and The Zone (jazz); Beatroot (speed garage, jazz & house); The Bomb does student nights and recently guested Irvine Welsh on the decks. I bet you never knew he mixed too...*
Music venues: Rock City is Nottingham's *main* indie/rock venue. The Royal Concert Hall has classical concerts, and more mainstream ents and Sam Fay's stages reggae events.
Cabaret: The Mad Dog Comedy Club at the Malt Cross Music Hall stars such satirists as Dylan Moran, Jo Brand and Lee Hurst every Saturday.
Eating out: *Plenty to satisfy the most jaded palate, including the usual run of franchises and dodgy kebabberies.* **push***plugs: Tequila, Muchacha's (Mexican); Severez, Sapnars (Indian); Mayflower (Chinese); San Rimo's, Antibo's (Italian); Fat Cats (gorgeous potato skins); Baltimore Exchange (for that parental visit).*

UNIVERSITY:
● <u>Price of a pint of beer: £1.25</u> ● <u>Glass of wine: 80p</u>
Bars: (15) There are well-patronised bars in the halls of residence and the sports centre but the focal points are the Buttery and DH Lawrence bars. The 'Campus 14' is a tried and tested bar crawl around halls which still goes on *despite*

being outlawed by the sheriffs of Nottingham University.

Theatres: The New Theatre (recently refurbished to the tune of £80,000) is used for 3 student productions each term, as are the Main Hall and Studio. 3 student shows trekked to the Edinburgh Fringe last year.

Cinema: 1 film a week in a converted lecture theatre.

Clubs/discos/music venues: There are 2 club nights a week and the Buttery Bar has been adapted for live music; Bucks Fizz and Dannii Minogue were recent *cutting-edge* visitors.

Cabaret: Titterworthy turns every two weeks.

Food: The Bars do *reasonable* sarnies to soak up the booze; the University-run Lakeside Diner and Food Court have a wider range but they're a bit pricey. The Ballroom is a rather swanky continental style cafe and the Portland Dining room has a good veggie variety.

Others: Several balls a year including the Graduation extravaganza and the Snowflake Ball for Rag. The University has its own art galleries, art bookshop, museum and a cafeteria (Café Lautrec).

social & political
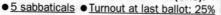

UNIVERSITY OF NOTTINGHAM UNION (UNU):

- 5 sabbaticals • Turnout at last ballot: 25%
- NUS member

It's a very moderate union, concentrating on slickly-run services rather than identifiable political commitment, though there have been complaints about the ents programme and venues. Relations between UNU and the University authorities are very good - almost too good?

SU FACILITIES:

In the Portland Building, UNU houses: 1 bar; travel agent; 2 shops; print shop and photocopying; record/CD/video library; car and minibus hire; NatWest and Midland Banks (with cashpoints); games and vending machines; Endsleigh Insurance office; library; photo booth; pool table; juke box; TV lounge; 8 meeting rooms; and car parking.

CLUBS (NON SPORTING):

Action For Earth; Afrikan-Caribbean; AIESEC; Alternative Film; Amateur Radio; American; Amnesty; Anglican; Arab; Asian Cultural; Baha'i; Ballroom Dancing; Bands; Bell Ringing; Blowsoc; Bridge; Buddhist; BUNAC; Catholic; Chess & Backgammon; Chinese; Chocolate; Christian; Classic & Cult Film; Classical; Cocktail; Conservation; Cymsoc (Welsh); Cyprus; Dance; Debating; Denning; Duke of Edinburgh; European; Feast; Football Supporters; Funk; Gaba (Going Abroad, Being Abroad); Gilbert & Sullivan; Gothic; Guinness; Hedonizm; Hellenic; High; Hispanic; Indian; Iranian; Jazz; Juggling; Kebab; Korean; Lager; Latin American; Law; Malaysian & Singapore; Methodist; Music; Mutant; Pakistan; Pasta; Photographic; Politics; Pro-Life (anti-abortion); Real Ale; Rock Music; Role Playing Games; Russian; Scout & Guide; Scribble; Sikh; Slavonic; Smug; Soul; Star; Table Football; Taiwan; Tequila; Thai; Theology; Travel; Turkish; Wine.

OTHER ORGANISATIONS:

'Impact' is the University's *pretty good* student magazine. University Radio Nottingham is constantly winning national prizes. Also Karnival, the charity Rag, is the country's biggest student-run (ie non-sabbatical) Rag, with a turnover of more than £100,000 last year. The University's tremendously successful Community Action group involves nearly 2,000 students in 75 projects and *can claim some responsibility for the excellent student/community relations.*

RELIGIOUS:
- 8 chaplains (CofE, RC, Methodist, Baptist, Jewish, Muslim).

There's a chapel and Muslim prayer room in the Portland Building. Locally, the city offers churches for most Christian denominations and worship shops for Muslims, Jews, Sikhs, Hindus and Buddhists.

PAID WORK:
The Union runs a job agency, 'Nucleus'. Apart from the usual money scrambles, students have been known to sell themselves as guinea pigs at the medical school (£120 for 3 days).

sports

- Recent successes: football

The SU has arranged blanket sponsorship for all sporting activities. *Facilities are outstanding and involvement and standards are high - Nottingham was 3rd overall in BUSA last year.*

SPORTS FACILITIES:
Most outdoor facilities are at Grove Farm, 1 mile from the campus, but some are also on campus. In all, there are 220 acres of playing fields, including a floodlit artificial hockey pitch and a croquet lawn/bowling green. There's also the University lake, a 2,000m rowing course near the campus and the University boathouse on the Trent. The sports centre on campus has the biggest and most efficient sports hall in the country, a 25m pool, 2 tennis courts, indoor sports courts, a smaller hall, 7 squash courts, a climbing wall, fitness room, table tennis, snooker room, bar and coffee shop. The membership fee is £15 a year and there are bursaries for the best.

SPORTING CLUBS:
Aikido; American Football; Archery; Bat Polo; Boat; Boxing; Caving; Exploring; Gliding; Hand Ball; Hang Gliding; Jiu Jitsu; Korfball; Kung Fu; KSBO; Lacrosse; Lifesaving; Mountaineering; Munro; Motorsport; Nin Jutsu; Parachuting; Paragliding; Rambling; Rifle & Pistol; Rugby League; Snowsports; Surfing; Tennis; Tai Chi; Ten Pin Bowling; Triathlon; Water Polo; Water Skiing; Weight Training; Windsurfing; Yawara Ryu.

ATTRACTIONS:
In addition to Nottingham Forest and Notts County FCs, the Rugby Club and the County Cricket, there are geegees and woof-woofs racing at Colwick, the ice rink (where Torvill and Dean learned their craft) and the National Watersports Centre.

accommodation

IN COLLEGE:
- Catered: 28% ● Cost: £71(31wks)
- Self-catering: 9% ● Cost: £35-72(44wks)

Availability: Every 1st year is offered the opportunity to live in college accommodation in one of the catered halls or self-catering flats (there are 300 places at the Sutton Bonington site). 80% of 1st years take up the opportunity, leaving space for about 20% of other students. 2% have to share. *The community atmosphere in halls is very strong and there is always a friendly rivalry with inter-hall competitions and so on.* 4 halls are single sex only (2 men's, 2 women's). In self-catering flats, each kitchen is shared by 5 students.

Car parking: At Sutton Bonington, there is some parking, but elsewhere a permit is needed and this is never allocated to 1st years.

EXTERNALLY:
● Ave rent: £39

Availability: *The bad news is that finding suitable housing in Nottingham is not easy. The good news is it is possible. Lenton and Dunkirk (not that Dunkirk) are good places to look, lying as they do between the campus and the city. Beeston is also a student spot, but slightly further out. Stapleford and Ilkeston are a bit far and Radford is none too safe.*

welfare

SERVICES:
● Nursery ● Nightline ● Lesbian & Gay Society
● Mature SA ● International SA ● Postgrad SA ● Minibus
● Women's Officer ● Self-defence classes

UNU's Student Advice Centre is its pride and joy, co-ordinating all its welfare work from advice and help for students, to the International Students Bureau (giving special aid to overseas students) to the Union solicitors which students can consult (free for the first session). The University employs 4 full- and 5 part-time counsellors in the Student Counselling Service. Cripps Health Centre has 4 doctors, an occupational health specialist and nurses and offers extra care for a £12 annual subscription. Physiotherapists are based in the Sports Centre. Free attack alarms are available to first years, £1 to others.

Disabled: There is a special mobility van and facilities for both hearing- and sight-impaired students, *but despite good intentions, access is a mixed bag. There is good learning support for dyslexic students.*

FINANCE:
● Ave debt per year: £1,250 ● Access fund: £278,234
● Successful applications (1997): 807

The Registrar's Necessitous Student Fund can offer limited assistance *to anyone who can say 'necessitous'* and the University gives £50 loans when needed.

Nottingham Trent University

● *Formerly Nottingham Polytechnic, Trent Polytechnic*
The Nottingham Trent University, Burton Street, Nottingham, NG1 4BU. Tel: (0115) 941 8418. Fax: (0115) 948 4266. E-mail: marketing@ntu.ac.uk
The Nottingham Trent University Union of Students, Byron House, Shakespeare Street, Nottingham, NG1 4GH. Tel: (0115) 848 6200. Fax: (0115) 848 6201.

general

Once upon a time there was Trent Poly, then it became Nottingham Poly, and now it's in its 3rd incarnation as a university. *Dr Who managed to survive 4 changes (until after Tom Baker) before it started to get crap, so there's hope for Notts Trent.* Docs come and go, but the Tardis remains the same. In the case of the University, there are 2 (or 3) Tardises: the City site in the city centre, the largest site and, if the truth be known, the main one; and the more modern Clifton site, 4 miles from the centre, and next to Clifton Hall, a *stunning* large Georgian manor, which houses the University's education faculty.

52% ♂♂♂♂♂♀♀♀♀♀ 48%

Sex ratio(M:F): 52%:48% **Founded: 1970**
Full time u'grads: 14,367 **Part time: 1,077**
Postgrads: 844 **Non-degree: 4,461**
Ave course: 3/4yrs **Ethnic: 7.6%**
Private school: n/a **Flunk rate: 11%**
Mature students: 56% **Overseas students: 9%**
Disabled students: 1.8% **Staff/student ratio: 1:17**
Clearing: 14%

ATMOSPHERE:
It's a right old mix of ages and backgrounds. Students are scattered geographically, because most live out and because they're spread across both sites. But students from the 2 sites mingle, despite the fact that both can look after themselves very well, thank you.

THE SITES:
City Site: (art, business, environmental, law, social sciences, engineering) Just on the edge of the city centre, the University's main campus is a jumble of *lovely* converted (3 and 4 storey) terraces, tower blocks (such as the main Newton Building) and slabs of *clean* concrete with *sparse* green areas between. The Union's main centre is in a block designed as a swimming pool complex. *It's an ugly building, but the lively atmosphere endears it to the regulars.*
Clifton Campus: (humanities, science) 4 miles away on a hill overlooking the River Trent and its valley, Clifton is *a small, friendly, modern site offering so many opportunities, students can get isolated from city life.* 5,500 students are based at this site near where D H Lawrence set 'Sons & Lovers'.
Clifton Hall: (education) Georgian manor with views of the Trent, ½ mile from the Clifton Campus.

THE CITY: see University of Nottingham

TRAVEL: see University of Nottingham
Nottingham Station is 1 mile from the City site. Buses cost between 50p and 80p (£1 return) from the City site to Clifton, with several companies running regular services.

LIBRARIES & COMPUTERS:
● Books: 400,000 ● Study places: 1,500
● Computer workstations: 1,500
Dryden Street and the Chaucer Library (business and law) are on the City Site, where a third *impressive* library has been built. There's a 4th library at Clifton, which has also been renovated and extended, *but it's still short of books.* There are 2 Computer Centres: the main one in the Arkwright Building at the City Site; 1 near the library on the Clifton Campus.

CAREER PROSPECTS:
- Careers Service ● No of staff: 7full/3part
- Unemployed after 6mths (1996): 5%

FAMOUS ALUMNI:
Simon Hodgkinson (rugby player); Paul Kaye (aka Dennis Pennis); Dame Laura Knight (artist); Alan Simpson MP (Lab, former Union President).

FURTHER INFO:
Prospectuses for undergrads and postgrads and a web site (http://www.ntu.ac.uk).

entertainment

THE CITY: see University of Nottingham

UNIVERSITY:
- Price of a pint of beer: £1.40 ● Glass of wine: £1.25

Bars: The Sub Bar & Diner (capacity 740) is fairly popular during the day at the City Site; Clifton has Peggy Sue's (795) a 50s style bar/club.

Theatres: 1 customised theatre and 2 lecture rooms with stages. 2 productions a year from the dram society, who have *as yet unrealised* ambitions to go to Edinburgh.

Clubs/discos/music venues: Once a week at Clifton and twice at the City site Shipwrecked washes the faithful safely to shore with its blend of charty/dancey/techno stuff; Tease in the Sub Bar. Bands don't happen unless they're a dreadful tribute band, but visiting DJs liven things up occasionally.

Food: The Sub Diner deals with all fast food requirements - *the legoland-like Uni Refectory's school dinner efforts pale by comparison.*

Others: Balls are mostly organised by societies but the SU does the big summer affair.

social & political

NOTTINGHAM TRENT UNIVERSITY UNION OF STUDENTS:

- 5 sabbaticals ● Turnout at last ballot: 17%
- NUS member

NTUUS shuns politics, preferring to stress its position as a commercial organisation. A University shutdown to protest against fees was observed, unsurprisingly since it's an easy statement to make, but very few got out of bed one Saturday to join a regional rally.

SU FACILITIES:
NTUUS has facilities on both sites: in Byron House on the City site and in the Benenson Building at Clifton. Byron provides 2 bars, cafe, 2 minibuses, 1 car, travel agent, photocopying, a shop, games and vending machines, pool tables, juke box,

> ❬ 20% of the medals won by Britain in the 1996 Olympics went to Loughborough University graduates. ❭

> ❝ When Philip Larkin was librarian at Hull University, he used to lock himself in his office to listen to jazz records, and abuse anybody who tried to disturb him. ❞

bank, recycling facilities, meeting and conference rooms, Midland bank, Endsleigh Insurance and STA Travel. Clifton offers a bar, coffee bar, shop, bookshop, printing service, pool tables, recycling facilities and games machines. Employment store and ticket agency at both sites.

CLUBS (NON SPORTING):
Band; Chinese; Cult Fiction; Duke of Edinburgh; Greek; Health & Safety; Hiking; Human Rights; Malaysian; Sikh; Wargames & Role-play; Wine.

OTHER ORGANISATIONS:
'Platform', the weekly NTUUS student newspaper, is distributed free as part of the local 'Evening Post'. KICK radio is applying for a full FM licence and currently transmits for 1 month twice a year. The Student Festival Week raised £23,000 for charity last year.

RELIGIOUS:
● 9 chaplains (CofE, RC, Free Church, Muslim, Jewish, Hindu)
The Christian Union is extremely forthright and influential. The chaplains organise worship groups. **Religion in Nottingham:** see University of Nottingham.

PAID WORK: see University of Nottingham

········ sports

● Recent successes: basketball, water-polo, football
The primary responsibility for the co-ordination of athletic endeavour is in the hands of NTUUS and goes under the title of 'recreation' rather than sports, betraying the emphasis on fun and fitness rather than goal-scoring and trophy-winning. There is a fee of £5 per year to use facilities, but thereafter charges are nominal.

SPORTS FACILITIES:
There are facilities on both sites and further provisions at Wilford, 2 miles from the city centre, where there are playing fields and a sports complex (free during the day).
City: A large sports hall; indoor cricket nets; climbing wall; badminton & volleyball courts; fitness suites; 2 squash courts; gym.
Clifton: Sports hall; 2 gyms; multigym; 2 squash courts; playing fields; all-weather sports pitch; athletics track; cricket pitch.

SPORTING CLUBS:
American Football; Belgrave Sports; Jiu Jitsu; Motorcycle; Mountaineering; Rowing; Sky Diving; Shotokan; Snowboarding; Surf; Tennis; Ultimate Frisbee; Water-ski; Yawara Ryu.

ATTRACTIONS: see University of Nottingham

accommodation

IN COLLEGE:
- Catered: 3% • Cost: £66(40wks)
- Self-catering: 17% • Cost: £38-54(41wks)

Availability: 65% of 1st years live in - 15% who want to can't. Most halls are near the City site (or on the main road that leads to it), with 2 at Clifton. Very few have to share. *Students who hope to get a place in college would be wise to apply early.* There is a University-run head tenancy scheme for 842 students.

Car parking: Parking permits for the limited spaces for a few really deserving cases.

EXTERNALLY: see University of Nottingham

Housing help: The University Accommodation Service has an office on each site and employs 5 full- and 2 part-time staff keeping a register of houses, helping with contracts and running a landlord accreditation scheme. NTUUS runs an introduction course to house-hunting for 1st years.

welfare

SERVICES:
- Nursery • Nightline • Lesbian & Gay Society
- Overseas SA • Minibus • Women's Officer
- Self-defence classes

The University offers 1 full-time and 2 part-time counsellors, and 4 outside counsellors have drop-in sessions. The medical centres (on both sites) have 4 doctors and nurses. There are day nurseries on both sites.

Disabled: There is a Disabled Students Society and the self-catering hall in Peel Street has suitable accommodation for students with wheelchairs. There are also hearing loops in some lecture theatres, and lessons can be scheduled around special needs. *However, with notable exceptions, access to most buildings is poor.* There is a Dyslexia Support Group.

Women: Free alarms available to all women.

FINANCE:
- Ave debt per year: £2,700 • Access fund: £313,006
- Successful applications (1996): 1,128

There's an Emergency Hardship Fund to which students can appeal and the Hillsborough Memorial Bursary is for part-time students.

> ❝If you have any comments about PUSH or fancy being involved in the next edition, please write to PUSH, McGraw-Hill Publishing Company, Shoppenhangers Road, Maidenhead, Berkshire SL6 2QL.❞

Open University

- Oriental Studies
  see SOAS

University of Oxford
Balliol College, Oxford
Brasenose College, Oxford
Christ Church, Oxford
Corpus Christi College, Oxford
Exeter College, Oxford
Greyfriars Hall, Oxford
Harris Manchester College, Oxford
Hertford College, Oxford
Jesus College, Oxford
Keble College, Oxford
Lady Margaret Hall, Oxford
Lincoln College, Oxford
Magdalen College, Oxford
Mansfield College, Oxford
Merton College, Oxford
New College, Oxford
Oriel College, Oxford
Pembroke College, Oxford
The Queen's College, Oxford
Regent's Park College, Oxford
St Anne's College, Oxford
St Catherine's College, Oxford
St Edmund Hall, Oxford
St Hilda's College, Oxford
St Hugh's College, Oxford
St John's College, Oxford
St Peter's College, Oxford
Somerville College, Oxford
Trinity College, Oxford
University College, Oxford
Wadham College, Oxford
Worcester College, Oxford

Oxford Brookes University

- Oxford Poly
  see Oxford Brookes University

❝Cranfield is the first University in Britain to hire out its own security guards.❞

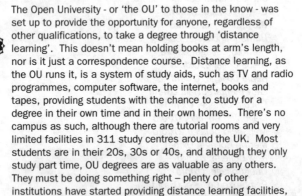

Open University

The Open University, Walton Hall, Milton Keynes, MK7 6AA.
Tel: (01908) 274066.
Open University Students' Association (OUSA), PO Box 397,
Walton Hall, Milton Keynes, MK7 6BE. Tel: (01908) 652026.

General

The Open University - or 'the OU' to those in the know - was
set up to provide the opportunity for anyone, regardless of
other qualifications, to take a degree through 'distance
learning'. This doesn't mean holding books at arm's length,
nor is it just a correspondence course. Distance learning, as
the OU runs it, is a system of study aids, such as TV and radio
programmes, computer software, the internet, books and
tapes, providing students with the chance to study for a
degree in their own time and in their own homes. There's no
campus as such, although there are tutorial rooms and very
limited facilities in 311 study centres around the UK. Most
students are in their 20s, 30s or 40s, and although they only
study part time, OU degrees are as valuable as any others.
They must be doing something right – plenty of other
institutions have started providing distance learning facilities,
but the OU is the original and probably the best.

48% ♂♂♂♂♂ ♀♀♀♀ 52%	
Sex ratio(M:F): 48%:52%	Founded: 1969
Full time u'grads: 0	Part time: 118,000
Postgrads: 39,000	Non-degree: 9,501
Ave course: 4/6yrs	Ethnic: 5%
Private school: n/a	Flunk rate: n/a
Mature students: 99%	Overseas students: 14%
Disabled students: 4.5%	Staff/student ratio: 1:19
Clearing: n/a	

ATMOSPHERE:
*The old image of middle-aged housewives watching strange
men with greasy trousers and flared corduroy hair
demonstrating thermodynamics at 3 in the morning made a
great Fry & Laurie sketch but it's well out of date. The
lecturers have cut their hair and the TV programmes are dead
trendy.*

*Still, the OU is not, and doesn't attempt to be, like
conventional colleges. Most students are studying while they
continue to work or raise a family or serve jail sentences or
whatever it is they normally do. OU students are usually very
committed to their studies and talk about the increased
confidence and opportunities they give them. Everything runs
at the student's own pace and even doing a whole degree is
optional. Shorter courses are available as refreshers (for*

teachers, doctors, business people and so on), for professional qualifications or just for fun. All this, inevitably, is at the expense of a more conventional student life. The contact between students is confined to seminars at the study centres and week-long summer schools, while personal contact and support comes through locally based tutors. Those who become active in the Students' Association (the exception rather than the rule) see each other a bit, but basically, as the car stickers say, OU students do it on their own.

The OU's unique approach lends itself especially to students that bit older than your standard spotty teenager; maybe they've got other commitments, like jobs or children, or just don't fancy spending 3 years in an institution. Many OU students left school at 16 and have very few qualifications, so wouldn't be able to study elsewhere even if they wanted to. *The OU has nibbled a special nîche for itself – students with disabilities, who may have access difficulties elsewhere.*

TRAVEL:
Working at home is a distinct advantage when it comes to travel, but the cost of travel to the local study centre for seminars and often long distances to summer schools comes out of the student's pocket. National Express decided that OU students are real students and so deserve discounts. ISIC and rail operators haven't been so generous.

LIBRARIES & COMPUTERS:
OU students may find this a particular problem, because, without a campus, the OU is without a library except for a 400,000 volume collection at the OU headquarters in Milton Keynes *which is great for those who can get to it (incidentally, Milton Keynes is strictly for those who think that life as a Fisher Price toy would be paradise).* OUSA has agreements with students' unions at other colleges so that OU students can use their libraries and other services. OU also provides an online gateway to a database of resources such as HE libraries who lend to OU students, plus electronic journals, guides and training material (http://www.oulib1.open.ac.uk/lib/). Many students make their own arrangements with local colleges (for which they often have to pay) or rely on public libraries and *excellent* course aids. The number of courses requiring computer access is increasing and students usually have to find their own - 40,000 students are currently studying online with OU.

CAREER PROSPECTS:
The OU solves the problem of how to take a degree and pursue a career at the same time. Over 70% of students are also in full-time employment and their employers are often extremely encouraging, particularly for students in the OU's Business School.

FAMOUS ALUMNI:
Connie Booth (actress); Micky Dolenz (ex-Monkee); Lord Gardiner (former Lord Chancellor); Sheila Hancock (actress); Dave Sexton (football manager); Susan Tully (ex-'EastEnders' actress). The Chancellor is Betty Boothroyd, Speaker of the House of Commons.

FURTHER INFO:
Various free course guides, brochures and web site
(http://www.open.ac.uk).

 social & political

OPEN UNIVERSITY STUDENTS' ASSOCIATION:
- <u>Turnout at OUSA National Conference: 400-500 delegates</u>

OUSA is not really a political union, and most of their campaigns
relate directly to academic and welfare issues as they affect OU
students (they're pushing for creche facilities at regional
centres, for example). The NUS won't accept OU students as
members. Of more than 80,000 students, about 12,000 apply
for their SA membership cards, but fewer are genuinely active.
OUSA is run by student volunteers and 17 full-time staff.

SA FACILITIES:
OUSA's main role is a campaigning and representative one and
there is no union building although they do sell stationery and
other products by mail and organise a few handy services such as
societies, back exam papers and ents at the Summer Schools.

CLUBS (NON SPORTING):
Change Ringers; London; London Arts; Music; OU Graduates; Poetry; Postal Chess;
Remote Students; Shakespeare.

OTHER ORGANISATIONS:
OUSA staff publish 'OU Student' and the University publishes
'Sesame', which both feature students' contributions. 'Open
Graduate' has been relaunched as 'Open Eye'. Students raise
OUSET funds (see below) and this takes the place of any Rag
organisation.

welfare

SERVICES:
- <u>Lesbian & Gay Society</u> - <u>Postgrad SA</u>

OUSA offers some advisers and there are full-time senior
counsellors at the 13 regional centres and at the Summer
Schools.

FINANCE:
- <u>Access fund: £830,000</u>
- <u>Successful applications (1996): 14,021</u>

Local authorities don't have to provide grants for OU students,
though that doesn't stop them applying, but students wanting
to take OU degrees often have to fork out about £500 a year
in fees themselves. Many turn to their employers who often
look on it as an investment, some take out loans (government
student loans aren't available). The University Admissions
Office sometimes offers some limited assistance packages
and OUSA runs a trust called OUSET, which had £70,000 to
distribute last year.

▶▶ Oriental Studies
see SOAS

University of Oxford

University of Oxford, University Offices, Wellington Square,
Oxford, OX1 2JD. Tel: (01865) 270208.
E-mail: undergraduate.admissions@ox.ac.uk
Oxford University Student Union (OUSU), New Barnett House,
28 Little Clarendon Street, Oxford, OX1 2HU.
Tel: (01865) 270777. Fax: (01865) 270778.
E-mail: president@ousu.ox.ac.uk

General

The oldest university in Britain and, along with Cambridge, probably the most famous in the world. It is split into 39 colleges and 6 private halls, which all have their own unique features - hence, Oxford's catch-phrase: '...except for some of the colleges'. Each college is self-managing, though applications are co-ordinated centrally and the University also provides many central facilities. In addition to the colleges described here (those who admit undergraduates) there are 3 more Catholic halls and 9 graduate colleges - for further info about these, please contact the University at the above address.

The citizens of Oxford manage to avoid virtually all contact with students despite their influence. It's a bit like one of those Escher drawings where faceless wraiths walk up and down the same set of stairs, but are completely ignorant of each other's existence. It is, however, impossible to ignore the stunning elegance of Oxford, the city of the 'dreaming spires' of colleges' chapels. Around every unassuming corner is a scene from everyone's stereotypical image of Oxford with the River Cherwell or the Thames (or Isis, as it's called around here) completing the picture. The buildings in the city centre date from every century since the years reached 4 figures. They are all connected with the University, but these are interspersed with shops, supermarkets, houses and all things civic. Just 10 miles out of the city are the villages and hills of the Cotswolds.

> ❝ 'I met a girl who was going to Oxford. I said to her, "Why can't you read bloody Pride and Prejudice in the f***ing kitchen? Why do you have to go to Oxford?" No answer.'
> —Jeffrey Bernard, writer and bon viveur ❞

60% ♂♂♂♂♂♂♀♀♀♀ 40%	
Sex ratio(M:F): 60%:40%	Founded: c1150
Full time u'grads: 10,823	Part time: 0
Postgrads: 4,413	Non-degree: 0
Ave course: 3yrs	Ethnic: 5%
Private school: 48%	Flunk rate: 3%
Mature students: 10%	Overseas students: 5%
Disabled students: 1%	Staff/student ratio: 1:10
Clearing: 0	

BEING A STUDENT IN OXFORD:
If someone says s/he's a student at Oxford, people will immediately think of intellectual superiority, gowns, punts, teddy-bears, jugs of Pimm's and re-runs of 'Inspector Morse'.

The stereotypes are - as are most stereotypes - true in part. Oxford is indeed a hive of tradition - it is the elephant's tusk from which the original ivory tower of academia was carved. It is full of pomposity and circumstance and some of the students are as intelligent, and some are as arrogant, as the myths tell. On the other hand, some are not so special nor so intimidating and nobody should assume that everyone will be brainier or posher or more deserving than them. The legends of excellence mainly spring from an utter intensity of activity. At Oxford, it is just not 'the done thing' to concentrate on your degree to the exclusion of all else. No one should underestimate the work involved but Oxford students are also constantly active in other ways too: in politics, debating, sports, drama, the media or worm-breeding. They almost all find some untrivial pursuit.

Life for many is centred around their colleges. Unless students live out, they eat, sleep, play and work in their college. In theory, it would actually be possible to avoid ever leaving and rumour has it that this is what some dons - as tutors are called (but not by students) - have been doing for centuries. Students, however, usually find the colleges, which range in size from 31 (Greyfriar's) to over 600 (St Anne's) are altogether too claustrophobic for 24 hours a day. The atmosphere varies enormously from college to college, from the supposedly stuffy Magdalen to the tentatively trendy Wadham. It would be almost as big a mistake to apply to any old college (or new college, for that matter), as it would be to apply to just any university without discretion and preparation. Features worth watching for are whether the college does the course you want to do, how big it is, the sex ratio, the accommodation, where it is and how it's designed (St Catherine's buildings are uncommonly modern for Oxford, and New College is, ironically, very old).

THE CITY:
● Population: 109,000 ● London: 55miles
● Bristol: 55miles ● Birmingham: 55miles
If tourists want to 'do' England properly, they must 'do' Oxford. They must tour the colleges, go for a punt on the river and possibly drop in to one of the city's many museums: the famous Ashmolean (archaeological & artistic treasures); the Bate Collection; Christ Church Gallery; History of Science

Museum; Museum of Modern Art; the Oxford Museum; the Pitt Rivers and the University Museum. However, it's not all atmospheric shots from 'Morse'; real people do also live in Oxford and for them there are plenty of shops (including 2 shopping malls), banks, a market, public libraries, and enough new and 2nd-hand bookshops *to fill a village on their own*. On the seedier side, there are also 2 brothels in Jericho, North Oxford. Also, *amongst Oxford's more dubious honours,* the city has one of the worst homelessness problems outside London.

TRAVEL:

Trains: Trains draw up at Oxford Station, close to the steps of the city's most central colleges. Mainline service to London (£9.75), Birmingham (£9.85) etc.

Coaches: As well as National Express serving London, Birmingham (£11.50) and all points beyond, there are 2 other coach companies (Oxford City Link & Oxford Tube) serving London and Heathrow only. *For London, the bus is much cheaper than the train.*

Car: 10 mins off the M40. Also on the A40, A34, A23, A43 and A420. However, there is very restricted access to the city centre and parking is either limited or expensive. Car theft is also a problem - remember the University is only a few miles from the *infamous* joyriders of Blackbird Leys.

Hitching: Pretty good on the M40 or the larger local A roads, but get out of the city by bus.

Local: Several local bus companies with frequent and cheap services (40p to get as far as digs in Jericho), *but they're not really worth it for shorter trips* and they give up at about 11pm.

Taxis: Enough of them, but they cost about £3 a mile.

Bicycles: *Ah yes. Paradise on pedals.* Oxford is flat, many roads are closed to cars and most colleges have sheds. *Two words of warning: (i) a good lock and a cheap bike is the safest defence against theft; and (ii) pedestrians, beware of pedal-powered hells angels. That's 21 words.*

LIBRARIES & COMPUTERS:
- <u>Books: 8million</u> ● <u>Study places: 2,457</u>
- <u>Computer workstations: 2,405</u>

Contrary to popular belief, Oxford students tend to spend more time in libraries than pubs. This isn't just because the opening hours are longer, but also because the choice of libraries is virtually unparalleled. The famous Bodleian Library is the collective title given to the University's main research libraries (including the Radcliffe Science Library, Hooke Library, Bodleian Law Library, Rhodes House Library and Indian Institute Library mainly housed in the Old and the New Library Buildings, the *architecturally astonishing* Radcliffe Camera and the Clarendon Building). It is one of the country's 5 copyright libraries which means that it can demand a copy of any book published in this country and, as a consequence, it has over 8 million books, including **push**. Only 859,000 of these - yup, a mere 859,000 - are on open shelves and most of them can't be borrowed. In fact, Oxford students don't have the right to use the Bodleian until they've undergone one of the University's many bizarre initiation rituals. Like so many others, this one involves wearing subfusc (gown and white tie) and swearing oddly practical oaths such as agreeing not to set fire to the buildings. Nude dancing and sacrificing virgin goats is not usually an essential part of this ceremony. *Pity.* Each college and each University department also has its own library, most of which lend books.

The story for computer facilities is less impressive although most colleges have woken up to the idea of an IT revolution and upgraded from their clapped-out Amstrads. There is also the Computer Teaching Centre with 100 networked terminals and the Computer Service which provides support for students' research where their departments fall short. There's some 24hr access to computers in the colleges.

CAREER PROSPECTS:
- Careers Service ● No of staff: 20full/15part
- Unemployed after 6mths (1996): 2.6%

There is a theory that certain fields of employment won't take anyone unless they've been to Oxford (or maybe Cambridge). The professions particularly pinpointed include politics, the civil service, journalism (the BBC especially), law and high finance. *Some say this is just paranoia, but that doesn't mean they're not out to get the non-Oxbridge types.* Whatever the truth, the Careers Service is *big* and offers a variety of services including vacancy lists, careers library, talks, counselling and so on.

SPECIAL FEATURES:
- Oxford has terms of just 8 weeks, *though it would be a tragic error to think that means long lazy days of vacant vacation.* Exams such as 'mods' (nothing to do with parka-wearing bike-riding Paul Weller fans), 'collections' (nothing to do with church plates and small change) and 'prelims' await students' return.
- Oxford is full of ritual, especially when it comes to exams where students have to dress in subfusc *and look like batman on the way to the Oscars.* It is rumoured that once a student turned up for his finals exams and demanded a glass of sherry in accordance with an ancient rite. After the exam, he was fined a shilling by his college authorities for not wearing his sword during his exam - another forgotten statute. *Rites like these seem positively sane when compared with some of the continuing traditions.*

FURTHER INFO:
Prospectuses for undergrads and postgrads. Also available are the Alternative Prospectus (£4.65 inc p&p) and the Oxford Handbook (£6) from OUSU - *both excellent.* Most colleges produce their own prospectuses and some JCRs also cobble together their own alternative guides. University and SU web sites (http://www.ox.ac.uk and http://www.ousu.ox.ac.uk) and most colleges also have their own.

.... entertainment

IN TOWN:
- Price of a pint of beer: £1.80 ● Glass of wine: £2

Cinemas: For standard blockbusters there are 2 ABC Cinemas (3 screens and 1 screen) and for the slightly higher brow, The Phoenix (2) and The Penultimate Picture Palace in Headington.

Theatres: The Apollo has standard family entertainment with pantos at Xmas and summer specials after the end of term. Occasionally it also hosts concerts. The Oxford Playhouse hosts more thespian offerings, including a few student productions. The Pegasus Theatre is on the fringe in every sense with experimental productions and a bit of a trek to get there. It also shows student productions.

Pubs: *Although expensive, Oxford's pubs have the same ubiquitous old world charm and the advantage of not being monopolised by students. It would be unfair not to mention a few of Oxford's most studenty haunts, although it's also unfair to mention only these: The King's Arms ('The K A' as it's affectionately known); The Turf; The Billingdon Arms; The Lamb & Flag; The Horse and Jockey; The Eagle and Child (CS Lewis and Tolkien used to quaff there). The Jolly Farmer is the main gay haunt.*

Clubs/discos: *Most clubs go for the lowest common denominator and then work downwards.* **push***plugs: Club Zoo at 5th Avenue (student night Tuesdays); Safari at Club Latino (indie).*

Music venues: *The music scene is booming, with dozens of hopefuls taking a lead from local boys made good Radiohead and Supergrass. Oxford also has Oxygen FM, the first UK student radio station to get a permanent FM licence (on 107.9FM). Check out the free mag 'Nightshift' for details of gigs etc.* **push***plugs: The Apollo (big, mainstream); The Point; The Zodiac (indie).*

Eating out: Carfax chippy, right in the centre of town is a bit of a landmark for students and there are various kebab vans *open till they run out of domestic animals or 3am whichever is sooner. Cowley Road in general is good for cheap eats.* **push***plugs: Brown's (perfect parent parlour); Jamal's (Indian); Queen's Lane Coffee House; George and Davis (Ice Cream); Radcliffe Arms (pub grub); La Cappanina (Italian, Supergrass eat here).*

UNIVERSITY:
● <u>Price of a pint of beer: £1.15</u> ● <u>Glass of wine: £1.20</u>

Bars: Each college has its own bar (see college entries following), some of which serve only their own students - officially, that is. *It is in these bars that students find their college identity. Some also find themselves talking to God and seeing indigo meerkats, but that's what comes of cheap alcohol.* 'The Union' (see later) has a bar - again, officially only for members, but **push** managed to get served.

Balls: No, not an unsubtle insult - most colleges (except for some - spot the Oxford catch-phrase) have an annual ball, which is a big dinner with everyone in ball dresses and penguin suits with loads of live bands, discos, cabarets, casinos, hypnotists, karaoke, in fact anything that becomes a lot more fun when completely pissed. *Sounds great? Well, for some, it's the lark of a lifetime. For others, balls are a sickening Sloane-swamped waste of about £80 in 1 night. Either way, balls are an Oxbridge institution. Some colleges have a cheaper alternative called an 'event', which usually doesn't involve the get-up or the grub and costs nearer £20.*

Theatres: If a room is large enough to fit in more audience than cast members, then the likelihood is that it has been, is being, or will be used as a theatre for student productions. In particular, there's the customised Burton-Taylor Room (above The Playhouse) and the larger Newman Rooms.

Clubs/discos: Frequent bops pop in almost every college.

Cabaret: Every week The Oxford Revue (student comedy group *which for several years now has out-jested Cambridge Footlights*) performs stand-up and impro at the Comedy Cellar at 'the Union' (see later) and does other special shows.

Music venues: The twice weekly Jazz Cellar at 'the Union' (wait for it) has, believe it or not, live jazz, but a capacity of only 80. Student bands play in any room large enough - bars usually - and the Sheldonian Theatre and Holywell Music rooms host classical concerts. However, because the University has no single big venue, it doesn't often attract big names, except at college balls *when old has-beens crawl out of their coffins, for example Desmond Dekker, Shawaddywaddy and so on. Crumblies they may be, but most of them have still got what it takes.*

Food: Oxford tends to go for formal meals *in a big way*, although the frequency, quality and number of *ludicrous* rituals differs from college to college. There are cafeterias, often known (*in true boarding school fashion*) as 'butteries'. Apart from these, there are few University facilities - no central refectory, although some faculties have caffs.

social & political

OXFORD UNIVERSITY STUDENT UNION (OUSU):

● 4 sabbaticals ● Turnout at last ballot: 33%

The big thing about OUSU is that it doesn't have a union building. Well, they feel really insecure about it anyway. Being a strongly collegiate University, the colleges provide most of the services that Students' Unions offer elsewhere. The purpose of OUSU is largely to step in at a University-wide level on representation and campaigning. It also provides a soap box for students who find their college's Junior Common Room ('JCRs' are mini Students' Unions) too parochial. The JCRs affiliate to OUSU and give it much of its funding and so OUSU isn't a member of NUS, but some JCRs are. Confused? Well, don't worry, it's not important. The important thing to know is that every student is a member of OUSU, but, like anywhere else, it is run by a collection of hack activists. It is also worth noting the phenomenal number of clubs OUSU co-ordinates and their excellent publications such as the Oxford Handbook, the Alternative Prospectus (see above), Freshers' Guide, a variety of handbooks and so on. Politically, OUSU is a bit to the left of many Oxford students.

CLUBS (NON SPORTING):

Acoustic Music; Air Squadron; Alice (Lewis Carroll appreciation); Alternative Classical; Apathy; Arcadian Singers (unaccompanied singing); Archaeological; Architectural; Art; Arthurian; Artificial Intelligence; Arts; Astronomical; Australia; Bach Choir; Ba'hai; Ballroom Dancing; Bell Ringing; Book-Lovers; Black Caucus; Bonn (Oxford's German twin town); Bow Group (Conservative ideology); Brazilian; Buddhist; Caledonian (Scottish dancing); Friend of Cambodia; Campaign for an Independent Europe (anti-EU); Canadian; Central America Support; Ceroc (French-style jive dancing); Chamber Choir; Champagne Socialists; Choice (teacher & pupil support); Christian Aid; Student Christian Movement; Christian Science; Classical; Classical Drama; Colombian; Comedy Cellar; Comic Books; Community Church; Computing; Contemporary Music; Cranmer (Anglican Christian); Creative Writing; Cribbage; C S Lewis Appreciation; Cypriot; Dangerous Sports; Diplomatic (tactical board games); Dr Who; Douglas

Adams ('Hitch Hikers' Guide to the Galaxy'); Early Music; East Asian Research; Educational Exchange (studying abroad); English-Speaking Union; Enterprise; Esperanto; European Community; Exploration; Film Foundation; Alternative Film; Food & Wine; Freedom (dance music); French; Gamelan (Javanese percussion); German; Gilbert & Sullivan; Go (oriental game); Greek; Guitar; History; History Alive!; Homeless Action; Hong Kong; Humanist; Hunt Sabs; Indie Music; Inner Temple (Law); International Political Economy; Investment; Israel; Italian; Japanese; Juggling; Kites; Laissez-Faire Dining (individual freedoms and food); Latin American; Law; L'Chaim (Jewish cultural); Legal Aid; Light Entertainment; Links (St John's Ambulance); Literary Society; Living Marxism; La Maison Française (French cultural); Malaysia-Singapore; Malaysian; Middle-East; Middle Temple (Law); Monty Python Appreciation; Motor Drivers; Natural History; Natural Philosophy; New Testament; Numismatic (Coins); Ockham (philosophical); Opera; Ornithology; Pacific Rim; Past & Present Historical; Pastorate (Christian); Peripheral Vision (film/Third World issues); Club de Petanque (French game); Philharmonia; Plough (bio-environmental); Poetry; Polish & Central European; Politics; Pooh Sticks (A A Milne appreciation); Practical Arts; Psychology; Railway; Reformed Church; Role-Playing Games; Russian; Save the Children; Schola Cantoram (Chamber Choir); Scientific; Scottish Dance; Scout & Guide; Sherlock Holmes; Sinfonietta (chamber orchestra); Soul Appreciation; Soviet Jewry Campaign; Space Exploration; Spanish; Star Trek; Strategic Studies; Tawney (discussion); Theatre-Going; Tolkein; Tory Reform; Turf (horse-racing & gambling); UNICEF; Upfront (soul/hip-hop/house disco); Vedic (Indian); Vegetarian; Visual Productions (film/video); Wagner (appreciation); Wargaming; Welsh; John Wesley (Christian); Wheatsheaf (pub philosophy); Wind Orchestra; Wine; WWF; Wychwood Warriors (dark ages); Yank (Americans).

OTHER ORGANISATIONS:

Students who spend their days at Oxford doing nothing but their degrees are made to feel like Gazza at a Mensa meeting. There are plenty fields of endeavour to choose from including various sports, OUSU and college JCRs as well as the following:

The Oxford Union Society: Not to be confused with OUSU (the Students' Union), 'The Union' is Oxford's world famous debating society. Ted Heath, Edwina Currie and Benazir Bhutto are among the many, many famous ex-presidents. Its high profile has attracted some of the world's most famous speakers to take part in debates and discussions, from Yasser Arafat to Vinny Jones. 'The Union' is also their HQ building which offers a social scene, a bar, restaurant, the Comedy and Jazz Cellars, a library and all the paraphernalia of traditional gentlemen's clubs - but women can join too. *That's the good news.* The bad news is that it costs £100 *and The Union is a nest for some of the University's most arrogant and obnoxious knob-ends.*

Oxford University Dramatic Society (OUDS): Almost every day of every term, the population of Oxford is faced with a choice of several student theatrical performances. Thesps visit each other's productions and thus the shows go on. *The standard often reaches a thoroughly professional level, but sometimes, well, it doesn't, and the selection is as diverse as any legal experience in a theatre can get. Whether the star of Spielberg's last pic or the third sheep in the primary school nativity effort, new talent is welcomed to auditions with open arms, kisses on both cheeks and the words 'lovely, daaarling'. The post-audition reception is more discriminating and bitter cries of 'clique!' have echoes of truth, although drama at Oxford is so widespread that even the most wooden pretenders get a chance to try their board-treading technique.* Meanwhile, there are just as many opportunities to play the non-singing part of unsung hero backstage. OUDS is the organisational body which co-ordinates and supports this plague of plays and runs the Cuppers drama competition.

The Media: Magazines come and go as fast as the tourists in

Oxford but there are several long-standing publications *with excellent reputations*. Primarily, there's 'Cherwell', Oxford's award-winning weekly student newspaper. There's also 'The Word' *which concentrates on more artsy, featuresy matters and most definitely plays second fiddle*. Last of the newspapers *and least*, is OUSU's 'Oxford Student'. For magazines, there's 'Isis', *the students' answer to 'Vogue' and verbosity*, and various others such as 'International Review', 'Amazon' (women's), 'Phoenix' (termly magazine of student writing - both poetry and prose) and a recycling binfull of college gossip/scandal rags and societies' newsletters.

Music: It would be unfair not to mention Oxford's many student bands and classical music groups, so now, we've mentioned them.

Rag: With its own sabbatical co-ordinator, Rag raises over £50,000 a year with all the standard pranks, stunts and events.

Student Volunteer Action: *The relationship between the students and the locals can't be described as nasty - they just tend to misunderstand or ignore each other*. Volunteer Action links students up with nearly 40 help groups both in the University and the local community, *going some way to improve matters in the process*.

RELIGIOUS:

Put any group of self-consciously intellectual people together - such as Oxford students - and within minutes they'll have established as many different religious groups as they can invent and then some. The fervour for activity amongst Oxford students extends to religion as much as anything else. Many of the colleges owe their existence to funding from Christian sinners in fear of hell and the religious rock rolls on...

Christianity: Students at Christ Church who say they're popping down to the college chapel are talking about Oxford's Anglican cathedral. The other colleges have less 'high church' chapels and most have at least one chaplain. Other Christian denominations are also catered for around town: Catholics, Baptists, Evangelicals, Methodists, URC, Seventh-Day Adventists, Christian Scientists, Pentecostals, Unitarians, Quakers, Orthodox, Cliff Richard Fan Club, and so on. The Inter-Collegiate Christian Union (ICCU) brings these Christian groups together *(Ireland could do with them)*.

Islam: Mosque and prayer room at the Islamic Studies centre.

Jews: Local synagogue and large Jewish student population.

PAID WORK:

With nearly 25,000 students (including <u>Oxford Brookes University</u>) living in - well, let's face it - not one of the world's great metropolitan centres, the number of job opportunities is somewhat limited. But with the hectic pace of academic and social life at Oxford, it'd be hard to find the time anyhow, although some students earn a bob in college bars. *If you really need the cash, rob a bank.*

sports

● <u>Recent successes: cycling, boxing</u>

One of the highest accolades in university sport (apart from being able to drink a pint of beer in under 3 seconds) is an Oxbridge 'blue'. To earn one of these, you've got to be selected for one of the University's major sports teams. These teams often compete on a first class level, *which doesn't necessarily mean that they're better than all the other university teams, just they're highly respected and they expect highly.* There are those of a cruel and malicious disposition who claim that the University admissions procedure becomes a whole lot more flexible if you have an international sporting reputation. **push** *would (for legal reasons) like to distance itself from any suggestion of the sort. Suffice it to say that the University places emphasis and funding on its impressive record in sports both minor and major. Sport at a college level is more geared to fun and fitness and is very welcoming, even to students who are't quite Olympians.*

SPORTS FACILITIES:

All colleges have their own facilities to varying degrees and the University has an *excellent* range of central amenities: playing fields; sports halls; squash courts; athletics field; bowls and croquet in the quads; tennis courts; gym (with multigym); and, of course, the rivers Isis and Cherwell. The town also has a golf course, ice rink and swimming pool.

SPORTING CLUBS:

Aerobics; Aikido; American Football; Board Sailing; Boxing; Bridge; Clay Pigeon Shooting; Croquet; Gliding; Gymnastics; Hang Gliding; Ice Hockey; Kayak; Korfball; Lacrosse; Mountain Bike; Pentathlon; Pistol; Polo; Rambling & Hill-walking; Real Tennis; Rifle; Rowing; Rugby League; Shoringo Kempo; Sky-Diving; Squash; Sul Ki Do; Table Football; Tiddlywinks; Triathlon; Water Polo; Yachting.

ATTRACTIONS:

Oxford United Football Club are the local round-ballers and the city also has its own ice hockey team.

accommodation

IN COLLEGE:
● <u>Catered: 83%</u>

Availability: One of the best features of the Oxford colleges is that accommodation is guaranteed in college rooms (*often of an excellent standard*) for all 1st years. Most colleges also provide for finalists and so, if they want, students can usually stay in college for all but one of their years. What's more, rooms are cleaned, beds are made and sleeping partners are frowned upon by 'bedders' or 'scouts' in most colleges. Each college has its own quirks and quiddities, for example, St Hilda's is all female and in some colleges most 1st years have to share, but all this stuff varies from college to college and details can be found in the entries following. Centrally, the University has no accommodation except for a few flats - about 390 places - for married and single graduates, *but you can offer to snog the Chancellor to get them and it won't help.*

EXTERNALLY:
● <u>Ave rent: £53</u>

Availability: *Most housing is organised by letting agencies which have a nasty policy of panicking students into snapping up property months before they need to move in - the agencies then suck up the interest from their hefty deposits. The flipside is that quality's pretty good - at that price, it should be. Cowley Road and Jericho are the preferred locations.*

Housing help: *The best way of finding a house is to get friendly with someone who's got one the year before you need it.* You can also turn to agencies who'll charge a supplement, or to ads on notice-boards around the colleges. The University-run Accommodation Office with 4 full-time staff, a vacancies list and bulletin board usually only points students in the right direction. The local Housing Rights Centre is much frequented by students, but, like OUSU, they can only offer free advice and don't have any vacancies to dish out.

welfare

SERVICES:
- Creche ● Lesbian & Gay Society
- Minibus ● Women's Officer ● Self-defence classes

The academic and social pressures of Oxford can seem overwhelming but the University is onto the problem. The University operates a counselling service with 3 full- and 8 part-time staff and individual colleges have their own arrangements. The OUSU Welfare Officer can advise and refer students with most problems. Law students give free advice at OUSU 2 days a week.

Women: St Hilda's is the last all-female college. *Life in the male-dominated colleges can often be just that.* The University has an harassment code, *to deal with the worst macho excesses.* A nightwalk service accompanies women walking alone at night, and there's a women-only bus.

Disabled: Over the past 8 centuries, access for people with disabilities has not been given a high priority by architects and Oxford suffers as a result. Efforts include OUSU's disabled access guide and Taylor House, an accommodation block with special facilities. Some colleges have Braille machines, etc.

FINANCE:
- Ave debt per year: £1,200 ● Access fund: £372,735
- Successful applications (1997): 444

The University operates the central Access Fund, while other hardship funds are run by the College. *Some of them are very well off and can provide support in the form of loans, grants, bursaries or prizes to a pocket-popping extent.*

• •

Balliol College, Oxford

▼ ● *The College is part of <u>University of Oxford</u> and students are entitled to use its facilities.*
Balliol College, Broad Street, Oxford, OX1 3BJ.
Tel: (01865) 277748. Fax: (01865) 277803.
Junior Common Room, Balliol College, Oxford, OX1 3BJ.
Tel: (01865) 721270. Fax: (01865) 240152.
Web site: http://www.balliol.ox.ac.uk

Balliol is one of the oldest, largest, *famous-est and central-est* colleges, just 370 yds from the Carfax chippy. *Academic standards are high, yet the atmosphere remains relatively*

relaxed, with a cosmopolitan flavour lent by the proportion of international students. Descriptions of the buildings range from 'idiosyncratically Gothic' through 'silly Disney' to 'unpleasant and stripey'.

| 60% | ♂♂♂♂♂♂♀♀♀♀ | 40% |

Sex ratio(M:F): 60%:40% **Founded: 1263**
Full time u'grads: 412 **Postgrads: 146**
Private school: 50% **Mature students: 1%**
Overseas students: 25% **Disabled students: 0**

1 bar; 2 or 3 *sweaty* bops per term in JCR Norway Rm (cap 250); May Event (<u>not</u> Ball) has a big name band, but no penguin suits. Recitals in dining hall (cap 450) and free student bands in bar; cabaret and karaoke. Weekly news sheet in loos, 'John de Balliol'; Anglican chapel. Library (110,000 books); 23 computers, 24hr access. *Good* sports facilities and *does okay in a variety of sports;* sports fields 5mins away. All students live in except 75% of 2nd years; pay-as-you-eat self service; *legendary* JCR pantry. Hardship funds, living-out grants; doctor, nurse. Taxi fund, rape alarms and free tampons.

FAMOUS ALUMNI:
Rabbi Lionel Blue (writer, broadcaster); Richard Dawkins (scientist); Graham Greene (writer); Sir Edward Heath MP (Con, ex-PM); Gerard Manley Hopkins (poet); Aldous Huxley (writer); Lord Jenkins (Oxford University Chancellor); Howard Marks (dope evangelist); Adam Smith (economist); Algernon Swinburne ('perverse' poet); Stephen Twigg MP (lab, Portillo-slayer); Hugo Young ('The Guardian').

● ●

Brasenose College, Oxford

▼ ● **The College is part of <u>University of Oxford</u> and students are entitled to use its facilities.**
Brasenose College, Radcliffe Square, Oxford, OX1 4AJ.
Tel: (01865) 277510. Fax: (01865) 275202.
E-mail: brasinfo@bnc.ox.ac.uk
Junior Common Room, Brasenose College, Oxford, OX1 4AJ.
Tel: (01865) 277510.
Web site: http://www.bnc.ox.ac.uk

Brasenose College is named after its brass door knocker (made in 1279 and now hanging over the high table) which is shaped like an animal's face with a pronounced snout (ie brazen nose). The College is *ideally situated* at the heart of the University in Radcliffe Square and 300 yards from Carfax. *The College is very sporty, with a bit of a rugby-lad feel to the place, but they're tolerant with it and an arty side comes out in their festival.* The students also provide the University with a steady stream of journalists for 'Cherwell' and so on.

60% 40%	
Sex ratio(M:F): 60%:40%	**Founded: 1509**
Full time u'grads: 353	**Postgrads: 167**
Private school: 65%	**Mature students: 1%**
Overseas students: 15%	**Disabled students: 1**

Excellent bar (cap 120). Student bands in the dining hall (200), JCR (100) and a basement room (100); bops 3 times per term; annual drama and arts mini-festival. Fortnightly news sheet and termly satirical mag, 'Noserag'. Anglican chapel. 2 libraries (60,000 books); 7 computers, 24hrs. Oldest rowing club, strong in rugby, hockey; sports fields 5 mins bike ride away. Everyone lives in; some cooking facilities for finalists. Doctor, nurse; attack alarms issued.

FAMOUS ALUMNI:
Jeffrey Archer (briefly); Colin Cowdrey (cricketer); Stephen Dorrell MP (Con); William Golding (writer); Field Marshall Earl Haig (WW1); Michael Palin (Monty Python etc); Lord Runcie (former Archbishop of Canterbury).

• •

Christ Church, Oxford

▼ ● *The College is part of* <u>University of Oxford</u> *and students are entitled to use its facilities.*
Christ Church, St Aldate's, Oxford, OX1 1DP.
Tel: (01865) 276181. Fax: (01865) 276488.
E-mail: tutor.admissions@christ-church.ox.ac.uk
Junior Common Room, Christ Church, Oxford, OX1 1DP.
Tel: (01865) 276166.
Web site: http://www.chch.ox.ac.uk

Christ Church ('The House'), just 200 yards from Carfax chippy, is the home of Oxford's Anglican cathedral. *When people dream about the dreaming spires of Oxford, the spires of Christ Church are the ones they remember when they wake up* - the 5 *fine* quads and the meadow stretching down to the river. *The architecture and tradition can be quite daunting to outsiders, but the natives are friendly, often arty or thespian with a high involvement in Oxygen FM.*

50% 50%	
Sex ratio(M:F): 50%:50%	**Founded: 1525**
Full time u'grads: 420	**Postgrads: 150**
Private school: 55%	**Mature students: 2%**
Overseas students: 7%	**Disabled students: 7**

1 bar; occasional theme discos in the 'Undercroft' (cap 120) or JCR with occasional student bands; annual Ball; own picture gallery with works by Michelangelo and Raphael. *JCR steers clear of political debate.* 'Chit Chat' bogsheet. 2 libraries

(100,000 books and other treasures); 12 computers. Q*uality* sports fields 5 mins away. Everyone lives in; *spacious* rooms; vacation accommodation feasible; evening meal either formal (*gown and tie with Latin and bigwigs sitting at high table*), or *the standard scoff scuffle; veggie opition. Generous* hardship fund; nurse, doctor and counsellor. *Limited* access for disabled students, *but they do try.*

FAMOUS ALUMNI:
WH Auden (poet); Lewis Carroll (writer); Alan Clark (ex-MP, diarist); David Dimbleby (broadcaster); Einstein (briefly); William Gladstone (Victorian PM); Lord Hailsham (ex-Lord Chancellor); Lord Nigel Lawson (slimming guru and ex-Chancellor); Anna Pasternak (Di 'n' Hewitt hack); Sir Robert Peel (founder of the police); Auberon Waugh (controversialist).

• •

Corpus Christi College, Oxford

● *The College is part of <u>University of Oxford</u> and students are entitled to use its facilities.*
Corpus Christi College, Merton Street, Oxford, OX1 4JF.
Tel: (01865) 276693. Fax: (01865) 793121.
E-mail: college.office@ccc.ox.ac.uk
Junior Common Room, Corpus Christi College, Merton Street, Oxford, OX1 4JF. Tel: (01865) 276690.
Web site: http://www.ccc.ox.ac.uk

500 yards from Carfax is one of Oxford's smallest colleges - *classic dreaming spire-type* buildings from the 16th, 18th, 19th and 20th centuries, around *standard pretty paved* quads backing onto Christ Church meadow. At the front of the College is a famous Pelican sundial and the main quad is bordered by an *elegant* Tudor building. *Corpus has a strong academic reputation but by no means is it stuffy or dull.*

60% ♂♂♂♂♂♂♀♀♀♀ 40%	
Sex ratio(M:F): 60%:40%	**Founded: 1517**
Full time u'grads: 218	**Postgrads: 104**
Private school: 55%	**Mature students: 1%**
Overseas students: 10%	**Disabled students: 1%**

The Beer Cellar Bar (cap 150, closed Saturday nights); 'sweaty bops' every fortnight; gigs in the bar, concerts in new music room; annual 'Mayhem' event; Burns night with haggis and pipes. 16th century library (60,000 books); reading rooms; 9 computers, 24hrs; 'Smallprint' magazine and weekly newsletter. Playing fields (5 acres) 15mins walk; shares a boathouse; *emphasis on participation and fun rather than sporting honours but football's strong.* Everyone can live in college in *pretty good* rooms on site and shares the *plush* Liddell housing complex in Iffley Rd with Christ Church; excellent food, veggie option. Doctors and nurse; dentist; *excellent* welfare.

❝ 'Political correctness is a
creature of silly women and people
badly educated at polytechnics
masquerading as universities.'
–Brian Sewell, art critic. ❞

FAMOUS ALUMNI:
Dr Arnold (of Rugby fame); Sir Isaiah Berlin (writer); Robert
Bridges (Poet Laureate); Brough Scott (racing commentator);
Vikram Seth (novelist); William Waldegrave MP (Con).

● ●

Exeter College, Oxford

● *The College is part of <u>University of Oxford</u> and students
are entitled to use its facilities.*
Exeter College, Turl Street, Oxford, OX1 3DP.
Tel: (01865) 279648. Fax: (01865) 279630.
E-mail: admissions@exeter.ox.ac.uk
The Stapledon Society, Exeter College, Turl Street, Oxford,
OX1 3DP. Tel: (01865) 279614.
Web site: http://www.exeter.ox.ac.uk

Oxford's 4th oldest college, Exeter is slap bang in the middle
of the academic heart of Oxford on semi-pedestrianised Turl
Street right next door to the Bodleian Library and 275 yards
from Carfax chippy. The buildings span 5 centuries *and afford
many a magnificent view.* Access to the high walls makes it
possible to snipe from on high at tourists below. *Despite the
location, interaction with the rest of the University isn't as
strong as it could be, although the location and compact layout
make it ideal for students allergic to walking. Occasional new
lad behaviour.*

60% ♂♂♂♂♂♂♀♀♀♀ 40%	
Sex ratio(M:F): 60%:40%	Founded: 1314
Full time u'grads: 323	Postgrads: 126
Private school: 15%	Mature students: 1%
Overseas students: 10%	Disabled students: 1%

Subterranean, medieval bar; fortnightly bops - free, mostly
house - in the bar (cap 200); student bands occasionally;
non-elitist summer 'Event'. Library (65,000 books); 8
computers, 24hrs. Anglican chapel. Sports fields and
boathouse 1½ miles. All 1st years live in; most others are
placed in college-owned accommodation; *odd* food, veggie
option, self catering available. Doctor, nurse; hardship fund,
travel grants.

FAMOUS ALUMNI:
Tariq Ali (journalist, activist); Martin Amis, Alan Bennett, Will Self, JRR Tolkein (writers); Roger Bannister (4 minute miler); Richard Burton (actor); William Morris (designer & socialist pioneer); Russell Harty, Robert Robinson, Ned Sherrin (broadcasters); Imogen Stubbs (actress).

Greyfriars Hall, Oxford

● **The College is part of _University of Oxford_ and students are entitled to use its facilities.**
Greyfriars Hall, Iffley Road, Oxford, OX4 1SB.
Tel: (01865) 250664. Fax: (01865) 727027.
Junior Common Room, Greyfriars Hall, Iffley Road, Oxford, OX4 1SB. Tel: (01865) 246665.
Web site: http://www.greyfriars.ox.ac.uk

Greyfriars, surrounded by _gorgeous_ Oxfordshire countryside, offers a limited number of places for academically successful lay candidates, apart from whom students are all Franciscans, members of other orders and priests. _There is a strong family atmosphere, but, like most families_, everyone leaves the college for fun and games (_Greyfriars is too small to offer any_ except the Summer Garden Party_) and for a breath of fresh air. This also applies to sport; most keen athletes attach themselves to Balliol or Keble for lively pursuits._ They accepted women for the first time in 1992.

50% ♂♂♂♂♂♀♀♀♀♀ 50%	
Sex ratio(M:F): 50%:50%	**Founded: 1953**
Full time u'grads: 31	**Postgrads: 5**
Private school: 36%	**Mature students: 0**
Overseas students: 14%	**Disabled students: 0**

No bar - just 1 _poorly stocked_ shelf of drinks and free Pimms at the summer party; Xmas and Mayday events planned. Pool table, Sky TV, weights room. Catholic church. _Well-equipped_ specialist library (10,000 volumes); 9 computers. Smart formal dinner every evening; bread and soup lunches on Fridays during lent. Women's counsellor.

Harris Manchester College, Oxford

● **The College is part of _University of Oxford_ and students are entitled to use its facilities.**
Harris Manchester College, Mansfield Road, Oxford, OX1 3TD.
Tel: (01865) 271006. Fax: (01865) 271012.
E-mail: info@hmc.ox.ac.uk
Junior Common Room, Harris Manchester College, Mansfield Rd, Oxford, OX1 3TD. Tel: (01865) 271006.
Web site: http://www.hmc.ox.ac.uk

Harris Manchester is an 18th century institution but only came to Oxford in 1889. The buildings are mainly late Victorian Gothic and there's some *lovely* Pre-Raphaelite stained glass in the chapel. *Its atmosphere is distinct from other Oxford colleges*, originally because of its Nonconformist Christian roots and more recently because it only accepts mature students. The students are *friendly* and have varied backgrounds *and there's still a liberal, worldly ethos*. It has just received its charter (making it a full college of the University) and added the Harris bit to its name - not after His Rolfness, *sadly*, but after Lord Harris of Peckham, *who's doubtless an excellent bloke but probably can't play the wobble-board.*

45%  55%

Sex ratio(M:F): 45%:55%	Founded: 1786
Full time u'grads: 107	Postgrads: 20
Private school: n/a	Mature students: 100%
Overseas students: 12%	Disabled students: n/a

Small bar; film club; ball every 3 years; 3 libraries (40,000 books); 8 computers, 24hrs; *cordial staff/student relations*; 'Mancunian' college newspaper; Unitarian chaplain; recent emergence in University football and cricket; all freshers and finalists who wish to can live in and most others, *excellent* food, veggie option, 2 formals a week; *poor* wheelchair access; doctor; *limited* hardship fund; Women's and LGB officers, chaplain.

Hertford College, Oxford

▼ ● **The College is part of <u>University of Oxford</u> and students are entitled to use its facilities.**

Hertford College, Catte Street, Oxford, OX1 3BW.
Tel: (01865) 279400. Fax: (01865) 279466.
Junior Common Room, Hertford College, Catte Street, Oxford OX1 3BU. Tel: (01865) 279400.
Web site: http://www.hertford.ox.ac.uk

Hertford is near the King's Arms in the very centre of Oxford. *It has had a rocky history*, going bankrupt, collapsing, changing name (previous incarnations include Hart Hall and Magdalen Hall) and going bankrupt again. Now, however, it's far from broke. It was one of the first colleges to admit women and make entrance exams optional. The college is built of mellow stone around 3 quads, *attractive* buildings, but *unremarkable by Oxford standards, although there is the famous and magnificent* Bridge of Sighs. There are also 2 more modern blocks, Abingdon House and Warnock House, residential blocks a few minutes walk away by the river. On a different note, The Spice Girls turned down honorary membership of the JCR.

51% ♂♂♂♂♂♀♀♀♀♀ **49%**

Sex ratio(M:F): 51%:49%	Founded: 1874
Full time u'grads: 355	Postgrads: 153
Private school: 34%	Mature students: 0.01%
Overseas students: 0.08%	Disabled students: 0

Bar; *strong* drama and music; Baring Room (cap 250) is 1 of the best venues in any Oxford college; bop cellar Saturday nights; floating black-tie party on Thames. College magazine 'Simpkins' (after the college cat); JCR considering affiliation to NUS. Anglican chapel; library (35,000 books); 16 computers, 24hrs. *Sporty, excelling* in football; boat-house 10mins by bike. All accommodated; self catering available; formals every day; food *poor;* cafeteria, new coffee bar. Doctor & nurse; Women's, LGB and 2 Welfare officers; *good security*.

FAMOUS ALUMNI:
John Donne (poet); David Elleray (football referee); Charles James Fox (18th century politician); Thomas Hobbes (philosopher); Jonathan Swift (writer); William Tyndale (translator of *global blockbuster* 'The Bible', *coming to a cinema near you*); Evelyn Waugh (writer).

• •

Jesus College, Oxford

▼ • *The College is part of <u>University of Oxford</u> and students are entitled to use its facilities.*
▼ Jesus College, Turl Street, Oxford, OX1 3DW.
Tel: (01865) 279790. Fax: (01865) 279687.
E-mail: admissions.tutor@jesus.ox.ac.uk
Junior Common Room, Jesus College, Turl Street, Oxford, OX1 3DW. Tel: (01865) 279720. Fax: (01865) 279687.
Web site: http://www.jesus.ox.ac.uk

Jesus is just 250 yards from both the Carfax chippy and the Bodleian. It was founded by Queen Elizabeth (the first one) and traditionally it was rumoured to be full of Welsh students (still *a little* true) and Old Etonians (less true). Nowadays, students from *all social backgrounds and levels of fondness for daffodils* sunbathe and revise (allegedly) in the small second quad.

60% ♂♂♂♂♂♂♀♀♀♀ **40%**

Sex ratio(M:F): 60%:40%	Founded: 1571
Full time u'grads: 320	Postgrads: 110
Private school: 40%	Mature students: 1%
Overseas students: 2.2%	Disabled students: 1%

Bar (cap 150), usually packed; hosts bops every Friday, usually themed, and occasional local bands; new ents pavilion underway; Friday night socials; annual event; lots of one-off events and trips; Thames boat cruise planned. Drinking and dining clubs; 'Sheepshagger' for gossip; *fortnightly JCR meetings popular, possibly due to the free booze*. 'Lizzie's' - banned drinking soc which carries on *regargless* in secret. Interdenominational chapel. Library (36,000 volumes); 22 computers, 24hrs. *Excellent* sports facilities 1½ miles from college, pavilion with multigym, conference rroms and bar; *good reputation in rugby, hockey, rowing and football*; multigym. All can live in; daily formals; food on a credit system and self-catering is available as are flats for couples. Doctor, nurse and LGB officer; hardship grants, scholarships.

FAMOUS ALUMNI:
Paul Jones (singer); TE Lawrence (of Arabia); Sian Lloyd (weatherperson); Magnus Magnusson (Mastermind inquisitor); Lord Wilson (former PM).

● ●

Keble College, Oxford

▼
▼ ● *The College is part of* <u>University of Oxford</u> *and students are entitled to use its facilities.*
Keble College, Parks Road, Oxford, OX1 3PG.
Tel: (01865) 272711. Fax: (01865) 272769.
E-mail: admissions@keb.ox.ac.uk
Junior Common Room, Keble College, Oxford, OX1 3PG.
(01865) 272755.
Web site: http://www.keble.ox.ac.uk

Keble is just under ½ mile north of Carfax chippy, right next to the University Science Area. It's very convenient for students in that faculty and also well placed for OUSU, 'The Lamb & Flag' and the *excellent* Maison Blanc patisserie. It's a big and relatively modern college - only 124 years old. The main buildings are Victorian redbrick, some of them resembling vast Battenburg cakes. These buildings contrast *almost violently* with the spaceship which landed one night in the rear quad and claimed it was the bar and Middle Common Room. *Students get out and about and are often involved in high profile University activities despite being fairly laid back.*

65% ♂♂♂♂♂♂♂♀♀♀ 35%

Sex ratio(M:F): 65%:35%	Founded: 1870
Full time u'grads: 435	Postgrads: 180
Private school: 40%	Mature students: 2
Overseas students: 9%	Disabled students: 0

Large *popular* purpose-built bar; bop room under JCR, 2 or 3 themed a term; big ball every other year; weekly ents eg karaoke, paintball. *Active* Rag and *strong* drama. Library (40,000 books); 25 computers, 24hrs; Anglican chapel. 'The

Brick' weekly for college news. *Very sporty* (loads of 'Blues') *and excellent* sports facilities, but most over 1 mile away. *Especially strong at rugby and hockey.* Keble can house most of its many undergrads due to new *conference-type* rooms; catered pay-as-you-eat credit system (you have to buy 30 meals in advance) and limited self-catering; 6 formals a week (no alternative); no shared rooms. Car parking close by, *not safe*. Nurse, doctor, LGB, Women's and welfare officers; scholarships, bursaries, hardship fund.

FAMOUS ALUMNI:
Michael Croft (founder, National Youth Theatre); Imran Khan (cricketer); Rev Chad Varah (founder of the Samaritans); Andreas Whittam Smith (founder of 'The Independent') - *yes Keble's your college if you're planning to found something.*

• •

Lady Margaret Hall, Oxford

▼ ● **The College is part of <u>University of Oxford</u> and students are entitled to use its facilities.**

Lady Margaret Hall, Norham Gardens, Oxford, OX2 6QA.
Tel: (01865) 274300. Fax: (01865) 511069.
Junior Common Room, Lady Margaret Hall, Oxford, OX2 6QA.
Web site: http://www.lmh.ox.ac.uk

Lady Margaret Hall is a 19th century red brick 'River' College set in extensive gardens. 2 purpose-built 5-floor residential blocks *slightly damage the idyllic setting and the handsome architecture.* Being ¾ mile from Oxford's centre *doesn't put a dampener on University level involvement. They are pretty informal and down to earth as Oxford goes.*

50% ♂♂♂♂♂♀♀♀♀♀ 50%	
Sex ratio(M:F): 50%:50%	Founded: 1878
Full time u'grads: 350	Postgrads: 120
Private school: 50%	Mature students: 5%
Overseas students: 7%	Disabled students: 0

Bar (cap 200); Talbot Hall (120) and Toynbee (100) for student bands/discos; 3 bops a term; rowing cocktail party. 2 libraries (1 for law only, 60,000 books total); 18 computers, 24hrs. Anglican chapel. Sports facilities 1 mile away; *strong on netball and rowing; undefeated University paintball champs.* 1st years and finalists live in, as do most 2nd years; pay-as-you-eat cafeteria and weekly formal hall dinner; *food excellent.* Doctor/nurse, Women's Officer.

FAMOUS ALUMNI:
Benazir Bhutto (ex-President, Pakistan); Caryl Churchill (writer); Lady Antonia Fraser (historian); Eglantyne Jebb (founder, Save the Children); Barbara Mills (Director of Public Prosecutions); Diana Quick (actress); Matthew Taylor MP (Lib Dem); Lady Warnock (educationalist).

Lincoln College, Oxford

▼ ● *The College is part of <u>University of Oxford</u> and students are entitled to use its facilities.*
Lincoln College, Turl Street, Oxford, OX1 3DR.
Tel: (01865) 279800. Fax: (01865) 279802.
Junior Common Room, Lincoln College, Oxford, OX1 3DR.
Tel: (01865) 724122.
Web site: http://www.linc.ox.ac.uk

Lincoln is *a miniature version of a picture-book Oxford college*, 200 yards from Carfax. Its small, old stone quads are just *dreamy. Students tend to stick to college affairs and this helps to maintain the impressive academic standard.*

65%	35%
Sex ratio(M:F): 65%:35%	**Founded: 1427**
Full time u'grads: 250	**Postgrads: 170**
Private school: 50%	**Mature students: 1%**
Overseas students: 5%	**Disabled students: 1%**

Annual pantomime; discos in Deep Hall Bar (cap 175, soon to be 200) 3 times a term; ball now biennial after last year's flop. *Big* college Rag; 'Imperative' newsletter; library (30,000); 12 computers, 24hrs; Anglican chapel. *Rowing and croquet are popular;* sports fields 10mins bike ride away. Everyone lives in and eats the formal and/or informal dinners; *best food in Oxford; self catering is limited.* Nurse; Women's Tutor; harassment support; generous financial support; book grant.

FAMOUS ALUMNI:
John le Carre (writer); Bill Cash MP (Con); Sir Peter Parker (ex-BR chief); Manfred von Richtofen (the Red Baron); Dr Seuss (writer); Edward Thomas (poet); John Wesley (founder of Methodism).

Magdalen College, Oxford

▼ ● *The College is part of <u>University of Oxford</u> and students are entitled to use its facilities.*
Magdalen College, High St, Oxford, OX1 4AU.
Tel: (01865) 276063. Fax: (01865) 276094.
E-mail: admissions@magd.ox.ac.uk
Junior Common Room, Magdalen College, Oxford, OX1 4AU.
Web site: http://www.magd.ox.ac.uk

Magdalen (pronounced 'Maudlin') is one of Oxford's biggest, richest colleges. Its *superb* buildings, ½ mile from Carfax, are set in 100 acres of grounds, which include over a mile of riverside walks, as well as a deer park. The surroundings attract a plague of tourists and plenty of film crews. The *old-fashioned* bar (crossed oars, etc) overlooks the river. The Magdalen May Morning celebration *is especially enchanting,* coming to a climax when the choir welcomes summer from the top of Magdalen Tower. *The students are a tolerant and friendly bunch, hard-working but not overly so (although they did win University Challenge in 97 and 98).*

59% ♂♂♂♂♂♂♀♀♀♀ 41%	
Sex ratio(M:F): 59%:41%	Founded: 1458
Full time u'grads: 400	Postgrads: 159
Private/state school: 51%	Mature students: 0.5%
Overseas students: 10%	Disabled students: 1.5%

Bar (cap 200) and JCR (150) used for student bands; classical concerts in the chapel (200); fortnightly bops; Commemoration Ball every 3 years, *one of the biggies;* new auditorium planned. 3 libraries (100,000 books); 25 computers, 24hrs; Anglican chapel; student mag ('The Ghost of Magdalen'). *Great* sports fields 10mins walk; 4 squash courts in College; Women's squash *strong.* Almost everyone lives in; 27 kitchens for undergrads, *lousy food - better in the bar but you ought to bring your garibaldi biscuits.* Doctor and nurse; LGB and Women's officers. *College is responsive to students' problems.* Walk scheme escorts women home till 2am; free attack alarms provided. Hardship funds, scholarships, book and travel grants.

FAMOUS ALUMNI:
John Betjeman (poet, sent down); Edward Gibbon (historian, described his time here as 'idle and unprofitable'); Darius Guppy (fraudster); William Hague MP, John Redwood MP (Con); Ian Hislop (editor, 'Private Eye'); CS Lewis (writer); Dudley Moore (actor/pianist); Desmond Morris (socio-anthropologist); David Rendel MP (LibDem); AJP Taylor (historian); Oscar Wilde (writer, wit); Cardinal Wolsey.

Mansfield College, Oxford

● *The College is part of <u>University of Oxford</u> and students are entitled to use its facilities.*
Mansfield College, Mansfield Road, Oxford, OX1 3TF.
Tel: (01865) 270999. Fax: (01865) 270970.
Junior Common Room, Mansfield College, Oxford, OX1 3TF.
Tel: (01865) 270889.
Web site: http://www.mansfield.ox.ac.uk

Mansfield was once a Free Church centre *and prides itself on a tradition of being the source of many a minister.* The main Victorian buildings are set around the huge circular lawn. Outside it *looks inspiring and spacious. Rowing is popular* and the College has its own boathouse, indeed Mansfield was the home of *True Blue and meaty* rower Donald McDonald; most sports amenities are run jointly with <u>Merton College</u>. *The atmosphere is friendly and down-to-earth and there's a strong tradition of supplying hacks to the SU and journos to Cherwell.*

65% ♂♂♂♂♂♂♂♀♀♀ **35%**

Sex ratio(M:F): 65%:35%	**Founded: 1886**
Full time u'grads: 194	**Postgrads: 70**
Private/state school: 32%	**Mature students: 1%**
Overseas students: 8.2%	**Disabled students: 1**

'Black Bottle' Bar, packed at the weekend; 2-3 bops termly and bands in the JCR (cap 225); cabaret; Sky TV; jazz & cocktail parties. 'Heaven's Boilers' news/gossip sheet; 'Heaven's Gate' student mag. 2 libraries (27,000 volumes); 10 computers, 24hrs; URC chapel. Sport: pool. *Varied* accommodation for all 1st, 3rd years and finalists; students eat in college dining halls except Sundays. 1 room for a wheelchair user; doctor and nurse; counselling team, Women's, LGB officers.

FAMOUS ALUMNI:
CH Dodd and Albert Schweitzer (theologians); Donald McDonald (mutinous rower); Von Trott (who tried to kill Hitler).

Merton College, Oxford

▼ **● The College is part of <u>University of Oxford</u> and students are entitled to use its facilities.**
▼ Merton College, Merton St, Oxford, OX1 4JD.
Tel: (01865) 276310. Fax: (01865) 276361.
E-mail clare.bass@melton.ox.ac.uk
Junior Common Room, Merton College, Oxford, OX1 4JD.
Tel: (01865) 286310. Fax: (01865) 286495.
Web site: http://www.merton.ox.ac.uk

Merton is *one of Oxford's prettier colleges,* 600 yards from Carfax, with *magical* gardens (where Tolkien wrote 'Lord of the Rings'), a *beautiful* chapel and *bizarre* gargoyles. The Mob Quad is the oldest quad in Oxford and home of the library (the oldest in England), which is supposedly haunted and contains Chaucer's Astrolabe. *The atmosphere is laid-back but standards are high and students have made their mark in University journalism, drama and music. Odd* traditions include walking backwards around the quad drinking port for an hour when the clocks go back.

60% ♂♂♂♂♂♂♀♀♀♀ **40%**

Sex ratio(M:F): 60%:40%	**Founded: 1264**
Full time u'grads: 271	**Postgrads: 151**
Private school: 50%	**Mature students: 0.3%**
Overseas students: 5%	**Disabled students: 0**

❝Lincoln College, Oxford, suffered a 10-year ban from 'University Challenge' for stripping the set bare.❞

Friendly bar; student bands and fortnightly bops in JCR (cap 200); Xmas Ball; *strong* Choral Society; *charmingly named* termly mag 'The Felcher'. 3 libraries (70,000 volumes); 16 computers, 24hrs; Interdenominational chapel. Sports facilities (10mins walk) shared with <u>Mansfield College</u>; *korfball is strong; emphasis on sports participation rather than achievement. JCR now have a Squirrel Rep who works tirelessly to protect trees in the Merton garden.* Almost everyone lives in; many *elegant* rooms; daily formals, *excellent* food. Shared doctor and nurse, LGB officer; hardship fund.

FAMOUS ALUMNI:
Roger Bannister (the original 4-minute miler); Frank Bough (broadcaster); Howard Davies (deputy Governor, Bank of England); TS Eliot (poet); Kris Kristofferson (singer); Robert Morley (actor); Crown Prince Naruhito (Japanese heir apparent); John Wycliffe (theologian).

•••

New College, Oxford

▼ **● The College is part of <u>University of Oxford</u> and students**
▼ **are entitled to use its facilities.**
New College, Oxford, OX1 3BN. Tel: (01865) 279555.
Fax: (01865) 279590. E-mail: admissions@new.ox.ac.uk
Junior Common Room, New College, Oxford, OX1 2BN.
Tel: (01865) 279577.
Web site: http://www.new.ox.ac.uk

New College, ironically one of the oldest colleges, is *so prettily Gothic that it wouldn't look out of place in Disneyland Paris*, with the city wall running through its *pleasant* grounds. The College is only 600 yards from Carfax, but it's hidden to a certain extent from the swarms of tourists. The social scene rotates around the Beer Cellar, a refurbished medieval cave attracting students from all over Oxford. New College (full name, never just 'New') students come from a wide geographical and social cross-section, *united by running round the college backwards three times at Hallowe'en to 'appease the ghosts', amongst other things.*

52% ♂♂♂♂♂♀♀♀♀♀ **48%**

Sex ratio(M:F): 52%:48%	**Founded: 1379**
Full time u'grads: 430	**Postgrads: 170**
Private school: 55%	**Mature students: 1%**
Overseas students: 5%	**Disabled students: 0.5%**

❝Merton College, Oxford, has an annual 'Time Ceremony'. When the clocks are turned back at 2am, students walk backwards in academic dress around the Fellows' Quad. ❞

Bar (cap 200); classical music in Anglican chapel; bops, jazz and student bands in the Long Room (200); student DJ nights *popular*, open to non-college members; *big* ball, 'social event of the year' according to 'The Times'. *Strong music and theatre; famous choir.* Fortnightly bogsheet. Library (70,000 books & 30,000 antiquarian items); 45 computers, 24hrs. 14 acres of playing fields on site. New accommodation for 99 will ensure everyone is housed. All students eat in halls; daily formal dinner in college hall; self catering in new buildings. Doctor, nurse; LGB, Women's and Harassment Officers - *welfare good*.

FAMOUS ALUMNI:
Tony Benn MP (Lab); Angus Deayton (before he was famous); John Fowles, John Galsworthy (writers); Hugh Grant (film star); Bryan Johnston (cricket commentator, after whom the new pavilion is named); Naomi Woolf (feminist writer).

Oriel College, Oxford

● The College is part of <u>University of Oxford</u> and students are entitled to use its facilities.
Oriel College, Oriel Square, Oxford, OX1 4EW.
Tel: (01865) 276543. Fax: (01865) 791823.
Junior Common Room, Oriel College, Oxford, OX1 4EW.
Tel: (01865) 276587.
Web site: http://www.oriel.ox.ac.uk/

One of the oldest and smallest Colleges, Oriel is 300 yards from Carfax and *despite the popular stereotype, it's no more of a public school stronghold than the rest of Oxford.* Its quiet and closed quads and tight, friendly communal spirit can be a bit suffocating. *It's had a reputation for sporting obsessions, but this is waning.* The bar, however, is great to hang out in if you're into pool, darts or table football. There is an *excellent* choir and a *famed* drama society.

65% ♂♂♂♂♂♂♂♀♀♀ **35%**

Sex ratio(M:F): 65%:35%	Founded: 1326
Full time u'grads: 303	Postgrads: 157
Private school: 50%	Mature students: 0.1%
Overseas students: 10%	Disabled students: n/a

Student bands and bops in the bar (cap 160); regular cabaret; ball every three years. Various news sheets and college mags; library (100,000 books); 12 computers. Anglican chapel. 6½ acres of playing fields 1 mile off site; ideally positioned for the river, rowing very strong; *sportsmania still leaves room for the musical and dramatic type.* All students live in; students eat in the dining hall; *moderate* food, but eat-as-much-as-you-like-breakfasts. Doctor, nurse. Scholarships, book and travel grants and *lots of* prizes.

FAMOUS ALUMNI:
Beau Brummel (dandy); Cardinal Newman; Sir Walter Raleigh; Cecil Rhodes (*dodgy* imperialist); AJP Taylor (historian).

• •

Pembroke College, Oxford

● The College is part of <u>University of Oxford</u> and students are entitled to use its facilities.
Pembroke College, St Aldgate's, Oxford, OX1 1DW.
Tel: (01865) 276412. Fax: (01865) 276418.
Junior Common Room, Pembroke College, Oxford, OX1 1DW.

Pembroke's quads, 300 yards from Carfax, range from medieval *marvels* to modern *misdemeanours,* but even Alan Titchmarsh could get some tips from their garden. *They're also known for sporting prowess and political hackery but academic achievement hovers around the 'adequate' mark. Still, as long as there's beer flowing, they're a happy bunch.*

60% ♂♂♂♂♂♂♀♀♀♀ **40%**

Sex ratio(M:F): 60%:40%	**Founded: 1624**
Full time u'grads: 397	**Postgrads: 90**
Private school: 50%	**Mature students: 2%**
Overseas students: 10%	**Disabled students: 0**

Bar (cap 120) and *refurbished* JCR (150) used for student bands; ball every 2 years (cap 1,000); regular bops (180). 2 newpapers: 'Broadsheet' (*run by wimmin*) and 'Endeavour' (*raucous*); yearbook; library (40,000 books); 10 computers, 24 hrs; Anglican chapel; music room. *Thriving* sports; high proportion of University sports players, *excellent rowing.* 1st and 3rd years guaranteed accommodation; no sharing; some single sex staircases; creeping 'conference effect' means rooms are gradually being tarted up; formal dinner in dining hall, *pretty much compulsory for 1st years*; food *pretty good. Good* disabled access in Geoffrey Arthur Building, where all finalists are guaranteed rooms. Doctor, nurse; hardship fund.

FAMOUS ALUMNI:
Denzil Davies MP (Lab); Michael Heseltine MP (Con); Samuel Johnson (writer, lexicographer); James Smithson (founded Smithsonian Institute).

The Queen's College, Oxford

● *The College is part of <u>University of Oxford</u> and students are entitled to use its facilities.*

The Queen's College, High Street, Oxford, OX1 4AW.
Tel: (01865) 279167. Fax: (01865) 790819.
E-mail: admissions@queens.ox.ac.uk
Junior Common Room, The Queen's College, Oxford, OX1 4AW.
Web site: http://www.queens.ox.ac.uk

Queen's is steeped in history and tradition. For example, under ancient lore, students have the right to send servants to the cellar to fetch them beer. Its *superb* buildings *dominate* the High Street, 600 yards from Carfax. The cupola and quad designed by Hawksmoor are *impressive. Queen's isn't typical of Oxford colleges. There is a larger northern contingent among the students than at most colleges and the atmosphere is refreshingly unpretentious. They don't often go beyond their own doorstep for entertainment.*

60% ♂♂♂♂♂♂♀♀♀♀ 40%	
Sex ratio(M:F): 60%:40%	Founded: 1341
Full time u'grads: 300	Postgrads: 100
Private school: 50%	Mature students: n/a
Overseas students: 10%	Disabled students: 1.5

Bar - The Beer Cellar (150) - With 'the friendliest bar manager in the world'. Queen's was the last college to brew its own beer; Queen's Hall (cap 350) and JCR (75) used for ents as above and bands, cabaret and fortnightly groove in The Beer Cellar; also slap-up dinners preceeded by trumpet fanfare, afternoon tea. Library (170,000 books); 8 computers, 24hrs; Anglican chapel. *Participation in sport stressed rather than success, but they're dead good at darts*; 6½ acres of playing fields, ¾ mile from College. Everyone lives in and eats (*food 'edible'*) in the dining hall. Doctor, nurse; bursaries and hardship fund.

FAMOUS ALUMNI:
Rowan Atkinson (comedian); Jeremy Bentham (philosopher); Edmund Halley (as in comet); Henry V (king); David Jenkins (ex-Bishop of Durham); Gerald Kaufman MP (Lab); Oliver Sacks (writer, psychiatrist); Brian Walden (journalist).

❝In 1881, the entire student body of University College, Oxford, was sent down, after the Dean's Room was screwed shut (with the Dean inside).❞

Regent's Park College, Oxford

▼ ● *The College is part of <u>University of Oxford</u> and students are entitled to use its facilities.*
Regent's Park College, Pusey Street, Oxford, OX1 2LB.
Tel: (01865) 288120. Fax: (01865) 228121.
Junior Common Room, Regent's Park College,
Pusey Street, Oxford, OX1 2LB.
Web site: http://www.rpc.ox.ac.uk/rpc

Regent's Park is a very small college and its *unassuming* entrance, a door off the street, is typical of the whole College. It was originally established in London to train Baptist ministers and missionaries, *but it's not solely for the spiritual - it has its fair share of typical Oxford rowers and hacks* and attracts many visiting students from the USA and elsewhere. The College has *a homely atmosphere* and welcomes those with families. *Tekkie boffins, however, need not apply,* as you can only read Arts subjects at Regent's Park. Lots of bursaries for the *theologically inclined.*

55% ♂♂♂♂♂♀ ♀♀♀♀ 45%	
Sex ratio(M:F): 55%:45%	Founded: 1810
Full time u'grads: 66	Postgrads: 26
Private school: 45%	Mature students: 12%
Overseas students: 2%	Disabled students: 2

Bar (*tiny with irregular hours*); 30s Helwys Hall (cap 300) and JCR (60) for bands, cabaret termly and discos 2 times a term; lots of ad hoc ents - quiz nights, picnics, punting parties; mini ball. *The JCR is very active* and votes about everything. *Good relations with staff; drama and charitable urges strong.* 2 libraries (25,000 books) - *good for theology, poo for anything else;* 5 computers; Baptist chapel. Snooker table, but no sports fields. Everyone lives in. Disabled access on ground floor. Nurse.

St Anne's College, Oxford

▼ ● *The College is part of <u>University of Oxford</u> and students are entitled to use its facilities.*
St Anne's College, Woodstock Road, Oxford, OX2 6HS.
Tel: (01865) 274800. Fax: (01865) 274899.
E-mail: sheila.sherlock@st-annes.ox.ac.uk
Junior Common Room, St Anne's College, Oxford, OX2 6HS.
Web site: http://www.stannes.ox.ac.uk

St Anne's is 10mins walk from the town centre. The main building is made of white stone with a battlement top and was built in the 30s. Most of the others were constructed *with a*

little less care for beauty in the 50s and 60s as well as a new building finished in 1992. *The students are a no-nonsense bunch - not much petty student politicking, they prefer to put their energies into charity Rag events or the wealth of drama societies. St Anne's claims to be particularly open to applications from minorities and its students are reputed to be 'normal'. Well that's comforting.*

58% ♂♂♂♂♂♂ ♀♀♀♀ 42%	
Sex ratio(M:F): 58%:42%	Founded: 1878
Full time u'grads: 436	Postgrads: 182
Private school: 50%	Mature students: 5%
Overseas students: 6%	Disabled students: n/a

Bar; big lecture theatre with screen and collapsible stage (cap 150); bops, bands in JCR (150); *fab* discos in dining hall (300); cabarets 1-3 times a term. 'Double Standards' and 'Agent Orange' mags; 'Bogsheet' for news/gossip; TV room; library (110,000 books); 17 computers. *Rowing and rugby pretty strong*; sports fields shared with St John's ½ mile away. Everyone lives in; meal card system, veggie option; *good* self-catering. Doctor, nurse; student counsellor. *Good* disabled access.

FAMOUS ALUMNI:
Maria Aitken (actress); Sister Wendy Beckett (art nun); Edwina Currie MP (Con); Penelope Lively, Iris Murdoch (writers); Libby Purves (broadcaster); Simon Rattle (conductor); Victor Ubogu (rugby player).

• •

St Catherine's College, Oxford

▼ ● *The College is part of <u>University of Oxford</u> and students are entitled to use its facilities.*
St Catherine's College, Manor Road, Oxford, OX1 3UJ.
Tel: (01865) 271700. Fax: (01865) 271768.
Junior Common Room, St Catherine's College, Oxford, OX1 3UJ.
Web site: http://www.stcatz.ox.ac.uk

Catz, as St Catherine's is known, looks unlike most other Oxford colleges being a modernist *brick, glass and concrete* environment 1¼ miles from Carfax. *The relatively progressive architecture doesn't look like an Oxbridge college, and the same is true of the forward-looking, unstuffy atmosphere inside. There are lots of ents and bops which pull in the crowds.* It's very big and has all the mod cons - warm rooms, showers, kitchens, purpose-built bars, even a grassy amphitheatre and water gardens. *For students who want to go to Oxford for the academic kudos, but want to steer clear of the Ivory Tower mentality, Catz is a good bet. It still has that one big happy family feel, though, mainly because of its comparatively detached setting.*

60% **40%**

Sex ratio(M:F): 60%:40%
Full time u'grads: 448
Private school: 45%
Overseas students: 1%
Founded: 1962
Postgrads: 166
Mature students: 1%
Disabled students: n/a

Lively bar; 2 theatres; JCR Courtyard (cap 400), Bernard Sunley theatre (250) and the Music House (30) used for bands; occasional impromptu cabaret but no balls; *very popular air-conditioned* weekly bops in JCR and MCR (250). Library (56,500 books). Some on site sports facilities, the rest 15mins walk away. New accomodation means all 1st years and finalists, plus 20% of 2nd years can live in; formal dining hall in the evenings; cafeteria; buttery. Doctor and nurse; hardship fund. *Good* disabled access.

FAMOUS ALUMNI:
John Birt (Director-General, BBC); Phil De Glanville (England rugby captain); Joseph Heller ('Catch 22' author); Richard Herring (of Lee & Herring fame); Peter Mandelson MP (Lab); Matthew Pinsent (rower); Jeanette Winterson (writer).

●●●●●●●●●●●●●●●●●●●●●●●●●●●●●●●●●●●●●●●

St Edmund Hall, Oxford

▼ ● *The College is part of <u>University of Oxford</u> and students are entitled to use its facilities.*
St Edmund Hall, Queen's Lane, Oxford, OX1 4AR.
Tel: (01865) 279000.
Junior Common Room, St Edmund Hall, Oxford, OX1 4AR.
Web site: http://www.seh.ox.ac.uk

Small, cute and cuddly, Teddy Hall, officially St Edmund Hall, is a blend of old and new buildings, 700yds from Carfax. The buildings include a Norman church (now the library) and its attached graveyard. *The students radiate freedom of spirit and intimacy and definitely know how to paaarty. They're strong in journalism, drama and, especially, sport, but always with an emphasis on 'team spirit'. For anyone particularly concerned about the punyness of their pounds, college charges are uniquely linked to the retail price index. Isn't that interesting.*

50% **50%**

Sex ratio(M:F): 50%:50%
Full time u'grads: 420
Private school: 30%
Overseas students: 5%
Founded: 1263
Postgrads: 120
Mature students: 5%
Disabled students: 0

Excellent tiny bar; bands and bops in Wolfson Hall, old dining hall (150) and the 2 JCR party rooms (100); 2 black tie dinners a term; theatre trips; annual summer Event. College mag,

'Closet Chronicles' and *informative* 'Hall Happenings' newsletter. Library (50,000 books); 20 computers; Anglican chapel. Sports facilities 5mins from site. All 1st and 3rd years live in; students eat in dining hall; daily formal meal; *good* self catering (microwaves). 'Chaps Tea' every weekday in Wolfson Hall. Doctor, nurse; hardship fund; 1 room equipped for wheelchair user.

FAMOUS ALUMNI:
Sir Robin Day (broadcaster); Terry Jones (Monty Python - his room is now a toilet); Graham Kentfield (Chief Cashier, Bank of England - the signature on all notes); Sir Michael Rose (UN Bosnia head honcho); John Wells (satirist).

FURTHER INFO:
No reports yet as to whether conditions in the college have improved following apointment of new principal - ex HM Prisons Inspector, Sir Stephen Tumin.

St Hilda's College, Oxford

● *The College is part of <u>University of Oxford</u> and students are entitled to use its facilities.*
St Hilda's College, Cowley Place, Oxford, OX4 1DY.
Tel: (01865) 276884. Fax: (01865) 276816.
Junior Common Room, St Hilda's College, Oxford, OX4 1DY.
Tel: (01865) 276846.
Web site: http://www.sthildas.ox.ac.uk

St Hilda's College, almost 1 mile from Carfax, is the last all-female college in Oxford. The mish-mash of detached buildings is not arranged around quads or linear corridors, but dotted about beside the river. *This is no nunnery; most students have come to an environment where macho attitudes don't impinge on academic life but they don't object to associating with blokes after hours, after all the only ones around have been hand picked. The high proportion of foreign students adds to the fun mix. There's a 'sister' programme, whereby each fresher 'Hildabeast' is assigned to a student on the same course in the year above.*

0%	♀♀♀♀♀♀♀♀♀♀	100

Sex ratio(M:F): 0%:100%	Founded: 1893
Full time u'grads: 403	Postgrads: 77
Private school: 40%	Mature students: 4%
Overseas students: 23%	Disabled students: 0

Bar; dining room (cap 200) and JCR (100) for student bands and jazz nights, theme bops; cheapest annual ball; annual arts festival week; new music building. Termly mag 'Hilda Guardian' and weekly 'Loo News'; keen recycling policies. 2 libraries (65,000 books); 16 computers, 24hrs; non-denominational chapel. Near Iffley Road Sports Centre; a few sports facilities on site, including punts, new boathouse;

strong on rowing, netball, rugby. All 1st and 3rd years and finalists live in; students eat in buttery and dining room; *damn fine food*; optional weekly formal meal; self catering kitchens on most floors. 2 doctors; nurse; hardship fund, travel grants.

FAMOUS ALUMNI:
Zeinab Badawi (newscaster); Helen Jackson MP (Lab); Rosalind Miles (writer); Kate Millett (writer, victim of live TV snog from Ollie Reed); Barbara Pym (writer); Gillian Shephard MP (Con). Jacqueline du Pre (cellist) was an Honorary Fellow and the music building is named after her.

●●

St Hugh's College, Oxford

● *The College is part of <u>University of Oxford</u> and students are entitled to use its facilities.*
St Hugh's College, St Margaret's Road, Oxford, OX2 6LE. Tel: (01865) 274900.
Junior Common Room, St Hugh's College, Oxford, OX2 6LE.
Web site: http://www.st-hughs.ox.ac.uk

St Hugh's red brick buildings are a mile from Carfax, the college was founded *almost by accident* by Elizabeth Wordsworth. It's known for its garden parties, firework party and ball, *its big booze ups at the start of each term and its general penchant for revelry, larks and laughs. Having survived for a century without them, St Hugh's admitted men in 1987; this apparently resulted in an increase of rugby songs and associated lewdness in the bar - though the women's football team give as good as they get - and the college is welcoming with a community atmosphere.* Hugh's students plague almost every activity at a University level.

60% ♂♂♂♂♂♂♀♀♀♀ 40%

Sex ratio(M:F): 60%:40%	**Founded: 1886**
Full time u'grads: 388	**Postgrads: 160**
Private school: 45%	**Mature students: 10%**
Overseas students: 5%	**Disabled students: 0.1%**

2 bars; Wordsworth Room (cap 50), Lee House (50) used for student bands, as well as Mordan Hall theatre (300); frequent, *popular* ents events in JCR (250); free annual Dean's Xmas Party. College news, 'Hughs News'; 2 libraries (79,000

❝In the mid-70s smarty pants at University College, Oxford who won too many times were banned from competing in University Challenge.❞

books); 25 computers. *Lots of enthusiastic sportswomen and rowers*, despite being quite far from the river; some sports facilities on site; joint college sports fields with <u>Wadham</u> ½ mile off site. Most live in for all 3 years; students head to the buttery for good food, the hall for cheapness; formal meal in dining hall weekly. Visiting doctor, nurse and counsellor; interdenominational chapel.

FAMOUS ALUMNI:
Baroness Barbara Castle (ex-Labour MP); Emily Davidson (suffragette martyr); Ruth Lawrence (mathematical prodigy); Mary Renault (historical novelist); Aung San Suu Kyi (Burmese human rights activist); Joanna Trollope (Aga saga writer).

• •

St John's College, Oxford

● *The College is part of <u>University of Oxford</u> and students are entitled to use its facilities.*
St John's College, St Giles', Oxford, OX1 3JP.
Tel: (01865) 277300.
Junior Common Room, St John's College, Oxford, OX1 3JP.
Web site: http://www.sjc.ox.ac.uk

St John's, one of the oldest and richest colleges in Oxford, is 800 yards from Carfax. Its 15th, 17th and 18th century buildings are arranged around 6 quads for the public gaze with *the largest garden in Oxford, while, like poor relations, the modern additions are kept wisely out of sight. The only sounds during the day are the busy jottings, the page flicking or the pencil chewing of diligent students. At night, though, students remove their thinking caps, let their hair down and get down to the bar, already full of the women rowers (alias 'The Sirens'). Reputation as an academically snooty workhouse isn't entirely justified.*

56% ♂♂♂♂♂♀ ♀ ♀ ♀ 44%	
Sex ratio(M:F): 56%:44%	**Founded: 1555**
Full time u'grads: 384	**Postgrads: 145**
Private school: 50%	**Mature students: 1%**
Overseas students: 5%	**Disabled students: 2**

Audoritium for St John's Mummers; student bands in *postmodern* Basement (cap 80), Prestwich Room (40) and Larkin Room (40); 1 bop a term; balls every 3 years. JCR has declared war on Luton *for less than apparent reasons*. Library (75,000 books); 20 computers, 24hrs; Anglican chapel. Squash courts; 10 acres of sports fields 1 mile. Everyone lives in (*high standard*); most eat in hall once a day; formal hall daily; *reasonable* self catering. Doctor, nurse, counsellor. *Money available for those who need/deserve it.*

FAMOUS ALUMNI:
Sir Kingsley Amis, Robert Graves, Philip Larkin, John Wain (all writers); Tony Blair (PM).

❝When mad Romantic poet Percy Shelley was at University College, Oxford he wired up his door-handle in an attempt to electrocute his scout.❞

• •

St Peter's College, Oxford

▼ ● *The College is part of <u>University of Oxford</u> and students are entitled to use its facilities.*
St Peter's College, New Inn Hall Street, Oxford, OX1 2DL.
Tel: (01865) 278900. Fax: (01865) 278855.
Junior Common Room, St Peter's College, Oxford, OX1 2DL.
Tel: (01865) 278900.

St Peter's is situated just off Oxford's main High Street, 800 yards from Carfax. It's small and cosy, with buildings from a variety of *modern* architectural styles arranged around 4 grass quads. The large JCR, *ideal for entertainments*, is on the ground floor of a 70s building, where some of the 1st years live, and next to the modern redbrick bar, which spills over onto a terrace, overlooking Oxford. *The word everybody uses to describe St Peter's is 'laidback' and most activities, including extreme manifestations of academic excellence, take second place to having a laugh.*

40% 60%

Sex ratio(M:F): 40%:60%	Founded: 1929
Full time u'grads: 330	Postgrads: 100
Private school: 50%	Mature students: 1%
Overseas students: 10%	Disabled students: 0

Bar; student bands and 3 bops per term in the JCR (cap 200); concerts in chapel (250); JCR sometimes hires local clubs in Oxford; black-tie dinners each term and ball every other year. 2 libraries (35,000 books); 15 computers, 24 hrs; Anglican chapel. *Sporty;* college shares a sports ground with Exeter and Hertford colleges; *women's sport strong; improved results means that the college is currently shaking off a reputation as a less academic college.* 1st years and 90% of 3rd years live in; 3 female-only corridors in 1st yr block; no self catering; everyone eats in dining hall; 5 *stuffy* formal dinners a week. Nurse, doctor; LGB, Women's officers; *poor* disabled access.

FAMOUS ALUMNI:

Rev W Awdry (writer of 'Thomas the Tank Engine'); Sir Rex Hunt (ex-Falklands Governor); Ken Loach (film director); Peter Wright (author, 'Spycatcher') .

> **Hungry diners at University College, Oxford might find themselves rumbling their way through the 122 word long Latin grace.**

• •

Somerville College, Oxford

● **The College is part of <u>University of Oxford</u> and students are entitled to use its facilities.**
Somerville College, Woodstock Road, Oxford, OX2 6HD.
Tel: (01865) 270600. Fax: (01865) 270620.
Junior Common Room, Somerville College, Oxford, OX2 6HD.
Tel: (01865) 270593.
Web site: http://www.som.ox.ac.uk

Somerville is ½ a mile from the town centre. *The architecture is mixed and the gardens are very peaceful. The small bar, with its merry happy hours, bonds the bits other bars cannot reach. Men are a recent addition but the atmosphere hasn't become as blokey as some hoped (feared). Informality and tolerance is the rule and Somervillians opt out of some of Oxford's dafter traditions, although they are ubiquitous in positions of authority across the University. Clearly the college to choose if your ambition is to be a Baroness when you grow up.*

50% ♂♂♂♂♂♀♀♀♀♀ **50%**

Sex ratio(M:F): 50%:50%   Founded: 1879
Full time u'grads: 360   Postgrads: 80
Private school: 60%   Mature students: 1%
Overseas students: 15%   Disabled students: 0

Bar; Wolfson Hall (cap 200) for bands, cabaret (1-2 times per term); summer event; ball every 3 years. Weekly bogsheet; high turnout against tuition fees. Library (100,000 books); 10 *ropey* computers. Shares sports facilities with <u>Wadham College</u>. All 1st yrs and finalists live in; *varied, but generally spacious rooms; lack of college houses a bone of contention;* students eat in the cafeteria and formal dinners once weekly in dining hall. Multi-denominational chapel. Doctor, nurse; hardship fund.

FAMOUS ALUMNI:
Sunethra Bandaranaike (Sri Lanka's ex-PM); Indira Ghandi (India's ex-PM); Dorothy Hodgkin (Nobel Prize winner); Iris Murdoch (writer); Baroness Park (spymaster); Esther Rantzen (TV celeb); Dorothy L Sayers (writer); Baroness Thatcher (*who she?*); Baroness Shirley Williams.

Trinity College, Oxford

● *The College is part of <u>University of Oxford</u> and students are entitled to use its facilities.*
Trinity College, Broad Street, Oxford, OX1 3BH.
Tel: (01865) 279910. Fax: (01865) 279911.
Junior Common Room, Trinity College, Oxford, OX1 3BH.
Tel: (01865) 279100
Web site: http://www.trinity.ox.ac.uk

Trinity College sits *very prettily* in extensive gardens, ¼ of a mile from Carfax and within easy walking distance from the University's main facilities, libraries, other colleges and shops. *The college is a generally moderate one (size, sporting and political activity, cost), though it has a slightly posh and academic hint about it. Trinity has its fair share of journos, politicos and thespos on the University scene too.*

55% ♂♂♂♂♂♂♀♀♀♀♀ 45%

Sex ratio(M:F): 55%:45%	Founded: 1555
Full time u'grads: 293	Postgrads: 107
Private school: 55%	Mature students: 3%
Overseas students: 3%	Disabled students: 0.3

Bar; student bands rarely and 3 bops a term in Beer Cellar (cap 120); small weekly ents events; ball every 3 years; drinking and dining socs. 1 library (46,000 books); 13 computers, 24hrs; Internet access in all rooms. 5 acres of shared sports fields 1½ miles away, *which puts students off sport a bit - though strong boat club and hockey.* All students live in college or college-owned housing and eat in the dining hall or in the Beer Cellar; *veggie options a bit naff; self-catering limited.* Doctor, nurse; Anglican chapel.

FAMOUS ALUMNI:
Sir Kenneth Clark (art historian); Robin Leigh-Pemberton (former 'Guvner' of Bank of England); Ross & Norris McWhirter (right-wing twins of 'Record Breakers' fame); Cardinal Newman (theologian); William Pitt and Lord North (ex-PMs); Terence Rattigan (playwright).

> ❦ 'What's wrong with the University of Oxford? President Clinton went there and failed to inhale; Tony Blair didn't even put his fingers to the smouldering sin.'
> –Julian Barnes. ❧

> **Get your money's worth... read 'PUSHover: how to use PUSH' at the front of the book.**

University College, Oxford

● **The College is part of <u>University of Oxford</u> and students are entitled to use its facilities.**
University College, High Street, Oxford, OX1 4BH.
Tel: (01865) 276602. Fax: (01865) 276790.
E-mail: postmaster@university-college.oxford.ac.uk
Junior Common Room, University College, Oxford, OX1 4BH.
Tel: (01865) 276606.
Web site: http://www.univ.ox.ac.uk

University College, the oldest Oxford College, claims to have been founded by King Alfred *the Bad Cook* in the 9th century. It presents an *imposing* facade to the High Street, but is *pleasantly habitable inside* with the massive marble Shelley memorial lurking down one of its quieter corridors. *The friendly environment tempts students not to stray too far from their college, which tends towards insularity. A tolerable level of things sporty and dramatic complement the strong academic record; JCR meetings are well attended.*

63% ♂♂♂♂♂♂♂♀♀♀ 37%	
Sex ratio(M:F): 63%:37%	Founded: 1249
Full time u'grads: 433	Postgrads: 110
Private school: 50%	Mature students: 0.4%
Overseas students: 17%	Disabled students: 1

Bar (cap 150); 3 sweaty bops per term; jazz evenings; *strong* drama soc puts on panto and annual revue; music soc performs regularly. JCR newsletter and 'News & Screws'. 2 libraries (Main, Law: 50,000 books); 9 computers, 24hrs; Inter-denominational chapel. *Strong in sports, women's teams especially.* 7 acres of sports fields and boat-house 1½ miles away; gym, squash court. 1st and 2nd yrs live in, 70% of 3rds, finalists in a *distant* annexe; *generally comfortable rooms; poor variety in dining room; limited self-catering.* Nurse; *reasonable disabled access.*

FAMOUS ALUMNI:
Clement Attlee, Harold Wilson (former Labour PMs); Bill Clinton (US President); Bob Hawke (former Australian PM); Stephen Hawking (physicist/cosmologist); Armando Ianucci (comedian, writer); Richard Ingrams (founder 'Private Eye', editor 'The Oldie'); VS Naipaul (writer); PB Shelley (poet); Peter Snow ('Tomorrow's World' presenter); Prince Youssoupov (Rasputin's murderer).

Wadham College, Oxford

● *The College is part of <u>University of Oxford</u> and students are entitled to use its facilities.*

Wadham College, Parks Road, Oxford, OX1 3PN.
Tel: (01865) 277949.
Wadham College Student Union, Parks Road, Oxford, OX1 3PN.
Tel: (01865) 277946.
Web site: http://www.wadham.ox.ac.uk

Opposite the Bod (the Bodleian Library), 300 yards from Carfax, are the golden grey stone buildings of Wadham College. *The College may look like the 'Brideshead' stereotype, but the atmosphere is more progressive* and it is perhaps significant that it was the first to be founded by a woman (Dorothy Wadham). The old main buildings centre around a large grassy Jacobean quad and are surrounded by gardens, the Ho Chi Minh Quad and newer buildings including some *dead dapper* new accommodation blocks, the library and SU. *The SU is an important part of Wadham which has a deservedly liberal and politically active (but not party political) reputation. We could almost say it was right on. It's certainly less stuffy than most colleges and has wild ents.*

50% ♂♂♂♂♂♀♀♀♀♀ 50%

Sex ratio(M:F): 50%:50%	**Founded: 1610**
Full time u'grads: 416	**Postgrads: 104**
Private school: 50%	**Mature students: 2%**
Overseas students: 9%	**Disabled students: 1**

Bar; theatre; King's Arms pub almost in grounds; classical concerts in Holywell Music Room (cap 150); fortnightly *top* bops, cabaret, bands and other regular events in the JCR (200); 'Wadstock' festival every summer. 'Wadham Sound' news sheet; 'Wadwords' termly slag mag; Library; 20 computers, 24hrs. Chapel. 6 acres of playing fields 1½ miles away; some sports facilities on site. Mainly 1st years and finalists live in, new block will house ⅓ of 2nd years; *good* self-catering amenities; livers in eat in cafeteria; informal meals in dining hall. College counsellors; nurse; minorities group; free safety alarms; tampon co-op; women's room.

FAMOUS ALUMNI:
Melvyn Bragg (writer, broadcaster); Alan Coren (columnist); Cecil Day Lewis (poet, Daniel's dad); Michael Foot (former Labour leader); Earl of Rochester (libertine, poet); Christopher Wren (architect).

❛The original Alice in Wonderland was the daughter of the Dean of Christ Church, Oxford.❜

Worcester College, Oxford

> ● *The College is part of <u>University of Oxford</u> and students are entitled to use its facilities.*

Worcester College, Worcester Street, Oxford, OX1 2HB.
Tel: (01865) 270060. Fax: (01865) 278387.
Junior Common Room, Worcester College, Oxford, OX1 2HB.
Tel: (01865) 278380.
Web site: http://www.worcester.ox.ac.uk

Worcester is a *beautiful* college, ½ mile from Carfax, with both medieval and modern buildings, some of which are *splendid and spacious,* all surrounded by *stunning* gardens, complete with a lake and ducks. *They're sporty and serious about music but still concentrate on having a good time, although hoorayism is being phased out in favour of hard work. The JCR reflects this attitude by not mentioning the P-word (politics)* and offering weekly bops and regular bands instead.

62% ♂♂♂♂♂♂♀♀♀♀ 38%	
Sex ratio(M:F): 62%:38%	Founded: 1714
Full time u'grads: 368	Postgrads: 140
Private school: 60%	Mature students: 1%
Overseas students: 8%	Disabled students: 0

Cellar bar (cap 100); theatre. For bops: the Hall (150), JCR (100), Rumpus Room (100); soundproof room; ball every 3 years; boat club cocktail party termly. Worcester Buskins drama soc. Newsletter 'Smurf's Babies' fortnightly. 2 libraries (120,000 books); 14 computers, 24hrs; Anglican chapel. 12 acres of sports fields on site; shares boat-house; *strong* football and mixed hockey. 1st and 2nd years live in, few others; *varied rooms* - en suite showers and heated towel rails in new block; most eat in hall or the Cellar; *limited* self-catering. Doctor, nurse; *very poor wheelchair access.*

FAMOUS ALUMNI:
Richard Adams (writer); Sir Alistair Burnett (newscaster); Sir Alastair Morton (former Chunnel boss); Rupert Murdoch (media mogul); John Sainsbury (of supermarket fame); Judge Stephen Tumin.

> ❛'If you go straight (to college) from school, unfortunately you turn into a student, and you go on pyjama jumps and talk in that student voice.'
> - Jarvis Cocker❜

Oxford Brookes University

▼
▼ ● *Formerly Oxford Polytechnic*
Oxford Brookes University, Gipsy Lane, Headington, Oxford,
OX3 0BP. Tel: (01865) 741111. Fax: (01865) 483616.
prosp@brookes.ac.uk
Oxford Brookes University Students' Union, Helena Kennedy
Student Centre, Headington Hill Campus, Oxford, OX3 0BP.
Tel: (01865) 484750. Fax: (01865) 484799.
E-mail: obsu@brookes.ac.uk

General

*Oxford Brookes is unlike its famous neighbour in many ways.
Despite being in the same city of ivory towers and dreaming
spires, Oxford Brookes dodges any of the dusty stuffiness of
<u>Oxford University</u>. The students, however, are just as partial to
punting pissed, falling in the river and strolling through
Christchurch meadows.* It has 3 modern campuses: the main site
at Gipsy Lane is 1 mile outside Oxford's centre in the suburbs,
away from that hazy churn of academic ritual. It is compressed
into a *cramped* 11 acres of 60s blocks of glass and concrete (*but
is not as bad as it sounds*). The newest site is Headington Hill, a
15-acre estate which used to belong to *dead fat crook* Robert
Maxwell, just across the road from Gipsy Lane. The other site is
at Wheatley, housing the education and business courses on its
65 acres, 5 miles further out into the countryside.

44% ♂♂♂♂♂♀♀♀♀♀ 56%

Sex ratio(M:F): 44%:56%	Founded: 1865
Full time u'grads: 8,350	Part time: 516
Postgrads: 1,182	Non-degree: 0
Ave course: 3yrs	Ethnic: 20%
Private school: 21%	Flunk rate: n/a
Mature students: 34%	Overseas students: 15%
Disabled students: 7%	Staff/student ratio: 1:17
Clearing: 10%	

ATMOSPHERE:
*Unlike many 'new' universities, there's a high proportion of
phone-wielding, privately-educated, GTi-driving students from
the Home Counties, possibly drawn by the 'Oxford' name-tag
(without such rigorous entry qualifications). That said, there
are plenty of mature students and others who don't
necessarily fit the mould, and everyone is included in the
sporty, boozy party that is social life at Brookes.*

THE CITY: see <u>University of Oxford</u>

TRAVEL: see <u>University of Oxford</u>
The University provides a free bus between the Gipsy Lane and
Wheatley sites every ½ hour, which takes about 15 minutes.

The modular course structure means that some students have academic commitments on both sites.

LIBRARIES & COMPUTERS:
- Books: 325,000 ● Study places: 1,050
- Computer workstations: 1,000

Library provision is one area where Brookes is in the shadow of its famous neighbour. Computer provision is probably better but it's still not good enough.

CAREER PROSPECTS:
- Careers Service ● No of staff: 3full/5part
- Unemployed after 6mths (1996): 5%

Those students who know the careers service exists are quite happy with it.

SPECIAL FEATURES:
- There's a no smoking rule in all areas of the University, except the SU Bars.
- The University's Chancellor is Helena Kennedy, the campaigning barrister.

FAMOUS ALUMNI:
Andrew Logan (creator of Alternative Miss World); John Pilkington (BBC); Tim Rodber (rugby player).

FURTHER INFO:
Prospectuses for undergrads and postgrads. There's also a web site (http://www.brookes.ac.uk).

entertainment

IN TOWN: see University of Oxford

UNIVERSITY:
- Price of a pint of beer: £1.35 ● Glass of wine: £1.10

Bars: (5) Morals at Morrell Hall is the largest bar (cap 550) and it doubles as a club venue. Hart's Lounge Bar (350 - so-called because it was opened by Tony Hart) at Headington Hill is also popular.

Theatres: The 2 drama societies are pretty popular, with at least 1 show usually going to the Edinburgh Fringe Festival each year.

Cinema: The Film Society shows mainstream and cult movies every week on a big digital screen.

Clubs/discos: The week is dominated by Crunchy on Fridays at Headington Hill (1,200). *The charty/dance mix may not win any plaudits for originality or cool, but it's the biggest club night in Oxford.* There are 2 discos a week at Morals. DJs such as Pete Tong have also spun their stuff in recent months.

Music venues: Headington Hill can also attract some *decent* live acts such as, recently, Lightning Seeds, Embrace, Spiritualized, Sleeper and The Longpigs. On Thursdays there's a new bands' night.

Cabaret: Every week sides split at the command of comedians such as Craig Charles and JoJo Smith.

Food: The University's refectory, contracted out to an external caterer, refects at lunchtime and early evenings. *Most students' comments about the food are unprintable, but suffice to say its overpriced and revolting, though the portions are mercifully tiny.*

Others: 3 balls a year, the biggest being the May do.

········ social & political

OXFORD BROOKES UNIVERSITY STUDENTS' UNION:
- 7 sabbaticals • Turnout at last ballot: 12%
- NUS member

The Students' Union based in the Helena Kennedy Students' Centre is surprisingly politically active for such a middle-class set. Recently they've been locked in arguments with the University authorities who they feel are encouraging only rich kids to apply. Also fell out with the NUS when they discovered that students on modular courses could possibly apply for Housing Benefit, but the NUS weren't interested in actually telling any students about it. OBSU took matters into their own hands and faxed details to all the University Students' Unions in the country. Smokin'.

SU FACILITIES:
Ents venue; shops; bars; pool table; vending and games machines; pool tables; photocopying; minibus; TV room; insurance; travel agents.

CLUBS (NON SPORTING):
Alternative Music; Bike; Brave New Dance; Bridge (volunteers); Cartography; CHAOS (Choral and Orchestral); Chinese; CHUFF (Casual Staff); Club Caribbean; Corkscrew; Dead Poets; Dyslexic; Fortune Players; Hellenic; Japanese; Jazz; Juggling; KEEN (volunteers); Law; Malaysian; Mature; MOLES (environmental); NEWTS (wildlife); ORBS (radio station); Pakistan; Salsa; Scandinavian; Spanish; Student Parents; Turkish; WUS (Wheatley Users); WARP (war games).

OTHER ORGANISATIONS:
The SU publishes a newsletter the '7 Day Bulletin' as well as the glossy student mag 'The Last Edition' 3 times a term.

RELIGIOUS:
- 4 chaplains (CofE, RC, Methodist, URC)

Prayer provisions in the University for Christians and Muslims.

········ sports

- Recent successes: rowing, rugby

Sport is one of the few things that can drag students out of the bar. Standards are pretty good and facilities are superb, especially by comparison with other former polys.

SPORTS FACILITIES:
There's a new, *superbly equipped* sports centre at Headington, including an astroturf pitch, gym, sports hall, climbing room and plush bar and social areas. Outdoor sports facilities are based at the Wheatley site.

SPORTING CLUBS:
Aerobics; Boxercise; Jiu Jitsu; Rowing; Tennis; Weights; Yoga.

ATTRACTIONS: see University of Oxford

> ❝The Vice-Chancellor of Staffordshire University is a leading authority on Elvis Presley.❞

❝'Have you seen how many people have gone back to school now? It just keeps the unemployment figures down and produces millions of half-educated old coots.'
—Mark E Smith (The Fall) holds forth on mature students.❞

·········· accommodation

IN COLLEGE:

● Catered: 6% ● Cost: £69-71(42wks)
● Self-catering: 24% ● Cost: £46-52(34-42wks)
Availability: The University can house 70% of 1st years but no other students. *Although a tad pricy, almost all the accommodation is of a high standard,* conveniently in or near the Headington campus *with good amenities.* Very few have to share rooms *and that's just at the start of term when everyone turns up and for some reason the University hasn't managed to allocate rooms properly - after all, you do need to know how to count, don't you?* There are limited provisions for couples and some single sex accommodation for female overseas students.
Car parking: Permit parking at 2 halls only.

EXTERNALLY: see University of Oxford
Housing help: Places in the University are allocated by pot luck, but those 1st years and other students who need to go it alone can get help from the University Accommodation Office which has a number of full-time staff providing bulletin boards and an approval scheme to help students check for roaches.

·········· welfare

SERVICES:

● Nightline ● Lesbian & Gay Society
● Mature SA ● Overseas SA ● Minibus ● Women's Officer
● Self-defence classes
The Health Centre on the Headington campus has 4 doctors and nurses and there are 3 full-time counsellors. There is a policy to help disadvantaged minorities and so there are support groups for dyslexics and students with eating disorders, local helplines, and specialist advisors for mature, disabled and overseas students.
Women: Safety bus and Officer; rape alarms given out free by SU. One or two *dingy* lanes near some of the halls of residence.
Disabled: There is a rolling programme of improvements to access including lifts and ramps *and all new developments are excellent.*

FINANCE:
- Ave debt per year: £1,900 ● Access fund: £255,000
- Successful applications (1997): 445

A small hardship fund is set aside, used mainly for those disadvantaged minorities (in particular, part-time and overseas students). There's also a debt counsellor.

● ●

▶▶ **Oxford Poly**
see Oxford Brookes University

Fold-out guide to symbols inside back cover

❛Get your money's worth... read 'PUSHover: how to use PUSH' at the front of the book.❜

 ❛Freaked out by finance? Why not pop into your local branch of Lloyds Bank and see what they have to offer.❜

University of Paisley

University of Paisley

● *Formerly Paisley College*
(1) University of Paisley, Paisley, PA1 2BE.
Tel: (0141) 848 3000. Fax: (0141) 887 0812.
University of Paisley Students' Association, 17 Hunter Street,
Paisley, PA1 1DN. Tel: (0141) 889 9940.
(2) University of Paisley, Craigie Campus, Beech Grove, Ayr,
KA8 0SR. Tel: (01292) 260321. Fax: (01292) 611705.

General

Paisley, to the west of Glasgow, is a town *in manufacturing
decline, but business growth* - long gone are those 18th
and 19th century days when it had a great weaving
industry. The town used to produce so many shawls, that
it even invented (*or nicked off some Indian bloke*) its own
pattern - the now familiar 'paisley' that appears on millions
of Tie Rack ties, M&S boxer shorts, and The Artist
Formerly Known As Mr Bumfluff. Spread around the centre
of town is the University campus, mostly a set of concrete
blocks, joined by walkways, *scoring zero on the eyeability
scale,* but also including lecture halls in converted
churches. The second campus is in Ayr, about 30 miles
away.

42% ♂♂♂♂♀♀♀♀♀♀ 58%	
Sex ratio(M:F): 42%:58%	Founded: 1897
Full time u'grads: 5,819	Part time: 2,158
Postgrads: 445	Non-degree: 988
Ave course: 4yrs	Ethnic: 3.8%
Private school: n/a	Flunk rate: n/a
Mature students: 30%	Overseas students: 4.8%
Disabled students: 5.8%	Staff/student ratio: 1:20
Clearing: 18%	

ATMOSPHERE:

Most students are drawn from Paisley and the surrounding area which creates a tight-knit community. They're a pretty level-headed bunch, concentrating on their vocationally oriented degrees and not leaving much time for hedonism, and they occasionally suffer from a slight but unwarranted inferiority complex due to the 3 big brother unis in Glasgow, which is 7 miles away. In the past, the hedonists had to head out to Glasgow to get their kicks, but these days the Glaswegians are popping over to Paisley.

CRAIGIE CAMPUS:

1,200 full-time students are based at the Craigie Campus in Ayr, 30 miles away and the home of Robbie Burns. Education and nursing courses are taught here and a new Management Training & Development Centre has been set up.

PAISLEY:

- Population: 100,000 ● London: 371miles
- Glasgow: 7miles ● Edinburgh: 51miles

You can't spend centuries making fine swirling shapes without a fair amount of artiness rubbing off on you. And indeed, despite everything else, Paisley remains a thriving arts centre. Right opposite the University are the town's museum and art gallery. Along with shops, banks and the like, there are other attractions such as Paisley Abbey (parts of which date back to the 12th century), the Coats Observatory and the Weaver's Cottage, *but Paisley isn't one of Scotland's tourist draws. It's also a noted drugs blackspot - unfortunately the Student's Union is in one of the most notorious areas.*

THE CITY: see University of Glasgow

TRAVEL:

Trains: The nearest mainline station is 5 minutes' walk to Gilmour St. It has a regular direct service to Glasgow (£2 return) with the last train at night at 11.46pm. London (£40).

Coaches: Served nationally by Scottish Citylink, via Glasgow. London (£27); Glasgow (£1.70).

Car: The M8 is 1 mile from the town, also the A737 and A726.

Taxis: Relatively cheap; there's a huge rank by the station.

Hitching: *Generally not recommended.*

Local: Local buses allow easy access to surrounding areas. A single bus fare to Glasgow at 85p is cheaper than the train and is available till 3am.

Bicycles: *Quite hilly* and nowhere to store bikes on campus, but quite a few students give it a go.

LIBRARIES & COMPUTERS:
- Books: 256,072 ● Study places: 768
- Computer workstations: 2,000

A new £6.8 million development will provide a new Library and Learning Resource Centre, *which should address the inadequate internet facilities.*

CAREER PROSPECTS:
- Careers Service ● No of staff: 5full/1part
- Unemployed after 6mths (1996): 11%

FAMOUS ALUMNI:
Gavin Hastings (rugby/American football legend); Graeme Obree (cyclist).

FURTHER INFO:
Undergrad & postgrad prospectuses. Course leaflets. Web site (http://www.paisley.ac.uk).

entertainment

THE CITY: see University of Glasgow

PAISLEY:
- Price of a pint of beer: £1.80 ● Glass of wine: £1.70

Paisley is starting to adapt to the student contingent and cater to their needs accordingly.

Cinemas: The CAC has 2 screens (adm £3.50) and the Arts Centre has regular screenings (£2).

Theatres: Paisley Arts Centre hosts popular touring companies.

Pubs: push*plugs: Café Borgia; Cellar Bar (very close to University); Fiddlers Green, O'Neill's and Paddy Malarkey's (Irish); Vodka Wodka (Scotland's only vodka bar).*

Clubs/discos: *Shag at Furry Murry's, Toledo (student nights are popular) and Utopia are the real booty-shakers.*

Music venues: *The Arts Centre is the only real hot-spot.*

Eating out: *Pub lunches are usually a reliable source of sustenance.* **push***plugs beyond that: Café Borgia in the Arts Centre (again); A Taste of Europe (bargain lunches); Kaldi's Coffee House; Vodka Wodka does excellent value student meals at £2 for 2 colossal courses.*

UNIVERSITY:
- Price of a pint of beer: £1.25 ● Glass of wine: £1.25

Bars: (2) The Main Bar is the most popular daytime quaff-stop and there's also the Union bar at Hunter Street.

Films: 1 film a week along arthouse and world cinema lines.

Clubs/discos/music venues: Friday night is charty dance night at the Union, Saturdays is live music night, although for anything beyond local and tribute bands Paisleyites have to go to Glasgow.

Food: *The University refectory food hardly deserves the name but the SU nosh is cheap and cheerful.*

Others: 1 formal ball a year and a big bash at a nightclub in Glasgow once a term. Major sports events every week in the Union.

social & political

UNIVERSITY OF PAISLEY STUDENTS' ASSOCIATION:

- 4 sabbaticals ● Turnout at last ballot: 16%

- NUS member

The SA is solidly left-wing, with strong nationalist tendencies, although this isn't reflected so strongly in the student body, although a recent referendum on Tuition Fees lured 20% of them into making a statement - 95% opposed the fees, naturally enough.

SU FACILITIES:
2 bars; cafe; a shop; Bank of Scotland cashpoint; pool tables; photocopiers; games and video machines; juke box; vending machines; TV lounge; a meeting room; advice centre; stationery shop; customised night club; launderette.

CLUBS (NON SPORTING):
Ayr & Craigie Film; SNP; Star Trek, plus many national societies.

OTHER ORGANISATIONS:
The SA has revamped 'The Associate', called it 'AM' and given it a glossy cover *to make it seem less like one of those earnest left-wing rags that intense people sell in shopping-centres on Saturday mornings.* The student TV club uses the Educational Development Unit's TV Studio to produce programmes by and for students. *For Rag, lunatics jump out of aeroplanes with nothing between them and the hard earth but a large piece of silk. Stranger still, other people give them money to do it.*

RELIGIOUS:
The town provides Catholic, Methodist, Baptist, Church of Scotland and Christian Fellowship worship shops. The University runs a multi-faith chaplaincy at the Thomas Coats Memorial Church.

PAID WORK:
The Student Advisory Service gives out information on job vacation vacancies and term-time tasks, *but the openings aren't out of the ordinary.*

sports

● Recent successes: hockey, mountaineering

Sport isn't a major obsession but the new Robertson Trust Sports Centre has got a few people dragging their Green Flash out of the closet, if only to lose that beer-belly.

SPORTS FACILITIES:
The Sports Centre two miles from campus includes rugby and football pitches, a sports hall and a fitness room. Students use the *extensive* local facilities and reciprocal agreements means that they may also use facilities in some other educational establishments nearby, including a lake, swimming pool, golf course, squash and tennis courts, croquet lawn, sauna/solarium and ice rink.

SPORTING CLUBS:
Aerobics; American Football; Gaelic Football; Mountain Bike; Self Defence.

ATTRACTIONS:
The local football heroes are St Mirren.

accommodation

IN COLLEGE:
● Catered: 1% ● Cost: £56(32wks)
● Self-catering: 15% ● Cost: £28-34(32/52wks)

Availability: The University has 967 places accommodating

30% of 1st years and 10-15% of each other year. Most places are within 10 mins of the campus, such as Underwood Residence, which has 171 places (165 single rooms). *Thornly Park is sociable and desirable.* There are also 116 catered places at the Craigie campus.

EXTERNALLY:
● Ave rent: £35

Availability: *It is reasonably easy to find accommodation in Paisley and the standard is usually OK. West End Park should be avoided on safety grounds and Ladylane and Storie Street are best left alone, not because they're rough, but because the houses have mould growing in them.*

Housing help: The Residential Accommodation Unit employs 3 full-time staff, offering residential places when available, a register of private accommodation in the area and gas safety checks.

········ welfare

SERVICES:
● Nursery ● Lesbian & Gay Society
● Overseas SA ● Women's Officer

There are various help organisations: the Student Advisory Service employing 4 counsellors; Student Welfare Association; the Student Health Service run by an occupational health nurse. Another counsellor is also employed in the SA, as is a full-time welfare advisor. There's also a dyslexia support group. The creche costs £3.50/session to students.

Drugs: Paisley is one of the hard drug blackspots of the UK *but the problem does not seem to have filtered through to the University.*

Disabled: *Standard of access and special facilities are pretty average, but with the appointment of a Special Needs Advisor things are improving. Facilities for the visually and hearing impaired are very good.*

FINANCE:
● Ave debt per year: £1,250 ● Access fund: £125,000
● Successful applications (1996): 1,500

There is a bursary system and student welfare has a Hardship fund (£10,000) which it gives out to those who would otherwise be missed (eg married women, where husbands would be expected to support them). Loans (but not grants) from the access fund can be made available in as little as 48 hours.

●●●

 ## PCL

see University of Westminster

●●●

 ## Pharmacy School

see School of Pharmacy, London

●●●

University of Plymouth

● *Formerly Polytechnic South West*

(1) University of Plymouth, Drake Circus, Plymouth, PL4 8AA.
Tel: (01752) 600600.
University of Plymouth Students' Union, Drake Circus,
Plymouth, PL4 8AA Tel: (01752) 663337.
Fax: (01752) 251669.
(2) Faculty of Arts & Education, University of Plymouth, Earl
Richards Road North, Exeter, EX2 6AS. Tel: (01392) 475022.
Fax: (01392) 475012.
(3) Faculty of Arts & Education, University of Plymouth, Douglas
Avenue, Exmouth, EX8 2AT. Tel: (01395) 255309.
Fax: (01395) 255303.
(4) Seale-Hayne Faculty of Agriculture, Food & Land Use,
University of Plymouth, Newton Abbot, Devon, TQ12 6NQ.
Tel: (01626) 325800. Fax: (01626) 325605.

General

If Plymouth were any further south-west, it would be
Cornwall. As it is, it's a port around the Plymouth Sound
(the bay) on the south coast of Devon. It was from here
that Sir Francis Drake sailed to kick the poo out of the
Spanish Armada - according to the myth, Frankie psyched
himself up by playing bowls on the Hoe, a patch of
greenery by the sea. The Hoe's still there near the city
centre and not far from the main site of the University.
The University's old name, Polytechnic South West, was
more accurate geographically, because, in fact, it has 4
sites spread around south Devon at Plymouth, Exeter,
Exmouth and just outside Newton Abbot. *To be fair,*
Plymouth does provide the focal point for the University.
However, all the sites have some of their own facilities.

52% ♂♂♂♂♂♀♀♀♀♀ **48%**

Sex ratio(M:F): 52%:48%	Founded: 1970
Full time u'grads: 15,660	Part time: 4,264
Postgrads: 630	Non-degree: 7,534
Ave course: 3yrs	Ethnic: 2.2%
Private school: n/a	Flunk rate: 21%
Mature students: 38.5%	Overseas students: 8.9%
Disabled students: 5.3%	Staff/student ratio: 1:18
Clearing: 18.6%	

ATMOSPHERE:
The South-West as a whole is a pretty mellow place but
Plymouth students are capable of perking up when it comes to
work (there's a strong sense of careerist zeal) and drinking
unfeasible quantities of beer. The smaller sites have their
own quirks.

THE SITES:

Plymouth: (Business, Human Sciences, Science, Technology) This is the main site housing 5 out of the University's 7 faculties and nearly 7,500 of the students. It's a city centre campus and *concrete is much in evidence.*

Exeter: (Art and Design, Health Studies) The campus is redbrick, 2 miles from the city centre, next to the hilly countryside that surrounds Exeter. It was purpose-built as Exeter Art College. For a more detailed low-down on the ups and downs of Exeter, see <u>University of Exeter</u>, which, *for students who are willing to mix with the Sloanes, is a social life-saver.*

Exmouth: (Arts & Education) The town of Exmouth is, unsurprisingly, at the mouth of the river Exe on the east bank of the wide estuary. *This is a small town, a bit of a baby brother to Exeter, 8 miles upstream. Exeter is very important for students who want more from life than pretty sea views.* There are 3,546 full- and part-time students across Exeter and Exmouth.

Seale-Hayne: (Agriculture, Food & Land Use) This site is 3 miles outside the tiny town of Newton Abbot, 30 miles from Plymouth, 16 from Exeter, and just round the corner from the middle of nowhere. It houses 1,042 students in *beautiful stately* buildings in *beautiful* countryside. *But the site is self-contained and, since travelling around is a hassle of the first degree, the student community is just so close-knit there's little escape. Some students find it all a bit suffocating; others love the close and closeted lifestyle.*

PLYMOUTH:

- <u>Population: 238,800</u> ● <u>London: 200miles</u>
- <u>Exeter: 37miles</u> ● <u>Bristol: 106miles</u>

Plymouth: Apart from a few buildings which date from the days of Drake, most of Plymouth has been rebuilt since the last World War, when it was trashed by bombing raids. *As a result, it has a great deal less rural charm than most West Country towns* and consequently fewer tourists. Instead, it's a functional city with amenities serving a large catchment area. The Hoe and Quay are *pleasant enough* and students wanting a little aesthetic distraction might stroll across the road to the City Art Gallery and Museum.

EXETER: see <u>University of Exeter</u>

TRAVEL:

Trains: The nearest station to the main site is Plymouth with services to London (£27.50), Bristol (£25) and all over. Newton Abbot is on the same line and most trains stop.

Coaches: National Express and Western National services from Plymouth to London (£27) and beyond.

Car: The A38 links Plymouth with Newton Abbot and Exeter.

Air: Flights inland and to Ireland from Plymouth airport.

Ferries: Services from Plymouth to France and Spain.

Hitching: *Okay along the A38, for he (and she) that wait.*

Local: Buses around Devon are *reliable and reasonably priced.* A return train ticket between Plymouth and Exeter is £10.80.

Taxis: *Plenty and they're comprehensive, but prices are high.*

Bicycles: *Plymouth is a bit hilly. At Seale-Hayne, a bike is handy for getting into Newton Abbot.*

LIBRARIES & COMPUTERS:
● <u>Books: 440,106</u> ● <u>Study places: 1,099</u>
● <u>Computer workstations: 1,030</u>
There are libraries at each site. *Major investment has improved computer provision but many students still find book facilities limited - except when it comes to marine biology for which they have one of the best libraries in the country.*

CAREER PROSPECTS:
● <u>Careers Service</u> ● <u>No of staff: 11full/2part</u>
● <u>Unemployed after 6mths (1996): 9%</u>

SPECIAL FEATURES:
● The only perfumery course in Europe.

FAMOUS ALUMNI:
Jonathan Haslam (Press Officer to John Major when he was PM - *not even Plymouth can train a man to make old John look good*); Diid Osman (Sleeper bassist); Pam St Clement (Pat in 'EastEnders'); Peter Winterbottom (rugby player).

FURTHER INFO:
Prospectuses for undergrads and postgrads, guides for overseas and mature students and a CD. Web site (http://www.plym.ac.uk).

·········· entertainment

PLYMOUTH:
● <u>Price of a pint of beer: £1.80</u> ● <u>Glass of wine: £1.25</u>
Cinemas: (3) There's the Cannon with 3 screens, The Drake Odeon (*an independent flea pit*) with 5, and arty flicks at the Plymouth Arts Centre.
Theatres: (4) There's the mainstream Theatre Royal and experimental productions at the Arts Centre, the Drum and Barbican Theatre.
Pubs: *Pubs range from the friendly and welcoming (some even sponsor sports teams) to those in Devonport where identifiably studenty behaviour isn't recommended.* **push***plugs: Kitty O'Hanlon's; The Fortescue (nice beer garden); Freebooter & Firkin (firkin firkin); The Ship (good grub and a pleasant pint). Places to avoid are listed in the booklet 'Student Watch' from the SU, which should be ignored at your limbs' peril.*
Clubs/discos: *Plymouth has more clubs than, by all rights, a city of its size should and, with admission costing around £2, most are worth checking out, but avoid the ones down Union Street where life is cheap yet students can't afford it.*
push*plugs: Oz (cap 1,500, very popular, often live music,*

p

❝Great exam excuses of our time — students at Anglia Poly University had their exams postponed because the hall didn't have enough desks to go round.❞

adm £1-£2); Ritzy's; The Dance Academy; Jelly Jazz at the Studio; Oscar's (gay).
Music venues: Classical at the Theatre Royal and Guildhall, pop at the Plymouth Pavilions. Recently: Sleeper, Prodigy, JK.
Eating out: Apart from the usual chains, *restaurants in Plymouth err on the pricey side.* **push***plugs: Café Cuba; Bomb Shelter Café; Cap'n Jasper's; Caffeine Club (chilled filling post). Exmouth's speciality is seafood restaurants.*

UNIVERSITY:

● <u>Price of a pint of beer: £1.10</u> ● <u>Glass of wine: £1.00</u>
Most of the University entertainments are at Plymouth.
Bars: The Main Bar at Plymouth is open until 2am at the weekend but fills up shortly after 10. *Both Union bars are nameless, which makes arranging to meet there a little hard.* There are smaller bars at the outlying sites.
Clubs/discos: The SU pounds to house and indie sounds twice a week (£1); Sub Sub Club Fridays & Saturdays at the Union. Clubs in town are often booked as well.
Music venues: The Pavilions in the town centre is the site for sore ears.
Cabaret: At the Union in Plymouth, there are occasional cabaret nights (recently Craig Charles and Lee & Herring).
Eating out: There's a total of 8 University-run refectories around the sites.
Others: Balls galore, especially the Rag Valentine Ball.

·······social & political

UNIVERSITY OF PLYMOUTH STUDENTS' UNION:

● <u>5 sabbaticals</u> ● <u>Turnout at last ballot: 20%</u>
● <u>NUS member</u>
The Union has facilities on all 4 sites, but usually in a building shared with the University. The notable exception is Plymouth where the Union building is a largely subterranean, modern maze. There's little sense of cross-site cooperation on Union matters and each place has its own Union officers, though it is hoped that a new SU building will unify the disparate masses.

SU FACILITIES:
2 bars; advice centre; games & vending machines; travel agency; Union shop; cafe; launderette; showers; pool tables; PO; print, fax and photocopying; meeting room; juke box; stationery shop; photobooth; ticket agency.

CLUBS (NON SPORTING):
Juggling; Little Goblins; Motorcycle; Muso; Terminal.

OTHER ORGANISATIONS:
'Fly', the weekly student newspaper, is produced by the SU. There is both a charity Rag and student Community Action Group.

RELIGIOUS:
● <u>1 chaplain</u>
A range of churches and places of worship in Plymouth (including a synagogue).

PAID WORK:
Apart from the usual bar work and all that, there are a few tourist and maritime based jobs in Plymouth. Hopping over the Tamar to Cornwall can be fruitful in the summer.

sports

● <u>Recent successes: yachting, netball</u>

The sports situation is going from good to gripeworthy despite the students' efforts. The housing shortage means that halls are planned on the site of Exmouth's facilities, and a campaign to free Wednesday afternoons of lectures was rejected by the University; all of which conspires to dampen the sporting spirit. For shame.

SPORTS FACILITIES:
Plymouth: Gym; multigym; squash courts; sports hall; playing fields; 5-hole golf-course; watersports centre. The town provides facilities for watersports, bowling green, swimming pools and ski slope.
Exmouth: 13 acres of fields; netball and tennis courts; multigym.
Seale-Hayne: Playing fields; sports hall; squash and tennis courts.
Exeter: Facilities are mainly hired.

SPORTING CLUBS:
Aikido; Boxercise; Caving; Chinese Kung-Fu; Flying; Handball; Kick-boxing; Life-saving; Octopush; Shooting; Sky Diving;; Surf; Tai Chi; Ultimate Frisbee; Water-Skiing; Windsurfing.

ATTRACTIONS:
Plymouth Argyle for footie fans, horse racing at Newton Abbot, regattas at Plymouth.

accommodation

IN COLLEGE:

● <u>Self-catering: 10%</u> ● <u>Cost: £40-61(33-39wks)</u>
Availability: Across all sites, 37% of 1st years have a place in college accommodation. At Plymouth the halls are all within 3 miles of the campus. There are further places at Seale-Hayne and 145 places in head tenancy schemes in Exeter. The university plans to build more halls at Exmouth.
Car parking: Limited but free with permit.

EXTERNALLY:
● <u>Ave rent: £40</u>
Availability in Plymouth: *There's just about enough for those who are quick off the mark, but students who bend down to tie their laces or check the mirror for zits may look round to find, to mix a metaphor or two, they've missed the boat.* Recommended areas include Mutley, Lipson, Stoke, Peverell and St Judes.
Housing help: The University runs an *efficient* accommodation office on each site with 16 staff, offering computerised vacancy lists and an approval scheme.

welfare

SERVICES:

● <u>Nursery</u> ● <u>Lesbian & Gay Society</u> ■ <u>Mature SA</u>
● <u>Overseas SA</u> ● <u>Minibus</u> ● <u>Women's Officer</u>
● <u>Self-defence classes</u>
There are 4 full- and 3 part-time counsellors overall, as well as a GP and nurse on each site, and a family planning unit. Late minibuses run you home.

Disabled: *Access could be better around the Plymouth campus, including the Union.* There are induction loops.

FINANCE:
- Ave debt per year: £1,250 ● Access fund: £335,000
- Successful applications (1997): 500

Small loans and vacation funds are available.

● ●

 PNL

see University of North London

● ●

University of Portsmouth

● ***Formerly Portsmouth Polytechnic***

University of Portsmouth, Winston Churchill Avenue, Portsmouth, PO1 2UP. Tel: (01705) 876543.
Fax: (01705) 842733. E-mail: admissions@port.ac.uk
University of Portsmouth Students' Union, Alexandra House, Museum Road, Southsea, Hants, PO1 2QH.
Tel: (01705) 843640. Fax: (01705) 843675.

 ## General

 Portsmouth sits by the Solent within champion spitting distance of the Isle of Wight. Built on Portsea Island, it is one of Europe's most densely populated cities. For 400 years, Portsmouth has been one of Britain's foremost naval ports and *the maritime influence is still unavoidable. Sailors, students and locals all walk the same streets but remain virtually oblivious of each other.* The other main campus, at Milton, is 2½ miles from the Guildhall site.

60% ♂♂♂♂♂♂ ♀♀♀ 40%	
Sex ratio(M:F): 60%:40%	Founded: 1969
Full time u'grads: 11,933	Part time: 3,771
Postgrads: 1,708	Non-degree: 756
Ave course: 3yrs	Ethnic: 11%
Private school: n/a	Flunk rate: 34%
Mature students: 15%	Overseas students: 7.9%
Disabled students: 5.6%	Staff/student ratio: 1:18
Clearing: n/a	

ATMOSPHERE:
The transition from polydom has been less fraught than with many of the other new universities. Student life still revolves around the battle of beer and brains with occasional sporting interludes. Horizons are firmly fixed on A Good Job.

THE SITES:
The Guildhall campus is definitely the dominant site and

students at Milton, which merged with the then Poly in 1976, can feel like lesser cousins (business studies and information science are based there).

TOWN:
- Population: 174,700 ● London: 70miles
- Southampton: 21miles

Portsmouth is compact, *if not bijou*. Small enough to walk around town, down to the beach or to pay a visit to all sorts of maritime sights: HMS Victory; The Mary Rose; The Warrior; The Royal Marines Museum and so on. *More useful but much more ugly*, there's the Cascades shopping centre. You can find most major branch stores here and in the other shopping streets and centres. There's also a daily fruit and veg market, plenty of supermarkets and late-night corner shops.

TRAVEL:
Trains: Mainline connections to, among other places, London Waterloo (£17.80), Bristol (£21.60), Manchester (£56).
Coaches: National Express services to many destinations including London (£14, 2:20hrs, 8/day), Manchester (£35, 7:45hrs, 1/day), Bristol (£15.50, 3:30hrs, 1/day).
Car: The A27, which runs along the south coast, becomes the M27 between Portsmouth and Southampton. The A3 connects the town with London.
Air: Southampton Airport is 22 miles away.
Ferries: Regular ferries to the Isle of Wight, Spain and France (St Malo, Cherbourg, Caen, Le Havre), and the IoW hovercraft.
Hitching: *Good opportunities from lorry drivers coming off the ferries on to the A3.*
Local: Bus services are *quite good*, but most distances are walkable.
Taxis: *An unnecessarily extravagant way of getting around, but it doesn't work out too expensive since the town's so small.*
Bicycles: *A bike loan scheme and Lottery-funded cycle lanes make for two wheels pretty good.*

LIBRARIES & COMPUTERS:
- Books: 560,000 ● Study places: 1,070
- Computer workstations: 710

The Frewen Library is on the main site with the smaller Goldsmith Library at Milton.

CAREER PROSPECTS:
- Careers Service ● No of staff: 8full/16part
- Unemployed after 6mths (1996): 7%

Efficient and effective service at University House on the Guildhall campus and an information room in Milton.

FAMOUS ALUMNI:
David Chidgey MP (Lib Dem); Shirley Conran (writer); Ron Davies MP (Lab); Nicky Wire (Manic Street Preachers) dropped out because he was 'having a thoroughly miserable time'.

❝Wallace and Gromit are honorary members of the University of Central Lancashire SU.❞

FURTHER INFO:
Prospectus, departmental brochures, video, web site (http://www.port.ac.uk).

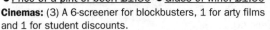 entertainment

THE CITY:
● Price of a pint of beer: £1.80 ● Glass of wine: £1.50

Cinemas: (3) A 6-screener for blockbusters, 1 for arty films and 1 for student discounts.

Theatres: The King's Theatre and the Theatre Royal *are decent mainstream thespitoria*; there's also the Southsea Arts Centre.

Pubs: *More than enough to turn a pub crawl into a night in the gutter and all friendly, especially in Old Portsmouth and along Albert Road (Southsea). Gales HSB, a local brew, is worth a tongue trial, if you're not doing anything tomorrow.*
pushplugs: *Wetherspoon's (near the Guildhall); Fuzz & Firkin; The Dog; The Hogshead; The Duke of Buckingham. The White Swan is best avoided, as is any pub packed with jolly jack tars.*

Clubs/discos: Plenty of clubs, particularly around the South Parade Pier. pushplugs: *Scandals (indie/house); Maggie Thatcher Experience (80s) at Fifth Avenue; Harry Lime's (funk/acid jazz); Route 66.*

Music venues: Portsmouth's *premiere* venue is the Guildhall *which hosts big old names and currently groovy popsters.* The Wedgewood Rooms is a *solid* indie haunt and the Pyramids *adds further to the aural palette.*

Eating out: There's more than enough in the way of fish'n'chip shops and burger joints, as well as curry houses (including balti) by the furnace-full. pushplugs: *Bombay Express; The Vaults (pub grub); Café Citrus; Fistful of Tacos (Mexican); Rickshaws (Mongolian).*

UNIVERSITY:
● Price of a pint of beer: £1.40 ● Glass of wine: £1

Bars: (4) The Dry Dock (cap 1,100) at Alexandra House is the main dive throughout the day. The Ranch House (300) *is quieter and more pubby* while the Garage (600) is used for ents. There are also bars at the Milton site and at the halls in Langstone.

Music venues: The Garage has recently coped with The Shire Horses and Michelle Gayle.

Clubs/discos: 5 club nights a week from the Amnesia (disco) in the Dry Dock to Contrast (drum & bass) and All Mod Cons (indie) at the Garage.

Food: The SU runs *an OK but pricey* Refectory at the main site; alternatively Al's snack bar and the Milton coffee bar do snackular-shaped stuff.

Other: Several balls, including the Freshers Ball, Alternative Xmas, Valentine, and the Graduation job which can pull in 3,000+ punters.

social & political

UNIVERSITY OF PORTSMOUTH STUDENTS' UNION:
● 6 sabbaticals ● Turnout at last ballot: 10%
● NUS member
The SU's main strength is as a focus for social life and political posturing rarely comes into the frame. Relations

between the SU and the University administration are practically at the intense snogging stage, a closeness which some students find peculiar. There are SU facilities on each site. 3,000 signed an anti-Tuition Fees petition.

SU FACILITIES:
Alexandra House contains bars, canteen, cash machines, Endsleigh Insurance office, employment bureau, travel agency, shop, ents halls, print shop, lift-sharing scheme, photo booth and fax.

CLUBS (NON SPORTING):
Batacuda; Big Band; Chinese; Fantasy Role Playing; Flute; French; Hellenic; Hispanic; Latin American; Literary; Malaysian; Pompogs; Real Ale; Resistance Sound.

OTHER ORGANISATIONS:
'Pugwash' is the SU's magazine, *and it means something rude in Australia, apparently.* Pure FM is the radio station, and 'Purple Wednesdays' is the weekly clubs & societies newsletter.

RELIGIOUS:
● 3 chaplains (CofE, RC, Free)
Most religions are represented in town (mosques and synagogues) where there are also Anglican and Catholic cathedrals.

PAID WORK:
What with the ferries, the bars, Southsea being a holiday resort and all, there's a better than average chance of finding something to line students' pockets during vacations. A Job Shop at Alex House puts students in touch with temp employers.

·········· sports

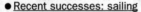

● Recent successes: sailing

University sports are pretty well organised by the SU and jockish attitudes are quite prevalent. Bursaries are available for rugby and will be extended to other sports soon.

SPORTS FACILITIES:
On the main site, there's the Nuffield Sports Centre with cricket bays, a gym, 2 weights rooms with multigym, netball, squash and tennis courts and a climbing wall. Near the halls, there are 4 acres of sports fields by Langstone Harbour. The University also has a host of facilities to be used on the Solent, *a flood of fun for those whose appetite is sharpened by water sports.* The public Pyramids Centre swimming complex opened just a couple of years ago on the sea front.

SPORTING CLUBS:
Airgun; Boxing; Caving; Gymnastics; Motorcycle; Mountain Bike; Paintball; Rowing; Surf; Ten Pin Bowling; Water Polo; Waterski; Windsurfing.

ATTRACTIONS:
Portsmouth FC (Pompey) is the biz, and don't you forget it, mush. Hampshire Cricket Club also has its No2 ground in town and there's also a dog track.

> ❝ Text in italics is PUSH's point of view – take it or leave it. ❞

accommodation

IN COLLEGE:

- Catered: 4% ● Cost: £56-66(39wks)
- Self-catering: 11% ● Cost: £40-50(39wks)

Availability: ¾ of the 1,778 places in the 10 halls are reserved for 1st years, but that's only enough to accommodate half of them. 7 of the halls are self-catered. There are limited provisions for students with children. There are also 700 places in a head tenancy scheme.

Car parking: Only feasible at QEQM and then a permit is needed. Bateson has an NCP car park opposite, but that costs. *Otherwise, it's virtually impossible throughout Portsmouth.*

EXTERNALLY:
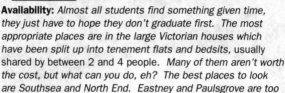
- Ave rent: £40

Availability: *Almost all students find something given time, they just have to hope they don't graduate first. The most appropriate places are in the large Victorian houses which have been split up into tenement flats and bedsits,* usually shared by between 2 and 4 people. *Many of them aren't worth the cost, but what can you do, eh? The best places to look are Southsea and North End. Eastney and Paulsgrove are too rough to be worth it.*

Housing help: The Accommodation Office publishes a daily bulletin, as well as assisting individual students. The University and SU run a 'Secure a Home' Day before the first year.

welfare

SERVICES:

- Creche ● Lesbian & Gay Society
- Mature SA ● Minibus

The University has a sick bay and arrangements with 2 local NHS practices. It also runs a *very good* Welfare Service with 6 part-time counsellors and a solicitor who visits once a week. The SU Rights & Advice Centre advises students on nitty-gritty stuff. There is a late-night minibus.

Disabled: *Wheelchair access is good in the newer, purpose-built areas, less so in the older parts.* The library has a braille computer and there's some accommodation for students with special needs, as well as a new Disability Co-ordinator.

FINANCE:
- Ave debt: £1,250 ● Access fund: £350, 647
- Successful applications (1996): 861

Short-term loans (£1K max) are available and financial workshops and debt counselling are organised.

● ●

▶▶ **Preston Polytechnic**
see University of Central Lancashire

● ●

▶▶ **Printing**
see The London Institute

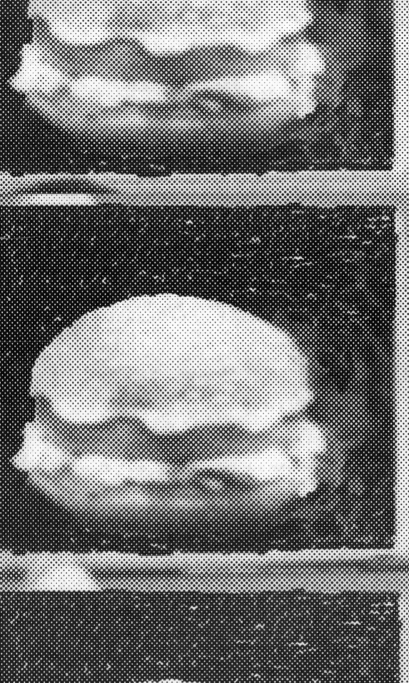

Queen Margaret College, Edinburgh

Queen Mary & Westfield College, London

- Queen's College, Glasgow
  see Glasgow Caledonian University

The Queen's University of Belfast

Queen Margaret College, Edinburgh

(1) Queen Margaret College, Corstorphine Campus, Edinburgh, EH12 8TS. Tel: (0131) 317 3000. Fax: (0131) 317 3256. E-mail: admissions@mail.qmced.ac.uk
Queen Margaret Students' Association, Clerwood Terrace, Edinburgh, EH12 8TS. Tel: (0131) 317 1990.
Fax: (0131) 317 3402. E-mail: qmcsa@mail.qmced.ac.uk
(2) Queen Margaret College, Leith Campus, Duke Street, Leith, Edinburgh, EH6 8HF.

General

QMC is based on 2 campuses, one in the Corstorphine area of Edinburgh, about 4 miles from the city centre and the other in Leith, a mile from the East End. The college specialises in business, theatre and healthcare subjects. The drama department is developing a studio workshop and theatre on a third site in the city centre.

20% ♂♂♂ ♀♀♀♀♀♀♀♀♀ 80%	
Sex ratio(M:F): 20%:80%	Founded: 1875
Full time u'grads: 2,588	Part time: 733
Postgrads: 42	Non-degree: 0
Ave course: 4yrs	Ethnic: 4.5%
Private/state school: n/a	Flunk rate: n/a
Mature students: 49%	Overseas students: 8%
Disabled students: 5.4%	Staff/student ratio: 1:15
Clearing: 16	

ATMOSPHERE:
It's a friendly, quite intimate place and the fact that some of the buildings conjure up the worst excesses of 60s comprehensive school architecture doesn't dampen the students' enthusiasm. Men are severely outnumbered, which can be an advantage or extra pressure for them, depending what mood they're in.

LEITH CAMPUS:

The Leith site, which houses 600 students on physiotherapy, occupational therapy, radiography and podiatry courses, is 7miles from Corstorphine. *Apart from a café, facilities are limited, but the ethos here is work-oriented anyway.*

THE CITY: see University of Edinburgh

TRAVEL: see University of Edinburgh

LIBRARIES & COMPUTERS:
- Books: 98,000 ● Study places: 438
- Computer workstations: 280

Students find the library facilities OK but there aren't enough computers to go round.

CAREER PROSPECTS:
- Careers Service ● No of staff: 1full/1part
- Unemployed after 6mths (1996): 7%

This must be the only institution where the Careers Advisor has been described (by students) as 'lovely', 'brilliant' and 'everyone's mum'.

SPECIAL FEATURES:

QMC is one of only 7 unis offering an undergraduate drama degree.

FAMOUS ALUMNI:

David Crystal (linguistics guru); Lloyd Quinan (Scottish weatherman); Andy Gray (actor).

FURTHER INFO:

Undergrad and postgrad prospectuses, video, web site (http://www.qmced.ac.uk).

entertainment

THE CITY: see University of Edinburgh

COLLEGE:
- Price of a pint of beer: £1.45 ● Glass of wine: £1.20

Bar/music venue/club: The Union Bar (cap 350) is open from 9am till late, Mon-Sat. *It's been refurbished, but unfortunately the students preferred its former seediness.* It's the only place in college where smoking is allowed. The bar doubles (triples?) as a gig venue (local and student bands only) and thrice-weekly *cheesy* disco.

Cinema: Video double features on Sundays.

Theatre: The college theatre hosts regular productions by the drama students; QMC doubles as a Fringe venue in the summer.

Food: The college provides 2 dining halls and a fast food bar

❝The installation ceremony for the Rector of Aberdeen University involves being wheeled around on the back of a model bull called Angus.❞

but it's pretty expensive. The Union offers an unimaginative but good-value selection of stodge.
Others: Games nights, hypnotists. Graduation ball in June, as well as various departmental beanos.

social & political

QUEEN MARGARET'S STUDENTS' ASSOCIATION:
● 2 sabbaticals ● Turnout at last ballot: 20%
● NUS member

Political activity has improved here, unsurprisingly since a) it was dead before and b) the introduction of tuition fees has stirred things up. There are no party political organisations or societies. Internally, everything's 'lovely and fluffy' apparently.

SU FACILITIES:
Bar; general shop; Royal Bank; photocopier; payphone; pool table; jukebox; TV lounge; meeting rooms.

CLUBS (NON SPORTING):
European; Film; Real Ale.

OTHER ORGANISATIONS:
A magazine, 'EH12', is published by the SA and a newsletter for the Leith campus is planned. Community relations are discussed with local reps twice a year. *Everything's just too nice.*

RELIGIOUS:
A new room has recently been provided for meetings of any persuasion.

PAID WORK: see University of Edinburgh

sports

● Recent successes: fencing, football
Sports provisions are limited at the moment, especially at Leith, but the level of enthusiasm has improved dramatically.

SPORTS FACILITIES:
Sports hall; pool; multigym; squash courts; all-weather playing field.

SPORTING CLUBS:
Aerobics; Aqua-Aerobics; Step; Weights; Mountaineering.

accommodation

IN COLLEGE:
● Catered: 6% ● Cost: £67(31wks)
● Self-catering: 14% ● Cost: £42-51(38wks)

About ½ of the 1st years can live in, but very few others. The Guthrie-Wright Halls are all-female, have single study bedrooms and offer 10 meals a week. *The fact that all catered accommodation is reserved for women is either a very right-on statement about domestic sex roles, a wry piece of Scots irony or a cock-up.* The self-catering halls and flats have kitchens shared between 3-13. *Also a new head tenancy scheme, for those who want private housing without the hassle of finding it.*

EXTERNALLY: see University of Edinburgh
The Accommodation Office is very helpful. Dalry, Corstorphine

q

and Haymarket are the most popular areas for students to rest their heads. Flats are cheaper and more plentiful around Leith.

······· welfare

SERVICES:
● Lesbian & Gay Society ● Overseas SA
● Equal Opportunities Officer

The college provides a part-time counsellor and nurse, plus 20 voluntary advisors who *finally* have their own room. *Recent welfare coups include teaching international students how to use irons.*

Disabled: *Access is pretty bad, with narrow, sloping paths and too many stairs*, but lecture theatres have loops, and there are a few ramps.

Women: There's an *increasingly active* women's group campaigning for improved provision, such as a sabbatical officer. *Plans are afoot to illuminate an 'eerie path'.*

FINANCE:
● Ave debt: £1,700 ● Access fund: £55,000
● Successful applications (1995): 116
Some bursaries.

●●●

Queen Mary & Westfield College, London

▼ ● *The College is part of University of London and students are entitled to use its facilities.*

(1) Queen Mary & Westfield College, University of London, Mile End Road, London, E1 4NS. Tel: (0171) 975 5555. Fax: (0171) 975 5500.

Queen Mary & Westfield Students' Union, Mile End Site, Benjamin Moloise Building, 432 Bancroft Road, London, E1 4DH. Tel: (0171) 975 5390. Fax: (0181) 981 0802. E-mail: su-genoff@qmw.ac.uk

(2) London Hospital Medical College, Turner Street, London, E1 2AD. Tel: (0171) 377 7000.

(3) The Medical College of St Bartholomew's Hospital, West Smithfield, London, EC1A 7BE. Tel: (0171) 601 8834.

······· general

Set in the multi-cultural melee of the East End, QMW is surrounded by the *bursting and buoyant* areas of Bethnal Green and Whitechapel, very close to Brick Lane Market and loads of East End pubs. QMW is the only campus college in London University - a campus which is *a sprawling mass* of buildings from many different periods - from the *fine* old Queens' Building (complete with clock tower) to some 50s art deco and 60s *eyesores, and strangely, a cemetery.* With 19th century origins, Queen Mary College was set up as a philanthropic institution for the education of East Enders, while

q

Westfield was a pioneering college for women. It's a 15min tube journey from the College to the city centre.

55% ♂♂♂♂♂♂♀♀♀♀ 45%	
Sex ratio(M:F): 55%:45%	Founded: 1934
Full time u'grads: 6,625	Part time: 0
Postgrads: 1,553	Non-degree: 0
Ave course: 3yrs	Ethnic: 38%
Private school: n/a	Flunk rate: 25%
Mature students: 19%	Overseas students: 20%
Disabled students: 2%	Staff/student ratio: 1:10
Clearing: 10%	

ATMOSPHERE:
The multi-racial, multi-national mix can be a learning experience in itself and its situation, in the bizarre bazaar that is the East End is worth something in itself. This rubs off on the students who mix with each other (and with the locals) like that very mixy thing we wanted to use for a simile but we forgot it temporarily.

THE MEDICAL SCHOOLS:
The medical schools of St Bartholomew's and the London Hospital have now merged to form a single school within QMW but they retain their 2 original sites.

Whitechapel: (170 students) *Friendly and approachable (at least by comparison with some other med schools),* the London Hospital is right opposite Whitechapel Tube in an *impressive* brick edifice, ½ a mile from the main QMW site.

West Smithfield: (730) Bart's is housed in a lovely Georgian-fronted building near Smithfield meat market (*don't bother, they've heard all the jokes about where the corpses end up*). It's got something of a reputation as a public school bastion, *but the merger's toned this down a bit.* It's a mile from QMW. Students at both sites are entitled to use the facilities at the main Mile End campus if they've got the time.

THE CITY: see University of London

TRAVEL: see University of London
Trains: Liverpool Street Station is very close.
Buses: Numbers 25, 106 and Night buses N76 and N98.
Underground: Nearest tubes are Mile End (Central, District, and Hammersmith & City Lines) and Stepney Green (District and Hammersmith & City). Whitechapel for the London Hospital, St Paul's and Barbican for Bart's.

LIBRARIES & COMPUTERS:
- Books: 570,000 ● Study places: 1,444
- Computer workstations: 700

The Law and Medical libraries are pretty impressive, the general one pretty average. Computer availability is good.

CAREER PROSPECTS:
- Careers Service ● No of staff: 3full/3part
- Unemployed after 6mths (1995): 6.3%

The Careers Service is helpful provided you know what you want to do. There is now a careers reference library, which is handy in a careers office.

q

SPECIAL FEATURES:
● All students can study a language with their degree and all *should* become computer literate.

FAMOUS ALUMNI:
Dr Barnardo; Bernard Butler (indie guitar deity); Graham Chapman (Monty Python); Bruce Dickinson (ex-Iron Maiden); Malcolm Bradbury, Eva Figes, Ruth Prawer Jhabvala, Andrea Newman (writers); Peter Hain MP (Lab); Sir Roy Strong (former Director, V&A Museum); David Sullivan (football/porn baron); Frederick Treves (treated the Elephant Man).

FURTHER INFO:
Prospectuses for undergrads and postgrads and a web site (http://www.qmw.ac.uk/).

entertainment

IN LONDON: see University of London
Local: *Pub prices in the East End are less ludicrous than in the centre of town but it still ain't cheap.* push*plugs: The Blind Beggar (Whitechapel); The Hayfield (now a theme pub, whatever that is); Rose & Punchbowl; Fountain; White Hart.*

COLLEGE:
● Price of a pint of beer: £1.40 ● Glass of wine: 90p
Bars: The SU runs 2 bars. *The e1 Venue Bar, unsurprisingly, comes into its own when there are ents on. The main focus for regular elbow-lifting is the shabby but comfortable Drapers Arms* (capacity 350).
Cinema: (1) Mainstream films shown every week.
Theatres: The *strong* drama department works in conjunction with the Central School of Speech & Drama and makes *good* use of the Harold Pinter Drama Studio. Regular trips to the Edinburgh Fringe are made by the students at the main campus and even the medics.
Clubs/discos/music venues: The e1 nightclub *serves a slamming selection of prime cuts* 3 nights a week and is also the base for occasional bands, *mostly tribute merchants.* The Drapers Bar hosts *lower-key* gigs.
Cabaret: *Top acts twice a term courtesy of QMW's new pals at Jongleurs, the famous comedy club.*
Food: *The college refectory spreads over 3 floors and quality and value have improved recently.* The SU has a Pizza bar in e1 and The Griddle in the Draper's Arms.
Others: The annual Valentine's Ball is very successful. There is a gallery in the College which exhibits local artists' work.

social & political

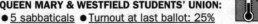

QUEEN MARY & WESTFIELD STUDENTS' UNION:
● 5 sabbaticals ● Turnout at last ballot: 25%
● NUS member
The SU is hard-working and popular with the students, but hardly radical. There was a recent campaign to boycott Nestlé products which was successful, although the campaign to boycott the boycott met with equal support. What a waste of time, eh? There's a £2m project afoot to renovate and extend the SU building, which should be finished in September 1998. *It needs it, too.*

SU FACILITIES:
Shop; STA travel branch; bars; photocopying; video games; 2nd-hand bookshop; cashpoint.

CLUBS (NON SPORTING):
More than 60, including: Arab; Circus; Cypriot; French; Hellenic; Ideological; Iranian; Korean; Malaysian; *F***in'* Manchester United; Pakistan; Sci-Fi; Sri Lanka; Tamil; Thinking.

OTHER ORGANISATIONS:
'CUB' is the monthly student mag. There's also 'The Sun' newspaper and 'Sweat' for sporty types. There's also a charity Rag and various Community Action projects.

RELIGIOUS:
The SU has a Muslim prayer room and the mega-dome of St Paul's Cathedral can be seen from the campus.

PAID WORK: see <u>University of London</u>

sports

● <u>Recent successes: fencing, football, hockey</u>

Sport is one of the few activities that binds the student body together and, for an inner-city college, QMW's record is pretty sound.

SPORTS FACILITIES:
In the SU Building there is a gym, a weights room, squash courts, a snooker room, sauna, multigym and other indoor sports. At Theydon Bois, on the north-east outskirts of London, there are sports fields and tennis courts. The Medical Association has facilities at Hale End and Chistlehurst, and there are watersports at Docklands. There are, of course, <u>London University</u>'s facilities.

SPORTING CLUBS:
Aikido; Boating; Kick boxing; Polo; Tennis; Turf Club (owns its own race horse); Wu Shu Kwan.

ATTRACTIONS:
West Ham is the local footie team. There's Leyton Orient as well, *but Andrew Lloyd Webber supports them, so they're rubbish.* There's also a dog track, indoor climbing wall and ice rink.

accommodation

IN COLLEGE:
● <u>Catered: 6%</u> ● <u>Cost: £60-70(31-38wks)</u>
● <u>Self-catering: 12%</u> ● <u>Cost: £60-73(38wks)</u>
Availability: The College's own accommodation includes 855 catered and *about* 900 self-catered places. Another 142 find a roof in the University's inter-collegiate halls. All 1st years who apply in time can live in (3% of them have to share), and over 20% of finalists. The accommodation on site is *new and very good looking* with a view of the Regent's Canal *but some of the other sites are depressing and too far away. The food in catered halls is dreadful.* Expansion of college accommodation is at the planning stage.
Car parking: Free permit parking outside office hours only.

EXTERNALLY: see <u>University of London</u>
Housing help: The College Accommodation Office offers full-

time staff and a bulletin board. *The East End is fun but quality can be variable and not all parts are safe. Millennium funding should see a good deal of tidying-up.*

welfare

SERVICES:
● Creche ● Nightline ● Lesbian & Gay Society
● Overseas SA ● Women's Officer

The College provides 5 full- and 2 part-time counsellors and the SU has 2 welfare officers. There's a Health Centre with 2 doctors and a senior nurse, and a visiting psychiatrist.
Disabled: *Access in University accommodation is OK, but it's variable in some of the other buildings.*

FINANCE:
● Ave debt: £650 ● Access fund: £260,000
● Successful applications (1996): 641

There are undergraduate bursaries of £1,500 p.a.

▶▶ Queen's College, Glasgow
see Glasgow Caledonian University

The Queen's University of Belfast

(1) The Queen's University of Belfast, University Road, Belfast, BT7 1NN. Tel: (01232) 245133. Fax: (01232) 247895.
Queen's University of Belfast Students' Union, University Road, Belfast, BT7 1PE. Tel: (01232) 324803.
Fax: (01232) 236900. E-mail: s.union@qub.ac.uk
(2) The Queen's University at Armagh, 39 Abbey Street, Armagh, BT61 7EB. Tel: (01861) 510678.
Fax: (01861) 510679.

general

On the River Lagan, where Belfast Lough opens out into the Irish Sea, lies Belfast, the largest city in Northern Ireland. The queen of Queen's University was the *unamused* Queen Vic and the *tasteful* University buildings date from her time to ours. The University has taken over much of the surrounding prosperous Belfast suburb, so that the houses of the nearby genuine Victorian terraces are more likely to contain one of the University's faculties (or Schools) than any Victorians. Given the surrounding greenery -

❝One of Bristol University's accommodation blocks used to be a Berni Inn.❞

many parks and the nearby Botanical Gardens - it can be hard to believe that Belfast city centre is only ½ mile away, with the Shankill and Falls Roads ½ mile beyond that.

44% ♂♂♂♂♂♀♀♀♀♀ 56%

Sex ratio(M:F): 44%:56%	Founded: 1845
Full time u'grads: 12,193	Part time: 2,177
Postgrads: 5,132	Non-degree: 3,394
Ave course: 3yrs	Ethnic: 3%
Private school: n/a	Flunk rate: 16%
Mature students: 16.8%	Overseas students: 10.8%
Disabled students: 1.8%	Staff/student ratio: 1:16
Clearing: 3.6%	

ATMOSPHERE:
It's beyond the scope of push *to comment in depth on the Northern Ireland situation. At the time of going to press, a peace deal had been made, and elections were in the wings. By the time you read this, you'll know better than we do whether there is a permanent ceasefire, an elected assembly, a big street party with all the factions doing the hokey-cokey or what. But whatever the state of play, it's fair to say that the worst of 'The Troubles' has bypassed students at Queen's, especially since it's in a prosperous suburb of South Belfast, away from the profoundly sectarian parts.* 87% of Queen's students are still locals and 7% are from the South of Ireland with a healthy mix of Catholic and Protestant students, *yet most of the tension on campus is reserved for essays and exams rather than sectarianism. The rest is reserved for being rude about* Ulster University *and hardcore drinking.*

OUTREACH SITES:
Queen's also has 2 subsidiary sites, 1 in Armagh, about 40 miles south-west of Belfast and one in Portaferry, also 40 miles from Belfast. Further Outreach sites are planned, which will concentrate on serving the local population, especially returners to education. All subsidiary centres have direct data links to the Belfast campus.

THE CITY:
● Population: 300,000
The first impression of Belfast city centre is of a collection of *earthy* Victorian civic buildings, with a *monstrously* modern shopping centre at its heart. Belfast lies in an *attractive* bay ringed by mountains and when the rain clears *(twice a year if you're lucky)*, it's quite possible to enjoy the city's gifts: shopping malls; supermarkets; the new and 2nd-hand bookshops; the Ulster Museum on the campus and the banks (mainly Irish). *The debris of the Troubles (soldiers, murals, protection rackets) may or may not persist but the locals are a happy bunch and there's a new air of fun and games, with clubs and pubs doing a roaring trade. Ironically,* the overall crime rate is among the lowest in the UK.

TRAVEL:
Trains: All of Ireland's main cities and towns, north and south, are just a Northern Ireland Railways' journey away, including

(London)Derry (£7.20) and Coleraine. A *fast* train, the Enterprise, goes to Dublin (£17).

Coaches: Translink serve most destinations in Northern Ireland, but it's somewhat difficult to catch a bus direct from the British mainland. National Express run a service to London (£48).

Car: *The centre of Belfast is a pain for driving in, although parking's easy enough.*

Air: Regular flights from all over the UK mainland and Europe to Belfast City and Aldergrove Airports, including London (£69).

Ferries: Services to Stranraer, Holyhead and Liverpool on mainland Britain and now a fast, new Sea Cat.

Hitching: *Better than most places in the UK, particularly heading south or west, but not to the ports or airport. The worst bit is heading for a crossing from the mainland and invariably being asked about The Troubles.*

Local: Frequent local buses provide a 10-minute journey into the city centre for 50p.

Taxis: Plenty of taxis and black cabs charging minimum fares of £2.50.

Bicycles: *Theft's not a problem, but the weather is dreadful.*

LIBRARIES & COMPUTERS:

● <u>Books: 1,100,000</u> ● <u>Study places: 2,530</u>
● <u>Computer workstations: 2,000</u>

Students are more than a little grumpy about limited book availability despite there being 5 libraries. There are usually enough computers to go round but they're not necessarily the most powerful or up-to-date models.

CAREER PROSPECTS:

● <u>Careers Service</u> ● <u>No of staff: 12 full</u>
● <u>Unemployed after 6mths (1996): 6%</u>

There is a high level of unemployment in Northern Ireland, *which casts an especially impressive light on the University's employment record.*

FAMOUS ALUMNI:

Dr John Alderdice (leader, Alliance Party); Simon Callow, James Ellis, Liam Neeson, Stephen Rea (actors); Seamus Heaney (Nobel-winning poet); Patrick Kielty ('Last Chance Lottery' presenter); Mary McAleese (President of Ireland); Bernadette McAliskey (née Devlin, former MP); Dr Brian Mawhinney MP (Con); Ian Paisley Jr (*chip off the old mouth*); Trevor Ringland (rugby player); Nick Ross (*don't have nightmares*); Dawson Stelfox (mountaineer); Mary Peters (Olympic pentathlete).

FURTHER INFO:

Prospectuses for undergrads and postgrads, newsletter for schools, CD-ROM. The SU is starting up an alternative prospectus. Web site (http://www.qub.ac.uk).

entertainment

CITY:
● <u>Price of a pint of beer: £1.80</u> ● <u>Glass of wine: £1.80</u>

Most Belfast nightlife takes place in the Golden Mile that stretches from Queen's to the city centre. For up-to-the-minute details, catch the bi-monthly 'Buzz' magazine, or 'That's Entertainment'.

Cinemas: (3) 2 mainstream and the *arty* Queen's Film Theatre.

Theatres: (7) *Plenty of choice and regular major touring productions including the Royal Shakespeare Company and An Culturlann, an innovative Irish language theatre company.*
Pubs: *What better reason for coming to Ireland than for a pint of stout strong enough to stand a pencil in? Guinness from any of the local hostelries will have a head you can draw a broad smile in.* pushplugs: *Botanic (aka The Bot); Lavery's Gin Palace (v. friendly and alternative); The Crown (Victorian boozer); The Fly; Eglantine's. The Parliament Bar and the Crow's Nest are the main gay venues.*
Clubs/discos: *Belfast is developing quite a reputation as a clubbers' paradise.* pushplugs: *Limelight (indie, retro and jazz nights); The Brunswick (soul and hardcore, 4 separate floors); Network Club (dance/hip-hop); M Club (student nights); Thompson's Garage (house); Ultimate rave, Saturdays at the Art College; the new Storm in Lisburn is the largest club in NI, 5 miles from Belfast.*
Music venues: *Ulster Hall for big names; Empire Music Hall for medium-sized and comedy nights; the newish Waterfront Hall (anything from Mozart to the Monkees); innumerable smaller-scale gigs in pubs and clubs.*
Eating out: *Plenty of eating experiences good and cheap enough to make Gary Rhodes' hair lie flat. Locals spend more on eating out than in any other UK city.* pushplugs: *Speranza's (pizzas, a student institution); Vincents, The Other Place (both bring your own booze); Giro's and Bookfinders (veggie); Revelations Internet Cafe (student concessions). Many of the pubs are good for a bite, too.*

UNIVERSITY:
● Price of a pint of beer: £1.50 ● Glass of wine: £1.85
Bars: The Union's 2 main bars, the Bunatee Bar (cap 250) and the Speakeasy (550, recently refurbished), *are packed by 7pm.*
Cinema: The QFT (Queen's Film Theatre) *offers an excellent mix of arty, culty and left-field celluloid.*
Clubs/discos: Every night the Mandela Hall or the snack bar quivers to a variety of sounds, *the most impressive being the Friday 'Shine' house/hip-hop event which attracts big-name guest DJs* although this can push the price above 10 quid.
Music venues: The renovated Mandela Hall has recently hosted Radiohead, Divine Comedy and Seahorses.
Cabaret: Every fortnight the Speakeasy is taken over *by some nutter or another* (Ed Byrne recently) as part of the National Comedy Network.
Food: *The Speakeasy undercuts the opposition when it comes to price but the range available leaves a bit to be desired.* The University also has several fuelling stations.
Other: Up to 7 balls a year, including Freshers', Rag and St Paddy's bashes. Most faculties also have some kind of formal. The annual Queen's International Arts Festival is now 2nd only to Edinburgh, with a bit of everything: ballet; theatre; alternative comedy; and the alternative to alternative comedy.

q

❛Rabbits outnumber students on the University of Essex campus.❜

········ social & political

**QUEEN'S UNIVERSITY OF BELFAST STUDENTS' UNION/
AONTAS NA MAC LÉINN OLLSCOIL NA BANRIONA:**

● 6 sabbaticals ● Turnout at last ballot: 10%
● NUS/USI member

*Most strands of political thought, NI-based or not, are
represented, which tends to balance things out, though
nationalists are in the majority. Recent introduction of bilingual
signs had a mixed response. The incestuous nature of the SU's
internal politics have alienated some students but the majority,
of course, just regard the SU as a source of cheap booze.*

SU FACILITIES:
Bars; refectories; advice centre; Bank of Ireland (with
cashpoint); launderette; showers; supermarket; writing room;
2nd-hand bookshops; sports shop; Endsleigh Insurance office;
travel centre; computer shop; hairdresser; snooker room; games
room; vending/games machines; photocopier; function rooms.

CLUBS (NON SPORTING):
AIESEC; Alliance; An Cumann Gaelach; Ballroom Dancing; Celtic Supporters;
Christian Democrats; Crucible; CS Lewis; Debating; Dragonslayers; Gaelic;
Hispanic; Hong Kong; Italian; Juggling; Malaysian; Media; Pro-Life; Radio; Rangers
Supporters; Russian; SDLP; Singapore; Ulster Unionist; Wine. *Plus many more than
we want to shake a stick at.*

OTHER ORGANISATIONS:
Queen's students run 2 newspapers: 'Gown' and 'Banter'.
Furthermore, the charity Rag clocks along actively, having
raised £19K in 96/7. Their *renowned* mag 'PTQ' had to
withdraw 20,000 copies which had Diana jokes in them, *but
not until after record sales were achieved.* The Community
Workshop does what it can for town/gown relations.

RELIGIOUS:
There are 16 chaplaincies at Queen's, from Catholic and
Church of Ireland to facilities for 5 flavours of Presbyterian,
Muslims and Jews and even a Church for the Deaf. Belfast
fills in any gaps there might be, including Mormons, Seventh
Day Adventists and Hare Krishna.

PAID WORK:
All the usual casual labour, but unemployment is high in
Northern Ireland and work can be hard to come by.

········ sports

● Recent successes: snooker, rowing
*The University's PE Centre has all the mod cons to get
students shaking their tail feathers. Blues are awarded, on the
Oxbridge model.*

SPORTS FACILITIES:
Apart from the many indoor facilities of the PE centre on
campus, Queen's is proud of the Mary Peters Track (named
after the Olympic athlete), but it's 400m long and goes round
in circles like everyone else's. The track and 20 playing fields
(4 all-weather) are a 2-mile bus ride away. The town offers a
further sprinkling of leisure centres and golf courses. *Worthy
of special mention* is the Dundonald Ice Bowl. Malone Sports
Facility (known as 'The Dub') is good for outdoor stuff.

SPORTING CLUBS:

Aikido; Boat; Camogie; Caving; Gaelic Football; Gliding; Handball; Hurling; Jiu Jitsu; Motorcycle; Mountain Bike; Parachuting; Racquetball; Snooker; Sub-Aqua; Surf; Tae Jitsu; Water Polo; Water Ski; Windsurfing; Wing Chun Kung Fu; Yoga.

accommodation

IN COLLEGE:

● Catered: 7% ● Cost: £49-57(32wks)
● Self-catering: 8% ● Cost: £34-43(35-39wks)

Availability: 48% of 1st years live in, with half of them sharing, mainly in 10 storey blocks ½ mile from campus *in attractive surrounds. Queen's Elms has a groovy 1,100 capacity, and Riddell is all female.* There are also a few places in associated halls (two with religious links) and flats for married couples.
Car parking: *Plentiful and permitless, if you really need wheels.*

EXTERNALLY:

● Ave rent: £33

Availability: *Many students are locals. For home hunters who look early in summer, there is little difficulty in finding accommodation, although by September the task is harder. Most student areas offer good quality terraced housing with high class amenities, particularly Stranmillis, Malone Road, Holylands and Lisburn Road. Some areas are obviously best avoided but previously untouchable parts, such as the Ormeau Road, are becoming increasingly popular, mainly because they're so cheap.*
Housing help: The Union Welfare Office and the University Accommodation Office are the roofing specialists, that is to say, they help make sure students have one over their heads, and they keep tabs on vacant rooms and houses. There are also a number of Housing Associations who accept student applications.

welfare

SERVICES:

● Nursery ● Nightline ● Lesbian & Gay Society
● Mature SA ● Overseas SA ● Minibus ● Women's Officer
● Self-defence classes

The Union's small counselling service meets most immediate needs for troubled souls, while troubled bodies are mended by the Student Health Centre. The legally troubled can ask the advice of the solicitor who visits 4 afternoons a week. There are also officers with responsibility for mature and overseas students. A new Sports Injury Clinic has started up.
Women: There are *excellent* services for women including the support magazine 'Shrewd', and a women's night-time minibus.
Disabled: *Ramps are all over the place, lifts less so. Serious efforts are being made to tackle some of the older buildings.*
Drugs: *Apart from the usual dangers, the drug trade has paramilitary connections, so watch it.*

FINANCE:

● Ave debt: £1,250 ● Access fund: £219,518
● Successful applications (1997): 517

There are several scholarships, including 15 Guinness sports bursaries.

q

University of Reading

- Ripon & York St John
  see Other Institutions

- RMCS
  see Cranfield University

Robert Gordon University

- Roehampton Institute
  see Other Institutions

- Rose Bruford
  see Other Institutions

Royal Academy of Music

- Royal Agricultural College
  see Other Institutions

Royal College of Music

Royal Free Hospital School of Medicine, London

Royal Holloway, London

- Royal Military College of Science
  see Cranfield University

Royal Veterinary College, London

University of Reading

University of Reading, Whiteknights, Reading, RG6 2AH.
Tel: (0118) 987 5123. Fax: (0118) 931 4404.
University of Reading Students' Union, Whiteknights, Reading, RG6 6AZ. Tel: (0118) 986 0222. Fax: (0118) 975 0337.

general

Reading is unfortunately pronounced 'redding' which somewhat scuppers those witticisms that friends of students' parents will come up with such as, 'So, what are you reading at Reading?'. *Apart from the potential for jokes about the*

name, there is little remotely remarkable about the town. It's a *nondescript* place close enough to London to be popular with commuters. *The surrounding area is more attractive, lots of pleasant Thames-side villages and small towns*, such as Henley, Hurley and Goring. The University is based on the large Whiteknights campus, just under 2 miles from the town centre, set in 300 acres of parkland, lake and wood. The buildings are a varied mixture, ranging from 19th century houses to the new microbiology building. There is a small 2nd campus about 1½ miles away at Bulmershe, housing about 2,000 students in the departments of Education and Film & Drama. *It has a closer knit community atmosphere, but fewer facilities.*

47% ♂♂♂♂♂ ♀♀♀♀♀ 53%	
Sex ratio(M:F): 47%:53%	Founded: 1892
Full time u'grads: 7,683	Part time: 3,376
Postgrads: 5,245	Non-degree: 0
Ave course: 3yrs	Ethnic: 3%
Private school: 17%	Flunk rate: n/a
Mature students: 22%	Overseas students: 13.9%
Disabled students: 3%	Staff/student ratio: 1:13
Clearing: n/a	

ATMOSPHERE:
The University has a cosy, sporty, self-contained atmosphere with a large proportion of students living on the green and quiet campus, or close to it. The students tend to be middle-class and from south-east England but there are plenty who buck the trend. The campus empties at the weekend.

THE TOWN:
- Population: 122,600 • London: 40miles
- Oxford: 25miles • Bristol: 74miles

The University often seems more fun than it really is, because the town's pretty bland and is dead on week nights. It is a large country town *with little more to recommend it than good shopping and opportunities for business.* There's a vast range of supermarkets, bookshops (including a very big Blackwells) and plenty of shops open into the night. Reading does have tourist attractions - *well, there has to be something to do on rainy bank holidays* - 3 museums (English Rural Life *(a pre-eminent museum of hand-ploughs and things)*, Reading Museum and Blakes Lock Museum) and the River Thames, the River Kennet, the Avon Canal and Reading Abbey ruins.

TRAVEL:
Trains: Reading station, about 1½ miles from campus, offers direct services to London Paddington and Waterloo (£12), and most points west.
Coaches: National Express services all over the country. There are also the Reading-London Link (Reading Transport - £7) and Bee-Line Coaches.
Car: The M4 and A4 run west out of London. The M25 and M40 lead onto the M1.
Air: Regular 45-minute coach service to Heathrow International Airport, the busiest airport in the world.

Hitching: The SU doesn't recommended it after recent attacks *and the area's not that good for getting lifts anyway.*
Local: *Buses between the University and town are reasonably good* (£1 rtn).
Taxis: Many taxi companies, but beware of those offering so-called 'student fares' - *they can be even more expensive.*
Bicycles: *The campus is bikeably flat. Bikes are especially useful for early morning lectures or for getting to Bulmershe.*

LIBRARIES & COMPUTERS:
● Books: 1,008,445 ● Study places: 954
● Computer workstations: 310
Apart from the main University Library at Whiteknights there's another at Bulmershe and various departmental libraries (eg Music, Education and Agriculture). *Students are very happy with their facilities.*

CAREER PROSPECTS:
● Careers Service ● No of staff: 9full/10part
● Unemployed after 6mths (1996): 11%

SPECIAL FEATURES:
● A flexible 1st year course structure is operated, giving students in some faculties a chance to experience other subjects and even change. *1st years get very wound up about their FUEs (First University Exams) and, unlike most universities, the 1st year is as academically demanding as any other.* However, many students don't see another exam paper till their finals.

FAMOUS ALUMNI:
Suzanne Charlton (BBC weatherperson, daughter of Sir Bobby); Nigel de Gruchy (general secretary, NASUWT); Glynn Ford MEP (Lab); Andy McKay (Roxy Music saxophonist). Gustav Holst, the composer of 'The Planets Suite', lectured here.

FURTHER INFO:
Prospectuses for undergrads, postgrads, part-timers and mature students, a handbook for students with special needs and a web site
(http://www.reading.ac.uk/schools/courses.html).

entertainment

THE TOWN:
● Price of a pint of beer: £2.20 ● Glass of wine: £1.80
Cinemas: (4) Including the 12-screen multiplex the Show Case and the *excellent and varied* Reading Film Theatre.
Theatres: The Hexagon stages everything from snooker to ballet, panto to opera as does the Millstream, on a smaller scale. For alternative drama, try the Progress Theatre.
Pubs: *Apart from the ridiculous prices, several pubs are a tad unwelcoming to students.* pushplugs: Monk's Retreat; Rising Sun; College Arms; Queen's Head.
Clubs/discos: *Reading doesn't have the hottest club scene in the world, in fact it's tepid. Purple Turtle and RGI do the straightforward chart/dance business and Level 1 does regular student nights.*
Music venues: Alleycat Live is a *good* indie venue and the Rivermead Centre has regular bands; it's also been the site of

the WOMAD Festival in recent years.

Eating out: All the usual chains and franchises you'd expect are present and politically incorrect *but Reading isn't exactly a gustatorial centre of excellence.* **push***plugs: JD Wetherspoons; Monk's Tree (cheap and cheerful); Muswell's (American-style diner); TGI Friday's (good for parties, but the joke wears thin eventually).*

Other: The Reading Festival, *the No 2 hang out (after Glastonbury) for all blitzed party people,* is held on the flood bank of the Thames over the August bank holiday weekend. Suede and the Manic Street Preachers were among the headliners at the 1997 fest.

UNIVERSITY:

● Price of a pint of beer: £1.60 ● Glass of wine: £1.25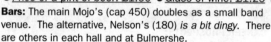

Bars: The main Mojo's (cap 450) doubles as a small band venue. The alternative, Nelson's (180) *is a bit dingy.* There are others in each hall and at Bulmershe.

Clubs/discos: There are 3 club nights a week in the Main Hall (cap 770) plus occasional specialist nights and guest DJs such as LTJ Bukem.

Music venues: The Main Hall is also the scene of live action from, recently, My Life Story, Sleeper, Teenage Fanclub and several tribute bands.

Food: There is an *OK* choice of chomping on campus including The Buttery or, *slightly better,* the pre-packed platters in the Blue and Orange Rooms. Most faculties have their own refectories, open all day. The SU provides the Servery and the Mojo's does *cheap* hot food at lunchtime.

Other: Several balls and lots of karaoke.

········ social & political

READING UNIVERSITY STUDENTS' UNION (RUSU):

● 5 sabbaticals ● Turnout at last ballot: 15%

  ● NUS member

RUSU has facilities at both the Bulmershe and Whiteknights sites, where it has its own big building with damn fine amenities. Students seem quite happy with things but they're probably more concerned with sport than anything else. A recent campaign about campus security roused enough people to get something done. Now there's a committee. Well, it's a start.

SU FACILITIES:

Travel shop; welfare office; 3 bars; stationery shop; bookshop; general/wholefood shop; Endsleigh Insurance office and other services such as photocopying and vending machines; launderette.

CLUBS (NON SPORTING):

Anglican; Brazilian; Bridge; Creative Writing; Debating; Duke of Edinburgh; Expeditionary; Paintball; Pooh; Sci Fi; Turkish; WARUS (wargames); Yoga.

OTHER ORGANISATIONS:

The SU publishes a weekly colour newspaper, 'Spark'. There is a charity Rag and the student Community Action group runs projects for children and people with disabilities. A radio station is planned soon, *as are all the other as-yet-non-existent student radio stations.*

RELIGIOUS:
There is a Chaplaincy centre on campus serving Christians, and a Muslim centre. In town, there are prayer places for Muslims, Hindus, Sikhs, Jews, and most Christians.

sports

● <u>Recent successes: ladies' football, fencing</u>

The University has *good* facilities, mostly on campus attached to the Wolfenden Sports Centre although the Thames is handy for watersports. After an initial payment of £4.50 each year, there is only a nominal fee for some facilities. *Standards are especially high in women's sports.*

SPORTS FACILITIES:
On campus the Wolfenden Sports Centre provides facilities for badminton, archery, basketball, cricket, fencing, five-a-side football, hockey, martial arts, netball, table tennis, trampolining and tennis and a brand new gym. Plans are afoot for an astroturf pitch. There's also a squash centre, gym and weights room at Bulmershe. Outdoor facilities include an athletics pavilion, playing fields for cricket, football and rugby, an all-weather surface and running track. In town, there are numerous swimming pools and rowing and sailing on the river.

SPORTING CLUBS:
Aikido; American Football; Boat (rowing); Caving; Clay Pigeon; Hot Air Balloon; Kick Boxing; Kung Fu; Lacrosse; Motor; Ninjutsu; Polo; Rifle & Pistol; Sky Diving; T'ai Chi; Trampoline; Weights.

ATTRACTIONS:
Henley Regatta; Ascot; Windsor Races; Newbury Races; Reading Football Club.

accommodation

IN COLLEGE:

● <u>Catered: 40%</u> ● <u>Cost: £75-88(30wks)</u>
● <u>Self-catering: 17%</u> ● <u>Cost: £38-56(30wks)</u>

Availability: All 1st years that apply in time (by June) are accommodated. 5% have to share. With the exception of Sibly (self-catering) and Mansfield (owned by a Japanese college, but not housing exclusively Japanese students), all halls are within a mile of the Whiteknights site. They range from brand new self-catering blocks to the redbrick Oxbridge-style Wantage Hall and Grade II-listed St Andrew's Hall. Many of the newest ones offer en suite facilities. There is accommodation for 465 students at Bulmershe.
Car parking: A permit is needed to park on campus and 1st years are dissuaded from bringing cars.

EXTERNALLY:
● <u>Ave rent: £50</u>

Availability: *With the help of the accommodation office, it is quite easy to find accommodation, although the quality varies from lucky luxury to dingy dives. There's a fair amount of housing available within a mile of campus, Donnington Gardens and Wokingham Road having the best selection. The rough stuff between London Road and the Railway and around Oxford Road is worth giving a miss.*
Housing help: The University Accommodation Office is willing

to do a cockroach check on accommodation within a mile of campus. The Welfare Office will also give contracts the once over. *The best places though, are usually passed down through generations of students via RUSU's notice board.*

 welfare

SERVICES: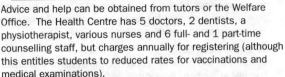
 ● <u>Creche</u> ● <u>Mature SA</u> ● <u>Overseas SA</u> ● <u>Minibus</u>
● <u>Women's Officer</u> ● <u>Self-defence classes</u>

Advice and help can be obtained from tutors or the Welfare Office. The Health Centre has 5 doctors, 2 dentists, a physiotherapist, various nurses and 6 full- and 1 part-time counselling staff, but charges annually for registering (although this entitles students to reduced rates for vaccinations and medical examinations).

Disabled: *The thought's there -* there's a Special Needs Co-ordinator, a handbook and some accommodation is specifically adapted for wheelchair users. *However, there are still gaps.*

FINANCE:
● <u>Ave debt: £950</u> ● <u>Access fund: £189,000</u>
● <u>Successful applications (1997): 560</u>

Hardship fund run by SU, emergency loans fund and various departmental prizes.

● ●

▶▶ Ripon & York St John

see Other Institutions

● ●

▶▶ RMCS

see Cranfield University

● ●

Robert Gordon University

▼ ● *Formerly Robert Gordon Institute of Technology*
The Robert Gordon University, Schoolhill, Aberdeen, AB10 1FR.
Tel: (01224) 262105. Fax: (01224) 263133.
Robert Gordon University Students' Association, 60 Schoolhill, Aberdeen, AB10 1JQ. Tel: (01224) 262262.
Fax: (01224) 262268. E-mail: rgusa@compuserve.com

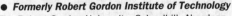 general

 The old Robert Gordon Institute (*but you can call it Bob's*) became a university in 1992. The student population of the city is large and *RGU's students mix affably with all the others. Perhaps this is helped by where they're situated,* because RGU is spread across 8 sites around the city (3 of which are residential sites only). Apart from the main site on Schoolhill in the city centre, the sites are on the outskirts, but all are within 3½ miles of the centre and set in small parks or gardens.

46% ♂♂♂♂♂♀♀♀♀♀ **54%**

Sex ratio(M:F): 46%:54%	**Founded: 1881**
Full time u'grads: 5,318	**Part time: 542**
Postgrads: 518	**Non-degree: 0**
Ave course: 3yrs	**Ethnic: 6.1%**
Private school: 3%	**Flunk rate: n/a**
Mature students: 16.6%	**Overseas students: 12.4%**
Disabled students: 2.9%	**Staff/student ratio: 1:17**
Clearing: n/a	

ATMOSPHERE:
This is no ivory tower, more of a modest bungalow - a damn sight more realistic but it can be a bit soul-destroying. The Union is the focus for social and political activity and is the bonding agent between such disparate sites. Students make the most of the limited facilities, but when they don't meet their needs, they're quick to take advantage of <u>Aberdeen University</u>'s *attractions and those of the wider city. The emphasis on hard work* (mostly vocational courses), *however, is never dropped completely. Students are referred to as 'customers' but they shouldn't have undue expectations about the level of services this entails.*

THE SITES:
Schoolhill/St Andrew Street: (1,630 students - applied sciences, engineering, electronics, computing, maths) The largest site and home of the Union.

Merkland/King Street: (c.350 students - librarianship, public administration & law) An *elegant* light stone building, 1 mile from Schoolhill near shops, accommodation and buses, but on a busy road. As of the 98-99 session there will be no teaching at King St or Hilton, and the libraries of the two sites will be merged. No decision has yet been made as to whether King Street will close.

Hilton: (c.1,300 students - business, librarianship) 2½ miles from Schoolhill, Hilton is a modern block set in parkland to the north of the city. This site belongs to the Northern College of Education who may be taking it back in the next few years. Students are being relocated to Garthdee.

Kepplestone: (c.1,000 students - applied social studies, food & consumer studies) A set of modern blocks surrounded by playing fields and landscaped grounds, 1¾ miles west of Schoolhill. Largely residential *with an amiable ambience.*

Foresterhill: (900 students - nursing) Large, grey bricked, 3 storey houses set in hospital grounds, 1½ miles from Schoolhill.

Woolmanhill: (c.350 - occupational therapy, radiography, physiotherapy) In the centre of town.

Garthdee: (c.3,500 students - art, architecture, surveying) The furthest site from Schoolhill, 3 miles to the south west, *but possibly the most attractive* - a large mansion overlooking the River Dee and encompassed by rolling parkland. *Less*

> ❧ The Sutra rave at BUWE is so popular that one punter, denied entry, tried to ram-raid the venue – in his own car. ❞

convenient, but peaceful and conducive to contemplative study. There are plans to shift the whole University out here, starting with the new Management Faculty in 1998.

THE CITY: see <u>University of Aberdeen</u>

TRAVEL: see <u>University of Aberdeen</u>
Aberdeen Station is a mile south of Schoolhill. Buses run every 20 minutes to most sites, *but feet are the most effective way of getting around.*

LIBRARIES & COMPUTERS:
- <u>Books: 208,135</u> ● <u>Study places: 841</u>
- <u>Computer workstations: 760</u>

There are 8 libraries around the sites. *Computer facilities aren't that hot, considering the large number of students doing IT-related courses.*

CAREER PROSPECTS:
- <u>Careers Service</u> ● <u>No of staff: 4full/2part</u>
- <u>Unemployed after 6mths (1996): 5%</u>

Vocational degrees make job prospects better, as do industrial placements and careers advice within courses.

FAMOUS ALUMNI:
Ena Baxter (maker of *wholesome and nutritious* soups); Donnie Munro (Runrig singer).

FURTHER INFO:
Prospectuses for undergrads and postgrads, school brochures, video, web site (http://www.rgu.ac.uk).

entertainment

THE CITY: see <u>University of Aberdeen</u>

UNIVERSITY:
- <u>Price of a pint of beer: £1.30</u> ● <u>Glass of wine: £1.50</u>

Bars: The Union offers the choice of the *raucous, slightly tacky* Asylum (cap 280, mainly a venue) or *the more mellow* Theo's Gallery (200) with hard church pews for seating.
Music venues/clubs/discos: The Asylum (£1) is the disco inferno twice a week but live bands aren't on the agenda, *except for the odd bit of folk and jazz.*
Theatre: One major production is put on every term by students, often penned by themselves.
Food: Theo's does *OK* snacks and Wilma's canteen *offers variants on fast food and meat 'n' 2 veg (ie chips).* Bar food till 11pm.
Others: Ceilidhs, quizzes, karaoke - there's something at least 3 nights a week. *But students are tending to drift away from the Union, preferring the increasingly groovy entertainments in town or maybe sneaking in to see what <u>Aberdeen University</u>*

has to offer. The SU is taking note, and planning to make RGU's facilities cater more for mature students and daytime events (big-screen sports etc).

sociaL & poLiticaL

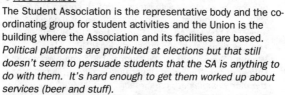

ROBERT GORDON UNIVERSITY STUDENTS' ASSOCIATION:
- 2 sabbaticals ● Turnout at last ballot: 5%
- NUS member

The Student Association is the representative body and the co-ordinating group for student activities and the Union is the building where the Association and its facilities are based. *Political platforms are prohibited at elections but that still doesn't seem to persuade students that the SA is anything to do with them. It's hard enough to get them worked up about services (beer and stuff).*

SU FACILITIES:
The Union, despite having some unexpectedly good facilities, is a bit shabby: 2 bars; 2 cafeterias; general shop; photocopying; vending and games machines; pool table; TV room with cable TV; launderette; showers; cashpoint (Clydesdale Bank); 2 meeting rooms.

CLUBS (NON SPORTING):
Ceramics; Chess; Duke of Edinburgh; International; KGB (role play); Line Dancing.

OTHER ORGANISATIONS:
There's a monthly paper, 'Cogno'.

RELIGIOUS:
Multi-denominational chaplaincy.

PAID WORK: see University of Aberdeen

sports

- Recent successes: skiing, fencing, rowing

Finally, something that gets students interested. Well, some of them. Sometimes. A bit.

SPORTS FACILITIES:
Sports facilities vary from site to site. Students have access to 4 acres of playing fields, 2 sports halls and tennis courts. Some use of the Council facilities.

SPORTING CLUBS:
Aerobics; Circuit Training; Curling; Fitness; Gaelic Athletic; Life-Saving; Surfing; Snowboarding; Ladies' Football; Zhuan Shu Huan (Chinese Boxing).

ATTRACTIONS: see University of Aberdeen

accommodation

IN COLLEGE:
- Self-catering: 25% ● Cost: £38-59(34-36wks)

Availability: About half the 1st years and 10% of others live in. Blocks of self-catering flats make more space at the King St, Woolmanhill and Kepplestone sites and at the Mearns all-male block near the harbour, ½ mile from Schoolhill. There is a head tenancy scheme.

EXTERNALLY: see University of Aberdeen

Housing help: The University Accommodation Office has 6 staff who help by offering a bulletin board and advice on contracts.

welfare

SERVICES:
● <u>Creche</u> ● <u>Lesbian & Gay Society</u>
● <u>Overseas SA</u> ● <u>Minibus</u> ● <u>Self-defence classes</u>

The Student Counselling Service (SCS), which employs 3 counsellors (*and is especially helpful for students from minorities and special needs groups*), is the main source of comfort for students with problems of all sorts. The SA's welfare department is willing to listen *and will do what little it can*. The Medical Advisory Service has nurses and administrative staff and links with local GPs.

Women: Subsidised attack alarms. The former Women's Officer is now the Equal Opportunities Officer, *which means the men complained, presumably.*

Disabled: *Changes have been taking place and most buildings are more-or-less accessible to wheelchair-users.*

FINANCE:
● <u>Ave debt: £1,950</u> ● <u>Access fund: £133,817</u>
● <u>Successful applications (1997): 400</u>

The hardship fund offers *small* short-term loans and there are a few scholarships.

▶▶ Roehampton Institute
see Other Institutions

▶▶ Rose Bruford
see Other Institutions

Royal Academy of Music

▼ ● *The Academy is part of <u>University of London</u>.*
Royal Academy of Music, Marylebone Road, London, NW1 5HT.
Tel: (0171) 873 7373. Fax: (0171) 873 7374.
Students' Union, Royal Academy of Music, Marylebone Road,
London, NW1 5HT. Tel: (0171) 837 7337.

general

Just south of Regent's Park, along Marylebone Road from Madame Tussaud's, stands the striking Edwardian edifice that houses the Royal Academy of Music (RAM to its many friends). *It's one of the pre-eminent music schools in the country, probably in the world, with the notes of current budding geniuses harmonising with the echoes of greats from the past. The RAM is proudly elitist, in the best possible sense, but the students are as financially downtrodden as any in London.*

| 45% | ♂♂♂♂♂♀♀♀♀♀ | 55% |

Sex ratio(M:F): 45%:55% **Founded: 1822**
Full time u'grads: 310 **Part time: 0**
Postgrads: 260 **Non-degree: 240**
Ave course: 4yrs **Ethnic: 20%**
Private school: 30% **Flunk rate: n/a**
Mature students: 2% **Overseas students: 25%**
Disabled students: 0.25% **Staff/student ratio: n/a**
Clearing: 0%

ATMOSPHERE:
The Academy is small, so everybody knows everyone else. The place is steeped in history and musical tradition, with big names from the musical world liable to pop in at any minute. It's friendly and frenetic but with a sense of purpose; this is vocational training for the cut-throat classical music biz, not art for art's sake.

CITY: see University of London

TRAVEL: see University of London
The Academy is near Baker Street tube, with easy access to Paddington, Euston and King's Cross mainline stations.

LIBRARIES & COMPUTERS:
● Books: 125,000 ● Study places: 29
● Computer workstations: 10
There's a modem link to the more substantial facilities of King's College, London.

CAREER PROSPECTS:
Employment figures are difficult to ascertain, since most graduates go freelance immediately. The Development Office runs the 'Music Box' for career-related help and advice.

SPECIAL FEATURES:
● Current professors include early music specialist Christopher Hogwood and conductor Sir Colin Davis.
● The excellent instrument collection includes Wagner's old piano.

FAMOUS ALUMNI:
Sir John Barbirolli (conductor); John Dankworth (jazz musician); Lesley Garrett (opera singer); Evelyn Glennie (percussionist); Dame Myra Hess (pianist); Elton John (*former wig-wearer extraordinaire*); Aled Jones (former chorister, *your gran loved him*); Annie Lennox (ex-Eurythmic); Joanna McGregor (pianist); Simon Rattle (conductor); Sir Arthur Sullivan (Gilbert and...)

FURTHER INFO:
Prospectus. Web site (http://www.ram.ac.uk).

entertainment

CITY: see University of London

ACADEMY:
● Price of a pint of beer: £1.80 ● Glass of wine: £1.20
Bar: *Small and comfy*, the RAM bar can accommodate 100. Open early evening until 9pm; later for special events.

Cinemas: 2 or 3 movies a term.
Food: The college runs a restaurant between 8 and 6, *serving up a high standard of grub which compares favourably for value with the local cafés and sarnie bars.*
Other: Much entertainment obviously centres around 'proper' music and there are countless recital and concert rooms geared up for this. RAMSU does, however, lay on discos, termly balls, international nights, regular jazz nights and everything from karaoke to didgeridoo workshops.

social & political

ROYAL ACADEMY OF MUSIC STUDENTS' UNION (RAMSU):

● 1 sabbatical ● Turnout at last ballot: 50%

RAMSU's facilities extend to an office, a pool table, a microwave oven and a TV lounge. *The union is apolitical; most students wave batons, not banners. Their baton waving did, however, win them Sundays off from rehearsals recently.*

CLUBS (NON SPORTING):
Bellydancing; Homeless Help Project; Tai Chi.

OTHER ORGANISATIONS:
The SU publishes 'RAMSU News'.

PAID WORK:
Students can steward at concerts or get box office work with the big London concert halls and opera houses. There is also help in obtaining paid performance work.

sports

● Recent successes: nothing special

RAM has no sports facilities of its own; students use ULU.

ATTRACTIONS: see University of London

accommodation

IN COLLEGE:
RAM has no accommodation of its own. Students can make use of the Accommodation Offices at King's College, London and the University of London. The Academy also advertises in London papers for landlords who are sympathetic to students – *presumably the ones with thick walls and double-glazing.*

EXTERNALLY: see University of London

welfare

SERVICES:
RAM shares a counsellor with King's College and RAMSU can provide another. Chaplains, deans, tutors are also available. The Academy also has links to medical specialists dealing with problems related to musical performance *(such as supporting Aston Villa and saying 'monstah' when you really come from the Home Counties).*
Disabled: *Access is poor,* although there's a lift to all floors.

FINANCE:
● Ave debt: £1,900 ● Access fund: £47,000
● Successful applications (1997): 46
Bursaries, prizes, trust funds.

Royal Agricultural College

see Other Institutions

Royal College of Music

● **The College is part of <u>University of London</u> and students are entitled to use its facilities.**

Royal College of Music, Prince Consort Road, London, SW7 2BS. Tel: (0171) 589 3643. Fax: (0171) 589 7740. Students' Association, Royal College of Music, Prince Consort Road, London, SW7 2BS. Tel: (0171) 584 8195.

 ## General

Right next to the Albert Hall, over the road from Kensington Gardens (where Peter Pan lives, honest...) is the *imposing* Victorian edifice of the Royal College of Music. It was founded by the Prince of Wales who went on to become the chubby, popular Timothy West lookalike Edward VII. He also had it off with numerous actresses *but we're drifting from the point.* We're talking music, not drama here. The RCM has a worldwide reputation, especially for chamber music.

45% ♂♂♂♂♂ ♀♀♀♀♀ 55%	
Sex ratio(M:F): 45%:55%	Founded: 1882
Full time u'grads: 380	Part time: 0
Postgrads: 190	Non-degree: 0
Ave course: 4yrs	Ethnic: 5%
Private school: 15%	Flunk rate: n/a
Mature students: 2%	Overseas students: 30%
Disabled students: 1%	Staff/student ratio: 1:3
Clearing: 0%	

ATMOSPHERE:
Things are quite laid back (although the workload isn't) and the whole college shuts down at weekends. Students are unified by a love of music, but little else.

CITY: see <u>University of London</u>

TRAVEL: see <u>University of London</u>
Locally, the nearest tubes are: South Kensington; Gloucester Road; Knightsbridge. Nearest rail station: Paddington.

❮Text in italics is PUSH's point of view – take it or leave it.❯

LIBRARIES & COMPUTERS:
- Books: 250,000 ● Study places: 82
- Computer workstations: 10

CAREER PROSPECTS:
- Careers Service ● No of staff: 1full

Employment rates are difficult to assess, since most musicians go straight into freelance work.

SPECIAL FEATURES:
- Exchange schemes are in place with the Universities of California and Western Ontario and numerous European conservatoires.
- There's a unique joint honours Physics and Music degree available in conjunction with Imperial College.

FAMOUS ALUMNI:
Janet Baker, Peter Pears, Joan Sutherland (singers); Julian Bream (guitarist); Benjamin Britten, Gustav Holst, Michael Tippet, Mark Anthony Turnage, Ralph Vaughan Williams (composers); Colin Davis, Neville Marriner (conductors); Barry Douglas (pianist); James Galway (flautist); Vanessa-Mae (*nymphet* violinist); Rick Wakeman (*weirdy beardy* keyboard bloke); Lord Lloyd Webber (*provide your own description*).

FURTHER INFO:
Prospectuses and video (£3.50) from the Registry, plus a web site (http://www.rcm.ac.uk).

entertainment

CITY: see University of London

COLLEGE:
- Price of a pint of beer: £1.50 ● Glass of wine: £1.20

Students tend to use the facilities at Imperial College, next door.

Bar: (1) *Small but lively*; students often indulge in spontaneous bursts of musical virtuosity.

Music venues: 3 halls for concerts and recitals, and an opera theatre.

Food: The college refectory is a popular meeting place, *although it's a bit pricey. The food isn't exactly symphonic, but neither is it cacophonous.*

Others: Discos every month; jazz evenings; theme nights; summer ball.

social & political

RCM STUDENTS' ASSOCIATION:
- 1 sabbatical ● Turnout at last ballot: 36%

Party politics is, if not a dirty word, a bit grubby round the edges.

SU FACILITIES:
Photocopier; games machines; pool table; TV lounge.

OTHER ORGANISATIONS:
The College publishes 'Obbligato', a termly newsletter and 'The Note'; the SU responds with 'Not The Note'. The SA promotes performances by students at schools and hospitals around Kensington.

RELIGIOUS:
- 1 chaplain

PAID WORK: see University of London

sports

- Recent successes: nothing special

Facilities and clubs are shared with Imperial College, London.

ATTRACTIONS: see University of London

accommodation

IN COLLEGE:

- Self-catering: 40% ● Cost: £65(36wks)

All first years who want can be housed in College Hall (a converted bank) and about 20% of other students. *One advantage to living in RCM accommodation is the 24-hr, soundproofed practice suite, to allow for the sort of spontaneous, nocturnal virtuosity that doesn't go down too well in a rented flat. Students who complain that it's a bit crap and noisy really ought to have thought about that beforehand, shouldn't they?*

EXTERNALLY: see University of London

The college welfare officer holds details of appropriate accommodation and maintains a notice board.

welfare

SERVICES:

- Overseas SA ● Postgrad SA

A counsellor is on hand, in addition to 3 Alexander Technique therapists. There's a student health centre at Imperial College with 4 doctors attached.

Disabled: *Access is mixed*; there are lifts and ramps in the theatre and concert halls, but no ramp at the main entrance.

FINANCE:
- Ave debt: n/a ● Access fund: £46,982
- Successful applications (1996): 91

Extensive scholarship and other financial resources are available, including an instrument loan fund.

Royal Free Hospital School of Medicine, London

- *The Medical College is part of University of London and students are entitled to use its facilities.*

Royal Free Hospital School of Medicine, University of London, Rowland Hill Street, London, NW3 2PF. Tel: (0171) 794 0500. Fax: (0171) 794 3505.

Royal Free Hospital School of Medicine Students' Union, Rowland Hill Street, London, NW3 2PF. Tel: (0171) 830 2275. Fax: (0171) 830 2275. E-mail: s.union@rfhsm.ac.uk

General

The Royal Free is about 3 miles as the proverbial crow flies from Trafalgar Square, *in one of London's more up-market, arty, beautiful and, to be frank, richer districts. Living in or near Hampstead takes more than a standard student grant.* The Royal Free Hospital (into which the School is integrated) is near Hampstead Heath (*a pleasant piece of inner-city parkland with fine views and nocturnal promiscuity*). The Royal Free was the first medical school to admit women as students and still maintains a *healthy* sex ratio. The School is due to merge with University College, London in the next few years.

50% ♂♂♂♂♂ ♀♀♀♀♀ 50%	
Sex ratio(M:F): 50%:50%	Founded: 1874
Full time u'grads: 582	Part time: 0
Postgrads: 166	Non-degree: 0
Ave course: 5yrs	Ethnic: n/a
Private school: n/a	Flunk rate: n/a
Mature students: 15%	Overseas students: 9%
Disabled students: n/a	Staff/student ratio: 1:5
Clearing: 0%	

ATMOSPHERE:
The hospital is an early 70s concrete building *and despite attempts to blend it with trees and greenery, it still reminds you of Australian afternoon soaps.* Inside, it's about as good as NHS hospitals get (not that that's saying much), and as relaxed as possible. *Students keep themselves to themselves not bothering much with other London colleges or the University. Instead, they have fostered a strong team spirit, put into practice on the sports fields.*

THE CITY: see University of London

TRAVEL: see University of London
Trains: Nearest station is Hampstead Heath.
Buses: Numbers 24, 46, 168, 268, C11.
Car: Parking is quite difficult (*especially parallel, that's really tough*). There are a few free places at the Hall, but they're *woefully inadequate for the number of students.*
Underground: Belsize Park (Northern Line).
Bicycles: *A lot of students rely on their bikes.* There is practically no theft and they can be locked in sheds.

LIBRARIES & COMPUTERS:
● Books: 27,000 ● Study places: 150
● Computer workstations: 30
24hr access to computing facilities. The library is closed on Sundays.

CAREER PROSPECTS:
As with most med schools, students have a fairly good career plan mapped out, provided they finish the course. The University of London careers service is available for any queries.

FAMOUS ALUMNI:
Drs Hilary Jones and Mark Porter (TV's *hunky yet reassuring medics*).

FURTHER INFO:
Prospectuses for undergrads and postgrads.

entertainment

IN LONDON: see <u>University of London</u>

HAMPSTEAD:
In Hampstead there is a fringe theatre and 3 cinemas including the *arty* Screen on the Hill. The *trendy* Camden Palais club has a student night (admission £4) and the Holly Bush offers live music. *Villa Maria and Ravel's are the best value for nosh but to have fun on a tight budget most students go to Camden (which isn't exactly cheap, either).*

COLLEGE :

● <u>Price of a pint of beer: £1.20</u> ● <u>Glass of wine: £1</u>
3 bars (Doctors' bar, Students' bar and Hospital bar). The Students' bar (cap 350), the Peter Samuel Hall (cap 300) and the New JCR (200) are used for bops and occasional live ents. The Hospital canteen is the main fuel source but the bars and the Servery (*a bit healthier*) provide options. 2 balls a year provide the entertainment highspots.

social & political

THE ROYAL FREE HOSPITAL SCHOOL OF MEDICINE STUDENTS' UNION:

● <u>Turnout at last ballot: 30%</u>
The Union provides a secretarial service for students, a shop, various games, a pool table, Lloyds cashpoint and satellite TV. No political clubs are allowed. 'The Free Press' gossip sheet provides entertainment for the libel lawyers every couple of weeks. Students are also entitled to use the facilities of ULU and <u>University College, London</u>.

CLUBS (NON SPORTING):
Choir; Expedition; Line dancing; Salsa.

sports

● <u>Recent successes: rugby, rowing</u>
Good facilities at the hospital: a swimming pool (equipped for scuba diving); squash courts; badminton; and a weights room. 24 acres of fields in Enfield. *Enthusiasm runs high and standards are excellent for somewhere so small.*

SPORTING CLUBS:
Bungee Jumping; Rowing.

accommodation

IN COLLEGE:
● <u>Self-catering: 20%</u> ● <u>Cost: £43-53</u>
Availability: All 1st years are housed, except those already living in London, some in <u>University of London</u> inter-collegiate accommodation, others in the Francis Gardner Hall; 60% share rooms. 10% of 2nd and 3rd years live in.

EXTERNALLY: see <u>University of London</u>
● <u>Ave rent: £70</u>
Kentish Town, Belsize Park and West Hampstead all have affordable property. Hampstead itself is too expensive for most real doctors, let alone student ones.

welfare

SERVICES:
The SU and tutors are available to deal with personal and academic problems and counselling is provided by the hospital's Department of Psychiatry, Stress Clinic and Occupational Health Clinic.

FINANCE:
- Ave debt: £1,100 ● Access fund: £34,000
- Successful applications (1997): 72

Royal Holloway, London

▼
▼
- *The College is part of <u>University of London</u> and students are entitled to use its facilities.*
Royal Holloway, Egham, Surrey, TW20 0EX.
Tel: (01784) 434455. Fax: (01784) 437520.
E-mail: liaison-office@rhbnc.ac.uk
Royal Holloway Student Union, Egham, Surrey, TW20 0EX.
Tel: (01784) 486300. Fax: (01784) 486312.
E-mail: reception@su.rhbnc.ac.uk

general

Royal Holloway is part of London University, despite being 20 miles away from the capital, a mile from Egham in Surrey, near Thorpe Park and Hampton Court. It is sometimes called London's country campus - *it's certainly as green as the University gets, even if it is all manicured and tamed splendour*. The *extensive* park grounds on a *steep* hill on the fringe of Windsor Park set off the College's *astoundingly beautiful* Founder's Building, an *ornate* red brick and stone structure, based on the Château Chambord in the Loire Valley in France, arranged as a square around grass courtyards with turrets, domes and ornamental carvings all over.

44% ♂♂♂♂♂♀♀♀♀♀♀ 56%	
Sex ratio(M:F): 44%:56%	Founded: 1886
Full time u'grads: 4,492	Part time: 13
Postgrads: 915	Non-degree: 0
Ave course: 3yrs	Ethnic: 15%
Private school: 25%	Flunk rate: 13%
Mature students: 18%	Overseas students: 22%
Disabled students: 4.5%	Staff/student ratio: 1:15
Clearing: 11%	

ATMOSPHERE:
Royal Holloway is starting to shrug off its right-wing past and become much more open and multi-cultural, though still somewhat middle-class. It's just the right size and location

> ❝Girton, Cambridge, has a weekly newsletter, called 'The Bog Sheet', distributed in all college toilets.❞

(small but not claustrophobic; close to London but still green) for fun and friendship and most of the students seem glad to be here.

THE CITY: see University of London

EGHAM:
The closest town to the campus is Egham, about 1 mile away. *It's a typically small, suburban, commutery-type place and it cannot truthfully be described as groovy or student-oriented.*

TRAVEL: see University of London

TRAVEL: EGHAM:
Trains: Trains to Waterloo from Egham every ¼ hour (£3.65).
Buses: *They are infrequent and dear* - 90p single for a 5min journey to the station - but there's a College service every half hour (35p for the same trip) and the SU bus is free to livers-out after 10pm.
Coaches: Egham's just a hop from Heathrow (which is useful if you want to catch a plane anywhere, oddly enough); coaches cost £2.30 to the airport and from there they go anywhere in the UK.
Car: Egham is just outside the M25 London ring road, north of where the M3 crosses it on the way south west. The A30 goes right through the town. *A car is obviously handier than at other London sites but there are clampers on campus.*
Bicycles: *If cycling up the slight hill doesn't put students off, bikes are useful.*

LIBRARIES & COMPUTERS:
● Books: 538,996 ● Study places: 634
● Computer workstations: 520
24-hr access to computing facilities with a swipe card.

CAREER PROSPECTS:
● Careers Service ● No of staff: 4full/7part
● Unemployed after 6mths (1996): 5.5%

SPECIAL FEATURES:
● Royal Holloway owns some of Britain's most valuable works of art. In 1993, amidst much controversy, it flogged a Turner painting to the Getty Museum in the USA for £11million. This money has been put in a trust, the interest will be used to pay towards the up-keep of the *beautiful* Founder's Building.
● The Drama Department has the only stage for Japanese Noh theatre in the UK.

FAMOUS ALUMNI:
David Bellamy (naturalist); Richmal Crompton (writer, 'Just William'); Emma Freud (broadcaster); Felicity Lott, Susan Bullock (opera singers); Francis Wheen (journalist).

FURTHER INFO:
Prospectuses for undergrads and postgrads, departmental brochures, video loan, guide for mature students, guide for international students, web site (http://www.rhbnc.ac.uk).

entertainment

EGHAM:

● <u>Price of a pint of beer: £2</u> ● <u>Glass of wine: £1.50</u>

Egham is about as lively as a hedgehog that got run over last Wednesday, although the Happy Man pub is aptly named, and run by ex-students. The Tap & Spile and Bar 163 are also worth a gargle. There's an OK selection of eateries here and in Englefield Green. **push***plugs: Beehive; Holly Tree; Armstrong Gun; Don Beni (Italian); Bengal Brasserie (Indian). Students looking for the high life go into London instead.*

CITY: see <u>University of London</u>

COLLEGE:

● <u>Price of a pint of beer: £1.40</u> ● <u>Glass of wine: £1.25</u>

Bars: There are 5 bars in all, the busiest being Tommy's (*perhaps because it's on the ground floor of the SU and not such an effort to reach*), the Stumble Inn and the Union Bar. Holloway's is popular with the sporty set.

Theatres: Not 1, but 2 theatres, including a Japanese one. The Touring Theatre group does what it says on the tin, including regular visits to the Edinburgh Fringe Festival.

Cinemas: 1 film a week, *nothing too esoteric.*

Clubs/discos/music venues: 4-5 nights a week there are all flavours of clubbing in the SU (cap 1250), with occasional bands on Fridays, recent examples being My Life Story, Lightning Seeds and *er..* Dannii Minogue.

Cabaret: About twice a term chuckle monsters like Lee & Herring *cause ribs to pop out at the least expected moments at Holloways or the Union.*

Food: The SU-run Gallery Bar *offers the best range* (including a *decent* vegetarian selection) *but some find it a bit pricey. Students who live on campus tend to prefer the University dining halls.*

Others: *Since there's little else to do around this part of the world,* the SU runs ents on virtually every night of the week. Clubs and societies hold functions and there are film nights and everything comes to a star-speckled, champagne-filled head at the Summer Ball (2,000 people, tickets £50 a throw).

social & political

ROYAL HOLLOWAY STUDENTS' UNION:

● <u>4 sabbaticals</u> ● <u>Turnout at last ballot: 27%</u>
● <u>NUS member</u>

The SU used to restrict its political teeth-baring to knotty questions like library opening hours while concentrating on a varied ents and welfare portfolio. It has recently been coming out of its shell, though, and an anti-tuition fee campaign got TV and radio coverage. Golly!

SU FACILITIES:
2nd-hand book stall; bars; coffee bar; satellite TV; photobooth; function halls; 3 minibuses and vans; games machines; bus

service; NatWest bank on campus; uni-run shop.

CLUBS (NON SPORTING):

Acid Jazz; Ballroom Dance; Battle Re-enactment; Beers, Wines & Spirits; Chinese; Chocoholics; Debating; Duke of Edinburgh; Expedition; Impure Science; Individualist; James Bond; Japanese; Pagan; Royal Brokers; Savoy Opera; Technoflux; Touring Theatre.

OTHER ORGANISATIONS:

'The Orbital' is published by the students. There is a Community Action Group and the last Rag raised over £15,000. Radio Station 'Insanity' is getting off the ground.

RELIGIOUS:

● 3 chaplains (CofE, RC, Free Church)

Within college there is a non-denominational chapel and a Muslim prayer room, as well as facilities for Jewish and other persuasions.

PAID WORK:

The SU has plenty of remunerative options.

sports

● Recent successes: cricket, netball, skiing

Enthusiasm and results are excellent, despite some serious inadequacies in facilities. However, a 5-year plan of improvements is underway *and the simple fact of having playing fields on site gives them the edge over other London colleges. Declared London's best sporting college by ULU.*

SPORTS FACILITIES:

There are playing fields on the campus, tennis and netball courts, a *small* gym and a sports hall and at Kingswood Halls of Residence there are new squash courts. There are sporting bursaries for the especially talented.

SPORTING CLUBS:

Aerobics; Caving; Lacrosse; Kick-Boxing; Ninjutsu; Softball; Sky-Diving; Surf; Thai Boxing.

ATTRACTIONS:

Horsey types can visit Ascot or watch polo in Windsor Great Park. Wentworth and Sunningdale are *easy* travelling distance too.

accommodation

IN COLLEGE:

● Catered: 38% ● Cost: £55-68(30-39wks)
● Self-catering: 10% ● Cost: £55-59(30-50wks)

Availability: All 1st years and about half the finalists can live in, but very few 2nd years. There are big and modern new halls or, for *spacious rooms and kudos*, there are rooms in the Founder's Building. 8% have to share (only in Founder's and Kingswood). In Reid Hall, solely for finalists, rooms have en suite showers and loos. Self-catering (for 3rd years and postgrads only) in the recently extended Runnymede Hall and Penrose Court. Students must vacate most rooms during the holidays so the College can host the lucrative conference trade. *The dining rooms have come in for criticism.*

EXTERNALLY:

● Ave rent: £55

Availability: *Students must expect to look early to find anywhere decent, but, for a price, there is just about enough.*

Englefield Green is the most convenient area but many go as far as Staines (4 to 5 miles) for the better social life it offers... better than Egham, that is.

Housing help: The College Accommodation Service provides vacancy sheets and standard contracts.

welfare

SERVICES:
- Nightline ● Lesbian & Gay Society
- Mature SA ● Overseas SA ● Self-defence classes

There are 4 counsellors employed by the College and the SU has a Welfare Officer. There is a nursery for 2-8 year olds. Other services include a legal aid solicitor, drug counselling and attack alarms.

Disabled: *Access is pretty bad in some parts of the campus - the older parts mainly. Things are improving but potential applicants are encouraged to contact the registrar before submitting an application.*

FINANCE:
- Ave debt: £1,450 ● Access fund: £130,819
- Successful applications (1997): 238

Loans from the Principal's Hardship Fund have to be repaid before students are allowed to graduate.

▶▶ Royal Military College of Science

see Cranfield University

Royal Veterinary College, London

- **The College is part of University of London.**

The Royal Veterinary College, Royal College Street, London, NW1 0TU. Tel: (0171) 468 5000. Fax: (0171) 388 2342. Royal Veterinary College Union Society, Hawkshead Campus, Hawkshead Lane, North Mimms, Hatfield, Herts, AL9 7TA. Tel: (01707) 666310. Fax: (01707) 652090.

general

You won't be surprised to learn that RVC (as its chums call it) only teaches students how to be vets. It's all to do with training people to make the sort of decisions that have Rolf Harris in floods of tears, so if you can't hack 5 years of that, stop reading now. The College's main site is 1¼ miles from Trafalgar Square in Camden, *one of the trendiest, buzziest areas of London.* The redbrick College buildings here are home to the pre-clinical teaching and administration. The College's Hawkshead campus, a couple of miles from Hatfield, is set in the *relaxed, commuter belt* countryside (see University of Hertfordshire). It is a large self-contained green site with

low buildings accommodating clinical students. In other words, students spend 2 years at Camden, *enjoying city life,* and then move out to *almost tediously tranquil* Hawkshead, *which is beautiful even if much of it smells of poo. The atmosphere is quite intense and geared to studying, although there is also a lot of sport going on.*

34% ♂♂♂♂♀♀♀♀♀♀ 66%

Sex ratio(M:F): 34%:66%	Founded: 1791
Full time u'grads: 532	Part time: 0
Postgrads: 124	Non-degree: 0
Ave course: 5yrs	Ethnic: n/a
Private school: n/a	Flunk rate: n/a
Mature students: 21%	Overseas students: 11%
Disabled students: 0	Staff/student ratio: 1:7
Clearing: 0%	

THE CITY: see <u>University of London</u>

TRAVEL: see <u>University of London</u>
Trains: Nearest stations are King's Cross, St Pancras, Euston and Camden Road for the Camden site. Two trains every hour between King's Cross and Potter's Bar (£3.05) for Hawkshead.
Buses: Numbers 46 and 214 pass close to the Camden site.
Car: A lot of students have cars at Hawkshead.
Underground: Camden Town or Mornington Crescent (Northern Line).
Bicycles: Racks are provided on both sites.
Hawkshead: See <u>University of Hertfordshire</u>.

LIBRARIES & COMPUTERS:
● <u>Books: 16,000</u> ● <u>Study places: 30</u>
● <u>Computer workstations: 50</u>
Library open till 8pm on Sundays for serious swotting.

CAREER PROSPECTS:
Students can use the careers facilities of <u>University of London</u>.

SPECIAL FEATURES:
● During vacations in the 1st and 2nd years, students have to work on farms.

FURTHER INFO:
Undergrad/postgrad prospectus, web site (http://www.rvc.ac.uk).

entertainment

IN LONDON: see <u>University of London</u>

CAMDEN & HAWKSHEAD:
Obviously there is a lot more going on near Camden than Hawkshead, but prices are higher. The famous weekend market is still pretty cool, especially for young, slightly alternative Japanese tourists. If you're not one, it can get a bit samey. pushplugged *pubs at Hawkshead: The Bridge; The Maypole; avoid Williots. In Camden: Prince Alfred; Lord John Russell.*

> **Loughborough University has warned its students that they could face 7 years' imprisonment for stealing traffic cones.**

COLLEGE:
● <u>Price of a pint of beer: £1.55</u> ● <u>Glass of wine: £1.30</u>
2 bars, one at each site. Occasional bands play at refectories on both sites. Discos every other Friday at Camden. 1 ball a year at each site. ULU facilities are open to RVC students. Both Hawkshead and Camden have refectories open from 10.30am to 2.30pm *but choice is poor.*

social & political

ROYAL VETERINARY COLLEGE UNION SOCIETY:

● <u>Turnout at last ballot: 65%</u>
The Union is low key and tends to concentrate on sports rather than other activities. It provides welfare services, a shop, a pool table and a minibus but there are very few non-sporting societies. There is, however, a Rag week. *For religious advice, one reverend is willing to help worshippers of any persuasion.*

sports

● <u>Recent successes: riding, sailing</u>
Sports provision is good, especially at Hawkshead, which has tennis and squash courts, a heated pool, etc. Unfortunately, nobody's discovered a way to make sticking your fist up a cow's bum a competitive sport.

SPORTING CLUBS:
Mountaineering; Rowing; Water Polo.

accommodation

IN COLLEGE:
● <u>Catered: 11%</u> ● <u>Cost: £73(45wks)</u>
● <u>Self-catering: 6%</u> ● <u>Cost: £53(45wks)</u>
Availability: In Camden students stay in London University accommodation for 2 years so the real scenario is better than the figures above might suggest. 85% of 1st years are housed here and 10% of finalists can also live in. The catered accommodation at Hawkshead has pool and snooker tables and computers on site. All accommodation is in single rooms.
Car parking: *In Camden, parking is a real problem,* but in Hawkshead it's free *and there is plenty of it.*

EXTERNALLY: see <u>University of London</u>
Camden: Most Camden students live in Kentish Town which is a bit cheaper than Camden. The College and SU keep details of housing.
Hawkshead: Potter's Bar is the best place to look for a place, but you'll have to compete with students from <u>University of Hertfordshire</u>.

········ welfare

SERVICES:
The SU and the College go halves on a bought-in counselling service.

FINANCE:
● Access fund: £24,000 ● Successful applications (1995): 20

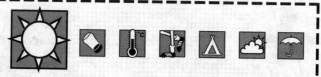

Fold-out guide to symbols inside back cover

❝If you have any comments about PUSH or fancy being involved in the next edition, please write to PUSH, McGraw-Hill Publishing Company, Shoppenhangers Road, Maidenhead, Berkshire SL6 2QL.❞

S

University of Salford

- Scarborough University College
  see Other Institutions

- School of Economics
  see LSE

- School of Oriental & African Studies
  see SOAS

School of Pharmacy, London

- School of Slavonic & East European
  Studies
  see SSEES

- Scottish College of Textiles
  see Heriot-Watt University

University of Sheffield

- Sheffield City Poly
  see Sheffield Hallam University

Sheffield Hallam University

- Shrivenham
  see Cranfield University

- Silsoe
  see Cranfield University

- Slavonic & East European Studies
  see SSEES

SOAS

South Bank University

- South West Poly
  see University of Plymouth

University of Southampton

Southampton Institute of Higher Education

SSEES

University of St Andrews

Continued next page ▶▶

▶▶ *Continued from last page*

- St David's University College
  see Lampeter, University of Wales

St George's Hospital Medical School,
London

- St Mark & St John
  see Other Institutions

- St Martin's University College
  see Other Institutions

- St Martin's College of Art
  see The London Institute

- St Mary's Hospital
  see Imperial College, London

- St Mary's University College
  see Other Institutions

- St Thomas's Hospital
  see King's College, London

Staffordshire University

University of Stirling

- Stockton
  see University of Durham

University of Strathclyde

University of Sunderland

University of Surrey

Surrey Institute of Art & Design

University of Sussex

Swansea, University of Wales

- Swansea Institute
  see Other Institutions

❝Liverpool University awarded
Arthur C Clarke an honorary degree
by satellite link to Sri Lanka.❞

· ·

University of Salford

▼ University of Salford, Salford, M5 4WT. Tel: (0161) 295 5000.
▼ Fax: (0161) 295 5999. E-mail: ug.prospectus@salford.ac.uk
Salford Students' Union, The Crescent, Salford, M5 4WT.
Tel: (0161) 736 7811. Fax: (0161) 737 1633.

General

At the western end of Manchester is the city of Salford, *but
screw up your eyes and you can't see the join. Salford isn't
magically different, nor is it sufficiently far to make it properly
distinct and so everything we said about Manchester (see
University of Manchester) applies equally to Salford with the
added benefit of* push*'s insights.* After all, it's only 2 miles
to the centre of Manchester. *It's certainly not the posh end of
Manchester*, but the 34-acre site of the University is quite
green and *less ugly* than many modern campuses. With a few
redbrick exceptions, the buildings have all been built in the
last 20 years. The University has strong links with industry,
particularly local firms.

55% ♂♂♂♂♂♂♀♀♀♀♀ **45%**

Sex ratio(M:F): 55%:45%	Founded: 1967
Full time u'grads: 11,692	Part time: 3,154
Postgrads: 849	Non-degree: 855
Ave course: 3-4yrs	Ethnic: 15%
Private school: n/a	Flunk rate: n/a
Mature students: 35%	Overseas students: 11%
Disabled students: 3%	Staff/student ratio: 1:15
Clearing: 20%	

ATMOSPHERE:
*The University's strong local links provide a real community
identity for students. Students get the best of both worlds: a
campus university in a small neighbourhood town at the same
time as the metropolitan high life of Manchester, although the
latter tends to overshadow any specifically Salfordian local
colour. There's a good mix of ages and backgrounds. The
recent merger with the local University College means the
student body is more spread out than before, putting a slight
strain on social cohesion.*

THE SITES:
Peel House/Bury Campus: (2,000 students) The school of
nursing is in Eccles, 2 miles from the main site while midwifery
is taught in Bury, 12 miles away.

THE CITY: see University of Manchester

SALFORD:
● Population: 217,900
Salford has its own small and friendly community. Occasionally,

it looks somewhat like a Lowry painting, full of matchstick men and matchstick cats and dogs, factory gates and the rest of it. Not surprising, really, since this is Lowry's home town. The City Art Gallery has the largest single collection of his works. *Occasionally, it also looks like a scene from 'Coronation Street'.* Again, no surprise, chuck, as this is where it is set. But far more often, it is the rebuilt Salford that shows its face, the docklands have been developed and right in the heart of *The Grim North* are all sorts of new constructions: high rise blocks; shopping malls and supermarkets; libraries; book shops; banks (including a Midland on campus); and everything else a town needs, including 3 museums, an 'urban heritage park' and its own nightlife.

TRAVEL: see University of Manchester
Local: Salford is covered by Manchester's bus and train networks which are reliable, comprehensive and generally cheap. Salford Crescent station is actually on the campus, although for some national services it may be necessary to change at one of Manchester's stations (trains every 15 mins). Buses go to Manchester city centre every 3 mins.

LIBRARIES & COMPUTERS:
- Books: 397,233 ● Study places: 1,347
- Computer workstations: 795

There are 7 libraries in all. Supply of both books and computers hasn't met the demand, especially from IT students.

CAREER PROSPECTS:
- Careers Service ● No of staff: 10full/2part
- Unemployed after 6mths (1996): 10%

FAMOUS ALUMNI:
Bill Beaumont (ex-England rugby captain); John Cooper Clarke (poet); Ieuan Evans (rugby player); LS Lowry (artist); Jonathon Morris (actor); Murray Lachlan Young (poet).

FURTHER INFO:
Prospectuses for undergrads and postgrads, part-time course brochures and a web site (http://www.salford.ac.uk).

entertainment

CITY: see University of Manchester

SALFORD:
- Price of a pint of beer: £1.65 ● Glass of wine: £1.25

Cinemas: Even Mancunians leave more local cinemas to come to the 8-screen multiplex at Salford Quays.
Pubs: The real Coronation St has been demolished long since, but the spirit of 'The Rover's Return' continues in many a local, although many are quite rough and you don't get Betty's hotpots. *pushplugs: The Old Pint Pot; The Crescent; The Black Horse; Wallness Tavern.*
Food: *pushplugs: Hanrahan's, Frankie & Benny's and Starvin' Marvin's offer good value and a student-friendly environment at Salford Quays; Punter's Bistro.*

UNIVERSITY:
- Price of a pint of beer: £1.60 ● Glass of wine: £1.20

Bars: *The Pavilion ('Pav') (cap 1,000) and the Wallness Tavern*

('Walley') are the main all-day drinking dens; the Lowry is pretty packed at lunchtimes. There's also the Sub Club Bar, mainly used for ents.

Theatres: The acquisition of UCS has seen a rise in the standard and quantity of drama.

Cinemas: The 'Culture Club' shows the latest *mainstream* vids 3 times a week.

Clubs/discos/music venues: The Pav is the Union's customised club venue where 3 times a week sound and visions rule (£1-3). There are regular house and indie nights but guest DJs raise the stakes every now and then. Live music tends to be restricted to local and cover bands.

Food: There's a restaurant, 6 cafeterias and 2 sandwich bars and the bars also do snacky type things. *While it's not going to earn a Michelin star, the customers seem quite happy with the quality and cost.*

Others: On campus, there's a gallery, sometimes exhibiting student work, and a campus pottery. 5 balls a year.

social & political

SALFORD STUDENTS' UNION:

● 4 sabbaticals ● Turnout at last ballot: 15%
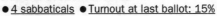
● NUS member

The Union's main thrust is its professionally handled services and entertainments. It even has its own company, SUPER Services, which runs the student pub among other things. Agitation isn't uncommon either, with the SU prodding the University over the quality of food and the library, while 2,000 (yes, count 'em) students got involved in recent anti-fees demonstrations.

SU FACILITIES:

The Union has *felicitous* facilities on 3 sites and a main Union building, called University House. Plans are afoot to put facilities in the nursing and midwifery colleges. The total gamut of provisions provided includes: 4 bars and a pub (see above); travel agency; print shop (including bookbinding); 3 shops (selling stationery, groceries and 2nd-hand books); hairdressers; computer shop; opticians; mortgage advisory service (*that's a unique one*); Interflora service; Endsleigh Insurance office; customised disco; cafeterias and snack bars; 2 minibuses (for hire); vending, video and games machines; photo booth; juke box; launderette; TV and function rooms.

CLUBS (NON SPORTING):

China & Hong Kong; Cyprus; Hellenic; Malaysian; Pakistan; Singapore; Turkish; Wine.

OTHER ORGANISATIONS:

The Union publishes 'Student Direct', a weekly newspaper, and 'Pulp', a monthly magazine. The charity Rag is part of MUSA (the umbrella spongers for all Manchester's universities). The Community Services Group involves a healthy 200 or so students in a range of local help projects and has a permanent member of staff.

RELIGIOUS:

● 4 chaplains (CofE, RC, Methodist, URC)

There is a chaplaincy in the main lecture hall building, a

Muslim prayer room on campus and Manchester's 2 rabbis act as chaplains to Jewish students in the area.

PAID WORK: see University of Manchester

sports

● Recent successes: cycling

While Salford may not be nationally famous for its sporting record, enthusiasm and facilities are above average. A campaign by the students successfully won them floodlights for their playing fields.

SPORTS FACILITIES:
There's a leisure centre right next to the Union building for indoor sports including a gym, sports hall, multigym, 4 squash courts and a snooker room. *Oh, and the best student climbing wall in the country.* On the campus, there are floodlit playing fields and all-weather pitches. New swimming pool with sauna, jacuzzi and sunbeds. There's also a local swimming pool a mile from the University. The Union employs an Outdoor Pursuits Officer who takes responsibility for encouraging involvement in the kinds of sports which make thermal pants popular, like canoeing, caving, mountaineering and so on.

SPORTING CLUBS:
Cave & Pothole; Kung Fu; Lawn Tennis; Mountaineering; Mountain Bike; Nin Jutsu; Paintball; Rowing; Rugby League; Tai Chi; Water Polo.

ATTRACTIONS: see University of Manchester

accommodation

IN COLLEGE:
● Catered: 5% ● Cost: £62-85(31wks)

● Self-catering: 28% ● Cost: £35-49(35-50wks)
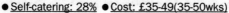
Availability: *None of the accommodation blocks is too far from the campus.* All 1st years who apply in time are guaranteed accommodation, and if self-catering, there's a choice of blocks of rooms, blocks of flats, courts of blocks of flats or rooms and the large Student Village (1,612 places in terraced single sex houses on the old race course at Castle Irwell). Catered accommodation is available at Peel Park. Nobody has to share. The University also operates a head tenancy scheme with 1,028 places.
Car parking: Although a permit is needed, there's *generally adequate* free parking around the student accommodation.

EXTERNALLY: see University of Manchester
Students who can't find anything closer than Eccles are not looking hard enough. The Union-run Accommodation Office can help students find housing with a vacancies board and newsletter. *Avoid Ordsall and Higher Broughton.*

welfare

SERVICES:
● Nightline ● Lesbian & Gay Society ● Mature SA

● Overseas SA ● Minibus ● Equal Opportunities Officer
● Self-defence classes
The Union runs its own advice centre with a visiting solicitor

every Thursday. The University Health Centre has male and female doctors, 3 nurses as well as 1 full- and 5 part-time counsellors. Each student also has a personal tutor. Overseas students can turn to the Overseas Student Secretary or the University's Overseas Students Counsellor for problems which relate particularly to them.

Disabled: *All new buildings have ramps and facilities are improving gradually.* There is a Learning Support Co-ordinator who helps with special needs.

FINANCE:
● Ave debt: £1,650 ● Access fund: £187,258
● Successful applications (1997): 279
The Registrar's Department can also offer loans of up to £150 from its hardship fund, but students cannot register for their next year of study until this has been repaid.

▶▶ **Scarborough University College**
see Other Institutions

▶▶ **School of Economics**
see LSE

▶▶ **School of Oriental & African Studies**
see SOAS

School of Pharmacy, London

● *The College is part of University of London and students are entitled to use its facilities.*
The School of Pharmacy, 29 Brunswick Square, London, WC1N 1AX. Tel: (0171) 753 5800. Fax: (0171) 753 5829. E-mail: registry@cua.ulsop.ac.uk
School of Pharmacy Student Union, 29 Brunswick Square, London, WC1N 1AX. Tel: (0171) 753 5809.

General

Close to Russell Square, ³⁄₄ mile from Trafalgar Square, is the School of Pharmacy, a *not unattractive* brown brick building with big and *austere* windows and an art deco interior. *The atmosphere is as much like a school as a university college; there is a strong work ethic and the really wild social animals have to look to ULU or UCL for a bestial howl. There's an unusually high proportion of women for a science-based college and there are also lots of students of Asian origin.*

40% ♂♂♂♂♀♀♀♀♀ 60%	
Sex ratio(M:F): 40%:60%	Founded: 1842
Full time u'grads: 430	Part time: 2
Postgrads: 115	Non-degree: 0
Ave course: 4yrs	Ethnic: 65%
Private school: n/a	Flunk rate: n/a
Mature students: 20%	Overseas students: 20%
Disabled students: 6%	Staff/student ratio: 1:9
Clearing: 5%	

THE CITY: see <u>University of London</u>

TRAVEL: see <u>University of London</u>
Trains: Nearest stations are Euston, King's Cross & St Pancras.
Buses: Numbers 17, 45, 46, 68 and 168 pass near by.
Car: *The only available parking is very expensive.*
Underground: Russell Square (Piccadilly line).
Bicycles: There are bike stands provided but *the traffic is horrendous so be warned.*

LIBRARIES & COMPUTERS:
- <u>Books: 50,000</u> ● <u>Study places: 75</u>
- <u>Computer workstations: 40</u>

The library has recently been extended. *Computer provision could be better* but students can use <u>UCL</u>'s facilities and a new IT room will open in Autumn 98.

CAREER PROSPECTS:
- <u>Unemployed after 6mths (1996): 1%</u>

If students really need help the University's Careers Service is available but there's little unemployment in this sector.

FURTHER INFO:
Prospectuses for undergrads. Web site (http://194.66.95.129).

entertainment

IN LONDON: see <u>University of London</u>

COLLEGE:
- <u>Price of a pint of beer: £1.50</u> ● <u>Glass of wine: £1.10</u>

The JCR Bar is a bit smoky - *you'd think this lot would be anti-nicotine zealots* - and is open 5-7pm Mon-Thurs and till midnight on Fridays for discos. There are occasional comedy and jazz performances but ULU is pretty close. The film club shows 1 video a fortnight. The popular cafeteria (open 8.30am to 4pm, no food served between 2pm and 3pm) serves *cheap, institutional* food, and is the hang-out for students during the day while the bar's closed. There's an

> ❝ The Sex Pistols played their first proper gig at St Martin's College (now part of London Institute). ❞

annual formal ball in a posh hotel and the summer-time Garden Party with sport, barbeques and a disco.

social & political

SCHOOL OF PHARMACY STUDENTS' UNION:
● Turnout at last ballot: 42%

The Union takes a completely apolitical stance. It runs the bar, a general shop (open about once a week), games room and *limited* ents. There is a *supposedly* fortnightly newsletter. *Surprisingly productive* Rag raised £2,500 last year.

CLUBS (NON SPORTING):
Chinese; Entertainment.

sports

● Recent successes: nothing special

The various playing fields in Enfield (rugby, hockey, football, tennis, netball) are shared with the Royal Free Hospital.

SPORTING CLUBS:
Kabbadi.

ATTRACTIONS: see University of London

accommodation

IN COLLEGE:
Availability: The School has no accommodation of its own but, with the University's intercollegiate housing, most 1st years from outside London can be housed, along with a good number of finalists.

EXTERNALLY: see University of London

welfare

SERVICES:
There's a pastoral care scheme run by the Registrar who doubles as Welfare Officer. Personal tutors are available to give help. Other welfare services are provided by ULU and the University Health Service.
Disabled: *Limited access in parts, but the buildings have lifts and ramps in places.*

FINANCE:
● Access fund: £14,100 ● Successful applications (1997): 29
Some postgraduate scholarships available and a small hardship fund.

● ●

▶▶ **School of Slavonic & East European Studies**
see SSEES

● ●

▶▶ **Scottish College of Textiles**

see Heriot-Watt University

● ●

University of Sheffield

The University of Sheffield, Sheffield, S10 2TN.
Tel: (0114) 222 2000. Fax: (0114) 272 8014.
E-mail: ug.admissions@sheffield.ac.uk
University of Sheffield Union of Students, Western Bank,
Sheffield, S10 2TG. Tel: (0114) 222 8606.
Fax: (0114) 275 2506. E-mail: union@sheffield.ac.uk

General

Sheffield, England's 4th largest city, is the closest city to the
north-east corner of the Derbyshire Peak District and 1 of the
furthest places from the coast in the whole of Britain. Most
people immediately connect it with the steel industry - knives,
forks and razor blades. Fair enough, that's what made the
place famous and to the east, there's still a *sordid* reminder of
industrial demise. Now the city is *a busy and bustling but
friendly place* with a modern centre and compact Victorian
suburbs. The University is 15 minutes walk (¾ mile) due west
from the city centre on a campus extending over about a mile
of buildings massaged into the surrounding urban setting.
Almost all the buildings are less than a century old and have
been constructed with some thought and care. Mostly they're
attractive redbrick buildings, although there are a few more
modern structures - the arts tower and library, which have just
been given a Grade II listing, are *quite appealing* glass high
rises.

50% ♂♂♂♂♂♀♀♀♀ 50%	
Sex ratio(M:F): 50%:50%	Founded: 1905
Full time u'grads: 14,171	Part time: 1,870
Postgrads: 2,512	Non-degree: 0
Ave course: 3/4yrs	Ethnic: n/a
Private school: n/a	Flunk rate: 12%
Mature students: 10%	Overseas students: 13.1%
Disabled students: 4.5%	Staff/student ratio: 1:14
Clearing: n/a	

ATMOSPHERE:
*Nearly ⅓ of students stay in Sheffield after graduation which
can't be bad. That's probably because, unlike some cities,
being a student in Sheffield is to 'live' here for 3 years rather
than just 'stay' here. The University accommodation has its
limitations in that only a small number live in after the first
year so students go out into the community which welcomes
them. It also means students form family groups for the
purpose of sharing a house, so they form strong friendships.
Student life is hectic and full of opportunities - the SU is wide
awake - throbbing with a heady mix of town and gown
activities. Sheffield has a good cultural and racial mix which is*

reflected among the students, who willingly jump headfirst onto any bandwagon in the belief that their actions might actually make a difference.

THE CITY:
- Population: 499,700 ● London: 147miles
- Manchester: 35miles ● Birmingham: 67miles

'WELCOME TO SHEFFIELD, THE HOME OF BRITISH CUTLERY' reads a sign on the outskirts of the city but, honestly, it's got a hell of a lot more than that, being the cultural core of a wide catchment, offering all sorts of entertainments and diversions. Cars are diverted from pedestrian parts of the modern city centre. It's a hilly, clean, litterless city, threaded by 3 rivers. The old industrial area has recently been redeveloped and includes the site for 1991's World Student Games, which left Sheffield well set for leisure and sports facilities. The suburbs in the south-west, where the University accommodation is based, were described by John Betjeman as one of 'England's prettiest suburbs'. *As far as amenities are concerned, Sheffield has it all, or almost: local luxuries like late-night shops, 52 parks, street markets, museums and galleries (the City Museum, the Mappin Art Gallery and so on). There are fewer bookshops than might be expected,* although 4 big ones and many 2nd hand. *Special mention must go to the vast Meadowhall Shopping Centre, 1 of Europe's largest. It's known as Meadowhell to some, but its sheer range and size is astonishing.*

TRAVEL:
Trains: Sheffield Station offers many routes nationally, including London (£29.35), Birmingham (£12.95), Edinburgh (£34.80) and more.
Coaches: Sheffield is served by South Yorkshire Transport as well as National Express whose services go to London (£12.50), Birmingham (£13.75) and other destinations.
Car: 10 mins off the M1, Sheffield is also visited by the A57, A61, A616 and A631. 20 mins off the end of the M18.
Air: Sheffield's own brand new airport is now open.
Hitching: *For getting out to the M1 a bus is needed, but then students can cruise by the rule of thumb.*
Local: Local buses run till about 11pm, but before then, they're *frequent, reliable and quite cheap.* The local minibuses are *even better,* not because they run any later, but because they go everywhere. *The Supertram is best of all, 'cos it's fun and cheap* (£1.80 all-day pass for students) with 3 out-of-town routes.
Taxis: *Worthy wheels for after 11pm.* Private companies are cheaper than the black cabs. Either way it's over £1 per mile.
Bicycles: *Everything may be within thigh power, but it's quite hilly and pedal pinchers prowl.* Endsleigh is considering withdrawing its insurance cover on bikes in Sheffield.

LIBRARIES & COMPUTERS:
- Books: 1,300,000 ● Study places: 2,230
- Computer workstations: 1,000

There are 2 main libraries and 10 of the 63 departments also have their own mini collections. The computer hardware includes 100 Apple Macs.

CAREER PROSPECTS:
- Careers Service ● No of staff: 18full/8part
- Unemployed after 6mths (1996): 7.6%

FAMOUS ALUMNI:
Carol Barnes (newsreader); David Blunkett MP (Lab); Eddie Izzard (comedian); Amy Johnson (aviator); Jack Rosenthal (writer); Richard Roberts (Nobel prize-winning scientist); Helen Sharman (Britain's first astronaut); Dave Weatherall (footballer).

FURTHER INFO:
Prospectuses for undergrads and postgrads. Further info on the web sites (http://www.shef.ac.uk and http://www.shef.ac.uk/~union).

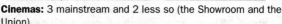

entertainment

THE CITY:
- Price of a pint of beer: £1.65 ● Glass of wine: £1.80

Cinemas: 3 mainstream and 2 less so (the Showroom and the Union).

Theatres: The Crucible may be famous for the World Snooker Championship, but also features *top* shows in its main theatre (cap 1,000) and more alternative productions in its studio. The Lyceum also hosts many plays and concerts. Both theatres offer student discounts. There are some smaller community theatres and several arts centres and galleries.

Pubs: *Dead friendly local pubs and remember, this is Yorkshire (South Yorkshire), so there's never a brew too few. The SU runs a couple of pubs itself, but* **push** *would also like to shove in quick plugs for the Frog & Parrot ('strongest beer in the world'); the Cavendish; Bar Coast, the Forum and the Halcyon (cool-as-fridge pre-club hangouts); and Scruffy Murphy's. Overall, 'Irish' pubs such as O'Neill's are in the ascendant and West Street is the area of biggest concentration.*

Clubs/discos: *The grooves are cut deep in the streets of Sheffield although the usual mob of lager-swilling bulletheads might want to get in your way (see 'Mis-Shapes' by local wordsmith J Cocker Esq for full sociological analysis).* **push** *plugs: Rise (indie) at the Leadmill; My Sushi at the Music Factory; Delirious (happy house) at Niche; Double Decade (retro) at Millionaires; Gatecrasher at Republic; and many more...*

Music venues: The Arena and Don Valley Stadium deal with the sort of acts punters are happy to watch through binoculars; City Hall copes with the mainstream; the Leadmill, the

> ❛The registrar and finance director of Hull University agreed to live on £10 each for a week, to see what life was like for hard-pressed students.❜

Roundhouse and Hallamshire Hotel are the major indie venues. Recently in Sheffield: Michael Jackson, Oasis and M-People.

Eating out: *As might be expected in a place this size, there's the usual range of fast grease franchises and BSE vans until the small hours but* **push** *plugs for the more discerning budget gourmet go to: Balti King and Butlers Balti Bar; Blue Moon (veggie); Fat Jack's (burgers). The Italian restaurants down West Street are also very popular.*

UNIVERSITY:

● <u>Price of a pint of beer: £1.25</u> ● <u>Glass of wine: £1.05</u>
SU facilities, already good, have been improved further by a new £4m extension.

Bars: Bar One (capacity 600) is packed most of the time, despite the fact it's not even on campus. The new Interval is *slightly more laid back* and is marketed as 'an eating and drinking experience'. The SU also runs the Fox & Duck in Broomhill and there are 5 bars whose opening hours revolve around gigs and other events.

Theatres: The University Theatre Company puts on 3 plays a term in the University Drama Studio and has also recently taken shows to the Edinburgh Fringe.

Film: 4-6 films a week in the new 400-seat auditorium; *a good mix of mainstream and alternative movies.*

Music venues: Concerts are held in the *fantastic* Octagon Centre (cap 1,500) - not only an 8-sided building, but also *an arts venue to run with the best.* Live jazz at the Interval on Sundays. Recent band appearances include the Chemical Brothers, Skunk Anansie, Bluetones, Fun Lovin' Criminals, Symposium and Placebo.

Clubs/discos: 6 club events a week including the *brazenly naff, astonishingly popular* Pop Tarts retro night and Fabulous, a 60s to 90s party night. *For those keen to hang onto their cred,* visiting clubs and DJs have included Megadog and Paul Oakenfold in recent months.

Cabaret: The SU hosts cabaret nights 3 or 4 times a term in The Foundry, with big names (eg recently, Sean Hughes and Eddie Izzard).

Food: The University-run Food Court supplies *satisfying* school dinners; the Interval bar does *posh* pasta and salady type stuff. Laxely's does a *fab* English breakfast. *These, and the numerous other eateries around the place, offer excellent value.*

Other: Balls and annual beer festival.

········· social & political

UNIVERSITY OF SHEFFIELD UNION OF STUDENTS:
● <u>7 sabbaticals</u> ● <u>Turnout at last ballot: 26.9%</u>
● <u>NUS member</u>
The SU's facilities are enough to have other unions drooling at the sweet-shop window but they don't lounge on their laurels. The exec is efficient and proactive and there's even a suggestion box for student complaints - which are usually restricted to bar prices and the mysterious veggieburger shortage. The Union's anti-fees demo was one of the largest in the country.

SU FACILITIES:

5 bars; 2 pubs; 2 snack bars; pizza kiosk; 1 staff canteen; travel agent; general shop; advice centre; NatWest Bank; Endsleigh Insurance; cinema; ticket agency; prayer rooms; creche; TV lounge; pool and snooker tables; daily stalls and Thursday market; computer suite; photocopiers; video games; juke boxes; vending machines; launderette and conference facilities.

CLUBS (NON SPORTING):

AIESEC; Anime Anonymous; Ballroom & Latin American; Bridge; Bangladesh; Birders; Ceilidh; Change Ringers; Contemporary Dance; Charter 88; Children's Education; Chinese; Chinese Students & Scholars; CND; Continental; Creative Writing; Cuban; Debating; Duke of Edinburgh; Dungeons & Dragons; Egyptian; Everton; Flying Teapots; Free Education; Guinness; Hellenic; Hemp; Hindu; Hispanic; Indian; Indonesian; International Students' Choir; Iranian; Iraqi; Irish; Israeli; Italian; Kenyan; Korean; Japanese; Journalism; Kenyan; Liverpool; Malaysian; Man City; Mauritian; Mexican & Latin; Mileage Marathon; Medieval; Music; Ozymandius Poetry; Pagan; Pakistan; Pantomime; Philippine Islands; Politics; Portuguese Speaking; Planet Morris; Radio; Real Ale; Reunion; Revolutionary Communists; Rocky Horror; Salsa; Scandinavian; Scout & Guides; Shiatsu; Sikh; Soccer Supporters; Sound; Sri Lankan and Maldivian; St John Ambulance; Star Trek; Student Christian Movement; Students Industrial; Taiwan; Tamil; Turkish; United Nations; Vegetarian; Vodka; Wargames; Wildlife; Young Socialists.

OTHER ORGANISATIONS:

'Steel Press' is the free, fortnightly newspaper published by, but independent of, the SU which also produces the weekly 'What's On' and 'Rubicon' arts magazine. A new campus radio station Sure also operates on a temporary FM license. The Student's Charity Fund has a full-time member of staff and raised over £10,000 last year. The Student Community Action group is *immense,* involving between 700 and 800 students in all sorts of community work (teaching English, helping the elderly, etc).

RELIGIOUS:
- ● 8 chaplains

There are centres for both Jews and Muslims in the SU. In town there is no shortage of places to pray including 2 cathedrals (Anglican & Catholic).

PAID WORK:

Sheffield may offer a lot of things to students, but employment is often hard to come by. Only the usual bar and restaurant work.

.... sports

- ● Recent successes: rugby, lacrosse, water polo

The amenities are possibly the best in the country but the prevailing attitude is that beginners and casual participants should be encouraged as well as thronging supermen and wonderwomen and, of course, many couldn't care less. Sheffield is nationally renowned for rock climbing with 4 climbing walls and some of the best crags in England nearby.

SPORTS FACILITIES:

The World Student Games left more than a large pile of litter and unnoticed publicity - although the facilities belong to the city, students are welcome to use them. There are 4 world class sports centres offering an Olympic pool and waterpolo pool, all-weather centre, artificially surfaced pitches, including a new expanse of astroturf, 130 acres of sports fields, a huge indoor sports hall and gymnasium. Slightly older and *only slightly less impressive* is The Goodwin Athletics Centre (a short walk from the campus) which would have been enough on its own and now there are 2 new astroturf pitches. The River Don provides for most water sports with Ogston reservoir (20 miles away) making up the weight. The Peak District covers rambling, mountaineering, caving and all that stuff. *The biggest challenge facing Sheffield students is finding a sport which isn't catered for,* and what's more, all the facilities are free.

SPORTING CLUBS:
Combat; Diving; Gymnastics; Hang Gliding; High Peaks; Jiu Jitsu; Korfball; Lacrosse; Mountaineering; Rowing; Rugby League; Shodokan Aikido; Skydiving; Snowboarding; Speleological (potholing); Swimming & Water Polo; Surfing; Tennis; Ten Pin Bowling; Triathlon; Ultimate Frisbee; Walking; Windsurfing.

ATTRACTIONS:
The local football clubs are well known: Sheffield Wednesday and United. Sheffield has been chosen as the centre for the United Kingdom Sports Institute. Also locally: Europe's biggest dry ski slope.

accommodation

IN COLLEGE:
● Catered: 17% ● Cost: £61-69(31wks)
● Self-catering: 13% ● Cost: £35-72(38wks)
Availability: Nearly all 1st years live in but the rapid expansion in recent years has put pressure on this provision. 17% of the rest of students get places in college, but they realise this early on and can start looking at their options. The halls of residence are collections of large brick buildings each housing between 380 and 670 students in the leafy south-west of the city, and 20 mins walk from the University. 11% have to share. There are also 39 units leased from the city council. Several hundred new en suite study bedrooms have been added recently *but this is as much to do with attracting the lucrative conference trade as keeping students* (many of whom can't afford the more expensive rooms) *happy.*
Car parking: *Just about adequate* (permit needed).

EXTERNALLY:
● Ave rent: £35
Availability: *There is little difficulty in finding accommodation,* usually in shared rented terraced houses for 4 or more, *especially in Crookes, Broomhill and Ecclesall Road. Car parking isn't a problem except in the city centre, partly because there's little need for cars for getting around.*
Housing help: The University accommodation office *does its best* to check out houses and match them up with students. Most students use word of mouth, notice boards in the Union and ads in shops.

welfare

SERVICES:
● Nursery ● Lesbian & Gay Society
● Mature SA ● International SA ● Postgrad SA ● Minibus
● Women's Officer ● Self-defence classes
The SU and University have 6 full- and 10 part-time advisers between them. The Health Service employs 4 doctors, 2

> **' 'How can you have student cool? It's like having student sex.' -David Quantick, NME. '**

nurses and a dentist and has 16 beds and in-patient facilities. The SU runs the Student Development Unit, an initiative to give undergraduates communication and other skills to complement their degrees for the outside world.

Women: The Women's Officer is sabbatical; there's a women-only room and a women's safety bus.

Disabled: *The policy is, of course, to encourage applications from disabled students, but access is poor and Sheffield's hills can give wheelchairs users the hump, but the Supertram is well equipped for them. The Union is 100% wheelchair accessible, though, and the library is well equipped for students with hearing and sight impairment.*

FINANCE:
- Ave debt: £2,250 ● Access fund: £322,000
- Successful applications (1995): 799

Hardship funds are available *without too much difficulty* and instalment payment schemes can be arranged for hall fees.

• •

▶▶ Sheffield City Poly
see Sheffield Hallam University

• •

Sheffield Hallam University

▼ ● *Formerly Sheffield City Polytechnic*

Sheffield Hallam University, City Campus, Pond Street, Sheffield, S1 1WB. Tel: (0114) 225 3587.
Fax: (0114) 225 2094.
Sheffield Hallam University Union of Students, Nelson Mandela Building, City Campus, Pond Street, Sheffield, S1 2BW.
Tel: (0114) 253 4111. Fax: (0114) 253 4140.
E-mail: hallam-union@shu.ac.uk

General

Sheffield Hallam is built around a glass atrium on the City Campus at Pond Street with 2 other sites in town and is undergoing a major redevelopment scheme. Different departments are based at each site and each is pretty much self-sufficient. Students don't need to hop constantly between sites, but, with free intersite transport, *it's not that difficult to do when necessary. Students should check on which site their course is based.*

56% ♂♂♂♂♂♂ ♀♀♀♀ **44%**

Sex ratio(M:F): 56%:44%	Founded: 1969
Full time u'grads: 13,348	Part time: 1,555
Postgrads: 926	Non-degree: n/a
Ave course: 4yrs	Ethnic: n/a
Private school: n/a	Flunk rate: n/a
Mature students: 57%	Overseas students: 2%
Disabled students: 1%	Staff/student ratio: 1:16
Clearing: n/a	

ATMOSPHERE:
The proportion of mature and local students gives a special flavour to the student body; Sheffield's their home patch, they don't need to prove anything to anybody and they enjoy themselves how they blimmin' well want. Meanwhile, most courses involve placements which make a change from academia and keep students' livelier interests alive.

THE SITES:
City Campus: (most subjects and SU) Main city centre site, at Pond Street.
Collegiate Crescent: (health, education, leisure and food management) The second largest site with 3,500 students, green space and a mix of buildings. The Union runs a shop in the Pearson Building. Also sports facilities, 3 halls (housing 520 students) and 65 houses.
Psalter Lane: (cultural studies, art, design, film) This is a little community of over 2,000 students, *generally artists and weirdos* (the two are not exclusive), 3 miles from Pond St. It has a Union Bar and a few facilities, including a library and a hall (cap 300) for discos.

TOWN: see University of Sheffield

TRAVEL: see University of Sheffield
The University provides free minibuses between sites during the day, although it's easy enough to walk or catch public transport between most of them.

LIBRARIES & COMPUTERS:
● Books: 500,000 ● Study places: 1,500
● Computer workstations: 2,300
There is a library on each site with a new 'Learning Centre' at Pond Street including TV recording studios, photography units, lecture theatres and more. It can get *marish* at peak times.

CAREER PROSPECTS:
● Careers Service ● No of staff: 3full/3part
● Unemployed after 6mths (1996): 6%

SPECIAL FEATURES:
● Most courses include a year's placement for work experience and the University offers more sandwich courses than any other.

FAMOUS ALUMNI:
David Kohler (footballer); Bruce Oldfield (fashion designer); Nick Park (animator, 'Wallace & Gromit'); Howard Wilkinson (FA bigwig).

FURTHER INFO:
Prospectuses for undergrads, postgrads, part-time and mature students from the Customer Services Office; web site (http://www.shu.ac.uk).

entertainment

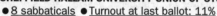

TOWN: see <u>University of Sheffield</u>

UNIVERSITY:

● <u>Price of a pint of beer: £1.00</u> ● <u>Glass of wine: £1.40</u>
Bars: (4) The main Sara Thornton Bar (named after the woman set free after killing her abusive and, um, alcoholic husband) has just been renovated; the Cooler has been refurbished and is now non-smoking, mainly a snack bar during the day; the Furnace is used for comedy nights and other small events; the Works (cap 1,000) opens for big-time ents.
Clubs/discos: The Works hosts 4 club nights a week, mostly chart and retro stuff.
Music venues: The main hall is also the University's top music venue recently hosting Longpigs and the Wannadies.
Food: The main campus houses the Atrium where a *wide* range of snacks and meals hit the various spots; the Union's main food stop is at the Sara Thornton Bar, *where the chip butties come particularly recommended, and the Cooler for sublime jacket spuds.*
Others: Annual Graduation, School and Sports Balls.

social 2 political

SHEFFIELD HALLAM UNIVERSITY UNION OF STUDENTS:

● <u>8 sabbaticals</u> ● <u>Turnout at last ballot: 11%</u>
 ● <u>NUS member</u>
The Union has tackled apathy with the XXX-Files, an 'opportunity profile pack' outlining how students can get involved in SU affairs. The message is that 'student life means more than study' and the students seem to be taking this on, however hesitantly. Support for women's rights and the Campaign for Free Education is strong.

SU FACILITIES:
4 bars; 1 cafeteria; 3 snack bars; shop; Endsleigh Insurance office; travel agency; optician; disco; gay room; ticket office; video games; vending machines; photocopier; function rooms.

CLUBS (NON SPORTING):
Campaign For Free Education; Chinese; Clubbers; Elastic Frontiers; Hellenic; Hindu; Malaysian.

OTHER ORGANISATIONS:
'S-Press', the student magazine, ran into controversy over non-

‘In a poll at Robert Gordon University 70% of students said that the communal fridge is the biggest cause of student flat disputes.’

disclosure of accounts, got taken over by the SU and was relaunched with a close guiding hand which means no more controversy. Forge FM is run by students. More than 500 students get involved in direct community help through the Community Action group.

RELIGIOUS:
● 2 chaplains

PAID WORK: see University of Sheffield

sports

● Recent successes: rugby, volleyball
Participation, facilities and the silverware collection are more than adequate, if slightly overshadowed by the other University in town.

SPORTS FACILITIES:
The University relies heavily on the hire of local amenities (see Sheffield University), *but it also has a fair few facilities of its own for a range of indoor and outdoor sports, including a magnificent indoor climbing wall, gym, squash courts, 20 acres of playing fields and 2 sports halls. There is a small charge for some of the facilities.*

SPORTING CLUBS:
Parachuting; Snowboarding.

ATTRACTIONS: see University of Sheffield

accommodation

IN COLLEGE:
● Catered: 3% ● Cost: £66(33wks)
● Self-catering: 6% ● Cost: £43-46(42wks)

Availability: At the moment half of 1st years can be housed but that's it. 50% of first years who want to, can't. The halls are outside the city centre and some halls have been purpose built (modern brick - *boring but comfy enough*). Most rooms are single and the halls are mixed. Most of the self-catered accommodation is in converted houses in and around the city for up to 10 students each and a few are reserved for single-sex groups. There are plans for a new hall with 800 places.
Car parking: *Difficult near the halls.*

EXTERNALLY: see University of Sheffield
Housing help: The University runs an Accommodation Office and advice service with 7 full-time staff. Packed notice boards and contract negotiation.

welfare

SERVICES:
● Creche ● Lesbian & Gay Society
● Mature SA ● Overseas SA ● Postgrad SA ● Minibus
● Women's Officer ● Self-defence classes

The Union Advice Centre and Financial Support Office offer free help to students. The University employs 8 counsellors. At the Pond Street complex, there is a student health centre with 3 doctors and a number of nurses. There are also daily surgeries at 2 sites.

Women: There's a sabbatical officer, a group, a room and a priority minibus.

Disabled: *Most of the more modern buildings (including the Union) have excellent access and there is some assistance available.* A Disability Development Project has been carried out to improve things further. Special facilities are provided for hearing-impaired students.

FINANCE:
- Ave debt: £1,800 ● Access fund: £314,502
- Successful applications (1997): 487

As well as the access fund, a loan of £50 is available in extreme emergencies to be repaid as soon as possible.

●●●

 Shrivenham
see Cranfield University

●●●

 Silsoe
see Cranfield University

●●●

 Slavonic & East European Studies
see SSEES

●●●

SOAS

 ● *The College is part of* University of London *and students are entitled to use its facilities.*
School of Oriental & African Studies, Thornhaugh Street, Russell Square, London, WC1H 0XG. Tel: (0171) 637 2388. Fax: (0171) 436 3844. E-mail: registrar@soas.ac.uk
SOAS Students' Union, Thornhaugh Street, Russell Square, London, WC1H 0XG. Tel: (0171) 580 0916.
E-mail: su@soas.ac.uk

 ## General

 SOAS is part of the central complex of London University in Bloomsbury, *which makes it convenient for students wanting to wallow in the luxury of ULU's services.* On one side is SSEES, directly over the road is the University's Senate House and Birkbeck College is just round the corner. The whole caboodle is on the roads parallel to Tottenham Court Rd, bang in the middle of London. SOAS itself is a 30s brick building, *hyper-depressingly uniform*, and overshadowed by the vast Brunei Gallery opposite, a gift from the *well-loaded* Sultan of Brunei. It's not called the School of Oriental & African Studies for nothing and courses all concentrate on subjects that fit the description. It was originally a training ground for those about to go off to look after the British Empire, *but the general tone now is definitely post-Imperial and right-on, although not as much as some students would wish.*

50% ♂♂♂♂♂♀♀♀♀♀ 50%	
Sex ratio(M:F): 50%:50%	Founded: 1916
Full time u'grads: 1,500	Part time: 0
Postgrads: 1,000	Non-degree: 400
Ave course: 3yrs	Ethnic: n/a
Private school: n/a	Flunk rate: n/a
Mature students: 45%	Overseas students: 23%
Disabled students: n/a	Staff/student ratio: 1:12
Clearing: 0	

ATMOSPHERE:
SOAS is small enough for everyone to know everyone else, by sight at least. There's a wide mix of religious and ethnic backgrounds which is a fascinating example of multi-culturalism. ULU offers an escape from the potential pressure cooker, as well as being the main facilitator of extra-curricular activity.

THE CITY: see University of London

TRAVEL: see University of London

LIBRARIES & COMPUTERS:
- Books: 900,000 ● Study places: 600
- Computer workstations: 150

The main library is *impressive* (housing a *well-stocked* section on Oriental and African music), *though provision for undergrads is a source of much complaint, as are the dated computers.* Many departments have their own smaller libraries.

CAREER PROSPECTS:
- Careers Service ● No of staff: 3part
- Unemployed after 6mths (1996): 8%

FAMOUS ALUMNI:
Zeinab Badawi (newsreader); Jomo Kenyatta (ex-President of Kenya); Enoch Powell (former MP); Paul Robeson (singer); Princess Sirindhorn of Thailand.

FURTHER INFO:
Undergrad and postgrad prospectuses, video, web site (http://www.soas.ac.uk).

entertainment

IN LONDON: see University of London

COLLEGE:
- Price of a pint of beer: £1.60

Bars: (1) *The bar has been taken out of the hands of the SU due to its lax attitude to drugs on the premises and it's now dead. Social life in the School can be a bit limited, but hell, London's out there.*

Clubs/discos/music venues: The bar (100), the Assembly Hall (500) and the SU building (250) host bands and there's a

> *The Northumberland Building at the University of Northumbria was going to be powered entirely by the biggest solar panels in Europe until a passing student pointed out they were facing the wrong way.*

world/music/bhangra/hip-hop type dance thing once a week.
Food: *The JCR Snack bar is the best value* but there's also a Refectory, another snack bar and a posh café in the Brunei Gallery.
Others: Many of the international student clubs provide ents which attract many people from outside college. There have been Indonesian Gamelan recitals, Laotian dancing, an African drum and dance group, food and music evenings and so on, plus 2 or 3 balls a year.

·······social & political

SOAS STUDENTS' UNION:

- 2 sabbaticals • Turnout at last ballot: 40%

- NUS member

The SU has been enjoying rather poor relations with the college authorities after being rapped on the knuckles and losing its bar, but things are improving slowly. An otherwise apathetic body occupied the library which they felt was inadequate and gained media coverage in the process. **Also ULU:** see University of London.

SU FACILITIES:
A shop; snack bar; creche; juke box; pool tables; games machines.

CLUBS (NON SPORTING):
African Drumming; Buddhist; Class War; Cuban; Gender Watch; Japanese; 1924; Pakistan; Palestinian; Workers' Liberty.

OTHER ORGANISATIONS:
'The New Spirit' is published independently.

RELIGIOUS:
- 2 chaplains (CofE, RC)
Muslim prayer room.

PAID WORK: see University of London

·······sports

- Recent successes: football

Budget and facilities are scarce - there are squash courts and a gym, but most make use of ULU.

accommodation

IN COLLEGE:
- Self-catering: 23% ● Cost: £73(30wks)

Availability: SOAS has two halls of residence, plus its allocation of University of London places, which means that 50% of 1st years and 20% of other students can be housed.

EXTERNALLY: see University of London
Housing help: The Student Accommodation Advisor helps those with roof-over-head-related traumas and there's always ULU.

welfare

SERVICES:
- Lesbian & Gay Society ● Mature SA ● Overseas SA
- Minibus ● Women's Officer ● Self-defence classes

The college offers 2 part-time counsellors, the Union 1 full-time.

Disabled: *Physical access is okay, but there are a lot of annoying little oversights. For instance, library shelves are too high for students in wheelchairs, and you need to get a key from the porter to use the modified toilets. There is a Disability Officer.*

Drugs: *CCTV and undercover police have been introduced as part of an effort to tone down SOAS's reputation as a soft drug den.*

FINANCE:
- Ave debt: £1,600

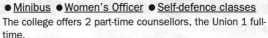

South Bank University

● *Formerly South Bank Polytechnic*
South Bank University, 103 Borough Road, Elephant & Castle, London, SE1 0AA. Tel: (0171) 815 8158.
Fax: (0171) 815 8273. E-mail: postmaster@sbu.ac.uk
South Bank Students' Union, Keyworth Street, Elephant & Castle, London, SE1. Tel: (0171) 815 6060.
Fax: (0171) 815 6061.

general

Southwark in south London is not London's most beautiful borough. And the Elephant & Castle, 2½ miles from Trafalgar Square, is not Southwark's most beautiful part. It is grey and drab until the garish pink shopping centre assaults your gaze. Apart from the precinct, the Elephant consists of 2 large roundabouts, surrounded by an indoor leisure pool, the enormous Metropolitan Tabernacle Church and various offices, shops and a halfway house for released criminals. *But it's not all urban psychosis* - the South Bank complex, *a honeytrap for culture cravers*, is within walking distance. *The buildings of*

the main site of South Bank University fall somewhere in between, architecturally and geographically. There's another site on the Wandsworth Road, just under 3 miles away. It houses the faculty of the Built Environment, *but doesn't set a very good example, looking rather like a big breeze-block.*

52% ♂♂♂♂♂♀♀♀♀ 48%	
Sex ratio(M:F): 52%:48%	**Founded: 1970**
Full time u'grads: 8,900	**Part time: 1,200**
Postgrads: 825	**Non-degree: 3,850**
Ave course: 3yrs	**Ethnic: n/a**
Private school: n/a	**Flunk rate: 36%**
Mature students: 38%	**Overseas students: 15%**
Disabled students: 5%	**Staff/student ratio: 1:15**
Clearing: n/a	

ATMOSPHERE:
Once you've shown your pass to get inside, South Bank is smart, upbeat and busy. Students, many of whom are returning to education, are down to earth and realistic - this is gritty south London stuff and they're proud of it. Most courses have a vocational element and there are close links with business and industry. The University has a strong cosmopolitan flavour with a broad ethnic and social mix so, in theory at least, nobody should feel out of place. The University has been expanding and resources are starting to feel the pinch.

THE CITY: see <u>University of London</u>

ELEPHANT & CASTLE:
The Old Kent Road costs just £60 on a Monopoly Board and is the cheapest property available. It starts at the Elephant & Castle. *This tells you something about the area.* The roundabouts are among the *busiest* London has to offer. Within a stone's throw there are shops and more shops, a council estate, the Labour Party headquarters on the Walworth Rd and, in fact, some *quite nice* Georgian terraced streets. *Local communications are good, for those who can find them.* The BR train connection involves a walk through the upstairs of the pink shopping centre and the tube is hidden in a cave-like entrance.

TRAVEL: see <u>University of London</u>
Local Trains: Elephant & Castle (ThamesLink) or for a mainline station, Waterloo.
Buses: Numbers 3, 44, 12, 45, 59 and 68 pass nearby the main site.
Underground: Elephant & Castle (Bakerloo, Northern Lines).

❝'Get off your backsides and do something!'
-Eco-activist Swampy, when asked if he had a message to students.❞

LIBRARIES & COMPUTERS:
- Books: 300,000 ● Study places: 1,500
- Computer workstations: 1,500

4 libraries in all. The Learning Resource Centre on Borough Road runs IT courses available to all students. *You might need cut-throat survival instincts at peak times.*

CAREER PROSPECTS:
- Careers Service ● No of staff: 7full/3part
- Unemployed after 6mths (1994): 15%

FAMOUS ALUMNI:
Ben Arogundade (editor, 'Extract'); Jimeoin (comedian); Norma Major; Umer Rashid (cricketer); Greg Searle (Olympic oarsman).

FURTHER INFO:
Undergraduate and postgrad/post-experience prospectuses. Web site (http://www.sbu.ac.uk).

entertainment

IN LONDON: see University of London

ELEPHANT & CASTLE:
Avoid the Elephant & Castle unless you fancy yourself as a small-time gangster and the Butts (pink pub that's part of the pink shopping centre *and where a student's life expectancy is short*). *The George & Firkin is a safer option.* There is also the NFT and all the other attractions of the South Bank arts complex, including The National Theatre and Royal Festival Hall. For music lovers, the Brixton Academy, the Fridge and the Vox are just a couple of miles down the road and Ministry of Sound is round the corner. *There are many good, cheap cafés around this part of London and some of the cafés at the South Bank arts complex are excellent.*

UNIVERSITY:
- Price of a pint of beer: £1.80 ● Glass of wine: £1.60

Bars: (6) *The most popular bars are in the SU at Keyworth Street. Upstairs is the Tavern which is pubby, smoky and backgammony, while downstairs is the Isobar in resplendent chrome which is cliquey when it's not empty.*

Clubs/discos/music venues: *The Void is used for small-scale high-jinks.* There are 2 club nights a week and visits from *big name* DJs occur less frequently than they used to. *An excellent venue is being wasted on noisy bands poking their noses out of obscurity.*

Food: There are canteens and snack bars all over. The Tavern does snacks, the Isobar fast food, *but the best bet for actual sustenance is the refectory.* New European Coffee Lounge has opened in Borough Road.

Others: 2 balls a year and fortnightly frivolity from funsters such as, recently, Junior Simpson.

social & political

SOUTH BANK UNIVERSITY STUDENTS' UNION:
- 4 sabbaticals ● Turnout at last ballot: 8%

- NUS member

SBUSU has had a hard few years, what with political infighting, limited resources and even more limited interest from the

> ❝The UEA Union Financial Officer for 1995–6 was John Holmes (aka Gonch Gardner from 'Grange Hill').❞

student body. It could get even worse with a new constitution drawn up which will put the SU in the pocket of the University. *Weep.*

SU FACILITIES:
6 bars; cafés; 3 shops; Midland Bank; Endsleigh Insurance; Campus Travel; the Arc; recreation and common rooms.

CLUBS (NON SPORTING):
Afrikan; Chinese; Industrial.

OTHER ORGANISATIONS:
The SU magazine, 'As It Goes', *is not bad.*

RELIGIOUS:
● <u>2 chaplains (CofE, RC)</u>
Catholic masses held on site. Muslim prayer room. **Religion in London:** see <u>University of London</u>.

PAID WORK: see <u>University of London</u>

·········· sports

● <u>Recent successes: rugby, basketball, football</u>
Considering the location, the sporting record is pretty good.

SPORTS FACILITIES:
The 21-acre fields in Dulwich offer 4 football, 2 rugby and 3 cricket pitches, a bar, pavilion, changing facilities and new scrummage machines, while at the other 2 sites there is a sports hall and gymnasium.

SPORTING CLUBS:
Aikido; Chinese Boxing; Dominos & Games; Jiu Jitsu; Kabbadi; Paintballing.

ATTRACTIONS:
The Elephant & Castle pool is too small for any serious swimming (unless treading water becomes an Olympic event) but is excellent fun with slides and a wave machine. The huge plastic elephant in the middle of the pool, unsurprisingly, causes problems. **Sports in London:** see <u>University of London</u>.

·········· accommodation

IN COLLEGE:
● <u>Self-catering: 13%</u> ● <u>Cost: £58-70(42wks)</u>
Availability: *Housing is not a serious problem,* since the majority of students are already sorted, though 5% of those who want to live in can't. Places are distributed according to who lives furthest away.
Car parking: *Limited, to say the least.*

EXTERNALLY: see <u>University of London</u>
Availability: *It's easier to find accommodation in south London than north of the river (The Thames) and it's cheaper.*
Housing help: The *excellent* service offers 3 housing advice

workers to help with house hunting. There are daily accommodation vacancy lists, often as long as 70 pages.

welfare

SERVICES:

- Creche ● Lesbian & Gay Society
- Overseas SA ● Postgrad SA ● Women's Officer

The University employs 2 full- and 2 part-time counsellors and an adviser and the Union has an Advice Bureau with 2 full-time advisers. All students have personal tutors assigned to them. 2 full-time nurses work on site in term-time.

Disabled: *Access is not very good* and only the Union building has ramps to the entrance and lifts. There's a booklet available, 'Enabling You'. There are induction loops plus a Dyslexia Support unit.

Women: There's always a female member of the welfare team available.

FINANCE:
- Ave debt: £2,100 ● Access fund: £440,000
- Successful applications (1995): 1,360

The University distributes a charitable fund of £12,000, mainly to those who wouldn't otherwise get financial assistance, such as part-time and overseas students. Student Services also provide a Money Management Guide and give out £50,000 in Fee Remissions, so that those who pay their own tuition costs can finish their courses.

• •

▶▶ South West Poly

see University of Plymouth

• •

University of Southampton

▼▼ University of Southampton, Southampton, SO17 1BJ.
Tel: (01703) 595000. Fax: (01703) 593037.
Southampton University Students' Union, Highfield, Southampton, SO17 1BJ. Tel: (01703) 595200.
Fax: (01703) 595252. E-mail: pres@soton.ac.uk

general

The chunk of the southern coast that fell off and became the Isle of Wight left a hole which was filled by a channel of water called The Solent. In the niche on the mainland to the north of the Solent is Southampton. During the 2nd World War, the Luftwaffe decided to pay a visit and drop a few hundred tonnes of explosives all over the place, so most of it has been rebuilt since. Despite destroying just about everything else, the bombs somehow managed to miss most of the 12th century city wall and various other historic relics. The University -

typical of the rest of the city - has redbrick buildings that survived the war, along with post-war geometric blocks that won awards in the 60s *and look pretty cruddy now*, mostly on a landscaped campus, 2 miles from the city centre. The main site is dotted with *bizarre* sculptures in the style of Henry Moore.

50% ♂♂♂♂♂♀♀♀♀♀ 50%	
Sex ratio(M:F): 50%:50%	Founded: 1952
Full time u'grads: 11,539	Part time: 2,645
Postgrads: 1,894	Non-degree: 158
Ave course: 3yrs	Ethnic: 3.2%
Private school: 30%	Flunk rate: 5%
Mature students: 16%	Overseas students: 8%
Disabled students: 4%	Staff/student ratio: 1:14
Clearing: 6%	

ATMOSPHERE:
It's probably fair to say that white, English, middle-class students aren't exactly thin on the ground. This doesn't, of course, mean that people who don't fall into these groups will come to any grief - indeed on arrival at Southampton students tend to turn into unpretentious, vaguely scruffy types no matter what their background. Sorry? What sweeping generalisation?

THE SITES:
Boldrewood: (1,000 students – medicine) Less than a mile from the main campus is this large, *squat Lego-box* building. *Even though it's within easy walking distance, this is a separate community, where the student medics make their own entertainment.*

Southampton Oceanography Centre: (600 – geology, oceanography) A purpose-built site taking advantage of Southampton's natural environment. It's 3 miles from the main campus but there's a regular shuttle bus service.

Avenue Campus: (3,000 - Faculty of Arts) A new development, a brisk walk from the main campus, housing most arts students, except musicians and...

Winchester School of Art: (1,000 students) This member of the Southampton family merged with the University in August 96. It's in the historic city of Winchester (12 miles from Southampton) and maintains its own separate identity (creative and predominantly female).

New College: (2,000 - combined honours and adult education) Previously known as La Sainte Union, this new acquisition to Southampton University is in the city centre rather than France.

THE CITY:
- Population: 194,400 ● London: 74miles
- Portsmouth: 16miles

Southampton used to revolve around its port, but since its pretty functional reconstruction after the war, it's become a city that's there simply because a lot of people were all in the same place at the same time. The centre is thoroughly modern and great for grant-gutting sprees. But Southampton has more to recommend it than the opportunity to buy anything from a continental quilt to one of those things you put eggs in to boil them in a microwave. There is a small *bohemian* quarter with good pubs and shops, and the outlying districts are *quaint* and worth exploring for cream teas and antiques. The town boasts a *very good* music and book library, various supermarkets and a few late night shops around the student areas. The docks are being developed and are worth a look. The city contains many parks, archaeological digs and 5 museums of varying size and obscurity of content. *Rumours that this is a cultural desert are probably put around by jealous people from Bognor or snooty Londoners. They're not to be believed.*

TRAVEL:
Trains: Southampton Central offers services to London (14.70), Bristol (£17.80), Manchester (£38.60)... the list goes on.
Buses: National Express services all over the country, including London (£4), Manchester (£21.50) and all points beyond.
Car: The A27 splits for a brief spell into the M27 and the continuing A27 around Southampton. There's also the A31, A33, A36 and A336.
Air: Flights inland, to Europe, Ireland and the Channel Islands from Southampton Airport.
Ferries: To France, the Isle of Wight and the Channel Islands.
Hitching: Good prospects to London, Oxford, the Midlands and Wales from the petrol station at the end of the A33. The Union also offers a lifts board for cadging off other students.
Local: Buses are cheap and reliable, but infrequent. Local trains are regular with connections all over Hampshire and there are 7 stations around the city, but it's not the cheapest or most practical way of getting around.
Bicycles: Good cycling, despite a couple of big hills.

LIBRARIES & COMPUTERS:
● Books: 1,000,000 ● Study places: 1,921
● Computer workstations: 630
7 libraries - the main one is the Hartley Library in the centre of the campus.

CAREER PROSPECTS:
● Careers Service ● No of staff: 10full/7part
● Unemployed after 6mths (1996): 6.8%

FAMOUS ALUMNI:
Roger Black (athlete, 'sex on legs'); John Denham MP (Lab, ex-SU President); Jeremy Hardy (comic); Jenni Murray (Radio 4,

❝A petition against a proposed hall of residence at Royal Holloway claimed that local businesses would decline as students do not require anything except cheap food.❞

Woman's Hour); John Nettles (actor, Bergerac); Chris Packman ('Really Wild Show'); John Sopel (BBC correspondent); Kathy Tayler (ex-athlete, TV *non*-personality); Lord Tonypandy (former speaker of House of Commons).

FURTHER INFO:
Prospectuses for undergrads, postgrads and part-timers and a web site (http://www.soton.ac.uk).

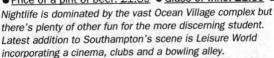

entertainment

CITY:

● Price of a pint of beer: £1.80 ● Glass of wine: £1.30

Nightlife is dominated by the vast Ocean Village complex but there's plenty of other fun for the more discerning student. Latest addition to Southampton's scene is Leisure World incorporating a cinema, clubs and a bowling alley.

Cinemas: (3) A 7-screen multiplex and the Harbour Lights art house. New 14-screen multiplex at Leisure World.

Theatres: (3) The Nuffield specialises in modern drama, the Mayflower in the touring blockbusters and the Gantry in arty and experimental theatre.

Pubs: A wide selection, many with extended opening. **push***plugs: Hobbit; Garden Arms; Talking Heads; O'Malley's; The Mitre. The Stoneham Arms is best avoided.*

Clubs/discos: *Southampton is trying to shake off its reputation as 'the arse end of our dance nation' (© 'Sky' magazine) and has a fair few nights to keep the more trend-conscious booty-shaker beaming. Ocean Village is a mainstay of mainstream glitz and Leisure World has added two new clubs.* **push***plugs: Magnum, Kaos (pop/chart); Rhinos, University of Sound, Menage a Trois at the Chantry (house/garage/techno).*

Music venues: The Joiners for middling indie; The Gantry for jazz and folk; The Mayflower and the Guildhall for bigger names.

Eating out: *Apart from several excellent pub-lunchy type places,* **push***plugs go to: Boozy Rouge, Bon Gusto (French/Italian); New Orleans (cajun); Rose of India; Mistang Sally's; Fatty Arbuckles. There are also some bearable restaurants in the Ocean Village development.* The kebab shops in Bedford Place keep on turning till 4am.

Others: The 'Bitterne Bowl' is the place for a spot of hi tech ten pin bowling and zap your pals at the Quasar Studio at Ocean Village.

UNIVERSITY:

● Price of a pint of beer: £1.32 ● Glass of wine: 70p

Bars: (6) The main Union Bar (cap 400) *is fairly pubby*; there's also a sports bar with board games and Twister *for those who need to flex their competitive instincts.* The School of Art at Winchester has another boozer and there are 3 additional University-run ones.

Theatres: (3) 2 of the theatres are temporary spaces used for between 1 and 3 weeks a term. The 3rd is The Nuffield, a professional theatre used once a year by students. Trips to Edinburgh are a common occurrence.

Cinemas: 6 movies a week are shown by the award-winning Union Films Society. It's a *very active* club with regular cult

movie nights and there are film-making opportunities as well.
Clubs/discos/music venues: The University's largest venue is the West Refectory (800) but the Bar and the Ballroom (400 each) can cope with smaller events. There are 1 or 2 club nights a week, covering the spectrum from indie to jungle. Recent live appearances include Gene, Echobelly and Mansun.
Cabaret: Most Sundays, there's a comedy gig, courtesy of the likes of Alan Davies, Sean Locke, Bill Bailey or some other mirthmonger.
Food: The Union runs the coffee bars and Gordon's, *offering excellent quality and VFM; the University's refectories are OK on the quality front but portions are small, prices high.*
Other: At least 7 annual balls.

social & political

SOUTHAMPTON UNIVERSITY STUDENTS' UNION:

● 9 sabbaticals   ● Turnout at last ballot: 8%
● NUS member

The Tories are the largest society and although the majority of students prefer their conservatism with a small 'c', Southampton isn't the ideal place to foment a proletarian uprising. The Union is trying valiantly to shake out the apathy but it's like trying to jumpstart a tub of cottage cheese.

SU FACILITIES:
Dry cleaners; hairdressers; guarded cloakroom; lockers; photo booth; pottery studio; minibus; 2 bars; café; cheap driving school; showers and baths; launderette; market stalls each Monday; sports equipment and hire service; Lloyds Bank with cashpoint; TV rooms; Interflora; dark room; meeting rooms; customised disco; ballroom; retail centre with a shop, travel agency, and sports shop.

CLUBS (NON SPORTING):
AIESEC; Alien; Arab; Art; Astronomical; Ballroom Dancing; Bangladesh; Bible Fellowship; Bike; Bridge; Buddhist; Chamber Choir; Change Ringers; Chaos; Chinese; Choral; Concert Band; Darts; Dining; Exploration; First Aid; Folk Dance; Games; Hellenic; Hindu; House Music; Human Potential; Hunt Sabs; Industrial; Iraqi; Jazz; Jazz Dance; Jazzmanix; Jocksoc; Juggling; Light Opera; Lodge; Mainland Chinese; Malaysian; Massage; Pakistan; Persian; Pink; Radio; Real Ale; Showstoppers; Singapore; Smoke; Spanish & Latin American; Sindicate; Students Against NUS; Students For NUS; Survival International; Transport; Turkish; UN; Wessex Films; Wine; Women's Safety.

OTHER ORGANISATIONS:
The SU produces the 'Wessex Scene' newspaper. Other campus media includes the Glen Eyre Hall radio station and 'Wessex Films' which makes films and documentaries. Rag raised £23,000 last year. The Community Interaction group runs 15 local help projects.

RELIGIOUS:
● 3 chaplains (CofE, RC, Free)
Provision for Muslims is poor although they can use a prayer room in the Union. Just about every religion is catered for in Southampton.

PAID WORK:
The boat show in summer offers some opportunities not available elsewhere.

❝The library at Queen Mary & Westfield is built on top of a cemetery.❞

sports

● Recent successes: cricket

The Athletic Union is an active student organisation but sport isn't dominant. There are good facilities for most activities on or near the campus.

SPORTS FACILITIES:
On campus, there are a large sports hall, multigym, 6 squash courts, climbing wall (outdoors), judo room, table tennis, aerobics room, tennis courts, snooker room and after all that, an injuries clinic. Off campus there are 90 acres of playing fields, a rifle range and a boatyard. The city adds a golf course, dry ski slope, bowling green and a cycle track.

SPORTING CLUBS:
Aikido; American Football; Boat; Boxing; Caving; Frisbee; Gliding; Hang Gliding; Hung Leng Kuen Kung Fu; Lacrosse; Life Saving; Motor; Mountain Bike; Nin Jutsu; Okinawan Shorin Ryu Karate; Parachute; Polo; Rambling & Hillwalking; Rifle; Shorinji Kenpo; Shotokai Karate; Snooker; Tai Chi Chuan; Ten Pin Bowling; Trampolining; Triathlon; Water Polo; Water Ski; Weightlifting; Windsurf.

ATTRACTIONS:
Southampton FC, *Saints to their friends, Scummers to others,* avoid relegation at the Dell and there's also Hampshire County Cricket ground. Cowes Week, when lots of people go messing about in boats on the Solent, is *one of the major events of the sailing calendar, but, sadly, few cows attend.*

accommodation

IN COLLEGE:
● Catered: 10% ● Cost: £70-85(30wks)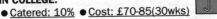
● Self-catering: 22% ● Cost: £34-78(30-50wks)

Availability: Almost all 1st years live in, but very few others can. *All the rooms are broadly similar with basic furnishings and fittings.* 7 of the 17 halls are catered (13 meals a week), just under a mile from the campus. The kitchens in the self-catering halls are shared by between 6 and 20 students. All halls are mixed, but sexes are split into floors or corridors according to each hall's layout. *Students who think the grass is significantly greener on the other side of the hall fence can switch without hassle.* Montefiore III and Glen Eyre II have ensuite facilities.
Car parking: Permit needed, 1st years not allowed cars.

EXTERNALLY:
● Ave rent: £40

Availability: *It's very easy to find accommodation - it will take 2 days search max to find somewhere (if it takes longer, don't come crying to us).* Good standard housing can be found, particularly around Portswood and Inner Avenue, within *staggering distance of the best student pubs.* Avoid Bassett Green and Bitterne which are *less welcoming than the Strangeways reception committee.* Students should also avoid letting anyone convince them to sort it out too long in advance. Landlords shove up prices and charge for renting over the summer. It takes guts, but this is the time to wait, to hold on till the landlords are a little more anxious to fill their places - don't worry, there are enough.

Housing help: The University Accommodation Office provides an approval service, legal advice and crashpads for house-hunters. The Union has a vacancies board.

welfare

SERVICES:
- Creche ● Nightline ● Lesbian & Gay Society
- Mature SA ● Overseas SA ● Postgrad SA ● Minibus
- Women's Officer ● Self-defence classes

For all manner of problems, SUSU has a Student Advice & Information Centre and the University runs a Counselling service with 1 full- and 5 part-time counsellors who not only arrange help on a individual basis, but also run group sessions on study skills, relaxation and so on. There is a University health centre with psychotherapists and 5 doctors running various clinics for family planning and sports injuries. There is an eating disorders support group and SUSU gives attack alarms to students, as well as running a Night Bus.

Disabled: *Access is improving all the time.* Most buildings have lifts and there's a residential hall for students who need care assistance.

FINANCE:
- Ave debt: £1,050 ● Access fund: £316,753
- Successful applications (1996): 801

In addition to the access fund, the University runs a hardship fund for people whose circumstances change mid-course. SUSU also gives short-term emergency loans.

Southampton Institute of Higher Education

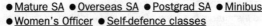

▼ Southampton Institute, East Park Terrace, Southampton, SO14 0YN. Tel: (01703) 319000. Fax: (01703) 222259. E-mail: ms@solent.ac.uk
Southampton Institute Students' Union, East Park Terrace, Southampton, SO14 0YN. Tel: (01703) 232154.

general

Southampton Institute is so keen to become a university, it received a rap across the knuckles for describing itself as such in an advert a couple of years ago. It's certainly expanding fast in preparation and is now the largest HE institution that still isn't a university (or part of one). It's just acquired a new site, giving a 50% increase in space. The other site, 9 miles away at Warsash right on the Solent coast, is halfway to the towns around Portsmouth Harbour.

60% ♂♂♂♂♂♂ ♀♀♀♀ 40%	
Sex ratio(M:F): 60%:40%	Founded: 1984
Full time u'grads: 11,410	Part time: 5,254
Postgrads: 514	Non-degree: 2,901
Ave course: 3yrs	Ethnic: 8.5%
Private school: n/a	Flunk rate: 21%
Mature students: 38%	Overseas students: 7%
Disabled students: 4.9%	Staff/student ratio: 1:15
Clearing: 38%	

ATMOSPHERE:
The Institute is busy and friendly, and a bit less cramped than it was. The students are a good friendly mix, from crazed skateboarders to mature returners to education all united in a vocational dream. Despite the size of the place, everyone seems to know everyone else.

WARSASH SITE:
This site is a 20-acre campus with about 800 undergraduates and its own pier. An old naval college was based here, overlooking the River Hamble in a *beautiful* landscaped setting, *quietly* tucked out of town. Departments of maritime study and engineering are based at this site, *which is essentially self-contained and maintains a completely separate existence from the main site. Entertainment is lacking and regular trips into town are needed to stave off boredom, unless you enjoy talking to old people about their time in the navy.*

THE CITY: see University of Southampton

TRAVEL: see University of Southampton

LIBRARIES & COMPUTERS:
● Books: 170,000 ● Study places: 1,000
● Computer workstations: 500
The Mountbatten Library and Design Library are on the city campus and Warsash has a small wing of the Mountbatten collection. Also the new Collins Library (business & law). *There are enough computers to go round but students complain that they tend to have inappropriate software, especially for media and design courses.* A new IT suite, due to open in late 98, should help address this.

CAREER PROSPECTS:
● Careers Service ● No of staff: 6full
● Unemployed after 6mths (1996): 35.6%

FURTHER INFO:
General and part-time prospectuses; web site (http://www.solent.ac.uk).

entertainment

TOWN: see University of Southampton

INSTITUTE:
● Price of a pint of beer: £1.40 ● Glass of wine: £1.10
Bars: There are 3 bars, one on top of the other, each with a capacity of 750. Biffa's and Bilbo's have DJs; the Brass Tap

is a sports bar *and the beer's better.*

Clubs/discos/music venues: 2 free club nights a week, open DJ spots and karaoke; a few *decent acts* such as Dodgy, a few *less so* such as Dannii Minogue and *the odd towering pinnacle of celebrity perfection* such as Rolf *'wacca wacca'* Harris have stopped off here recently.

Food: Bilbo's serves breakfast, lunch and tea *at rockbottom prices; the Institute refectory has improved since being contracted to outside caterers.*

Others: The SU organises 5 balls a year.

social & political
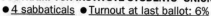

SOUTHAMPTON INSTITUTE STUDENTS' UNION:

- 4 sabbaticals ● Turnout at last ballot: 6%
- NUS member

SISU has facilities in the Student Union building on the main site and in another small building at Warsash. Student officers are basically apolitical and the students themselves are apathy personified.

SU FACILITIES:
City: 3 bars; 4 minibuses for hire; 2 shops (books, stationery, sweets); cash machine (Barclays, NatWest); photo booth; games and vending machines; pool tables; juke boxes; 2 meeting rooms; satellite TV.
Warsash: Shop; bar; refectory.

CLUBS (NON SPORTING):
2d Painting; Karting; Record; Roleplay; Sculpture; Transoc.

OTHER ORGANISATIONS:
'Havit' is a three-weekly mag. There's a student community organisation (arranging youth clubs, decorating flats and helping at local special needs schools) which will be transformed into a fully fledged Community Action Group with the arrival of a full-time officer.

RELIGIOUS:
- 1 chaplain (CofE)

PAID WORK :
There's the usual jobs offered by the SU such as bar-work and stewardiong, plus a job shop on campus. Also see University of Southampton

sports

- Recent successes: nothing special
Overall participation is greater than the somewhat thin facilities would suggest.

SPORTS FACILITIES:
Main site: Sports hall; a health suite; sailing facilities; fitness centre; multigym; circuit training; 12 acres of playing fields 3 miles away; use of squash and tennis courts.
Warsash: Small sports hall; multigym; sailing/water sports on the Hamble and Itchen.

SPORTING CLUBS:
Surf; Tennis; Waterski; Windsurfing; Yachts.

ATTRACTIONS: see University of Southampton

accommodation

IN COLLEGE:
● Self-catering: 21% ● Cost: £51-74(38wks)

Availability: 70% of 1st years are accommodated but the large proportion of local and mature students means that this is pretty much everyone who wants. *The halls, especially the new ones, appear to be pretty good although they're very expensive and the fire alarms keep going off.* It can actually be cheaper to live out.
Car parking: With a permit (£215pa).

EXTERNALLY: see University of Southampton
Housing help: The Institute has an Accommodation Office with 12 full-time staff, providing a vacancies notice board, safety checks, emergency housing and listings.

welfare

SERVICES:
● Lesbian & Gay Society ● Mature SA ● Overseas SA
● Minibus ● Women's Officer ● Self-defence classes

The Institute has 2 full- and 3 part-time counsellors. There is an NHS medical practice near the city campus and a visiting nurse. Warsash has its own nurse and visiting doctor. Each site has a 'student assistance base', to provide help with revision, time management and other study problems.
Disabled: 75% of the Institute is wheelchair accessible; there are induction loops and a Disabilities Co-ordinator.

FINANCE:
● Ave debt: £2,100 ● Access fund: £152,000
● Successful applications (1997): 368

The SU provides hardship loans up to £30 and the Principal's Discretionary Fund (£10,000) lends £150 to students waiting for their grants to arrive.

SSEES

● **The College is part of University of London and students are entitled to use its facilities.**
School of Slavonic and East European Studies, University of London, Senate House, Malet Street, London, WC1E 7HU.
Tel: (0171) 636 8000. Fax: (0171) 862 8641.
SSEES Union Association, 21-22 Russell Square, London.
Tel: (0171) 637 4934. Fax: (0171) 436 8916.

general

SSEES (along with SOAS, Birkbeck College and numerous others) is part of the central complex of London University colleges in Bloomsbury in central London. This is one of the smallest and doesn't even have a separate building. Instead it squats in the 2nd and 3rd floors of Senate House, the administrative centre of

London University, an enormous white art deco building *that looks as much like an ocean liner as a university - it's probably the University's most imposing building*. The School has further space in the annexe building at 21 Russell Square, *which by comparison, is a dreary Georgian place, but by normal standards is an elegant part of inner London*. Since the annexe includes the SU, canteen and bar, *it's as important to students as the academic side of things in Senate House*.

49% ♂♂♂♂♂♀♀♀♀♀ 51%	
Sex ratio(M:F): 49%:51%	Founded: 1915
Full time u'grads: 330	Part time: 0
Postgrads: 200	Non-degree: 20
Ave course: 3yrs	Ethnic: 6%
Private school: 30%	Flunk rate: n/a
Mature students: 40%	Overseas students: 8%
Disabled students: 1%	Staff/student ratio: 1:10
Clearing: 10%	

ATMOSPHERE:
Being such a small school, staff/student interaction is all very cosy and informal. Everyone knows everyone, who they're going out with, what their underwear size is and so on. For some students it can feel a bit claustrophobic - depending on whether the gossip is directed at them or not and whether it's in a language they understand. For most though, London offers ample opportunity to escape. SSEES provides comfort and friendship (but few amenities of its own) in an otherwise vast and impersonal University.

THE CITY: see University of London

TRAVEL: see University of London

LIBRARIES & COMPUTERS:
- Books: 318,000 ● Study places: 116
- Computer workstations: 10

The University of London library is also available in Senate House. Students have to pay a deposit to use the *inadequate* computer facilities (*only* 1 printer and 1 internet connection).

CAREER PROSPECTS:
- No of staff: 1part

There are weekly, *well-attended* careers 'surgeries'.

SPECIAL FEATURES:
- As the only centre for East European Studies, students get to meet people from relevant embassies, governments and academics who have written definitive works. Students get access to relevant sources and resources not available anywhere else.
- 10% of students have an Eastern European background.

FAMOUS ALUMNI:
Jonathan Ross (TV celebwity).

FURTHER INFO:
Prospectuses for undergrads and postgrads and a web site (http://www.ssees.ac.uk).

❝In 1994 students at Portsmouth were housed temporarily in a naval barracks and subjected to naval discipline.❞

entertainment

IN LONDON: see University of London

COLLEGE :
● Price of a pint of beer: £1.40 ● Shot of vodka: £1

Bars: The *cosy* bar has variously been called the Oliver Reed and the Des Lynam but it's now the Hammer & Sickle. There's a pool table, a darts board and an *intriguing* selection of Eastern European beverages.

Cinemas: The Stanley Kubrick society shows Polish and Russian films on a large TV screen.

Food: The School runs Irene's canteen (open 9.30am to 4.15pm) and *the indomitable Irene knows what's happening to who, with whom, when and where and she even remembers Jonathan Ross.*

Others: Regular parties and a summer barbie.

social & political

SSEES STUDENTS' UNION:
● Turnout at last ballot: 50% ● NUS member

Beacuse of the nature of the courses, SSEES students tend to be more politically switched-on than their colleagues at other colleges.

SU FACILITIES:
In the basement of 21 Russell Square (a listed building, no less) the SU runs the Hammer & Sickle Bar, the SU office, the Rainbow Room (TV, video etc) and a pool room.

CLUBS (NON SPORTING):
Debating; Film; Masaryk (Czech/Slovak); Polish; Post-Yugoslav; Romanian; Russian Singing/Poetry.

OTHER ORGANISATIONS:
Students independently publish a student newspaper, 'SSEESfire' twice a term, plus the weekly newsletter 'Samizdat'.

sports

● Recent successes: Nothing special
No facilities other than London University's.

accommodation

IN COLLEGE:
Availability: The School has no accommodation of its own although 50% of 1st years live in the University's intercollegiate accommodation.
Car parking: No parking is available.

EXTERNALLY: see <u>University of London</u>
Availability: *Most students live around Manor House, Finsbury Park and Hackney – not great areas but cheaper than most.*
Housing help: The University has an accommodation office.

ᴡelfare

SERVICES:

● <u>Lesbian & Gay Society</u> ● <u>Women's Officer</u>

Students are assigned personal tutors from the academics; in addition to the small Welfare Service, trained counsellors are available from the <u>University of London</u>.
Disabled: *Access is poor, especially to the Russell Square annexe.* There are ramps and lifts at Senate House.

FINANCE:
● <u>Ave debt: £1,656</u> ● <u>Access fund: £15,000</u>
● <u>Successful applications (1996): 70</u>

University of St Andrews

▼ University of St Andrews, College Gate, St Andrews, Fife,
KY16 9AJ. Tel: (01334) 476161. Fax: (01334) 462543.
E-mail: admissions@st-andrews.ac.uk
St Andrews University Students' Association, St Mary's Place,
St Andrews, Fife, KY16 9JZ. Tel: (01334) 462700.
Fax: (01334) 462740. E-mail: union@st-andrews.ac.uk

general

The city of St Andrews is situated on the east coast of Scotland. St Andrews, the University, is the oldest in Scotland, the third oldest in the UK (after Oxford and Cambridge) and, quite naturally, tradition plays a large part in the lives of the students. The University buildings reflect the heritage, dating from the 15th century until the modern day, with many *tasteful* examples from the 16th and 17th centuries. Neither the city nor the University are very big - in fact, more than a ¼ of the local population are students. Apart from making this a university city (as opposed to a city with a university), it means that, although the University buildings are scattered all over the place, they are all still within walking distance of each other.

S

48% ♂♂♂♂♂ ♀♀♀♀ **52%**

Sex ratio(M:F): 48%:52%	Founded: 1410
Full time u'grads: 4,673	Part time: 44
Postgrads: 711	Non-degree: 180
Ave course: 4yrs	Ethnic: n/a
Private school: n/a	Flunk rate: n/a
Mature students: 9%	Overseas students: 15%
Disabled students: n/a	Staff/student ratio: 1:14
Clearing: 7%	

ATMOSPHERE:

Everywhere there are rituals, ceremonies, customs and students wearing groovy red gowns but they have staggered into the 20th century. Relations between students and the local population are generally good, partly because the University is the major local employer. Among students themselves, there's a happy atmosphere; even the state school/private school and English/Scottish divides are expressed more as healthy rivalry than as bitter antagonism.

THE CITY:

- Population: 16,000 ● London: 371miles
- Edinburgh: 45miles ● Dundee: 13miles

Never mind Florida, this is the world's golfing capital. There's not only the Royal & Ancient Golf Club, the oldest in the world, but 5 others, attracting 1,000s of people in peach and purple plaid pants. It's not just golfers who come here, though; it's a natural tourist town, like a theme park, with museums, enchanting architecture and scenery to die for. The cathedral and castle are the most famous of St Andrews' many historic buildings. For the tourist trade, there are many quaint shops and cafés, but nothing of particular note aimed at students. The city consists of 3 main streets with interlocking alleys and side streets. It's all fairly isolated, enclosed by a rock coast to the north, sandy beaches to the east and countryside the rest of the way round.

TRAVEL:

The University Travel Service provides info and sells tickets.
Trains: Leuchars station is 5 miles from the main group of the University buildings with direct lines to London (£44.20), Dundee and Edinburgh. For other services, passengers (sorry, customers) must change at Edinburgh or Dundee.
Coaches: National Express coaches run from Dundee, 13 miles away, to London (£26.99), Glasgow (£7.20) and beyond.
Car: A915 south, A91 west to M90 (to Edinburgh).
Hitching: *Difficult to get from St Andrews to anywhere. Better from Edinburgh (A1) or Dundee if thumbsters can get there.*
Local: *Buses every ½ hour but rarer at night, although they're quite cheap. In general, St Andrews is small enough to walk round.*
Taxis: Works out about £1 a mile (£5 to Leuchars).
Bicycles: *The best way to get around short of a chauffeur-driven limo. St Andrews is small and flat with limited traffic.*

LIBRARIES & COMPUTERS:

- Books: 1,050,000 ● Study places: 1,300
- Computer workstations: 625

University Library is the main library with well over 750,000 books - *massive for a university this size.* The North Haugh, the Buchanan Building and St Mary's College areas of University buildings also offer libraries as do some departments.

CAREER PROSPECTS:

- Careers Service ● No of staff: 7full/1part
- Unemployed after 6mths (1996): 4.4%

The Careers Service is great if you want to be shoe-horned into marketing.

SPECIAL FEATURES:
● Students get free admission to the castle while wearing their gowns.

FAMOUS ALUMNI:
Sir James Black (Nobel Prize scientist); Madsen Pirie (Adam Smith Institute); Siobhan Redmond (actress); Alex Salmond MP (SNP); Fay Weldon (writer). Former Rectors (elected by students) include Rudyard Kipling and John Cleese, who advised students not to let their degrees get in the way of their education.

FURTHER INFO:
Prospectuses for undergrads and postgrads, video loans. CD-ROM and web site (http://www.st-andrews.ac.uk).

entertainment

TOWN:

● Price of a pint of beer: £1.90 ● Glass of wine: £1.50

Cinemas: There's 1 cinema with 2 screens.
Theatres: 2 *small* theatres and the Castle sometimes doubles up.
Pubs: *Pubs tend to be geared towards the summer tourist trade more than students. Some (such as Ma Bell's) are monopolised by the privately educated yahs.* **push***plugs: The Cellar Bar; Whey Pat Tavern; Bert's Bar; Ogston's; The Central.*
Music venues: Jazz swings its stuff at Younger Hall and the Vic Café, which also hosts blues and folk music.
Eating out: *Considering the city's size, the range and quality is impressive - again, this has much to do with the tourist trade. Pubs are often a good bet.* **push***plugs: Balaka, Babur (Indian); Vine Leaf (for romantic liaisons à deux); Ma Brown's (tea shop); Coffee House (15 blends and hotly tipped bacon sarnies); The Doll's House (vfm).*

UNIVERSITY:

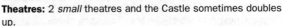

● Price of a pint of beer: £1.40 ● Glass of wine: £1.30

Bars: (3) The Union's Main Bar provides the cheapest eating and drinking in town; the Beer Bar is used as a venue; the Fraser Suite is quieter and more intimate.
Theatres: There's an immense selection of thespian goings on going on (mostly in the Union Theatre, cap 500) and every student is automatically a member of the Mermaids University Dramatic Society which usually performs at the Edinburgh Fringe Festival, the National Student Drama Festival and the Scottish Drama Festival.
Clubs/discos: The city doesn't have any real nightclubs and so the Union's 3 weekly club nights do wonders for local relations. Friday is the Bop and Saturdays rotate between house and retro disco.
Music venues: When the Union Theatre isn't being used for discos, plays or whatever, it's often used for live music, including ceilidhs.
Cabaret: A major stopover for touring talent, such as Rhona Cameron, Craig Charles and Bill Bailey.
Food: The Main Bar includes a restaurant which doles out everything from snacks to full feasts. The Old Union coffee bar also doles out the nibbles.

Others: These posh student types love their balls - the black tie variety - and so they have over a dozen a term, some of them full Scottish kilt-and-sporran jobs.

social & political

UNIVERSITY OF ST ANDREWS STUDENTS' ASSOCIATION:

● <u>4 sabbaticals</u> ● <u>Turnout at last ballot: 25%</u>

The Students' Association is made up of 2 parts, the Student Representative Council (SRC), which does all the shouting, and the Students' Union which dishes out services. The SRC opted out of NUS in 1979. Political stances tend to be supine, although a rent rise was successfully fought off last year.

SU FACILITIES:

The Union has facilities at St Mary's Place: 3 bars; cafeteria; travel agency; general shop; Clydesdale cashpoint; TV lounge; launderette; photocopying; photo booth; fax service; 2 minibuses for hire; sexual health clinic; games and vending machines; pool table; juke box; 5 meeting rooms; 2 conference halls; 2 nightclub/discos; parking.

CLUBS (NON SPORTING):

Anglican; Arab; Arts; Astronomy; Ballroom Dancing; Basement Films; Beats Working; Breakaway; Celtic; Chinese; Christian Music & Drama; Christian Socialist; Classical; Dead Parrots; Developing Nations; Duke of Edinburgh; Dyslexic; Early Music; Entertainment Enterprises; Friends of Fondue; Gilbert & Sullivan; Hispanic; Juggling; Just So (musical theatre); Kites; Methodist; One World; Progress (women's group); Real Ale; Retro; Role Play; Scouts & Guides; Scottish Romania Language Link; Shire of Caer Caledon; Slappers; Spectrum Management; St Andrews Chorus; Tiddlywinks; Tunnocks Caramel Wafer Appreciation; Wargames; Women in Art Festival.

OTHER ORGANISATIONS:

'The Saint' is the *readily readable read* that won The Guardian/NUS Student Newspaper of the Year award in 97. 'Squib' is an arts magazine and 'Gryphon' features student poetry. The charity campaign raised £62,000 last year, but there's also the Kate Kennedy Club (named after the niece of the University's founder), which is an all-male charitable club which raised an additional £3,000 last year. Each year, they hold a parade with horse-drawn carriages and costumed characters. There's also the Union Debating Society, a (*pompous*) talk shop.

RELIGIOUS:

● <u>1 chaplain</u>

The University chaplaincy, city churches and cathedral cater for most versions of Christianity.

PAID WORK:

A bit in the local tourist and golfing trade - hotels, golf bars and so on. *Caddying isn't as easy as you'd think, though.*

sports

● <u>Recent successes: football, athletics</u>

Excellent facilities (especially for golf) considering that, as far as universities go, this ain't one of the big boys. Maybe this is why participation is so high.

SPORTS FACILITIES:
Sports halls; 60 acres of playing fields; squash courts; athletics tracks and field; croquet lawn; floodlit all-weather tennis courts; multigym; gym; running track; cricket nets; boat house (and other rowing facilities); sauna; and, of course, a reduced fee golf course. Locally there's also the sea, hills for hilly-type sports, ski slopes and 5 golf courses.

SPORTING CLUBS:
Aikido; Boat; Clay Pigeon; Lacrosse; Life Saving; Mountaineering; Parachute; Rifle; Shinty; Tennis; Ultimate Frisbee; Water Polo; Wind-surfing.

ATTRACTIONS:
There's golf, watersports, golf, walking, golf, climbing, golf. Oh, and golf, for which students pay only the same as local residents (less than £100 a year).

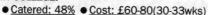 accommodation

IN COLLEGE:
- Catered: 48% ● Cost: £60-80(30-33wks)
- Self-catering: 8% ● Cost: £31-49(37wks)

Availability: All 1st years who want to live in can do so and there's room for nearly half of other years. 22% of students have to share rooms. There's a large mixture of old and new buildings, including the self-catered flats in Fife Park and Albany Park (on the beach).

EXTERNALLY:
- Ave rent: £50

Availability: *There are no specific student areas because it's so small. The available places are generally good, a reflection of local prosperity. It's slightly easier to sell condoms in a convent than to park in St Andrews - even in the residential areas it is fairly bad. Bikes are recommended. A few students resort to local villages.*

Housing help: Help is available from the Head of University Accommodation which employs 4 staff to help with house hunting and the problems that inevitably will occur, even to the most optimistic. *After all, the difference between an optimist and a pessimist is that an optimist isn't in possession of all the facts.*

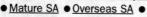 welfare

SERVICES:
- Playgroup ● Lesbian & Gay Society
- Mature SA ● Overseas SA ● Equal Opportunities Officer
- Self-defence classes

The Student Association Welfare Adviser helps with legal, financial and academic problems. So too do the University's 3 part-time student counsellors and the 'Hebdomadar' (welfare/discipline officer). The local health centre has a dedicated student practice.

Disabled: Ramps are provided where practical *but access is pretty hopeless. Part of the problem is the design of the old buildings. Residences are better.* There is a Special Needs Co-ordinator.

Women: *Although female students are now in the majority, many feel that this is still a male-dominated enclave and that specific welfare provision is limited.*

FINANCE:
- <u>Ave debt: £1,100</u> ● <u>Access fund: £134,235</u>
- <u>Successful applications (1997): 643</u>

In addition to the access fund, the University can provide interest-free loans in extreme cases through Hebdomadars.

 # St David's University College

see Lampeter, University of Wales

St George's Hospital Medical School, London

● **The Medical College is part of <u>University of London</u> and students are entitled to use its facilities.**

St George's Hospital Medical School, Cranmer Terrace, Tooting, London, SW17 ORE. Tel: (0181) 725 5992. Fax: (0181) 725 3426.
St George's School Club, Cranmer Terrace, Tooting, London, SW17 ORE. Tel: (0181) 725 2709. Fax: (0181) 767 0217.
E-mail: stuuni@sghms.ac.uk

 ## General

6 miles from Trafalgar Square is St George's Hospital, situated in the Tooting district of South London, *famed for 'Citizen Smith' and, well, not a lot else.* The Medical School is in a 1970s redbrick building, adjoined by other older buildings. *Undergraduates are less alienated from the rest of the hospital than those in other medical schools, but are distanced from the rest of the <u>University of London</u>.*

57% ♂♂♂♂♂♂ ♀♀♀♀ 43%

Sex ratio(M:F): 57%:43%	Founded: 1751
Full time u'grads: 928	Part time: 0
Postgrads: 60	Non-degree: 0
Ave course: 5yrs	Ethnic: 45%
Private school: 40%	Flunk rate: n/a
Mature students: 10%	Overseas students: 5%
Disabled students: 0	Staff/student ratio: 1:2
Clearing: 0	

ATMOSPHERE:
George's has a much more relaxed feel and informal atmosphere than the other London medical schools, and the students miss it when they're sent off on assignments in other hospitals. For example, one wall has been coated in a *graffiti-style* mural. *Because of the teaching structure, there is also much better mixing between years.*

THE CITY: see <u>University of London</u>

TRAVEL: see <u>University of London</u>
Local Trains: Nearest stations are Tooting and Earlsfield.
Underground: Tooting Broadway (Northern Line).
Buses: Numbers 44, 57, 77, 131, 133, 155, 220, 264, 280, N87, N88.
Bicycles: ½ the students have bikes. *Theft is rare - racks are available at the hospital and sheds at the halls of residence.*

LIBRARIES & COMPUTERS:
● <u>Books: 40,000</u> ● <u>Study places: 400</u>
● <u>Computer workstations: 150</u>
There is 24hr access to the computer facilities.

CAREER PROSPECTS:
● <u>Careers Service</u> ● <u>No of staff: 2full</u>

FAMOUS ALUMNI:
Henry Gray (author, Gray's Anatomy); Harry Hill (neckless comic); Edward Jenner (invented smallpox vaccination); Edward Wilson (accompanied Scott to the Antarctic); Mike Stroud (Antarctic explorer).

FURTHER INFO:
Prospectuses for undergrads and postgrads and an alternative prospectus (all available from the Registry). Web site (http://www.sghms.ac.uk).

entertainment

IN LONDON: see <u>University of London</u>

TOOTING:
The Theatre is the local night spot. It has a student night, *but little else going for it.* JJ Moon's is a good local boozer, part of the Wetherspoon operation. *Prices are cheaper than elsewhere in town but for any variety of thrills, students head to Clapham, Brixton or, better still, the city centre.*

COLLEGE:
● <u>Price of a pint of beer: £1.25</u> ● <u>Glass of wine: 70p</u>
Bar/clubs/music venues: The longest med school bar in the country has a capacity of 650 and stages live music, fortnightly discos, student DJ nights and lunchtime food, with regular cut-price promotions.
Theatre & cinema: There's a 400-seat theatre for the thesps – musicals are popular. 1 cult film or recent realease every week in a lecture theatre.
Food: The bar only does lunch; *the hospital canteen is pretty poor,* the Queen Vic over the road usually soaks up the resulting hungry custom.
Others: 7 black tie extravaganzas a year.

social & political

THE SCHOOL CLUB:
● <u>1 sabbatical</u> ● <u>Turnout at last ballot: 30%</u>
 ● <u>NUS member</u>
The Union is apolitical, maybe even conservative (but with a small 'c'). It has reasonable facilities on 1 floor in the School. Rag raised £84,000 last year; there's a fortnightly newsletter revelling compellingly in its lack of political correctness and the

> ❝ The Trent Park Site of Middlesex University originally belonged to poet Siegfried Sassoon, who held orgies in the surrounding woods. ❞

slightly more reverent 'Gazette'. **Also ULU:** see <u>University of London</u>.

CLUBS (NON SPORTING):
Christmas Revue; Spectrum; Wine.

sports

● <u>Recent successes: cricket, rugby, hockey, tennis</u>

Although sport isn't an all-consuming passion, there's been several minor successes recently. Sport tends to be a social scene thing, though. Students have access to 35 acres of playing field and (as part of the Hospital/School complex) a sports hall, climbing wall, 6 squash courts and a multigym. They also have free entry to Tooting Leisure Centre swimming pool.

SPORTING CLUBS:
Boxing; Climbing; Edward Wilson (outdoor pursuits); Paintball; Parachute; Rowing; Tennis; Windsurfing.

accommodation

IN COLLEGE:
● <u>Self-catering: 28%</u> ● <u>Cost: £41(30-50wks)</u>

Availability: 90% of 1st years and a few of the others live in college accommodation. The rooms are clean and modern and set in large grounds. Kitchens equipped with pots and pans are provided, as is a condom machine, laundry and tennis courts. No female students are housed on the ground floor.
Car parking: *Loads of free parking, but only because no-one uses it.*

EXTERNALLY: see <u>University of London</u>
Local accommodation is slightly cheaper and easier to find than in central London, *but some of it's a bit grotty.*

welfare

SERVICES:
● <u>Self-defence classes</u>
There are 2 part-time counsellors for students' non-physical ailments.

FINANCE:
● <u>Ave debt: £2,100</u> ● <u>Access fund: £40,000</u>
● <u>Successful applications (1997): 93</u>
Bursaries, grants and prizes all over the place.

▶▶ St Mark & St John
see Other Institutions

▶▶ **St Martin's University College**
see Other Institutions

▶▶ **St Martin's College of Art**
see The London Institute

▶▶ **St Mary's Hospital**
see Imperial College, London

▶▶ **St Mary's University College**
see Other Institutions

▶▶ **St Thomas's Hospital**
see King's College, London

Staffordshire University

▼ ● *Formerly Staffordshire Polytechnic*
▼ (1) Staffordshire University, College Road, Stoke-on-Trent,
ST4 2DE. Tel: (01782) 292752. Fax: (01782) 745422.
E-mail: admissions@staffs.ac.uk
Staffordshire University Union of Students, College Road,
Stoke-on-Trent, ST4 2DE. Tel: (01782) 294629.
Fax: (01782) 744568. E-mail: suame@staffs.ac.uk
(2) Staffordshire University, Beaconside Campus, Stafford,
ST18 0AD. Tel: (01782) 294000. Fax: (01782) 745422.

General

Staffordshire University is named after the county not the town
of Stafford - students might find themselves in either of 2
towns depending on where their course is based. Stafford is
one of them and Stoke the other *and never the twain shall
meet. They may as well be separate institutions, having their
own identities and loyalties. Both look down on the other,* but
what they have in common is that they are towns in the north-
west Midlands, 17 miles apart. The Stafford campus on a
green-field site in the outskirts of the small and *pretty* county
town. It is a former technical college made of 1960s concrete.
*It's a bit bleak in winter, but great for lazy days in summer
marred only by the looming doom of exams.* The Stoke part of
the University is on 2 sites at College Road and Leek Road in

the town centre of Stoke-on-Trent. *Leek Road has more of the feeling of a self-contained campus with playing fields and accommodation on site.*

57% ♂♂♂♂♂♂ ♀♀♀♀ 43%

Sex ratio(M:F): 57%:43% | **Founded: 1970**
Full time u'grads: 11,600 | **Part time: 3,400**
Postgrads: 1,700 | **Non-degree: 1,108**
Ave course: 3yrs | **Ethnic: 11%**
Private school: n/a | **Flunk rate: 34%**
Mature students: 36% | **Overseas students: 4.5%**
Disabled students: 12% | **Staff/student ratio: 1:20**
Clearing: n/a

ATMOSPHERE:

Many students are on part-time or professional courses *and the University as a whole is developing very rapidly. Stoke and Stafford have totally different atmospheres despite plucky attempts by the University to unite them: Stoke is proactive and radical, while Stafford is dominated by male engineers with more interest in study and beer than anything more creative or political.*

THE SITES:

Stoke: (social sciences, business, art & design, sciences, law) Made up of 2 sites of *tightly packed* post-war buildings, *Stoke is a bit more radical and groovy. The 2 sites have less of the closeness of the community at Stafford although the snack bars are busy and bustling.*

Stafford: (4,397 students - engineering, computing, business, health) *The site is small and students mix between subject groups and across other boundaries often imposed elsewhere. It can get claustrophobic since there's nowhere much to escape to.*

STOKE-ON-TRENT:

● Population: 244,800 ● London: 165miles
● Birmingham: 44miles ● Manchester: 38miles

Stoke has suffered for the last couple of decades from urban decline and the closure of many local industries but, *never mind, it's also the hometown of Anthea Turner and Robbie Williams.* In Hanley, there is a new shopping centre and Festival Park, once the site of the National Garden Festival, now has an *excellent* swimming pool and various other attractions. *Most Stoke students here love it, but they didn't apply for the scenery; whoever painted this place forgot to wash his brush out between colours.* The University has its own art gallery, the Flaxman, on site. See also Keele University.

STAFFORD:

● Population: 117,000 ● London: 131 miles
● Birmingham: 32 miles

Stafford is a market town. The livestock has all gone though and been replaced by an indoor market instead. There are a couple of *pleasant* streets, *but much of the town has been ruined by a blight of town planning.* A new complex of shops near the church *has brought in more attractions for trendy young things.*

TRAVEL:

Trains: Stafford and Stoke are on the Merseyside and Manchester services to London (£18.50). The main Stoke site is right next to the station.

Coaches: National Express services from both towns include London (£12) and more.

Car: The M6 and A34 connect the 2 towns. Stafford is also served by the A518 and A513. The new A50 provides handy links to Derby and Nottingham.

Hitching: *In Stoke a hike may be hitched from the nearby ringroad and the M6 provides a launch pad for both towns. The University and SU discourage this, though, for safety reasons.*

Local: The University runs a free minibus between sites 6 times a day but priority goes to staff and its impossible to get to a 9am lecture. *The 20-minute train journey might offer better odds.* Local buses run by the bizarrely named PMT are also handy and cheap.

Taxis: *With many firms working in both towns, prices are competitive.* Some offer student discounts *which are worth remembering for late nights.*

Bicycles: *For those with thighs like tree trunks, bikes are useful.*

LIBRARIES & COMPUTERS:
- Books: 309,000 • Study places: 1,331
- Computer workstations: 2,400

3 libraries: Leek Rd, College Rd and Beaconside (Stafford). At Stafford, *which is renowned as a centre of computing expertise,* the new, *well-equipped* Octagon Centre has opened - home of the School of Computing. *Students are less impressed with library facilities - limited opening times at the weekends means there's a Friday stampede.*

CAREER PROSPECTS:
- Careers Service • No of staff: 4full/8part
- Unemployed after 6mths (1996): 10.4%

SPECIAL FEATURES:
- Any student under 21 who is resident in Staffordshire, Shropshire or Cheshire is guaranteed an offer, provided they meet the normal entry requirements.
- Staffordshire recently became the first University in the UK to open an Art Gallery in New York, *which the kids in Stoke and Stafford will doubtless appreciate enormously.*

FAMOUS ALUMNUS:
Jim Davies (auxiliary Chemical Brother).

FURTHER INFO:
Prospectuses for undergrads, postgrads and part timers. Also a video guide and a web site (http://www.staffs.ac.uk/welcome.html).

entertainment

TOWNS:
- Price of a pint of beer: £1.70 • Glass of wine: £1.40

The Hanley Cultural Initiative has just received £14.8m of Lottery funding for a theatre/concert venue in the area, *which will stop people having to hike to Birmingham or Manchester for their aesthetic delights.*

Pubs: *Stafford has a slight edge on Stoke as far as variety goes. Most pubs are student-friendly but the general rule is, the closer to the University, the safer.* **push***plugs: Stoke: The Terrace; Fawn & Firkin; Corner Cupboard; the Roebuck. Stafford: Bird in Hand; Telegraph; Wagon & Horses; Potterhouse.*

Cinemas: 2 in Stoke, 1 in Stafford.

Theatres: The Stoke Repertory Theatre, the New Vic in Newcastle-under-Lyme near Stoke and the Gatehouse in Stafford *are the prime spots for luvvie-viewing.*

Clubs/discos: *The University is probably the best place for serious clubbing but Uropa in Hanley has student nights on Mondays.* **push***plug: Swoon (hardcore rave) at the Void (Stafford).*

Music venues: The Stage, the Royal and the Victoria Hall (Hanley) all have *decent* touring indie bands stopping off. *Nothing to speak of in Stoke or Stafford since Wetherspoons and their no-music policy took over the Wheatsheaf in Stoke.*

Eating out: *Not a bad selection, especially for curry-nuts.* **push***plugs: Al Sheikh's (balti); Shaka's (Indian); Dillon's (veggie); Dreadheads (hippy/crusty hangout).*

UNIVERSITY:

● <u>Price of a pint of beer: £1.15</u> ● <u>Glass of wine: £1.20</u>

Bars: There are 4 SU-run bars. Club 1866 in Stoke (named after its capacity) doubles as the prime ents venue; the pink-and-purple Odyssey (cap 500) at College Road is an alternative. Stafford has Sleepers (350), the day-to-day boozer, and Legends (550) as a nightclub bar.

Cinemas: *Arty/culty tendencies are on show at the Stoke regional film theatre on the College Road site.*

Theatre: *Small but moderately active student drama society who put on 2 shows a term.*

Clubs/discos: 8 club events per week across the sites; *highlights include* Scandal Wax (jungle/funk) at the Odyssey and the monthly Reverence (house) at Legends. Guest clubs such as Ministry of Sound and Megadog are also regular events.

Music venues: All the bars double as venues of some description but Club 1866 is the obvious choice for major acts. Recent players have included Louise, Mark Owen and *even* Carter.

Cabaret: Every Saturday Odyssey is turned over to the funnymen; recently, Brendan Burns.

Food: The SU and University compete for the tastebuds of students across the sites. There are traditional refectories as well as the Universe-City fast food operation (Leek Road) and the *smart* Terrace Café and American Graffiti for fast food (Stafford). The bars can also *fill an 'ole.*

Others: Apart from club and society dos there are 3 *major* events crammed together at the end of the year; the May, Summer and AU balls.

·········· sociaL 2 politicaL

STAFFORDSHIRE UNIVERSITY UNION OF STUDENTS:

● <u>7 sabbaticals</u> ● <u>Turnout at last ballot: 10%</u>

● <u>NUS member</u>

University, Union and student body appear to operate on a level of mutual respect; the Union recently persuaded the administration

to shelve its plans to restructure the academic year. Political interest has risen lately, thanks to that old chestnut, student finance; the Campaign for Free Education is strong.

CLUBS (NON SPORTING):
Art About; Computer; Classic Cars; Cult TV; Environmental Protection; Ernest Borgnine Film Society; HIV/Aids Awareness; Hard Rock Beer Drinking; Kebab; Malaysian; Melvyn Bragg; Multicultural; Northern Bastards; Performing Musicians; Role-Playing; Swinging Sculptors; Vampire; Vinyl Only; Welsh.

OTHER ORGANISATIONS:
The 'Get Knotted' newspaper was shortlisted for a 'Guardian' award. The radio station Zone FM has been granted a license to broadcast 28 days a year.

RELIGIOUS:
The University has a Christian Chaplaincy and both towns have churches for all the main denominations. There are places of worship in Stoke for Jews, Muslims, Hindus and Sikhs.

PAID WORK:
Locally there's the usual kind of shop work and the University hires students for work such as mailing and decorating. Union Ents employs 250-300 students.

sports

● <u>Recent successes: athletics, football</u>

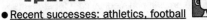

Sport is a major preoccupation for some of the students. A Sport & Recreation degree is offered at Stoke and consequently, the facilities are much better than at Stafford. There are small charges for some of the newest facilities (eg 50p).

SPORTS FACILITIES:
Stoke: 40 acres of fields; 5 floodlit synthetic pitches; sports hall; squash courts; activities studio; fitness suite.
Stafford: 30 acres of fields; 2 synthetic pitches; sports hall; squash court; fitness suite.

SPORTING CLUBS:
American Football; Caving; Gun; Mountain Bike; Mountain Walking; Parachute; Rollerskate; Rowing; Rugby League; Snowboarding.

ATTRACTIONS:
Stoke City FC; Port Vale FC; Crewe Alexandra FC; Uttoxeter Race Course; Northwood Stadium for international athletics.

accommodation

IN COLLEGE:
● <u>Self-catering: 16%</u> ● <u>Cost: £38-53(40wks)</u>

Availability: ½ of the 1st years can be housed, but still very few from other years. 10% of new undergrads don't get a place. However, many of the local, mature and part-time students aren't interested anyway. The University runs a head tenancy scheme offering 50 places.
Car parking: There are limited spaces, but at least it's free. Permits are needed in Stoke.

EXTERNALLY:
● <u>Ave rent: £35</u>
Availability: Hanley and Shelton are popular areas for Stoke students and Highfields is convenient for the Stafford site.

Stafford is marginally more expensive than Stoke but still very affordable.

Housing help: Each site has an Accommodation Office which keeps registers of landlords.

welfare

SERVICES:
- Nurseries ● Nightline ● Lesbian & Gay Society
- Mature SA ● Overseas SA ● Women's Officer
- Self-defence classes

There is a University-run counselling service with 2 full- and 4 part-time *helpful* counsellors. There's also an on-site GP, a harassment network and legal advice.

Women: There is a Women's Group. Free attack alarms are provided by the Union.

Disabled: *Access is excellent in Stoke and in Stafford it's vastly improved (new lifts, etc).* There are 19 rooms adapted for mobility-impaired students, 12 rooms fitted with trembler alarms for hearing-impaired students and every reception area has minicom phones. Main lecture theatres have induction loops and there's a portable loop for smaller rooms. The University and students were the 1st to operate a support worker scheme to provide non-medical care for students with disabilities.

FINANCE:
- Ave debt: £1,000 ● Access fund: £234,567
- Successful applications (1996): 333

University of Stirling

University of Stirling, Stirling, FK9 4LA. Tel: (01786) 467044.
Fax: (01786) 466800. E-mail: admissions@stir.ac.uk
Stirling University Students' Association, The Robbins Centre,
University of Stirling, Stirling, FK9 4LA. Tel: (01786) 467166.
E-mail: susa-president@stir.ac.uk

general

Stirling is nestled in the centre of Scotland, surrounded by the Highlands and Trossachs. The castle, on a cliff face, dominates the landscape and was the royal home in Scotland until 1600. The Old Town has much historic architecture surviving. The University is 2 miles out of town and, like Stirling itself, is small. The students, who account for 1 in 8 of the local population, have a campus reputed to be the 2nd most beautiful in Europe. Which begs 2 questions: which is the most beautiful? and, how do you measure? It is set in 350 acres of landscaped grounds, complete with Airthrey Castle (a different castle - *the place is plagued with the things*), a golf course and a loch with a bridge, separating the University residences from the academic buildings and providing a home for wild fowl and a *fun feature for wild students*. The University buildings are *less impressive* than the setting, apart, that is, from the castle which is used by University departments and offices. Most of the buildings are grey or white flat-topped oblongs, usually 3 or 4 floors high, but, shaded with trees, t*hey blend in somehow*. Meanwhile, the towering Wallace Monument (dedicated to William 'Braveheart' Wallace) presides over the goings on, *not looking much like Mel Gibson, oddly - lacks the blue face paint and the rubbish accent.*

50% ♂♂♂♂♂♀♀♀♀♀ 50%	
Sex ratio(M:F): 50%:50%	Founded: 1967
Full time u'grads: 5,000	Part time: 800
Postgrads: 800	Non-degree: 1,500
Ave course: 4yrs	Ethnic: n/a
Private school: n/a	Flunk rate: n/a
Mature students: 18%	Overseas students: 10%
Disabled students: 2%	Staff/student ratio: 1:13
Clearing: 5%	

ATMOSPHERE:
There's a busy, bustling feel to the place, as if everyone knows exactly where they're going, although they're always prepared to take a detour for a coffee and a slice of gossip. The campus is self-sufficient and the relatively small student body is cosy and welcoming; as a result, many students don't ever feel the need to leave.

THE SITES:
There are two other sites, which are both part of the Department of Nursing and Midwifery.
Highland Campus: (370 students) On the outskirts of Inverness in the grounds of Raigmore Hospital is the medical school. There is a regular bus service into Inverness.
Western Isles Campus: (60 students) *Somewhat isolated (you can only reach it by boat)*, this site is a part of Lewis Hospital in Stornoway on the island of Lewis. Almost all students are local since its purpose is to serve the Western Highlands and Islands.

THE TOWN:
● Population: 35,000 ● London: 378miles
● Glasgow: 27miles ● Edinburgh: 33miles
The University is placed between a very small town, Bridge of Allan, and Stirling itself. Lots of 17th and 18th century architecture, craft and antique shops *give Stirling that historical feel*. There's also an indoor shopping centre and all the essential shops. *It has something of a small town atmosphere, which may have something to do with the fact that it's a small town.*

TRAVEL:
Trains: Stirling Station, 2 miles from the campus, has direct services to London (£42.25) and Edinburgh (£4.35) which is a good place to change for most Scottish destinations.
Coaches: National Express services to London (£24.50),

Edinburgh (£2.50), Newcastle (£12.50) and all points beyond.
Car: Just off the A9 and M9.
Hitching: *Fairly easy to Edinburgh, if you start from the outskirts of town.*
Local: *Cheap* bus service connects the campus with the town centre, running till midnight *but the timetables appear to have been created by someone with a somewhat tenuous grasp on reality.*
Taxis: Stirling is a taxi-infested town, but they're no cheaper than most places (£2.50ish city-campus).
Bicycles: *Except for the strong wind, there are no good reasons why students shouldn't cycle, but then again, there's no good reason why they should.*

LIBRARIES & COMPUTERS:
● Books: 500,000 ● Study places: 1,025
● Computer workstations: 500
Main library and Pathfoot education library (5,000 books).
Facilities are impressive if a little congested, though 24hr access to computers should help.

CAREER PROSPECTS:
● Careers Service ● No of staff: 4full/3part
● Unemployed after 6mths (1995): 5.3%
Good prospects on vocational courses.

SPECIAL FEATURES:
● Stirling was the first UK university to operate a semester system where there are 2 terms (semesters) of 15 weeks each per year. There's also a continuous assessment policy. Both these ideas have been taken up by many other universities since.

FAMOUS ALUMNI:
Iain Banks (writer); Michael Connarty MP, John Reid MP (Lab); Stuart Hepburn, Shelley Jofre, Andrew Miller (TV personalities); Tommy Sheridan (poll tax campaigner); Gordon Sherry (golfer).

FURTHER INFO:
Prospectuses for undergrads and postgrads, course leaflets, web site (http://www.stir.ac.uk).

·········· entertainment

TOWN:
● Price of a pint of beer: £1.60 ● Glass of wine: £1.70
Before you judge harshly, remember Edinburgh and Glasgow are only an hour away.
Cinemas: 1 with 2 screens, *but it's not up to much.*
Theatres: 2 theatres providing anything from panto to opera. *Artistic yearnings tend to be focused on the MacRobert Arts Centre, a cultural nexus for aesthetes from all over central Scotland; when it's not showing blockbusters, that is.*
Pubs: *Quite a few are tolerant of, even friendly to, students but some, such as the Rob Roy, deserve a wide berth if you've got an English accent.* **push***plugs: Hog's Head; O'Neill's; Courtyard.*
Clubs/discos: A couple of *tacky* clubs in town where, for £3, students don't usually bother. *The FU Bar and Rocks have student nights on Thursdays.*

Music venues: Several of the pubs have folk nights and the Albert Bar hosts jazz. The MacRobert also has classical and jazz nights.

Eating out: *The best food in town is probably to be found in the pubs* but there's the standard range of Indian, Italian and fast food feeders as well. **push***plugs: Smilin' Jack's (Mexican); the Bistro.*

UNIVERSITY:

● <u>Price of a pint of beer: £1.45</u> ● <u>Glass of wine: £1.05</u>

Bars: (5) In the Robbins Student Centre, there's a choice of floors upon which to fall face down: the Alehouse (*rustic/pubby*, no music); Shankies (disco bar, events-driven); Long Bar (newly refurbished); Maisies (*good food*); and the Gannochy (sports bar).

Cinemas: The MacRobert Arts Centre on campus shows 4 films a week; *lots of subtitled stuff with aesthetically justifiable nudity.*

Theatres: The MacRobert also has *a very well-equipped* 450 seat theatre and smaller studio (140), both open to the people of Stirling as well as students. It features drama, opera, ballet and modern dance as well as *highly regarded* student efforts.

Clubs/discos: Shankies plays party host 5 times a week, the *highspots* being the fortnightly house/techno night, Carrera.

Music venues: Robbins, the small bar (cap 200) and the Union bar throb with the vibes of live sounds, recent ones coming from the Supernaturals and No Way Sis.

Food: McBob, the university canteen, serves *unexciting but cheap* grub. The Alehouse does pies, Oscars does snacks, Julienne's Vegetarian Cafe at the Gannocky Sports Centre does - *you guessed it* - veggie food.

Others: 3 balls a year and the anarchic 'Final Fling'.

······· social & political

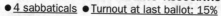

STIRLING UNIVERSITY STUDENTS' ASSOCIATION:

● <u>4 sabbaticals</u> ● <u>Turnout at last ballot: 15%</u>
● <u>NUS member</u>

After a spell of frost, relations between the SA and the University administration are quite positive again. Political interest is on the up; Labour is the dominant political group with a substantial SNP presence.

SU FACILITIES:
5 bars, 3 serving food; 1 disco; general shop; academic support centre; photocopying; photo booth; 2 meeting rooms.

CLUBS (NON SPORTING):
Birding; Chinese; Film Circle; Hellenic; Japanese; Maisies; Malaysian; Musical; Role Play; SNP; Strategic Games; Video Works.

OTHER ORGANISATIONS:
The monthly student paper, 'Brig', has been nominated for a 'Guardian' award; there's also an unofficial mag, 'Mental Block'. SUSA runs Airthrey 963, the campus radio station. There's also a *thriving* student community organisation.

RELIGIOUS:
● <u>6 chaplains (Baptist, Methodist, Anglican, RC, Congregationalist, CofS)</u>
There's a Christian chaplaincy on campus and a Muslim prayer

room. In town there are 9 holy watering holes for those thirsty for Christianity. There's a Jewish chaplain in Glasgow...

PAID WORK:
Usual stuff in Stirling, *but limited*. During vacations, try Glasgow or Edinburgh, a daily train journey away. Within SUSA, there's bar work and the University sometimes needs gaps filled in the library.

sports

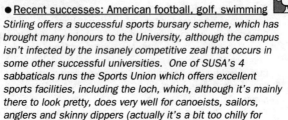

● Recent successes: American football, golf, swimming

Stirling offers a successful sports bursary scheme, which has brought many honours to the University, although the campus isn't infected by the insanely competitive zeal that occurs in some other successful universities. One of SUSA's 4 sabbaticals runs the Sports Union which offers excellent sports facilities, including the loch, which, although it's mainly there to look pretty, does very well for canoeists, sailors, anglers and skinny dippers (actually it's a bit too chilly for that). The Scottish National Tennis Centre is also on campus.

SPORTS FACILITIES:
23 acres of playing fields; sports hall; squash courts; athletics field; loch; croquet lawn/bowling green; swimming pool; tennis courts; all-weather pitch; multigym; running track; 9-hole golf course; sauna & solarium. The town also adds a curling and skating rink, ten pin bowling and the River Forth. Skiing facilities are close by.

SPORTING CLUBS:
Aikido; American Football; Croquet; Gaelic Football; Lacrosse; Rowing; Senokai; Ten Pin Bowling; Tennis; Tenshikan.

ATTRACTIONS:
The local teams are, for rugby, Stirling County, and for football, Stirling Albion. There's also local greyhound racing.

accommodation

IN COLLEGE:
● Self-catering: 72% ● Cost: £39-54(30-37wks)

Availability: The campus accommodation consists of 4 halls: 3 mixed sex and 1 divided into single sex sections. They are all *blessed with unimaginative* breeze blocks, which quickly get smothered in posters. This is enough to accommodate all the 1st years who want to live in. Over 50% of 3rd years, finalists and postgrads can be housed as well, but 2nd years are more likely to fend for themselves. Overseas students can live in for the whole of their course if they want. Nobody has to share and there are facilities for married couples, mainly in the 130 off-campus flats maintained by the University. There's also a flat for women only. After 11pm on campus, students must show their student ID.
Car parking: Free and *sufficient*.

EXTERNALLY:
● Ave rent: £40

Availability: *Stirling is a small place and it ain't easy to find housing locally. Bridge of Allan is the best nest. Raploch and Cornton can be scary. A car can be parked, but students won't need one unless they fancy regular jaunts to the Highlands.*

Housing help: Help is at hand from 7 full- and 3 part-time staff. They issue a vacancies newsletter, advertising lodging listings and bulletin boards, and vet all recommended gaffs.

welfare

SERVICES:
- Nursery ● Nightline ● Lesbian & Gay Society
- Mature SA ● Overseas SA ● Minibus ● Women's Officer
- Self-defence classes

The University employs 2 counsellors. There's a Student & Staff Health Centre, which employs a sister and consulting doctor, and a medical practice on campus.

Disabled: The campus is one of the few designed with disabled access in mind and some rooms and facilities have been adapted. There are induction loops in lecture theatres and help is available for dyslexics. *Students with severe disabilities may still face problems but the Disabilities Officer irons out many creases.*

FINANCE:
- Access fund: £139,900
- Successful applications (1996): 365

● ●

▶▶ Stockton

see University of Durham

● ●

University of Strathclyde

University of Strathclyde, 16 Richmond Street, Glasgow, G1 1XQ. Tel: (0141) 548 2803. Fax: (0141) 552 5860. Strathclyde University Students' Association, 90 John Street, Glasgow, G1 1JH. Tel: (0141) 567 5000. Fax: (0141) 567 5050.

general

Strathclyde University is situated on a number of hills in the middle of Glasgow, right in the city's central business district. The campus is modern and *fairly ugly, but blends inconspicuously with the rest of the city.* The original University building, an *out of place* redbrick affair, is *rather lost* among the more modern structures built since the 1960s. The *compact* campus consists of large department buildings and tower blocks and is fast expanding. *But when it comes to greenery, you wouldn't find much less in an underground car park* (however, the University gardens did win an award in 1994 from the Incorporation of Gardeners of Glasgow). The University has recently 'merged' with Jordanhill College *(ie the University swallowed it)*, which created a second site housing the Faculty of Education.

49% ♂♂♂♂♂♀♀♀♀♀ 51%

Sex ratio(M:F): 49%:51%	Founded: 1796
Full time u'grads: 11,000	Part time: 300
Postgrads: 3,600	Non-degree: 0
Ave course: 4yrs	Ethnic: 1.5%
Private school: n/a	Flunk rate: n/a
Mature students: 21%	Overseas students: 8%
Disabled students: 2%	Staff/student ratio: 1:13
Clearing: 8%	

ATMOSPHERE:
Strathclyde was originally a non-residential University and the students all lived locally. There's still a high proportion of Glaswegians who regard the University as an extension of school and don't hang around more than is necessary. Despite this, and the uninspiring architecture, there's a lot of fun to be had, a large proportion of it generated by the SA.

JORDANHILL:
The Faculty of Education at Jordanhill has 2,000 students. In cheesey-chalk contrast with the main campus 5 miles away, it's a pleasant leafy site, lovely in summer. It has good sports facilities and accommodation for 180 students. Students don't really need to travel between sites, but it's possible anyway by free University bus.

THE CITY: see University of Glasgow

TRAVEL: see University of Glasgow
Strathclyde University is 5mins walk from Queen Street Station and 10mins from Central Station.

LIBRARIES & COMPUTERS:
● Books: 850,000 ● Study places: 2,143
● Computer workstations: 600
The Andersonian is the main library, but there's also the Fleck Library (housing chemistry), the Law Library, the Business & Information Centre and the Jordanhill Library. *Computing standards are good but there aren't enough to go round.*

CAREER PROSPECTS:
● Careers Service ● No of staff: 13full/5part
● Unemployed after 6mths (1997): 7.7%
In addition to information about job availability, the Careers Service offers CV clinics and workshops.

SPECIAL FEATURES:
● There are 33 weeks in the academic year (which does mean a bigger grant).

❝ Space at Luton University is so tight that some exams have taken place in a disused lorry factory in Dunstable. ❞

FAMOUS ALUMNI:
Malcom Bruce MP (Lib Dem); Michael Connarty, Ian Davidson, Maria Fyfe, John McFall, Jim Murphy (Labour MPs); Dougie Donnelly (sports commentator); James Kelman (Booker-winning author); Helena Kennedy QC; Lord Reith (founder of the BBC); Elaine Smith (actress); Teenage Fanclub.

FURTHER INFO:
Prospectuses for undergrads and departmental leaflets. CD-ROM and web sites (http://www.strath.ac.uk and http://www.strath.ac.uk/ussa).

entertainment

THE CITY: see University of Glasgow

UNIVERSITY:
● Price of a pint of beer: £1.30 ● Glass of wine: £1.00
Bars: There are 5 bars in the *vast* Union Building. The *pubby* Barony Bar *is the most popular;* the others include the Cavern *(baguettes by day, bops by night)*; and the Dark Room.
Theatres: The Eclipse drama group presents 3 or 4 productions a year in the Drama Centre and performs at the Edinburgh Fringe.
Clubs/discos: The Dark Room is the main venue, with 3 club nights a week. There are also regular visits from *big name* DJs such as Paul Oakenfold, Leftfield and the Propellerheads.
Music venues: The Union *has a good reputation*, especially for giving a kick-start to local bands and it's also hosted the likes of No Way Sis and Leftfield recently. Every bar in the Union building is equipped for big sounds.
Food: The Food Court in the Dark Room offers traditional stodge and curries, while Delice de France does *healthy* baguettes. The *best bet* is the Cavern which does baked spuds and the like *and value for money is very good.*

social & political

STRATHCLYDE UNIVERSITY STUDENTS' ASSOCIATION:
● 6 sabbaticals ● Turnout at last ballot: 25%
● NUS member
The Union is very well organised and provides a phenomenal number of commercial services. Political activists might feel a little aghast but then you can't have everything.

SU FACILITIES:
5 bars; 5 cafeterias; travel agency; printing shop; general shop; bank and cash machines; Endsleigh Insurance office; TV lounge; photocopier; free playgroup (for offspring of students, sadly, not the studes themselves); games and vending machines; snooker and pool tables; juke box; nightclub; launderette; 8 meeting and function rooms including LGB room; 2 conference rooms.

CLUBS (NON SPORTING):
AIESEC; Anja (Norwegian); Anti-Trainspotters; Cads and Boundahs; Chorus; Federation of Student Nationalists; Hellenic; Hong Kong; Indian; Iranian; Jewish; Kilt; Malaysian/Chinese; Millionaires; Monate (South African); North American; Pakistani; S4 (SF films); Singapore; SNP; Surge; Thai; Websoc.

OTHER ORGANISATIONS:
'Telegraph' is the student newspaper published by, but

editorially independent of, the Union. The University Rag, 'Outrageous', raised £55,063, their most successful year to date. They're also hoping to have Fusion FM on air by November 98.

RELIGIOUS:
There is a team of chaplains who cater to most shades of biblical taste, as well as Jewish and Muslim persuasions. **Religion in Glasgow**, see <u>University of Glasgow</u>.

PAID WORK: see <u>University of Glasgow</u>

sports

● <u>Recent successes: badminton</u>
The University has provided much for the energetic type - sport has become quite a social as well as a physical activity - many of those who can't bring themselves to compete are quite prepared to yell from the sidelines. Nature has also been quite generous, throwing in the River Clyde for watersports. There are 5 golf scholarships, worth £1,250 a year each.

SPORTS FACILITIES:
45 acres of playing fields; sports centre; 2 small gyms; 2 swimming pools; all-weather pitch; squash courts; climbing wall; weight-training room and multigym.

SPORTING CLUBS:
Aikido; American Football; Boxing; Curling; Hang Gliding/Paragliding; Life-saving; Parachuting; Shinty.

ATTRACTIONS: see <u>University of Glasgow</u>

accommodation

IN COLLEGE:
● <u>Catered: 3%</u> ● <u>Cost: £63(35wks)</u>
● <u>Self-catering: 13%</u> ● <u>Cost: £42-57(37-50wks)</u>
Availability: 46% of 1st years can live in and then 17% of 2nd years. 11% of 1st years in halls have to share. Baird Hall, 20mins from the campus, is the only catered hall and houses mainly 1st years. The University provides housing for some married couples, but it's 15 miles away. Self-catered flats make up the student village next to the campus. *There have been complaints about the size of rooms and the fact that it's impossible to control the heating.* The most expensive self-catered places are in new blocks where rooms have en suite facilities and TVs. The other self-catered flats, not far from the student village, *can suffer from a lack of social mingling because they are separated into flats - they are a bit stuffy and lacking in character, even the Waterfront ones, in Yuppieville.*

EXTERNALLY: see <u>University of Glasgow</u>
Housing help: The Accommodation Office has 7 full- and 1

❝Past competitors on 'University Challenge' include Stephen Fry, David Mellor, Clive James, John Simpson and Malcolm Rifkind.❞

part-time staff who keep lists of vacancies and recommended and blacklisted landlords. Help also from the Students' Association.

welfare

SERVICES:

- Nursery ● Lesbian & Gay Society
- Mature SA ● Overseas SA ● Postgrad SA ● Minibus
- Women's Officer ● Self-defence classes

The University Student Advisory & Counselling Service provides 1 full- and 6 part-time counsellors. The Student Health Service runs a daily clinic on campus with a consultant psychiatrist. There are student advisers and the Welfare Officer at the Students' Union Welfare Office. There's also a Centre for Academic Practice for academic advice and an International Office for overseas students. All these bodies work closely together.

Disabled: *The hilly campus is a problem for access.* Individual arrangements can be made with the part-time adviser. The Union Building has disabled access to 6 of its 10 levels, and there's a Co-ordinator for Special Needs. For sight-impaired students, there's a support group ('Outreach') and a Braille translator/transcriber.

Women: Attack alarms and CCTV on campus help on the security front.

FINANCE:
- Ave debt: £550 ● Access fund: £300,000
- Successful applications (1997): 1,500

University of Sunderland

● *Formerly Sunderland Polytechnic*
University of Sunderland, Ryhope Road, Sunderland, SR2 7PS. Tel: (0191) 515 3000. Fax: (0191) 515 3805.
E-mail: student-helpline@sunderland.ac.uk
University of Sunderland Students' Union, Wearmouth Hall, Chester Road, Sunderland, SR1 3SD. Tel: (0191) 514 5512. Fax: (0191) 515 2441.

general

Sunderland is England's newest city, a port forming part of the Tyne & Wear conurbation. Buildings almost all date from the 60s and onwards and *the centre is only just old enough to have started to look shabby.* Although it is industrial, the Northumbrian coast and moors and the rural city of Durham to the south-west are all close, as are 2 of Europe's largest shopping complexes - the Metro Centre in Gateshead and Eldon Square in Newcastle (see Newcastle University). The University has 3 areas that you might call campuses, but, in fact, has splinters all over the city - more than 40 buildings.

The Chester Road campus in the city centre is mostly composed of early 60s tower blocks *which match the city architecture in style and complete lack of aesthetic appeal.* The newer St Peter's campus, by the river, *is more attractive.*

49% ♂♂♂♂♂♀♀♀♀♀ 51%	
Sex ratio(M:F): 49%:51%	Founded: 1969
Full time u'grads: 9,414	Part time: 1,763
Postgrads: 365	Non-degree: 633
Ave course: 3yrs	Ethnic: 4.8%
Private school: n/a	Flunk rate: 26%
Mature students: 41%	Overseas students: 7%
Disabled students: 4.3%	Staff/student ratio: 1:19
Clearing: 25%	

ATMOSPHERE:
The University has made a specific point of attracting local students and for many people in this once deprived corner of the country it can be a life-changing experience. Neither the city nor the Uni will win any beauty contests (they've won architecture awards, but then that's something different altogether) but they make up for it in friendliness and enthusiasm.

ST PETER'S CAMPUS:
4,000 students in the Business and IT departments are based here, a mile from the main site. *It's a far more attractive setting for study, being a coherent mix of wood and concrete.* In the long run, the University aims to base ½ of all students here.

THE CITY:
- Population: 286,800 ● London: 257miles
- Newcastle: 10miles ● Durham: 13miles

No-one would claim this is an architecturally appealing city - unless they were architects. It doesn't have a wide range of shops, just repetitive branch stores, although Newcastle and the Metro Centre make up for that. However, there are 2 museums, some *interesting* bridges and, a little way inland, the Penshaw Monument, a massive folly that looks like a Greek temple and can be seen for miles around. A new £70m development project should do some good.

TRAVEL:
Trains: Sunderland station is 10 mins walk from the Chester Road campus. There are direct trains to Newcastle, Middlesborough and London (£37.05) and connections to the rest of the country.
Coaches: Blueline and National Express services to many destinations including London (£20) and Manchester.
Car: 8 miles off the A1(M) on the A123, A19 and A690.
Air: Newcastle International and Teesside Airports are both under an hour's drive away.
Ferries: The nearest ferries are from Newcastle and Hull, serving Europe and Scandinavia.
Hitching: *Good prospects once out of Sunderland, particularly on the A1 north or south.*

Local: The buses are *cheap* (fares from 20p) *and quite reliable, although deregulation in Wearside has complicated the timetables.* A free campus bus service runs between all key University buildings and halls of residence. Trains run to Newcastle and Middlesborough every ½ hour, costing £2.60. Development of an underground system is imminent.

Taxis: *Since Sunderland's small, the taxis can't charge too much to get anywhere. Even so, they're cheap anyway.*

Bicycles: *There are bike lanes between Consett and the coast and between Sunderland and Whitehaven in Cumbria. Problems with theft are decreasing, but there aren't many places to leave them in town.*

LIBRARIES & COMPUTERS:
- Books: 350,000 ● Study places: 1,800
- Computer workstations: 679

The main library is on the Chester Road campus, and there are further departmental libraries. 24hr access to computer facilities.

CAREER PROSPECTS:
- Careers Service ● No of staff: 3full/3part
- Unemployed after 6mths (1996): 9.3%

FAMOUS ALUMNI:
Steve Cram (runner); Alan Donnelly MEP (Lab); Ian Wilson (swimmer). Sunderland FC has a collective honorary degree.

FURTHER INFO:
Prospectus, course literature, leaflets, web site (http://www.sunderland.ac.uk).

·········· entertainment

THE CITY:
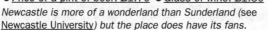
- Price of a pint of beer: £1.70 ● Glass of wine: £1.30

Newcastle is more of a wonderland than Sunderland (see Newcastle University) but the place does have its fans.

Cinemas: A 3-screen mainstream house and a new 12-screen Virgin cinema 10 miles out of town.

Theatres: (2) The Empire shows mainstream plays, pantos and concerts; the Royalty is for local offerings. The Seaburn Centre hosts visits from the RSC.

Pubs: *Cheap, cheerful and mostly friendly.* **push***plugs: Fitzgeralds; Stone Bridge; Rosie Malone's; Royalty Museum Vaults; The Windsor Castle is a cool gay hangout.*

Clubs/discos/music venues: *Not too many clubs, but the* **push***plugs go to The Palace (charty), Annabels (dance/retro) and Pzazz (Britpop). Local bands play at Rosie Malone's and live jazz jives at the Ground Floor Café.*

Eating out: *Fancy food isn't a Sunderland specialism but, apart from a large selection of burger bars and kebab joints,* **push***plugs go to: Marcello's, Capanella (Italian; NUS discount); Johnny Ringo's and Café Divine (Mexican).*

UNIVERSITY:
- Price of a pint of beer: £1.20 ● Glass of wine: £1

Bars: (3) The Manor Quay Bar is the main ents venue; the Roker Bar at St Peter's and the Wearmouth Bar at Chester

Road are the prime daytime haunts. A new bar opening in September 98 at the Pann's Bank residence will *almost certainly* be called the Bonded Warehouse.

Theatre: *Strong* performing arts courses and access to the Sunderland Empire.

Clubs/discos: Manor Quay (cap 1,200) gets somewhat funky 4 nights a week and can lure the likes of Judge Jules and Alistair Whitehead as guests. There's a termly LGB night too.

Music venues: Manor Quay is also developing as a *good* source of live sounds, recently hosting Jools Holland, Wannadies and Bizarre Inc.

Cabaret: Once a term stand-up nights.

Food: The University provides food-stops at all sites and the Roker and Wearmouth bars provide sustenance as well. A new addition is the Cybernet Connection on the Chester Road campus with fast food next to online access.

Others: The Summer Ball is popular *but they don't tend to go for the old dinner-jacket-and-strawberries-and-champagne-darling thing round these parts.*

social & political
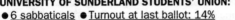

UNIVERSITY OF SUNDERLAND STUDENTS' UNION:

● 6 sabbaticals ● Turnout at last ballot: 14%
● NUS member

The Union arranges enough to keep a large number of the students busy and motivated, if not on a political wavelength, although a recent push by the SU may put a few more ants in their pants. As it were.

SU FACILITIES:
Bars; pool tables; games machines; vending machine; quiet room; shops; travel agency; minibus service; photocopier; print shop.

CLUBS (NON SPORTING):
Cheerleading; Chinese; Day Trippers; Duke of Edinburgh; Games; Hellenic; Indian; Juggling; Live Action Role Play; Malaysian; National Hat Society; Real Ale; Sikh; Spanish; Stop the Fees; Youth Rights in Europe.

OTHER ORGANISATIONS:
'Degrees North' is the monthly student newspaper, with a sabbatical editor. There's also a charity Rag and a student Community Action group.

RELIGIOUS:
● 2 chaplains (CofE)

The Islamic Society has its own mosque. Most brands of Christianity, as well as Judaism, have outlets in town.

PAID WORK:
Unemployment in the area has dropped substantially since the dim days of grim recession, so opportunities crop up. There are also about 150 casual posts with USSU, who are starting a jobshop in 1998.

sports

● Recent successes: netball, rugby

The University has an OK range of sporting clubs and the council facilities compensate for any gaps. £5 membership fee to use all facilities.

SPORTS FACILITIES:
The sports centre on Chester Road has a 25m pool, sports hall and 2 gyms. St George's House has a dance studio and training room. Bede Tower has a gym and hard area and there are 10 acres of playing fields at Seaburn and Hendon. The town adds squash, badminton and basketball courts, a dry ski-slope, football, rugby and cricket pitches; the Crowtree Centre has a pool, ice skating and hockey and boxing facilities; Silksworth outdoor complex has a tennis centre, dry ski-slope, running track, lake and orienteering courses; Sunderland Harbour offers water sports.

SPORTING CLUBS:
Aikido; American Football; Caving; Combative Arts; Gaelic Football; Ice Hockey; Mountaineering; Ri Tae Kwon Do; Rowing; Surfing; Tennis.

ATTRACTIONS:
Support for Sunderland FC (and loathing for their Newcastle neighbours) is endemic. There are also ice hockey and basketball teams.

accommodation

IN COLLEGE:

● Catered: 4% ● Cost: £53-57(40wks)
● Self-catering: 20% ● Cost: £35-43(40wks)

Availability: All 1st years who want university accommodation can have it (1 in 4 say 'no, ta') and about 20% of other undergraduates should be in luck. No one has to share. The facilities range from purpose-built halls to tower blocks to the new *swish* self-catering flats with en suite facilities. There are also 700 places under the head tenancy scheme.

Car parking: Permit parking, £30 a year (free to disabled users).

EXTERNALLY:
● Ave rent: £33

Availability: *As the University grows apace, it's becoming harder to find suitable housing. Recommended areas include Millfield, Ashbrooke, Chester Road and Hylton Road. Avoid Pennywell and Ford - not safe.*

Housing help: The University's Student Services organisation runs an accommodation finding service.

welfare

SERVICES:

● Creche ● Nightline ● Lesbian Gay & Bisexual Society
● Mature SA ● Overseas SA ● Minibus ● Women's Officer
● Self-defence classes

Help is at hand from Student Services and the welfare department, which has 2 counsellors (1 full- and 1 part-time), 2 health advisers, a nurse and a legal service provided by a local solicitor. 2 bobbies from Northumbria Police are permanently attached to the campus *but not by electrodes to the genitals or copydex glue or anything.* The Union adds 5 full-time welfare and academic advisers.

Disabled: *The older buildings are not wheelchair-friendly* but efforts are being made; there's a 3-person disability support team and special course modules for students with dyslexia.

Women: Sunderland has one of the few female Vice-Chancellors and there is a lot of concentration on careers for women.

FINANCE:
- Ave debt: £1,950 ● Access fund: £190,289
- Successful applications (1996): 1,326

Student Services has debt counsellors and financial help-books.

University of Surrey

University of Surrey, Guildford, Surrey, GU2 5XH.
Tel: (01483) 300800. Fax: (01483) 300803.
University of Surrey Students' Union, Union House, University of Surrey, Guildford, Surrey, GU2 5XH. Tel: (01483) 259223.
E-mail: su-comms@surrey.ac.uk

General

On the edge of the North Downs, in the heart of London's commuter country is the town of Guildford. Around the outskirts, it's a post-war invasion of modern architecture (not least the cathedral, where Gregory Peck met a sticky end in 'The Omen') and shopping malls, but the city centre is a *quaint* old place with its cobbled main street *and rural feel.* The University campus is on Stag Hill, 10 minutes walk away. It was built in the late 60s, before which the University had been Battersea Poly. *The campus is a bit cramped and confusing and suffers from looking like a sandy grey Lego set. But, from certain viewpoints over the man-made lakes and landscape gardening, it's just about possible to hide the concrete with greenery and occasional migrant wildlife (rabbits, ducks and the like). These are the only views the prospectus offers, but they're not the bleakly functional impression you get from ground level.*

48% ♂♂♂♂♂♀♀♀♀♀ 52%	
Sex ratio(M:F): 48%:52%	Founded: 1966
Full time u'grads: 5,107	Part time: 33
Postgrads: 3,332	Non-degree: 0
Ave course: 4yrs	Ethnic: n/a
Private school: n/a	Flunk rate: n/a
Mature students: 17%	Overseas students: 30%
Disabled students: 2.5%	Staff/student ratio: 1:17
Clearing: 11%	

ATMOSPHERE:
Being campus-based and with such a large proportion of students living in, Surrey University is a close-knit community, which from the outside seems insular, but is friendly enough

from within. Most courses being 4 years, with part of the 3rd year spent in vocational training (ie. a job), there are some seriously career-minded individuals around and a fairly business-like attitude to study; they do, however, loosen up a bit when night falls. Surrey originally specialised in science and engineering but recently arts and social studies have expanded greatly, taming a previously bloke-heavy atmosphere.

THE TOWN:
- Population: 121,500 ● London: 30miles
- Southampton: 45miles ● Birmingham: 106miles

One of the best things about Guildford is that it is close to London. For serious spending and furious fun, it's best to hop on the next train out of town. However, for your daily needs, Guildford is well equipped with supermarkets (a Tesco's within walking distance of the campus), shops (a few open till late), banks with cashpoints, bookshops (including 2nd hand), public libraries and a street market. The Spectrum Leisure Centre has an ice rink, bowling alley, pool and gym. Guildford also offers the River Wey, 2 museums and the castle keep.

TRAVEL:
Trains: From Guildford Station (½ mile from campus) mainline connections to London (£9.80).
Coaches: National Express from Guildford to London (£4.20) and elsewhere.
Car: 5 mins from A3 (look for the mortar board sign posts), A25 and Junction 10 of the M25 also near.
Air: ½hr by car to both Heathrow & Gatwick (inland and international).
Hitching: Okay for the A3 for London or to the M25 if you can find somewhere to stand.
Local: Good bus service around town, including a minibus every 12 mins from campus to the centre (60p return).
Bicycles: *Not too hilly and cycle lanes are proposed for the town.*

LIBRARIES & COMPUTERS:
- Books: 405,000 ● Study places: 900
- Computer workstations: 626

CAREER PROSPECTS:
- Careers Service ● No of staff: 3full
- Unemployed after 6mths (1996): 0.9%

SPECIAL FEATURES:
- Most of 1 year (usually 3rd) or 2 half years are spent on professional placements. Although some are optional, it's generally seen as an advantage.
- Students (regardless of their own course) are encouraged to learn a language for which extra classes are laid on.

FAMOUS ALUMNI:
Jasmine Dotiwala (former 'Word' presenter); Robert Earl (restauranteur, Planet Hollywood); Alec Issigonis (designed the Mini); Nabil Shaban (actor, founder Greae Theatre).

FURTHER INFO:
Prospectuses for undergrads and postgrads, alternative prospectus from the SU, a video and a web site (http://www.surrey.ac.uk).

❮ 'It was a time when the number of times one could get laid was exceeded only by the number of job opportunities – a state of affairs which applies only in the House of Commons. And to think we did it on local authority grants!'
–Tony Banks MP on his student days. ❯

·········· entertainment

TOWN:
● Price of a pint of beer: £2.20 ● Glass of wine: £2

Pubs: *In the city, the pubs represent a fairly broad and uninspired mix, although around the local countryside, pubs are a sight more real - real ale, real log fires, real pub grub.* push*plugs: The Hogshead; Scruffy Murphy's; The Forger & Firkin; Star Inn; George Abbott. Avoid the less than student-friendly Robin Hood.*

Cinemas: (2) Odeon with 10 screens and an arthouse.

Theatres: (2) The Yvonne Arnaud Theatre is sometimes a springboard for West End shows and the new Electric Theatre stages am dram.

Clubs/discos: (3) *Bojanglez, Cinderellas, The Drink and Bar Mambo are the main outlets for dance insanity but none of them can be described as cutting-edge.*

Music venues: The Civic Hall hosts everything from indie to the Band of the Royal Marines.

Eating out: There's an *OK* range of cosmopolitan eateries, as well as the usual greasebuckets. push*plugs: Bombay Spice (Indian); Bamboo Garden (Chinese); Mississippi Exchange (diner); King's Head; Cafés Uno and Tote; El Sombrero.*

UNIVERSITY:
● Price of a pint of beer: £1.70 ● Glass of wine: 95p

Bars: (6) The *vast* Lounge Bar is open lunchtimes and evenings *and is the main drinking den.* Chancellors is *slightly posher* and the Helyn Rose Bar is mainly used for functions. Horry's bar is the new one.

Theatres: (1) The *well-equipped* Performing Arts Technology studios are used by dance and music students as well as student drama *which is fairly low-key by most standards.*

Cinemas: 2 film clubs, *showing mainstream stuff 3 times a week.*

Clubs/discos: There are 3 discos a week: Shag night (dance); Citrus (swing, soul and R'n'B) and the Friday Night Out. Funk nights every 4 weeks.

Music venues: The Union has recently hosted the likes of Lightning Seeds and Space.

Cabaret: Occasional silliness in the Union from Lee & Herring, Craig Charles and more.

Food: The University refectory is the main face-filler but there's more besides: the Helyn Rose Bar does pasta and baguettes; Chancellor's has waitress service (*at a price*); and the new Lakeside restaurant is run by Hotel and Catering Management undergraduates.

Balls: Apart from the annual Graduation Ball, the Colours Ball celebrates sports awards and the Charter Ball celebrates the granting of the University's charter and is used to announce the results of Union elections.

social & political

UNIVERSITY OF SURREY STUDENTS' UNION:

● 5 sabbaticals ● Turnout at last ballot: 10%
● NUS member

Students have a good level of say within the University through USSU which has representatives on most major committees, partly because the University can rest assured the students aren't likely to get militant. There are no political societies and everyone stands for election on an independent slate. Campaigning tends to be a bit localised - a boycott of a local club forced them to review their policy on doormen.

SU FACILITIES:
4 bars; 2 cafeterias; 7 minibuses (for hire); travel agency; photocopying; market stalls; photo booth; pool and snooker tables; juke box; vending machines. NatWest bank with cash machine on campus.

CLUBS (NON SPORTING):
Amateur Radio; Biker; Conker; Cyprus; Electronic; Folk; Games; Gilbert & Sullivan; Hellenic; Hong Kong; Malaysian; Schools Link; Sri Lankan; Taiwanese; Tamil; Thai; Turkish; Venture Scouts; Welsh; Women's Engineering.

OTHER ORGANISATIONS:
The student newspaper is 'Bare Facts' and GCR is the award-winning student radio station based on campus. There's also a charity Rag.

RELIGIOUS:
There are no places of worship on campus, but meetings are held among most Christian denominations. Right next to the campus is the famous modern cathedral. Hindus and Sikhs are also catered for locally.

PAID WORK:
Standard bar, shop and restaurant work.

sports

● Recent successes: golf

Students can buy a sports and classes card for £30 a year which gives them annual use of the extensive facilities. It's £30 annually for the Quantum Fitness Club, or £40 for both services.

SPORTS FACILITIES:
Sports hall; 60 acres of playing fields; squash courts; astroturf; croquet lawn; tennis courts; climbing wall; gymnasium; multigym; sunbeds and the River Wey (suitable for a variety of water sports). The city also has a swimming pool, the new Spectrum Leisure Centre and athletics field.

SPORTING CLUBS:

Aikido; American Football; Boxing; Gliding; Gymnastics; Hiking; Rifle; Tai Itsu; Water Polo; Windsurfing.

ATTRACTIONS:

Sandown Park Race Course is near enough for a day's outing as are Ascot and Twickenham.

accommodation

IN COLLEGE:

● Self-catering: 42% ● Cost: £36-53(28/38wks)

Availability: All 1st years and most (65%) of finalists have the chance to live in. 3rd years, who for the most part are on placements, don't really need to. That only leaves the 2nd years to fend for themselves. On campus there are 7 'courts' which are accommodation blocks *of a generally adequate standard*. Between them they house 2,117 students in single rooms with shared kitchens, sometimes even an en suite bathroom. A further 208 places are available about 2½ miles away at Hazel Farm which are, in effect, terraced houses for 6 to 7 students let by the University. Students share 'KUBs' (Kitchen/Utility/Breakfast rooms with fridge/freezers and cookers) with about a dozen others, *great for coffee and gossip*. 6% of 1st years have to share split level rooms. Some floors and houses are single sex, but it's mostly mixed. There are a few flats for married students only. An *infrequent* shuttle bus runs to and from Hazel Farm and when the Union shuts at night.

Car-parking: Parking on campus is a problem and a permit (not readily available to residents) is required on weekdays.

EXTERNALLY:

● Ave rent: £52

Availability: *It's hard to find anything, even if you've got the dosh. The students lucky enough to own a car probably won't be lucky enough to find a parking place, foiling the point. Park Barn and Park Avenue are reasonably close but expensive. Hard cheese generally.*

Housing help: To the rescue comes the University-run Accommodation Office to guide students through the vacancy bulletin board and standard renting contracts.

welfare

SERVICES:

● Creche ● Lesbian & Gay Society
● Mature SA ● Overseas SA ● Postgrad SA ● Minibus
● Women's Officer ● Self-defence classes

USSU's Student Advice Service employs a welfare advice officer and personal tutors may also be helpful. The University

> ❛UMIST's collection of modern art includes a sculpture of Pacioli, the hugely interesting creator of double-entry book-keeping.❜

health centre has doctors, nurses and 2 full- and 5 part-time counsellors, as well as a 24-hour sick bay.

Disabled: *Wheelchair access isn't much cop - the campus is on a hill and covered in steps.* Special hearing equipment is available.

FINANCE:
- Ave debt: £700 ● Access fund: £147,043
- Successful applications (1996): 761

The access fund is largely used to help with accommodation problems. Undergrads living out can apply for a flat rate housing grant of £145 per year (£195 for postgrads).

● ●

Surrey Institute of Art & Design

● *Formerly West Surrey College of Art and Design*

(1) Surrey Institute of Art and Design, Falkner Road, Farnham, Surrey, GU9 7DS. Tel: (01252) 722441.
Fax: (01252) 733869. E-mail: registry@surrart.ac.uk
Students' Union, Surrey Institute of Art and Design, Falkner Road, Farnham, Surrey, GU9 7DS. Tel: (01252) 710263.
Fax: (01252) 713591. E-mail: su@surrart.ac.uk
(2) Surrey Institute of Art and Design, Epsom Campus, Ashley Road, Epsom, Surrey, KT18 5BE. Tel (01372) 728811.
Fax: (01372) 726233.

general

Farnham, on the home counties trail from London to Southampton, is an old rural market town, *full of quaint shops and beige jackets.* Not all, but many of those who live here commute to the big city and give the town a suburban (rather than a village) feel. Epsom is 32 miles away, *but a Martian would be hard-pressed to spot the difference.* The main Farnham site is on a small redbrick, prefabricated, *well-equipped*, campus with a village on one side and *gently* rolling fields on the other. (There's also an FE site 300 yards away.) The Epsom building, designed by the same bloke, holds 451 undergrads, and 301 other students, in the Faculty of Fashion and Communication.

57% ♂♂♂♂♂♂ ♀♀♀♀ 43%	
Sex ratio(M:F): 57%:43%	**Founded: 1969**
Full time u'grads: 2,400	**Part time: 150**
Postgrads: 28	**Non-degree: 600**
Ave course: 3yrs	**Ethnic: 10%**
Private school: n/a	**Flunk rate: n/a**
Mature students: 30%	**Overseas students: 2.5%**
Disabled students: n/a	**Staff/student ratio: 1:27**
Clearing: 1.5%	

ATMOSPHERE:
Like all art colleges, the students are utter trend monsters. To dress unobtrusively is a fashion faux pas. Nerds are few and far between and everybody is friendly. Local reactions are a bit mixed; this is green welly/commuter country and the concept of purple-haired, multiply-pierced arty farties doesn't really appeal to some. Farnham is quite buzzy socially but at Epsom work seems to come first.

FARNHAM:
- London: 42miles ● Reading: 9miles
- Southampton: 31miles

Farnham has a weekly street market, a large theatre (the Redgrave) and a large arts centre (the Maltings). It also provides the regular panoply of suburban amenities (public library, supermarket, book shops, major banks, cashpoints, a shopping mall, a street market, etc).

EPSOM:
Epsom is close enough to London to feel a bit like a suburb of the Big Smoke. The area's nothing to get excited over but with the city so accessible, who needs local excitement?

TRAVEL:
Trains: Farnham station is ¾ of a mile from the College, on the line to London (£11.50) and Guildford. Epsom station is 5 minutes walk from the Institute site - London (£4.10).
Car: Both towns are *bedevilled* by one-way systems. Farnham is best approached from the A325, Epsom from the A24.
Air: Heathrow and Gatwick both less than 30 miles.
Hitching: *Don't bother, no one's going anywhere useful even if they would give you a lift.*
Local: *Local buses in Farnham are erratic, to say the least; Epsom, being closer to London, has more co-ordinated services.*
Bicycles: No hills, lots of places to leave bikes and only small amounts of theft.
Others: Just west of Farnham is Alton, where the Watercress Line steam trains run in the summer. *Very pretty, but useless if you actually want to go anywhere.*

LIBRARIES & COMPUTERS:
- Books: 78,000 ● Study places: 180
- Computer workstations: 236

The library also has 150,000 slides and 3,500 videotapes. 22,000 of the books above are at Epsom.

CAREER PROSPECTS:
- Careers Service ● No of staff: 1full/1part
- Unemployed after 6mths (1996): 25%

SPECIAL FEATURES:
● The Institute provides the only Animation degree course in Europe.

❝Staffordshire University has pioneered the use of sewage for making bricks and floor tiles.❞

FAMOUS ALUMNI:
Daniel Greaves (animator); Alex Keshishian (director who got
'In Bed with Madonna'); Sadie Lee (artist); Nick Park (Oscar-
laden animator).

FURTHER INFO:
Prospectuses for undergrads and postgrads; alternative
prospectus 'The Gospel' from the Union. Web site
(http://www.surrart.ac.uk).

entertainment

TOWN:

● Price of a pint of beer: £2 ● Glass of wine: £1.60
*There isn't really much happening in Farnham, nor really in
Aldershot (4 miles up the road). Nor Guildford (11 miles) for
that matter (see* University of Surrey*). London's not too far,
especially for Epsom students.*
Pubs: *Many local boozers are bunged up by old buffers in
Barbours but some are equally stuffed with students.*
push*plugs: The Plough, The Hogshead (Farnham); Rising Sun
(Epsom).*
Theatres: The Redgrave Theatre in Farnham has a national
reputation and shows a mixture of touring and local
productions. The Playhouse in Epsom hosts comedy, films
and concerts as well as some *low-brow* theatre.
Clubs/discos/music venues: The Maltings and the Blues
Tavern field local tunesters. *For serious clubbing (or any
clubbing, really) Guildford's the nearest option, as clubs in
Farnham are rarer than hen's teeth.* In Epsom, Greens
provides *mild doses of almost-hedonism
(disco/house/garage).*
Food: There are cheap Italian pizza and pasta stops in
Farnham. Epsom has the Rising Sun for pub grub *but that's
about it.*

COLLEGE:

● Price of a pint of beer: £1.50 ● Glass of wine: £1.15
Bars/venues: (2) *The Grapes Bar (cap 275) is the centre of
social life.* Epsom's bar the Retreat has been recently
refurbished.
Cinemas: 2 film societies in College; the Roxy and the
Incredibly Strange Film Club, *both tending to culty/studenty
showings.*
Music venues/clubs/discos: 3 dance nights a week in the
bar, ranging from house to 80s sounds. Drum'n'bass nights
once a month. This is also the site for live noise of a
congenial calibre (eg 808 State and My Life Story).
Cabaret: 3 or 4 doses of chuckle a term in the Grapes.
Food: The Farnham canteen is open from 9am-11pm.
Other: 3 balls a year, plus a Leavers' Event.

social & political

**SURREY INSTITUTE OF ART AND
DESIGN STUDENTS' UNION:**

● 3 sabbaticals ● Turnout at last ballot: 35%
● NUS member
The SU is not a big force although ents are picking up. Political

heart-rending is limited, but a recent coup was successfully lobbying for better disabled access to the Union.

SU FACILITIES:
In a shared building the SU runs the bar, cafeteria, games, video and vending machines.

CLUBS (NON SPORTING):
Drawing; Film Societies; Fleece Wearing (drinking).

OTHER ORGANISATIONS:
'DAIS' magazine comes out *sporadically*. Their first Rag raised £500 last year.

RELIGIOUS:
Local CofE and Baptist churches.

PAID WORK:
The college employs students as cleaners and security staff and the SU takes them on in the bar.

sports

- <u>Recent successes: football</u>

Sports aren't really a huge part of College life and the only facility is an indoor games hall, which, it has to be said, is free to use. Local facilities are better: a sports centre (where Jet from 'Gladiators' is an instructor) and playing fields; a swimming pool and golf course; squash and tennis courts; sauna and solarium.

SPORTING CLUBS:
Skiing; Surfing.

ATTRACTIONS:
Local rugby team. Epsom has, *as you may have heard*, a race course. Local schoolkids often get a half-day holiday for the Derby.

accommodation

IN COLLEGE:
- <u>Self-catering: 19%</u> ● <u>Cost: £31-53(30wks)</u>

Availability: 30% of 1st years can be accommodated, spread between 2 halls and the award-winning student village. 25% have to share and 40% of 1st year who want to live in can't. There's no Institute-owned housing at Epsom.
Car parking: Very limited.

EXTERNALLY:
- <u>Ave rent: £58</u>

Availability: *Suitable accommodation isn't too hard to find. Wrecclesham, Upper Hale and Tilford Road are all convenient. Even though walking to College may be a shlepp, a car really is an unnecessary luxury.*
Housing help: The Accommodation Office has offices at Epsom and Farnham.

welfare

SERVICES:
- <u>Lesbian & Gay Society</u> ● <u>Mature SA</u>
- <u>Minibus</u> ● <u>Women's Officer</u> ● <u>Self-defence classes</u>

There are 2 full-time and 3 part-time counsellors, provided by the University.

Disabled: *Access is pretty poor. There's a Disabled Students' Officer, who provides lots of literature. BSL interpreters are also available.*

Women: Self-defence classes cost 50p per session.

FINANCE:
- Ave debt: £1,500 ● Access fund: £76,279
- Successful applications (1997): 287

Also a small (*and we mean small*) SU welfare fund.

●●

University of Sussex

University of Sussex, Falmer, Brighton, BN1 9RH.
Tel: (01273) 678416. Fax: (01273) 678545.
E-mail: ug.admissions@sussex.ac.uk
University of Sussex Students' Union, Falmer House, Falmer,
Brighton, BN1 9QF. Tel: (01273) 678555.
Fax: (01273) 670230.

General

3½ miles inland from Brighton town centre, before the land rises onto the Downs, is the thoroughly modern, 200-acre campus of Sussex University, set in rolling green land near the village of Falmer. The Basil Spence design of courtyards, arches, concrete pillars and redbrick buildings *could so easily have been hideous, but, in context, it works - it really does -* and it has awards to prove it. The campus is isolated, but virtually self-sufficient with a chemist, greengrocer, health centre and so on, all on site.

47% ♂♂♂♂♂ ♀♀♀♀♀ 53%	
Sex ratio(M:F): 47%:53%	**Founded: 1961**
Full time u'grads: 6,752	**Part time: 52**
Postgrads: 2,266	**Non-degree: n/a**
Ave course: 3yrs	**Ethnic: 45%**
Private school: n/a	**Flunk rate: n/a**
Mature students: 31%	**Overseas students: 25%**
Disabled students: 7%	**Staff/student ratio: 1:15**
Clearing: n/a	

ATMOSPHERE:
It's a laid-back campus and people tend to allow a good time to happen to them; the SU obliges and then some. For further fun, Brighton's nearby-ish, although quite a few find the 7-mile round trip too much of an effort.

TOWN: see University of Brighton

TRAVEL: see University of Brighton
Falmer is the closest station with frequent trains into Brighton and providing a comprehensive local service (£9.60 to

> ❝ 'Spice', the Cardiff SU dance night, was closed down when all the sweaty bodies set off the fire alarms and nobody paid any attention because they thought it was a techno record. ❞

London). *Local buses are reliable both when it comes to turning up and when it comes to taking the longest route into town* and charging a quid for the privilege. There are late night buses until 2am.

LIBRARIES & COMPUTERS:
- Books: 750,000 ● Study places: 1,000
- Computer workstations: 900

There's 24-hour computer access and a library extension is being built.

CAREER PROSPECTS:
- Career Development Unit ● No of staff: 4full/8part
- Unemployed after 6mths (1996): 10%

FAMOUS ALUMNI:
Simon Fanshawe (comedian); Nick Fisher ('Just 17' agony uncle); Brendan Foster (athlete); Peter Hain MP (Lab); Billy Idol (bleached rock *prat*); Ian McEwan (writer); Simon Jenkins (journalist); Bob Mortimer (*the sexier one*); Andrew Morton (royal writer); Dermot Murnaghan (ITN reporter); Nigel Planer (Neil from 'The Young Ones'); Julia Somerville (newsreader); Virginia Wade (the last Briton to win a Wimbledon singles title).

FURTHER INFO:
Prospectuses for undergrads and postgrads, alternative prospectus from the SU, a video and a web site (http://www.sussex.ac.uk).

entertainment

TOWN: see University of Brighton

UNIVERSITY:
- Price of a pint of beer: £1.30 ● Glass of wine: £1

Bars: (7) The East Slope (cap 280) *is the most popular*; Park Village Bar (100) is usually packed as well; the Falmer Pub *is more relaxed*.

Theatres: The purpose-built theatre hosts student productions and touring shows. It also displays art exhibitions.

Cinema: There's a thriving Film Society and the Gardner Arts Centre also shows *non-mainstream* flicks 3 times a week.

Clubs/discos: 6 nights a week, the Hothouse (250, adm £2-£3) keeps the tunes churning.

Music venues: The Mandela Hall is the largest music venue, recently hosting Space, Symposium, Urusei Yatsura, No Way Sis and the Mike Flowers Pops among others. The East Slope has local and student bands.

Food: The campus is dotted with a *wide* range of Uni and SU-run grub stops and each school of study has a snack bar.
Others: 5 balls a year.

social & political

UNIVERSITY OF SUSSEX STUDENTS' UNION:
● 6 sabbaticals ● Turnout at last ballot: 25%
● NUS member

The laidback nature of the student body extends to politics, although environmental matters can get them going; appropriately since so many seem to spend the summer sprawled on the grass. The SU has its own trading company which runs the commercial services.

SU FACILITIES:
In USSU's Falmer House, there are 2 bars (1 university-run), a print shop and photocopying, general shop, 2nd-hand bookshop, Endsleigh Insurance office, photo booth, kids' club, volunteer bureau and games room. There's another bar in Mandela Hall.

CLUBS (NON SPORTING):
Africa Forum; Autonomous Students; Bell Ringing; Campaign For Free Education; Chocolate; Creative Arts; Current Affairs; Debating; Eco-Action; Film-Making; Gay Ballroom Dancing; Internet; Jazz; Latin American; Literary; Living Marxism; Malaysia & Singapore; Musicals; Norwegian; Radio; Spanish; Sri Lankan; Turkish; Vegetarian; Yoga.

OTHER ORGANISATIONS:
'Badger' is the weekly newspaper and 'Pulse' magazine comes out every term. University Radio Falmer *gives students a chance to surf the wheels of steel (or play Menswear b-sides).*

RELIGIOUS:
● 4 chaplains (CofE, RC, Free Church, Jewish)
Interdenominational Meeting House chapel.
Religion in Brighton: see University of Brighton.

PAID WORK:
The University has a Student Employment Office, providing part-time and vacation work for students locally.

sports

● Recent successes: trampolining
The facilities are good and conveniently placed on campus but there are small charges for using them (eg 60p for the badminton court). *Sport isn't an all-enveloping obsession.*

SPORTS FACILITIES:
The sports complex contains: 2 sports halls; fitness room with multigym; 4 squash courts; sauna & solarium; café bar; sports shop; injury clinic with physiotherapists. Outdoor facilities include 14 acres of playing fields, a floodlit training area, a floodlit all-weather pitch, 6 tennis courts and 5 more squash courts.

SPORTING CLUBS:
Aikido; Aerobics; Boxing; Snooker; Tang Soo Do; Tennis; Ultimate Frisbee; Windsurfing.

ATTRACTIONS: see University of Brighton

accommodation

IN COLLEGE:
- Self-catering: 35% ● Cost: £46(30/38wks)

Availability: The University is able to accommodate all 1st years who request a place and about 30% of the others. The campus accommodation is in halls, houses and flats in groups of between 5 and 12 rooms. 105 flats cater for families. 10% of rooms are shared and there are some segregated areas for female Muslims.

Car parking: Permit needed *and a car which can nip into small spaces quickly. Or a tank.*

EXTERNALLY: see University of Brighton
- Ave rent: £50

Housing help: The University lends a particular hand allotting students into the places they manage but also helps in the general home hunt, which is increasingly fraught. Lewes Road and London Road (near the train station) are favoured haunts. Several local agencies also make a quick buck getting in on the act.

welfare

SERVICES:

- Creche ● Nightline ● Lesbian & Gay Society
- Mature SA ● Overseas SA ● Postgrad SA ● Minibus
- Women's Officer ● Self-defence classes

USSU runs a Welfare Advice Unit with 2 welfare advisers complementing the University-run counselling service which employs 7 counsellors and 2 advisers. The NHS runs the University health service on campus with doctors, nurses, maternity care and family planning and a dentist.

Disabled: *With the embarrassingly bad exception of Falmer House (the SU building), wheelchair access is fairly good and arrangements are made for the special needs of students with most forms of disability.* Falmer House is due for a refit, but the Council are kicking up a fuss about planning permission. There's also Kulukundis House which is specially adapted accommodation for disabled students.

FINANCE:
- Ave debt: £1,100 ● Access fund: £190,258
- Successful applications (1997): 954

Students can also apply for a Vice-Chancellor's Loan of £75 if their grants are late.

❮ The Sloane Ranger Handbook list of approved UK universities is: Oxford, Cambridge, Bristol, Exeter, Durham, the Courtauld, UCL, Reading, St Andrews, UEA and Edinburgh. ❯

Swansea, University of Wales

▼▼ ● *The College is part of <u>University of Wales</u> and students are entitled to use its facilities.*
University of Wales Swansea, Singleton Park, Swansea,
SA2 8PP. Tel: (01792) 295784. Fax: (01792) 295510.
E-mail: admissions@swan.ac.uk
Swansea Students' Union, Singleton Park, Swansea, SA2 8PP,
Wales. Tel: (01792) 295466/7. Fax: (01792) 206029.

General

Swansea, Wales's 2nd largest city, site of the invention of
instant custard and home of the world's only commercial leech
farm, squats on the south coast on the Gower peninsula - the
country's 1st designated Area of Outstanding Natural Beauty
and *a cool place to have beach parties. The city centre's not
bad* - a more modern and *not unpleasant* selection of slate
and stone houses and brick and concrete shopping malls. Out
west is better still, for there, about 2½ miles out of town,
among the rolling parkland overlooking the bay (*which looks
good from a distance*), is the University of Wales, Swansea.
Its buildings are almost exclusively concrete blocks with
concrete paths interspersed with concrete. But the
surrounding park is *very pleasant* and about 350 yards on the
other side of the coast road (which runs through the park) is a
beautiful sandy beach with dunes stretching into the distance.
Meanwhile, the climate's mild but wet.

45% ♂♂♂♂♂ ♀♀♀♀♀ 55%	
Sex ratio(M:F): 45%:55%	Founded: 1920
Full time u'grads: 6,365	Part time: 371
Postgrads: 1,212	Non-degree: 717
Ave course: 3yrs	Ethnic: 2.8%
Private school: n/a	Flunk rate: 6%
Mature students: 24%	Overseas students: 6.8%
Disabled students: n/a	Staff/student ratio: 1:15
Clearing: 6%	

ATMOSPHERE:
It's a very laid-back atmosphere and serious academic high-fliers appear to be thin on the ground (or maybe they're just working underground somewhere). There's a close-knit atmosphere, but relations with the locals are perfectly cordial and most thrill-seeking goes on in town.

THE CITY:
● <u>Population: 182,100</u> ● <u>London: 160miles</u>
● <u>Cardiff: 40miles</u> ● <u>Bristol: 60miles</u>
Dylan Thomas described Swansea as the 'graveyard of
ambition' because people just never bring themselves to leave
and pursue their wilder dreams - they love it here so much.

Although Swansea itself may not be a tourist attraction, the surrounding countryside is beautiful and brings in the holiday trade. They have to be fed and housed and so Swansea does the business. The locals are very friendly *and will talk you into the next world if you let them.* There's a *good* level of tourist facilities as well as all the amenities for the local residents: shops (some open till midnight); 1st and 2nd hand book shops; supermarkets; 3 large shopping malls; banks; a market and a street market once a week; libraries and museums (notably the Swansea Museum). In the summertime, tourists and students descend to bask on the beaches near The Mumbles, the *oddly* named but *pretty* village on the Gower peninsular 1½ miles west of the campus. *But beware - you may never leave...*

TRAVEL:
Trains: Direct trains from Swansea station, 3 miles from the campus, to Cardiff (£8.30), London (£24.40), Shrewsbury and beyond.
Coaches: Services to London (£18.50), Cardiff (£4.35), Birmingham (£15).
Car: A465, A48 and 5 miles off the M4.
Hitching: *Catch a bus to the M4 and then lifts are pretty easy.*
Local: Regular buses between the student village and the rail station, encompassing the campus, city centre and off-campus halls - £1.40 return to you, *boyo.*
Taxis: Free phone at the campus for students with flammable cash - *not as expensive as many places.*
Bicycles: *The hills inland from the coast have some crazy contours, but for the journey between campus and the city centre, a bike's an asset.*

LIBRARIES & COMPUTERS:
- Books: 700,000 ● Study places: 1,475
- Computer workstations: 972

6 libraries, *which students say are overcrowded, although book provision is OK. Computer facilities give less satisfaction.*

CAREER PROSPECTS:
- Careers Service ● No of staff: 22full
- Unemployed after 6mths (1996): 7%

The careers service is very well-organised and friendly and appears to be pretty efficient if the above figures are anything to go by. They arrange joblink and work shadowing schemes.

SPECIAL FEATURES:
- 50% of students are Welsh and many are Welsh-speakers.
- The campus includes the new 'Egypt Centre', containing a considerable collection of Egyptian artefacts.

FAMOUS ALUMNI:
Donald Anderson MP (Lab); Ian Bone (founder of Class War); Richey Edwards, Nicky Wire (Manics); Nigel Evans MP, Rod Richards MP (Con); Robert Howley, Paul Thorburn (Welsh rugby players); Mavis Nicholson (TV interviewer).

FURTHER INFO:
Prospectuses for undergrads and postgrads, video, web sites (http://www.swan.ac.uk and http://www.swan.ac.uk/uwssu) and an annual 6th form newsletter called 'Baywatch'.

entertainment

TOWN:
● <u>Price of a pint of beer: £1.70</u> ● <u>Glass of wine: £1.30</u>

Cinemas: Apart from the 10-screen multiplex the Taliesin (on campus) and Ty Llen arts centres provide *less mainstream* celluloid.

Theatres: The Grand Theatre *is very popular and successful, if not exactly radical.*

Pubs: *Pubs along the 'Mumbles Mile' are very popular with students and there are very few hostile ones in town. Theme pubs are taking over like anywhere else.* **push***plugs: Smokin' Dog (indie hangout); Vincent's; Knab Rock; Bar Oz; Fineleg & Firkin; Rhydding's; Rasputin.*

Clubs/discos: *Swansea is something of a clubber-magnet in an area ill-served for dance fans and serious party punters come from all over South Wales. Neptune's, on the seafront is pretty popular.* **push***plugs: Popstars at The Zone (Britpop); Carwash at Icon (70s funk/disco); Bubbaclub (drum & bass).*

Music venues: Apart from the campus refectory, Swansea doesn't have a major venue but dozens of pubs and clubs put on smaller-scale gigs, so there's always something on. **push***plugs: Coach House (local rockers); Ellington's (jazz and blues); Singleton, Mumbles Fishing Club and Celtic Pride (indie); Duke of York (jazz and blues).*

Eating out: *Come the evening, all your wildest greeds catered for. The Indian restaurants, in particular on St Helens Rd, are worth a mention. The range, quality and price are second only to Bradford, Rusholme and Delhi.* Night-time nibbles available till at least 2am and deliveries till midnight, but only 10pm in The Mumbles. **push***plugs: Café Mambo (Mexican); Baguette du Jour (sandwich bar); Mozart's (the only Austrian restaurant in Wales); Viceroy (Indian); Jubbly's (American).*

UNIVERSITY: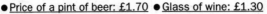
● <u>Price of a pint of beer: £1.15</u> ● <u>Glass of wine: £1.05</u>

The Taliesin Arts Centre is the crown of the campus with a whole host of entertainment facilities (from exhibitions to film and music). *It makes up in part for the city's musical and arty cultural limitations.* Most of the events aren't exclusively by or for students even though the College owns the place. *There's no denying that it's a very handy feature.* In October it's the focus of the Swansea Fringe Festival - the 2nd biggest in Britain after Edinburgh. *However, unlike Edinburgh it has the advantage of being during term time.*

Bars: (4)The main SU bar is Diva's (capacity 500); JC's and Idols are slightly smaller. There is also a bar in the Taliesin Arts Centre.

Theatres: The theatre in the Taliesin has a capacity of 350 where student productions get a look-in between the touring pros. *The Drama Society is a hotbed of actors acting actively, with a major production every term and an annual panto, as well as trips to the Edinburgh Fringe.*

Cinemas: Each week the Taliesin shows 3 or 4 films that may have been missed in mainstream cinemas and has arty and cult screenings.

Clubs/discos: Diva's is used for charty disco type action every Friday (50p-£1) and the SU also hires clubs in town for events.

Music venues: The Refectory is the largest venue (800) playing host to Space, Mansun and the Stereophonics in recent months. Branwyn Hall is also used for gigs.

Food: Angles Food Hall offers good value and a wide selection, including an *extensive* veggie range. *The grub in Diva's is less easy on the pocket.* There's also an internet café called Impressions, but it only has 6 workstations.

Others: Several major balls, culminating in the midsummer bash at, *of all places,* Swansea Airport. 5 marquees are set up on one of the runways.

·······social & political

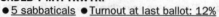

SWANSEA STUDENTS' UNION/
UNDEB Y MYFYRWYR:

● 5 sabbaticals ● Turnout at last ballot: 12%
● NUS member

The SU wags the ear of the college administration and manages to keep the punters fairly happy at the same time - no mean achievement. Fun and facilities abound like their genes are fused with rabbits and they even find time to campaign against fees. Groo-oo-oo-vy.

SU FACILITIES:

There are 3 bars, travel agency, media centre, general shop (including 2nd-hand books), print shop, nursery, Endsleigh Insurance, launderette, 4 pool and 4 snooker tables, photo booth, video and vending machines and pay phones. It also has the marginally more originally named Student Amenities Centre at Hendrefoilan Student Village which has a general shop, a bar, licensed diner, vending machines, a launderette and pay phones. By the way, the College signed away their soul to Lloyds Bank (but then again, so has **push**) and consequently theirs is the only bank and cashpoint on campus.

CLUBS (NON SPORTING):

Aquarian; Arabic; Chess & Diplomacy; Creative Writing; Choral; Club W (women's); Cult TV; Duke of Edinburgh; Eurosoc; 2 Left Feet (dancing); Greek; Gym Gym (Welsh language); Iranian; Militant Students; Malaysian; Marxist; Macabre; Open Door Meditation; Palestinian; Plaid Cymru; Travel; Yellow River (Chinese and Malaysian).

OTHER ORGANISATIONS:

'Waterfront' is the student newspaper which went daily during the recent meningitis scare; Xtreme 963 radio runs on an induction loop around campus. Rag has a very high profile, as does the student community group with over 500 people involved and a full-time co-ordinator organising 24 projects run every week with the young, the old, the disabled and the deprived.

RELIGIOUS:

● 5 chaplains (CofE, RC, URC, Methodist, Baptist)
On campus, there's an inter-denominational chapel, mosque and in town, churches of most orientations and places of worship for Jews and Jehovah's Witnesses.

PAID WORK:

Students looking for work often end up in bars, but only sometimes working there. Engineers and select scientists may find a little vocational vacation work in the local oil industry, but otherwise it's tourism that brings in the loot.

sports

● Recent successes: swimming, football

The College has attractive facilities and has achieved a considerable level of success on a national level as well as creating an enjoyable diversion from studies for those with less Olympian - Olympic, even - talents. Sports scholarships of £700 per year are available for applicants with a national level of prowess or potential in a particular sport. There is a £3 annual fee to join the Athletics Union which organises student sports. Thereafter there are minimal charges (eg 50p for the sports centre) to use facilities.

SPORTS FACILITIES:

On and around the campus there are 20 acres of playing fields, an astroturf pitch, an athletics track and field, sports hall, swimming pool, 5 squash, 6 tennis and 2 netball courts, a gymnasium and multigym, a climbing wall, rifle range and a lake. Off campus the College offers another 70 acres. The city supplements all this with several repetitions and a bowling green, an *excellent* dry ski slope, golf course, leisure centre, sauna and solarium. There's sailing at the Mumbles, and surfing on the Gower peninsula.

SPORTING CLUBS:

Aikido; Caving; Chinese Kick-boxing; Hang-gliding; Lacrosse; Lifesaving; Jiu Jitsu; Parachuting; Rifle; Rowing; Surfing; Tai Chi; Tennis.

ATTRACTIONS:

Within just 2 miles of the campus, students can watch rugby at St Helens and can see Swansea City FC at Vetch Field.

accommodation

IN COLLEGE:

● Catered: 15% ● Cost: £52-67(31wks)
● Self-catering: 29% ● Cost: £35-38(40wks)

Availability: 90% of freshers are accommodated and some other students, with 10% sharing. The 2 Clyne Halls, one for the ladies and one for the gents, provide nearly 350 catered places a mile further west out of town. One *prize* feature is the student village at Hendrefoilan which accommodates 989 students in attractive specially built houses, often split into flats. All these places are self-catering, occupied by between 4 and 11 people, sharing a kitchen and bathroom in noisy harmony. The Clyne Halls and Hendrefoilan are very much self-contained communities with some of their own amenities and organisations.

Car parking: To park on campus one of the 50 available permits is needed *and even with one, it ain't easy. At the other halls and at Hendrefoilan, though, it's not a problem.*

EXTERNALLY:

● Ave rent: £36

Availability: *Most students who end up looking for their own accommodation find it without too much difficulty,* usually sharing in the Victorian terraced houses and flats on the west side of town or in The Mumbles. *Other good areas include Brynmill, Uplands and Sketchy although the east side of town is a bit too distant.*

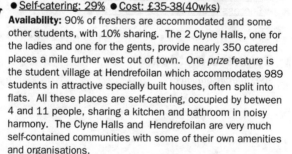

❝Jesus College, Oxford, has a summer Custard Vote, in which students are elected to be splattered.❞

Housing help: The 11 full-time staff of the Accommodation Office offer lists of recommended vacancies, a bulletin board, contract negotiation and an approval scheme.

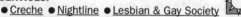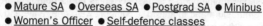

welfare

SERVICES:
- ● Creche ● Nightline ● Lesbian & Gay Society
- ● Mature SA ● Overseas SA ● Postgrad SA ● Minibus
- ● Women's Officer ● Self-defence classes

The College-run Health Centre and Counselling Service employs a medical officer, a sister, receptionist and 3 counsellors providing help with all sorts of personal and health problems. The Students' Union also has a *valuable* advice and information service with 5 advisers.

Women: *Active* women's group, offering free alarms, women-only room, etc although they've had to battle to keep the SU Women's Officer. Avoid Singleton Park at night *unless you want to get flashed at.*

Disabled: There are some specific modifications which help things along, such as a recording centre for visually-impaired students (opened by David Blunkett MP) *but overall, wheelchair access could be a lot better.*

FINANCE:
- ● Ave debt: £950 ● Access fund: £193,815
- ● Successful applications (1996): 951

● ●

▶▶ Swansea Institute

see Other Institutions

❝'I think that's the problem with a University education. You just end up thinking too much.' - Ed O'Brien (Radiohead).❞

Fold-out guide to symbols inside back cover

❛There's more to student life than poverty and fun... see the courses tables at the back of the book.❜

 ❛Freaked out by finance? Why not pop into your local branch of Lloyds Bank and see what they have to offer.❜

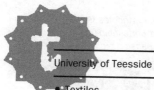

University of Teesside

- ***Formerly Teesside Polytechnic***
University of Teesside, Middlesbrough, TS1 3BA.
Tel: (01642) 218121. Fax: (01642) 342067.
University of Teesside Students' Union, Southfield Road,
Middlesbrough, TS1 3BW. Tel: (01642) 342234.
Fax: (01642) 342241.

General

On the edge of the *glorious* Yorkshire moors, on the north-east
coast of England and not far from the ancient city of Durham,
lies Cleveland, which was only created as a county in 1974
and has recently been abolished again. It's a large industrial
conurbation encompassing the towns of Middlesbrough,
Stockton, Redcar and Hartlepool, squeezing in over a million

**'Blur are Chas and Dave for
students.'
- Owen Morris, Oasis producer.**

people. One of Middlesbrough's newer attributes is the University, staggering out of its earlier portakabin-bound existence into the 'Campus 2000' expansion project.

49% ♂♂♂♂♂♀♀♀♀ **51%**	
Sex ratio(M:F): 49%:51%	Founded: 1970
Full time u'grads: 7,725	Part time: 2,792
Postgrads: 315	Non-degree: 4,122
Ave course: 3/4yrs	Ethnic: 1.8%
Private school: n/a	Flunk rate: 24%
Mature students: 36%	Overseas students: 4.5%
Disabled students: 5.5%	Staff/student ratio: 1:19
Clearing: 13.6%	

ATMOSPHERE:
The emphasis on business, health and vocational courses has attracted career-oriented students who appreciate the opportunities to study part time or on sandwich courses and don't mind the unattractive surroundings. It's very much a local university; the campus has a village-like air, and the locality is generally friendly and cheap.

MIDDLESBROUGH:
● <u>Population: 143,600</u> ● <u>London: 256miles</u>
● <u>York: 49miles</u> ● <u>Newcastle: 39miles</u>

Middlesbrough's a true northern town: mile upon mile of back-to-back Victorian terraces; massive (now largely silent) industrial plants; *strangely,* still active docks; and an *inconsistent* football team. Furthermore, the town's large enough to provide more shopping opportunities than any student can reasonably afford, including a sprinkling of bookshops, a couple of shopping malls and late night shopping past 10pm. *Potential students will be uninterested to note that the town's most attractive building is the 19th-century Central Library, and probably they couldn't care less that* Teesside was the birthplace of the railway (Stockton-Darlington, 1825). *Unless they like trains.*

TRAVEL:
Trains: Middlesbrough station offers direct links to Newcastle (£5.15), Manchester (£17.30) and other major interchanges. For London (£40.25) change at Darlington.
Coaches: Coach services courtesy of Blue Line, City Link, Swiftline and National Express to London (£20), Manchester (£11.75) and all over.
Car: The A19 south to York and north to Newcastle runs straight through Middlesbrough. Also, there's the A66, cross country to the lakes, and the A1 runs through Darlington, 15 miles to the west.
Air: Teesside airport, 12 miles away - domestic flights and to Europe and Scandinavia.
Local: Buses are *cheap* (50p max), but stop running after 11pm *and are not always reliable.* Trains run *regularly* all over the Teesside conurbation.
Taxis: *Reasonably priced (£2 across town) and readily available.*
Bicycles: *The town is flat, but small enough to render pedalling recreational.*

LIBRARIES & COMPUTERS:
- Books: 297,392 ● Study places: 1,300
- Computer workstations: 1,000+

A spanking new Learning Resource Centre *is visually and qualitatively impressive.*

CAREER PROSPECTS:
- Careers Service ● No of staff: 5full/1part
- Unemployed after 6mths (1996): 11.7%

FAMOUS ALUMNI:
David Bowe and Steve Hughes (MEPs); Paul Marsden (MP); Skin (singer, Skunk Anansie).

FURTHER INFO:
Prospectuses for undergrads, part timers and postgrads, CD-ROM, video, web sites (http://www.tees.ac.uk and http://www.utu.org.uk).

entertainment

THE CITY:
- Price of a pint of beer: £1.70 ● Glass of wine: £1.50

Cinemas: In addition to the 4-screen Odeon in Middlesbrough and the arts cinema in Stockton, there's the Teesside Park development, including a drive-in McDonald's and a 14-screen cinema.

Theatres: *The Little Theatre is mostly mainstream but Dovecot Arts Centre offers a wider range.*

Pubs: push*plugs: Dickens Inn; Cornerhouse; Scruffy Murphy's; Star & Garter. The Shakespeare and the Zetland are definitely to be avoided.*

Clubs/discos: *It would be unfair to say that all of Middlesbrough's large selection of clubs are tacky, but as generalisations go, it's fair enough. Grudging* push*plugs are awarded to: Wobble at Madisons (mainstream); Empire.*

Music venues: The Town Hall stages everything from popular to classical, country to more country. Sessions Jazz Bar *does just what it says on the tin.*

Eating out: *The choice is surprisingly good, including several value veggie joints and any number of curry houses. Above all, Roy's Café is a student institution – Roy is an honorary life member of the SU. Further* push*plugs: Savini's (Italian); Royal Palace and Khan's (Indian); Pierre Victoire.*

UNIVERSITY:
- Price of a pint of beer: £1.40 ● Glass of wine: £1.15

Bars: (3) Union Central (capacity 600) has a *publike* atmosphere with Sky TV and pool hall; the Zoo doubles as a nightclub venue and is open until 2am.

Cinema: 1 blockbuster a week on a big screen.

Clubs/discos: The Zoo (1,000) is also the venue for shaking your body down and swinging it all around twice a week. *It's usually mainstream dance stuff* but noted DJs like Danny Rampling aren't unknown. The SU promotes the Monday night bash at the Empire nightclub in town.

Music venues: The Zoo hosts occasional bands, such as Happy Clappers and several tribute acts.

Cabaret: Mirthmakers on Mondays include David Gorman and Andrew Maxwell.

Food: The Central Café, the Coffee Stop and the Gallery Restaurant all provide *decent if unexciting food* at sensible prices.

Others: The May Ball is the biggest event in the social calendar, attracting up to 1,500 people, but there are several other dos that require more sartorial effort than putting on a clean tee-shirt.

social & political

UNIVERSITY OF TEESSIDE STUDENTS' UNION:
- 4 sabbaticals ● Turnout at last ballot: 10%
- NUS member

The SU is increasingly concerned with recreation rather than revolution. Relations with the relatively young and happening Vice-Chancellor are very cordial. The SU building is very big and well-equipped, virtually a cube and looks from the outside as if it's made of plastic, and the students are largely unaware of the SU as anything other than this pseudo box cum beer dispenser.

SU FACILITIES:

There are 3 bars, 1 cafeteria, general shop, cash machine (Midland), Endsleigh Insurance office, advice centre, pool tables, vending machines, market stalls and other general services such as phones, photocopiers and photo booths.

CLUBS (NON SPORTING):

Arts; Cultural; Design; Interlink; Malaysian; Musicians; Mystic.

OTHER ORGANISATIONS:

The SU produces the fortnightly 'TNT' newsletter and there's also the monthly 'Universe'. There's an on-line info service on televisions around the campus.

RELIGIOUS:

In Middlesbrough there's the cathedral and Christians, Muslims and Jews are well served locally.

PAID WORK:

Ha, bloody ha. The Union is opening a Jobshop this year, although what they really need is a job factory first.

sports

- Recent successes: tennis, badminton, golf

Teesside was a major player among the polytechnics and its standing is improving within BUSA competitions. With a sports card (£15), almost all facilities are free. The University offers an honours degree in Sports Science and Leisure Management.

SPORTS FACILITIES:

The University's Sports and Recreation Unit provides 48 acres of playing fields, a sports hall, a new pavilion, tennis courts, an all-weather pitch, a climbing wall, gym, multigym and sauna. All facilities are off-site, but there is a free bus to get you there. The Health & Fitness Centre costs £15 for annual membership and gets you discounts on local facilities. Overall, 1/3 of the block grant goes on sport.

SPORTING CLUBS:

American Football; Gaelic Football; Handball; Jeet Kune Do; Rowing; Scuba-diving; Surf; Ten Pin Bowling.

ATTRACTIONS:
Middlesbrough FC; West Hartlepool Rugby Union; horse-racing at Redcar; speedway at Stockton. Tees Barage is is an 11-mile stretch of *worldclass* white-watercourse for rafting and canoeing.

accommodation

IN COLLEGE:
- Catered: 3% ● Cost: £42-45(33wks)
- Self-catering: 10% ● Cost: £38-46(33wks)

Availability: Woodlands and Parkside Halls are *popular* with their en suite bathrooms and landscaped gardens, and King Edward's Square, a converted Victorian terrace, *is OK, if a bit battered.* Catered places are in Linthorpe Hall *(famous for its Linthorpe Louts).* 75% of accommodation is reserved for 1st years and 20% of the rooms are shared. *The University accommodation, if not plentiful or pretty, is cheap and weatherproof,* and the worst of the housing problems are alleviated by a 398-place head tenancy scheme (where it rents from landlords and sublets to students on favourable terms).
Car parking: Permit required. Improved security on campus *means you might even find it in one piece when you go back to it.*

EXTERNALLY:
- Ave rent: £30

Availability: The large mature and local student population tends to live at home and *the private sector is far from saturated. It's pretty easy to find a place and some nice houses are available. Anywhere within the town centre is liable to be suitable; the area near the station probably isn't.*
Housing Help: The Accommodation Office has 7 staff who provide a notice-board, lists of vacancies and recommended landlords, legal advice, emerging housing and safety checks.

welfare

SERVICES:
- Nursery ● Lesbian & Gay Society ● Mature SA
- Overseas SA ● Minibus ● Women's Officer
- Self-defence classes

The University employs 3 full- and 1 part-time counsellors, but most students with problems call first at the Union's very *good* Advice Centre. Campus has CCTV and a late-night minibus.
Disabled: *Access is much improved now, with specially adapted accommodation, computing rooms and a dedicated SU Special Needs Advisor. Induction loops are installed.*

FINANCE:
- Ave debt: £2,200 ● Access fund: £148,000
- Successful applications (1996): 273

▶▶ Textiles

see Heriot-Watt University

▶▶ **Thames Poly**

see University of Greenwich

Thames Valley University

● *Formerly Polytechnic of West London, Ealing College.*
(1) Thames Valley University, St Mary's Road, Ealing, London, W5 5RF. Tel: (0181) 579 5000. Fax: (0181) 566 1353.
E-mail: learning.advice@tvu.ac.uk
Thames Valley University Students' Union, St Mary's Road, Ealing, London, W5 5RF. Tel: (0181) 231 2267.
Fax: (0181) 231 2359.
(2) Thames Valley University, Wellington Street, Slough, Berkshire, SL1 1YG. Tel: (01753) 534585.

˙˙˙˙˙˙˙˙General

In 1991, Ealing College, Thames Valley College Slough, London College of Music and Queen Charlotte's College of Healthcare Study amalgamated to form the Polytechnic of West London, which consequently had 4 sites. 1 year later it changed again and became Thames Valley University. There was a bit of fuss about this - a considerable faction preferred the name 'University of West London'; *we preferred 'Kylie', but no-one asked us. The University has a strong commitment to the local area and to encouraging entry through non-traditional routes.* Most students are in Ealing, 10 miles from Trafalgar Square, with Slough (pronounced to rhyme with 'cow'), currently housing 40% of courses.

36% ♂♂♂♂♀♀♀♀♀♀ 64%

Sex ratio(M:F): 36%:64%
Full time u'grads: 5,164
Postgrads: 629
Ave course: 3/4yrs
Private school: n/a
Mature students: 75%
Disabled students: 8%
Clearing: 50%

Founded: 1991
Part time: 2,767
Non-degree: 17,431
Ethnic: 40%
Flunk rate: n/a
Overseas students: 39%
Staff/student ratio: 1:13

ATMOSPHERE:

TVU's a real melting pot, taking a high proportion of mature and overseas students and reflecting the local ethnically diverse community. There's also a large number of students on part-time, day-release and evening courses, and plenty who rolled in off the roulette wheel of clearing, so it's quite far removed from many people's perception of a 'normal' University. Students always seem to be going somewhere, as if standing still makes them a target for paintball snipers.

THE SITES:

Ealing: The *airport lounge-style* reception area is just the frontage of buildings that resemble the High School in 'Grease'.

Slough: (hotel & catering, science, computing, accounting, business & finance) The Slough site, 17 miles away, now has the new Paul Hamlyn Learning Resource Centre. There is much more available space and fewer students on this site than Ealing, though Slough itself, a commuter satellite town, *is probably best described by John Betjeman: 'Come friendly bombs and fall on Slough. It's not fit for humans now'.*

THE CITY: see University of London

EALING:

Ealing is a usefully accessible part of west London. It is mostly affluent with designer dress shops and patisseries alongside the more sensible, basic shops. This part of town is renowned as a haunt for would-be celebs - the National Film & Television School is just opposite the college. South Ealing, however, is much less well-to-do. The main campus is between these 2 parts, amidst a *busy* private estate, *which has led to a bit of local friction. Matters are improving following a threatened ents and bar ban by the University authorities.*

TRAVEL: see University of London

Local travel: The nearest tube stations are Ealing Broadway (District and Central Lines) and South Ealing (Piccadilly Line).

LIBRARIES & COMPUTERS:
- Books: 221,300 ● Study places: 767
- Computer workstations: 360

There are 5 libraries in all, the new facilities in Slough being the most useful.

CAREER PROSPECTS:
- Careers Service ● No of staff: 8full/2part
- Unemployed after 6mths (1996): 10%

Careers centres at both sites and careers tutors in each School.

SPECIAL FEATURES:
- An 'electronic campus' has been created, with its central hub at the new Paul Hamlyn LRC in Slough, designed to facilitate distance learning. *Many students were afraid this might mean they were to be taught by robots, until Tony Blair's appearance at the opening when he blustered forth inane platitudes about it being something 'new', which of course meant that it would be the same as what they'd had for 18 years before but with a different name. Boom boom.*

FAMOUS ALUMNI:

Emma Anderson (Lush guitarist); Holly Hotlips (Chris Evans' posse pal); Jamiroquai (*the cat in the hat*); James Larlett (British hockey captain); Freddie Mercury (of Queen); Pete Townshend (of The Who); Ron Wood (of The Rolling Stones). Honorary Professorships have been awarded to figures as diverse as David Frost, Neil Kinnock and Alexei Sayle. But not Sporty Spice. *Yet.*

FURTHER INFO:
Undergrad and postgrad prospectuses, fact sheets for part-time programmes, web site (http://www.tvu.ac.uk).

entertainment

IN LONDON: see University of London

EALING:
● Price of a pint of beer: £2.15 ● Glass of wine: £2
Students tend not to bother with central London that often (it's more expensive and hassle to get back from late). Ealing itself offers quite enough by way of entertainments, pricey though they can be.
Cinemas: 2 local mainstream cinemas (Virgin, 3 screens and Warner, 8), and the Bellevue Asian cinema is nearby.
Theatres: Questors is the nearest (about 5 mins) hosting *quality* rep. Also the *unpretentious, but arty* Waterman's Centre (Brentford).
Pubs: push*plugs: Yates; The Townhouse; Muswell's; Old Orleans; Crispian's; Old Goa; Photographer & Firkin.*
Clubs/discos/music venues: *The Broadway Boulevard is Ealing's classiest venue, with a student night on Tuesdays. Live music is mainly pub-based but the Labbats Apollo (Hammersmith) and the Shepherds Bush Empire are within easy reach.*
Food: *Ealing has a good multi-cultural mix of food foundries.* push*plugs: Nando's (Mexican); La Cucina (sandwiches); Tandoori Villa; Minsky's (American diner).*

UNIVERSITY:
● Price of a pint of beer: £1.50 ● Glass of wine: £1

Bars: The Ealing alcoholeries consist of Freddie's (named after the late Mr Mercury), *a packed, functional boozer*; the *rather more comfy* DB's (changed it name from Dog's Bollocks cos it's a bit rude); and Artwoods Hall, the dance venue. 2 bars in Slough.
Cinema: Videos in Freddies once or twice a week.
Clubs/discos/music venues: Artwoods Hall (cap 800) has been done up with a new soundsystem and lights and hosts lots of tribute bands and the weekly 'Lollipop' and 'Lost It?' club nights. Recent acts include Cantaloup and LTJ Bukem.
Balls: Each site holds an annual ball.
Food: *The Dinermite canteen scores highly for value nosh but rather blows it on the sensible name front.* There are also 3 training restaurants at Slough and 1 at Ealing, *for above average scoff at below average prices.*
Other: Cultural societies stage events at the SU throughout the year. Annual May Ball is a 10-hour *extravaganzathon.*

social & political

THAMES VALLEY UNIVERSITY STUDENTS' UNION:
● 4 sabbaticals ● Turnout at last ballot: 10%
● NUS member

Slough and Ealing have separate facilities and sabbaticals, *but seem united in not taking politics too seriously. In a recent boycott of lectures to protest about tuition fees, only 50% of students stayed away and who's to say they wouldn't have*

> **'Legend has it that students who are standing under the Birmingham University's Old Joe clock tower when it chimes will fail their finals.'**

done anyway? The University is good at listening though and holds open meetings with the departmental student reps and the Student Council.

SU FACILITIES:
The main SU building is a converted Victorian grammar school. 3 bars; 2 minibuses; photocopying; printing facilities; travel agency; catering facilities; vending and games machines.

CLUBS (NON SPORTING):
Beer Appreciation (Martin Clunes is an honorary lifetime member); Law; Radio.

OTHER ORGANISATIONS:
The bi-monthly student magazine, 'Undergrad', was shortlisted for a 'Guardian' award after only 3 issues. TUBE radio station has a temporary license. Tomfoolery twice a year for Rag.

RELIGIOUS:
- 3 chaplains (CofE, RC, Jewish)

The chaplains are based at the chaplaincy part-time. *So if you're a part-time believer...*

PAID WORK:
TVU tries to offer part-time and temp vacancies to students.

⋯⋯⋯ sports

- Recent successes: tae kwon do

A growing interest in sporting pursuits is hampered by the lack of facilities.

SPORTS FACILITIES:
4-5 acres: apart from one football field, squash courts and a gym at Slough, the University has to hire facilities. *The gym, however, is amazing*: piped music videos all day, fitness and toning and heavy duty rooms, trained staff, indoor jogging track, exercise bikes, rowing machines, ergometers, saunas, sunbeds, a masseur and osteopath. Locally there is an all-weather pitch, golf course, squash, tennis and swimming baths.

SPORTING CLUBS:
Ladies' and Mixed Basketball; Ladies' Football; Ladies' and Mixed Hockey; Ladies' Rugby; Rowing; Skiing; Snowboarding; Softball; Tennis.

ATTRACTIONS:
Locally, Brentford FC; QPR FC; Wasps Rugby Union.

⋯⋯⋯ accommodation

IN COLLEGE:
TVU has no accommodation, although there are plans for a few hundred places at Slough. *This isn't quite as disastrous as it may seem, when you consider the number of local students.*

❛The Queen's College, Oxford, is allowed to shut down the High Street for archery practice.❜

EXTERNALLY: see <u>University of London</u>
● <u>Ave rent: £60</u>
Slough: There are worse places to live than Slough *such as Mars;* Windsor is close by but very expensive.
Housing help: The Administration Department runs an *excellent* accommodation service with 4 full-time officers. They have contacts with over 600 local landlords and last year housed about 1,500 students within 4 miles.

·········welfare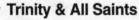

SERVICES:
● <u>Lesbian & Gay Society</u> ● <u>Minibus</u>
 ● <u>Women's Officer</u> ● <u>Self-defence classes</u>
There are nurses at both sites and a visiting doctor and the University employs 2 part-time counsellors, *a reduction in service which has left it inadequate.*
Women: The women's group is called the Betty Boothroyd Appreciation Society.
Disabled: *Access is good already and getting better.* The new SU Building is completely wheelchair friendly and there are ramps to the main site and disabled parking. Facilities for hearing- and sight-impaired students have been revamped recently. A guide to disabled facilities is produced each year.

FINANCE:
● <u>Ave debt: £1,550</u> ● <u>Access fund: £240,000</u>
● <u>Successful applications (1997): 411</u>
There are bursaries of up to £500 and some funding for overseas students.

● ●

▶▶ **Trent University**
see Nottingham Trent University

● ●

▶▶ **Trinity & All Saints**
see Other Institutions

● ●

❛2,000 students at Nottingham Trent signed a petition protesting at the award of an Honorary Degree to Kenneth Clarke MP.❜

Trinity College, Carmarthen
see Other Institutions

 Trinity College of Music
see Other Institutions

❝If you have any comments about PUSH or fancy being involved in the next edition, please write to PUSH, McGraw-Hill Publishing Company, Shoppenhangers Road, Maidenhead, Berkshire SL6 2QL.❞

- UCE
  see University of Central England

- UCL
  see University College, London

University of East Anglia

- UEL
  see University of East London

University of Ulster

- UMDS
  see King's College, London

UMIST

- United Medical and Dental Schools
  see King's College, London

University College, London

- University College, Stockton
  see University of Durham

- UNL
  see University of North London

- Uxbridge
  see Brunel University

●●

 UCE

see University of Central England

●●

 UCL

see University College, London

●●

u

❝Text in italics is PUSH's point
of view – take it or leave it.❞

University of East Anglia

University of East Anglia, Norwich, NR4 7TJ.
Tel: (01603) 456161. Fax: (01603) 458553.
E-mail: admissions@uea.ac.uk
Union of UEA Students, Union House, University of East Anglia,
Norwich, NR4 7TJ. Tel: (01603) 503711.
Fax: (01603) 250144. E-mail: su.comm@uea.ac.uk

General

East Anglia is flat as a pancake after Jo Brand has sat on it for
a week. Norfolk, the northern half, also has the Broads:
canals and rivers running all over the county like maple syrup.
The county's largest city is Norwich, which a couple of hundred
years ago was also the 2nd biggest in England. But it was
somewhat left behind by the Industrial Revolution and while
other cities cottoned on to cotton or coined it in with coal,
Norwich developed a mustard industry, still thriving today.
Now Norwich is a tourist attraction, market town and
administrative centre for Norfolk. The University's 270-acre
campus, known as University Plain, is 2½ miles from the city
centre between a 1940s council estate and the Yare Valley
conservation area. Most of the buildings are concrete, *but it's
not a jungle.* In fact, the campus is very green, but still flat as
a pancake. A green one.

The teaching hospitals at Hellesden (4 miles) and King's
Lynn (40 miles) are officially part of UEA and the nursing and
midwifery students here still have some teaching on the main
campus, *which must be a real pain in the Colman's.*

49% ♂♂♂♂♂♀♀♀♀♀ 51%	
Sex ratio(M:F): 49%:51%	Founded: 1963
Full time u'grads: 6,093	Part time: 1,908
Postgrads: 1,385	Non-degree: 0
Ave course: 3yrs	Ethnic: n/a
Private school: 13%	Flunk rate: 9%
Mature students: 20%	Overseas students: 9%
Disabled students: 1.9%	Staff/student: 1:16
Clearing: 13%	

ATMOSPHERE:
*There's an easy-going, informal atmosphere, but cliques still
exist in this largely white, middle-class environment. Those who
can overcome this, the lousy weather and the morgue-like
atmosphere that descends at weekends will find it a great place
to work and play. If it does get a bit claustrophobic, however, the
town's 2½ miles away, so you need to plan your escape. This
is, after all, a green field campus in the truest sense. Don't
come looking for cutting edge street style; quite clever people
having fun in a pleasant environment is closer to the mark.*

TOWN:

- <u>Population: 120,700</u> ● <u>London: 103miles</u>
- <u>Birmingham: 139miles</u> ● <u>Cambridge: 62miles</u>

Local people insist that Norwich is a city not a town. It does, after all, have 2 cathedrals and contains all the usual amenities such as a whole range of supermarkets, late-night shops, bookshops, banks and well-located cashpoints. As well as the Cathedral, tourist attractions include a Norman Castle, which has been converted into a museum and art gallery, and a small agricultural museum. *For UEA students, Norwich is like a warm duvet, nice and cosy, but down the road, so it doesn't really belong to them. The town's also far from an ethnic melting pot and non-white students have been known to elicit funny looks, if not outright hostility.*

TRAVEL:

Trains: Nearest BR station is Norwich, 3 miles from the University campus. Direct services to London (2hrs, £18.80) and change there for most other destinations.

Coaches: Services to, among other places, London (£11.75) and Glasgow (£35.25).

Car: The A11, A47, A140 and A146 all go via Norwich.

Air: Flights inland and also to Amsterdam from Norwich Airport.

Local: *Buses are reliable and wide ranging.* Campus to town centre £1.60 return.

Taxis: *Many students have problems with taxis not arriving.*

Bicycles: Some provision of cycle lanes near UEA, *but it's advisable to wear a gas mask on the ring road. Otherwise, it's good territory for 2-wheelers, since Norfolk is, as Noël Coward remarked, very flat.*

LIBRARIES & COMPUTERS:

- <u>Books: 750,000</u> ● <u>Study places: 1,000</u>
- <u>Computer workstations: 667</u>

The library has 'Silence Is Golden' plastered all over the walls. *Which is nice.*

CAREER PROSPECTS:

- <u>Careers Service</u> ● <u>No of staff: 7full/4part</u>
- <u>Unemployed after 6mths (1996): 6.9%</u>

FAMOUS ALUMNI:

Jenny Abramsky (Radio 5 Live controller); Malcolm Bradbury, Angela Carter, Kazuo Ishiguro, Ian McEwan, Clive Sinclair, Rose Tremain (writers); Jack Davenport (actor); Charlie Higson, Arthur Smith, Paul Whitehouse (comedians); Selina Scott (TV celebrity). The decision a few years ago to award Salman Rushdie an honorary degree aroused the wrath of UEA Muslims.

FURTHER INFO:

Official prospectuses from Admissions Office. There's also a web site (http://www.uea.ac.uk/welcome.html) and a CD-ROM.

u

entertainment

TOWN:

- <u>Price of a pint of beer: £2.05</u> ● <u>Glass of wine: £1.80</u>

Cinemas: (3) A Cannon, an Odeon and the *more interesting* Cinema City.

Theatres: The Theatre Royal is the largest with a capacity of

> ❝ The murals in the Sivell's Bar at Aberdeen University were originally nudes, but they were thought a bit racy for the 1930s, so clothes were added. ❞

2,000, *providing mainstream fare, opera and Shakespeare. The Norwich Playhouse is a bit more radical and Norwich Arts Centre is yet more diverse.*

Pubs: *Norwich has a massive choice of pubs; over 300 in all. The best concentration is in the Golden Triangle, the main student area.* **push***plugs: Garden House; Unthank Arms; Belle Vue; Mad Moose (rugger buggers). Best to avoid hostelries on some of the less friendly estates (eg the Larkman).*

Clubs/discos: *A varied selection, which is nurturing Norwich's hitherto nugatory nightlife.* **push***plugs: Zoom (indie/garage); Marvel (hip-hop/acid jazz) and Gas Station (soul/funk) at The Loft; Ikon (student nights); Mojo's Club (trip-hop/drum'n'bass).*

Music venues: The Arts Centre (cap 350) offers an *eclectic* selection and indeed comedy, *but the University is probably the best venue in East Anglia.* Some pubs are good for rock and local bands, especially the Oval.

Eating out: *Again, nothing too extraordinary, but who cares when you're out to celebrate, pull, or just soak up the beer?* **push***plugs: Tree House (wholefood); Cafe Rouge; Anchor Quay; Pedro's (Mexican); Earlham Cafe and Unthank Kitchen (greasy spoons).*

UNIVERSITY:
● Price of a pint of beer: £1.40 ● Glass of wine: £1.20

Bars: The Hive is open all day, although The Pub (with its booths *for discreet assignations*) soaks up some of the lunchtime trade. Others are Carol's and the LCR.

Theatres: The UEA Studio is the site of some *damn fine* work; trips to the Fringe.

Cinemas: 3 *mainstream and art* films each week are shown in a lecture theatre. The Film Soc manages to get movies very soon after release.

Music venues: The LCR, voted best student venue by 'Live' industry magazine, is a major tour date for some of the top name bands, such as, in the past year, Del Amitri, Supergrass, Robbie Williams, Ocean Colour Scene and Space. Local and obscure indie bands play the SU-run Waterfront. For more classical *and conventional* tastes, the site for sound is the small concert hall (cap 150) in the University Music Centre.

Clubs/discos: The Waterfront in Norwich is the base for regular dance and Britpop nights on Fridays and Saturdays as well as other moves and grooves such as the monthly 'Eat This' gay night.

Food: On campus there are 8 main food stops, ranging from the *cheap and cheerful* fast food in The Diner to the *right-on (but still reasonable)* SASSF sandwich bar, from which all profits go to charity. *All outlets are run by the University except for one wee pizza bar.*

Other: The *incredible* Sainsbury Centre for Visual Arts on campus has *a very impressive array of* tribal and other art, built in 1978 by the guy who owns the supermarkets. *Fortunately*, it's got a different colour-scheme. There are also 3 balls a year, and occasional cabaret from the likes of Mark Lamarr and Alan Parker.

social & political

THE UNION OF UEA STUDENTS:

● 4 sabbaticals ● Turnout at last ballot: 17%
● NUS member

UEA has lost its past reputation as a left-wing hotbed. The apathy ague (mistaking indifference for impartiality) has spread here too. Student antipathy to tinpot politicians is pretty common.

SU FACILITIES:

In Union House and elsewhere on campus, there's the campus convenience store, newsagent, a post office, travel shop, 2nd-hand bookshop, games room, common rooms, print room, dark room, photocopying, advice centre, women's room, snack-bar, vending machines, minibus hire, snooker tables, launderette, ticket agency, banks (Barclays, Lloyds, NatWest, Midland, Co-Op) and a bar.

CLUBS (NON SPORTING):

AIESEC; Alternative Music; Ballroom & Latin American Dance; Bell-ringing; Bird Club; Buddhist; Cannabis Awareness; Chinese; Pub Crawl; Creative Writing; English Football Supporters; Games; Healing; Hellenic; Jazz & Blues; Juggling; Kite; Klustaflux (comedy); Latin; Malaysian; Morris Dancing; Motorcycle; Movement (clubbing); Peace; Politics; Racing; Skan Clan (Scandinavian); Thursday Club (mutual help and friendliness); Travel & Exploration; Village People (*for those living in the Village halls, not a gay iconic disco demons appreciation club*); Undaground Music (*ravers who can't spell*); Wine.

OTHER ORGANISATIONS:

'Concrete', the fortnightly newspaper, is a regular award-winner and there's also 'Bacchus' and 'Bucket of Tongues' magazines. Livewire Radio has also picked up gongs *but Nexus TV is hampered by the fact it can only be seen in The Hive.* There's also the Student Community Action group, a Rag and SASSAF (South African Student Support and Aid Fund).

RELIGIOUS:

There is a non-denominational chaplaincy on campus and a worship room for Muslims. In the city, there is a *splendid* Anglican Cathedral and another for Catholics, as well as prayer lairs for Jews, Muslims and Buddhists.

PAID WORK:

There's less unemployment in East Anglia than in most of the country and apart from the usual bar work, students can get better paid jobs in local government and other areas.

sports

● Recent successes: basketball, volleyball
The campus is big enough to support sports facilities to stretch eyes as well as limbs and athletic activity is a mass participation thing.

SPORTS FACILITIES:

Most facilities are on campus, including a sports hall, gym, badminton courts, multigym, weight-training and indoor football facilities, baseball diamond, 6 squash courts (for which there's a small charge), 12 tennis courts, cricket nets, artificial pitch, the county athletics track and 2 new hockey pitches. On the edge of University Plain, are 30 acres of playing fields. Locally, there are the Norfolk Broads for water sports and the city provides a pool and golf course. UEA has been awarded over £7m lottery money to build a new sports hall with training pool, due to open in 1999.

SPORTING CLUBS:

American Football; Billiards & Snooker; Boat; Fell & Cave; Kayak; Korfball; Parachuting; Rowing; Skating; Tennis; Windsurfing.

ATTRACTIONS:

2 miles from the University is the massive Norwich Sports Village - a multi-million quid sports centre. There's a dry ski slope at Trowse (4 miles away) and a Quasar laser skirmish in the city. Norwich City is the local soccer team (with Delia Smith on the board).

accommodation

IN COLLEGE:

● <u>Self-catering: 49%</u> ● <u>Cost: £37-53(34-38wks)</u>

Availability: All 1st years (so long as they normally live further than 20 miles away) can live in and about a quarter of other years have a chance. Overseas and disabled students have priority for all 3 years. Most rooms are on campus in mixed halls (ground floors rooms are all male) and only about 1% share. *Don't bring a cat, there isn't room to swing one in most rooms (and it's cruel, anyway),* but Norfolk and Suffolk Terraces *(which won awards from architects who don't actually have to live there)* have *great* views of University Broad *(a lake, not the local floozy).*

Car parking: A hi-tech card (for which there is a charge) and barrier system operates.

EXTERNALLY:

● <u>Ave rent: £40</u>

Availability: *Students can usually find accommodation in Norwich. An area known as the Golden Triangle revolves around Unthank Road, Earlham Road and Dereham Road. It's a bit of a yuppie ghetto but that's where the good pubs and the 24-hour shops are, so, funnily enough, that's where the students go. Avoid the estates at Larkham and West Earlham.*

Housing help: The Housing Bureau keeps details of vacancies, a property index and offers advice on contracts.

welfare

SERVICES:

● <u>Nursery</u> ● <u>Nightline</u> ● <u>Lesbian & Gay Society</u>
● <u>Mature SA</u> ● <u>Overseas SA</u> ● <u>Minibus</u> ● <u>Women's Officer</u>

The University provides 3 full- and 1 part-time counsellors. There's a 24-hour Health Centre on campus, including GPs, a dentist and a psychiatrist. Societies include Race Awareness, Women's and Mature Student.

Disabled: *Wheelchair access is pretty good, mainly because the campus is so flat, but there are also plenty of lifts and ramps and all that good stuff, as well as a Special Needs Awareness society.*

FINANCE:
- Ave debt: £1,250 ● Access fund: £184,558
- Successful applications (1996): 673

There are 5 hardship funds, the VC's fund and a Nursery Fund. A recent rent strike has persuaded UEA to improve its financial provision.

▶▶ **UEL**

see University of East London

University of Ulster

(1) The University of Ulster (Coleraine), Cromore Road, Coleraine, BT52 1SA. Tel: (01265) 44141.
Fax: (01265) 40947.
Students' Union, South Buildings, The University of Ulster at Coleraine, Cromore Road, Coleraine, BT52 ISA.
Tel: (01265) 43664.
(2) The University of Ulster (Jordanstown), Shore Road, Newtownabbey, Co Antrim, BT37 OQB. Tel: (01232) 365131.
Students' Union, The University of Ulster (Jordanstown), Co Antrim, BT37 OQB. Tel: (01232) 365121.
Fax: (01232) 362817.
(3) The University of Ulster (Belfast), York Street, Belfast, BT15 1ED. Tel: (01232) 328515.
(4) The University of Ulster (Magee College), Northland Road, Londonderry, BT48 7JL. Tel: (01504) 371371.
Fax: (01504) 375410.

General

Once upon a time, there was a university and a polytechnic in Northern Ireland. Then, in 1984, they merged and became one large University with 4 distinctly different sites, thinly spread across 3 of the 6 counties. The largest is the Jordanstown Site - the former poly site on the hills above Belfast overlooking the Lough (bay) - and the smallest (housing art & design) is in the city centre. The University HQ is on the outskirts of Coleraine, nearly 60 miles north of Belfast (as the crow with a compass flies) on the *beautiful* Antrim coast. 30 miles to the west of that, is the 4th site, Magee College in (London)Derry. Each site is distinct and retains its own atmosphere and administration. *Indeed, all that Jordanstown and Coleraine seem to have in common are a beautiful isolated setting and monstrously ugly modern concrete buildings.*

43% ♂♂♂♂♂♀♀♀♀♀ **57%**

Sex ratio(M:F): 43%:57%	Founded: 1968
Full time u'grads: 11,835	Part time: 3,853
Postgrads: 4,255	Non-degree: 2,187
Ave course: 3yrs	Ethnic: 1%
Private school: n/a	Flunk rate: 6%
Mature students: 40%	Overseas students: 15%
Disabled students: 6%	Staff/student ratio: 1:18
Clearing: 8%	

ATMOSPHERE & SITES:

We're dealing with 4 different sites here, which despite the University's best efforts towards integration are still stubbornly up to 80 miles apart. Failing divine intervention, they will remain geographically distinct so that's the way to treat them.
Coleraine: (5,000 students) The original site of the University and its HQ. The campus is on the edge of the small and quiet market town of Coleraine and less than 5 miles from the lively coastal resorts of Portrush and Portstewart, where most students live. The campus is surrounded by green countryside and nearby the Giant's Causeway reaches out across the Irish Sea towards Scotland. *It is a peaceful place without being stifling. It would be unfair to describe the students as apathetic, but every night at 6pm the campus dies completely. The students can, however, be moved to groove in the lively nightclubs of the nearby seaside resorts of Portrush and Portstewart.*
Jordanstown: (11,680 students) The largest site is attended by over ½ the University's students and is still expanding fast. Belfast, 7 miles away, *is the nearest town of any size, so you might expect students to complain of isolation, but the campus is well-connected and the attractive grounds, buildings and views over the Lough provide compensation. Anyway, 80% of the students go home each weekend, so there's no room for claustrophobia. Relaxed, friendly and vacant just about sums up Jordanstown.*
Magee: There are 2,799 students based at this *attractive* campus on the River Foyle, just north of the old walled city of (London)Derry.
Belfast: 943 Art and Design students are housed on York Street just a mile away from <u>Queen's University</u>, *whose facilties they share and which is the focus of their social life.*

CITY: see <u>Queen's University Belfast</u>

TOWNS:

Coleraine/Portrush/Portstewart: The 3 towns form a triangle with the 2 ports to the north providing accommodation, jobs and nightlife, and Coleraine at the southern tip providing the amenities. A town of 20,721 give or take a few, Coleraine has a fair sprinkling of supermarkets, Irish and UK banks and bookshops. *It's an isolated coastal (touristy) outpost.*
(London)Derry: It's an ancient *and scenic* city and Northern Ireland's 2nd largest. The city walls show *a different concern for security from those that trouble the city today, but as you might expect, people's lives are ruled not by terrorism, but the more mundane concerns of life. They are immensely friendly*

and the social scene is similarly inviting. (NB. Use of the prefix 'London' labels a person as pro-Unionist to the largely Catholic locals. Calling the city simply 'Derry' ruffles the feathers of Her Majesty's armed forces. *Either way, students are stuffed.* No wonder most of the students are from Northern Ireland - *at least they understand the questions, even if they don't know the answers.)*

TRAVEL: see Queen's University Belfast

Trains: Direct lines from Coleraine to Belfast and (London)Derry only on Northern Ireland Railways, frequent and *frequently dirty* trains. Trains from (London)Derry to Belfast and most other local destinations, and to Dublin from Belfast.

Coaches: Goldline Express and Ulsterbus link Belfast, Coleraine and (London)Derry regularly. National Express to London (£52, 14hrs, 1/day).

Air: Flights to the UK mainland and the rest of Europe from Belfast International (London: £72). Also other flights to the UK mainland from Belfast City Airport.

Hitching: *Good between Coleraine and the ports, otherwise only with the greatest care. A bad idea to the airport or ferries.*

Local: *Comprehensive, but expensive* local buses, but ½ price fares for students around Coleraine.

Taxis: *Readily available and very cheap if shared.*

Bicycles: *Only for those most hardy with hills and inclement weather although theft is not a problem*

LIBRARIES & COMPUTERS:
- Books: 646,808 ● Study places: 1,914
- Computer workstations: 1,476

There are libraries on all campuses and loans can be made between sites from the Arts collection at Belfast (35,000 books) or the Irish collection at Magee (70,000 books). Each faculty has its own computing facilities and there are up to 4 computer centres on each campus. 24hr access to computers except at Belfast.

CAREER PROSPECTS:
- Careers Services ● No of staff: 12full
- Unemployed after 6mths (1996): 9%

The Jordanstown, Coleraine and Magee sites all have their own careers advisory services.

SPECIAL FEATURES:
- *Travel between sites is rarely needed,* but for those occasions when the gap has to be bridged a video-conferencing facility is available currently linking 3 campuses with further extension planned to the Belfast site.

FAMOUS ALUMNI:
Gerry Anderson (radio presenter); Brian Friel (Eurovision songwriter); Kate Hoey MP (Lab); Brian Keenan (ex-hostage); Brian Robinson (Irish rugby player).

u

❛Bangor have been the British wargames champions for five of the last six years. ❜

FURTHER INFO:
Prospectuses for undergrads, part timers, and postgrads and a video. Also web site (http://www.ulst.ac.uk).

entertainment

CITY: see Queen's University Belfast

(LONDON)DERRY:
Cinemas: 2, including a multiplex.
Pubs: (London)Derry has 3 parallel streets running from Magee to the town centre and they're all lined with pubs.
pushplugs: *The Gweedore/Peadar O'Donnell's (2 pubs in one, very studenty, traditional music every week); The Strand (very close to the Uni); The Anchor (more locals, but mainly the cool ones).*
Music venues: The Rialto and the Guildhall sometimes host big names.
Clubs: The only purpose-built club is Squires but many of the pubs have upstairs rooms for a bit more than an Irish jig.
Eating out: pushplugs: *Paolo's Pizza; Leprechaun (coffee shop); Mandarin Palace.*

COLERAINE:
● Price of a pint of beer: £1.80 ● Glass of wine: £2.30
Coleraine itself is far from the beating heart of the fun rhythm, and what laughs there are are jealously guarded by the locals (not the most student-friendly bunch). The real nightlife is in Portrush and Portstewart where the majority of students live.
Cinemas: 4 screens at the Jet Centre in Coleraine and The Playhouse in Portrush.
Pubs: *Burberry's is the only pub of note in Coleraine itself but The Derry and the Harbour Inn in Portrush and The Anchor and O'Hara's in Portstewart are pretty student-friendly. The Bushmills distillery is nearby and does guided tours.*
Clubs/discos: pushplugs: *in Portrush, Trax (Student Mania on Mondays).*
Music venues: Many of the bars and clubs host bands.
pushplug: *O'Hara's in Portstewart (traditional music).*
Eating out: *Portrush and Portstewart have all the chips and candyfloss you'd associate with seaside resorts.* pushplug: *Morelli's in Portstewart (great pizza and ice cream).*

UNIVERSITY:
● Price of a pint of beer: £1.15 ● Glass of wine: £1.30
Bars: Jordanstown has 3 bars, including the newly renovated Arthur's; Club Bar at Coleraine; Bunker Bar at Magee; Conor Hall at Belfast.
Theatres: The School of Performing Arts at Coleraine keeps the thespy flag flying and there's a small drama society at Jordanstown.
Music venues: *Jordanstown comes out best with its Assembly Hall but Coleraine's Biko Hall ain't bad either. Recent rockers include The Untouchables and Mansun.*
Clubs/discos: The Saturday night raves at Conor Hall (Belfast) are *very popular, despite the lack of air-conditioning,* and open to non-students. *Big-time* DJs such as David Holmes are regular attractions. There's usually something, *however low-key,* going on at all campuses every night.

Food: All sites except Belfast have *cheap but basic* (burger & chips variants) canteens run by the SU. Belfast has no catering outlets, *much to the consternation of skint and starving students.* Banside canteen at Coleraine serves *revolting* tuck.

social & political

UNIVERSITY OF ULSTER STUDENTS' UNION:

● 9 sabbaticals ● NUS/USI member

Politics isn't really an issue with the apathetic student body. The SU co-ordinates ents and facilities across all the sites, but can seem distant and unapproachable to the point that many students think the SU is just a bar and stuff. There are 3 global sabbaticals and each site has 1 or 2 as well.

SU FACILITIES:
All sites have bars and snack bar or cafeteria facilities as well as music venues, clubs and societies. Also in the South Building at Coleraine, there is a general shop, cashpoint, travel agent, hairdresser, launderette and printing facilities. At Jordanstown, there's a shop, travel agency, cashpoint, insurance office, 2nd-hand bookshop, car and van hire, photobooth and photocopying. The Belfast SU runs a free shuttle after SU ents. There is an art shop and games room in Belfast and a general store, photocopier and photobooth in the new SU building at Magee.

CLUBS (NON SPORTING):
There are different clubs on each campus but many duplicate and all are open to all Ulster students, whatever site. Accounting; An Cumann Gaelach; Bio-chemical; Craft & Art; Cross-Cultural; Mature; Peace People; Spanish.

OTHER ORGANISATIONS:
Each campus has its own magazine and there's an all-site publication called - *wait for it* - 'Foursite'. The combined charity Rag raises vast sums each year with wacky stunts, and students do many good works in the local community surrounding each of the sites.

RELIGIOUS:
● Chaplains (Christian).
Non-Christians must go into town for a wider choice of gods and creeds.

PAID WORK:
The usual bar jobs and so on in Coleraine and the tourist trade brings summer opportunities with the National Trust among others. The Union employs 70-80 students on a casual basis.

sports

● Recent successes: pool, gaelic football, canoeing
Sport is an enthusiasm on a campus basis, rather than University-wide. The best facilities are inevitably centred on Jordanstown and Coleraine. 10 £500 bursaries are available for sports players.

SPORTS FACILITIES:
Coleraine and Jordanstown offer 40 acres of playing fields (collectively), sports centres, athletic tracks, steam rooms and squash and tennis courts. In addition, at Coleraine

there are floodlit hockey and soccer pitches, a new fitness suite and the Antrim coast offers plenty of opportunities for scenery destroying golf courses, sinking and swimming, bobbing and boating. At Jordanstown, there's an *excellent* swimming and diving pool.

SPORTING CLUBS:
Camogie; Gaelic Football; Gymnastics; Hurling; Jiu Jitsu; Parachtuing; Rowing; Surf; Tennis.

accommodation

IN COLLEGE:
● <u>Self-catering: 12%</u> ● <u>Cost: £31-35(32-37wks)</u>
Availability: *The figures look a bit limited but remember that a high proportion of students are locals. All 1st years who require accommodation will be housed.* Jordanstown has 6-bedroom houses and flats; Coleraine offers 4 halls; and Magee has 3 blocks and a student village. Belfast art studes have to find their own *bohemian* garretts. There's a head tenancy scheme with 874 places.

EXTERNALLY:
● <u>Ave rent: £30</u>
Availability: Most students at Coleraine actually live in Portrush or Portstewart *where housing is exceptionally cheap,* although more affluent students can choose to spend up to £50 per week on a single flat. *Most are more than happy with a comfortable room in a shared house.* The University's renting scheme SHAC (Student Housing Association) provides 37-week leases (66 places at Coleraine, 4 at Magee), with Portrush and Portstewart houses being surrendered to tourists over the summer. *Cars make life a little simpler at Coleraine and parking presents few problems.*
Belfast: see <u>Queen's University Belfast</u>
Housing help: Both the SU and Accommodation Office are ready with advice. The accommodation list can be helpful to those housed in cardboard, *but SHAC is the real life-saver.*

welfare

SERVICES:
● <u>Creche</u> ● <u>Nightline</u> ● <u>Lesbian & Gay Society</u>
● <u>Mature SA</u> ● <u>Overseas SA</u> ● <u>Minibus</u> ● <u>Women's Officer</u>
● <u>Self-defence classes</u>
There's a Parent Support group and the University is *justifiably* proud of its child-care provision with *well-run* creches at all sites. It also employs 7 counsellors and the SU adds 2 welfare officers. The SU solicitor is on hand once a week with free legal advice. The chaplains run a non-alcoholic bar at Jordanstown.
Disabled: *There's a concerted effort to improve facilities and they're getting there, but things still aren't that great.*

FINANCE:
● <u>Ave debt per year: £1,650</u> ● <u>Access fund: £227,000</u>
● <u>Successful applications (1997): 1,709</u>
Financial help is also available from the Hardship Fund, Endowment Awards and the Hardship Loan Fund.

▶▶ UMDS

see King's College, London

UMIST

University of Manchester Institute of Science & Technology,
PO Box 88, Manchester, M60 1QD. Tel: (0161) 236 3311.
Fax: (0161) 228 7040. E-mail: ug.prospects@umist.ac.uk
UMIST Union, Barnes Wallis Building, Sackville Street,
Manchester, M60 1QD. Tel: (0161) 200 3270.
Fax: (0161) 200 3268. E-mail: president@umist.ac.uk

General

UMIST, the University of Manchester Institute of Science &
Technology occupies a 16-hectare site in Western Europe's
largest education precinct. UMIST and its students have
informal links with the <u>University of Manchester</u>, although
recently, the two institutions have formally separated *(but
they're still good friends and Helena Bonham Carter is not
involved)*. UMIST's Main Building, which was built in 1902
just before it was first allowed to award degrees, is an art
nouveau redbrick block. But most of the architecture is 60s
and 70s concrete blocks, white fronts, straight lines and
glass. *Useful rather than beautiful.* Once upon a time, it was
only possible to study sciences and engineering, but these
days, social sciences and even arts are available, but still it's
test tubes and all that stuff which dominate.

65% ♂♂♂♂♂♂♀♀♀ **35%**

Sex ratio(M:F): 65%:35%	Founded: 1824
Full time u'grads: 4,405	Part time: 0
Postgrads: 1,611	Non-degree: 0
Ave course: 3yrs	Ethnic: n/a
Private school: n/a	Flunk rate: 21%
Mature students: 15%	Overseas students: 21%
Disabled students: n/a	Staff/student ratio: 1:13
Clearing: 22%	

ATMOSPHERE:
*UMIST students are a hard-working crowd, with their noses in
books or their faces reflected in computer screens as often as
not. Non-science courses have been introduced alongside the
tekkie stuff for which UMIST is famous but it's probably fair to
say that those blessed by trendiness or creative style don't
tend to make this their first choice; it's overwhelmingly male
and, dare we say it, a bit nerdy. Still, they're a nice bunch and
everyone seems to appreciate a pint or seven.*

THE CITY: see <u>University of Manchester</u>

TRAVEL: see <u>University of Manchester</u>

LIBRARIES & COMPUTERS:
● <u>Books: 261,000</u> ● <u>Study places: 605</u>
● <u>Computer workstations: 7,000</u>
There are enough computers to go round but sometimes they're not powerful enough for the academic hoops the students make them jump through.

CAREER PROSPECTS:
● <u>Careers Service</u> ● <u>No of staff: 13full</u>
● <u>Unemployed after 6mths (1995): 12%</u>
The careers service is shared with <u>Manchester University</u>. A *phenomenal proportion of UMIST students are sponsored by companies to study there.*

FAMOUS ALUMNI:
Margaret Beckett MP, David Clark MP (Lab cabinet ministers); Sir John Cockcroft (scientist); John Dalton (chemist - not the type that stocks condoms); Ian Gibson (Chief Executive, Nissan); Sophie Grigson (TV cook); Terry Leahy (Chief Executive, Tesco); Keith Oates (Chief Executive, M&S); Sir Arthur Whitten-Brown (trans-Atlantic pilot).

FURTHER INFO:
Prospectuses for undergrads and postgrads and web site (http://www.umist.ac.uk).

entertainment

TOWN: see <u>University of Manchester</u>

UNIVERSITY:
● <u>Price of a pint of beer: £1.35</u> ● <u>Glass of wine: £1.20</u>
The 2 universities host some pretty swinging times and UMIST students often take their funky stuff strutting off to them. In return, other students often strut down to UMIST ents.
Bars: (2) Harry's Bar is open all day but students are just as likely to head into town.
Clubs/discos/music venues: Saturday night and all memories of bloody Whigfield are banished by Kudos, the *highly successful* techno/hard house club, Return to the Source and Sonic Eight, all of which invade the Underground (cap 600). There's no live music beyond the occasional organ recital but <u>Manchester University</u>'s *excellent* Academy is nearby.
Food: The Refectory offers a *wide* choice at lunchtimes (including halal food); Renold Tavern is open from 11 - 4 and the Cafe does snacks and butties until 9pm.
Other: Freshers' Ball.

social & political

UMIST UNION:
● <u>5 sabbaticals</u> ● <u>Turnout at last ballot: 10%</u>
● <u>NUS member</u>
UMIST Union's main impact on the student in the 'hood is through the clubs and services it runs rather than its representative role. Politics just doesn't intrude – if Jennifer

Aniston were elected President on a 'Haircuts For All' ticket here, very few people would notice.

SU FACILITIES:

In the Barnes Wallis Building (named after the Michael Redgrave look-alike who invented the bouncing bomb and who was immortalised in the 'The Dambusters'), UMIST Union offers 2 bars, a general shop, print shop, cafe, dark room, TV rooms, Barclay's cash point, women's room, t-shirt printing service, meeting room, showers and pool tables.

CLUBS (NON SPORTING):

Students are also entitled to join <u>University of Manchester</u> clubs and societies and vice versa. Bangladesh; Chinese; On-Line Computing; Cyprus; Gilbert & Sullivan; Hellenic; Hindu; Indonesian; Iranian; Korean; Juggling; Links; Live Action Role Play; Malaysian; Mandarin; Mexican; New Music; Norwegian; Pakistan; Rally '98; Revue; Sikh; Singapore; Storm; Talmud; Thai; Turkish.

OTHER ORGANISATIONS:

The Union publishes the student fortnightly magazine 'GRIP' which can also be found online. The Rag organises the annual Bogle Stroll, a 55-mile sponsored walk, and will also host the national Rag conference in 2000. UMIST also has its own Community Action group which employs permanent staff as well as enlisting student volunteers.

RELIGIOUS:

UMIST shares religious facilities with <u>Manchester University</u>, but does also have a Muslim prayer room of its own, as well as a quiet room.

PAID WORK: see <u>University of Manchester</u>

sports

● <u>Recent successes: nothing special</u>

Students are entitled to use <u>Manchester University's</u> facilities, so they have some mean amenities at their disposal. On their own, UMIST competitions and involvement aren't quite so pulse-straining. Students can play for Manchester University's teams in sports where UMIST hasn't got a team of its own.

SPORTS FACILITIES:

Most facilities are shared with <u>Manchester University</u>. At Fallowfield, 2½ miles from the campus, UMIST has a 10-acre sports ground called MUTECH, *which sounds frighteningly like something you might find on a used hanky* and where students can use the various playing fields, the tennis courts, the pavilion and its bar. Rowing facilities are being developed. On the campus, on the top floor of the Main Building, there are facilities for 5-a-side football, badminton and basketball. At the Sugden Sports Centre just 150yds from the campus, there's more sporty gear, including a multigym, squash and tennis courts and more 5-a-side football. A *frighteningly flash* pool is currently being built for the Commonwealth Games in 2002 *and on campus as luck would have it.*

SPORTING CLUBS:

Gliding; Hiking; Motor; Thai Fighting; Windsurfing.

ATTRACTIONS: see <u>University of Manchester</u>

accommodation

IN COLLEGE:

- Catered: 12% ● Cost: £56(31wks)
- Self-catering: 38% ● Cost: £38-56(31-38wks)

Availability: All 1st years are guaranteed housing in halls and a few finalists come back as well. An unlucky few have to share. UMIST pools its accommodation resources with the University; for more on the score, see University of Manchester.

EXTERNALLY: see University of Manchester

welfare

SERVICES:

- Creche ● Lesbian & Gay Society ● Mature SA
- Overseas SA ● Minibus ● Equal Opportunities Officer

Apart from the joint University counselling service, help is available from the SU advice centre.

Disabled: UMIST has a Special Needs tutor *and the general provision for students with all kinds of disabilities is positive;* ramps, adapted rooms and computer suites for sight-impaired students.

FINANCE:

- Ave debt per year: £1,850 ● Access fund: £130,000
- Successful applications (1996): 500

The Union employs an adviser who points students in the right direction with financial problems (as well as housing and some other welfare matters).

▬▬▬▬▬▬▬▬▬▬▬▬▬▬▬▬▬▬▬▬▬▬▬▬▬

▶▶ United Medical and Dental Schools

see King's College, London

▬▬▬▬▬▬▬▬▬▬▬▬▬▬▬▬▬▬▬▬▬▬▬▬▬

University College, London

● *The College is part of University of London and students are entitled to use its facilities.*
University College London, Gower Street, London, WC1E 6BT.
Tel: (0171) 387 7365. Fax: (0171) 380 7380.
E-mail: degree-info@ucl.ac.uk
University College London Union, 25 Gordon Street, London, WC1H 0AH. Tel: (0171) 387 3611. Fax: (0171) 383 3937.

general

University College London, or 'UCL', is the largest college (*big enough to be a whopper university on its own*) in London University. Faculties and accommodation are concentrated in Bloomsbury, *so, in effect, this is the nearest thing London University has to a campus in the city.* It was founded by a group of worthies influenced by the ideas of Jeremy Bentham, the famous Utilitarian philosopher (*but, of course, you knew that already*), to promote equality and the crossing of class barriers. It had no religious leanings - which was unique in those days - and was also the 1st university college to admit women. The main building is *very beautiful* with steps leading to an *impressive* portico at the main entrance. The library dome can be seen behind it. 3 stone cloisters edge a big grass lawn. It's all a bit like an inner city stately home. *Unfortunately, the other buildings, humdrum brick, are as impressive as Paula Yates next to Lily Savage.*

50% ♂♂♂♂♂♀♀♀♀♀ 50%	
Sex ratio(M:F): 50%:50%	Founded: 1826
Full time u'grads: 9,596	Part time: 246
Postgrads: 3,797	Non-degree: 464
Ave course: 3yrs	Ethnic: 27%
Private school: 27%	Flunk rate: 18%
Mature students: 16%	Overseas students: 20%
Disabled students: 3%	Staff/student ratio: 1:13
Clearing: 5%	

ATMOSPHERE:
There's a hectic atmosphere consisting mainly of drinking beer, contemplating navels and putting off that library stint for another hour. The size of the college and its proximity to all the temptations of the West End combine to dilute a specific 'college spirit' but it's not an unfriendly place.

THE CITY: see University of London

TRAVEL: see University of London

LIBRARIES & COMPUTERS:
● Books: 1,400,000 ● Study places: 1,514
● Computer workstations: 1,275
Apart from the Main and Science libraries there are 12 specialist book barns. Advance booking for computers.

CAREER PROSPECTS:
● Careers Service ● No of staff: 7full
● Unemployed after 6mths (1996): 5.8%
UCL's careers service is separate from the University's.

SPECIAL FEATURES:
● UCL includes the Slade School of Fine Art - *dead prestigious and nothing to do with a cup-a-soup-loving yob-rock quartet from Wolverhampton.*
● UCL still has 'Beadles' (a sort of college caretaker) who wear maroon uniforms *and pay £250 for transparently staged videos of small dogs falling into swimming pools. Probably.*

FAMOUS ALUMNI:
Brett Anderson (Suede); Rabbi Lionel Blue (writer/broadcaster); Raymond Briggs (writer/illustrator); AS Byatt (novelist); Jonathan Dimbleby (broadcaster); Ken Follet (writer); Justine Frischmann (Elastica); Hugh Gaitskell (former Labour leader); Mahatma Gandhi; David Gower (cricketer); Margaret Hodge MP (Lab); Derek Jarman (film director);

Jonathan Miller (writer and director); Sir Eduardo Paolozzi (artist/sculptor); Stanley Spencer (artist); Marie Stopes (birth control pioneer).

FURTHER INFO:
Prospectuses for undergrads and postgrads from Admissions Enquiries and a video. Alternative prospectus available from Union. Web sites (http://www.ucl.ac.uk and http://www.ucl.ac.uk/ucl-union).

entertainment

IN LONDON: see University of London

COLLEGE:
● Price of a pint of beer: £1.50 ● Glass of wine: £1.20

Bars: There are 7 bars around the College and in its halls of residence, the central one being the *pub-like* Phineas. Others include the *sporty* 2nd floor Bar, the *vast* Windeyer and Gordon's Café Bar.

Cinema: 2 films a week, *a good mix* of art films, golden oldies and blockbusters only recently in the West End.

Theatre: The Bloomsbury Theatre (cap 550) hosts UCL productions for 10 weeks a year and the Drama Society makes regular trips to the Edinburgh Fringe. *Opera and musical theatre are also strong.*

Clubs/discos: There's something dance-oriented every night, *major* events being the Thursday Cocktails night (3 rooms of varied sounds) and Slap'n'Tickle in the Windeyer Bar, with guest DJs, such as, recently, Peshay, Norman Jay and Judge Jules.

Music venues: There are occasional theme nights (eg Irish, salsa) with live bands *but no big-name acts.*

Cabaret: Shows at the Bloomsbury theatre have recently starred Greg Proops and John Hegley.

Food: There are 3 University refectories but students tend to prefer the SU facilities, which include snack and sandwich bars, Pizza Plus and food served in 6 of the bars.

Others: At least 3 balls a year, drinks promotions, quizzes, Blind Date - *a lorra lorra laffs all round.*

social & political

UCL UNION:
● 5 sabbaticals ● Turnout at last ballot: 15%
● NUS member
UCLU is not renowned for its political activity but it is very close to ULU, so those desperate for a soap box or frantic for fantastic facilities don't have far to go. The purpose of a recent march to Frank Dobson's house was to protest against tuition fees, rather than simply to laugh at his beard.

SU FACILITIES:
In UCL's main building: 4 bars; pizza and sandwich bars; 'Bear Necessities' (poster shop); a print shop; sweet shop; stationery shop; travel agency; advice centre; hairdresser; games machines and pool tables.

CLUBS (NON SPORTING):
Arabic; Bloomsbury TV; Chinese; Cypriot; Hindu; Human Powered Flight; Jazz; Lotus Eaters; Malaysian; Music; Pakistan; Persian; Roller-blading; Sikh; Singapore; Spanish; Stage Committee; Supine Recumbent; Welsh.

OTHER ORGANISATIONS:

'Pi' is the official mag. The award-winning Bloomsbury TV is broadcast by the Union at least once a week and the all-new Rare FM will broadcast twice a year. Rag raised £4,000 last year.

RELIGIOUS:

Despite UCL's godless foundations, the CU is one of London's largest. In the Union there is a multi-purpose meditation room and the University's church (the Church of Christ the King) is in Byng Place.

sports

● Recent successes: fencing

Many faculties keep Wednesday afternoons free for sports, although facilities are not so free - there's a £31 annual charge for the Bloomsbury Fitness Centre.

SPORTS FACILITIES:

In the Bloomsbury Fitness Centre, which is also open to the public, there are squash courts, aerobics, fencing and dance halls and weights gym. A brand new sports centre at Somers Town is 10 minutes' walk from campus.

SPORTING CLUBS:

Dangerous Sports; Kendo; Shorinji Kempo; Tiger Krane; Wing Chun.

ATTRACTIONS: see University of London

accommodation

IN COLLEGE:
● Catered: 12% ● Cost: £79-82(30wks)
● Self-catering: 20% ● Cost: £51-77(40wks)

Availability: All 1st years who apply in time get college accommodation, 15% of them sharing. 2nd years are almost certainly on their own but a few finalists come back. Those who do get housed will be in 1 of UCL's halls of residence or in the University's inter-collegiate accommodation. Catered halls provide breakfast and evening meals every day, except in Ifor Evans, which doesn't at weekends and has cooking facilities instead. The cost of electricity is extra. Self-catering halls have *good big* kitchens with a couple of cookers and fridges between 10 people.

EXTERNALLY: see University of London
Availability: Many UCL students live in Stoke Newington (the number 73 bus runs to UCL) and the Finsbury Park/Manor House ghetto or Camden *if they're feeling flush.*
Housing help: UCL keeps information on private and College accommodation and they publish a regular bulletin.

welfare

SERVICES:
● Creche ● Lesbian & Gay Society ● Mature SA
● Overseas SA ● Minibus ● Women's Officer
● Self-defence classes

UCLU has a rights advice office with 3 advisors, where weekly sessions are held with solicitors. On campus is a health centre with 3 trained counsellors (and part-time psychiatrists).

❝Students at the University of Essex have staged an exhibition of 70s glam rock clothing including one of Freddie Mercury's jumpsuits.❞

The Dean of Students is responsible for student welfare.
Disabled: *Provision varies greatly depending on departments* and some changes can be made if required on an individual basis.

FINANCE:
● Ave debt per year: £1,800 ● Access fund: £401,468
● Successful applications (1997): 844
The SU has a hardship fund of £20,000 and special bursaries are available to non-EU students.

●●

▶▶ **University College, Stockton**
see University of Durham

●●

▶▶ **UNL**
see University of North London

●●

▶▶ **Uxbridge**
see Brunel University

❝A former Vice-President of John Moores Students' Union was hypnotised on 'Richard & Judy' by a dog called Oscar.❞

‘Freaked out by finance? Why not pop into your local branch of Lloyds Bank and see what they have to offer.’

‘Get your money's worth... read 'PUSHover: how to use PUSH' at the front of the book.’

Fold-out guide to symbols inside back cover

University of Wales

University of Wales College of Medicine

- Wales Poly
  see University of Glamorgan

- University College Warrington
  see Other Institutions

University of Warwick

- West London Poly
  see Thames Valley University

- University of the West of England
  see Bristol, University of the West of England

- West Surrey College of Art & Design
  see Surrey Institute of Art & Design

- Westfield
  see Queen Mary & Westfield College, London

- Westhill College of HE
  see Other Institutions

University of Westminster

- Westminster College, Oxford
  see Other Institutions

- Wimbledon School of Art
  see Other Institutions

- Winchester College of Art
  see University of Southampton

University of Wolverhampton

- University College, Worcester
  see Other Institutions

- Writtle College
  see Other Institutions

Wye College, London

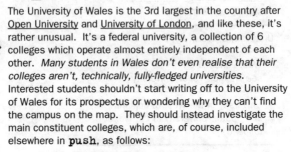

University of Wales

▼ University of Wales, University Registry, Cathays Park, Cardiff,
CF1 3NS. Tel: (01222) 382656.

general

The University of Wales is the 3rd largest in the country after
<u>Open University</u> and <u>University of London</u>, and like these, it's
rather unusual. It's a federal university, a collection of 6
colleges which operate almost entirely independent of each
other. *Many students in Wales don't even realise that their
colleges aren't, technically, fully-fledged universities.*
Interested students shouldn't start writing off to the University
of Wales for its prospectus or wondering why they can't find
the campus on the map. They should instead investigate the
main constituent colleges, which are, of course, included
elsewhere in **push**, as follows:

<u>Aberystwyth, University of Wales</u>

<u>Bangor, University of Wales</u>

<u>Cardiff, University of Wales</u>

<u>Lampeter, University of Wales</u>

<u>Swansea, University of Wales</u>

<u>University of Wales, College of Medicine</u>

Some of the colleges in the 'Other Institutions' chapter also
award University of Wales degrees. UCAS applications are
made to the individual colleges.

University of Wales College of Medicine

▼ ● *The Medical College is part of <u>University of Wales</u> and
students are entitled to use its facilities.*
University of Wales College of Medicine, Heath Park, Cardiff,
CF4 4XN. Tel: (01222) 742027. Fax: (01222) 742914.
UWCM Students' Club, Neuadd Meirionnydd, Heath Park,
Cardiff, CF4 4YS. Tel: (01222) 742125.
Fax: (01222) 743619. E-mail: uwcm_su_president@cf.ac.uk

general

UWCM is on the outskirts of Cardiff with the countryside in
sight but still no more than 3 miles from the city centre. Being
a medical school, the College is attached to a hospital next
door and only offers courses in healthcare subjects. The
College is made up of low-rise 70s blocks, and is small with

> ❝The Abertay Students' Association Handbook was withdrawn after threats of libel action from local publicans.❞

few student facilities of its own. If students want more, they get down to the larger and completely separate <u>Cardiff, University of Wales</u>, whose facilities they're allowed to use. In 1995 the College took over the Institute of Health Care Studies, expanding the range of courses with physiotherapy, radiology and other subjects related to medicine.

28% ♂♂♂♀♀♀♀♀♀♀ 72%	
Sex ratio(M:F): 28%:72%	Founded: 1931
Full time u'grads: 1,740	Part time: 0
Postgrads: 280	Non-degree: 609
Ave course: 5yrs	Ethnic: n/a
Private school: n/a	Flunk rate: n/a
Mature students: 13%	Overseas students: 8%
Disabled students: n/a	Staff/student ratio: 1:17
Clearing: n/a	

ATMOSPHERE:
Medical types take a professional, serious-minded and quiet attitude to study, working closely together and with hospital staff, except when boozing like there's no tomorrow. The College trots along on a friendly plane, but it's small and a tad cliquey, with social life very much alcohol-based. Escape into town is possible and students can take a less quiet attitude to fun there. Locals like to stay on the right side of those who may be stitching them up or fiddling with their most valued attachments tomorrow.

THE CITY: see <u>Cardiff, University of Wales</u>

TRAVEL: see <u>Cardiff, University of Wales</u>
Heath High Level and Heath Low Level stations are ¾ mile away. *Reliable* local buses (Nos 8 & 9) run from the city centre through the campus every 20mins till around midnight. Taxis to or from the city centre cost about £4.

LIBRARIES & COMPUTERS:
● <u>Books: 150,000</u> ● <u>Study places: 582</u>
● <u>Computer workstations: 110</u>
7 libraries and a 24-hour reading room.

CAREER PROSPECTS:
Unemployment is always rare for graduates from any medical school but there is a careers service, operated by staff of the postgraduate departments.

SPECIAL FEATURES:
● All 4th year medical, dental and Bachelor of Nursing students do an 'elective' - an opportunity to spend time on a research project for 6 to 8 weeks, often abroad.

> ❛Text in italics is PUSH's point of view – take it or leave it.❜

FAMOUS ALUMNI:
Prof Bernard Knight (Home Office pathologist, crime writer); Dr Thomas Stamps (Health Minister, Zimbabwe).

FURTHER INFO:
Prospectuses for undergrads and postgrads, and loan of a video. Web site (http://www.uwcm.ac.uk).

entertainment

THE CITY: see <u>Cardiff, University of Wales</u>

COLLEGE:
● <u>Price of a pint of beer: £1.30</u>
Teetotallers may feel a little isolated here.
Bars: (2) The students-only Med Club Bar (cap 500) *is the hub of all social activity, especially on Friday nights.* The Sports & Social Club on the hospital site, is used by hospital staff as well as students, although it charges a £15 annual membership fee.
Clubs/discos/venues: Discos every Thursday and Friday in the Med Club and occasional tribute bands.
Cabaret: Occasional hypnotists and contortionists.
Food: *The food in the refectories is pretty dull but it is cheap.* The hospital canteen is open all day *and the food is always hospital food.*
Others: At least 5 balls a year, beer fests, toga parties *and other spiritually and intellectually uplifting pastimes.*

social & political

UNIVERSITY OF WALES COLLEGE OF MEDICINE STUDENTS' CLUB:
● <u>1 sabbatical</u> ● <u>Turnout at last ballot: 32%</u>
● <u>NUS member</u>
Med Club is the home of (among other things) the Students' Club, *which is apolitical and then some. Apart from its representative role, it's mainly ents-based.*

SU FACILITIES:
In the Med Club: Bars (with TV); pool table; disco area with equipment; games and video machines. The Students' Club also has 3 minibuses for student clubs to hire and a snooker room. The hospital has several shops and a NatWest Bank.

CLUBS (NON SPORTING):
Choir; Welsh.

OTHER ORGANISATIONS:
The independent student paper is called 'Leech', or 'Y Gelen' to its Welsh fans. It can also be found online (http://www.uwcm.ac.uk/uwcmsc/leech). *More effort is put into their online identity than most other unis put together, despite the fact they're a small college. Nice one.* Charity Groups Revue organises marathons, charity balls and bed pushes.

sports

- <u>Recent successes: rugby</u>

Med Club runs about 20 clubs and despite its size, the College has its own sports teams and facilities (which students can use by joining The Sports & Social Club at £15 a year).

SPORTS FACILITIES:
A sports hall; squash courts; swimming pool; 2 gyms; badminton court; weights room. Students can also use the facilities of <u>Cardiff, University of Wales</u>.

SPORTING CLUBS:
Boating; Caving.

accommodation

IN COLLEGE:

- <u>Self-catering: 12%</u> ● <u>Cost: £32-51(46wks)</u>

Availability: All 1st years are housed, many of them in <u>Cardiff, University of Wales</u> accommodation - single study bedrooms in modern purpose built halls with 8 people to a kitchen and single sex corridors. After the 1st year, about 20% of students get places, often in College-owned flats and houses. The Medical School accommodation, Neuadd Meirionnydd, is a *pretty basic* 70s tower block, overlooking the Med Club bar.
Car parking: *Inadequate* permit parking space.

EXTERNALLY: see <u>Cardiff, University of Wales</u>
Housing help: The Accommodation Office provides lists of landlords and houses.

welfare

SERVICES:

- <u>Nightline</u> ● <u>Overseas SA</u>
- <u>Postgrad SA</u>

There are 2 independent counsellors and an occupational health service on site.
Disabled: *While access is good - patients need to get in as well as students - medicine is not a profession in which there are many opportunities for students with disabilities.*

FINANCE:
- <u>Ave debt: £1,100</u> ● <u>Access fund: £38,696</u>
- <u>Successful applications (1997): 112</u>

There's an emergency loan fund of £8,000. Selective scholarships.

Wales Poly
see University of Glamorgan

University College Warrington
see Other Institutions

University of Warwick

University of Warwick, Coventry, CV4 7AL.
Tel: (01203) 523523. Fax: (01203) 461606.
E-mail: ugadmissions@admin.warwick.ac.uk
Warwick University Students' Union, Coventry, CV4 7AL.
Tel: (01203) 417220. Fax: (01203) 692083.
E-mail: enquiries@sunion.warwick.ac.uk

general

Warwick University isn't actually in Warwick. In fact, Warwick, just over 9 miles south, isn't even the nearest town. Royal Leamington Spa is bigger than Warwick and only 7 miles away. Coventry, bigger still, is just 3 miles north, or there's Kenilworth about 1½ miles west. *But the University of Somewhere-In-The-South-East-Midlands was a bit of a mouthful and, under the title that was chosen, it's earned a very good name for itself.* It's on a 500-acre site hiding from Leamington Spa and Coventry amidst rolling hills and *seeming deceptively remote*, although Birmingham is within 25 miles. *The campus looks extraordinary: wildly modern with lots of sculptures and 3 man-made lakes, all surrounded by nature. The buildings are white or as brightly coloured as children's crayons and just as weirdly shaped. It's not unpleasant, so long as you don't mind living in an episode of 'The Jetsons'.* The smaller Westwood campus is about 10 minutes walk away and houses the Institute of Education and some halls.

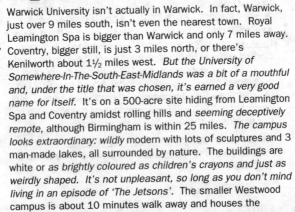

50% ♂♂♂♂♂♀♀♀♀ 50%	
Sex ratio(M:F): 50%:50%	Founded: 1965
Full time u'grads: 7,575	Part time: 420
Postgrads: 2,276	Non-degree: 0
Ave course: 3/4yrs	Ethnic: 7%
Private school: 19%	Flunk rate: 14%
Mature students: 10%	Overseas students: 9%
Disabled students: 0.1%	Staff/student ratio: 1:15
Clearing: 1.5%	

ATMOSPHERE:
Although it's a favourite with middle-class people from the Home Counties, in no way is Warwick a cliquey den of snobbery. In fact, it's a buzzing, friendly campus with students who can balance high academic standards with having a good time, whether on the gym floor, the dancefloor or the pub floor. In the summer the whole site turns into one big sun lounge.

LEAMINGTON SPA:
Many Warwick students live in Leamington Spa - more than in Coventry, although this trend is changing as Coventry gets cheaper. *Leamington Spa is an attractive little town, belonging more to the Cotswolds to the south than to the Midlands,*

which might be a more accurate geographic description. It has enough by way of shops for daily fodder, but foraging for clothes or major purchases, Coventry or even Birmingham would be a better bet. It's not too hot on local entertainments either.

COVENTRY: see <u>Coventry University</u>

TRAVEL:
Trains: The nearest main station is 2½ miles away in Coventry, but there is a line that runs south through to Leamington Spa and Warwick.
Cars: *Cars are not the answer to Warwick's isolation (push reserves the right to describe the suburbs of Coventry as isolated).* As the University is quick to point out, they're less environmentally friendly than public transport. *This is a genuine concern, but it also happens to coincide conveniently with a need to reduce pressure on the campus' limited parking.* Only 70 students are allowed permits for overnight parking, but during term, up to 1,000 cars can park on campus during the day.
Local: From the bus stops on campus, the numbers 12, 12A, 12B, 12C and 112 run into Coventry centre via the train station every 15 mins until 11pm (50-72p) and other services go to other parts of town. There are similar services to Leamington (£1.35) and Kenilworth (70p). Late night services during term time.
Taxis: At some point as a student living out at Warwick University, most students are likely to get caught on campus after the last bus and without a lift. Then it's time to dig deep in the pocket for £6 to Coventry or £9 to Leamington.
Bicycles: *Quite handy for getting around the campus, especially for livers in, but think of that ride twice a day for the students living in Leamington. A big lock's a good idea, as are big legs.*

TRAVEL: see <u>Coventry University</u>

LIBRARIES & COMPUTERS:
● <u>Books: 890,000</u> ● <u>Study places: 1,890</u>
● <u>Computer workstations: 1000</u>
Library facilities have come in for some student criticism over space, book availability and the cost of photocopying.

CAREER PROSPECTS:
● <u>Careers Service</u> ● <u>No of staff: 10full/5part</u>
● <u>Unemployed after 6mths (1996): 2.8%</u>

SPECIAL FEATURES:
● The University does a roaring trade in conferences which means there are some *excellent* facilities and accommodation manages to be better at a cheaper rate. *It also means students can feel like they're an inconvenience stuck between the real business of travelling salesmen's piss-ups worthy of a Steve Coogan sketch and dandruffy, navel-gazing academics reading logarithms at each other.*
● Warwick has over 14,000 students doing Open Studies Certificates and post-experience training, but no HND courses.

FAMOUS ALUMNI:
Jenny Bond (BBC correspondent); David Davis MP; Timmy

Mallett (hammer-wielding *prat*); Simon Mayo (DJ); Sheila McKechnie (campaigner); Dave Nellist (Militant ex-MP); Stephen Pile (writer); Jeff Rooker MP (Lab); Frank Skinner (comedian); Gary Sinyor & Vadim Jean (film-makers); Sting (for a term); Tony Wheeler (author, 'Lonely Planet' guides). Lenny Henry has an honorary degree.

FURTHER INFO:
Prospectuses for undergrads, postgrads and part-timers, video and web site (http://www.warwick.ac.uk). Alternative prospectus (£1) from SU.

entertainment

COVENTRY: see <u>Coventry University</u>

LEAMINGTON:
● <u>Price of a pint of beer: £1.70</u> ● <u>Glass of wine: £1.40</u>
The excellent facilities on campus compensate for Leamington's sparseness.
Pubs: push*plugs: Benjamin Satchwell's, Jug & Jester, and Scholars (made for students). Don't win on the bandit in The Guardsman - it upsets the locals.*
Cinemas: 2, with 7 screens between them. *The Rubin Cinema is a bit artier than the Apollo.*
Theatre: *The Royal Spa is a standard regional rep house but Leamington is on a direct rail route to Stratford-upon-Avon.*
Clubs/discos/music venues: *Monroe's has a student night on Thurdays but it still plays the same Top 40 stuff. Brown's Cow attracts bands and DJs from out of town.*
Eating out: *Again, not a huge deal, although, this being the Midlands, there's a number of excellent value balti houses. Further* **push***plugs: Mongolian Wok Bar (£7.50 buffet lunch); Pierre Victoire. Spun End Balti does deliveries to campus.*

UNIVERSITY:
● <u>Price of a pint of beer: £1.50</u> ● <u>Glass of wine: £1.25</u>
Bars: The principal bars are Cholo's (cap 750) and the Cooler (850) which doubles as a venue. Others include Lynam's (300, no smoking), Grumpy John's (270, *pub-like*) and Zippy's (270, mainly used by societies). There are also supping stops at the Arts Centre, in the Athletic Union and some University bars which tend to be frequented more by staff.
Arts Centre: *The Arts Centre on campus is fantastic in every respect - it looks as though it's sprung from some futuristic fantasy and has facilities to dream about:* 2 theatres; conference hall; film theatre; art gallery; sculpture court; concert hall; music centre and bookshop.
Theatres: (3) In the Arts Centre, the main theatre (cap 570) attracts touring companies (drama, dance, opera, etc), as well as big student shows. The studio theatre (200) lends itself to smaller scale productions. *Students enter into the dramatic fray with thespian gusto,* including some prize-winning efforts at the Edinburgh Fringe.
Cinemas: A purpose-built and a customised cinema show around 20 films a week, with the Arts Centre providing a *less commercial* counterbalance.
Clubs/discos: *The Cooler is developing quite a name for clubular antics.* There are 6 events a week, from the acid jazz

of Mojo, via Supersonic's indie feedback, to Saturday night's Culture, which takes over the Market Place as well with its blend of techno and dance sounds. Guest DJs have included Carl Cox, Paul Oakenfold and Danny Rampling.

Music venues: The Union's Market Place is the vastest venue, featuring names such as, recently, Stereophonics, Catatonia and *the brilliant* Super Furry Animals. Butterworth Hall (1,500) in the Arts Centre features a variety of music, mostly classical, attracting top national and international performers. The University Chorus and orchestra, among other University and student music groups, perform here in between world tours.

Food: The Union caters for student tastes (if not pockets) at Harvey's, the Snack Bar and the Deli counter. The University counters with the hi-tech Rootes restaurant and Air Fair for quick snacks. There's also the restaurant in the Arts centre, a coffee bar in the library and a few other outlets on campus.

Others: At least 7 balls a year, February Real Ale Festival, May Week Festival (*4 days of silliness*), The Hurst Party (mini-Glastonbury) and plenty more debauchery.

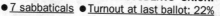

social & political

UNIVERSITY OF WARWICK STUDENTS' UNION:
- <u>7 sabbaticals</u> ● <u>Turnout at last ballot: 22%</u>
- <u>NUS member</u>

Hacks hang to what we used to call the left, full of sensible moderation and concentrating on student issues and campus concerns rather than party labels. In this post-80s culture, commercialism is the principle prong - students are shareholders in the company which is their Union, but they are also social satellites to its solar services which stay open late.

SU FACILITIES:

In the Union Building and elsewhere: bars; cafeteria; 2 coffee bars; restaurants; 3 minibuses and 2 cars for hire; travel agency; print shop; DTP suite; dark room; bookshop; 2 big shops (general and supermarket); computer and typewriters for sale; all 4 major banks with cash machines; Endsleigh Insurance office; photocopying; fax; photo booth; games and vending machines; pool tables; juke boxes; 5 TVs; 5 meeting rooms; conference hall; customised nightclub; launderette; opticians; hairdresser; post office; and snooker tables. A *brand spanking new* SU building is being constructed which *should* be ready for entry in '98.

CLUBS (NON SPORTING):

The dafter names are mostly music/club related. AIESEC; All Things Considered; Amateur Radio; Badd-Ass Phunk; Band; Big Band; Blues & Roots; Boar; Boomshanka; Brass; Bridge; Campaign Against the Arms Trade; Ceramics; Change Ringing; Chill Out; Chinese; Chorus; Club 205; Codpiece Theatre; Contemporary Dance; Da Muthafunkas; Debating; Dirty Fat Beatz; Disability Rights; Duke of Edinburgh Award; East Timor; Endangered Species; Eurotalk; Film Making; Football Fans; Fresh Blood Theatre; Gettin' Hectic; Gilbert & Sullivan; Greek; Greek Cypriot; High Society; Highlife; Hunt Sabs; Italian; Juggling; Ko-Labs; Latinos; Live Action Role Play; Malaysian; Motorbike; Nigerian; Nightline; Northern Ireland Children's Welfare; Not So Historical; Offbeat; One World; Ovation; Poetry; Pooh Bear; Portuguese Speaking; Radio Drama; Real Ale; Revelation; Russian; Saville Row; Scandinavian; Shaft; Sikh; Singapore; Skirmish (paintball); Socialist Labour; Sri Lanka; St John's; Star Trek; Synergy; Tai Chi; Taiwan; Tap Dance; Theatre 4 All; Tribe of the Trout; Turkish Delights; 2+2; Underground; UN; W963; Welsh; Wind Orchestra; Wine; Workers' Power; Ya Mama's So Fat.

OTHER ORGANISATIONS:

There's the *award-hogging* 'Warwick Boar' student newspaper, a listings sheet called 'The Word' and the radio station, W963, broadcasting 18hrs a day. The Warwick Boar is online (http://www.warwick.ac.uk/boar). The charity Rag raised £10,000 last year. The Community Volunteers Group gets students involved in local help projects and owns Dippy, an inflatable dragon.

RELIGIOUS:

● <u>4 chaplains (CofE, RC, Free Church, Jewish)</u>

Multi-faith chaplaincy on campus and Muslim prayer room.

PAID WORK:

At such a major conference venue there's plenty of vacation work. The Union runs a service publishing an opportunities list and linking students with jobs and vice versa both on and off campus. The Union itself employs over 300 students on a casual basis, and the University runs a Temp Agency.

sports

● <u>Recent successes: badminton, archery</u>

Plenty of clubs and goings on. Almost all sport is based on campus, split into 2 areas. 40% take part in regular activity.

SPORTS FACILITIES:

There are 2 sports centres with 7 squash courts, 2 swimming pools, 2 sports halls, fitness room, weights, dance studios, 2 gyms/activities rooms, climbing wall and a sauna. The playing fields include: 1 all weather pitch; 2 grass hockey, 7 football, 1 ladies' football, 2 netball, 1 American football and 4 rugby pitches; 3 cricket squares; 9 tennis courts; 1 lacrosse pitch and an athletics track. There's also a climbing centre which recently hosted the British Climbing Championships.

SPORTING CLUBS:

Aerobics; Aikido; American Football; Autosport; Ballroom Dance; Baseball; Christians in Sport; Gliding; Hang-Gliding; Ken Yu Kiai; Lacrosse; Life Saving; Mountain Bike; Parachute; Paragliding; Pistol & Rifle; Pool; Rambling; Rowing; Rugby League; Shotokan Karate; Snooker; Snowboarding; Street Hockey; Surf; Ten Pin Bowling; Thai Boxing; Trampoline; Triathlon; Ultimate Frisbee; Windsurfing; Wing Chun; Yoga; Zhuan Shu Kuan.

ATTRACTIONS: see <u>Coventry University</u>

accommodation

IN COLLEGE:

● <u>Catered: 6%</u> ● <u>Cost: £63(30wks)</u>

● <u>Self-catering: 50%</u> ● <u>Cost: £38-52(30-39wks)</u>

Availability: Almost everyone lives in during their 1st year, usually in the 6 halls (5% in shared rooms) although the few students who enter through clearing aren't guaranteed a place. About 40% of finalists are also allowed back in. *Some of the accommodation is very nice:* luxury rooms with en suite bathrooms, *not built for the better comfort of students but to attract conference guests* - still, students can't complain, except that rents for the better rooms are higher. There may be problems, however, if they want to stay over the vacation. There are also 1,642 places off campus, organised by the University under head tenancy arrangements. A new accommodation block will be largely reserved for postgrads.

EXTERNALLY: see <u>Coventry University</u>
Central Leamington is the preferred roost for the majority but South Coventry and Earlsdon are cheap and near enough to be worthy of consideration.
Housing help: The Accommodation Office has 14 staff who approve vacancies on their list and help negotiate contracts. The SU can also assist.

welfare

SERVICES:
● <u>Creche</u> ● <u>Nightline</u> ● <u>Lesbian & Gay Society</u>
● <u>Mature SA</u> ● <u>Overseas SA</u> ● <u>Minibus</u> ● <u>Women's Officer</u>
● <u>Self-defence classes</u>

The Union runs an *effective* Rights & Advice Service with 6 staff and a student sabbatical Welfare Officer. The University has 6 part-time counselling staff of its own and further help with personal problems can be found through Nightline's phone and drop-in service. Each hall has a resident tutor, *who often isn't a tutor at all, so you don't need to worry about doing your homework before looking for some sympathy.*
Women: Personal alarms are available and there's a minibus to get around campus.
Drugs: *There has been fairly strong dope (cannabis) culture at Warwick. The University is very tough on users if they're discovered.*
Disabled: *Wheelchair access is among the best in the country including lifts in the Union. There are induction loops, and accommodation for carers if necessary. The SU and the newer academic buildings also have Braille signs.*

FINANCE:
● <u>Ave debt: £2,100</u> ● <u>Access fund: £190,000</u>
● <u>Successful applications (1997): 260</u>
There's also a hardship fund, as well as postgrad bursaries and music scholarships.

• •

▶▶ West London Poly
see Thames Valley University

• •

▶▶ University of the West of England
see Bristol, University of the West of England

• •

▶▶ West Surrey College of Art & Design
see Surrey Institute of Art & Design

• •

▶▶ Westfield
see Queen Mary & Westfield College, London

• •

▶▶ Westhill College of HE

see Other Institutions

University of Westminster

● *Formerly Polytechnic of Central London*
University of Westminster, 309 Regent Street, London,
W1R 8AL. Tel: (0171) 911 5000. Fax: (0171) 911 5118.
University of Westminster Students' Union, 32-38 Wells Street,
London, W1P 3HG. Tel: (0171) 636 6271.
Fax: (0171) 911 5192. E-mail: supresi@wmin.ac.uk

General

The University was founded as the Royal Polytechnic Institute
to give lectures on science and engineering to the general
public. It's changed a bit since then - there are 4 main sites
plus numerous additional buildings, built in a real mixture of
old and new architectural styles. They are mostly in the 2
miles north of Trafalgar Square so all that London's West End
has to offer is within easy reach. The exception is the site at
Harrow, which used to be the separate Harrow College of HE,
9 miles away or ½ hour by tube.

50% ♂♂♂♂♂ ♀♀♀♀♀ 50%	
Sex ratio(M:F): 50%:50%	Founded: 1838
Full time u'grads: 8,400	Part time: 7,135
Postgrads: 900	Non-degree: 355
Ave course: 3yrs	Ethnic: n/a
Private school: n/a	Flunk rate: n/a
Mature students: 60%	Overseas students: 10%
Disabled students: n/a	Staff/student ratio: 1:14
Clearing: n/a	

ATMOSPHERE:
*The students are a mixed crowd with a great ethnic diversity
and a high proportion of mature students. Although the
campuses are relatively close together, students tend to stick
to their own site's bars and facilities and there's little sense of
a big cohesive family. Still, with all the fun of the West End on
their doorsteps, nobody's got any excuse to be bored.*

HARROW SITE:
Over 4,000 full- and part-time students are based here,
studying Communications, Design & Media, Management and
Computer Science. Major investment is being ploughed into
the site: recent additions have included 2 TV/film studios, a
new computer centre, 4 radio production suites,
accommodation for 400 students - oh, and a bar.

THE CITY: see <u>University of London</u>

TRAVEL: see <u>University of London</u>
Trains: Euston station is closest.
Buses: If you think we're going to list all the buses that go to all the sites, you've got another bus coming.
Underground: Baker Street (Bakerloo, Circle, Jubilee, Metropolitan and Hammersmith & City Lines), Oxford Circus (Bakerloo, Victoria and Central Lines) and so on... For Harrow, Northwick Park (Metropolitan) and Kenton (Bakerloo).

LIBRARIES & COMPUTERS:
- <u>Books: 380,600</u> ● <u>Study places: 1,400</u>
- <u>Computer workstations: 1,600</u>

There are 6 libraries distributed around the campuses, plus an Information Resource Centre *(which isn't the same thing at all, oh no sirree)* at Harrow.

CAREER PROSPECTS:
- <u>Careers Service</u> ● <u>No of staff: 9full/3part</u>
- <u>Unemployed after 6mths (1996): 9.9%</u>

The careers service is very efficient. Part-time jobs are regularly posted on the internet.

SPECIAL FEATURES:
- More than 75% of undergraduates undertake 'enterprise' activities as an assessed part of their courses. *Sadly, this does not involve learning Klingon, how to set your phasers on 'stun', or making corsets for William Shatner.*

FAMOUS ALUMNI:
Baroness Chalker (Tory peer); Jasper Conran (designer); Quentin Crisp (writer, wit); the Emmanuels (designers who rustled up Princess Di's wedding frock); Lisa l'Anson (TV presenter, DJ); Michael Jackson (Channel 4 controller, not Wacko); Julian Metcalfe (sandwich entrepreneur); some of Pink Floyd; Jonathan Porritt (environmentalist).

FURTHER INFO:
Prospectuses for undergrads and postgrads, video. Web site (http://www.wmin.ac.uk).

entertainment

IN LONDON: see <u>University of London</u>

UNIVERSITY:
- <u>Price of a pint of beer: £1.20</u> ● <u>Glass of wine: £1</u>

Bars: Around the University sites, there are 7 bars of which 3 are run by students and the rest are run by outside caterers, making them more expensive. The Studio Bar has opened at Harrow, while The Bar Formerly Known As... at Bolsover St *is now The Reopened-at-Wells-St Bar Formerly Known As The Closed-Down Bar Formerly Known As The Bar Formerly Known As...*

Cinemas: There's a big screen at Harrow. Student-made films are often run *and Manga flicks are pretty popular.*

Clubs/discos/music venues: There are 2 dancey type things a week, one at each bar.

Food: The University offers contract catering at each site; *students complain about the cost but it tastes OK.*

Others: The Union runs 3 big events a year, including a Freshers' extravaganza at the Ministry of Sound nightclub.

social & political

UNIVERSITY OF WESTMINSTER STUDENTS' UNION:

● <u>5 sabbaticals</u> ● <u>Turnout at last ballot: 3.5%</u>
● <u>NUS member</u>

The exec tends to be hardworking and prepared to stand up to the administration but the students don't seem to know or care what's going on. The SU is trying to address this by revamping its style, but the kids still find them slightly distant. The sabbatical officer for entertainments has been dropped for a professional, although functions still seem to be few and far between nonetheless.

SU FACILITIES:
The Union building is part of the main student and staff centre in Wells St near Regent's Park. It provides a bar, common rooms and vending and games machines. Harrow has a bar, shop and common room. There are Union offices on all sites.

CLUBS (NON SPORTING):
Chinese; Da'Wah (Islamic Education); Disability; Friends of Palestine; Future Media; Hellenic; Hispanic; Ideological; Oriental; Sikh; Tamil.

OTHER ORGANISATIONS:
The fortnightly 'Smoke' student mag is *pretty damn good.*

RELIGIOUS:
● <u>1 chaplain (CofE)</u>

PAID WORK: see <u>University of London</u>

sports

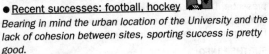

● <u>Recent successes: football, hockey</u>

Bearing in mind the urban location of the University and the lack of cohesion between sites, sporting success is pretty good.

SPORTS FACILITIES:
The Regent Street site has badminton, snooker, a gym, a sauna, solarium and multigym. At Harrow there's a fitness centre and a sports hall, and there's a sports ground at Chiswick, complete with running track, boathouse, bar and 55 acres of pitches. New gym and all-weather pitches are now open.

SPORTING CLUBS:
Rowing; Kick-Boxing; Parachuting; Roller-Blading; Rowing; Skate Boarding; Water Polo.

ATTRACTIONS: see <u>University of London</u>

accommodation

IN COLLEGE:

● <u>Self-catering: 15%</u> ● <u>Cost: £59-67(34-42wks)</u>

Availability: Only 18% of 1st years and a few others can be housed by the University, although the high proportion of local students should put this into perspective. There are 8 halls, with kitchens shared by 6-12 students.

EXTERNALLY: see <u>University of London</u>

Housing help: The University advisory scheme at the Marylebone Road and Harrow sites provides a notice board, newsletter, an approval scheme and advice on various housing matters. Temporary accommodation is available in September while students house hunt.

 welfare

SERVICES:

 ● Creche ● Nightline ● Lesbian & Gay Society ● Mature SA ● Overseas SA ● Women's Officer

The Student Services Department provides 1 part-time and 3 full-time counsellors and the SU also offers advisors and help. A nurse and doctor are assigned to the Bolsover Street site and to Harrow. An International Student Officer helps overseas students. There's also an Exam Anxiety Group - *other universities take note.*

Disabled: Toilets, ramps and lifts are provided, although the lifts often don't work. *Access is pretty poor, although Harrow's OK.* Dyslexia advice is available.

FINANCE:
● Ave debt per year: £2,550 ● Access fund: £330,000
● Successful applications (1996): 721

A booklet called 'Housing & Money Matters' is distributed free to students. There are also short-term loans available.

▶▶ Westminster College, Oxford

see Other Institutions

▶▶ Wimbledon School of Art

see Other Institutions

▶▶ Winchester College of Art

see University of Southampton

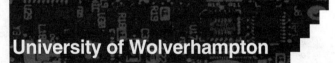

University of Wolverhampton

● *Formerly Wolverhampton Polytechnic*

University of Wolverhampton, Wulfruna Street, Wolverhampton, WV1 1SB. Tel: (01902) 321000. Fax: (01902) 322680.
E-mail: enquiries@wlv.ac.uk
University of Wolverhampton Students' Union, St Peter's Square Site, Wulfruna Street, Wolverhampton, WV1 1LY.
Tel: (01902) 322026. Fax: (01902) 322020.
E-mail: suexecutive@wlv.ac.uk

University of Wolverhampton, Telford Campus, Shifnal Road,
Priorslee, Telford, Shropshire, TF2 9NT.
Tel: (01902) 323400.

general

It will probably offend every one of Wolverhampton's 266,000
inhabitants to say that it's a bulbous mass sprouting out of
the north west of Birmingham. From the centre of Wolves (as
it's called) to the centre of Brum (as it's called) is 13 miles,
with Walsall, Dudley and West Bromwich in between and no
break in the urban crush and crawl. Each of these towns in
The Birmingham Conurbation is distinctly different: for
example, Wolves is on a hill. It is more residential *and has a
slower pace than Brum itself and is, frankly, more depressing.*
As for the University, Wolves is simply one of its bases.
Humanities & Social Sciences are based on a campus in
Dudley, and Education is on the Walsall Campus. And even
further flung, is the University's Business School near Telford,
a town of 28,000 souls, 16 miles away.

44% ♂♂♂♂♂♀♀♀♀♀ 56%	
Sex ratio(M:F): 44%:56%	Founded: 1983
Full time u'grads: 13,301	Part time: 3,226
Postgrads: 730	Non-degree: 2,910
Ave course: 3yrs	Ethnic: 29%
Private school: n/a	Flunk rate: 26
Mature students: 45%	Overseas students: 14%
Disabled students: 3%	Staff/student ratio: 1:14
Clearing: n/a	

ATMOSPHERE:
*The high proportion of mature, local and non-degree students,
many with their own lives and responsibilities beyond the
University, means the atmosphere is as distinct from the
boater-doffing, champagne-swigging stereotype as you can get.
One survey identified this part of the Midlands as the least
popular UK region for prospective applicants but the locals are
still flocking in and they don't need anybody else, ta very
much. So many students from the local area means
town/gown relations are unusually mellow.*

THE SITES:
Wolverhampton Campus: This is the main campus, consisting
of a number of modern buildings. *It may not be too ugly, but
the main building is seriously big and does look distinctly
institutional, as if it used to be a hospital. Inside, the floors
are so clean there's not a skirt or trouser leg you can't look
up. The reception looks like the entrance to a law court or
something similarly official and smart.* Being in the centre of
Wolves, it is useful for the shopping centre and other civic
amenities.

Compton Park Campus: (1,000 students - Business Studies)
*Business Schools always get the best-looking site and this is
not the exception that proves the rule.* This is the leafy smart
part of Wolves, 1½ miles from the main site, but connected by
public transport.

Dudley Campus: (1,805 students - Humanities, Social Sciences, Continuing Education) 7 miles from the main site, this campus is just under a mile from Dudley town centre in a *pleasantly* green suburb. *The best things about this campus are the facilities and the real ale in the local pubs, but it is not so good for shops or transport connections.* Dudley itself is a small market town dominated by a castle.

Walsall Campus: (3,403 students - School of Education) 9 miles from the main site, this campus is about ¾ of a mile from Walsall town centre - *more of a suburb of Brum than a town in itself - but is okay for shops and stuff like that.* The campus, a set of geometric modern purpose-built blocks, also has a few facilities of its own for sports and fun.

Telford: (2,781 students - Business, Engineering, Social Work) Out on a limb, 16 miles from Wolverhampton, this site was set up for students who wanted to live and study in their own locality. It's the smallest and newest site, but offers most of the courses available elsewhere. *It's based around a stately home, but is lacking quite a lot by way of atmosphere and facilities.*

WOLVERHAMPTON:

Wolves is the biggest town (ie not a city) in the UK. *For so long in the shadow of the Brum Beast, it's now possible to buy decent clothes and records, get your hair cut, have a pint or two somewhere without sawdust on the floor then go to a nightclub and tongue-wrestle with someone half-decent looking all within the (ill-defined) town limits. Of course, if you want to do something really spectacular, Birmingham's just down the road.*

THE CITY: see University of Birmingham

TRAVEL:

Trains: Wolverhampton Station is 5 minutes' walk from the main site and operates services all over the country and into Brum (£2.40) - other destinations include London (£19.80), Newcastle (£30.85) and Exeter (£27.35). There are also British Rail stations at Walsall and Telford.

Coaches: National Express services to London (£11), Newcastle (£24.95), Edinburgh and beyond.

Car: Wolverhampton, Walsall and Dudley can be reached on the M5, M54, M6. The A41 and M54 also connect with Telford.

Local: The many *cheap* buses are *the best way of getting anywhere* and connect with Brum too, *although there are the unreliable trains too. A new Supertram service is supposed to open by summer '99.* The University also provides a free, popular, *but less than dependable,* inter-site shuttle bus for staff and students, between all the sites.

Bicycles: Secure bike sheds on the main campus. *Unless you're in training for the Tour de France, cycling between the sites is not on.*

THE CITY: see University of Birmingham

LIBRARIES & COMPUTERS:
● Books: 400,000 ● Study places: 1,948
● Computer workstations: 1,327

There's a library on each site - including the main

Wolverhampton Learning Centre (a new multi-million pound development which has improved working conditions no end, *but failed somewhat to address limited book availability*) which also houses most of the computer service.

CAREER PROSPECTS:
● <u>Careers Service</u> ● <u>No of staff: 8 full</u>
● <u>Unemployed after 6mths (1996): 10.3%</u>
There are many vocational degrees, and the university arranges work placements which may soon be accredited on courses.

FAMOUS ALUMNI:
Trevor Beattie (advertising guru, *so they say*); Sir Terence Beckett (deputy chairman, CEGB); Vernie (Eternal).

FURTHER INFO:
Full- and part-time, and postgrad prospectuses. Video. Alternative prospectus. Uni web site (http://www.wlv.ac.uk); SU web site (http://www.wlv.ac.uk/su).

entertainment

TOWN:

● <u>Price of a pint of beer: £1.65</u> ● <u>Glass of wine: £1.40</u>
Cinemas & theatres: There's a number of theatres and cinemas in Wolves, most notably the Grand Theatre, the *fringe-ish* Arena Theatre on campus, 10-screen multiplexes at Dudley, Walsall and Telford and the *arty* Lighthouse Arts & Media Centre.
Pubs: *Cheap and cheery, putting the real back into real ale.* **push***plugs: Varsity; Posada. The students' own bars are more popular, given that the Uni is hard by the Wanderer's Molyneux Park.*
Clubs/discos: There's a choice of studenty clubs. **push***plugs: student night at the Canal Club; 'Stumpjuice' (Britpop) at the Connaught; 'Pooh Your Pants' (indie/house) at Zone II.* **push** *reckons the best thing about the latter is that you can chat someone up with a casual 'Are you going to pooh your pants tonight?' Actually, maybe not such a good idea.*
Music venues: The Varsity is getting onto the map as a *damned fine indie hangout, pulling in the kids from Brum.* The Civic/Wulfrun Hall (2 venues under one roof) *has sounds to stomp to as does JBs in Dudley.*
Eating out: *The multi-ethnic mix of the whole West Midlands affects Wolves restaurants as much as anywhere else, but, as with most things, for serious choice of eats it's best to go closer to the centre of Brum.* **push***plugs: Dilshad Tandoori; Gondola (Italian); Moon Under Water.*
Others: The West Midlands Safari & Leisure Park *is a relief to those who like seeing animals so long as they're not behind bars*, unlike the zoo in Dudley. Boating on the canal *can get you moist with excitement.*

CITY: see <u>University of Birmingham</u>

UNIVERSITY:

● <u>Price of a pint of beer: £1.30</u> ● <u>Glass of wine: £1.15</u>
Bars: 5 bars around the SU's sites, *the most important being* Fat Mick's at the main site.

Clubs/discos: Some sort of dance thang somewhere every night; regulars include Crunchy (house) and Donut (easy listening).
Music venues: Fat Mick's and Dudley host live gigs, recent examples being My Life Story and Silver Sun.
Theatre and cinema: Screwed Up and Clueless Theatre Group is run by drama students *and is making a splash;* free video showings once a week.
Cabaret: There's occasional cabaret at Fat Mick's.
Food: *The University Refectory offers a good range but at a price.* The SU café does snacks.
Others: Rag Ball, AU Ball at each site.

social & political
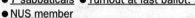

UNIVERSITY OF WOLVERHAMPTON STUDENTS' UNION:
● <u>7 sabbaticals</u> ● <u>Turnout at last ballot: 18%</u>
● <u>NUS member</u>
The SU does its best on the welfare and ents fronts, within the constraints of pretty limited resources. Politics is usually either strongly left-wing or non-existent, with non-existent well on top, despite the efforts of the SU exec to rouse the masses. Only 200 of over 12,000 students turned up to the last Tuition Fees rally.

SU FACILITIES:
Most facilities are in the SU Building on the main campus and at the Dudley campus, but the SU also has centres at Walsall and Telford. In all, the SU offers 5 bars, 5 minibuses, a travel agency, printing & photocopying services, 4 shops, library, games, vending & video machines, photo developing, pool tables, juke box, TV lounge, nightclub, function rooms (cap 600) and conference facilities.

CLUBS (NON SPORTING):
Asian; Bhangra; Biko Trust; Brunei; Chaplaincy; Creative Aid; Cult TV; Dance; Eastern; Great Escape; Hunt Sabs; Jazz; Juggling; Malaysian; Pagan; Punjabi; Real Ale; Role Playing; Sikh; Singapore; Signing; Vegan and Vegetarian; War Games.

OTHER ORGANISATIONS:
The SU's magazine, 'Cry Wolf', has been in the running for national awards recently. *Cry Wolf tries to rally the students but they're frustratingly apathetic.* The SU has started up a Skills Training Scheme which covers *useful potential CV fillers.*

RELIGIOUS:
Ecumenical chaplains.

sports

● <u>Recent successes: squash, football</u>
Most sites have their own facilities which add up to an okay level of service, but since they're spread out there's very little focus for sporting activity. Recent additions to the trophy cabinet may galvanise things a bit, though. A Sports Card costs £5 per year and with one of these, *facilities are fairly cheap,* generally no more than £1.

SPORTS FACILITIES:
Main campus: sports hall, multigym and squash courts. Compton Park: local public sports centre. Dudley: playing

> ❝Bradford University offers the country's only degree course in Yorkshire Studies.❞

field, sports hall, tennis courts. Walsall: swimming pool, playing fields, gym, floodlit tennis courts, running track, dance studio. Telford: football, netball, tennis facilities.

SPORTING CLUBS:
Aerobics; Aikido; Bowling; Caving; Frisbee; Hiking; Jiu Jitsu; Surfing; Windsurfing; Yoga.

ATTRACTIONS:
Apart from the famous Wolverhampton Wanderers FC, 100 yards from the SU building, and the nearby West Bromwich Albion (the Baggies) and Walsall, there's a race course, a dog track and a local athletics club.

accommodation

IN COLLEGE:

- Catered: 1% ● Cost: £44(38wks)
- Self-catering: 14% ● Cost: £37-43(38wks)

Some students have felt let down by allegedly misleading college brochures.
Availability: All sites have some form of accommodation. What there is gets snapped up mostly by 1st years, accommodating about ½ of them. Main campus: 1075 single self-catering rooms. Compton Park: 130 single self-catering rooms. Dudley: 360 rooms with some meals catered, mostly single, but some shared. Walsall: 380 single rooms with evening meals only during the week. Telford: 300 new single rooms with en suite facilities (£38/wk). All halls have shared kitchens and bathrooms and single sex corridors Overall, 4% share.
Car parking: *Free, but inadequate.*

EXTERNALLY:
- Ave rent: £32

Availability: *No problem about finding a place in Wolves and the prices aren't extortionate, however, Walsall and Dudley are less easy and more expensive, but still well under £40. Whitmore Reans is the studey ghetto.* The University has about 100 places in 40 houses and flats which it also rents to students on a private basis, *but on more sympathetic terms than the open market.*
Housing help: The University Residential Services at the main campus run by the University help find and arrange student housing for almost all students who don't get hall places.

welfare

SERVICES:
- Nursery ● Lesbian & Gay Sector ● Mature SA
- Overseas SA ● Minibus ● Women's Officer
- Self-defence classes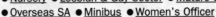

The University has 5 counsellors and the chaplains are also to hand. Medical problems are dealt with by the health centres near each of the main 4 sites. At the main Wolves site, the health centre is within the campus bounds. The nurseries are based at the main campus and Dudley. The University provides free rape/attack alarms for all students. The subway between North and South sides of Wolves campus is *rather dingy and dangerous.*

Disabled: There is a Disabilities Officer based at Dudley and a Disabled Students' Council providing advice and representation. For more practical help, there are lifts, ramps and *generally okay access to* most places, *although accommodation is a little lacking. Good* facilities for students with hearing problems.

FINANCE:
- Ave debt per year: £1,950 ● Access fund: £231,685
- Successful applications (1997): 391

Hardship Funds are appallingly advertised and therefore undersubscribed. *Go get that cash!* Also bursaries and a fund for black South African students.

• •

 University College, Worcester
see Other Institutions

• •

 Writtle College
see Other Institutions

• •

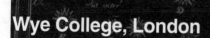

Wye College, London

 ● *The College is part of University of London and students are entitled to use its facilities.*
Wye College, Wye, Ashford, Kent, TN25 5AH. Tel: (01233) 812401. Fax: (01233) 813320. E-mail: registry@wye.ac.uk
Wye College JCR, Wye, Ashford, Kent, TN25 5AH.
Tel: (01233) 812091.

 General

Wye College specialises in the teaching of science, business, environmental and related subjects. Until just recently it was big on agriculture, so although it's a part of London University, it is set in rural Kent, worlds away from the capital's polluted centre. Established in the 15th century, *the College has a definite Oxbridge air*, with long traditions and built around grassy quads. There are many 19th century additions and new redbrick sections. Wye itself is nothing more than a village and the nearest town Ashford, 4 miles away, isn't much more, *although the International Rail Terminal has woken things up a bit.*

44% ♂♂♂♂♂♀♀♀♀♀ 56%	
Sex ratio(M:F): 44%:56%	Founded: 1894
Full time u'grads: 500	Part time: 0
Postgrads: 300	Non-degree: 0
Ave course: 3yrs	Ethnic: n/a
Private school: 25%	Flunk rate: n/a
Mature students: 30%	Overseas students: 10%
Disabled students: 4 %	Staff/student ratio: 1:12
Clearing: 11%	

ATMOSPHERE:
With so few students, in an area pretty remote from thrills and spills, a cosy atmosphere in which everyone knows everyone else has developed. This can be very comforting at times but it's not to everyone's taste and often the urge to escape (especially to London) becomes irresistible. Lots of the students have cars, so it is quite easy to do, especially at weekends. Wye is suffering from an agricultural hangover, though the cliquey farming contingent is being increasingly alka-seltzered by business and environmental students.

TOWN:
- Population (Ashford): 15,000 ● London: 52miles
- Canterbury: 10miles

The College is in the heart of the Kent countryside, surrounded by small villages, such as Wye, and next to a conservation area. This is the Garden of England - *indeed it is very beautiful, if rather quiet.* Ashford, the nearest town, has plenty of shops for daily needs, *but it's not a lively place. Canterbury is the nearest student-oriented settlement*; see University of Kent for details.

TRAVEL:
Trains: BR station at Wye, ¼ mile from college, with regular services to and from London (£13.60) and Canterbury (£2.80).
Coaches: National Express to London (£11rtn, 1:35hrs, 7/day).
Buses: Buses from Ashford to the campus run till 8pm and cost £1.
Car: *Very handy for going out in the evening* as the last train from Ashford leaves at 11pm. Ashford is connected to London by the A20 and to Folkestone on the coast, by the M20. The A28 runs to Canterbury and then south towards Hastings.
Bicycles: Bike sheds are provided and the surrounding area is very flat. *Theft is pretty minimal.*

LIBRARIES & COMPUTERS:
- Books: 40,000 ● Study places: 200
- Computer workstations: 100

❛Students from Bangor Rag once 'closed' the island of Anglesey by erecting an 'Anglesey Full' sign.❜

The Kemp Centre library has recently undergone *excellent* major expansion.

CAREER PROSPECTS:
● No of staff: 3part ● Unemployed after 6mths (1996): 11%

FAMOUS ALUMNI:
Sir Roy Griffiths (author, 'Care in the Community'); Rebecca Stevens (first UK woman to climb Everest); *and many celebrated farmers.*

FURTHER INFO:
Prospectuses for undergrads and postgrads. 'Wye World' for overseas students and a web site (http://www.wye.ac.uk).

entertainment

TOWN:

● Price of a pint of beer: £1.85 ● Glass of wine: £1.60

Ashford is quiet but the influx of cross-channel punters is waking things up a bit, the main development being a new shopping mall. For less laid-back larks, students still go to Canterbury.
Cinemas: The mall in Ashford has a 10-screen multiplex, *but students still prefer to go to Canterbury for movies.*
Pubs: *An ample supply of country pubs and traditional free-houses serving good food and better beer. They do tend to cater for tourists rather than the meagre number of students.* pushplugs: *The Compasses; New Flying Horse; The Camel; The Tiger.*
Eating out: pushplugs: *Joshan of Wye (Indian); August Moon (Chinese) in Ashford.*

COLLEGE:

● Price of a pint of beer £1.40 ● Glass of wine: £1.20

Bars: *The main SU bar is open lunchtimes and evenings 6 days a week as is the rather nicer and therefore more popular postgrad bar. All students can use both and are desperately trying to mingle more.*
Theatre and cinemas: *Occasional student productions and video nights, but both activities aren't what they used to be.*
Clubs/discos/music venues: Friday night discos in the Union Venue (capacity 460), discos in the Sports Hall and a new rave event, Toxic. Occasional bands - recent highlights: The Worzels, *just to confound all you stereotypists. Woodland raves are rumoured to have been staged in the vicinity.*
Food: The Canteen offers *reasonable value* meals and the Wheel Room is *good* for snacks. *Snack vans proliferate like proliferating things do.*
Others: 5 balls a year, including the 12-hour summer Commemoration *monster.* There's also Cricket Week, a post-exam binge of barbies, beer tents and even cricket.

social & political

WYE COLLEGE JCR:

● Turnout at last ballot: 60% ● NUS member

The JCR is constitutionally required to be apolitical, but there is a blueish tinge among the students, counterbalanced by a strong environmental movement. Students recently roused themselves to protest at Dover against the beef ban, and ²/₃ of

> *Every year, a tortoise race takes place between Corpus Christi and Balliol Colleges, Oxford.*

the students attended the London Countryside March. The environmentalists for obvious reasons, the farmers to parade their beagles, and the rest because the college would be a bit dead with everyone else gone, presumably. Students often owe more allegiance to their private drinking clubs than to a political creed.

SU FACILITIES:
1 bar; photocopiers; printing; vending and games machines; minibus for hire; juke box; pool table; TV room; meeting room; shop.

CLUBS (NON SPORTING):
Beaus (*snobby* exclusive drinking); Choral; Debating; Druids (secret exclusive drinking, practical jokers); Film; Garters (women's exclusive drinking); Juggling; JSF (rugby and exclusive drinking); Ploughing and Machinery (*tractors and exclusive drinking?*).

OTHER ORGANISATIONS:
There's no regular student media but a gossip mag, 'Odds', goes out annually and 'Wye Life' is distributed to freshers. *The recent strengthening of the Gay, Lesbian and Bisexual Group was considered somewhat radical for Wye JCR.*

RELIGIOUS:
● 1 chaplain (CofE)
Places of worship for Anglicans, Methodists and Muslims.

PAID WORK:
Agricultural work during vacations. *Opportunities are good and include fire-fighting for all you crusaders out there.*

sports

● Recent successes: football, hockey
Results are pretty good for somewhere so small. Unsurprisingly, many sporting activities are booze-related.

SPORTS FACILITIES:
There are rugby, football, cricket, hockey and lacrosse pitches in nearby Withersdane. Locally, there is a leisure centre, all-weather pitch and croquet lawn. The Sailing Club uses a nearby reservoir. The new mall in Ashford will have a sports hall and 10-pin bowling.

SPORTING CLUBS:
Beagles (*recently disowned by the college authorities*); Chess (*postgrads only, apparently*); Clay Pigeon; Darts (*groovy*); Fellwalking; Gun; Powerlifting; Rifle.

ATTRACTIONS:
Kent cricket at Canterbury; Ashford FC; Folkestone Races.

accommodation

IN COLLEGE:
● Catered: 31% ● Cost: £69-85(30wks)
● Self-catering: 9% ● Cost: £44-56(52wks)
Availability: All 1st years who request it and 12% of finalists

live in. At Withersdane, *the rooms are big, but uniform and peaceful*. Self-catering rooms have fully equipped, shared kitchens with freezers. Storage of guns and ammunition in bedrooms is not permitted, *in case you were interested*.
Car parking: Free permit parking.

EXTERNALLY:
● Ave rent: £50

Availability: *Students can expect a good standard of accommodation from the private sector. The only problem is that it is hard to come by, given that this is a rural place - students are advised to start looking early. Ashford is cheaper than Wye itself and the surrounding villages.*
Housing help: Accommodation office and bulletin board.

welfare

SERVICES:
● Mature SA ● Overseas SA

There is a family common room in College for use by students with children. On site nurse and 3 part-time trained counsellors, 1 welfare advisor.
Disabled: *Wheelchair access and special facilities are poor. There is currently only one disabled student (and these are their 15 minutes of fame), but needs are dealt with on an individual basis: for example, lecturers wrote out notes for a profoundly deaf student, ramps were fitted for the disabled student.* 15% of students are dyslexic.

FINANCE:
● Ave debt: £1,700 ● Access fund: £28,000
● Successful applications (1995): 160

The College which has a *generous* hardship fund, providing up to £140 per student per term to help with housing costs. There are also 5 academic scholarships of £1,000 each.

❝If you have any comments about PUSH or fancy being involved in the next edition, please write to PUSH, McGraw-Hill Publishing Company, Shoppenhangers Road, Maidenhead, Berkshire SL6 2QL.❞

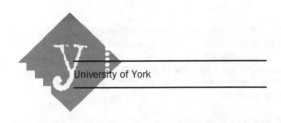

University of York

University of York

University of York, Heslington, York, YO1 5DD.
Tel: (01904) 430000. Fax: (01904) 433433.
E-mail: admissions@york.ac.uk
York University Students' Union, The Daw Suu Centre,
Goodricke College, Heslington, York, YO1 5DD.
Tel: (01904) 433723. Fax: (01904) 433724.

General

The Romans came to York. So did the Vikings and Dick Turpin. The builders of *magnificent* Minsters also came, and the cathedral they left dominates the city both culturally and physically. However, all this historical importance has more to do with the fact that York, coursed by the *beautiful* River Ouse, is midway between London and Edinburgh, 35 miles from the coast, than with the University, because that didn't pop up until 1963. It is 2 miles south-east of the city centre at the village of Heslington. It is a largely concrete campus round a man-made lake, complete with ducks, a stately manor and some *pleasant* landscaping, *albeit with a giant replica UFO in the middle of it all*. It was designed as a 'concept' campus - the concept in question being 'discovery around every corner', *which explains why everywhere looks the same and it's easy to get lost*.

49% ♂♂♂♂♂♀♀♀♀♀ **51%**

Sex ratio(M:F): 49%:51%	**Founded: 1963**
Full time u'grads: 5,238	**Part time: 754**
Postgrads: 1,298	**Non-degree: 526**
Ave course: 3yrs	**Ethnic: 6.25%**
Private school: 15.2%	**Flunk rate: 16%**
Mature students: 18.8%	**Overseas students: 8%**
Disabled students: 3.2%	**Staff/student ratio: 1:16**
Clearing: 6.5%	

ATMOSPHERE:
York is a collegiate University - cynics claim this is an unsuccessful attempt to copy Oxbridge. There are 7 colleges, each with 900-1,000 members, *which don't vary enormously. Students don't get to choose their own college, but it's not difficult to switch if they feel the need.* The collegiate system *isn't all that strong (especially compared to Oxbridge) - college spirit can mostly be found when served with ice in college*

bars. *The University may not be enormously happening (and positively moribund at weekends), but it's cosy and friendly (some find it almost suffocating) and many find it hard to leave. Anybody who's seen 60s cult TV show 'The Prisoner' will have an idea. The town swarms with graduates which must mean something positive.*

THE CITY:

- Population: 100,600 ● London: 205miles
- Edinburgh: 205miles ● Leeds: 23miles

Apart from London, York is Britain's top tourist city and offers a host of traps and treats, including museums such as the Jorvik Viking Centre (free admission with a Blue Peter badge). *It is quaint in the extreme* with city walls, tea shops, a castle and what claims to be the oldest street in Britain, The Shambles. The shortest street in the city also has the longest name: Whip-ma-Whop-ma Gate. In York, as locals love to explain to American visitors, streets are called 'gates', city gates are called 'bars' and bars are called 'pubs', of which there are a *huge* number. Got that? There is also a daily market, supermarkets and numerous bookshops (new and 2nd hand), but there's not much for the late night shopper.

TRAVEL:

Trains: Mainline connections from York Station (2 miles from the campus) to many destinations including London King's X (£33.40), Glasgow (£30.35) and Birmingham (£18.95).
Coaches: National Express to most destinations, including London (£20), Newcastle and beyond.
Car: A19; 10 miles from the A1 and 20 from the M62.
Air: Nearest airport of any size is Leeds/Bradford (40mins by car) and there is a direct train link to and from Manchester Airport.
Hitching: *Good north/south, once hitchers reach M1 or A1.*
Local: York is too small and compact for local trains except regionally to Leeds, Hull and Bradford. Frequent bus services run everywhere (80p from campus to city centre) but they don't run late at night.
Taxis: *Unreliable and expensive despite some companies offering student discounts, although students still use them for late night journeys.*
Bicycles: *Pretty good, flat with plenty of cycle lanes, but also a few light-fingered would-be bike-owners.*

LIBRARIES & COMPUTERS:

- Books: 750,000 ● Study places: 983
- Computer workstations: 500

Main JB Morrell Library plus smaller specialist outposts and individual college libraries. York recently won a Queen's Award for work in computer science *and we all know what a whizz at Torosaurus Her Maj is.*

CAREER PROSPECTS:

- Careers Service ● No of staff: 7full/1part
- Unemployed after 6mths (1995): 10%

FAMOUS ALUMNI:

Tony Banks MP, Harriet Harman MP, Oona King (all Lab); Greg Dyke (*the man who gave us Roland Rat. Thanks. Now CEO of*

Channel 5. Thanks again); Harry Enfield (comedian); Jung Chang (writer); Christine Hamilton (loyal Tory spouse); Victor Lewis-Smith (comedian/journalist); Genista McIntosh (theatre director); Dominic Muldowney (composer); John Witherow (editor, Sunday Times).

FURTHER INFO:
Prospectuses for undergrads and postgrads. Alternative prospectus £2.00 from SU. Web site (http://www.york.ac.uk).

entertainment

THE CITY:
● <u>Price of a pint of beer: £1.50</u> ● <u>Glass of wine: £1.60</u>
Cinemas: A choice of 4, ranging from a 12-screen multiplex to the *arty* City Screen.
Theatres: (4) *Mostly quite straight but the Arts Centre makes up for it with weirder stuff.*
Pubs: Supposedly, there's a pub (*mostly student-friendly*) for every day of the year, playing hosts to such Yorkshire favourites as the 3 Smiths - Samuel, John and Tom - Theakston's, Tetley and Timothy Taylor; *enough to make any southern blouse renounce his/her lager shandy past.*
pushplugs: *The Charles; Rose & Crown; The Firkin; The Lowther; The Deramore Arms.*
Clubs/discos: There's a number of *popular* nights *with mainstream student leanings*; Mondays at The Gallery (70s/80s); Tuesdays at Toffs (indie); weekends at the Arts Centre (*bohemian posing and dancing*). *There's an underground rave scene in York and nearby Selby but students don't tend to get involved; for serious clubbers the nearest prime site is Leeds.*
Music venues: *Not a great deal.* Fibbers is a *fair-to-middling* indie hangout and The Cells is popular with jazz fiends. The Spotted Cow is good for local hopefuls.
Eating out: *A good range of cheap eats, including some excellent Indians, if nothing to get you drooling puddles. Other* **push**plugs: *Oscar's wine bar; Caesar's (Italian); Rubicon (pricey veggie); The Willow (Chinese restaurant becomes cheesy disco at midnight).*

UNIVERSITY:
● <u>Price of a pint of beer: £1.30</u> ● <u>Glass of wine: £1.50</u>
Bars: Each college has a bar. *Vanburgh and Goodricke get quite groovy.*
Theatres: (2) The Drama Barn or The Audio Visual Studio for University drama on campus and regular trips to Edinburgh and the National Student Drama Festival at Scarborough.
Cinema: York Student Cinema presents a *cheap, high-quality*, student-orientated alternative to the city multi-screens.
Clubs/discos/music venues: *The SU has had trouble enticing big name acts to play,* although Three Colours Red and Audioweb have made the trip lately. Otherwise, it's mostly local bands and cover acts, doing their stuff in the college bars. The SU has recently persuaded the University to rescind its 12.30 curfew for ents, *so things may pick up shortly.*
Cabaret: Fortnightly comic capers, most recently Alan Parker and Phil Kaye.
Food: Each college has a snack bar and most have a dining

hall, *a fair bet for daytime nosh and natter. Vanburgh does excellent sandwiches, Langwith has a veggie snack bar and Goodricke is noted for its hot chocolate - is that food or drink? Answers on a Cadbury's Options sachet, please.*

Others: Annual balls in colleges. *The lack of a dedicated music venue means it's a struggle to get big names.*

···social & political

YORK UNIVERSITY STUDENTS' UNION:

- 6 sabbaticals ● Turnout at last ballot: 30%
- NUS member

YUSU survived for many years without its own building and it still lacks a central SU bar or music venue. Because of the collegiate system, many students operate day-to-day without much awareness of the SU, but it's there when they want it. YUSU is not as radical as it used to be, with the dubious exception of a Pepsi boycott which they seem to think was the main cause for the corporation pulling out of Burma.

SU FACILITIES:

A shop; 2nd-hand bookshop; cashpoint (Link); essay bank; vending machines; minibus hire; printing and typing services; travel agency.

CLUBS (NON SPORTING):

Aaardvark (comedy); Africa; Ballroom Dancing; Bloke Soc; Brecht/Weill; Cake; Debating; Dionysian; Discordia; Duke of Edinburgh; European; Film; Football Supporters; FoE; Frog Soc (cuddly toys); Gilbert & Sullivan; Glee; Goth Hippy Groovers; Guys & Dolls; Hellenic; Hindu; Hong Kong & China; Juggling; Latin American Dancing; Lunatics; Methodist-Anglican; Modern Dancing; Multimedia (cult TV); Natural History; Outdoor; Rocky Horror; Socialist Organiser; Spooky; Thomas More; Visual Arts; Wind Band; Wine; Wrist; WWFF; Yoga.

OTHER ORGANISATIONS:

2 independent student newspapers, 'Nouse' (inevitably nicknamed 'no use') and 'Vision', which compete for the top student journo hacks. There are also 4 mags (feminist, arts, Christian and environmental). The University radio station (URY) was one of the first *and is among the most respected* with a recent graduate going straight to producing the Radio 1 Chart Show. YSTV - the twice daily award-winning television station - broadcasts to snack bars and JCRs across campus and its SU election night specials are *enough to get Peter Snow fidgeting with his swingometer.* The North Yorkshire NUS Rag based at the University raised over £46,000 last year with stunts such as gnoming - students pay to have their friends tailed and annoyed by someone dressed in red and green with a fishing rod. The Community Action Project (known as 'CAP'), organised by a dedicated sabbatical officer, runs over 30 community projects, especially holidays for disadvantaged kids.

RELIGIOUS:

- 7 chaplains

For Anglicans, the Minster, home to one of England's 2 Archbishops, has an *inspiring influence, which has rubbed off on other Christian denominations.* Following an incident involving a Jewish massacre nearly 1,000 years ago, there is no synagogue in York. There is a mosque.

PAID WORK:

Plenty of pubs and a few restaurants during term time, and the

> ❝York University hasn't had a central music venue since the Boomtown Rats (Bob Geldof's old band) played in 1979. The fans danced so hard the building began to slip into the lake.❞

conference trade brings opportunities during vacations. The SU has a vacancy board.

sports

● <u>Recent successes: badminton, hockey</u>

It's not up with the really big boys and girls but plenty muck in and keep trim, without the killer competitive instinct. The Athletics Union - which, including membership of the sports centre, costs £6 to join - has its own sabbatical officer.

SPORTS FACILITIES:
57.5 acres of playing fields; new Astroturf pitch; climbing wall; gym; multigym; sports hall; sauna; 6 new tennis courts; athletics track. The city also has 3 public swimming pools and the River Ouse.

SPORTING CLUBS:
Aikido; American Football; Ben Lairig; Boules; Bridge; Caving & Potholing; Gliding; Hang Gliding; Kabbadi; Jiu-Jitsu; Lacrosse; Octopush; Parachuting; Rifle; Rowing; Rugby League; Tennis; Windsurfing; Yoga.

ATTRACTIONS:
York Race Course, Rugby League or York FC (*if you can call them an attraction*).

accommodation

IN COLLEGE:

● <u>Catered: 37%</u> ● <u>Cost: £35-37(30/38wks)</u>
● <u>Self-catering: 14%</u> ● <u>Cost: £35(30wks)</u>

Availability: All 1st years can be accommodated, in the *Major-grey* blocks by the lake, as can over ¹/₂ the finalists. *The major problem with living on campus is having to ensure you don't fall in the lake when drunk because of the toxic levels of duck-droppings in it.* Another 538 places are *still pending* - slightly more expensive but still well below the national average. About 3% of residents have to share.

Car parking: Parking is limited (permit required) and 1st years aren't allowed cars on campus, unless medically necessary. Firing weapons in halls is also prohibited, apparently.

EXTERNALLY:

● <u>Ave rent: £40</u>

Availability: *Finding accommodation is easy enough, especially in Fulford and Heslington, but some council estates are best avoided. Cars are difficult to park around town and unnecessary for getting around.*

Housing help: The University Accommodation Office runs a

‘Text in italics is PUSH's point of view – take it or leave it.’

Property Rental Scheme, where inspected houses are tied to a recommended rent. There are also housing lists and tenancy advice on offer.

········ welfare

SERVICES:
● Creche ● Nightline ● Mature SA ● Overseas SA
● Lesbian, Gay & Bisexual Society ● Postgrad SA ● Minibus
● Women's Officer ● Self-defence classes

There is a health centre and students can always register with local NHS practices. The SU employs a Welfare Information Officer and the University employs 3 part-time counsellors. The SU can arrange a free consultation with a solicitor. Special provisions for those with dyslexia.

Women: The SU maintains an abortion fund and the night bus gives priority to women. *Some dingy areas on the fringes of campus should be avoided at night.*

Disabled: James College was built with disabled access in mind and *generally the campus is pretty good.* There is a new Disabled Officer and some hearing loops installed.

FINANCE:
● Ave debt per year: £1,750 ● Access fund: £138,219
● Successful applications (1996): 498

There are some University bursaries available and YUSU hardship loans.

Fold-out guide to symbols inside back cover

‘Freaked out by finance? Why not pop into your local branch of Lloyds Bank and see what they have to offer.’

other institutions

▶▶ **OR EVEN MORE PLACES TO CONFUSE YOU...**
In addition to the main institutions in push, there are a number
of other colleges, usually those that don't award their own
degrees but confer them on behalf of a larger university. *It
shouldn't be presumed that these colleges are in any way inferior
to the other institutions but they do tend to have certain things in
common.* They're usually smaller, *which can create a sense of
community and/or claustrophobia according to the mood you're
in.* Several have links to particular Christian denominations,
although they all accept applications from people of any religious
background or none. Many have a high proportion of students
training to be teachers – this tends to affect the gender balance
and in many of these colleges men are heavily outnumbered.

ENTITLED TITLES
Many of these institutions are called 'University Colleges' or
'University Sector Colleges'. The rules regarding these labels and
who can actually use them are currently being tightened up, but,
to the student on the ground, there's no real difference in quality
between somewhere that calls itself a University College and one
that's a College or Institute of HE.

DEPTH WARNING
A word of warning - unlike the colleges and universities in the
main chapters, these institutions have not been visited by our
gallant band of push researchers and most of the data comes
direct from the colleges themselves. It's as accurate as we can
make it but the entries are, by definition, not as in-depth as those
in other chapters.

Bishop Grosseteste College

University College Bretton Hall

Canterbury Christ Church College

University of Wales Institute, Cardiff

University College Chester

Chichester Institute

Dartington College of Arts

Edge Hill University College

Falmouth College of Arts

Farnborough College of Technology

Harper Adams

Kent Institute of Art & Design

King Alfred's, Winchester

Liverpool Hope University College

NESCOT

University of Wales College, Newport

North East Wales Institute of HE

Northern College

University College of Ripon & York St John

Roehampton Institute, London

Rose Bruford College

Royal Agricultural College

College of St Mark & St John

University College of St Martin

St Mary's University College

University College, Scarborough

Swansea Institute of HE

Trinity & All Saints

Trinity College, Carmarthen

Trinity College of Music

University College, Warrington

Westhill College of HE

Westminster College, Oxford

o t h e r i n s t s

Wimbledon School of Art

University College, Worcester

Writtle College

● ●

Bishop Grosseteste University College

o
t
h
e
r

i
n
s
t
s

▼▼ Bishop Grosseteste University College, Lincoln, LN1 3DY.
Tel: (01522) 527347. Fax: (01522) 530243.
E-mail: registry@bgc.ac.uk Web site: http://www.bgc.ac.uk

General

Formerly Lincoln Training College, until it changed its name in 1962, Bishop Grosseteste College is set on single site in the centre of Lincoln. The college specialises in initial teacher training but also offers courses in Arts in the Community, Heritage Studies and English Literature. Teaching has a firmly practical bent and the college has strong links with local primary schools. The college is named after one of 13th-century Europe's foremost scientists and scholars and the first ever Chancellor of Oxford University, Bishop Big Head. For information about being a student in Lincoln, see the University of Lincolnshire & Humberside.

14% ♂♂♀♀♀♀♀♀♀♀ 86%	
Sex ratio(M:F): 14%:86%	**Founded: 1862**
Full time u'grads: 791	**Part time: 0**
Postgrads: 21	**Non-degree: 0**
Ave course: 4yrs	**Ethnic: 0.9%**
Private school: n/a	**Flunk rate: n/a**
Mature students: 14%	**Overseas students: 0.4%**
Disabled students: 14.8%	**Staff/student ratio: 1:20**
Clearing: 16%	

Library (135,109 volumns, 247 study places, open 5 days); IT suite. SU Bar (12noon-11pm); college dining hall (7.45am-6.45pm); theatre/cinema (cap 200); TV lounge; SU ents most nights. SU (no sabbs, NUS member); Rag. Gym; tennis courts; football and hockey pitches; local Sports & Leisure

❮ The lighting rig at the Surrey SU Bar is made of shopping trolleys 'borrowed' from Tesco's. ❯

Centre 5mins walk away. All first years accommodated (200 catered places, £60/34wks, 3 meals a day, 5 days a week); small kitchens with microwaves; non-smoking accommodation available; cheap local rents (£33/wk) for the rest. CofE chaplain; nurse; SU welfare officer; personal tutors; access fund £14,000 (49 successful applications 1997); cathedral scholarships. U/g and p/g prospectuses, course leaflets, 2 sixth form and 2 family open days a year.

●●

University College Bretton Hall

▼ University College Bretton Hall, West Bretton, Wakefield,
▼ W Yorkshire, WF4 4LG. Tel: (01924) 830261.
Fax: (01924) 830521. E-mail: bretton@mailhost.bretton.ac.uk

general

Bretton Hall is within 20 miles of Leeds, Sheffield and Bradford *so* the *idyllic* 500-acre campus, also home to the Yorkshire Sculpture Park and full of lakes, woodland and generally nice stuff *comes as something of a surprise.* The college has a *strong* reputation in teacher training and performing arts, including one of the few degree courses in pop music. There are 2 smaller outposts in Wakefield itself, 6 miles away - Powerhouse 2 (some education and arts teaching) and the Smythe Street Studio (90 students - Theatre Design & Technology). Wakefield itself boasts the *usual student-friendly* Firkins et al, a couple of *ok* clubs and, *for the more cultured*, the Wakefield Opera House. Celluloid junkies head for the 12-screen Cineworld nearby.

30% ♂♂♂♂♀♀♀♀♀♀♀ 70%	
Sex ratio(M:F): 30%:70%	Founded: 1949
Full time u'grads: 2,000	Part time: 300
Postgrads: 300	Non-degree: n/a
Ave course: 3yrs	Ethnic: n/a
Private school: 5%	Flunk rate: n/a
Mature students: 12%	Overseas students: 5%
Disabled students: 3.8%	Staff/student ratio: n/a
Clearing: 5.5%	

Library (100,000 volumes); 50 computers; access to Leeds and Leeds Met facilities. Studios, gallery and theatre; 2 bars (open lunchtimes and evenings); club/music venue (cap 300); 1 main club night/wk (Weds, *cheesy* party music); SU (1 sabb, NUS member), SU-run paper, Bretton Butter, and independent Bretton Underground Magazine (BUM to its friends). All 1st years who want it accommodated (55% in total) and some others (150 part-catered, £62/33wks; 500 self-catered, including the *popular* Manygates, £46-52/40 wks; 200 head tenancy, £34-44/40 wks). 4 chaplains; prayer room; counsellor; nurse (5 days/wk) and doctor (1 morning/wk); creche; late-night minibus (Weds only); college and SU disability officers; access fund £36,000 (200 successful applications 1997), hardship fund and bursaries. Prospectuses and video available.

Canterbury Christ Church College

▼▼ Canterbury Christ Church College, Canterbury, Kent, CT1 1QU.
Tel: (01227) 767700. Fax: (01227) 470442.
E-mail: admissions@cant.ac.uk
Web site http://www.cant.ac.uk

§eneral

CCCC or C4 (but without 'Brookside') is near the centre of Canterbury, near the cathedral. There are 3 other sites, none more than 20mins walk from the main one. As with many CHEs, it was originally a teacher training college and a quarter of 1st degree students are still on education courses but its main academic selling point is its combined honours system – TV and tourism, anyone? 40% of students are locals. For info on Canterbury, see University of Kent.

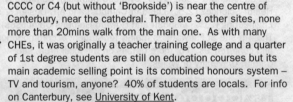

35% ♂♂♂♂♀♀♀♀♀♀ 65%	
Sex ratio(M:F): 35%:65%	Founded: 1962
Full time u'grads: 3,309	Part time: n/a
Postgrads: 510	Non-degree: 34
Ave course: 3yrs	Ethnic: 5%
Private school: n/a	Flunk rate: n/a
Mature students: 45%	Overseas students: 3%
Disabled students: 5%	Staff/student ratio: n/a
Clearing: 8%	

Library (231,000 volumes, 374 study places, open 7 days) and access to University of Kent facilities; 440 computer workstations. 2 bars; *good* ents; SU bar doubles as music/club venue (cap 400) hosting 3 club nights a week (dance, retro, party), live bands (eg Bluetones) and comedians (1/mth). SU (3 sabbs, NUS member); student paper, Eye Eye, radio and TV stations; Rag (£3,000 in 1997). *Strong* sport (football, rugby, cricket, hockey); 12 acres playing fields; all-weather pitch; multigym; tennis courts; fitness centre. 38% of 1st years in hall (£47-78), boosted by a number of head-leases. Chapel; 2 counsellors; Medical Centre; Overseas SA; Postgrad SA; Welfare Officer; access fund £77,059 (340 successful applications 1997). U/g and p/g prospectuses.

> ❛'Keele' is Old English for 'Cow-Hill'.❜

University of Wales Institute, Cardiff

▼▼ University of Wales Institute Cardiff, Western Avenue, Cardiff, CF5 2SG. Tel: (01222) 506070. Fax: (01222) 506928. E-mail: uwicinfo@uwic.ac.uk Web site http://www.uwic.ac.uk

General

On 4 sites, all within a 3-mile radius of the centre of Cardiff, *we find this contender for the 'Most Convoluted Name in Higher Education' award.* UWIC offers a mixed palette of courses, all with a vocational edge. The largest faculty, with 31% of all undergraduates, is Business, Leisure and Food, based at the Colchester Avenue campus. The other faculties are Education & Sport (26% - Cyncoed Campus), Community Health Sciences (22% - Llandaff Campus) and Art, Design & Engineering (21% - Llandaff and Howard Gardens Campuses). The 4th site at Fairwater is mainly for student accommodation and conferences. For more details on the local area, see Cardiff, University of Wales.

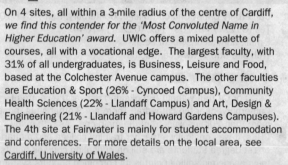

Sex ratio(M:F): 45%:55%	Founded: 1976
Full time u'grads: 5,684	Part time: 417
Postgrads: 944	Non-degree: 2,398
Ave course: 3yrs	Ethnic: 7.8%
Private school: n/a	Flunk rate: n/a
Mature students: 32%	Overseas students: 1.9%
Disabled students: 2.5%	Staff/student ratio: 1:25
Clearing: n/a	

4 libraries (255,000 volumes, 712 study places); 486 computer workstations. 3 bars - *Taffy's is the place to be seen on Friday nights* while Tommys at Howard Gardens is the main venue (Dust Junkies, Cantaloop and Space have all called in recently). SU (3 sabbs, NUS member, 10% turnout); shop at each campus; 40 clubs & societies; SU-run paper, 'Retro'. *Excellent* sports facilities and results, recent successes: squash, rugby, netball, gymnastics and trampolining; facilities include an astro-turf pitch, tennis centre, 2 rugby and 2 football pitches, a new indoor athletics centre will open in 1999. 95% of 1st years accommodated (£41-65) plus a few others. 1 chaplain; Health Clinic; access fund £115,362. Course leaflets, video, open days.

❛Queens' College, Cambridge hosts the world tiddlywinks championships.❜

o t h e r i n s t s

University College Chester

University College Chester, Parkgate Road, Chester CH1 4BJ.
Tel: (01244) 375444. Fax: (01244) 373379.
E-mail: b.reg@chester.ac.uk

𝔾eneral

Chester, home of 'Hollyoaks' and Mansun, is 25 miles from
Liverpool, near the Welsh border. *Apart from smug bad actors
and second rate indie bands* there's the University College, a
compact 30-acre campus containing a mix of Victorian and
modern buildings, about 10 minutes walk from the city centre.
¼ of undergraduates are trainee teachers, with the rest on
various science and humanities courses, often with a
vocational emphasis, and 20% are locals. The college is hot
on small-group teaching with around 30 students to a lecture
and tutorials for groups as small as 4. Chester itself is also
famous for still having its medieval walls. Liverpool and
Manchester aren't *too* far *for those after brighter lights than
Chester can muster*, as are the *stunning* Welsh hills *if even
Chester's subdued illuminations get too much.*

33% ♂♂♂♀♀♀♀♀♀♀ 67%	
Sex ratio(M:F): 33%:67%	Founded: 1839
Full time u'grads: 2,500	Part time: 250
Postgrads: 500	Non-degree: 250
Ave course: 3yrs	Ethnic: 5%
Private school: 5%	Flunk rate: 22%
Mature students: 29%	Overseas students: 5%
Disabled students: 5%	Staff/student ratio: 1:22
Clearing: 10%	

Library (200,000 volumes, 484 study places, open 7 days) and
access to <u>University of Liverpool</u> facilities (25 miles away); 100
computer workstations; 3 f-t careers advisors (8% 1996 grads
unemployed after 6 mths). 1 bar; plenty of nosh stops including
2 college dining halls, SU Bistro and several coffee bars; Molloy
Hall is the college's main venue, hosting the RSC and Radio 4's
'Any Question's' recently. SU (2 sabbs); SU-run paper 'The
Collegian'; Action into the Community group; Rag. *Good*
reputation in sport helped by *strong* PE Department; sports hall;
pool; multigym; squash and tennis courts; athletics field; all-
weather pitch; climbing wall; the local area adds an ice rink, dry-
ski slope and the Welsh mountains. Most 1st years who want
it, bar a few who get in via Clearing, and a few from other years
can live in college accommodation (400 catered, £60-65
termtime only; 300 self-catered, £40-45 full year, 3 or 4 to a
kitchen); 10% share rooms; also head tenancy scheme run by
good accommodation office. 3 counsellors; nursery; Medical
Centre; late-night minibus through City Council's Women's Safe

Transport Scheme; Overseas SA; Mature SA; Postgrad SA; SU-run Student Guidance & Support Services add welfare and job-hunting advice. U/g and p/g prospectuses, including the alternative variety (from SU).

Chichester Institute

▼ (1) Chichester Institute of Higher Education, Bishop Otter Campus, College Lane, Chichester, West Sussex, PO19 4PE. (2) Chichester Institute of Higher Education, Bognor Regis Campus, Upper Bognor Road, Bognor Regis, West Sussex, PO21 1HR. Tel: (01243) 816000. Fax: (01243) 816080. E-mail: admissions@chihe.ac.uk Web site: www.chihe.ac.uk

General

Despite the name, only one of this college's 2 sites is in Chichester itself. The Bishop Otter Campus, named after the 19th-century religious leader and freshwater mammal, is a 38 acre site just outside the centre of this *pretty* cathedral city, 20 miles from Portsmouth, founded in 1839 as Bishop Otter College. The other campus dates from 1947 and is centred on a Georgian mansion terrace in the seaside resort of Bognor Regis, 6 miles away. They merged in 1977 and both sites have several modern additions. Nearly ½ the students are on teaching-related courses and Sports Studies and Arts are also popular options.

30% ♂♂♂ ♀♀♀♀♀♀♀ 70%

Sex ratio(M:F): 30%:70%	Founded: 1977
Full time u'grads: 2,900	Part time: 300
Postgrads: 200	Non-degree: 0
Ave course: 3/4yrs	Ethnic: 2.2%
Private school: n/a	Flunk rate: 31%
Mature students: 35%	Overseas students: 6%
Disabled students: n/a	Staff/student ratio: 1:30
Clearing: 5-20%	

Library at each campus including new Learning Resources Centre at Bishop Otter (200,000 volumes in all, open 7 days); 100 computers; f-t careers officer. Free shuttle bus between campuses. SU bar and College refectory at each campus; shop; regular ents; Rag week; College-run Jobshop. S*trong* on sport and arts, boosted by relevant courses and attendant facilties. Several BUSA successes and *excellent* rugby team. 35% of 1st years accommodated (330 catered, £61-83/36wks, 12 meals/wk) but no others; accommodation at both campuses with more rooms being added at Bognor for 1999. 2 counsellors; chaplain and chapel (Bishop Otter); prayer room (Bognor); nurse on each campus; Learning Support Service; nursery at Bognor Regis; access fund; rugby scholarship.

Dartington College of Arts

Dartington College of Arts, Totnes, Devon TQ9 6EJ.
Tel: (01803) 861620. Fax: (01803) 863569.
E-mail: registry@dartington.ac.uk
Web site: http://www.dartington.ac.uk

General

The *dinky* (pop 7,020) townlet of Totnes is on the South
Devon coast and 2 miles from Totnes, by the River Dart, is
the beautiful Dartington Hall estate, the site of this unique
college. Dartington concentrates on contemporary visual
and performance arts and arts management and has a high
academic reputation in these areas, with its teaching
described *with uncharacteristic enthusiasm* by the HEFCE as
"inspirational" and "charismatic". All students study the
same core programme, including arts management for
artists, and there are 5 specialist subject areas available.
*The location is relatively isolated and Totnes doesn't have
that much to offer crazy funseekers*, though it has *the usual
market town accoutrements* of supermarkets, leisure centre,
pubs and restaurants. However, Dartington Arts, a year-
round programme of concerts, exhibitions, film and more,
together with its famous International Summer School of
Music, is on the same estate, *and Dartington's creative
students are more than capable of making their own
entertainment. For those after more conventional student
kicks* the cities and universities of Exeter and Plymouth are
less than 30miles away in each direction.

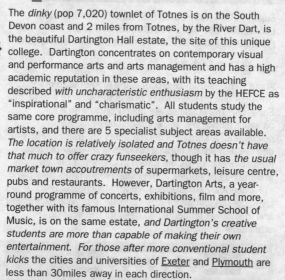

47% ♂♂♂♂♂ ♀♀♀♀♀ **53%**

Sex ratio(M:F): 47%:53%	Founded: 1961
Full time u'grads: 443	Part time: 0
Postgrads: 0	Non-degree: 0
Ave course: 3yrs	Ethnic: 0.5%
Private school: 10%	Flunk rate: n/a
Mature students: 35%	Overseas students: 3%
Disabled students: 10%	Staff/student ratio: 1:15
Clearing: 13%	

Library (46,000 volumes, open 7 days); 36 computer
workstations. SU Higher Close Club Bar serves snacks; BFI
supported cinema on campus; the Barn Theatre and Great
Hall for live performances of all varieties plus *more
workshops, studios and practice rooms than you can poke
a stick at* including a digital audio and video suite. The SU
provides social rather than political focus. *As un-sporty as
you'd expect*. No accommodation of its own though the
Dartington Hall Trust offers 70 self-catered places on
campus; *reasonable* local rents (£37/wk). Welfare issues

others insts

tackled on an individual basis; 1 counsellor; 1 f-t Welfare & Accommodation Officer; Health Centre (nurse; doctors twice weekly); Women's Officer; access fund £14,000 plus a few bursaries to help with instrumental tuition. U/g prospectus.

• •

Edge Hill University College

▼▼ Edge Hill University College, St Helen's Road, Ormskirk, Lancashire, L39 4QP. Tel: (01695) 575171. Fax: (01695) 579997. Web site: http://www.ehche.ac.uk

𝔤eneral

About 17miles from Liverpool is the market town of Ormskirk and on the edge of that is the 45 acre site of Edge Hill. The buildings are mainly brick, with a few concrete blocks and some *interesting* wrought iron sculptures. A third of undergraduates are trainee teachers and the rest are on nursing courses or modular degrees. Professional courses are based in Chorley, 17 miles away and the health studies and nursing programmes take place in Fazakerley, near Liverpool. Both <u>Manchester</u> and <u>Liverpool</u> *are just about close enough to provide excitement* and in summer students can head for the seaside attractions of Southport.

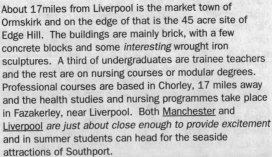

28% ♂♂♂ ♀♀♀♀♀♀♀ 72%	
Sex ratio(M:F): 28%:72%	Founded: 1885
Full time u'grads: 3,652	Part time: 1,558
Postgrads: 463	Non-degree: 0
Ave course: 3yrs	Ethnic: 2.6%
Private school: n/a	Flunk rate: n/a
Mature students: 34%	Overseas students: 2.2%
Disabled students: 3.5%	Staff/student ratio: n/a
Clearing: 22%	

1 library (220,000 volumes); 600 computers. SU bar, discos, etc; burgers and pizzas from the Diner until 9pm. SU-run paper, Community Action group and RAG. New £4m sports development Sporting Edge (*boom! boom!*) adding playing fields, running track, weights room, squash, 5-a-side and badminton courts; pool on campus All 1st years who want to can live in (around 80%) but only a handful of others (400 catered, £58/38wks, 2 meals/day; 370 self-catered, £40/38wks); 2 all-female halls; 24hr security; local rents *average* (£40/wk). 1 f-t, 3 p-t counsellors; multi-faith prayer room; creche (2-5yrs, 20 places); 2 Financial/Welfare Rights Officers; *ok* wheelchair access; access fund £20,000 (200 successful applications 1997). U/g and p/g prospectuses, video loan.

Falmouth College of Arts

▼▼▼ Falmouth College of Arts, Woodlane, Falmouth, Cornwall, TR11 4RA. Tel: (01326) 211077. Fax: (01326) 211205.

General

In the remote, *close-knit* town of Falmouth, almost at the pointiest bit of Cornwall, sits this large college, now affiliated to <u>Plymouth University</u>. Originally founded as an Art School, Falmouth now covers various aspects of media and journalism as well as painting and stuff. There's an annexe at Redruth, about 9miles away. *Falmouth can be a bit of a tourist trap in summer, but this does help swell the facilities.* There's a *decent* live music venue, the Pirate (recent melody makers include Ash, Reef, Dodgy and the Supernaturals), and the Paradox nighclub provides the sounds every night (dance, indie, retro, party) including a *popular* student-night on Wednesdays. The nearest cinema is the Old Regal in Redruth *but we're not talking 12-screen multiplex here.*

40% ♂♂♂♂♀♀♀♀♀♀ 60%	
Sex ratio(M:F): 40%:60%	Founded: 1938
Full time u'grads: 453	Part time: 0
Postgrads: 58	Non-degree: 864
Ave course: 3yrs	Ethnic: 1.5%
Private school: 4%	Flunk rate: n/a
Mature students: 10%	Overseas students: 1%
Disabled students: 1%	Staff/student ratio: 1:22
Clearing: 5%	

Library (20,000 volumes); 140 PCs and Macs; neither accessible on Sundays. Refectory/bar (food 10am-7pm Mon-Thurs, 10am-5pm Fri; booze 12.30-1.30pm and 6-11pm) which doubles as a *decent* club/music venue (cap 240); comedians 1/term; 1 or 2 films a week, either in a lecture theatre (cap 120) or in the refectory/bar/venue, mostly new releases or old classics. SU (1 sabb, NUS member) *active for its size*, with 10% turning out over tuition fees and *dodgy* goings-on in a local store; SU-run paper, 'Mouth'; Flavour Radio broadcasts at lunchtimes to the refectory (*slightly bizarrely* through TV sets). No sports facilities of its own, though students can use local facilties which, Falmouth being on the coast, are *especially good* for watersports. No accommodation of its own, either, *and local rents aren't the cheapest (£45/wk), but it's usually possible to get something within walking distance of campus* and new Halls should be ready for Autumn 99. Accommodation, welfare and counselling services are provided by Student Services, along with an orientation and induction programme for new students; 1 counsellor; nurse; creche; *limited* wheelchair access; access fund £37,000. Prospectus.

other insts

Farnborough College of Technology

▼ Farnborough College of Technology, Boundary Road,
Farnborough, Hants GU14 6SB. Tel: (01252) 405555.
Fax: (01252) 407041. E-mail: info@farn-ct.ac.uk
Web site: http://www.farn-ct.ac.uk

General

35 miles from London is the commuter town of Farnborough.
The College of Technology is mainly inhabited by non-degree
students (A-levels, HND etc) but it offers degree courses in
various vocational areas, including business, computing,
engineering and media technology, all on a concrete-and-glass
site about 500yds from the town centre, and boasts 2
Gladiators among its famous offspring (Jet and Trojan *if you
really must know*). Farnborough offers enough for a *basic*
night-out (clubs, pubs, restaurants), with a cinema, bowling
alley and dry-ski slope 4 miles away and the teeming
metropolis just a short train-ride up the mainline to Waterloo.

44% ⚲⚲⚲⚲⚲♀♀♀♀♀ 56%	
Sex ratio(M:F): 44%:56%	Founded: 1957
Full time u'grads: 546	Part time: 30
Postgrads: 23	Non-degree: 5,749
Ave course: 3yrs	Ethnic: 2.5%
Private school: n/a	Flunk rate: n/a
Mature students: 42%	Overseas students: 1.2%
Disabled students: 2.8%	Staff/student ratio: 1:15
Clearing: 13.4%	

2 libraries (56,000 volumes, 400 study places, open 6 days);
300 computer workstations; new Teaching and Learning
Technologies Resources Centre. New SU building opened in
1997 with *top quality* club/music venue (cap 550). Student-run
newspaper, 24hr radio station 1mth/yr and Genesis TV.
Accommodation for 30% of 1st years, 25% of 2nd years and a
few finalists (200 catered, £50-77/36wks, half-board), with a
number of those sharing *and rumblings about quality*; commuter-
belt rents (£50/wk). 2 counsellors; chaplains; occupational

❝Baywatch icon Pamela Anderson Lee
has turned down an invitation to
stand for the Presidency of
Stirling University Students'
Association.❞

o t h e r   i n s t s

health nurse; nursery (40 places, 6mths-5yrs); Disabilities Co-ordinator; access fund £42,271, Sky TV sponsorships (£2,000 total) and bursaries for locals. Prospectuses, accommodation pack, a number of open days, video.

Harper Adams

▼
▼ Harper Adams, Newport, Shropshire, TF10 8NB.
Tel: (01952) 820280. Fax: (01952) 814783.
E-mail: gpodmore@haac.ac.uk
Web site: http://www.haac.ac.uk

General

Harper Adams, in the heart of rural Shropshire, offers courses related to land-based industries. 42% of undergraduates are studying agriculture but the college also offers such *oddities* as an HND in golf course management. It's a 500 acre site, with its own 650 acre working farm, 2 miles outside Newport and 36 from Birmingham. 95% of students are on sandwich courses and 10% come from Northern Ireland or the Irish Republic. *It's a bit isolated* and the nearest train station is 10 miles away in Telford, *so a car comes in handy.*

65% ♂♂♂♂♂♂♂♀♀♀ 35%	
Sex ratio(M:F): 65%:35%	Founded: 1901
Full time u'grads: 1,557	Part time: 10
Postgrads: 41	Non-degree: 588
Ave course: 4yrs	Ethnic: 2%
Private school: 40%	Flunk rate: n/a
Mature students: 10%	Overseas students: 11%
Disabled students: 1%	Staff/student ratio: 1:20
Clearing: 7%	

Library (38,000 volumes, 63 study places, open 7 days); 120 computer workstations (not available at weekends). 2 bars; Harper Adams Cafe open all day, including weekends; regular club nights and *grand* end of session ball. SU; student paper, 'Cat-a-Mountain'; RAG. *Strong* sporting reputation, regularly taking on sporting *giants* like Loughborough and Durham, especially at rugby, which is top of the BUSA league; 40 acres playing fields; sports hall; pool; multigym; squash and tennis courts; athletics field; climbing wall; croquet pitch *for the more sedate*; the local area adds plenty for climbers, hikers, canoeists, horse-riders and other outward-bound folk plus the National Sports Centre at Lilleshall, 5 miles away. All 1st years and most finalists accommodated (500 catered, £66-81, all meals Mon-Fri, 180 en suite). Student Services provide accommodation and welfare advice; 1 counsellor; access fund £27,000 (22 successful applications 1997). U/g and p/g prospectuses, video.

Kent Institute of Art & Design

▼▼ Kent Institute of Art & Design, Oakwood Park, Maidstone,
Kent, ME16 8AG. Tel: (01622) 757286.
Fax: (01622) 621100. E-mail: kiadmarketing@kiad.ac.uk
Web site: http://www.kiad.ac.uk/kiad.htm

General

KIAD was formed from the merger of 3 art colleges and
different courses are based at each one: Canterbury (65miles
from London) for Fine Art and Architecture; Rochester
(40miles) for 3D Design, Jewellery, Fashion and Photography;
Maidstone (45miles) for Graphic Design, Illustration and Visual
Communication. All sites are concrete constructions amidst
pleasant greenery on the outskirts of town. Canterbury has a
built-in student population from the University of Kent which
validates all degrees; *the other areas are quieter.*

48% ♂♂♂♂♂ ♀♀♀♀♀ **52%**

Sex ratio(M:F): 48%:52%	Founded: 1987
Full time u'grads: 1,407	Part time: 143
Postgrads: 29	Non-degree: 739
Ave course: 3yrs	Ethnic: 5%
Private school: n/a	Flunk rate: n/a
Mature students: 14%	Overseas students: 25%
Disabled students: 12%	Staff/student ratio: 1:21
Clearing:	

Library at each site (70,000 volumes, 150 study places
between them, closed weekends); 25 PCs in library, more
should arrive in 98. SU bar/canteen facilities at each site. SA
organises ents and sport; student paper 'Impress/Express'.
No sports facilities but access to local facilities with student
discounts. 52% of 1st years housed in college-owned or
managed housing plus a fair few from other years (438 self-
catered, £55/43wks, 5-7 share *good* kitchens; 130 head
tenancy); *local rents above average (£45/wk) but not bad for
commuter-country and there's enough of it.* 1 careers adviser;

> ❝The Jesus and Mary Chain appeared
> at the Poly (now University) of
> North London in the mid 80s. They
> performed for 15 minutes and
> refused to do an encore. The
> crowd rioted.❞

3 p-t counsellors; Welfare Officers; wheelchair access improving; access fund £64,836 (192 successful applications 1997), small number of bursaries. U/g and p/g prospectus, course leaflets, video.

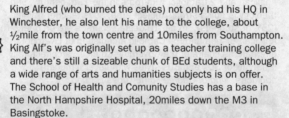

King Alfred's College, Winchester

King Alfred's College Winchester, Sparkford Road, Winchester, Hants, SO22 4NR. Tel: (01962) 841515.
Fax: (01962) 842280. E-mail: A.Childs@wkac.ac.uk
Web site: http://www.wkac.ac.uk

General

King Alfred (who burned the cakes) not only had his HQ in Winchester, he also lent his name to the college, about ½mile from the town centre and 10miles from Southampton. King Alf's was originally set up as a teacher training college and there's still a sizeable chunk of BEd students, although a wide range of arts and humanities subjects is on offer. The School of Health and Comunity Studies has a base in the North Hampshire Hospital, 20miles down the M3 in Basingstoke.

25% ♂♂♂♀♀♀♀♀♀♀ 75%	
Sex ratio(M:F): 25%:75%	Founded: 1840
Full time u'grads: 3,058	Part time: 165
Postgrads: 97	Non-degree: 0
Ave course: 3yrs	Ethnic: 1%
Private school: n/a	Flunk rate: n/a
Mature students: 36%	Overseas students: 2%
Disabled students: 3%	Staff/student ratio: 1:31
Clearing: 10%	

Library (170,000 volumes, 375 study places, open 7 days); refurbished IT centre; 265 computer workstations. 3 bars (open all day); John Stripe theatre for luvs (both student and pro). SU; student paper, 'Harder Times', and radio station; Rag; SU-run Job Shop. *Limited* sports facilities including sports hall, squash courts, athletics field, gym and dance studio. 80% of 1st years accommodated but few others (235 catered, £71-74/30wks, some meals; 793 self-catered, £55-59/40wks); accommodation for single parents and married couples (£70-80); a *devilish* 666 places in the new student village with 24hr security (*armed with holy-water?*). 1 f-t, 5 p-t counsellors; chapel and Muslim facilities; nurse; Disability Officer and facilities for students with mobility, sight and hearing problems and dyslexia; access fund £68,000 (91 successful applications 1997). U/g, p/g and part-time prospectuses, video, course leaflets and accommodation brochure.

Liverpool Hope University College

▼▼ Liverpool Hope University College, Hope Park, Liverpool
L16 9JD. Tel: (0151) 291 3295. Fax: (0151) 291 3048.
Web site: http://www.livhope.ac.uk/

General

4 miles (*or a cheap bus ride*) from the centre of Liverpool is
the city's 3rd HE institution, formerly Liverpool Institute *and (by
the sound of the new name) rather 'Hope'-ful to gain University
status soonish.* In the meantime its degrees are validated by
Liverpool University. Appropriately in this strongly ecumenical
city, it was formed from the federation of 3 colleges, 1
Anglican and 2 Catholic, with roots in the 19th century, and
theology is still a strong subject area, as is teacher training
(25% of students). In all, 16 degree courses are on offer. The
Anglican Bishop and the Catholic Archbishop of Liverpool
alternate as chairs of the Governing Council. Architecturally,
it's a mix of 30s and 60s styles with several modern
additions, *kind of George Fornby does Britpop.*

28% ♂♂♂♀♀♀♀♀♀♀ **72%**

Sex ratio(M:F): 28%:72%	Founded: 1980
Full time u'grads: 3,378	Part time: 252
Postgrads: 278	Non-degree: 353
Ave course: 3yrs	Ethnic: 4%
Private/state school: n/a	Flunk rate: 19%
Mature students: 37%	Overseas students: 2%
Disabled students: 8%	Staff/student ratio: 1:20
Clearing: 18.5%	

New library/learning resources centre (225,000 volumes,
500 study places, open 7 days); 65 computer
workstations. 2 bars; refectory (9am-5pm), snack bar
(10am-3pm, 8-11pm/4days) and pizza kitchen (8-11pm);
the massed entertainments of Liverpool are *practically on
your doorstep.* SU; student paper; community action group.
Good at sport (especially rugby and football); flood-lit astroturf; squash courts; 2 football pitches; gym; new sports
hall; sports injury clinic and 2 scientific sports laboratories;
outdoor pursuits centre in N Wales. Accommodation for
nearly 40% of 1st years, with priority to non-Liverpudlians
who make Hope their 1st choice, and some of the rest
(822 catered, £59/31wks, 12 meals/wk; 12 self-catered,
£45/31wks) but Liverpool rents *won't break the bank.* 3
counsellors; nurse; twice weekly GP surgery; 2 chaplains (1
RC, 1 Anglican); multi-faith prayer room; *good* wheelchair
access and a disability officer; welfare advice from SU;
access fund £70,000 (239 successful applications 1997),
Hillsborough Bursary for local students, other subject

o t h e r i n s t s

specific prizes and bursaries, hardship loans. U/g and p/g
prospectuses, programme and subject leaflets, quarterly
mag 'Hope Direct', online prospectus, 'Hope on the
Waterfront' computerised-info-centre-cum-cafe at Liverpool's
Albert Dock.

● ●

NESCOT

▼ NESCOT, Reigate Road, Ewell, Epsom, Surrey, KT17 3DS.
▼ Tel: (0181) 394 1731. Fax: (0181) 394 3030.

General

Based near Epsom, about 15 miles from central London, is
the former North East Surrey College Of Technology, now
called NESCOT (*which sounds like a whisky-flavour
milkshake, but don't worry*). It's a classic example of the
way the Higher Ed market has exploded in the last few years;
it offers everything from GCSEs to postgrad qualifications
and the vast majority of the degree-level students are local
returners to education. It's strongly vocational in emphasis,
with courses in technology, business, design and performing
arts. *Epsom (also home to part of <u>Surrey Institute of Art &
Design</u>) cannot truthfully be called the entertainment capital
of the UK, but it's close enough to London to keep serious
withdrawl symptoms at bay.*

51% ♂♂♂♂♂♀♀♀♀♀ **49%**

Sex ratio(M:F): 51%:49%	Founded: 1953
Full time u'grads: 419	Part time: 417
Postgrads: 12	Non-degree: 4,368
Ave course: 3yrs	Ethnic: 28%
Private school: 5%	Flunk rate: n/a
Mature students: 72%	Overseas students: 3%
Disabled students: 1%	Staff/student ratio: 1:20
Clearing: 35%	

Library (46,500 volumes, 170 study places, closed at
weekends); 40 PCs (24:7 access). 1 bar doubles as
club/music venue (cap 400); refectory open 10am-8.30pm;
Adrian Mann Drama Studio. SU (no sabbs, NUS member,
turnout 5%) provides snack bar, shop, pool table, photocopier
and video games. Sports hall; multigym; tennis courts; athletics
field and running track; Epsom Races in summer. Only 22
accommodation places (£50/39wks, mainly for overseas
students) and *extortionate* local rents (up to £100/wk). 2
counsellors; CofE chaplain; nurse; Welfare & Student Services
provide welfare, legal and accommodation advice; access fund
£33,000 (120 successful applications 1997); hardship fund.
Prospectus and course sheets available.

University of Wales College, Newport

▼▼ University of Wales College, Newport, Caerleon
Campus, PO Box 179, Newport, NP6 1YG.
Tel:(01633) 432432. Fax: (01633) 432850.
E-mail: uic@newport.ac.uk
Web site: http://www.newport.ac.uk

general

UWCN is on 2 main sites, 5 miles apart, in the town of
Newport, SE Wales. Caerleon, the larger campus, is a village
on the outskirts of town *and was a pretty happening place in
Roman times*, housing the administration and accommodation
buildings and much of the teaching premises, except for 3
departments (Business & Management, Health & Social Care
and Engineering) which are in Allt-yr-yn, in the town centre.
*Newport itself is looking pretty happening these days, with
local boyz 60ft Dolls, Catatonia, Manics and Super Furry
Animals generating a load of 'New Seattle' hype.* Overall,
business and management students provide the single biggest
chunk of the undergraduate body, but non-degree (eg HND,
professional courses) students outnumber them all. 11% are
on teacher training courses.

47% ♂♂♂♂♂ ♀♀♀♀♀ 53%	
Sex ratio(M:F): 47%:53%	Founded: 1975
Full time u'grads: 2,252	Part time: 494
Postgrads: 898	Non-degree: 4,219
Ave course: 3yrs	Ethnic: 3.9%
Private school: n/a	Flunk rate: n/a
Mature students: 56%	Overseas students: 4%
Disabled students: 7%	Staff/student ratio: n/a
Clearing: 30%	

Libraries at each site (150,000 volumes, 130 study places
in all, open 7 days); 371 computers. TV studio; SU bar.
35% of 1st years accommodated (678 self-catered, £39-
46/37wks, up to 16 share a kitchen, 465 en suite rooms)
but around 50% of undergrads live at home. 4 p-t
counsellors; Medical Service (doctor, 2 nurses); Student
Support Services; access fund £56,262 (222 successsful
applications 1997). Prospectus.

> ❝Six of the MPs elected in
> Labour's 1997 landslide were
> former Presidents of the National
> Union of Students❞

Anthrozoologists at Southampton University have discovered that one of the most immature and antisocial dog breeds is the cocker spaniel.

• •

North East Wales Institute of HE

▼ North East Wales Institute of HE, Plas Coch, Mold Road,
▼ Wrexham, LL11 2AW. Tel: (01978) 290666.
Fax: (01978) 290008. E-mail: enquiries@newi.ac.uk
Web site: http://www.newi.ac.uk

General

NEWI is in the centre of Wrexham, a town of 123,000 people near the England/Wales border, 30 miles from Liverpool. The main site on the Mold Road houses most academic departments but the School of Art & Design (350 students) is 500 yards down the road and there's a further site on the other side of town at Cartrefle. There's a bilingual policy in the Institute and the SU, although the vast majority of students have English as a first or only language. 21% of students are trainee teachers.

49% ♂♂♂♂♂♀♀♀♀♀ 51%

Sex ratio(M:F): 49%:51%	Founded: 1975
Full time u'grads: 1,930	Part time: 412
Postgrads: 34	Non-degree: 1,851
Ave course: 3yrs	Ethnic: 2.5%
Private school: n/a	Flunk rate: n/a
Mature students: 47%	Overseas students: 6%
Disabled students: 2.4%	Staff/student ratio: 1:11
Clearing: 20%	

Library (90,000 volumes, 200 study places, open 6 days); 300 computers; careers advisor (9% 1996 grads unemployed after 6mths). Bar; SU (3 sabbs, NUS member); student paper; Rag. 40% of 1st years and a few finalists accommodated in self-catering hostels (480 places, £37-52/37wks), 40% en suite, 15% shared. Welfare and accommodation services provided by Information & Student Support; 2 counsellors; nurse; GP surgery 1 day/wk; Disability Co-ordinator; nursery (24 places); SU also offers welfare advice; access fund £41,750 (180 successful applications 1997). Full- and part-time prospectuses.

other insts

Northern College

▼▼▼ Northern College, Aberdeen Campus, Hilton Place, Aberdeen,
AB24 4FA. Tel: (01224) 283500. Fax: (01224 283900).
Web site: http://www.norcol.ac.uk

General

Northern College was formed by the merger of the teacher
training colleges in Aberdeen and Dundee. The resulting 2-site
college still specialises in initial teacher training and also
offers courses in community education and social work. Many
of its courses are validated by the Open University and there is
a strong programme of off-campus, distance learning and
professional development studies. Most courses take place
at either campus, with the exception of community education,
which is based at Dundee, and the BEd in Music and BSc in
Maths & Computing which are based at Aberdeen. For
information about the towns, see Aberdeen University and
Dundee University.

20% ♂♂♀♀♀♀♀♀♀♀ 80%	
Sex ratio(M:F): 20%:80%	Founded: 1987
Full time u'grads: 960	Part time: 100
Postgrads: 200	Non-degree: 110
Ave course: 4yrs	Ethnic: 2%
Private school: n/a	Flunk rate: n/a
Mature students: 20%	Overseas students: 2%
Disabled students: 1%	Staff/student ratio: n/a
Clearing: 30%	

Library on each site (160,000 volumnes, 230 study places,
open 6 days); 350 computer workstations. Bar on each site;
SU (2 sabbs, NUS member). Pool, football pitch and sports
hall on each site. All 1st years who want to live in can (about
45%) plus 10-20% from other years (135 catered, £62/31wks;
145 self-catered, £43/42wks). Counselling service and
medical officer. U/g prospectus, course brochures.

> ❝UCL has removed the preserved
> head of philosopher Jeremy
> Bentham from its display case
> after a group of King's College
> students 'borrowed' it for a game
> of football.❞

University College of Ripon & York St John

University College of Ripon & York St John,
Lord Mayor's Walk, York, YO31 7EX.
Tel: (01904) 656771. Fax: (01904) 612512.
E-mail: i.waghorn@ucrysj.ac.uk
Web site: http://www.ucrysj.ac.uk

General

The main site of *the mouthful that is* UCRYSJ is in the centre of historic York right by its *impressive* medieval walls (see University of York for local info) but awards degrees from the University of Leeds. There's also a site in the quieter market town of Ripon, 25 miles away with about 900 students. The college was historically a centre for teacher training and education courses still make up 25% of the student body, although the college has expanded its brief to cover creative and performing arts, health & life sciences and humanities courses as well.

35% ♂♂♂♀♀♀♀♀♀♀ 65%

Sex ratio(M:F): 35%:65%	Founded: 1841
Full time u'grads: 3,031	Part time: 7
Postgrads: 124	Non-degree: 915
Ave course: 3yrs	Ethnic: 1%
Private school: n/a	Flunk rate: 23%
Mature students: 27%	Overseas students: 5%
Disabled students: 3%	Staff/student ratio: 1:21
Clearing: 18%	

Library at each site (180,000 volumes, 300 study places in total, open 6 days); 130 computers. SU bars at both sites, club/music venue (cap 200), live bands (inc Shawaddywaddy) and 2 clubs nights a week; 2 snack bars (9am-4pm); health food shop; drama (fringe regulars) and musical production (non-luvs) socs; theatre; 1 film a week. SU (3 sabbs, NUS member, turnout 26%); SU-run paper, 'Scoop'; Rag on each site. *Good* sports record; sports hall; pool; multigym; tennis courts; athletics field and running track; climbing wall; gym; access to University of York facilities. Most 1st years in college accommodation and around 15% from other years (York: 371 catered, £65/31wks, 21 meals; 497 self-catered, £40-43/39-48wks; 122 head tenancy. Ripon: 390 catered, £65-75/31wks, 112 en suite); accommodation office. 3 f-t and 7 p-t counsellors; Health Centre on each site; chaplains at each site; *poor* wheelchair access; access fund £52,000 (108 successful applications 1997). U/g, p/g, overseas and part-time prospectuses, videos, subject leaflets.

Roehampton Institute London

▼ Roehampton Institute London, Senate House, Roehampton Lane,
London, SW15 5PU. Tel: (0181) 392 3000.
Fax: (0181) 392 3131. E-mail: admissions@roehampton.ac.uk
Web site: http://www.roehampton.ac.uk

ⓘ General

Roehampton Institute comprises 4 separate colleges, on 2
sites in the genteel suburban area of South West London,
about 10 miles from the city centre. The colleges are Digby
Stuart, a Catholic foundation, Froebel, founded on the
teachings of Friedrich Froebel (who invented kindergartens)
and Southlands, a Methodist foundation, all in Roehampton;
and Whitelands, an Anglican college in Putney. There are no
religious restrictions to applicants and students can attend
one college and take courses at another. 25% of students are
on education courses of some description. Bus nos 72, 33
and 265, or the District Line from Whitelands, will take you to
central London in ½hr. For more information about being a
student in London, see University of London. The Institute
awards degrees from the University of Surrey

26% ♂♂♂♀♀♀♀♀♀♀ 74%	
Sex ratio(M:F): 26%:74%	Founded: 1975
Full time u'grads: 4,800	Part time: 250
Postgrads: 500	Non-degree: 700
Ave course: 3yrs	Ethnic: 13%
Private school: n/a	Flunk rate: n/a
Mature students: 34%	Overseas students: 9%
Disabled students: 5%	Staff/student ratio: 1:20
Clearing: 26%	

Library at each site, including *high-spec* new Learning
Resource Centre (300,000 books, 888 study places in all,
open 7 days); 250 PCs; 3 careers advisors (5.8% 1996 grads
unemployed after 6mths). 4 bars open all day; each college
has a canteen and there are a couple of cafes for lunch and
snacks; the Montefiore Hall for classical concerts. SUs at
each college and Joint Union; student paper, 'Scream'. 1996
BUSA Football Champions; 4 acres of playing fields; sports
hall; multigym; tennis courts; gym. Free bus service between
colleges. 60% of 1st years accommodated but hardly any from
other years (1,480 catered, £67-75, 12 meals/wk, 3 all-
female halls; 421 self-catered, £58-63, some en suite); 15%
have to share; 24hr security. 3 counsellors; welfare office;
nursery (30 places, 5mths-3yrs); *good* support for students
with disabilities; Overseas SA; Mature SA; Postgrad SA;
access fund £171,309 (710 successful applications 1997).
U/g and p/g prospectuses, video, course leaflets, open days.

Rose Bruford College

Rose Bruford College, Lamorbey Park, Sidcup, Kent,
DA15 9DF. Tel: (0181) 300 3024. Fax: (0181) 308 0542.
E-mail: admiss@bruford.ac.uk

General

In a green commuter-belt setting, 30mins by train from central
London, stands the main site of Rose Bruford College, which is
entirely concerned with offering degrees (validated by
University of Manchester) related to all aspects of the theatre,
including the only opera studies degree course in Europe.
Gary Oldman, *Hollywood bad-guy extraordinaire* and *top* Brit
director, is among its former students. There's another site in
Deptford, 8 miles away, based in a former secondary school;
see Goldsmiths and Greenwich for details of the local area.

20% ♂♂♀♀♀♀♀♀♀♀ 80%	
Sex ratio(M:F): 20%:80%	Founded: 1950
Full time u'grads: 482	Part time: 0
Postgrads: 19	Non-degree: 44
Ave course: 3yrs	Ethnic: 4%
Private school: n/a	Flunk rate: n/a
Mature students: 36%	Overseas students: 8%
Disabled students: 4%	Staff/student ratio: 1:15
Clearing: 10%	

Libraries on each site (35,000 volumes in all); 30 computers;
new 450-seat theatre; limited SU facilities (no bar); 40% of 1st
years housed in University of Greenwich accommodation; free
parking; counsellor; access fund £11,873; prospectus.

Royal Agricultural College

The Royal Agricultural College, Cirencester, Gloucestershire,
GL7 6JS. Tel: (01285) 652531. Fax: (01285) 650219.
E-mail: gail.young@royagcol.ac.uk
Web site: http://www.royagcol.ac.uk

General

About a mile from the country town of Cirencester is the (other)
RAC, the world's oldest agricultural college and, since 1995,
the first to award its own degrees. It's a private institution, so
full fees are payable (£3,282-£6,291 for undergraduate

other insts

courses, although LEAs usually contribute £1,590 of this). The College farms 2,000 acres nearby, to which students have access. College alumni between them are said to own, manage or administer over 80% of the UK. *Conspiracy-theorist heaven or what?*

68% ♂♂♂♂♂♂♂ ♀♀♀ 32%	
Sex ratio(M:F): 68%:32%	Founded: 1845
Full time u'grads: 393	Part time: 0
Postgrads: 59	Non-degree: 67
Ave course: 3yrs	Ethnic: 0
Private school: 65.1%	Flunk rate: n/a
Mature students: 17.8%	Overseas students: 10.7%
Disabled students: 0	Staff/student ratio: 1:13
Clearing: 1%	

Library (31,000 volumes, 160 study places, open 6 days); 50 PCs; 1 careers advisor (8% 1996 grads unemployed after 6mths). SU common room and bar (open 12.30-2pm, 7-11pm); 5 balls a year; disco night till 2am on Fris; canteen (8.30am-4pm, 7.30-10pm). Strong sports ethos (particularly rugby, polo and other equestrian sports); 20 acres of playing fields; all-weather pitch; tennis and squash courts; multigym; clay-pigeon shooting range. 98% of 1st years in catered halls (245 places, £100-120/30wks, 3 meals/day, some en suite). 1 counsellor; nightline; GP surgery (4 days); access fund £30,000 (50 successful applications 1997); scholarships. U/g and p/g prospectuses, video, 'The Cirencester Experience' brochure.

College of St Mark & St John

▼ College of St Mark and St John, Derriford Road, Plymouth, PL6 8BH. Tel: (01752) 636827. Fax: (01752) 636849.

General

Quick quiz: Marjon is 1) A Chinese version of dominoes; 2) how some people like their toast; or 3) the popular name for an Anglican college 5 miles from the centre of Plymouth, pretty close to the airport and the *gorgeous* wilderness of Dartmoor. Although the constituent colleges were founded in London over 150 years ago, and merged in 1923, Marjon has only been in Plymouth since 1973. It's still primarily a teacher training college, with 60% on related courses – the others are studying for modular BA degrees.

> ❝Imperial College, London has its own nuclear reactor.❞

o t h e r   i n s t s

33% ♂♂♂♀♀♀♀♀♀ 67%

Sex ratio(M:F): 33%:67%
Full time u'grads: 3,000
Postgrads: 550
Ave course: 4yrs
Private school: n/a
Mature students: 40%
Disabled students: 3%
Clearing: 79%

Founded: 1840
Part time: 7
Non-degree: 12
Ethnic: 5%
Flunk rate: 9%
Overseas students: 20%
Staff/student ratio: 1:20

Learning Resources Centre (120,000+ volumes, 250 study places); 200 computers; SU bar and own pub; sports centre; 80% of 1st years accommodated and 5% of finalists (£42-56pw); *good* sports facilities and results, especially women's; 3 counsellors; access fund £58,000; prospectus and video.

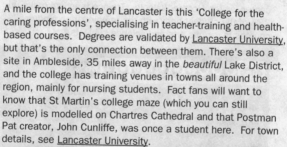

University College of St Martin

▼ University College of St Martin, Bowerham Road, Lancaster, LA1 3JD. Tel: (01524) 384444. Fax: (01524) 384567.
E-mail: admissions@ucsm.ac.uk
Web site: http://www.ucsm.ac.uk

General

A mile from the centre of Lancaster is this 'College for the caring professions', specialising in teacher-training and health-based courses. Degrees are validated by <u>Lancaster University</u>, but that's the only connection between them. There's also a site in Ambleside, 35 miles away in the *beautiful* Lake District, and the college has training venues in towns all around the region, mainly for nursing students. Fact fans will want to know that St Martin's college maze (which you can still explore) is modelled on Chartres Cathedral and that Postman Pat creator, John Cunliffe, was once a student here. For town details, see <u>Lancaster University</u>.

25% ♂♂♂♀♀♀♀♀♀ 75%

Sex ratio(M:F): 25%:75%
Full time u'grads: 3,470
Postgrads: 529
Ave course: 3/4yrs
Private school: n/a
Mature students: 28.6%
Disabled students: 1.1%
Clearing: 20%

Founded: 1963
Part time: 1,913
Non-degree: 1,226
Ethnic: 1.9%
Flunk rate: n/a
Overseas students: 0.7%
Staff/student ratio: 1:21

7 libraries (237,427 volumes, 475 study places, open 6 days) and students can also use <u>Lancaster University's</u> library; 160 computer

workstations (24hr access); 3 careers advisors (10% 1996 grads unemployed after 6mths). 2 bars (open 6-11pm); 2 dining rooms; 2 snack bars; various ents every week night at Lancaster plus 4 major events a year; *good* student drama. SU (NUS member); fortnightly paper, 'The Saint', with its own sabb editor; charity group; SU-run jobshop. *Strong* sports; sports hall; multigym; squash and tennis courts; all-weather pitch; gym; new £1.4m sports complex under development. 95% of 1st years accommodated plus a few finalists (640 catered, £63-74/34wks, all meals; 89 self-catered, £40-43/42wks; 86 head tenancies); 25% have to share; 24hr security. 3 counsellors; accommodation office; SU welfare officer; late-night minibus; creche (44 places, 2-4yrs); access fund £67,956 (148 successful applications 1997); bursaries and scholarships. U/g prospectus, department and course leaflets.

St Mary's University College

St Mary's University College, Waldegrave Road, Strawberry Hill, Twickenham, TW1 4SX. Tel: (0181) 240 4000.
Fax: (0181) 240 4255.

General

Apart from being the HQ of English rugby, Twickenham, in the *attractive* London borough of Richmond, is the site of St Mary's, a Catholic college of the University of Surrey, based in a Grade I listed Gothic mansion originally built by the 18th-century writer, Horace Walpole. Trainee teachers make up 33% of the student body with the remainder on modular courses in various arts and science subjects.

34% ♂♂♂♂♀♀♀♀♀♀ 66%	
Sex ratio(M:F): 34%:66%	Founded: 1850
Full time u'grads: 2,100	Part time: 25
Postgrads: 250	Non-degree: 25
Ave course: 3/4yrs	Ethnic: 4%
Private school: n/a	Flunk rate: n/a
Mature students: 17%	Overseas students: 12%
Disabled students: 6%	Staff/student ratio: 1:20
Clearing: 10%	

1 library (150,000 volumes); most 1st years accommodated (11% sharing) but under 10% of other years (£63-85); access fund £70,000; 2 counsellors (plus chaplains); prospectus.

> **Researchers at Sheffield University have developed a contraceptive pill for squirrels.**

University College, Scarborough

University College Scarborough, Filey Road, Scarborough,
N Yorks, YO11 3AZ. Tel: (01723) 362392.
Fax: (01723) 370815. E-mail: external@ucscarb.ac.uk
Web site: http://www.ucscarb.ac.uk

General

Scarborough's a windy *but pleasant* seaside town on the North Yorkshire coast, 42 miles from York. About a mile from the town centre, very near the coast is the Edwardian building which provides the centrepiece for University College, which offers modular courses in a range of subjects, including environmental sciences and teacher training, validated by the University of York. *Drama is also particularly strong*; some modules make use of Alan Ayckbourn's nearby Stephen Joseph Theatre and the National Student Drama Festival is based here. *Scarborough's a more lively place than you might imagine.* As well as the Stephen Joseph, there's a *fair smartering* of theatres and small cinemas, enough *student-friendly* pubs with *cheap* beer to go round, a couple of clubs and the nearby Bridlington Spa pulls in name acts like Ocean Colour Scene, the Levellers and Portishead. Then there's always the beach and the local surfing scene *for those who get a kick out of watching their extremities turn blue and drop off.*

35% ♂♂♂♀♀♀♀♀♀♀ 65%	
Sex ratio(M:F): 35%:65%	Founded: 1948
Full time u'grads: 1,327	Part time: 17
Postgrads: 40	Non-degree: 0
Ave course: 3yrs	Ethnic: 1.7%
Private school: n/a	Flunk rate: n/a
Mature students: 31%	Overseas students: 1.2%
Disabled students: 6.1%	Staff/student ratio: 1:21
Clearing: 41%	

Library (110,000 volumes; open 6 days); 60 PCs; 2 p-t careers advisors. Bar (*cheap* beer, open all day); *strong* student drama sent 3 productions to the Fringe last year; live music in Calvino's (cap 300, mostly local bands); several club nights a week in SU (*cheesy party music a speciality*); food until 6pm. SU (2 sabbs, NUS member, turnout 20%); shop; fax and copying service; payphone; pool table; RAG. Sports hall; tennis courts; gym; 4 acres of playing fields; *surfing, surfing, surfing.* Catered accommodation for 95% of 1st years (£69-75/30wks, includes £5 worth of meals a day) some en suite. 1 counsellor; 3 chaplains (Baptist, RC, Anglican); SU advice centre; nurse (5 days); doctor (4 days); access fund £2,190 (64 successful applications 1997). Prospectus and course leaflets.

> ❝Nirvana played their first UK gig at SOAS.❞

....

Swansea Institute of HE

▼▼ Swansea Institute of Higher Education, Townhill Road,
Swansea SA2 0UT. Tel: (01792) 481000.
Fax: (01792) 208683. E-mail: enquiry@sihe.ac.uk

general

Athrofa Addysg Uwch Abertawe, as it's known by some, is based on 2 main sites on the west side of Wales's 2nd largest city (see <u>Swansea, University of Wales</u> for more details) and is an associate college of the University of Wales. Townhill houses the artists and trainee teachers while Mount Pleasant is for computer boffins, lawyers, engineers and the rest.

55% ♂♂♂♂♂♂♀♀♀♀ 45%	
Sex ratio(M:F): 55%:45%	Founded: 1976
Full time u'grads: 2,800	Part time: 1,200
Postgrads: 350	Non-degree: 950
Ave course: 3yrs	Ethnic: 4%
Private school: n/a	Flunk rate: n/a
Mature students: 48%	Overseas students: 4.7%
Disabled students: 1%	Staff/student ratio: 1:18
Clearing: n/a	

3 libraries (130,000 volumes between them, open 6 days); 450 computers; careers advisor. Small bar (open 12-2pm, 7-11pm); 3 college refectories (8.30am-6pm); 2 SU coffee bars (9am-4pm); main hall (cap 350) for live bands; no club nights; student drama coming on, with one show heading Fringe-wards this summer. SU (3 sabbs, NUS member, turnout 20%); input into <u>Swansea University</u> SU paper. Surfing team in BUSA finals 2 years running; multigym and fitness suite. 25% of 1st years accommodated in self-catering halls (300 places, £38-46/33wks, some en suite); 1 all-female hall. 2 counsellors; chapel; prayer rooms 'by arrangement'; nurse; SU welfare service; accommodation office; access fund c£50,000; emergency fund. Prospectus.

> ❝A 17ft condom publicising a Safe Sex campaign was stolen from outside the Leeds University Student Union.❞

‘The law department at Warwick University has admitted the former military dictator of Sierra Leone.’

Trinity & All Saints

▼▼ Trinity & All Saints College, Brownberrie Lane, Horsforth, Leeds, LS18 5HD. Tel: (0113) 283 7150.
Fax: (0113) 283 7200. E-mail: s.sellars@tasc.ac.uk
Web site: http://www.tasc.ac.uk

General

6 miles from the centre of Leeds is the northern suburb of Horsforth and on a rural 43-acre campus is Trinity & All Saints, a Catholic foundation and a college of the University of Leeds. The college concentrates on combining academic and vocational subjects; 39% of undergraduates are on media-related courses and 34% are studying towards teaching qualifications.

37% ♂♂♂♂♂♀♀♀♀♀♀ 63%

Sex ratio(M:F): 37%:63%	Founded: 1966
Full time u'grads: 1,922	Part time: 10
Postgrads: 191	Non-degree: 0
Ave course: 3/4yrs	Ethnic: 6%
Private school: n/a	Flunk rate: n/a
Mature students: 11%	Overseas students: 1%
Disabled students: 0%	Staff/student ratio: 1:21
Clearing: 16%	

Library (129,000 volumes, 200 study places, open 7 days) plus access to University of Leeds facilities; 174 computers; 2 careers advisors (16.9% 1996 grads unemployed after 6mths). College bar (10am-2pm, 5.30-11.30pm) serves food; SU discos and live bands (cap 300; Beatlemania, Champagne Supernova and the Tarantinos recently). SU (2 sabbs, NUS member, turnout 25%); SU-run paper, 'Saint & Sinner'; Rag. Successes in football and golf; gym; football and rugby pitches; all-weather pitch; squash and tennis courts; pool; athletics field; multigym. Most 1st years who want to can live in (catered, £58-62/34wks, 8 to a kitchen, some en suite rooms); accommodation officer helps the rest. 2 counsellors; chapel and RC chaplain; nursery (20 places); surgery; access fund £42,000; golf bursaries and hardship fund. Prospectus.

other insts

Trinity College, Carmarthen

▼ Trinity College, Carmarthen, Ceredigion, SA31 3EP.
Tel: (01267) 676767. Fax: (01267) 676766.
E-mail: registry@trinity-cm.ac.uk

general

Carmarthen's a market town in West Wales, about 25 miles from Swansea, with a population of 30,000 and *good* access to the *splendid* countryside of the Gower peninsula and Pembrokeshire and the surf-friendly Carmarthen Bay. There's also, a mile outside town, Trinity College, mainly a teacher-training college (60% of undergraduates) with a special emphasis on Welsh language education. The main building dates from the college's Victorian foundation, while various modern additions are dotted around the green campus.

35% ♂♂♂♂♀♀♀♀♀♀♀♀ 65%	
Sex ratio(M:F): 35%:65%	Founded: 1848
Full time u'grads: 1,308	Part time: 0
Postgrads: 150	Non-degree: 190
Ave course: 3yrs	Ethnic: 2%
Private school: n/a	Flunk rate: n/a
Mature students: 15%	Overseas students: 1%
Disabled students: n/a	Staff/student ratio: 1:16
Clearing: 10%	

Library (50 study places, open 7 days); careers advisor; 2 bars; strong sports, especially rugby; 90% of 1st years accommodated (£48-64pw); visiting counsellor; Church of Wales chaplain; prospectus.

Trinity College of Music

▼ Trinity College of Music, 11 Mandeville Place, London
W1M 6AQ. Tel: (0171) 935 5773. Fax: (0171) 224 6278.
E-mail: info@tcm.ac.uk Web site: http://www.tcm.ac.uk

general

In the heart of London's West End, close to Oxford Street, Trinity is the oldest music college in the UK, offering 4 year degree courses in all areas of classical music. There are practice rooms in Blandford Street and the library and academic studies centre are in Bulstrode Place, each a few

minutes' walk away. As with all music colleges, students get
one-to-one tuition on their chosen instrument.

38% ♂♂♂♂♀♀♀♀♀♀ 62%	
Sex ratio(M:F): 38%:62%	Founded: 1872
Full time u'grads: 351	Part time: 0
Postgrads: 115	Non-degree: 33
Ave course: 3yrs	Ethnic: 14%
Private school: n/a	Flunk rate: n/a
Mature students: 17%	Overseas students: 16%
Disabled students: 2%	Staff/student ratio: 1:4
Clearing: n/a	

Library (60,000 volumes, 50 study places, open 5 days); 7
PCs. SU common room. SU (no sabbs, NUS member); Rag
week. Virtually no sport. No college accommodation but
advice available from college and SU. Methodist chaplain;
college welfare officer; college doctor; osteopathy and
physiotherapy sessions; free self-defence classes; access
fund £26,000 (40 successful applications 1997); limited
bursaries and scholarships. Prospectus.

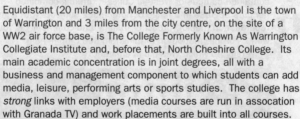

University College, Warrington

University College Warrington, Padgate Campus, Crab Lane,
Warrington, WA2 0DB. Tel: (01925) 494494.
Fax: (01925) 816077. E-mail: registry.he@warr.ac.uk
Web site: http://www.warr.ac.uk/unicoll.html

General

Equidistant (20 miles) from Manchester and Liverpool is the town
of Warrington and 3 miles from the city centre, on the site of a
WW2 air force base, is The College Formerly Known As Warrington
Collegiate Institute and, before that, North Cheshire College. Its
main academic concentration is in joint degrees, all with a
business and management component to which students can add
media, leisure, performing arts or sports studies. The college has
strong links with employers (media courses are run in assocation
with Granada TV) and work placements are built into all courses.

49% ♂♂♂♂♂♂♀♀♀♀ 51%	
Sex ratio(M:F): 49%:51%	Founded: 1946
Full time u'grads: 640	Part time: 110
Postgrads: 20	Non-degree: 205
Ave course: 3yrs	Ethnic: 2%
Private school: 30%	Flunk rate: n/a
Mature students: 30%	Overseas students: 2%
Disabled students: 0.5%	Staff/student ratio: 1:20
Clearing: 21%	

2 libraries (95,000 volumes, 400 study places, open 7 days); 134 computer workstations; 2 careers advisors (10% 1996 grads unemployed after 6mths). 2 bars (open lunchtimes and evenings); lots of eateries for a range of tastes and pockets; 2 club nights a week at the Bunker (cap 300); 1 video a week on the big screen; NOMADS drama and ents group; theatre. SU (3 sabbs, NUS member, turnout 15%); SU-paper, 'Shrapnel'; online paper, 'Xpansion'; student radio; Rag. Good reputation in rugby and football; national-standard facilities including sports hall, fitness centre, football, rugby and hockey pitches and sports laboratories. Self-catered accommodation for 85% of 1st years and finalists and a few 2nd years (480 places, £28-36/34wks, 20 share a kitchen); 24hr security and CCTV. Student services for accommodation and welfare advice; 4 counsellors; 3 chaplains (CofE, RC, methodist); 2 nurses; nursery (34 places, 0-5yrs); wheelchair access to main buildings; access fund £42,699 (169 successful applications 1997); bursaries from Granada TV for media courses; emergency fund. U/g and p/g prospectuses, alternative prospectus (from SU), course leaflets.

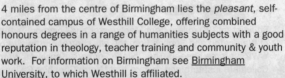

Westhill College of HE

Westhill College of HE, Weoley Park Road, Selly Oak, Birmingham, B29 6LL. Tel: (0121) 472 7245. Fax: (0121) 415 5399. E-mail: publicity@westhill.ac.uk Web site: http://www.westhill.ac.uk

General

4 miles from the centre of Birmingham lies the *pleasant*, self-contained campus of Westhill College, offering combined honours degrees in a range of humanities subjects with a good reputation in theology, teacher training and community & youth work. For information on Birmingham see Birmingham University, to which Westhill is affiliated.

25% ♂♂♀♀♀♀♀♀♀♀ 75%

Sex ratio(M:F): 25%:75%	Founded: 1907
Full time u'grads: 900	Part time: 78
Postgrads: 94	Non-degree: 116
Ave course: 3yrs	Ethnic: n/a
Private school: n/a	Flunk rate: n/a
Mature students: 45%	Overseas students: 0.5%
Disabled students: 7%	Staff/student ratio: n/a
Clearing: n/a	

New learning resources centre (150,000 volumnes, 200 study places, open 5 days); 100+ computer workstations. Yard & Bucket SU bar; restaurant, sandwich bar and shop; regular ents. Guild of Students (2 sabbs, NUS member). Gym; pool;

sports field. All 1st years are guaranteed a room on campus (200 catered, £70/33wks, 17 meals a week); *limited* cooking facilities. Health Centre; accommodation officer; 2 chaplains; Muslim prayer room; the Guild of Students and Dean of Students add other support; access fund £19,288 (80 successful applications 1997). U/g and p/g prospectuses, course leaflets, video.

Westminster College, Oxford

▼
▼ Westminster College, Oxford, OX2 9AT. Tel: (01865) 247644. Fax: (01865) 251847. E-mail: marketing@ox-west.ac.uk Web site: http://www.ox-west.ac.uk

⁞⋯⋯⋯ General

Originally a Methodist institution in London, founded to train teachers for the inner cities, since 1959 Westminster College has been in a *slightly more relaxed* environment, a *pleasant* 100 acre site about 2 miles from the centre of Oxford, near to the ring-road. 55% of undergrads are on BEd courses but Theology and other humanities degrees are also available. Students become members of OUSU. Regular shuttle buses run into the city. For details on Oxford, see University of Oxford.

20% ♂♂♀♀♀♀♀♀♀♀ 80%	
Sex ratio(M:F): 20%:80%	Founded: 1851
Full time u'grads: 1018	Part time: 196
Postgrads: 193	Non-degree: 1070
Ave course: 3/4yrs	Ethnic: 5%
Private school: 11%	Flunk rate: n/a
Mature students: 25%	Overseas students: 3%
Disabled students: 7%	Staff/student ratio: 1:18
Clearing: 30%	

Library (100,000 volumes, 100 study places, open 7 days) plus access to Oxford University libraries; 70 computer workstations, more to be added shortly; careers advisor (15% 1996 grads unemployed after 6mths). SU bar (12-2pm, 6-11pm); refectory; theatre; 2 ents a week plus 2 balls a year. Union Society; SU-paper, 'The Watertower'; community action and Rag groups. Sports hall; pool; squash and tennis courts; athletics field; golf course; gym. 65% of 1st years accommodated with places guaranteed to school-leavers (catered, £68-78, termtime only) and 50% of others; 15% have to share. Access to Oxford University counselling service; chapel; 6 chaplains; surgery (nurse and doctors); late-night minibus to and from city; limited wheelchair access; access fund £30,000. F-t and p-t prospectuses, course leaflets.

Wimbledon School of Art

▼ Wimbledon School of Art, Merton Hall Road, London,
SW19 3QA. Tel: (0181) 408 5000. Fax: (0181) 408 5050.
E-mail: art@wimbledon.ac.uk

general

Situated in suburbia, but a ½hr train or tube ride to central
London, Wimbledon includes the country's largest centre for
Theatre Design degree courses as well as Fine Art courses. A
mile from the main site is the Terry Bruen Building where
foundation courses are based. Degrees are awarded by Surrey
University. For more information about being a student in
London, see University of London.

30% ♂♂♂♀♀♀♀♀♀♀ 70%	
Sex ratio(M:F): 30%:70%	Founded: 1890
Full time u'grads: 425	Part time: 0
Postgrads: 124	Non-degree: 198
Ave course: 3yrs	Ethnic: 20%
Private school: n/a	Flunk rate: n/a
Mature students: 52%	Overseas students: 15%
Disabled students: n/a	Staff/student ratio: 1:10
Clearing: 0%	

Library (28,000 volumes, 40 study places, open 5 days); 40
computer workstations. State-of-the-art theatre/workshop and
studio; small SU common room; no bar; college canteen. No
college accommodation; local rents around £55 a week.
Welfare office (4 f-t staff); 2 counsellors; access fund £13,000
(45 successful applications 1997). Prospectus and open days.

University College Worcester

▼ University College Worcester, Henwick Grove, Worcester,
WR2 6AJ. Tel: (01905) 855000. Fax: (01905) 855132.
Web site: http://www.worc.ac.uk

general

Worcester College is on a single site in a rural setting, 2 miles
from the city centre. Worcester has a number of student-
friendly pubs, a 7-screen Odeon and Thursday night is the
night to try out the 2 local clubs. It's within easy reach of
glorious countryside but any gaps in entertainment have to be
met by Birmingham, 30 miles away.

31% ♂♂♂♀♀♀♀♀♀♀ 69%

Sex ratio(M:F): 31%:69%	Founded: 1946
Full time u'grads: 2,742	Part time: 1,101
Postgrads: 218	Non-degree: 1,169
Ave course: 3yrs	Ethnic: 1.8%
Private school: n/a	Flunk rate: 25%
Mature students: 59%	Overseas students: 1%
Disabled students: 5%	Staff/student ratio: 1:23
Clearing: n/a	

Recently extended library (200,000 volumnes, 630 study places, open 6 days); 160 computer workstations; 2 careers advisors. 2 SU bars, Hanger bar (12noon-11pm) doubles as club/music venue (cap 634), smaller Sports bar opens some nights; Henwicks college canteen (8.30am-7.30pm) and SU-run Snack Attack (11am-3pm, 9pm-11.30pm) for cheap eats; drama studio; 2 films a week in SU bar. SU (3 sabbs, NUS member, turnout 30%); Student Community Action; Rag raised £25,000 last year. Good showing in athletics and hockey; tennis courts; gym; all-weather pitch. 50% of 1st years and 25% of finalists live in self-catered accommodation (580 places, £34-40/35-40wks), cheaper rooms have no cooking facilties, otherwise 5/6 to a kitchen; some sharing at the start of the year; 24hr security. Counselling service; 1 chaplain; accommodation office (2 staff); nursery (25 places, 3mths-5yrs); SU advice bureau; equal opportunities co-ordinator; access fund £50,147; bursaries and sports scholarships. Prospectus, course leaflets, video, open days.

University College Writtle

University College Writtle, Lordship Road, Writtle, Chelmsford, Essex, CM1 3RR. Tel: (01245) 424200. Fax: (01245) 420456. E-mail: postmaster@writtle.ac.uk Web site: http://www.writtle.ac.uk

General

2 miles west of Chelmsford lies the historic village of Writtle where, if you take a right at the village green, you will also find the 220-hectare estate of Writtle College, which specialises in vocational courses for the land, countryside, amenity and related industries. It's degrees are validated by the University of Essex, with which the College has strong links. For

❛ Sussex University has the sunniest campus in Britain. ❜

'Text in italics is PUSH's point of view – take it or leave it.'

information on the attractions of Chelmsford see <u>Anglia Polytechnic University</u>.

51% ♂♂♂♂♂♀♀♀♀♀ 49%	
Sex ratio(M:F): 51%:49%	Founded: 1893
Full time u'grads: 633	Part time: 0
Postgrads: 40	Non-degree: >1000
Ave course: 3yrs	Ethnic: n/a
Private school: n/a	Flunk rate: n/a
Mature students: 39%	Overseas students: 2%
Disabled students: 7%	Staff/student ratio: 1:10
Clearing: n/a	

New library (60,000 volumnes). Recreation Centre with bar (disco every fortnight), snooker and pool tables, TV lounge and big screen; the *wittily named* Writz, Writtle Chef and Cow Watering Cafe for food. SU (2 sabbs, NUS member); Rag committee. The Recreation Centre also contains a large indoor hall for sport, 2 squash courts, fitness room and multigym; outdoors there are playing fields, pitches for rugby, football, hockey and cricket and several tennis courts. Around 40% of 1st years and 20% from other years can live-in (340 catered, £57-68/39wks, 1 main meal/day termtimes only); ½ rooms en suite; basic cooking facilities; lockable cages for bikes. Student Support Unit; accommodation office; 3 chaplains (CofE, RC, inter-denominational); chapel in Recreation Centre; access fund £16,167 (87 successful applications 1997); special support fund for part-time and overseas students. U/g and p/g prospectuses, video.

Fold-out guide to symbols inside back cover

 'Freaked out by finance? Why not pop into your local branch of Lloyds Bank and see what they have to offer.'

push, of course

How to use 'push, of course':

▶▶ **CHOOSING A COURSE**
There's probably a different way to choose a course for every potential student. Many gaze in awe at the list of courses available and run screaming into the night. Many others stick to their 'best' subject at A-level, without realising that Maths at A-level and Maths at degree-level can be about as similar as Arnie and Julian Clary. Others pick a degree based on the career they want to follow. This can be a sound move but don't forget that you can get a career in the media without a Media Studies degree and not all accountants studied Accountancy at University. The best tip is to pick a course you think you'll enjoy. You'll find it much easier to cope with that 3am essay crisis if you get some kind of satisfaction from the obscure fragment of an Assyrian limerick you're deconstructing.

FINDING A COURSE
If you've a rough idea of the course you're looking for, look for the general heading it would come under. So, for example, if Civil Engineering is the bag you're into, turn to Engineering and there it is, sure enough, with the names of all the colleges which run undergraduate Civil Engineering courses.

CHECKING UP
Although every endeavour has been made to keep this list up to date, always check details with the college in question. 'push, of course' is only intended as a first stop and should not be used as a be-all-and-end-all, end-of-the-road, finite, eat-the-dust checklist.

COURSE NAMES
If 80 colleges do approximately the same course, they'll give it 112 different names - so push has cut through the wrapping and gone straight for the prize. To do this, we've had to standardise many names and group them together. As a result, we may inadvertently have dumped a course into a

category which wouldn't have been the choice of the academics who teach it. But then again, they'd probably think it merited a section all of its own, so who gives a toss?

JOINT COURSES

Don't think you've got to commit yourself to one subject for the duration of your academic career. Many universities offer combinations of courses; obvious ones are language courses (eg French and German) or social studies mixes (history and politics) but other, less likely combos are available – physics and music for example. Don't presume, however, that just because two separate subjects are available at one institution that you can do both. Check with the prospectus and in the UCAS Handbook. Some students find the workload on joint courses is heavier than on single honours equivalents, because they have to do more than half a course in each subject.

MODULAR COURSES

As an extension of joint courses, many universities now offer modular courses; this means you can pick and choose a range of options across the academic spectrum. Successful completion of a certain number of courses gives you enough credits for a degree. This is particularly good for students with outside commitments, since you can often accumulate credits, go back to full-time work for a year and pick up again where you left off. It's also good for people who don't know at the time of application what sort of subjects will interest them.

OMISSIONS

The courses available at almost all the colleges featured in **push** are listed. However, regrettably, we cannot bring you the courses at Birkbeck College, the Open University or the Other Institutions on pages 725 to 760.

••

Accountancy Aberdeen, Abertay, Aberystwyth, Anglia, Aston, Bangor, Birmingham, Bolton, Bournemouth, Brighton, BUWE, Cardiff, CEngland, CLancs, De Montfort, Derby, Dundee, Durham, E London, Essex, Exeter, Glamorgan, Glasgow, Glasgow Cal, Greenwich, Herts, Huddersfield, Hull, Kent, Kingston, Lancaster, Leeds, Leeds Met, Lincs & Humbs, Liverpool, Liverpool JM, London Guildhall, Luton, Manchester, Man Met, Middlesex, Napier, Nene, Newcastle, N London, Northumbria, Nott Trent, Oxford Brookes, Paisley, Plymouth, Portsmouth, Queen's Belfast, Robert Gordon, Salford, Sheffield, Sheffield Hallam, South Bank, Southampton Inst, Staffs, Stirling, Strathclyde, Sunderland, Teesside, Thames Valley, UEA, Ulster, Wolves

• **Financial Management** Abertay, Aberystwyth, Anglia, Bangor, Birmingham, Bournemouth, Brighton, BUWE, Buckingham, Cardiff, CEngland, CLancs, Chelt & Gloucs, City, De Montfort, Dundee, Glamorgan, Glasgow Cal, Greenwich, Heriot-Watt, Kent, Lancaster, London Guildhall, Loughborough, LSE, Luton, Manchester, Man Met, Middlesex, N London, Northumbria, Nott Trent, Oxford Brookes, Paisley, Portsmouth, Queen's Belfast, Reading, Salford, Sheffield Hallam, Southampton Inst, Stirling, Ulster, Ulster

African Languages Birmingham, SOAS

Agriculture Aberdeen, Aberystwyth, Bangor, Bath, Bolton, Bournemouth, Brighton, BUWE, CEngland, CLancs, Chelt & Gloucs, Cranfield, De Montfort, Derby, E London, Edinburgh, Essex, Glamorgan, Glasgow, Greenwich, Herts, Leeds, Lincs & Humbs, Liverpool JM, Nene, Newcastle, Northumbria, Nottingham, Nott Trent, Plymouth, Queen's Belfast, Reading, Sheffield Hallam, South Bank, Staffs, Stirling, Strathclyde, Sunderland, UEA, Wolves, Wye

- **Forestry** Aberdeen, Bangor, Brighton, CLancs, De Montfort, Edinburgh
- **Land and Property Management** Anglia, CEngland, CLancs, City, De Montfort, Glamorgan, Glasgow Cal, Greenwich, Kingston, Luton, Napier, Nott Trent, Oxford Brookes, Paisley, Plymouth, Portsmouth, Reading, Sheffield Hallam, South Bank, Southampton Inst, Staffs, Westminster

American Studies Aberystwyth, Birmingham, Brunel, CLancs, De Montfort, Derby, Dundee, Edinburgh, Essex, Glamorgan, Hull, Kent, King's Coll, Lampeter, Lancaster, Leicester, Middlesex, Nene, Nottingham, Queen's Belfast, Reading, Sheffield, Staffs, Swansea, UEA, Ulster, Warwick, Wolves

Anatomy/Physiology Aberdeen, Abertay, Bradford, Bristol, Cambridge, Cardiff, CLancs, Dundee, E London, Edinburgh, Glasgow, Greenwich, Herts, Huddersfield, King's Coll, Leeds, Leeds Met, Leicester, Lincs & Humbs, Liverpool, Loughborough, Luton, Manchester, Middlesex, Newcastle, N London, Nottingham, Oxford, Oxford Brookes, Plymouth, Queen's Belfast, Reading, Royal Holloway, Salford, Sheffield, South Bank, Southampton, St Andrews, Staffs, Strathclyde, Sunderland, Sussex, Teesside, UCL, Westminster, Wolves

Ancient Languages Cambridge, Edinburgh, Jew's Coll, Liverpool, Oxford, SOAS

Anthropology Aberdeen, Derby, Durham, E London, Edinburgh, Glamorgan, Glasgow, Goldsmith's, Greenwich, Hull, Kent, Lampeter, Lancaster, Leeds Met, Liverpool, LSE, Manchester, Nott Trent, Oxford, Queen's Belfast, Sheffield Hallam, SOAS, St Andrews, Staffs, Swansea, UEA, UCL

Archaeology Birmingham, Bournemouth, Bradford, Bristol, Cardiff, Durham, E London, Edinburgh, Exeter, Glasgow, King's Coll, Lampeter, Leicester, Liverpool, Manchester, Newcastle, Nottingham, Queen's Belfast, Reading, Sheffield, SOAS, Southampton, UEA, UCL, York

Architecture Bath, Brighton, Cambridge, Cardiff, CEngland, De Montfort, Derby, Dundee, E London, Edinburgh, Glasgow, Greenwich, Heriot-Watt, Huddersfield, Kingston, Leeds Met, Lincs & Humbs, Liverpool, Liverpool JM, Luton, Manchester, Man Met, Middlesex, Newcastle, N London, Northumbria, Nottingham, Nott Trent, Oxford Brookes, Plymouth, Portsmouth, Queen's Belfast, Robert Gordon, Sheffield, Sheffield Hallam, South Bank, Strathclyde, UCL, Westminster

- **Building/Construction** Abertay, Anglia, Bolton, Brighton, BUWE, CEngland, CLancs, Coventry, De Montfort, Derby, Glamorgan, Glasgow Cal, Greenwich, Heriot-Watt, Herts, Huddersfield, Kingston, Leeds Met, Lincs & Humbs, Liverpool, Liverpool JM, Loughborough, Luton, Napier, Nene, Northumbria, Nott Trent, Oxford Brookes, Paisley, Plymouth, Portsmouth, Queen's Belfast, Reading, Robert Gordon, Salford, Sheffield Hallam, South Bank, Southampton Inst, Staffs, Strathclyde, Teesside, Ulster, UMIST, UCL, Westminster, Wolves
- **Town & Country Planning** Aberdeen, Anglia, Bangor, BUWE, Cardiff, CEngland, Coventry, De Montfort, Dundee, Glamorgan, Greenwich, Heriot-Watt, Leeds Met, Liverpool, Liverpool JM, Luton, Manchester, Napier, Newcastle, Northumbria, Nottingham, Nott Trent, Oxford Brookes, Queen's Belfast, Reading, Salford, Sheffield, Sheffield Hallam, South Bank, Strathclyde, Ulster, UCL, Westminster, Wolves

Arts
Anglia, Bangor, Bath Spa, Bolton, Brighton, Brunel, BUWE, Coventry, De Montfort, Durham, Glamorgan, Glasgow, Greenwich, Heriot-Watt, Herts, Kent, Lancaster, Leicester, Lincs & Humbs, Luton, Manchester, Man Met, Middlesex, N London, Nott Trent, Oxford Brookes, Portsmouth, Southampton, Staffs, Sunderland,Thames Valley, Ulster, Ulster, Westminster

- **Ceramics & Glass** De Montfort, Leeds, Sheffield, Staffs
- **Craft** Brighton, CEngland, De Montfort, Dundee, London Guildhall, London Inst, Loughborough, Man Met, Middlesex, Sheffield Hallam, Staffs, Westminster
- **Design** Anglia, Bath Spa, Bolton, Bournemouth, Brighton, BUWE, CEngland, CLancs, Chelt & Gloucs, Coventry, De Montfort, Derby, Dundee, E London, Glamorgan, Glasgow Cal, Goldsmith's, Greenwich, Heriot-Watt, Herts, Huddersfield, Kingston, Leeds Met, Lincs & Humbs, Liverpool JM, London Guildhall, London Inst, Loughborough, Luton, Man Met, Middlesex, Napier, Nene, N London, Northumbria, Nott Trent, Plymouth, Portsmouth, Reading, Robert Gordon, Salford, Sheffield Hallam, Southampton, Southampton Inst, Staffs, Sunderland, Surrey Inst, Teesside, Ulster, Westminster, Wolves
- **Fine Art** Aberystwyth, Anglia, Bath Spa, Bolton, Brighton, BUWE, CEngland, CLancs, Chelt & Gloucs, Coventry, De Montfort, Derby, Dundee, E London, Edinburgh, Glamorgan, Goldsmith's, Herts, Kingston, Lancaster, Leeds, Leeds Met, Lincs & Humbs, Liverpool JM, London Guildhall, London Inst, Loughborough, Luton, Man Met, Middlesex, Nene, Newcastle, Northumbria, Nott Trent, Oxford, Oxford Brookes, Plymouth, Portsmouth, Reading, Salford, Sheffield Hallam, Southampton, Southampton Inst, Staffs, Sunderland, Surrey Inst, UCL, Wolves

Asian Languages
CLancs, Hull, Newcastle, Sheffield, SOAS

Astronomy
Cambridge, Cardiff, CLancs, Edinburgh, Glamorgan, Herts, Keele, Liverpool, Liverpool JM, Newcastle, QMW, Royal Holloway, St Andrews, Sussex, UCL

Biology
Aberdeen, Abertay, Aberystwyth, Anglia, Aston, Bangor, Bath, Bath Spa, Birmingham, Bolton, Brighton, Bristol, BUWE, Brunel, Cambridge, Cardiff, CLancs, Coventry, De Montfort, Derby, Dundee, Durham, E London, Edinburgh, Essex, Exeter, Glamorgan, Glasgow, Glasgow Cal, Greenwich, Heriot-Watt, Herts, Huddersfield, Hull, Imperial, Keele, Kent,

King's Coll, Kingston, Lancaster, Leeds, Leicester, Liverpool, Liverpool JM, Luton, Manchester, Man Met, Napier, Newcastle, N London, Northumbria, Nottingham, Nott Trent, Oxford, Oxford Brookes, Paisley, Plymouth, Portsmouth, QMW, Queen's Belfast, Reading, Robert Gordon, Royal Holloway, Salford, Sheffield, Sheffield Hallam, South Bank, Southampton, St Andrews, Staffs, Stirling, Strathclyde, Sunderland, Sussex, Swansea, UEA, Ulster, UMIST, UCL, Warwick, Westminster, Wolves, Wye, York

- **Biotechnology** Aberdeen, Birmingham, Cardiff, De Montfort, E London, Glamorgan, Greenwich, Herts, Imperial, King's Coll, Leeds, Liverpool JM, Paisley, Portsmouth, Reading, South Bank, Teesside, UCL, Westminster, Wolves

- **Botany** Aberdeen, Aberystwyth, Bangor, Birmingham, Bristol, Cambridge, Dundee, Durham, Edinburgh, Glasgow, Imperial, Leeds, Leicester, Liverpool, Luton, Manchester, Newcastle, Plymouth, Queen's Belfast, Reading, Royal Holloway, Sheffield, Southampton, UEA, Wye

- **Food Science** Anglia, Bath Spa, Bournemouth, Cranfield, Dundee, Glamorgan, Glasgow Cal, Huddersfield, Leeds, Lincs & Humbs, Liverpool JM, Man Met, Newcastle, N London, Nottingham, Nott Trent, Oxford Brookes, Plymouth, Queen Margaret, Queen's Belfast, Reading, Robert Gordon, Sheffield Hallam, South Bank, Staffs, Teesside, Ulster, Wolves, Wye

- **Genetics** Aberdeen, Aberystwyth, Birmingham, Cambridge, Cardiff, Dundee, Edinburgh, Glasgow, Huddersfield, King's Coll, Leeds, Leicester, Liverpool, Manchester, Newcastle, Nottingham, Oxford, QMW, Queen's Belfast, Sheffield, Swansea, UCL, York

- **Microbiology** Aberdeen, Aberystwyth, Anglia, Birmingham, Bradford, Bristol, BUWE, Cardiff, CLancs, Dundee, E London, Edinburgh, Glamorgan, Glasgow, Heriot-Watt, Herts, Huddersfield, Imperial, Kent, King's Coll, Leeds, Leicester, Liverpool, Liverpool JM, Luton, Manchester, Napier, Newcastle, N London, Nottingham, Plymouth, Portsmouth, Queen's Belfast, Reading, Sheffield, South Bank, Staffs, Strathclyde, Sunderland, Surrey, Teesside, UEA, UCL, Warwick, Wolves

- **Molecular Biology/Biophysics** Anglia, Bangor, Cambridge, Cardiff, Coventry, De Montfort, Dundee, Edinburgh, Glasgow, Greenwich, Herts, Kent, King's Coll, Leicester, Liverpool, Liverpool JM, Luton, Manchester, Newcastle, N London, Portsmouth, QMW, Queen's Belfast, Reading, Sheffield, Sheffield Hallam, Sunderland, Surrey, UEA, UCL

●●●

Business & Management
Aberdeen, Abertay, Aberystwyth, Anglia, Aston, Bath, Bath Spa, Birmingham, Bolton, Bournemouth, Bradford, Brighton, BUWE, Brunel, Buckingham, Cardiff, CEngland, CLancs, Chelt & Gloucs, City, Coventry, Cranfield, De Montfort, Derby, Dundee, Durham, E London, Edinburgh, Exeter, Glamorgan, Glasgow, Glasgow Cal, Greenwich, Heriot-Watt, Herts, Huddersfield, Hull, Kent, King's Coll, Kingston, Lampeter, Lancaster, Leeds, Leeds Met, Lincs & Humbs, Liverpool, Liverpool JM, London Guildhall, London Inst, Loughborough, LSE, Luton, Manchester, Man Met, Middlesex, Napier, Nene, Newcastle, N London, Northumbria, Nottingham, Nott Trent, Oxford, Oxford Brookes, Paisley, Plymouth, Portsmouth, Queen Margaret, Queen's Belfast, Reading, Robert Gordon, Royal Holloway, Salford, Sheffield, Sheffield Hallam, South Bank, Southampton, Southampton Inst, St Andrews, Staffs, Stirling, Strathclyde, Sunderland, Surrey, Swansea, Teesside, Thames Valley, UEA, Ulster, UMIST, Warwick, Westminster

- **Industrial Relations** CLancs, E London, Glamorgan, Greenwich, Herts, Kent, Lincs & Humbs, Luton, Middlesex, Nott Trent, Salford, Wolves

- **Institutional Management** Anglia, Bath, Bath Spa, Bolton,

Bournemouth, Brighton, Brunel, Buckingham, CEngland, CLancs, Chelt & Gloucs, Coventry, De Montfort, Derby, Dundee, Glamorgan, Glasgow Cal, Greenwich, Huddersfield, Leeds Met, Lincs & Humbs, Liverpool JM, London Inst, Loughborough, Luton, Man Met, Middlesex, Napier, N London, Nott Trent, Oxford Brookes, Plymouth, Portsmouth, Queen Margaret, Robert Gordon, Salford, Sheffield Hallam, South Bank, Southampton Inst, Strathclyde, Surrey, Teesside, Thames Valley, Ulster, Westminster, Wolves

Celtic Languages
Aberdeen, Aberystwyth, Bangor, Bath Spa, Cardiff, Edinburgh, Glamorgan, Glasgow, Lampeter, Liverpool, N London, Queen's Belfast, Swansea, Ulster, Ulster

Chemistry
Aberdeen, Abertay, Anglia, Aston, Bangor, Bath, Birmingham, Bradford, Bristol, BUWE, Cambridge, Cardiff, CLancs, Coventry, De Montfort, Derby, Dundee, Durham, Edinburgh, Exeter, Glamorgan, Glasgow, Greenwich, Heriot-Watt, Herts, Huddersfield, Hull, Imperial, Keele, Kent, King's Coll, Kingston, Lancaster, Leeds, Leicester, Liverpool, Liverpool JM, Loughborough, Manchester, Man Met, Napier, Newcastle, N London, Northumbria, Nottingham, Nott Trent, Oxford, Paisley, Plymouth, QMW, Queen's Belfast, Reading, Robert Gordon, Salford, Sheffield, Sheffield Hallam, Southampton, St Andrews, Staffs, Stirling, Strathclyde, Surrey, Sussex, Swansea, Teesside, UEA, UMIST, UCL, Warwick, Wolves, York

- **Biochemistry** Aberdeen, Aberystwyth, Bangor, Bath, Birmingham, Bradford, Bristol, Brunel, Cambridge, Cardiff, CLancs, Coventry, Dundee, E London, Edinburgh, Essex, Glasgow, Greenwich, Heriot-Watt, Herts, Huddersfield, Imperial, Keele, Kent, King's Coll, Kingston, Lancaster, Leeds, Leicester, Liverpool, Liverpool JM, Luton, Manchester, Man Met, Newcastle, N London, Nottingham, Oxford, Paisley, Portsmouth, QMW, Queen's Belfast, Reading, Royal Holloway, Salford, Sheffield, South Bank, Southampton, St Andrews, Stirling, Strathclyde, Surrey, Sussex, Swansea, UEA, Ulster, UMIST, UCL, Warwick, Wolves, Wye, York
- **Materials Science** Bath, Liverpool, London Guildhall, Man Met, UMIST
- **Minerals Technology** Cambridge, Exeter, Glamorgan, Imperial, Leeds, Nottingham, QMW, Westminster
- **Metallurgy** Brunel, Cambridge, Leeds, Liverpool, Oxford, Sheffield, Surrey, Wolves

Chinese
CLancs, De Montfort, Durham, Edinburgh, Leeds, Newcastle, N London, Oxford, Sheffield, SOAS

Classics
Birmingham, Bristol, Cambridge, Durham, Edinburgh, Exeter, Glasgow, King's Coll, Lampeter, Leeds, Liverpool, Manchester, Newcastle, Nottingham, Oxford, Queen's Belfast, Reading, Royal Holloway, St Andrews, Swansea, UCL, Warwick

- **Classical Greek** Edinburgh, Glasgow, Lampeter, Leeds, Manchester, Newcastle, Royal Holloway, St Andrews
- **Latin** Birmingham, Durham, Edinburgh, Exeter, Glasgow, Lampeter, Leeds, Manchester, Newcastle, Nottingham, Reading, Royal Holloway, St Andrews, Swansea

Computer Science
Aberdeen, Abertay, Aberystwyth, Anglia, Aston, Bath, Bolton, Bournemouth, Bradford, Brighton, Bristol,

BUWE, Brunel, Buckingham, Cambridge, Cardiff, CEngland, CLancs, Chelt & Gloucs, City, Coventry, De Montfort, Derby, Dundee, Durham, E London, Edinburgh, Essex, Exeter, Glamorgan, Glasgow, Glasgow Cal, Goldsmith's, Greenwich, Heriot-Watt, Herts, Huddersfield, Hull, Imperial, Keele, Kent, King's Coll, Kingston, Lampeter, Lancaster, Leeds, Leeds Met, Leicester, Lincs & Humbs, Liverpool, Liverpool JM, London Guildhall, Loughborough, Luton, Manchester, Man Met, Middlesex, Napier, Nene, Newcastle, N London, Northumbria, Nottingham, Nott Trent, Oxford, Oxford Brookes, Paisley, Plymouth, Portsmouth, QMW, Queen's Belfast, Reading, Robert Gordon, Royal Holloway, Salford, Sheffield, Sheffield Hallam, South Bank, Southampton, Southampton Inst, St Andrews, Staffs, Stirling, Strathclyde, Sunderland, Surrey, Sussex, Swansea, Teesside, Thames Valley, UEA, Ulster, UMIST, UCL, Warwic

- **Artificial Intelligence** Anglia, Derby, Durham, Essex, Herts, Imperial, Luton, Manchester, Middlesex, Oxford Brookes, Staffs, Sussex, UMIST, Westminster

- **Computer Systems Engineering** Anglia, Bolton, CEngland, CLancs, City, Coventry, Cranfield, Essex, Greenwich, Hull, Liverpool JM, London Guildhall, Luton, Manchester, Middlesex, Napier, Newcastle, N London, Northumbria, Nottingham, Nott Trent, Oxford Brookes, Paisley, Plymouth, Portsmouth, Sheffield, Sheffield Hallam, South Bank, Southampton Inst, Staffs, Sunderland, UEA, Westminster

- **Software Engineering** Aberystwyth, Anglia, Bath, Bolton, Bournemouth, Bradford, Brighton, BUWE, CEngland, CLancs, City, Coventry, Cranfield, De Montfort, Derby, Durham, E London, Edinburgh, Essex, Glamorgan, Greenwich, Heriot-Watt, Herts, Huddersfield, Hull, Imperial, Kent, Kingston, Leeds Met, Lincs & Humbs, Liverpool JM, London Guildhall, Luton, Manchester, Man Met, Napier, Newcastle, Northumbria, Oxford Brookes, Paisley, Portsmouth, Queen's Belfast, Salford, Sheffield, Sheffield Hallam, South Bank, Southampton, Southampton Inst, Staffs, Stirling, Sunderland, Teesside, Thames Valley, Ulster, UMIST, Westminster, Wolves

Drama
Aberystwyth, Bath Spa, Birmingham, Bristol, Brunel, CLancs, Coventry, De Montfort, Derby, E London, Exeter, Glamorgan, Goldsmith's, Greenwich, Heriot-Watt, Herts, Huddersfield, Hull, Kent, Lancaster, Liverpool JM, London Inst, Loughborough, Luton, Manchester, Man Met, Middlesex, Nene, N London, Northumbria, Nott Trent, Plymouth, Queen Margaret, Reading, Royal Holloway, Salford, Staffs, Surrey, UEA, Ulster, Warwick, Wolves

Economics
Aberdeen, Abertay, Aberystwyth, Anglia, Bangor, Bath, Birmingham, Bradford, Bristol, BUWE, Brunel, Buckingham, Cambridge, Cardiff, CEngland, CLancs, City, Coventry, De Montfort, Derby, Dundee, Durham, E London, Edinburgh, Essex, Exeter, Glamorgan, Glasgow, Glasgow Cal, Greenwich, Heriot-Watt, Herts, Huddersfield, Hull, Kent, Kingston, Lancaster, Leeds, Leeds Met, Leicester, Lincs & Humbs, Liverpool, Liverpool JM, London Guildhall, Loughborough, LSE, Manchester, Man Met, Middlesex, Napier, Newcastle, N London, Northumbria, Nottingham, Nott Trent, Oxford, Oxford Brookes, Paisley, Plymouth, Portsmouth, QMW, Queen's Belfast, Reading, Royal Holloway, Salford, Sheffield, SOAS, Southampton, St Andrews, Staffs, Stirling, Strathclyde, Sunderland, Surrey, Swansea, Teesside, UEA, Ulster, UCL, Warwick, Wolves, York

Education

- **Nursery (Pre-School)** Chelt & Gloucs
- **Nursery & Infants (Nursery & Lower Primary)** Brighton, Chelt & Gloucs, Leeds Met, Man Met
- **Infants Only (Lower Primary)** Bath Spa, Chelt & Gloucs, Goldsmith's, Nene, Plymouth, Sunderland
- **Junior Only (Upper Primary)** Brighton, Chelt & Gloucs, Goldsmith's, Leeds Met, Man Met, Nene, Sunderland
- **Primary (All Ages)** Anglia, Brunel, CEngland, De Montfort, Greenwich, Herts, Man Met, Middlesex, N London, Northumbria, Nott Trent, Oxford Brookes, Paisley, Strathclyde, Wolves
- **Junior/Middle (Upper Primary & Middle)** Leeds Met, Sunderland
- **Secondary** Man Met, Wolves
- **Physical Education** Chelt & Gloucs, Newcastle
- **Other Educational Subjects** Bath, Bath Spa, Bristol, Cardiff, CLancs, De Montfort, Derby, E London, Exeter, Glamorgan, Herts, Huddersfield, Lancaster, Leeds, Leeds Met, Liverpool, Liverpool JM, Luton, Manchester, Man Met, Middlesex, Newcastle, N London, Northumbria, Nott Trent, Plymouth, Sheffield Hallam, Stirling, Strathclyde, Sunderland, Wolves, York

Engineering
Aberdeen, Abertay, Anglia, Bath, Birmingham, Bolton, Bournemouth, Brighton, BUWE, Brunel, Cambridge, Cardiff, CEngland, CLancs, Coventry, Cranfield, De Montfort, Durham, E London, Edinburgh, Exeter, Glamorgan, Glasgow, Glasgow Cal, Greenwich, Heriot-Watt, Herts, Huddersfield, Hull, Kingston, Lancaster, Leeds, Leeds Met, Leicester, Lincs & Humbs, Liverpool, Liverpool JM, Loughborough, Luton, Man Met, Middlesex, Napier, Nene, Northumbria, Nott Trent, Oxford, Oxford Brookes, Paisley, Plymouth, Portsmouth, QMW, Reading, Salford, Sheffield Hallam, South Bank, Southampton, Staffs, Sunderland, Surrey, Swansea, Teesside, Ulster, UMIST, Warwick, Wolves

- **Aeronautical Engineering** Bath, Bristol, BUWE, City, Coventry, Cranfield, Glasgow, Herts, Imperial, Kingston, Lincs & Humbs, Liverpool, Loughborough, Manchester, QMW, Queen's Belfast, Salford, Sheffield, Southampton, UMIST
- **Chemical Engineering** Aston, Bath, Birmingham, Bradford, Brighton, Cambridge, CLancs, Edinburgh, Heriot-Watt, Imperial, Leeds, Loughborough, Newcastle, Nottingham, Oxford, Paisley, Queen's Belfast, Sheffield, South Bank, Strathclyde, Surrey, Swansea, Teesside, UMIST, UCL
- **Civil Engineering** Aberdeen, Abertay, Anglia, Aston, Bath, Birmingham, Bolton, Bradford, Brighton, Bristol, BUWE, Cardiff, City, Coventry, Cranfield, Dundee, Durham, E London, Edinburgh, Exeter, Glamorgan, Glasgow, Glasgow Cal, Greenwich, Heriot-Watt, Herts, Imperial, Kingston, Leeds, Leeds Met, Liverpool, Liverpool JM, Loughborough, Manchester, Napier, Newcastle, Northumbria, Nottingham, Nott Trent, Oxford, Oxford Brookes, Paisley, Plymouth, Portsmouth, QMW, Queen's Belfast, Salford, Sheffield, Sheffield Hallam, South Bank, Southampton, Southampton Inst, Strathclyde, Surrey, Swansea, Teesside, Ulster, UMIST, UCL, Warwick, Westminster, Wolves
- **Electrical Engineering** Aberdeen, Bangor, Bath, Bolton, Brighton, CEngland, Cranfield, De Montfort, Durham, Edinburgh, Glasgow Cal, Greenwich, Heriot-Watt, Herts, Imperial, Liverpool, Luton, Napier, Northumbria, Nottingham, Oxford, QMW, Sheffield, Sheffield Hallam, Southampton, Staffs, Teesside, Warwick, Wolves
- **Electronic Engineering** Abertay, Anglia, Aston, Bangor, Bath,

Birmingham, Bolton, Bournemouth, Bradford, Brighton, Bristol, BUWE, Brunel, Cardiff, CEngland, CLancs, City, Coventry, Cranfield, De Montfort, Derby, Durham, E London, Edinburgh, Essex, Exeter, Glamorgan, Glasgow Cal, Greenwich, Herts, Huddersfield, Hull, Kent, King's Coll, Kingston, Lancaster, Leeds, Leeds Met, Lincs & Humbs, Liverpool, Liverpool JM, Loughborough, Luton, Manchester, Man Met, Middlesex, Napier, Newcastle, N London, Northumbria, Nottingham, Nott Trent, Oxford, Oxford Brookes, Paisley, Plymouth, Portsmouth, QMW, Reading, Robert Gordon, Royal Holloway, Salford, Sheffield, Sheffield Hallam, Southampton, Southampton Inst, Staffs, Strathclyde, Sunderland, Surrey, Sussex, Swansea, Teesside, UEA, Ulster, UMIST, UCL, Warwick, Westminster, Wolves, York

- **Mechanical Engineering** Aberdeen, Abertay, Aston, Bath, Birmingham, Bolton, Bradford, Brighton, Bristol, BUWE, Brunel, Cardiff, CEngland, CLancs, City, Coventry, Cranfield, De Montfort, Derby, Dundee, Durham, Edinburgh, Exeter, Glamorgan, Glasgow, Glasgow Cal, Greenwich, Heriot-Watt, Herts, Huddersfield, Hull, Imperial, Kingston, Lancaster, Leeds, Leicester, Lincs & Humbs, Liverpool, Liverpool JM, Loughborough, Luton, Manchester, Man Met, Middlesex, Napier, Newcastle, Northumbria, Nottingham, Nott Trent, Oxford, Oxford Brookes, Paisley, Plymouth, Portsmouth, QMW, Queen's Belfast, Reading, Robert Gordon, Salford, Sheffield, Sheffield Hallam, South Bank, Southampton, Southampton Inst, Staffs, Strathclyde, Sunderland, Surrey, Sussex, Swansea, Teesside, Ulster, UMIST, UCL, Warwick, Westminster, Wolves

- **Production/Manufacturing Engineering** Abertay, Anglia, Aston, Bath, Birmingham, Bolton, Bournemouth, Bradford, Brighton, BUWE, Brunel, Cardiff, CEngland, CLancs, Coventry, De Montfort, Derby, Durham, E London, Exeter, Glamorgan, Glasgow Cal, Greenwich, Herts, Huddersfield, Hull, King's Coll, Kingston, Leeds Met, Lincs & Humbs, Liverpool JM, Loughborough, Luton, Man Met, Middlesex, Napier, Newcastle, Northumbria, Nottingham, Nott Trent, Plymouth, Portsmouth, Queen's Belfast, Salford, Sheffield Hallam, South Bank, Southampton, Southampton Inst, Staffs, Strathclyde, Sunderland, Swansea, Teesside, Ulster, UMIST, Warwick, Westminster, Wolves

•••

English Aberdeen, Aberystwyth, Anglia, Bangor, Bath Spa, Birmingham, Bristol, BUWE, Brunel, Buckingham, Cambridge, Cardiff, CEngland, CLancs, De Montfort, Dundee, Durham, E London, Edinburgh, Essex, Exeter, Glamorgan, Glasgow, Goldsmith's, Greenwich, Herts, Huddersfield, Hull, Kent, King's Coll, Kingston, Lampeter, Lancaster, Leeds, Leicester, Lincs & Humbs, Liverpool, Liverpool JM, London Guildhall, Loughborough, Luton, Manchester, Man Met, Middlesex, Newcastle, N London, Northumbria, Nottingham, Nott Trent, Oxford, Oxford Brookes, QMW, Queen's Belfast, Reading, Royal Holloway, Salford, Sheffield, Sheffield Hallam, South Bank, Southampton, St Andrews, Staffs, Stirling, Strathclyde, Sunderland, Swansea, Teesside, UEA, Ulster, UCL, Warwick, Westminster, Wolves, York

•••

Environmental Science Aberdeen, Abertay, Aberystwyth, Anglia, Bangor, Bath, Bath Spa, Birmingham, Bolton, Bournemouth, Bradford, Brighton, BUWE, Brunel, Cambridge, CLancs, Chelt & Gloucs, Coventry, De Montfort, Derby, Dundee, Durham, E London, Exeter, Glamorgan, Glasgow Cal, Greenwich, Herts, Huddersfield, Hull, Imperial, King's Coll, Kingston, Lampeter, Lancaster, Leeds, Leeds Met, Lincs & Humbs, Liverpool, Liverpool JM, LSE, Luton, Manchester, Man Met, Middlesex, Napier, Nene, Newcastle, N London, Northumbria, Nottingham, Nott Trent, Oxford Brookes, Paisley, Plymouth, Portsmouth, QMW, Reading, Robert Gordon, Royal Holloway, Salford, Sheffield, Sheffield Hallam,

Southampton, Southampton Inst, Staffs, Stirling, Sunderland, Sussex, UEA, Ulster, Wolves, Wye
- **Environmental Technologies** Aberdeen, Bangor, Bolton, CEngland, CLancs, Chelt & Gloucs, Derby, Dundee, Glamorgan, Greenwich, Heriot-Watt, Kingston, Leeds Met, Luton, Man Met, N London, Nott Trent, Oxford Brookes, Staffs

European Languages Aberdeen, Aberystwyth, Anglia, Aston, Bangor, Bath Spa, Birmingham, Bradford, Cardiff, CLancs, Coventry, De Montfort, Derby, Dundee, Durham, E London, Glamorgan, Goldsmith's, Herts, Huddersfield, Hull, Kent, King's Coll, Lancaster, Leeds, Liverpool, Liverpool JM, London Guildhall, Loughborough, Luton, N London, Northumbria, Nottingham, Portsmouth, Queen's Belfast, Reading, Royal Holloway, Salford, Sheffield Hallam, South Bank, Southampton, Stirling, Strathclyde, Sunderland, Thames Valley, UEA, Ulster, UCL, Wolves

French Aberdeen, Aberystwyth, Aston, Bangor, Bath, Birmingham, Bradford, Bristol, Cardiff, CLancs, De Montfort, Derby, Durham, E London, Edinburgh, Exeter, Glamorgan, Glasgow, Goldsmith's, Hull, Kent, King's Coll, Kingston, Lampeter, Lancaster, Leeds, Leicester, Liverpool, London Guildhall, Manchester, Man Met, Middlesex, Newcastle, N London, Northumbria, Nottingham, Nott Trent, Oxford Brookes, Portsmouth, QMW, Queen's Belfast, Reading, Royal Holloway, Sheffield, Southampton, St Andrews, Stirling, Strathclyde, Swansea, UEA, Ulster, UMIST, UCL, Warwick, Wolves

Geography
- **Physical** Aberdeen, Aberystwyth, Anglia, Bath Spa, Birmingham, Bournemouth, Bradford, Brighton, Bristol, Brunel, Cardiff, Coventry, Cranfield, Derby, Dundee, Durham, E London, Edinburgh, Exeter, Glamorgan, Glasgow, Greenwich, Herts, Huddersfield, Hull, King's Coll, Kingston, Lampeter, Lancaster, Leeds, Leicester, Liverpool, Liverpool JM, Loughborough, Luton, Manchester, Middlesex, Nene, Newcastle, Northumbria, Nottingham, Oxford Brookes, Plymouth, Portsmouth, QMW, Queen's Belfast, Reading, Royal Holloway, Salford, Sheffield, Southampton, Southampton Inst, St Andrews, Staffs, Sussex, Swansea, Ulster, UCL, Wolves
- **Social** Aberdeen, Aberystwyth, Anglia, Bath Spa, Birmingham, Bristol, BUWE, Brunel, Cambridge, CLancs, Coventry, De Montfort, Dundee, Durham, E London, Edinburgh, Exeter, Glamorgan, Glasgow, Greenwich, Huddersfield, Hull, King's Coll, Kingston, Lampeter, Lancaster, Leeds, Leeds Met, Leicester, Liverpool, Liverpool JM, LSE, Luton, Manchester, Man Met, Middlesex, Newcastle, N London, Northumbria, Nottingham, Nott Trent, Oxford, Plymouth, Portsmouth, QMW, Queen's Belfast, Reading, Royal Holloway, Salford, Sheffield, Sheffield Hallam, SOAS, South Bank, Southampton, St Andrews, Staffs, Strathclyde, Sunderland, Swansea, UCL, Westminster, Wolves

Geology Aberdeen, Aberystwyth, Anglia, Bangor, Bath Spa, Birmingham, Bournemouth, Bristol, Cambridge, Cardiff, Derby, Durham, Edinburgh, Exeter, Glamorgan, Glasgow, Greenwich, Herts, Imperial, Keele, Kingston, Lancaster, Leeds, Leicester, Liverpool, Luton, Manchester, Oxford, Oxford Brookes, Plymouth, Portsmouth, Queen's Belfast, Reading, Royal Holloway, Sheffield, Southampton, St Andrews, Staffs, Sunderland, UEA, UCL, Wolves

courses

German Aberdeen, Aston, Bangor, Bath, Birmingham, Bradford, Bristol, Cardiff, CLancs, De Montfort, Derby, Durham, E London, Edinburgh, Exeter, Glamorgan, Glasgow, Goldsmith's, Hull, Kent, King's Coll, Lampeter, Lancaster, Leeds, Leicester, Liverpool, London Guildhall, Manchester, Man Met, Middlesex, Newcastle, N London, Nottingham, Oxford Brookes, Portsmouth, QMW, Queen's Belfast, Reading, Royal Holloway, Sheffield, Southampton, St Andrews, Stirling, Strathclyde, Sussex, Swansea, UEA, Ulster, UMIST, UCL, Warwick, Wolves

History Aberdeen, Aberystwyth, Anglia, Bangor, Bath Spa, Birmingham, Bolton, Brighton, Bristol, BUWE, Brunel, Buckingham, Cambridge, Cardiff, CLancs, De Montfort, Derby, Dundee, Durham, E London, Edinburgh, Essex, Exeter, Glamorgan, Glasgow, Goldsmith's, Greenwich, Herts, Huddersfield, Hull, Keele, Kent, King's Coll, Kingston, Lampeter, Lancaster, Leeds, Leicester, Lincs & Humbs, Liverpool, London Guildhall, LSE, Luton, Manchester, Man Met, Middlesex, Nene, Newcastle, N London, Northumbria, Nottingham, Nott Trent, Oxford, Oxford Brookes, Portsmouth, QMW, Queen's Belfast, Reading, Royal Holloway, Sheffield, Sheffield Hallam, SOAS, Southampton, SSEES, St Andrews, Staffs, Stirling, Strathclyde, Sunderland, Sussex, Swansea, Teesside, UEA, Ulster, UCL, Warwick, Westminster, Wolves, York

- **Economic & Social History** Aberystwyth, Birmingham, Bristol, Derby, Edinburgh, Essex, Glasgow, Hull, Kent, Lampeter, Lancaster, Leeds, Leicester, Liverpool, LSE, Luton, Manchester, Man Met, Plymouth, Portsmouth, Queen's Belfast, Southampton Inst, Sussex, Swansea, UEA, Wolves
- **History & Philosophy of Science** Cambridge, Leeds, UCL
- **History of Art** Aberdeen, Anglia, Brighton, Bristol, Buckingham, Cambridge, CLancs, Courtauld, De Montfort, Derby, E London, Edinburgh, Essex, Glamorgan, Glasgow, Goldsmith's, Kent, Kingston, Leeds, Leicester, Liverpool, Liverpool JM, Loughborough, Manchester, Man Met, Middlesex, Newcastle, Nottingham, Oxford Brookes, Reading, Sheffield Hallam, SOAS, Southampton, St Andrews, Staffs, UEA, UCL, Warwick, York

Humanities Aberdeen, Edinburgh, Essex, Leeds Met, Newcastle

Italian Birmingham, Bristol, Cardiff, CLancs, Durham, E London, Edinburgh, Exeter, Glasgow, Hull, Kent, Leeds, Leicester, Liverpool, Manchester, Man Met, Queen's Belfast, Reading, Royal Holloway, Strathclyde, Sussex, Swansea, UCL, Wolves

Japanese CLancs, Durham, Edinburgh, Newcastle, Oxford, Sheffield, SOAS, Stirling, Ulster, Wolves

Latin American Languages Aberdeen, Essex, King's Coll, Liverpool, Middlesex, Newcastle, Portsmouth, Wolves

Law Aberdeen, Abertay, Aberystwyth, Anglia, Aston, Bangor, Birmingham, Bournemouth, Bristol, BUWE, Brunel, Buckingham, Cambridge, Cardiff, CEngland, CLancs, City, Coventry, De Montfort, Derby, Dundee, Durham, E London, Edinburgh, Essex, Exeter, Glamorgan, Glasgow, Glasgow Cal,

c o u r s e s

Greenwich, Herts, Huddersfield, Hull, Keele, Kent, King's Coll, Kingston, Lancaster, Leeds, Leeds Met, Leicester, Lincs & Humbs, Liverpool, Liverpool JM, London Guildhall, LSE, Luton, Manchester, Man Met, Middlesex, Napier, Nene, Newcastle, N London, Northumbria, Nottingham, Nott Trent, Oxford, Oxford Brookes, Paisley, Plymouth, Portsmouth, QMW, Queen's Belfast, Reading, Robert Gordon, Sheffield, Sheffield Hallam, SOAS, South Bank, Southampton, Southampton Inst, Staffs, Stirling, Strathclyde, Sussex, Swansea, Teesside, Thames Valley, UEA, UCL, Warwick, Westminster, Wolves

Librarianship
Leeds Met, Man Met, Napier, N London, Staffs
- **Information Science** Aberystwyth, CEngland, Loughborough, N London, Northumbria, Queen Margaret, Queen's Belfast

Linguistics
Bangor, BUWE, CLancs, Derby, Durham, E London, Edinburgh, Essex, Glamorgan, Herts, Lancaster, Leeds, Luton, Manchester, Newcastle, Northumbria, Nott Trent, Portsmouth, Reading, SOAS, UEA, Ulster, UCL, Westminster, Wolves, York

Literature (Comparative)
Bolton, Bradford, Derby, E London, Edinburgh, Glasgow, Jew's Coll, Kent, Leeds Met, Luton, Nene, Portsmouth, Stirling, UEA, Ulster, Ulster

Maritime Technology
Glamorgan, Glasgow, Heriot-Watt, Liverpool JM, Newcastle, Plymouth, Southampton, Southampton Inst, Strathclyde

Marketing/Market Research
Abertay, Anglia, Aston, Bolton, Bournemouth, Brighton, BUWE, CEngland, CLancs, Chelt & Gloucs, Coventry, De Montfort, Derby, Glamorgan, Glasgow Cal, Greenwich, Herts, Huddersfield, Lancaster, Lincs & Humbs, London Guildhall, London Inst, Luton, Man Met, Middlesex, N London, Northumbria, Oxford Brookes, Paisley, Plymouth, Queen Margaret, Salford, Sheffield Hallam, South Bank, Southampton Inst, Staffs, Stirling, Teesside, Wolves

Maths
Aberdeen, Aberystwyth, Bangor, Bath, Bath Spa, Birmingham, Bolton, Brighton, Bristol, Brunel, Cambridge, Cardiff, CLancs, City, Coventry, De Montfort, Derby, Dundee, Durham, E London, Edinburgh, Essex, Exeter, Glamorgan, Glasgow, Glasgow Cal, Goldsmith's, Greenwich, Heriot-Watt, Herts, Huddersfield, Hull, Imperial, Keele, Kent, King's Coll, Kingston, Lancaster, Leeds, Leicester, Liverpool, London Guildhall, Loughborough, LSE, Luton, Manchester, Man Met, Middlesex, Newcastle, N London, Northumbria, Nottingham, Nott Trent, Oxford, Oxford Brookes, Paisley, Plymouth, Portsmouth, QMW, Queen's Belfast, Reading, Royal Holloway, Salford, Sheffield, Sheffield Hallam, Southampton, St Andrews, Staffs, Stirling, Strathclyde, Surrey, Sussex, Swansea, Teesside, UEA, UMIST, UCL, Warwick, Westminster, Wolves, York
- **Statistics** Aberdeen, Aberystwyth, Bath, BUWE, Cardiff, CLancs, City, Derby, E London, Glamorgan, Glasgow, Glasgow Cal, Greenwich, Heriot-Watt, Herts, Lancaster, Liverpool, Liverpool JM, LSE, Luton, Middlesex, Newcastle, N London, Nott Trent, Plymouth, Portsmouth, QMW, Reading, Sheffield, Sheffield Hallam, St Andrews, Strathclyde, Sussex, Swansea, UMIST, UCL, Warwick

- **Other Mathematical and Informatics Sciences** BUWE, Coventry, De Montfort, Derby, E London, Exeter, Greenwich, Kingston, Liverpool JM, Luton, Man Met, N London, Portsmouth, QMW, Sheffield Hallam, Ulster, Wolves

....

Media Studies
Birmingham, CEngland, CLancs, Chelt & Gloucs, De Montfort, E London, Glamorgan, Glasgow Cal, Goldsmith's, Greenwich, Huddersfield, Lancaster, Lincs & Humbs, Liverpool JM, London Inst, Luton, Middlesex, Nene, Oxford Brookes, Paisley, Sheffield Hallam, Southampton Inst, Staffs, Stirling, Sunderland, Surrey Inst, Thames Valley, UEA, Ulster, Wolves

- **Communication Studies** Anglia, Bangor, Bath Spa, Bournemouth, Bradford, Brunel, Cardiff, CEngland, CLancs, Chelt & Gloucs, Coventry, Derby, E London, Glamorgan, Leeds, Leeds Met, Leicester, Lincs & Humbs, Liverpool, Loughborough, Luton, Man Met, Middlesex, Napier, N London, Nott Trent, Queen Margaret, Robert Gordon, Sheffield Hallam, Southampton Inst, Sunderland, Ulster, Wolves
- **Cinematics** Aberystwyth, Anglia, Bournemouth, Brighton, BUWE, Brunel, CEngland, CLancs, Chelt & Gloucs, Derby, Greenwich, Heriot-Watt, Kent, London Inst, Middlesex, Napier, Newcastle, N London, Northumbria, Nott Trent, Royal Holloway, Sheffield Hallam, Southampton Inst, Staffs, Sunderland, Surrey Inst, UEA, Warwick, Westminster, Wolves
- **Journalism** Bournemouth, Cardiff, CLancs, Lincs & Humbs, Liverpool JM, London Inst, Middlesex, Napier, Nott Trent, Sheffield, Southampton Inst, Staffs, Surrey Inst
- **Publishing** Luton, Middlesex, Napier, Oxford Brookes, Robert Gordon

....

Medicine
Aberdeen, Birmingham, Bristol, Cambridge, Dundee, Edinburgh, Glasgow, Imperial, King's Coll, Leeds, Leicester, Liverpool, Manchester, Newcastle, Nottingham, Oxford, QMW, Queen's Belfast, Royal Free, Sheffield, Southampton, St Andrews, St George's, UCL, Wales Coll Med

- **Dentistry** Birmingham, Bristol, Dundee, Glasgow, King's Coll, Leeds, Liverpool, Manchester, Newcastle, QMW, Queen's Belfast, Sheffield, Wales Coll Med
- **Other Subjects Related to Medicine** Aberdeen, Anglia, Bath Spa, Birmingham, Bournemouth, Bradford, Brighton, BUWE, Brunel, CEngland, CLancs, City, Coventry, De Montfort, Derby, Durham, E London, Edinburgh, Glamorgan, Glasgow, Glasgow Cal, Greenwich, Herts, Huddersfield, Hull, Keele, King's Coll, Kingston, Leeds Met, Lincs & Humbs, Liverpool, Liverpool JM, London Inst, Manchester, Man Met, Middlesex, Napier, Nene, Newcastle, N London, Northumbria, Nottingham, Nott Trent, Oxford Brookes, Paisley, Plymouth, Portsmouth, Queen Margaret, Queen's Belfast, Reading, Robert Gordon, Salford, Sheffield, Sheffield Hallam, South Bank, Southampton, St George's, Staffs, Strathclyde, Sunderland, Teesside, Thames Valley, UEA, Ulster, UCL, Wales Coll Med, Westminster, Wolves, York

....

Middle-Eastern Languages
Durham, Edinburgh, Exeter, Lampeter, Leeds, Manchester, Oxford, Salford, SOAS, St Andrews, UCL

....

Modern Languages
Aston, Cambridge, CLancs, Derby, Durham, Edinburgh, Essex, Exeter, Heriot-Watt, Huddersfield, Hull, Lampeter, Leeds Met, Leicester, Liverpool, Nottingham, Oxford, Plymouth, Sheffield, Sheffield Hallam, St Andrews, Surrey, UEA, Ulster, Wolves

Music Anglia, Bangor, Bath Spa, Birmingham, Brighton, Bristol, Brunel, Cambridge, Cardiff, City, Coventry, Derby, Durham, Edinburgh, Exeter, Glasgow, Glasgow Cal, Goldsmith's, Herts, Huddersfield, Hull, King's Coll, Kingston, Lancaster, Leeds, Leeds Met, Lincs & Humbs, Liverpool, London Inst, Manchester, Middlesex, Napier, Nene, Newcastle, Nottingham, Oxford, Oxford Brookes, Queen's Belfast, Reading, Royal Holloway, Salford, Sheffield, SOAS, Southampton, Staffs, Strathclyde, Sunderland, Surrey, Thames Valley, UEA, Ulster, Westminster, Wolves, York

Nursing Abertay, Anglia, Bangor, Birmingham, Bournemouth, Brighton, BUWE, CEngland, CLancs, City, De Montfort, E London, Edinburgh, Glamorgan, Glasgow, Glasgow Cal, Greenwich, Herts, Huddersfield, Hull, King's Coll, Leeds, Leeds Met, Liverpool, Liverpool JM, Luton, Manchester, Middlesex, Nene, N London, Northumbria, Nottingham, Oxford Brookes, Plymouth, Queen Margaret, Reading, Robert Gordon, Salford, Sheffield Hallam, South Bank, Southampton, Stirling, Sunderland, Surrey, Swansea, Thames Valley, Ulster, Wales Coll Med

Nutrition Coventry, Glasgow Cal, Greenwich, Huddersfield, King's Coll, Kingston, Leeds Met, Luton, N London, Nottingham, Oxford Brookes, Queen Margaret, Robert Gordon, Sheffield Hallam, South Bank, Southampton, Surrey, Ulster, Westminster

Oceanography Bangor, Birmingham, Greenwich, Huddersfield, Liverpool JM, Luton, Plymouth, QMW, Sheffield Hallam, Southampton, Stirling, Wolves

Ophthalmics/Audiology Anglia, Aston, Bradford, Cardiff, CLancs, City, Glasgow Cal, Liverpool, N London, Sheffield, Sheffield Hallam, Ulster, UMIST, Westminster

Pharmacy/Pharmacology Aberdeen, Aston, Bath, Bradford, Brighton, Bristol, Cambridge, Cardiff, CLancs, Coventry, De Montfort, Dundee, E London, Edinburgh, Glasgow, Greenwich, Herts, King's Coll, Leeds, Liverpool, Liverpool JM, Luton, Manchester, Middlesex, Napier, Newcastle, N London, Nottingham, Oxford Brookes, Portsmouth, Queen's Belfast, Robert Gordon, Salford, School of Pharmacy, Sheffield, Southampton, Strathclyde, Sunderland, UCL, Westminster, Wolves

Philosophy Aberdeen, Anglia, Birmingham, Bolton, Bradford, Brighton, Bristol, Cambridge, Cardiff, CLancs, Dundee, Durham, Edinburgh, Essex, Glamorgan, Glasgow, Greenwich, Herts, Heythrop, Hull, Kent, King's Coll, Lampeter, Lancaster, Leeds, Liverpool, London Guildhall, LSE, Manchester, Man Met, Middlesex, N London, Nottingham, Oxford, Queen's Belfast, Reading, Sheffield, Southampton, St Andrews, Staffs, Stirling, Swansea, UEA, Ulster, UCL, Warwick, Wolves, York

Physics Aberdeen, Aberystwyth, Bath, Birmingham, Bristol, Cambridge, Cardiff, CLancs, De Montfort, Dundee, Durham, Edinburgh, Exeter, Glamorgan, Glasgow, Glasgow Cal, Heriot-Watt, Herts, Hull, Imperial,

Keele, Kent, King's Coll, Kingston, Lancaster, Leeds, Leicester, Liverpool, Loughborough, Manchester, Man Met, Napier, Newcastle, Northumbria, Nottingham, Nott Trent, Oxford, Paisley, Portsmouth, QMW, Queen's Belfast, Reading, Robert Gordon, Royal Holloway, Salford, Sheffield, Sheffield Hallam, Southampton, St Andrews, Staffs, Strathclyde, Surrey, Sussex, Swansea, UMIST, UCL, Warwick, York

Politics Aberdeen, Aberystwyth, Birmingham, Bradford, Brighton, Bristol, BUWE, Brunel, Buckingham, Cardiff, CEngland, CLancs, De Montfort, Derby, Dundee, Durham, E London, Edinburgh, Essex, Exeter, Glamorgan, Glasgow, Greenwich, Herts, Huddersfield, Hull, Keele, Kent, Kingston, Lancaster, Leeds, Leeds Met, Leicester, Lincs & Humbs, Liverpool, London Guildhall, LSE, Luton, Manchester, Man Met, Middlesex, Newcastle, N London, Northumbria, Nottingham, Nott Trent, Oxford, Paisley, Plymouth, Portsmouth, QMW, Queen's Belfast, Reading, Robert Gordon, Sheffield, Sheffield Hallam, SOAS, South Bank, Southampton, Southampton Inst, St Andrews, Staffs, Stirling, Strathclyde, Swansea, Teesside, UEA, Ulster, Warwick, Westminster, Wolves, York

Portuguese King's Coll, Liverpool, Newcastle

Psychology
- **As a Biological Science** Aberdeen, Abertay, Anglia, Bangor, Bath Spa, Birmingham, Bolton, Bournemouth, Bristol, BUWE, Brunel, Cambridge, Cardiff, CLancs, City, Coventry, De Montfort, Derby, Dundee, Durham, E London, Edinburgh, Essex, Exeter, Glamorgan, Glasgow, Goldsmith's, Greenwich, Herts, Hull, Kent, Lancaster, Leeds, Leicester, Lincs & Humbs, Liverpool, Liverpool JM, London Guildhall, Loughborough, Luton, Manchester, Middlesex, Nene, Newcastle, Northumbria, Nottingham, Nott Trent, Oxford, Plymouth, Portsmouth, Queen's Belfast, Reading, Royal Holloway, Sheffield, Sheffield Hallam, South Bank, Southampton, Southampton Inst, St Andrews, Staffs, Stirling, Strathclyde, Surrey, Sussex, Swansea, Thames Valley, UEA, Ulster, UCL, Warwick, Westminster, Wolves, York
- **As a Social Science** Abertay, Aston, Bradford, Bristol, CLancs, De Montfort, Dundee, Durham, E London, Edinburgh, Exeter, Glamorgan, Glasgow Cal, Heriot-Watt, Huddersfield, Kent, Leeds Met, Leicester, London Guildhall, Loughborough, Luton, Man Met, Middlesex, N London, Queen Margaret, Sheffield Hallam, Sunderland, Swansea, Teesside, Thames Valley

Radiography Bangor, Bradford, BUWE, CEngland, City, Cranfield, Derby, Glasgow Cal, Herts, Leeds, Liverpool, Portsmouth, Queen Margaret, Robert Gordon, Salford, Sheffield Hallam, South Bank, St George's, Staffs, Teesside, Ulster, Wales Coll Med

Russian Birmingham, Bradford, Bristol, Durham, Essex, Glasgow, Leeds, Liverpool, Nottingham, Portsmouth, QMW, Sheffield, SSEES, St Andrews, Strathclyde, Sussex, Wolves

Science (Combined or General) Aberdeen, Anglia, Bath, Birmingham, Bolton, BUWE, Brunel, Cambridge, Cardiff, CLancs,

Cranfield, De Montfort, Derby, Dundee, Durham, E London, Exeter, Glamorgan, Glasgow, Glasgow Cal, Greenwich, Heriot-Watt, Herts, Huddersfield, Kingston, Lancaster, Leeds, Leicester, Liverpool, Liverpool JM, Luton, Man Met, Napier, Newcastle, N London, Nott Trent, Oxford Brookes, Paisley, Plymouth, QMW, Reading, Royal Holloway, Salford, Sheffield, Sheffield Hallam, Southampton, St Andrews, Strathclyde, Teesside, UEA, UCL, Wolves

Social Science
Bradford, CLancs, De Montfort, Durham, E London, Edinburgh, Essex, Glasgow, King's Coll, Lancaster, Leeds, Leeds Met, Liverpool, Liverpool JM, LSE, Luton, Manchester, Middlesex, N London, Northumbria, Nott Trent, Queen's Belfast, Salford, Sheffield, St Andrews, Staffs, Sussex, Swansea, UEA, Ulster, Westminster, Wolves

•**Social Policy & Administration** Anglia, Bath, Bath Spa, Birmingham, Bolton, Bradford, Brighton, Bristol, Brunel, Buckingham, Cardiff, CLancs, De Montfort, Durham, E London, Edinburgh, Glamorgan, Glasgow, Goldsmith's, Herts, Hull, Kent, Lancaster, Leeds, Leeds Met, Lincs & Humbs, London Guildhall, Loughborough, LSE, Luton, Manchester, Man Met, Middlesex, Napier, Newcastle, N London, Nottingham, Paisley, Plymouth, Portsmouth, Queen Margaret, Queen's Belfast, Royal Holloway, Salford, Sheffield Hallam, South Bank, Southampton, Staffs, Stirling, Swansea, Teesside, Thames Valley, Ulster, Wolves, York

•**Social Work** Anglia, Bath, Bournemouth, Bradford, Brighton, BUWE, Brunel, CEngland, CLancs, Chelt & Gloucs, Coventry, De Montfort, Derby, Dundee, Durham, E London, Edinburgh, Glamorgan, Glasgow Cal, Goldsmith's, Greenwich, Herts, Huddersfield, Kingston, Lancaster, Leeds Met, Lincs & Humbs, Liverpool JM, Luton, Man Met, Middlesex, N London, Northumbria, Nott Trent, Oxford Brookes, Paisley, Plymouth, Reading, Salford, Sheffield Hallam, Southampton Inst, Staffs, Stirling, Strathclyde, Sunderland, Teesside, Ulster, Ulster

Sociology
Aberdeen, Abertay, Anglia, Bangor, Bath, Bath Spa, Birmingham, Bolton, Bradford, Bristol, BUWE, Brunel, Cardiff, CEngland, CLancs, City, Coventry, De Montfort, Derby, Durham, E London, Edinburgh, Essex, Exeter, Glamorgan, Glasgow, Glasgow Cal, Goldsmith's, Greenwich, Herts, Huddersfield, Hull, Kent, Kingston, Lancaster, Leeds, Leeds Met, Leicester, Lincs & Humbs, Liverpool, Liverpool JM, London Guildhall, Loughborough, LSE, Luton, Manchester, Man Met, Middlesex, Nene, Newcastle, N London, Northumbria, Nottingham, Nott Trent, Oxford, Oxford Brookes, Paisley, Plymouth, Portsmouth, Queen's Belfast, Reading, Robert Gordon, Royal Holloway, Salford, Sheffield, Sheffield Hallam, South Bank, Southampton, Southampton Inst, Staffs, Stirling, Strathclyde, Sunderland, Surrey, Swansea, Teesside, Thames Valley, UEA, Ulster, Warwick, Westminster, Wolves, York

Scandinavian Languages
Edinburgh, Hull, UEA, UCL

Slavonic and East-European Languages
Glasgow, Nottingham, SSEES

Spanish
Aberdeen, Aberystwyth, Birmingham, Bradford, Bristol, Cardiff, CLancs, De Montfort, Derby, Durham, E London, Edinburgh, Exeter, Hull, Kent, King's Coll, Leeds, Leicester, Liverpool, London Guildhall, Man

Met, Middlesex, Newcastle, N London, Nottingham, Portsmouth, QMW, Queen's Belfast, Sheffield, Southampton, St Andrews, Stirling, Strathclyde, Swansea, Ulster, UCL, Wolves

Sports Science Aberdeen, Anglia, Bangor, Birmingham, Bolton, Brighton, Brunel, CLancs, Chelt & Gloucs, Coventry, De Montfort, Durham, E London, Essex, Exeter, Glamorgan, Greenwich, Herts, Kingston, Leeds, Leeds Met, Liverpool JM, Luton, Man Met, Middlesex, N London, Portsmouth, Sheffield Hallam, South Bank, Staffs, Stirling, Strathclyde, Sunderland, Swansea, Teesside, Westminster, Wolves

Textiles & Polymers Bolton, De Montfort, E London, Leeds, London Guildhall, London Inst, Man Met, Napier, Nene, N London, Sheffield, UMIST

Theology/Religious Studies Aberdeen, Bangor, Bath Spa, Birmingham, Bristol, BUWE, Cambridge, Cardiff, Chelt & Gloucs, Derby, Durham, Edinburgh, Exeter, Glasgow, Greenwich, Heythrop, Hull, Kent, King's Coll, Lampeter, Lancaster, Leeds, Manchester, Middlesex, Newcastle, Nottingham, Oxford, Queen's Belfast, Sheffield, SOAS, St Andrews, Stirling, Sunderland, Wolves

Tourism Abertay, Anglia, Bolton, Bournemouth, Brighton, CLancs, Coventry, Derby, Glamorgan, Glasgow Cal, Herts, Leeds Met, Lincs & Humbs, Luton, Napier, N London, Northumbria, Paisley, Plymouth, Queen Margaret, Sheffield Hallam, South Bank, Southampton Inst, Sunderland, Thames Valley, Wolves

Veterinary Science Bristol, Cambridge, Edinburgh, Glasgow, Liverpool, Royal Vet

Zoology Aberdeen, Aberystwyth, Bangor, Birmingham, Bristol, Cambridge, Cardiff, Dundee, Durham, E London, Edinburgh, Glasgow, Imperial, Leeds, Leicester, Liverpool, Liverpool JM, Manchester, Newcastle, Nottingham, QMW, Queen's Belfast, Reading, Royal Holloway, Sheffield, Southampton, Swansea, UCL

c
o
u
r
s
e
s

pu s h tables

Where would education be without tables? There is a great tradition from the the Periodic Table, times tables, time-tables, log tables, until most recently, the government's own league tables. And, of course, school desks, which are tables. Sort of.

Never one to buck a trend, push introduces the tables to end all tables - the crucial guides to clubs and sports and the controversial reality of hard facts.

 CLUBS

Some clubs and societies are available at most colleges. So, rather than bore you rigid listing them in every college profile, push has detailed them in the following pages (780 to 785), so you can see if there's rock at Reading or karate at Keele.

 VITAL STATISTICS

What you want to do is get those colleges up against the wall and see how they look side by side. So on pages 786 to 791 push has distilled its finest facts and charted them: the sex ratio; the founding year; the student numbers; the level of care; the numbers who enter through clearing; the numbers who flunk; the cost and availability of housing; the cost of booze (average cost of a pint of beer/glass of wine); the employment prospects; and the bill of debt at the end of the day (including student loans).

NB Some smaller colleges have been left out of the clubs tables because they've hardly got any anyway. For a fuller explanation of the statistical data see 'How to use push' (page 9).

Column headers (universities, left to right):

1. UNIVERSITY OF ABERDEEN
2. UNIVERSITY OF ABERTAY DUNDEE
3. ABERYSTWYTH U OF WALES
4. ANGLIA POLYTECHNIC UNIVERSITY
5. ASTON UNIVERSITY
6. BANGOR U OF WALES
7. UNIVERSITY OF BATH
8. BATH SPA UNIVERSITY COLLEGE
9. BIRKBECK COLLEGE LONDON
10. UNIVERSITY OF BIRMINGHAM
11. BOLTON UNIVERSITY
12. BOURNEMOUTH UNIVERSITY
13. UNIVERSITY OF BRADFORD
14. UNIVERSITY OF BRIGHTON
15. BRISTOL, UNIV OF W OF ENGLAND
16. UNIVERSITY OF BRISTOL
17. BRUNEL UNIVERSITY
18. UNIVERSITY OF BUCKINGHAM
19. BUCKINGHAMSHIRE UNIV COLLEGE
20. UNIVERSITY OF CAMBRIDGE
21. CARDIFF U OF WALES

clubs

NON-SPORTING

- African-Caribbean
- Amnesty
- Animal Rights
- Anti-racist/Anti-nazi
- Asian
- BUNAC
- Catholic
- Christian Union
- Conservation
- Conservative
- Dance
- Debating
- Drama
- Film making
- Green/Environment
- Industrial Society
- Irish Society
- Islamic
- Jewish
- Labour
- Lesbian/Gay/Bisexual
- Lib Dem
- Orchestra(s)
- Photography
- Rock/Indie Music
- SF & Fantasy
- Socialist Worker (SWSS)
- Third World First

SPORTING

- Archery
- Athletics
- Badminton
- Basketball
- Canoeing
- Chess
- Climbing
- Cricket
- Cross country
- Cycling
- Fencing
- Football
- Golf
- Hill-walking
- Hockey
- Horse-riding
- Judo
- Karate
- Netball
- Orienteering
- Rugby
- Sailing
- Skiing
- Squash
- Sub-aqua
- Swimming
- Table tennis
- Tae Kwan Do
- Trampolining
- Volleyball

780

Directory of university clubs and societies. Columns (left to right):

1. UNIV OF CENTRAL ENGLAND
2. UNIV OF CENTRAL LANCASHIRE
3. CHELTENHAM & GLOUCESTER
4. CITY UNIVERSITY
5. COURTAULD INSTITUTE, LONDON
6. COVENTRY UNIVERSITY
7. CRANFIELD UNIVERSITY
8. DE MONTFORT UNIVERSITY
9. UNIVERSITY OF DERBY
10. UNIVERSITY OF DUNDEE
11. UNIVERSITY OF DURHAM
12. UNIVERSITY OF EAST LONDON
13. UNIVERSITY OF EDINBURGH
14. UNIVERSITY OF ESSEX
15. UNIVERSITY OF EXETER
16. UNIVERSITY OF GLAMORGAN
17. UNIVERSITY OF GLASGOW
18. GLASGOW CALEDONIAN UNIVERSITY
19. GOLDSMITH'S COLLEGE, LONDON
20. UNIVERSITY OF GREENWICH
21. HERIOT-WATT UNIVERSITY

NON-SPORTING

- African-Caribbean
- Amnesty
- Animal Rights
- Anti-racist/Anti-nazi
- Asian
- BUNAC
- Catholic
- Christian Union
- Conservation
- Conservative
- Dance
- Debating
- Drama
- Film making
- Green/Environment
- Industrial Society
- Irish Society
- Islamic
- Jewish
- Labour
- Lesbian/Gay/Bisexual
- Lib Dem
- Orchestra(s)
- Photography
- Rock/Indie Music
- SF & Fantasy
- Socialist Worker (SWSS)
- Third World First

SPORTING

- Archery
- Athletics
- Badminton
- Basketball
- Canoeing
- Chess
- Climbing
- Cricket
- Cross country
- Cycling
- Fencing
- Football
- Golf
- Hill-walking
- Hockey
- Horse-riding
- Judo
- Karate
- Netball
- Orienteering
- Rugby
- Sailing
- Skiing
- Squash
- Sub-aqua
- Swimming
- Table tennis
- Tae Kwan Do
- Trampolining
- Volleyball

clubs

c
l
u
b
s

	University of Hertfordshire	Heythrop College London	University of Huddersfield	University of Hull	Imperial College London	Keele University	Univ of Kent at Canterbury	King's College London	Kingston University	Lampeter U of Wales	Lancaster University	Leeds Metropolitan University	University of Leeds	University of Leicester	University of Lincs & Humbs	Liverpool University	Liverpool John Moores Univ	University of Liverpool	London Guildhall University	London Institute	Loughborough University
NON-SPORTING																					
African-Caribbean	●		●	●	●	●	●	●		●		●	●		●	●		●		●	●
Amnesty		●		●	●	●	●	●	●			●		●		●		●	●	●	
Animal Rights			●								●			●	●	●					
Anti-racist/Anti-nazi		●						●	●									●			
Asian	●		●	●	●	●	●	●			●		●		●	●	●				●
BUNAC				●				●						●				●			
Catholic			●	●	●	●	●	●			●		●		●	●	●	●		●	
Christian Union	●	●	●	●	●	●	●	●	●	●	●	●	●	●	●	●	●	●	●	●	●
Conservation						●						●						●			
Conservative			●	●		●	●				●		●		●						
Dance	●						●					●						●			●
Debating		●	●	●	●	●	●	●		●			●		●			●			
Drama			●	●	●	●	●	●	●	●	●	●	●	●	●	●	●	●			●
Film making	●				●		●									●				●	
Green/Environment	●		●	●		●	●	●		●	●		●		●	●	●		●		●
Industrial Society			●	●		●			●			●		●						●	
Irish Society		●	●				●	●		●	●							●			
Islamic		●	●	●	●	●	●	●	●		●		●	●	●	●	●	●	●		●
Jewish	●			●	●	●	●	●				●	●	●		●	●	●			●
Labour			●	●		●	●		●		●		●								
Lesbian/Gay/Bisexual	●	●	●	●	●	●	●	●	●		●	●	●	●		●	●	●	●	●	●
Lib Dem			●	●							●		●								
Orchestra(s)		●	●	●	●		●			●			●					●			
Photography	●				●	●		●		●			●				●				●
Rock/Indie Music			●	●	●	●	●				●		●	●	●	●	●				●
SF & Fantasy			●	●	●	●	●	●			●		●	●		●		●			●
Socialist Worker (SWSS)			●	●	●	●	●				●		●		●			●	●		
Third World First			●	●			●						●								
SPORTING																					
Archery	●		●		●		●				●		●	●		●		●			●
Athletics			●	●	●	●	●	●	●		●	●	●	●	●	●	●		●		●
Badminton	●		●	●	●	●	●	●	●	●	●	●	●	●	●	●	●	●	●		●
Basketball	●		●	●	●	●	●	●	●		●	●	●	●		●	●	●	●		●
Canoeing	●		●		●	●	●	●			●		●	●		●		●			●
Chess	●		●	●		●	●		●		●			●		●			●		●
Climbing	●		●	●	●		●	●			●		●	●		●		●	●	●	●
Cricket	●	●	●	●	●	●	●	●	●	●	●	●	●	●	●	●	●	●	●	●	●
Cross country			●	●	●	●	●	●			●		●	●	●	●		●			●
Cycling	●		●	●	●	●	●				●		●	●		●		●	●		●
Fencing	●			●	●	●	●	●			●		●	●		●		●			●
Football	●	●	●	●	●	●	●	●	●	●	●	●	●	●	●	●	●	●	●	●	●
Golf	●		●	●	●	●	●	●			●		●	●		●		●	●		●
Hill-walking			●	●	●	●	●				●		●	●		●		●			●
Hockey	●		●	●	●	●	●	●	●		●	●	●	●	●	●	●	●			●
Horse-riding	●				●	●	●				●		●	●		●		●			●
Judo	●		●	●		●	●	●			●		●	●		●		●			●
Karate	●		●	●	●	●	●	●			●		●	●		●		●			●
Netball	●		●	●	●	●	●	●	●		●	●	●	●	●	●	●	●			●
Orienteering			●	●	●	●					●		●	●		●		●			●
Rugby	●		●	●	●	●	●	●	●	●	●	●	●	●	●	●	●	●	●		●
Sailing	●		●	●	●	●	●	●	●		●		●	●		●		●			●
Skiing	●		●	●	●	●	●	●	●		●		●	●	●	●	●	●			●
Squash	●		●	●	●	●	●	●	●		●	●	●	●	●	●	●	●			●
Sub-aqua	●		●	●	●	●	●	●			●		●	●		●	●	●			●
Swimming	●		●	●	●	●	●	●	●		●	●	●	●	●	●	●	●	●		●
Table tennis			●	●	●	●	●	●	●		●		●	●	●	●	●	●			●
Tae Kwan Do	●		●	●	●	●	●	●			●		●	●		●	●	●	●		
Trampolining			●		●	●	●	●			●		●	●		●		●			●
Volleyball	●		●	●	●	●	●	●	●		●	●	●	●	●	●	●	●			●

(782)

	LSE	Luton University	University of Manchester	Manchester Metropolitan	Middlesex University	Napier University	Nene University College	University of Newcastle	University of North London	University of Northumbria	University of Nottingham	Nottingham Trent University	University of Oxford	Oxford Brookes University	University of Paisley	University of Plymouth	University of Portsmouth	Q Mary & Westfield College	Queen Margaret College	Queen's University Belfast	University of Reading
NON-SPORTING																					
African-Caribbean	•		•	•			•		•				•				•	•	•		•
Amnesty	•		•	•			•		•				•				•	•		•	•
Animal Rights	•	•	•			•			•		•		•				•			•	•
Anti-racist/Anti-nazi	•		•					•													•
Asian	•		•	•	•	•		•		•		•	•				•		•	•	•
BUNAC				•					•				•								•
Catholic	•		•					•			•						•		•	•	•
Christian Union	•	•	•	•			•	•			•	•	•	•			•	•	•	•	•
Conservation		•	•		•		•				•		•				•		•	•	•
Conservative	•		•	•				•			•		•				•	•	•	•	•
Dance	•	•	•	•			•				•		•				•	•	•		•
Debating	•	•	•	•	•						•		•					•	•	•	•
Drama	•	•	•	•			•	•			•	•	•				•	•	•	•	•
Film making	•		•	•	•						•		•							•	•
Green/Environment	•		•	•			•			•	•		•	•		•		•		•	•
Industrial Society			•								•		•			•					
Irish Society	•		•	•		•		•			•		•				•			•	•
Islamic	•	•	•	•	•	•		•	•	•	•	•	•	•			•		•	•	•
Jewish	•	•	•	•				•			•		•						•	•	•
Labour	•		•						•				•				•	•	•	•	•
Lesbian/Gay/Bisexual	•	•	•	•				•	•		•		•				•	•	•	•	•
Lib Dem	•		•					•			•		•				•		•	•	•
Orchestra(s)	•		•	•	•						•		•	•			•			•	•
Photography			•					•			•		•						•	•	•
Rock/Indie Music		•	•			•			•				•				•	•		•	
SF & Fantasy			•	•				•	•				•	•					•	•	•
Socialist Worker (SWSS)	•	•	•		•	•		•			•		•				•	•	•	•	•
Third World First			•								•		•							•	•
SPORTING																					
Archery			•		•			•			•		•			•			•	•	•
Athletics		•	•	•	•			•		•	•		•	•			•		•	•	•
Badminton	•	•	•	•	•			•		•	•	•	•	•		•	•	•	•	•	•
Basketball	•	•	•	•	•	•		•	•	•	•	•	•	•		•	•	•	•	•	•
Canoeing		•	•	•	•		•	•	•		•		•			•	•		•	•	•
Chess	•	•	•					•			•		•			•	•	•	•	•	•
Climbing	•	•	•	•	•			•			•		•			•	•	•	•	•	•
Cricket	•	•	•	•	•	•		•		•	•	•	•			•	•	•	•	•	•
Cross country		•	•								•		•					•	•	•	•
Cycling		•	•					•			•		•					•	•	•	•
Fencing		•	•	•				•	•		•	•	•			•	•	•	•	•	•
Football	•	•	•	•	•	•	•	•	•	•	•	•	•	•	•	•	•	•	•	•	•
Golf	•	•	•	•	•	•		•		•	•	•	•			•	•		•	•	•
Hill-walking		•	•								•		•							•	•
Hockey	•	•	•	•	•	•		•		•	•	•	•			•	•	•	•	•	•
Horse-riding			•					•			•		•				•		•	•	•
Judo	•	•	•	•	•			•	•	•	•	•	•			•	•	•	•	•	•
Karate	•	•	•	•	•	•		•	•	•	•	•	•	•		•	•	•	•	•	•
Netball	•	•	•	•	•	•		•		•	•	•	•			•	•	•	•	•	•
Orienteering			•			•					•		•				•			•	•
Rugby	•	•	•	•	•	•		•		•	•	•	•			•	•	•	•	•	•
Sailing	•	•	•	•				•			•		•			•	•	•	•	•	•
Skiing		•	•	•	•			•		•	•	•	•			•	•	•	•	•	•
Squash	•	•	•	•	•	•		•		•	•	•	•			•	•	•	•	•	•
Sub-aqua	•	•	•	•				•			•		•			•	•	•	•	•	•
Swimming	•	•	•	•	•	•		•	•	•	•	•	•			•	•	•	•	•	•
Table tennis		•	•	•	•	•		•			•		•			•	•	•	•	•	•
Tae Kwan Do	•	•	•	•	•	•		•			•		•			•	•	•	•	•	•
Trampolining		•	•	•	•			•			•		•			•	•		•	•	•
Volleyball	•	•	•	•	•	•	•	•	•	•	•	•	•	•	•	•	•	•	•	•	•

c l u b s

783

clubs

Column key:
1. Robert Gordon University
2. Royal Academy of Music
3. Royal College of Music
4. Royal Free Hospital
5. Royal Veterinary College
6. Royal Holloway, London
7. University of St Andrews
8. St George's Hospital
9. School of Pharmacy, London
10. University of Salford
11. Sheffield Hallam University
12. University of Sheffield
13. University of Southampton
14. Southampton Institute
15. SOAS
16. South Bank University
17. Staffordshire University
18. SSEES
19. University of Stirling
20. University of Strathclyde
21. University of Sunderland

NON-SPORTING

	1	2	3	4	5	6	7	8	9	10	11	12	13	14	15	16	17	18	19	20	21
African-Caribbean							•			•		•	•		•	•		•	•		•
Amnesty							•		•	•		•	•		•	•			•		•
Animal Rights												•			•	•					
Anti-racist/Anti-nazi										•		•			•				•		•
Asian							•			•		•	•		•	•		•	•		•
BUNAC	•						•			•		•	•		•	•		•	•		•
Catholic										•		•	•		•			•	•		•
Christian Union	•	•	•	•			•			•		•	•		•	•			•		•
Conservation					•		•			•		•							•		
Conservative	•											•			•			•	•		•
Dance							•			•		•	•		•			•	•		•
Debating	•						•		•	•		•			•	•		•	•		
Drama	•			•		•	•			•			•		•	•		•	•		•
Film making							•			•		•			•				•		
Green/Environment	•						•			•		•	•		•	•		•	•		•
Industrial Society	•									•		•			•			•			
Irish Society							•			•		•	•		•			•	•		•
Islamic	•						•		•	•	•	•	•	•	•	•	•	•	•		•
Jewish				•			•			•		•	•		•	•	•	•			
Labour							•			•		•	•		•				•	•	
Lesbian/Gay/Bisexual	•						•			•		•	•		•	•		•	•		•
Lib Dem							•			•		•			•				•		
Orchestra(s)		•	•	•			•		•	•		•									•
Photography	•						•		•	•		•						•	•		•
Rock/Indie Music										•		•						•			
SF & Fantasy	•						•			•	•	•	•						•	•	•
Socialist Worker (SWSS)										•		•			•				•		
Third World First																					

SPORTING

	1	2	3	4	5	6	7	8	9	10	11	12	13	14	15	16	17	18	19	20	21
Archery							•			•		•			•				•	•	•
Athletics							•			•	•	•			•				•	•	•
Badminton	•			•		•	•		•	•	•	•			•				•	•	•
Basketball	•			•			•			•	•	•	•	•	•				•	•	•
Canoeing	•						•			•	•	•	•		•				•	•	•
Chess	•				•		•			•	•	•		•	•		•	•	•	•	•
Climbing	•			•		•	•	•	•	•	•	•	•		•				•	•	•
Cricket	•						•			•	•	•	•		•				•	•	•
Cross country							•			•		•	•		•				•	•	•
Cycling							•			•	•	•	•		•				•	•	•
Fencing	•						•		•	•		•	•		•				•	•	•
Football	•	•	•	•		•	•		•	•	•	•	•	•	•	•			•	•	•
Golf	•			•		•	•			•	•	•	•		•				•	•	•
Hill-walking	•			•			•			•		•	•		•				•	•	•
Hockey	•			•		•	•	•	•	•	•	•	•		•		•		•	•	•
Horse-riding	•						•			•		•	•		•				•	•	•
Judo	•						•			•		•	•		•				•		•
Karate	•						•			•	•	•	•		•	•			•	•	•
Netball	•	•	•	•		•	•	•	•	•	•	•	•		•	•			•	•	•
Orienteering	•			•			•			•		•	•		•				•	•	•
Rugby				•		•	•	•	•	•	•	•	•		•		•		•	•	•
Sailing				•			•	•		•		•	•		•				•	•	•
Skiing	•						•			•		•	•		•				•	•	•
Squash	•			•		•	•		•	•	•	•	•		•				•	•	•
Sub-aqua	•			•		•	•		•	•	•	•	•		•				•	•	•
Swimming	•						•			•	•	•	•		•	•			•	•	•
Table tennis				•			•			•	•	•	•		•	•		•	•	•	•
Tae Kwan Do	•						•			•		•	•		•	•			•	•	•
Trampolining	•						•			•		•							•	•	•
Volleyball				•			•		•	•		•	•		•	•		•	•	•	•

c
l
u
b
s

	Surrey	Surrey Inst.	Sussex	Swansea	Teesside	Thames Valley	UEA	Ulster	UMIST	UC London	UW Coll Medicine	Warwick	Westminster	Wolverhampton	Wye College	York
NON-SPORTING																
African-Caribbean	●	●	●		●	●		●		●	●	●	●			
Amnesty	●		●	●			●		●		●	●	●	●		
Animal Rights			●	●					●		●	●	●			
Anti-racist/Anti-nazi			●	●					●							
Asian	●		●	●	●		●		●	●		●				
BUNAC			●						●			●				
Catholic	●		●	●					●	●		●				
Christian Union	●		●	●		●	●	●	●	●		●				
Conservation			●		●			●	●							
Conservative			●	●					●		●	●	●			
Dance		●	●	●			●	●	●		●		●			
Debating			●						●			●				
Drama		●	●	●				●	●		●		●			
Film making		●					●		●							
Green/Environment	●		●		●			●	●		●	●	●			
Industrial Society								●	●				●			
Irish Society				●		●	●	●								
Islamic	●		●	●	●	●		●	●		●	●				
Jewish		●	●	●				●	●	●	●	●				
Labour			●	●		●		●	●			●				
Lesbian/Gay/Bisexual	●	●	●	●	●		●	●	●	●	●	●	●	●		
Lib Dem			●	●				●	●		●	●				
Orchestra(s)		●	●	●			●	●	●		●	●				
Photography			●				●		●			●	●			
Rock/Indie Music	●	●	●		●			●	●			●	●			
SF & Fantasy			●	●					●			●	●			
Socialist Worker (SWSS)			●	●				●	●			●				
Third World First			●	●			●		●			●				
SPORTING																
Archery	●	●	●	●		●			●		●		●			
Athletics	●	●	●	●		●		●	●	●		●	●			
Badminton	●	●	●	●	●	●	●	●	●	●	●	●	●			
Basketball	●	●	●	●	●	●	●	●	●	●	●	●	●			
Canoeing	●	●	●	●	●		●	●	●	●	●	●	●			
Chess	●	●	●			●		●	●			●	●			
Climbing	●	●	●					●	●			●	●			
Cricket	●	●	●	●		●	●	●	●	●	●	●	●			
Cross country	●	●	●						●			●				
Cycling	●	●	●				●		●			●	●	●		
Fencing	●	●	●	●	●	●	●	●	●		●	●	●			
Football	●	●	●	●	●	●	●	●	●	●	●	●	●	●		
Golf	●		●	●				●	●		●	●	●			
Hill-walking			●		●			●	●			●				
Hockey		●	●	●		●	●	●	●	●	●	●	●			
Horse-riding	●		●	●		●		●		●		●	●	●		
Judo	●	●	●		●		●	●	●		●	●	●			
Karate	●		●	●		●	●	●	●		●	●	●			
Netball			●	●	●	●	●	●	●		●	●	●			
Orienteering	●								●							
Rugby	●		●	●	●		●	●	●	●	●	●	●			
Sailing	●	●	●	●	●		●	●	●	●		●	●			
Skiing	●	●	●	●	●		●	●	●	●	●	●	●			
Squash	●	●	●	●	●		●	●	●	●	●	●	●			
Sub-aqua	●		●	●	●		●	●	●		●	●	●			
Swimming		●	●	●	●		●	●		●	●	●	●			
Table tennis		●	●	●		●		●	●			●	●			
Tae Kwan Do	●		●	●			●		●			●				
Trampolining			●		●		●		●			●				
Volleyball	●		●	●	●	●	●	●	●	●	●	●	●			

	SEX RATIO	YEAR FOUNDED	NUMBER OF UNDERGRADS	NUMBER OF PART TIME STUDENTS	NUMBER OF POSTGRADS	% IN VIA CLEARING
University of Aberdeen	49:51	1495	8,351	115	1,250	12
University of Abertay Dundee	50:50	1994	3,316	349	206	n/a
Aberystwyth	49:51	1872	5,335	365	859	17
Anglia Polytechnic University	40:60	1989	7,000	3,843	330	22
Aston University	52:48	1966	4,403	0	504	8
Bangor	49:51	1884	5,223	97	854	11
University of Bath	59:41	1966	5,108	0	1,097	2
Bath Spa	27:73	1983	2,274	38	262	2
University of Birmingham	51:49	1900	13,197	529	3,250	0
Bolton Institute	54:46	1982	4,000	3,000	950	10
Bournemouth University	53:47	1976	7,714	2,813	454	14
University of Bradford	54:46	1966	6,300	250	1,460	18
University of Brighton	42:58	1976	7,929	875	641	20
University of Bristol	52:48	1876	9,112	975	3,465	1
Bristol, W of E	49:51	1969	11,992	1,917	988	n/a
Brunel University	57:43	1966	7,886	678	1,171	24.5
University of Buckingham	55:45	1976	544	41	116	5.5
Buckinghamshire	50:50	1893	6,000	2,000	600	20
University of Cambridge	56:44	1284	11,223	0	4,688	n/a
Cardiff	49:51	1883	11,468	0	2,404	3
University of Central Lancashire	43:57	1828	11,581	7,304	409	n/a
Cheltenham & Gloucester CHE	41:59	1990	4,413	702	366	13.5
City University	50:50	1893	4,465	279	1,692	12
Courtauld Institute of Art	25:75	1932	115	0	125	0
Coventry University	55:45	1970	9,785	3,694	1,576	n/a
Cranfield	75:25	1975	613	0	642	3
De Montfort University	49:51	1969	15,650	3,100	1,500	19.5
University of Derby	45:55	1851	9,300	3,500	1,000	30
University of Dundee	43:57	1967	7,524	424	749	10
University of Durham	50:50	1832	7,843	553	1,214	2
University of East London	50:50	1970	8,400	2,900	1,820	n/a
University of Edinburgh	53:47	1583	13,228	379	3,560	0
University of Essex	53:47	1964	4,175	35	1,535	n/a
University of Exeter	46:54	1955	6,943	35	1,462	6
University of Glamorgan	60:40	1913	10,879	6,269	1,607	n/a
Glasgow University	45:55	1451	15,721	2,932	1,948	2
Glasgow Caledonian University	41:59	1971	9,564	1,960	883	16
Goldsmiths College	34:66	1891	3,797	1,141	992	17
University of Greenwich	50:50	1890	8,577	3,067	1,244	n/a
Heriot-Watt University	71:29	1966	4,750	465	900	10

% OF MATURE STUDENTS	% OF OVERSEAS STUDENTS	STUDENTS PER COUNSELLOR	FLUNK RATES	AVERAGE COST OF ACCOMMODATION PER WEEK	% IN COLLEGE ACCOMMODATION	BOOZE INDEX	% OF GRADS UNEMPLOYED AFTER 6 MONTHS	STUDENT'S AVERAGE DEBT PER YEAR
21	12	2386	n/a	£57	39	£1.40	5.5	£1,400
31	11.3	1096	n/a	£42	24	£1.25	6.2	£1,350
17	12	2134	9	£45	37	£1.17	5.8	£1,850
48	10.8	1400	n/a	£52	30	£1.30	5.1	£1,350
5	16	1100	n/a	£45	47	£1.25	5.3	£1,850
20	4.7	2,612	n/a	£50	37	£1.33	7.4	£3,450
10.6	14	1,659	30	£57	29	£1.20	11	£2,400
40	7	2,274	n/a	£41	26	£1.18	10	£2,250
14	10.6	1,320	n/a	£69	37	£1.28	3.6	£1,600
72	n/a	1,333	n/a	£41	18	£1.20	5.1	£1,700
25	8	n/a	n/a	£56	9	£1.20	9.8	£1,950
20	16	3,150	5	£51	36	£1	9.6	£950
48	14	1,982	39	£56	20	£1.20	10	£1,700
11	16	868	5	£53	40	£1.15	3.7	£1,050
56.5	5	922	n/a	£41	9	£1.25	11.4	£2,600
36	7.5	1,314	n/a	£48	36	£1.60	8	£3,050
40	70	701	n/a	£58	83	£1.53	5	n/a
20	12	1,500	33	£58	23	£1.23	6.9	£2,600
5.2	6.3	n/a	11	£43	95	£1.25	5	£800
16	11	3,277	24	£51	38	£1.28	6	£1,350
53	6	2,106	n/a	£49	13	£1.40	15	£1,900
52	1.7	1,261	23	£64	13	£1.20	7.9	£1,700
35	15	1,276	28	£75	20	£1.30	6.5	£1,600
16	2	340	n/a	n/a	n/a	n/a	n/a	n/a
47	15	1,957	24	£58	18	£1.57	8	£1,200
32	13	623	n/a	£55	100	£1.37	6	n/a
25	9	3,913	n/a	£57	19	£1.10	7.5	£2,150
52	5	930	30	£47	28	£1.25	24	£2,250
32	9	3762	n/a	£50	21	£1.10	4.8	£1,400
13	4	1,307	n/a	£59	58	99p	6	£1,650
80	16	1,400	n/a	£44	10	£1.20	15	£1,950
13	10	2,646	n/a	£67	43	£1.30	8	n/a
28	37	2,088	16	£47	65	£1.10	8.8	£1,600
11.8	7	1,542	17	£67	61	£1.18	6.3	£1,750
n/a	9.1	5,628	17	£52	9	£1.20	7.2	£2,100
18	7	8,549	n/a	£50	23	£1.35	6.8	£900
24	5.2	2,733	n/a	£57	5	£1.25	8.6	£1,350
40	17.5	2,531	27	£54	32	£1.43	9	£3,950
58	n/a	2,144	n/a	£56	28	£1.20	14	£2,800
18	15	6,115	n/a	£52	23	£1.25	7.8	n/a

Stats

	SEX RATIO	YEAR FOUNDED	NUMBER OF UNDERGRADS	NUMBER OF PART TIME STUDENTS	NUMBER OF POSTGRADS	% IN VIA CLEARING
University of Hertfordshire	50:50	1952	10,655	4,342	2,269	12
Heythrop College	60:40	1614	140	0	345	20
University of Huddersfield	50:50	1841	10,012	5,339	2,142	19
University of Hull	45:55	1927	6,466	868	1,080	5
Imperial College	69:31	1907	6,240	0	2,532	3.4
Keele University	48:52	1949	4,164	36	877	10
University of Kent	43:57	1965	5,898	111	1,103	n/a
King's College, London	41:59	1829	11,500	190	4,500	n/a
Kingston University	49:51	1971	10,743	1,470	833	15
Lampeter	50:50	1822	1,542	182	252	35
Lancaster University	49:51	1964	6,981	121	2,103	12
University of Leeds	48:52	1887	16,981	943	5,193	4
Leeds Metropolitan University	50:50	1970	11,000	12,000	690	20
University of Leicester	48:52	1921	7,164	64	1,493	9.7
University of Lincs & Humbs	50:50	1983	9,727	2,474	1,421	18
University of Liverpool	51:49	1881	10,200	250	1,650	4
Liverpool John Moores	48:52	1970	13,652	6,748	680	15.4
London Guildhall University	50:50	1970	7,541	1,145	400	20
London Institute	37:63	1986	5,942	575	555	5
Loughborough University	64:36	1966	8,657	84	1,047	5.8
LSE	55:45	1895	2,698	56	2,537	n/a
University of Luton	46:54	1957	8,200	1,800	860	30
University of Manchester	50:50	1851	15,557	669	3,072	n/a
Manchester Metropolitan	44:56	1970	18,513	6,186	1,640	20
Middlesex University	44:56	1973	16,657	698	1,027	n/a
Napier University	51:49	1964	7,966	1,965	684	n/a
Nene	44:56	1975	7,365	520	690	25
University of Newcastle	53:47	1834	10,063	45	1,859	4.6
University of North London	44:56	1896	8,232	2,465	724	29
University of Northumbria	47:53	1969	11,237	1,850	832	33
University of Nottingham	48:52	1881	11,990	6,430	4,530	3
Nottingham Trent University	52:48	1970	14,367	1,077	844	14
University of Oxford	60:40	c1150	10,823	0	4,413	0
Oxford Brookes University	44:56	1865	8,350	516	1,182	10
University of Paisley	42:58	1897	5,819	2,158	445	18
University of Plymouth	52:48	1970	15,660	4,264	630	18.6
University of Portsmouth	60:40	1969	11,933	3,771	1,708	n/a
Queen Margaret College	20:80	1875	2,588	733	42	16
Queen Mary & Westfield College	55:45	1934	6,625	0	1,553	10
Queen's University, Belfast	44:56	1845	12,193	2,177	5,132	3.6

% OF MATURE STUDENTS	% OF OVERSEAS STUDENTS	STUDENTS PER COUNSELLOR	FLUNK RATES	AVERAGE COST OF ACCOMMODATION PER WEEK	% IN COLLEGE ACCOMMODATION	BOOZE INDEX	% OF GRADS UNEMPLOYED AFTER 6 MONTHS	STUDENT'S AVERAGE DEBT PER YEAR
39	6	3,044	n/a	£45	33	£1.15	9.1	£3,500
75	4	510	n/a	£55	n/a	n/a	n/a	n/a
29	3.3	1,540	n/a	£51	22	£1.30	6	£950
17	12	2,155	n/a	£51	30	98p	3.8	n/a
44	27.6	2,080	23	£57	37	£1.25	4.6	£2,150
18	9	641	10	£34	76	£1.20	8.4	£1,500
25	23	1,685	8	£66	54	£1.10	4.3	£1,000
33.7	18	639	n/a	£80	32	£1.40	6.4	£1,500
22	9.8	1343	n/a	£53	21	£1.30	5	£2,250
42	7.3	1,542	n/a	£53	38	£1.40	9.6	£3,050
18	14	997	19	£44	52	£1.30	6.1	£950
16.2	10.1	2,612	15	£59	41	£1.33	10.5	£1,850
54	2	3,667	n/a	£49	20	£1.34	9.8	£2,400
14	10	1,791	n/a	£57	55	£1.25	4.6	£2,200
57	11	4,864	n/a	£50	35	£1.20	14	£2,200
19	10	2,914	10	£55	23	£1.38	7	£1,100
39	8	1,950	26	£46	13	£1.16	8.1	£1,550
49	12	1,885	n/a	£64	6	£1.33	9	£1,850
35	26	2,377	18	£63	9	£1.15	17	n/a
12.5	10	2,266	5	£56	64	£1.30	3.6	£1,500
n/a	51.7	1,349	3	£74	39	£1.20	6.8	n/a
14	14	631	n/a	£46	13	£1.20	9	£1,550
11.5	12	1,945	14	£61	56	£1.15	6.8	£1,900
53	6	3,702	21	n/a	n/a	n/a	9.4	£2,050
70	20	3,331	22	£53	14	£1.41	11	£2,650
30	9	3,186	n/a	£42	13	£1.45	7.4	£1,700
32	1.5	3,683	34	£40	20	£1.20	7.5	£2,050
13	8	2,875	31	£51	38	£1.10	7.8	£1,750
73	28	2,352	n/a	£59	11	£1.30	12.5	n/a
32	14	2,247	14	£50	18	£1.15	8.7	£1,450
9.1	11	1,845	17	£53	37	£1.03	1.9	£1,250
56	9	7,184	11	£52	20	£1.33	5	£2,700
10	5	1,546	3	£55	83	£1.18	2.6	£1,200
34	15	2,448	n/a	£59	30	£1.23	5	£1,900
30	4.8	1,455	n/a	£42	16	£1.25	11	£1,250
38.5	8.9	2,847	21	£51	10	£1.05	9	£1,250
15	7.9	3,978	34	£53	15	£1.20	7	£1,250
49	8	2,588	n/a	£55	20	£1.33	7	£1,700
19	20	1,104	25	£67	18	£1.15	6.3	£650
16.8	10.8	6,097	16	£46	15	£1.68	6	£1,250

Stats

	SEX RATIO	YEAR FOUNDED	NUMBER OF UNDERGRADS	NUMBER OF PART TIME STUDENTS	NUMBER OF POSTGRADS	% IN VIA CLEARING
University of Reading	47:53	1892	7,683	3,376	5,245	n/a
Robert Gordon University	46:54	1881	5,318	542	518	n/a
Royal Academy of Music	45:55	1822	310	0	260	0
Royal College of Music	45:55	1882	380	0	190	0
Royal Free Hospital	50:50	1874	582	0	166	0
Royal Holloway	44:56	1886	4,492	13	915	11
Royal Veterinary College	34:66	1791	532	0	124	0
University of Salford	55:45	1967	11,692	3,154	849	20
School of Pharmacy	40:60	1842	430	2	115	5
University of Sheffield	50:50	1905	14,171	1,870	2,512	n/a
Sheffield Hallam	56:44	1969	13,348	1,555	926	n/a
SOAS	50:50	1916	1,500	0	1,000	0
South Bank University	52:48	1970	8,900	1,200	825	n/a
University of Southampton	50:50	1952	11,539	2,645	1,894	6
Southampton Institute	60:40	1984	11,410	5,254	514	38
SSEES	49:51	1915	330	0	200	10
University of St Andrews	48:52	1410	4,673	44	711	7
St George's Hospital	57:43	1751	928	0	60	0
Staffordshire University	57:43	1970	11,600	3,400	1,700	n/a
University of Stirling	50:50	1967	5,000	800	800	5
University of Strathclyde	49:51	1796	11,000	300	3,600	8
University of Sunderland	49:51	1969	9,414	1,763	365	25
University of Surrey	48:52	1966	5,107	33	3,332	11
Surrey Institute	57:43	1969	2,400	150	28	1.5
University of Sussex	47:53	1961	6,752	52	2,266	n/a
Swansea	45:55	1920	6,365	371	1,212	6
University of Teesside	49:51	1970	7,725	2,792	315	13.6
Thames Valley University	36:64	1991	5,164	2,767	629	50
UCE	43:57	1971	10,111	9,014	3,474	4.2
University of East Anglia	49:51	1963	6,093	1,908	1,385	13
University of Ulster	43:57	1968	11,835	3,853	4,255	8
UMIST	65:35	1824	4,405	0	1,611	22
University College, London	50:50	1826	9,596	246	3,797	5
Wales College of Medicine	28:72	1931	1,740	0	280	n/a
University of Warwick	50:50	1965	7,575	420	2,276	1.5
University of Westminster	50:50	1838	8,400	7,135	900	n/a
University of Wolverhampton	44:56	1983	13,301	3,226	730	n/a
Wye College	44:56	1894	500	0	300	11
University of York	49:51	1963	5,238	754	1,298	6.5
UK Averages	49:51	n/a	7,691	2,167	1,749	12.5

% OF MATURE STUDENTS	% OF OVERSEAS STUDENTS	STUDENTS PER COUNSELLOR	FLUNK RATES	AVERAGE COST OF ACCOMMODATION PER WEEK	% IN COLLEGE ACCOMMODATION	BOOZE INDEX	% OF GRADS UNEMPLOYED AFTER 6 MONTHS	STUDENT'S AVERAGE DEBT PER YEAR
22	13.9	1,182	12	£63	57	£1.42	11	£950
16.6	12.4	1,773	n/a	£52	25	£1.40	5	£1,950
2	25	310	n/a	n/a	0	£1.50		£1,900
2	30	380	n/a	£65	40	£1.35		n/a
15	9	n/a	n/a	£48	20	£1.10		£1,100
18	22	1,123	13	£62	48	£1.33	5.5	£1,450
21	11	n/a	n/a	£63	17	£1.43		n/a
35	11	3,341	n/a	£60	33	£1.40	10	£1,650
20	20	547	n/a	£60	3	£1.30	1	£1,800
10	13.1	1,288	12	£54	30	£1.15	7.6	£2,250
57	2	1,669	n/a	£55	9	£1.20	6	£1,800
45	23	2,500	n/a	£73	23	£1.65	8	£1,600
38	15	2,967	36	£64	13	£1.70	15	£2,100
16	8	3,297	5	£60	32	£1.01	6.8	£1,050
38	7	3,260	21	£63	21	£1.25	35.6	£2,100
40	8	n/a	n/a	£62	37	£1.20	12	n/a
9	15	3,115	n/a	£40	56	£1.35	4.4	£1,100
10	5	988	n/a	£41	28	97p		£2,100
36	4.5	3,913	34	£46	16	£1.18	10.4	£1,000
18	10	2,300	n/a	£47	72	£1.25	5.3	n/a
21	8	2,750	n/a	£53	16	£1.15	8.4	£550
41	7	6,276	26	£46	24	£1.10	9.3	£1,950
17	30	1,119	n/a	£45	42	£1.33	0.9	£700
30	2.5	686	n/a	£42	19	£1.33	25	£1,500
31	25	965	18	£46	35	£1.15	10	£1,100
24	6.8	1,273	6	£51	44	£1.10	7	£950
36	4.5	2,207	24	£42	13	£1.28	11.7	£2,200
75	39	5,164	n/a	£55	0	£1.25	10	£1,550
61	4.7	2,528	n/a	£46	15	£1.35	7.4	£1,400
20	9	1,741	9	£45	49	£1.30	6.9	£1,250
40	15	1,691	6	£33	12	£1.23	9	£1,650
15	21	3008	21	£47	50	£1.28	12	£1,850
16	20	3,199	18	£67	32	£1.35	5.8	£1,800
13	8	870	n/a	£42	12	£1.30		£1,100
10	9	2,576	14	£51	56	£1.38	2.8	£2,100
60	10	3,360	n/a	£63	15	£1.10	9.9	£2,550
45	14	2,660	26	£41	14	£1.23	10.3	£1,950
30	10	500	n/a	£65	40	£1.30	11	£1,700
18.8	8	2,095	16	£36	51	£1.40	10	£1,750
31.2	11	2,638	19	£52.70	28.6	£1.20	8.4	£1,732

S
t
a
t
s

When p u s h comes to shove

Glossary

In the world of higher education, there's a whole language of weird words and interminable terminology. Ever true to our no nonsense, cut-the-brown-smelly-stuff approach, push takes you on a ramble through the jargon jungle, explaining all the terms to help anyone pass themselves off as a student. We've even highlighted some of the more confusing course terms that don't tend to crop up in pre-university education – they're the ones in italics.

Accountancy/Accounting: Not a professional qualification, just a background course giving prospective accountants the necessary insight into finance, investment, tax, management and business. These courses do not, however, give you a life.

Alumni: 'Old-boys' and 'Old-girls', but they're not called that in case they don't give the college any money when they leave. Singular: alumnus.

American Studies: Often dismissed as a doss subject (eg 'you just watch films and listen to old jazz records') this is a multi-disciplinary subject, covering the culture, history and current affairs of the US. Usually includes a period spent in the States – a big draw for people who like Oreo cookies, country music and drive-by shootings.

Archaeology: You might think 3 years risking the wrath of disturbed Egyptian mummies is a cool way to spend a degree course, but archaeology courses are more 'Time Team' than 'Indiana Jones', using a combination of history, science, languages and other disciplines, as well as practical fieldwork.

Architecture: Architecture requires a combination of technical knowledge of forms and structures (sciencey) with creative and aesthetic talents (arty), as well as history, economics, environmental studies and upsetting Prince Charles.

Art(s): Arts subjects include pretty much anything creative. You know, painting, drama, music and all that. It often overlaps with humanities.

Athletics Union/Sports Union: The student organisation that runs student sports clubs and sometimes sports facilities. They're usually hot-beds of sexism, alcohol abuse and hairy chests... and that's just the women.

Botany: The plant bit of Biology.

Business Studies: The study of business, obviously (doh!), but it also includes maths and economics and, less predictably, bits of psychology and sociology. And what with Europe and all that stuff, languages are becoming increasingly unavoidable.

Campaign for Free Education: Unlike the NUS, who are only committed to stopping tuition fees, these guys have also been out trying to save the maintenance grant. Nice try but, we fear, no cigar.

Campus: The area of land on which a collection of college buildings are built. So, a campus university is one built entirely or mainly on a single campus. A civic campus is a campus in a town. And a greenfield campus is not. Just to confuse things, some universities use 'campus' as a synonym for 'site' and vice versa, so it could mean anything from a single building to an almost entirely separate college.

Court: The Cambridge term for a quad.

Economics: Economists will tell you that their subject is 'the study of the allocation of scarce resources'. In fact, they mean it's about the way money changes hands, affecting society (and managing never to reach you and me).

Education: A Bachelor of Education degree trains teachers to teach, within a specialised field at any rate (usually determined by age group, academic subject, or both). Some take a 'normal' first degree (BA, BSc, etc) instead and study for a further year to get a Postgraduate Certificate of Education (PGCE). Either way, after four years of being a student, they know how to work for low pay and look moth-eaten.

Engineering: Engineering is the study of how to create things that make people's lives easier/healthier/safer/better. There are sub-divisions such as: Chemical Engineering (studying how materials change); Civil Engineering (transport, sewage, public buildings, etc); Electrical Engineering and so on. Engineers usually work phenomenally hard, play 'Quake' for hours, and tell you that their subject is 'really interesting, actually'.

Ents: Short for entertainments, which are usually run by the students' union and include such larks as gigs, hypnotists and, if you're unlucky, karaoke.

Environmental Studies: A relatively new discipline that takes bits of biology, chemistry, geology and social sciences and investigates how environmental problems occur, how to prevent them and how to chain yourself to a bulldozer.

European Studies: French, Spanish and Italian aren't just languages, nowadays there are courses which combine learning how to talk with learning something to talk about. A German course might include bits about German culture, business, law, history and Klinsmann's diving techniques.

Faculty: Universities are usually divided into departments. Just in case these departments feel lonely, they're allowed to club together into faculties. So, the physicists join their chemistry and biology chums in a Science Faculty and the musicians get together with the drama luvvies in an Arts Faculty and everybody's happy. Except the lawyers, who usually have a Faculty on their own. Maybe they smell funny.

Finals/Finalists: Finals are the exams in the final year of study, that decide whether or not the last 3 or 4 years have been worth living in abject poverty for. Hence, finalists are students in their final year with their heads on the exam block.

Freshers: Freshers are first year students in their first few weeks - when the pace is faster than curry through a dog with diarrhoea and the main topics of conversation are home towns, A-level grades and UCAS codes. During students' time as freshers, they are likely to spend 99% of their grant cheque, join student clubs whose events they never attend and get stupidly drunk most nights. After 3 weeks of this, they are hungover, broke and wiser - fully-fledged students.

Geology: Geologists study the structure of the earth and the rocks, fossils, minerals and all the general gunk that's in it.

Guild of Students/Students' Guild: Another name for a students' union.

Hack: Not the sound of a bad cough or a lozenge to cure it, but a person who is utterly committed to their extra-curricular activities. Usually refers to those in involved in SUs or student journalism. You can tell a hack because they are the ones claiming everyone else is apathetic.

Halls: At most colleges, when students talk about halls, they mean 'halls of residence', the accommodation blocks, which traditionally provide catered meals (but increasingly are becoming self-catered), cleaners, heat, light and electricity and a variety of amenities such launderettes, common rooms and TV lounges. Oxbridge, of course, has to be different. At Oxford or Cambridge, halls are the formal dining rooms.

Head tenancy scheme: Rather than handing out cardboard boxes or have students cluttering up the gym floor, some colleges have started to do the house-hunting themselves. They get a group of landlords together, rent all their brick boxes that pretend to be homes and then sublet them to students, often at cheaper rates or on better terms.

Humanities: The study of human creative endeavour, whether it's literature, art, music or whatever. It's arguable whether Richard & Judy counts, though. Humanities aren't quite the same as actually doing the creative bit, ie The Arts (which includes almost anything likely to get Lottery funding).

Junior Common Room (JCR): Another name for a students' union, but usually quite a modest affair such as in a hall.

Law: An LLB course will not qualify a student to don a silly wig and act like Kavanagh QC. In theory, it teaches the workings of the legal system (usually the English one) and how laws are applied. It also includes the skills and methods that the legal profession requires (eg cross-examination). To actually become a barrister or solicitor requires further study at Bar or Law School.

Learning Resources Centre (LRC): In the old days (when there were Tories in Scotland) universities used to have libraries (which had books in them) and computer rooms (which had computers). Now they're just as likely to have LRCs which are vast buildings with books <u>and</u> computers in them. Crikey.

Mature students: It is not necessarily true that mature students behave any more maturely than conventional ones. Nor are they necessarily old fogeys - some are as young as 21, but, generally, they are older than most other students and are probably returning to education rather than being fresh out of school. (Having a year out counts as being fresh, having 10 years out living in a brothel doesn't.) See also 'pushing on a bit' (page 25).

Media Studies: A heavily over-subscribed course, often by students who think (i) it'll get them straight into the BBC or Hollywood or (ii) it's a doss course. Both are wrong. Media courses usually cover practical and theoretical training in all areas of mass communication and while the experience and contacts might give students an edge in pursuit of a glittering career full of men with pony-tails, unfortunately, life-membership of the Groucho Club is not automatic and there are many other routes to media infamy.

Modular: A sort of pick 'n' mix course of study comprising a number of components (modules), either just within one department or across a range of subjects.

Nightline: All students have times when the skin on the cup of cocoa of life is just a bit too thick and Nightline services, available in most colleges worth their salt, are there for those times. They are telephone counselling services, a bit like the Samaritans, run (usually) by students for students.

NUS: The National Union of Students, run by students who never grew up, provides research, welfare information and services to SUs which are affiliated. NUS is also the national body which represents and campaigns on behalf of students.

Oxbridge: The collective term for the 2 oldest universities in the country, Oxford and Cambridge, which have a style and prestige all of their own. Why did Camford never catch on?

Personal Tutors/Moral Tutors: At many, if not most, colleges, students are assigned to a personal tutor who is charged with responsibilities beyond the purely academic. The extent of their remit and of their usefulness varies enormously. Some have regular meetings to discuss everything from exams to sex, others introduce themselves to their tutees at the beginning of their college career with some Piat D'Or and limp cheese and don't see them again till graduation day. Sometimes they're called moral tutors, but expecting academics to give moral guidance is like asking a fish to ride a bike. In wellies.

Philosophy: 'What is philosophy?' is a philosophical question, but, ever ready to ponder the even the deepest mysteries, push's definition is that it's about asking the complex questions behind other subjects. Without necessarily expecting an answer. So, when philosophers ask 'Does God exist?', they're more interested in the ideas and argument involved, than His fax number (for that you want theology).

Politics: Of course, nobody with the intelligence and decency to read **push** would want to become anything as vile as a politician, but you might wish to study how these creatures operate. Politics (aka Political Studies, Government, etc) uses elements of history, economics, statistics and more to investigate how people govern themselves and each other and whether William Hague polishes his head.

Polytechnic: Once upon a time there was something called 'the binary divide' which distinguished between universities and polytechnics. It never meant much anyway and now it means nothing at all. Polytechnics tended to have a slant towards vocational courses and an often unfair reputation for lower academic standards than universities. Now they've all become universities themselves, but the old poly prejudices seem to linger about like last week's dirty socks, again somewhat unfairly.

Psychology: If, at university, you ever get pestered by students wielding clipboards and asking intimate questions about sexuality and your favourite colour, chances are they're either chatting you up or they're psychologists (or both). Psychology is the study of the way people think and behave, using elements of biology, sociology, maths and other disciplines. And sometimes they experiment on rats.

Quad: A square surrounded by buildings, usually covered in grass and commonly found in Oxbridge colleges. Only at Cambridge they call them courts, just to be difficult.

Rag: Rag is an excuse to dress up in stupid clothing and get up to wacky, irresponsible and often illegal antics - and all in the name of charity. Collectively, student charity Rags raise millions of pounds with stunts like parachute jumps, sponsored hitch-hikes and so-called Rag raids where students (usually dressed as rabbits, Spice Girls, characters from Rocky Horror, etc) accost strangers in the street and try to sell them 'Rag magazines'. Rag mags are tackily printed joke books, which usually fulfil 1 of 2 conditions: either, they are not very funny or they're in appalling bad taste, or both.

Redbrick: A redbrick building or campus does not necessarily have to have a single red brick. Instead, it refers to a style of building, or a period from around the turn of the century through to the 2nd World War. What redbrick means is not very precise, but what it doesn't mean is easier to explain. A campus is described as redbrick if it isn't an Oxbridge rip-off or a modern concrete monstrosity.

Sabbatical: Every year at most colleges, a few students either take a year off their studies or hang around after them because they've got nothing better to do. In the meantime they are employed (sub-peanut wages) by various student bodies, such as SUs, Rags, newspapers, athletics unions and so on. Not just anyone can do this though; they almost always

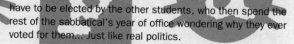

have to be elected by the other students, who then spend the rest of the sabbatical's year of office wondering why they ever voted for them... Just like real politics.

Sandwich course: The bread in a sandwich course is academic study. The filling is vocational experience, usually on an industrial work placement. Usually it takes a year to fill a sandwich (as a result many last 4 years), but there are thin and thick versions with different amounts of filling. push eagerly awaits the introduction of toasted and club sandwich courses.

Semester: A semester is the American word for a term and is used in this country to describe American-style college terms which are longer (usually about 15 weeks) than British ones (between 8 and 11 weeks). Generally speaking, universities have either 2 semesters or 3 terms.

Social science: A social science is any subject which uses scientific methods to study human society, rather than the natural world. Originally regarded as a soft option, some social scientists can now earn big wads by going on the telly and talking lots.

Sociology: The study of how people operate within social groups (eg families, schools, football crowds). Sociologists have to use a variety of skills, such as dealing with data and statistics. Sociology still has an undeserved reputation as a dumping ground for left-wing under-achievers, but it's as intellectually rigorous (and attractive to employers) as any other social science subject.

Socs: Short for 'societies', these are the student clubs which range from serious political battlegrounds to sporting teams, from cultural groups to seriously silly socs, such as the Rolf Harris Appreciation Club and Up Shit Creek Without A Paddle Soc – both genuine.

Students' Association (SA): Just another name for a students' union really. Common in Scotland.

Student Representative Council (SRC): Yet another name for a students' union.

Students' Union (SU): Almost all colleges have a students' union and students are usually automatically members, though they can opt out if they wish. As a rule, an SU is usually a services and representative organisation run by students for students or the building in which such services are housed. See also 'United we push' (page 30).

Theology: The study of God, gods and religion. Often largely Christian-based, theology tends to attract Bible-bashers, ardent atheists and little in between.

Thesp: An arty-farty acting type.

Town/Gown: An expression which describes the juxtaposition of the local populace with the student and academic staff community. This is why people say 'town/gown', even though students these days are more at home in a Manics T-shirt and a pair of scuffed Vans than gown and mortar boards. Come Graduation Day, though, students are geared up in 'subfusc', as the outfit is called, and photos are taken of them. Embarrassment guaranteed.

University College: Once upon a time, there were Colleges of Higher Education, but then they decided that was a bit of a naff title and decided to start calling themselves University Colleges instead. Officially, a University College is either a college which has the power to award its own degrees, but isn't a fully-fledged university, or a college attached to and run by a fully-fledged university. In practice, the waters are somewhat muddier, though the Government looks set to install a state-of-the-art filtration system sometime soon.

Vice-Chancellor: Aka principals, wardens, masters etc. These are the big cheeses - the Stilton amongst the Dairyleas of academia. Students rarely get to meet them, but basically they run the place. Where there are vice-chancellors, there are also chancellors, who are the token heads of the institutions but usually don't do much more than shake students' hands at the graduation ceremony. The allegations that vice-chancellors have anything to do with vice are entirely unfounded.

***Women's Studies (aka Gender Studies)* :** A multi-disciplinary subject that studies how women (and men) are treated in fields as diverse as law, history and health and the reasons for gender differences in behaviour, communication, pay and more. Oh, and men are allowed to apply.

Zoology: The animal bit of biology.

Short, sharp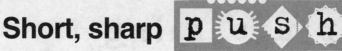

The abbreviations used in push:

 AU: Athletics Union

BUNAC: British Universities North America Club

BUSA: British Universities Sports Association

cap: capacity

CDL: Career Development Loan

CofE: Church of England

CofS: Church of Scotland

CVCP: The Committee of Vice-Chancellors & Principals

DfEE: Department for Education and Employment

ents: entertainments

HND: Higher National Diploma

HE: higher education (ie degree/HND-level or above)

JCR: Junior Common/Combination Room (usually Oxbridge)

LEA: Local Education Authority

LGB: Lesbian, Gay, Bisexual

LRC: Learning Resources Centre

MCR: Middle Common Room

NHS: National Health Service

NUS: The National Union of Students

Poly: Polytechnic

Postgrads: postgraduates

RC: Roman Catholic

SA: Students' Association (usually Scottish)

sabb: sabbatical officer

SCR: Senior Common Room

SNP: Scottish Nationalist Party

soc: society or club

SRC: Student Representative Council

SU: Students' Union

SWSS: Socialist Workers' Student Society

u'grads: undergraduates

UCAS: The Universities and Colleges Admissions Service

URC: United Reform Church

USI: Union of Students in Ireland

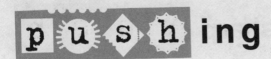

books

A guide to useful publications and recommended reading:

GENERAL
Everything you Need to Know About Going to University, Sally
   Lonson, Kogan Page, £8.99.
Fresher Pressure, Aidan Macfarlane & Ann McPherson, Oxford
   Paperbacks, £4.99.
A Parent's Guide to Higher Education, Trotman/UCAS, £7.99.
   A condensed version is available free from UCAS.

TAKING A YEAR OFF/TRAVELLING
The Gap Year Guide Book, Peridot Press, £8.95.
Let's Go Guides.
Lonely Planet Guides.
Rough Guides.

ACADEMIC GUIDES & APPLICATIONS PROCEDURE
Individual colleges publish prospectuses for admissions and
many students' unions produce alternative prospectuses. Use
the contact details in the **push** entries, see your careers
adviser or call HEIST on (01623) 421622 to get all the
prospectuses you need.
The Big Official UCAS Guide to University & College Entrance,
   UCAS, £18.95.
How to Complete your UCAS Form, Tony Higgins, Trotman,
   £7.99.
How to Choose Your Degree Course, Brian Heap, Trotman,
   £13.95.
Degree Course Offers, Brian Heap, Trotman, £17.99.

NEW MEDIA
push *CD: The Multimedia Guide to UK Universities,* McGraw
   Hill/PUSH, £39.99. A real groundbreaker which allows you
   to make your choice of university on the basis of what it's
   really like, with a unique function that enables you to create
   your 'ideal' university and see how far the real universities
   come up to scratch. The only CD-ROM to give you a virtual
   tour of every university in the UK, now with official UCAS
   course listings
push *Online.* Lots more information on student life and
   issues plus links to university and college web sites and
   other useful stuff. http://www.push.co.uk
UCAS web site. http://www.ucas.co.uk

UK Course Discover, ECCTIS+, computerised information service, covering over 100,000 courses at universities and colleges throughout the country. CD and subscription web site available at schools, colleges, careers offices and training access points (TAP). http://www.ecctis.co.uk

FINANCE, GRANTS AND SPONSORSHIP
Student Grants and Loans, Department for Education and Employment, Publications Centre, PO Box 2193, London, E15 ZEU. Tel: (0181) 533 2000.
Sponsorships for Students, Hobsons, £8.99.
Students' Money Matters, Trotman, £8.99
Form AB11 from the Department of Social Security has information about student entitlement to help with prescriptions, dental and eye care charges. Claims can be made on form AG1.

OVERSEAS STUDENTS
Study UK Handbook, CRAC/Hobsons, £24.99.

MATURE STUDENTS
The Mature Students' Guide, Trotman, £7.95.
A condensed version is available free from UCAS.

POSTGRADUATE STUDY
How to Get a PhD, Open University Press, £14.99.
Postgrad: The Student's Guide, 4 volumes by subject area, Hobsons, £5.99 each or £19.99 for all 4.

DISABLED STUDENTS
Higher Education & Disability, SKILL, £1.50 to students.
Financial Assistance for Students with Disabilities in Higher Education, SKILL, free. (This booklet contains information about social security entitlements).

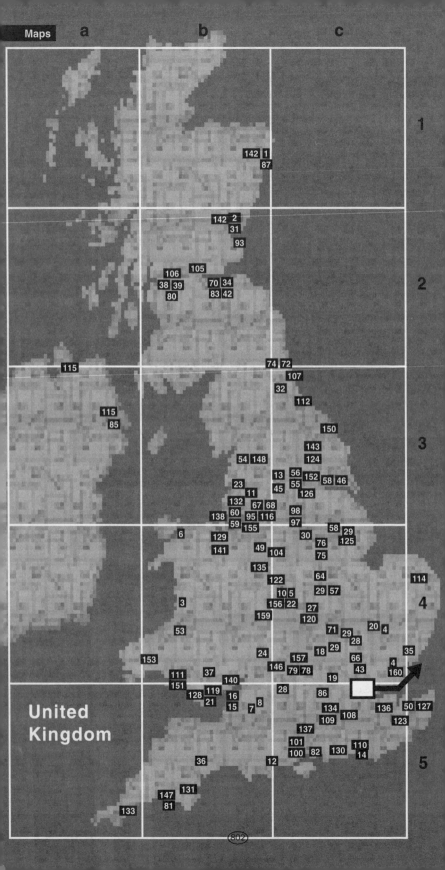

a

b

c

1

2

3

4

5

United Kingdom

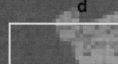

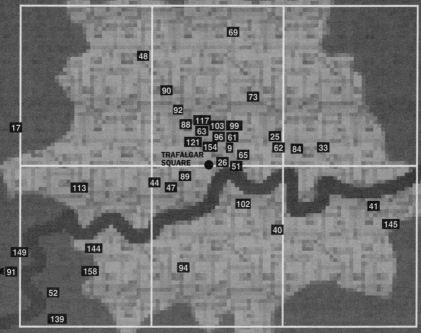

Greater London

TRAFALGAR SQUARE

5 miles

Number	Institution	Number	Institution
1	University of Aberdeen *b1*	29	De Montfort University *c4*
2	University of Abertay Dundee *b2*	30	University of Derby *c4*
3	Aberystwyth, University of Wales *b4*	31	University of Dundee *b2*
4	Anglia Polytechnic University *c4*	32	University of Durham *c3*
5	Aston University *c4*	33	University of East London *f1*
6	Bangor, University of Wales *b4*	34	University of Edinburgh *b2*
7	University of Bath *b5*	35	University of Essex *c4*
8	Bath Spa University College *b5*	36	University of Exeter *b5*
9	Birkbeck College, London *e1*	37	University of Glamorgan *b4*
10	University of Birmingham *c4*	38	University of Glasgow *b2*
11	Bolton Institute *b3*	39	Glasgow Caledonian University *b2*
12	Bournemouth University *b5*	40	Goldsmiths College, London *e2*
13	University of Bradford *b3*	41	University of Greenwich *f2*
14	University of Brighton *c5*	42	Heriot-Watt University *b2*
15	University of Bristol *b5*	43	University of Hertfordshire *c4*
16	Bristol, Univ of the West of England *b5*	44	Heythrop College, London *e2*
17	Brunel University *d1*	45	University of Huddersfield *c3*
18	University of Buckingham *c4*	46	University of Hull *c3*
19	Buckinghamshire Chilterns UC *c4*	47	Imperial College, London *e2*
20	University of Cambridge *c4*	48	Jews' College, London *d1*
21	Cardiff, University of Wales *b5*	49	Keele University *b4*
22	University of Central England *c4*	50	University of Kent at Canterbury *c5*
23	University of Central Lancashire *b3*	51	King's College London *e1*
24	Cheltenham & Gloucester College *b4*	52	Kingston University *d2*
25	City University *e1*	53	Lampeter, University of Wales *b4*
26	Courtauld Institute, London *e1*	54	Lancaster University *b3*
27	Coventry University *c4*		
28	Cranfield University *c4, c5*		*Continued next page* ▶▶

▶▶ *Continued from last page*

55 University of Leeds *c3*
56 Leeds Metropolitan University *c3*
57 Leicester University *c4*
58 Univ of Lincolnshire & Humberside *c3, c4*
59 Liverpool John Moores University *b3*
60 University of Liverpool *b3*
61 University of London *e1*
62 London Guildhall University *e1*
63 The London Institute *e1*
64 Loughborough University *c4*
65 LSE *e1*
66 Luton University *c4*
67 University of Manchester *b3*
68 Manchester Metropolitan University *b3*
69 Middlesex University *e1*
70 Napier University *b2*
71 Nene, UC Northampton *c4*
72 University of Newcastle Upon Tyne *b2*
73 University of North London *e1*
74 University of Northumbria at Newcastle *b2*
75 University of Nottingham *c4*
76 Nottingham Trent University *c4*
77 Open University *not marked on map*
78 University of Oxford *c4*
79 Oxford Brookes University *c4*
80 University of Paisley *b2*
81 University of Plymouth *b5*
82 University of Portsmouth *c5*
83 Queen Margaret College *b2*
84 Queen Mary & Westfield College *f1*
85 Queen's University Belfast *a3*
86 University of Reading *c5*
87 Robert Gordon University *b1*
88 Royal Academy of Music *e1*
89 Royal College of Music *e2*
90 Royal Free Hospital, London *e1*
91 Royal Holloway, London *d2*
92 Royal Veterinary College, London *e1*
93 University of St Andrews *b2*
94 St George's Hospital, London *e2*
95 University of Salford *b3*
96 School of Pharmacy, London *e1*
97 University of Sheffield *c3*
98 Sheffield Hallam University *c3*
99 SOAS *e1*
100 University of Southampton *c5*
101 Southampton Institute *c5*
102 South Bank University *e2*
103 SSEES *e1*
104 Staffordshire University *c4*
105 University of Stirling *b2*
106 University of Strathclyde *b2*
107 University of Sunderland *c3*
108 University of Surrey *c5*
109 Surrey Institute of Art & Design *c5*
110 University of Sussex *c5*
111 Swansea, University of Wales *b4*
112 University of Teesside *c3*
113 Thames Valley University *d2*

114 UEA *c4*
115 University of Ulster *a3*
116 UMIST *b3*
117 University College London *e1*
118 University of Wales *not marked on map*
119 University of Wales College of Medicine *b5*
120 University of Warwick *c4*
121 University of Westminster *e1*
122 University of Wolverhampton *b4*
123 Wye College, London *c5*
124 University of York *c3*
125 Bishop Grosseteste University College *c4*
126 University College, Bretton Hall *c3*
127 Canterbury Christ Church College *c5*
128 Cardiff UWI *b5*
129 University College, Chester *b4*
130 Chichester Institute *c5*
131 Dartington College of Arts *b5*
132 Edge Hill University College *b3*
133 Falmouth College of Arts *a5*
134 Farnborough College of Technology *c5*
135 Harper Adams *b4*
136 Kent Institute of Art & Design *c5*
137 King Alfred's, Winchester *c5*
138 Liverpool Hope University College *b3*
139 NESCOT *d2*
140 Univ of Wales College, Newport *b4*
141 North East Wales Institute of HE *b4*
142 Northern College *b1, b2*
143 University College of Ripon & York St John *c3*
144 Roehampton Institute, London *d2*
145 Rose Bruford College *f2*
146 Royal Agricultural College *c4*
147 College of St Mark & St John *b5*
148 University College of St Martin *b3*
149 St Mary's College, Twickenham *d2*
150 University College, Scarborough *c3*
151 Swansea Institute of HE *b4*
152 Trinity & All Saints *c3*
153 Trinity College, Carmarthen *b4*
154 Trinity College of Music *e1*
155 University College, Warrington *b3*
156 Westhill College *c4*
157 Westminster College, Oxford *c4*
158 Wimbledon School of Art *d2*
159 University College, Worcester *b4*
160 Writtle College *c4*

p u s h index